Merrill

Advanced Mathematical Concepts

Precalculus with Applications

SOLUTIONS MANUAL

GLENCOE

McGraw-Hill

New York, New York
Columbus, Ohio
Mission Hills, California
Peoria, Illinois

Contents

The copy in this text was word processed using ChiWriter Software from Horstmann Software, P.O. Box 5039, San Jose, California 95192

Send all inquires to:
Glencoe/McGraw-Hill
936 Eastwind Drive
Westerville, OH 43081

ISBN 0-02-824280-7

Printed in the United States of America

4 5 6 7 8 9 10 11 12 BAW 01 00 99 98 97 96

Unit 1 Relations, Functions, and Graphs

Chapter 1 Linear Relations and Functions

1-1 Relations and Functions

PAGES 9–10 CHECKING FOR UNDERSTANDING

1. Relations and functions can both be represented by sets of ordered pairs. Unlike a relation, however, a function cannot pair any member of the domain with more than one member of the range.

2. The vertical line test is a quick visual way of determining whether or not a graph of a relation is a function. If a vertical line drawn on the graph of a relation passes through no more than one point of the graph, then the relation is a function.

3. See students' work.

4. Since a relation can be represented by a set of ordered pairs, a function is always a relation. However, in a function, there is exactly one y-value for every x-value. Not all relations have this constraint.

5. yes   6. no   7. yes

8. $f(0) = 7 - 0^2$
    $= 7$

9. $f(4) = 7 - 4^2$
    $= -9$

10. $f(-3) = 7 - (-3)^2$
     $= -2$

11. $f(11) = 7 - 11^2$
     $= -114$

12. $f\left(\frac{1}{2}\right) = 7 - \left(\frac{1}{2}\right)^2$
     $= \frac{27}{4}$
     $= 6\frac{3}{4}$

13. $f(3.7) = 7 - 3.7^2$
     ≈ -6.69

14. $f(2a) = 7 - (2a)^2$
     $= 7 - 4a^2$

15. $f(6 + n) = 7 - (6 + n)^2$
     $= 7 - (36 + 12n + n^2)$
     $= -29 - 12n - n^2$

16. $4x = 0$
     $x = 0$

17. $x - 4 \le 0$
     $x \le 4$

PAGES 10 – 11 EXERCISES

18. {–3, 2, 4}, {–6, –2, 0}, yes
19. {–3, 0, 1, 2}, {–6, 0, 2, 4}, yes
20. {0, 2, 5, 6}, {3}, yes
21. {–2}, {7, 8, 9}, no
22. {5, 6}, {5, 6}, yes
23. {1, 2, 3, 4}, {5, 6, 7, 8}, yes
24. {4, 9}, {–3, –2, 2, 3}, no
25. {6, 7, 8}, {–3, 3}, yes
26. {(1, 0), (2, 3), (3, 6), (4, 9), (5, 12)}, yes
27. {(4, 10), (5, 12.5), (6, 15), (7, 17.5), (8, 20)}, yes
28. {(4, 5), (5, 5), (6, 5), (7, 5), (8, 5), (9, 5)}, yes
29. {(11, 3), (11, –3)}, no
30. {(4, 2), (4, –2)}, no
31. {(–2, 0.5), (–1, –0.5), (0, –1.5), (1, –0.5), (2, 0.5), (3, 1.5)}, yes

32. $f(-4) = [-4] + 4$
     $= -4 + 4$
     $= 0$

33. $f(2.5) = [2.5] + 4$
     $= 2 + 4$
     $= 6$

34. $f(-6.3) = [-6.3] + 4$
     $= -7 + 4$
     $= -3$

35. $f(\sqrt{2}) = [\sqrt{2}] + 4$
     $= 1 + 4$
     $= 5$

36. $f(-\sqrt{3}) = [-\sqrt{3}]$
     $= -2 + 4$
     $= 2$

37. $f(\pi) = [\pi] + 4$
     $= 3 + 4$
     $= 7$

38. $f(-4 + t) = [-4 + t] + 4$
     $= -4 + [t] + 4$
     $= [t]$

39. $f(q + 1) = [q + 1] + 4$
     $= [q] + 1 + 4$
     $= [q] + 5$

40. $f(0) = |0^2 - 13|$
     $= 13$

41. $f(-4) = |(-4)^2 - 13|$
     $= 3$

42. $f(-\sqrt{13}) = |(-\sqrt{13})^2 - 13|$
     $= 0$

43. $f(2) = |2^2 - 13|$
     $= 9$

44. $f(4.8) = |4.8^2 - 13|$
     $= 10.04$

45. $f\left(1\frac{1}{2}\right) = \left|\left(1\frac{1}{2}\right)^2 - 13\right|$
     $= \frac{43}{4} = 10\frac{3}{4}$

46. $f(n + 4) = |(n + 4)^2 - 13|$
     $= |n^2 + 8n + 16 - 13|$
     $= |n^2 + 8n + 3|$

47. $f(5m) = |(5m)^2 - 13|$

$= |25m^2 - 13|$

48. $x - 1 = 0$
$x = 1$

49. $5 + x = 0$
$x = -5$

50. $32 - x^2 = 0$
$32 = x^2$
$\pm\sqrt{32} = x$
$\pm 4\sqrt{2} = x$

51. $|2x| - 9 = 0$
$|2x| = 9$
$2x = \pm 9$
$x = \pm \dfrac{9}{2}$
$x = \pm 4\dfrac{1}{2}$

52. $x^2 - 9 < 0$
$x^2 < 9$
$-3 < x < 3$

53. $x^2 - 7 \leq 0$
$x^2 \leq 7$
$-\sqrt{7} \leq x \leq \sqrt{7}$

54. function

55. function

56. relation

57. relation

58. $P(4) = \dfrac{(1)(2) + 1}{3} = 1$

$P(5) = \dfrac{(2)(3) + 1}{1} = 7$

$P(6) = \dfrac{(3)(1) + 1}{7} = \dfrac{4}{7}$

59. If the x-coordinate represents the pounds of aluminum produced and the y-coordinate represents the number of cans recycled, the relation is a function. If the x-coordinate represents the number of cans recycled and the y-coordinate represents the pounds of aluminum produced, the relation is not a function because the x-coordinate, 75,000, would be paired with 2 y-coordinates, 3000 and 3100.

60. a. year 1: $I = (5000)(0.08)(1) = \$400$
year 2: $I = (5400)(0.08)(1) = \$432$
year 3: $I = (5832)(0.08)(1) = \$466.56$
year 4: $I = (6298.56)(0.08)(1) = \$503.88$
year 5: $I = (6802.44)(0.08)(1) = \$544.20$

b. domain = {1, 2, 3, 4, 5}
range = {\$400, \$432, \$466.56, \$503.88, \$544.20}

c. Yes, the relation is a function. For each member of the domain, there is only one corresponding element in the range.

Case Study Follow-Up

PAGE 11

1. yes; yes

2. $f(1986) = -240(1986) + 482,640 = 6000$
$f(1993) = -240(1993) + 482,640 = 4320$
$f(2006) = -240(2006) + 482,640 = 1200$

a. 1986, 2006

b. yes

3. See students' work.

1-2 Composition and Inverses of Functions

PAGES 16-17 CHECKING FOR UNDERSTANDING

1. No. In fact, $(f \circ g)(x)$ and $(g \circ f)(x)$ are almost never equal.

2. The equation does not represent a function because each value of x has two values of $y = f^{-1}(x)$. For example, let $x = 2$. Then $y = +\sqrt{3}$ and $-\sqrt{3}$.

3. See students' graphs; $f(x)$ and $f^{-1}(x)$ are reflections of each other about the line $y = x$.

4. $(f + g)(x) = \dfrac{x}{x + 1} + x^2 - 1$

$= \dfrac{x}{x + 1} + \dfrac{(x^2 - 1)(x + 1)}{x + 1}$

$= \dfrac{x}{x + 1} + \dfrac{x^3 + x^2 - x - 1}{x + 1}$

$= \dfrac{x^3 + x^2 - 1}{x + 1}, \; x \neq -1$

5. $(f - g)(x) = \dfrac{x}{x + 1} - (x^2 - 1)$

$= \dfrac{x}{x + 1} - \dfrac{(x^2 - 1)(x + 1)}{x + 1}$

$= \dfrac{x}{x + 1} - \dfrac{x^3 + x^2 - x - 1}{x + 1}$

$= \dfrac{-x^3 - x^2 + 2x + 1}{x + 1}, \; x \neq -1$

6. $(f \circ g)(x) = \dfrac{x}{x + 1} \cdot (x^2 - 1)$

$= \dfrac{x(x + 1)(x - 1)}{x + 1}$

$= x^2 - x$

7. $\left(\dfrac{f}{g}\right)(x) = \dfrac{\dfrac{x}{x + 1}}{x^2 - 1}$

$= \dfrac{x}{x + 1} \cdot \dfrac{1}{x^2 - 1}$

$= \dfrac{x}{x^3 + x^2 - x - 1}, \; x \neq 1$

8. $(f \circ g)(x)$
$= f(g(x))$
$= 2x + 5 + 3$
$= 2x + 8$

$(g \circ f)(x)$
$= g(f(x))$
$= 2(x + 3) + 5$
$= 2x + 11$

2

9. $(f \circ g)(x)$ $(g \circ f)(x)$

   $= f(g(x))$ $= g(f(x))$

   $= (x + 4)^2 - 9$ $= x^2 - 9 + 4$

   $= x^2 + 8x + 16 - 9$ $= x^2 - 5$

   $= x^2 + 8x + 7$

10. $(f \circ g)(x)$ $(g \circ f)(x)$

   $= f(g(x))$ $= g(f(x))$

   $= 3\left(\dfrac{x - 1}{3}\right) + 1$ $= \dfrac{3x + 1 - 1}{3}$

   $= x - 1 + 1$ $= \dfrac{3x}{3}$

   $= x$

   yes $= x$

11. $(f \circ g)(x)$ $(g \circ f)(x)$

   $= f(g(x))$ $= g(f(x))$

   $= \frac{1}{2}(2x + 5) - 5$ $= 2(\frac{1}{2}x - 5) + 5$

   $= x + \dfrac{5}{2} - 5$ $= x - 10 + 5$

                     $= x - 5$

   $= x - \dfrac{5}{2}$

   no

PAGES 17–18   EXERCISES

12. $(f + g)(x) = \dfrac{3}{x - 7} + x^2 + 5x$

             $= \dfrac{3}{x - 7} + \dfrac{(x^2 + 5x)(x - 7)}{x - 7}$

             $= \dfrac{3}{x - 7} + \dfrac{x^3 - 7x^2 + 5x^2 - 35x}{x - 7}$

             $= \dfrac{x^3 - 2x^2 - 35x + 3}{x - 7}$, $x \neq 7$

13. $(f - g)(x) = \dfrac{3}{x - 7} - (x^2 + 5x)$

             $= \dfrac{3}{x - 7} - \dfrac{(x^2 + 5x)(x - 7)}{x - 7}$

             $= \dfrac{3}{x - 7} - \dfrac{x^3 - 7x^2 + 5x^2 - 35x}{x - 7}$

             $= -\dfrac{x^3 - 2x^2 - 35x - 3}{x - 7}$, $x \neq 7$

14. $(f \cdot g)(x) = \dfrac{3}{x - 7} \cdot (x^2 + 5x)$

             $= -\dfrac{3x^2 + 15x}{x - 7}$, $x \neq 7$

15. $\left(\dfrac{f}{g}\right)(x) = \dfrac{\dfrac{3}{x - 7}}{x^2 + 5x}$

         $= \dfrac{3}{x - 7} \cdot \dfrac{1}{x^2 + 5x}$

         $= \dfrac{3}{x^3 - 2x^2 - 35x}$, $x \neq -5, 0, 7$

16. $(f \circ g)(x)$ $(g \circ f)(x)$

   $= f(g(x))$ $= g(f(x))$

   $= \frac{1}{2}(x + 6) - 7$ $= \frac{1}{2}x - 7 + 6$

   $= \frac{1}{2}x + 3 - 7$ $= \frac{1}{2}x - 1$

   $= \frac{1}{2}x - 4$

17. $(f \circ g)(x)$ $(g \circ f)(x)$

   $= f(g(x))$ $= g(f(x))$

   $= 3(x - 4)^2$ $= 3x^2 - 4$

   $= 3(x^2 - 8x + 16)$

   $= 3x^2 - 24x + 48$

18. $(f \circ g)(x)$ $(g \circ f)(x)$

   $= f(g(x))$ $= g(f(x))$

   $= (x + 1)^3$ $= x^3 + 1$

   $= x^3 + 3x^2 + 3x + 1$

19. $(f \circ g)(x)$ $(g \circ f)(x)$

   $= f(g(x))$ $= g(f(x))$

   $= 5(x^2 - 1)^2$ $= (5x^2)^2 - 1$

   $= 5(x^4 - 2x^2 + 1)$ $= 25x^4 - 1$

   $= 5x^4 - 10x^2 + 5$

20. $(f \circ g)(x)$ $(g \circ f)(x)$

   $= f(g(x))$ $= g(f(x))$

   $= (2x)^3 + (2x)^2 + 1$ $= 2(x^3 + x^2 + 1)$

   $= 8x^3 + 4x^2 + 1$ $= 2x^3 + 2x^2 + 2$

21. $(f \circ g)(x)$ $(g \circ f)(x)$

   $= f(g(x))$ $= g(f(x))$

   $= (x + 1)^2 + 5(x + 1) + 6$ $= x^2 + 5x + 6 + 1$

   $= x^2 + 2x + 1 + 5x + 5 + 6$ $= x^2 + 5x + 7$

   $= x^2 + 7x + 12$

22. $(f \circ g)(x)$ $(g \circ f)(x)$

   $= f(g(x))$ $= g(f(x))$

   $= 5\left(\dfrac{x + 6}{5}\right) - 6$ $= \dfrac{5x - 6 + 6}{5}$

   $= x + 6 - 6$ $= \dfrac{5x}{5}$

   $= x$

   yes $= x$

23. $(f \circ g)(x)$ $(g \circ f)(x)$

   $= f(g(x))$ $= g(f(x))$

   $= x - 5 + 5$ $= x + 5 - 5$

   $= x$ $= x$

   yes

24. $(f \circ g)(x)$ $(g \circ f)(x)$

$= f(g(x))$ $= g(f(x))$

$= \dfrac{2x + 1 - 1}{2}$ $= 2\left(\dfrac{x - 1}{2}\right) + 1$

$= \dfrac{2x}{2}$ $= x - 1 + 1$

$= x$ $= x$

yes

25. $(f \circ g)(x)$ $(g \circ f)(x)$

$= f(g(x))$ $= g(f(x))$

$= -x$ $= -x$

no

26. $(f \circ g)(x)$ $(g \circ f)(x)$

$= f(g(x))$ $= g(f(x))$

$= -3(3x - 7) + 7$ $= 3(-3x + 7) - 7$

$= -9x + 21 + 7$ $= -9x + 21 - 7$

$= -9x + 28$ $= -9x + 14$

no

27. $(f \circ g)(x)$ $(g \circ f)(x)$

$= f(g(x))$ $= g(f(x))$

$= \dfrac{1}{3}(3(x - 2)) + 2$ $= 3\left(\dfrac{1}{3}x + 2 - 2\right)$

$= x - 2 + 2$ $= 3\left(\dfrac{1}{3}x\right)$

$= x$

yes $= x$

28. $y = 4x + 4$

$x = 4y + 4$

$x - 4 = 4y$

$\dfrac{x - 4}{4} = y$

$\dfrac{x - 4}{4} = f^{-1}(x)$

$\dfrac{1}{4}x - 1 = f^{-1}(x)$

function

29. $y = x^3$

$x = y^3$

$\sqrt[3]{x} = y$

$\sqrt[3]{x} = f^{-1}(x)$

function

30. $y = x^2 - 9$

$x = y^2 - 9$

$x + 9 = y^2$

$\pm\sqrt{x + 9} = y$

$\pm\sqrt{x + 9} = f^{-1}(x)$

not a function

31. See students' work.

32. a. $f(2) = 2(2) + 1$

$= 5$

$f(f(2)) = 2(5) + 1$

$= 11$

b. $f(-1) = 2(-1) + 1$

$= -1$

$f(f(-1)) = 2(-1) + 1$

$= -1$

$f(f(f(-1))) = 2(-1) + 1$

$= -1$

c. $f(3) = 2(3) + 1 = 7$

$f(f(3)) = 2(7) + 1 = 15$

$f(f(f(3))) = 2(15) + 1 = 31$

33.

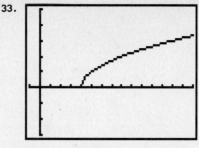

domain: $x \geq 4$

range: $y \geq 0$

34.

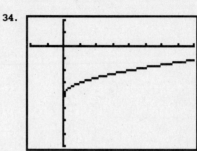

domain: $x \geq 0$

range: $y \geq -4$

35. $(f \circ g)(x) = f(g(x))$

$= f(1 - x^2)$

$= \dfrac{x^2(x^2 + 1)}{1 + x^2}$

$= x^2$

$= -(1 - x^2) + 1$

So, $f(x) = -x + 1$ and $f\left(\dfrac{1}{2}\right) = -\dfrac{1}{2} + 1 = \dfrac{1}{2}$.

36. $T(x) = 1.07x$ where $x = $ original price.

$S(x) = 0.75x$ (cost of an item with 25% discount)

$(T \circ S)(x) = T(S(x))$

$= 1.07(0.75x)$

$(T \circ S)(59.99) = 1.07(0.75(59.99))$

$\approx \$48.14$

37. $T(x) = 1.055x$ where $x = $ original price.

$S(x) = 0.67x$ (cost of an item with 33% discount)

$(T \circ S)(x) = T(S(x))$

$= 1.055(0.67x)$

$45.95 = 1.055(0.67x)$

$45.95 = 0.70685x$

$\$65.00 \approx x$

38. No, most elements in the domain are paired with two elements in the range.

39. {(-3, 14), (-2, 13), (-1, 12), (0, 11)}, yes

40. $f(14) = 4 + 6(14) - 14^3$

$= 4 + 84 - 2744$

$= -2656$

41. $x^2 - 6 = 0$

$x^2 = 6$

$x = \pm\sqrt{6}$

42. $\dfrac{9^5 - 9^4}{8} = \dfrac{9^4(9 - 1)}{8}$

$= \dfrac{9^4(8)}{8}$

$= 9^4$

The best answer is D.

Graphing Calculators:
Graphing Linear Equations
and Inequalities

1.

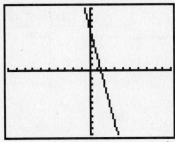

[-10, 10] Xscl:1, [-10, 10] Yscl:1

2.

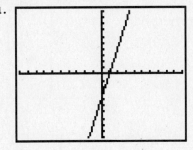

[-10, 10] Xscl:1, [-10, 10] Yscl:1

3.

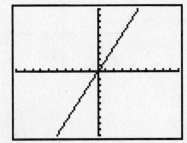

[-10, 10] Xscl:1, [-0.1, 0.1] Yscl:0.01

4.

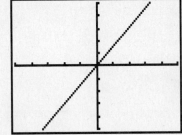

[-5, 5] Xscl:1, [-500, 500] Yscl:100

5.

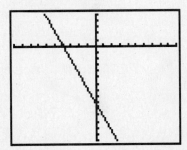

[-10, 10] Xscl:1, [-150, 150] Yscl:10

6.

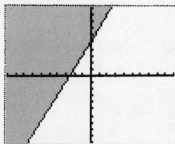

[-20, 100] Xscl:10, [-50, 50] Yscl:10

7.

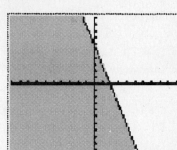

8.

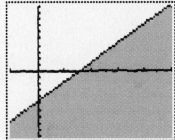

9.

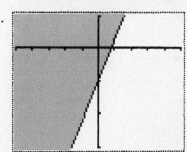

10.

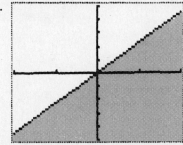

11.

5

12.

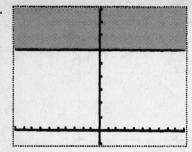

1-3 Linear Functions and Inequalities

PAGES 24-25   CHECKING FOR UNDERSTANDING

1. Graph the lines $-5 = x - 5y$ and $x - 5y = 6$. Test points to determine which region(s) should be shaded. Then, shade the correct region(s).

2. Replace m with 186 and c with 72.45 in the inequality $c < 35 + 0.30m$. Then see if the inequality is true. If it is, Mike would be reimbursed for his rental car travel.

3. 2   **4.** -2   **5.** none

6. $3(0) - 4(0) = 0 \geq -5$
   $3(3) - 4(2) = 1 \geq -5$
   $3(-4) - 4(2) = -20 < -5$
   $3(-2) - 4(4) = -22 < -5$
   $(0, 0), (3, 2)$

7. $0 \neq 0 - 5$
   $2 \neq 3 - 5$
   $2 \neq -4 - 5$
   $4 \neq -2 - 5$
   all points

8. $0 < 4(0) + 3$
   $3 < 4(2) + 3$
   $-4 < 4(2) + 3$
   $-2 < 4(4) + 3$
   none

9. $x > 2$

10. $y \leq 3$

11. $y \leq x + 2$

12.

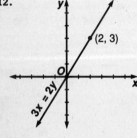

13.

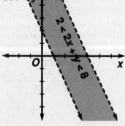

PAGES 25-27   EXERCISES

14. $y > -2x - 3$

15. $1 \leq y \leq 4$

16. $-2 \leq -x + y \leq 3$

17. $0.5x + 6 = 0$
   $0.5x = -6$
   $x = -12$

18. $14x = 0$
   $x = 0$

19. $9x + 5 = 0$
   $9x = -5$
   $x = -\dfrac{5}{9}$

20. $5x - 8 = 0$
   $5x = 8$
   $x = \dfrac{8}{5}$

21. $19 \neq 0$
   none

22. $3x + 1 = 0$
   $3x = -1$
   $x = -\dfrac{1}{3}$

23.

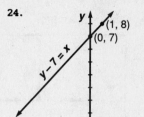

24.

25.

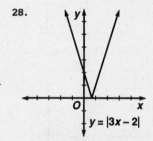

26.

27.

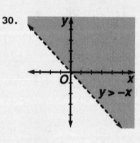

28.

29.

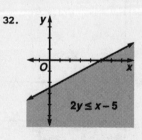

30.

31.

32.

33.

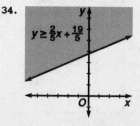

34.

35.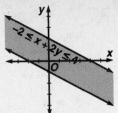

36.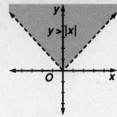

37.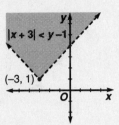

38. See students' work.

39.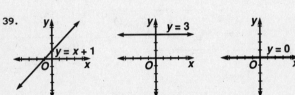

40. a. $D(6.15) = \dfrac{560}{6.15} \approx 91.06$

b. $D(6.15)$ represents the demand for soybeans, given that the price of soybeans for that month is $6.15 per bushel.

41. a.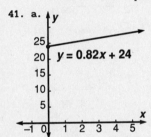

b. $24 billion

c. If the nation had no disposable income, personal consumption expenditures would be $24 billion.

42. $\{(-4, 16), (-3, 9), (-2, 4)\}$, yes

43. $f(2 + a) = 4 + 6(2 + a) - (2 + a)^3$

$\qquad = 4 + 12 + 6a - (a^3 + 6a^2 + 12a + 8)$

$\qquad = 8 - 6a - 6a^2 - a^3$

44. $(f + g)(x) = 2x + x^2 - 4$

$\qquad = x^2 + 2x - 4$

$(f - g)(x) = 2x - (x^2 - 4)$

$\qquad = 2x - x^2 + 4$

$\qquad = -x^2 + 2x + 4$

45. $(f \circ g)(x) = f(g(x))$

$\qquad = \dfrac{2}{5}(40x - 10)$

$\qquad = 16x - 4$

46. $(f \circ g)(x) = f(g(x)) \qquad\qquad (g \circ f)(x) = g(f(x))$

$\qquad = 3\left(\dfrac{x + 5}{3}\right) + 5 \qquad\qquad = \dfrac{3x + 5 + 5}{3}$

$\qquad = x + 5 + 5 \qquad\qquad\qquad = \dfrac{3x + 10}{3}$

$\qquad = x + 10 \qquad\qquad\qquad\quad = x + \dfrac{10}{3}$

no

47. $\qquad \dfrac{2x - 3}{x} = \dfrac{3 - x}{2}$

$\qquad 2(2x - 3) = x(3 - x)$

$\qquad\quad 4x - 6 = 3x - x^2$

$\qquad x^2 + x - 6 = 0$

$\qquad (x + 3)(x - 2) = 0$

$\qquad x + 3 = 0 \qquad x - 2 = 0$

$\qquad\quad x = -3 \qquad\quad x = 2$

The best answer is A.

Mid-Chapter Review

PAGE 27

1. a. domain: $\{2, 3, 5, 6\}$

range: $\{-1, 0, 1, 2, 3\}$

b. No, the element 5 in the domain is paired with both 2 and −1 in the range.

2. $f(0) = 4 + 6(0) - 0^3 = 4$

3. $f(-1) = 4 + 6(-1) - (-1)^3 = -1$

4. $f\left(\dfrac{1}{2}\right) = 4 + 6\left(\dfrac{1}{2}\right) - \left(\dfrac{1}{2}\right)^3 = 6\dfrac{7}{8}$

5. $f(3k) = 4 + 6(3k) - (3k)^3$

$\qquad = 4 + 18k - 27k^3$

6. $x^2 - 5 = 0$

$\qquad x^2 = 5$

$\qquad x = \pm\sqrt{5}$

7. $(f \circ g)(x) = f(g(x)) \qquad\qquad (g \circ f)(x) = g(f(x))$

$\qquad = \left(\dfrac{1}{x}\right)^2 \qquad\qquad\qquad = \dfrac{1}{x^2}$

$\qquad = \dfrac{1}{x^2}$

8. $\qquad y = \dfrac{7 - x}{4}$

$\qquad\quad x = \dfrac{7 - y}{4}$

$\qquad\quad 4x = 7 - y$

$\qquad\quad y = 7 - 4x$

$\qquad f^{-1}(x) = 7 - 4x$

9.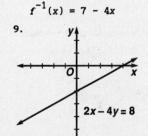

10.

7

Technology: Graphing Linear Relations

1. yes   2. yes   3. no

4. If $g(x)$ and $f(x)$ are inverses and one of the graphs intersects the line $y = x$, the other graph will also intersect the line at the same point.

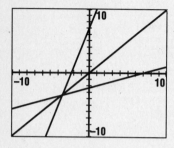

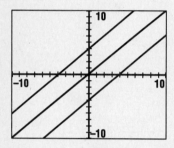

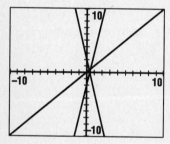

1-4   Distance and Slope

1. Answers will vary.

2. It does not matter which point is (x_1, y_1) and which point is (x_2, y_2). Either way, the slope is $-\frac{4}{3}$.

3. Disposable income is the money that households have left to spend or save after taxes have been paid.

4. $d = \sqrt{(7 - 4)^2 + (1 - 1)^2}$ $m = \frac{1 - 1}{7 - 4}$

   $ = \sqrt{9 + 0}$ $ = \frac{0}{3}$

   $ = 3$ $ = 0$

---

5. $d = \sqrt{(5 - 5)^2 + (11 - 1)^2}$ $m = \frac{11 - 1}{5 - 5}$

   $ = \sqrt{0 + 100}$ $ = \frac{10}{0}$

   $ = 10$ undefined

6. $d = \sqrt{(-1 - 1)^2 + (-3 - 3)^2}$ $m = \frac{-3 - 3}{-1 - 1}$

   $ = \sqrt{4 + 36}$ $ = \frac{-6}{-2}$

   $ = \sqrt{40}$ $ = 3$

   $ = 2\sqrt{10}$

7. $d = \sqrt{(-4 - 0)^2 + (-3 - 0)^2}$ $m = \frac{-3 - 0}{-4 - 0}$

   $ = \sqrt{16 + 9}$ $ = \frac{-3}{-4}$

   $ = 5$ $ = \frac{3}{4}$

8. $d = \sqrt{(4 - (-1))^2 + (13 - 1)^2}$ $m = \frac{13 - 1}{4 - (-1)}$

   $ = \sqrt{25 + 144}$ $ = \frac{12}{5}$

   $ = \sqrt{169}$

   $ = 13$

9. $d = \sqrt{(0 - (-2))^2 + (4 - 2)^2}$ $m = \frac{4 - 2}{0 - (-2)}$

   $ = \sqrt{4 + 4}$ $ = \frac{2}{2}$

   $ = \sqrt{8}$ $ = 1$

   $ = 2\sqrt{2}$

10. distance between (2, 3) and (14, 3)

    $= \sqrt{(14 - 2)^2 + (3 - 3)^2} = \sqrt{144 + 0} = 12$

    distance between (14, 3) and (14, 8)

    $= \sqrt{(14 - 14)^2 + (8 - 3)^2} = \sqrt{0 + 25} = 5$

    distance between (14, 8) and (2, 3)

    $= \sqrt{(2 - 14)^2 + (3 - 8)^2} = \sqrt{144 + 25} = 13$

    perimeter = 12 + 5 + 13 = 30

11. distance between (2, 2) and (5, 2)

    $= \sqrt{(5 - 2)^2 + (2 - 2)^2} = \sqrt{9 + 0} = 3$

    distance between (5, 2) and (2, 6)

    $= \sqrt{(2 - 5)^2 + (6 - 2)^2} = \sqrt{9 + 16} = 5$

    distance between (2, 6) and (2, 2)

    $= \sqrt{(2 - 2)^2 + (2 - 6)^2} = \sqrt{0 + 16} = 4$

    perimeter = 3 + 5 + 4 = 12

12. distance between (1, -1) and (1, 3)

    $= \sqrt{(1 - 1)^2 + (3 - (-1))^2} = \sqrt{0 + 16} = 4$

    distance between (1, 3) and (-2, -1)

    $= \sqrt{(-2 - 1)^2 + (-1 - 3)^2} = \sqrt{9 + 16} = 5$

    distance between (-2, -1) and (1, -1)

    $= \sqrt{(1 - (-2))^2 + (-1 - (-1))^2} = \sqrt{9 + 0} = 3$

    perimeter = 4 + 5 + 3 = 12

13. distance between (3, 3) and (3, -9)

$$= \sqrt{(3 - 3)^2 + (-9 - 3)^2} = \sqrt{0 + 144} = 12$$

distance between (3, -9) and (-2, 3)

$$= \sqrt{(-2 - 3)^2 + (3 - (-9))^2} = \sqrt{25 + 144} = 13$$

distance between (-2, 3) and (3, 3)

$$= \sqrt{(3 - (-2))^2 + (3 - 3)^2} = \sqrt{25 + 0} = 5$$

perimeter = 12 + 13 + 5 = 30

14. length $= \sqrt{(3 - (-1))^2 + (-1 - 3)^2}$

$$= \sqrt{16 + 16}$$
$$= \sqrt{32}$$
$$= 4\sqrt{2}$$

width $= \sqrt{(1 - 3)^2 + (-3 - (-1))^2}$

$$= \sqrt{4 + 4}$$
$$= \sqrt{8}$$
$$= 2\sqrt{2}$$

area $= (4\sqrt{2})(2\sqrt{2})$
$$= 16$$

15. midpoint of leg from (5, 0) to (-3, 2)

$$= \left(\frac{5 - 3}{2}, \frac{0 + 2}{2}\right) = (1, 1)$$

midpoint of leg from (-3, 2) to (-1, -4)

$$= \left(\frac{-3 - 1}{2}, \frac{2 - 4}{2}\right) = (-2, -1)$$

midpoint of leg from (-1, -4) to (5, 0)

$$= \left(\frac{-1 + 5}{2}, \frac{-4 + 0}{2}\right) = (2, -2)$$

PAGES 33-35   EXERCISES

16. $d = \sqrt{(-1 - 5)^2 + (-6 - (-3))^2}$ $m = \frac{-6 - (-3)}{-1 - 5}$

$$= \sqrt{36 + 9}$$ $= \frac{-3}{-6}$
$$= \sqrt{45}$$ $= \frac{1}{2}$
$$= 3\sqrt{5}$$

17. $d = \sqrt{(0 - 6)^2 + (6 - 0)^2}$ $m = \frac{6 - 0}{0 - 6}$

$$= \sqrt{36 + 36}$$ $= \frac{6}{-6}$
$$= \sqrt{72}$$ $= -1$
$$= 6\sqrt{2}$$

18. $d = \sqrt{(0 - 5)^2 + (0 - 7)^2}$ $m = \frac{0 - 7}{0 - 5}$

$$= \sqrt{25 + 49}$$ $= \frac{-7}{-5}$
$$= \sqrt{74}$$ $= \frac{7}{5}$

19. $d = \sqrt{(-7 - 1)^2 + (11 - (-5))^2}$ $m = \frac{11 - (-5)}{-7 - 1}$

$$= \sqrt{64 + 256}$$ $= \frac{16}{-8}$
$$= \sqrt{320}$$ $= -2$
$$= 8\sqrt{5}$$

20. $d = \sqrt{(8 - 3)^2 + (a - a)^2}$ $m = \frac{a - a}{8 - 3}$

$$= \sqrt{25 + 0}$$ $= \frac{0}{5}$
$$= 5$$ $= 0$

21. $d = \sqrt{(b - b)^2 + (a + 3 - (6 + a))^2}$

$$= \sqrt{0 + 9}$$
$$= 3$$

$$m = \frac{a + 3 - (6 + a)}{b - b}$$

$$= \frac{-3}{0}$$

undefined

22. $d = \sqrt{(r + 2 - r)^2 + (s + 1 - s)^2}$
$$= \sqrt{4 + 1}$$
$$= \sqrt{5}$$

$$m = \frac{s - 1 - s}{r + 2 - r}$$

$$= -\frac{1}{2}$$

23. $d = \sqrt{(n + 1 - n)^2 + (n - 4n)^2}$

$$= \sqrt{1 + 9n^2}$$

$$m = \frac{n - 4n}{n + 1 - n}$$

$$= \frac{-3n}{1}$$

$$= -3n$$

24. slope between (3, 4) and (6, 2)

$$= \frac{2 - 4}{6 - 3} = \frac{-2}{3}$$

slope between (5, 9) and (8, 7)

$$= \frac{7 - 9}{8 - 5} = \frac{-2}{3}$$

slope between (6, 2) and (8, 7)

$$= \frac{7 - 2}{8 - 6} = \frac{5}{2}$$

slope between (5, 9) and (3, 4)

$$= \frac{4 - 9}{3 - 5} = \frac{-5}{-2} = \frac{5}{2}$$

yes

25. slope between (4, 11) and (8, 14)

$$= \frac{14 - 11}{8 - 4} = \frac{3}{4}$$

slope between (0, 15) and (4, 19)

$$= \frac{19 - 15}{4 - 0} = \frac{4}{4} = 1$$

slope between (4, 11) and (0, 15)

$$= \frac{15 - 11}{0 - 4} = \frac{4}{-4} = -1$$

slope between (4, 19) and (8, 14)

$$= \frac{14 - 19}{8 - 4} = \frac{-5}{4}$$

no

26. slope between $(-2, 1)$ and $(-1, 5)$

$= \dfrac{5 - 1}{-1 - (-2)} = \dfrac{4}{1} = 4$

slope between $(-6, 2)$ and $(-5, 6)$

$= \dfrac{6 - 2}{-5 - (-6)} = \dfrac{4}{1} = 4$

slope between $(-6, 2)$ and $(-2, 1)$

$= \dfrac{1 - 2}{-2 - (-6)} = \dfrac{-1}{4}$

slope between $(-5, 6)$ and $(-1, 5)$

$= \dfrac{5 - 6}{-1 - (-5)} = \dfrac{-1}{4}$

yes

27. slope between $(-3, -2)$ and $(2, -3)$

$= \dfrac{-3 - (-2)}{2 - (-3)} = \dfrac{-1}{5}$

slope between $(-2, 3)$ and $(3, 2)$

$= \dfrac{2 - 3}{3 - (-2)} = \dfrac{-1}{5}$

slope between $(-3, -2)$ and $(-2, 3)$

$= \dfrac{3 - (-2)}{-2 - (-3)} = \dfrac{5}{1} = 5$

slope between $(2, -3)$ and $(3, 2)$

$= \dfrac{2 - (-3)}{3 - 2} = \dfrac{5}{1} = 5$

yes

28. $m = \dfrac{-3 - 0}{4 - 4}$ $\qquad m = \dfrac{3 - 0}{k - 4}$

$\quad = \dfrac{-3}{0}$ $\qquad\qquad = \dfrac{3}{k - 4}$

undefined $\qquad\qquad$ undefined when $k = 4$

29. $m = \dfrac{-11 - (-5)}{-4 - 2}$ $\qquad 1 = \dfrac{1 - (-11)}{k - (-4)}$

$\quad = \dfrac{-6}{-6}$ $\qquad\qquad = \dfrac{12}{k + 4}$

$\quad = 1$ $\qquad\qquad\quad k = 8$

30. $m = \dfrac{5 - (-2)}{0 - 7}$ $\qquad -1 = \dfrac{k - 5}{3 - 0}$

$\quad = \dfrac{7}{-7}$ $\qquad\qquad\quad = \dfrac{k - 5}{3}$

$\quad = -1$ $\qquad\qquad\quad k = 2$

31. $m = \dfrac{-8 - 1}{-3 - 15}$ $\qquad \dfrac{1}{2} = \dfrac{k - (-8)}{3 - (-3)}$

$\quad = \dfrac{-9}{-18}$ $\qquad\qquad = \dfrac{k + 8}{6}$

$\quad = \dfrac{1}{2}$ $\qquad\qquad\quad k = -5$

32. a. $BD = \sqrt{(c - 0)^2 + (a - 0)^2} = \sqrt{c^2 + a^2}$

$AC = \sqrt{(c - 0)^2 + (0 - a)^2} = \sqrt{c^2 + a^2}$

Thus, $\overline{AC} \cong \overline{BD}$

b. The midpoint of $\overline{AC}$ is $\left(\dfrac{c}{2}, \dfrac{a}{2}\right)$. The midpoint of

$\overline{BD}$ is $\left(\dfrac{c}{2}, \dfrac{a}{2}\right)$. Therefore, the diagonals

intersect at their common midpoint, $E\left(\dfrac{c}{2}, \dfrac{a}{2}\right)$.

Thus, $\overline{AE} \cong \overline{EC}$ and $\overline{BE} \cong \overline{ED}$.

c. The diagonals of a rectangle bisect each

other.

33.

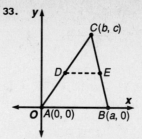

Prove that $DE = \frac{1}{2}AB = \frac{1}{2}a$.

$D = \left(\dfrac{b + 0}{2}, \dfrac{c + 0}{2}\right) = \left(\dfrac{b}{2}, \dfrac{c}{2}\right)$

$E = \left(\dfrac{a + b}{2}, \dfrac{0 + c}{2}\right) = \left(\dfrac{a + b}{2}, \dfrac{c}{2}\right)$

$DE = \sqrt{\left(\dfrac{b}{2} - \dfrac{a + b}{2}\right)^2 + \left(\dfrac{c}{2} - \dfrac{c}{2}\right)^2} = \sqrt{\left(\dfrac{-a}{2}\right)^2} = \dfrac{a}{2}$

34.

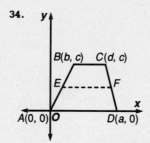

Prove that $EF = \frac{1}{2}(AD + BC)$.

The coordinates of E are $\left(\dfrac{b}{2}, \dfrac{c}{2}\right)$. The coordinates

of F are $\left(\dfrac{a + d}{2}, \dfrac{c}{2}\right)$. $AD = a$; $BC = d - b$.

Therefore, $EF = \sqrt{\left(\dfrac{a + d}{2} - \dfrac{b}{2}\right)^2 + \left(\dfrac{c}{2} - \dfrac{c}{2}\right)^2}$

$\qquad\qquad\quad = \dfrac{a + d - b}{2}$

$\qquad\qquad\quad = \dfrac{1}{2}(a + (d - b))$

$\qquad\qquad\quad = \dfrac{1}{2}(AD + BC)$

35.

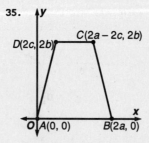

Let the vertices of the isosceles trapezoid

have the coordinates $A(0, 0)$, $B(2a, 0)$,

$C(2a - 2c, 2b)$, $D(2c, 2b)$.

The coordinates of the midpoints are:

$P(a, 0)$, $Q(2a - c, b)$, $R(a, 2b)$, $S(c, b)$.

$$PQ = \sqrt{(2a - c - a)^2 + (b - 0)^2}$$
$$= \sqrt{(a - c)^2 + b^2}$$
$$QR = \sqrt{(2a - c - a)^2 + (b - 2b)^2}$$
$$= \sqrt{(a - c)^2 + b^2}$$
$$RS = \sqrt{(a - c)^2 + (2b - b)^2}$$
$$= \sqrt{(a - c)^2 + b^2}$$
$$PS = \sqrt{(a - c)^2 + (0 - b)^2}$$
$$= \sqrt{(a - c)^2 + b^2}$$

So, all of the sides are congruent and quadrilateral $PQRS$ is a rhombus.

36. a. $\dfrac{60 - 44}{68 - 48} = \dfrac{16}{20} = 0.8$

b. $(1805)(0.8) = \$1444$

37. a. $MPS = 1 - 0.8 = 0.2$

b. $(1805)(0.2) = \$361$

38. a. $m = \dfrac{565 - 295}{80 - 40}$ We know: $295 = 6.75(40) + b$

$\qquad = \dfrac{270}{40}$ $\qquad\qquad\qquad 295 = 270 + b$

$\qquad = 6.75$ $\qquad\qquad\qquad\quad 25 = b$

So, $y = 6.75x + 25$.

b. $\$6.75$

c. $\$25$

39. $f(3) = 5 - 3^2 = -4$

40. $(f \circ g)(x)$ $\qquad\qquad (g \circ f)(f(x))$

$= f(g(x))$ $\qquad\qquad\quad = g(f(x))$

$= -2(x - 6) + 11$ $\qquad = -2x + 11 - 6$

$= -2x + 12 + 11$ $\qquad = -2x + 5$

$= -2x + 23$

41. $(f \cdot g)(x) = x^3(x^2 - 3x + 7)$

$\qquad\qquad\quad = x^5 - 3x^4 + 7x^3$

$\left(\dfrac{f}{g}\right)(x) = \dfrac{x^3}{x^2 - 3x + 7}$

42. $5x - 3 = 0$

$\quad 5x = 3$

$\quad\; x = \dfrac{3}{5}$

43.

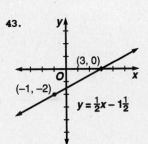

$y = \frac{1}{2}x - 1\frac{1}{2}$

44. Since the area is 2, each side has length $\sqrt{2}$ and the radius of the circle has length equal to the side of the square, $\sqrt{2}$.

So, $A = \pi r^2 = \pi(\sqrt{2})^2 = \pi(2) = 2\pi$.

The best answer is C.

PAGES 39-40   CHECKING FOR UNDERSTANDING

1. The gross national product is the total value of the goods and services produced by the residents of a nation during a specified period, like a year.

2. 5.5 represents the hourly wage and –10 represents a fixed amount taken from the paycheck, like taxes or insurance.

3. Solve the equation for y and use the slope-intercept form to graph the line. Graph the y-intercept and use the slope to find a second point, then sketch a line through them.

4. Use the slope-intercept form when you know the slope and the coordinates of a point. Use the point-slope form when you know the coordinates of two points.

5. Overhead costs include rent, utilities, office supplies, and so on. They are fixed costs, and are often paid monthly.

6. $3x - 2y = 7$ $\qquad\qquad$ **7.** $\quad 8x = 2y - 1$

$\quad -2y = -3x + 7$ $\qquad\qquad \quad 8x + 1 = 2y$

$\qquad y = \dfrac{3}{2}x - \dfrac{7}{2}$ $\qquad\qquad \quad 4x + \dfrac{1}{2} = y$

$m = \dfrac{3}{2},\; b = \dfrac{-7}{2}$ $\qquad\qquad m = 4,\; b = \dfrac{1}{2}$

8. $4x + 3y = 0$ $\qquad\qquad$ **9.** $y - 2 = 4(x - 3)$

$\quad\; 3y = -4x$ $\qquad\qquad\qquad\quad y = 4x - 12 + 2$

$\quad\;\; y = -\dfrac{4}{3}x$ $\qquad\qquad\qquad\; y = 4x - 10$

$m = -\dfrac{4}{3},\; b = 0$

10. $y - 7 = 0(x - 5)$ $\qquad$ **11.** $y - (-4) = -6(x - (-3))$

$\quad y - 7 = 0$ $\qquad\qquad\qquad\quad y + 4 = -6(x + 3)$

$\qquad\; y = 7$ $\qquad\qquad\qquad\qquad\quad y = -6x - 18 - 4$

$\qquad\qquad\qquad\qquad\qquad\qquad\qquad y = -6x - 22$

12. $m = \dfrac{-6 - 6}{-6 - 6}$ $\qquad$ **13.** $m = \dfrac{-3 - 0}{1 - (-2)}$

$\quad = \dfrac{-12}{-12}$ $\qquad\qquad\qquad = \dfrac{-3}{3}$

$\quad = 1$ $\qquad\qquad\qquad\qquad = -1$

$y - 6 = 1(x - 6)$ $\qquad\quad y - 0 = -1(x + 2)$

$\quad y = x - 6 + 6$ $\qquad\qquad\; y = -x - 2$

$\quad y = x$

14. $\quad m = \dfrac{2 - 2}{7 - 4}$

$\qquad\; = \dfrac{0}{3}$

$\qquad\; = 0$

$y - 2 = 0(x - 4)$

$\quad y - 2 = 0$

$\qquad\; y = 2$

15. $y - 2 = 8(x - (-6))$

  $y - 2 = 8x + 48$

  $y = 8x + 50$

16. $y - (-12) = 5(x - (-5))$

  $y + 12 = -5x - 25$

  $y = -5x - 37$

17. $y - 5 = -3(x - 3)$

  $y - 5 = -3x + 9$

  $y = -3x + 14$

18. $y - 4 = \frac{3}{4}(x - (-10))$

  $y - 4 = \frac{3}{4}x + \frac{30}{4}$

  $y = \frac{3}{4}x + \frac{46}{4}$

  $y = \frac{3}{4}x + \frac{23}{2}$

19. $y - 3 = -\frac{1}{4}(x - (-7))$

  $y - 3 = -\frac{1}{4}x - \frac{7}{4}$

  $y = -\frac{1}{4}x + \frac{5}{4}$

20. $y - 11 = \frac{2}{3}(x - 9)$

  $y - 11 = \frac{2}{3}x - 6$

  $y = \frac{2}{3}x + 5$

21. $m = \frac{7 - (-4)}{-1 - (-1)}$

  $= \frac{11}{0}$

  undefined

  Point-slope form is

  undefined. $x = -1$

22. $m = \frac{-1 - (-5)}{2 - 3}$

  $= \frac{4}{-1}$

  $= -4$

  $y - (-5) = -4(x - 3)$

  $y + 5 = -4x + 12$

  $y = -4x + 7$

23. $m = \frac{9 - 2}{7 - 5}$

  $= \frac{7}{2}$

  $y - 2 = \frac{7}{2}(x - 5)$

  $y - 2 = \frac{7}{2}x - \frac{35}{2}$

  $y = \frac{7}{2}x - \frac{31}{2}$

24. $m = \frac{8 - 5}{7 - 2}$

  $= \frac{3}{5}$

  $y - 5 = \frac{3}{5}(x - 2)$

  $y - 5 = \frac{3}{5}x - \frac{6}{5}$

  $y = \frac{3}{5}x + \frac{19}{5}$

25. $m = \frac{4 - 1}{-2 - 3}$

  $= \frac{3}{-5}$

  $y - 1 = -\frac{3}{5}(x - 3)$

  $y - 1 = -\frac{3}{5}x + \frac{9}{5}$

  $y = -\frac{3}{5}x + \frac{14}{5}$

26. $m = \frac{-2 - (-1)}{4 - (-7)}$

  $= \frac{-1}{11}$

  $y - (-1) = -\frac{1}{11}(x - (-7))$

  $y + 1 = -\frac{1}{11}x - \frac{7}{11}$

  $y = -\frac{1}{11}x - \frac{18}{11}$

27.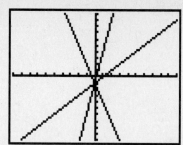

The graphs are all lines. When m is positive, the graph slopes up to the right. When m is negative, the graph slopes down to the right. All three graphs cross the y-axis at $(0, -1)$.

28.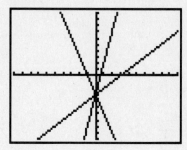

The graphs are all lines. When m is positive, the graph slopes up to the right. When m is negative, the graph slopes down to the right. All three graphs cross the y-axis at $(0, -3)$.

29.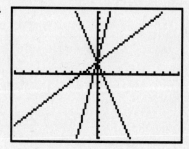

The graphs are all lines. When m is positive, the graph slopes up to the right. When m is negative, the graph slopes down to the right. All three graphs cross the y-axis at $(0, 2)$.

30.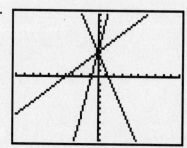

The graphs are all lines. When m is positive, the graph slopes up to the right. When m is negative, the graph slopes down to the right. All three graphs cross the y-axis at $(0, 4)$.

31. AB: $m = \dfrac{1 - (-7)}{5 - 2} = \dfrac{8}{3}$

$$y - (-7) = \dfrac{8}{3}(x - 2)$$

$$y + 7 = \dfrac{8}{3}x - \dfrac{16}{3}$$

$$y = \dfrac{8}{3}x - \dfrac{37}{3}$$

BC: $m = \dfrac{2 - 1}{-3 - 5} = -\dfrac{1}{8}$

$$y - 1 = -\dfrac{1}{8}(x - 5)$$

$$y - 1 = -\dfrac{1}{8}x + \dfrac{5}{8}$$

$$y = -\dfrac{1}{8}x + \dfrac{13}{8}$$

AC: $m = \dfrac{2 - (-7)}{-3 - 2} = -\dfrac{9}{5}$

$$y - (-7) = -\dfrac{9}{5}(x - 2)$$

$$y + 7 = -\dfrac{9}{5}x + \dfrac{18}{5}$$

$$y = -\dfrac{9}{5}x - \dfrac{17}{5}$$

32. PQ: $m = \dfrac{-1 - 4}{4 - 1} = -\dfrac{5}{3}$

$$y - 4 = -\dfrac{5}{3}(x - 1)$$

$$y - 4 = -\dfrac{5}{3}x + \dfrac{5}{3}$$

$$y = -\dfrac{5}{3}x + \dfrac{17}{3}$$

RS: $m = \dfrac{1 - (-4)}{-4 - (-1)} = -\dfrac{5}{3}$

$$y - (-4) = -\dfrac{5}{3}(x - (-1))$$

$$y + 4 = -\dfrac{5}{3}x - \dfrac{5}{3}$$

$$y = -\dfrac{5}{3}x - \dfrac{17}{3}$$

QR: $m = \dfrac{-4 - (-1)}{-1 - 4} = \dfrac{-3}{-5} = \dfrac{3}{5}$

$$y - (-1) = \dfrac{3}{5}(x - 4)$$

$$y + 1 = \dfrac{3}{5}x - \dfrac{12}{5}$$

$$y = \dfrac{3}{5}x - \dfrac{17}{5}$$

PS: $m = \dfrac{1 - 4}{-4 - 1} = \dfrac{-3}{-5} = \dfrac{3}{5}$

$$y - 4 = \dfrac{3}{5}(x - 1)$$

$$y - 4 = \dfrac{3}{5}x - \dfrac{3}{5}$$

$$y = \dfrac{3}{5}x + \dfrac{17}{5}$$

33. a. $m = \dfrac{1250 - 1050}{500 - 100} = \dfrac{200}{400} = \dfrac{1}{2}$

$$y - 1250 = 0.5(x - 500)$$

$$y - 1250 = 0.5x - 250$$

$$y = 0.5x + 1000$$

b. fixed cost = \$1000

variable cost per box = \$0.50

c.

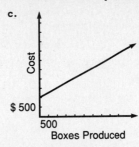

34. a. $m = \dfrac{188 - 173}{44.125 - 38.5}$

$\quad = \dfrac{15}{5.625}$

$\quad = 2\dfrac{2}{3}$

$$y - 188 = 2\dfrac{2}{3}\left(x - 44\dfrac{1}{8}\right)$$

$$y - 188 = \dfrac{8}{3}x - \dfrac{2824}{24}$$

$$y = \dfrac{8}{3}x + \dfrac{1688}{24}$$

$$y = \dfrac{8}{3}x + \dfrac{211}{3}$$

$$y = 2\dfrac{2}{3}x + 70\dfrac{1}{3}$$

b. $y = 2\dfrac{2}{3}(40) + 70\dfrac{1}{3}$

$\quad = \dfrac{320}{3} + \dfrac{211}{3}$

$\quad = \dfrac{531}{3}$

$\quad = 177$ cm

35. a. $m = \dfrac{174 - 160}{26 - 22}$

$\quad = \dfrac{14}{4}$

$\quad = \dfrac{7}{2}$

$$y - 174 = \dfrac{7}{2}(x - 26)$$

$$y - 174 = \dfrac{7}{2}x - 91$$

$$y = \dfrac{7}{2}x + 83$$

b. $157.5 = \dfrac{7}{2}x + 83$

$\quad 74.5 = \dfrac{7}{2}x$

$\quad x \approx 21.286$ cm

36. yes

37. $(f \circ g)(x) = f(g(x))$ $(g \circ f)(x) = g(f(x))$

$\qquad\qquad\quad = 4x^2 - 7$ $\qquad\qquad\quad = 4x^2 - 7$

38.

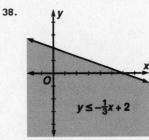

39. $m = \dfrac{3{,}885{,}000 - 2{,}352{,}000}{1990 - 1970}$

$\quad = \dfrac{1{,}533{,}000}{20}$

$\quad = 76{,}650$ people per year

40. $5 \times 6^{12} > 6 \times 5^{12}$

The best answer is A.

Parallel and Perpendicular Lines

1. The definition says that the slopes of any two parallel lines are equal. Vertical lines have no slope, yet they are parallel.

2. $267,000; This makes the proportion
$\frac{24}{30} = \frac{213,600}{267,000}$ true.

3. No; the slopes must be negative reciprocals and thus, their signs must be opposite.

4. All vertical lines have undefined slope and only horizontal lines are perpendicular to them. The slope of all horizontal lines is 0.

5. 3, -3, neither   6. 6, 6, parallel

7. $y = x - 9$, $m = 1$
   $x + y + 9 = 0$
   $\qquad y = -x - 9$, $m = -1$
   perpendicular

8. $y = 2x + 4$, $m = 2$
   $x + 2y + 10 = 0$
   $\qquad 2y = -x - 10$
   $\qquad\qquad y = -\frac{1}{2}x - 5$, $m = -\frac{1}{2}$
   perpendicular

9. $y + 4x - 2 = 0$
   $\qquad y = -4x + 2$, $m = -4$
   $y + 4x + 1 = 0$
   $\qquad y = -4x - 1$, $m = -4$
   parallel

10. $y = 8x - 1$, $m = 8$
    $7x - y - 1 = 0$
    $\qquad 7x - 1 = y$, $m = 7$
    neither

11. parallel: $m = 2$ perpendicular: $m = -\frac{1}{2}$
    $y - 2 = 2(x - 4)$
    $y - 2 = 2x - 8$ $y - 2 = -\frac{1}{2}(x - 4)$
    $\qquad 0 = 2x - y - 6$ $2y - 4 = -x + 4$
    $\qquad\qquad\qquad\qquad x + 2y - 8 = 0$

12. parallel: $m = 2$ perpendicular: $m = -\frac{1}{2}$
    $y - 6 = 2(x - (-3))$
    $y - 6 = 2x + 6$ $y - 6 = -\frac{1}{2}(x - (-3))$
    $\qquad 0 = 2x - y + 12$ $2y - 12 = -x - 3$
    $\qquad\qquad\qquad\qquad x + 2y - 9 = 0$

13. parallel: $m = 2$ perpendicular: $m = -\frac{1}{2}$
    $y - (-2) = 2(x - 8)$
    $\qquad y + 2 = 2x - 16$ $y - (-2) = -\frac{1}{2}(x - 8)$
    $\qquad\qquad 0 = 2x - y - 18$ $2y + 4 = -x + 8$
    $\qquad\qquad\qquad\qquad x + 2y - 4 = 0$

14. parallel: $m = 2$
    $y - (-7) = 2(x - (-5))$
    $\qquad y + 7 = 2(x + 5)$
    $\qquad y + 7 = 2x + 10$
    $\qquad\qquad 0 = 2x - y + 3$
    perpendicular: $m = -\frac{1}{2}$
    $\qquad y - (-7) = -\frac{1}{2}(x - (-5))$
    $\qquad\qquad 2y + 14 = -x - 5$
    $x + 2y + 19 = 0$

15. $WZ = \sqrt{(2 + 1)^2 + (-1 - 3)^2} = \sqrt{9 + 16} = 5$
    $YZ = \sqrt{(2 - 6)^2 + (-1 - 2)^2} = \sqrt{16 + 9} = 5$
    $XY = \sqrt{(6 - 3)^2 + (2 - 6)^2} = \sqrt{9 + 16} = 5$
    $WX = \sqrt{(3 + 1)^2 + (6 - 3)^2} = \sqrt{16 + 9} = 5$
    Thus, $WXYZ$ is a rhombus.
    The slope of $\overline{WX} = \frac{6 - 3}{3 + 1} = \frac{3}{4}$ and the slope of
    $\overline{WZ} = \frac{3 + 1}{-1 - 2} = -\frac{4}{3}$. Thus, $\overline{WX}$ is perpendicular to
    $\overline{WZ}$ and $WXYZ$ is a square.

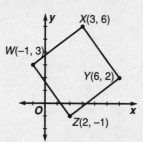

16. slope of $\overline{AC} = \frac{a - 0}{a - 0} = 1$
    slope of $\overline{BD} = \frac{0 - a}{a - 0} = -1$
    Since the slope of $\overline{BD}$ is the negative reciprocal of the slope of $\overline{AC}$, $\overline{AC}$ is perpendicular to $\overline{BD}$.

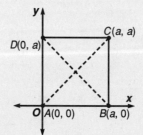

17. $m = 3$
    $y - 6 = 3(x - 0)$
    $\qquad y - 6 = 3x$
    $\qquad\qquad 0 = 3x - y + 6$

18. $m = 2$
    $y - (-2) = 2(x - (-1))$
    $\qquad y + 2 = 2x + 2$
    $\qquad\qquad 0 = 2x - y$

19. $m = 6$

$y - (-3) = 6(x - 0)$

$y + 3 = 6x$

$0 = 6x - y - 3$

20. $m = -4$

$y - (-7) = -4(x - 5)$

$y + 7 = -4x + 20$

$4x + y - 13 = 0$

21. $3y = -2x + 5$

$y = -\frac{2}{3}x + \frac{5}{3}, \ m = -\frac{2}{3}$

$y - 4 = -\frac{2}{3}(x - 2)$

$3y - 12 = -2x + 4$

$2x + 3y - 16 = 0$

22. $-7y = -2x + 3$

$y = \frac{2}{7}x - \frac{3}{7}, \ m = \frac{2}{7}$

$y - 0 = \frac{2}{7}(x - 8)$

$7y = 2x - 16$

$0 = 2x - 7y - 16$

23. $m = \frac{1}{2}$

$y - (-3) = \frac{1}{2}(x - 0)$

$2y + 6 = x$

$0 = x - 2y - 6$

24. $m = -\frac{1}{4}$

$y - 4 = -\frac{1}{4}(x - 3)$

$4y - 16 = -x + 3$

$x + 4y - 19 = 0$

25. $5y = 4x + 10$

$y = \frac{4}{5}x + 2$

$m = -\frac{5}{4}$

$y - 8 = -\frac{5}{4}(x - (-15))$

$4y - 32 = -5x - 75$

$5x + 4y + 43 = 0$

26. $3y = -2x + 3$

$y = -\frac{2}{3}x + 1$

$m = \frac{3}{2}$

$y - (-6) = \frac{3}{2}(x - (-9))$

$2y + 12 = 3x + 27$

$0 = 3x - 2y + 15$

27. $6x + 8 = 4y$

$\frac{3}{2}x + 2 = y$

$m = -\frac{2}{3}$

$y - 12 = -\frac{2}{3}(x - 2)$

$3y - 36 = -2x + 4$

$2x + 3y - 40 = 0$

28. $3x - 8 = y$

$m = -\frac{1}{3}$

$y - 5 = -\frac{1}{3}(x - (-1))$

$3y - 15 = -x - 1$

$x + 3y - 14 = 0$

29. parallel: $kx + 10 = 7y \qquad 8x + 3 = 14y$

$\frac{k}{7}x + \frac{10}{7} = y \qquad \frac{4}{7}x + \frac{3}{14} = y$

$\frac{k}{7} = \frac{4}{7} \ \rightarrow \ k = 4$

perpendicular: $\frac{k}{7} = -\frac{7}{4}$

$4k = -49$

$k = -\frac{49}{4}$

30. parallel: $2x + 5 = ky \qquad 7y = -3x - 15$

$\frac{2}{k}x + \frac{5}{k} = y \qquad y = -\frac{3}{7}x - \frac{15}{7}$

$\frac{2}{k} = -\frac{3}{7}$

$14 = -3k$

$-\frac{14}{3} = k$

perpendicular: $\frac{2}{k} = \frac{7}{3}$

$7k = 6$

$k = \frac{6}{7}$

31. slope of $\overline{AB} = \frac{2 - (-3)}{-1 - 4} = \frac{5}{-5} = -1$

slope of $\overline{BC} = \frac{-1 - (-3)}{-2 - 4} = \frac{2}{-6} = -\frac{1}{3}$

slope of $\overline{CA} = \frac{-1 - 2}{-2 - (-1)} = \frac{-3}{-1} = 3$

The slopes of $\overline{BC}$ and $\overline{CA}$ have a product of -1, so the lines are perpendicular. Therefore, $\triangle ABC$ is a right triangle.

32. $PQ = \sqrt{(3 - 8)^2 + (1 - 1)^2} = \sqrt{(-5)^2 + 0^2} = 5$

$QR = \sqrt{(12 - 8)^2 + (4 - 1)^2} = \sqrt{4^2 + 3^2} = 5$

$RS = \sqrt{(12 - 7)^2 + (4 - 4)^2} = \sqrt{5^2 + 0^2} = 5$

$SP = \sqrt{(7 - 3)^2 + (4 - 1)^2} = \sqrt{4^2 + 3^2} = 5$

slope of $\overline{PQ} = \dfrac{1 - 1}{3 - 8}$ slope of $\overline{QR} = \dfrac{4 - 1}{12 - 8}$

$= \dfrac{0}{-5}$ $= \dfrac{3}{4}$

$= 0$

slope of $\overline{RS} = \dfrac{4 - 4}{12 - 7}$ slope of $\overline{SP} = \dfrac{4 - 1}{7 - 3}$

$= \dfrac{0}{5}$ $= \dfrac{3}{4}$

$= 0$

Since opposite sides are parallel, and all sides are congruent, the figure must be a rhombus.

33. The coordinates of E are $\left(\dfrac{b}{2}, \dfrac{c}{2}\right)$.

The coordinates of F are $\left(\dfrac{a + d}{2}, \dfrac{c}{2}\right)$.

slope of $\overline{EF} = \dfrac{\dfrac{c}{2} - \dfrac{c}{2}}{\dfrac{b}{2} - \dfrac{a + d}{2}} = 0$

Since the slopes of $\overline{BC}$ and $\overline{AD}$ are also zero, $\overline{BC}$, $\overline{AD}$, and $\overline{EF}$ are parallel.

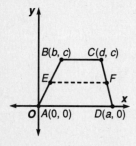

34. first day: $520x + 280y = 1410$

$280y = -520x + 1410$

$y = -\dfrac{13}{7}x + \dfrac{141}{28}$

second day: $390x + 210y = 1057.50$

$210y = -390x + 1057.50$

$y = -\dfrac{13}{7}x + \dfrac{423}{42}$

Since they have the same slope, the graphs are parallel lines. As a result, the ratio of the total sales should be proportional to the ratio of calzones sold from day to day. Since $\dfrac{1057.50}{1410} = \dfrac{210}{280}$, her sales on the second day could have been $1057.50.

35. No, they are riding along parallel lines or the same line, 5 miles apart.

36. $(f \circ g)(4) = f(g(4))$ $(g \circ f)(4) = g(f(4))$

$= 3(21)^2 - 4$ $= 5(44) + 1$

$= 1319$ $= 221$

37.

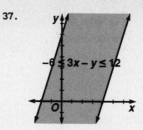

$-6 \leq 3x - y \leq 12$

38. $d = \sqrt{(-2 - 4)^2 + (6 - (-3))^2}$

$= \sqrt{36 + 81}$

$= \sqrt{117}$

39. a. $m = \dfrac{5000 - 3000}{60 - 20} = \dfrac{2000}{40} = 50$

$y - 3000 = 50(x - 20)$

$y = 50x - 1000 + 3000$

$y = 50x + 2000$

So, $C(x) = 50x + 2000$.

b. fixed cost = $2000

variable cost per unit = $50

c.

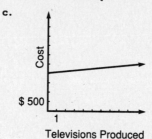

40. $y = 12 - 2x$ $y = 12 - 2(10)$

So, $x + 2(12 - 2x) = -6$ $= -8$

$x + 24 - 4x = -6$

$-3x = -30$

$x = 10$

Therefore, $2x + 2y = 2(10) + 2(-8)$

$= 20 - 16$

$= 4.$

Chapter 1 Summary and Review

PAGES 48-50   SKILLS AND CONCEPTS

1. {(0, -7), (1, -2), (2, 3), (3, 8)}; yes

2. {(-1, -3), (0, 0), (1, 3), (2, 24)}; yes

3. {(5, 1), (5, -1), (6, 2), (6, -2)}; no

4. {(-8, 4), (-7, 3), (-6, 2), (-5, 1), (-4, 0), (-3, 1)}; yes

5. $x = 0$ **6.** $x^2 - 3 = 0$

$x^2 = 3$

$x = \pm\sqrt{3}$

7. $x + 3 = 0$

$\quad x = -3$

8. $2|x| - 5 = 0$

$\quad 2|x| = 5$

$\quad |x| = \dfrac{5}{2}$

$\quad x = \pm\dfrac{5}{2}$

9. $(f \circ g)(x)$
$= f(g(x))$
$= 3(x + 2) - 5$
$= 3x + 6 - 5$
$= 3x + 1$

$(g \circ f)(x)$
$= g(f(x))$
$= 3x - 5 + 2$
$= 3x - 3$

10. $(f \circ g)(x)$
$= f(g(x))$
$= -3(2x^3)^2$
$= -3(4x^6)$
$= -12x^6$

$(g \circ f)(x)$
$= g(f(x))$
$= 2(-3x^2)^3$
$= 2(-27x^6)$
$= -54x^6$

11. $(f \circ g)(x)$
$= f(g(x))$
$= (x + 1)^2 + 2(x + 1) + 3$
$= x^2 + 2x + 1 + 2x + 2 + 3$
$= x^2 + 4x + 6$

$(g \circ f)(x)$
$= g(f(x))$
$= x^2 + 2x + 3 + 1$
$= x^2 + 2x + 4$

12. $(f \circ g)(x) = f(g(x))$

$\quad = \dfrac{1}{2\left(\frac{1}{2}x - 1\right)}$

$\quad = \dfrac{1}{x - 2}$

$(g \circ f)(x) = g(f(x))$

$\quad = \dfrac{1}{2}\left(\dfrac{1}{2}x\right) - 1$

$\quad = \dfrac{1}{4x} - 1$

13.
$y = x^2 - 12$
$x = y^2 - 12$
$x + 12 = y^2$
$\pm\sqrt{x + 12} = y$
$f^{-1}(x) = \pm\sqrt{x + 12}$
no

14.
$y = 6 - 3x$
$x = 6 - 3y$
$x - 6 = -3y$
$-\dfrac{1}{3}x + 2 = y$
$f^{-1}(x) = -\dfrac{1}{3}x + 2$
yes

15.
$y = 8x^3$
$x = 8y^3$
$\dfrac{x}{8} = y^3$
$\dfrac{\sqrt[3]{x}}{2} = y$
$f^{-1}(x) = \dfrac{1}{2}\sqrt[3]{x}$
yes

16.
$y = 3x^3 - 2$
$x = 3y^3 - 2$
$x + 2 = 3y^3$
$\dfrac{x + 2}{3} = y^3$
$\sqrt[3]{\dfrac{x + 2}{3}} = y$
$f^{-1}(x) = \sqrt[3]{\dfrac{x + 2}{3}}$
yes

17. $3x - 8 = 0$

$\quad 3x = 8$

$\quad x = \dfrac{8}{3}$

18. $19 \neq 0$, none

19. $0.25x - 5 = 0$

$\quad 0.25x = 5$

$\quad x = 20$

20. $7x + 1 = 0$

$\quad 7x = -1$

$\quad x = -\dfrac{1}{7}$

21. $d = \sqrt{(5 - 0)^2 + (12 - 0)^2}$
$\quad = \sqrt{25 + 144}$
$\quad = 13$

22. $d = \sqrt{(-3 - 1)^2 + (-4 - (-6))^2}$
$\quad = \sqrt{16 + 4}$
$\quad = \sqrt{20}$
$\quad = 2\sqrt{5}$

23. $d = \sqrt{(a + 3 - a)^2 + (b + 4 - b)^2}$
$\quad = \sqrt{9 + 16}$
$\quad = 5$

24. $d = \sqrt{(3k - 2k)^2 + (6k - 4k)^2}$
$\quad = \sqrt{k^2 + 4k^2}$
$\quad = \sqrt{5k^2}$
$\quad = |k|\sqrt{5}$

25. $y - 5 = 2(x - 5)$
$\quad y = 2x - 10 + 5$
$\quad y = 2x - 5$

26. $y - 3 = -1(x - (-2))$
$\quad y = -x - 2 + 3$
$\quad y = -x + 1$

27. $y - 0 = \dfrac{3}{5}(x - 0)$
$\quad y = \dfrac{3}{5}x$

28. $y - 4 = -\dfrac{4}{3}(x - 1)$
$\quad y = -\dfrac{4}{3}x + \dfrac{4}{3} + 4$
$\quad y = -\dfrac{4}{3}x + \dfrac{16}{3}$

29. $m = \dfrac{10 - 7}{6 - 3}$
$\quad = \dfrac{3}{3}$
$\quad = 1$

$y - 7 = 1(x - 3)$
$\quad y = x - 3 + 7$
$\quad y = x + 4$

30. $m = \dfrac{9 - 0}{5 - (-1)}$
$\quad = \dfrac{9}{6}$
$\quad = \dfrac{3}{2}$

$y - 0 = \dfrac{3}{2}(x - (-1))$
$\quad y = \dfrac{3}{2}x + \dfrac{3}{2}$

31. $m = \dfrac{-3 - 4}{2 - 4}$
$\quad = \dfrac{-7}{-2}$
$\quad = \dfrac{7}{2}$

$y - 4 = \dfrac{7}{2}(x - 4)$
$\quad y = \dfrac{7}{2}x - 14 + 4$
$\quad y = \dfrac{7}{2}x - 10$

32. $m = \dfrac{-9 - (-6)}{10 - 11}$
$\quad = \dfrac{-3}{-1}$
$\quad = 3$

$y - (-6) = 3(x - 11)$
$\quad y = 3x - 33 - 6$
$\quad y = 3x - 39$

33. $m = 4$
$\quad y - 3 = 4(x - (-2))$
$\quad 0 = 4x + 8 - y + 3$
$\quad 0 = 4x - y + 11$

34. $3y = 2x + 5$
$\quad y = \dfrac{2}{3}x + \dfrac{5}{3}, \ m = \dfrac{2}{3}$
$\quad y - 4 = \dfrac{2}{3}(x - 2)$
$\quad 3y - 12 = 2x - 4$
$\quad 0 = 2x - 3y + 8$

35. $6x + 4 = 2y$

$3x + 2 = y$, $m = -\frac{1}{3}$

$y - 4 = -\frac{1}{3}(x - 0)$

$3y - 12 = -x$

$x + 3y - 12 = 0$

36. $y = \frac{4}{5}x + \frac{2}{5}$, $m = -\frac{5}{4}$

$y - 0 = -\frac{5}{4}(x - 5)$

$4y = -5x + 25$

$5x + 4y - 25 = 0$

PAGE 50   APPLICATIONS AND PROBLEM SOLVING

37. a. at $t = 1$, $d = \frac{1}{2}(20)(1)^2 = 10$ m

at $t = 2$, $d = \frac{1}{2}(20)(2)^2 = 40$ m

at $t = 3$, $d = \frac{1}{2}(20)(3)^2 = 90$ m

at $t = 4$, $d = \frac{1}{2}(20)(4)^2 = 160$ m

at $t = 5$, $d = \frac{1}{2}(20)(5)^2 = 250$ m

b. Yes, each element of the domain is paired with exactly one element of the range.

38. The midpoint of $\overline{AC}$ is $\left(\dfrac{a + b + 0}{2}, \dfrac{0 + c}{2}\right)$ or $\left(\dfrac{a + b}{2}, \dfrac{c}{2}\right)$.

The midpoint of $\overline{BD}$ is $\left(\dfrac{a + b}{2}, \dfrac{c + 0}{2}\right)$ or $\left(\dfrac{a + b}{2}, \dfrac{c}{2}\right)$.

Since the coordinates of the midpoint of $\overline{AC}$ are the same as those of $\overline{BD}$, the diagonals bisect each other.

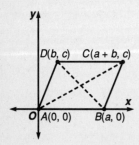

39. $m = \dfrac{200 - 150}{600 - 100} = \dfrac{50}{500} = 0.10$

$y - 200 = 0.10(x - 600)$

$y = 0.10x - 60 + 200$

$y = 0.10x + 140$

fixed cost = \$140

variable cost per candy bar = \$0.10

Chapter 1 Test

PAGE 51

1. {(-2, -7), (-1, -4), (0, -1), (1, 2), (2, 5)}; yes

2. {(0, 5), (0, -5), (1, 7), (1, -7), (2, 9), (2, -9), (3, 11), (3, -11), (4, 13), (4, -13)}; no

3. $f(0) = 0 - 3(0)^2$
   $= 0$

4. $f(4) = 4 - 3(4)^2$
   $= -44$

5. $f(-6) = -6 - 3(-6)^2$
   $= -114$

6. $f(7.1) = 7.1 - 3(7.1)^2$
   $= -144.13$

7. $(f \circ g)(x)$
   $= f(g(x))$
   $= \sqrt{2x^2 - 5}$

   $(g \circ f)(x)$
   $= g(f(x))$
   $= 2(\sqrt{x})^2 - 5$
   $= 2x - 5$

8. $(f \circ g)(x)$
   $= f(g(x))$
   $= 2(5x + 6)^2$
   $= 2(25x^2 + 60x + 36)$
   $= 50x^2 + 120x + 72$

   $(g \circ f)(x)$
   $= g(f(x))$
   $= 5(2x^2) + 6$
   $= 10x^2 + 6$

9. $(f \circ g)(x) = f(g(x))$
   $= -(-3x) - 7$
   $= 3x - 7$

   $(g \circ f)(x)$
   $= g(f(x))$
   $= -3(-x - 7)$
   $= 3x + 21$

10.
$y = \dfrac{x^2 + 5}{3}$

$x = \dfrac{y^2 + 5}{3}$

$3x = y^2 + 5$

$3x - 5 = y^2$

$\pm\sqrt{3x - 5} = y$

$f^{-1}(x) = \pm\sqrt{3x - 5}$

no

11.
$y = \dfrac{1}{4}x + 1$

$x = \dfrac{1}{4}y + 1$

$x - 1 = \dfrac{1}{4}y$

$4x - 4 = y$

$f^{-1}(x) = 4x - 4$

yes

12.
$y = -2(x^3 - 1)$

$x = -2(y^3 - 1)$

$-\dfrac{x}{2} = y^3 - 1$

$-\dfrac{x}{2} + 1 = y^3$

$\sqrt[3]{-\dfrac{x}{2} + 1} = y$

$f^{-1}(x) = \sqrt[3]{-\dfrac{x}{2} + 1}$ yes

13.

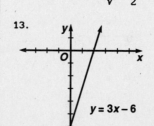

$y = 3x - 6$

14.

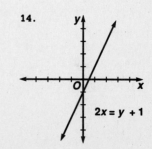

$2x = y + 1$

15.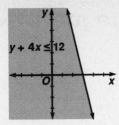

$y + 4x \leq 12$

16.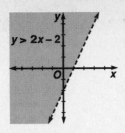

$y > 2x - 2$

17. $d = \sqrt{(3 - (-1))^2 + (1 - 2)^2}$ $m = \dfrac{1 - 2}{3 - (-1)}$

$= \sqrt{16 + 1}$ $= -\dfrac{1}{4}$

$= \sqrt{17}$

18. $d = \sqrt{(12 - 5)^2 + (12 - 11)^2}$ $m = \dfrac{12 - 11}{12 - 5}$

$= \sqrt{49 + 1}$ $= \dfrac{1}{7}$

$= \sqrt{50}$

$= 5\sqrt{2}$

19. $d = \sqrt{(2k - 3k)^2 + (k - 1 - (k + 1))^2}$

$= \sqrt{k^2 + 4}$

$m = \dfrac{k - 1 - (k + 1)}{2k - 3k}$

$= \dfrac{-2}{-k}$

$= \dfrac{2}{k}$

20. $y - 3 = \dfrac{5}{3}(x - (-1))$

$y = \dfrac{5}{3}x + \dfrac{5}{3} + 3$

$y = \dfrac{5}{3}x + \dfrac{14}{3}$

21. $m = \dfrac{-2 - 4}{8 - 0} = -\dfrac{6}{8} = -\dfrac{3}{4}$

$y - 4 = -\dfrac{3}{4}(x - 0)$

$y = -\dfrac{3}{4}x + 4$

22. $2y = -3x + 3$

$y = -\dfrac{3}{2}x + \dfrac{3}{2}, \quad m = -\dfrac{3}{2}$

$y - 4 = -\dfrac{3}{2}(x - 3)$

$2y - 8 = -3x + 9$

$3x + 2y - 17 = 0$

23. $5y = x - 3$

$y = \dfrac{1}{5}x - \dfrac{3}{5}, \quad m = -5$

$y - 0 = -5(x - 0)$

$y = -5x$

$5x + y = 0$

24. D is the midpoint of hypotenuse $\overline{AB}$.

The coordinates of D are $\left(\dfrac{a}{2}, \dfrac{b}{2}\right)$.

$BD = \sqrt{\left(0 - \dfrac{a}{2}\right)^2 + \left(b - \dfrac{b}{2}\right)^2} = \sqrt{\dfrac{a^2}{4} + \dfrac{b^2}{4}}$

$AD = \sqrt{\left(a - \dfrac{a}{2}\right)^2 + \left(0 - \dfrac{b}{2}\right)^2} = \sqrt{\dfrac{a^2}{4} + \dfrac{b^2}{4}}$

$CD = \sqrt{\left(\dfrac{a}{2} - 0\right)^2 + \left(\dfrac{b}{2} - 0\right)^2} = \sqrt{\dfrac{a^2}{4} + \dfrac{b^2}{4}}$

$BD = AD = CD$

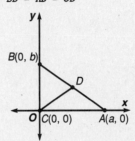

25. $E = \dfrac{750}{4\pi d^2}$

a. $E = \dfrac{750}{4\pi(2.5)^2}$

$= 9.55 \text{ lm/m}^2$

b. d cannot be negative or zero.

PAGE 51   **BONUS**

$f(f(x)) = \dfrac{k\left(\dfrac{kx}{4x + 2}\right)}{4\left(\dfrac{kx}{4x + 2}\right) + 2}$

$= \dfrac{\dfrac{k^2 x}{4x + 2}}{\dfrac{4kx + 8x + 4}{4x + 2}}$

$= \dfrac{k^2 x}{4kx + 8x + 4}$

$x = \dfrac{k^2 x}{4kx + 8x + 4}$

$4kx^2 + 8x^2 + 4x = k^2 x$

$xk^2 - 4x^2 k - 8x^2 - 4x = 0$

$k = \dfrac{4x^2 \pm \sqrt{16x^4 - 4x(-8x^2 - 4x)}}{2x}$

$= \dfrac{4x^2 \pm 4x\sqrt{x^2 + 2x + 1}}{2x}$

$= \dfrac{4x^2 \pm 4x\sqrt{(x + 1)^2}}{2x}$

$= 2x \pm 2(x + 1)$

$= 2x + (2x + 2) \text{ or } 2x - (2x + 2)$

$= 4x + 2 \text{ or } -2$

$k = -2$

Chapter 2   Systems of Equations and Inequalities

**Graphing Calculators:
Graphing Systems
of Linear Equations**

PAGE 55   EXERCISES

1. $(-0.78, -1.67)$

2. $(-0.92, -3.37)$

3. $(-0.88, -2.86)$

4. $(3.93, 7.19)$

5. $4.9x + 0.3y = 1.6$

$\quad 0.3y = -4.9x + 1.6$

$\quad\quad y = -16.3x + 5.3$

$\quad -6.2x + 3.2y = -4.4$

$\quad\quad 3.2y = 6.2x - 4.4$

$\quad\quad\quad y = 1.9x - 1.4$

$\quad (0.37, -0.70)$

6. $8.33x + 3.492y = 3.8$

$\quad\quad 3.492y = -8.33x + 3.8$

$\quad\quad\quad\quad y = -2.39x + 1.1$

$\quad 4.8x - 1.074y = 2.3$

$\quad\quad -1.074y = -4.8x + 2.3$

$\quad\quad\quad\quad y = 4.5x - 2.1$

$\quad (0.46, -0.01)$

Solving Systems of Equations

PAGES 59-60   CHECKING FOR UNDERSTANDING

1. The substitution method is usually easier whenever one or both of the equations are already solved for one variable in terms of the other (for example, $y = 2x - 7$).

2. break-even point

3. A system of equations is inconsistent when it represents two parallel lines; since they have no points in common, there is no solution.

4. Answers may vary.

5. $4\left(\frac{1}{2}\right) + 6 \overset{?}{=} 8$

$\quad\quad 8 = 8$

$6\left(\frac{1}{2}\right) - 2(6) \overset{?}{=} -9$

$\quad\quad -9 = -9$

yes

6. $2\left(\frac{1}{3}\right) + 3\left(\frac{2}{3}\right) \overset{?}{=} 3$

$\quad\quad 2 + 6 \overset{?}{=} 9$

$\quad\quad 8 \neq 9$

$12\left(\frac{1}{3}\right) - 15\left(\frac{2}{3}\right) \overset{?}{=} -4$

$\quad\quad 4 - 10 \overset{?}{=} -4$

$\quad\quad -6 \neq -4$

no

7. $-3(2) + 10(5) \overset{?}{=} 5$

$\quad\quad 44 \neq 5$

$2(2) + 7(5) \overset{?}{=} 24$

$\quad\quad 4 + 35 \overset{?}{=} 24$

$\quad\quad 39 \neq 24$

no

8. $\frac{1}{2}(4) + 5(3) \overset{?}{=} 17$

$\quad\quad 17 = 17$

$3(4) + 2(3) \overset{?}{=} 18$

$\quad\quad 18 = 18$

yes

9. $\frac{1}{3}(-6) - \frac{3}{2}(-4) \overset{?}{=} -4$

$\quad\quad -2 + 6 \overset{?}{=} -4$

$\quad\quad 4 \neq -4$

$5(-6) - 4(-4) \overset{?}{=} 14$

$\quad\quad -30 + 16 \overset{?}{=} 14$

$\quad\quad -14 \neq 14$

no

10. $1.5(4) + 2(7) \overset{?}{=} 20$

$\quad\quad 20 = 20$

$2.5(4) - 5(7) \overset{?}{=} -25$

$\quad\quad -25 = -25$

yes

11.

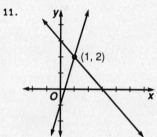

(1, 2)

$y = 3x - 1$

$y = -x + 3$

$\quad (1, 2)$

12. $5x - y = 16 \longrightarrow (5x - 4 = 16) \times 3$

$\quad 2x + 3y = 3 \longrightarrow \quad 2x + 3y = 3$

$\quad 15x - 3y = 48 \quad\quad\quad 5x - y = 16$

$\quad \underline{2x + 3y = 3} \quad\quad\quad 5(3) - y = 16$

$\quad 17x \quad\quad = 51 \quad\quad 15 - y = 16$

$\quad\quad x \quad\quad = 3 \quad\quad\quad y = -1 \quad (3, -1)$

PAGES 60-61   EXERCISES

13. $y = \frac{5}{7}x - 10$

$\quad y = \frac{5}{7}x + \frac{60}{7}$

inconsistent

14. $y = \frac{7}{8}x + \frac{11}{8}$

$\quad y = \frac{7}{8}x + \frac{11}{8}$

consistent and dependent

15. $y = 0.4x - 1.3$

$\quad y = 0.5x - 2.3$

consistent and independent

16.

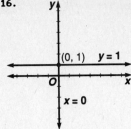

(0, 1) $y = 1$

$x = 0$

(0, 1)

17.

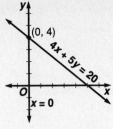

(0, 4)

$4x + 5y = 20$

$x = 0$

(0, 4)

18.

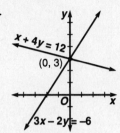

$x + 4y = 12$

(0, 3)

$3x - 2y = -6$

(0, 3)

19.

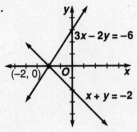

$3x - 2y = -6$

(−2, 0)

$x + y = -2$

(−2, 0)

20.

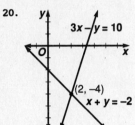

$3x - y = 10$

(2, −4)

$x + y = -2$

(2, −4)

21.

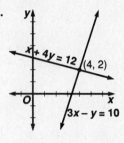

$x + 4y = 12$ (4, 2)

$3x - y = 10$

(4, 2)

22. By substitution,

$x = -2y + 1$ $x + 2(1) = 1$

$3(-2y + 1) - 5y = -8$ $x + 2 = 1$

$-6y + 3 - 5y = -8$ $x = -1$

$-11y = -11$ (−1, 1)

$y = 1$

23. By elimination,

$2x - y = -7 \longrightarrow (2x - y = -7) \times -2$

$x = 2y - 8 \longrightarrow x - 2y = -8$

$-4x + 2y = 14$ $2x - y = -7$

$\underline{\quad x - 2y = -8\quad}$ $2(-2) - y = -7$

$-3x = 6$ $-4 - y = -7$

$x = -2$ $y = 3$ (−2, 3)

24. By elimination,

$3x + 5y = 7 \longrightarrow (3x + 5y = 7) \times -2$

$2x - 6y = 11 \longrightarrow (2x - 6y = 11) \times 3$

$-6x - 10y = -14$ $3x + 5\left(-\dfrac{19}{28}\right) = 7$

$\underline{6x - 18y = 33\quad}$

$-28y = 19$ $3x - \dfrac{95}{28} = 7$

$y = -\dfrac{19}{28}$ $3x = \dfrac{291}{28}$

$x = \dfrac{97}{28}$

$\left(\dfrac{97}{28}, -\dfrac{19}{28}\right)$

25. By elimination,

$3x + 2y = 40 \longrightarrow 3x + 2y = 40$

$x - 7y = -2 \longrightarrow (x - 7y = -2) \times -3$

$3x + 2y = 40$ $3x + 2(2) = 40$

$\underline{-3x + 21y = 6\quad}$ $3x + 4 = 40$

$23y = 46$ $3x = 36$

$y = 2$ $x = 12$ (12, 2)

26. By elimination,

$2x + 3y = 8 \longrightarrow 2x + 3y = 8$

$x - y = 2 \longrightarrow (x - y = 2) \times 3$

$2x + 3y = 8$ $x - y = 2$

$\underline{3x - 3y = 6\quad}$ $\dfrac{14}{5} - y = 2$

$5x = 14$

$x = \dfrac{14}{5}$ $\dfrac{14}{5} - \dfrac{10}{5} = y$

$\dfrac{4}{5} = y$ $\left(\dfrac{14}{5}, \dfrac{4}{5}\right)$

27. By elimination,

$x + y = 6 \longrightarrow x + y = 6$ $5.25 + y = 6$

$x = y + 4.5 \longrightarrow \underline{x - y = 4.5\quad}$ $y = 6 - 5.25$

$2x = 10.5$ $y = 0.75$

$x = 5.25$ (5.25, 0.75)

28. See students' programming work.

  a. (1, 0)   **b.** inconsistent or dependent

  c. (−3, −3)

29. Solve each equation for y.

$4x + 3y + 1 = 0$ $4x - 3y - 17 = 0$

$y = -\dfrac{4}{3}x - \dfrac{1}{3}$ $y = \dfrac{4}{3}x - \dfrac{17}{3}$

$4x - 9y + 13 = 0$

$y = \dfrac{4}{9}x + \dfrac{13}{9}$

Pair each equation with each of the others and solve each system.

$y = -\dfrac{4}{3}x - \dfrac{1}{3}$ $y = -\dfrac{4}{3}x - \dfrac{1}{3}$ $y = \dfrac{4}{3}x - \dfrac{17}{3}$

$y = \dfrac{4}{3}x - \dfrac{17}{3}$ $y = \dfrac{4}{9}x + \dfrac{13}{9}$ $y = \dfrac{4}{9}x + \dfrac{13}{9}$

  (2, −3)   (−1, 1)   (8, 5)

30. a. Let y = monetary value.   **b.** 201 sweatshirts

  Let x = number of sweatshirts.

  cost function: $y = 5x + 2000$

  revenue function: $y = 15x$

  (200, 3000)

31. Let s = acres of soybeans and c = acres of corn.

$6s + 8c = 660$

$s + c = 100 \rightarrow s = -c + 100$

$6(-c + 100) + 8c = 660$

$2c + 600 = 660$

$c = 30$

$s = -30 + 100 = 70$

(70, 30)

70 acres of soybeans, 30 acres of corn

32. Let x = number of three-bedroom homes.

Let y = number of four-bedroom homes.

profit function: $2,500,000 = 6000x + 7000y$

ratio function: $3y = x$

By substitution,

$2,500,000 = 6000(3y) + 7000y$ $3(100) = x$

$2,500,000 = 18,000y + 7000y$ $300 = x$

$2,500,000 = 25,000y$

       $100 = y$

300 three-bedroom homes and 100 four-bedroom

homes

33. The domain is {16}. The range is {-4, 4}. no

34. (0, 0): $0 + 0 \not\geq 3$

(-4, 2): $-4 + 2 \not\geq 3$

(3, 2): $3 + 2 \geq 3$

(-2, 4): $-2 + 4 \not\geq 3$ (3, 2)

35. $m = \dfrac{y_2 - y_1}{x_2 - x_1}$ $4 = \dfrac{3}{4}(1) + b$ $y = \dfrac{3}{4}x + 3\dfrac{1}{4}$

     $= \dfrac{7 - 4}{5 - 1}$ $\dfrac{16}{4} = \dfrac{3}{4} + b$

     $= \dfrac{3}{4}$ $\dfrac{13}{4} = b$

               $3\dfrac{1}{4} = b$

36.

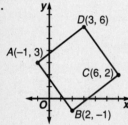

$AB = \sqrt{(2 + 1)^2 + (-1 - 3)^2} = 5$

$BC = \sqrt{(2 - 6)^2 + (-1 - 2)^2} = 5$

$CD = \sqrt{(6 - 3)^2 + (2 - 6)^2} = 5$

$DA = \sqrt{(3 + 1)^2 + (6 - 3)^2} = 5$

Thus, $ABCD$ is a rhombus. The slope of $\overline{AD}$ =

$\dfrac{6 - 3}{3 + 1} = \dfrac{3}{4}$, and the slope of $\overline{AB} = \dfrac{3 + 1}{-1 - 2} = -\dfrac{4}{3}$.

Thus, $\overline{AD}$ is perpendicular to $\overline{AB}$ and $ABCD$ is a

square.

37. The present age is the sum of y, the former age,

and x, the intervening years: $x + y$. A year

ago, the person's age would be the present age,

$x + y$, minus 1 year: $y + x - 1$. The best

answer is D.

Graphing Calculators: Matrices

PAGE 63   EXERCISES

See students' programming work.

1. $\begin{bmatrix} -10 & -4 & -8 \\ -2 & 8 & 6 \\ 0 & -12 & -6 \end{bmatrix}$ **2.** 48

3. $\begin{bmatrix} 0.125 & 0.375 & 0.2083 \\ -0.0625 & 0.3125 & 0.39583 \\ 0.125 & -0.625 & -0.4583 \end{bmatrix}$

4. $\begin{bmatrix} 6 & 24 \\ 21 & -15 \\ 6 & 3 \end{bmatrix}$ **5.** $\begin{bmatrix} 32 & 34 \\ -32 & 25 \\ 48 & -27 \end{bmatrix}$

6. $\begin{bmatrix} 56 & -34 & 50 \\ -35 & 46 & -23 \\ 7 & 1 & 8 \end{bmatrix}$ **7.** 0

8. $\begin{bmatrix} 23 & -14 \\ -9 & 87 \end{bmatrix}$ **9.** 1875

10. $\begin{bmatrix} 3 & -6 & -6 \\ 30 & 70 & 61 \end{bmatrix}$ **11.** $\begin{bmatrix} 3 & -3 & -5 \\ 37 & 65 & 67 \end{bmatrix}$

12. $\begin{bmatrix} 51 & -36 & 46 \\ -36 & 50 & -20 \\ 7 & -5 & 5 \end{bmatrix}$ **13.** $\begin{bmatrix} 655 & -1540 \\ -990 & 7695 \end{bmatrix}$

14. $\begin{bmatrix} 0.0464 & 0.00746 \\ 0.0048 & 0.01226 \end{bmatrix}$ **15.** $\begin{bmatrix} 61 & -32 & 54 \\ -34 & 42 & -26 \\ 7 & 7 & 11 \end{bmatrix}$

16. $\begin{bmatrix} 238 & -74 & 236 \\ 175 & -221 & 118 \\ -189 & 279 & -114 \end{bmatrix}$ **17.** $\begin{bmatrix} 34 & 42 \\ -25 & 20 \\ 50 & -26 \end{bmatrix}$

18. $\begin{bmatrix} 224 & -136 & 200 \\ -140 & 184 & -92 \\ 28 & 4 & 32 \end{bmatrix}$

Introduction to Matrices

PAGE 68   CHECKING FOR UNDERSTANDING

1. The dimensions of a matrix are given by $m \times n$,

where m is the number of rows in the matrix and

n is the number of columns.

2. b_{45} **3.** Answers will vary.

4. Answers will vary.

5. $A + B = \begin{bmatrix} 3 & 0 \\ -1 & 5 \end{bmatrix} + \begin{bmatrix} 5 & 1 \\ -3 & 4 \end{bmatrix}$

     $= \begin{bmatrix} 3 + 5 & 0 + 1 \\ -1 + (-3) & 5 + 4 \end{bmatrix} = \begin{bmatrix} 8 & 1 \\ -4 & 9 \end{bmatrix}$

6. $A - B = A + (-B)$

     $= \begin{bmatrix} 3 & 0 \\ -1 & 5 \end{bmatrix} + \begin{bmatrix} -5 & -1 \\ 3 & -4 \end{bmatrix}$

     $= \begin{bmatrix} 3 + (-5) & 0 + (-1) \\ -1 + 3 & 5 + (-4) \end{bmatrix} = \begin{bmatrix} -2 & -1 \\ 2 & 1 \end{bmatrix}$

7. $B - A = B + (-A)$

     $= \begin{bmatrix} 5 & 1 \\ -3 & 4 \end{bmatrix} + \begin{bmatrix} -3 & 0 \\ 1 & -5 \end{bmatrix}$

     $= \begin{bmatrix} 5 + (-3) & 1 + 0 \\ -3 + 1 & 4 + (-5) \end{bmatrix} = \begin{bmatrix} 2 & 1 \\ -2 & -1 \end{bmatrix}$

8. $5C = 5\begin{bmatrix} 3 \\ -1 \end{bmatrix} = \begin{bmatrix} 5(3) \\ 5(-1) \end{bmatrix} = \begin{bmatrix} 15 \\ -5 \end{bmatrix}$

9. $-3B = -3\begin{bmatrix} 5 & 1 \\ -3 & 4 \end{bmatrix} = \begin{bmatrix} -3(5) & -3(1) \\ -3(-3) & -3(4) \end{bmatrix} = \begin{bmatrix} -15 & -3 \\ 9 & -12 \end{bmatrix}$

10. $AC = \begin{bmatrix} 3 & 0 \\ -1 & 5 \end{bmatrix}\begin{bmatrix} 3 \\ -1 \end{bmatrix} = \begin{bmatrix} 3(3) + 0(-1) \\ -1(3) + 5(-1) \end{bmatrix} = \begin{bmatrix} 9 \\ -8 \end{bmatrix}$

11. $AB = \begin{bmatrix} 3 & 0 \\ -1 & 5 \end{bmatrix}\begin{bmatrix} 5 & 1 \\ -3 & 4 \end{bmatrix}$

$= \begin{bmatrix} 3(5) + 0(-3) & 3(1) + 0(4) \\ -1(5) + 5(-3) & -1(1) + 5(4) \end{bmatrix} = \begin{bmatrix} 15 & 3 \\ -20 & 19 \end{bmatrix}$

12. $AB = \begin{bmatrix} 3 & 0 \\ -1 & 5 \end{bmatrix}\begin{bmatrix} 5 & 1 \\ -3 & 4 \end{bmatrix}$

$= \begin{bmatrix} 3(5) + 0(-3) & 3(1) + 0(4) \\ -1(5) + 5(-3) & -1(1) + 5(4) \end{bmatrix} = \begin{bmatrix} 15 & 3 \\ -20 & 19 \end{bmatrix}$

$ABC = \begin{bmatrix} 15 & 3 \\ -20 & 19 \end{bmatrix}\begin{bmatrix} 3 \\ -1 \end{bmatrix} = \begin{bmatrix} 15(3) + 3(-1) \\ -20(3) + 19(-1) \end{bmatrix} = \begin{bmatrix} 42 \\ -79 \end{bmatrix}$

13. $BB = \begin{bmatrix} 5 & 1 \\ -3 & 4 \end{bmatrix}\begin{bmatrix} 5 & 1 \\ -3 & 4 \end{bmatrix}$

$= \begin{bmatrix} 5(5) + 1(-3) & 5(1) + 1(4) \\ -3(5) + 4(-3) & -3(1) + 4(4) \end{bmatrix} = \begin{bmatrix} 22 & 9 \\ -27 & 13 \end{bmatrix}$

14. $\begin{bmatrix} y \\ x \end{bmatrix} = \begin{bmatrix} 2x - 6 \\ 2y \end{bmatrix}$ $\quad y = 2x - 6$ $\quad x = 2y$

By substitution, $y = 2(2y) - 6$ $\quad x = 2(2)$

$\qquad\qquad\qquad y = 4y - 6$ $\qquad x = 4$

$\qquad\qquad\qquad 6 = 3y$ $\qquad\qquad (4, 2)$

$\qquad\qquad\qquad 2 = y$

15. $\begin{bmatrix} 5x - 3y \\ 3y \end{bmatrix} = \begin{bmatrix} 8 \\ 27 \end{bmatrix}$ $\quad 5x - 3y = 8$

$\qquad\qquad\qquad\qquad\qquad 3y = 27 \longrightarrow y = 9$

By substitution, $5x - 3(9) = 8$

$\qquad\qquad\qquad 5x - 27 = 8$

$\qquad\qquad\qquad 5x = 35$

$\qquad\qquad\qquad x = 7 \qquad (7, 9)$

PAGES 68-70   EXERCISES

16. $A + B = \begin{bmatrix} 1 & 5 & 7 \\ 5 & 2 & -6 \\ 3 & 0 & -2 \end{bmatrix} + \begin{bmatrix} -3 & 6 & -9 \\ 4 & -3 & 0 \\ 8 & -2 & 3 \end{bmatrix}$

$= \begin{bmatrix} 1 + (-3) & 5 + 6 & 7 + (-9) \\ 5 + 4 & 2 + (-3) & -6 + 0 \\ 3 + 8 & 0 + (-2) & -2 + 3 \end{bmatrix}$

$= \begin{bmatrix} -2 & 11 & -2 \\ 9 & -1 & -6 \\ 11 & -2 & 1 \end{bmatrix}$

17. $A + C = \begin{bmatrix} 1 & 5 & 7 \\ 5 & 2 & -6 \\ 3 & 0 & -2 \end{bmatrix} + \begin{bmatrix} 6 & 9 & -4 \\ -11 & 13 & -8 \\ 20 & 4 & -2 \end{bmatrix}$

$= \begin{bmatrix} 1 + 6 & 5 + 9 & 7 + (-4) \\ 5 + (-11) & 2 + 13 & -6 + (-8) \\ 3 + 20 & 0 + 4 & -2 + (-2) \end{bmatrix}$

$= \begin{bmatrix} 7 & 14 & 3 \\ -6 & 15 & -14 \\ 23 & 4 & -4 \end{bmatrix}$

18. $B + C = \begin{bmatrix} -3 & 6 & -9 \\ 4 & -3 & 0 \\ 8 & -2 & 3 \end{bmatrix} + \begin{bmatrix} 6 & 9 & -4 \\ -11 & 13 & -8 \\ 20 & 4 & -2 \end{bmatrix}$

$= \begin{bmatrix} -3 + 6 & 6 + 9 & -9 + (-4) \\ 4 + (-11) & -3 + 13 & 0 + (-8) \\ 8 + 20 & -2 + 4 & 3 + (-2) \end{bmatrix}$

$= \begin{bmatrix} 3 & 15 & -13 \\ -7 & 10 & -8 \\ 28 & 2 & 1 \end{bmatrix}$

19. $(A + B) + C$

$= \begin{bmatrix} 1 & 5 & 7 \\ 5 & 2 & -6 \\ 3 & 0 & -2 \end{bmatrix} + \begin{bmatrix} -3 & 6 & -9 \\ 4 & -3 & 0 \\ 8 & -2 & 3 \end{bmatrix} + \begin{bmatrix} 6 & 9 & -4 \\ -11 & 13 & -8 \\ 20 & 4 & -2 \end{bmatrix}$

$= \begin{bmatrix} 1 + (-3) & 5 + 6 & 7 + (-9) \\ 5 + 4 & 2 + (-3) & -6 + 0 \\ 3 + 8 & 0 + (-2) & -2 + 3 \end{bmatrix} +$

$\begin{bmatrix} 6 & 9 & -4 \\ -11 & 13 & -8 \\ 20 & 4 & -2 \end{bmatrix}$

$= \begin{bmatrix} -2 & 11 & -2 \\ 9 & -1 & -6 \\ 11 & -2 & 1 \end{bmatrix} + \begin{bmatrix} 6 & 9 & -4 \\ -11 & 13 & -8 \\ 20 & 4 & -2 \end{bmatrix}$

$= \begin{bmatrix} -2 + 6 & 11 + 9 & -2 + (-4) \\ 9 + (-11) & -1 + 13 & -6 + (-8) \\ 11 + 20 & -2 + 4 & 1 + (-2) \end{bmatrix}$

$= \begin{bmatrix} 4 & 20 & -6 \\ -2 & 12 & -14 \\ 31 & 2 & -1 \end{bmatrix}$

20. $B + (-A) = \begin{bmatrix} -3 & 6 & -9 \\ 4 & -3 & 0 \\ 8 & -2 & 3 \end{bmatrix} + \begin{bmatrix} -1 & -5 & -7 \\ -5 & -2 & 6 \\ -3 & 0 & 2 \end{bmatrix}$

$= \begin{bmatrix} -3 + (-1) & 6 + (-5) & -9 + (-7) \\ 4 + (-5) & -3 + (-2) & 0 + 6 \\ 8 + (-3) & -2 + 0 & 3 + 2 \end{bmatrix}$

$= \begin{bmatrix} -4 & 1 & -16 \\ -1 & -5 & 6 \\ 5 & -2 & 5 \end{bmatrix}$

21. $C - B = C + (-B)$

$= \begin{bmatrix} 6 & 9 & -4 \\ -11 & 13 & -8 \\ 20 & 4 & -2 \end{bmatrix} + \begin{bmatrix} 3 & -6 & 9 \\ -4 & 3 & 0 \\ -8 & 2 & -3 \end{bmatrix}$

$= \begin{bmatrix} 6 + 3 & 9 + (-6) & -4 + 9 \\ -11 + (-4) & 13 + 3 & -8 + 0 \\ 20 + (-8) & 4 + 2 & -2 + (-3) \end{bmatrix}$

$= \begin{bmatrix} 9 & 3 & 5 \\ -15 & 16 & -8 \\ 12 & 6 & -5 \end{bmatrix}$

22. $B - C = B + (-C)$

$= \begin{bmatrix} -3 & 6 & -9 \\ 4 & -3 & 0 \\ 8 & -2 & 3 \end{bmatrix} + \begin{bmatrix} -6 & -9 & 4 \\ 11 & -13 & 8 \\ -20 & -4 & 2 \end{bmatrix}$

$= \begin{bmatrix} -3 + (-6) & 6 + (-9) & -9 + 4 \\ 4 + 11 & -3 + (-13) & 0 + 8 \\ 8 + (-20) & -2 + (-4) & 3 + 2 \end{bmatrix}$

$= \begin{bmatrix} -9 & -3 & -5 \\ 15 & -16 & 8 \\ -12 & -6 & 5 \end{bmatrix}$

23. $C - A = C + (-A)$

$= \begin{bmatrix} 6 & 9 & -4 \\ -11 & 13 & -8 \\ 20 & 4 & -2 \end{bmatrix} + \begin{bmatrix} -1 & -5 & -7 \\ -5 & -2 & 6 \\ -3 & 0 & 2 \end{bmatrix}$

$= \begin{bmatrix} 6 + (-1) & 9 + (-5) & -4 + (-7) \\ -11 + (-5) & 13 + (-2) & -8 + 6 \\ 20 + (-3) & 4 + 0 & -2 + 2 \end{bmatrix}$

$= \begin{bmatrix} 5 & 4 & -11 \\ -16 & 11 & -2 \\ 17 & 4 & 0 \end{bmatrix}$

24. $B - A = B + (-A)$

$= \begin{bmatrix} -3 & 6 & -9 \\ 4 & -3 & 0 \\ 8 & -2 & 3 \end{bmatrix} + \begin{bmatrix} -1 & -5 & -7 \\ -5 & -2 & 6 \\ -3 & 0 & 2 \end{bmatrix}$

$= \begin{bmatrix} -3 + (-1) & 6 + (-5) & -9 + (-7) \\ 4 + (-5) & -3 + (-2) & 0 + 6 \\ 8 + (-3) & -2 + 0 & 3 + 2 \end{bmatrix}$

$= \begin{bmatrix} -4 & 1 & -16 \\ -1 & -5 & 6 \\ 5 & -2 & 5 \end{bmatrix}$

25. $x = y + 5$ By substitution,

$2y = x - 3$ $2y = (y + 5) - 3$ $x = 2 + 5$

$2y = y + 2$ $x = 7$

$y = 2$ $(7, 2)$

26. $5 = 2x \longrightarrow \dfrac{5}{2} = x$ By substitution,

$4x = 5y$

$$4\left(\dfrac{5}{2}\right) = 5y$$

$$10 = 5y$$

$$2 = y \qquad \left(\dfrac{5}{2},\ 2\right)$$

27. $2x = 8 - y$ By substitution, Check:

$0 = y$ $2x = 8 - 0$ $16 \overset{?}{=} 4(4)$

$16 = 4x$ $x = 4$ $16 = 16 \quad (4, 0)$

28. $y = 15 + x$ By substitution,

$8x = 2y$ $8x = 2(15 + x)$ $y = 15 + 5$

$8x = 30 + 2x$ $y = 20$

$6x = 30$ $(5, 20)$

$x = 5$

29. $3D = 3\begin{bmatrix} 7 & 0 \\ 5 & 3 \end{bmatrix} = \begin{bmatrix} 3(7) & 3(0) \\ 3(15) & 3(3) \end{bmatrix} = \begin{bmatrix} 21 & 0 \\ 15 & 9 \end{bmatrix}$

30. $4E = 4\begin{bmatrix} 2 & 4 \\ 8 & -4 \\ -2 & 6 \end{bmatrix} = \begin{bmatrix} 4(2) & 4(4) \\ 4(8) & 4(-4) \\ 4(-2) & 4(6) \end{bmatrix} = \begin{bmatrix} 8 & 16 \\ 32 & -16 \\ -8 & 24 \end{bmatrix}$

31. $2F = 2\begin{bmatrix} 3 & -3 & 6 \\ 5 & 4 & -2 \end{bmatrix}$

$= \begin{bmatrix} 2(3) & 2(-3) & 2(6) \\ 2(5) & 2(4) & 2(-2) \end{bmatrix} = \begin{bmatrix} 6 & -6 & 12 \\ 10 & 8 & -4 \end{bmatrix}$

32. $-5D = -5\begin{bmatrix} 7 & 0 \\ 5 & 3 \end{bmatrix} = \begin{bmatrix} -5(7) - 5(0) \\ -5(5) - 5(3) \end{bmatrix} = \begin{bmatrix} -35 & 0 \\ -25 & -15 \end{bmatrix}$

33. $ED = \begin{bmatrix} 2 & 4 \\ 8 & -4 \\ -2 & 6 \end{bmatrix} \begin{bmatrix} 7 & 0 \\ 5 & 3 \end{bmatrix}$

$= \begin{bmatrix} 2(7) + 4(5) & 2(0) + 4(3) \\ 8(7) + [-4(5)] & 8(0) + [-4(3)] \\ -2(7) + 6(5) & -2(0) + 6(3) \end{bmatrix}$

$= \begin{bmatrix} 34 & 12 \\ 36 & -12 \\ 16 & 18 \end{bmatrix}$

34. $EF = \begin{bmatrix} 2 & 4 \\ 8 & -4 \\ -2 & 6 \end{bmatrix} \begin{bmatrix} 3 & -3 & 6 \\ 5 & 4 & -2 \end{bmatrix}$

$= \begin{bmatrix} 2(3) + 4(5) & 2(-3) + 4(4) & 2(6) + 4(-2) \\ 8(3) + [-4(5)] & 8(-3) + [-4(4)] & 8(6) + [-4(-2)] \\ -2(3) + 6(5) & -2(-3) + 6(4) & -2(6) + 6(-2) \end{bmatrix}$

$= \begin{bmatrix} 26 & 10 & 4 \\ 4 & -40 & 56 \\ 24 & 30 & -24 \end{bmatrix}$

35. $FE = \begin{bmatrix} 3 & -3 & 6 \\ 5 & 4 & -2 \end{bmatrix} \begin{bmatrix} 2 & 4 \\ 8 & -4 \\ -2 & 6 \end{bmatrix}$

$= \begin{bmatrix} 3(2) + [-3(8)] + 6(-2) & 3(4) + [-3(-4)] + 6(6) \\ 5(2) + 4(8) + [-2(-2)] & 5(4) + 4(-4) + [-2(6)] \end{bmatrix}$

$= \begin{bmatrix} -30 & 60 \\ 46 & -8 \end{bmatrix}$

36. $DF = \begin{bmatrix} 7 & 0 \\ 5 & 3 \end{bmatrix} \begin{bmatrix} 3 & -3 & 6 \\ 5 & 4 & -2 \end{bmatrix}$

$= \begin{bmatrix} 7(3) + 0(5) & 7(-3) + 0(4) & 7(6) + 0(-2) \\ 5(3) + 3(5) & 5(-3) + 3(4) & 5(6) + 3(-2) \end{bmatrix}$

$= \begin{bmatrix} 21 & -21 & 42 \\ 30 & -3 & 24 \end{bmatrix}$

37. $DD = \begin{bmatrix} 7 & 0 \\ 5 & 3 \end{bmatrix} \begin{bmatrix} 7 & 0 \\ 5 & 3 \end{bmatrix}$

$= \begin{bmatrix} 7(7) + 0(5) & 7(0) + 0(3) \\ 5(7) + 3(5) & 5(0) + 3(3) \end{bmatrix} = \begin{bmatrix} 49 & 0 \\ 50 & 9 \end{bmatrix}$

38. $(FE)D$

$= \begin{bmatrix} 3 & -3 & 6 \\ 5 & 4 & -2 \end{bmatrix} \begin{bmatrix} 2 & 4 \\ 8 & -4 \\ -2 & 6 \end{bmatrix} \begin{bmatrix} 7 & 0 \\ 5 & 3 \end{bmatrix}$

$= \begin{bmatrix} 3(2)+[-3(8)]+6(-2) & 3(4)+[-3(-4)]+6(6) \\ 5(2)+4(8)+[-2(-2)] & 5(4)+4(-4)+[-2(6)] \end{bmatrix} \begin{bmatrix} 7 & 0 \\ 5 & 3 \end{bmatrix}$

$= \begin{bmatrix} -30 & 60 \\ 46 & -8 \end{bmatrix} \begin{bmatrix} 7 & 0 \\ 5 & 3 \end{bmatrix}$

$= \begin{bmatrix} -30(7) + 60(5) & -30(0) + 60(3) \\ 46(7) + [-8(5)] & 46(0) + [-8(3)] \end{bmatrix}$

$= \begin{bmatrix} 90 & 180 \\ 282 & -24 \end{bmatrix}$

39. $E(DF)$

$= \begin{bmatrix} 2 & 4 \\ 8 & -4 \\ -2 & 6 \end{bmatrix} \begin{bmatrix} 7 & 0 \\ 5 & 3 \end{bmatrix} \begin{bmatrix} 3 & -3 & 6 \\ 5 & 4 & -2 \end{bmatrix}$

$= \begin{bmatrix} 2 & 4 \\ 8 & -4 \\ -2 & 6 \end{bmatrix} \begin{bmatrix} 7(3)+0(5) & 7(-3)+0(4) & 7(6)+0(-2) \\ 5(3)+3(5) & 5(-3)+3(4) & 5(6)+3(-2) \end{bmatrix}$

$= \begin{bmatrix} 2 & 4 \\ 8 & -4 \\ -2 & 6 \end{bmatrix} \begin{bmatrix} 21 & -21 & 42 \\ 30 & -3 & 24 \end{bmatrix}$

$= \begin{bmatrix} 2(21)+4(30) & 2(-21)+4(-3) & 2(42)+4(24) \\ 8(21)+[-4(30)] & 8(-21)+[-4(-3)] & 8(42)+[-4(24)] \\ -2(21)+6(30) & -2(-21)+6(-3) & -2(42)+6(24) \end{bmatrix}$

$= \begin{bmatrix} 162 & -54 & 180 \\ 48 & -156 & 240 \\ 138 & 24 & 60 \end{bmatrix}$

40. $-4EF$

$= -4\begin{bmatrix} 2 & 4 \\ 8 & -4 \\ -2 & 6 \end{bmatrix} \begin{bmatrix} 3 & -3 & 6 \\ 5 & 4 & -2 \end{bmatrix}$

$= \begin{bmatrix} -4(2) & -4(4) \\ -4(8) & -4(-4) \\ -4(-2) & -4(6) \end{bmatrix} \begin{bmatrix} 3 & -3 & 6 \\ 5 & 4 & -2 \end{bmatrix}$

$= \begin{bmatrix} -8 & -16 \\ -32 & 16 \\ 8 & -24 \end{bmatrix} \begin{bmatrix} 3 & -3 & 6 \\ 5 & 4 & -2 \end{bmatrix}$

$= \begin{bmatrix} -8(3)+[-16(5)] & -8(-3)+[-16(4)] & -8(6)+[-16(-2)] \\ -32(3)+16(5) & -32(-3)+16(4) & -32(6)+16(-2) \\ 8(3)+[-24(5)] & 8(-3)+[-24(4)] & 8(6)+[-24(-2)] \end{bmatrix}$

$= \begin{bmatrix} -104 & -40 & -16 \\ -16 & 160 & -224 \\ -96 & -120 & 96 \end{bmatrix}$

41. $2A - 3B = 2A + (-3B)$

$= 2\begin{bmatrix} 1 & -7 \\ 3 & 2 \end{bmatrix} + (-3)\begin{bmatrix} -4 & 5 \\ 1 & -1 \end{bmatrix}$

$= \begin{bmatrix} 2(1) & 2(-7) \\ 2(3) & 2(2) \end{bmatrix} + \begin{bmatrix} -3(-4) & -3(5) \\ -3(1) & -3(-1) \end{bmatrix}$

$= \begin{bmatrix} 2 & -14 \\ 6 & 4 \end{bmatrix} + \begin{bmatrix} 12 & -15 \\ -3 & 3 \end{bmatrix}$

$= \begin{bmatrix} 2 + 12 & -14 + (-15) \\ 6 + (-3) & 4 + 3 \end{bmatrix}$

$= \begin{bmatrix} 14 & -29 \\ 3 & 7 \end{bmatrix}$

42. Let $A = \begin{bmatrix} a_{11} & a_{12} \\ a_{21} & a_{22} \end{bmatrix}$ and $B = \begin{bmatrix} b_{11} & b_{12} \\ b_{21} & b_{22} \end{bmatrix}$.

$$A + B = \begin{bmatrix} a_{11} & a_{12} \\ a_{21} & a_{22} \end{bmatrix} + \begin{bmatrix} b_{11} & b_{12} \\ b_{21} & b_{22} \end{bmatrix}$$

$$= \begin{bmatrix} a_{11} + b_{11} & a_{12} + b_{12} \\ a_{21} + b_{21} & a_{22} + b_{22} \end{bmatrix}$$

$$= \begin{bmatrix} b_{11} + a_{11} & b_{12} + a_{12} \\ b_{21} + a_{21} & b_{22} + a_{22} \end{bmatrix}$$

$$= \begin{bmatrix} b_{11} & b_{12} \\ b_{21} & b_{22} \end{bmatrix} + \begin{bmatrix} a_{11} & a_{12} \\ a_{21} & a_{22} \end{bmatrix}$$

$$= B + A$$

Addition of 2×2 matrices is commutative.

43. Let $A = \begin{bmatrix} a_{11} & a_{12} \\ a_{21} & a_{22} \end{bmatrix}$, $B = \begin{bmatrix} b_{11} & b_{12} \\ b_{21} & b_{22} \end{bmatrix}$, $C = \begin{bmatrix} c_{11} & c_{12} \\ c_{21} & c_{22} \end{bmatrix}$.

$$(A + B) + C = \begin{bmatrix} a_{11} + b_{11} & a_{12} + b_{12} \\ a_{21} + b_{21} & a_{22} + b_{22} \end{bmatrix} + \begin{bmatrix} c_{11} & c_{12} \\ c_{21} & c_{22} \end{bmatrix}$$

$$= \begin{bmatrix} (a_{11} + b_{11}) + c_{11} & (a_{12} + b_{12}) + c_{12} \\ (a_{21} + b_{21}) + c_{21} & (a_{22} + b_{22}) + c_{22} \end{bmatrix}$$

$$= \begin{bmatrix} a_{11} + (b_{11} + c_{11}) & a_{12} + (b_{12} + c_{12}) \\ a_{21} + (b_{21} + c_{21}) & a_{22} + (b_{22} + c_{22}) \end{bmatrix}$$

$$= A + (B + C)$$

Addition of 2×2 matrices is associative.

44. Let $A = \begin{bmatrix} a_{11} & a_{12} \\ a_{21} & a_{22} \end{bmatrix}$ and $B = \begin{bmatrix} b_{11} & b_{12} \\ b_{21} & b_{22} \end{bmatrix}$.

$$AB = \begin{bmatrix} a_{11}b_{11} + a_{12}b_{21} & a_{11}b_{12} + a_{12}b_{22} \\ a_{21}b_{11} + a_{22}b_{21} & a_{21}b_{12} + a_{22}b_{22} \end{bmatrix}$$

$$BA = \begin{bmatrix} b_{11}a_{11} + b_{12}a_{21} & b_{11}a_{12} + b_{12}a_{22} \\ b_{21}a_{11} + b_{22}a_{21} & b_{21}a_{12} + b_{22}a_{22} \end{bmatrix}$$

Thus, $AB \neq BA$ since $a_{12}b_{21} \neq b_{12}a_{21}$.

Multiplication of two second-order matrices is <u>not</u> commutative.

45. Let $A = \begin{bmatrix} a_{11} & a_{12} \\ a_{21} & a_{22} \end{bmatrix}$, $B = \begin{bmatrix} b_{11} & b_{12} \\ b_{21} & b_{22} \end{bmatrix}$ and $C = \begin{bmatrix} c_{11} & c_{12} \\ c_{21} & c_{22} \end{bmatrix}$.

$$(AB)C = \begin{bmatrix} a_{11}b_{11} + a_{12}b_{21} & a_{11}b_{12} + a_{12}b_{22} \\ a_{21}b_{11} + a_{22}b_{21} & a_{21}b_{12} + a_{22}b_{22} \end{bmatrix} \begin{bmatrix} c_{11} & c_{12} \\ c_{21} & c_{22} \end{bmatrix}$$

$$= \begin{bmatrix} a_{11}b_{11}c_{11} + a_{12}b_{21}c_{11} + a_{11}b_{12}c_{21} + a_{12}b_{22}c_{21} \\ a_{21}b_{11}c_{11} + a_{22}b_{21}c_{11} + a_{21}b_{12}c_{21} + a_{22}b_{22}c_{21} \end{bmatrix}$$
$$\begin{bmatrix} a_{11}b_{11}c_{12} + a_{12}b_{21}c_{12} + a_{11}b_{12}c_{22} + a_{12}b_{22}c_{22} \\ a_{21}b_{11}c_{12} + a_{22}b_{21}c_{12} + a_{21}b_{12}c_{22} + a_{22}b_{22}c_{22} \end{bmatrix}$$

$$A(BC) = \begin{bmatrix} a_{11} & a_{12} \\ a_{21} & a_{22} \end{bmatrix} \begin{bmatrix} b_{11}c_{11} + b_{12}c_{21} & b_{11}c_{12} + b_{12}c_{22} \\ b_{21}c_{11} + b_{22}c_{21} & b_{21}c_{12} + b_{22}c_{22} \end{bmatrix}$$

$$= \begin{bmatrix} a_{11}b_{11}c_{11} + a_{11}b_{12}c_{21} + a_{12}b_{21}c_{11} + a_{12}b_{22}c_{21} \\ a_{21}b_{11}c_{11} + a_{21}b_{12}c_{21} + a_{22}b_{21}c_{11} + a_{22}b_{22}c_{21} \end{bmatrix}$$
$$\begin{bmatrix} a_{11}b_{11}c_{12} + a_{11}b_{12}c_{22} + a_{12}b_{21}c_{12} + a_{12}b_{22}c_{22} \\ a_{21}b_{11}c_{12} + a_{21}b_{12}c_{22} + a_{22}b_{21}c_{12} + a_{22}b_{22}c_{22} \end{bmatrix}$$

Therefore $(AB)C = A(BC)$. Multiplication of three second-order matrices is associative.

46. Only columns 2 and 4 contain even numbers. By extending their patterns slightly, one can see that only column 2 contains multiples of 8. Since 1992 is a multiple of 8, it will be in column 2.

47. $\begin{matrix} TF \\ FG \\ BR \end{matrix} \begin{bmatrix} 1021 & 523 \\ 2547 & 785 \\ 3652 & 2456 \end{bmatrix} \begin{bmatrix} 6 & 4 \end{bmatrix} = \begin{bmatrix} 1021(6) + 523(4) \\ 2547(6) + 785(4) \\ 3652(6) + 2456(4) \end{bmatrix}$

$$= \begin{bmatrix} 8218 \\ 18,422 \\ 31,736 \end{bmatrix}$$

TF = \$8218, FG = \$18,422, BR = \$31,736

48. $3\begin{bmatrix} 2 & 5 \\ -4 & 5 \\ 3 & -7 \end{bmatrix} = \begin{bmatrix} 6 & 15 \\ -12 & 15 \\ 9 & -21 \end{bmatrix}$

$D(6, 15)$, $E(-12, 15)$, $F(9, -21)$

49. $[f \circ g](x) = f(g(x))$

$$= f(x - 1)$$

$$= (x - 1)^2 + 3(x - 1) + 2$$

$$= (x^2 - 2x + 1) + (3x - 3) + 2$$

$$= x^2 + x$$

$[g \circ f](x) = g(f(x))$

$$= g(x^2 + 3x + 2)$$

$$= (x^2 + 3x + 2) - 1$$

$$= x^2 + 3x + 1$$

50.

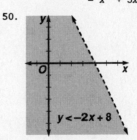

$y < -2x + 8$

51. $d = \sqrt{(5t - 2t)^2 + (5t - t)^2}$ $m = \dfrac{5t - t}{5t - 2t}$

$\quad = \sqrt{(3t)^2 + (4t)^2}$ $\quad = \dfrac{4t}{3t}$

$\quad = \sqrt{9t^2 + 16t^2}$ $\quad = \dfrac{4}{3}$

$\quad = \sqrt{25t^2}$

$\quad = 5|t|$

52. $y = mx + b$

$5 = -2(1) + b$

$5 = -2 + b$

$7 = b$

Thus, $y = -2x + 7$.

53. By elimination,

$3x + 4y = 375$	$\longrightarrow$	$3x + 4y = 375$
$(5x + 2y = 345)(-2)$	$\longrightarrow$	$-10x - 4y = -690$

$\begin{array}{r} 3x + 4y = 375 \\ -10x - 4y = -690 \\ \hline -7x \quad\quad = -315 \\ x \quad\quad = 45 \end{array}$ $\qquad$ $\begin{array}{r} 3(45) + 4y = 375 \\ 135 + 4y = 375 \\ 4y = 240 \\ y = 60 \quad (45, 60) \end{array}$

54. If x is the reciprocal of y, then $x = \frac{1}{y}$.

arithmetic mean of x and y

$$= \frac{y + \frac{1}{y}}{2} = \frac{\frac{y^2 + 1}{y}}{2} = \frac{y^2 + 1}{y} \times \frac{1}{2} = \frac{y^2 + 1}{2y}$$

The best answer is A.

2-3 Determinants and Multiplicative Inverses of Matrices

PAGE 75   CHECKING FOR UNDERSTANDING

1. No, a matrix must be square in order for it to have a determinant.

2. A matrix is nonsingular when its determinant is nonzero.

3. All elements are 0s except for the elements on the main diagonal, which are 1s.

4. If the determinant is zero, then part of the inverse is $\frac{1}{0}$, which is undefined.

5. $3(9) - [-5(7)] = 62$ 6. $10(25) - 50(-5) = 500$

7. $7 \begin{vmatrix} -1 & 4 \\ 3 & 0 \end{vmatrix} - 1 \begin{vmatrix} 3 & 4 \\ -2 & 0 \end{vmatrix} + 6 \begin{vmatrix} 3 & -1 \\ -2 & 3 \end{vmatrix}$

$= 7(-12) - 1(8) + 6(7)$

$= -84 - 8 + 42 = -50$

8. $2 \begin{vmatrix} 2 & 3 \\ -1 & 4 \end{vmatrix} - 4 \begin{vmatrix} 1 & 3 \\ 3 & 4 \end{vmatrix} + 6 \begin{vmatrix} 1 & 2 \\ 3 & -1 \end{vmatrix}$

$= 2(11) - 4(-5) + 6(-7) = 22 + 20 - 42 = 0$

9. $\frac{1}{10} \begin{vmatrix} 1 & -3 \\ 4 & -2 \end{vmatrix}$ 10. $\frac{1}{0}$; does not exist

11. $-\frac{1}{28} \begin{bmatrix} -3 & -8 \\ -2 & 4 \end{bmatrix} \begin{bmatrix} 4 & 8 \\ 2 & -3 \end{bmatrix} \begin{bmatrix} x \\ y \end{bmatrix} = -\frac{1}{28} \begin{bmatrix} -3 & -8 \\ -2 & 4 \end{bmatrix} \begin{bmatrix} 7 \\ 0 \end{bmatrix}$

$\begin{bmatrix} x \\ y \end{bmatrix} = -\frac{1}{28} \begin{bmatrix} -3(7) + (-8(0)) \\ -2(7) + 4(0) \end{bmatrix}$

$\begin{bmatrix} x \\ y \end{bmatrix} = -\frac{1}{28} \begin{bmatrix} -21 \\ -14 \end{bmatrix}$

$\begin{bmatrix} x \\ y \end{bmatrix} = \begin{bmatrix} \frac{3}{4} \\ \frac{1}{2} \end{bmatrix}$ $\left(\frac{3}{4}, \frac{1}{2}\right)$

12. $-\frac{1}{37} \begin{bmatrix} -5 & -4 \\ -3 & 5 \end{bmatrix} \begin{bmatrix} 5 & 4 \\ 3 & -5 \end{bmatrix} \begin{bmatrix} x \\ y \end{bmatrix} = -\frac{1}{37} \begin{bmatrix} -5 & -4 \\ -3 & 5 \end{bmatrix} \begin{bmatrix} -3 \\ -24 \end{bmatrix}$

$\begin{bmatrix} x \\ y \end{bmatrix} = -\frac{1}{37} \begin{bmatrix} -5(-3) + (-4)(-24) \\ -3(-3) + 5(-24) \end{bmatrix}$

$\begin{bmatrix} x \\ y \end{bmatrix} = -\frac{1}{37} \begin{bmatrix} 111 \\ -111 \end{bmatrix}$

$\begin{bmatrix} x \\ y \end{bmatrix} = \begin{bmatrix} -3 \\ 3 \end{bmatrix}$ $(-3, 3)$

PAGE 75-77   EXERCISES

13. $7(8) - 16(3) = 8$ 14. $-4(2) - 8(0) = -8$

15. $16(16) - 17(15) = 1$

16. $6 \begin{vmatrix} -4 & 3 \\ 1 & 1 \end{vmatrix} - 7 \begin{vmatrix} -2 & 3 \\ 1 & 1 \end{vmatrix} + 4 \begin{vmatrix} -2 & -4 \\ 1 & 1 \end{vmatrix}$

$= 6(-7) - 7(-5) + 4(2) = -42 + 35 + 8 = 1$

---

17. $3 \begin{vmatrix} -1 & 5 \\ 7 & 0 \end{vmatrix} - 0 \begin{vmatrix} 0 & 5 \\ 6 & 0 \end{vmatrix} + 2 \begin{vmatrix} 0 & -1 \\ 6 & 7 \end{vmatrix}$

$= 3(-35) - 0(-11) + 2(6) = -105 - 0 + 12 = -93$

18. $4 \begin{vmatrix} 1 & 0 \\ 1 & 11 \end{vmatrix} - 2 \begin{vmatrix} 5 & 0 \\ -2 & 11 \end{vmatrix} + (-3) \begin{vmatrix} 5 & 1 \\ -2 & 1 \end{vmatrix}$

$= 4(11) - 2(55) - 3(7) = 44 - 110 - 21 = -87$

19. $\begin{bmatrix} -1 & 2 \\ 0 & -1 \end{bmatrix}$ 20. $\frac{1}{0}$; does not exist   21. $-\frac{1}{5} \begin{bmatrix} -3 & -1 \\ -2 & 1 \end{bmatrix}$

22. $\frac{1}{32} \begin{bmatrix} 1 & 5 \\ -6 & 2 \end{bmatrix}$ 23. $\frac{1}{7} \begin{bmatrix} 1 & -1 \\ 4 & 3 \end{bmatrix}$ 24. $-\frac{1}{3} \begin{bmatrix} 1 & -2 \\ -2 & 1 \end{bmatrix}$

25.

$\begin{bmatrix} 5 & 1 \\ 2 & -3 \end{bmatrix} \begin{bmatrix} x \\ y \end{bmatrix} = \begin{bmatrix} 26 \\ 41 \end{bmatrix}$

$-\frac{1}{17} \begin{bmatrix} -3 & -1 \\ -2 & 5 \end{bmatrix} \begin{bmatrix} 5 & 1 \\ 2 & -3 \end{bmatrix} \begin{bmatrix} x \\ y \end{bmatrix} = -\frac{1}{17} \begin{bmatrix} -3 & -1 \\ -2 & 5 \end{bmatrix} \begin{bmatrix} 26 \\ 41 \end{bmatrix}$

$\begin{bmatrix} x \\ y \end{bmatrix} = -\frac{1}{17} \begin{bmatrix} -3(26) + (-1)(41) \\ -2(26) + 5(51) \end{bmatrix}$

$\begin{bmatrix} x \\ y \end{bmatrix} = -\frac{1}{17} \begin{bmatrix} -119 \\ 153 \end{bmatrix}$

$\begin{bmatrix} x \\ y \end{bmatrix} = \begin{bmatrix} 7 \\ -9 \end{bmatrix}$ $(7, -9)$

26.

$\begin{bmatrix} 5 & 1 \\ 9 & 3 \end{bmatrix} \begin{bmatrix} x \\ y \end{bmatrix} = \begin{bmatrix} 1 \\ 1 \end{bmatrix}$

$\frac{1}{6} \begin{bmatrix} 3 & -1 \\ -9 & 5 \end{bmatrix} \begin{bmatrix} 5 & 1 \\ 9 & 3 \end{bmatrix} \begin{bmatrix} x \\ y \end{bmatrix} = \frac{1}{6} \begin{bmatrix} 3 & -1 \\ -9 & 5 \end{bmatrix} \begin{bmatrix} 1 \\ 1 \end{bmatrix}$

$\begin{bmatrix} x \\ y \end{bmatrix} = \frac{1}{6} \begin{bmatrix} 3(1) + (-1)(1) \\ -9(1) + 5(1) \end{bmatrix}$

$\begin{bmatrix} x \\ y \end{bmatrix} = \frac{1}{6} \begin{bmatrix} 2 \\ -4 \end{bmatrix}$

$\begin{bmatrix} x \\ y \end{bmatrix} = \begin{bmatrix} \frac{1}{3} \\ -\frac{2}{3} \end{bmatrix}$ $\left(\frac{1}{3}, -\frac{2}{3}\right)$

27. $-\frac{1}{9} \begin{bmatrix} -1 & -10 & 4 \\ -3 & -3 & 3 \\ -1 & 8 & -5 \end{bmatrix} \begin{bmatrix} 1 & 2 & 2 \\ 2 & -1 & 1 \\ 3 & -2 & 3 \end{bmatrix} \begin{bmatrix} x \\ y \\ z \end{bmatrix}$

$= -\frac{1}{9} \begin{bmatrix} -1 & -10 & 4 \\ -3 & -3 & 3 \\ -1 & 8 & -5 \end{bmatrix} \begin{bmatrix} 0 \\ -1 \\ -4 \end{bmatrix}$

$\begin{bmatrix} x \\ y \\ z \end{bmatrix} = -\frac{1}{9} \begin{bmatrix} -1(0) + (-10)(-1) + 4(-4) \\ -3(0) + (-3)(-1) + 3(-4) \\ -1(0) + 8(-1) + (-5)(-4) \end{bmatrix}$

$\begin{bmatrix} x \\ y \\ z \end{bmatrix} = -\frac{1}{9} \begin{bmatrix} -6 \\ -9 \\ 12 \end{bmatrix} = \begin{bmatrix} \frac{2}{3} \\ 1 \\ -\frac{4}{3} \end{bmatrix}$ $\left(\frac{2}{3}, 1, -\frac{4}{3}\right)$

28. $-\frac{1}{9} \begin{bmatrix} 1 & -1 & -2 \\ 21 & -12 & -15 \\ -33 & 15 & 21 \end{bmatrix} \begin{bmatrix} 3 & 1 & 1 \\ -6 & 5 & 3 \\ 9 & -2 & -1 \end{bmatrix} \begin{bmatrix} x \\ y \\ z \end{bmatrix}$

$= -\frac{1}{9} \begin{bmatrix} 1 & -1 & -2 \\ 21 & -12 & -15 \\ -33 & 15 & 21 \end{bmatrix} \begin{bmatrix} -1 \\ -9 \\ 5 \end{bmatrix}$

$\begin{bmatrix} x \\ y \\ z \end{bmatrix} = -\frac{1}{9} \begin{bmatrix} 1(-1) + (-1)(-9) + (-2)(5) \\ 21(-1) + (-12)(-9) + (-15)(5) \\ -33(-1) + 15(-9) + 21(5) \end{bmatrix}$

$\begin{bmatrix} x \\ y \\ z \end{bmatrix} = -\frac{1}{9} \begin{bmatrix} -2 \\ 12 \\ 3 \end{bmatrix} = \begin{bmatrix} \frac{2}{9} \\ -\frac{4}{3} \\ -\frac{1}{3} \end{bmatrix}$ $\left(\frac{2}{9}, -\frac{4}{3}, -\frac{1}{3}\right)$

29. $\begin{vmatrix} 1 & 2 & 3 & 1 \\ 4 & 3 & -1 & 0 \\ 2 & -5 & 4 & 4 \\ 1 & -2 & 0 & 2 \end{vmatrix} = 1\begin{vmatrix} 3 & -1 & 0 \\ -5 & 4 & 4 \\ -2 & 0 & 2 \end{vmatrix} - 2\begin{vmatrix} 4 & -1 & 0 \\ 2 & 4 & 4 \\ 1 & 0 & 2 \end{vmatrix} +$

$\qquad\qquad 3\begin{vmatrix} 4 & 3 & 0 \\ 2 & -5 & 4 \\ 1 & -2 & 2 \end{vmatrix} - 1\begin{vmatrix} 4 & 3 & -1 \\ 2 & -5 & 4 \\ 1 & -2 & 0 \end{vmatrix}$

$\begin{vmatrix} 3 & -1 & 0 \\ -5 & 4 & 4 \\ -2 & 0 & 2 \end{vmatrix} = 3\begin{vmatrix} 4 & 4 \\ 0 & 2 \end{vmatrix} - (-1)\begin{vmatrix} -5 & 4 \\ -2 & 2 \end{vmatrix} + 0\begin{vmatrix} -5 & 4 \\ 2 & 0 \end{vmatrix}$

$= 3(8 - 0) + 1(-10 + 8) + 0(0 - 8) = 22$

$\begin{vmatrix} 4 & -1 & 0 \\ 2 & 4 & 4 \\ 1 & 0 & 2 \end{vmatrix} = 4\begin{vmatrix} 4 & 4 \\ 0 & 2 \end{vmatrix} - (-1)\begin{vmatrix} 2 & 4 \\ 1 & 2 \end{vmatrix} + 0\begin{vmatrix} 2 & 4 \\ 1 & 0 \end{vmatrix}$

$= 4(8 - 0) + 1(4 - 4) + 0(0 - 4) = 32$

$\begin{vmatrix} 4 & 3 & 0 \\ 2 & -5 & 4 \\ 1 & -2 & 2 \end{vmatrix} = 4\begin{vmatrix} -5 & 4 \\ -2 & 2 \end{vmatrix} - 3\begin{vmatrix} 2 & 4 \\ 1 & 2 \end{vmatrix} + 0\begin{vmatrix} 2 & -5 \\ 1 & -2 \end{vmatrix}$

$= 4(-10 + 8) - 3(4 - 4) + 0(-4 + 5) = -8$

$\begin{vmatrix} 4 & 3 & -1 \\ 2 & -5 & 4 \\ 1 & -2 & 0 \end{vmatrix} = 4\begin{vmatrix} -5 & 4 \\ -2 & 0 \end{vmatrix} - 3\begin{vmatrix} 2 & 4 \\ 1 & 0 \end{vmatrix} + (-1)\begin{vmatrix} 2 & -5 \\ 1 & -2 \end{vmatrix}$

$= 4(0 + 8) - 3(0 - 4) - 1(-4 + 5) = 43$

$\begin{vmatrix} 1 & 2 & 3 & 1 \\ 4 & 3 & -1 & 0 \\ 2 & -5 & 4 & 4 \\ 1 & -2 & 0 & 2 \end{vmatrix} = 1(22) - 2(32) + 3(-8) - 1(43)$
$\qquad\qquad\qquad = -109$

30. $\begin{vmatrix} 7 & 0 & 9 & 5 \\ 8 & 2 & -1 & 2 \\ -5 & 3 & 7 & 9 \\ 0 & -1 & -4 & -6 \end{vmatrix} = 7\begin{vmatrix} 2 & -1 & 2 \\ 3 & 7 & 9 \\ -1 & -4 & -6 \end{vmatrix} - 0\begin{vmatrix} 8 & -1 & 2 \\ -5 & 7 & 9 \\ 0 & -4 & -6 \end{vmatrix} +$

$\qquad\qquad 9\begin{vmatrix} 8 & 2 & 2 \\ -5 & 3 & 9 \\ 0 & -1 & -6 \end{vmatrix} - 5\begin{vmatrix} 8 & 2 & -1 \\ -5 & 3 & 7 \\ 0 & -1 & -4 \end{vmatrix}$

$\begin{vmatrix} 2 & -1 & 2 \\ 3 & 7 & 9 \\ -1 & -4 & -6 \end{vmatrix} = 2\begin{vmatrix} 7 & 9 \\ -4 & -6 \end{vmatrix} - (-1)\begin{vmatrix} 3 & 9 \\ -1 & -6 \end{vmatrix} + 2\begin{vmatrix} 3 & 7 \\ -1 & -4 \end{vmatrix}$

$= 2(-42 + 36) + 1(-18 + 9) + 2(-12 + 7) = -31$

$\begin{vmatrix} 8 & -1 & 2 \\ -5 & 7 & 9 \\ 0 & -4 & -6 \end{vmatrix} = 8\begin{vmatrix} 7 & 9 \\ -4 & -6 \end{vmatrix} - (-1)\begin{vmatrix} -5 & 9 \\ 0 & -6 \end{vmatrix} + 2\begin{vmatrix} -5 & 7 \\ 0 & 4 \end{vmatrix}$

$= 8(-6) + 1(21) + 2(-20) = -67$

$\begin{vmatrix} 8 & 2 & 2 \\ -5 & 3 & 9 \\ 0 & -1 & -6 \end{vmatrix} = 8\begin{vmatrix} 3 & 9 \\ -1 & -6 \end{vmatrix} - 2\begin{vmatrix} -5 & 9 \\ 0 & -6 \end{vmatrix} + 2\begin{vmatrix} -5 & 3 \\ 0 & -1 \end{vmatrix}$

$= 8(-18 + 9) - 2(30 - 0) + 2(5 - 3) = -122$

$\begin{vmatrix} 8 & 2 & -1 \\ -5 & 3 & 7 \\ 0 & -1 & -4 \end{vmatrix} = 8\begin{vmatrix} 3 & 7 \\ -1 & -4 \end{vmatrix} - 2\begin{vmatrix} -5 & 7 \\ 0 & -4 \end{vmatrix} + (-1)\begin{vmatrix} -5 & 3 \\ 0 & -1 \end{vmatrix}$

$= 8(-12 + 7) - 2(20 - 0) - 1(5 - 0) = -85$

$\begin{vmatrix} 7 & 0 & 9 & 5 \\ 8 & 2 & -1 & 2 \\ -5 & 3 & 7 & 9 \\ 0 & -1 & -4 & -6 \end{vmatrix} = 7(-31) - 0(-67) + 9(-122)$
$\qquad\qquad\qquad - 5(-85) = -890$

31. $\begin{vmatrix} 3 & 0 & 0 & 4 & 0 \\ 6 & -3 & 2 & 0 & 7 \\ 0 & 4 & 3 & 0 & 5 \\ 0 & 2 & 1 & 3 & -4 \\ 6 & 0 & -2 & -3 & 0 \end{vmatrix} = 3\begin{vmatrix} -3 & 2 & 0 & 7 \\ 4 & 3 & 0 & 5 \\ 2 & 1 & 3 & -4 \\ 0 & -2 & -3 & 0 \end{vmatrix} - 4\begin{vmatrix} 6 & -3 & 2 & 7 \\ 0 & 4 & 3 & 5 \\ 0 & 2 & 1 & -4 \\ 6 & 0 & -2 & 0 \end{vmatrix}$

$\begin{vmatrix} -3 & 2 & 0 & 7 \\ 4 & 3 & 0 & 5 \\ 2 & 1 & 3 & -4 \\ 0 & -2 & -3 & 0 \end{vmatrix} = -3\begin{vmatrix} 3 & 0 & 5 \\ 1 & 3 & -4 \\ -2 & -3 & 0 \end{vmatrix} - 2\begin{vmatrix} 4 & 0 & 5 \\ 2 & 3 & -4 \\ 0 & -3 & 0 \end{vmatrix} + 0 -$

$\qquad\qquad 7\begin{vmatrix} 4 & 3 & 0 \\ 2 & 1 & 3 \\ 0 & -2 & -3 \end{vmatrix}$

$\qquad = -3(-21) - 2(-78) - 7(30) = 9$

$\begin{vmatrix} 6 & -3 & 2 & 7 \\ 0 & 4 & 3 & 5 \\ 0 & 2 & 1 & -4 \\ 6 & 0 & -2 & 0 \end{vmatrix} = 6\begin{vmatrix} 4 & 3 & 5 \\ 2 & 1 & -4 \\ 0 & -2 & 0 \end{vmatrix} + 3\begin{vmatrix} 0 & 3 & 5 \\ 0 & 1 & -4 \\ 6 & -2 & 0 \end{vmatrix} +$

$\qquad\qquad 2\begin{vmatrix} 0 & 4 & 5 \\ 0 & 2 & -4 \\ 6 & 0 & 0 \end{vmatrix} - 7\begin{vmatrix} 0 & 4 & 3 \\ 0 & 2 & 1 \\ 6 & 0 & -2 \end{vmatrix}$

$= 6(-52) + 3(-102) + 2(-156) - 7(-12) = -846$

$\begin{vmatrix} 3 & 0 & 0 & 4 & 0 \\ 6 & -3 & 2 & 0 & 7 \\ 0 & 4 & 3 & 0 & 5 \\ 0 & 2 & 1 & 3 & -4 \\ 6 & 0 & -2 & -3 & 0 \end{vmatrix} = 3(9) - 4(-846) = 3411$

32. $[A] = \begin{bmatrix} 3 & -3 & 6 \\ 1 & -3 & 10 \\ -1 & 3 & -5 \end{bmatrix}$ Input coefficient matrix $[A]$

$[B] = \begin{bmatrix} 30 \\ 50 \\ 40 \end{bmatrix}$ Input answer matrix $[B]$

Find inverse of $[A]$ and multiply by $[B]$.

$(26, 52, 18)$

33. Let $A = \begin{bmatrix} a_{11} & a_{12} \\ a_{21} & a_{22} \end{bmatrix}$ and $I = \begin{bmatrix} 1 & 0 \\ 0 & 1 \end{bmatrix}$.

$AI = \begin{bmatrix} a_{11} & a_{12} \\ a_{21} & a_{22} \end{bmatrix}\begin{bmatrix} 1 & 0 \\ 0 & 1 \end{bmatrix} = \begin{bmatrix} a_{11} + 0 & 0 + a_{12} \\ a_{21} + 0 & 0 + a_{22} \end{bmatrix}$

$\qquad = \begin{bmatrix} a_{11} & a_{12} \\ a_{21} & a_{22} \end{bmatrix} = A$

$IA = \begin{bmatrix} 1 & 0 \\ 0 & 1 \end{bmatrix}\begin{bmatrix} a_{11} & a_{12} \\ a_{21} & a_{22} \end{bmatrix} = \begin{bmatrix} a_{11} + 0 & a_{12} + 0 \\ 0 + a_{21} & 0 + a_{22} \end{bmatrix}$

$\qquad = \begin{bmatrix} a_{11} & a_{12} \\ a_{21} & a_{22} \end{bmatrix} = A$

Therefore, $AI = IA = A$ for second-order matrices.

34.

Let $A = \begin{bmatrix} a_{11} & a_{12} \\ a_{21} & a_{22} \end{bmatrix}$ and $I = \begin{bmatrix} 1 & 0 \\ 0 & 1 \end{bmatrix}$.

$$A^{-1} = \begin{bmatrix} \dfrac{a_{22}}{a_{11}a_{22} - a_{21}a_{12}} & \dfrac{-a_{12}}{a_{11}a_{22} - a_{21}a_{12}} \\[4mm] \dfrac{-a_{21}}{a_{11}a_{22} - a_{21}a_{12}} & \dfrac{a_{11}}{a_{11}a_{22} - a_{21}a_{12}} \end{bmatrix}$$

$$AA^{-1} = \begin{bmatrix} \dfrac{a_{11}a_{22} - a_{12}a_{21}}{a_{11}a_{22} - a_{21}a_{12}} & \dfrac{-a_{11}a_{12} + a_{12}a_{11}}{a_{11}a_{22} - a_{21}a_{12}} \\[4mm] \dfrac{a_{21}a_{22} - a_{21}a_{22}}{a_{11}a_{22} - a_{21}a_{12}} & \dfrac{-a_{21}a_{12} + a_{11}a_{22}}{a_{11}a_{22} - a_{21}a_{12}} \end{bmatrix}$$

$$= \begin{bmatrix} 1 & 0 \\ 0 & 1 \end{bmatrix} = I$$

Thus, $AA^{-1} = I$.

35. Let x = amount of 60% solution in mL.

Let y = amount of 40% solution in mL.

$x + y = 200$, since 200 mL of 48% solution is needed.

$0.60x + 0.40y = 0.48(x + y)$

$0.60x + 0.40y = 0.48x + 0.48y$

$0.12x - 0.08y = 0$

$12x - 8y = 0$

$x + y = 200$
$12x - 8y = 0$

$$\begin{bmatrix} 1 & 1 \\ 12 & -8 \end{bmatrix}\begin{bmatrix} x \\ y \end{bmatrix} = \begin{bmatrix} 200 \\ 0 \end{bmatrix}$$

$$-\frac{1}{20}\begin{bmatrix} -8 & -1 \\ -12 & 1 \end{bmatrix}\begin{bmatrix} 1 & 1 \\ 12 & -8 \end{bmatrix}\begin{bmatrix} x \\ y \end{bmatrix} = -\frac{1}{20}\begin{bmatrix} -8 & -1 \\ -12 & 1 \end{bmatrix}\begin{bmatrix} 200 \\ 0 \end{bmatrix}$$

$$\begin{bmatrix} x \\ y \end{bmatrix} = -\frac{1}{20}\begin{bmatrix} -8(200) - 1(0) \\ -12(200) + 1(0) \end{bmatrix}$$

$$\begin{bmatrix} x \\ y \end{bmatrix} = \begin{bmatrix} 80 \\ 120 \end{bmatrix}$$

80 ml of the 60% solution and 120 ml of the 40% solution

36. Let x = number of trips taken by 10-ton truck.

Let y = number of trips taken by 12-ton truck.

$x + y = 20$

$10x + 12y = 226$

$$\begin{bmatrix} 1 & 1 \\ 10 & 12 \end{bmatrix}\begin{bmatrix} x \\ y \end{bmatrix} = \begin{bmatrix} 20 \\ 226 \end{bmatrix}$$

$$\frac{1}{2}\begin{bmatrix} 12 & -1 \\ -10 & 1 \end{bmatrix}\begin{bmatrix} 1 & 1 \\ 10 & 12 \end{bmatrix}\begin{bmatrix} x \\ y \end{bmatrix} = \frac{1}{2}\begin{bmatrix} 12 & -1 \\ -10 & 1 \end{bmatrix}\begin{bmatrix} 20 \\ 226 \end{bmatrix}$$

$$\begin{bmatrix} x \\ y \end{bmatrix} = \frac{1}{2}\begin{bmatrix} 12(20) - 226 \\ -10(20) + 226 \end{bmatrix}$$

$$\begin{bmatrix} x \\ y \end{bmatrix} = \begin{bmatrix} 7 \\ 13 \end{bmatrix}$$

7 trips by the 10-ton truck and 13 trips by the 12-ton truck

37. $[f \circ g](4) = f(g(4))$ $[g \circ f](4) = g(f(4))$

$\qquad\qquad = f(4 + 1) \qquad\qquad\quad = g(4^2 - 1)$

$\qquad\qquad = (4 + 1)^2 - 1 \qquad\quad = g(15)$

$\qquad\qquad = 25 - 1 \qquad\qquad\quad = 15 + 1$

$\qquad\qquad = 24 \qquad\qquad\qquad\; = 16$

38. $y = mx + b$

$\quad 6 = (2)(1) + b$

$\quad 6 = 2 + b$

$\quad 4 = b$

$\quad y = 2x + 4$

39. By substitution,

$3(5y - 2) + y = 10 \qquad\qquad x = 5(1) - 2$

$15y - 6 + y = 10 \qquad\qquad x = 5 - 2$

$\qquad 16y = 16 \qquad\qquad\qquad x = 3$

$\qquad\quad y = 1 \qquad\qquad (3, 1)$

40. Answers may vary.

41. (A) $3^2 + 4^2 = 9 + 16$ (B) $7^2 = 49$

$\qquad\qquad\qquad = 25$

Quantity B is greater.   B

Mid-Chapter Review

PAGE 77

1. $y = 3x - 1$
   $\quad y = -x + 3$
   $\qquad (1, 2)$

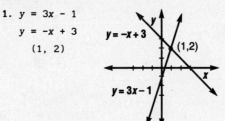

2. $2y = 3x - 5 \qquad\qquad 7y = -x - 6$
   $\quad y = 1.5x - 2.5 \qquad\quad y = -0.143x - 0.857$
   $\qquad\qquad\qquad (1, -1)$

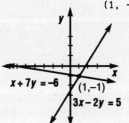

3. By elimination,

   $5x - y - 16 = 0 \rightarrow 15x - 3y = 48$

   $2x + 3y - 3 = 0 \rightarrow 2x + 3y = 3$

   $\quad 15x - 3y = 48 \qquad\quad 5(3) - y = 16$

   $\underline{\quad 2x + 3y = \;\;3\quad} \qquad\quad 15 - y = 16$

   $\quad 17x \qquad\quad = 51 \qquad\qquad\quad y = -1 \qquad (3, -1)$

   $\qquad x \qquad\quad = 3$

4. By elimination,

   $-2x + 4y = 3 \rightarrow -10x + 20y = 15$

   $5x - 7y = 11 \rightarrow 10x - 14y = 22$

   $-10x + 20y = 15 \qquad -2x + 4\left(\dfrac{37}{6}\right) = 3$

   $\underline{\;\;10x - 14y = 22\;\;} \qquad$

   $\qquad\qquad 6y = 37 \qquad\quad -2x + \dfrac{148}{6} = \dfrac{18}{6}$

   $\qquad\qquad\; y = \dfrac{37}{6} \qquad\qquad -2x = -\dfrac{130}{6}$

   $\qquad\qquad\qquad\qquad\qquad\qquad x = \dfrac{65}{6} \qquad \left(\dfrac{65}{6}, \dfrac{37}{6}\right)$

5. $A + B = \begin{bmatrix} 3 & 0 \\ -1 & 5 \end{bmatrix} + \begin{bmatrix} 5 & 1 \\ -3 & 4 \end{bmatrix} = \begin{bmatrix} 8 & 1 \\ -4 & 9 \end{bmatrix}$

6. $A - B = A + (-B) = \begin{bmatrix} 3 & 0 \\ -1 & 5 \end{bmatrix} + \begin{bmatrix} -5 & -1 \\ 3 & -4 \end{bmatrix} = \begin{bmatrix} -2 & -1 \\ 2 & 1 \end{bmatrix}$

7. $AB = \begin{bmatrix} 3 & 0 \\ -1 & 5 \end{bmatrix} \begin{bmatrix} 5 & 1 \\ -3 & 4 \end{bmatrix}$

$= \begin{bmatrix} 3(5) + 0(-3) & 3(1) + 0(4) \\ -1(5) + 5(-3) & -1(1) + 5(4) \end{bmatrix} = \begin{bmatrix} 15 & 3 \\ -20 & 19 \end{bmatrix}$

8. $\begin{vmatrix} 5 & 3 & 2 \\ 6 & 1 & 8 \\ 4 & 2 & 2 \end{vmatrix} = 5 \begin{vmatrix} 1 & 8 \\ 2 & 2 \end{vmatrix} - 3 \begin{vmatrix} 6 & 8 \\ 4 & 2 \end{vmatrix} + 2 \begin{vmatrix} 6 & 1 \\ 4 & 2 \end{vmatrix}$

$= 5(2 - 16) - 3(12 - 32) + 2(12 - 4) = 6$

9. $\frac{1}{2}\begin{bmatrix} 3 & 4 \\ -2 & -2 \end{bmatrix} \begin{bmatrix} -2 & -4 \\ 2 & 3 \end{bmatrix} \begin{bmatrix} x \\ y \end{bmatrix} = \frac{1}{2}\begin{bmatrix} 3 & 4 \\ -2 & -2 \end{bmatrix} \begin{bmatrix} 6 \\ 5 \end{bmatrix}$

$\begin{bmatrix} x \\ y \end{bmatrix} = \frac{1}{2}\begin{bmatrix} 3(6) + 4(5) \\ -2(6) + (-2)(5) \end{bmatrix}$

$\begin{bmatrix} x \\ y \end{bmatrix} = \begin{bmatrix} 19 \\ -11 \end{bmatrix} \qquad (19, -11)$

10. $-\frac{1}{96}\begin{bmatrix} 12 & -14 \\ -6 & -1 \end{bmatrix} \begin{bmatrix} -1 & 14 \\ 6 & 12 \end{bmatrix} \begin{bmatrix} x \\ y \end{bmatrix} = -\frac{1}{96}\begin{bmatrix} 12 & -14 \\ -6 & -1 \end{bmatrix} \begin{bmatrix} 4 \\ 0 \end{bmatrix}$

$\begin{bmatrix} x \\ y \end{bmatrix} = -\frac{1}{96}\begin{bmatrix} 12(4) + (-14)(0) \\ -6(4) + (-1)(0) \end{bmatrix}$

$\begin{bmatrix} x \\ y \end{bmatrix} = \begin{bmatrix} -\frac{1}{2} \\ \frac{1}{4} \end{bmatrix} \qquad \left(-\frac{1}{2}, \frac{1}{4}\right)$

Technology:
Finding Determinants of Matrices

PAGE 78   EXERCISES

1-3. See students' work.

1. -39   **2.** -114   **3.** 917

2-4

Solving Systems of Equations by Using Matrices

PAGE 82   CHECKING FOR UNDERSTANDING

1. The objective is to get the identity matrix to appear on the left side of the augmented matrix by using row operations. When you have done this, the solution can be read directly from the resulting augmented matrix.

2. Answers may vary.

3. Multiply row 2 by 5 and add it to row 1.
Multiply row 1 by -2 and add it to row 2.

4. Multiply row 1 by 2 and row 2 by 7.
Add row 2 to row 1.
Multiply row 2 by -4 and add row 1 to it.

5. Multiply row 1 by 2. Add row 2 to row 1.
Multiply row 1 by -3 and row 2 by 5.
Add row 1 to row 2.

6. $\begin{bmatrix} 5 & -2 & 5 \\ 1 & 1 & 8 \end{bmatrix} \rightarrow \begin{bmatrix} 7 & 0 & 21 \\ 1 & 1 & 8 \end{bmatrix} \rightarrow \begin{bmatrix} 7 & 0 & 21 \\ 0 & -7 & -35 \end{bmatrix} \rightarrow$

$\begin{bmatrix} 1 & 0 & 3 \\ 0 & 1 & 5 \end{bmatrix} \qquad (3, 5)$

7. $\begin{bmatrix} 2 & 1 & -2 & 7 \\ 1 & -2 & -5 & -1 \\ 4 & 1 & 1 & -1 \end{bmatrix} \rightarrow \begin{bmatrix} 2 & 1 & -2 & 7 \\ 0 & 5 & 8 & 9 \\ 4 & 1 & 1 & -1 \end{bmatrix} \rightarrow \begin{bmatrix} 2 & 1 & -2 & 7 \\ 0 & 5 & 8 & 9 \\ 0 & -1 & 5 & -15 \end{bmatrix} \rightarrow$

$\begin{bmatrix} 2 & 0 & 3 & -8 \\ 0 & 5 & 8 & 9 \\ 0 & -1 & 5 & -15 \end{bmatrix} \rightarrow \begin{bmatrix} 2 & 0 & 3 & -8 \\ 0 & 5 & 8 & 9 \\ 0 & 0 & 33 & -66 \end{bmatrix} \rightarrow \begin{bmatrix} 2 & 0 & 3 & -8 \\ 0 & 5 & 8 & 9 \\ 0 & 0 & 1 & -2 \end{bmatrix} \rightarrow$

$\begin{bmatrix} 2 & 0 & 0 & -2 \\ 0 & 5 & 8 & 9 \\ 0 & 0 & 1 & -2 \end{bmatrix} \rightarrow \begin{bmatrix} 1 & 0 & 0 & -1 \\ 0 & 5 & 0 & 25 \\ 0 & 0 & 1 & -2 \end{bmatrix} \rightarrow \begin{bmatrix} 1 & 0 & 0 & -1 \\ 0 & 1 & 0 & 5 \\ 0 & 0 & 1 & -2 \end{bmatrix}$

$(-1, 5, -2)$

PAGES 82-83   EXERCISES

8. $\begin{bmatrix} 3 & 5 & 7 \\ 6 & -1 & -8 \end{bmatrix} \rightarrow \begin{bmatrix} 33 & 0 & -33 \\ 6 & -1 & -8 \end{bmatrix} \rightarrow \begin{bmatrix} 1 & 0 & -1 \\ 6 & -1 & -8 \end{bmatrix} \rightarrow$

$\begin{bmatrix} 1 & 0 & -1 \\ 0 & -1 & -2 \end{bmatrix} \rightarrow \begin{bmatrix} 1 & 0 & -1 \\ 0 & 1 & 2 \end{bmatrix} \qquad (-1, 2)$

9. $\begin{bmatrix} 4 & -7 & -2 \\ 1 & 2 & 7 \end{bmatrix} \rightarrow \begin{bmatrix} 4 & -7 & -2 \\ 0 & -15 & -30 \end{bmatrix} \rightarrow \begin{bmatrix} 4 & -7 & -2 \\ 0 & 1 & 2 \end{bmatrix} \rightarrow$

$\begin{bmatrix} 4 & 0 & 12 \\ 0 & 1 & 2 \end{bmatrix} \rightarrow \begin{bmatrix} 1 & 0 & 3 \\ 0 & 1 & 2 \end{bmatrix} \qquad (3, 2)$

10. $\begin{bmatrix} 3 & 3 & -9 \\ -2 & 1 & -4 \end{bmatrix} \rightarrow \begin{bmatrix} 3 & 3 & -9 \\ 0 & 9 & -30 \end{bmatrix} \rightarrow \begin{bmatrix} 3 & 3 & -9 \\ 0 & 1 & -\frac{10}{3} \end{bmatrix} \rightarrow$

$\begin{bmatrix} 3 & 0 & 1 \\ 0 & 1 & -\frac{10}{3} \end{bmatrix} \rightarrow \begin{bmatrix} 1 & 0 & \frac{1}{3} \\ 0 & 1 & -\frac{10}{3} \end{bmatrix} \qquad \left(\frac{1}{3}, -\frac{10}{3}\right)$

11. $5x - 3y = -50$
$3x - 2y = 1$

$\begin{bmatrix} 5 & -3 & -50 \\ 3 & 2 & 1 \end{bmatrix} \rightarrow \begin{bmatrix} 19 & 0 & -97 \\ 3 & 2 & -1 \end{bmatrix} \rightarrow \begin{bmatrix} 1 & 0 & -\frac{97}{19} \\ 3 & 2 & -1 \end{bmatrix} \rightarrow$

$\begin{bmatrix} 1 & 0 & -\frac{97}{19} \\ 0 & 2 & \frac{310}{19} \end{bmatrix} \rightarrow \begin{bmatrix} 1 & 0 & -\frac{97}{19} \\ 0 & 1 & \frac{155}{19} \end{bmatrix} \qquad \left(-\frac{97}{19}, \frac{155}{19}\right)$

12. $\begin{bmatrix} 1 & -1 & 1 & 3 \\ 0 & 2 & -1 & 1 \\ -1 & 2 & 0 & -1 \end{bmatrix} \rightarrow \begin{bmatrix} 2 & 0 & 1 & 7 \\ 0 & 2 & -1 & 1 \\ -1 & 2 & 0 & -1 \end{bmatrix} \rightarrow \begin{bmatrix} 2 & 0 & 1 & 7 \\ 0 & 2 & -1 & 1 \\ -1 & 0 & 1 & -2 \end{bmatrix} \rightarrow$

$\begin{bmatrix} 3 & 0 & 0 & 9 \\ 0 & 2 & -1 & 1 \\ -1 & 0 & 1 & -2 \end{bmatrix} \rightarrow \begin{bmatrix} 1 & 0 & 0 & 3 \\ 0 & 2 & -1 & 1 \\ 0 & 0 & 1 & 1 \end{bmatrix} \rightarrow \begin{bmatrix} 1 & 0 & 0 & 3 \\ 0 & 2 & 0 & 2 \\ 0 & 0 & 1 & 1 \end{bmatrix} \rightarrow$

$\begin{bmatrix} 1 & 0 & 0 & 3 \\ 0 & 1 & 0 & 1 \\ 0 & 0 & 1 & 1 \end{bmatrix} \qquad (3, 1, 1)$

13. $\begin{bmatrix} 1 & 1 & 1 & -2 \\ 2 & -3 & 1 & -11 \\ -1 & 2 & -1 & 8 \end{bmatrix} \rightarrow \begin{bmatrix} 1 & 1 & 1 & -2 \\ 0 & -5 & -1 & -7 \\ -1 & 2 & -1 & 8 \end{bmatrix} \rightarrow$

$\begin{bmatrix} 1 & 1 & 1 & -2 \\ 0 & -5 & -1 & -7 \\ 0 & 3 & 0 & 6 \end{bmatrix} \rightarrow \begin{bmatrix} 1 & 1 & 1 & -2 \\ 0 & -5 & -1 & -7 \\ 0 & -2 & -1 & -1 \end{bmatrix} \rightarrow \begin{bmatrix} 1 & -1 & 0 & -3 \\ 0 & -5 & -1 & -7 \\ 0 & -2 & -1 & -1 \end{bmatrix} \rightarrow$

$\begin{bmatrix} 1 & -1 & 0 & -3 \\ 0 & -5 & -1 & -7 \\ 0 & 0 & 3 & -9 \end{bmatrix} \rightarrow \begin{bmatrix} 1 & -1 & 0 & -3 \\ 0 & -5 & -1 & -7 \\ 0 & 0 & 1 & -3 \end{bmatrix} \rightarrow \begin{bmatrix} 1 & -1 & 0 & -3 \\ 0 & -5 & 0 & -10 \\ 0 & 0 & 1 & -3 \end{bmatrix} \rightarrow$

$\begin{bmatrix} 1 & -1 & 0 & -3 \\ 0 & 1 & 0 & 2 \\ 0 & 0 & 1 & -3 \end{bmatrix} \rightarrow \begin{bmatrix} 1 & 0 & 0 & -1 \\ 0 & 1 & 0 & 2 \\ 0 & 0 & 1 & -3 \end{bmatrix} \qquad (-1, 2, -3)$

14. $\begin{bmatrix} 2 & 6 & 8 & 5 \\ -2 & 9 & -12 & -1 \\ 4 & 6 & -4 & 3 \end{bmatrix} \to \begin{bmatrix} 2 & 6 & 8 & 5 \\ 0 & 15 & -4 & 4 \\ 4 & 6 & -4 & 3 \end{bmatrix} \to \begin{bmatrix} 2 & 6 & 8 & 5 \\ 0 & 15 & -4 & 4 \\ 0 & -6 & -20 & -7 \end{bmatrix} \to$

$\begin{bmatrix} 2 & 6 & 8 & 5 \\ 0 & -81 & 0 & -27 \\ 0 & -6 & -20 & -7 \end{bmatrix} \to \begin{bmatrix} 2 & 6 & 8 & 5 \\ 0 & 1 & 0 & \frac{1}{3} \\ 0 & -6 & -20 & -7 \end{bmatrix} \to$

$\begin{bmatrix} 2 & 0 & -12 & -2 \\ 0 & 1 & 0 & \frac{1}{3} \\ 0 & -6 & -20 & -7 \end{bmatrix} \to \begin{bmatrix} 2 & 0 & -12 & -2 \\ 0 & 1 & 0 & \frac{1}{3} \\ 0 & 0 & -20 & -5 \end{bmatrix} \to \begin{bmatrix} 2 & 0 & -12 & -2 \\ 0 & 1 & 0 & \frac{1}{3} \\ 0 & 0 & 1 & \frac{1}{4} \end{bmatrix} \to$

$\begin{bmatrix} 2 & 0 & 0 & 1 \\ 0 & 1 & 0 & \frac{1}{3} \\ 0 & 0 & 1 & \frac{1}{4} \end{bmatrix} \to \begin{bmatrix} 1 & 0 & 0 & \frac{1}{2} \\ 0 & 1 & 0 & \frac{1}{3} \\ 0 & 0 & 1 & \frac{1}{4} \end{bmatrix}$ $\left(\frac{1}{2}, \frac{1}{3}, \frac{1}{4} \right)$

15. $\begin{bmatrix} 1 & 1 & 1 & 6 \\ 2 & -3 & 4 & 3 \\ 4 & -8 & 4 & 12 \end{bmatrix} \to \begin{bmatrix} 1 & 1 & 1 & 6 \\ -2 & 5 & 0 & -9 \\ 4 & -8 & 4 & 12 \end{bmatrix} \to \begin{bmatrix} 1 & 1 & 1 & 6 \\ -2 & 5 & 0 & -9 \\ 0 & 2 & 4 & -6 \end{bmatrix} \to$

$\begin{bmatrix} -4 & -2 & 0 & 30 \\ -2 & 5 & 0 & -9 \\ 0 & 2 & 4 & -6 \end{bmatrix} \to \begin{bmatrix} -24 & 0 & 0 & -168 \\ 2 & 5 & 0 & -9 \\ 0 & 2 & 4 & -6 \end{bmatrix} \to \begin{bmatrix} 1 & 0 & 0 & 7 \\ -2 & 5 & 0 & -9 \\ 0 & 2 & 4 & -6 \end{bmatrix} \to$

$\begin{bmatrix} 1 & 0 & 0 & 7 \\ 0 & 5 & 0 & 5 \\ 0 & 2 & 4 & -6 \end{bmatrix} \to \begin{bmatrix} 1 & 0 & 0 & 7 \\ 0 & 1 & 0 & 1 \\ 0 & 2 & 4 & -6 \end{bmatrix} \to \begin{bmatrix} 1 & 0 & 0 & 7 \\ 0 & 1 & 0 & 1 \\ 0 & 0 & 4 & -8 \end{bmatrix} \to$

$\begin{bmatrix} 1 & 0 & 0 & 7 \\ 0 & 1 & 0 & 1 \\ 0 & 0 & 1 & -2 \end{bmatrix}$ $(7, 1, -2)$

16. $\begin{bmatrix} 0 & 1 & 2 & 0 & 5 \\ 0 & 3 & 0 & 4 & 2 \\ 3 & 0 & 2 & 0 & -2 \\ -2 & 0 & 0 & 3 & 1 \end{bmatrix} \to \begin{bmatrix} 0 & 0 & -6 & 4 & -13 \\ 0 & 3 & 0 & 4 & 2 \\ 3 & 0 & 2 & 0 & -2 \\ -2 & 0 & 0 & 3 & 1 \end{bmatrix} \to$

$\begin{bmatrix} 9 & 0 & 0 & 4 & -19 \\ 0 & 3 & 0 & 4 & 2 \\ 3 & 0 & 2 & 0 & -2 \\ -2 & 0 & 0 & 3 & 1 \end{bmatrix} \to \begin{bmatrix} -35 & 0 & 0 & 0 & 61 \\ 0 & 3 & 0 & 4 & 2 \\ 3 & 0 & 2 & 0 & -2 \\ -2 & 0 & 0 & 3 & 1 \end{bmatrix} \to$

$\begin{bmatrix} 1 & 0 & 0 & 0 & -\frac{61}{35} \\ 0 & 3 & 0 & 4 & 2 \\ 3 & 0 & 2 & 0 & -2 \\ -2 & 0 & 0 & 3 & 1 \end{bmatrix} \to \begin{bmatrix} 1 & 0 & 0 & 0 & -\frac{61}{35} \\ 0 & 3 & 0 & 4 & 2 \\ 0 & 0 & 2 & 0 & \frac{113}{35} \\ -2 & 0 & 0 & 3 & 1 \end{bmatrix} \to$

$\begin{bmatrix} 1 & 0 & 0 & 0 & -\frac{61}{35} \\ 0 & 3 & 0 & 4 & 2 \\ 0 & 0 & 1 & 0 & \frac{113}{70} \\ -2 & 0 & 0 & 3 & 1 \end{bmatrix} \to \begin{bmatrix} 1 & 0 & 0 & 0 & -\frac{61}{35} \\ 0 & 3 & 0 & 4 & 2 \\ 0 & 0 & 1 & 0 & \frac{113}{70} \\ 0 & 0 & 0 & 3 & -\frac{87}{35} \end{bmatrix} \to$

$\begin{bmatrix} 1 & 0 & 0 & 0 & -\frac{61}{35} \\ 0 & 3 & 0 & 4 & 2 \\ 0 & 0 & 1 & 0 & \frac{113}{70} \\ 0 & 0 & 0 & 1 & -\frac{29}{70} \end{bmatrix} \to \begin{bmatrix} 1 & 0 & 0 & 0 & -\frac{61}{35} \\ 0 & 3 & 0 & 0 & \frac{186}{35} \\ 0 & 0 & 1 & 0 & \frac{113}{70} \\ 0 & 0 & 0 & 1 & -\frac{29}{35} \end{bmatrix} \to$

$\begin{bmatrix} 1 & 0 & 0 & 0 & -\frac{61}{35} \\ 0 & 1 & 0 & 0 & \frac{62}{35} \\ 0 & 0 & 1 & 0 & \frac{113}{70} \\ 0 & 0 & 0 & 1 & -\frac{29}{35} \end{bmatrix}$ $\left(-\frac{61}{35}, \frac{62}{35}, \frac{113}{70}, -\frac{29}{35} \right)$

17. $\begin{bmatrix} 1 & 1 & 1 & 1 & 10 \\ 2 & 1 & -1 & -1 & 1 \\ -1 & -1 & 1 & 1 & 0 \\ 0 & 2 & 1 & 0 & 0 \end{bmatrix} \to \begin{bmatrix} 3 & 2 & 0 & 0 & 1 \\ 2 & 1 & -1 & -1 & 1 \\ -1 & -1 & 1 & 1 & 0 \\ 0 & 2 & 1 & 0 & 0 \end{bmatrix} \to$

$\begin{bmatrix} 3 & 2 & 0 & 0 & 1 \\ 1 & 0 & 0 & 0 & 1 \\ -1 & -1 & 1 & 1 & 0 \\ 0 & 2 & 1 & 0 & 0 \end{bmatrix} \to \begin{bmatrix} 3 & 2 & 0 & 0 & 1 \\ 0 & 2 & 0 & 0 & -2 \\ -1 & -1 & 1 & 1 & 0 \\ 0 & 2 & 1 & 0 & 0 \end{bmatrix} \to$

$\begin{bmatrix} 3 & 2 & 0 & 0 & 1 \\ 0 & 1 & 0 & 0 & -1 \\ -1 & -1 & 1 & 1 & 0 \\ 0 & 2 & 1 & 0 & 0 \end{bmatrix} \to \begin{bmatrix} 3 & 0 & 0 & 0 & 3 \\ 0 & 1 & 0 & 0 & -1 \\ -1 & -1 & 1 & 1 & 0 \\ 0 & 2 & 1 & 0 & 0 \end{bmatrix} \to$

$\begin{bmatrix} 1 & 0 & 0 & 0 & 1 \\ 0 & 1 & 0 & 0 & -1 \\ -1 & -1 & 1 & 1 & 0 \\ 0 & 2 & 1 & 0 & 0 \end{bmatrix} \to \begin{bmatrix} 1 & 0 & 0 & 0 & 1 \\ 0 & 1 & 0 & 0 & -1 \\ -1 & -1 & 1 & 1 & 0 \\ 1 & 3 & 0 & -1 & 0 \end{bmatrix} \to$

$\begin{bmatrix} 1 & 0 & 0 & 0 & 1 \\ 0 & 1 & 0 & 0 & -1 \\ -1 & -1 & 1 & 1 & 0 \\ 1 & 0 & 0 & -1 & 3 \end{bmatrix} \to \begin{bmatrix} 1 & 0 & 0 & 0 & 1 \\ 0 & 1 & 0 & 0 & -1 \\ -1 & -1 & 1 & 1 & 0 \\ 0 & 0 & 0 & -1 & 2 \end{bmatrix} \to$

$\begin{bmatrix} 1 & 0 & 0 & 0 & 1 \\ 0 & 1 & 0 & 0 & -1 \\ -1 & -1 & 1 & 1 & 0 \\ 0 & 0 & 0 & 1 & -2 \end{bmatrix} \to \begin{bmatrix} 1 & 0 & 0 & 0 & 1 \\ 0 & 1 & 0 & 0 & -1 \\ -1 & -1 & 1 & 0 & 2 \\ 0 & 0 & 0 & 1 & 2 \end{bmatrix} \to$

$\begin{bmatrix} 1 & 0 & 0 & 0 & 1 \\ 0 & 1 & 0 & 0 & -1 \\ -1 & 0 & 1 & 0 & 1 \\ 0 & 0 & 0 & 1 & -2 \end{bmatrix} \to \begin{bmatrix} 1 & 0 & 0 & 0 & 1 \\ 0 & 1 & 0 & 0 & -1 \\ 0 & 0 & 1 & 0 & 2 \\ 0 & 0 & 0 & 1 & -2 \end{bmatrix}$ $(1, -1, 2, -2)$

18. $a(1)^2 + b(1) + c = 4 \longrightarrow a + b + c = 4$

$a(5)^2 + b(5) + c = 40 \longrightarrow 25a + 5b + c = 40$

$a(3)^2 + b(3) + c = 14 \longrightarrow 9a + 3b + c = 14$

$\begin{bmatrix} 1 & 1 & 1 & 4 \\ 25 & 5 & 1 & 40 \\ 9 & 3 & 1 & 14 \end{bmatrix} \to \begin{bmatrix} 1 & 1 & 1 & 4 \\ 0 & -20 & -24 & -60 \\ 9 & 3 & 1 & 14 \end{bmatrix} \to$

$\begin{bmatrix} 1 & 1 & 1 & 4 \\ 0 & -20 & -24 & -60 \\ 0 & -6 & -8 & -22 \end{bmatrix} \to \begin{bmatrix} 1 & 1 & 1 & 4 \\ 0 & -2 & 0 & 6 \\ 0 & -6 & -8 & -22 \end{bmatrix} \to$

$\begin{bmatrix} 1 & 1 & 1 & 4 \\ 0 & 1 & 0 & -3 \\ 0 & -6 & -8 & -22 \end{bmatrix} \to \begin{bmatrix} 1 & 0 & 1 & 7 \\ 0 & 1 & 0 & -3 \\ 0 & -6 & -8 & -22 \end{bmatrix} \to$

$\begin{bmatrix} 1 & 0 & 1 & 7 \\ 0 & 1 & 0 & -3 \\ 0 & 0 & -8 & -40 \end{bmatrix} \to \begin{bmatrix} 1 & 0 & 1 & 7 \\ 0 & 1 & 0 & -3 \\ 0 & 0 & 1 & 5 \end{bmatrix} \to \begin{bmatrix} 1 & 0 & 0 & 2 \\ 0 & 1 & 0 & -3 \\ 0 & 0 & 1 & 5 \end{bmatrix}$

$y = 2x^2 - 3x + 5$

19. $a(2)^2 + b(2) + c = 3 \longrightarrow 4a + 2b + c = 3$

$a(3)^2 + b(3) + c = 6 \longrightarrow 9a + 3b + c = 6$

$a(-2)^2 + b(-2) + c = 31 \longrightarrow 4a - 2b + c = 31$

$\begin{bmatrix} 4 & 2 & 1 & 3 \\ 9 & 3 & 1 & 6 \\ 4 & -2 & 1 & 31 \end{bmatrix} \to \begin{bmatrix} 8 & 0 & 2 & 34 \\ 9 & 3 & 1 & 6 \\ 4 & -2 & 1 & 31 \end{bmatrix} \to \begin{bmatrix} 8 & 0 & 2 & 34 \\ 5 & 5 & 0 & -25 \\ 4 & -2 & 1 & 31 \end{bmatrix} \to$

$\begin{bmatrix} 8 & 0 & 2 & 34 \\ 5 & 5 & 0 & -25 \\ 30 & 0 & 5 & 105 \end{bmatrix} \to \begin{bmatrix} 8 & 0 & 2 & 34 \\ 5 & 5 & 0 & -25 \\ 0 & 0 & -10 & -90 \end{bmatrix} \to \begin{bmatrix} 8 & 0 & 2 & 34 \\ 5 & 5 & 0 & -25 \\ 0 & 0 & 1 & 9 \end{bmatrix} \to$

$\begin{bmatrix} 8 & 0 & 0 & 16 \\ 5 & 5 & 0 & -25 \\ 0 & 0 & 1 & 9 \end{bmatrix} \to \begin{bmatrix} 1 & 0 & 0 & 2 \\ 5 & 5 & 0 & -25 \\ 0 & 0 & 1 & 9 \end{bmatrix} \to \begin{bmatrix} 1 & 0 & 0 & 2 \\ 0 & 5 & 0 & -35 \\ 0 & 0 & 1 & 9 \end{bmatrix} \to$

$\begin{bmatrix} 1 & 0 & 0 & 2 \\ 0 & 1 & 0 & -7 \\ 0 & 0 & 1 & 9 \end{bmatrix}$ $y = 2x^2 - 7x + 9$

20. The system is dependent; there is no unique solution.

21. The system is inconsistent; there is no solution.

22. Let x = price of prime rib. $x + 2y + z = 36$

Let y = price of side dish. $x + 3y + 2z = 44$

Let z = price of roll. $x - 3y + 0z = 0$

$$\begin{bmatrix} 1 & 2 & 1 & 36 \\ 1 & 3 & 2 & 44 \\ 1 & -3 & 0 & 0 \end{bmatrix} \rightarrow \begin{bmatrix} 1 & 2 & 1 & 36 \\ 1 & 3 & 2 & 44 \\ 0 & -5 & -1 & -36 \end{bmatrix} \rightarrow \begin{bmatrix} 1 & 2 & 1 & 36 \\ 0 & 1 & 1 & 8 \\ 0 & -5 & -1 & -36 \end{bmatrix} \rightarrow$$

$$\begin{bmatrix} 1 & 2 & 1 & 36 \\ 0 & -4 & 0 & -28 \\ 0 & -5 & -1 & -36 \end{bmatrix} \rightarrow \begin{bmatrix} 1 & 2 & 1 & 36 \\ 0 & 1 & 0 & 7 \\ 0 & -5 & -1 & -36 \end{bmatrix} \rightarrow$$

$$\begin{bmatrix} 1 & -3 & 0 & 0 \\ 0 & 1 & 0 & 7 \\ 0 & -5 & -1 & -36 \end{bmatrix} \rightarrow \begin{bmatrix} 1 & -3 & 0 & 0 \\ 0 & 1 & 0 & 7 \\ 0 & 0 & -1 & -1 \end{bmatrix} \rightarrow \begin{bmatrix} 1 & -3 & 0 & 0 \\ 0 & 1 & 0 & 7 \\ 0 & 0 & 1 & 1 \end{bmatrix} \rightarrow$$

$$\begin{bmatrix} 1 & 0 & 0 & 21 \\ 0 & 1 & 0 & 7 \\ 0 & 0 & 1 & 1 \end{bmatrix}$$ prime rib: \$21
side dish: \$7
roll: \$1

23. Let x = price of blouse.

Let y = price of shirt.

Let z = price of jeans.

$3x + 2y + 4z = 292 \rightarrow 3x + 2y + 4z = 292$

$4x + 1y + 3z = 252 \rightarrow 4x + 1y + 3z = 252$

$z = y + 4 \qquad\qquad \rightarrow -y + 1z = 4$

$$\begin{bmatrix} 3 & 2 & 4 & 292 \\ 4 & 1 & 3 & 252 \\ 0 & -1 & 1 & 4 \end{bmatrix} \rightarrow \begin{bmatrix} 3 & 2 & 4 & 292 \\ 4 & 4 & 0 & 240 \\ 0 & -1 & 1 & 4 \end{bmatrix} \rightarrow \begin{bmatrix} 3 & 6 & 0 & 276 \\ 4 & 4 & 0 & 240 \\ 0 & -1 & 1 & 4 \end{bmatrix} \rightarrow$$

$$\begin{bmatrix} 3 & 6 & 0 & 276 \\ 0 & -12 & 0 & -384 \\ 0 & -1 & 1 & 4 \end{bmatrix} \rightarrow \begin{bmatrix} 3 & 6 & 0 & 276 \\ 0 & 1 & 0 & 32 \\ 0 & -1 & 1 & 4 \end{bmatrix} \rightarrow \begin{bmatrix} 3 & 0 & 0 & 84 \\ 0 & 1 & 0 & 32 \\ 0 & -1 & 1 & 4 \end{bmatrix} \rightarrow$$

$$\begin{bmatrix} 1 & 0 & 0 & 28 \\ 0 & 1 & 0 & 32 \\ 0 & 0 & 1 & 36 \end{bmatrix}$$ blouse: \$28
skirt: \$32
jeans: \$36

24. yes

25. By substitution,

$x = 11 - 2y$

$3(11 - 2y) - 5y = 11 \qquad\qquad x = 11 - 2(2)$

$33 - 6y - 5y = 11 \qquad\qquad x = 11 - 4$

$33 - 11y = 11 \qquad\qquad x = 7$

$-11y = -22 \qquad\qquad (7, 2)$

$y = 2$

26. $\begin{bmatrix} 3 + 1 & 8 + 5 \\ -2 + (-2) & 4 + 8 \end{bmatrix} = \begin{bmatrix} 4 & 13 \\ -4 & 12 \end{bmatrix}$

27. $\begin{vmatrix} 2 & 3 & 4 \\ 5 & 6 & 7 \\ 8 & 9 & 10 \end{vmatrix} = 2\begin{vmatrix} 6 & 7 \\ 9 & 10 \end{vmatrix} - 3\begin{vmatrix} 5 & 7 \\ 8 & 10 \end{vmatrix} + 4\begin{vmatrix} 5 & 6 \\ 8 & 9 \end{vmatrix}$

$= 2(-3) - 3(-6) + 4(-3) = 0$

28. $\dfrac{a + b + c + d}{4} = 15$

$a + b + c + d = 60$

PAGES 84-85

1.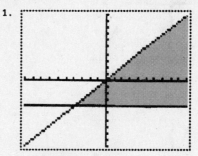

2.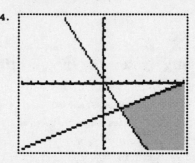

3.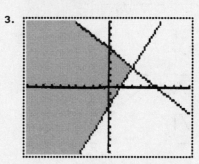

4.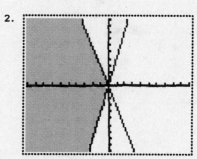

5.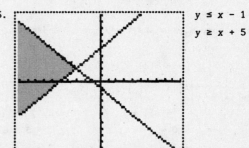

$y \le x - 1$
$y \ge x + 5$

31

6.

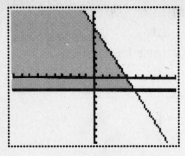

$y \geq -2$
$y \leq -2x + 8$

7. $-2y \geq -2x + 9$ $\quad -y \leq 3x - 4$
$\quad\quad y \leq x - 4.5$ $\quad y \geq -3x + 4$

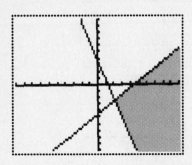

8. $3y \leq -3x + 6$ $\quad -y \leq -2x + 5$
$\quad\quad y \leq -x + 2$ $\quad y \geq 2x - 5$

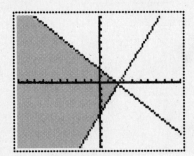

2-5 Solving Systems of Inequalities

PAGES 88-89 CHECKING FOR UNDERSTANDING

1. Yes, if the function passes through two vertices or coincides with an edge of the convex polygonal set representing the constraints in the problem.

2. Yes, there may not be a maximum if the region is not bounded.

3. $f(3, 2) = 3(3) + 2(2) + 1 = 14$

4. $f\left(\frac{1}{3}, \frac{1}{2}\right) = 3\left(\frac{1}{3}\right) + 2\left(\frac{1}{2}\right) + 1 = 3$

5. $f(-1.5, 4) = 3(-1.5) + 2(4) + 1 = 4.5$

6. $f(0, 0) = 0 + 0 = 0$ $\quad\quad f(3, 5) = 3 + 5 = 8$
$\quad f(4, 0) = 4 + 0 = 4$ $\quad\quad f(0, 5) = 0 + 5 = 5$
$\quad (8, 0)$

7. $f(0, 0) = 8(0) + 0 = 0$ $\quad f(3, 5) = 8(3) + 5 = 29$
$\quad f(4, 0) = 8(4) + 0 = 32$ $\quad f(0, 5) = 8(0) + 5 = 5$
$\quad (32, 0)$

8. $f(0, 0) = 4(0) - 3(0) = 0$
$\quad f(4, 0) = 4(0) - 3(4) = -12$
$\quad f(3, 5) = 4(5) - 3(3) = 11$
$\quad f(0, 5) = 4(5) - 3(0) = 20$
$\quad (20, -12)$

9.

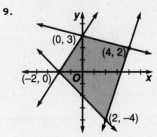

$(0, 3), (4, 2), (2, -4), (-2, 0)$
$f(0, 3) = 0 - 3 + 2 = -1$
$f(4, 2) = 4 - 2 + 2 = 4$
$f(2, -4) = 2 - (-4) + 2 = 8$
$f(-2, 0) = -2 - 0 + 2 = 0$
maximum at $(2, -4) = 8$, minimum at $(0, 3) = -1$

10.

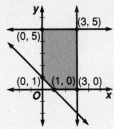

$(1, 0), (3, 0), (3, 5), (0, 5), (0, 1)$
$f(1, 0) = 2(1) + 8(0) + 10 = 12$
$f(3, 0) = 2(3) + 8(0) + 10 = 16$
$f(0, 5) = 2(0) + 8(5) + 10 = 50$
$f(0, 1) = 2(0) + 8(1) + 10 = 18$
$f(3, 5) = 2(3) + 8(5) + 10 = 56$
maximum at $(3, 5) = 56$, minimum at $(1, 0) = 12$

PAGES 89-90 EXERCISES

11.

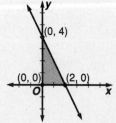

$(0, 0), (2, 0), (0, 4)$
$f(0, 0) = 0 - 0 = 0$ $\quad\quad$ maximum at $(0, 4) = 4$
$f(2, 0) = 0 - 2 = -2$ $\quad\quad$ minimum at $(2, 0) = -2$
$f(0, 4) = 4 - 0 = 4$

12.

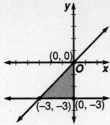

$(0, 0)$, $(0, -3)$, $(-3, -3)$

$f(0, 0) = 0 + 2(0) = 0$

$f(0, -3) = 0 + 2(-3) = -6$

$f(-3, -3) = -3 + 2(-3) = -9$

maximum at $(0, 0) = 0$

minimum at $(-3, -3) = -9$

13.

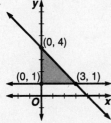

$(0, 1)$, $(3, 1)$, $(0, 4)$

$f(0, 1) = 4(0) + 2(1) + 7 = 9$

$f(3, 1) = 4(3) + 2(1) + 7 = 21$

$f(0, 4) = 4(0) + 2(4) + 7 = 15$

maximum at $(3, 1) = 21$

minimum at $(0, 1) = 9$

14.

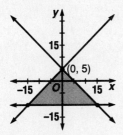

$(0, 5)$, $(15, -10)$, $(-15, -10)$

$f(0, 5) = \frac{1}{2}(0) - \frac{1}{3}(5) = -\frac{5}{3}$

$f(15, -10) = \frac{1}{2}(15) - \frac{1}{3}(-10) = \frac{65}{6}$

$f(-15, -10) = \frac{1}{2}(-15) - \frac{1}{3}(-10) = -\frac{25}{6}$

maximum at $(15, -10) = \frac{65}{6}$

minimum at $(-15, -10) = -\frac{25}{6}$

15.

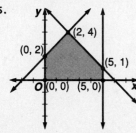

$(0, 0)$, $(5, 0)$, $(5, 1)$, $(2, 4)$, $(0, 2)$

$f(0, 0) = 3(0) - 5(0) = 0$

$f(5, 0) = 3(5) - 5(0) = 15$

$f(5, 1) = 3(5) - 5(1) = 10$

$f(2, 4) = 3(2) - 5(4) = -14$

$f(0, 2) = 3(0) - 5(2) = -10$

maximum at $(5, 0) = 15$

minimum at $(2, 4) = -14$

16.

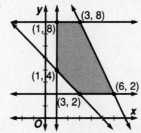

$(1, 4)$, $(3, 2)$, $(6, 2)$, $(3, 8)$, $(1, 8)$

$f(1, 4) = 4 - 2(1) + 5 = 7$

$f(3, 2) = 2 - 2(3) + 5 = 1$

$f(6, 2) = 2 - 2(6) + 5 = -5$

$f(3, 8) = 8 - 2(3) + 5 = 7$

$f(1, 8) = 8 - 2(1) + 5 = 11$

maximum at $(1, 8) = 11$

minimum at $(6, 2) = -5$

17. The equation of the line through $(0, 0)$ and $(6, 1)$:

$m = \frac{6 - 0}{1 - 0} = 6$

$y = mx + c$

$6 = 6(1) + c$

$0 = c$

$y = 6x$

$-6x + y = 0$

The equation of the line through $(6, 4)$ and $(6, 1)$:

$m = \frac{6 - 4}{1 - 6} = -\frac{2}{5}$

$y = mx + c$

$6 = \left(-\frac{2}{5}\right)(1) + c$

$\frac{32}{5} = c$

$y = -\frac{2}{5}x + \frac{32}{5}$

$2x + 5y - 32 = 0$

The equation of the line through $(5, 1)$ and $(6, 4)$:

$m = \frac{4 - 1}{6 - 5} = 3$

$y = mx + c$

$4 = 3(6) + c$

$-14 = c$

$y = 3x - 14$

$3x - y - 14 = 0$

The equation of the line through $(0, 0)$ and $(5, 1)$:

$m = \frac{1 - 0}{5 - 0} = -\frac{1}{5}$

$y = mx + c$

$1 = 5\left(-\frac{1}{5}\right) + c$

$0 = c$

$y = -\frac{1}{5}x$

$x - 5y = 0$

The system of equalities may be written as follows:

$-6x + y \leq 0$ $3x - y - 14 \leq 0$

$2x + 5y - 32 \leq 0$ $x - 5y \leq 0$

18. See students' work.   **19.** See students' work.

33

20.

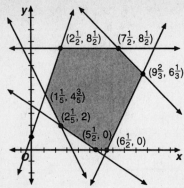

$$\begin{cases} 2y = 0 \\ 3x = -2x + 11 \end{cases} \qquad \begin{cases} 2y = 0 \\ y = 2x - 13 \end{cases}$$

$$x = 5\tfrac{1}{2}, \ y = 0 \qquad\qquad x = 6\tfrac{1}{2}, \ y = 0$$

$$\begin{cases} y = 2x - 13 \\ y = 16 - x \end{cases} \qquad \begin{cases} y = 16 - x \\ 2y = 17 \end{cases}$$

$$x = \tfrac{29}{3}, \ y = \tfrac{19}{3} \qquad x = 7\tfrac{1}{2}, \ y = 8\tfrac{1}{2}$$

$$\begin{cases} 2y = 17 \\ y = 3x + 1 \end{cases} \qquad \begin{cases} y = 3x + 1 \\ y = 7 - 2x \end{cases}$$

$$x = 2\tfrac{1}{2}, \ y = 8\tfrac{1}{2} \qquad x = \tfrac{6}{5}, \ y = \tfrac{23}{5}$$

$$\begin{cases} y = 7 - 2x \\ 3y = -2x + 11 \end{cases}$$

$$x = 2\tfrac{1}{2}, \ y = 2$$

$$f(x, y) = 5x + 6y$$

$$f\left(5\tfrac{1}{2}, 0\right) = 5\left(5\tfrac{1}{2}\right) + 6(0) = 27\tfrac{1}{2}$$

$$f\left(6\tfrac{1}{2}, 0\right) = 5\left(6\tfrac{1}{2}\right) + 6(0) = 32\tfrac{1}{2}$$

$$f\left(\tfrac{29}{3}, \tfrac{19}{3}\right) = 5\left(\tfrac{29}{3}\right) + 6\left(\tfrac{19}{3}\right) = 86\tfrac{1}{3}$$

$$f\left(7\tfrac{1}{2}, 8\tfrac{1}{2}\right) = 5\left(7\tfrac{1}{2}\right) + 6\left(8\tfrac{1}{2}\right) = 88\tfrac{1}{2}$$

$$f\left(2\tfrac{1}{2}, 8\tfrac{1}{2}\right) = 5\left(2\tfrac{1}{2}\right) + 6\left(8\tfrac{1}{2}\right) = 63\tfrac{1}{2}$$

$$f\left(\tfrac{6}{5}, \tfrac{23}{5}\right) = 5\left(\tfrac{6}{5}\right) + 6\left(\tfrac{23}{5}\right) = 33\tfrac{3}{5}$$

$$f\left(2\tfrac{1}{2}, 2\right) = 5\left(2\tfrac{1}{2}\right) + 6(2) = 24\tfrac{1}{2}$$

The maximum is at $\left(7\tfrac{1}{2}, 8\tfrac{1}{2}\right) = 88\tfrac{1}{2}$ and the minimum is at $\left(2\tfrac{1}{2}, 2\right) = 24\tfrac{1}{2}$.

21. Let s = SAT score. $\qquad s \geq 1200$

Let a = ACT score. $\qquad a \geq 30$

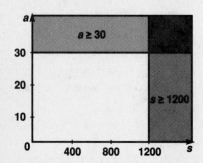

22.

Let x = number of tires.

Let y = income in dollars.

$$y \geq 3000 + 2x$$

$$y \leq 5x \qquad (1000, 5000)$$

23. $-2y = -4x + 7 \qquad 6y = 12x - 21$

$$y = 2x - \tfrac{7}{2} \quad \Rightarrow \quad y = 2x - \tfrac{7}{2}$$

consistent and dependent

24. $4x + y = 6 \qquad$ By substitution,

$$x = 2y - 12 \qquad y = -4x + 6 \qquad\qquad 0 = 2y - 12$$

$$x = 2(-4x + 6) - 12 \qquad 12 = 2y$$

$$x = -8x + 12 - 12 \qquad 6 = y$$

$$9x = 0$$

$$x = 0 \qquad\qquad (0, 6)$$

25. $(1 \times 5) - (3 \times 2) = -1 = $ determinant

Yes, an inverse exists: $-\begin{vmatrix} 5 & -3 \\ -2 & 1 \end{vmatrix}$.

26. $\begin{vmatrix} 4 & 2 & 3 & 6 \\ 2 & 7 & -3 & 0 \\ -3 & -9 & 2 & -13 \end{vmatrix} \rightarrow \begin{vmatrix} 4 & 2 & 3 & 6 \\ 0 & -12 & 9 & 6 \\ -3 & -9 & 2 & -13 \end{vmatrix} \rightarrow$

$\begin{vmatrix} 4 & 2 & 3 & 6 \\ 0 & -12 & 9 & 6 \\ 0 & -30 & 17 & -34 \end{vmatrix} \rightarrow \begin{vmatrix} 24 & 0 & 27 & 42 \\ 0 & -12 & 9 & 6 \\ 0 & -30 & 17 & -34 \end{vmatrix} \rightarrow$

$\begin{vmatrix} 24 & 0 & 27 & 42 \\ 0 & -12 & 9 & 6 \\ 0 & 0 & 22 & 196 \end{vmatrix} \rightarrow \begin{vmatrix} 24 & 0 & 27 & 42 \\ 0 & -12 & 9 & 6 \\ 0 & 0 & 1 & \tfrac{98}{11} \end{vmatrix} \rightarrow$

$\begin{vmatrix} 24 & 0 & 0 & -\tfrac{2184}{11} \\ 0 & -12 & 9 & 6 \\ 0 & 0 & 1 & \tfrac{98}{11} \end{vmatrix} \rightarrow \begin{vmatrix} 1 & 0 & 0 & -\tfrac{91}{11} \\ 0 & -12 & 9 & 6 \\ 0 & 0 & 1 & \tfrac{98}{11} \end{vmatrix} \rightarrow$

$\begin{vmatrix} 1 & 0 & 0 & -\tfrac{91}{11} \\ 0 & -12 & 0 & -\tfrac{816}{11} \\ 0 & 0 & 1 & \tfrac{98}{11} \end{vmatrix} \rightarrow \begin{vmatrix} 1 & 0 & 0 & -\tfrac{91}{11} \\ 0 & 1 & 0 & \tfrac{68}{11} \\ 0 & 0 & 1 & \tfrac{98}{11} \end{vmatrix}$

$\left(-\tfrac{91}{11}, \tfrac{68}{11}, \tfrac{98}{11}\right)$

27.

$y < x$ cannot be true

The best answer is B.

2-6   Linear Programming

1. Answers will vary, but most should say that linear programming is the process used to find the maximum and minimum values of a function under certain constraints.

2. Answers will vary, but students should focus on the fact that only the vertices of the region have to be checked to find the maximum or minimum values.

3. Answers will vary, but students should say that a linear programming problem has alternate optimal solutions when the function to be maximized or minimized is parallel to one side of the polygonal convex set.

4. $x + y \leq 800$

5. $x \geq 200$

6. $y \geq 300$

7. $P(x, y) = 20x + 30y$

8.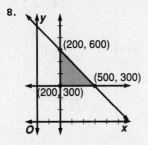

9. (200, 600), (500, 300), (200, 300)

10. $P(x, y) = 20x + 30y$

   $P(200, 600) = 20(200) + 30(600) = 22,000$

   $P(500, 300) = 20(500) + 30(300) = 19,000$

   200 units of lumber and 600 units of plywood

11. maximum profit = $22,000

12.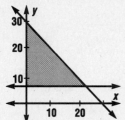

   alternate optimal

13.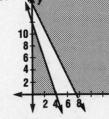

   infeasible

14.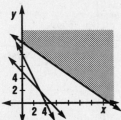

   unbounded solution

15. Let x = number of Travelers.

   Let y = number of Touristers.

   $x + y \leq 300$

   $x + 3y \leq 360$

   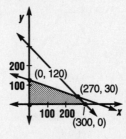

   $f(x, y) = 200x + 600y$

   (0, 0), (0, 120), (270, 30), (300, 0)

   $f(0, 0) = 200(0) + 600(0) = 0$

   $f(0, 120) = 200(0) + 600(120) = 72,000$

   $f(270, 30) = 200(270) + 600(30) = 72,000$

   $f(300, 0) = 200(300) + 600(0) = 60,000$

   alternate optimal solutions

16. Let x = number of widgets.

   Let y = number of gadgets.

   $1200 \geq x \geq 500$

   $1400 \geq y \geq 700$

   $x + y \leq 2300$

   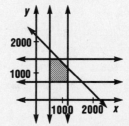

   (500, 700), (500, 1400), (900, 1400), (1200, 700), (1200, 1100)

   a. $f(x, y) = 0.40x + 0.50y$

   $f(500, 700) = 0.40(500) + 0.50(700) = 550$

   $f(500, 1400) = 0.40(500) + 0.50(1400) = 900$

   $f(900, 1400) = 0.40(900) + 0.50(1400) = 1060$

   $f(1200, 700) = 0.40(1200) + 0.50(700) = 830$

   $f(1200, 1100) = 0.40(1200) + 0.50(1100) = 1030$

   900 widgets and 1400 gadgets for a maximum daily income of $1060

   b. $P(x, y) = 0.40x - 0.07x + 0.50y - 0.18y$

   $P(x, y) = 0.33x + 0.32y$

   $P(500, 700) = 0.33(500) + 0.32(700) = 389$

   $P(500, 1400) = 0.33(500) + 0.32(1400) = 613$

   $P(900, 1400) = 0.33(900) + 0.32(1400) = 745$

   $P(1200, 700) = 0.33(1200) + 0.32(700) = 620$

   $P(1200, 1100) = 0.33(1200) + 0.32(1100) = 748$

   1200 widgets and 1100 gadgets for a maximum daily profit of $748

17. Let x = Type X food.

Let y = Type Y food.

$10x + 30y \geq 140$

$20x + 15y \geq 145$

$\left(0, 9\frac{2}{3}\right)$, $(5, 3)$, $(14, 0)$

$f(x, y) = 12x + 8y$

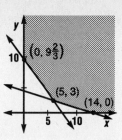

$f\left(0, 9\frac{2}{3}\right) = 12(0) + 8\left(9\frac{2}{3}\right) = 17.67$

$f(5, 3) = 12(5) + 8(3) = 84$

$f(14, 0) = 12(14) + 8(0) = 168$

$9\frac{2}{3}$ Type Y food and 0 Type X food should be

purchased.

18. Let x = number of Drivers.

Let y = number of Masters.

$2x + 2y \leq 10,000$

$x + 3y \leq 9000$

$2x + 3y \leq 12,000$

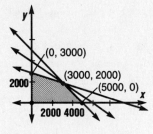

$(0, 0)$, $(0, 3000)$, $(3000, 2000)$, $(5000, 0)$

$f(x, y) = 30x + 40y$

$f(0, 0) = 30(0) + 40(0) = 0$

$f(0, 3000) = 30(0) + 40(3000) = 120,000$

$f(3000, 2000) = 30(3000) + 40(2000) = 170,000$

$f(5000, 0) = 30(5000) + 40(0) = 150,000$

$170,000$ is the maximum revenue for the coming

month.

19. Let x = number of masters.

Let y = number of apprentices.

$x + y \geq 30$

$3x \geq 25$

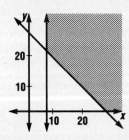

$f(x) = 750x + 350y$

The solution is unbounded.

20. Let x = light fixture A.

Let y = light fixture B.

$12x + 18y \leq 14,400$

$2x + y \leq 1200$

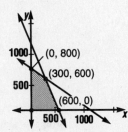

$(0, 0)$, $(0, 800)$, $(300, 600)$, $(600, 0)$

a. $f(x, y) = 1.50x + 1.70y$

$f(0, 0) = 1.50(0) + 1.70(0) = 0$

$f(0, 800) = 1.50(0) + 1.70(800) = 1360$

$f(300, 600) = 1.50(300) + 1.70(600) = 1470$

$f(600, 0) = 1.50(600) + 1.70(0) = 900$

300 Type A and 600 Type B; maximum income of

$1470

b. $P(x, y) = 1.50x - 0.75x + 1.70y - 0.85y$

$= 0.75x + 0.85y$

$P(0, 0) = 0.75(0) + 0.85(0) = 0$

$P(0, 800) = 0.75(0) + 0.85(800) = 680$

$P(300, 600) = 0.75(300) + 0.85(600) = 735$

$P(600, 0) = 0.75(600) + 0.85(0) = 450$

300 Type A and 600 Type B; maximum profit of

$735

21. Let x = number of gallons of #1 crude.

Let y = number of gallons of #2 crude.

$x + y \geq 3800$

$0.02x + 0.05y \geq 120$

$0.06x + 0.01y \geq 136$

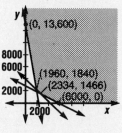

$(0, 13,600)$, $(1960, 1840)$, $(2334, 1466)$,

$(6000, 0)$

$f(x, y) = 1.50x + 1.10y$

$f(0, 13,600) = 1.50(0) + 1.10(13,600) = 14,960$

$f(1960, 1840) = 1.50(1960) + 1.10(1840) = 4964$

$f(2334, 1466) = 1.50(2334) + 1.10(1466) = 5113.60$

$f(6000, 0) = 1.50(6000) + 1.10(0) = 9000$

1960 gallons of crude #1 and 1840 gallons of

crude #2

22. Let x = number of letter-size file cabinets.

Let y = number of legal-size file cabinets.

$36x + 54y \leq 120,000$

$42x + 52y \leq 375,000$

$18x + 21y \leq 194,500$

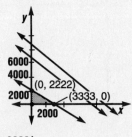

$(0, 0)$, $(3333, 0)$, $(0, 2222)$

$f(x, y) = 138x + 176.50y$

$f(0, 0) = 138(0) + 176.50(0) = 0$

$f(3333, 0) = 138(3333) + 176.50(0) = 459,954$

$f(0, 2222) = 138(0) + 176.50(2222) = 392,183$

3333 letter-size filing cabinets only

23. Let x = gallons of black walnut.
Let y = gallons of tutti frutti.
$x + y \leq 45,000$
$y \geq 20,000$
$x \geq 3y$
$f(x) = 2.95(x + y)$
infeasible

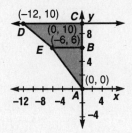

24. Graph the boundaries of the closed figure and extend a line from point (-6, 6) to point (0, 6). Now, $\triangle ABE$ is a right triangle of area = $\frac{1}{2}(6)(6) = 18$. The trapezoid $BCDE$ has area = $\frac{1}{2}(12 + 6)(4) = 36$. Therefore, the area of the closed figure is $18 + 36 = 54$ square units.

25. $\begin{bmatrix} 8 & -7 \\ -4 & 0 \end{bmatrix} \frac{3}{4} = \begin{bmatrix} 8\left(\frac{3}{4}\right) & -7\left(\frac{3}{4}\right) \\ -4\left(\frac{3}{4}\right) & -0\left(\frac{3}{4}\right) \end{bmatrix} = \begin{bmatrix} 6 & -\frac{21}{4} \\ -3 & 0 \end{bmatrix}$

26. $\frac{1}{7}\begin{bmatrix} 2 & -1 \\ 3 & 2 \end{bmatrix}$

27. Multiply row 2 by -3 and add it to row 1.
Multiply row 1 by 2 and row 2 by 3 and add row 1 to row 2.

28. $f(0, 0) = 0 + 2(0) = 0$
$f(4, 0) = 4 + 2(0) = 4$
$f(3, 5) = 3 + 2(5) = 13$
$f(0, 5) = 0 + 2(5) = 10$ 13, 0

29. $\sqrt{\dfrac{\sqrt{25}}{5}} = \sqrt{\dfrac{5}{5}} = \sqrt{1} = 1$
The best answer is A.

Case Study Follow-Up

PAGE 97

1. Let x = rent.
Let y = mortgage payment before deductions.
$x \leq 800$
$x + 0.75y \leq 2000$
(800, 1600), (2000, 0)
$f(x, y) = x + 0.75y$
$f(800, 1200) = 800 + 0.75(1200) = 1700$
$f(2000, 0) = 2000 + 0.75(0) = 2000$
\$800 in rent + \$900 in mortgage payments (after deductions) = \$1700

2. about \$120,000

3. See students' work.

Chapter 2 Summary and Review

PAGES 98-100   SKILLS AND CONCEPTS

1. By substitution,
$x + (-2x) = -2$ $y = -2(2)$
$-x = -2$ $y = -4$
$x = 2$ (2, -4)

2. By substitution,
$(6y) - y = 5$ $x = 6(1)$
$5y = 5$ $x = 6$
$y = 1$ (6, 1)

3. By substitution,
$5y - 2(-1 - 3y) = 0$ $3\left(-\dfrac{2}{11}\right) + x = -1$
$5y + 2 + 6y = 0$ $-\dfrac{6}{11} + x = -1$
$11y = -2$
$y = -\dfrac{2}{11}$ $x = -\dfrac{5}{11}$
$\left(-\dfrac{5}{11}, -\dfrac{2}{11}\right)$

4. By substitution,
$-15x + 2(6x + 1) = -4$ $y - 6(2) = 1$
$-15x + 12x + 2 = -4$ $y - 12 = 1$
$-3x + 2 = -4$ $y = 13$
$-3x = -6$
$x = 2$ (2, 13)

5. $\begin{bmatrix} 7 & 8 \\ 0 & -4 \end{bmatrix} + \begin{bmatrix} -3 & -5 \\ 2 & -2 \end{bmatrix} = \begin{bmatrix} 7-3 & 8-5 \\ 0+2 & -4-2 \end{bmatrix} = \begin{bmatrix} 4 & 3 \\ 2 & -6 \end{bmatrix}$

6. $\begin{bmatrix} -3 & -5 \\ 2 & -2 \end{bmatrix} + (-1)\begin{bmatrix} 7 & 8 \\ 0 & -4 \end{bmatrix} = \begin{bmatrix} -3 + (-7) & -5 + (-8) \\ 2 + 0 & -2 + 4 \end{bmatrix}$
$= \begin{bmatrix} -10 & -13 \\ 2 & 2 \end{bmatrix}$

7. $3\begin{bmatrix} -3 & -5 \\ 2 & -2 \end{bmatrix} = \begin{bmatrix} 3(-3) & 3(-5) \\ 3(2) & 3(-2) \end{bmatrix} = \begin{bmatrix} -9 & -15 \\ 6 & -6 \end{bmatrix}$

8. $-4\begin{bmatrix} 2 \\ -5 \end{bmatrix} = \begin{bmatrix} -4(2) \\ -4(-5) \end{bmatrix} = \begin{bmatrix} -8 \\ 20 \end{bmatrix}$

9. $AB = \begin{bmatrix} 7 & 8 \\ 0 & -4 \end{bmatrix}\begin{bmatrix} -3 & -5 \\ 2 & -2 \end{bmatrix}$

$= \begin{bmatrix} 7(-3) + 8(2) & 7(-5) + 8(-2) \\ 0(-3) + (-4)(2) & 0(-5) + (-4)(-2) \end{bmatrix} = \begin{bmatrix} -5 & -51 \\ -8 & 8 \end{bmatrix}$

10. $BC = \begin{bmatrix} -3 & -5 \\ 2 & -2 \end{bmatrix}\begin{bmatrix} 2 \\ -5 \end{bmatrix} = \begin{bmatrix} -3(2) + (-5)(-5) \\ 2(2) + (-2)(-5) \end{bmatrix} = \begin{bmatrix} 19 \\ 14 \end{bmatrix}$

11. $\begin{vmatrix} 7 & -4 \\ 5 & -3 \end{vmatrix} = (7)(-3) - (-4)(5) = -21 + 20 = -1$

12. $\begin{vmatrix} 8 & -4 \\ -6 & 3 \end{vmatrix} = (8)(3) - (-4)(-6) = 0$

13. $\begin{vmatrix} 5 & 0 & 4 \\ 7 & 3 & -1 \\ 2 & -2 & 6 \end{vmatrix} = 5\begin{vmatrix} 3 & -1 \\ -2 & 6 \end{vmatrix} + 4\begin{vmatrix} 7 & 3 \\ 2 & -2 \end{vmatrix}$

$= 5(18 - 2) + 4(-14 - 6) = 0$

14. $\begin{vmatrix} 3 & -1 & 4 \\ 5 & -2 & 6 \\ 7 & 3 & -4 \end{vmatrix} = 3\begin{vmatrix} -2 & 6 \\ 3 & -4 \end{vmatrix} - (-1)\begin{vmatrix} 5 & 6 \\ 7 & -4 \end{vmatrix} + 4\begin{vmatrix} 5 & -2 \\ 7 & 3 \end{vmatrix}$

$= 3(8 - 18) + 1(-20 - 42) + 4(15 + 14)$

$= -30 - 62 + 116 = 24$

15. $-1\begin{bmatrix} -3 & -5 \\ 1 & 2 \end{bmatrix}\begin{bmatrix} 2 & 5 \\ -1 & -3 \end{bmatrix}\begin{bmatrix} x \\ y \end{bmatrix} = -1\begin{bmatrix} -3 & -5 \\ 1 & 2 \end{bmatrix}\begin{bmatrix} 1 \\ 2 \end{bmatrix}$

$\begin{bmatrix} x \\ y \end{bmatrix} = -1\begin{bmatrix} -3 - 10 \\ 1 + 4 \end{bmatrix}$

$\begin{bmatrix} x \\ y \end{bmatrix} = \begin{bmatrix} 13 \\ -5 \end{bmatrix} \qquad (13, -5)$

16. $\frac{1}{24}\begin{bmatrix} 4 & -2 \\ 6 & 3 \end{bmatrix}\begin{bmatrix} 3 & 2 \\ -6 & 4 \end{bmatrix}\begin{bmatrix} x \\ y \end{bmatrix} = \frac{1}{24}\begin{bmatrix} 4 & -2 \\ 6 & 3 \end{bmatrix}\begin{bmatrix} -3 \\ 6 \end{bmatrix}$

$\begin{bmatrix} x \\ y \end{bmatrix} = \frac{1}{24}\begin{bmatrix} -12 - 12 \\ -18 + 18 \end{bmatrix}$

$\begin{bmatrix} x \\ y \end{bmatrix} = \begin{bmatrix} -1 \\ 0 \end{bmatrix} \qquad (-1, 0)$

17. $-\frac{1}{2}\begin{bmatrix} 4 & -5 \\ 2 & -3 \end{bmatrix}\begin{bmatrix} -3 & 5 \\ -2 & 4 \end{bmatrix}\begin{bmatrix} x \\ y \end{bmatrix} = -\frac{1}{2}\begin{bmatrix} 4 & -5 \\ 2 & -3 \end{bmatrix}\begin{bmatrix} 1 \\ -2 \end{bmatrix}$

$\begin{bmatrix} x \\ y \end{bmatrix} = -\frac{1}{2}\begin{bmatrix} 4 + 10 \\ 2 + 6 \end{bmatrix}$

$\begin{bmatrix} x \\ y \end{bmatrix} = \begin{bmatrix} -7 \\ -4 \end{bmatrix} \qquad (-7, -4)$

18. $\begin{bmatrix} 1 & -2 & -3 & 2 \\ 1 & -4 & 3 & 14 \\ -3 & 5 & 4 & 0 \end{bmatrix} \rightarrow \begin{bmatrix} 1 & -2 & -3 & 2 \\ 0 & -2 & 6 & 12 \\ -3 & 5 & 4 & 0 \end{bmatrix} \rightarrow$

$\begin{bmatrix} 1 & -2 & -3 & 2 \\ 0 & -2 & 6 & 12 \\ 0 & -1 & -5 & 6 \end{bmatrix} \rightarrow \begin{bmatrix} 1 & -2 & -3 & 2 \\ 0 & -2 & 6 & 12 \\ 0 & 0 & 16 & 0 \end{bmatrix} \rightarrow \begin{bmatrix} 1 & -2 & -3 & 2 \\ 0 & -2 & 6 & 12 \\ 0 & 0 & 1 & 0 \end{bmatrix} \rightarrow$

$\begin{bmatrix} 1 & -2 & -3 & 2 \\ 0 & -2 & 0 & 12 \\ 0 & 0 & 1 & 0 \end{bmatrix} \rightarrow \begin{bmatrix} 1 & -2 & -3 & 2 \\ 0 & 1 & 0 & -6 \\ 0 & 0 & 1 & 0 \end{bmatrix} \rightarrow \begin{bmatrix} 1 & 0 & -3 & -10 \\ 0 & 1 & 0 & -6 \\ 0 & 0 & 1 & 0 \end{bmatrix} \rightarrow$

$\begin{bmatrix} 1 & 0 & 0 & -10 \\ 0 & 1 & 0 & -6 \\ 0 & 0 & 1 & 0 \end{bmatrix} \qquad (-10, -6, 0)$

19. $\begin{bmatrix} 2 & 3 & -4 & 5 \\ 1 & 1 & 2 & 3 \\ -1 & 2 & -6 & 4 \end{bmatrix} \rightarrow \begin{bmatrix} 2 & 3 & -4 & 5 \\ 0 & 1 & -8 & -1 \\ -1 & 2 & -6 & 4 \end{bmatrix} \rightarrow \begin{bmatrix} 2 & 3 & -4 & 5 \\ 0 & 1 & -8 & -1 \\ 0 & 7 & -16 & 13 \end{bmatrix} \rightarrow$

$\begin{bmatrix} 2 & 3 & -4 & 5 \\ 0 & 5 & 0 & 15 \\ 0 & 7 & -16 & 13 \end{bmatrix} \rightarrow \begin{bmatrix} 2 & 3 & -4 & 5 \\ 0 & 1 & 0 & 3 \\ 0 & 7 & -16 & 13 \end{bmatrix} \rightarrow \begin{bmatrix} 2 & 3 & -4 & 5 \\ 0 & 1 & 0 & 3 \\ 0 & 0 & -16 & -8 \end{bmatrix} \rightarrow$

$\begin{bmatrix} 2 & 3 & -4 & 5 \\ 0 & 1 & 0 & 3 \\ 0 & 0 & 1 & \frac{1}{2} \end{bmatrix} \rightarrow \begin{bmatrix} 2 & 0 & -4 & -4 \\ 0 & 1 & 0 & 3 \\ 0 & 0 & 1 & \frac{1}{2} \end{bmatrix} \rightarrow \begin{bmatrix} 2 & 0 & 0 & -2 \\ 0 & 1 & 0 & 3 \\ 0 & 0 & 1 & \frac{1}{2} \end{bmatrix} \rightarrow$

$\begin{bmatrix} 1 & 0 & 0 & -1 \\ 0 & 1 & 0 & 3 \\ 0 & 0 & 1 & \frac{1}{2} \end{bmatrix} \qquad \left(-1, 3, \frac{1}{2}\right)$

20.

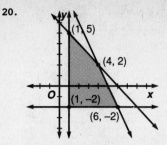

(1, -2), (1, 5), (4, 2), (6, -2)

$f(x, y) = 3y + 2x - 4$

$f(1, -2) = 3(-2) + 2(1) - 4 = -8$

$f(1, 5) = 3(5) + 2(1) - 4 = 13$

$f(4, 2) = 3(2) + 2(4) - 4 = 10$

$f(5, 1) = 3(1) + 2(5) - 4 = 9$

maximum at $(1, 5) = 13$

minimum at $(1, -2) = -8$

21.

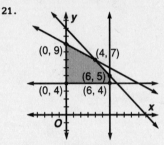

(0, 4), (0, 9), (4, 7), (6, 4), (6, 5)

$f(x, y) = 3y + 2x - 4$

$f(0, 4) = 3(4) + 2(0) - 4 = 8$

$f(0, 9) = 3(9) + 2(0) - 4 = 23$

$f(4, 7) = 3(7) + 2(4) - 4 = 25$

$f(6, 4) = 3(4) + 2(6) - 4 = 20$

$f(6, 5) = 3(5) + 2(6) - 4 = 23$

maximum at $(4, 7) = 25$

minimum at $(0, 4) = 8$

22.   **23.**

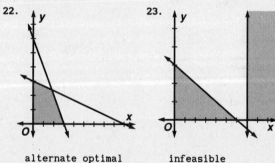

alternate optimal   infeasible

PAGE 100   APPLICATIONS AND PROBLEM SOLVING

24. $\begin{bmatrix} 2 & 5 & 5 \\ 8 & 2 & 3 \\ 6 & 4 & 1 \end{bmatrix}\begin{bmatrix} 5 \\ 3 \\ 1 \end{bmatrix} = \begin{bmatrix} 2(5) + 5(3) + 5(1) \\ 8(5) + 2(3) + 3(1) \\ 6(5) + 4(3) + 1(1) \end{bmatrix} = \begin{bmatrix} 39 \\ 49 \\ 43 \end{bmatrix}$

Boardman: 30; Girard: 49; Niles: 43

25. Let x = shortest side, y = middle-length side, z = longest side.

$$x + y + z = 83 \longrightarrow x + y + z = 83$$
$$z = 3x \longrightarrow 3x \qquad - z = 0$$
$$\tfrac{1}{2}(x + y) + 17 = z \longrightarrow x + y + 34 = 2z$$

$$\begin{bmatrix} 1 & 1 & 1 & 83 \\ 3 & 0 & -1 & 0 \\ 1 & 1 & -2 & -34 \end{bmatrix} \rightarrow \begin{bmatrix} 1 & 1 & 1 & 83 \\ 0 & -3 & -4 & -249 \\ 1 & 1 & -2 & -34 \end{bmatrix} \rightarrow$$

$$\begin{bmatrix} 1 & 1 & 1 & 83 \\ 0 & -3 & -4 & -279 \\ 0 & 0 & 3 & 117 \end{bmatrix} \rightarrow \begin{bmatrix} 1 & 1 & 1 & 83 \\ 0 & -3 & -4 & -279 \\ 0 & 0 & 1 & 39 \end{bmatrix} \rightarrow$$

$$\begin{bmatrix} 4 & 1 & 0 & 83 \\ 0 & -3 & -4 & -249 \\ 0 & 0 & 1 & 39 \end{bmatrix} \rightarrow \begin{bmatrix} 4 & 1 & 0 & 83 \\ 0 & -3 & 0 & -93 \\ 0 & 0 & 1 & 39 \end{bmatrix} \rightarrow$$

$$\begin{bmatrix} 4 & 1 & 0 & 83 \\ 0 & 1 & 0 & 31 \\ 0 & 0 & 1 & 39 \end{bmatrix} \rightarrow \begin{bmatrix} 4 & 0 & 0 & 52 \\ 0 & 1 & 0 & 31 \\ 0 & 0 & 1 & 39 \end{bmatrix} \rightarrow \begin{bmatrix} 1 & 0 & 0 & 13 \\ 0 & 1 & 0 & 31 \\ 0 & 0 & 1 & 39 \end{bmatrix}$$

$x = 13$ inches; $y = 31$ inches; $z = 39$ inches

26. Let x = number of Voyagers.
Let y = number of Explorers.

$$5x + 6y \leq 240$$
$$3x + 2y \leq 120$$
$$5x + 18y \leq 540$$

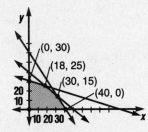

$(0, 0)$, $(0, 30)$, $(18, 25)$, $(30, 15)$, $(40, 0)$

a. $P(x, y) = 2.40x + 5.00y$

$P(0, 0) = 240(0) + 5.00(0) = 0$

$P(0, 30) = 2.40(0) + 5.00(30) = 150$

$P(18, 25) = 2.40(18) + 5.00(25) = 168.20$

$P(30, 15) = 2.40(30) + 5.00(15) = 147$

$P(40, 0) = 2.40(40) + 5.00(0) = 96$

18 Voyagers and 25 Explorers

b. $168.20 maximum daily profit

Chapter 2 Test

PAGE 101

1. By substitution,

$x = y + 4$

$y = 2(y + 4) - 8$ $\qquad$ $x = 0 + 4$

$y = 2y$ $\qquad$ $x = 4$

$0 = y$ $\qquad$ $(4, 0)$

2. By substitution,

$x = y - 5$

$3(y - 5) = y - 1$ $\qquad$ $x = 7 - 5$

$3y - 15 = y - 1$ $\qquad$ $x = 2$

$2y = 14$

$y = 7$ $\qquad$ $(2, 7)$

3. By substitution,

$y = 8 + 3x$

$x + (8 + 3x) = 4$ $\qquad$ $y = 8 + 3(-1)$

$4x + 8 = 4$ $\qquad$ $y = 8 - 3$

$4x = -4$ $\qquad$ $y = 5$

$x = -1$ $\qquad$ $(-1, 5)$

4. By substitution,

$2x + 7(5 - 6x) = 5$ $\qquad$ $5 - 6\left(\dfrac{3}{4}\right) = y$

$2x + 35 - 42x = 5$ $\qquad$ $\dfrac{20}{4} - \dfrac{18}{4} = y$

$-40x = -30$ $\qquad$ $\dfrac{2}{4} = y$

$x = \dfrac{3}{4}$ $\qquad$ $\left(\dfrac{3}{4}, \dfrac{1}{2}\right)$

5. $5D = 5\begin{bmatrix} 1 & -2 \\ 0 & 4 \\ -3 & 4 \end{bmatrix} = \begin{bmatrix} 5(1) & 5(-2) \\ 5(0) & 5(4) \\ 5(3) & 5(4) \end{bmatrix} = \begin{bmatrix} 5 & -10 \\ 0 & 20 \\ -15 & 20 \end{bmatrix}$

6. $2A + B = 2\begin{bmatrix} 5 & 4 \\ -1 & -2 \end{bmatrix} + \begin{bmatrix} -1 & -2 \\ 5 & 4 \end{bmatrix}$

$= \begin{bmatrix} 2(5) - 1 & 2(4) - 2 \\ 2(-1) + 5 & 2(-2) + 4 \end{bmatrix} = \begin{bmatrix} 9 & 6 \\ 3 & 0 \end{bmatrix}$

7. $2B - A = 2\begin{bmatrix} -1 & -2 \\ 5 & 4 \end{bmatrix} + (-1)\begin{bmatrix} 5 & 4 \\ -1 & -2 \end{bmatrix}$

$= \begin{bmatrix} 2(-1) - 5 & 2(-2) - 4 \\ 2(5) + 1 & 2(4) + 2 \end{bmatrix} = \begin{bmatrix} -7 & -8 \\ 11 & 10 \end{bmatrix}$

8. $CD = \begin{bmatrix} -2 & 4 & 6 \\ 5 & -7 & -1 \end{bmatrix}\begin{bmatrix} 1 & -2 \\ 0 & 4 \\ -3 & 4 \end{bmatrix}$

$= \begin{bmatrix} -2(1)+4(0)+6(-3) & -2(-2)+4(4)+6(4) \\ 5(1)+-7(0)+(-1)(-3) & 5(-2)+(-7)(4)+(-1)(4) \end{bmatrix}$

$= \begin{bmatrix} -20 & 44 \\ 8 & -42 \end{bmatrix}$

9. $AB + CD = \begin{bmatrix} 5 & 4 \\ -1 & -2 \end{bmatrix}\begin{bmatrix} -1 & -2 \\ 5 & 4 \end{bmatrix} + \begin{bmatrix} -2 & 4 & 6 \\ 5 & -7 & -1 \end{bmatrix}\begin{bmatrix} 1 & -2 \\ 0 & 4 \\ -3 & 4 \end{bmatrix}$

$= \begin{bmatrix} 5(-1)+4(5) & 5(-2)+4(4) \\ -1(-1)+(-2)(5) & -1(-2)+(-2)(4) \end{bmatrix} +$

$\begin{bmatrix} -2(1)+4(0)+6(-3) & -2(-2)+4(4)+6(4) \\ 5(1)+(-7)(0)+(-1)(-3) & 5(-2)+(-7)(4)+(-1)(4) \end{bmatrix}$

$= \begin{bmatrix} 15 & 6 \\ -9 & -6 \end{bmatrix}\begin{bmatrix} -20 & 44 \\ 8 & -42 \end{bmatrix} = \begin{bmatrix} -5 & 50 \\ -1 & -48 \end{bmatrix}$

10. $\begin{vmatrix} -3 & 5 \\ 1 & -4 \end{vmatrix} = -3(-4) - (5)(1) = 7$

11. $\begin{vmatrix} 8 & 5 \\ -3 & -2 \end{vmatrix} = 8(-2) - (5)(-3) = -1$

12. $\begin{vmatrix} 2 & 1 & -1 \\ 6 & 4 & -3 \\ 0 & 2 & -2 \end{vmatrix} = 2\begin{vmatrix} 4 & -3 \\ 2 & -2 \end{vmatrix} - 1\begin{vmatrix} 6 & -3 \\ 0 & -2 \end{vmatrix} + (-1)\begin{vmatrix} 6 & 4 \\ 0 & 2 \end{vmatrix}$

$= 2(-2) - 1(-12) - 1(12) = -4$

13. $\begin{vmatrix} 3 & 1 & 2 \\ -2 & 0 & 4 \\ 3 & 5 & 2 \end{vmatrix} = 3\begin{vmatrix} 0 & 4 \\ 5 & 2 \end{vmatrix} - 1\begin{vmatrix} -2 & 4 \\ 3 & 2 \end{vmatrix} + 2\begin{vmatrix} -2 & 0 \\ 3 & 5 \end{vmatrix}$

$= 3(-20) - 1(-16) + 2(-10) = -64$

14. $-\dfrac{1}{28}\begin{bmatrix} 0 & -4 \\ -7 & -1 \end{bmatrix}\begin{bmatrix} -1 & 4 \\ 7 & 0 \end{bmatrix}\begin{bmatrix} x \\ y \end{bmatrix} = -\dfrac{1}{28}\begin{bmatrix} 0 & -4 \\ -7 & -1 \end{bmatrix}\begin{bmatrix} -1 \\ -14 \end{bmatrix}$

$\begin{bmatrix} x \\ y \end{bmatrix} = -\dfrac{1}{28}\begin{bmatrix} 56 \\ 21 \end{bmatrix}$

$\begin{bmatrix} x \\ y \end{bmatrix} = \begin{bmatrix} -2 \\ -\dfrac{3}{4} \end{bmatrix}$ $\qquad$ $\left(-2, -\dfrac{3}{4}\right)$

15. $\begin{bmatrix} 1 & 2 & 1 & 3 \\ 2 & -3 & 2 & -1 \\ 1 & -3 & 2 & 1 \end{bmatrix} \rightarrow \begin{bmatrix} 1 & 2 & 1 & 3 \\ 2 & -3 & 2 & -1 \\ 0 & -5 & 1 & -2 \end{bmatrix} \rightarrow \begin{bmatrix} 1 & 2 & 1 & 3 \\ 0 & -7 & 0 & -7 \\ 0 & -5 & 1 & -2 \end{bmatrix} \rightarrow$

$\begin{bmatrix} 1 & 2 & 1 & 3 \\ 0 & 1 & 0 & 1 \\ 0 & -5 & 1 & -2 \end{bmatrix} \rightarrow \begin{bmatrix} 1 & 2 & 1 & 3 \\ 0 & 1 & 0 & 1 \\ 0 & 0 & 1 & 3 \end{bmatrix} \rightarrow \begin{bmatrix} 1 & 0 & 1 & 1 \\ 0 & 1 & 0 & 1 \\ 0 & 0 & 1 & 3 \end{bmatrix} \rightarrow$

$\begin{bmatrix} 1 & 0 & 0 & -2 \\ 0 & 1 & 0 & 1 \\ 0 & 0 & 1 & 3 \end{bmatrix}$ $(-2, 1, 3)$

16. $\begin{bmatrix} -3 & 1 & 1 & 2 \\ 5 & 2 & -4 & 21 \\ 1 & -3 & -7 & -10 \end{bmatrix} \rightarrow \begin{bmatrix} -3 & 1 & 1 & 2 \\ 5 & 2 & -4 & 21 \\ 0 & -8 & -20 & -28 \end{bmatrix} \rightarrow$

$\begin{bmatrix} -3 & 1 & 1 & 2 \\ 0 & 11 & -7 & 73 \\ 0 & -8 & -20 & -28 \end{bmatrix} \rightarrow \begin{bmatrix} -3 & 1 & 1 & 2 \\ 0 & 11 & -7 & 73 \\ 0 & 0 & -276 & 276 \end{bmatrix} \rightarrow$

$\begin{bmatrix} -3 & 1 & 1 & 2 \\ 0 & 11 & -7 & 73 \\ 0 & 0 & 1 & -1 \end{bmatrix} \rightarrow \begin{bmatrix} 33 & 0 & -18 & 51 \\ 0 & 11 & -7 & 73 \\ 0 & 0 & 1 & -1 \end{bmatrix} \rightarrow$

$\begin{bmatrix} 33 & 0 & -18 & 51 \\ 0 & 11 & 0 & 66 \\ 0 & 0 & 1 & -1 \end{bmatrix} \rightarrow \begin{bmatrix} 33 & 0 & -18 & 51 \\ 0 & 1 & 0 & 6 \\ 0 & 0 & 1 & -1 \end{bmatrix} \rightarrow$

$\begin{bmatrix} 33 & 0 & 0 & 33 \\ 0 & 1 & 0 & 6 \\ 0 & 0 & 1 & -1 \end{bmatrix} \rightarrow \begin{bmatrix} 1 & 0 & 0 & 1 \\ 0 & 1 & 0 & 6 \\ 0 & 0 & 1 & -1 \end{bmatrix}$ $(1, 6, -1)$

17.

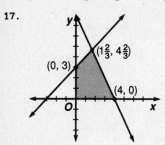

$(0, 0)$, $(0, 3)$, $\left(1\frac{2}{3}, 4\frac{2}{3}\right)$, $(4, 0)$

$f(x, y) = 5y + 3x$

$f(0, 0) = 5(0) + 3(0) = 0$

$f(0, 3) = 5(3) + 3(0) = 15$

$f\left(1\frac{2}{3}, 4\frac{2}{3}\right) = 5\left(4\frac{2}{3}\right) + 3\left(1\frac{2}{3}\right) = 28\frac{1}{3}$

$f(4, 0) = 5(0) + 3(4) = 12$

maximum at $\left(1\frac{2}{3}, 4\frac{2}{3}\right) = 28\frac{1}{3}$

minimum at $(0, 0) = 0$

18.

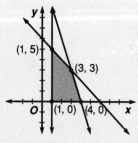

$(1, 0)$, $(1, 5)$, $(3, 3)$, $(4, 0)$

$f(x, y) = 5y + 3x$

$f(1, 0) = 5(0) + 3(1) = 3$

$f(1, 5) = 5(5) + 3(1) = 28$

$f(3, 3) = 5(3) + 3(3) = 24$

$f(4, 0) = 5(0) + 3(4) = 12$

maximum at $(1, 5) = 28$

minimum at $(0, 0) = 3$

19.

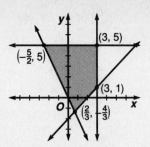

$\left(-\frac{5}{2}, 5\right)$, $(3, 5)$, $(3, 1)$, $\left(\frac{2}{3}, -\frac{4}{3}\right)$

$f(x, y) = 5y + 3x$

$f\left(-\frac{5}{2}, 5\right) = 5(5) + 3\left(-\frac{5}{2}\right) = 7\frac{1}{2}$

$f(3, 5) = 5(5) + 3(3) = 34$

$f(3, 1) = 5(1) + 3(3) = 14$

$f\left(\frac{2}{3}, -\frac{4}{3}\right) = 5\left(-\frac{4}{3}\right) + 3\left(\frac{2}{3}\right) = -4\frac{2}{3}$

maximum at $(3, 5) = 34$

minimum at $\left(\frac{2}{3}, -\frac{4}{3}\right) = -4\frac{2}{3}$

20. Let x = number of large bookcases.

Let y = number of small bookcases.

$6x + 2y \leq 24$

$x \geq 2$

$y \geq 2$

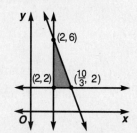

The vertices of the convex polygon are $(2, 2)$, $(2, 6)$, and $\left(\frac{10}{3}, 2\right)$. If P is the profit function, then $P(x, y) = 80x + 50y$.

$P(2, 2) = 80(2) + 50(2) = 260$

$P(2, 6) = 80(2) + 50(6) = 460$

$P\left(\frac{10}{3}, 2\right) = 80\left(\frac{10}{3}\right) + 50(2) = 366.67$

The maximum weekly profit is $460 when 2 large bookcases and 6 small bookcases are made.

PAGE 101   BONUS

The polygonal area is a pentagon as seen by graphing the given condition for n = any positive unit.

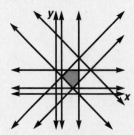

40

Chapter 3   The Nature of Graphs

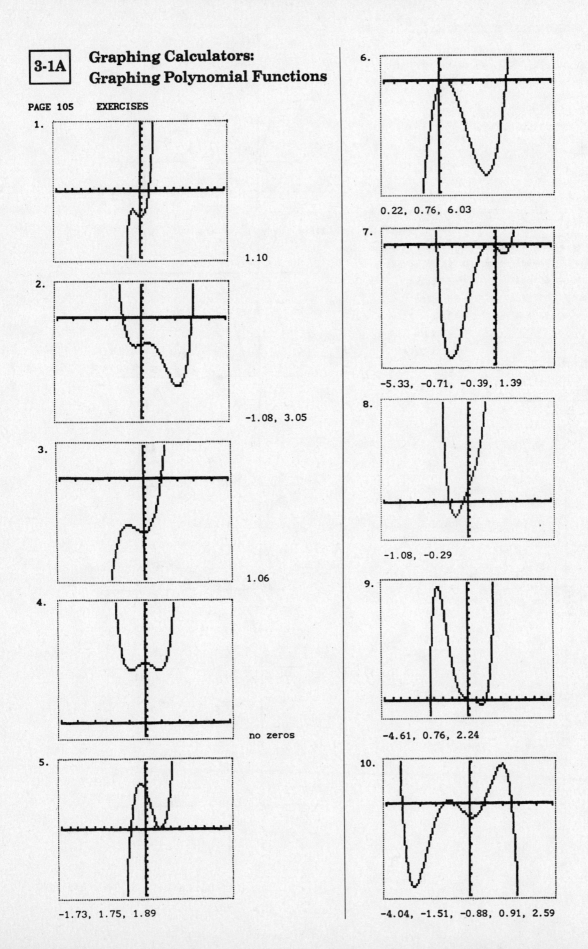

3-1A   **Graphing Calculators:**
Graphing Polynomial Functions

PAGE 105   EXERCISES

1.

1.10

2.

−1.08, 3.05

3.

1.06

4.

no zeros

5.

−1.73, 1.75, 1.89

6.

0.22, 0.76, 6.03

7.

−5.33, −0.71, −0.39, 1.39

8.

−1.08, −0.29

9.

−4.61, 0.76, 2.24

10.

−4.04, −1.51, −0.88, 0.91, 2.59

PAGE 113   CHECKING FOR UNDERSTANDING

1. the origin

2.

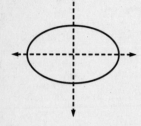

3. a. $-f(x)$
   b. $f(x)$
   c. $45°$

4. Each term containing x has an even power. When evaluating the function, this always results in a positive number. A positive number is added to this. This result must always be positive.

5. both   6. neither   7. point
8. both   9. line   10. line
11. $x = 2$ 12. $y = -5$ 13. $x = 2, y = -2$

14.
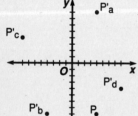

a. $(3, -4)$
b. $(-3, 4)$
c. $(4, 3)$
d. $(-4, -3)$

15.

a. $(-2, 5)$
b. $(2, -5)$
c. $(-5, -2)$
d. $(5, 2)$

16.

a. $(4, 8)$
b. $(-4, -8)$
c. $(-8, 4)$
d. $(8, -4)$

17. $P'(4, 4)$ 18. $P'(3, -2)$ 19. $P'(-3, -5)$

20. a.   b.
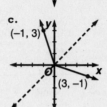

c.   d.
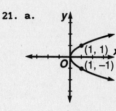

21. a.   b.
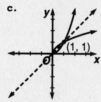

c.   d.
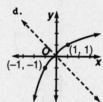

22. a.   b.
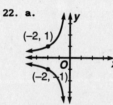

c.   d.
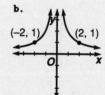

23. a.   b.
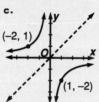

c.   d.
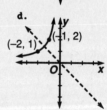

24. a. 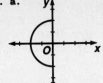 **b.**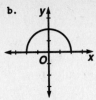

c. 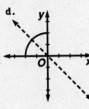 **d.**

25. a. **b.**

c. **d.**

26. $f(-x) = (-x)^5 - 4(-x)$

$\qquad = -x^5 + 4x$

$\qquad = -f(x)$

odd

27. $f(-x) = 6(-x)^3 - 3(-x) + 5$

$\qquad = -6x^3 + 3x + 5$

neither

28. $f(-x) = (-x)^2 - 64$

$\qquad = x^2 - 64$

$\qquad = f(x)$

even

29. $f(-x) = 6 - 6(-x)^2 + (-x)^8$

$\qquad = 6 - 6x^2 + x^8$

$\qquad = f(x)$

even

30. $f(-x) = 5(-x)^2 + 6(-x) - 9$

$\qquad = 5x^2 - 6x - 9$

neither

31. $f(-x) = -3(-x)^9 + 4(-x)^5$

$\qquad = 3x^9 - 4x^5$

$\qquad = -f(x)$

odd

32. origin;

For a: $b = -6a$

For $-a$: $b = -6(-a)$

$\qquad = 6a$

So, in general, point $(-a, -b)$ is on the graph if and only if point (a, b) is on the graph.

33. y-axis;

For a: $b = 6a^4 - 3a^2 + 1$

For $-a$: $b = 6(-a)^4 - 3(-a)^2 + 1$

$\qquad = 6a^4 - 3a^2 + 1$

So, in general, point $(-a, b)$ is on the graph if and only if point (a, b) is on the graph.

34. x-axis;

For b: $a = b^2 + 4$

For $-b$: $a = (-b)^2 + 4$

$\qquad = b^2 + 4$

So, in general, point $(a, -b)$ is on the graph if and only if point (a, b) is on the graph.

35. no symmetry;

For a: $b = 2a^9 - 7a^2 + 4$

For $-a$: $b = 2(-a)^9 - 7(-a)^2 + 4$

$\qquad = -2a^9 - 7a^2 + 4$

36. all;

If (a, b) is on the graph then so is $(-a, b)$, $(a, -b)$, (b, a), and $(-b, -a)$.

37. x-axis, y-axis, origin;

If (a, b) is on the graph, then so is $(a, -b)$, $(-a, b)$, and $(-a, -b)$.

38.

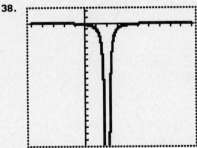

$x = 2$

39.

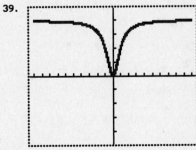

$x = 0$

40.

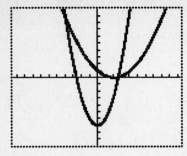

Answer is approximate: (-3.9, 8.2), (2.8, 0.8).

41.

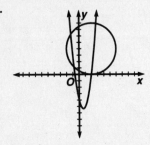

No, neither the parabola nor the circle are symmetric with respect to the y-axis, so they do not follow the rules for points with that symmetry.

42. a. neither   **b.** odd

43. x-intercept: $\dfrac{x^2}{4} = 1$

$$x^2 = 4$$
$$x = \pm 2$$
$$(2, 0)$$

other points:

when x = -3,

$$\frac{9}{4} - \frac{y^2}{16} = 1$$
$$-\frac{y^2}{16} = -\frac{5}{4}$$
$$y^2 = 20$$
$$y \approx \pm 4.5$$

(-3, 4.5) and (-3, -4.5)

when x = 3,

$$\frac{9}{4} - \frac{y^2}{16} = 1$$
$$-\frac{y^2}{16} = -\frac{5}{4}$$
$$y^2 = 20$$
$$y \approx \pm 4.5$$

(3, -4.5)

44. Since both the circle and the parabola are symmetric with respect to the y-axis, the coordinates of the position of the other two poles are (-3.2, 3.9) and (-1.1, -4.9).

45. $(f \circ g)(x) = f(g(x))$

$$= (x - 2)^2 - 4(x - 2) + 5$$
$$= x^2 - 4x + 4 - 4x + 8 + 5$$
$$= x^2 - 8x + 17$$

So, $(f \circ g)(4) = 4^2 - 8(4) + 17 = 1.$

$(g \circ f)(x) = g(f(x))$

$$= x^2 - 4x + 5 - 2$$
$$= x^2 - 4x + 3$$

So, $(g \circ f)(4) = 4^2 - 4(4) + 3 = 3.$

46. $\left(\dfrac{-3 + 8}{2},\ \dfrac{-2 + 4}{2}\right) = \left(\dfrac{5}{2},\ 1\right) = (2.5,\ 1)$

47. Parallel; the lines have the same slope.

48. $\dfrac{1}{-40 - (-12)} \begin{bmatrix} -5 & 3 \\ -4 & 8 \end{bmatrix} = -\dfrac{1}{28} \begin{bmatrix} -5 & 3 \\ -4 & 8 \end{bmatrix}$

$$= \dfrac{1}{28} \begin{bmatrix} 5 & -3 \\ 4 & -8 \end{bmatrix}$$

49. $\begin{bmatrix} 8 & -3 & -4 & 6 \\ 4 & 9 & -2 & -4 \\ 6 & 12 & 5 & -1 \end{bmatrix} \rightarrow \begin{bmatrix} 1 & -\frac{3}{8} & -\frac{1}{2} & \frac{3}{4} \\ 0 & \frac{21}{2} & 0 & -7 \\ 0 & \frac{57}{4} & 8 & -\frac{11}{2} \end{bmatrix} \rightarrow$

$\begin{bmatrix} 1 & 0 & -\frac{1}{2} & \frac{1}{2} \\ 0 & 1 & 0 & -\frac{2}{3} \\ 0 & 0 & 8 & 4 \end{bmatrix} \rightarrow \begin{bmatrix} 1 & 0 & 0 & \frac{3}{4} \\ 0 & 1 & 0 & -\frac{2}{3} \\ 0 & 0 & 1 & \frac{1}{2} \end{bmatrix}$

$\left(\dfrac{3}{4},\ -\dfrac{2}{3},\ \dfrac{1}{2}\right)$

50. a. $a \geq 0,\ b \geq 0,\ 4a + b \leq 32,\ a + 6b \leq 54$

b. (0, 0), (8, 0), (0, 9), and (6, 8) are the vertices.

M(a, b) = a + b

M(0, 0) = 0   M(0, 9) = 9

M(8, 0) = 8   M(6, 8) = 14

14 gallons is the maximum.

51. Student B = $\dfrac{4}{3}$(15) = 20 years old.

Let x = number of years.

$$20 - x = 2(15 - x)$$
$$20 - x = 30 - 2x$$
$$x = 10$$

3-2   Families of Graphs

PAGES 122-123   CHECKING FOR UNDERSTANDING

1. Reflection flips the figure over a line of symmetry. The shape remains the same. Translations move the figure from one location to another. The shape and orientation of the figure remains the same. Dilations change the shape of the figure.

2. It is closer to the axis than the graph of $f(x) = x^4$.

3. It moves 2 units right and 7 units up, resulting in (6, 12).

4. See students' work.

5. a. shrunk vertically

b. moved 2 units up

c. shrunk horizontally

6. a. reflected over x-axis and moved 3 units up

b. moved 1 unit left

c. moved 3 units right

7. f(x) + 2   **8.** f(x - 6)   **9.** -f(x - 4)

10. -f(x) - 2   **11.** f(x + 5) - 2   **12.** -f(x + 6) - 3

13.

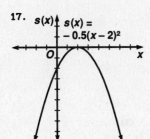

$g(x)$

$g(x) = (x + 1)^2$

O x

14.

$h(x)$

$h(x) = (x - 2)^2 - 4$

O x

15.

$j(x)$

$j(x) = -(x - 2)^2$

O x

16.

$k(x)$

$k(x) = 3(x - 2)^2$

O x

17.

$s(x)$

$s(x) = -0.5(x - 2)^2$

O x

18.

$m(x)$

$m(x) = 2(x - 2)^2 + 3$

O x

19.

$n(x)$

$n(x) = (x - 7)^2 + 4$

O x

20.

$p(x)$

$p(x) = 3x^2 - 7$

O x

21. a. narrower than the parent

    b. narrower and reflected over the *x*-axis

    c. narrower and moved 2 units right

    d. wider and moved 1 unit left

    e. narrower and moved 5 units down

22. a. moved down 5 units

    b. moved left 7 units

    c. narrower

    d. narrower, moved up 4 units

    e. inverted

23. a. moved up 6 units

    b. moved right 4 units

    c. wider

    d. narrower, moved 3 units left and 8 units down

    e. inverted, moved 3 units right and 6 units up

24.

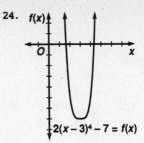

$f(x)$

O x

$2(x - 3)^4 - 7 = f(x)$

25.

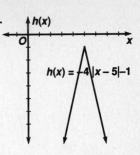

$h(x)$

O x

$h(x) = -4|x - 5| - 1$

26.

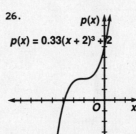

$p(x)$

$p(x) = 0.33(x + 2)^3 + 2$

O x

27.

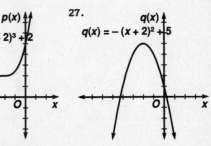

$q(x)$

$q(x) = -(x + 2)^2 + 5$

O x

28.

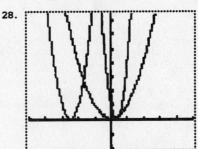

$0, \ -\dfrac{5}{2}, \ \dfrac{1}{3}$

29.

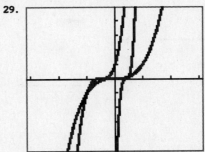

$0, \ -\dfrac{1}{2}, \ \dfrac{2}{5}$

30.

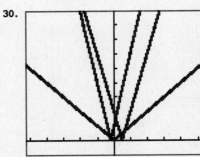

$0, \ \dfrac{1}{2}, \ -\dfrac{1}{5}$

31. The *x*-intercept will be $-\dfrac{b}{a}$.

32. a. (1) $y = x^2$

(2) $y = x^3$

(3) $y = -x^2$

(4) $y = -x^3$

b. (1) 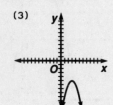 (2)

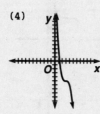

(3) 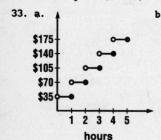 (4)

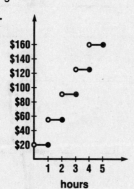

c. (1) $y = (x - 3)^2 - 5$

(2) $y = (x - 3)^3 - 5$

(3) $y = -(x - 3)^2 - 5$

(4) $y = -(x - 3)^3 - 5$

33. a. **b.**

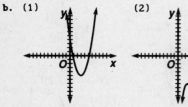

c. $4(35) - 15 = \$125$

34. a. $V(w) = w(w + 3)(w - 2)$

$= w(w^2 + w - 6)$

$= w^3 + w^2 - 6w$

b. **c.**

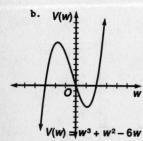
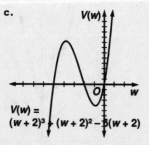

$V(w) = w^3 + w^2 - 6w$

$V(w) = (w + 2)^3 + (w + 2)^2 - 3(w + 2)$

d. $w < 0$ because the width cannot be negative and $0 \le w \le 2$ because the volume cannot be negative.

35. not a function

36. $15y - x = 1$

$15y = x + 1$

$y = \frac{1}{15}x + \frac{1}{15}$

37. $5(-3) - 7(9) = -15 - 63$

$= -78$, yes

38. y-axis;

For a: $b = 6(a)^4 - 3(a)^2 + 1$

$= 6a^4 - 3a^2 + 1$

For $-a$: $b = 6(-a)^4 - 3(-a)^2 + 1$

$= 6a^4 - 3a^2 + 1$

So, in general, point $(-a, b)$ is on the graph if and only if point (a, b) is on the graph.

39. $(75^3)(75^7) = 75^{3+7} = 75^{10}$

The best answer is B.

3-3A   Graphing Calculators: Graphing Radical Functions

PAGE 125   EXERCISES

1.

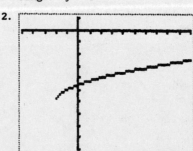

domain: $x \ge 1$

range: $y \ge 5$

2.

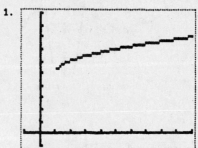

domain: $x \ge -2$

range: $y \ge -6$

3.

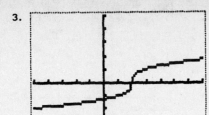

domain: all real numbers
range: all real numbers

4.

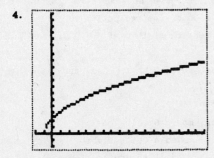

domain: $x \geq -\dfrac{5}{6}$

range: $y \geq 0$

5.

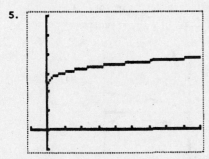

domain: $x \geq 0$

range: $y \geq 2$

6.

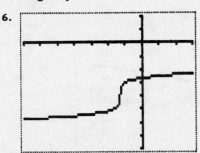

domain: all real numbers
range: all real numbers

PAGES 129-130   CHECKING FOR UNDERSTANDING

1. The ordered pair (a, b) corresponds to the ordered pair (b, a) in the inverse.

2. Graph $y = x^3$. Reflect over line $y = x$, move 2 units right and 3 units up.

3. Sample answer: The inverse of $f(x) = x^2$ is $f^{-1}(x) = \pm\sqrt{x}$, which is not a function.

4. If you can draw a horizontal line through the function and it intersects the graph more than once, the inverse of the function will not be a function.

5. $P'(5, -4)$ **6.** $P'(-2, -3)$ **7.** $P'(8, -2)$

8. $P'(8u, 3t)$ **9.** yes   **10.** yes

11. no

12.
$$y = x^2 - 7$$
$$x = y^2 - 7$$
$$x + 7 = y^2$$
$$\pm\sqrt{x + 7} = y$$

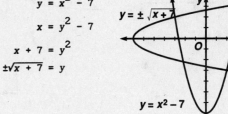

$y = \pm\sqrt{x + 7}$

$y = x^2 - 7$

PAGES 130-131   EXERCISES

13.
$$y = 2x + 3$$
$$x = 2y + 3$$
$$x - 3 = 2y$$
$$\frac{x - 3}{2} = y$$

14.
$$y = 0.5x - 8$$
$$x = 0.5y - 8$$
$$x + 8 = 0.5y$$
$$2(x + 8) = y$$

15.
$$y = 4 - 3x^2$$
$$x = 4 - 3y^2$$
$$x - 4 = -3y^2$$
$$-\frac{1}{3}(x - 4) = y^2$$
$$\frac{1}{3}(4 - x) = y^2$$
$$\pm\sqrt{\frac{1}{3}(4 - x)} = y$$
$$\pm\frac{1}{3}\sqrt{3(4 - x)} = y$$

16.
$$y = x^2 + 4$$
$$x = y^2 + 4$$
$$x - 4 = y^2$$
$$\pm\sqrt{x - 4} = y$$

17.
$$y = (x - 2)^3$$
$$x = (y - 2)^3$$
$$\sqrt[3]{x} = y - 2$$
$$\sqrt[3]{x} + 2 = y$$

18.
$$y = (x + 3)^4 - 5$$
$$x = (y + 3)^4 - 5$$
$$x + 5 = (y + 3)^4$$
$$\pm\sqrt[4]{x + 5} = y + 3$$
$$\pm\sqrt[4]{x + 5} - 3 = y$$

19.
$$y = x^2 + 2$$
$$x = y^2 + 2$$
$$x - 2 = y^2$$
$$\pm\sqrt{x - 2} = y; \text{ no}$$

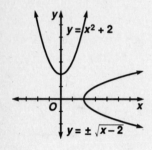

20.
$$y = (x + 3)^3$$
$$x = (y + 3)^3$$
$$\sqrt[3]{x} = y + 3$$
$$\sqrt[3]{x} - 3 = y; \text{ yes}$$

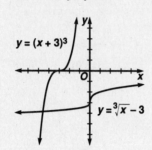

21.
$$y = (x - 4)^4$$
$$x = (y - 4)^4$$
$$\pm\sqrt[4]{x} = y - 4$$
$$\pm\sqrt[4]{x} + 4 = y; \text{ no}$$

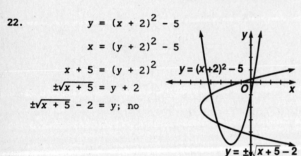

22.
$$y = (x + 2)^2 - 5$$
$$x = (y + 2)^2 - 5$$
$$x + 5 = (y + 2)^2$$
$$\pm\sqrt{x + 5} = y + 2$$
$$\pm\sqrt{x + 5} - 2 = y; \text{ no}$$

23.
$$y = (x - 3)^3 + 6$$
$$x = (y - 3)^3 + 6$$
$$x - 6 = (y - 3)^3$$
$$\sqrt[3]{x - 6} = y - 3$$
$$\sqrt[3]{x - 6} + 3 = y; \text{ yes}$$

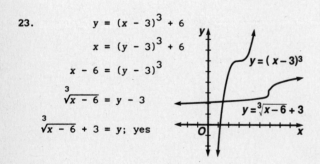

24.
$$y = x^5 + 5$$
$$x = y^5 + 5$$
$$x - 5 = y^5$$
$$\sqrt[5]{x - 5} = y; \text{ yes}$$

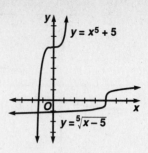

25. a. reflection

b. reflection, moved 3 units right

c. reflection, moved 6 units up

d. wider version of the reflection

e. narrower version of the reflection, moved 4 units up

f. reflection, moved 5 units right and 3 units up

26. a. reflection

b. reflection, moved 6 units up

c. reflection, moved 4 units right

d. narrower version of the reflection

e. reflection, moved 3 units left and 8 units down

f. reflection; then reflected over the x-axis, moved 3 units right and 6 units up

27.

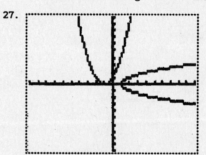

no, $y = \sqrt{x} - 1$

28.

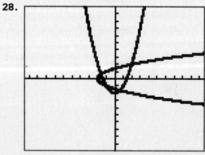

yes

29.

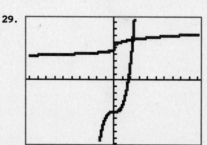

no, $y = \sqrt[3]{x + 5}$

48

30. $f(x) = x$, $f(x) = -x$

31. x = lab work score

$$\frac{75 + 80 + 72 + x}{4} = 80$$

$$227 + x = 320$$

$$x = 93$$

32. a. $v = \sqrt{2(32)h}$

$= \sqrt{64h}$

$= 8\sqrt{h}$

b.

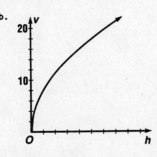

c. 88 feet   **d.** yes

e. $70 = 8\sqrt{h}$

$8.75 = \sqrt{h}$

$76.6 \approx h$

No, it only propels water up to 76.6 feet.

33.   **34.**

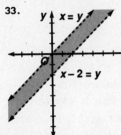   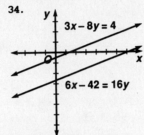

no solution

35. both

36. wider than the parent graph, moved 1 unit left

37. m will increase in value and $\frac{50}{m}$ will decrease in value. Therefore, the difference will increase in value. The best answer is A.

3-4A Graphing Calculators: Graphing Rational Functions

PAGE 133   EXERCISES

1.

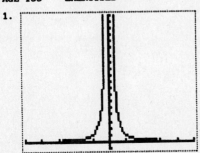

vertical asymptote: $x = 0$

horizontal asymptote: $y = 0$

2.

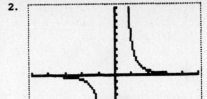

vertical asymptote: $x = 0$

horizontal asymptote: $y = 0$

3.

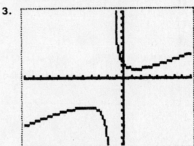

vertical asymptote: $x = -\frac{3}{2}$

4.

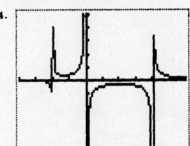

$$x^3 - 2x^2 - 8x = 0$$

$$x(x^2 - 2x - 8) = 0$$

$$x(x - 4)(x + 2) = 0$$

vertical asymptotes: $x = 0$, $x = 4$, $x = -2$

horizontal asymptote: $y = 0$

5.

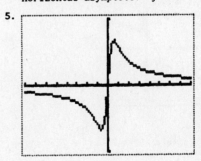

6.

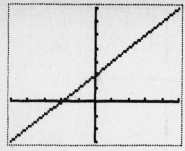

point discontinuity: $x = 2$

7.

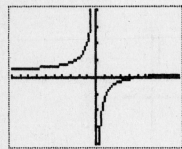

vertical asymptote: $x = 0$

horizontal asymptote: $y = \frac{1}{3}$

8.

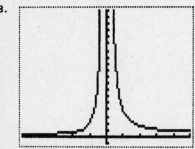

vertical asymptote: $x = 0$

horizontal asymptote: $y = \frac{1}{2}$

9.

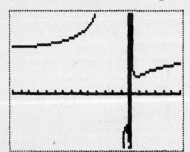

vertical asymptote: $x = 2, x = 0$

horizontal asymptote: $y = 6$

10.

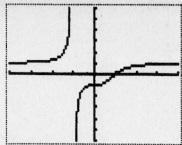

vertical asymptote: $x = -1$

horizontal asymptote: $y = 1$

<table>
<tr><td>3-4</td><td>

Rational Functions and Asymptotes

</td></tr>
</table>

1. As the graph approaches the asymptote, it gets closer and closer but never intersects the line, no matter how great or how small the value of x gets.

2. A slant asymptote occurs when the greatest exponent of the numerator is greater than the greatest exponent of the denominator and the difference of the 2 exponents is 1. First use long division to rewrite the rational expression as a quotient. The fractional part approaches 0. The rest of the quotient describes the line which is the slant asymptote.

3.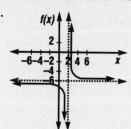
   a. $x = 2$; $y = -6$
   b. $f(x) = \dfrac{1}{x - 2} - 6$

4. At 6400, you are at sea level. Values less would put you below sea level.

5. $f(x) = \dfrac{1}{x - 1}$ 6. $f(x) = \dfrac{1}{x + 4}$

7. $f(x) = \dfrac{1}{x} + 5$ 8. $f(x) = \dfrac{1}{x - 2} - 3$

9. $f(x) = -\dfrac{1}{x}$ 10. $f(x) = \dfrac{-1}{x + 5}$

11. $x = -1$, $y = 0$ 12. $x = 2$, $y = 1$

13. $x = -5$ 14. $y = \dfrac{(x + 7)(x - 4)}{x(x - 7)(x - 4)}$

   $x = 4$

15. $x^2 + x - 6 = (x + 3)(x - 2)$

   vertical asymptotes: $x = -3, x = 2$

   horizontal asymptote: $y = 0$

16. $x^5 - 3x^3 = x^3(x^2 - 3)$

vertical asymptotes: $x = 0$, $x = \pm\sqrt{3}$

$\approx \pm1.7$

horizontal asymptote: $y = 0$

17. vertical asymptote: $x = 0$

slant asymptote:

$$2x^2 \overline{\smash{\big)}\,3x^3 - 2x + 1} \quad \frac{\frac{3}{2}x}{}$$

$$\underline{3x^3}$$

$$-2x + 1$$

So, $y = \dfrac{3}{2}x + \dfrac{-2x + 1}{2x^2}$ and $y = \dfrac{3}{2}x$ is a slant

asymptote.

18. $x^2 - 11x + 30 = (x - 6)(x - 5)$

vertical asymptotes: $x = 5$, $x = 6$

horizontal asymptote: $y = 1$

19.

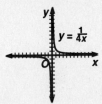

a. translated
   1 unit down

b. translated
   5 units left

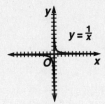

c. closer to
   the axes

d. wider, translated
   8 units up

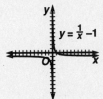

e. translated 3 units right, 7 units up

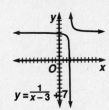

20.

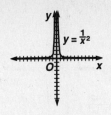

a. translated
   3 units up

b. translated
   9 units right

c. wider

d. translated
   5 units left,
   1 unit down

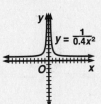

e. reflected, translated 2 units right,
   4 units up

21. $y = \dfrac{x}{x(x - 4)}$

22. $y = \dfrac{x + 1}{(x + 1)(x + 5)(x - 1)}$

23. $y = \dfrac{x(x - 3)(x + 7)}{(x - 3)(x + 7)}$

24.

25.

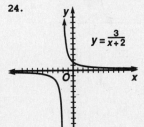

26.

27.

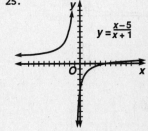

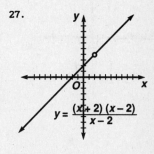

51

28.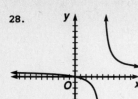

$$y = \frac{x}{x-5}$$

29.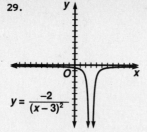

$$y = \frac{-2}{(x-3)^2}$$

30.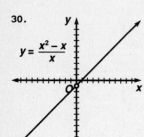

$$y = \frac{x^2 - x}{x}$$

31.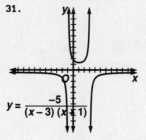

$$y = \frac{-5}{(x-3)(x+1)}$$

32.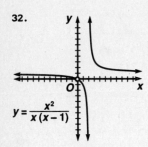

$$y = \frac{x^2}{x(x-1)}$$

33.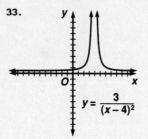

$$y = \frac{3}{(x-4)^2}$$

34.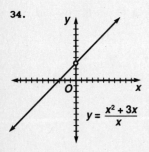

$$y = \frac{x^2 + 3x}{x}$$

35.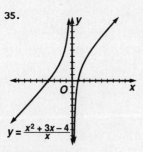

$$y = \frac{x^2 + 3x - 4}{x}$$

36.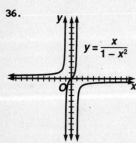

$$y = \frac{x}{1 - x^2}$$

37.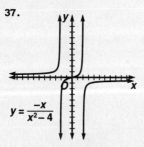

$$y = \frac{-x}{x^2 - 4}$$

38.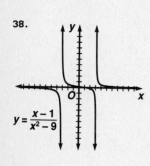

$$y = \frac{x - 1}{x^2 - 9}$$

39.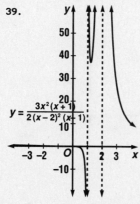

$$y = \frac{3x^2(x+1)}{2(x-2)^2(x-1)}$$

40. a. $w_1 d_1 = w_2 d_2$

$(30)(6) = w_2 d_2$

$\dfrac{180}{d_2} = w_2$

b.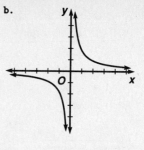

c. $\dfrac{180}{d_2} = 45$

$\dfrac{180}{45} = d_2$

$4 = d_2 \qquad 4$ feet

d. If a person is heavier than the other person, that person should sit closer to the center of the seesaw.

41. a.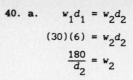

b. It increases.

c. It is half.

x- and y-axes.

42. a. $t + 3 = 0$ when $t = -3$.

b. $v = \dfrac{2(2)^2 + 7(2) + 5}{2 + 3}$

$= \dfrac{8 + 14 + 5}{5}$

$= \dfrac{27}{5} = 5.4$

c. It has a vertical asymptote at $t = -3$ and seems to also have a slant asymptote approximated by $y = 2t$.

43. Sample answer:

$\{(2, 4), (2, -4), (1, 2), (1, -2), (0, 0)\}$; because there is more than one member of the domain paired with the range.

44. $AB = \sqrt{(-1 - (-1))^2 + (-3 - 3)^2}$

$= \sqrt{0 + 36}$

$= 6$

$BC = \sqrt{(3 - (-1))^2 + (0 - (-3))^2}$

$= \sqrt{16 + 9}$

$= 5$

$AC = \sqrt{(3 - (-1))^2 + (0 - 3)^2}$

$= \sqrt{16 + 9}$

$= 5$

45. $-4y = -3x$

$y = \dfrac{3}{4}x \qquad$ Slope of $3x - 4y = 0$ is $\dfrac{3}{4}$.

Slope of perpendicular line is $-\dfrac{4}{3}$.

46. $f(0, 0) = 0 - 0 = 0$

$f(4, 0) = 0 - 4 = -4 \leftarrow$ minimum

$f(3, 5) = 5 - 3 = 2$

$f(0, 5) = 5 - 0 = 5 \leftarrow$ maximum

47. $x^2 - 9 = y$

$y^2 - 9 = x$

$y^2 = x + 9$

$y = \pm\sqrt{x + 9}$

48. Volume of cube is x^3.

Volume of rectangular solid is

$x(x + 1)(x - 1) = x^3 - x$.

$x^3 > x^3 - x$ for $x > 1$

Quantity A is greater.   A

Technology:
Graphing Rational Functions

1.

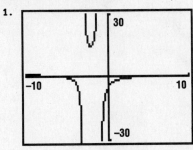

$x = -1$, $x = -3$, $y = 1$

2.

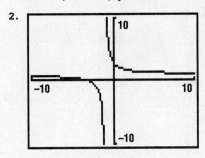

$x = -1$, $y = 1$

3.

$x = -4$, $x = 3$, $y = 0$

1. After graphing the boundary function, test a point not on the boundary. If the point satisfies the inequality, shade that region. If not, test a point in the other region.

2. Sample answer: $|x| < -4$

3. $3 \overset{?}{\gtrless} 2^4 - 5(2)^2 + 2$

   $3 \overset{?}{\gtrless} 16 - 20 + 2$

   $3 > -2$, yes

4. $20 \overset{?}{\lessgtr} -0.2(10)^2 + 9(10) - 7$

   $20 \overset{?}{\lessgtr} -20 + 90 - 7$

   $20 < 63$, yes

5. $8 \overset{?}{\lessgtr} |3 - 2| + 7$

   $8 \overset{?}{\lessgtr} 1 + 7$

   $8 \not< 8$, no

6. $-4 \overset{?}{\gtrless} -\sqrt{-2 + 11} + 1$

   $-4 \overset{?}{\gtrless} -\sqrt{9} + 1$

   $-4 \not> -2$, no

7.

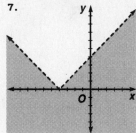

8.

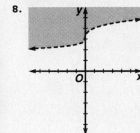

9.

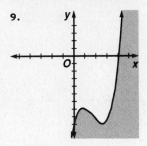

10.

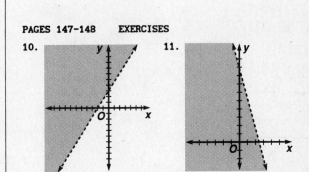

11.

12.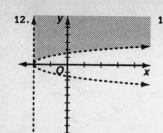

13.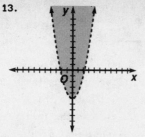

14.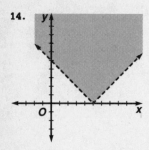

15.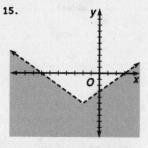

16.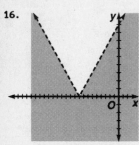

17.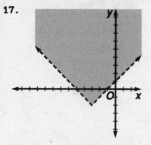

18.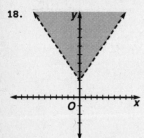

19.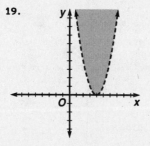

20.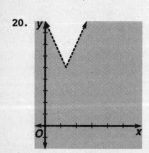

21.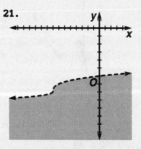

22. $x + 2 > 3$ $x + 2 < -3$

       $x > 1$ $x < -5$

   $\{x \mid x < -5 \text{ or } x > 1\}$

23. $\varnothing$, absolute value can never be < 0.

24. $3x + 12 > 42$ $3x + 12 < -42$

       $3x > 30$ $3x < -54$

        $x > 10$ $x < -18$

   $\{x \mid x < -18 \text{ or } x > 10\}$

25. $x \leq x$ $x \geq -x$

   all x $2x \geq 0$

             $x \geq 0$

   $\{x \mid x \geq 0\}$

26. $x > x$ $x < -x$

   $\varnothing$ $2x < 0$

             $x < 0$ $\{x \mid x < 0\}$

27. $x + 2 \geq x$ $x + 2 \leq -x$

       $0 \geq -2$ $2x \leq -2$

   all real numbers $x \leq -1$

   all real numbers

28.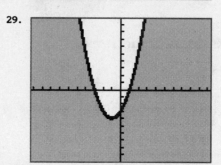

29.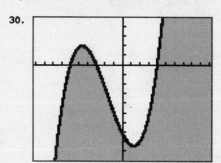

30.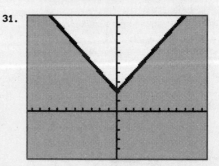

31.

32. In order for $|x + 1| + |x - 1| \leq 2$, $|x + 1| \leq 2$
and $|x - 1| \leq 2$ because absolute value can never
be negative.

   If $|x + 1| \leq 2$,

   $x + 1 \leq 2$ $x + 1 \geq -2$

     $x \leq 1$ $x \geq -3$

   If $|x - 1| \leq 2$,

   $x - 1 \leq 2$ $x - 1 \geq -2$

     $x \leq 3$ $x \geq -1$

   $\{x \mid -1 \leq x \leq 1\}$

33.

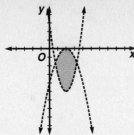

34. Let x = length of crest with frame.

$$(x - 3)^2 \le \frac{2}{3}x^2$$

$$x^2 - 6x + 9 \le \frac{2}{3}x^2$$

$$\frac{1}{3}x^2 - 6x + 9 \le 0$$

35. $35 - 3.3 < v < 35 + 3.3$

$31.7\% < v < 38.3\%$

36. $(f \circ g)(x) = f(g(x))$

$= (x - 0.3x) - 0.2(x - 0.3x)$

$= x - 0.3x - 0.2x + 0.06x$

$= 0.56x$

37. $x - 2y - 4 = 0$

$-2y = -x + 4$

$y = \frac{1}{2}x - 2$

$m = \frac{1}{2}, \ b = -2$

38. $3\begin{bmatrix} 4 & -2 \\ 5 & 7 \end{bmatrix} + 2\begin{bmatrix} -3 & 5 \\ -4 & 3 \end{bmatrix} = \begin{bmatrix} 12 & -6 \\ 15 & 21 \end{bmatrix} + \begin{bmatrix} -6 & 10 \\ -8 & 6 \end{bmatrix}$

$= \begin{bmatrix} 6 & 4 \\ 7 & 27 \end{bmatrix}$

39. Inverse of $\begin{bmatrix} -1 & 2 \\ -4 & 3 \end{bmatrix} = \frac{1}{-3 - (-8)}\begin{bmatrix} 3 & -2 \\ 4 & -1 \end{bmatrix}$

$= \frac{1}{5}\begin{bmatrix} 3 & -2 \\ 4 & -1 \end{bmatrix}$

$= \begin{bmatrix} \frac{3}{5} & -\frac{2}{5} \\ \frac{4}{5} & -\frac{1}{5} \end{bmatrix}$

$\begin{bmatrix} x \\ y \end{bmatrix} = \begin{bmatrix} \frac{3}{5} & -\frac{2}{5} \\ \frac{4}{5} & -\frac{1}{5} \end{bmatrix}\begin{bmatrix} 0 \\ 15 \end{bmatrix}$

$= \begin{bmatrix} -6 \\ -3 \end{bmatrix} \qquad (-6, -3)$

40.

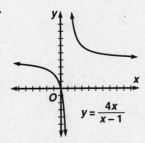

$y = \frac{4x}{x - 1}$

41. $5w = 4\ell \longrightarrow w = \frac{4}{5}\ell$

$$(\ell + w)(4\ell) = 180$$

$$\left(\ell + \frac{4}{5}\ell\right)(4\ell) = 180$$

$$\left(\frac{9}{5}\ell\right)(4\ell) = 180$$

$$\frac{36}{5}\ell^2 = 180$$

$$\ell^2 = \frac{900}{36}$$

$$\ell^2 = 25$$

$$\ell = 5, \ w = \frac{4}{5}(5)$$

$$= 4$$

$P = 6\ell + 7w = 30 + 28 = 58$ in.

The best answer is B.

Mid-Chapter Review

PAGE 148

1. y-axis;

For a: $b = |a| + 1$

$= a + 1$

For $-a$: $b = |-a| + 1$

$= a + 1$

So, in general, point $(-a, b)$ is on the graph if and only if point (a, b) is on the graph.

2. a. moved up 3 units

b. moved left 2 units

c. narrower and moved down 4 units

3.

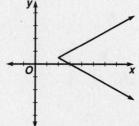

4. $y = x^2 + 6$

$x = y^2 + 6$

$x - 6 = y^2$

$\pm\sqrt{x - 6} = y$

$y = \pm\sqrt{x - 6}$

5. $y = \frac{x(x - 1)}{(x + 1)(x - 1)}$

hole at $x = 1$

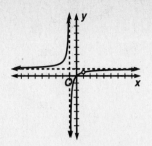

6.

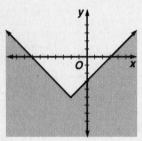

13. $f'(x) = 2(2)x^{2-1}$
   $= 4x$
   $f'(0) = 4(0)$
   $= 0$

14. $f'(x) = 2x^{2-1}$
   $= 2x$
   $f'(2) = 2(2)$
   $= 4$
   $y - 4 = 4(x - 2)$
   $y - 4 = 4x - 8$
   $y = 4x - 4$

15. $f'(x) = 3x^{3-1} - 2(2)x^{2-1} + 1(4)x^{1-1}$
   $= 3x^2 - 4x + 4$

16. $f'(x) = 2(3)x^{2-1} - 1(8)x^{1-1} + 0$
   $= 6x - 8$

17. $f'(x) = 3(0.3)x^{3-1} - 2(4)x^{2-1} + 0$
   $= 0.9x^2 - 8x$

18. $f'(x) = -2(4)x^{-2-1} + (-3)(2)x^{-3-1} + 0$
   $= -8x^{-3} - 6x^{-4}$

19. $f'(x) = 5(-4)x^{5-1} + 3(7)x^{3-1} + 1(x^{1-1})$
   $= -20x^4 + 21x^2 + 1$

20. $f(x) = 3x^{-4} + x^2 - \frac{6}{13}$

   $f'(x) = -4(3)x^{-4-1} + 2x^{2-1} - 0$

   $= -12x^{-5} + 2x$

21. $f'(x) = 2(2)x^{2-1} = 4x$
   $f'(-2) = 4(-2) = -8$

22. $f'(x) = 2\left(\frac{1}{2}\right)x^{2-1} + 0 = x$
   $f'(-3) = -3$

23. $f'(x) = 2(-2)x^{2-1} + 3x^{1-1} + 0 = -4x + 3$
   $f'(1) = -4(1) + 3 = -1$

24. $f'(x) = 2(0.5)x^{2-1} - 0.4x^{1-1} - 0 = x - 0.4$
   $f'(1) = 1 - 0.4 = 0.6$

25. $f'(x) = 2x^{2-1} + \frac{1}{6}x^{1-1} + 0 = 2x + \frac{1}{6}$

   $f'\left(\frac{1}{2}\right) = 2\left(\frac{1}{2}\right) + \frac{1}{6} = 1\frac{1}{6}$

26. $f'(x) = 3\left(\frac{1}{6}\right)x^{3-1} - 0 = \frac{1}{2}x^2$

   $f'(2) = \frac{1}{2}(2)^2 = 2$

27. $f'(x) = 2(2)x^{2-1} - 3x^{1-1} - 0 = 4x - 3$
   $f'(-2) = 4(-2) - 3 = -11$

28. $f'(x) = 2\left(\frac{1}{2}\right)x^{2-1} + \frac{1}{4}x^{1-1} + 0 = x + \frac{1}{4}$

   $f'(x) = \frac{1}{2} + \frac{1}{4} = \frac{3}{4}$

3-6   Tangent to a Curve

1. A secant line intersects a graph in one or more points. If often lies in more than one region defined by the graph. A tangent touches a curve at a single point and usually lies in one region of the graph.

2. For each term, multiply the exponent of the variable by the coefficient and then write the variable with an exponent one less than the original. If the term is a constant, the derivative is zero.

3. the point at the top of the hill

4. $f'(x)$

5. $f'(x) = 2x^{2-1} + 0$
   $= 2x$

6. $f'(x) = 2(2)x^{2-1} - 0$
   $= 4x$

7. $f'(x) = 4\left(\frac{1}{2}\right)x^{4-1}$

   $= 2x^3$

8. $f'(x) = 2(-2)x^{2-1} + 1(3)x^{1-1} + 0$
   $= -4x + 3$

9. $f'(x) = 4(0.6)x^{4-1} - 2(0.4)x^{2-1} - 0$
   $= 2.4x^3 - 0.8x$

10. $f'(x) = 6(2)x^{6-1} + 3(8)x^{3-1} + 1(4)x^{1-1} - 0$
   $= 12x^5 + 24x^2 + 4$

11. $f'(x) = 2x^{2-1}$
   $= 2x$
   $f'(3) = 2(3)$
   $= 6$

12. $f'(x) = 2x^{2-1} + 0$
   $= 2x$
   $f'(0) = 2(0)$
   $= 0$

29. $f'(x) = 2x$

$\quad f'(3) = 2(3) = 6$

$\quad y - 6 = 6(x - 3)$

$\quad y - 6 = 6x - 18$

$\quad\quad\quad y = 6x - 12$

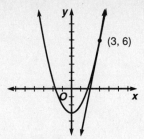

30. $f'(x) = 2x - 3$

$\quad f'(1) = 2(1) - 3 = -1$

$\quad y - 0 = -1(x - 1)$

$\quad\quad\quad y = -x + 1$

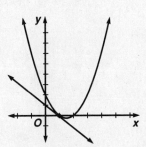

31. $f'(x) = -2x - 1$

$\quad f'(0.5) = -2(0.5) - 1$

$\quad\quad\quad\quad = -2$

$\quad y - 1.25 = -2(x - 0.5)$

$\quad y - 1.25 = -2x + 1$

$\quad\quad\quad\quad y = -2x + 2.25$

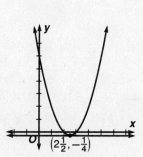

32. $f'(x) = 2x - 5$

$\quad f'(2.5) = 2(2.5) - 5$

$\quad\quad\quad\quad = 0$

$\quad y + 0.25 = 0(x - 2.5)$

$\quad\quad\quad y = -0.25$

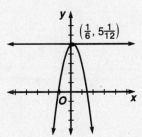

33. $f'(x) = x + 1$

$\quad f'(-4) = -4 + 1 = -3$

$\quad y - 3 = -3(x + 4)$

$\quad y - 3 = -3x - 12$

$\quad\quad\quad y = -3x - 9$

34. $f'(x) = -6x + 1$

$\quad f'\left(\frac{1}{6}\right) = -6\left(\frac{1}{6}\right) + 1 = 0$

$\quad y - \frac{61}{12} = 0\left(x - \frac{1}{6}\right)$

$\quad y - \frac{61}{12} = 0$

$\quad\quad\quad y = \frac{61}{12} = 5\frac{1}{12}$

35. $f'(x) = 2x + 4$

$\quad -2 = 2x + 4$

$\quad -6 = 2x$

$\quad -3 = x$

$\quad f(-3) = (-3)^2 + 4(-3) + 4 = 1$

$\quad (-3, 1)$

36. $f'(x) = 9x^2 - 36$

$\quad 0 = 9x^2 - 36$

$\quad 36 = 9x^2$

$\quad 4 = x^2$

$\quad \pm 2 = x$

$\quad f(2) = 3(2)^3 - 36(2) = -48$

$\quad f(-2) = 3(-2)^3 - 36(-2) = 48$

$\quad (2, -48),\ (-2, 48)$

37. $f'(x) = -1(-4)x^{-1-1}$

$\quad\quad\quad = 4x^{-2}$

$\quad\quad\quad 1 = 4x^{-2}$

$\quad\quad\quad x^2 = 4$

$\quad\quad\quad x = \pm 2$

$\quad f(2) = \frac{-4}{2} = -2$

$\quad f(-2) = \frac{-4}{-2} = 2$

$\quad (2, -2),\ (-2, 2)$

38. $f'(x) = 16x^3 - 16x$

$\quad 0 = 16x^3 - 16x$

$\quad 0 = 16x(x^2 - 1)$

$\quad\quad = 16x(x + 1)(x - 1)$

$\quad x = 0, -1, 1$

$\quad f(0) = 4(0)^4 - 8(0)^2 - 5 = -5$

$\quad f(-1) = 4(-1)^4 - 8(-1)^2 - 5 = -9$

$\quad f(1) = 4(1)^4 - 8(1)^2 - 5 = -9$

$\quad (0, -5),\ (-1, -9),\ (1, -9)$

39.

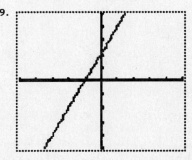

pos: $\quad x > -1$

neg: $\quad x < -1$

zero: $\quad x = -1$

40.

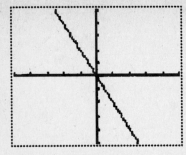

pos: $x < 0$

neg: $x > 0$

zero: $x = 0$

41.

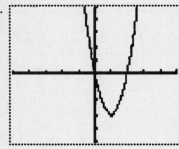

pos: $x < 0$, $x > 6$

neg: $0 < x < 6$

zero: $x = 6$, $x = 0$

42. Let $f(x) = c$. This can also be written as

$f(x) = cx^0$. Take the derivative.

43. B and D, because at each of these points, the tangent line appears to be horizontal.

44. $f'(t) = 2(2)t^{2-1} - 8t^{1-1} + 0 = 4t - 8$

$f'(5) = 4(5) - 8 = 12$ m/s

45. $V = \frac{4}{3}\pi r^3$

$V'(r) = 3\left(\frac{4}{3}\pi\right)r^{3-1} = 4\pi r^2$

$V'(2) = 4\pi(2)^2 = 16\pi$ in^3

46.

47. $x + y = 1 \quad\longrightarrow\quad y = 1 - x$

$3x + 5y = 7$

$3x + 5(1 - x) = 7$

$3x + 5 - 5x = 7$

$-2x = 2$

$x = -1 \qquad y = 1 - x$

$= 1 - (-1)$

$= 2 \qquad (-1, 2)$

48. $\begin{bmatrix} 2 & 1 & 1 & 0 \\ 3 & -2 & -3 & -21 \\ 4 & 5 & 3 & -2 \end{bmatrix} \rightarrow \begin{bmatrix} 1 & \frac{1}{2} & \frac{1}{2} & 0 \\ 0 & -\frac{7}{2} & -\frac{9}{2} & -21 \\ 0 & 3 & 1 & -2 \end{bmatrix} \rightarrow$

$\begin{bmatrix} 1 & 0 & -\frac{1}{7} & -3 \\ 0 & 1 & \frac{9}{7} & 6 \\ 0 & 0 & -\frac{20}{7} & -20 \end{bmatrix} \rightarrow \begin{bmatrix} 1 & 0 & 0 & -2 \\ 0 & 1 & 0 & -3 \\ 0 & 0 & 1 & 7 \end{bmatrix}$

$(-2, -3, 7)$

49. $f(-7, 4) = 5(-7) - 2(-1) + 1 = -42$

50.

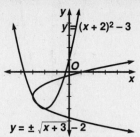

51.

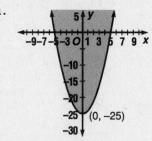

52. Volume xyz weighs 3 oz. So volume

$(2x)(2y)(2z) = 8xyz$ weighs $8(3) = 24$ oz.

The best answer is E.

3-7A

Graphing Calculators: Locating Critical Points of Polynomial Functions

PAGE 155   EXERCISES

1.

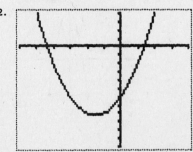

rel. min. $(0, 2)$

2.

rel. min. $(-1.5, -8.25)$

3.

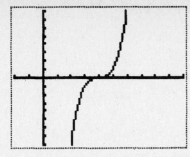

inflection pt. (4, 0)

4.

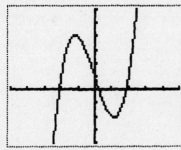

rel. min. (1.15, -2.08)

rel. max. (-1.15, 4.08)

5.

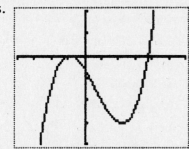

rel. min. (2.23, -15.22)

rel. max. (-0.91, 0.04)

6.

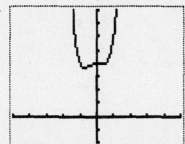

rel. min. (-0.71, 3.69), (0.31, 3.93)

rel. max. (0, 4)

7.

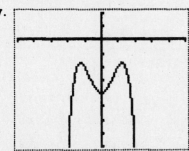

rel. min. (0, -4)

rel. max. (-1.23, -1.75), (1.23, -1.75)

8.

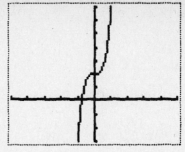

inflection pt. (0, 2)

| 3-7 | **Graphs and Critical Points of Polynomial Functions** |

PAGES 161-162   CHECKING FOR UNDERSTANDING

1. maximum: a point where the y-value is the maximum for the function; minimum: a point where the y-value is the minimum for the function; point of inflection: a point where the graph of the function changes curvature.

2. After determining the coordinates of the critical points, test values on each side of the point to determine if it is a maximum, minimum, or point of inflection.

3.

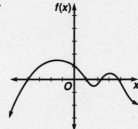

4. $f(x) = x^2 + 4x - 12$

$f'(x) = 2x + 4$

$0 = 2x + 4$

$-4 = 2x$

$-2 = x$

$f''(x) = 2$

$f(-2) = (-2)^2 + 4(-2) - 12 = -16$

critical point (-2, -16)

$f(-2.01) = (-2.01)^2 + 4(-2.01) - 12 \approx -15.9999$

$f(-1.99) = (-1.99)^2 + 4(-1.99) - 12 \approx -15.9999$

So (-2, -16) is a minimum.

5. $f(x) = -2x^2 - 6x + 5$

$f'(x) = -4x - 6$

$0 = -4x - 6$

$6 = -4x$

$-\dfrac{3}{2} = x$

$f''(x) = -4$

$f\left(-\dfrac{3}{2}\right) = -2\left(-\dfrac{3}{2}\right)^2 - 6\left(-\dfrac{3}{2}\right) + 5 = \dfrac{19}{2}$

critical point $\left(-\dfrac{3}{2}, \dfrac{19}{2}\right)$

$f(-1.51) = -2(-1.51)^2 - 6(-1.51) + 5 \approx 9.4998$

$f(-1.49) = -2(-1.49)^2 - 6(-1.49) + 5 \approx 9.4998$

So, $\left(-\dfrac{3}{2}, \dfrac{19}{2}\right)$ is a maximum.

6. $f(x) = x^2 - x - 6$

$f'(x) = 2x - 1$

$0 = 2x - 1$

$1 = 2x$

$\dfrac{1}{2} = x$

$f''(x) = 2$

$f\left(\dfrac{1}{2}\right) = \left(\dfrac{1}{2}\right)^2 - \dfrac{1}{2} - 6 = -6\dfrac{1}{4}$

critical point $(0.5, -6.25)$

$f(0.49) = 0.49^2 - 0.49 - 6 \approx -6.2499$

$f(0.51) = 0.51^2 - 0.51 - 6 \approx -6.2499$

So, $(0.5, -6.25)$ is a minimum.

7. $f(x) = 12x^3$

$f'(x) = 36x^2$ $f''(x) = 72x$

$0 = 36x^2$ $0 = 72x$

$0 = x$ $0 = x$

$f(0) = 12(0)^3 = 0$

critical point $(0, 0)$

$f(-0.01) = 12(-0.01)^3 = -0.000012$

$f(0.01) = 12(0.01)^3 = 0.000012$

So, $(0, 0)$ is a point of inflection.

8. $f(0) = 3(0)^2 - 8(0) + 5$

     $= 5$ y-intercept

$3x^2 - 8x + 5 = 0$

$(3x - 5)(x - 1) = 0$

$x = \dfrac{5}{3}, 1$ x-intercepts

9. $f(0) = 0^2 - 0$

     $= 0$ y-intercept

$x^2 - x = 0$

$x(x - 1) = 0$

$x = 0, 1$ x-intercepts

10. $f(x) = x^2 - 8x + 10$

$f'(x) = 2x - 8$

$0 = 2x - 8$

$8 = 2x$

$4 = x$

$f''(x) = 2$

$f(4) = 4^2 - 8(4) + 10 = -6$

critical point $(4, -6)$

$f(3.99) = 3.99^2 - 8(3.99) + 10 \approx -5.9999$

$f(4.01) = 4.01^2 - 8(4.01) + 10 \approx -5.9999$

So, $(4, -6)$ is a minimum.

11. $g(t) = t^2 + 2t - 15$

$g'(t) = 2t + 2$

$0 = 2t + 2$

$-2 = 2t$

$-1 = t$

$g''(t) = 2$

$g(-1) = (-1)^2 + 2(-1) - 15 = -16$

critical point $(-1, -16)$

$g(-1.01) = (-1.01)^2 + 2(-1.01) - 15 \approx -15.9999$

$g(-0.99) = (-0.99)^2 + 2(-0.99) - 15 \approx -15.9999$

So, $(-1, -16)$ is a minimum.

12. $D(r) = -r^2 - 2r + 8$

$D'(r) = -2r - 2$

$0 = -2r - 2$

$2 = -2r$

$-1 = r$

$D''(r) = -2$

$D(-1) = -(-1)^2 - 2(-1) + 8 = 9$

critical point $(-1, 9)$

$D(-1.01) = -(-1.01)^2 - 2(-1.01) + 8 \approx 8.9999$

$D(-0.99) = -(-0.99)^2 - 2(-0.99) + 8 \approx 8.9999$

So, $(-1, 9)$ is a maximum.

13. $f(x) = 3x^2 - 4x + 1$

$f'(x) = 6x - 4$

$0 = 6x - 4$

$4 = 6x$

$\dfrac{2}{3} = x$

$f''(x) = 6$

$f\left(\dfrac{2}{3}\right) = 3\left(\dfrac{2}{3}\right)^2 - 4\left(\dfrac{2}{3}\right) + 1 = -\dfrac{1}{3}$

critical point $\left(\dfrac{2}{3}, -\dfrac{1}{3}\right)$

$f(0.65) = 3(0.65)^2 - 4(0.65) + 1 \approx -0.3325$

$f(0.68) = 3(0.68)^2 - 4(0.68) + 1 \approx -0.3328$

So, $\left(\dfrac{2}{3}, -\dfrac{1}{3}\right)$ is a minimum.

14. $S(w) = w^3 - w^2 + 3$

$S'(w) = 3w^2 - 2w$ $\qquad$ $S''(w) = 6w - 2$

$0 = 3w^2 - 2w$ $\qquad$ $0 = 6w - 2$

$0 = w(3w - 2)$ $\qquad$ $2 = 6w$

$w = 0, \dfrac{2}{3}$ $\qquad$ $\dfrac{1}{3} = w$

$S(0) = 0^3 - 0^2 + 3 = 3$

$S\left(\dfrac{2}{3}\right) = \left(\dfrac{2}{3}\right)^3 - \left(\dfrac{2}{3}\right)^2 + 3 = \dfrac{77}{27}$

$S\left(\dfrac{1}{3}\right) = \left(\dfrac{1}{3}\right)^3 - \left(\dfrac{1}{3}\right)^2 + 3 = \dfrac{79}{27}$

critical points: $(0, 3)$, $\left(\dfrac{2}{3}, \dfrac{77}{27}\right)$, $\left(\dfrac{1}{3}, \dfrac{79}{27}\right)$

$S(-0.01) = (-0.01)^3 - (-0.01)^2 + 3 \approx 2.9999$

$S(0.01) = (0.01)^3 - (0.01)^2 + 3 \approx 2.9999$

$S(0.32) = (0.32)^3 - (0.32)^2 + 3 \approx 2.9304$

$S(0.34) = (0.34)^3 - (0.34)^2 + 3 \approx 2.8978$

$S(0.65) = (0.65)^3 - (0.65)^2 + 3 \approx 2.8521$

$S(0.68) = (0.68)^3 - (0.68)^2 + 3 \approx 2.8520$

So, $(0, 3)$ is a maximum, $\left(\dfrac{2}{3}, \dfrac{77}{27}\right)$ is a minimum,

and $\left(\dfrac{1}{3}, \dfrac{79}{27}\right)$ is an inflection point.

15. $f(x) = 2x^3 - x^2 + 1$

$f'(x) = 6x^2 - 2x$ $\qquad$ $f''(x) = 12x - 2$

$0 = 6x^2 - 2x$ $\qquad$ $0 = 12x - 2$

$= 2x(3x - 1)$ $\qquad$ $2 = 12x$

$x = 0, \dfrac{1}{3}$ $\qquad$ $\dfrac{1}{6} = x$

$f(0) = 2(0)^3 - 0^2 + 1 = 1$

$f\left(\dfrac{1}{6}\right) = 2\left(\dfrac{1}{6}\right)^3 - \left(\dfrac{1}{6}\right)^2 + 1 = \dfrac{53}{54}$

$f\left(\dfrac{1}{3}\right) = 2\left(\dfrac{1}{3}\right)^3 - \left(\dfrac{1}{3}\right)^2 + 1 = \dfrac{26}{27}$

critical points: $(0, 1)$, $\left(\dfrac{1}{6}, \dfrac{53}{54}\right)$, $\left(\dfrac{1}{3}, \dfrac{26}{27}\right)$

$f(-0.01) = 2(-0.01)^3 - (-0.01)^2 + 1 \approx 0.9999$

$f(0.01) = 2(0.01)^3 - (0.01)^2 + 1 \approx 0.9999$

$f(0.15) = 2(0.15)^3 - (0.15)^2 + 1 \approx 0.9843$

$f(0.18) = 2(0.18)^3 - (0.18)^2 + 1 \approx 0.9793$

$f(0.32) = 2(0.32)^3 - (0.32)^2 + 1 \approx 0.9631$

$f(0.34) = 2(0.34)^3 - (0.34)^2 + 1 \approx 0.9630$

So, $(0, 1)$ is a maximum, $\left(\dfrac{1}{6}, \dfrac{53}{54}\right)$ is a point of

inflection, and $\left(\dfrac{1}{3}, \dfrac{26}{27}\right)$ is a minimum.

16. $D(r) = r^4 - 8r^2 + 16$

$D'(r) = 4r^3 - 16r$ $\qquad$ $D''(r) = 12r^2 - 16$

$0 = 4r^3 - 16r$ $\qquad$ $0 = 12r^2 - 16$

$0 = 4r(r^2 - 4)$ $\qquad$ $16 = 12r^2$

$0 = 4r(r - 2)(r + 2)$ $\qquad$ $r^2 = \dfrac{4}{3}$

$r = 0, 2, -2$

$\qquad\qquad\qquad\qquad$ $r = \dfrac{\pm 2\sqrt{3}}{3} \approx \pm 1.15$

$D(0) = 0^4 - 8(0)^2 + 16 = 16$

$D(-2) = (-2)^4 - 8(-2)^2 + 16 = 0$

$D(2) = (2)^4 - 8(2)^2 + 16 = 0$

$D(1.15) = (1.15)^4 - 8(1.15)^2 + 16 \approx 7.17$

$D(-1.15) = (-1.15)^4 - 8(-1.15)^2 + 16 \approx 7.17$

critical points: $(0, 16)$, $(\pm 2, 0)$, $(\pm 1.15, 7.17)$

$D(-0.01) = (-0.01)^4 - 8(-0.01)^2 + 16 \approx 15.9992$

$D(0.01) = (0.01)^4 - 8(0.01)^2 + 16 \approx 15.9992$

$D(-2.01) = (-2.01)^4 - 8(-2.01)^2 + 16 \approx 0.001608$

$D(-1.99) = (-1.99)^4 - 8(-1.99)^2 + 16 \approx 0.001592$

$D(1.99) = (1.99)^4 - 8(1.99)^2 + 16 \approx 0.001592$

$D(2.01) = (2.01)^4 - 8(2.01)^2 + 16 \approx 0.001608$

$D(-1.16) = (-1.16)^4 - 8(-1.16)^2 + 16 \approx 7.0458$

$D(-1.14) = (-1.14)^4 - 8(-1.14)^2 + 16 \approx 7.2922$

$D(1.14) = (1.14)^4 - 8(1.14)^2 + 16 \approx 7.2922$

$D(1.16) = (1.16)^4 - 8(1.16)^2 + 16 \approx 7.0458$

So, $(0, 16)$ is a maximum, $(\pm 2, 0)$ are minimums,

$(\pm 1.15, 7.17)$ are points of inflection.

17. $V(w) = w^5 - 28$

$V'(w) = 5w^4$ $\qquad\qquad$ $V''(w) = 20w^3$

$0 = 5w^4$ $\qquad\qquad$ $0 = 20w^3$

$0 = w$ $\qquad\qquad$ $0 = w$

$V(0) = 0^5 - 28 = -28$

critical point $(0, -28)$

$V(-0.1) = (-0.1)^5 - 28 = -28.00001$

$V(0.1) = (0.1)^5 - 28 = -27.99999$

So, $(0, -28)$ is a point of inflection.

18. $f(0) = 0^2 + 12(0) + 32$

$= 32$ $\qquad$ y-intercept

$x^2 + 12x + 32 = 0$

$(x + 4)(x + 8) = 0$

$x = -4, -8$ $\qquad$ x-intercepts

19. $f(0) = 4(0)^2 + 16(0) + 15$

$= 15$ $\qquad$ y-intercept

$4x^2 + 16x + 15 = 0$

$(2x + 5)(2x + 3) = 0$

$x = -\dfrac{5}{2}, -\dfrac{3}{2}$ $\qquad$ x-intercepts

20. $f(0) = (0 + 3)(0 - 3)(0 + 1)$
　　　　$= -9$　　　y-intercept
　　$(x + 3)(x - 3)(x + 1) = 0$
　　$x = -3, 3, -1$　x-intercepts

21. $f(0) = 0^3 - 12(0)^2 + 35(0)$
　　　　$= 0$　　　　y-intercept
　　$x^3 - 12x^2 + 35x = 0$
　　$x(x^2 - 12x + 35) = 0$
　　$x(x - 5)(x - 7) = 0$
　　$x = 0, 5, 7$　　x-intercepts

22. $f(0) = (0 + 7)^5$
　　　　$= 16,807$　y-intercept
　　$(x + 7)^5 = 0$
　　$x = -7$　　　x-intercept

23. $f(0) = (0)^4 - 13(0)^2 + 36$
　　　　$= 36$　　　y-intercept
　　　　$x^4 - 13x^2 + 36 = 0$
　　　　$(x^2 - 9)(x^2 - 4) = 0$
　　$(x + 3)(x - 3)(x + 2)(x - 2) = 0$
　　$x = \pm 3, \pm 2$　　x-intercepts

24.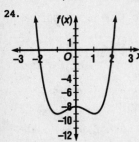

25.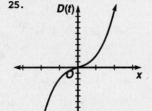

26.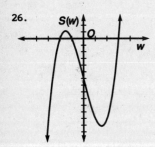

27.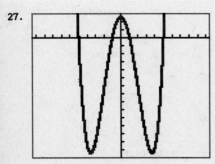

x: 1, -1, 5, -5; y: 25
rel. max. (0, 25)
rel. min. (3.6, -144), (-3.6, -144)

28.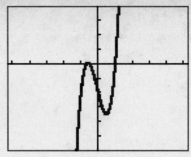

x: $-\dfrac{1}{2}$, 1, $-\dfrac{2}{3}$; y: -2
rel. max. (-0.6, 0.07)
rel. min. (0.5, -3.5)

29.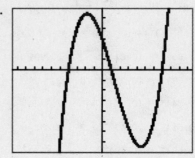

x: 1, -4, 7; y: 28
rel. max. (-1.8, 54)
rel. min. (4.5, -74.4), (3.1, -52.1)

30.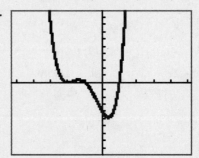

x: -2, -1, 1; y: -4
rel. max. (-1.4, 0.35)
rel. min. (-2, 0), (0.4, -4.8)

31. $f(x) = 2x^{\frac{1}{2}} + 3x^{\frac{2}{3}} - 4x^{\frac{1}{4}}$

$f'(x) = x^{-\frac{1}{2}} + 2x^{-\frac{1}{3}} - x^{-\frac{3}{4}}$

32. equations in the form $y = (x + a)^n + b$ where n is odd and a and b are real numbers

33. Let w = width, $\frac{125,000}{w}$ = length.

$$10w + 10w + 20\left(\frac{125,000}{w}\right) + 20\left(\frac{125,000}{w}\right) = C(w)$$

$$20w + \frac{5,000,000}{w} = C(w)$$

$$20 - 5,000,000w^{-2} = C'(w)$$

$$20 - 5,000,000w^{-2} = 0$$

$$5,000,000w^{-2} = 20$$

$$w^2 = \frac{5,000,000}{20}$$

$$w^2 = 250,000$$

$$w = 500$$

$$\ell = \frac{125,000}{500} = 250$$

34. $P(w) = (0.48 - 0.03w)(120 + 10w)$

$P(w) = 57.6 + 1.2w - 0.3w^2$

$P'(w) = 1.2 - 0.6w$

$0 = 1.2 - 0.6w$

$0.6w = 1.2$

$w = 2$ weeks

$P(w) = 57.6 + 1.2(2) - 0.3(2)^2$

$= \$58.80$ per acre

35. P lies on $\overline{AB}$.

$$AP \overset{?}{=} PB$$

$$\sqrt{(9-4)^2 + (3-2)^2} \overset{?}{=} \sqrt{(4+1)^2 + (2-1)^2}$$

$$\sqrt{26} = \sqrt{26} \quad \text{true}$$

36. Multiply each element of the matrix by the scalar. $2\begin{bmatrix} 1 & 2 \\ 3 & 4 \end{bmatrix} = \begin{bmatrix} 2 & 4 \\ 6 & 8 \end{bmatrix}$

37. $(-15)(3) - (-9)(5) = 0$, no

38. 4 units left and 8 units down

39. $f'(x) = 4x - 3$

$f'(-1) = 4(-1) - 3 = -7$

$y - 5 = -7(x + 1)$

$y - 5 = -7x - 7$

$y = -7x - 2$

40. $A = \frac{1}{2}bh$

$12 = \frac{1}{2}bh$

$24 = bh$

Since the legs are in ratio 2:3, they must have lengths 4 and 6 ($4 \cdot 6 = 24$).

Using the pythagorean theorem,

$4^2 + 6^2 = c^2$

$52 = c^2$

$\sqrt{52} = c$

$2\sqrt{13} = c$

The best answer is C.

Case Study Follow-Up

PAGE 163

1. a. $R(20) = 160(20) - \frac{1}{5}(20)^2 = \$3120$

   b. $R(100) = 160(100) - \frac{1}{5}(100)^2 = \$14,000$

   c. $R(500) = 160(500) - \frac{1}{5}(500)^2 = \$30,000$

2. $R'(x) = 160 - \frac{2}{5}x$

   $0 = 160 - \frac{2}{5}x$

   $\frac{2}{5}x = 160$

   $x = 400$ destroyers

   $R(400) = 160(400) - \frac{1}{5}(400)^2 = \$32,000$

   $\frac{32,000}{400} = \$80$

3. $\frac{41,000,000,000}{32,000} = 1,281,250$ times

4. See students' work.

3-8 **Continuity and End Behavior**

PAGES 169-170   CHECKING FOR UNDERSTANDING

1. Infinite discontinuity occurs when a graph has an asymptote. Jump discontinuity occurs when the the graph is defined for all values of x, but the graph itself is broken for a given value of x. Point discontinuity occurs when the function is defined for all values of x, except one, and would be continuous if that point were included.

2. If $a > b$, and $f(a) > f(b)$, the function is increasing. If $a < b$, and $f(a) < f(b)$, the function is decreasing.

3. If you can trace a graph without lifting your pencil, it is continuous.

4. The end behavior of the function is similar to the end behavior of the parent function defined by the first term.

5. point discontinuity

   $x \to \infty, f(x) \to -\infty$

   $x \to -\infty, f(x) \to -\infty$

6. jump discontinuity

   $x \to \infty, f(x) \to \infty$

   $x \to -\infty, f(x) \to -\infty$

7. infinite discontinuity

   $x \to \infty, f(x) \to \pm\infty$

   $x \to -\infty, f(x) \to \pm\infty$

8. continuous

   $x \to \infty, f(x) \to -\infty$

   $x \to -\infty, f(x) \to \infty$

9. infinite discontinuity

   $x \to \infty, f(x) \to 0$

   $x \to -\infty, f(x) \to 0$

10. jump discontinuity

    $x \to \infty, f(x) \to -\infty$

    $x \to -\infty, f(x) \to \infty$

11. $y = 2x + 5$ is a line having positive slope.

    all reals: increasing

12. asymptote at $x = 0$

    $x > 0$: decreasing, $x < 0$: decreasing

13. minimum at $x = 0$

    $x < 0$: decreasing, $x > 0$: increasing

PAGES 170-171   EXERCISES

14.

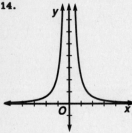

For $x > 0$, as $x \to 0$, $f(x) \to \infty$.

For $x < 0$, as $x \to 0$, $f(x) \to -\infty$.

infinite discontinuity

15.

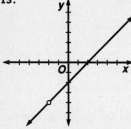

undefined at $x = -2$

point discontinuity

16.

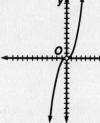

undefined at $x = 0$

point discontinuity

17.

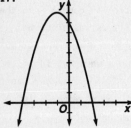

continuous

18.

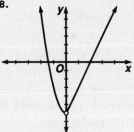

undefined at $x = 0$

point discontinuity

19.

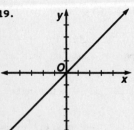

continuous

20.

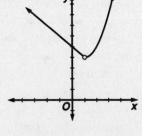

undefined at $x = 1$

point discontinuity

21.

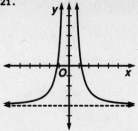

For $x > 0$, as $x \to 0$, $f(x) \to \infty$.

For $x < 0$, as $x \to 0$, $f(x) \to \infty$.

infinite discontinuity

22.

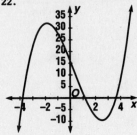

continuous

23.

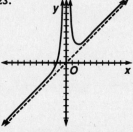

For $x > 0$, as $x \to 0$, $f(x) \to \infty$.

For $x < 0$, as $x \to 0$, $f(x) \to \infty$.

infinite discontinuity

24. $x \to \infty$, $f(x) \to \infty$; $x \to -\infty$, $f(x) \to -\infty$

25. $x \to \infty$, $f(x) \to \infty$; $x \to -\infty$, $f(x) \to \infty$

26. $x \to \infty$, $f(x) \to -\infty$; $x \to -\infty$, $f(x) \to \infty$

27. $\dfrac{x^2 - 11x + 28}{x - 4} = \dfrac{(x - 7)(x - 4)}{x - 4} = x - 7$

    If $x = 4$, $y = -3$. $-3, 4$

28. $\dfrac{x^2 - 11}{x + \sqrt{11}} = \dfrac{(x + \sqrt{11})(x - \sqrt{11})}{x + \sqrt{11}} = x - \sqrt{11}$

    If $x = -\sqrt{11}$, $y = -2\sqrt{11}$. $-2\sqrt{11}, -\sqrt{11}$

29. If $x = 4$, $x^3 = 64$.

    If $x = 4$, $68 - x = 64$. $64, 4$

30. $\dfrac{x^3 + 27}{x + 3} = \dfrac{(x + 3)(x^2 - 3x + 9)}{(x + 3)}$

    $= x^2 - 3x + 9$

    If $x = -3$, $y = (-3)^2 - 3(-3) + 9$

              $= 27$ $27, -3$

31.

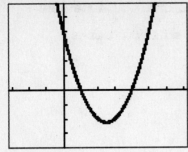

a. continuous

b. decreasing: $-\infty < x < -2.5$

 increasing: $-2.5 < x < \infty$

32.

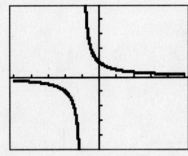

a. no

b. decreasing for all x, $x \neq -1$

33.

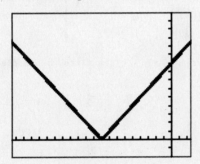

a. continuous

b. decreasing $-\infty < x < -9$

 increasing $-9 < x < \infty$

34. When $x = 2$, $f(x) = 2 - 2 = 0$.

So, $\sqrt{p - x^2} = 0$ at $x = 2$

$\sqrt{p - 4} = 0$

$p = 4$

When $x = -2$, $\sqrt{p - x^2} = \sqrt{4 - (-2)^2} = 0$.

So, $q - (-2) = 0$

$q + 2 = 0$

$q = -2$

35. $V = \pi r^2 h$

$300 = \pi r^2 h$

$\dfrac{300}{\pi r^2} = h$

Let $f(x) =$ surface area.

$f(x) = 2\pi r^2 + 2\pi r h$

$= 2\pi r^2 + 2\pi r \left(\dfrac{300}{\pi r^2}\right)$

$= 2\pi r^2 + \dfrac{600}{r}$

Since the minimum is a critical point, it can be found using the first derivative.

$f'(x) = 4\pi r + 600r^{-2}$

$0 = 4\pi r + 600r^{-2}$

$r^2(0) = 4\pi r(r^2) + 600r^{-2}(r^2)$

$0 = 4\pi r^3 + 600$

$\sqrt[3]{\dfrac{150}{\pi}} = r$

$3.6 \approx r$

$300 = \pi r^2 h$

$300 = \pi(3.6)^2 h$

$h \approx 7.4$ cm

$S = 2\pi r^2 + 2\pi r h$

$= 2\pi(3.6)^2 + 2\pi(3.6)(7.4)$

≈ 248.8 cm^2

36. a. $f(x) =$

$\begin{cases} 0.15x & \text{if } 0 < x \le 34{,}000 \\ 0.28(x - 34{,}000) + 5100 & \text{if } 34{,}000 < x \le 82{,}150 \\ 0.31(x - 82{,}150) + 18{,}582 & \text{if } x > 82{,}150 \end{cases}$

b.

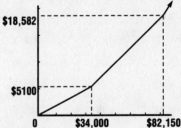

c. It is continuous.

d. (1) If $x = 73{,}000$, $f(x) = \$16{,}020$.

 (2) If $x = 32{,}050$, $f(x) = \$4807.50$.

 (3) If $x = 22{,}174$, $f(x) = \$3326.10$.

 (4) If $x = 87{,}234$, $f(x) = \$20{,}158.04$.

37. $(f \circ g)(x) = f(g(x))$

$= 5(0.5x - 1) + 9$

$= 2.5x + 4$

$(f \circ g)(4) = 2.5(4) + 4$

$= 14$

38. a. Let c = number of console TVs, w = number of
wide-screen TVs.

$0 \leq c \leq 450$

$0 \leq w \leq 200$

$600c + 900w \leq 3,600,000$

possible solutions: $(0, 200)$, $(450, 0)$,
$(0, 0)$, and $(450, 200)$

$P(c, w) = 125c + 200w$

$P(0, 200) = \$40,000$

$P(450, 0) = \$56,250$

$P(0, 0), = \$0$

$P(450, 200) = \$96,250$

maximum at $(450, 200)$

b. $\$96,250$

39.
$y = (x - 9)^2$

$x = (y - 9)^2$

$\pm\sqrt{x} = y - 9$

$\pm\sqrt{x} + 9 = y$

40.

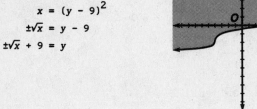

41. $f'(x) = 3x^2 - 2x \qquad f''(x) = 6x - 2$

$0 = 3x^2 - 2x \qquad\qquad 0 = 6x - 2$

$= x(3x - 2) \qquad\qquad 2 = 6x$

$x = 0, \dfrac{2}{3} \qquad\qquad x = \dfrac{1}{3}$

$f(0) = 0^3 - 0^2 + 3 = 3$

$f\left(\dfrac{2}{3}\right) = \left(\dfrac{2}{3}\right)^3 - \left(\dfrac{2}{3}\right)^2 + 3 \approx 2.85$

$f\left(\dfrac{1}{3}\right) = \left(\dfrac{1}{3}\right)^3 - \left(\dfrac{1}{3}\right)^2 + 3 \approx 2.93$

critical points: $(0, 3)$, $(0.67, 2.85)$,
$(0.33, 2.93)$

$f(-0.01) = (-0.01)^3 - (-0.01)^2 + 3 \approx 2.9999$

$f(0.01) = (0.01)^3 - (0.01)^2 + 3 \approx 2.9999$

$f(0.65) = (0.65)^3 - (0.65)^2 + 3 \approx 2.8521$

$f(0.68) = (0.68)^3 - (0.68)^2 + 3 \approx 2.8520$

$f(0.32) = (0.32)^3 - (0.32)^2 + 3 \approx 2.9304$

$f(0.34) = (0.34)^3 - (0.34)^2 + 3 \approx 2.9237$

So, $(0, 3)$ is a maximum, $(0.67, 2.85)$ is a
minimum, and $(0.33, 2.93)$ is a point of
inflection.

42. started at $\$x$

cut to $\$0.90x$

raised to $(1.1)(0.90x) = \$0.99x$

The best answer is B.

Chapter 3 Summary and Review

PAGES 172-174   SKILLS AND CONCEPTS

1.
$y = \dfrac{8}{x}$

$f(-x) = \dfrac{8}{-x}$

$= -\dfrac{8}{x}$

$= -f(x)$

origin, $y = \pm x$, odd

2.
$y^2 = -x - 3$

$y = \pm\sqrt{-x - 3}$

$f(-x) = \pm\sqrt{x - 3}$

x-axis; neither

3. $f(-x) = -2(-x)^3 + (-x)^2 - 3$

$= 2x^3 + x^2 - 3$

none, neither

4. $f(-x) = 8 - 4(-x)^2$

$= 8 - 4x^2$

$= f(x)$

y-axis, even

5.

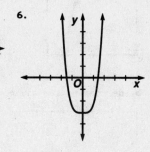

reflect across
x-axis

6.

translate down 3 places

7.

translate left
5 places

8.

thinner, reflect across
y-axis

9.
$y = 6 - 2x$

$x = 6 - 2y$

$x - 6 = -2y$

$\dfrac{6 - x}{2} = y$

yes

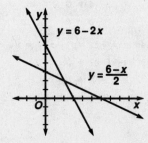

$y = 6 - 2x$

$y = \dfrac{6 - x}{2}$

10.

$y = \frac{1}{4}(x - 3)^2$

$x = \frac{1}{4}(y - 3)^2$

$4x = (y - 3)^2$

$\pm\sqrt{4x} = y - 3$

$3 \pm 2\sqrt{x} = y$

no

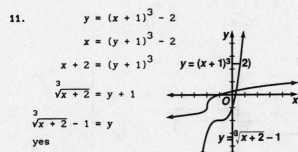

$y = \frac{1}{4}(x-3)^2$

$y = \pm2\sqrt{x} + 3$

11.

$y = (x + 1)^3 - 2$

$x = (y + 1)^3 - 2$

$x + 2 = (y + 1)^3$

$\sqrt[3]{x + 2} = y + 1$

$\sqrt[3]{x + 2} - 1 = y$

yes

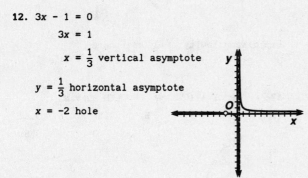

$y = (x + 1)^3 - 2$

$y = \sqrt[3]{x + 2} - 1$

12. $3x - 1 = 0$

$3x = 1$

$x = \frac{1}{3}$ vertical asymptote

$y = \frac{1}{3}$ horizontal asymptote

$x = -2$ hole

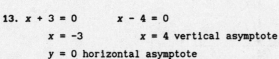

13. $x + 3 = 0 \qquad x - 4 = 0$

$x = -3 \qquad x = 4$ vertical asymptote

$y = 0$ horizontal asymptote

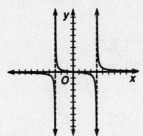

14. $y = \frac{(x + 3)(x - 3)}{x - 3}$

$x = 3$ hole

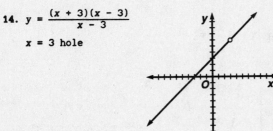

15.

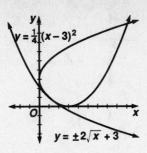

16.

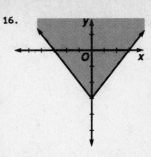

17.

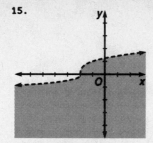

18.

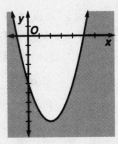

19. $f'(x) = 2x + 5$

$f'(1) = 2(1) + 5$

$\quad = 7$

$y - 4 = 7(x - 1)$

$y - 4 = 7x - 7$

$\quad y = 7x - 3$

20. $f'(x) = -2x + 6$

$f'(-2) = -2(-2) + 6$

$\quad = 10$

$y - 3 = 10(x + 2)$

$y - 3 = 10x + 20$

$\quad y = 10x + 23$

21. $f'(x) = 6x + 4$

$f'(1) = 6(1) + 4$

$\quad = 10$

$y - 5 = 10(x - 1)$

$y - 5 = 10x - 10$

$\quad y = 10x - 5$

22. $f'(x) = 4x - 9$

$f'(2) = 4(2) - 9$

$\quad = -1$

$y + 5 = -1(x - 2)$

$y + 5 = -x + 2$

$\quad y = -x - 3$

23. $f'(x) = 1 - 2x$

$0 = 1 - 2x$

$2x = 1$

$x = \frac{1}{2}$

$f'(x) = -2$

$f\left(\frac{1}{2}\right) = 4 + \frac{1}{2} - \left(\frac{1}{2}\right)^2 = \frac{17}{4}$

critical point $\left(\frac{1}{2}, \frac{17}{4}\right)$

$f(0.49) = 4 + 0.49 - (0.49)^2 = 4.2499$

$f(0.51) = 4 + 0.51 - (0.51)^2 = 4.2499$

So, $\left(\frac{1}{2}, \frac{17}{4}\right)$ is a maximum.

24. $f'(x) = 3x^2 - 12x + 9 \qquad f''(x) = 6x - 12$

$\qquad 0 = 3x^2 - 12x + 9 \qquad\qquad 0 = 6x - 12$

$\qquad 0 = x^2 - 4x + 3 \qquad\qquad 12 = 6x$

$\qquad 0 = (x - 3)(x - 1) \qquad\qquad 2 = x$

$\qquad x = 3, 1$

$f(3) = 3^3 - 6(3)^2 + 9(3) = 0$

$f(1) = 1^3 - 6(1)^2 + 9(1) = 4$

$f(2) = 2^3 - 6(2)^2 + 9(2) = 2$

critical points: (3, 0), (1, 4), (2, 2)

$f(2.99) = 2.99^3 - 6(2.99)^2 + 9(2.99) \approx 0.000299$

$f(3.01) = (3.01)^3 - 6(3.01)^2 + 9(3.01) \approx 0.000301$

$f(0.99) = (0.99)^3 - 6(0.99)^2 + 9(0.99) \approx 3.9997$

$f(1.01) = (1.01)^3 - 6(1.01)^2 + 9(1.01) \approx 3.9997$

$f(1.99) = (1.99)^3 - 6(1.99)^2 + 9(1.99) \approx 2.0300$

$f(2.01) = (2.01)^3 - 6(2.01)^2 + 9(2.01) \approx 1.9700$

So, (3, 0) is a minimum, (1, 4) is a maximum, and (2, 2) is a point of inflection.

25. $f'(x) = 3x^2 + 6x \qquad f''(x) = 6x + 6$

$\qquad 0 = 3x^2 + 6x \qquad\qquad 0 = 6x + 6$

$\qquad 0 = 3x(x + 2) \qquad\qquad -6 = 6x$

$\qquad x = 0, -2 \qquad\qquad -1 = x$

$f(0) = 0^3 + 3(0)^2 - 4 = -4$

$f(-2) = (-2)^3 + 3(-2)^2 - 4 = 0$

$f(-1) = (-1)^3 + 3(-1)^2 - 4 = -2$

critical points: (0, -4), (-2, 0), (-1, -2)

$f(-0.01) = (-0.01)^3 + 3(-0.01)^2 - 4 \approx -3.9997$

$f(0.01) = (0.01)^3 + 3(0.01)^2 - 4 \approx -3.9997$

$f(-2.01) = (-2.01)^3 + 3(-2.01)^2 - 4 = -0.000301$

$f(-1.99) = (-1.99)^3 + 3(-1.99)^2 - 4 = -0.000299$

$f(-1.01) = (-1.01)^3 + 3(-1.01)^2 - 4 \approx -1.9700$

$f(-0.99) = (-0.99)^3 + 3(-0.99)^2 - 4 \approx -2.0300$

So, (0, -4) is a minimum, (-2, 0) is a maximum, and (-1, -2) is a point of inflection.

26. $f'(x) = 6x^2 \qquad\qquad f''(x) = 12x$

$\qquad 0 = 6x^2 \qquad\qquad\quad 0 = 12x$

$\qquad 0 = x \qquad\qquad\qquad x = 0$

$f(0) = 2(0)^3 - 5 = -5$

critical point (0, -5)

$f(-0.1) = 2(-0.1)^3 - 5 \approx -5.002$

$f(0.1) = 2(0.1)^3 - 5 \approx -4.998$

So, (0, -5) is a point of inflection.

27.

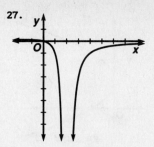

For $x < 2$, as $x \to 2$, $f(x) \to \infty$.

For $x > 2$, as $x \to 2$, $f(x) \to -\infty$.

infinite discontinuity

28.

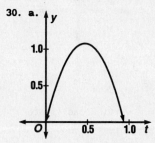

jump discontinuity

29.

continuous

PAGE 174   APPLICATIONS AND PROBLEM SOLVING

30. a.

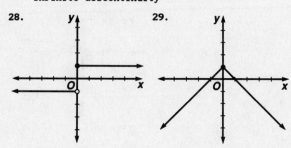

b. $h'(t) = 4.6 - 9.8t$

$\qquad 0 = 4.6 - 9.8t$

$\qquad 9.8t = 4.6$

$\qquad t \approx 0.47$

$\qquad h(0.47) \approx 1.08$ m

31. a. $f'(t) = 6t + 5$

$\qquad f'(4.29) = 30.74$ m/s

b. $f''(t) = 6$ m/s^2

Chapter 3 Test

PAGE 175

1.

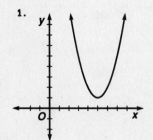

shift 5 units right

2.

reflected and shifted 2 units up

68

3.

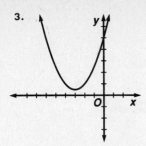

wider and shifted 3 units left

4.
$$y = (x - 4)^2$$
$$x = (y - 4)^2$$
$$\pm\sqrt{x} = y - 4$$
$$\pm\sqrt{x} + 4 = y, \text{ no}$$

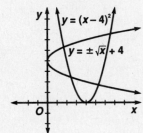

5.
$$y = 8x^3 + 1$$
$$x = 8y^3 + 1$$
$$x - 1 = 8y^3$$
$$\frac{x - 1}{8} = y^3$$
$$\sqrt[3]{\frac{x - 1}{8}} = y$$
$$\frac{1}{2}\sqrt[3]{x - 1} = y, \text{ yes}$$

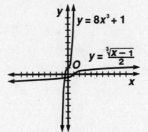

6.
$$y = (x + 3)^4 - 7$$
$$x = (y + 3)^4 - 7$$
$$x + 7 = (y + 3)^4$$
$$\pm\sqrt[4]{x + 7} = y + 3$$
$$\pm\sqrt[4]{x + 7} - 3 = y, \text{ no}$$

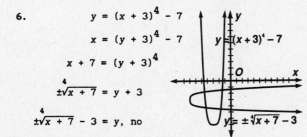

7. $x = 3, -1$ vertical asymptotes

$y = 0$ horizontal asymptote

$$f(-x) = \frac{-x + 5}{(-x - 3)(-x + 1)}$$

neither

8.
$$x^2 - 4 = 0$$
$$(x + 2)(x - 2) = 0$$

$x = -2, 2$ vertical asymptotes

$y = 0$ horizontal asymptote

$$f(-x) = \frac{-x}{(-x)^2 - 4}$$
$$= \frac{-x}{x^2 - 4}$$
$$= -f(x), \text{ odd}$$

9. no asymptotes

$$f(-x) = (-x)^7 - 5(-x)^3 - 8$$
$$= -x^7 + 5x^3 - 8, \text{ neither}$$

10.

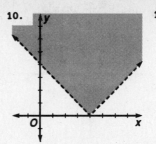

11.

12. $f'(x) = 2x - 4$

$f'(1) = 2(1) - 4 = -2$

$y + 2 = -2(x - 1)$

$y + 2 = -2x + 2$

$y = -2x$

13. $f'(x) = 6x - 2$

$f'(2) = 6(2) - 2 = 10$

$y - 9 = 10(x - 2)$

$y - 9 = 10x - 20$

$y = 10x - 11$

14. $f'(x) = 2x - 8$

$0 = 2x - 8$

$8 = 2x$

$4 = x$

$f''(x) = 2$

$f(4) = 4^2 - 8(4) + 4 = -12$

critical point $(4, -12)$

$f(3.99) = 3.99^2 - 8(3.99) + 4 = -11.9999$

$f(4.01) = 4.01^2 - 8(4.01) + 4 = -11.9999$

So, $(4, -12)$ is a minimum.

15. $f'(x) = -3x^2 - 6x$ $\qquad f''(x) = -6x - 6$

$\quad 0 = -3x^2 - 6x \qquad\qquad 0 = -6x - 6$

$\quad\quad = -3x(x + 2) \qquad\qquad 6 = -6x$

$\quad x = 0, -2 \qquad\qquad\qquad -1 = x$

$f(0) = -(0)^3 - 3(0)^2 + 3 = 3$

$f(-2) = -(-2)^3 - 3(-2)^2 + 3 = -1$

$f(-1) = -(-1)^3 - 3(-1)^2 + 3 = 1$

critical points: $(0, 3)$, $(-2, -1)$, $(-1, 1)$

$f(-0.01) = -(-0.01)^3 - 3(-0.01)^2 + 3 \approx 2.9997$

$f(0.01) = -(0.01)^3 - 3(0.01)^2 + 3 \approx 2.9997$

$f(-2.01) = -(-2.01)^3 - 3(-2.01)^2 + 3 \approx -0.9997$

$f(-1.99) = -(-1.99)^3 - 3(-1.99)^2 + 3 \approx -0.9997$

$f(-1.01) = -(-1.01)^3 - 3(-1.01)^2 + 3 \approx 0.9700$

$f(-0.99) = -(-0.99)^3 - 3(-0.99)^2 + 3 \approx 1.0300$

So, $(0, 3)$ is a maximum, $(-2, -1)$ is a minimum, and $(-1, 1)$ is a point of inflection.

16.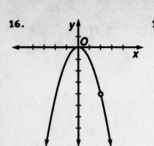

undefined at $x = 2$

point discontinuity

17.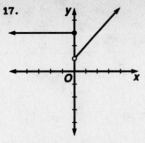

jump discontinuity

at $x = 0$

18. $f(0) = 3(0)^3 - 2(0)^2 - 5(0)$

$\qquad = 0 \qquad$ y-intercept

$3x^3 - 2x^2 - 5x = 0$

$x(3x^2 - 2x - 5) = 0$

$x(3x - 5)(x + 1) = 0$

$x = 0, \dfrac{5}{3}, -1 \qquad$ x-intercepts

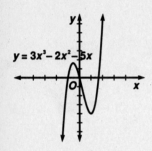

$y = 3x^3 - 2x^2 - 5x$

19. As $x \to \infty$, $y \to \infty$.

As $x \to -\infty$, $y \to \infty$.

20. a.

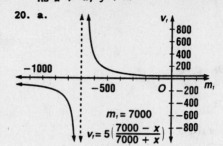

$m_t = 7000$

$v_t = 5\left(\dfrac{7000 - x}{7000 + x}\right)$

b. $v_f = \dfrac{7000 - 50}{7000 + 50} \cdot 5$

$\qquad = \dfrac{6950}{7050} \cdot 5$

$\qquad = \dfrac{695}{141} \approx 4.93$ m/s

PAGE 175   BONUS

When $x = 1$,

$1 + 1 = 1^2 + b(1) + c$

$2 = 1 + b + c$

$1 = b + c$

When $x = 3$,

$3 + 1 = 3^2 + b(3) + c$

$4 = 9 + 3b + c$

$-5 = 3b + c$

$b + c = 1 \longrightarrow b = 1 - c$

$3b + c = -5 \qquad 3(1 - c) + c = -5$

$\qquad\qquad\qquad 3 - 3c + c = -5$

$\qquad\qquad\qquad\qquad -2c = -8$

$\qquad\qquad\qquad\qquad\quad c = 4$

$\qquad\qquad b = 1 - c = -3$

Chapter 4   Polynomial and Rational Functions

PAGES 181-182   CHECKING FOR UNDERSTANDING

1. The solutions to a polynomial equation are the values for which the function $P(x) = 0$.

2. A complex number is any number in the form $a + bi$, where a and b are real numbers and i is the imaginary unit. A complex number is a real number when $b = 0$.

3.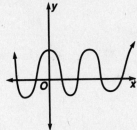

4. 55 feet is greater than the width of the entire area on which the pool is to be built.

5. yes, 3   6. no because $\frac{1}{x} = x^{-1}$ and $\frac{1}{2x} = (2x)^{-1}$

7. yes, 7

8. $P(2) = 2^4 - 4(2)^3 - 2^2 + 4(2)$
   $= 16 - 32 - 4 + 8$
   $= -12$, no

9. $P(0) = 0^4 - 4(0)^3 - 0^2 + 4(0)$
   $= 0 - 0 - 0 + 0$
   $= 0$, yes

10. $P(-1) = (-1)^4 - 4(-1)^3 - (-1)^2 + 4(-1)$
    $= 1 + 4 - 1 + (-4)$
    $= 0$, yes

11. $P(-2) = (-2)^4 - 4(-2)^3 - (-2)^2 + 4(-2)$
    $= 16 + 32 - 4 + (-8)$
    $= 36$, no

12. $P(4) = 4^4 - 4(4)^3 - 4^2 + 4(4)$
    $= 64 - 64 - 16 + 16$
    $= 0$, yes

13. $(x - 1)(x - (-1))(x - 2)(x - (-2)) = 0$
    $(x - 1)(x + 1)(x - 2)(x + 2) = 0$
    $(x^2 - 1)(x^2 - 4) = 0$
    $x^4 - 5x^2 + 4 = 0$

14. $(u + 2)(u^2 - 4) = 0$
    $(u + 2)(u - 2)(u + 2) = 0$
    $u + 2 = 0 \qquad u - 2 = 0 \qquad u + 2 = 0$
    $u = -2 \qquad u = 2 \qquad u = -2$

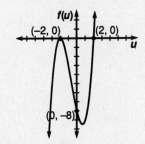

PAGES 182-184   EXERCISES

15. 1 root
    $x - 2 = 0$
    $x = 2$

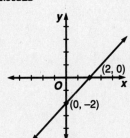

16. 2 roots
    $x^2 - 144 = 0$
    $(x - 12)(x + 12) = 0$
    $x - 12 = 0 \qquad x + 12 = 0$
    $x = 12 \qquad x = -12$

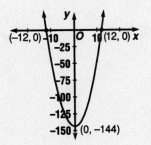

17. 2 roots
    $r^2 - 14r + 49 = 0$
    $(r - 7)(r - 7) = 0$
    $r - 7 = 0 \qquad r - 7 = 0$
    $r = 7 \qquad r = 7$

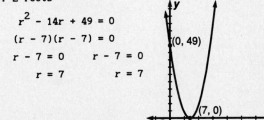

18. 2 roots

$$x^2 + 25 = 0$$
$$(x - 5i)(x + 5i) = 0$$
$$x - 5i = 0 \qquad x + 5i = 0$$
$$x = 5i \qquad x = -5i$$

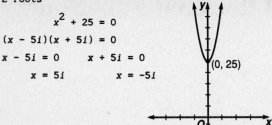

19. 2 roots

$$12x^2 + 8x - 15 = 0$$
$$x^2 + \frac{8}{12}x - \frac{15}{12} = 0$$
$$\left(x - \frac{10}{12}\right)\left(x + \frac{18}{12}\right) = 0$$
$$\left(x - \frac{5}{6}\right)\left(x + \frac{3}{2}\right) = 0$$
$$x - \frac{5}{6} = 0 \qquad x + \frac{3}{2} = 0$$
$$x = \frac{5}{6} \qquad x = -\frac{3}{2}$$

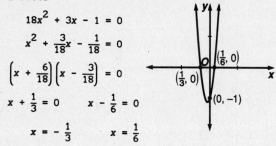

20. 2 roots

$$18x^2 + 3x - 1 = 0$$
$$x^2 + \frac{3}{18}x - \frac{1}{18} = 0$$
$$\left(x + \frac{6}{18}\right)\left(x - \frac{3}{18}\right) = 0$$
$$x + \frac{1}{3} = 0 \qquad x - \frac{1}{6} = 0$$
$$x = -\frac{1}{3} \qquad x = \frac{1}{6}$$

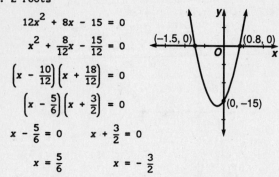

21. 3 roots

$$6c^3 - 3c^2 - 45c = 0$$
$$c(6c^2 - 3c - 45) = 0$$
$$c(c - 3)(6c + 15) = 0$$
$$c = 0 \qquad c - 3 = 0 \qquad 6c + 15 = 0$$
$$c = 3 \qquad c = -\frac{15}{6} = -\frac{5}{2}$$

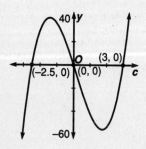

22. 3 roots

$$n^3 - 9n = 0$$
$$n(n^2 - 9) = 0$$
$$n(n - 3)(n + 3) = 0$$
$$n = 0 \qquad n - 3 = 0 \qquad n + 3 = 0$$
$$n = 3 \qquad n = -3$$

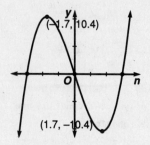

23. $(x - (-3))(x - 2) = 0$

$$(x + 3)(x - 2) = 0$$
$$x^2 + x - 6 = 0$$

24. $(x - (-2))(x - (-0.5))(x - 4) = 0$

$$(x + 2)(x + 0.5)(x - 4) = 0$$
$$(x^2 + 2.5x + 1)(x - 4) = 0$$
$$x^3 - 4x^2 + 2.5x^2 - 10x + x - 4 = 0$$
$$x^3 - 1.5x^2 - 9x - 4 = 0$$
$$2x^3 - 3x^2 - 18x - 8 = 0$$

25. $(x - (-1))(x - (-1))(x - 4)(x - 4)(x - 4) = 0$

$$(x + 1)(x + 1)(x - 4)(x - 4)(x - 4) = 0$$
$$(x^2 + 2x + 1)(x^2 - 8x + 16)(x - 4) = 0$$
$$(x^2 + 2x + 1)(x^3 - 12x^2 + 48x - 64) = 0$$
$$x^5 - 12x^4 + 48x^3 - 64x^2 + 2x^4 -$$
$$24x^3 + 96x^2 - 128x + x^3 - 12x^2 + 48x - 64 = 0$$
$$x^5 - 10x^4 + 25x^3 + 20x^2 - 80x - 64 = 0$$

26. $(x - (-5i))(x - 5i)(x - i)(x - (-i)) = 0$

$$(x + 5i)(x - 5i)(x - i)(x + i) = 0$$
$$(x^2 + 25)(x^2 + 1) = 0$$
$$x^4 + 26x^2 + 25 = 0$$

27. $(x - 1)(x - (-1))(x - (1 + i))(x - (1 - i)) = 0$

$$(x - 1)(x + 1)(x - 1 - i)(x - 1 + i) = 0$$
$$(x^2 - 1)(x^2 - x + xi - x + 1 - i - xi + i - i^2) = 0$$
$$(x^2 - 1)(x^2 - 2x + 2) = 0$$
$$x^4 - 2x^3 + 2x^2 - x^2 + 2x - 2 = 0$$
$$x^4 - 2x^3 + x^2 + 2x - 2 = 0$$

28.

$$(x - 2)(x - (2 + 3i))(x - (2 - 3i))$$
$$(x - (-1 + i))(x - (-1 - i)) = 0$$
$$(x - 2)(x - 2 - 3i)(x - 2 + 3i)(x + 1 - i)$$
$$(x + 1 + i) = 0$$
$$(x - 2)(x^2 - 2x + 3xi - 2x + 4 - 6i - 3xi + 6i -$$
$$9i^2)(x^2 + x + xi + x + 1 + i - xi - i - i^2) = 0$$
$$(x - 2)(x^2 - 4x + 13)(x^2 + 2x + 2) = 0$$
$$(x^3 - 4x^2 + 13x - 2x^2 + 8x - 26)(x^2 + 2x + 2) = 0$$
$$(x^3 - 6x^2 + 21x - 26)(x^2 + 2x + 2) = 0$$
$$x^5 + 2x^4 + 2x^3 - 6x^4 - 12x^3 - 12x^2 + 21x^3 +$$
$$42x^2 + 42x - 26x^2 - 52x - 52 = 0$$
$$x^5 - 4x^4 + 11x^3 + 4x^2 - 10x - 52 = 0$$

29.

$$x^3 - 6x^2 + 10x - 8 = 0$$
$$(x - 4)(x^2 - 2x + 2) = 0$$
$$(x - 4)(x - (1 + i))(x - (1 - i)) = 0$$
$$x = 4, 1 \pm i$$

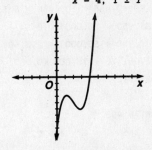

30.

$$x^4 - 10x^2 + 9 = 0$$
$$(x^2 - 9)(x^2 - 1) = 0$$
$$(x - 3)(x + 3)(x - 1)(x + 1) = 0$$

$x - 3 = 0$	$x + 3 = 0$	$x - 1 = 0$	$x + 1 = 0$
$x = 3$	$x = -3$	$x = 1$	$x = -1$

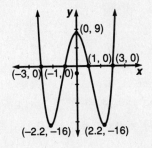

31.

$$x^4 + x^2 - 2 = 0$$
$$(x^2 + 2)(x^2 - 1) = 0$$
$$(x^2 + 2)(x - 1)(x + 1) = 0$$

$x^2 + 2 = 0$	$x - 1 = 0$	$x + 1 = 0$
$x^2 = -2$	$x = 1$	$x = -1$
$x = \pm\sqrt{-2}$		
$x = \pm i\sqrt{2}$		

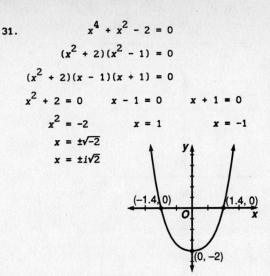

32.

$$4m^4 + 17m^2 + 4 = 0$$
$$(4m^2 + 1)(m^2 + 4) = 0$$

$4m^2 + 1 = 0$	$m^2 + 4 = 0$
	$m = \pm\sqrt{-4}$
$m = \pm\sqrt{\dfrac{-1}{4}}$	$m = \pm 2i$
$m = \pm\frac{1}{2}i$	

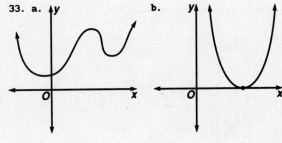

33. a. **b.**

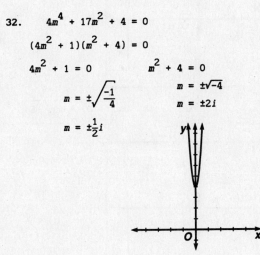

c. **d.**

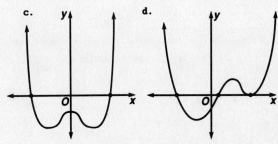

e. **f. not possible**

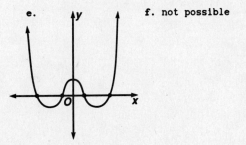

34. -2; Xmin: -10, Xmax: 10, Ymin: -10, Ymax: 10

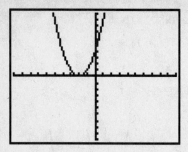

35. 0, 20, -16; Xmin: -20, Xmax: 25, Ymin: -400, Ymax: 400

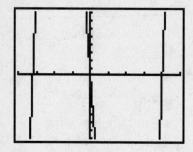

36. -1, -5, 1, 5; Xmin: -10, Xmax: 10, Ymin: -50, Ymax: 50

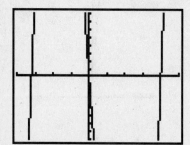

37.

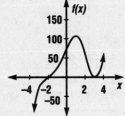

  a. 5   **b.** 2; -2, 3

  c. There are 5 real roots. However, there is a triple root at -2 and a double root at 3.

38. $(x - B)(x - C) = 0$

$x^2 - Cx - Bx + BC = 0$

$x^2 - (C + B)x + BC = 0$

$\left.\begin{array}{l}-C - B = B \\ BC = C\end{array}\right\}$ from $x^2 + Bx + C = 0$

  $B = 1$

  $-C - 1 = 1$

    $-C = 2$

     $C = -2$

  $B \times C = -2$

39. a. 30   **b.** -25   **c.** -3.5625

40. a. $d(30) = (1341)(30) + \frac{1}{2}(16.4)(30)^2$

             $= 40,230 + 7380$

             $= 47,610$ ft

  b. $d(1 \text{ min} = 60 \text{ sec}) = 1341(60) + \frac{1}{2}(16.4)(60)^2$

                      $= 80,460 + 29,520$

                      $= 109,980$ ft

  c. $d(2 \text{ min} = 120 \text{ sec}) = 1341(120) + \frac{1}{2}(16.4)(120)^2$

                      $= 160,920 + 118,080$

                      $= 279,000$ ft

  d. No, the relationship is not linear.

41. $A = P(1 + R)^t$

  a. $R = 0.13$; Let $x = 1 + R = 1.13$.

    $T(x) = 30,000(x)^3 + 55,000(x)^2 + 75,000(x)^1$

    $T(1.13) = 30,000(1.13)^3 + 55,000(1.13)^2 +$
             $75,000(1.13)$

         $= \$198,266.41$

  b. first year: $30,000(0.065) + 30,000 = \$31,950$

    second year: $(31,950 + 55,000)(0.065) +$
                $(31,950 + 55,000) = \$92,601.75$

    third year: $(92,601.75 + 75,000)(0.065) +$
              $(92,601.75 + 75,000) \approx$
              $\$178,495.86$

    total amount: $\$178,495.86$

    difference: $198,266.41 - 178,495.86 =$
              $\$19,770.55$ less

42. Let x = width of window.

Let $x + 6$ = height of window.

  $A = \ell w$

$315 = x(x + 6)$

$315 = x^2 + 6x$

$0 = x^2 + 6x - 315$

$0 = (x + 21)(x - 15)$

$x + 21 = 0$ $x - 15 = 0$

    $x = -21$ $x = 15$

Since distance cannot be negative, $x = 15$ and $x + 6 = 21$. The window should be 15 in. × 21 in.

43. $[g \circ h](x) = g(h(x)) = g(x^2) = x^2 - 1$

44. $m = \dfrac{7 - 2}{0 - 5} = \dfrac{5}{-5} = -1$

$y = mx + b$

$7 = -1(0) + b$

$7 = b$

$y = -x + 7$

45. $x - 2y = -1 \longrightarrow 2x + 4y = 2$

   $2x + 3y = -16$ $\underline{2x + 3y = -16}$

                           $7y = -14$

                               $y = -2$

      $x - 2(-2) = -1$

         $x + 4 = -1$

             $x = -5$ $(-5, -2)$

46. $x^2 = 25$ $y = 9$ $2z = 12$

   $x = \pm 5$ $z = 6$

47.

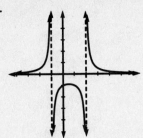

48. $y = \dfrac{x^2 - 1}{x + 1}$

The function is undefined
at $x = -1$. So it has
point discontinuity at
$x = 3$.

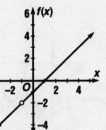

49. (A) $2x + 3y = 7$ **(B)** $3x - 2y = 7$

$3y = -2x + 7$ $3x - 7 = 2y$

$y = -\dfrac{2}{3}x + \dfrac{7}{3}$ $\dfrac{3}{2}x - \dfrac{7}{2} = y$

$\text{slope} = -\dfrac{2}{3}$ $\text{slope} = \dfrac{3}{2}$

$$B > A$$

The best answer is B.

Case Study Follow-Up

PAGE 184

1. $(1.8 \text{ million}) \times (82\%) = 1{,}800{,}000 \times 0.82$

$\phantom{(1.8 \text{ million}) \times (82\%) } = 1{,}476{,}000$

$\phantom{(1.8 \text{ million}) \times } 1.5 \text{ million}$

2. a. $A(5) = -0.0015(5)^2 + 0.1058(5)$

$ = -0.0375 + 0.529$

$ = 0.4915$

b. $A(0.2) = -0.0015(0.2)^2 + 0.1058(0.2)$

$ \approx 0.0211$

$A(0.4) = -0.0015(0.4)^2 + 0.1058(0.4)$

$ \approx 0.0421$

$A(0.6) = -0.0015(0.6)^2 + 0.1058(0.6)$

$ \approx 0.0629$

$A(0.8) = -0.0015(0.8)^2 + 0.1058(0.8)$

$ \approx 0.0837$

$ \text{after } 0.8 \text{ hours}$

3. See students' work.

PAGE 186   EXERCISES

1.

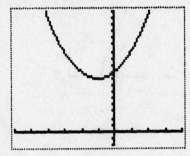

2.

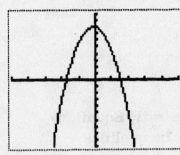

3.

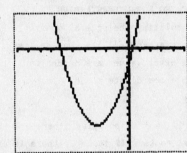

4.

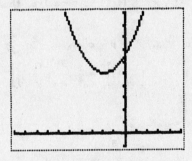

5.

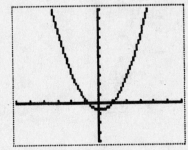

6.

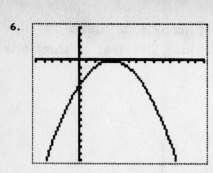

Answers for Exercises 7-12 are approximate.

7. −7.36, 1.36	**8.** −1.06, 0.81
9. −28.91, −7.24	**10.** −2.02, 0.43
11. −0.23, 0.98	**12.** −1.66, 2.31

4-2	**Quadratic Equations and Inequalities**

PAGE 192   **CHECKING FOR UNDERSTANDING**

1. Graphing, completing the square, quadratic formula; The graphing solution may be less exact, since exact values are harder to determine on a coordinate plane.

2. $b^2 - 4ac$

3. If the discriminant is positive, there are two distinct real roots. If it is 0, there is one distinct real root. If it is negative, there are two imaginary roots.

4. $x^2 + 4x + c$ **5.** $p^2 - p + c$ **6.** $y^2 + \frac{3}{2}y + c$

$\left[\frac{1}{2}(4)\right]^2 = 4$ $\left[\frac{1}{2}(-1)\right]^2 = \frac{1}{4}$ $\left[\frac{1}{2}\left(\frac{3}{2}\right)\right]^2 = \frac{9}{16}$

7. $x^2 - 5x + 9 = 0$

$$x^2 - 5x = -9$$

$$x^2 - 5x + \left(\frac{5}{2}\right)^2 = -9 + \left(\frac{5}{2}\right)^2$$

$$\left(x - \frac{5}{2}\right)^2 = -\frac{11}{4}$$

$$x - \frac{5}{2} = \pm i\sqrt{\frac{11}{4}}$$

$$x = \frac{5}{2} \pm \frac{i\sqrt{11}}{2}$$

$$x = \frac{5 \pm i\sqrt{11}}{2}$$

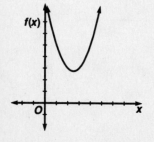

8. $z^2 - 10z + 10 = -11$

$$z^2 - 10z = -21$$

$$z^2 - 10z + 25 = -21 + 25$$

$$(z - 5)^2 = 4$$

$$z - 5 = \pm 2$$

$$z = 5 \pm 2$$

$$z = 3,\ 7$$

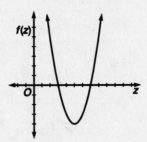

9. $b^2 - 4ac$

$= 6^2 - 4(4)(25)$

$= -364$

2 imaginary roots

10. $b^2 - 4ac$

$= 12^2 - 4(1)(36)$

$= 0$

1 distinct real root

11. $5 + i\sqrt{2}$

12. $t^2 - 3t - 28 = 0$

$$t = \frac{-(-3) \pm \sqrt{(-3)^2 - 4(1)(-28)}}{2(1)}$$

$$= \frac{3 \pm \sqrt{121}}{2}$$

$$= \frac{3 \pm 11}{2}$$

$$t = \frac{14}{2} = 7,\ t = \frac{-8}{2} = -4$$

13. $3x^2 - 5x + 9 = 0$

$$x = \frac{-(-5) \pm \sqrt{(-5)^2 - 4(3)(9)}}{2(3)}$$

$$= \frac{5 \pm \sqrt{-83}}{6}$$

$$x = \frac{5 \pm i\sqrt{83}}{6}$$

14.

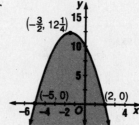

76

15. $x^2 - 3x - 88 = 0$

$x^2 - 3x = 88$

$x^2 - 3x + (1.5)^2 = 88 + (1.5)^2$

$(x - 1.5)^2 = 90.25$

$x - 1.5 = \pm 9.5$

$x = 1.5 + 9.5 \qquad x = 1.5 - 9.5$

$x = 11 \qquad\qquad x = -8$

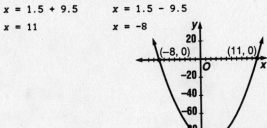

16. $x^2 - \frac{3}{4}x + \frac{1}{8} = 0$

$x^2 - \frac{3}{4}x + \left(\frac{3}{8}\right)^2 = -\frac{1}{8} + \left(\frac{3}{8}\right)^2$

$\left(x - \frac{3}{8}\right)^2 = \frac{1}{64}$

$x - \frac{3}{8} = \pm\frac{1}{8}$

$x = \frac{3}{8} + \frac{1}{8} \qquad x = \frac{3}{8} - \frac{1}{8}$

$x = \frac{1}{2} \qquad\qquad x = \frac{1}{4}$

17. $2x^2 + 11x - 21 = 0$

$x^2 + \frac{11}{2}x - \frac{21}{2} = 0$

$x^2 + \frac{11}{2}x = \frac{21}{2}$

$x^2 + \frac{11}{2}x + \left(\frac{11}{4}\right)^2 = \frac{21}{2} + \left(\frac{11}{4}\right)^2$

$\left(x + \frac{11}{4}\right)^2 = \frac{289}{16}$

$x + \frac{11}{4} = \pm\frac{17}{4}$

$x = \frac{-11}{4} + \frac{17}{4} \qquad x = \frac{-11}{4} - \frac{17}{4}$

$x = \frac{3}{2} \qquad\qquad x = -7$

18. $x^2 - 3x - 7 = 0$

$x^2 - 3x = 7$

$x^2 - 3x + \left(\frac{3}{2}\right)^2 = 7 + \left(\frac{3}{2}\right)^2$

$\left(x - \frac{3}{2}\right)^2 = \frac{37}{4}$

$x - \frac{3}{2} = \pm\frac{\sqrt{37}}{2}$

$x = \frac{3}{2} + \frac{\sqrt{37}}{2}, \quad x = \frac{3}{2} - \frac{\sqrt{37}}{2}$

$x = \frac{3 \pm \sqrt{37}}{2}$

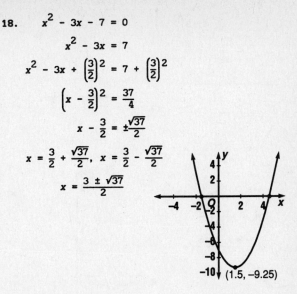

19. $z^2 - 2z = 24$

$z^2 - 2z + 1^2 = 24 + 1^2$

$(z - 1)^2 = 25$

$z - 1 = \pm 5$

$z = 1 + 5 \qquad z = 1 - 5$

$z = 6 \qquad\qquad z = -4$

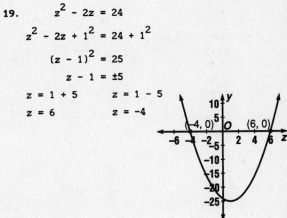

20. $3x^2 - 12x = -4$

$x^2 - 4x = -\frac{4}{3}$

$x^2 - 4x + 4 = -\frac{4}{3} + 4$

$(x - 2)^2 = \frac{8}{3}$

$x - 2 = \frac{\pm 2\sqrt{2}}{\sqrt{3}}$

$x = 2 \pm \frac{2\sqrt{6}}{3}$

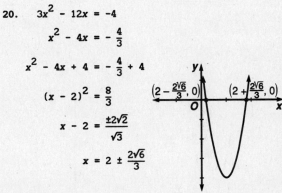

21. $19^2 - 4(4)(-5)$

$= 441$

2 real distinct roots

$x = \frac{-19 \pm \sqrt{441}}{2(4)}$

$= \frac{-19 \pm 21}{8}$

$x = \frac{1}{4}, \; -5$

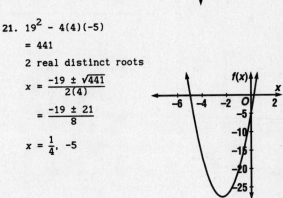

77

22. $(-7)^2 - 4(-6)(3)$

= 121

2 real distinct roots

$m = \dfrac{-(-7) \pm \sqrt{121}}{2(-6)}$

$= \dfrac{7 \pm 11}{-12}$

$m = \dfrac{1}{3}, -\dfrac{3}{2}$

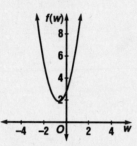

23. $3^2 - 4(2)(3) = -15$

2 imaginary roots

$w = \dfrac{-3 \pm \sqrt{-15}}{2(2)}$

$= \dfrac{-3 \pm i\sqrt{15}}{4}$

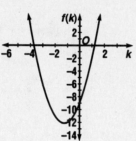

24. $5^2 - 4(2)(-9) = 97$

2 real distinct roots

$k = \dfrac{-5 \pm \sqrt{97}}{2(2)}$

$= \dfrac{-5 \pm \sqrt{97}}{4}$

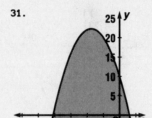

25. $(-39)^2 - 4(6)(45)$

= 441

2 real distinct roots

$b = \dfrac{-(-39) \pm \sqrt{441}}{2(6)}$

$= \dfrac{39 \pm 21}{12}$

$b = 5, \dfrac{3}{2}$

26. $(-2)^2 - 4(4)(9)$

= -140

2 imaginary roots

$x = \dfrac{2 \pm \sqrt{-140}}{2(4)}$

$= \dfrac{2 \pm 2i\sqrt{35}}{8}$

$x = \dfrac{1 \pm i\sqrt{35}}{4}$

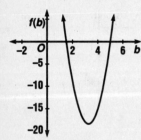

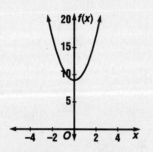

27.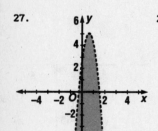

28.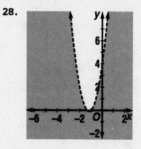

29.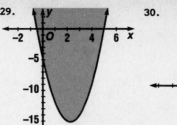

30.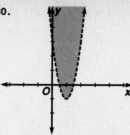

31.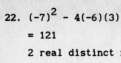

32.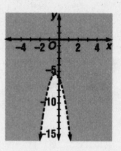

33. $f(x) = x^3 - 2x^2 - 35x$

$f'(x) = 3x^2 - 4x - 35$

$0 = 3x^2 - 4x - 35$

$x = \dfrac{2 \pm \sqrt{109}}{3}$ or about 4.1, -2.8

$f(4.1) = (4.1)^3 - 2(4.1)^2 - 35(4.1)$

≈ -108.2

$f(-2.8) = (-2.8)^3 - 2(-2.8)^2 - 35(-2.8)$

≈ 60.4

rel. min. at (4.1, -108.2)

rel. max. at (-2.8, 60.4)

$f''(x) = 6x - 4$

$0 = 6x - 4$

$x = \dfrac{2}{3}$ or about 0.7

$f(0.7) = (0.7)^3 - 2(0.7)^2 - 35(0.7)$

≈ -24.3

point of inflection at (0.7, -24.3)

34. $f(x) = 15x^3 - 16x^2 - x + 2$

$f'(x) = 45x^2 - 32x - 1$

$0 = 45x^2 - 32x - 1$

$x = \dfrac{32 \pm \sqrt{1204}}{90}$ or about 0.7, -0.03

$f(0.7) = 15(0.7)^3 - 16(0.7)^2 - 0.7 + 2$

≈ -1.4

$f(-0.03) = 15(-0.03)^3 - 16(-0.03)^2 - (-0.03) + 2$

≈ 2.0

rel. min. at (0.7, -1.4)

rel. max. at (-0.03, 2.0)

$f''(x) = 90x - 32$

$0 = 90x - 32$

$x = 0.4$

$f(0.4) = 15(0.4)^3 - 16(0.4)^2 - 0.4 + 2 \approx 0$

point of inflection at (0.4, 0)

35. $f(x) = x^3 - 9x^2 + 23x - 15$

$f'(x) = 3x^2 - 18x + 23$

$0 = 3x^2 - 18x + 23$

$x = \dfrac{18 \pm \sqrt{48}}{6}$ or about 4.2, 1.8

$f(4.2) = (4.2)^3 - 9(4.2)^2 + 23(4.2) - 15$

≈ -3.1

$f(1.8) = (1.8)^3 - 9(1.8)^2 + 23(1.8) - 15$

≈ 3.1

rel. min. at (4.2, -3.1)

rel. max. at (1.8, 3.1)

$f''(x) = 6x - 18$

$0 = 6x - 18$

$x = 3$

$f(3) = 3^3 - 9(3)^2 + 23(3) - 15$

≈ 0

point of inflection at (3, 0)

36. $f(x) = x^3 + 6x^2 + 8x$

$f'(x) = 3x^2 + 12x + 8$

$0 = 3x^2 + 12x + 8$

$x = \dfrac{-12 \pm \sqrt{48}}{6}$ or about -0.8, -3.2

$f(-0.8) = (-0.8)^3 + 6(-0.8)^2 + 8(-0.8)$

≈ -3.1

$f(-3.2) = (-3.2)^3 + 6(-3.2)^2 + 8(-3.2)$

≈ 3.1

rel. min. at (-0.8, -3.1)

rel. max. at (-3.2, 3.1)

$f''(x) = 6x + 12$

$0 = 6x + 12$

$x = -2$

$f(-2) = (-2)^3 + 6(-2)^2 + 8(-2)$

$= 0$

point of inflection at (-2, 0)

37. a. $0 = x^2 - 3x - 54$ $\qquad 0 = 54 + 3x - x^2$

$0 = (x - 9)(x + 6)$ $\qquad 0 = (9 - x)(6 + x)$

$x = 9, -6$ $\qquad\qquad x = 9, -6$

$\qquad\qquad$ (9, 0), (-6, 0)

b.

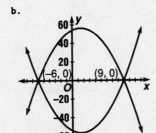

c. The two graphs have the same shape and the same x-intercepts. However, they are reflections of each other over the x-axis.

38. 3; Xmin: -10, Xmax: 10, Ymin: -10, Ymax: 10

39. 28, -25; Xmin: -30, Xmax: 30, Ymin: -800, Ymax: 800

40. ±1, ±7; Xmin: -20, Xmax: 20, Ymin: -400, Ymax: 400

41. $(3 + 2\sqrt{2})x^2 + (1 + \sqrt{2})x - 2 = 0$

$x = \dfrac{-1 - \sqrt{2} \pm \sqrt{3 + 2\sqrt{2} - 4(3 + 2\sqrt{2})(-2)}}{2(3 + 2\sqrt{2})}$

$x = \dfrac{-1 - \sqrt{2} \pm \sqrt{3 + 2\sqrt{2} + 24 + 16\sqrt{2}}}{6 + 4\sqrt{2}}$

$= \dfrac{-1 - \sqrt{2} \pm \sqrt{27 + 18\sqrt{2}}}{6 + 4\sqrt{2}}$

$= \dfrac{-1 - \sqrt{2} \pm 3\sqrt{3 + 2\sqrt{2}}}{2(3 + 2\sqrt{2})}$

Now find the difference of the roots.

$\dfrac{-1 - \sqrt{2} + 3\sqrt{3 + 2\sqrt{2}}}{2(3 + 2\sqrt{2})} - \left(\dfrac{-1 - \sqrt{2} - 3\sqrt{3 + 2\sqrt{2}}}{2(3 + 2\sqrt{2})} \right)$

$= \dfrac{6\sqrt{3 + 2\sqrt{2}}}{2(3 + 2\sqrt{2})} = \dfrac{3}{\sqrt{3 + 2\sqrt{2}}}$

42. $ax^2 + bx + c = 0 \qquad (a \neq 0)$

$x^2 + \dfrac{b}{a}x + \dfrac{c}{a} = 0$

$x^2 + \dfrac{b}{a}x = -\dfrac{c}{a}$

$x^2 + \dfrac{b}{a}x + \left(\dfrac{b}{2a}\right)^2 = -\dfrac{c}{a} + \left(\dfrac{b}{2a}\right)^2$

$\left(x + \dfrac{b}{2a}\right)^2 = -\dfrac{c}{a} + \dfrac{b^2}{4a^2}$

$\left(x + \dfrac{b}{2a}\right)^2 = \dfrac{b^2 - 4ac}{4a^2}$

$\left|x + \dfrac{b}{2a}\right| = \sqrt{\dfrac{b^2 - 4ac}{4a^2}}$

$x + \dfrac{b}{2a} = \pm \dfrac{\sqrt{b^2 - 4ac}}{2a}$

$x = -\dfrac{b}{2a} \pm \dfrac{\sqrt{b^2 - 4ac}}{2a}$

$x = \dfrac{-b \pm \sqrt{b^2 - 4ac}}{2a}$

43. Let x = width.

Let $x + 6$ = length.

$(x + 12)(x + 6) - (x + 6)(x) = 288$

$x^2 + 18x + 72 - x^2 - 6x = 288$

$12x + 72 = 288$

$x = 18$

$x + 6 = 24$

width: 18 feet, length: 24 feet

44. $-1750 = 4t - \frac{1}{2}(9.8)t^2$

$0 = -4.9t^2 + 4t + 1750$

$t = \dfrac{-4 \pm \sqrt{16 - 4(-4.9)(1750)}}{-9.8}$

$= \dfrac{-4 \pm \sqrt{34,316}}{-9.8}$

$\approx \dfrac{-4 \pm 185.2}{-9.8}$

≈ 19.3 seconds

45. $d(t) = v_0 t - \frac{1}{2}gt^2$

$d(t) = 80t - \frac{1}{2}(32)t^2$

$0 = 80t - 16t^2$

$0 = t(80 - 16t)$

$0 = 80 - 16t$

$-80 = -16t$

$5 = t$

5 seconds

46.

47. $y = 2x - 4$

$2x - y - 4 = 0$

$-\dfrac{A}{B} = \dfrac{-2}{(-1)} = 2$

The slope is 2.

$y - 2 = 2(x - 4)$

$y - 2 = 2x - 8$

$-2x + y + 6 = 0$

$2x - y - 6 = 0$

48. $\begin{bmatrix} 6 & 1 & 9 \\ 3 & 2 & 0 \end{bmatrix} \rightarrow \begin{bmatrix} 6 & 1 & 9 \\ 0 & -3 & 9 \end{bmatrix} \rightarrow \begin{bmatrix} 18 & 0 & 36 \\ 0 & -3 & 9 \end{bmatrix} \rightarrow$

$\begin{bmatrix} 1 & 0 & 2 \\ 0 & 1 & -3 \end{bmatrix}$ $(2, -3)$

49. $y = |x| + 1$

x-axis: $-y = |x| + 1$, no

y-axis: $y = |-x| + 1$, yes

line $y = x$: $x = |y| + 1$, no

line $y = -x$: $-y = |-x| + 1$, no

origin: $-y = |-x| + 1$, no

50. $f(x) = 3x^2 + 5$

$f'(x) = -6x$

$f'(-2) = -6(-2) = 12$

Slope at $(-2, 7)$ is 12.

$y + 7 = 12(x + 2)$

$y + 7 = 12x + 24$

$y = 12x + 17$

51. $(x + 5)(x + 6)(x - 10) = 0$

$(x^2 + 11x + 30)(x - 10) = 0$

$x^3 - 10x^2 + 11x^2 - 110x + 30x - 300 = 0$

$x^3 + x^2 - 80x - 300 = 0$

52. (A) $p + q$ (B) $p - q$

Try $p = 4$, $q = -3$.

$p + q = 1$ $p - q = 7$

Quantity B is greater. B.

4-3 The Remainder and Factor Theorems

1. $P(r)$

2. A depressed polynomial is the quotient resulting from dividing a polynomial by one of its binomial factors of degree 1.

3. Synthetic division is a shorthand version of long division of a polynomial, when the divisor is a binomial in the form $x - r$. This process uses only the coefficients of the dividend.

4. $P(3) = 3^2 - 6(3) + 0$
$= 9 - 18$
$= -9$, no

5. $P(3) = 3^2 + 2(3) - 15$
$= 9 + 6 - 15$
$= 0$, yes

6. $P(3) = 3^2 - 5(3) + 6$
$= 9 - 15 + 6$
$= 0$, yes

7. $P(3) = 3^4 + 3^2 - 2$
$= 81 + 9 - 2$
$= 88$, no

8. a. 12   **b.** 12   **c.** 11

d. $f(x) = x^7 + x^9 + x^{12} - 2x^2$

$= x^{12} + x^9 + x^7 - 2x^2$

$= x(x^{11} + x^8 + x^6 - 2x)$

$= x^2(x^{10} + x^7 + x^5 - 2)$

factors: x, x^2, $x^{10} + x^7 + x^5 - 2$

9.

r	1	7	-1	-7
1	1	8	7	0
2	1	9	17	27
4	1	11	43	165
-1	1	6	-7	0
-2	1	5	-11	15
-7	1	0	-1	0

$(x + 1)(x - 1)(x + 7)$

10. $\underline{-7|}$ 1 -1 -56

 -7   56

$\overline{1 \quad -8 \;|\; 0}$

$x - 8$

11. $\underline{2|}$ 1 -1 4

 2   2

$\overline{1 \quad 1 \;|\; 6}$

$x + 1$, R6

12. $\underline{-5|}$ 1 1 -17 15

 -5   20 -15

$\overline{1 \quad -4 \quad 3 \;|\; 0}$

$x^2 - 4x + 3$

13. $\underline{2|}$ 1 1 0 0 -1

 2   6 12 24

$\overline{1 \quad 3 \quad 6 \quad 12 \;|\; 23}$

$x^3 + 3x^2 + 6x + 12$, R23

14. $\underline{3|}$ 1 -9 27 -28

 3   -18   27

$\overline{1 \quad -6 \quad 9 \;|\; -1}$

$x^2 - 6x + 9$, R-1

15. $\underline{1|}$ 2 0 -2 -3

 2   2   0

$\overline{2 \quad 2 \quad 0 \;|\; -3}$

$2x^2 + 2x$, R1

16. $\underline{-5|}$ 1 0 -30 0

 -5   25   25

$\overline{1 \quad -5 \quad -5 \;|\; 25}$

25, no

17. $\underline{\sqrt{2}|}$ 1 0 -6 0 8

 $\sqrt{2}$ 2 $-4\sqrt{2}$ -8

$\overline{1 \quad \sqrt{2} \quad -4 \quad -4\sqrt{2} \;|\; 0}$

0, yes

18. $\frac{2}{5}$ | 5 -2   6

$\phantom{\frac{2}{5}|}$ 2   0

$\phantom{\frac{2}{5}|}$ 5   0 | 6

6, no

19. -2 | 1   0   0   0   32

  -2 4 -8 16 -32

 1 -2 4 -8 16 | 0

0, yes

20. $P(-1) = (-1)^2 + 1$

$ = 2$, no

21. $P(-5)^2 = (-5) + 5(-5) - 2$

$ = 25 - 25 - 2$

$ = -2$, no

22. $P(3) = 2(3)^2 - 3 + 3$

$ = 18$, no

23. $P(1) = 2(1)^3 - 3(1) + (1)$

$ = 2 - 3 + 1$

$ = 0$, yes

24. $P(3) = 3^4 + 3^2 + 2$

$ = 81 + 9 + 2$

$ = 92$, no

25. $P(-3) = 2(-3)^4 - (-3)^3 + 1$

$ = 162 + 27 + 1$

$ = 190$, no

26. $P(-2) = 0$

$0 = (-2)^3 + 8(-2)^2 + k(-2) + 4$

$ = -8 + 32 - 2k + 4$

$ = 28 - 2k$

$ = 14 - k$

$k = 14$

27. $P(-1) = 0$

$0 = (-1)^3 + k(-1)^2 + 4(-1) + 1$

$ = (-1) + k - 4 + 1$

$ = k - 4$

$k = 4$

28. 1 | 1   0 -3   2 $\qquad$ 1 | 1   1   -2

  1   1 -2 $\qquad$ 1   2

 1   1 -2 | 0 $\qquad$ 1   2 | 0

$x^2 + x - 2$ $\qquad\qquad$ $x + 2$

$\qquad\qquad\qquad$ twice

29. 2 | 1   0 -9   0   24   0   -16

  2   4 -10 -20   8   16

 1   2 -5 -10   4   8 | 0

$x^5 + 2x^4 - 5x^3 - 10x^2 + 4x + 8$

2 | 1   2 -5 -10   4   8

  2   8   6   -8   -8

 1   4   3   -4   -4 | 0

$x^4 + 4x^3 + 3x^2 - 4x - 4$

2 | 1   4   3   -4   -4

  2   12   30   -52

 1   6   15   -26 | -56

twice

30. -1 | 1   2 -1   -2

  -1 -1   2

 1   1 -2 | 0

$x^2 + x - 2$

$(x + 2)(x - 1)$

once; -2, 1

31. $P(3 + 4i) = 0$ and $P(3 - 4i) = 0$ implies that these are both roots of $ax^2 + bx + c$. Since this polynomial is of degree 2 it has only these two roots.

$\qquad x = 3 \pm 4i$

$\qquad x - 3 = \pm 4i$

$\qquad (x - 3)^2 = -16$

$\qquad x^2 - 6x + 9 = -16$

$\qquad x^2 - 6x + 25 = 0$

$\qquad a = 1,\ b = -6,\ c = 25$

32. $\qquad (R + r)^2 = \dfrac{R^2 \cdot w_E}{w_S}$

$\qquad (3960 + r)^2 = \dfrac{3960^2 (200)}{175}$

$\qquad (3960 + r)^2 = 17{,}921{,}828.57$

$\qquad 3960 + r = \sqrt{17{,}921{,}828.57}$

$\qquad 3960 + r \approx 4233.42$

$\qquad\qquad r \approx 273.4$ miles

33. $V = \pi r^2 h;\ h = r + 4,\ V = 15.71$

$\qquad 15.71 = \pi r^2 (r + 4)$

$\qquad \dfrac{15.71}{\pi} = r^3 + 4r^2$

$\qquad\qquad 5 \approx r^3 + 4r^2$

$\qquad\qquad 0 \approx r^3 + 4r^2 - 5$

1 | 1   4   0   -5

  1   5   5

 1   5   5 | 0

$r \approx 1$ inch, $h \approx 5$ inches

34. $g[f(-2)] = g[(-2)^3] = g(-8) = 3(-8) = -24$

35. $f(x) = x^5 - 32$

$\qquad f'(x) = 5x^4$

$\qquad\qquad 0 = 5x^4$

$\qquad\qquad x = 0$

$\qquad f(-0.5) = (-0.5)^5 - 32 \approx 32.0313$

$\qquad\quad f(0) = 0^5 - 32 = -32$

$\qquad f(0.5) = (0.5)^5 - 32 \approx -31.9688$

point of inflection: $(0, -32)$

36.

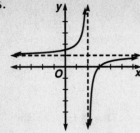

37.
$$z^2 + 4z = 96$$
$$z^2 + 4z + 2^2 = 96 + 2^2$$
$$(z + 2)^2 = 100$$
$$z + 2 = \pm 10$$
$$z = -2 + 10 \qquad z = -2 - 10$$
$$z = 8 \qquad\qquad z = -12$$

38. $6 \times (150) = 90 \times 10$
$$900 = 900$$

The best answer is B.

4-4 The Rational Root Theorem

1. You can often use the depressed polynomial to find the other zeros of the function. If it is a quadratic, the zeros can be found by using the quadratic formula.

2.

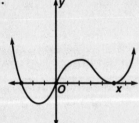

3. The rational root theorem states that $\frac{p}{q}$ is a possible root if p is a factor of a_n and q is a factor of a_0. If the polynomial has a leading coefficient of 1, the value of q is always 1. Thus, $\frac{p}{q}$ becomes p, which is always a factor of a_0.

4. The number of changes in signs in $f(x)$ correlates to the number of positive real zeros. The number of changes in signs in $f(-x)$ correlates to the number of negative real zeros. Samples will vary.

5. $p = \pm 1$

$q = \pm 1, \pm 2, \pm 3, \pm 6$

$\frac{p}{q} = \pm 1, \pm 2, \pm 3, \pm 6$

r	1	2	-5	-6
1	1	3	-2	-8
-1	1	1	-6	0
2	1	4	3	0
-2	1	0	-5	4
3	1	5	10	24
-3	1	-1	-2	0

rational zeros:

-1, 2, -3

6. $f(x) = 2x^3 + 3x^2 - 8x + 3$

p: $\pm 1, \pm 3$

q: $\pm 1, \pm 2$

$\frac{p}{q}$: $\pm 1, \pm \frac{1}{2}, \pm 3, \pm \frac{3}{2}$

r	2	3	-8	3
1	2	5	-3	0
-1	2	1	-9	12
0.5	2	4	-6	0
-0.5	2	2	-9	-1.5
3	2	9	19	60
-3	2	-3	1	0

rational zeros:

1, 0.5, -3

7. 1 positive

$f(-x) = -x^3 + 2x^2 + 5x - 6$

0 or 2 negative

r	1	2	-5	-6
1	1	3	-2	-8
-1	1	1	-6	0
2	1	4	3	0
-2	1	0	-5	4
3	1	5	10	24
-3	1	-1	-2	0

rational zeros: -1, 2, -3

8. 2 or 0 positive

$f(-x) = -2x^3 + 3x^2 + 8x + 3$

1 negative

r	2	3	-8	3
1	2	5	-3	0
-1	2	1	-9	12
0.5	2	4	-6	0
-0.5	2	2	-9	7.5
3	2	9	19	60
-3	2	-3	1	0

rational zeros: 1, 0.5, -3

9. 2 or 0 positive

$f(-x) = -6x^3 - 11x^2 + 24x + 9$

1 negative

r	6	-11	-24	9
1	6	-5	-29	-20
-1	6	-17	-7	16
$\frac{1}{3}$	6	-9	-27	0
1.5	6	-2	-27	-31.5
-1.5	6	-20	6	0
3	6	7	-3	0

rational zeros: $\frac{1}{3}$, -1.5, 3

10. 1 positive

$$f(-x) = -4x^3 + 5x^2 - 2x - 6$$

0 or 2 negative

r	4	5	2	-6
$\frac{3}{4}$	4	8	8	0
-4	4	-11	46	190
-6	4	-19	112	678

rational zero: $\frac{3}{4}$

PAGES 206-207   EXERCISES

11. $\frac{p}{q}$: ±1, ±2, ±3, ±6

r	1	5	5	-5	-6
1	1	6	11	6	0
-1	1	4	1	-6	0
2	1	7	19	33	60
-2	1	3	-1	-3	0
3	1	8	29	82	240
-3	1	2	-1	-2	0

rational zeros: 1, -1, -2, -3

12. $\frac{p}{q}$: ±1, ±2

r	1	-4	1	2
1	1	-3	-2	0

$$x^2 - 3x - 2 = 0$$

$$x = \frac{-(-3) \pm \sqrt{9 - 4(1)(-2)}}{2(1)}$$

$$x = \frac{3 \pm \sqrt{17}}{2}$$

rational zero: 1

13. $\frac{p}{q}$: ±1, ±2, ±4, ±5, ±10, ±20

r	1	-5	-4	20
1	1	-4	-8	12
-1	1	-6	2	18
2	1	-3	-10	0

$$x^2 - 3x - 10 = 0$$

$$(x - 5)(x + 2) = 0$$

$$x = 5, \ x = -2$$

rational zeros: 2, 5, -2

14. $\frac{p}{q}$: ±1, ±2, ±3, ±6, ±9, ±18

r	1	-2	1	18
2	1	0	1	20
-2	1	-4	9	0

$$x^2 - 4x + 9$$

$$b^2 - 4ac = 16 - 4(1)9 = -20$$

2 imaginary roots

rational zero: -2

15. $\frac{p}{q}$: ±1, ±2

r	1	-5	9	-7	2
1	1	-4	5	-2	0

$$x^3 - 4x^2 + 5x - 2$$

r	1	-4	5	-2
2	1	-2	1	0

$$x^2 - 2x + 1 = 0$$

$$(x - 1)(x - 1) = 0$$

rational zeros: 1, 2

16. p: ±1, ±3

q: ±1, ±2

$\frac{p}{q}$: ±1, ±$\frac{1}{2}$, ±3, ±$\frac{3}{2}$

r	2	-1	0	-6	3
$\frac{1}{2}$	2	0	0	-6	0

$$2x^3 - 6 = 0$$

$$x^3 = 3$$

$$x = \sqrt[3]{3}$$

rational zero: $\frac{1}{2}$

17. 1 positive

$$f(-x) = -x^3 - 2x^2 + 8$$

1 negative

$$f(x) = x^3 - 2x^2 - 8x$$

$$0 = x(x^2 - 2x - 8)$$

$$= x(x - 4)(x + 2)$$

$$x = 0, \ x = 4, \ x = -2$$

rational zeros: 0, 4, -2

18. 1 positive

$$f(-x) = -x^3 + 7x^2 - 7x - 15$$

0 or 2 negative

r	1	7	7	-15
1	1	8	15	0

$$x^2 + 8x + 15 = 0$$

$$(x + 5)(x + 3) = 0$$

$$x = -5, \ x = -3$$

rational zeros: 1, -3, -5

19. 0 or 2 positive

$f(-x) = -8x^3 - 6x^2 + 23x + 6$

1 negative

r	8	-6	-23	6
2	8	10	-3	0

$8x^2 + 10x - 3 = 0$

$x^2 + \frac{5}{4}x = \frac{3}{8}$

$x^2 + \frac{5}{4}x + \left(\frac{5}{8}\right)^2 = \frac{3}{8} + \left(\frac{5}{8}\right)^2$

$\left(x + \frac{5}{8}\right)^2 = \frac{49}{64}$

$x + \frac{5}{8} = \pm\frac{7}{8}$

$x = -\frac{5}{8} \pm \frac{7}{8}$

$x = \frac{1}{4}, \ x = -\frac{3}{2}$

rational zeros: $2, \frac{1}{4}, -\frac{3}{2}$

20. 0 or 2 positive

$f(-x) = -2x^3 - 5x^2 + 28x + 15$

1 negative

r	2	-5	-28	15
$\frac{1}{2}$	2	-4	-30	0

$2x^2 - 4x - 30 = 0$

$x^2 - 2x - 15 = 0$

$(x - 5)(x + 3) = 0$

$x = 5, \ x = -3$

rational zeros: $\frac{1}{2}, 5, -3$

21. 1 positive

$f(-x) = -6x^3 + 19x^2 - 2x - 3$

0 or 2 negative

r	6	19	2	-3
$\frac{1}{2}$	6	22	13	3.5
$-\frac{1}{2}$	6	16	-6	0

$6x^2 + 16x - 6 = 0$

$x^2 + \frac{8}{3}x = 1$

$x^2 + \frac{8}{3}x + \left(\frac{4}{3}\right)^2 = 1 + \left(\frac{4}{3}\right)^2$

$\left(x + \frac{4}{3}\right)^2 = \frac{25}{9}$

$x + \frac{4}{3} = \pm\frac{5}{3}$

$x = -\frac{4}{3} \pm \frac{5}{3}$

$x = \frac{1}{3}, \ x = -3$

rational zeros: $-\frac{1}{2}, \frac{1}{3}, -3$

22. 1 positive

$f(-x) = -x^3 + 7x - 6$

0 or 2 negative

r	1	0	-7	-6
1	1	1	-6	-12
-1	1	-1	-6	0

$x^2 - x - 6 = 0$

$(x - 3)(x + 2) = 0$

$x = 3, \ x = -2$

rational zeros: $-1, -2, 3$

23. 0 or 2 positive

$f(-x) = x^4 - 5x^2 + 4$

0 or 2 negative

r	1	0	-5	0	4
1	1	1	-4	-4	0

$x^3 + x^2 - 4x - 4$

r	1	1	-4	-4
-1	1	0	-4	0

$x^2 - 4 = 0$

$(x - 2)(x + 2) = 0$

$x = 2, \ x = -2$

rational zeros: $1, -1, 2, -2$

24. 0 or 2 positive

$f(-x) = x^4 - 2x^3 - 9x^2 + 2x + 8$

0 or 2 negative

r	1	2	-9	-2	8
1	1	3	-6	-8	0

$x^3 + 3x^2 - 6x - 8$

r	1	3	-6	-8
-1	1	2	-8	0

$x^2 + 2x - 8 = 0$

$(x + 4)(x - 2) = 0$

$x = -4, \ x = 2$

rational zeros: $1, -1, -4, 2$

25. $\frac{p}{q}$: $\pm 1, \pm\frac{1}{2}, \pm\frac{1}{3}, \pm\frac{1}{4}, \pm\frac{1}{6}, \pm\frac{1}{8}, \pm\frac{1}{12}, \pm\frac{1}{24}$

1 or 3 positive roots:, 0 negative roots

roots: $0.5, 0.\overline{3}, 0.25$

26. p: $\pm 1, \pm 2, \pm 4, \pm 5, \pm 10, \pm 20$; q: $\pm 1, \pm 5, \pm 25$

$\frac{p}{q}$: $\pm 1, \pm\frac{1}{5}, \pm\frac{1}{25}, \pm 2, \pm\frac{2}{5}, \pm\frac{2}{25}, \pm 4, \pm\frac{4}{5}, \pm\frac{4}{25}, \pm 5,$

$\pm 10, \pm 20$

0 or 2 positive roots, 1 negative root

roots: $0.4, -5$

27. $\frac{p}{q}$: $\pm 1, \pm\frac{1}{2}, \pm\frac{1}{3}, \pm\frac{1}{6}, \pm 2, \pm\frac{2}{3}, \pm 3, \pm\frac{3}{2}, \pm 4, \pm\frac{4}{3}, \pm 6,$

± 12

1 positive root, 0 or 2 negative roots

roots: $-0.5, 3, -1.\overline{3}$

28. $\frac{p}{q}$: $\pm 1, \pm 2, \pm 3, \pm 4, \pm 6, \pm 8, \pm 12, \pm 24$

0, 2, or 4 positive roots; 0 negative roots

roots: $1, 2, 3, 4$

29. a. To have zero positive real roots, according to Descartes' rule of signs, there must be no sign changes in the polynomial. Sample answer: $f(x) = x^3 + 2x^2 + 3x + 53$

   b. To have zero negative real roots, according to Descartes' rule of signs, there must be no sign changes in the function $f(-x)$. Sample answer: $f(x) = x^3 - 2x^2 + 3x - 7$

30. a. deceleration

   b. $D(t) = v_i t + 0.5at^2$

   $$43 = 12t + 0.5(-1.6)t^2$$
   $$43 = 12t - 0.8t^2$$
   $$0 = 0.8t^2 - 12t + 43$$
   $$0 = t^2 - 15t + 54$$
   $$0 = (t - 9)(t - 6)$$
   $$t = 9, \; t = 6$$

   6 seconds or 9 seconds

   c. 6 seconds is the car rolling up the hill. It reaches a maximum point at 7.5 seconds and rolls back down the hill. At 9 seconds the car is at the same point it was going up the hill.

31. a.

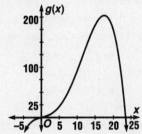

   b. $g(x) = -0.006x^4 + 0.140x^3 - 0.053x^2 + 1.79x$

   $\quad = x(-0.006x^3 + 0.140x^2 - 0.053x + 1.79)$

   $\quad = x(x^3 - 23.\overline{3}x^2 + 8.8\overline{3}x - 298.\overline{3})$

r	1	-23.333	8.833	-298.333
1	1	-22.333	-13.503	-311.836
5	1	-18.333	-82.835	-712.508
23.5	1	0.167	12.758	≈ 0

   rational zeros: 0, 23.5

32. $h = r + 6$

   $V = \frac{1}{3}\pi r^2 h$

   $\quad = \frac{1}{3}\pi r^2(r + 6)$

   $84.82 = \frac{\pi}{3}r^3 + 6r^2$

   $0 = \frac{\pi}{3}r^3 + 6r^2 - 84.82$

   $0 = r^3 + \frac{18}{\pi}r^2 - \frac{254.46}{\pi}$

r	1	$\frac{18}{\pi}$	0	$\frac{-254.46}{\pi}$
3	1	8.7296	26.189	≈ 0

   $r \approx 3$ cm, $h \approx 9$ cm

33. The three types of discontinuity are point, jump, and infinite. Point discontinuity means the function displays all the characteristics of continuity except for one point. Jump continuity occurs when a function is defined for all values of x, but at one point the graph jumps from (x, a) to (x, b). Infinite discontinuity occurs for functions whose graphs have asymptotes.

a. 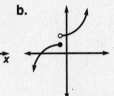 b.

c.

   a. point

   b. jump

   c. infinite

34. $f(x) = x^2 + 4x - 5$

   $f'(x) = 2x + 4$

   $f'(1) = 2(1) + 4 = 6$

   Slope of tangent at (1, 0) is 6.

35. $b^2 - 4ac$

   $= 5^2 - 4(3)(10)$

   $= 25 - 120$

   $= -95$

   2 imaginary roots

36.
```
-2| 1  6  12  12
     -2 -8  -8
   ────────────
   1  4   4   4
```
   No, there is a remainder of 4.

37.

   (area of $\triangle PAT$) + (area of $\triangle STB$) = area of $\triangle STR$)

   area of $\triangle STR = \frac{1}{4}$(area of rectangle)

   So the shaded region is 25% the area of the rectangle.

   The best answer is B.

Mid-Chapter Review

1. $x^3 + 2x^2 - 80x = 0$

    $x(x^2 + 2x - 80) = 0$

    $x(x + 10)(x - 8) = 0$

    $x = 0 \qquad x + 10 = 0 \qquad x - 8 = 0$

    $\qquad\qquad\quad x = -10 \qquad x = 8$

2. $p^2 + 6p + 3 = 0$

    $p^2 + 6p + 3^2 = -3 + 3^2$

    $(p + 3)^2 = 6$

    $p + 3 = \pm\sqrt{6}$

    $p = -3 \pm \sqrt{6}$

3. $b^2 - 4ac = (-13)^2 - 4(7)(2) = 113$

    2 real roots

    $m = \dfrac{-(-13) \pm \sqrt{113}}{2(7)}$

    $= \dfrac{13 \pm \sqrt{113}}{14}$

4. $P(4) = 4^3 - 4(4)^2 + 2(4) - 6 = 2$

    Since $R = 2$, $x - 4$ is not a factor.

5. p: ± 1, ± 2, ± 3, ± 4, ± 6, ± 12

    q: ± 1, ± 2

    $\dfrac{p}{q}$: ± 1, $\pm\dfrac{1}{2}$, ± 2, ± 3, $\pm\dfrac{3}{2}$, ± 4, ± 6, ± 12

r	2	-13	-17	12
0.5	2	-12	-23	0.5
-0.5	2	-14	-10	17
1	2	-11	-28	-16
-1	2	-15	-2	14
1.5	2	-10	-32	-36
-1.5	2	-16	7	1.5
2	2	-9	-35	-58
-2	2	-17	17	-22
3	2	-7	-38	-102
-3	2	-19	40	-108
4	2	-5	-37	136
-4	2	-21	67	-256
6	2	-1	-23	-126
-6	2	-25	133	-786
12	2	11	115	1392
-12	2	-37	427	-5112

no rational zeros

Graphing Calculators: Locating Zeros of Polynomial Functions

Answers for Exercises 1-6 are approximate.

1. -2, 0, 2   2. 2.88

3. 0.28, 1.32   4. -2.17, 0.34, 1.17

5. -1.26, 1.26   6. 0.24

4-5 Locating the Zeros of a Function

1. The location principle is a method of estimation by which the zero of a function can be approximated. Repeated applications of the technique can produce an estimate to the decimal place desired. It works because zero is the place where $f(x) = 0$. Values of $f(x)$ evaluated for x greater than and less than the target zero indicate the direction the graph is taking without graphing the function.

2. Volume cannot be negative.

3. First find between which two integers each zero is found. Use the two nearest integers to find between which two tenths the zero is found. Then find the zero to the nearest hundredth using the numbers between the tenths.

4. Use synthetic division to test values of r for $f(x)$ until there are no sign changes in the row. This value of r is the least positive upper bound. Repeat the process for values of r for $f(-x)$. When you find this upper bound, you can say that $-r$ is the greatest negative lower bound.

5. 3 zeros; between -2 and -1, at 1, and between 3 and 4; upper bound: 4

6. 4 zeros; between -3 and -2, -2 and -1, 1 and 2, 2 and 3; upper bound: 3

7.
r	1	3	1
-3	1	0	1
-2	1	1	-1

	1	2	-1
-1	1	2	-1
0	1	3	1

x	$f(x)$		x	$f(x)$
-2.9	0.71		-0.5	-0.25
-2.8	0.44		-0.4	-0.04
-2.7	0.19		-0.3	0.19
-2.6	-0.04		-0.2	0.44
-2.5	-0.25		-0.1	0.71

The zeros are approximately -2.6 and -0.4.

8.
r	1	-1	-1
1	1	0	-1
2	1	1	1

upper bound: 2

$f(-x) = x^2 + x - 1$

r	1	1	-1
1	1	2	1

lower bound: -1

9. 2 zeros

r	1	-4	-2
-2	1	-6	10
-1	1	-5	3]
0	1	-4	-2]
1	1	-3	-5
2	1	-2	-6
3	1	-1	-5
4	1	0	-2]
5	1	1	3]

between -1 and 0,

and 4 and 5

10. 2 zeros

r	2	-5	1
-1	2	-7	8
0	2	-5	1]
1	2	-3	-2]
2	2	-1	-1]
3	2	1	4]

between 0 and 1, and

2 and 3

11. 3 zeros

r	1	0	0	-2
-1	1	-1	1	-3
0	1	0	0	-2
1	1	1	1	-1]
2	1	2	4	6]
3	1	3	9	25

between 1 and 2

12. 3 zeros

r	1	0	-3	1
-2	1	-2	1	-1]
-1	1	-1	-2	3]
0	1	0	-3	1]
1	1	1	-2	-1
2	1	2	1	3]

between -2 and -1,

0 and 1, 1 and 2

13. 4 zeros

r	1	-2	0	1	-2
-2	1	-4	8	-15	28
-1	1	-3	3	-2	0
0	1	-2	0	1	-2
1	1	-1	-1	0	-1
2	1	0	0	1	0

at -1, at 2

14. 4 zeros

r	2	0	1	-3	3
-3	2	-6	19	-60	183
-1.5	2	-3	5.5	-11.25	19.875
-1	2	-2	3	0	3
0	2	0	1	-3	3
1	2	2	3	0	3
1.5	2	3	5.5	5.25	10.875
3	2	6	19	54	165

no real zeros

15.

r	1	3	2
-2	1	1	0
-1	1	2	0

zeros: -2, -1

16.

r	2	-4	0	-3
0	2	-4	0	-3
1	2	-2	-2	-5
2	2	0	0	-3]
3	2	2	6	15]

x	f(x)
2.1	-2.12
2.2	-1.06
2.3	0.17
2.4	1.61

approximate zero: 2.3

17.

r	1	0	-4	6
-3	1	-3	5	-9]
-2	1	-2	0	6]
-1	1	-1	-3	9
0	1	0	-4	6

x	f(x)
-2.9	-6.79
-2.8	-4.75
-2.7	-2.88
-2.6	-1.18
-2.5	0.38
-2.4	1.78

approximate zero: -2.5

18.

r	3	0	1	0	-1
-1	3	-3	4	-4	3]
0	3	0	1	0	-1]
1	3	3	4	4	3]
2	3	6	13	26	51

x	f(x)
-0.9	1.78
-0.8	0.87
-0.7	0.21
-0.6	-0.25

x	f(x)
0.9	1.78
0.8	0.87
0.7	0.21
0.6	-0.25

approximate zeros: 0.7, -0.7

19.

r	2	-1	0	1	-2
-2	2	-5	10	-19	36
-1	2	-3	3	-2	0
0	2	-1	0	1	-2
1	2	1	1	2	0
2	2	3	6	13	24

zeros: -1, 1

20.

r	-1	1	-1	1
-1	-1	2	-3	4
0	-1	1	-1	1
1	-1	0	-1	0
2	-1	-1	-3	-5

zero: 1

21.

r	1	3	-5	-10
1	1	4	-1	-11
2	1	5	5	0

upper bound: 2

$f(-x) = -x^3 + 3x^2 + 5x - 10$

r	-1	3	5	-10
1	-1	2	7	-3
2	-1	1	7	4
3	-1	0	5	5
4	-1	-1	1	-6
5	-1	-2	-5	-35

lower bound: -5

22.

r	1	0	0	-8	2
1	1	1	1	-7	-5
2	1	2	4	0	4

upper bound: 2

$f(-x) = x^4 + 8x + 2$

r	1	0	0	8	2
0	1	0	0	8	2

lower bound: 0

23.

r	3	-2	5	-1
1	3	1	6	5

upper bound: 1

$f(-x) = -3x^3 - 2x^2 - 5x - 1$

r	-3	-2	-5	-1
0	-3	-2	-5	-1

lower bound: 0

24.

r	1 5 -3 20 0	-15
1	1 6 3 23 23	8

upper bound: 1

$f(-x) = -x^5 + 5x^4 + 3x^3 + 20x^2 - 15$

r	-1 5 3 20 0	-15
1	-1 4 7 27 27	8
2	-1 3 9 38 76	137
3	-1 2 9 47 141	408
4	-1 1 7 48 192	753
5	-1 0 3 35 175	860
6	-1 -1 -3 2 12	57
7	-1 -2 -11 -57 -399	-2778

lower bound: -7

25. $f(x) = 2x^3 + 9x^2 - 12x - 40$

3 complex zeros

1 positive, 2 or 0 negative

r	2 9 -12	-40
-5	2 -1 -7	-5
-4	2 1 -16	24
-3	2 3 -21	23
-2	2 5 -22	4
-1	2 7 -19	-21
0	2 9 -12	-40
1	2 11 -1	-41
2	2 13 14	-12
3	2 15 33	59

x	f(x)	x	f(x)	x	f(x)
-4.9	-0.41	-1.9	1.57	2.1	-6.99
-4.8	3.78	-1.8	-0.9	2.2	-1.54
-4.7	7.56	-1.7	-3.42	2.3	4.34

approximate zeros: -4.9, -1.8, 2.2

$f(x) = 2x^3 + 9x^2 - 12x - 40$

$f'(x) = 6x^2 + 18x - 12$

$0 = 6x^2 + 18x - 12$

$0 = x^2 + 3x - 2$

$x = \dfrac{-3 \pm \sqrt{9 - 4(1)(-2)}}{2}$

$\quad = \dfrac{-3 \pm \sqrt{17}}{2}$

$x \approx 0.6, \ x \approx -3.6$

$f(0.6) \approx -43.5$

$f(-3.6) \approx 26.5$

rel. max. at (-3.6, 26.5)

rel. min. at (0.6, -43.5)

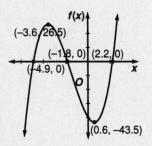

26. $f(x) = x^4 - 3x^2 - 9$

4 complex zeros

1 positive, 1 negative

r	1 0 -3 0	-9
-3	1 -3 6 -18	45
-1	1 -1 -2 2	-11
0	1 0 -3 0	-9
1	1 1 -2 -2	-11
3	1 3 6 18	45

x	f(x)
2.1	-2.78
2.2	-0.09
2.3	3.11

approximate zeros: 2.2, -2.2

$f(x) = x^4 - 3x^2 - 9$

$f'(x) = 4x^3 - 6x$

$0 = x(4x^2 - 6)$

$x = 0 \qquad 4x^2 - 6 = 0$

$\qquad\qquad\qquad x^2 = \dfrac{3}{2}$

$\qquad\qquad x = \pm\sqrt{\dfrac{3}{2}} \approx \pm 1.2$

$f(0) = 0^4 - 3(0)^2 - 9 = -9$

$f(1.2) = (1.2)^4 - 3(1.2)^2 - 9 \approx -11.3$

$f(-1.2) = (-1.2)^4 - 3(-1.2)^2 - 9 \approx -11.3$

rel. max. at (0, -9)

rel. min. at (-1.2, -11.3), (1.2, -11.3)

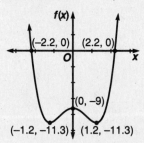

27. a. There will be at least 2 points of inflection on the graph. This means that the minimum degree of the second derivative of $g(x)$ is 2. The minimum degree of $g(x)$, then, is 4.

b.

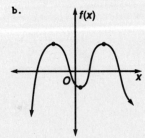

88

28. a.

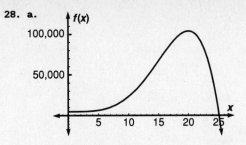

b.

r						
	−0.125	3.125	0	0	0	4000
5	−0.125	2.5	12.5	62.5	312.5	5562.5
10	−0.125	1.875	18.75	187.5	1875	22,750
15	−0.125	1.25	18.75	281.25	4218.75	63,281.25
20	−0.125	0.625	12.5	250	5000	104,000
25	−0.125	0	0	0	0	4000

The population stayed relatively steady from 1905 to 1910. Then it rose rapidly until it reached its maximum at (20, 104,000), which represents the population in 1925. Then it fell rapidly to 4000 at (25, 4000) which represents 1930. The deer population reached zero in the year 1930.

29. area = 6 × 4 = 24 meters, new area = 2(24) = 48
length = 6 meters, new length = 6 + x meters
width = 4 meters, new width = 4 + x meters
area = ℓw

$$48 = (6 + x)(4 + x)$$
$$48 = 24 + 10x + x^2$$
$$0 = x^2 + 10x - 24$$
$$= (x + 12)(x - 2)$$

$x = -12$, $x = 2$

Since there is no negative distance, the correct answer is 2 meters.

30. r_a = distance Io

$r_a + 6.5$ = distance of Ganymede

$$\left(\frac{T_a}{T_b}\right)^2 = \left(\frac{r_a}{r_b}\right)^3 = \left(\frac{r_a}{r_a + 6.5}\right)^3$$

$$\left(\frac{1.8}{7.3}\right)^2 = \left(\frac{r_a}{r_a + 6.5}\right)^3$$

$$0.061 \approx \left(\frac{r_a}{r_a + 6.5}\right)^3$$

$$0.394 \approx \frac{r_a}{r_a + 6.5}$$

$$0.394 r_a + 2.56 \approx r_a$$

$$2.56 \approx 0.606$$

$$4.2 \approx r_a$$

$r_a + 6.5 = 10.7$

Io: 4.2 units; Ganymede: 10.7 units

31. $3y + 8x = 12$

$$3y = -8x + 12$$
$$y = -\frac{8}{3}x + 4$$
$$m = -\frac{8}{3}$$

32.

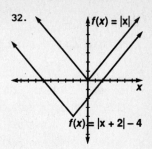

$f(x) = |x|$

$f(x) = |x + 2| - 4$

33.

34.

r	1	−4	−25	28
1	1	−3	−28	0

$$x^2 - 3x - 28 = 0$$
$$(x - 7)(x + 4) = 0$$
$$x = 7, \; x = -4$$
zeros: 1, 7, −4

$f'(x) = 3x^2 - 8x - 25$ $f''(x) = 6x - 8$

$0 = x^2 - \frac{8}{3}x - \frac{25}{3}$ $0 = 6x - 8$

$$\left(\frac{4}{3}\right)^2 + \frac{25}{3} = x^2 - \frac{8}{3}x + \left(\frac{4}{3}\right)^2 \qquad x = \frac{4}{3} \approx 1.3$$

$$\frac{91}{9} = \left(x - \frac{4}{3}\right)^2$$

$$\pm\sqrt{\frac{91}{9}} = x - \frac{4}{3}$$

$$\frac{4}{3} \pm 3.18 \approx x$$

$x \approx 4.5, \; x \approx -1.8$

$f(-1.8) = (-1.8)^3 - 4(-1.8)^2 - 25(-1.8) + 28 \approx 54.2$

$f(4.5) = (4.5)^3 - 4(4.5)^2 - 25(4.5) + 28 \approx -74.4$

$f(1.3) = (1.3)^3 - 4(1.3)^2 - 25(1.3) + 28 \approx -9.1$

rel. max. at (−1.8, 54.2)

rel. min. at (4.5, −74.4)

pt. of inf. at (1.3, −9.1)

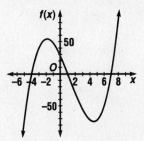

35. 15 cans for 7 men for 2 days is equal to 7.5 cans for 7 men for 1 day, or $\frac{7.5}{7}$ cans per man per day. Four men in one day need $4 \times \left(\frac{7.5}{7}\right)$. For 7 days, they need $7 \times 4 \times \left(\frac{7.5}{7}\right)$ or 30 cans.

Technology:
Locating Zeros and Critical Points

1. zeros: -2, 1, 2; critical points:

   (1.535184, -0.879420), (0.333333, 2.592593),

   (-0.868517, 6.065605)

2. zeros: -2, 2; no real critical points

3. zero: 0.865244; critical point: (0, -8)

4-6 Rational Equations and Partial Fractions

PAGES 220-221   CHECKING FOR UNDERSTANDING

1. For an equation $\frac{1}{a} + \frac{1}{b} = \frac{1}{c}$, the LCD is the

   product of the factors of a, b and c with no

   duplication of common factors.

2. All solutions must be checked because some may

   result in a zero in the denominator.

3. Decomposing a rational expression into partial

   fractions means to use factors and solving

   rational equations to find what terms were

   added/subtracted to arrive at that expression.

4. In both examples you are testing values for

   which the inequality is true. However, in

   Example 4, an expression less than 0 means a

   negative expression. Since the expression

   involves factors, you need only consider the

   combinations of signs that produce a negative

   rather than the exact numerical value of the

   function.

5. LCD: $2m^2$

   $$\frac{1}{m} = \frac{m - 34}{2m^2}$$

   $$m^2 - 34m = 2m^2$$

   $$0 = m^2 + 34m$$

   $$0 = m(m + 34)$$

   $$m = 0, \quad m = -34$$

   m cannot equal 0, so

   $m = -34$.

6. LCD: $(b + 5)(b - 3)$

   $$\frac{9}{b + 5} = \frac{3}{b - 3}$$

   $$9(b - 3) = 3(b + 5)$$

   $$9b - 27 = 3b + 15$$

   $$6b - 42 = 0$$

   $$b = 7$$

7. LCD: $12(a + 1)(a - 1)$

   $$\frac{7a}{3(a + 1)} - \frac{5}{4(a - 1)} = \frac{3a}{2(a + 1)}$$

   $$4(a - 1)7a - 3(a + 1)5 = 6(a - 1)3a$$

   $$28a^2 - 28a - 15a - 15 = 18a^2 - 18a$$

   $$10a^2 - 25a - 15 = 0$$

   $$2a^2 - 5a - 3 = 0$$

   $$(2a + 1)(a - 3) = 0$$

   $$a = -\frac{1}{2}, \quad a = 3$$

8. $\frac{3}{x} + \frac{7}{x} = 8$

   $$3 + 7 = 8x$$

   $$10 = 8x$$

   $$\frac{5}{4} = x$$

9. $1 + \frac{5}{a - 1} = \frac{7}{6}$

   $$6(a - 1) + 6 \cdot 5 = 6(a - 1)\frac{7}{6}$$

   $$6a - 6 + 30 = 7a - 7$$

   $$31 = a$$

10. $\frac{3y + 2}{4} = \frac{9}{4} - \frac{3 - 2y}{6}$

    $$6(3y + 2) = 6(9) - 4(3 - 2y)$$

    $$18y + 12 = 54 - 12 + 8y$$

    $$10y = 30$$

    $$y = 3$$

11. $\frac{-x + 5}{(x - 1)(x + 1)} = \frac{A}{(x - 1)} + \frac{B}{(x + 1)}$

    $$-x + 5 = A(x + 1) + B(x - 1)$$

    $$1 + 5 = A(-1 + 1) + B(-1 - 1)$$

    $$6 = -2B$$

    $$-3 = B$$

    $$-1 + 5 = A(1 + 1) + B(1 - 1)$$

    $$4 = 2A$$

    $$2 = A$$

    $$\frac{-x + 5}{(x - 1)(x + 1)} = \frac{2}{(x - 1)} - \frac{3}{(x + 1)}$$

12. $\frac{2}{w} + 3 > \frac{29}{w}$

    $$2 + 3w = 29$$

    $$w = 9$$

    Test $w = -1$: $\frac{2}{-1} + 3 > \frac{29}{-1}$

    $$1 > -29 \quad \text{true}$$

    $$w < 0 \text{ is a solution.}$$

    Test $w = 1$: $\frac{2}{1} + 3 > \frac{29}{1}$

    $$5 > 29 \quad \text{false}$$

    $$0 < w < 9 \text{ is not a solution.}$$

    Test $w = 10$: $\frac{2}{(10)} + 3 > \frac{29}{10}$

    $$\frac{32}{10} > \frac{29}{10} \quad \text{true}$$

    $$w > 9 \text{ is a solution.}$$

    The solutions are $w < 0$, $w > 9$.

PAGES 221-222   EXERCISES

13. $b - \frac{5}{b} = 4$

    $$b^2 - 5 = 4b$$

    $$b^2 - 4b - 5 = 0$$

    $$(b - 5)(b + 1) = 0$$

    $$b = 5, \quad b = -1$$

14.

$$\frac{6}{p+3} + \frac{p}{p-3} = 1$$

$$6(p-3) + p(p+3) = (p-3)(p+3)$$

$$6p - 18 + p^2 + 3p = p^2 - 9$$

$$9p - 9 = 0$$

$$p - 1 = 0$$

$$p = 1$$

15.

$$\frac{2}{x+2} + \frac{3}{x} = \frac{-x}{x+2}$$

$$2x + 3(x+2) = -x^2$$

$$2x + 3x + 6 = -x^2$$

$$x^2 + 5x + 6 = 0$$

$$(x+3)(x+2) = 0$$

$$x = -3, \; x = -2$$

x cannot equal -2,
so the only solution
is $x = -3$.

16.

$$\frac{12}{t} + t - 8 = 0$$

$$12 + t^2 - 8t = 0$$

$$t^2 - 8t + 12 = 0$$

$$(t-6)(t-2) = 0$$

$$t = 6, \; t = 2$$

17.

$$1 = \frac{1}{1-y} + \frac{y}{y-1}$$

$$(1-y)(y-1) = (y-1) + y(1-y)$$

$$y - 1 - y^2 + y = y - 1 + y - y^2$$

$$2y - 1 - y^2 = 2y - 1 - y^2$$

$$0 = 0$$

Solution: all reals except 1

18.

$$\frac{1}{3m} + \frac{6m-9}{3m} = \frac{3m-3}{4m}$$

$$4 + 4(6m-9) = 3(3m-3)$$

$$4 + 24m - 36 = 9m - 9$$

$$15m = 23$$

$$m = \frac{23}{15}$$

19.

$$1 + \frac{n+6}{n+1} = \frac{4}{n-2}$$

$$(n+1)(n-2) + (n-2)(n+6) = 4(n+1)$$

$$n^2 - n - 2 + n^2 + 4n - 12 = 4n + 4$$

$$2n^2 - n - 18 = 0$$

$$n = \frac{1 \pm \sqrt{1 - 4(2)(-18)}}{2 \cdot 2}$$

$$= \frac{1 \pm \sqrt{145}}{4}$$

20.

$$\frac{2q}{2q+3} - \frac{2q}{2q-3} = 1$$

$$2q(2q-3) - 2q(2q+3) = (2q+3)(2q-3)$$

$$4q^2 - 6q - 4q^2 - 6q = 4q^2 - 9$$

$$0 = 4q^2 + 12q - 9$$

$$q = \frac{-12 \pm \sqrt{144 - 4(4)(-9)}}{2 \cdot 4}$$

$$= \frac{-12 \pm \sqrt{288}}{8}$$

$$= \frac{-12 \pm 12\sqrt{2}}{8}$$

$$= \frac{-3 \pm 3\sqrt{2}}{2}$$

21.

$$5 + \frac{1}{x} > \frac{16}{x}$$

$$5x + 1 = 16$$

$$5x = 15$$

$$x = 3$$

Test -1: $\quad 5 + \frac{1}{(-1)} > \frac{16}{(-1)}$

$$4 > -16 \quad \text{true}$$

Test 1: $\quad 5 + \frac{1}{1} > \frac{16}{1}$

$$6 > 16 \quad \text{false}$$

Test 4: $\quad 5 + \frac{1}{4} > \frac{16}{4}$

$$5\frac{1}{4} > 4 \quad \text{true}$$

Solution: $\; x < 0, \; x > 3$

22.

$$\frac{2y+1}{5} - \frac{2+7y}{15} < \frac{2}{3}$$

$$3(2y+1) - 2 - 7y = 10$$

$$6y + 3 - 2 - 7y = 10$$

$$-y = 9$$

$$y = -9$$

Test (-10): $\quad \frac{2(-10)+1}{5} - \frac{2+7(-10)}{15} < \frac{2}{3}$

$$\frac{19}{5} + \frac{68}{15} < \frac{2}{3}$$

$$\frac{125}{15} < \frac{2}{3}$$

$$\frac{25}{3} < \frac{2}{3} \quad \text{false}$$

Test (-1): $\quad \frac{2(-1)+1}{5} - \frac{2+7(-1)}{15} < \frac{2}{3}$

$$-\frac{1}{5} + \frac{5}{15} < \frac{2}{3}$$

$$\frac{2}{15} < \frac{2}{3} \quad \text{true}$$

Solution: $\; y > -9$

23.

$$1 + \frac{5}{a-1} < \frac{7}{6}$$

$$6(a-1) + 30 = 7(a-1)$$

$$6a - 6 + 30 = 7a - 7$$

$$31 = a$$

Test -1: $\quad 1 + \frac{5}{-1-1} < \frac{7}{6}$

$$-\frac{3}{2} < \frac{7}{6} \quad \text{true}$$

Test 2: $\quad 1 + \frac{5}{2-1} < \frac{7}{6}$

$$6 < \frac{7}{6} \quad \text{false}$$

Test 36: $\quad 1 + \frac{5}{36-1} < \frac{7}{6}$

$$1 + \frac{1}{7} < \frac{7}{6}$$

$$\frac{48}{42} < \frac{49}{42} \quad \text{true}$$

Solutions: $\; a < 1, \; a > 31$

24. $\dfrac{2a - 5}{6} - \dfrac{(a - 5)}{4} < \dfrac{3}{4}$

$2(2a - 5) - 3(a - 5) = 9$

$4a - 10 - 3a + 15 = 9$

$a = 4$

Test 1: $\dfrac{2 - 5}{6} - \dfrac{1 - 5}{4} < \dfrac{3}{4}$

$\dfrac{-3}{6} + \dfrac{4}{4} < \dfrac{3}{4}$

$\dfrac{1}{2} < \dfrac{3}{4}$ **true**

Test 5: $\dfrac{2(5) - 5}{6} - \dfrac{5 - 5}{4} < \dfrac{3}{4}$

$\dfrac{5}{6} < \dfrac{3}{4}$ **false**

Solution: $a < 4$

25. $x^3 - 11x^2 + 18x \geq 0$

$x(x^2 - 11x + 18) = 0$

$x(x - 9)(x - 2) = 0$

$x = 0,\ x = 9,\ x = 2$

Test -1: $(-1)^3 - 11(-1)^2 + 18(-1) \geq 0$

$-1 - 11 - 18 \geq 0$

$-30 \geq 0$ **false**

Test 1: $1^3 - 11(1)^2 + 18(1) \geq 0$

$1 - 11 + 18 \geq 0$

$8 \geq 0$ **true**

Test 3: $3^3 - 11(3)^2 + 18(3) \geq 0$

$27 - 99 + 54 \geq 0$

$-18 \geq 0$ **false**

Test 10: $10^3 - 11(10)^2 + 18(10) \geq 0$

$1000 - 1100 + 180 \geq 0$

$80 \geq 0$ **true**

Solutions: $0 \leq x \leq 2,\ x \geq 9$

26. $x^5 + x^4 - 16x - 16 < 0$

r	1	1	0	0	-16	-16
-1	1	0	0	0	-16	0

$x^4 - 16 = 0$

$x^4 = 16$

$x = \pm 2$

$x = -1,\ x = \pm 2$

Test (-3): $(-3)^5 + (-3)^4 - 16(-3) - 16 < 0$

$-130 < 0$ true

Test 0: $-16 < 0$ true

Test 3: $3^5 + 3^4 - 16(3) - 16 < 0$

$260 < 0$ **false**

Solutions: $x < -2,\ -1 < x < 2$

27. $\dfrac{3p - 1}{p^2 - 1} = \dfrac{3p - 1}{(p - 1)(p + 1)}$

$\dfrac{3p - 1}{p^2 - 1} = \dfrac{A}{p - 1} + \dfrac{B}{p + 1}$

$3p - 1 = A(p + 1) + B(p - 1)$

Let $p = -1$.

$3(-1) - 1 = A(-1 + 1) + B(-1 - 1)$

$-4 = -2B$

$2 = B$

Let $p = 1$.

$3(1) - 1 = A(1 + 1) + B(1 - 1)$

$1 = A$

$\dfrac{3p - 1}{p^2 - 1} = \dfrac{1}{p - 1} + \dfrac{2}{p + 1}$

28. $\dfrac{-4y}{3y^2 - 4y + 1} = \dfrac{-4y}{(y - 1)(3y - 1)}$

$\dfrac{-4y}{3y^2 - 4y + 1} = \dfrac{A}{y - 1} + \dfrac{B}{3y - 1}$

$-4y = A(3y - 1) + B(y - 1)$

Let $y = \dfrac{1}{3}$.

$-4\left(\dfrac{1}{3}\right) = A\left(3\left(\dfrac{1}{3}\right) - 1\right) + B\left(\dfrac{1}{3} - 1\right)$

$-\dfrac{4}{3} = -\dfrac{2}{3}B$

$2 = B$

Let $y = 1$.

$-4(1) = A(3 \cdot 1 - 1) + B(1 - 1)$

$-4 = 2A$

$-2 = A$

$\dfrac{-4y}{3y^2 - 4y + 1} = \dfrac{-2}{y - 1} + \dfrac{2}{3y - 1}$

29. $\dfrac{2m + 1}{m^2 + m} = \dfrac{2m + 1}{m(m + 1)}$

$\dfrac{2m + 1}{m^2 + m} = \dfrac{A}{m} + \dfrac{B}{m + 1}$

$2m + 1 = A(m + 1) + B(m)$

Let $m = -1$.

$2(-1) + 1 = A(-1 + 1) + B(-1)$

$-1 = -B$

$1 = B$

Let $m = 0$.

$2(0) + 1 = A(0 + 1) + B(0)$

$1 = A$

$\dfrac{2m + 1}{m^2 + m} = \dfrac{1}{m} + \dfrac{1}{m + 1}$

30. $\dfrac{1}{2a - 2} = \dfrac{a}{a^2 - 1} + \dfrac{2}{a + 1}$

$\dfrac{1}{2(a - 1)} = \dfrac{a}{(a - 1)(a + 1)} + \dfrac{2}{a + 1}$

$a + 1 = 2a + 4(a - 1)$

$a + 1 = 2a + 4a - 4$

$5 = 5a$

$1 = a$

Since a cannot equal 1 there are no real solutions.

92

31. $\dfrac{x^2 - 16}{x^2 - 4x - 5} > 0$

$\dfrac{x^2 - 16}{(x - 5)(x + 1)} = 0$

$x^2 - 16 = 0$

$x^2 = 16$

$x = \pm 4$

Test (-5): $\dfrac{(-5)^2 - 16}{(-5 - 5)(-5 + 1)} > 0$

$\dfrac{9}{40} > 0$ true

Test (-2): $\dfrac{(-2)^2 - 16}{(-2 - 5)(-2 + 1)} > 0$

$\dfrac{-12}{7} > 0$ false

Test 0: $\dfrac{0 - 16}{0^2 - 4(0) - 5} > 0$

$\dfrac{-16}{-5} > 0$ true

Test 6: $\dfrac{6^2 - 16}{6^2 - 24 - 5} > 0$

$\dfrac{20}{7} > 0$ true

Solutions: $x < -4$, $-1 < x < 4$, $x > 5$

32. Graph the function $f(x)$. Anywhere the graph is above the x-axis, the value of $f(x)$ is positive. Those values where $f(x)$ is positive are solutions to the inequality.

33. $\dfrac{7}{y + 1} > 7$

$7 = 7(y + 1)$

$0 = y + 1$

$-1 = y$

Test -2: $\dfrac{7}{-2 + 1} > 7$

$-7 > 7$ false

Test 1: $\dfrac{7}{1 + 1} > 7$

$\dfrac{7}{2} > 7$ false

Solution: $-1 < y < 0$

34. Let c = cashews.
Let p = peanuts.

$\dfrac{c}{c + (p + 2)} = \dfrac{1}{5}$

$5c = c + p + 2$

$4c - p = 2$

$\dfrac{c + 2}{(c + 2) + (p + 2)} = \dfrac{1}{3}$

$3(c + 2) = (c + 2) + (p + 2)$

$2c - p = -2$

$\underline{4c - p = 2}$

$-2c = -4$

$c = 2, \ p = 6$

Original mixture was 25% cashews.

35. Let x = the number.

$4\left(\dfrac{1}{x}\right) + x = 10\dfrac{2}{5}$

$20 + 5x^2 = 52x$

$5x^2 - 52x + 20 = 0$

$(5x - 2)(x - 10) = 0$

$x = \dfrac{2}{5}, \ x = 10$

36. Let t = amount of time.

So, $\dfrac{1}{6}t$ = amount of beeswax burned in t hours,

$\dfrac{1}{9}t$ = amount of paraffin burned in t hours.

$2\left(1 - \dfrac{1}{6}t\right) = 1 - \dfrac{1}{9}t$

$2 - \dfrac{1}{3}t = 1 - \dfrac{1}{9}t$

$t = 4.5$ hours

37. Let t = amount of time.

So, $\dfrac{t}{10}$ = distance for Rosea after t minutes,

$\dfrac{t}{6}$ = distance for Tai after t minutes.

$\dfrac{t}{10} + \dfrac{t}{6} = 1$

$\dfrac{8t}{30} = 1$

$t = 3.75$ minutes

38. A relation relates a member of a set called the domain to a member of a set called the range. In a function, the relation must be such that each member of the domain is related to one and only one member of the range.

39. Let x = multiple-choice, y = essay.

$x \geq 0, \ y \geq 0$

$x + y \leq 30$

$x + 12y \leq 96$

possible solutions: $(0, 0)$, $(30, 0)$

$(0, 8)$, $(24, 6)$

$M(x, y) = 5x + 20y$ 　　　　$M(30, 0) = 150$

$M(0, 0) = 0$ 　　　　　　　$M(0, 8) = 160$

$M(24, 6) = 240 \longleftarrow$ max.

24 multiple-choice, 6 essay

40.

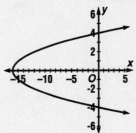

41. p: $\pm 1, \ \pm 2$

q: $\pm 1, \ \pm 2, \ \pm 3, \ \pm 6$

$\dfrac{p}{q}$: $\pm 1, \ \pm\dfrac{1}{2}, \ \pm\dfrac{1}{3}, \ \pm\dfrac{1}{6}, \ \pm 2, \ \pm\dfrac{2}{3}$

42.

r	3	-16	12	6
-1	3	-19	31	-25
0	3	-16	12	6
1	3	-13	-1	5
2	3	-10	-8	-10
3	3	-7	-9	-21
4	3	-4	-4	-10
5	3	-1	7	41

x	f(x)	x	f(x)	x	f(x)
-0.4	-1.55	1.3	1.15	4.2	-3.58
-0.3	0.88	1.4	-0.3	4.3	0.28
-0.2	2.94	1.5	-1.87	4.4	4.59

approximate zeros: -0.3, 1.4, 4.3

43. $d = rt = \frac{m}{h} \cdot x = \frac{mx}{h}$

The best answer is E.

4-7A **Graphing Calculators:
Solving Radical Equations
and Inequalities**

PAGES 223-224   EXERCISES

1-12. See students' programming work.

1.
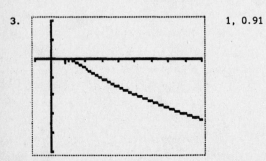
5

2.
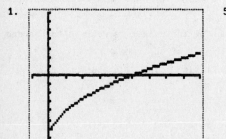
3

3.
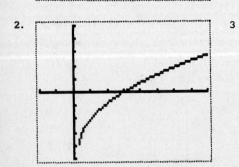
1, 0.91

4.
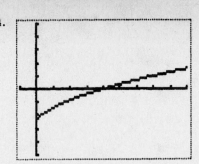
4

5.
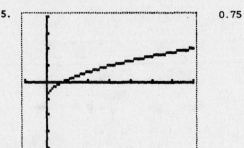
0.75

6.
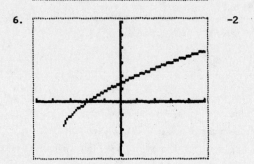
-2

7.
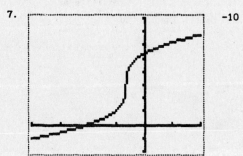
-10

8.
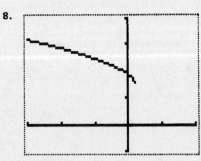
no real
solutions

9.
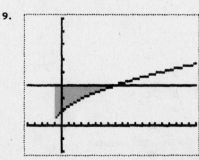

10.
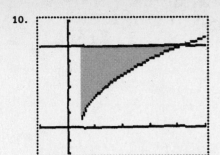

11.
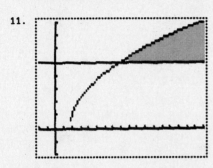

12.
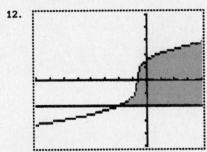

7. $\sqrt[4]{3x} - 2 = 0$ 　　Check:

$\qquad \sqrt[4]{3x} = 2$

$\qquad 3x = 16$ 　　$\sqrt[4]{3\left(\frac{16}{3}\right)} - 2 \overset{?}{=} 0$

$\qquad x = \frac{16}{3}$ 　　$\sqrt[4]{16} - 2 \overset{?}{=} 0$

$\qquad\qquad\qquad\qquad 2 - 2 = 0$

8. $\sqrt{8n - 5} - 1 = 2$ 　　Check:

$\qquad \sqrt{8n - 5} = 3$ 　　$\sqrt{8\left(\frac{7}{4}\right) - 5} - 1 \overset{?}{=} 2$

$\qquad 8n - 5 = 9$

$\qquad 8n = 14$ 　　$\sqrt{14 - 5} - 1 \overset{?}{=} 2$

$\qquad n = \frac{7}{4}$ 　　$3 - 1 = 2$

9. $\sqrt{1 - 4t} = 2$ 　　Check:

$\qquad 1 - 4t = 4$ 　　$\sqrt{1 - 4\left(-\frac{3}{4}\right)} \overset{?}{=} 2$

$\qquad -4t = 3$

$\qquad t = -\frac{3}{4}$ 　　$\sqrt{1 + 3} \overset{?}{=} 2$

$\qquad\qquad\qquad\qquad 2 = 2$

10. $\sqrt{7v - 2} + 12 = 7$ 　　Check:

$\qquad \sqrt{7v - 2} = -5$ 　　$\sqrt{7\left(\frac{27}{7}\right) - 2} + 12 \overset{?}{=} 7$

$\qquad 7v - 2 = 25$

$\qquad 7v = 27$ 　　$\sqrt{25} + 12 \overset{?}{=} 7$

$\qquad v = \frac{27}{7}$ 　　$19 \neq 7$

no real solution

11. $\sqrt[3]{6u - 5} + 2 = -3$ 　　Check:

$\qquad \sqrt[3]{6u - 5} = -5$ 　　$\sqrt[3]{6(-20) - 5} + 2 \overset{?}{=} -3$

$\qquad 6u - 5 = -125$

$\qquad 6u = -120$ 　　$\sqrt[3]{-125} + 2 \overset{?}{=} -3$

$\qquad u = -20$ 　　$-5 + 2 = -3$

12. $\sqrt{6x - 4} = \sqrt{2x + 10}$ 　　Check:

$\qquad 6x - 4 = 2x + 10$ 　　$\sqrt{6\left(\frac{7}{2}\right) - 4} = \sqrt{2\left(\frac{7}{2}\right) + 10}$

$\qquad 4x = 14$

$\qquad x = \frac{7}{2}$ 　　$\sqrt{21 - 4} = \sqrt{7 + 10}$

$\qquad\qquad\qquad\qquad \sqrt{17} = \sqrt{17}$

13. $\sqrt{9u - 4} = \sqrt{7u - 20}$ 　　Check:

$\qquad 9u - 4 = 7u - 20$ 　　$\sqrt{9(-8) - 4} \overset{?}{=} \sqrt{7(-8) - 20}$

$\qquad 2u = -16$ 　　$\sqrt{-76} = \sqrt{-76}$

$\qquad u = -8$

no real solutions

14. $\sqrt{k + 9} - \sqrt{k} = \sqrt{3}$

$\qquad \sqrt{k + 9} = \sqrt{3} + \sqrt{k}$

$\qquad k + 9 = 3 + 2\sqrt{3k} + k$

$\qquad 6 = 2\sqrt{3k}$

$\qquad 36 = 4(3k)$

$\qquad 36 = 12k$

$\qquad 3 = k$

Check: $\sqrt{3 + 9} - \sqrt{3} \overset{?}{=} \sqrt{3}$

$\qquad \sqrt{12} - \sqrt{3} \overset{?}{=} \sqrt{3}$

$\qquad 2\sqrt{3} - \sqrt{3} = \sqrt{3}$

4-7　Radical Equations and Inequalities

1. **a.** $T = 2\pi\sqrt{\dfrac{1}{9.8}}$ 　　**b.** $T = 2\pi\sqrt{\dfrac{1}{8.9}}$

$\qquad \approx 2.01$ 　　　　　≈ 2.11

2. First square each side of the equation. Then solve for x.

3. When there is more than one radical expression in an equation, you isolate one of the radicals and then square each side. Then you isolate the radical again and square each side. Then solve for the variable.

4. Check each possible solution.

5. $\sqrt{x + 8} - 5 = 0$ 　　Check:

$\qquad \sqrt{x + 8} = 5$ 　　$\sqrt{17 + 8} - 5 \overset{?}{=} 0$

$\qquad x + 8 = 25$

$\qquad x = 17$ 　　$5 - 5 = 0$

6. $\sqrt[3]{y - 7} = 4$ 　　Check:

$\qquad y - 7 = 64$ 　　$\sqrt[3]{71 - 7} \overset{?}{=} 4$

$\qquad y = 71$ 　　$\sqrt[3]{64} \overset{?}{=} 4$

$\qquad\qquad\qquad\qquad 4 = 4$

15. $\sqrt{x + 10} + \sqrt{x - 6} = 8$

$\qquad\sqrt{x + 10} = 8 - \sqrt{x - 6}$

$\qquad x + 10 = 64 - 16\sqrt{x - 6} + x - 6$

$\qquad -48 = -16\sqrt{x - 6}$

$\qquad 2304 = 256(x - 6)$

$\qquad 9 = x - 6$

$\qquad 15 = x$

Check: $\sqrt{15 + 10} + \sqrt{15 - 6} \overset{?}{=} 8$

$\qquad\qquad 5 + 3 = 8$

16. $\qquad\sqrt{x + 2} - 7 = \sqrt{x + 9}$

$x + 2 - 14\sqrt{x + 2} + 49 = x + 9$

$\qquad -14\sqrt{x + 2} = -42$

$\qquad 196(x + 2) = 1764$

$\qquad x + 2 = 9$

$\qquad x = 7$

Check: $\sqrt{7 + 2} - 7 \overset{?}{=} \sqrt{7 + 9}$

$\qquad\qquad 3 - 7 = 4$

no real solution

17. $\sqrt{4x^2 - 3x + 2} - 2x - 5 = 0$

$\qquad\sqrt{4x^2 - 3x + 2} = 2x + 5$

$\qquad 4x^2 - 3x + 2 = 4x^2 + 20x + 25$

$\qquad -23 = 23x$

$\qquad -1 = x$

Check: $\sqrt{4(-1)^2 - 3(-1) + 2} - 2(-1) - 5 \overset{?}{=} 0$

$\qquad\qquad\qquad \sqrt{9} + 2 - 5 \overset{?}{=} 0$

$\qquad\qquad\qquad 3 + 2 - 5 = 0$

18. $\sqrt{x + 4} + \sqrt{x - 3} = 7$

$\qquad\sqrt{x + 4} = 7 - \sqrt{x - 3}$

$\qquad x + 4 = 49 - 14\sqrt{x - 3} + x - 3$

$\qquad -42 = -14\sqrt{x - 3}$

$\qquad 1764 = 196(x - 3)$

$\qquad 9 = x - 3$

$\qquad 12 = x$

Check: $\sqrt{12 + 4} + \sqrt{12 - 3} \overset{?}{=} 7$

$\qquad\qquad \sqrt{16} + \sqrt{9} \overset{?}{=} 7$

$\qquad\qquad 4 + 3 = 7$

19. $\sqrt{x - 9} - \sqrt{x + 7} = 2$

$\qquad\sqrt{x - 9} = 2 + \sqrt{x + 7}$

$\qquad x - 9 = 4 + 4\sqrt{x + 7} + x + 7$

$\qquad -20 = 4\sqrt{x + 7}$

$\qquad 400 = 16(x + 7)$

$\qquad 25 = x + 7$

$\qquad 18 = x$

Check: $\sqrt{18 - 9} - \sqrt{18 + 7} \overset{?}{=} 2$

$\qquad\qquad \sqrt{9} - \sqrt{25} \overset{?}{=} 2$

$\qquad\qquad 3 - 5 \neq 2$

no real solution

20. $\sqrt{x + 4} \leq 6$

$\qquad x + 4 \leq 36$

$\qquad x \leq 32$

$\qquad x + 4 \geq 0$

$\qquad x \geq -4$

$\qquad -4 \leq x \leq 32$

Test 0: $\sqrt{0 + 4} \overset{?}{\leq} 6$

$\qquad\qquad \sqrt{4} \overset{?}{\leq} 6$

$\qquad\qquad 2 \leq 6$

21. $\sqrt{2x - 7} \geq 5$

$\qquad 2x - 7 \geq 25$

$\qquad 2x \geq 32$

$\qquad x \geq 16$

$\qquad 2x - 7 \geq 0$

$\qquad 2x \geq 7$

$\qquad x \geq \dfrac{7}{2}$

Test 4: $\sqrt{2(4) - 7} \overset{?}{\geq} 5$

$\qquad\qquad \sqrt{8 - 7} \overset{?}{\geq} 5$

$\qquad\qquad 1 \not\geq 5$

solution: $x \geq 16$

22. $\sqrt[3]{3x - 8} \geq 1$

$\qquad 3x - 8 \geq 1$

$\qquad 3x \geq 9$

$\qquad x \geq 3$

Test 4: $\sqrt[3]{3(4) - 8} \overset{?}{\geq} 1$

$\qquad\qquad \sqrt[3]{12 - 8} \overset{?}{\geq} 1$

$\qquad\qquad \sqrt[3]{4} \geq 1$

23. $\sqrt[4]{5x - 9} \leq 2$

$\qquad 5x - 9 \leq 16$

$\qquad 5x \leq 25$

$\qquad x \leq 5$

$\qquad 5x - 9 \geq 0$

$\qquad 5x \geq 9$

$\qquad x \geq \dfrac{9}{5} = 1.8$

$\qquad 1.8 \leq x \leq 5$

Test 2: $\sqrt[4]{5 \cdot 2 - 9} \overset{?}{\leq} 2$

$\qquad\qquad \sqrt[4]{1} \leq 2$

24. $\qquad\sqrt{3x + 10} = \sqrt{x + 11} - 1$

$\qquad 3x + 10 = x + 11 - 2\sqrt{x + 11} + 1$

$\qquad 2x - 2 = -2\sqrt{x + 11}$

$\qquad x - 1 = -\sqrt{x + 11}$

$\qquad x^2 - 2x + 1 = -x - 11$

$\qquad 2x^2 - 2x + 12 = 0$

$\qquad x^2 - x + 6 = 0$

$\qquad (x - 3)(x + 2) = 0$

$\qquad x = 3, \ x = -2$

Check: $\sqrt{3(3) + 10} \overset{?}{=} \sqrt{3 + 11} - 1$

$\qquad\qquad \sqrt{19} \neq \sqrt{14} - 1$

$\qquad\qquad \sqrt{3(-2) + 10} \overset{?}{=} \sqrt{-2 + 11} - 1$

$\qquad\qquad \sqrt{4} \overset{?}{=} \sqrt{9} - 1$

$\qquad\qquad 2 = 2$

Solution: $x = -2$

25. $\sqrt{2x + 1} + \sqrt{2x + 6} = 5$

$$\sqrt{2x + 1} = 5 - \sqrt{2x + 6}$$
$$2x + 1 = 25 - 10\sqrt{2x + 6} + 2x + 6$$
$$-30 = -10\sqrt{2x + 6}$$
$$3 = \sqrt{2x + 6}$$
$$9 = 2x + 6$$
$$3 = 2x$$
$$x = \frac{3}{2}$$

Check: $\sqrt{2\left(\frac{3}{2}\right) + 1} + \sqrt{2\left(\frac{3}{2}\right) + 6} \overset{?}{=} 5$

$$\sqrt{4} + \sqrt{9} \overset{?}{=} 5$$
$$2 + 3 = 5$$

26. a. $T = 2\pi\sqrt{\dfrac{0.5}{9.8}} \approx 1.419$ oscillations/second

If the length is doubled, $T \approx 2.01$ oscillations/second, which is not $2(1.419)$.

b. $2.838 \approx 2\pi\sqrt{\dfrac{\ell}{9.8}}$

$$8.054 \approx 4\pi^2 \frac{\ell}{9.8}$$

$\ell \approx 2.0$ meters

If you double the period, the length is 4 times the original.

c. $4.257 \approx 2\pi\sqrt{\dfrac{\ell}{9.8}}$

$\ell \approx 4.5$ meters

If you triple the period, the length is 9 times the original.

d. For $n(T)$, the length of the new pendulum equals n^2 times the original length.

27. $1.6 = 2\pi\sqrt{\dfrac{\ell}{9.8}}$

$$2.56 \approx 4\pi^2 \frac{\ell}{9.8}$$

$\ell \approx 0.64$ meters

28. $0.5 = 2\pi\sqrt{\dfrac{14}{g}} \times 60$

$$0.25 = 4\pi^2\left(\frac{14}{g}\right)60$$

$$g = \frac{56\pi^2}{0.25} \times 60$$

$$\approx 132,647.5$$

29.
$$y = -7x + 2$$
$$7x + y = 2$$

30. $\begin{bmatrix} 5 & -4 \\ 8 & 2 \end{bmatrix} = 5(2) - 8(-4) = 10 + 32 = 42$

31. $f(x) = x^3 - 3x + 5$ $\qquad$ $f'(x) = 6x$

$$f'(x) = 3x^2 - 3 \qquad\qquad 0 = 6x$$
$$0 = 3x^2 - 3 \qquad\qquad\quad x = 0$$
$$x = \pm 1$$

$f(-1.01) = (-1.01)^3 - 3(-1.01) + 5 \approx 6.9997$

$f(-1) = (-1)^3 - 3(-1) + 5 = 7$

$f(-0.99) = (-0.99)^3 - 3(-0.99) + 5 \approx 6.9997$

$f(-0.01) = (-0.01)^3 - 3(-0.01) + 5 \approx 5.0300$

$f(0) = 5$

$f(0.01) - (0.01)^3 - 3(0.01) + 5 \approx 4.9700$

$f(0.99) = (0.99)^3 - 3(0.99) + 5 \approx 3.0003$

$f(1) = 1^3 - 3(1) + 5 = 3$

$f(1.01) = (1.01)^3 - 3(1.01) + 5 \approx 3.0003$

max: $(-1, 7)$, min: $(1, 3)$,

point of inflection: $(0, 5)$

32.
$$\frac{x - 4}{x - 2} = \frac{x - 2}{x + 2} + \frac{1}{x - 2}$$
$$(x + 2)(x - 4) = (x - 2)^2 + (x + 2)$$
$$x^2 - 2x - 8 = x^2 - 4x + 4 + x + 2$$
$$x - 14 = 0$$
$$x = 14$$

33. $x = $ John $+ 4$ years

$x - 4 = $ John's age now

$\dfrac{x - 4}{3} = $ Pat's age now

The best answer is E.

Chapter 4 Summary and Review

PAGES 230-232 SKILLS AND CONCEPTS

1. $a + 4 = 0$

$a = -4$

2. $0 = t^2 + 6t + 9$

$0 = (t + 3)(t + 3)$

$t = -3$

3. $6y^2 + y - 2 = 0$

$(2y - 1)(3y + 2) = 0$

$y = \frac{1}{2}, \ y = -\frac{2}{3}$

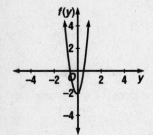

4. $x^3 + 2x^2 - 3x = 0$

$x(x^2 + 2x - 3) = 0$

$x(x + 3)(x - 1) = 0$

$x = 0, \ x = -3, \ x = 1$

5. $b^2 - 4ac$

$= (-7)^2 - 4(2)(-4)$

$= 81$

2 distinct real roots

$x = \dfrac{7 \pm \sqrt{81}}{2 \cdot 2}$

$= \dfrac{7 \pm 9}{4}$

$= 4, \ -\dfrac{1}{2}$

6. $b^2 - 4ac$

$= (-10)^2 - 4(3)(5)$

$= 40$

2 distinct real roots

$m = \dfrac{10 \pm \sqrt{40}}{6}$

$= \dfrac{10 \pm 2\sqrt{10}}{6}$

$= \dfrac{5 \pm \sqrt{10}}{3}$

7. $b^2 - 4ac$

$= 1^2 - 4(4)(4)$

$= -63$

no real roots

$a = \dfrac{-1 \pm \sqrt{-63}}{8}$

$= \dfrac{-1 \pm 3i\sqrt{7}}{8}$

8. $b^2 - 4ac$

$= 9 - 4(-2)8$

$= 73$

2 distinct real roots

$y = \dfrac{-3 \pm \sqrt{73}}{-4}$

$= \dfrac{3 \pm \sqrt{73}}{4}$

9. $P(-2) = (-2)^3 - (-2)^2 - 10(-2) - 8 = 0$; yes

10. $P(5) = 2(5)^3 - 5(5)^2 + 7(5) + 1 = 161$; no

11. $P\left(-\dfrac{1}{2}\right) = 4\left(-\dfrac{1}{2}\right)^3 - 7\left(-\dfrac{1}{2}\right) + 1 = 4$; no

12. $P(3) = 3^4 - 10(3)^2 + 9 = 0$; yes

13. 3 complex zeros

1 pos; 0 or 2 neg

r	1	-1	-34	-56
-2	1	-3	-28	0

$x^2 - 3x - 28 = 0$

$(x - 7)(x + 4) = 0$

$x = 7, \ x = -4$

rational zeros:

$-2, \ -4, \ 7$

14. 3 complex zeros

0 or 2 pos; 1 neg

r	2	-11	12	9
-3	2	-5	-3	0

$(2x^2 - 5x - 3) = 0$

$(2x + 1)(x - 3) = 0$

$x = -\dfrac{1}{2}, \ x = 3$

rational zeros:

$3, \ 3, \ -\dfrac{1}{2}$

15. 4 complex zeros

0 or 2 pos; 0 or 2 neg

r	1	0	-13	0	36
2	1	2	-9	-18	0
-2	1	-2	-9	18	0
3	1	3	-4	-12	0
-3	1	-3	-4	12	0

rational zeros: 2, -2, 3, -3

16. 4 complex zeros

1 pos; 1 or 3 neg

r	1	1	-9	-17	-8
-1	1	0	-9	-8	0
1	1	2	-7	-24	-32
2	1	3	-3	-23	-54
-2	1	-1	-7	-3	-2
-3	1	-2	-3	-8	16

rational zero: -1

17.

r	1	-3	-3
-1	1	-4	1
0	1	-3	-3
1	1	-2	-5
2	1	-1	-5
3	1	0	-3
4	1	1	1

between -1 and 0,

3 and 4

18.

r	1	-1	0	1
-1	1	-2	2	-1
0	1	-1	0	1
1	1	0	0	1
2	1	1	2	5

between -1 and 0

19.

r	4	1	-11	3
-2	4	-7	3	-3
-1	4	-3	-8	11
0	4	1	-11	3
1	4	5	-6	-3
2	4	9	7	17

between -2 and -1, 0 and 1, and 1 and 2

20.

r	1	-9	25	-24	6
0	1	-9	25	-24	6
1	1	-8	17	-7	-1
2	1	-7	11	-2	2
3	1	-6	7	-3	-3
4	1	-5	5	-4	-10
5	1	-4	5	1	11

between 0 and 1, 1 and 2, 2 and 3, 4 and 5

21. $n + 5 = \dfrac{6}{n}$

$n^2 + 5n = 6$

$n^2 + 5n - 6 = 0$

$(n + 6)(n - 1) = 0$

$n = -6, \ n = 1$

Check:

$-6 + 5 \overset{?}{=} \dfrac{6}{-6}$

$-1 = -1$

$1 + 5 \overset{?}{=} \dfrac{6}{1}$

$6 = 6$

22.
$$\frac{5}{6} - \frac{2m}{2m + 3} = \frac{19}{6}$$

$$5(2m + 3) - 6(2m) = 19(2m + 3)$$

$$10m + 15 - 12m = 38m + 57$$

$$-42 = 40m$$

$$\frac{-42}{40} = m$$

$$-\frac{21}{20} = m$$

Check: $\dfrac{5}{6} - \dfrac{2\left(-\dfrac{21}{20}\right)}{2\left(-\dfrac{21}{20}\right) + 3} \overset{?}{=} \dfrac{19}{6}$

$$\frac{5}{6} + \frac{14}{6} = \frac{19}{6}$$

23.
$$3x^2 - x - 4 \geq 0$$

$$(3x - 4)(x + 1) = 0$$

$$x = \frac{4}{3}, \ x = -1$$

Test -2: $3(4) + 2 - 4 \geq 0$

$$10 \geq 0 \qquad \text{true}$$

Test 0: $-4 \geq 0 \qquad \text{false}$

Test 2: $3(4) - 2 - 4 \geq 0$

$$6 \geq 0 \qquad \text{true}$$

$$x \leq -1, \ x \geq \frac{4}{3}$$

24.
$$\frac{2}{x + 1} - 1 < \frac{1}{6}$$

$$12 - 6(x + 1) - (x + 1) = 0$$

$$12 - 6x - 6 - x - 1 = 0$$

$$5 - 7x = 0$$

$$x = \frac{5}{7}$$

Test -2: $\dfrac{2}{-2 + 1} - 1 < \dfrac{1}{6}$

$$-3 < \frac{1}{6} \qquad \text{true}$$

Test 0: $2 - 1 < \dfrac{1}{6} \qquad \text{false}$

Test 2: $\dfrac{2}{3} - 1 < \dfrac{1}{6}$

$$-\frac{2}{6} < \frac{1}{6} \qquad \text{true}$$

$$x < -1, \ x > \frac{5}{7}$$

25. $5 - \sqrt{x + 2} = 0$ 　　　Check:

$$5 = \sqrt{x + 2} \qquad 5 - \sqrt{23 + 2} \overset{?}{=} 0$$

$$25 = x + 2 \qquad\qquad 5 - 5 = 0$$

$$23 = x$$

26. $\sqrt[3]{4a - 1} - 3 = 0$ 　　Check:

$$\sqrt[3]{4a - 1} = 3 \qquad \sqrt[3]{28 - 1} - 3 \overset{?}{=} 0$$

$$4a - 1 = 27 \qquad\qquad 3 - 3 = 0$$

$$4a = 28$$

$$a = 7$$

27. $\sqrt{x + 8} - \sqrt{x + 35} = -3$

$$\sqrt{x + 8} = \sqrt{x + 35} - 3$$

$$x + 8 = x + 35 - 6\sqrt{x + 35} + 9$$

$$-36 = -6\sqrt{x + 35}$$

$$6 = \sqrt{x + 35}$$

$$36 = x + 35$$

$$1 = x$$

Check: $\sqrt{1 + 8} - \sqrt{1 + 35} \overset{?}{=} -3$

$$3 - 6 = -3$$

28. $\sqrt{x - 5} - 7 < 0$ 　　　Test 9:

$$\sqrt{x - 5} < 7 \qquad\qquad \sqrt{9 - 5} - 7 \overset{?}{<} 0$$

$$x - 5 < 49 \qquad\qquad\quad 2 - 7 < 0$$

$$x < 54$$

Also, $x - 5 \geq 0$

$$x \geq 5$$

$$5 \leq x < 54$$

PAGE 232　　APPLICATIONS AND PROBLEM SOLVING

29. Substitute values for x and $h(x)$;

$30 \neq -460.3$; the ball hits the ground about 337 feet from the plate.

30. Let w = width and ℓ = length.

$$P = 2\ell + 2w$$

$$6 = 2\ell + 2w$$

$$\ell = \frac{6 - 2w}{2} = 3 - w$$

$$A(w) = (3 - w)w$$

$$A(w) = -w^2 + 3w$$

w	$A(w)$
1	2
1.5	2.25
2	2

The area is maximized when the width is 1.5 feet and the length is $3 - 1.5$ or 1.5 feet.

Chapter 4 Test

PAGE 233

1. $\quad n^2 - 5n + 4 = 0$ 　　　**2.** $\quad 6z^3 - 7z^2 - 3z = 0$

$$(n - 4)(n - 1) = 0 \qquad\qquad z(6z^2 - 7z - 3) = 0$$

$$n = 4, \ n = 1 \qquad\qquad\qquad z(3z + 1)(2z - 3) = 0$$

$$z = 0, \ z = -\frac{1}{3}, \ z = \frac{3}{2}$$

3. $2a^2 - 5a + 4 = 0$ 　　　**4.** $\dfrac{1}{80} + \dfrac{1}{a} = \dfrac{1}{10}$

$$a = \frac{5 \pm \sqrt{25 - 4 \cdot 4 \cdot 2}}{4} \qquad\qquad a + 80 = 8a$$

$$\qquad\qquad\qquad\qquad 80 = 7a$$

$$= \frac{5 \pm \sqrt{-7}}{4} \qquad\qquad\qquad \frac{80}{7} = a$$

$$= \frac{5 \pm i\sqrt{7}}{4}$$

5. $3y^2 + 4y - 15 \le 0$

$(3y - 5)(y + 3) \le 0$

$y = \frac{5}{3}, \ y = -3$

Test -4: $\ 3(16) + 4(-4) - 15 \le 0$

$17 \le 0 \qquad$ false

Test 0: $\ -15 \le 0 \qquad$ true

Test 2: $\ 3(4) + 8 - 15 \le 0$

$5 \le 0 \qquad$ false

$-3 \le y \le \frac{5}{3}$

6. $\frac{5}{x + 2} > \frac{5}{x} + \frac{2}{3x}$

$15x = 3(x + 2)5 + 2(x + 2)$

$15x = 15x + 30 + 2x + 4$

$-34 = 2x$

$-17 = x$

Test -20: $\ \frac{5}{-10} > \frac{5}{-20} + \frac{2}{-60}$

$\frac{30}{-60} > \frac{17}{-60} \qquad$ true

Test 1: $\ \frac{5}{3} > 5 + \frac{2}{3} \qquad$ false

Test -1: $\ 5 > -5 + \frac{2}{3} \qquad$ true

$x < -17, \ -2 < x < 0$

7. $\sqrt{y - 2} - 3 = 0$

$\sqrt{y - 2} = 3$

$y - 2 = 9$

$y = 11$

Check: $\sqrt{11 - 2} - 3 \overset{?}{=} 0$

$3 - 3 = 0$

8. $\sqrt{2x + 2} = \sqrt{3x - 5}$

$2x + 2 = 3x - 5$

$7 = x$

Check:

$\sqrt{14 + 2} \overset{?}{=} \sqrt{21 - 5}$

$\sqrt{16} = \sqrt{16}$

9. $\sqrt{11 - 10m} > 9$

$11 - 10m > 81$

$-10m > 70$

$m < -7$

Test -10:

$\sqrt{11 - 10(-10)} \overset{?}{>} 9$

$\sqrt{11 + 100} \overset{?}{>} 9$

$10.53 > 9$

10.

11.
$\underline{2|}\ \ 2\ -3\ \ 3\ -4$

$\qquad\quad \underline{4\ \ 2\ 10}$

$\qquad 2\ \ \ 1\ \ 5\ \ 6$

$2x^2 + x + 5 \quad$ R6

12.
$\underline{-1|}\ \ 1\ -5\ -13\ \ 53\ \ 60$

$\qquad\qquad \underline{-1\ \ \ 6\ \ \ 7\ -60}$

$\qquad\ 1\ -6\ \ -7\ \ 60\ \ \ 0$

$x^3 - 6x^2 - 7x + 60$

13. $P(-2) = (-2)^3 + 8(-2)^2 + 2(-2) - 11 = 9;$ no

14. $P(1) = 4(1)^4 - 2(1)^2 + 1 - 3 = 0;$ yes

15. 3; 1 pos, 0 or 2 neg

r	6	11	-3	-2
0	6	11	-3	-2
$\frac{1}{2}$	6	14	4	0

$6x^2 + 14x + 4 = 0$

$(6x + 2)(x + 2) = 0$

$x = -\frac{1}{3}, \ x = -2$

rational zeros:

$\frac{1}{2}, \ -\frac{1}{3}, \ -2$

16. 4; 1 pos, 1 or 3 neg

r	1	1	-9	-17	-8
-1	1	0	-9	-8	0

$x^3 - 9x - 8$

r	1	0	-9	-8
-1	1	-1	-8	0

rational zeros:

$-1, \ -1$

17. 4; 1 pos, 0 or 2 neg

$h(x) = x(x^3 - 3x^2 - 53x - 9)$

r	1	-3	-53	-9
9	1	6	1	0

$x^2 + 6x + 1 \qquad$ no rational zeros

rational zeros: 0, 9

18. 3; 0 or 2 pos, 1 neg

r	8	-36	22	21
$-\frac{1}{2}$	8	-40	42	0

$8x^2 - 40x + 42 = 0$

$4x^2 - 20x + 21 = 0$

$(2x - 3)(2x - 7) = 0$

$x = \frac{3}{2}, \ x = \frac{7}{2}$

rational zeros: $\ -\frac{1}{2}, \ \frac{3}{2}, \ \frac{7}{2}$

19. $\frac{5z - 11}{2z^2 + z - 6} = \frac{5z - 11}{(z + 2)(2z - 3)}$

$5z - 11 = \frac{A}{z + 2} + \frac{B}{2z - 3}$

$5z - 11 = A(2z - 3) + B(z + 2)$

Let $z = \frac{3}{2}$: $\ 5\left(\frac{3}{2}\right) - 11 = A\left(2 \cdot \frac{3}{2} - 3\right) + B\left(\frac{3}{2} + 2\right)$

$\frac{15}{2} - \frac{22}{2} = B\left(\frac{7}{2}\right)$

$\frac{-7}{2} = \frac{7}{2}B$

$-1 = B$

Let $z = -2$: $\ 5(-2) - 11 = A(2(-2) - 3) + B(-2 + 2)$

$-21 = -7A$

$3 = A$

$\frac{5z - 11}{2z^2 + z - 6} = \frac{3}{z + 2} - \frac{1}{2z - 3}$

100

20. $\dfrac{7x^2 + 18x - 1}{(x^2 - 1)(x + 2)} = \dfrac{7x^2 + 18x - 1}{(x - 1)(x + 1)(x + 2)}$

$$7x^2 + 18x - 1 = \dfrac{A}{(x - 1)} + \dfrac{B}{(x + 1)} + \dfrac{C}{(x + 2)}$$

$$7x^2 + 18x - 1 = A(x + 1)(x + 2) + B(x - 1)$$
$$(x + 2) + C(x - 1)(x + 1)$$

Let $x = 1$:
$$7 + 18 - 1 = A(1 + 1)(1 + 2) + B(1 - 1)$$
$$(1 + 2) + C(1 - 1)(1 + 1)$$
$$24 = 6A$$
$$4 = A$$

Let $x = -1$:
$$7 - 18 - 1 = A(-1 + 1)(-1 + 2) + B(-1 - 1)$$
$$(-1 + 2) + C(-1 - 1)(-1 + 1)$$
$$-12 = B(-2)$$
$$6 = B$$

Let $x = -2$:
$$28 + 18(-2) - 1 = A(-2 + 1)(-2 + 2) + B(-2 - 1)$$
$$(-2 + 2) + C(-2 - 1)(-2 + 1)$$
$$-9 = 3C$$
$$-3 = C$$

$$\dfrac{7x^2 + 18x - 1}{(x^2 - 1)(x + 2)} = \dfrac{4}{x - 1} + \dfrac{6}{x + 1} - \dfrac{3}{x + 2}$$

21.

r	1	-3	-3
-1	1	-4	1
0	1	-3	-3
1	1	-2	-5
2	1	-1	-5
3	1	0	-3
4	1	1	1

x	$f(x)$
3.7	-0.41
3.8	0.04
3.9	0.51

x	$f(x)$
-0.7	-0.41
-0.8	0.04
-0.9	0.51

approximate zeros: 3.8, -0.8

22.

r	1	0	-1	1
-2	1	-2	3	-5
-1	1	-1	0	1
0	1	0	-1	1
1	1	1	0	1

x	$f(x)$
-1.4	-0.44
-1.3	0.1
-1.2	0.47

approximate zero: -1.3

23.

r	-1	3	5	-10
0	-1	3	5	-10
1	-1	2	7	-3
2	-1	1	7	4
3	-1	0	5	5
4	-1	-1	1	-6
5	-1	-2	-5	-35

lower bound: -5

24. Let ℓ = length, $\ell - 7$ = width, $\dfrac{\ell}{6}$ = height.

$$V = \ell wh$$
$$120 = \ell(\ell - 7)\left(\dfrac{1}{6}\ell\right)$$
$$720 = \ell^3 - 7\ell^2$$
$$0 = \ell^3 - 7\ell^2 - 720$$

r	1	-7	0	-720
10	1	3	30	-420
12	1	5	60	0

length = 12 cm, width = 5 cm, height = 2 cm

25. $r = (r + 20)$

$$d = rt$$
$$t = \dfrac{d}{r}$$
$$t_{car} = \dfrac{300}{r + 20} \qquad t_{train} = \dfrac{200}{r}$$
$$\dfrac{300}{r + 20} = \dfrac{200}{r}$$
$$300r = 200(r + 20)$$
$$300r = 200r + 4000$$
$$100r = 4000$$
$$r = 40 \text{ km/h}$$

PAGE 233   BONUS

$P(-1) = -3 + k; \ P(-2) = -20 + k$

$-3 + k > 0$ and $-20 + k < 0$

$\quad k > 3 \qquad\qquad k < 20$

Therefore, $3 < k < 20$.

Unit 1 Review

PAGES 234-235

1. {(-1, -2), (0, 1), (1, 4), (2, 7), (3, 10)}; yes

2. {(-1, 3), (0, 2), (1, 1), (2, 0)}; yes

3. $[f \circ g](x) = f(x + 3)$
$$= 2(x + 3) - 1$$
$$= 2x + 5$$
$[g \circ f](x) = g(2x - 1)$
$$= (2x - 1) + 3$$
$$= 2x + 2$$

4. $[f \circ g](x) = f(-2x^3)$
$$= 4(-2x^3)^2$$
$$= 16x^6$$
$[g \circ f](x) = g(4x^2)$
$$= -2(4x^2)^3$$
$$= -128x^6$$

101

5. $[f \circ g](x) = f(2x - 4)$

$\qquad = (2x - 4)^2 - 25$

$\qquad = 4x^2 - 16x - 9$

$[g \circ f](x) = g(x^2 - 25)$

$\qquad = 2(x^2 - 25) - 4$

$\qquad = 2x^2 - 54$

6. $4x - 10 = 0$

$\qquad 4x = 10$

$\qquad x = \dfrac{5}{2}$

7. $15x = 0$

$\qquad x = 0$

8. $0.75x + 3 = 0$

$\qquad 0.75x = -3$

$\qquad x = -4$

9.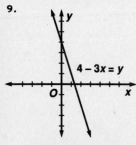

10.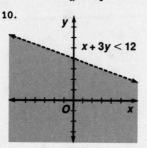

$x + 3y < 12$

11.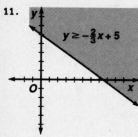

$y \geq -\dfrac{2}{3}x + 5$

12. $d = \sqrt{(3 - 5)^2 + (-1 - 2)^2}$

$\qquad = \sqrt{(-2)^2 + (-3)^2}$

$\qquad = \sqrt{13}$

$m = \dfrac{3 - 5}{-1 - 2} = \dfrac{-2}{-3} = \dfrac{2}{3}$

$y - 5 = \dfrac{2}{3}(x - 2)$

$\qquad y = \dfrac{2}{3}x + \dfrac{11}{3}$

13. $d = \sqrt{(0 - (-3)^2 + (-5 - 2)^2}$

$\qquad = \sqrt{3^2 + (-7)^2}$

$\qquad = \sqrt{58}$

$m = \dfrac{-5 - 2}{0 - (-3)} = -\dfrac{7}{3}$

$y - 2 = -\dfrac{7}{3}(x - (-3))$

$\qquad y = -\dfrac{7}{3}(x + 3) + 2$

$\qquad y = -\dfrac{7}{3}x - 5$

14. $d = \sqrt{(6 - 4)^2 + (-10 - (-4))^2}$

$\qquad = \sqrt{2^2 + (-6)^2}$

$\qquad = \sqrt{40}$ or $2\sqrt{10}$

$m = \dfrac{-10 - (-4)}{6 - 4} = \dfrac{-6}{2} = -3$

$y - (-4) = -3(x - 4)$

$\qquad y + 4 = -3x + 12$

$\qquad y = -3x + 8$

15. $m = 3$

$\qquad y - 4 = 3(x - (-1))$

$\qquad y = 3x + 7$

$3x - y + 7 = 0$

16. $2x - 3y = 6$

$\qquad -3y = -2x + 6$

$\qquad y = \dfrac{2}{3}x - 2$

$m = -\dfrac{3}{2}$

$\qquad y - 0 = -\dfrac{3}{2}(x - 2)$

$\qquad y = -\dfrac{3}{2}x + 3$

$\qquad 2y = -3x + 6$

$3x + 2y - 6 = 0$

17. $x - y = 5$

$\qquad x - (-4x) = 5$

$\qquad 5x = 5$

$\qquad x = 1$

$\qquad y = -4x$

$\qquad = -4(1)$

$\qquad = -4$

$\qquad (1, -4)$

18. $x + y = 12$

$\qquad \dfrac{2x - y = -4}{3x \qquad = 8}$

$\qquad x = \dfrac{8}{3}$

$x + y = 12$

$\dfrac{8}{3} + y = 12$

$\qquad y = \dfrac{28}{3}$

$\qquad \left(\dfrac{8}{3}, \dfrac{28}{3}\right)$

19. $3x - 2y = 10 \qquad 9x - 6y = 30$

$4x + 3y = 2 \Rightarrow \dfrac{8x + 6y = 4}{17x \qquad = 34}$

$\qquad x = 2$

$3x - 2y = 10$

$3(2) - 2y = 10$

$\qquad -2y = 4$

$\qquad y = -2$

$\qquad (2, -2)$

20. $A + B = \begin{bmatrix} 6 + (-4) & 2 + 6 \\ 3 + 5 & -3 + 7 \end{bmatrix} = \begin{bmatrix} 2 & 8 \\ 8 & 4 \end{bmatrix}$

21. $2A - B = \begin{bmatrix} 2(6) & 2(2) \\ 2(3) & 2(-3) \end{bmatrix} - \begin{bmatrix} -4 & 6 \\ 5 & 7 \end{bmatrix}$

$\qquad = \begin{bmatrix} 12 & 4 \\ 6 & -6 \end{bmatrix} - \begin{bmatrix} -4 & 6 \\ 5 & 7 \end{bmatrix}$

$\qquad = \begin{bmatrix} 12 - (-4) & 4 - 6 \\ 6 - 5 & -6 - 7 \end{bmatrix} = \begin{bmatrix} 16 & -2 \\ 1 & -13 \end{bmatrix}$

22. $CD = \begin{bmatrix} 3(2)+2(6)+(-1)(-5) & 3(0)+2(-3)+(-1)(-1) \\ -5(2)+(-8)(6)+1(-5) & -5(0)+(-8)(-3)+1(-1) \end{bmatrix}$

$\qquad = \begin{bmatrix} 23 & -5 \\ -63 & 23 \end{bmatrix}$

23. $AB + CD = \begin{bmatrix} 6(-4) + 2(5) & 6(6) + 2(7) \\ 3(-4) + (-3)(5) & 3(6) + (-3)(7) \end{bmatrix} +$

$\qquad \begin{bmatrix} 23 & -5 \\ -63 & 23 \end{bmatrix}$

$\qquad = \begin{bmatrix} -14 & 50 \\ -27 & -3 \end{bmatrix} + \begin{bmatrix} 23 & -5 \\ -63 & 23 \end{bmatrix}$

$\qquad = \begin{bmatrix} -14 + 23 & 50 + (-5) \\ -27 + (-63) & -3 + 23 \end{bmatrix}$

$\qquad = \begin{bmatrix} 9 & 45 \\ -90 & 20 \end{bmatrix}$

24. $\begin{vmatrix} 6 & 2 \\ 3 & -3 \end{vmatrix} = 6(-3) - 3(2) = -24$

25. $\begin{vmatrix} -3 & 1 & 5 \\ -1 & -4 & -2 \\ 3 & 2 & -1 \end{vmatrix} = -3\begin{vmatrix} -4 & -2 \\ 2 & -1 \end{vmatrix} - 1\begin{vmatrix} -1 & -2 \\ 3 & -1 \end{vmatrix} + 5\begin{vmatrix} -1 & -4 \\ 3 & 2 \end{vmatrix}$

$= -3(8) - 1(7) + 5(10)$

$= 19$

26. $\begin{vmatrix} -4 & 6 \\ 5 & 7 \end{vmatrix} = -4(7) - 5(6) = -58$

$B^{-1} = -\dfrac{1}{58}\begin{bmatrix} 7 & -6 \\ -5 & -4 \end{bmatrix} = \begin{bmatrix} -\dfrac{7}{58} & \dfrac{3}{29} \\ \dfrac{5}{58} & \dfrac{2}{29} \end{bmatrix}$

27. $\begin{bmatrix} 1 & -3 & 1 & 0 \\ 1 & 3 & -1 & 2 \\ -2 & 6 & 2 & 1 \end{bmatrix} \rightarrow \begin{bmatrix} 1 & -3 & 1 & 0 \\ 2 & 0 & 0 & 2 \\ -2 & 6 & 2 & 1 \end{bmatrix} \rightarrow \begin{bmatrix} 2 & 0 & 0 & 2 \\ 1 & -3 & 1 & 0 \\ -2 & 6 & 2 & 1 \end{bmatrix} \rightarrow$

$\begin{bmatrix} 1 & 0 & 0 & 1 \\ 1 & -3 & 1 & 0 \\ 0 & 0 & 4 & 1 \end{bmatrix} \rightarrow \begin{bmatrix} 1 & 0 & 0 & 1 \\ 1 & -3 & 1 & 0 \\ 0 & 0 & 1 & \frac{1}{4} \end{bmatrix} \rightarrow \begin{bmatrix} 1 & 0 & 0 & 1 \\ 0 & -3 & 1 & -1 \\ 0 & 0 & 1 & \frac{1}{4} \end{bmatrix} \rightarrow$

$\begin{bmatrix} 1 & 0 & 0 & 1 \\ 0 & -3 & 0 & -\frac{5}{4} \\ 0 & 0 & 1 & \frac{1}{4} \end{bmatrix} \rightarrow \begin{bmatrix} 1 & 0 & 0 & 1 \\ 0 & 1 & 0 & \frac{5}{12} \\ 0 & 0 & 1 & \frac{1}{4} \end{bmatrix}$ $\left(1, \dfrac{5}{12}, \dfrac{1}{4}\right)$

28. $\begin{bmatrix} 2 & 2 & -2 & 3 \\ 3 & -1 & 1 & 2 \\ 1 & -3 & -1 & 5 \end{bmatrix} \rightarrow \begin{bmatrix} 8 & 0 & 0 & 7 \\ 3 & -1 & 1 & 2 \\ 1 & -3 & -1 & 5 \end{bmatrix} \rightarrow \begin{bmatrix} 1 & 0 & 0 & \frac{7}{8} \\ 3 & -1 & 1 & 2 \\ 1 & -3 & -1 & 5 \end{bmatrix} \rightarrow$

$\begin{bmatrix} 1 & 0 & 0 & \frac{7}{8} \\ 0 & 8 & 4 & -13 \\ 1 & -3 & -1 & 5 \end{bmatrix} \rightarrow \begin{bmatrix} 1 & 0 & 0 & \frac{7}{8} \\ 0 & 8 & 4 & -13 \\ 0 & -3 & -1 & \frac{33}{8} \end{bmatrix} \rightarrow$

$\begin{bmatrix} 1 & 0 & 0 & \frac{7}{8} \\ 0 & -4 & 0 & \frac{7}{2} \\ 0 & -3 & -1 & \frac{33}{8} \end{bmatrix} \rightarrow \begin{bmatrix} 1 & 0 & 0 & \frac{7}{8} \\ 0 & 1 & 0 & -\frac{7}{8} \\ 0 & -3 & -1 & \frac{33}{8} \end{bmatrix} \rightarrow \begin{bmatrix} 1 & 0 & 0 & \frac{7}{8} \\ 0 & 1 & 0 & -\frac{7}{8} \\ 0 & 0 & -1 & \frac{3}{2} \end{bmatrix} \rightarrow$

$\begin{bmatrix} 1 & 0 & 0 & \frac{7}{8} \\ 0 & 1 & 0 & -\frac{7}{8} \\ 0 & 0 & 1 & -\frac{3}{2} \end{bmatrix}$ $\left(\dfrac{7}{8}, -\dfrac{7}{8}, -\dfrac{3}{2}\right)$

29.

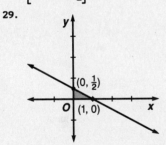

vertices: $(0, 0)$, $(1, 0)$, $\left(0, \dfrac{1}{2}\right)$

$f(0, 0) = 2(0) - 2(0) - 3 = -3$

$f(1, 0) = 2(0) - 2(1) - 3 = -5$

$f\left(0, \dfrac{1}{2}\right) = 2\left(\dfrac{1}{2}\right) - 2(0) - 3 = -2$

maximum at $\left(0, \dfrac{1}{2}\right) = -2$; minimum at $(1, 0) = -5$

30.

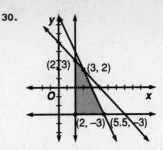

vertices: $(2, -3)$, $\left(\dfrac{11}{2}, -3\right)$, $(2, 3)$, $(3, 2)$

$f(2, -3) = 2(-3) - 2(2) - 3 = -13$

$f\left(\dfrac{11}{2}, -3\right) = 2(-3) - 2\left(\dfrac{11}{2}\right) - 3 = -20$

$f(2, 3) = 2(3) - 2(2) - 3 = -1$

$f(3, 2) = 2(2) - 2(3) - 3 = -5$

maximum at $(2, 3) = -1$;

minimum at $\left(\dfrac{11}{2}, -3\right) = -20$

31. Let $f(x) = y = -3x^3$.

$f(-x) = -3(-x)^3$

$= 3x^3$

$f(-x) = -f(x)$, so $y = -3x^3$ is odd.

32. Let $f(x) = y = 2x^4 - 5$.

$f(-x) = 2(-x)^4 - 5$

$= 2x^4 - 5$

$f(-x) = f(x)$, so $y = 2x^4 - 5$ is even.

33. Let $f(x) = y = x^3 + 3x^2 - 6x - 8$.

$f(-x) = (-x)^3 + 3(-x)^2 - 6(-x) - 8$

$= -x^3 + 3x^2 + 6x - 8$

$f(-x) \neq f(x)$ and $f(-x) \neq -f(x)$, so

$y = x^3 + 3x^2 - 6x - 8$ is neither even nor odd.

34.

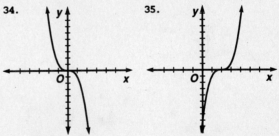

The graph is reflected over the x-axis.

35.

The graph is moved 2 units right.

36. $x = \frac{1}{2}y - 5$

$2x = y - 10$

$y = 2x + 10$

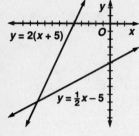

yes

37. $x = (y - 1)^3 + 2$

$x - 2 = (y - 1)^3$

$\sqrt[3]{x - 2} = y - 1$

$y = \sqrt[3]{x - 2} + 1$

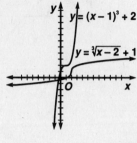

yes

38. $f\left(-\frac{1}{2}\right)$ and $f(-2)$ are not defined, so there are

vertical asymptotes at $x = -\frac{1}{2}$ and $x = -2$.

There are no horizontal or slant asymptotes.

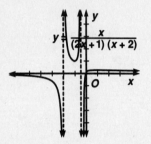

39. $y = \frac{x^2 - 9}{x + 3} = \frac{(x - 3)(x + 3)}{x + 3}$

Since the numerator and denominator have a
common factor, $x + 3$, there is a hole at $x = -3$.

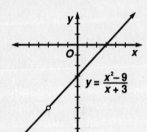

40.

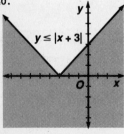

41.

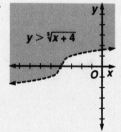

42. $f(x) = x^2 + 3x - 7$

$f'(x) = 2x + 3$

$f'(1) = 2(1) + 3 = 5$

Slope of the tangent at $(1, -3)$ is 5.

$y - (-3) = 5(x - 1)$

$y = 5x - 8$

43. $f(x) = -2x^2 + 5x + 1$

$f'(x) = -4x + 5$

$f'(-1) = -4(-1) + 5 = 9$

Slope of the tangent at $(-1, -6)$ is 9.

$y - (-6) = 9(x - (-1))$

$y = 9x + 3$

44. $f(x) = 2 + x + x^2$ $\qquad f(-0.51) = 1.7501$

$f'(x) = 1 + 2x$ $\qquad f(-0.50) = 1.75$

$0 = 1 + 2x$ $\qquad f(-0.49) = 1.7501$

$-1 = 2x$ $\qquad \left(-\frac{1}{2}, 1\frac{3}{4}\right)$ is a minimum.

$-\frac{1}{2} = x$

45. $f(x) = x^3 - 3x + 4$ $\qquad f(-1.01) \approx 5.9997$

$f'(x) = 3x^2 - 3$ $\qquad f(-1) = 6$

$0 = 3x^2 - 3$ $\qquad f(-0.99) \approx 5.9997$

$3 = 3x^2$ $\qquad f(0.99) \approx 2.0003$

$1 = x^2$ $\qquad f(1) = 2$

$x = \pm 1$ $\qquad f(1.01) \approx 2.0003$

$f''(x) = 6x$ $\qquad f(-0.01) \approx 4.0300$

$0 = 6x$ $\qquad f(0) = 4$

$0 = x$ $\qquad f(0.01) \approx 4.0300$

$(-1, 6)$ is a maximum; $(1, 2)$ is a minimum;
$(0, 4)$ is a point of inflection.

46. $y = \frac{x^2 - 1}{x + 1} = \frac{(x - 1)(x + 1)}{(x + 1)}$

Since the numerator and denominator have a
common factor, $x + 1$, there is a hole at $x = -1$.
So, the graph has point discontinuity.

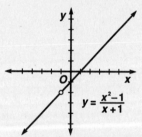

47. The graph jumps at $x = 0$, so it has jump
discontinuity.

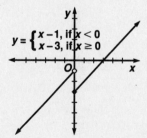

48. $x^2 - 8x + 16 = 0$

$(x - 4)(x - 4) = 0$

$x = 4$

49. $4x^2 - 4x - 10 = 0$

$2x^2 - 2x - 5 = 0$

$x = \dfrac{2 \pm \sqrt{4 - 4(2)(-5)}}{2(2)}$

$x = \dfrac{2 \pm \sqrt{44}}{4}$

$x = \dfrac{1 \pm \sqrt{11}}{2}$

50. $\dfrac{x + 2}{4} + \dfrac{x - 3}{4} = 6$

$x + 2 + x - 3 = 24$

$2x = 25$

$x = \dfrac{25}{2}$

51. $2 + \dfrac{1}{x - 1} = \dfrac{1}{2}$

$\dfrac{1}{x - 1} = -\dfrac{3}{2}$

$-3(x - 1) = 2$

$x - 1 = -\dfrac{2}{3}$

$x = \dfrac{1}{3}$

The value $x = 1$ is a point of discontinuity.

Test $x = 0$:

$2 + \dfrac{1}{0 - 1} > \dfrac{1}{2}$

$1 > \dfrac{1}{2}$ true

Test $x = \dfrac{1}{2}$:

$2 + \dfrac{1}{\frac{1}{2} - 1} > \dfrac{1}{2}$

$0 > \dfrac{1}{2}$ false

Test $x = 2$:

$2 + \dfrac{1}{2 - 1} > \dfrac{1}{2}$

$1 > \dfrac{1}{2}$ true

The solution set is $x < \dfrac{1}{3}$ or $x > 1$.

52. $9 + \sqrt{x - 1} = 1$

$\sqrt{x - 1} = -8$

$x - 1 = 64$

$x = 65$

Check:

$9 + \sqrt{65 - 1} \overset{?}{=} 1$

$9 + 8 \overset{?}{=} 1$

$17 \neq 1$

The equation has no real solution.

53. $\sqrt{x + 8} - \sqrt{x + 35} \leq -3$

$\sqrt{x + 8} \leq \sqrt{x + 35} - 3$

$x + 8 \leq x + 35 - 2(3)\sqrt{x + 35} + 9$

$-36 \leq -6\sqrt{x + 35}$

$6 \geq \sqrt{x + 35}$

$36 \geq x + 35$

$1 \geq x$

$x + 8 \geq 0$

$x \geq -8$

Check:

Test $x = 0$: $\sqrt{0 + 8} - \sqrt{0 + 35} \leq -3$

$\sqrt{8} - \sqrt{35} \leq -3$

$-3.088 \leq -3$ true

The solution set is $-8 \leq x \leq 1$.

54.
```
6│  1 -1   4
  │     6  30
  ─────────────
     1  5  34
```
$R = 34$

55.
```
2│  2  0 -3   1
  │     4  8  10
  ─────────────────
     2  4  5  11
```
$R = 11$

56. $f(x) = 3x^2 + x - 2$

There is 1 sign change, so there is 1 positive real zero.

$f(-x) = 3x^2 - x - 2$

There is 1 sign change, so there is 1 negative real zero.

$f(x) = 3x^2 + x - 2$

$= (3x - 2)(x + 1)$

The rational zeros are $\dfrac{2}{3}$ and -1.

57. $f(x) = x^4 + x^3 - 2x^2 + 3x - 1$

There are 3 sign changes, so there are 3 or 1 positive real zeros.

$f(-x) = x^4 - x^3 - 2x^2 - 3x - 1$

There is 1 sign change, so there is 1 negative real zero.

The possible rational zeros are ± 1.

r	1	1	-2	3	-1
-1	1	0	-2	5	-6
1	1	2	0	3	2

There are no rational zeros.

58. The function must have 1 positive real zero and 1 negative real zero. The possible rational zeros are ± 1, ± 5.

r	1	-2	-5
-5	1	-7	30
-4	1	-6	19
-3	1	-5	10
-2	1	-4	3
-1	1	-3	-2
0	1	-2	-5

r	1	-2	-5
1	1	-1	-6
2	1	0	-5
3	1	1	-2
4	1	2	3
5	1	3	10

There is a zero between -1 and -2 and a zero between 3 and 4.

x	$f(x)$
-1.3	-0.71
-1.4	-0.24
-1.5	0.25

x	$f(x)$
3.3	-0.71
3.4	-0.24
3.5	0.25

The real zeros are approximately -1.4 and 3.4.

59. The function must have 1 positive real zero and 2 or 0 negative real zeros. The possible rational zeros are ± 1, ± 2.

r	1	4	1	-2
2	1	6	13	24
1	1	5	6	4
0	1	4	1	-2

r	1	4	1	-2
-1	1	3	-2	0
-2	1	2	-3	4
-3	1	1	-2	4
-4	1	0	1	-6

There is a zero between 0 and 1, a zero between -3 and -4, and a zero at -1.

x	$f(x)$
0.5	-0.375
0.6	0.256

x	$f(x)$
-3.5	0.625
-3.6	-0.416

The real zeros are -1 and approximately 0.6 and -3.6.

Unit 2   Trigonometry
Chapter 5   The Trigonometric Functions

 5-1   **Angles and Their Measure**

PAGES 244-245   CHECKING FOR UNDERSTANDING

1. Sample answer: A positive angle is formed when the terminal side of an angle is rotated in a counterclockwise direction. A negative angle is formed when the terminal side of an angle is rotated in a clockwise direction.

2. If you know the degree measure of an angle and you need to find the radian measure, multiply the number of degrees by $\frac{\pi}{180°}$. If you know the radian measure of an angle and you need to find the degree measure, multiply the number of radians by $\frac{180°}{\pi}$.

3.
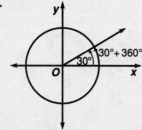

4. If θ is the degree measure of an angle, then $\theta + 360k°$, where k is an integer, is the measure of all angles that are coterminal with the angle. If θ is the radian measure of an angle, then $\theta + 2k\pi$, where k is an integer, is the measure of all angles that are coterminal with the angle.

5. IV   6. III   7. II   8. IV

9. II   10. I   11. II   12. III

13. $18° = 18° \times \frac{\pi}{180°}$
    $= \frac{\pi}{10}$

14. $240° = 240° \times \frac{\pi}{180°}$
    $= \frac{4\pi}{3}$

15. $1° = 1° \times \frac{\pi}{180}$
    $= \frac{\pi}{180°}$

16. $-45° = -45° \times \frac{\pi}{180°}$
    $= -\frac{\pi}{4}$

17. $\pi = \pi \times \frac{180°}{\pi}$
    $= 180°$

18. $\frac{3\pi}{2} = \frac{3\pi}{2} \times \frac{180°}{\pi}$
    $= 270°$

19. $-\frac{7\pi}{6} = -\frac{7\pi}{6} \times \frac{180°}{\pi}$
    $= -210°$

20. $\frac{5\pi}{4} = \frac{5\pi}{4} \times \frac{180°}{\pi}$
    $= 225°$

21. $\frac{9\pi}{4} - 2\pi \stackrel{?}{=} \frac{\pi}{4}$
    $\frac{\pi}{4} = \frac{\pi}{4}$; yes

22. $390° - 360° \stackrel{?}{=} -30°$
    $30° \neq -30°$; no

23. $\frac{14\pi}{3} = \frac{14\pi}{3} \times \frac{180°}{\pi} = 840°$
    $840° - 720° \stackrel{?}{=} 120°$
    $120° = 120°$; yes

PAGES 245-246   EXERCISES

24. III   25. III   26. II   27. III

28. I   29. IV   30. III   31. IV

32. $200° = 200° \times \frac{\pi}{180°}$
    $= \frac{10\pi}{9}$

33. $-150° = -150° \times \frac{\pi}{180°}$
    $= -\frac{5\pi}{6}$

34. $75° = 75° \times \frac{\pi}{180°}$
    $= \frac{5\pi}{12}$

35. $105° = 105° \times \frac{\pi}{180°}$
    $= \frac{7\pi}{12}$

36. $570° = 570° \times \frac{\pi}{180°}$
    $= \frac{19\pi}{6}$

37. $-450° = -450° \times \frac{\pi}{180°}$
    $= -\frac{5\pi}{2}$

38. $405° = 405° \times \frac{\pi}{180°}$
    $= \frac{9\pi}{4}$

39. $-1250° = -1250° \times \frac{\pi}{180°}$
    $= -\frac{125\pi}{18}$

40. $\frac{\pi}{3} = \frac{\pi}{3} \times \frac{180°}{\pi}$
    $= 60°$

41. $-3.5 = -3.5 \times \frac{180°}{\pi}$
    $\approx 200.54°$
    $\approx 200°32'$

42. $\frac{4\pi}{3} = \frac{4\pi}{3} \times \frac{180°}{\pi}$
    $= 240°$

43. $-\frac{\pi}{2} = -\frac{\pi}{2} \times \frac{180°}{\pi}$
    $= -90°$

44. $1.75 = 1.75 \times \frac{180°}{\pi}$
    $\approx 100.27°$
    $\approx 100°16'$

45. $-\frac{7\pi}{12} = -\frac{7\pi}{12} \times \frac{180°}{\pi}$
    $= -105°$

46. $17.46 = 17.46 \times \frac{180°}{\pi}$
    $\approx 1000.38°$
    $\approx 1000°23'$

47. $\frac{17\pi}{6} = \frac{17\pi}{6} \times \frac{180°}{\pi}$
    $= 510°$

48. $-60° + 360° = 300°$
    $-60° - 360° = -420°$

49. $\frac{5\pi}{12} + 2\pi = \frac{29\pi}{12}$
    $\frac{5\pi}{12} - 2\pi = -\frac{19\pi}{12}$

50. $\frac{11\pi}{6} + 2\pi = \frac{23\pi}{6}$
    $\frac{11\pi}{6} - 2\pi = -\frac{\pi}{6}$

51. $-310° + 360° = 50°$
    $-310° - 360° = -670°$

52. $-30°$ is coterminal with $330°$ in Quadrant IV.
    $\alpha' = 360° - \alpha = 360° - 330° = 30°$

53. $\frac{12\pi}{5}$ is coterminal with $\frac{2\pi}{5}$ in Quadrant I.

$\alpha' = \frac{2\pi}{5}$

54. $\alpha' = 180° - \alpha = 180° - 130° = 50°$

55. $-210°$ is coterminal with $150°$ in Quadrant II.

$\alpha' = 180° - \alpha = 180° - 150° = 30°$

56. $\frac{9\pi}{4}$ is coterminal with $\frac{\pi}{4}$ in Quadrant I.

$\alpha' = \frac{\pi}{4}$

57. $-420°$ is coterminal with $300°$ in Quadrant IV.

$\alpha' = 360° - \alpha = 360° - 300° = 60°$

58. $\frac{23\pi}{6}$ is coterminal with $\frac{11\pi}{6}$ in Quadrant IV.

$\alpha' = 2\pi - \alpha = 2\pi - \frac{11\pi}{6} = \frac{\pi}{6}$

59. $-\frac{5\pi}{3}$ is coterminal with $\frac{\pi}{3}$ in Quadrant I.

$\alpha' = \frac{\pi}{3}$

60. $22' \times \frac{1°}{60'} \approx 0.3667$

So, $55°22' \approx 55.3667°$.

$55.3667° \times \frac{\pi}{180°} \approx 0.966$

61. $28'' \times \frac{1'}{60''} \times \frac{1°}{60'} \approx 0.00778$

$50' \times \frac{1°}{60'} \approx 0.83333$

So, $-110°50'28'' \approx -110.840°$.

$-110.841° \times \frac{\pi}{180°} \approx -1.935$

62. $15'' \times \frac{1'}{60''} \times \frac{1°}{60'} \approx 0.00417$

$49' \times \frac{1°}{60'} \approx 0.81667$

So, $250°49'15'' \approx 250.821°$.

$250.821° \times \frac{\pi}{180°} \approx 4.378$

63. $\frac{360°}{24} = 15°$

$360° \times 7 = 2520°$

64. $154°15' - 35° = 119°15'$

$180° - 119°15' = 60°45'$

65. a. $\frac{2.22 \times 10^4 \text{ degrees}}{\text{second}} \times \frac{1 \text{ revolution}}{360 \text{ degrees}}$

$\times \frac{60 \text{ seconds}}{1 \text{ minute}} = 3700$ rev/min

b. $\frac{2.22 \times 10^4 \text{ degrees}}{\text{second}} \times \frac{60 \text{ seconds}}{1 \text{ minute}} \times \frac{\pi}{180°}$

$= 7400\pi$ rad/min

66. $f(3) = 4 + 6(3) - 3^3$

$= -5$

67. $m = \frac{7 - 2}{5 - (-3)}$

$= \frac{5}{8}$

68. $3x - y + 7 = 0$

$y = 3x + 7$

$m = \frac{y_2 - y_1}{x_2 - x_1}$

$3 = \frac{y - (-2)}{x - 3}$

$3(x - 3) = y + 2$

$3x - y - 11 = 0$

69. $3x + y = 6$ $3(1) + y = 6$

$\underline{4x + y = 7}$ $y = 3$

$\frac{-x}{} = -1$

$x = 1$ $(1, 3)$

70.

$$\begin{bmatrix} 1 & 1 \\ 1 & 1 \end{bmatrix} \begin{bmatrix} 3 & 5 \\ -3 & -5 \end{bmatrix} = X$$

$$\begin{bmatrix} 1(3) + 1(-3) & 1(5) + 1(-5) \\ 1(3) + 1(-3) & 1(5) + 1(-5) \end{bmatrix} = X$$

$$\begin{bmatrix} 0 & 0 \\ 0 & 0 \end{bmatrix} = X$$

71. Let $b =$ the number of bicycles.

Let $t =$ the number of tricycles.

$b \geq 0$

$t \geq 0$

$3b + 4t \leq 450$

$5b + 2t \leq 400$

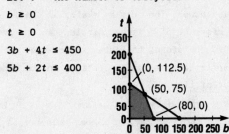

Profit function: $P(b, t) = 6b + 4t$

$P(0, 0) = 6(0) + 4(0) = 0$

$P(80, 0) = 6(80) + 4(0) = 480$

$P(0, 112.5) = 6(0) + 4(112.5) = 450$

$P(50, 75) = 6(50) + 4(75) = 600$

Fifty bicycles and 75 tricycles should be produced to maximize profit.

72. Sample answer: $y = \frac{x}{x(x - 5)}$

73. $P(3) = 6^3 - 5(6)^2 - 3(6) - 18$

$= 216 - 180 - 18 - 18$

$= 0$; yes

74. $\frac{3}{x} + \frac{5}{x} = 10$

$x\left(\frac{3}{x} + \frac{5}{x}\right) = x(10)$

$3 + 5 = 10x$

$\frac{8}{10} = x$

$x = \frac{4}{5}$

75. $5 - \sqrt{b + 2} = 0$

$5 = \sqrt{b + 2}$

$5^2 = b + 2$

$b = 23$

76. $\frac{2 \text{ miles}}{25 \text{ minutes}} \times \frac{60 \text{ minutes}}{1 \text{ hour}} = 4.8$ mph

1. If s equals the length of a circular arc and C equals the circumference, then $s:C = r\theta:2\pi r$ or $\theta:2\pi$ where θ is the measure of the angle in radians when 2π is the total number of radians in the sum of the central angle of a circle. The ratio of the area of a sector to the area of a circle is $0.5r^2\theta:\pi r^2$ or $\theta:2\pi$. Therefore, the area of the sector is proportional to the area of the circle in the same ratio as the angle is proportional to 2π, the number of radians in a circle.

2. Sample answer: Linear velocity is the movement along the arc with respect to time while angular velocity is the change in the angle with respect to time.

3. Sample answer: Multiply the number of revolutions by 6.

4. Sample answer: The outside skater is skating the circumference of a larger circle than the inner skater. Therefore, the outer skater must skate faster to cover a longer distance in the same amount of time.

5. Let $R = 2r$. For length of an arc, $S = R\theta$ or $2r\theta$ which is $2(r\theta)$ or $2s$. For linear velocity, $V = R\frac{\theta}{t}$ or $\frac{2r\theta}{t}$ which is $2\left(\frac{r\theta}{t}\right)$ or $2v$.

6. $s = r\theta$
$= 2\left(\frac{\pi}{2}\right)$
$= \pi$

7. $50° = 50° \times \frac{\pi}{180°}$
$= \frac{5\pi}{18}$
$s = r\theta$
$= 9\left(\frac{5\pi}{18}\right)$
$= \frac{5\pi}{2}$

8. $120° = 120° \times \frac{\pi}{180°}$
$= \frac{2\pi}{3}$
$s = r\theta$
$= 3\left(\frac{2\pi}{3}\right)$
$= 2\pi$

9. $\frac{60 \text{ mi}}{1 \text{ h}} \cdot \frac{5280 \text{ ft}}{1 \text{ mi}} \cdot \frac{1 \text{ h}}{3600 \text{ s}} = 88 \text{ ft/s}$

10. $\frac{8 \text{ rev}}{1 \text{ min}} \cdot \frac{2\pi \text{ rad}}{1 \text{ rev}} \cdot \frac{1 \text{ min}}{60 \text{ s}} = \frac{4\pi}{15} \text{ rad/s}$

11. $\frac{10 \text{ ft}}{1 \text{ min}} \cdot \frac{12 \text{ in.}}{1 \text{ ft}} \cdot \frac{1 \text{ min}}{60 \text{ s}} = 2 \text{ in./s}$

12. $\frac{15 \text{ cm}}{1 \text{ s}} \cdot \frac{1 \text{ m}}{100 \text{ cm}} \cdot \frac{60 \text{ s}}{1 \text{ min}} = 9 \text{ m/min}$

13. $A = \frac{1}{2}r^2\theta$
$= \frac{1}{2}(7)^2\left(\frac{\pi}{8}\right)$
$\approx 9.6 \text{ m}^2$

14. $48° = 48° \times \frac{\pi}{180°}$
$= \frac{4\pi}{15}$
$A = \frac{1}{2}r^2\theta$
$= \frac{1}{2}(22)^2\left(\frac{4\pi}{15}\right)$
$\approx 202.7 \text{ in}^2$

15. $270° = \frac{3\pi}{2}$
$A = \frac{1}{2}r^2\theta$
$= \frac{1}{2}(15)^2\left(\frac{3\pi}{2}\right)$
$\approx 530.1 \text{ cm}^2$

16. $s = r\theta$
$= 10\left(\frac{\pi}{4}\right)$
$= \frac{5\pi}{2} \text{ cm}$

17. $s = r\theta$
$= 10\left(\frac{2\pi}{3}\right)$
$= \frac{20\pi}{3} \text{ cm}$

18. $s = r\theta$
$= 10\left(\frac{5\pi}{6}\right)$
$= \frac{25\pi}{3} \text{ cm}$

19. $s = r\theta$
$= 10\left(\frac{2\pi}{5}\right)$
$= 4\pi \text{ cm}$

20. $30° = \frac{\pi}{6}$
$s = r\theta$
$= 15\left(\frac{\pi}{6}\right)$
$= \frac{5\pi}{2} \text{ in.}$

21. $5° = \frac{\pi}{36}$
$s = r\theta$
$= 15\left(\frac{\pi}{36}\right)$
$= \frac{5\pi}{12} \text{ in.}$

22. $77° = \frac{77\pi}{180}$
$s = r\theta$
$= 15\left(\frac{77\pi}{180}\right)$
$= \frac{77\pi}{12} \text{ in.}$

23. $18' = 18' \times \frac{1°}{60'}$
$= 0.3°$
So, $57°18' = 57.3°$.
$57.3° = 57.3° \times \frac{\pi}{180°}$
$= \frac{57.3\pi}{180}$
$s = r\theta$
$= 15\left(\frac{57.3\pi}{180}\right)$
$= \frac{859.5\pi}{180}$ or $\frac{191\pi}{40}$ in.

24. $s = r\theta$
$5 = 8\theta$
$\frac{5}{8} = \theta$
$\frac{5}{8} = \frac{5}{8} \times \frac{180°}{\pi}$
$\approx 35.8°$

25. $s = r\theta$
$14 = 8\theta$
$\frac{14}{8} = \theta$
$\frac{14}{8} = \frac{14}{8} \times \frac{180°}{\pi}$
$\approx 100.3°$

26. $s = r\theta$

$24 = 8\theta$

$3 = \theta$

$3 = 3 \times \dfrac{180°}{\pi}$

$\approx 171.9°$

27. $s = r\theta$

$12.5 = 8\theta$

$\dfrac{12.5}{8} = \theta$

$\dfrac{12.5}{8} = \dfrac{12.5}{8} \times \dfrac{180°}{\pi}$

$\approx 89.5°$

28. $A = \dfrac{1}{2}r^2\theta$

$= \dfrac{1}{2}(10)^2\left(\dfrac{5\pi}{12}\right)$

$\approx 65.4 \text{ ft}^2$

29. $54° = 54° \times \dfrac{\pi}{180°}$

$= \dfrac{3\pi}{10}$

$A = \dfrac{1}{2}r^2\theta$

$= \dfrac{1}{2}(6)^2\left(\dfrac{3\pi}{10}\right)$

$\approx 17.0 \text{ in}^2$

30. $A = \dfrac{1}{2}r^2\theta$

$= \dfrac{1}{2}(1.36)^2\left(\dfrac{2\pi}{3}\right)$

$\approx 1.9 \text{ m}^2$

31. $82° = 82° \times \dfrac{\pi}{180°}$

$= \dfrac{41\pi}{90}$

$A = \dfrac{1}{2}r^2\theta$

$= \dfrac{1}{2}(7.3)^2\left(\dfrac{41\pi}{90}\right)$

$\approx 38.1 \text{ km}^2$

32. $45° = \dfrac{\pi}{4}$

$A = \dfrac{1}{2}r^2\theta$

$= \dfrac{1}{2}(9.75)^2\left(\dfrac{\pi}{4}\right)$

$\approx 37.3 \text{ mm}^2$

33. $12° = \dfrac{\pi}{15}$

$A = \dfrac{1}{2}r^2\theta$

$= \dfrac{1}{2}(14)^2\left(\dfrac{\pi}{15}\right)$

$\approx 20.5 \text{ yd}^2$

34. $45° = \dfrac{\pi}{4}$

$s = r\theta$

$6.5 = r\left(\dfrac{\pi}{4}\right)$

$r \approx 8.3 \text{ cm}$

35. $s = r\theta$

$70.7 = r\left(\dfrac{2\pi}{7}\right)$

$r \approx 78.77$

$d = 2r$

$\approx 2(78.77)$

$\approx 157.5 \text{ m}$

36. $s = r\theta$

$6 = r(1.2)$

$r = 5 \text{ ft}$

$A = \pi r^2$

$= \pi(5)^2$

$\approx 78.5 \text{ ft}^2$

37. $A = \dfrac{1}{2}r^2\theta$

$15 = \dfrac{1}{2}r^2(0.2)$

$150 = r^2$

$r \approx 12.2 \text{ in.}$

$s = r\theta$

$\approx 12.2(0.2)$

$\approx 2.4 \text{ in.}$

38. $20° = \dfrac{\pi}{9}$

$s = r\theta$

$3.5 = r\left(\dfrac{\pi}{9}\right)$

$r \approx 10.0 \text{ mm}$

$A = \pi r^2$

$\approx \pi(10.0)^2$

$\approx 314.2 \text{ mm}^2$

39. $v_r = \dfrac{r\theta_r}{t}$ $\qquad$ $v_R = \dfrac{R\theta_R}{t}$

$\qquad\qquad\qquad v_R = Ra$

The linear velocity is the same for both gears.

$V_r = V_R$

$\dfrac{r\theta_r}{t} = Ra$

$\dfrac{\theta_r}{t} = \dfrac{R}{r}a$

The angular velocity of the gear with radius r is $\dfrac{R}{r}$ times a.

40. a. $v = r\dfrac{\theta}{t}$

$= (9.3 \times 10^7)\dfrac{2\pi}{364.25}$

$\approx 1{,}604{,}218 \text{ miles per day}$

$\dfrac{1{,}604{,}218 \text{ miles}}{1 \text{ day}} \cdot \dfrac{5280 \text{ feet}}{1 \text{ mile}} \cdot \dfrac{1 \text{ day}}{24 \text{ hours}} \cdot$

$\dfrac{1 \text{ hour}}{3600 \text{ seconds}} \approx 9.80 \times 10^4 \text{ ft/s}$

b. $0.5° = \dfrac{\pi}{360}$

$s = r\theta$

$= (9.3 \times 10^7)\left(\dfrac{\pi}{360}\right)$

$\approx 8.1 \times 10^5 \text{ miles}$

41. $130° = 130° \times \dfrac{\pi}{180°}$

$= \dfrac{13\pi}{18}$

$s = r\theta$

$= 3.5\left(\dfrac{13\pi}{18}\right)$

$\approx 8 \text{ feet}$

42. a. $38°37' - 32°17' = 6°20'$

$20' = 20' \times \dfrac{1°}{60'} \approx 0.333°$

So, $6°10' \approx 6.333° \times \dfrac{\pi}{180°}$

≈ 0.1105

$s = r\theta$

$\approx (4000)(0.1105)$

≈ 442 miles

b. $v = r\dfrac{\theta}{t}$

$= 4000\left(\dfrac{2\pi}{24}\right)$

≈ 1050 miles

43. $\theta = \dfrac{\pi}{4}$

$A_A = \dfrac{1}{2}\left(r_A\right)^2\theta$

$= \dfrac{1}{2}(1)^2\left(\dfrac{\pi}{4}\right)$

$\approx 0.39 \text{ ft}^2$

$A_B = \dfrac{1}{2}(r_{AB})^2\theta - A_A$

$\approx \dfrac{1}{2}(2)^2\left(\dfrac{\pi}{4}\right) - 0.39$

$\approx 1.18 \text{ ft}^2$

$A_C = \dfrac{1}{2}(r_{ABC})^2\theta - A_A - A_B$

$\approx \dfrac{1}{2}(3)^2\left(\dfrac{\pi}{4}\right) - 0.39 - 1.18$

$\approx 1.96 \text{ ft}^2$

44. a. 1 mile = 63,360 inches

$s = r\theta$

$63,360 = 13\theta$

$4874 \approx \theta$

$4874 \cdot \dfrac{1 \text{ rev}}{2\pi} \approx 776$ times

b. $v = r\dfrac{\theta}{t}$

$= 13\left(\dfrac{2.5 \cdot 2\pi}{1}\right)$

≈ 204 in./s

$\dfrac{204 \text{ inches}}{1 \text{ second}} \cdot \dfrac{1 \text{ foot}}{12 \text{ inches}} \approx 17$ ft/s

$\dfrac{17 \text{ feet}}{1 \text{ second}} \cdot \dfrac{1 \text{ mile}}{5280 \text{ feet}} \cdot \dfrac{3600 \text{ seconds}}{1 \text{ hour}}$

≈ 11.6 mph

45. $80° = \dfrac{4\pi}{9}$ $84.5° = \dfrac{84.5\pi}{180}$

$s_{BC} = r\theta$ $s_{DE} = r\theta$

$= (0.67)\left(\dfrac{4\pi}{9}\right)$ $= (0.70)\left(\dfrac{84.5\pi}{180}\right)$

≈ 0.94 ≈ 1.03

$1.8 + 0.94 + 1.46 + 1.03 \approx 5.23$ miles

46. $5° = \dfrac{\pi}{36}$

$s = r\theta$

$= 2.5\left(\dfrac{\pi}{36} + \dfrac{\pi}{36}\right)$

≈ 0.436

$\dfrac{0.436 \text{ meters}}{2 \text{ seconds}} \times \dfrac{3600 \text{ seconds}}{1 \text{ hour}} \approx 785$ m

47. a. B, clockwise; C, counterclockwise

b. $v_A = r_A\left(\dfrac{\theta}{t}\right)_A$

$v_A = 3.0\left(\dfrac{120}{1}\right)$

$= 360$

The linear velocity of each of the three rollers is the same.

$v_B = r_B\left(\dfrac{\theta}{t}\right)_B$ $v_C = r_C\left(\dfrac{\theta}{t}\right)_C$

$360 = 2.0 \cdot \dfrac{\theta_B}{1}$ $360 = 4.8 \cdot \dfrac{\theta_C}{1}$

$180 = \theta_B$ $75 = \theta_C$

180 rpm   75 rpm

48. $[f \circ g](x) = f(x + 1)$

$= \dfrac{1}{(x + 1) - 1}$

$= \dfrac{1}{x}$

49. $\begin{vmatrix} 4 & 3 \\ 8 & 6 \end{vmatrix} = 4(6) - 8(3) = 0$

No, an inverse does not exist because $\dfrac{1}{0}$ is undefined.

50. $f(x) = 2x^2 - 3x + 3$

$f'(x) = 4x - 3$

$f(-2) = 4(-2) - 3$

$= -11$

The slope is -11.

51. $x = \dfrac{-7 \pm \sqrt{(7)^2 - 4(6)(2)}}{2(6)}$

$= \dfrac{-7 \pm \sqrt{49 - 48}}{12}$

$= \dfrac{-7 \pm 1}{12}$

$x = -\dfrac{8}{12}$ or $x = -\dfrac{6}{12}$

$= -\dfrac{2}{3}$ $= -\dfrac{1}{2}$

52. Let x = the time it would take the landscaper to do the job alone.

$\dfrac{16}{x} + \dfrac{6}{30} = 1$

$5x\left(\dfrac{16}{x} + \dfrac{1}{5}\right) = 5x(1)$

$80 + x = 5x$

$-4x = -80$

$x = 20$ days

53. $\sqrt[3]{3y - 1} - 2 = 0$

$\sqrt[3]{3y - 1} = 2$

$3y - 1 = 8$

$3y = 9$

$y = 3$

54. $60° = 60° \times \dfrac{\pi}{180°}$

$= \dfrac{\pi}{3}$

55. $V = \pi r^2 h$

$= \pi(4)^2(18)$

$= 288\pi$ inches

The best answer is A.

5-3 Circular Functions

PAGES 259-260   CHECKING FOR UNDERSTANDING

1. Since $a + 360k°$ is coterminal with a, $\sin(a° + 360k°)$ is the same as $\sin a°$. For example, $\sin 90° = 1$ and $\sin(90° + 720°)$ $= \sin 810° = 1$.

2. first quadrant

3. By definition $\cos \theta = \dfrac{x}{r}$. Let $r = 1$. If the measure of θ is $0°$, $x = r$. Thus $\cos \theta = \dfrac{1}{1}$ or 1. As θ increases, r remains 1 and x decreases. Therefore, $\dfrac{x}{r}$ decreases. When r is vertical, $x = 0$. Thus $\cos \theta = \dfrac{0}{1}$ or 0.

4. $\sin 13°$

5.

	Quadrant			
	I	II	III	IV
sin α or csc α	+	+	−	−
cos α or sec α	+	−	−	+
tan α or cot α	+	−	+	−

6. $r = \sqrt{x^2 + y^2} = \sqrt{3^2 + (-4)^2} = 5$

$\sin \theta = \dfrac{y}{r}$ or $-\dfrac{4}{5}$ $\csc \theta = \dfrac{r}{y}$ or $-\dfrac{5}{4}$

$\cos \theta = \dfrac{x}{r}$ or $\dfrac{3}{5}$ $\sec \theta = \dfrac{r}{x} = \dfrac{5}{3}$

$\tan \theta = \dfrac{y}{x}$ or $-\dfrac{4}{3}$ $\cot \theta = \dfrac{x}{y} = -\dfrac{3}{4}$

7. $r = \sqrt{x^2 + y^2} = \sqrt{3^2 + 3^2} = 3\sqrt{2}$

$\sin \theta = \dfrac{y}{r}$ $\csc \theta = \dfrac{r}{y}$

$= \dfrac{3}{3\sqrt{2}}$ or $\dfrac{\sqrt{2}}{2}$ $= \dfrac{3\sqrt{2}}{3}$ or $\sqrt{2}$

$\cos \theta = \dfrac{x}{r}$ $\sec \theta = \dfrac{r}{x}$

$= \dfrac{3}{3\sqrt{2}}$ or $\dfrac{\sqrt{2}}{2}$ $= \dfrac{3\sqrt{2}}{3}$ or $\sqrt{2}$

$\tan \theta = \dfrac{y}{x}$ or 1 $\cot \theta = \dfrac{x}{y}$ or 1

---

8. $r = \sqrt{x^2 + y^2} = \sqrt{(-4)^2 + 0^2} = 4$

$\sin \theta = \dfrac{y}{r}$ $\csc \theta = \dfrac{r}{y}$

$= \dfrac{0}{4}$ or 0 $= \dfrac{4}{0}$ undefined

$\cos \theta = \dfrac{x}{r}$ $\sec \theta = \dfrac{r}{x}$

$= \dfrac{-4}{4}$ or -1 $= \dfrac{4}{-4}$ or -1

$\tan \theta = \dfrac{y}{x}$ $\cot \theta = \dfrac{x}{y}$

$= \dfrac{0}{-4}$ or 0 $= \dfrac{-4}{0}$ undefined

9. $\sin \theta = \dfrac{y}{r} = \dfrac{1}{2}$

So, r is 2 and y is 1.

$r = \sqrt{x^2 + y^2}$

$4 = x^2 + 1$

$3 = x^2$

$\pm\sqrt{3} = x$

Since θ is in the second quadrant, x must be negative. Thus, $\cos \theta = \dfrac{x}{r}$ or $-\dfrac{\sqrt{3}}{2}$.

10. From Exercise 9, we know that $y = 1$ and $x = -\sqrt{3}$. So, $\tan \theta = \dfrac{y}{x} = \dfrac{1}{-\sqrt{3}}$ or $-\dfrac{\sqrt{3}}{3}$.

11. From Exercise 9, we know that $x = -\sqrt{3}$ and $r = 2$. So, $\sec \theta = \dfrac{r}{x} = \dfrac{2}{-\sqrt{3}}$ or $-\dfrac{2\sqrt{3}}{3}$.

12. I, II   **13.** II, IV   **14.** II   **15.** III

For Exercises 16-21, sample answers given.

16. $0°, 360°$ **17.** $90°, 450°$ **18.** $90°, 270°$

19. $0°, 180°$ **20.** $180°, 540°$ **21.** $270°, -90°$

PAGES 260-262   EXERCISES

22. $r = \sqrt{x^2 + y^2} = \sqrt{5^2 + 12^2} = 13$

$\sin \theta = \dfrac{y}{r}$ or $\dfrac{12}{13}$ $\csc \theta = \dfrac{r}{y}$ or $\dfrac{13}{12}$

$\cos \theta = \dfrac{x}{r}$ or $\dfrac{5}{13}$ $\sec \theta = \dfrac{r}{x}$ or $\dfrac{13}{5}$

$\tan \theta = \dfrac{y}{x}$ or $\dfrac{12}{5}$ $\cot \theta = \dfrac{x}{y}$ or $\dfrac{5}{12}$

23. $r = \sqrt{x^2 + y^2} = \sqrt{15^2 + 8^2} = 17$

$\sin \theta = \dfrac{y}{r}$ or $\dfrac{8}{17}$ $\csc \theta = \dfrac{r}{y}$ or $\dfrac{17}{8}$

$\cos \theta = \dfrac{x}{r}$ or $\dfrac{15}{17}$ $\sec \theta = \dfrac{r}{x}$ or $\dfrac{17}{15}$

$\tan \theta = \dfrac{y}{x}$ or $\dfrac{8}{15}$ $\cot \theta = \dfrac{x}{y}$ or $\dfrac{15}{8}$

24. $r = \sqrt{x^2 + y^2} = \sqrt{3^2 + 4^2} = 5$

$\sin \theta = \dfrac{y}{r}$ or $\dfrac{4}{5}$ $\qquad$ $\csc \theta = \dfrac{r}{y}$ or $\dfrac{5}{4}$

$\cos \theta = \dfrac{x}{r}$ or $\dfrac{3}{5}$ $\qquad$ $\sec \theta = \dfrac{r}{x}$ or $\dfrac{5}{3}$

$\tan \theta = \dfrac{y}{x}$ or $\dfrac{4}{3}$ $\qquad$ $\cot \theta = \dfrac{x}{y}$ or $\dfrac{3}{4}$

25. $r = \sqrt{x^2 + y^2} = \sqrt{1^2 + (-8)^2} = \sqrt{65}$

$\sin \theta = \dfrac{y}{r}$ $\qquad$ $\csc \theta = \dfrac{r}{y}$

$\quad = \dfrac{-8}{\sqrt{65}}$ or $-\dfrac{8\sqrt{65}}{65}$ $\qquad = -\dfrac{\sqrt{65}}{8}$

$\cos \theta = \dfrac{x}{r}$ $\qquad$ $\sec \theta = \dfrac{r}{x}$

$\quad = \dfrac{1}{\sqrt{65}}$ or $\dfrac{\sqrt{65}}{65}$ $\qquad = \sqrt{65}$

$\tan \theta = \dfrac{y}{x}$ or -8 $\qquad$ $\cot \theta = \dfrac{x}{r}$ or $-\dfrac{1}{8}$

26. $r = \sqrt{x^2 + y^2} = \sqrt{(-3)^2 + 0^2} = 3$

$\sin \theta = \dfrac{y}{r}$ or 0 $\qquad$ $\csc \theta = \dfrac{r}{y}$

$\cos \theta = \dfrac{x}{r}$ or -1 $\qquad \quad = \dfrac{3}{0}$ undefined

$\tan \theta = \dfrac{y}{x}$ or 0 $\qquad$ $\sec \theta = \dfrac{r}{x}$ or -1

$\qquad\qquad\qquad\qquad$ $\cot \theta = \dfrac{x}{y}$

$\qquad\qquad\qquad\qquad\quad = \dfrac{-3}{0}$ undefined

27. $r = \sqrt{x^2 + y^2} = \sqrt{(-\sqrt{2})^2 + (\sqrt{2})^2} = 2$

$\sin \theta = \dfrac{y}{r}$ or $\dfrac{\sqrt{2}}{2}$ $\qquad$ $\csc \theta = \dfrac{r}{y}$

$\cos \theta = \dfrac{x}{r}$ or $-\dfrac{\sqrt{2}}{2}$ $\qquad = \dfrac{2}{\sqrt{2}}$ or $\sqrt{2}$

$\tan \theta = \dfrac{y}{x}$ or -1 $\qquad$ $\sec \theta = \dfrac{r}{x}$

$\qquad\qquad\qquad\qquad\quad = \dfrac{2}{-\sqrt{2}}$ or $-\sqrt{2}$

$\qquad\qquad\qquad\qquad$ $\cot \theta = \dfrac{x}{y}$ or -1

28. $r = \sqrt{x^2 + y^2} = \sqrt{5^2 + (-3)^2} = \sqrt{34}$

$\sin \theta = \dfrac{y}{r}$ $\qquad$ $\csc \theta = \dfrac{r}{y}$

$\quad = \dfrac{-3}{\sqrt{34}}$ or $\dfrac{-3\sqrt{34}}{34}$ $\qquad = -\dfrac{\sqrt{34}}{3}$

$\cos \theta = \dfrac{x}{r}$ $\qquad$ $\sec \theta = \dfrac{r}{x}$

$\quad = \dfrac{3}{\sqrt{34}}$ or $\dfrac{5\sqrt{34}}{34}$ $\qquad = \dfrac{\sqrt{34}}{5}$

$\tan \theta = \dfrac{y}{x}$ $\qquad$ $\cot \theta = \dfrac{x}{y}$

$\quad = -\dfrac{3}{5}$ $\qquad\qquad\qquad = -\dfrac{5}{3}$

29. $r = \sqrt{x^2 + y^2} = \sqrt{0^2 + 2^2} = 2$

$\sin \theta = \dfrac{y}{r}$ or 1 $\qquad$ $\csc \theta = \dfrac{r}{y}$ or 1

$\cos \theta = \dfrac{x}{r}$ or 0 $\qquad$ $\sec \theta = \dfrac{r}{x}$

$\tan \theta = \dfrac{y}{x}$ $\qquad\qquad\quad = \dfrac{2}{0}$ undefined

$\quad = \dfrac{2}{0}$ undefined $\qquad$ $\cot \theta = \dfrac{x}{y}$ or 0

30. $\sin \theta = \dfrac{y}{r} = -\dfrac{4}{5}$ $\qquad$ So, $r = 5$ and $y = -4$.

$r = \sqrt{x^2 + y^2}$

$5 = \sqrt{x^2 + 4^2}$

$25 = x^2 + 16$

$x = \pm 3$

Since θ is in Quadrant IV, $x = 3$.

$\cos \theta = \dfrac{x}{r}$ $\quad$ $\csc \theta = \dfrac{r}{y}$ $\quad$ $\cot \theta = \dfrac{x}{y}$

$\quad = \dfrac{3}{5}$ $\qquad\quad = -\dfrac{5}{4}$ $\qquad\quad = -\dfrac{3}{4}$

$\tan \theta = \dfrac{y}{x}$ $\quad$ $\sec \theta = \dfrac{r}{x}$

$\quad = -\dfrac{4}{3}$ $\qquad\quad = \dfrac{5}{3}$

31. $\cos \theta = \dfrac{x}{r} = -\dfrac{1}{2}$ $\qquad$ So, $r = 2$ and $x = -1$.

$r = \sqrt{x^2 + y^2}$

$2 = \sqrt{(-1)^2 + y^2}$

$4 = 1 + y^2$

$y = \pm\sqrt{3}$

Since θ is in Quadrant II, $y = \sqrt{3}$.

$\sin \theta = \dfrac{y}{r}$ $\qquad$ $\csc \theta = \dfrac{r}{y}$

$\quad = \dfrac{\sqrt{3}}{2}$ $\qquad\qquad = \dfrac{2}{\sqrt{3}}$ or $\dfrac{2\sqrt{3}}{3}$

$\tan \theta = \dfrac{y}{x}$ $\qquad$ $\sec \theta = \dfrac{r}{x}$

$\quad = \dfrac{\sqrt{3}}{-1}$ or $-\sqrt{3}$ $\qquad = \dfrac{2}{-1}$ or -2

$\qquad\qquad\qquad\qquad$ $\cot \theta = \dfrac{x}{y}$

$\qquad\qquad\qquad\qquad\quad = \dfrac{-1}{\sqrt{3}}$ or $-\dfrac{\sqrt{3}}{3}$

32. $\tan \theta = \dfrac{y}{x} = 2$

Since θ is in Quadrant I, $x = 1$ and $y = 2$.

$r = \sqrt{x^2 + y^2} = \sqrt{1^2 + 2^2} = \sqrt{5}$

$\sin \theta = \dfrac{y}{r}$ $\qquad$ $\csc \theta = \dfrac{r}{y}$

$\quad = \dfrac{2}{\sqrt{5}}$ or $\dfrac{2\sqrt{5}}{5}$ $\qquad = \dfrac{\sqrt{5}}{2}$

$\cos \theta = \dfrac{x}{r}$ $\qquad$ $\sec \theta = \dfrac{r}{x}$

$\quad = \dfrac{1}{\sqrt{5}}$ or $\dfrac{\sqrt{5}}{5}$ $\qquad = \dfrac{\sqrt{5}}{1}$ or $\sqrt{5}$

$\qquad\qquad\qquad\qquad$ $\cot \theta = \dfrac{x}{y} = \dfrac{1}{2}$

33. $\sec \theta = \dfrac{r}{x} = \sqrt{3}$ So, $r = \sqrt{3}$ and $x = 1$.

$$r = \sqrt{x^2 + y^2}$$
$$\sqrt{3} = \sqrt{1^2 + y^2}$$
$$3 = 1 + y^2$$
$$2 = y^2$$
$$\pm\sqrt{2} = y$$

Since θ is in Quadrant IV, $y = -\sqrt{2}$.

$$\sin \theta = \frac{y}{r} \qquad\qquad \csc \theta = \frac{r}{y}$$
$$= \frac{-\sqrt{2}}{\sqrt{3}} \text{ or } -\frac{\sqrt{6}}{3} \qquad = \frac{\sqrt{3}}{-\sqrt{2}} \text{ or } -\frac{\sqrt{6}}{2}$$

$$\cos \theta = \frac{x}{r} \qquad\qquad \cot \theta = \frac{x}{y}$$
$$= \frac{1}{\sqrt{3}} \text{ or } \frac{\sqrt{3}}{3} \qquad = \frac{1}{-\sqrt{2}} \text{ or } -\frac{\sqrt{2}}{2}$$

$$\tan \theta = \frac{y}{x}$$
$$= \frac{-\sqrt{2}}{1} \text{ or } -\sqrt{2}$$

34. zero **35.** positive **36.** negative

37. negative **38.** positive **39.** undefined

40. zero **41.** negative

42-45. See students' work.

46. If $\sin \theta = 2$, then $y = 2$ and $r = 1$. Since $r^2 = x^2 + y^2$, $1 = x^2 + 4$ or $x^2 = -3$ which is not possible.

47. Let $k = 2n$, where n is any integer. Then, $\sin (k90°) = \sin (2n \cdot 90°) = \sin (180° \cdot n)$. But $\sin (180° \cdot n) = \sin 0°$ for all integers n. Since $\sin 0° = 0$, $\sin (k90°) = 0$.

48. Let $k = 2n + 1$ where n is any integer. Then
$$\cos (k90°) = \cos ((2n + 1)90°)$$
$$= \cos (180°n + 90°).$$
The related angle for $(180°n + 90°) = 90°$
Thus, $\cos (180°n + 90°) = \cos 90° = 0$.

49. $\tan 35° = \dfrac{d}{250}$ **50.** $\sin \theta = \dfrac{y}{r}$
$$\sin 12° = \frac{v}{16}$$

51. $x^2 - 5 = 0$
$$x^2 = 5$$
$$x = \pm\sqrt{5}$$

52. $\begin{bmatrix} 6 & 5 \\ 8 & 4 \end{bmatrix} + \begin{bmatrix} a & b \\ c & d \end{bmatrix} = \begin{bmatrix} 0 & 0 \\ 0 & 0 \end{bmatrix}$

$$\begin{bmatrix} a & b \\ c & d \end{bmatrix} = \begin{bmatrix} -6 & -5 \\ -8 & -4 \end{bmatrix}$$

53. $x = \dfrac{-(7) \pm \sqrt{(-7)^2 - 4(3)(-20)}}{2(3)}$
$$= \frac{7 \pm \sqrt{49 + 240}}{6}$$
$$= \frac{7 \pm 17}{6}$$
$$x = \frac{24}{6} \text{ or } x = \frac{-10}{6}$$
$$= 4 \qquad\qquad = -\frac{5}{3}$$

54. $f(x) = x^4 - 8x^2 + 16$

$f'(x) = 4x^3 - 16x$ $\qquad\qquad$ $f''(x) = 12x^2 - 16$

$0 = 4x^3 - 16x$ $\qquad\qquad$ $0 = 12x^2 - 16$

$0 = 4x(x^2 - 4)$ $\qquad\qquad$ $0 = 3x^2 - 4$

$0 = x(x - 2)(x + 2)$ $\qquad\qquad$ $x^2 = \dfrac{4}{3}$

$x = 2, \; x = -2, \; x = 0$ $\qquad\qquad$ $x = \pm\dfrac{2\sqrt{3}}{3}$

$f(2) = (2)^4 - 8(2)^2 + 16 = 0$

$f\left(\dfrac{2\sqrt{3}}{3}\right) = \left(\dfrac{2\sqrt{3}}{3}\right)^4 - 8\left(\dfrac{2\sqrt{3}}{3}\right)^2 + 16 = \dfrac{64}{9}$

$f(-2) = (-2)^4 - 8(-2)^2 + 16 = 0$

$f\left(-\dfrac{2\sqrt{3}}{3}\right) = \left(-\dfrac{2\sqrt{3}}{3}\right)^4 - 8\left(-\dfrac{2\sqrt{3}}{3}\right)^2 + 16 = \dfrac{64}{9}$

$f(0) = (0)^4 - 8(0)^2 + 16 = 16$

The critical points are $(2, 0)$, $(-2, 0)$, $(0, 16)$, $\left(\dfrac{2\sqrt{3}}{3}, \dfrac{64}{9}\right)$, and $\left(-\dfrac{2\sqrt{3}}{3}, \dfrac{64}{9}\right)$.

$f(\pm2.01) \approx 0.00161$ $\qquad$ $f(\pm1.15) \approx 7.18$

$f(\pm2) = 0$ $\qquad\qquad$ $f\left(\pm\dfrac{2\sqrt{3}}{3}\right) = 7.11$

$f(\pm1.99) \approx 0.00159$

$f(0.01) \approx 15.999$ $\qquad$ $f(\pm1.16) \approx 7.05$

$f(0) = 16$

$f(-0.01) \approx 15.999$

minimums: $(\pm2, 0)$; maximum: $(0, 16)$; points of inflection: $\left(\pm\dfrac{2\sqrt{3}}{3}, \dfrac{64}{9}\right)$

55. $\underline{2|} \quad 1 \quad\;\; 0 \quad\;\; 2 \quad\;\; 3$

$\qquad\qquad \underline{\;\; 2 \quad 4 \quad 12}$

$\qquad\quad\;\; 1 \quad\;\; 2 \quad\;\; 6 \quad\; 15$

$x^2 + 2x + 6$ R15

56. $\dfrac{5\pi}{6} = \dfrac{5\pi}{6} \times \dfrac{180°}{\pi}$ $\qquad$ **57.** $v = r\dfrac{\theta}{t}$
$$= 150° \qquad\qquad\qquad = (0.10)\left(\frac{5 \cdot 2\pi}{1}\right)$$
$$\qquad\qquad\qquad\qquad\quad \approx 3.14 \text{ m/s}$$

58. Let n = the number of boxes.

(A) $2.98n \leq 15$ $\qquad$ (B) $3.25n \leq 20$
$\quad\;\; n \leq 5$ $\qquad\qquad\qquad n \leq 6$

Quantity B is greater. B

113

Mid-Chapter Review

1. $-\dfrac{3\pi}{4} = -\dfrac{3\pi}{4} \times \dfrac{180°}{\pi}$

$\qquad = -135°$

2. $405° = 405° \times \dfrac{\pi}{180°}$

$\qquad = \dfrac{9\pi}{4}$

3. $225° + 360° = 585°$

$225° - 360° = -135°$

4. $\dfrac{5\pi}{8}$ is in Quadrant II.

$\alpha' = \pi - \alpha$

$\quad = \pi - \dfrac{5\pi}{8}$

$\quad = \dfrac{3\pi}{8}$

5. $32° = 32° \times \dfrac{\pi}{180°}$

$\quad = \dfrac{8\pi}{45}$

$s = r\theta$

$\quad = 11\left(\dfrac{8\pi}{45}\right)$

$\quad \approx 6.1 \text{ cm}$

6. $A = \dfrac{1}{2}r^2\theta$

$\quad = \dfrac{1}{2}(7.5)^2(0.8)$

$\quad = 22.5 \text{ cm}^2$

7. $100° = 100° \times \dfrac{\pi}{180°}$

$\quad = \dfrac{5\pi}{9}$

$A = \dfrac{1}{2}r^2\theta$

$\quad = \dfrac{1}{2}(100)^2\left(\dfrac{5\pi}{9}\right)$

$\quad \approx 8700 \text{ ft}^2$

8. $r = \sqrt{x^2 + y^2}$ $\sin \alpha = \dfrac{y}{r}$ or $\dfrac{3}{5}$ $\csc \alpha = \dfrac{r}{y}$ or $\dfrac{5}{3}$

$\quad = \sqrt{4^2 + 3^2}$ $\cos \alpha = \dfrac{x}{r}$ or $\dfrac{4}{5}$ $\sec \alpha = \dfrac{r}{x}$ or $\dfrac{5}{4}$

$\quad = 5$ $\tan \alpha = \dfrac{y}{x}$ or $\dfrac{3}{4}$ $\cot \alpha = \dfrac{x}{y}$ or $\dfrac{4}{3}$

5. $\tan 60° = \sqrt{3}$

6. $450°$ is coterminal with $90°$.

$\cos 450° = \cos 90° = 0$

7. $-\dfrac{3\pi}{4}$ is coterminal with $\dfrac{5\pi}{4}$ in Quadrant III.

$\alpha' = \alpha - \pi$

$\quad = \dfrac{5\pi}{4} - \pi$

$\quad = \dfrac{\pi}{4}$

$\sin\left(-\dfrac{3\pi}{4}\right) = -\sin\dfrac{\pi}{4}$

$\qquad\qquad = -\dfrac{\sqrt{2}}{2}$

8. $\csc\dfrac{\pi}{2} = \dfrac{1}{\sin\dfrac{\pi}{2}}$

$\qquad = \dfrac{1}{1}$ or 1

9. $\sec 30° = \dfrac{1}{\cos 30°}$

$\qquad = \dfrac{1}{\dfrac{\sqrt{3}}{2}}$

$\qquad = \dfrac{2}{\sqrt{3}}$ or $\dfrac{2\sqrt{3}}{3}$

10. $\dfrac{8\pi}{3}$ is coterminal with $\dfrac{2\pi}{3}$ in Quadrant II.

$\alpha' = \pi - \alpha$

$\quad = \pi - \dfrac{2\pi}{3}$

$\quad = \dfrac{\pi}{3}$

$\cot\dfrac{8\pi}{3} = -\cot\dfrac{\pi}{3}$

$\qquad = -\dfrac{\cos\dfrac{\pi}{3}}{\sin\dfrac{\pi}{3}}$

$\qquad = -\dfrac{\dfrac{1}{2}}{\dfrac{\sqrt{3}}{2}}$

$\qquad = -\dfrac{\sqrt{3}}{3}$

11. 0.7431 12. 1.6733 13. 0.5774

14. $\sin\dfrac{3\pi}{2} = -1$

$\cos\dfrac{3\pi}{2} = 0$

$\tan\dfrac{3\pi}{2} = \dfrac{-1}{0}$ undefined

$\csc\dfrac{3\pi}{2} = \dfrac{1}{\sin\dfrac{3\pi}{2}}$

$\qquad = \dfrac{1}{-1}$ or -1

$\sec\dfrac{3\pi}{2} = \dfrac{1}{\cos\dfrac{3\pi}{2}}$

$\qquad = \dfrac{1}{0}$ undefined

$\cot\dfrac{3\pi}{2} = \dfrac{0}{-1}$

$\qquad = 0$

5-4   Trigonometric Functions of Special Angles

1. Some of the trigonometric functions for quadrantal angles are undefined because division by zero is undefined. For example, if $\theta = 90°$, $\tan\theta = \dfrac{1}{0}$ which is undefined.

2. Sample answer: Using a TI-34, enter 79 COS 1/x.

3. Choose $P(x, y)$ on the terminal side of the $45°$ angle so that $r = \sqrt{2}$. It follows that $x = 1$ and $y = 1$. Therefore, $\sin 45° = \dfrac{\sqrt{2}}{2}$, $\cos 45° = \dfrac{\sqrt{2}}{2}$, $\tan 45° = 1$, $\csc 45° = \sqrt{2}$, $\sec 45° = \sqrt{2}$, $\cot 45° = 1$.

4. Sample answer: $90°$, $270°$, $450°$

15. $\csc 90° = \dfrac{1}{\sin 90°}$

$\qquad = \dfrac{1}{1}$ or 1

16. $\cos 60° = \dfrac{1}{2}$

114

17. $\sin \frac{\pi}{3} = \frac{\sqrt{3}}{2}$

18. $\frac{9\pi}{4}$ is coterminal with $\frac{\pi}{4}$ in Quadrant I.

$\tan \frac{9\pi}{4} = \tan \frac{\pi}{4}$

$= 1$

19. $\frac{7\pi}{3}$ is coterminal with $\frac{\pi}{3}$ in Quadrant 1.

$\sec \frac{7\pi}{3} = \sec \frac{\pi}{3}$

$= \frac{1}{\cos \frac{\pi}{3}}$

$= \frac{1}{\cos \frac{\pi}{3}}$

$= \frac{1}{\frac{1}{2}}$

$= 2$

20. $\cot 45° = \frac{1}{\tan 45°}$

$= \frac{1}{1}$ or 1

21. $\sec 270° = \frac{1}{\cos 270°}$

$= \frac{1}{0}$

undefined

22. $\alpha' = \pi - \alpha$

$= \pi - \frac{5\pi}{6}$

$= \frac{\pi}{6}$

$\cos \frac{5\pi}{6} = -\cos \frac{\pi}{6}$

$= -\frac{\sqrt{3}}{2}$

23. $\alpha' = \alpha - \pi$

$= \frac{7\pi}{6} - \pi$

$= \frac{\pi}{6}$

$\sin \frac{7\pi}{6} = -\sin \frac{\pi}{6}$

$= -\frac{1}{2}$

24. $-\frac{7\pi}{2}$ is coterminal with $\frac{\pi}{2}$.

$\csc \left(-\frac{7\pi}{2} \right) = \csc \frac{\pi}{2}$

$= \frac{1}{\sin \frac{\pi}{2}}$

$= \frac{1}{1}$ or 1

25. 3π is coterminal with π.

$\tan 3\pi = \tan \pi$

$= \frac{0}{-1}$

$= 0$

26. $\frac{19\pi}{3}$ is coterminal with $\frac{\pi}{3}$.

$\cot \frac{19\pi}{3} = \cot \frac{\pi}{3}$

$= \frac{\cos \frac{\pi}{3}}{\sin \frac{\pi}{3}}$

$= \frac{\frac{1}{2}}{\frac{\sqrt{3}}{2}}$

$= \frac{\sqrt{3}}{3}$

27. -0.1763 28. -0.1736 29. -2.6695

30. 0.6570 31. -0.1584 32. 1.7531

33. $115°40' = 115.6667°$

$\tan 115.6667° \approx -2.0809$

34. $72°30'30'' = 72.5083°$

$\cos 72.5083° \approx 0.3006$

35. 0.8288

36. $r = \sqrt{x^2 + y^2}$

$1 = \sqrt{x^2 + y^2}$

$1 = x^2 + y^2$

$x = \pm\sqrt{1 - y^2}$

Substitute into $y = 5x$.

$y = 5x$

$y = 5\left(\pm\sqrt{1 - y^2} \right)$

$y^2 = 25(1 - y^2)$

$y^2 = 25 - 25y^2$

$26y^2 = 25$

$y^2 = \frac{25}{26}$

$y = \pm\frac{5\sqrt{26}}{26}$

Since θ is in Quadrant III, $y = -\frac{5\sqrt{26}}{26}$.

$x = \pm\sqrt{1 - y^2}$

$= \pm\sqrt{1 - \left(-\frac{5\sqrt{26}}{26} \right)^2}$

$= \pm\sqrt{1 - \frac{25}{26}}$

$= \pm\frac{\sqrt{26}}{26}$

Since θ is in Quadrant III, $x = -\frac{\sqrt{26}}{26}$.

Now, find six trigonometric functions.

$\sin \theta = -\frac{5\sqrt{26}}{26}$

$\csc \theta = \frac{1}{\sin \theta}$

$= -\frac{\sqrt{26}}{5}$

$\cos \theta = -\frac{\sqrt{26}}{26}$

$\tan \theta = \frac{-\frac{5\sqrt{26}}{26}}{-\frac{\sqrt{26}}{26}}$

$= 5$

$\sec \theta = \frac{1}{\cos \theta}$

$= -\sqrt{26}$

$\cot \theta = \frac{1}{\tan \theta}$

$= \frac{1}{5}$

37. $\frac{\sin \theta_1}{\sin \theta_2} = k$

$\frac{\sin 52°}{\sin 31.3°} = k$

$1.52 \approx k$

38. $x = t\left(\frac{\sin (B - A)}{\cos A} \right)$

$= 10\left(\frac{\sin (60° - 41°)}{\cos 41°} \right)$

≈ 4.31 cm

115

39. $m = \dfrac{3-5}{6-2}$

$\quad = \dfrac{-2}{4}$ or $-\dfrac{1}{2}$

$y = mx + b$

$3 = -\dfrac{1}{2}(6) + b$

$3 = -3 + b$

$6 = b$

$y = -\dfrac{1}{2}x + 6$

40. $f(x) = 2x^2$

$f'(x) = 4x$

$f'(2) = 4(2)$

$\qquad = 8$

The slope is 8.

41. $\dfrac{1}{9} + \dfrac{1}{2a} = \dfrac{1}{a}$

$18a\left(\dfrac{1}{9} + \dfrac{1}{2a}\right) = 18a\left(\dfrac{1}{a}\right)$

$2a + 9 = 18$

$a = \dfrac{9}{2}$

42. $35°20'55'' = 35° + 20'\left(\dfrac{1°}{60'}\right) + 55''\left(\dfrac{1°}{3600''}\right)$

$\qquad \approx 35.349°$

43. $v = r\dfrac{\theta}{t}$

$\quad = 75\left(\dfrac{2\pi}{6}\right)$

$\quad = 25\pi$ m/h

44. $\tan \theta = \dfrac{y}{x} = -\dfrac{3}{4}$

Since θ is in Quadrant IV,

$y = -3$ and $x = 4$.

$r = \sqrt{x^2 + y^2}$

$\quad = \sqrt{4^2 + (-3)^2}$

$\quad = 5$

$\sin \theta = \dfrac{y}{r} = -\dfrac{3}{5}$

45. If $\dfrac{x}{y}$ and $\dfrac{y}{z}$ are positive integers, then y is a divisor of x and z is a divisor of y. Thus, z must be a divisor of x. Therefore, $\dfrac{x}{z}$ is also a positive integer. However, since z is a divisor of x and by definition, they are not the same number, $\dfrac{z}{x}$ cannot be a positive integer. Thus, the best answer is C.

5-5 Right Triangles

PAGE 273 CHECKING FOR UNDERSTANDING

1. $\sin A = \cos B$; for two angles in a right triangle, neither of which is a right angle, the sine of one angle is equal to the cosine of the other.

2.

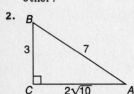

3. Answers may vary.

4. $\sin 20° = \dfrac{a}{35}$

5. $\tan 76° = \dfrac{a}{13}$

---

6. $\cos B = \dfrac{1}{2}$

7. $\tan A = \dfrac{21.2}{9}$

8. $\cos 16° = \dfrac{a}{13}$

9. $\tan 49°13' = \dfrac{10}{b}$

10. $7^2 + b^2 = 16^2$

11. $\tan A = \dfrac{7}{12}$

12. $5^2 + 6^2 = c^2$

13. $57°30' = 57.5°$

$\cos 57.5° = \dfrac{\frac{1}{2}(7.5)}{C}$

$c \approx 7.0$ cm

$\tan 57.5° = \dfrac{a}{\frac{1}{2}(7.5)}$

$a \approx 5.9$ cm

14. $\tan \theta = \dfrac{250}{176}$

$\theta \approx 54.85°$

$54.85° = 54° + 0.85°\left(\dfrac{60'}{1°}\right)$

$\approx 54°51'$

15. $B = 90° - 41° = 49°$

$\sin 49° = \dfrac{7.44}{c}$, $c \approx 9.9$

$\tan 41° = \dfrac{a}{7.44}$, $a \approx 6.5$

16. $A = 47°50'$

$\sin 47°50' = \dfrac{9}{c}$, $c \approx 12.1$

$\sin 42°10' = \dfrac{b}{12.1}$, $b \approx 8.1$

17. $B = 67°38'$

$\sin 67°38' = \dfrac{22}{c}$, $c \approx 23.8$

$\sin 22°22' = \dfrac{a}{23.8}$, $a \approx 9.1$

18. $\sin A = \dfrac{21}{30}$, $A \approx 44°25'$

$B \approx 45°35'$

$\sin 45°35' \approx \dfrac{b}{30}$, $b \approx 21.4$

19. $B = 45°$

$\sin 45° = \dfrac{a}{7\sqrt{2}}$

$a = 7$, $b = 7$

20. $\sin A = \dfrac{31.2}{42.4}$, $A \approx 47°22'$

$B \approx 42°38'$

$\sin 42°38' \approx \dfrac{b}{42.4}$, $b \approx 28.7$

21. $B = 52°45'$

$\tan 37°15' = \dfrac{a}{11}$, $a \approx 8.4$

$\cos 37°15' = \dfrac{11}{c}$, $c \approx 13.8$

22. $\tan A = \dfrac{11}{21}$, $A \approx 27°38'$

$B \approx 62°22'$

$\sin 27°38' \approx \dfrac{11}{c}$, $c \approx 23.7$

23. $B = 34°5'$

$\sin 55°55' = \dfrac{a}{16}$, $a \approx 13.3$

$\sin 34° = \dfrac{b}{16}$, $b \approx 9.0$

24. $A = 11°52'$

$\cos 78°8' = \dfrac{41}{c}$, $c \approx 199.4$

$\tan 78°8' = \dfrac{b}{41}$, $b \approx 195.1$

25. side: $\tan 36° = \dfrac{\frac{1}{2}s}{7.43}$

$\dfrac{1}{2}s \approx 5.40$

$s \approx 10.80$ cm

radius: $\cos 36° = \dfrac{7.43}{r}$

$r \approx 9.18$ cm

26. $\tan a = \dfrac{17.5}{26.2}$

$\tan a \approx 0.6679$

$a \approx 33°44'$

27. $\sin \dfrac{41°}{2} = \dfrac{3.7}{r}$

$r = \dfrac{3.7}{\sin 20°30'}$

≈ 10.57 cm

28. Let M represent the point of intersection of the altitude and $\overline{AB}$. Since $\triangle ABC$ is isosceles, the altitude bisects $\overline{AB}$. Thus, $\triangle AMC$ is a right triangle. Therefore, $\sin \theta = \dfrac{x}{a}$ or $a \sin \theta = x$ and $\tan \theta = \dfrac{x}{0.5b}$ or $\dfrac{b \tan \theta}{2} = x$.

29. $c^2 = a^2 + b^2$

$6^2 = a^2 + 4^2$

$a = \sqrt{6^2 - 4^2}$

$= \sqrt{20}$ or about 4.47 m

30. a. altitude = $70t$

b. $70(3.5) = 245$ ft

$70(22) = 1540$ ft

$70(60) = 4200$ ft

$\tan \theta = \dfrac{70t}{420}$

c. $\tan \theta = \dfrac{245}{420}$

$\theta \approx 30°15'$

$\tan \theta = \dfrac{1540}{420}$

$\theta \approx 74°45'$

$\tan \theta = \dfrac{4200}{420}$

$\theta \approx 84°17'$

31. $\tan \theta = \dfrac{169.29}{201.2}$

$\theta \approx 40°$

32. $\tan 49°42' = \dfrac{1235}{c}$

$c \approx 1047$

$\tan 26°27' = \dfrac{1235}{d}$

$d \approx 2482$

$2482 - 1047 = 1435$ ft

33. $\tan \theta = \dfrac{1.7}{3}$

$\theta \approx 29°32'$

34. $\tan \angle QCP = \dfrac{23,300}{3963}$

≈ 5.8794

$m\angle QCP \approx 80°21'$

$\sin 80°21' = \dfrac{x}{3963}$

$0.9859 \approx \dfrac{x}{3963}$

$3907 \approx x$

35. $P(-2) = (-2)^3 - 3(-2)^2 - 2(-2) + 4$

$= -8 - 12 + 4 + 4$

$= -12$

-2 is not a root.

36. $210°$ is in Quadrant III.

$\alpha' = \alpha - 180°$

$= 210° - 180°$

$= 30°$

37. I, III

38. $\sin \dfrac{\pi}{4} = \dfrac{\sqrt{2}}{2}$

$\cos \dfrac{\pi}{4} = \dfrac{\sqrt{2}}{2}$

$\tan \dfrac{\pi}{4} = 1$

39. $A = \pi\left(\dfrac{1}{2}\right)^2 + \pi(1)^2$

$= \dfrac{5\pi}{4}$

The best answer is C.

Case Study Follow-Up

PAGE 275

1. $\tan 28° = \dfrac{b}{\frac{1}{2}(48)}$

$b \approx 12.8$ ft

2. $A = s^2$

$2080 = s^2$

$s \approx 45.6$

$\tan 20° \approx \dfrac{b}{\frac{1}{2}(45.6)}$

$b \approx 8.3$ feet

3. See students' work.

5-6	**The Law of Sines**

PAGE 280   CHECKING FOR UNDERSTANDING

1. Sample answer: One condition for which the law of sines can be used to solve $\triangle ABC$ is when the measure of A is known and the measure of a and b is also known.

2. Sample answer: When the measures of a, b, and A are known, $m\angle A < 90°$, and $a < b \sin A$, the triangle has no solution. If $m\angle A \geq 90°$ and $a \leq b$, the triangle also has no solution.

3.

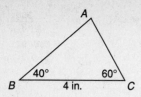

4. $\dfrac{20}{\sin 40^\circ} = \dfrac{b}{\sin 60^\circ}$ 5. $\dfrac{2.8}{\sin 61^\circ} = \dfrac{a}{\sin 53^\circ}$

6. $\dfrac{14}{\sin 50^\circ} = \dfrac{10}{\sin B}$ 7. $\dfrac{16}{\sin 42^\circ} = \dfrac{12}{\sin C}$

8. none, since $3 \le 10$

9. one, since $11 > 10 \sin 17^\circ$ and $11 > 10$

$$\dfrac{11}{\sin 17^\circ} = \dfrac{10}{\sin A}$$

$$\sin A = \dfrac{10 \sin 17^\circ}{11}$$

$$\sin A \approx 0.2658$$

$$A \approx 15^\circ 25'$$

$$\dfrac{11}{\sin 17^\circ} = \dfrac{b}{\sin 147^\circ 35'}, \; b \approx 20.2$$

$$B \approx 180^\circ - 17^\circ - 15^\circ 25' \approx 147^\circ 35'$$

10. one, since $4 = 8 \sin 30^\circ$

It is a 30°-60° right triangle. So, $B = 90^\circ$.

$C = 90^\circ - 30^\circ$ $8^2 = 4^2 + c^2$

$\quad = 60^\circ$ $c \approx 6.9$

11. none, since $A + B > 180^\circ$

12. one, since $\sqrt{3} = 2 \sin 60^\circ$

It is a 30°-60° right triangle. So, $B = 90^\circ$.

$C = 90^\circ - 60^\circ$ $2^2 = (\sqrt{3})^2 + c^2$

$\quad = 30^\circ$ $c = 1$

13. two, since $10 \sin 38^\circ < 8 < 10$

$$\dfrac{8}{\sin 38^\circ} = \dfrac{10}{\sin B}$$

$$\sin B = \dfrac{10 \sin 38^\circ}{8}$$

$$B \approx 50^\circ 19' \text{ or } 129^\circ 41'$$

$$C_1 \approx 180^\circ - 38^\circ - 50^\circ 19' \approx 91^\circ 41'$$

$$\dfrac{8}{\sin 38^\circ} \approx \dfrac{c_1}{\sin 91^\circ 41'}$$

$$c_1 \approx 13.0$$

$$C_2 \approx 180^\circ - 38^\circ - 129^\circ 41' \approx 12^\circ 19'$$

$$\dfrac{8}{\sin 38^\circ} \approx \dfrac{c_2}{\sin 12^\circ 19'}$$

$$c_2 \approx 2.8$$

One solution is $B \approx 50^\circ 19'$, $C_1 \approx 91^\circ 41'$,
$C_1 \approx 13.0$.
Another solution is $B \approx 129^\circ 41'$, $C_2 \approx 12^\circ 19'$,
$C_2 \approx 2.8$.

14. one; $C = 74^\circ$

$$\dfrac{8}{\sin 49^\circ} = \dfrac{b}{\sin 57^\circ} = \dfrac{c}{\sin 74^\circ}$$

$$b = \dfrac{8 \sin 57^\circ}{\sin 49^\circ} \approx \dfrac{8(0.8387)}{(0.7547)} \approx 8.9$$

$$c = \dfrac{8 \sin 74^\circ}{\sin 49^\circ} \approx \dfrac{8(0.9613)}{(0.7547)} \approx 10.2$$

15. $A \ge 90^\circ$ and $6 \le 8$, therefore no solution exists.

16. two; $\dfrac{26}{\sin 58^\circ} = \dfrac{29}{\sin B}$

$$\sin B = \dfrac{29 \sin 58^\circ}{26}$$

$$B \approx 71^\circ 4' \text{ or } 108^\circ 56'$$

$$C_1 \approx 180^\circ - 58^\circ - 71^\circ 4' \approx 50^\circ 56'$$

$$\dfrac{c_1}{\sin 50^\circ 56'} \approx \dfrac{26}{\sin 58^\circ}$$

$$c_1 \approx \dfrac{26 \sin 50^\circ 56'}{\sin 58^\circ} \approx 23.8$$

$$C_2 \approx 180^\circ - 58^\circ - 108^\circ 56' \approx 13^\circ 4'$$

$$\dfrac{c_2}{\sin 13^\circ 4'} \approx \dfrac{26}{\sin 58^\circ}$$

$$c_2 \approx \dfrac{26 \sin 13^\circ 4'}{\sin 58^\circ} \approx 6.9$$

One solution is $B \approx 71^\circ 4'$, $C \approx 50^\circ 56'$, $c \approx 23.8$.
Another solution is $B \approx 108^\circ 56'$, $C \approx 13^\circ 4'$,
$c \approx 6.9$.

17. one; $C = 80^\circ$

$$\dfrac{a}{\sin 40^\circ} = \dfrac{b}{\sin 60^\circ} = \dfrac{20}{\sin 80^\circ}$$

$$a = \dfrac{20 \sin 40^\circ}{\sin 80^\circ} \approx 13.1 \qquad b = \dfrac{20 \sin 60^\circ}{\sin 80^\circ} \approx 17.6$$

18. one; $A = 52^\circ$

$$\dfrac{84}{\sin 52^\circ} = \dfrac{b}{\sin 70^\circ} = \dfrac{c}{\sin 58^\circ}$$

$$b = \dfrac{84 \sin 70^\circ}{\sin 52^\circ} \approx 100.2$$

$$c = \dfrac{84 \sin 58^\circ}{\sin 52^\circ} \approx 90.4$$

19. none

20. two; $\dfrac{125}{\sin 25^\circ} = \dfrac{150}{\sin B}$

$$\sin B = \frac{150 \sin 25^\circ}{125}$$

$$B \approx 30^\circ 28' \text{ or } 149^\circ 32'$$

$$C_1 \approx 180^\circ - 25^\circ - 30^\circ 28' \approx 124^\circ 32'$$

$$\frac{c_1}{\sin 124^\circ 32'} \approx \frac{125}{\sin 25^\circ}$$

$$c_1 \approx 243.7$$

$$C_2 \approx 180^\circ - 25^\circ - 149^\circ 32' \approx 5^\circ 28'$$

$$\frac{c_2}{\sin 5^\circ 28'} \approx \frac{125}{\sin 25^\circ}$$

$$c_2 \approx 28.2$$

One solution is $B \approx 30^\circ 28'$, $C \approx 124^\circ 32'$, $c \approx 243.7$.

Another solution is $B \approx 149^\circ 32'$, $C \approx 5^\circ 28'$, $c \approx 28.2$.

21. none

22. one; $C = 180^\circ - 37^\circ 20' - 51^\circ 30' = 91^\circ 10'$

$$\frac{a}{\sin 37^\circ 20'} = \frac{b}{\sin 51^\circ 30'} = \frac{125}{\sin 91^\circ 10'}$$

$$a = \frac{125 \sin 37^\circ 20'}{\sin 91^\circ 10'} \approx 75.8$$

$$b = \frac{125 \sin 51^\circ 30'}{\sin 91^\circ 10'} \approx 97.8$$

23. none

24. one; $\dfrac{17.2}{\sin 107^\circ 13'} = \dfrac{12.2}{\sin C}$

$$\sin C = \frac{12.2 \sin 107^\circ 13'}{17.2}$$

$$C \approx 42^\circ 39'$$

$$B \approx 180^\circ - 107^\circ 13' - 42^\circ 39' \approx 30^\circ 8'$$

$$\frac{b}{\sin 30^\circ 8'} \approx \frac{17.2}{\sin 107^\circ 13'},$$

$$b \approx 9.0$$

25.
$$\frac{\sin A}{a} = \frac{\sin C}{c}$$

$$\frac{\sin A}{\sin C} = \frac{a}{c}$$

$$\frac{\sin A}{\sin C} - 1 = \frac{a}{c} - 1$$

$$\frac{\sin A - \sin C}{\sin C} = \frac{a - c}{c}$$

26. By the results of Exercise 25,

$$\frac{\sin B - \sin B}{\sin C} = \frac{b - c}{c},$$

so $\dfrac{\sin B - \sin C}{b - c} = \dfrac{\sin C}{c}.$

Also, $\dfrac{\sin B}{b} = \dfrac{\sin C}{c}$, so $\dfrac{\sin B}{\sin C} = \dfrac{b}{c}.$

Thus, $\dfrac{\sin B}{\sin C} + 1 = \dfrac{b}{c} + 1$

$$\frac{\sin B + \sin C}{\sin C} = \frac{b + c}{c}.$$

$$\frac{\sin B + \sin C}{b + c} = \frac{\sin C}{c}.$$

Therefore, $\dfrac{\sin B + \sin C}{b + c} = \dfrac{\sin B - \sin C}{b - c}$ and

$$\frac{b + c}{b - c} = \frac{\sin B + \sin C}{\sin B - \sin C}.$$

27. $\dfrac{\sin A}{a} = \dfrac{\sin B}{b}$

$$\frac{a}{\sin A} = \frac{b}{\sin B}$$

$$\frac{a}{b} = \frac{\sin A}{\sin B}$$

28. $\dfrac{\sin B}{b} = \dfrac{\sin A}{a}$

$$\frac{a}{b} = \frac{\sin A}{\sin B}$$

$$\frac{a}{b} + 1 = \frac{\sin A}{\sin B} + 1$$

$$\frac{a + b}{b} = \frac{\sin A + \sin B}{\sin B}$$

$$\frac{b}{a + b} = \frac{\sin B}{\sin A + \sin B}$$

29. Let $\angle A \cong \angle X$, $\angle B \cong \angle Y$, and $\angle C \cong \angle Z$. Applying the law of sines, $\dfrac{a}{\sin A} = \dfrac{b}{\sin B} = \dfrac{c}{\sin C}$ and $\dfrac{x}{\sin X} = \dfrac{y}{\sin Y} = \dfrac{z}{\sin Z}$. Thus, $\sin A = \dfrac{a \sin B}{b}$ and $\sin X = \dfrac{x \sin Y}{y}$. Since $A = X$, $\dfrac{a \sin B}{b} = \dfrac{x \sin Y}{y}$. However, $B = Y$ so $\dfrac{a}{b} = \dfrac{x}{y}$ or $\dfrac{a}{x} = \dfrac{b}{y}$. Similar proportions can be derived for c and z.

30. a. Since $450 \sin 12^\circ < 316 < 450$, there are two possible solutions.

$$\frac{316}{\sin 12^\circ} = \frac{450}{\sin \theta}$$

$$\theta \approx 17^\circ 13' \text{ or } 162^\circ 47'$$

turn angle $\approx 180^\circ - 162^\circ 47'$

$\approx 17^\circ 13'$ east of north

b. $180^\circ - 12^\circ - 162^\circ 47' \approx 5^\circ 13'$

$$\frac{316}{\sin 12^\circ} \approx \frac{a}{\sin 5^\circ 13'}$$

$$a \approx 138.19$$

$$d = rt$$

$$138.19 \approx 23t$$

$$t \approx 6 \text{ hours}$$

c. $180^\circ - 160^\circ - 12^\circ = 8^\circ$

$$\frac{200}{\sin 8^\circ} = \frac{c}{\sin 160^\circ}$$

$$c \approx 491.5 \text{ miles}$$

Since $491.5 \neq 450$, the ship will not reach port.

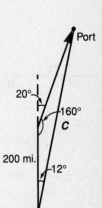

31. $180° = 85° + 2\theta$

$\theta = 47.5°$

$$\frac{60}{\sin 47.5°} = \frac{a}{\sin 85°}$$

$a \approx 81.1$

perimeter $\approx 60 + 60 + 81.1$

≈ 201.1 ft

32.
$$\frac{8}{x - 3} = \frac{x + 5}{x - 3}$$

$$(x - 3)\left(\frac{8}{x - 3}\right) = (x - 3)\left(\frac{x + 5}{x - 3}\right)$$

$$8 = x + 5$$

$$x = 3$$

But x cannot equal 3 because you cannot have 0 in the denominator. So there is no solution.

33. $45° + 360k°$, where k is an integer

34. $\frac{13\pi}{6}$ is coterminal with $\frac{\pi}{6}$.

$$\sin \frac{13\pi}{6} = \sin \frac{\pi}{6}$$

$$= \frac{1}{2}$$

35. $\tan 27° = \frac{h}{25}$

$h \approx 12.7$ meters

36. first month: $500

second month: $500 + (0.1)(500) = \$550$

third month: $550 + (0.1)(550) = \$605$

fourth month: $605 + (0.1)(605) = \$665.50$

The best answer is D.

Technology: Solving Triangles

PAGE 282   EXERCISES

1. $C = 79°$, $b = 21$, $c = 24$
2. $C = 80°$, $b = 27$, $c = 31$
3. $C = 66°$, $b = 4$, $c = 3$

5-7   The Law of Cosines

PAGES 285-286   CHECKING FOR UNDERSTANDING

1. Sample answer: In any triangle, the length of a side squared is the sum of the squares of the other two sides minus the product of twice the other two sides and the cosine of the angle opposite the first side.

2. Sample answer: If the included angle measures 90°, the equation becomes $c^2 = a^2 + b^2 - 2ab \cos 90°$. Since $\cos 90° = 0$, $c^2 = a^2 + b^2 - 2ab(0)$ or $c^2 = a^2 + b^2$.

3. Use the law of cosines to find a. Then use the law of sines to find C.

4. a.

b. no

5. law of cosines

$14^2 = 15^2 + 16^2 - 2 \cdot 15 \cdot 16 \cos A$, $A \approx 53°35'$

$$\frac{14}{\sin 53°35'} = \frac{15}{\sin B}, \ B \approx 59°33'$$

$C \approx 180° - 53°35' - 59°33' \approx 66°52'$

6. law of cosines

$c^2 = 11^2 + 10.5^2 - 2 \cdot 11 \cdot 10.5 \cos 35°$

$c \approx 6.5$

$$\frac{6.5}{\sin 35°} \approx \frac{11}{\sin A}, \ A \approx 76°5'$$

$B \approx 180° - 76°5' - 35° \approx 68°55'$

7. law of sines

$\sin C = \frac{8 \sin 40°}{10}$, $C \approx 30°57'$

$B \approx 109°3'$

$b \approx \frac{10 \sin 109°3'}{\sin 40°} \approx 14.7$

8. law of cosines

$a^2 = 6^2 + 7^2 - 2 \cdot 6 \cdot 7 \cos 40°$, $a \approx 4.5$

$\sin B \approx \frac{6 \sin 40°}{4.5}$, $B \approx 58°59'$

$C \approx 81°1'$

9. law of cosines

$b^2 = 14^2 + 21^2 - 2 \cdot 14 \cdot 21 \cos 60°$, $b \approx 18.5$

$\sin C \approx \frac{21 \sin 60°}{18.5}$, $C \approx 79°3'$

$A \approx 40°57'$

10. law of sines

$$\frac{14}{\sin 70°} = \frac{a}{\sin 40°}, \ a \approx 9.6$$

$B = 70°$

$$\frac{14}{\sin 70°} = \frac{14}{\sin 70°}, \ b \approx 14$$

11. law of sines

$$\frac{17}{\sin 45°28'} = \frac{12}{\sin A}, \quad A \approx 30°13'$$

$$C \approx 104°19'$$

$$c \approx \frac{17 \sin 104°19'}{\sin 45°28'} \approx 23.1$$

12. law of cosines

$$a^2 = 4^2 + 2.9^2 - 2 \cdot 4 \cdot 2.9 \cos 28°50', \quad a \approx 2.0$$

$$\sin B \approx \frac{4 \sin 28°50'}{2.0}, \quad B \approx 105°18'$$

$$C \approx 45°52'$$

13. $a^2 = 75^2 + 319^2 - 2(75)(319) \cos 15°$

$$a \approx 247.3 \text{ miles}$$

PAGES 286-287   EXERCISES

14. $4^2 = 5^2 + 7^2 - 2 \cdot 5 \cdot 7 \cos A, \quad A \approx 34°3'$

$$\frac{4}{\sin 34°3'} = \frac{5}{\sin B}, \quad B \approx 44°25'$$

$$C \approx 101°32'$$

15. $a^2 = 7^2 + 10^2 - 2 \cdot 7 \cdot 10 \cos 51°, \quad a \approx 7.8$

$$\frac{7.8}{\sin 51°} \approx \frac{7}{\sin B}, \quad B \approx 44°13'$$

$$C \approx 84°47'$$

16. $a^2 = 540^2 + 490^2 - 2 \cdot 540 \cdot 490 \cos 52°40'$

$$a \approx 459.1$$

$$\frac{459.1}{\sin 52°40'} \approx \frac{540}{\sin B}, \quad B \approx 69°16'$$

$$C \approx 58°4'$$

17. $5^2 = 6^2 + 7^2 - 2 \cdot 6 \cdot 7 \cos A, \quad A \approx 44°25'$

$$\frac{5}{\sin 44°25'} \approx \frac{6}{\sin B}, \quad B \approx 57°7'$$

$$C \approx 78°28'$$

18. $a^2 = 191^2 + 205^2 - 2 \cdot 191 \cdot 205 \cos 61°25'$

$$a \approx 202.6$$

$$\frac{202.6}{\sin 61°25'} \approx \frac{191}{\sin B}, \quad B \approx 55°53'$$

$$C \approx 62°42'$$

19. $3^2 = 7^2 + 5^2 - 2 \cdot 7 \cdot 5 \cos A, \quad A \approx 21°47'$

$$\frac{3}{\sin 21°47'} \approx \frac{7}{\sin B}, \quad B \approx 120°$$

$$C \approx 38°13'$$

20. $c^2 = 13^2 + (21.5)^2 - 2 \cdot 13 \cdot 21.5 \cos 39°20'$

$$c \approx 14.1$$

$$\frac{14.1}{\sin 39°20'} \approx \frac{21.5}{\sin A}, \quad A \approx 104°53'$$

$$B \approx 35°47'$$

21. $(11.4)^2 = (13.7)^2 + (12.2)^2 - 2(13.7)(12.2)\cos A$

$$A \approx 51°50'$$

$$\frac{11.4}{\sin 51°50'} \approx \frac{13.7}{\sin B}, \quad B \approx 70°53'$$

$$C \approx 57°17'$$

22. $C = 81°$

$$\frac{a}{\sin 40°} = \frac{b}{\sin 59°} = \frac{14}{\sin 81°}, \quad a \approx 9.1; \; b \approx 12.1$$

23. $b^2 = 9^2 + 5^2 - 2 \cdot 9 \cdot 5 \cos 120°, \quad b \approx 12.3$

$$\frac{12.3}{\sin 120°} \approx \frac{9}{\sin A}, \quad A \approx 39°19'$$

$$C \approx 20°41'$$

24. $(4.9)^2 = (6.8)^2 + (8.4)^2 - 2(6.8)(8.4)(\cos A)$

$$A \approx 35°41'$$

25. $d_1^2 = 71^2 + 55^2 - 2 \cdot 71 \cdot 55 \cos 106°,$

$$d_1 \approx 101.1 \text{ cm}$$

$$d_2^2 = 55^2 + 71^2 - 2 \cdot 55 \cdot 71 \cos 74°$$

$$d_2 \approx 76.9 \text{ cm}$$

26.

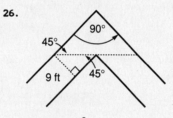

$$\sin 45° = \frac{9}{c}$$

$$c \approx 12.73$$

length of board $\approx 2(12.73) = 25.5$ feet

27. $x^2 = 165^2 + 220^2 - 2 \cdot 165 \cdot 220 \cos 130°$

$$x \approx 349.7 \text{ nautical miles}$$

28. $a^2 = (4275)^2 + (6336)^2 - (4275)(6336) \cos 37°$

$$a \approx 6065.34 \text{ feet}$$

$$a^2 = (4275)^2 + (6336)^2 - (4275)(6336) \cos 36.95°$$

$$a \approx 6064.17 \text{ feet}$$

$$6065.34 - 6064.17 = 1.17 \text{ feet}$$

29. $m = \dfrac{7 - 2}{5 - (-3)} = \dfrac{5}{8}$

30. $\begin{vmatrix} 7 & 9 \\ 3 & 6 \end{vmatrix} = 7(6) - 3(9) = 15$

31. $\alpha' = 180° - \alpha$

$$= 180° - 150°$$

$$= 30°$$

32. $r = \sqrt{x^2 + y^2}$

$$= \sqrt{(-7)^2 + 24^2}$$

$$= 25$$

$$\sin \theta = \frac{y}{r}$$

$$= \frac{24}{25}$$

33. $C = 180° - 38° - 27° = 115°$

$$\frac{560}{\sin 115°} = \frac{a}{\sin 27°}$$

$$a \approx 280.52$$

$$\sin 38° \approx \frac{x}{280.52}$$

$$x \approx 172.7 \text{ yards}$$

34. Let x = Sue's score in the first game.

$$\frac{x + (x - 10) + (x - 10 - 13)}{3} = 162$$

$$3x - 33 = 486$$

$$x = 173$$

5-8 Area of Triangles

1. Separate the parallelogram into two triangles, $\triangle ABC$ and $\triangle ACD$. Use the law of cosines to find the length of $\overline{AC}$. Then use Hero's formula to find the area of $\triangle ACD$ and double it to find the area of the parallelogram.

2. Sample answer: Let K be the measure of the area of $\triangle ABC$ and let b and c be the two known lengths. Substitute K, B, and c into the formula $K = \frac{1}{2}bc \sin A$ and solve for A. Then use the law of cosines to find the length of the third side, a.

3. Answers may vary; see students' work.

4. $K = \frac{1}{2}(3)(4) \sin 120° \approx 5.2 \text{ units}^2$

5. $K = \frac{1}{2}(20)^2\left(\dfrac{\sin 45° \cdot \sin 30°}{\sin 105°}\right) = 73.2 \text{ units}^2$

6. $s = \frac{1}{2}(4 + 6 + 8) = 9$

   $K = \sqrt{9(9 - 4)(9 - 6)(9 - 8)} \approx 11.6 \text{ units}^2$

7. $K = \frac{1}{2}(16)(12) \sin 43° \approx 65.5 \text{ units}^2$

8. $K = \frac{1}{2}(6)(4) \sin 52° \approx 9.5 \text{ units}^2$

9. $K = \frac{1}{2}(12)^2\left(\dfrac{\sin 30° \cdot \sin 15°}{\sin 135°}\right) \approx 13.2 \text{ units}^2$

10. $S = \frac{1}{2}r^2(\alpha - \sin \alpha)$

    $= \frac{1}{2} \cdot 16^2\left(\dfrac{81\pi}{180} - \sin \dfrac{81\pi}{180}\right)$

    $\approx 54.5 \text{ units}^2$

11. $S = \frac{1}{2}r^2(\alpha - \sin \alpha)$

    $= \frac{1}{2} \cdot 15^2\left(\dfrac{5\pi}{6} - \sin \dfrac{5\pi}{6}\right)$

    $\approx 238.3 \text{ units}^2$

12. $K = \frac{1}{2}(3.2)^2 \cdot \dfrac{\sin 16° \cdot \sin 31°45'}{\sin 132°15'} \approx 1.0 \text{ units}^2$

13. $s = \frac{1}{2}(2 + 7 + 8) = 8.5$

    $K = \sqrt{8.5(8.5 - 2)(8.5 - 7)(8.5 - 8)} \approx 6.4 \text{ units}^2$

14. $K = \frac{1}{2}(2^2) \cdot \dfrac{\sin 75° \cdot \sin 45°}{\sin 60°} \approx 1.6 \text{ units}^2$

15. $s = \frac{1}{2}(174 + 138 + 188) = 250$

    $K = \sqrt{250 \cdot 76 \cdot 112 \cdot 62} \approx 11,486.3 \text{ units}^2$

16. $K = \frac{1}{2}(8^2) \cdot \dfrac{\sin 60° \cdot \sin 75°}{\sin 45°} \approx 37.9 \text{ units}^2$

17. $K = \frac{1}{2} \cdot 11 \cdot 5 \sin 50°6' \approx 21.1 \text{ units}^2$

18. $s = \frac{1}{2}(17 + 13 + 19) = 24.5$

    $K = \sqrt{24.5(24.5 - 17)(24.5 - 13)(24.5 - 19)}$

    $\approx 107.8 \text{ units}^2$

19. $K = \frac{1}{2}(146.2)(209.3) \sin 62°12' \approx 13,533.9 \text{ units}^2$

20. $K = \frac{1}{2}(19.42)(19.42) \sin 31°16' \approx 97.9 \text{ units}^2$

21. $S = \frac{1}{2} \cdot 24^2\left(\dfrac{3\pi}{4} - \sin \dfrac{3\pi}{4}\right)$

    $\approx 288\left(\dfrac{3\pi}{4} - 0.707\right)$

    $\approx 474.9 \text{ units}^2$

22. $S = \frac{1}{2} \cdot 8^2\left(\dfrac{2\pi}{3} - \sin 120°\right)$

    $\approx 32\left(\dfrac{2\pi}{3} - 0.866\right)$

    $\approx 39.3 \text{ units}^2$

23. $S = \frac{1}{2} \cdot (2.1)^2\left(\dfrac{85\pi}{180} - \sin 85°\right)$

    $\approx 2.205\left(\dfrac{85\pi}{180} - 0.996\right)$

    $\approx 1.1 \text{ units}^2$

24. $S = \frac{1}{2} \cdot 6^2\left(\dfrac{5\pi}{8} - \sin \dfrac{5\pi}{8}\right)$

    $\approx 18\left(\dfrac{5\pi}{8} - 0.924\right)$

    $\approx 18.7 \text{ units}^2$

25. $S = \frac{1}{2} \cdot 42^2\left(\dfrac{26\pi}{180} - \sin 26°\right)$

    $\approx 882\left(\dfrac{26\pi}{180} - 0.438\right)$

    $\approx 13.6 \text{ units}^2$

26. $S = \frac{1}{2}(16.25)^2\left(\dfrac{\pi}{5} - \sin \dfrac{\pi}{5}\right)$

    $\approx 132.03\left(\dfrac{\pi}{5} - 0.588\right)$

    $\approx 5.4 \text{ units}^2$

27. area $= 2K = 2 \cdot \frac{1}{2} \cdot 8 \cdot 12 \sin 60° \approx 83.1 \text{ cm}^2$

28. area $= 2K = 2\sqrt{8(8 - 6)(8 - 5)(8 - 5)} = 24 \text{ cm}^2$

29. area $= 5\left(\frac{1}{2} \cdot 7 \cdot 7 \sin 72°\right) \approx 116.5 \text{ cm}^2$

30. area = $8\left(\frac{1}{2} \cdot 5 \cdot 5 \sin 45°\right) \approx 70.7 \text{ cm}^2$

31. a. $c^2 = 17.7^2 + 21^2 - 2(17.7)(21) \cos 78°10'$

    $c \approx 24.53$

    area $\approx 181.9 \text{ units}^2$

    b. $\dfrac{10}{\sin 75°20'} = \dfrac{b}{\sin 49°40'}$

    $b \approx 7.88$

    $C = 180° - 75°20' - 49°40' = 55°$

    $\dfrac{10}{\sin 75°20'} = \dfrac{c}{\sin 55°}$

    $c \approx 8.47$

    area $\approx 32.3 \text{ units}^2$

32. $K = \frac{1}{2}b\left(\dfrac{b \sin c}{\sin B}\right) \sin (180° - (m\angle B + m\angle C))$

    $= \dfrac{b^2 \sin C}{2 \sin B} \sin (180° - (m\angle B + m\angle C))$

33. a. $K_1 = \frac{1}{2}(16.5)(26) \sin 75° \approx 207.2$

    $a^2 = 16.5^2 + 26^2 - 2(16.5)(26) \cos 75°$

    $a \approx 26.9$

    $s \approx \frac{1}{2}(12.5 + 18 + 26.9) \approx 28.7$

    $K_2 \approx \sqrt{28.7(28.7 - 12.5)(28.7 - 18)(28.7 - 26.9)}$

    ≈ 94.6

    area of sail $\approx 207.2 + 94.6 \approx 302 \text{ in}^2$

    b. $\dfrac{\frac{1}{4} \text{ in}^2}{302 \text{ in}^2} = \dfrac{1 \text{ ft}^2}{x \text{ ft}^2}$

    $x = 1208 \text{ ft}^2$

34. $s = \frac{1}{2}(15 + 22.5 + 23) = 30.25$

    $K = \sqrt{30.25(30.25 - 15)(30.25 - 22.5)(30.25 - 23)}$

    ≈ 161

    $\cos \theta = \dfrac{3}{22.5}$

    $\theta \approx 82.34°$

    $K = \frac{1}{2}(22.5)(46) \sin 82.34° \approx 512.9$

    total area $\approx 2(161) + 2(512.9) \approx 1348 \text{ ft}^2$

35. a. $a^2 = 5^2 + 5.4^2 - 2(5)(5.4) \cos 24°$

    $a \approx 2.20$

    $s_1 = \frac{1}{2}(5 + 5.4 + 2.2) = 6.3$

    $K_1 \approx \sqrt{6.3(6.3 - 5)(6.3 - 5.4)(6.3 - 2.2)}$

    ≈ 5.5

    $s_2 = \frac{1}{2}(1.7 + 2.25 + 2.2) \approx 3.075$

    $K_2 \approx \sqrt{3.1(3.1 - 1.7)(3.1 - 2.25)(3.1 - 2.2)}$

    ≈ 1.8

    total area $\approx 2(5) + 5.5 + 1.8 \approx 17 \text{ ft}^2$

    b. total volume $\approx 17(8.6) \approx 146 \text{ ft}^3$

36. $3x - y + 7 = 0$

    $y = 3x + 7$

    slope = 3

    $y - y_1 = m(x - x_1)$

    $y - (-2) = 3(x - 3)$

    $y + 2 = 3x - 9$

    $3x - y - 11 = 0$

37. For a: $b = a^4 + 3a^2 + 2$

    For $-a$: $b = (-a)^4 + 3(-a)^2 + 2$

    $= a^4 + 3a^2 + 2$

    $(-a, b)$ is on the graph if and only if (a, b) is on the graph. So, the graph is symmetric with respect to the y - axis.

38.
$$\begin{array}{c|cccc} 2 & 1 & 0 & 8 & 1 \\ & & 2 & 4 & 24 \\ \hline & 1 & 2 & 12 & 25 \end{array}$$

    The remainder is 25.

39. $v = r\dfrac{\theta}{t}$

    $= 9.2\left(\dfrac{2400 \cdot 2\pi}{1}\right)$

    $\approx 139{,}000 \text{ cm/s}$

40. $a^2 = 13^2 + 6^2 - (13)(6) \cos 36°$

    $a \approx 11.9$

    $\dfrac{13}{\sin B} = \dfrac{11.9}{\sin 36°}$, $B \approx 39°57'$

    $C \approx 180° - 36° - 39°57' \approx 104°3'$

41. $x - y = 4$ $3.5 - y = 4$

    $\dfrac{x + y = 3}{2x \quad\quad = 7}$ $y = -0.5$

    $x = 3.5$

    Since $3.5 > -0.5$, $x > y$.

    Therefore, quantity A is greater. A

Chapter 5 Summary and Review

PAGES 296-298   SKILLS AND CONCEPTS

1. $\dfrac{\pi}{3} = \dfrac{\pi}{3} \times \dfrac{180°}{\pi}$

    $= 60°$

2. $-\dfrac{5\pi}{12} = -\dfrac{5\pi}{12} \times \dfrac{180°}{\pi}$

    $= -75°$

3. $\dfrac{4\pi}{3} = \dfrac{4\pi}{3} \times \dfrac{180°}{\pi}$

    $= 240°$

4. $150° = 150° \times \dfrac{\pi}{180°}$

    $= \dfrac{5\pi}{6}$

5. $-315° = -315° \times \dfrac{\pi}{180°}$

    $= -\dfrac{7\pi}{4}$

6. $270° = 270° \times \dfrac{\pi}{180°}$

    $= \dfrac{3\pi}{2}$

7. $\alpha' = 2\pi - \alpha$

    $= 2\pi - \dfrac{7\pi}{4}$

    $= \dfrac{\pi}{4}$

8. $405°$ is coterminal with $45°$ is Quadrant I.

    $\alpha' = 45°$

9. $-\frac{4\pi}{3}$ is coterminal with $\frac{2\pi}{3}$ in Quadrant II.

$\alpha' = \pi - \alpha$

$= \pi - \frac{2\pi}{3}$

$= \frac{\pi}{3}$

10. $-60°$ is coterminal with $300°$ in Quadrant IV.

$\alpha' = 360° - \alpha$

$= 360° - 300°$

$= 60°$

11. $\alpha' = 2\pi - \alpha$

$= 2\pi - \frac{11\pi}{6}$

$= \frac{\pi}{6}$

12. $870°$ is coterminal with $150°$ in Quadrant II.

$\alpha' = 180° - \alpha$

$= 180° - 150°$

$= 30°$

13. $s = r\theta$

$= 15\left(\frac{3\pi}{4}\right)$

$= \frac{45\pi}{4}$

14. $s = r\theta$

$= 15\left(\frac{\pi}{5}\right)$

$= 3\pi$

15. $s = r\theta$

$= 15\left(\frac{5\pi}{12}\right)$

$= \frac{25\pi}{4}$

16. $s = r\theta$

$= 15\left(\frac{5\pi}{6}\right)$

$= \frac{25\pi}{2}$

17. $r = \sqrt{x^2 + y^2}$

$= \sqrt{3^2 + 3^2}$

$= 3\sqrt{2}$

$\sin \theta = \frac{y}{r}$

$= \frac{3}{3\sqrt{2}}$

$= \frac{1}{\sqrt{2}}$ or $\frac{\sqrt{2}}{2}$

18. $r = \sqrt{x^2 + y^2}$

$= \sqrt{(-5)^2 + 12^2}$

$= 13$

$\cos \theta = \frac{x}{r}$

$= \frac{-5}{13}$

19. $\cot \theta = \frac{x}{y}$

$= \frac{8}{-2}$ or -4

20. $r = \sqrt{x^2 + y^2}$

$= \sqrt{(-2)^2 + 0^2}$

$= 2$

$\sec \theta = \frac{r}{x}$

$= \frac{2}{-2}$ or -1

21. $\cos \frac{3\pi}{4} = -\cos \frac{\pi}{4}$

$= -\frac{\sqrt{2}}{2}$

22. $\tan \frac{7\pi}{3} = \tan \frac{\pi}{3}$

$= \sqrt{3}$

23. $\csc 120° = \csc 60°$

$= \frac{1}{\sin 60°}$

$= \frac{1}{\frac{\sqrt{3}}{2}}$

$= \frac{2\sqrt{3}}{3}$

24. $\cot 315° = -\cot 45°$

$= -1$

25. $\sin \frac{18\pi}{4} = \sin \frac{\pi}{2}$

$= 1$

26. $\sec \left(-\frac{5\pi}{6}\right) = -\sec \frac{\pi}{6}$

$= -\frac{1}{\cos \frac{\pi}{6}}$

$= -\frac{1}{\frac{\sqrt{3}}{2}}$

$= -\frac{2\sqrt{3}}{3}$

27. $B = 27°$

$\sin 63° \approx \frac{9.7}{c}$, $c \approx 10.9$

$\cos 63° \approx \frac{b}{10.9}$, $b \approx 4.9$

28. $c = \sqrt{2^2 + 7^2} = \sqrt{53} \approx 7.3$

$\tan A = \frac{2}{7}$, $A \approx 15°57'$

$B \approx 74°3'$

29. $A = 7°$

$\sin 83° \approx \frac{\sqrt{31}}{c}$, $c \approx 5.6$

$\sin 7° \approx \frac{a}{5.6}$, $a \approx 0.7$

30. $A = 45°16'$

$\sin 45°16' = \frac{44}{c}$, $c \approx 61.9$

$\sin 44°44' \approx \frac{b}{61.9}$, $b \approx 43.6$

31. two; $\frac{172}{\sin 38°42'} = \frac{203}{\sin C}$, $C \approx 47°33'$ or $132°27'$

$B \approx 93°45'$ or $8°51'$

$\frac{172}{\sin 38°42'} = \frac{b_1}{\sin 93°45'}$, $b_1 \approx 274.5$

$\frac{172}{\sin 38°42'} \approx \frac{b_2}{\sin 8°51'}$, $b_2 \approx 42.3$

One solution is $C \approx 47°33'$, $B \approx 93°45'$, and $b \approx 274.5$.

Another solution is $C \approx 132°27'$, $B \approx 8°51'$, and $b \approx 42.3$.

32. none

33. two; $\frac{12}{\sin 29°} = \frac{15}{\sin B}$, $B \approx 37°18'$ or $142°42'$

$C \approx 113°42'$ or $8°18'$

$\frac{c_1}{\sin 113°42'} \approx \frac{12}{\sin 29°}$, $c_1 \approx 22.7$

$\frac{c_2}{\sin 8°18'} \approx \frac{12}{\sin 29°}$, $c_2 \approx 3.6$

One solution is $B \approx 37°18'$, $C \approx 113°42'$, and $c \approx 22.7$.

Another solution is $B \approx 142°42'$, $C \approx 8°18'$, and $c \approx 3.6$.

34. one; $\dfrac{83}{\sin 45°} = \dfrac{79}{\sin B}$, $B \approx 42°18'$

$C \approx 92°42'$

$\dfrac{83}{\sin 45°} \approx \dfrac{c}{\sin 92°42'}$, $c \approx 117.2$

35. $a = 40^2 + 45^2 - 2 \cdot 40 \cdot 45 \cos 51°$, $a \approx 36.9$

$\dfrac{36.9}{\sin 51°} \approx \dfrac{40}{\sin B}$, $B \approx 57°24'$

$C \approx 71°36'$

36. $b^2 = 51^2 + 61^2 - 2 \cdot 51 \cdot 61 \cos 19°$, $b \approx 21.0$

$\dfrac{21.0}{\sin 19°} \approx \dfrac{51}{\sin A}$, $A \approx 52°15'$

$C \approx 108°45'$

37. $11^2 = 13^2 + 20^2 - 2 \cdot 13 \cdot 20 \cos A$, $A \approx 30°31'$

$\dfrac{11}{\sin 30°31'} \approx \dfrac{13}{\sin B}$, $B \approx 36°53'$

$C \approx 112°36'$

38. $b^2 = 42^2 + (6.5)^2 - 2 \cdot 42 \cdot 6.5 \cos 24°$

$b \approx 36.2$

$\dfrac{36.2}{\sin 24°} \approx \dfrac{42}{\sin A}$, $A \approx 151°52'$

$C \approx 4°9'$

39. $K = \dfrac{1}{2} \cdot 19^2 \dfrac{\sin 64° \cdot \sin 96°}{\sin 20°} \approx 471.7$ units^2

40. $K = \sqrt{10.5(10.5 - 5)(10.5 - 7)(10.5 - 9)}$

≈ 17.4 units^2

41. $K = \dfrac{1}{2}(11.7)(13.5) \sin 81°20' \approx 78.1$ units^2

42. $K = \dfrac{1}{2} \cdot 63^2 \dfrac{\sin 65° \cdot \sin 73°}{\sin 42°} \approx 2570.5$ units^2

PAGE 298   APPLICATIONS AND PROBLEM SOLVING

43. $v = r\dfrac{\theta}{t}$

$= 15\left(\dfrac{12 \cdot 2\pi}{3}\right)$

≈ 376.99

$\dfrac{376.49 \text{ ft}}{\min} \times \dfrac{1 \text{ mi}}{5280 \text{ ft}} \times \dfrac{60 \min}{h} \approx 4.3$ mph

44. a. $S = \dfrac{1}{2}r^2(\alpha - \sin \alpha)$

$= \dfrac{1}{2}(4)^2\left(\dfrac{2\pi}{3} - \sin \dfrac{2\pi}{3}\right)$

≈ 9.8 ft^2

b. $3\left[9.8 \text{ ft}^2 \cdot \dfrac{3 \text{ plants}}{\text{ft}^2} \cdot \dfrac{\text{flat}}{24 \text{ plants}}\right] \approx 4$ flats

Chapter 5 Test

PAGE 299

1. $135° = 135° \times \dfrac{\pi}{180°}$

$= \dfrac{3\pi}{4}$

2. $-\dfrac{\pi}{5} = -\dfrac{\pi}{5} \times \dfrac{180°}{\pi}$

$= -36°$

3. $480° = 480° \times \dfrac{\pi}{180°}$

$= \dfrac{8\pi}{3}$

4. $\dfrac{7\pi}{12} = \dfrac{7\pi}{12} \times \dfrac{180°}{\pi}$

$= 105°$

5. $s = r\theta$

$= 6.3\left(\dfrac{5\pi}{6}\right)$

≈ 16.5 cm

6. $A = \dfrac{1}{2}r^2\theta$

$= \dfrac{1}{2}(6.3)^2\left(\dfrac{5\pi}{6}\right)$

≈ 52.0 cm^2

7. $S = \dfrac{1}{2}r^2(\alpha - \sin \alpha)$

$= \dfrac{1}{2}(6.3)^2\left(\dfrac{5\pi}{6} - \sin \dfrac{5\pi}{6}\right)$

≈ 42.0

8. $\sin \dfrac{5\pi}{6} = \sin \dfrac{\pi}{6}$

$= \dfrac{1}{2}$

9. $\cot 210° = \cot 30°$

$= \dfrac{\frac{\sqrt{3}}{2}}{\frac{1}{2}}$

$= \sqrt{3}$

10. $\sec 135° = -\sec 45°$

$= -\dfrac{1}{\frac{\sqrt{2}}{2}}$

$= -\dfrac{2}{\sqrt{2}}$ or $-\sqrt{2}$

11. $\cos\left(-\dfrac{\pi}{6}\right) = \cos \dfrac{\pi}{6}$

$= \dfrac{\sqrt{3}}{2}$

12. $\tan 225° = \tan 45°$

$= 1$

13. $B = 13°$

$\sin 13° = \dfrac{42}{c}$, $c \approx 186.7$

$\tan 13° = \dfrac{42}{a}$, $a \approx 181.9$

14. $\sin A = \dfrac{12}{13}$, $A \approx 67°23'$

$B \approx 22°37'$

$b = \sqrt{13^2 - 12^2} = 5$

15. $A = 58°$

$\sin 32° = \dfrac{b}{14}$, $b \approx 7.4$

$\sin 58° = \dfrac{a}{14}$, $a \approx 11.9$

16. one; $\dfrac{64}{\sin A} = \dfrac{90}{\sin 98°}$, $A \approx 44°46'$

$B \approx 37°14'$

$\dfrac{b}{\sin 37°14'} \approx \dfrac{90}{\sin 98°}$, $b \approx 55.0$

17. none

18. one;

$15^2 = 13^2 + 7^2 - 2 \cdot 13 \cdot 7 \cos C$, $C \approx 92°12'$

$\dfrac{15}{\sin 92°12'} \approx \dfrac{13}{\sin A}$, $A \approx 60°$

$B \approx 27°48'$

19. one;

$b^2 = 20^2 + 24^2 - 2 \cdot 20 \cdot 24 \cos 47°$, $b \approx 17.9$;

$\dfrac{17.9}{\sin 47°} \approx \dfrac{24}{\sin C}$, $C \approx 78°41'$

$A \approx 54°19'$

20. $K = \dfrac{1}{2}(16.7)^2 \dfrac{\sin 70°11' \sin 65°54'}{\sin 43°55'} \approx 172.7$ units^2

21. $K = \dfrac{1}{2}(11.5)(14) \sin 20° \approx 27.5$ units^2

22. $v = r\dfrac{\theta}{t}$

$2300 = (2.4 \times 10^5)\left(\dfrac{2\pi}{t}\right)$

$t \approx 656$ h

656 h $\cdot \dfrac{1 \text{ day}}{24 \text{ h}} \approx 27.3$ days

23. $\sin 70° = \dfrac{x}{65}$, $x \approx 61.08$ meters

24. $x^2 = 70^2 + 130^2 - 2 \cdot 70 \cdot 130 \cos 130°$

$x \approx 183.0$

The transmitters are about 183.0 miles apart.

25. $\cos 72° = \dfrac{11}{c}$, $c \approx 35.597$ cm

perimeter $\approx 2(35.597) + 22$

≈ 93.2 cm

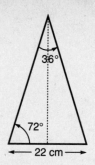

PAGE 299   BONUS

$$\dfrac{a + b + c}{2 + \sqrt{3}} = \dfrac{ab}{a + b - c}$$

$$(a + b + c)(a + b - c) = (2 + \sqrt{3})ab$$

$$a^2 + ab - ac + ab + b^2 - bc + ac + bc - c^2$$
$$= 2ab + \sqrt{3}ab$$
$$a^2 + b^2 - c^2 = \sqrt{3}ab$$
$$c^2 = a^2 + b^2 - \sqrt{3}ab$$

So, $2 \cos \theta = \sqrt{3}$

$\theta = 30°$ or $\dfrac{\pi}{6}$.

Chapter 6 Graphs and Inverses of the Trigonometric Functions

<table><tr><td>**6-1**</td><td>**Graphs of the Trigonometric Functions**</td></tr></table>

PAGES 304-305 CHECKING FOR UNDERSTANDING

1. shift to the right 90° or shift to the left 270°

2. $f(\theta)$ is undefined for that value of θ.

3. at θ = -270°, -90°, 90°, and 270°

4. reflection and translation

5. 0   6. 1   7. 0   8. 0   9. 0   10. 0

11. 0   12. 1   13. -1

14. 360k°, k is any integer

15. 45° + 180k°, k is any integer

16. 180k°, k is any integer

17. 90° + 180k°, k is any integer

18.

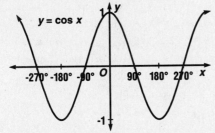

PAGES 305-307 EXERCISES

19. 1   20. -1   21. 1   22. -1   23. -1   24. 1

25. 0   26. -1   27. undefined

28. 90° + 360k°, k is any integer

29. 180° + 360k°, k is any integer

30. 270° + 360k°, k is any integer

31. 315° + 180k°, k is any integer

32. 360k°, k is any integer

33. 315° + 180k°, k is any integer

34. real numbers; $-1 \le y \le 1$

35. real numbers; $-1 \le y \le 1$

36. real numbers except $\theta = k \cdot 180°$; real numbers

37. real numbers except $\theta = k \cdot 180° + 90°$;
    $y \le -1$, $y \ge 1$, k is any integer

38. real numbers except $\theta = k \cdot 180° + 90°$;
    real numbers

39. real numbers except $\theta = k \cdot 180°$; $y \le -1$, $y \ge 1$,
    k is any integer

40.

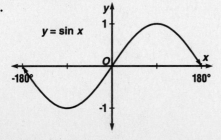

41.

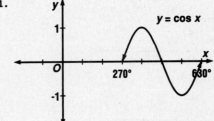

42.

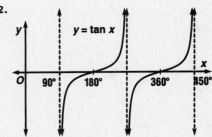

43.

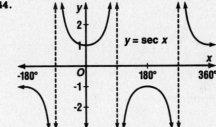

44.

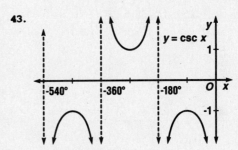

45.

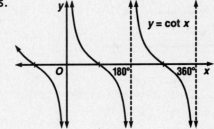

46.

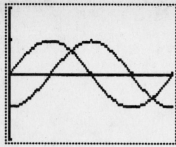

$x = 135°, 315°$

47.

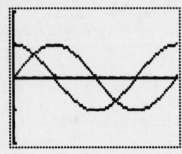

$0° \leq x \leq 45°, 225° \leq x \leq 360°$

48.

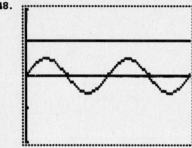

49.

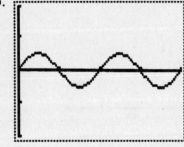

$90° \leq x \leq 180°, 270° \leq x \leq 360°$

50.

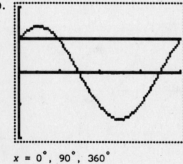

$x = 0°, 90°, 360°$

51.

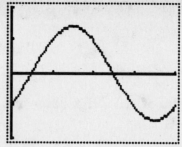

$x = 45°, 225°$

52.

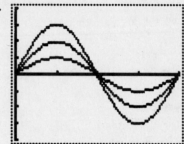

The graphs of $y = \sin x$ and $y = 2 \sin x$ have the same x-intercepts, but different maximum and minimum values, 1 to -1 and 2 to -2, respectively. The graph of $y = 3 \sin x$ has the same x-intercepts as the other two graphs but its maximum is 3 and its minimum is -3.

53. a. $I_{eff} = 110\sqrt{2} \sin (120\pi t)$

b.

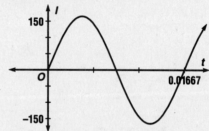

c. $t = \frac{1}{30}k$, where k is any integer

54. a. $\theta = \frac{\pi}{4} \cos \pi t$

b. $0 = \frac{\pi}{4} \cos \pi t$

$0 = \cos \pi t$

$0.5, 1.5 = t$

55. $m = \dfrac{4 - 2}{-1 - 5}$ $\qquad y - 2 = -\frac{1}{3}(x - 5)$

$\quad = \dfrac{2}{-6}$ $\qquad\qquad y - 2 = -\frac{1}{3}x + \frac{5}{3}$

$\quad = -\dfrac{1}{3}$ $\qquad\qquad y = -\frac{1}{3}x + \frac{11}{3}$

56. $\begin{bmatrix} 4 & 2 & 10 \\ 1 & 1 & 6 \end{bmatrix} \rightarrow \begin{bmatrix} 1 & 1 & 6 \\ 4 & 2 & 10 \end{bmatrix} \rightarrow \begin{bmatrix} 1 & 1 & 6 \\ 0 & -2 & -14 \end{bmatrix} \rightarrow$

$\begin{bmatrix} 1 & 1 & 6 \\ 0 & 1 & 7 \end{bmatrix} \rightarrow \begin{bmatrix} 1 & 0 & -1 \\ 0 & 1 & 7 \end{bmatrix}$ $\qquad (-1, 7)$

57. For each of the x-values in the domain of the graph, there exist a +y and -y value. Therefore, the graph is symmetric with respect to the x-axis.

58. $(-4)^4 + 3(-4)^3 + 10(-4) - 20 = 4$
$\neq 0$, no

59. $4(x - 3) = 6(x + 1)$
$4x - 12 = 6x + 6$
$-18 = 2x$
$-9 = x$

60. $\frac{5\pi}{16} \cdot \frac{180}{\pi} = 56.25°$
$= 56° \; 15'$

61. $\frac{9}{\sin 40°} = \frac{16}{\sin B}$
$9 \sin B = 16 \sin 40°$
$\sin B = \frac{16 \sin 40°}{9}$
≈ 1.14
No angle has sine > 1, so no solution exists.

62. $b^2 = (24)^2 + (32)^2 - 2(24)(32) \cos 45°$
$b^2 = 513.88$
$b \approx 22.67$ mi

63. $s = \frac{1}{2}(17 + 13 + 19) = 24.5$
$K = \sqrt{24.5(24.5 - 17)(24.5 - 13)(24.5 - 19)}$
≈ 108 units^2

64. $\frac{2}{5}, \frac{4}{10}, \frac{6}{15}, \frac{8}{20}, \cdots$
$\uparrow$
$\frac{6 - 2}{15 + 1} = \frac{4}{16} = \frac{1}{4}$ ✓
The numerator is 6.

Technology:
Ordered Pairs for Graphing
Trigonometric Functions

1.   **2.**

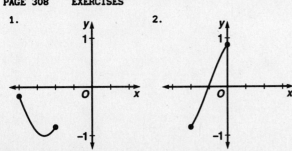

3.   **4.**

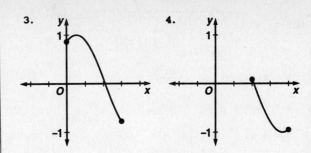

6-2   Amplitude, Period, and Phase Shift

1. They coincide.

2. The "peaks and valleys" of the graph become taller.

3. See students' work.

4. 4, 360°, 0°

5. 2, $\frac{360°}{5} = 72°$, 0°

6. 2, $\frac{360°}{2} = 180°$, 0°

7. none, $\frac{\pi}{2}$, $\frac{-(-\pi)}{2} = \frac{\pi}{2}$

8. 2, $\frac{360°}{4} = 90°$, 0°

9. 3, 360°, $\frac{-(-90°)}{1} = 90°$

10. none, $\frac{180°}{2} = 90°$, $\frac{-(-360°)}{2} = 180°$

11. 243, $\frac{360°}{15} = 24°$, $\frac{-(-40°)}{15} = 2\frac{2}{3}$

12. $y = \pm 3 \sin\left(\frac{1}{2}\theta + 30°\right)$

13. $y = \pm 4 \cos\left(\frac{1}{2}\theta + \frac{\pi}{4}\right)$

14. $y = \tan(\theta - 25°)$

15. 2, 360°, 0°

16. none, $\frac{180°}{4} = 45°$, 0°

17. 110, $\frac{360°}{20} = 18°$, 0°

18. 2, 360°, 0°

19. 7, $\frac{360°}{6} = 60°$, 0°

20. 4, $\frac{360°}{\frac{1}{2}} = 720°$, 0°

21. $\frac{1}{4}$, $\frac{360°}{\frac{1}{2}} = 720°$, 0°

22. 12, $\frac{2\pi}{3}$, $\frac{-\left(\frac{-3\pi}{2}\right)}{3} = \frac{\pi}{2}$

23. 6, -360°, $\frac{-(180°)}{-1} = 180°$

24. 10, $\frac{360°}{\frac{1}{3}} = 1080°$, $\frac{-(-300°)}{\frac{1}{3}} = 900°$

25. $y = \pm 5 \sin(x - 60°)$

26. $y = \pm\frac{2}{3} \sin\left(2x - \frac{\pi}{2}\right)$

27. $y = \pm 17 \sin(8x + 480°)$

28. $y = \pm\frac{1}{2} \sin\left(\frac{4}{3}x + \frac{\pi}{3}\right)$

29. $y = \pm 7 \sin\left(\frac{8}{5}x + 144°\right)$

30. $y = \pm\frac{1}{3} \cos 2x$

31. $y = \pm 3 \cos (2x - 240°)$

32. $y = \pm 100 \cos \left(\frac{4}{7}x + \frac{360°}{7}\right)$

33. $y = \pm\frac{7}{3} \cos \left(\frac{12}{5}x - 648°\right)$

34. $y = \pm\cos \left(\frac{8}{3}x + \frac{8\pi}{9}\right)$

35.

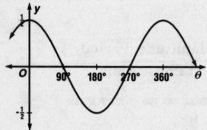

36.

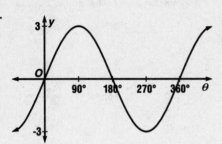

37.

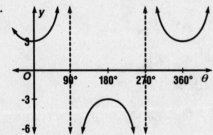

38.

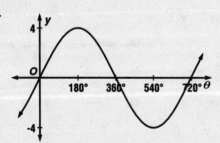

39.

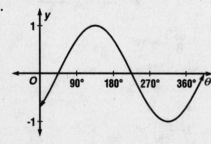

40.

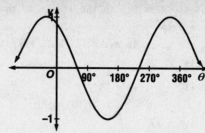

41.

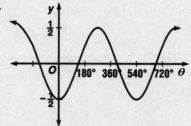

42.

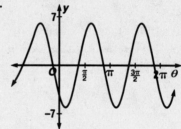

43. a. $90° + 45° = 135°$

   b. $\frac{90°}{3} = 30°$

   c. $\frac{90° + 90°}{2} = 90°$

   d. $\frac{90° + c}{k}$

44-45.

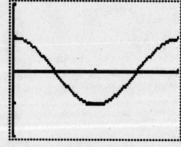

$\sin\left(x + \frac{\pi}{2}\right) = \cos x$

130

46.

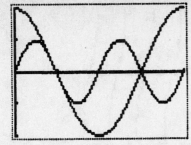

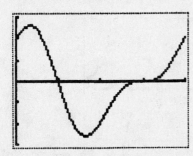

See students' work for conjecture.

47. a. $P = 500 + 200 \sin 0.4(15 - 2)$

≈ 323

$D = 1500 + 400 \sin 0.4(15)$

≈ 1388

b.

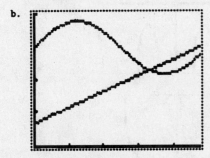

c. See students' work.

48. a. $y = -19 \cos \left(\frac{2\pi}{15}t\right) + 19$

b. 37.6 feet from the minimum height, or

37.6 − 19 = 18.6 feet from the equilibrium point

c. $24 = -19 \cos \left(\frac{2\pi}{15}t\right) + 19$

$5 = -19 \cos \left(\frac{2\pi}{15}t\right)$

$-\frac{5}{19} = \cos \left(\frac{2\pi}{15}t\right)$

$105.26 \approx \frac{2\pi}{15}t$

$4.4 \approx t$

49. a.

```
  8000

   O    45°    90°   θ
```

b. $\frac{150}{0.02} = 7500$

c. See students' work.

50.

```
<---o---------o--->
  0 1 2 3 4 5
```

51. $\begin{bmatrix} 4 & -3 & 2 \\ 8 & -2 & 0 \\ 9 & 6 & -3 \end{bmatrix} + \begin{bmatrix} -2 & 2 & -2 \\ -5 & 1 & 1 \\ -7 & 2 & -2 \end{bmatrix} = \begin{bmatrix} 2 & -1 & 0 \\ 3 & -1 & 1 \\ 2 & 8 & -5 \end{bmatrix}$

52. $f'(x) = 12x^3 - 24x^2 - 288x$

$0 = 12x^3 - 24x^2 - 288x$

$= 12x(x^2 - 2x - 24)$

$= 12x(x - 6)(x + 4)$

$x = 0, 6, -4$

$f''(x) = 36x^2 - 48x - 288$

$0 = 36x^2 - 48x - 288$

$= 3x^2 - 4x - 24$

$x = \frac{4 \pm \sqrt{16 + 288}}{6}$

$= \frac{4 \pm \sqrt{304}}{6}$

$= \frac{4 \pm 4\sqrt{19}}{6}$

$= \frac{2 \pm 2\sqrt{19}}{3}$

$f(0) = 6$

$f(6) = -3018$

$f(-4) = -1018$

$f\left(\frac{2 + 2\sqrt{19}}{3}\right) \approx -1708.01$

$f\left(\frac{2 - 2\sqrt{19}}{3}\right) \approx -550.80$

critical points: $(0, 6)$, $(6, -3018)$,

$(-4, -1018)$, $\left(\frac{2 + 2\sqrt{19}}{3}, -1708.01\right)$,

$\left(\frac{2 - 2\sqrt{19}}{3}, -550.80\right)$

$f(-4.01) \approx -1017.98$ $f(3.56) \approx -1698.08$

$f(-3.99) \approx -1017.98$ $f(3.58) \approx -1713.84$

$f(-2.25) \approx -554.99$ $f(5.99) \approx -3017.96$

$f(-2.23) \approx -547.19$ $f(6.01) \approx -3017.96$

$f(-0.01) \approx 5.99$

$f(0.01) \approx 5.99$

$x = 0$, max; $x = 6$, min; $x = -4$, min;

$x = \frac{2 \pm 2\sqrt{19}}{3}$, point of inflection.

53. 1 positive real zero, 0 negative real zeros

possible rational zeros: ±1, ±2, ±4

r	1 0 3 0 0	−4
1	1 1 4 4 4	0

The real zero is 1.0.

54. $7° \times \frac{\pi}{180°} = 0.12$

$s = r\theta$

$= 20(7°)$

$\approx 20(0.12)$

≈ 2.44 cm

131

55. Quadrant IV angle, $r = \sqrt{7^2 + (-3)^2}$
$= \sqrt{58}$

$\sin x = -\dfrac{3}{\sqrt{58}}$, $\cos x = \dfrac{7}{\sqrt{58}}$, $\tan x = -\dfrac{3}{7}$

$\csc x = -\dfrac{\sqrt{58}}{3}$, $\sec x = \dfrac{\sqrt{58}}{7}$, $\cot x = -\dfrac{7}{3}$

56. $x = 180°$ or $270°$

57. $d = \sqrt{(6 - (-6))^2 + 0^2}$ $12 = \sqrt{(0 - 6)^2 + (y - 0)^2}$

$\qquad = \sqrt{144}$ $12 = \sqrt{36 + y^2}$

$\qquad = 12$ $144 = 36 + y$

$\qquad\qquad\qquad\qquad\qquad\quad y^2 = 108$

$\qquad\qquad\qquad\qquad\qquad\quad\ y = \sqrt{108}$

$\qquad\qquad\qquad\qquad\qquad\qquad = 6\sqrt{3}$

The best answer is C.

Case Study Follow-Up

PAGE 318

1. $1085 = 7000\lambda$

$\qquad \lambda = 0.155$ ft

2. $c = 450 \sin \left[\left(\dfrac{7000}{20,000} \right) 90° \right]$

$\qquad = 450 \sin (31.5°)$

$\qquad \approx \$235.12/\text{room}$

$\qquad 7 \times 235.12 \approx \$1,645.87$

3. See students' work.

6-3A   Graphing Calculators: Graphing Trigonometric Functions

PAGE 320   **EXERCISES**

1.

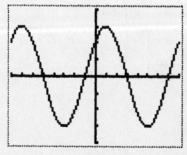

1, 2π, $0°$

2.

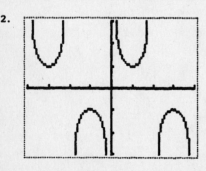

none, 2π, $0°$

3.

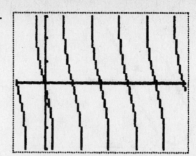

none, $\dfrac{\pi}{2}$, $0°$

4.

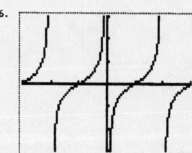

none, 2π, $0°$

5.

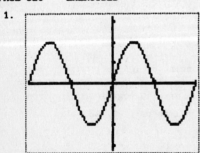

none, $\dfrac{2\pi}{3}$, $0°$

6.

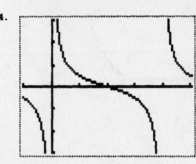

none, $\dfrac{\pi}{3}$, $30°$

7.

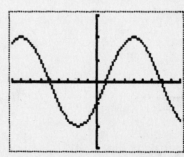

3, 2π, $-45°$

8.

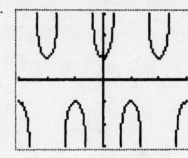

4, $\dfrac{2\pi}{3}$, $-20°$

9.

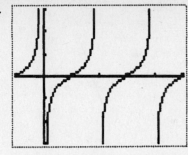

none, π, 0°

10.

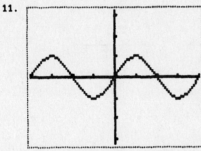

none, 2π, 45°

11.

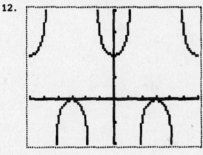

$\frac{1}{2}$, π, 45°

12.

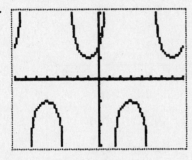

none, π, −90°

4.

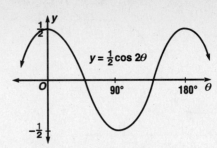

$y = \frac{1}{2} \cos 2\theta$

5.

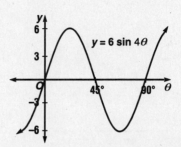

$y = 6 \sin 4\theta$

6.

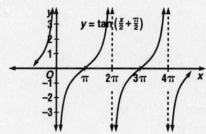

$y = \tan\left(\frac{x}{2} + \frac{\pi}{2}\right)$

7.

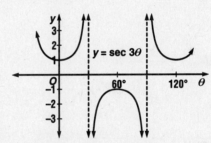

$y = \sec 3\theta$

8.

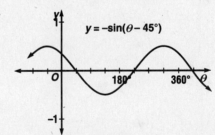

$y = -\sin(\theta - 45°)$

9.

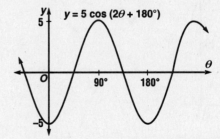

$y = 5 \cos(2\theta + 180°)$

6-3 Graphing Trigonometric Functions

PAGES 325-326   CHECKING FOR UNDERSTANDING

1. **a.** increase $|A|$ **b.** decrease h
   c. increase $|k|$ **d.** increase c

2. The ordinate of the sum will be the sum of the ordinates.

3. The graph of $y = 3 \sin 2x + 4$ is the graph of $y = 3 \sin 2x$ shifted 4 units upward.

10.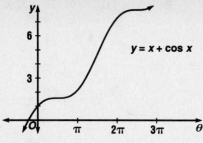

$y = x + \cos x$

11.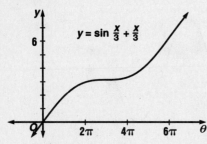

$y = \sin \frac{x}{3} + \frac{x}{3}$

12.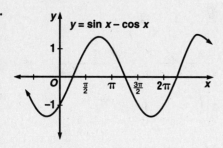

$y = \sin x - \cos x$

PAGES 326-327   EXERCISES

13.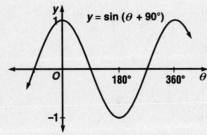

$y = \sin(\theta + 90°)$

14.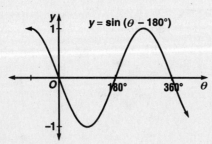

$y = \sin(\theta - 180°)$

15.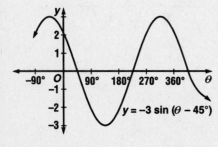

$y = -3 \sin(\theta - 45°)$

16.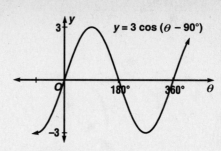

$y = 3 \cos(\theta - 90°)$

17.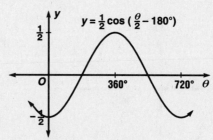

$y = \frac{1}{2} \cos\left(\frac{\theta}{2} - 180°\right)$

18.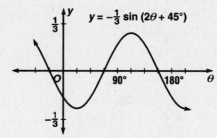

$y = -\frac{1}{3} \sin(2\theta + 45°)$

19.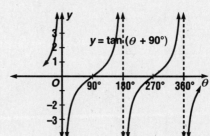

$y = \tan(\theta + 90°)$

20.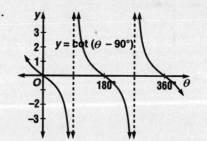

$y = \cot(\theta - 90°)$

21.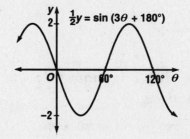

$\frac{1}{2} y = \sin(3\theta + 180°)$

134

22.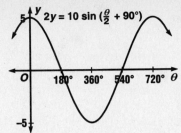

$2y = 10 \sin \left(\frac{\theta}{2} + 90°\right)$

23.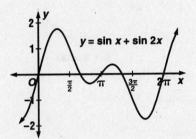

$y = \sin x + \sin 2x$

24.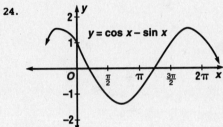

$y = \cos x - \sin x$

25.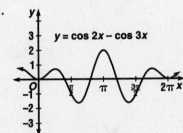

$y = \cos 2x - \cos 3x$

26.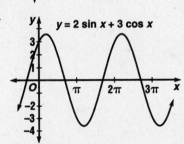

$y = 2 \sin x + 3 \cos x$

27.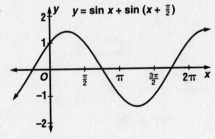

$y = \sin x + \sin \left(x + \frac{\pi}{2}\right)$

28.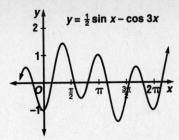

$y = \frac{1}{2} \sin x - \cos 3x$

29.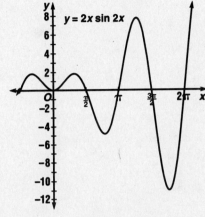

$y = 2x \sin 2x$

30.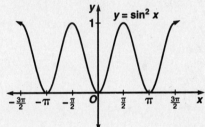

$y = \sin^2 x$

31.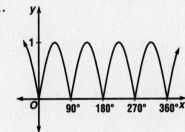

32. a. $2,\ 160°,\ y = -2 \sin \frac{9\theta}{4}$

　b. $2,\ 80°,\ y = 2 \sin \frac{9\theta}{2}$

33. There is a $45°$ phase difference.

34. a.

$y = -\sin t - \frac{1}{2} \sin 2t$

　b. See students' work.

135

35. $3x + 5y = 4 \rightarrow 5y = 4 - 3x \rightarrow y = \frac{4}{5} - \frac{3}{5}x$

$$14x - 35\left(\frac{4}{5} - \frac{3}{5}x\right) = 21$$

$$14x - 28 + 21x = 21$$

$$35x = 59$$

$$x = \frac{49}{35}$$

$$x \approx 1.4$$

$$y \approx \frac{4}{5} - \frac{3}{5}(1.4)$$

$$y \approx -0.04$$

36. $f(3) = 3^3 - 7(3^2) - 3k + 6$

$\qquad = -30 - 3k$

$\qquad 0 = -30 - 3k$

$\qquad 3k = -30$

$\qquad k = -10$

37. a. $5(2\pi) = 10\pi$ radians per second

$\quad$ **b.** $v = 0.5(10\pi) = 15.7$ ft/s

38. $\quad \tan 73° = \frac{h}{4}$

$\quad 4 \tan 73° = h$

$\qquad\qquad h \approx 13.1$ m

$\quad (13.1)^2 + 4^2 \approx c^2$

$\qquad\qquad 187.61 \approx c^2$

$\qquad\qquad\qquad c \approx 13.7$ m

39. $y = \pm 4 \cos(2x - 40°)$

40. $x + y = 180°$

$\quad x + z = 180°$

The quantities are equal. C

6-4 Inverse Trigonometric Functions

PAGE 331 CHECKING FOR UNDERSTANDING

1. $y = \sin^{-1} x$ is the inverse relation of $y = \sin x$; $y = (\sin x)^{-1}$ is the function $y = \frac{1}{\sin x}$; and $y = \sin(x^{-1})$ is the function $y = \sin \frac{1}{x}$.

2. Many values of y will be generated for each x value and a function must be one-to-one.

3. $\theta = \arcsin x$

4. $\alpha = \arccos \frac{1}{3}$

5. $y = \arctan -3$

6. $\theta = \arctan \frac{4}{3}$

7. $x = \arccos y$

8. $x = \arcsin 1$

9. $\sin x = 0$ when $x = 0°, 180°, 360°$

10. $\tan x = 1$ when $x = 45°, 225°$

11. $\sin x = \frac{\sqrt{3}}{2}$ when $x = 60°, 120°$

12. $\frac{4}{5}$

13. $\sec(0) = 1$

14. $\tan(53.13°) = \frac{4}{3}$

PAGES 331-333 EXERCISES

15. $\theta = \arcsin n$

16. $\beta = \arccos \frac{1}{3}$

17. $\delta = \arctan \frac{3}{2}$

18. $\alpha = \arcsin 1$

19. $\theta = \arccos y$

20. $A = \arctan \sqrt{3}$

21. $\cos x = 0$ when $x = 90°, 270°$

22. $\sin x = \frac{1}{\sqrt{2}}$ when $x = 45°, 135°$

23. $\tan x = \frac{\sqrt{3}}{2}$ when $x = 30°, 210°$

24. $\sec x = 2$ when $x = 60°, 300°$

25. $\tan x = 0$ when $x = 0°, 180°$

26. $\sin x = \frac{1}{2}$ when $x = 30°, 150°$

27. $\cot x = 2.1445$ when $x = 25°, 205°$

28. $\sin x = -0.5$ when $x = 210°, 330°$

29. $\cot x = 0$ when $x = 90°, 270°$

30. $\sin\left(\sin^{-1}\frac{1}{2}\right) = \frac{1}{2}$

31. $\cot\left(\arctan\frac{4}{5}\right) = \frac{5}{4}$

32. $\sin\left(\cos^{-1}\frac{\sqrt{3}}{2}\right) = \sin(30°)$

$$= \frac{1}{2}$$

33. $\sec\left(\cos^{-1}\frac{1}{2}\right) = \sec 60°$

$$= 2$$

34. $\cos\left(\text{arccot}\frac{4}{3}\right) = \cos(36.87°)$

$$= \frac{4}{5}$$

35. $\tan(\sec^{-1} 2) = \tan 60°$

$$= \sqrt{3}$$

36. $\sin(\arctan\sqrt{3} + \text{arccot}\sqrt{3}) = \sin(60° + 30°)$

$$= \sin(90°) \text{ or } 1$$

37. $\sin(\tan^{-1} 1) + \cos(\cos^{-1} 0.5)$

$\quad = \sin(45°) + 0.5$

$\quad = \frac{\sqrt{2}}{2} + \frac{1}{2} \text{ or } \frac{\sqrt{2} + 1}{2}$

38. $\tan\left(\arcsin\frac{\sqrt{2}}{2}\right) - \cot\left(\arccos\frac{\sqrt{2}}{2}\right)$

$\quad = \tan 45° - \cot(45°)$

$\quad = 1 - 1 \text{ or } 0$

39. $\tan\left(\sin^{-1}\frac{\sqrt{3}}{2} - \cos^{-1}\frac{\sqrt{3}}{2}\right) = \tan(60° - 30°)$

$$= \tan 30° \text{ or } \frac{\sqrt{3}}{3}$$

40. $\sin^{-1}\dfrac{\sqrt{2}}{2} + \cos^{-1}\dfrac{\sqrt{2}}{2} \stackrel{?}{=} \tan^{-1}\dfrac{\sqrt{3}}{3} + \tan^{-1}\sqrt{3}$

$$45° + 45° \stackrel{?}{=} 30° + 60°$$
$$90° = 90°$$

41. $\arccos\dfrac{\sqrt{3}}{2} + \arcsin\dfrac{\sqrt{3}}{2} \stackrel{?}{=} \arctan 1 + \operatorname{arccot} 1$

$$30° + 60° \stackrel{?}{=} 45° + 45°$$
$$90° = 90°$$

42. $\arcsin\dfrac{2}{5} + \arccos\dfrac{2}{5} \stackrel{?}{=} 90°$

$$23.6° + 66.4° \stackrel{?}{=} 90°$$
$$90° = 90°$$

43. $\tan^{-1}1 + \cos^{-1}\dfrac{\sqrt{3}}{2} \stackrel{?}{=} \sin^{-1}\dfrac{1}{2} + \sec^{-1}\sqrt{2}$

$$45° + 30° \stackrel{?}{=} 30° + 45°$$
$$75° = 75°$$

44. $\tan^{-1}\dfrac{3}{4} + \tan^{-1}\dfrac{5}{12} \stackrel{?}{=} \tan^{-1}\dfrac{56}{33}$

$$36.9° + 22.6° \stackrel{?}{=} 59.5°$$
$$59.5° = 59.5°$$

45. $\arcsin\dfrac{3}{5} + \arccos\dfrac{15}{17} \stackrel{?}{=} \arctan\dfrac{77}{36}$

$$36.9° + 28.1° \stackrel{?}{=} 65°$$
$$65° = 65°$$

46. See students' explanations; yes, $0° \leq x \leq 360°$.

47. a.
$$5543 = 2\pi(6400)\cos\theta$$
$$0.1378 \approx \cos\theta$$
$$\cos^{-1}(0.1378) \approx \theta$$
$$82° \approx \theta$$

b. $2\pi(6400)\cos 90° = 0$ km; it is the north or south pole.

48. a. $\cos\theta = \sqrt{\dfrac{1}{4}}$

$$\cos\theta = \dfrac{1}{2}$$
$$\theta = \cos^{-1}\left(\dfrac{1}{2}\right)$$
$$\theta = 60°$$

b. $\cos\theta = \sqrt{0}$

$$\cos\theta = 0$$
$$\theta = \cos^{-1}(0)$$
$$\theta = 90°$$

49. $v = 55$ mi/hr
$$\approx 80.67 \text{ ft/sec}$$
$$\tan\theta = \dfrac{(80.67)^2}{(32)(1000)}$$
$$\tan\theta \approx 0.2034$$
$$\theta \approx \tan^{-1}(0.2034)$$
$$\theta \approx 11.5°$$

50. First prove that P is on segment AB. It is sufficient to show that segments AP and AB have the same slope.

slope of $\overline{AP} = \dfrac{3-2}{9-4} = \dfrac{1}{5}$

slope of $\overline{AB} = \dfrac{3-1}{9-(-1)} = \dfrac{2}{10}$ or $\dfrac{1}{5}$

Now show that $AP = BP$.

$$AP = \sqrt{(9-4)^2 + (3-2)^2} = \sqrt{26}$$
$$BP = \sqrt{(-1-4)^2 + (1-2)^2} = \sqrt{26}$$

51. $-2(-5-0) - 1(20+4) - 3(0-1) = 10 - 24 + 3$
$$= -11$$

52.
$$y = \dfrac{3}{2}x - 2$$
$$x = \dfrac{3}{2}y - 2$$
$$x + 2 = \dfrac{3}{2}y$$
$$\dfrac{2}{3}(x+2) = y$$
$$\dfrac{2}{3}x + \dfrac{4}{3} = y$$

53.
$$x = \dfrac{7 \pm \sqrt{49-24}}{6}$$
$$= \dfrac{7 \pm \sqrt{25}}{6}$$
$$= \dfrac{7 \pm 5}{6}$$
$$x = \dfrac{7+5}{6} \qquad x = \dfrac{7-5}{6}$$
$$x = 2 \qquad\quad x = \dfrac{1}{3}$$

54. $\sin 360° = 0$

55. $B = 180° - 90° - 20°$

$= 70°$

$$\frac{\sin 70°}{b} = \frac{\sin 90°}{35}$$

$$b = \frac{(\sin 70°)(35)}{\sin 90°}$$

$b \approx 32.9$

$a^2 + (32.9)^2 \approx (35)^2$

$a^2 \approx 142.59$

$a \approx 11.9$

56. $\cos 70° \approx 0.34$

$\cos 170° \approx -0.98$

$\cos 70°$ is greater.

57.

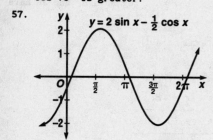

58. area of $\triangle ABE$ + area of $\triangle ECD$

$= \frac{1}{2}hx + \frac{1}{2}hy$

$= \frac{1}{2}h(x + y)$

$= \frac{1}{2}hz$

= area of $\triangle BEC$

The ratio of shaded area

to unshaded area is 1:1.

The best answer is B.

Mid-Chapter Review

PAGE 333

1. $180k°$ **2.** $180k° + 90°$ **3.** $360k° + 90°$

4. $1, 2\pi, -\frac{\pi}{2}$

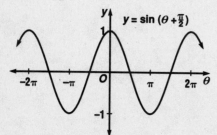

5. none, $180°$, $-60°$

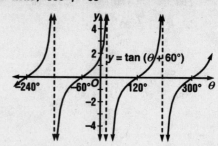

6. $5, \frac{360°}{2} = 180°, 0°$

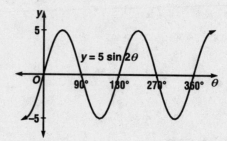

7.

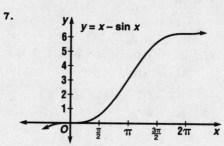

8.

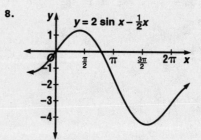

9.

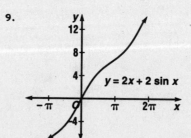

10. $\cos^{-1} \frac{\sqrt{2}}{2} = 45°$, $\tan^{-1} 1 = 45°$;

thus, $\cos^{-1} \frac{\sqrt{2}}{2} = \tan^{-1} 1$.

| **6-5** | **Principal Values of the Inverse Trigonometric Functions** |

PAGE 337   CHECKING FOR UNDERSTANDING

1. They are inverse functions.

2. The trigonometric functions are not one-to-one functions. So if the domains were not restricted, the inverses would not be functions.

3. Restricted domains are denoted with a capital letter.

4. yes; The angle is the same if it is measured in degrees or radians.

5. Let $\theta = \text{Sin}^{-1}\left(-\frac{\sqrt{3}}{2}\right)$.

$\text{Sin }\theta = -\frac{\sqrt{3}}{2}$

$\theta = -60°$

6. Let $\theta = \text{Arctan } 1$.

$\text{Tan }\theta = 1$

$\theta = 45°$

7. Let $\theta = \text{Sin}^{-1} 0$.

$\text{Sin }\theta = 0$

$\theta = 0°$

8. Let $\theta = \text{Sin}^{-1}\left(-\frac{1}{2}\right)$.

$\text{Sin }\theta = -\frac{1}{2}$

$\theta = -30°$

9. Let $\theta = \text{Tan}^{-1}\left(\frac{\sqrt{3}}{3}\right)$.

$\text{Tan }\theta = \frac{\sqrt{3}}{3}$

$\theta = 30°$

10. Let $\theta = \text{Arcsin } 1$.

$\text{Sin }\theta = 1$

$\theta = 90°$

11. Let $\theta = \text{Arccos } 0$.

$\text{Cos }\theta = 0$

$\theta = 90°$

12. Let $\theta = \text{Cos}^{-1} \frac{4}{5}$.

$\text{Cos }\theta = \frac{4}{5}$

13. Let $\theta = \text{Cos}^{-1}\left(-\frac{3}{5}\right)$.

$\text{Cos }\theta = -\frac{3}{5}$

$\text{Sin }\theta = \sqrt{1 - \left(-\frac{3}{5}\right)^2} = \frac{4}{5}$

$\tan \theta = -\frac{4}{3}$

14. Let $\theta = \text{Tan}^{-1} \sqrt{3}$.

$\text{Tan }\theta = \sqrt{3}$

$\theta = 60°$

$\cos (2(60)) = \cos 120°$

$= -\frac{1}{2}$

15. Let $\alpha = \text{Arctan}\left(-\frac{3}{4}\right)$ and $\beta = \text{Arccot}\left(-\frac{4}{3}\right)$.

$\text{Tan }\alpha = -\frac{3}{4}$ $\qquad$ $\text{Cot }\beta = -\frac{4}{3}$

$\alpha \approx -36.9°$ $\qquad$ $\beta \approx -36.9°$

$\sin (\alpha + \beta) = \sin (-73.8)$

$= -0.96$

$= -\frac{24}{25}$

PAGES 337-338 **EXERCISES**

16. Let $\theta = \text{Arctan } 1$.

$\text{Tan }\theta = 1$

$\theta = 45°$

17. Let $\theta = \cos^{-1}\left(-\frac{\sqrt{3}}{2}\right)$.

$\text{Cos }\theta = -\frac{\sqrt{3}}{2}$

$\theta = 150°$

18. Let $\theta = \text{Arcsin }\left(-\frac{\sqrt{2}}{2}\right)$.

$\text{Sin }\theta = -\frac{\sqrt{2}}{2}$

$\theta = -45°$

19. Let $\theta = \text{Arctan } \frac{3}{4}$.

$\text{Tan }\theta = \frac{3}{4}$

$\theta \approx 36.87°$

$\approx 36° \, 52'$

20. Let $\theta = \text{Cos}^{-1}\left(-\frac{1}{2}\right)$.

$\text{Cos }\theta = -\frac{1}{2}$

$\theta = 120°$

21. Let $\theta = \text{Arctan } \sqrt{3}$.

$\text{Tan }\theta = \sqrt{3}$

$\theta = 60°$

22. Let $\theta = \text{Sin}^{-1} \frac{1}{2}$.

$\text{Sin }\theta = \frac{1}{2}$

23. $\cos \frac{\pi}{2} = 0$

$\text{Sin}^{-1} 0 = 0°$

24. Let $\theta = \text{Cos}^{-1} \frac{1}{2}$.

$\cos \theta = \frac{1}{2}$

25. Let $\theta = \text{Tan}^{-1} \sqrt{3}$

$\text{Tan }\theta = \sqrt{3}$

$\theta = 60°$

$\cos 60° = \frac{1}{2}$

26. Let $\theta = \text{Sin}^{-1} \frac{5}{13}$.

$\text{Sin }\theta = \frac{5}{13}$

$\tan \theta = \frac{5}{12}$

27. Let $\theta = \text{Sin}^{-1} \frac{\sqrt{3}}{2}$.

$\sin \theta = \frac{\sqrt{3}}{2}$

28. Let $\theta = \text{Cos}^{-1} \frac{3}{5}$.

$\text{Cos }\theta = \frac{3}{5}$

$\theta \approx 53.13°$

$\sin 2\theta = \sin (106.26°)$

$= 0.96$

$= \frac{24}{25}$

29. Let $\theta = \text{Arcsin }\left(-\frac{1}{2}\right)$.

$\text{Sin }\theta = -\frac{1}{2}$

$\theta = -30°$

$\cos - 30° = \frac{\sqrt{3}}{2}$

30. Let $\theta = \text{Sin}^{-1} \frac{1}{2}$.

$\text{Sin }\theta = \frac{1}{2}$

$\theta = 30°$

$2\theta = 60°$

$\sin 60° = \frac{\sqrt{3}}{2}$

31. Let $\theta = \text{Arctan } (-\sqrt{3})$.

$\text{Tan }\theta = -\sqrt{3}$

$\theta = -60°$

$\sin (-60°) = -\frac{\sqrt{3}}{2}$

32. Let $\theta = \text{Tan}^{-1} 1$.

$\text{Tan }\theta = 1$

$\theta = 45°$

$\cos 45° = \frac{\sqrt{2}}{2}$

33. Let $\theta = \text{Sin}^{-1} \frac{\sqrt{3}}{2}$.

$\text{Sin }\theta = \frac{\sqrt{3}}{2}$

$\theta = 60°$

$2\theta = 120°$

$\sin 2\theta = \frac{\sqrt{3}}{2}$

34. Let $\theta = \text{Sin}^{-1} \frac{15}{17}$.

$\text{Sin } \theta = \frac{15}{17}$

$\theta \approx 61°56'$

$\frac{1}{2}\theta \approx 30°58'$

$\tan 30°58' \approx 0.6 \text{ or } \frac{3}{5}$

35. Let $\theta = \text{Arctan } \frac{3}{5}$.

$\text{Tan } \theta = \frac{3}{5}$

$\theta \approx 30.96°$

$\frac{1}{2}\theta \approx 15.48°$

$\sin 15.48° \approx 0.2669$

36. Let $\alpha = \text{Tan}^{-1} \sqrt{3}$ and $\beta = \text{Sin}^{-1} \frac{1}{2}$.

$\text{Tan } \alpha = \sqrt{3} \qquad \text{Sin } \beta = \frac{1}{2}$

$\alpha = 60° \qquad\qquad \beta = 30°$

$\cos (60° - 30°) = \cos 30°$

$\qquad\qquad = \frac{\sqrt{3}}{2}$

37. Let $\alpha = \text{Cos}^{-1} 0$ and $\beta = \text{Sin}^{-1} \frac{1}{2}$.

$\text{Cos } \alpha = 0 \qquad \text{Sin } \beta = \frac{1}{2}$

$\alpha = 90° \qquad\qquad \beta = 30°$

$\cos (90° + 30°) = \cos 120°$

$\qquad\qquad = -\frac{1}{2}$

38. Let $\alpha = \text{Tan}^{-1} 1$ and $\beta = \text{Sin}^{-1} 1$.

$\text{Tan } \alpha = 1 \qquad \text{Sin } \beta = 1$

$\alpha = 45° \qquad\qquad \beta = 90°$

$\sin (45° - 90°) = \sin (-45°)$

$\qquad\qquad = -\frac{\sqrt{2}}{2}$

39. Let $\alpha = \text{Cos}^{-1} \left(-\frac{1}{2}\right)$ and $\beta = \text{Sin}^{-1} 2$.

$\text{Cos } \alpha = -\frac{1}{2} \qquad \text{Sin } \beta = 2$

$\alpha = 120° \qquad\qquad \text{not possible}$

40. Let $\theta = \text{Cos}^{-1} \left(-\frac{\sqrt{2}}{2}\right)$.

$\text{Cos } \theta = -\frac{\sqrt{2}}{2}$

$\theta = 135°$

$\theta = \frac{3\pi}{4}$

$\cos \left(\frac{3\pi}{4} - \frac{\pi}{2}\right) = \cos \frac{\pi}{4}$

$\qquad\qquad = \frac{\sqrt{2}}{2}$

41. Let $\theta = \text{Cos}^{-1} \left(-\frac{1}{2}\right)$.

$\text{Cos } \theta = -\frac{1}{2}$

$\theta = 120°$

$\theta = \frac{2\pi}{3}$

$\cos \left(\frac{4\pi}{3} - \frac{2\pi}{3}\right) = \cos \frac{2\pi}{3}$

$\qquad\qquad = -\frac{1}{2}$

42. Let $\theta = \text{Cos}^{-1} \left(\frac{1}{2}\right)$.

$\text{Cos } \theta = \frac{1}{2}$

$\theta = 60°$

$\theta = \frac{\pi}{3}$

$\sin \left(\frac{\pi}{2} - \frac{\pi}{3}\right) = \sin \frac{\pi}{6}$

$\qquad\qquad = \frac{1}{2}$

43. Let $\alpha = \text{Cos}^{-1} \frac{3}{5}$ and $\beta = \text{Sin}^{-1} \frac{5}{13}$.

$\text{Cos } \alpha = \frac{3}{5} \qquad \text{Sin } \beta = \frac{5}{13}$

$\alpha = 53.13° \qquad \beta = 22.62°$

$\tan (53.13° - 22.62°) = \tan 30.51°$

$\qquad\qquad = 0.59$

$\qquad\qquad = \frac{33}{56}$

44.

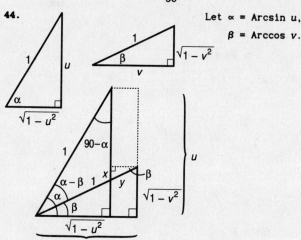

Let $\alpha = \text{Arcsin } u$, $\beta = \text{Arccos } v$.

$\sin (\text{Arcsin } u - \text{Arccos } v) = \sin (\alpha - \beta)$

By similar triangles,

$\frac{x}{\sqrt{1 - v^2}} = \frac{v - \sqrt{1 - u^2}}{v}$

$x = \frac{\left(v - \sqrt{1 - u^2}\right)\sqrt{1 - v^2}}{v}$

$\frac{y}{1} = \frac{v - \sqrt{1 - u^2}}{v}$

$y = \frac{v - \sqrt{1 - u^2}}{v}$

Use the law of sines.

$\frac{\sin (\alpha - \beta)}{x + u - \sqrt{1 - v^2}} = \frac{\sin (90 - \alpha)}{1 - y}$

$\frac{\sin (\alpha - \beta)}{x + u - \sqrt{1 - v^2}} = \frac{\sqrt{1 - u^2}}{1 - y}$

$$\sin(\alpha - \beta) = \frac{\sqrt{1 - u^2}\left(x + u - \sqrt{1 - v^2}\right)}{1 - y}$$

$$= \frac{\sqrt{1 - u^2}\left[\left(\dfrac{\left(v - \sqrt{1 - u^2}\right)\sqrt{1 - v^2}}{v}\right) + u - \sqrt{1 - v^2}\right]}{1 - \dfrac{v - \sqrt{1 - u^2}}{v}}$$

$$= \frac{\sqrt{1 - u^2}\left[\dfrac{v\sqrt{1 - v^2} - \sqrt{(1 - u^2)(1 - v^2)}}{v} + u - \sqrt{1 - v^2}\right]}{1 - \left(1 - \dfrac{\sqrt{1 - u^2}}{v}\right)}$$

$$= \frac{\dfrac{v\sqrt{(1 - v^2)(1 - u^2)} - (1 - u^2)\sqrt{1 - v^2}}{v} + uv\sqrt{1 - u^2} - \sqrt{(1 - u^2)(1 - v^2)}}{\dfrac{\sqrt{1 - u^2}}{v}}$$

$$= \frac{\dfrac{\sqrt{(1 - v^2)(1 - u^2)} - (1 - u^2)\sqrt{1 - v^2}}{v} + u\sqrt{1 - u^2} - \sqrt{(1 - u^2)(1 - v^2)}}{\dfrac{\sqrt{1 - u^2}}{v}}$$

$$= \frac{v\sqrt{(1 - u^2)(1 - v^2)} - (1 - u^2)\sqrt{1 - v^2} + uv\sqrt{1 - u^2} - v\sqrt{(1 - u^2)(1 - v^2)}}{\sqrt{1 - u^2}}$$

$$= v\sqrt{1 - v^2} - \sqrt{(1 - u^2)(1 - v^2)} + uv - v\sqrt{1 - v^2}$$

$$= uv - \sqrt{(1 - u^2)(1 - v^2)}$$

45. $P = VI \cos \phi$

$7.2 = (120)(0.75) \cos \phi$

$0.08 = \cos \phi$

$85.4° = \phi$

46. a. $0°$, the light is pointed along the perpendicular to the surface of the water.

b. See students' work.

47. no

48. Let x = number of units of newsprint.

Let y = number of units of notebook paper.

$x + y \le 200$

$x \ge 80, \ y \ge 10$

profit = $350x + 500y$

possible solutions: (80, 10), (190, 10), (80, 120)

at (80, 10), profit = \$33,000

at (190, 10), profit = \$71,500

at (80, 120), profit = \$88,000 ← max

120 units of notebook paper and 80 units of newsprint

49. As $x \to \infty$, $y \to \infty$, as $x \to -\infty$, $y \to -\infty$.

50. possible rational roots: $\pm 7, \ \pm \dfrac{7}{3}, \ \pm \dfrac{1}{3}, \ \pm 1$

$f(7) = 49,412,517 \qquad f(-7) = 0$

$f\left(\dfrac{7}{3}\right) = 360.89 \qquad f\left(-\dfrac{7}{3}\right) = -240.59$

$f\left(\dfrac{1}{3}\right) = 0 \qquad f\left(-\dfrac{1}{3}\right) = -14.81$

$f(1) = 32 \qquad f(-1) = -8 \qquad$ roots: $-7, \dfrac{1}{3}$

51. no solution

52. $s = \dfrac{1}{2}(7 + 9 + 12) = 14$

$K = \sqrt{14(14 - 7)(14 - 9)(14 - 12)} \approx 31.3 \ \text{in}^2$

53. Let $\theta = \text{Sin}^{-1} \dfrac{1}{2}$.

$\sin \theta = \dfrac{1}{2}$

$\theta = 30°$

$2\theta = 60°$

$\sin 60° = \dfrac{\sqrt{3}}{2}$

54. $\left(\dfrac{2x^2}{y}\right)^3 = \dfrac{2^3(x^2)^3}{y^3}$

$= \dfrac{8x^6}{y^3}$

The best answer is A.

Graphing Calculators: Graphing Inverses of Trigonometric Functions

PAGE 339   EXERCISES

1.

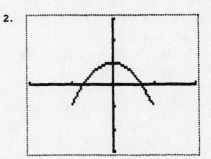

2.

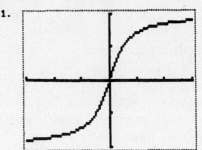

3.

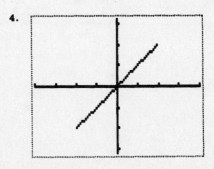

4.

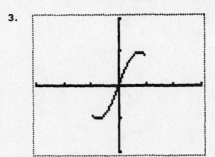

5.

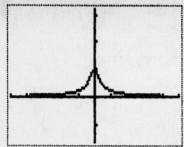

6.

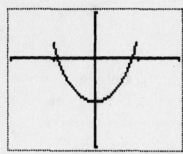

Graphing Inverses of Trigonometric Functions

PAGE 342   CHECKING FOR UNDERSTANDING

1. The graph of the inverse is the graph of the function reflected across the line $y = x$.

2. Sample answer: Exchange the roles of x and y and solve for y.

3. The domain of the relation is the range of the inverse and the range of the relation is the domain of the inverse.

4. all real numbers; $-1 \leq y \leq 1$

5. all real numbers except $90° + n \cdot 180°$; all real numbers

6. $0° \leq x \leq 180°$; $-1 \leq y \leq 1$

7. $-1 \leq x \leq 1$; all real numbers

8. $-1 \leq x \leq 1$; $0° \leq y \leq 180°$

9. all real numbers; $-90° < y < 90°$

10. $y = \arccos x$

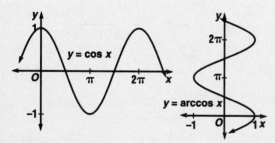

11. true

12. false; Answers may vary.

PAGES 343-344   EXERCISES

13. all real numbers; $-1 \leq y \leq 1$

14. $-90° \leq x \leq 90°$, $-1 \leq y \leq 1$

15. $-90° < x < 90°$; all real numbers

16. $-1 \leq x \leq 1$; all real numbers

17. $-1 \leq x \leq 1$; $-90° \leq y \leq 90°$

18. all real numbers; all real numbers except $90° + n \cdot 180°$

19. $y = \text{Tan } x$

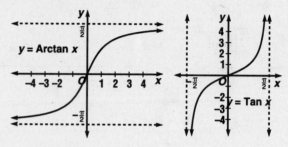

20. $y = \text{Sin } x$

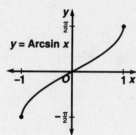
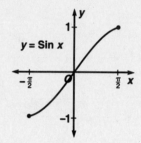

21. $y = \text{Arcsin } x$

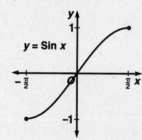
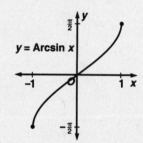

22.
$$x = \frac{\pi}{2} + \text{Arcsin } y$$
$$x - \frac{\pi}{2} = \text{Arcsin } y$$
$$\text{Sin}\left(x - \frac{\pi}{2}\right) = y$$

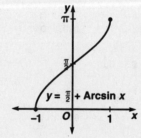
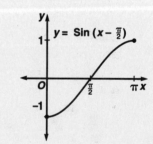

23.

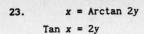

$x = \text{Arctan } 2y$

$\text{Tan } x = 2y$

$\frac{1}{2} \text{Tan } x = y$

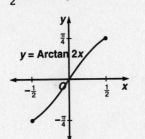

$y = \text{Arctan } 2x$

$y = \frac{1}{2}\text{Tan } x$

24.

$x = \text{Cos } (y + 90°)$

$\text{Arccos } x = y + 90°$

$\text{Arccos } (x - 90°) = y$

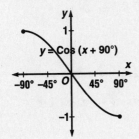

$y = \text{Cos } (x + 90°)$

$y = \text{Arccos } (x - 90°)$

25. true

26. False; when $x = -1$, $\text{Arccos } (-1) = 180°$,

$\text{Arccos } (-(-1)) = 0$.

27. False; when $x = 1$, $\cos^{-1} (-1) = 180°$,

$\cos^{-1} (1) = 0$.

28. true

29. False; when $x = \frac{\pi}{2}$, $\cos^{-1} x = $ undefined,

$\cos x = 0$.

30. False; when $x = 0$, $\text{Tan}^{-1} x = 0$, $\text{Tan } 0 = 0$.

31.

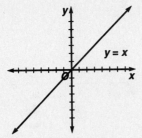

$y = x$

32.

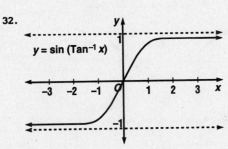

$y = \sin (\text{Tan}^{-1} x)$

33.

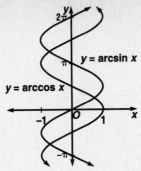

$y = \text{arcsin } x$

$y = \text{arccos } x$

$\frac{\pi}{4} + k\pi$, where k is any integer

34. a.

$\ell = 6077 - 31 \cos 2\theta$

$\ell - 6077 = -31 \cos 2\theta$

$\frac{6077 - \ell}{31} = \cos 2\theta$

$\text{arccos } \left(\frac{6077 - \ell}{31}\right) = 2\theta$

$\frac{1}{2} \text{arccos } \left(\frac{6077 - \ell}{31}\right) = \theta$

b. $\ell = 6077 - 31 \cos (2(40))$

≈ 6071.6 ft

c. $\theta = \frac{1}{2} \text{arccos } \left(\frac{6077 - 6060}{31}\right)$

$\approx$ 28th parallel

35. a.

$\tan 37° = \frac{m_2 - 2}{1 + 2m_2}$

$\tan 37° (1 + 2m_2) = m_2 - 2$

$\tan 37° + 2m_2 \tan 37° = m_2 - 2$

$\tan 37° + 2 = m_2 - 2m_2 \tan 37°$

$\frac{\tan 37° + 2}{1 - 2 \tan 37°} = m_2$

$-5.43 \approx m_2$

b. $\tan \theta = \dfrac{\frac{3}{4} - \left(-\frac{1}{2}\right)}{1 + \left(\frac{3}{4}\right)\left(-\frac{1}{2}\right)}$

$= \dfrac{\frac{5}{4}}{\frac{5}{8}}$

$= 2$

$\theta \approx 63°$

from t to s: about $-63°$

36. a. Answers may vary. Sample answers:

0.1973955598; 0.004184076

b. Answers may vary. See students' work.

c. See students' work.

37. $(f \circ g)(x) = f(g(x))$ $(g \circ f)(x) = g(f(x))$

$= (3x)^3 - 1$ $= 3(x^3 - 1)$

$= 27x^3 - 1$ $= 3x^3 - 3$

38. $2x - 6y = -3$

$\qquad -6y = -2x - 3$

$\qquad y = \frac{1}{3}x + 2, \ m = \frac{1}{3}$

$\qquad y + 4 = \frac{1}{3}(x - 9)$

$\qquad 3y + 12 = x - 9$

$\qquad 0 = x - 3y - 21$

39. $\sqrt{2y - 3} = -1 + \sqrt{2y + 3}$

$\qquad 2y - 3 = 1 - 2\sqrt{2y + 3} + 2y + 3$

$\qquad -7 = -2\sqrt{2y + 3}$

$\qquad 49 = 4(2y + 3)$

$\qquad 49 = 8y + 12$

$\qquad 37 = 8y$

$\qquad \frac{37}{8} = y$

40. $x = 4, \ y = 3, \ r = \sqrt{16 + 9}$

$\qquad\qquad\qquad\qquad = 5$

$\qquad \cos \alpha = \frac{x}{r}$

$\qquad\qquad = \frac{4}{5}$

41. Let $\alpha = \text{Tan}^{-1} \sqrt{3}$ and $\beta = \text{Sin}^{-1} \frac{1}{2}$.

$\qquad \tan \alpha = \sqrt{3} \qquad\qquad \sin \beta = \frac{1}{2}$

$\qquad\quad \alpha = 60° \qquad\qquad\quad \beta = 30°$

$\qquad \cos (60° - 30°) = \cos 30°$

$\qquad\qquad\qquad\qquad\quad = \frac{\sqrt{3}}{2}$

42. $\dfrac{120a^5b^6}{8a^3b^2} = 15a^2b^4$

$\qquad \dfrac{120a^4b^{\frac{13}{2}}}{6a^0b^{\frac{1}{2}}} = 20a^4b^6$

Quantity B is greater. B

6-7 Simple Harmonic Motion

1. See students' work.

2. They are reciprocals.

3. $\frac{1}{330} \approx 0.003$ second

4. $7, \ \dfrac{2\pi}{\frac{\pi}{2}} = 4, \ \dfrac{1}{4}, \ \dfrac{-\frac{\pi}{4}}{\frac{\pi}{2}} = -\dfrac{1}{2}$

5. $8, \ \dfrac{2\pi}{4} = \dfrac{\pi}{2}, \ \dfrac{2}{\pi}, \ \dfrac{\pi}{4}$

6. $120, \ \dfrac{2\pi}{100\pi} = \dfrac{1}{50}, \ 50, \ 0$

7. $4, \ \dfrac{2\pi}{3}, \ \dfrac{3}{2\pi}, \ \dfrac{-\frac{3\pi}{4}}{3} = -\dfrac{\pi}{4}$

8. $y = -3 \cos \pi t$ 　　　9. $y = 5 \sin \pi t$

10. $y = 7 \sin \dfrac{\pi t}{5}$ 　　　11. $y = 7 \cos \dfrac{\pi t}{5}$

12. $y = 6 \sin \dfrac{\pi}{3}t$ 　　　13. $y = -5 \cos \dfrac{\pi t}{6}$

14. $5, \ \dfrac{2\pi}{\pi} = 2, \ \dfrac{1}{2}, \ \dfrac{-\left(-\frac{\pi}{2}\right)}{\pi} = \dfrac{1}{2}$

15. $15, \ \dfrac{2\pi}{\frac{\pi}{3}} = 6, \ \dfrac{1}{6}, \ 0$

16. $10, \ \dfrac{2\pi}{2\pi} = 1, \ 1, \ \dfrac{\pi}{2\pi} = \dfrac{1}{2}$

17. $150, \ \dfrac{2\pi}{80\pi} = \dfrac{1}{40}, \ 40, \ 0$

18. $0.1, \ \dfrac{2\pi}{\frac{\pi}{4}} = 8, \ \dfrac{1}{8}, \ \dfrac{-\frac{\pi}{4}}{\frac{\pi}{4}} = -1$

19. $25, \ \dfrac{2\pi}{8} = \dfrac{\pi}{4}, \ \dfrac{4}{\pi}, \ 0$

20. $y = -7 \cos \dfrac{\pi}{2}t$ 　　　21. $y = 0.5 \sin 2\pi t$

22. $y = 22 \sin \dfrac{\pi}{6}t$ 　　　23. $y = 10 \cos 4\pi t$

24. They are not affected.

25. a. frequency $= \dfrac{14 \text{ rev}}{\text{min}}$

$\qquad\qquad\qquad = \dfrac{14 \text{ rev}}{60 \text{ s}}$

$\qquad\qquad\qquad = \dfrac{7}{30} \dfrac{\text{rev}}{\text{s}}$

$\qquad$ period $= \dfrac{30}{7}$ second

b. $\left(3.5 \cos \dfrac{7}{15}\pi t, \ 3.5 \sin \dfrac{7}{15}\pi t \right)$

c. $(3.20, -1.42)$

d. $(-3.50, 0.18)$

e. $3.5 \cos \left(\dfrac{7}{15}\pi t + \dfrac{\pi}{2} \right), \ 3.5 \sin \left(\dfrac{7}{15}\pi t + \dfrac{\pi}{2} \right)$

f. $2.2^2 + x^2 = 3.5^2$

$\qquad\qquad x^2 = 7.41$

$\qquad\qquad x \approx \pm 2.72$

26. a. $h = 2.2 \cos 30° + \sqrt{5.8^2 + 2.2^2 (\sin 30°)^2}$

$\qquad\quad \approx 1.91 + 5.90$

$\qquad\quad \approx 7.81$ in.

b.

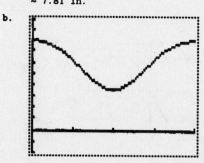

27. a. pulled down

b. at $t = 0$, $y = 3 \sin \left(-\frac{\pi}{2} \right)$

$\qquad = -3$

$\qquad 3 + 5 = 8$ ft

c. $10 - 8 = 2$ ft

d. $0 = 3 \sin \left(\pi t - \frac{\pi}{2} \right)$

$\qquad \sin \left(\pi t - \frac{\pi}{2} \right) = 0$ when $\pi t - \frac{\pi}{2} = 0$

$\qquad\qquad\qquad\qquad\qquad \pi t = \frac{\pi}{2}$

$\qquad\qquad\qquad\qquad\qquad t = \frac{1}{2}$ s

e. 8 ft $\qquad\qquad$ **f.** $\frac{2\pi}{\pi} = 2$ seconds

g. 3 ft $\qquad\qquad$ **h.** $\frac{1}{2}$ cycle/second

i. at $t = 2.5$, $y = 3 \sin \left(2.5\pi - \frac{\pi}{2} \right)$

$\qquad = 0$

$\qquad 5$ ft

28. a. at $t = 0$, $m = 1200 + 300 \sin 0$

$\qquad = 1200$

b. at $t = 0$, $H = 250 + 25 \sin \left(-\frac{\pi}{4} \right)$

$\qquad = 232$

c. 1500 when $t = 1$, and 275 when $t = \frac{3}{2}$; no

d. when $t = 1$, January 1, 1971

e. when $\frac{\pi t}{2} - \frac{\pi}{4} = \frac{3\pi}{2}$

$\qquad\qquad\quad \frac{\pi t}{2} = \frac{7\pi}{4}$

$\qquad\qquad\quad t = \frac{7}{2} = 3\frac{1}{2}$, $H = 225$

$\qquad$ occurred on July 1, 1973

f. See students' work.

29.

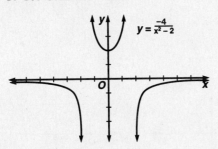

$y = \frac{-4}{x^2 - 2}$

30. -1.1, -0.6, 0.6, 1.1

31. yes, $-15° + 360° = 345°$

32. $\sin 60° = \frac{a}{6.4}$

$\qquad 5.5 = a$

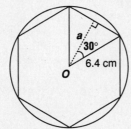

33. $\frac{1}{a} + \frac{1}{b} = 7$ $\qquad$ $\left(\frac{1}{a} + \frac{1}{b} \right)\left(\frac{1}{a} - \frac{1}{b} \right) = 7 \cdot 3$

$\quad \frac{1}{a} - \frac{1}{b} = 3$ $\quad \rightarrow \quad$ $\frac{1}{a^2} - \frac{1}{b^2} = 21$

Chapter 6 Summary and Review

PAGES 352–354 $\qquad$ SKILLS AND CONCEPTS

1. 0 $\quad$ **2.** 1 $\quad$ **3.** undefined $\quad$ **4.** -1

5.

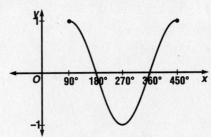

6.

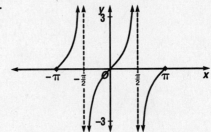

7.

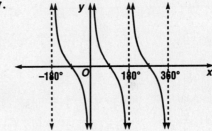

8. 4, $\frac{360°}{2} = 180°$, 0°

9. 15, $\frac{360°}{\frac{3}{2}} = 240°$, $\frac{-90°}{\frac{3}{2}} = -60°$

10. none, $\frac{180°}{\frac{1}{2}} = 360°$, $\frac{45°}{\frac{1}{2}} = 90°$

11. none, $\frac{180°}{5} = 36°$, 0°

12.

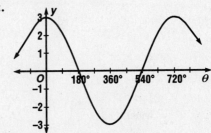

13.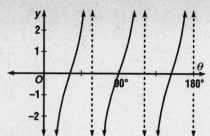

14.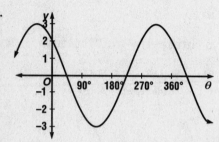

15.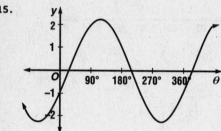

16.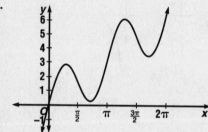

17. $\alpha = \arcsin y$

18. $y = \arctan x$

19. $\theta = \arccos n$

20. $\theta = \text{arcsec } y$

21. Let $\theta = \arccos \frac{1}{2}$.

$\cos \theta = \frac{1}{2}$

22. Let $\theta = \text{arccot } \frac{4}{5}$.

$\cot \theta = \frac{4}{5}$

$\tan \theta = \frac{5}{4}$

23. Let $\alpha = \tan^{-1} 1$ and $\beta = \sin^{-1} 1$.

$\tan \alpha = 1 \qquad \sin \beta = 1$

$\alpha = 45° \qquad\quad \beta = 90°$

$\sin 45° + \cos 90° = \frac{\sqrt{2}}{2} + 0$

$\qquad\qquad\qquad = \frac{\sqrt{2}}{2}$

24. Let $\alpha = \arcsin \frac{\sqrt{3}}{2}$ and $\beta = \arccos \frac{\sqrt{3}}{2}$.

$\sin \alpha = \frac{\sqrt{3}}{2} \qquad \cos \beta = \frac{\sqrt{3}}{2}$

$\alpha = 60° \qquad\quad \beta = 30°$

$\tan (60° + 30°) = \tan 90°$

$\qquad\qquad\qquad = \text{undefined}$

25. Let $\theta = \text{Sin}^{-1} \frac{1}{2}$.

$\text{Sin } \theta = \frac{1}{2}$

$\theta = 30°$

$\cos 30° = \frac{\sqrt{3}}{2}$

26. Let $\theta = \text{Sin}^{-1} \frac{\sqrt{3}}{2}$.

$\text{Sin } \theta = \frac{\sqrt{3}}{2}$

$\theta = 60°$

$3\theta = 180°$

$\sin 180° = 0$

27. Let $\theta = \text{Arcsin } \frac{1}{2}$.

$\text{Sin } \theta = \frac{1}{2}$

$\theta = 30°$

$2\theta = 60°$

$\sin 60° = \frac{\sqrt{3}}{2}$

28. Let $\theta = \text{Cos}^{-1} \frac{\sqrt{2}}{2}$.

$\text{Cos } \theta = \frac{\sqrt{2}}{2}$

$\theta = 45° \text{ or } \frac{\pi}{4}$

$\cos \left(\frac{\pi}{2} - \frac{\pi}{4} \right) = \cos \frac{\pi}{4}$

$\qquad\qquad\qquad = \frac{\sqrt{2}}{2}$

29. Let $\alpha = \text{Arctan } \sqrt{3}$ and $\beta = \text{Arcsin } \frac{1}{2}$.

$\text{Tan } \alpha = \sqrt{3} \qquad \text{Sin } \beta = \frac{1}{2}$

$\alpha = 60° \qquad\qquad \beta = 30°$

$\cos (60° + 30°) = \cos 90°$

$\qquad\qquad\qquad = 0$

30. $\qquad y = \text{Arcsin } x$

$\qquad x = \text{Arcsin } y$

$\quad \text{Sin } x = y$

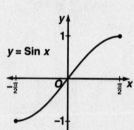

31. $\qquad y = \text{Csc } x$

$\qquad x = \text{Csc } y$

$\text{Csc}^{-1} x = y$

32.
$$y = \cot x$$
$$x = \cot y$$
$$\cot^{-1} x = y$$

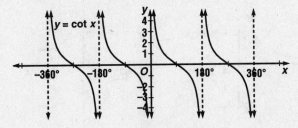

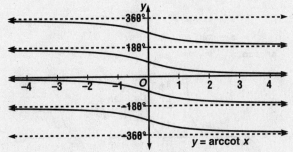

$y = \text{arccot } x$

33.
$$y = \text{arcsec } x$$
$$x = \text{arcsec } y$$
$$\sec x = y$$

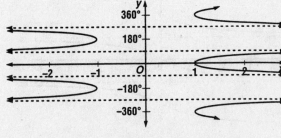

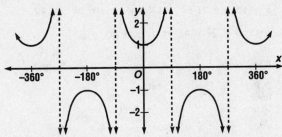

34. $x = 5 \cos 8\pi t$
$y = 5 \sin 8\pi t$

35. 4 cycles per second

36. $x = 5 \cos \left(8\pi \cdot \dfrac{1}{6}\right) = -\dfrac{5}{2}$

$y = 5 \sin \left(8\pi \cdot \dfrac{1}{6}\right) = -\dfrac{5\sqrt{3}}{2}$

37. a. $122 - 46 = 76; \dfrac{76}{2} = 38$ (amplitude)

period $= 2(3) = 6$

$y = -38 \cos \dfrac{\pi}{3} t$

b. $122 - 38 = 84$

$y = -38 \cos \dfrac{\pi}{3} t - 84$

c. at $t = 30$, $y = -38 \cos \dfrac{\pi}{3}(30) - 84$

$= -122$

122 feet below the ledge

38. $0.04 = \dfrac{0.2}{(5)(1) \sin \theta}$

$\sin \theta = \dfrac{0.2}{(0.04)(5)(1)}$

$\sin \theta = 1$

$\theta = \dfrac{\pi}{2}$ or $90°$

Chapter 6 Test

PAGE 355

1. $180k°$, k is any integer

2. $270° + 360k°$, k is any integer

3. $45° + 360k°$ and $315° + 360k°$, k is any integer

4.

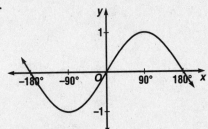

5.

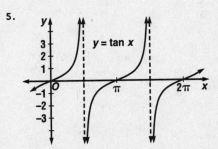

6. $3, \dfrac{360°}{4} = 90°, 0°$ **7.** $110, \dfrac{360°}{15} = 24°, \dfrac{40}{15} = 2\dfrac{2}{3}°$

8. $10, 360°, \dfrac{-\pi}{-1} = \pi$ or $180°$

147

9.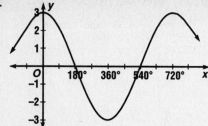

10.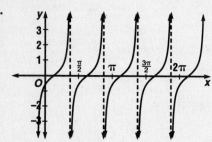

11.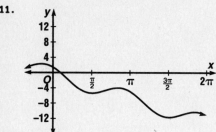

12. Let $\theta = \arccos \frac{\sqrt{3}}{2}$.

$\cos \theta = \frac{\sqrt{3}}{2}$

$\theta = 30°$

$\sin 30° = \frac{1}{2}$

13. Let $\theta = \cos^{-1} \frac{5}{13}$.

$\cos \theta = \frac{5}{13}$

$\theta \approx 67.4°$

$\tan \theta = 2.4$

$\tan \theta = \frac{12}{5}$

14. Let $\alpha = \arctan \sqrt{3}$ and $\beta = \text{arccot} \sqrt{3}$.

$\tan \alpha = \sqrt{3}$ $\cot \beta = \sqrt{3}$

$\alpha = 60°$ $\beta = 30°$

$\cos (60° + 30°) = \cos 90°$

$= 0$

15. Let $\theta = \text{Arccos} \frac{1}{2}$.

$\text{Cos} \theta = \frac{1}{2}$

$\theta = 60°$

$\sin 60° = \frac{\sqrt{3}}{2}$

16. Let $\theta = \text{Tan}^{-1} \frac{3}{4}$.

$\text{Tan} \theta = \frac{3}{4}$

$\theta = 36.9°$

$\frac{1}{2}\theta = 18.45°$

$\cos 18.45° = 0.95$

$= \frac{3\sqrt{10}}{10}$

17. Let $\theta = \text{Arcsin} \frac{2}{3}$

$\text{Sin} \theta = \frac{2}{3}$

$\theta = 41.8°$

$\tan (\pi + \theta) = 0.89$

$= \frac{2\sqrt{5}}{5}$

18. $y = \text{Arccsc } x$

        $x = \text{Arccsc } y$

   $\text{Csc } x = y$

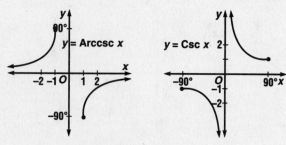

19. $y = \tan x$

        $x = \tan y$

  $\arctan x = y$

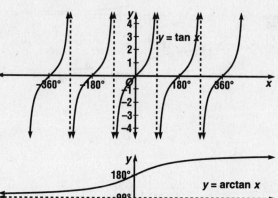

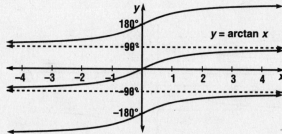

20. $x = 10 \cos 2t$ **21.** $y = 10 \sin 2t$ **22.** 10

23. period $= \frac{2\pi}{2} = \pi$, so frequency $= \frac{1}{\pi}$

24. amplitude $= \frac{6 - 2}{2} = 2$ ft   period $= \frac{2\pi}{k} = 12$ h

2 P.M. is the fourteenth $k = \frac{\pi}{6}$
hour of the day.
Since the low point is 2 ft, the
equation is $y = 2 \cos (\frac{\pi}{6}t) + 4$.

Thus, at $t = 14$, $y = 5$ ft.

25. 65 mph ≈ 95.33 ft/s

$\tan \theta \approx \frac{(95.33)^2}{(32)(1200)}$

$\tan \theta \approx 0.24$

$\theta \approx 13.31°$

PAGE 355   **BONUS**

The graph of $y = x^2 - \cos x$ is symmetric with
respect to the y-axis. So the function is even.

Chapter 7   Trigonometric Identities and Equations

7-1   Basic Trigonometric Identities

PAGES 361-362   CHECKING FOR UNDERSTANDING

1. Simplifying an expression that contains trigonometric functions means that the expression is written as a numerical value or in terms of a single trigonometric function, if possible.

2. The secant, cosecant, and cotangent can be found by finding the multiplicative inverse of the cosine, sine, or tangent.

3. The identity does not hold true for values of θ for which any of the ratios are undefined.

$\cot \theta = \dfrac{\cos \theta}{\sin \theta}$ is undefined for $\theta = 0°$ or $180°$.

4. $\cos^2 A + \sin^2 A = 1$

$\cos^2 A = 1 - \sin^2 A$

$\cos^2 A = 1 - \left(\dfrac{4}{5}\right)^2$

$\quad = 1 - \dfrac{16}{25}$

$\quad = \dfrac{9}{25}$

$\cos A = \sqrt{\dfrac{9}{25}} = \dfrac{3}{5}$

5. $\tan A = \dfrac{\sin A}{\cos A}$

$= \dfrac{\sin A}{\sqrt{1 - \sin^2 A}}$

$= \dfrac{\dfrac{4}{5}}{\sqrt{1 - \left(\dfrac{4}{5}\right)^2}}$

$= \dfrac{\dfrac{4}{5}}{\dfrac{3}{5}}$

$= \dfrac{4}{3}$

6. $\csc A = \dfrac{1}{\sin A}$

$= \dfrac{1}{\dfrac{4}{5}}$

$= \dfrac{5}{4}$

7. $\cot \theta = \dfrac{1}{\tan \theta}$

$= \dfrac{1}{3}$

8. $\cos \theta = \sqrt{1 - \sin^2 \theta}$

$= \sqrt{1 - \left(\dfrac{5}{13}\right)^2}$

$= \sqrt{1 - \dfrac{25}{169}}$

$= \sqrt{\dfrac{144}{169}}$

$= \dfrac{12}{13}$

9. $\tan \theta = \dfrac{\sin \theta}{\cos \theta}$

$= \dfrac{\sqrt{1 - \cos^2 \theta}}{\cos \theta}$

$= \dfrac{\sqrt{1 - \left(\dfrac{2}{3}\right)^2}}{\dfrac{2}{3}}$

$= \dfrac{\sqrt{\dfrac{5}{9}}}{\dfrac{2}{3}}$

$= \dfrac{\sqrt{5}}{2}$

10. $\sec \theta = \dfrac{1}{\cos \theta}$

$= \dfrac{1}{\sqrt{1 - \sin^2 \theta}}$

$= \dfrac{1}{\sqrt{1 - \left(\dfrac{1}{\csc \theta}\right)^2}}$

$= \dfrac{1}{\sqrt{1 - \left(\dfrac{1}{5}\right)^2}}$

$= \dfrac{1}{\sqrt{\dfrac{24}{25}}}$

$= \dfrac{1}{\dfrac{2\sqrt{6}}{5}}$

$= \dfrac{5}{2\sqrt{6}} \cdot \dfrac{\sqrt{6}}{\sqrt{6}}$

$= \dfrac{5\sqrt{6}}{12}$

11. $\sin 400° = \sin (40° + 360°)$

$\quad = \sin 40°$

12. $\tan 475° = \dfrac{\sin 475°}{\cos 475°}$

$= \dfrac{\sin (540 - 65)°}{\cos (540 - 65)°}$

$= \dfrac{\sin 180°(3) - 65°}{\cos 180°(3) - 65°}$

$= \dfrac{\sin 65°}{-\cos 65°}$

$= -\tan 65°$

13. $\cos 220° = \cos (40° + 180°)$

$\quad = -\cos 40°$

14. $\csc^2 \theta - \cot^2 \theta = 1 + \cot^2 \theta - \cot^2 \theta$

$\quad = 1$

15. $\dfrac{\sin x + \cos x}{\cos^2 x} = \dfrac{1}{\cos^2 x}$

   $\qquad = \sec^2 x$

16. $\cos y \csc y = \cos y \left(\dfrac{1}{\sin y}\right)$

   $\qquad = \dfrac{\cos y}{\sin y}$

   $\qquad = \cot y$

17. $2 \csc^2 \alpha - \csc^4 \alpha + \cot^4 \alpha$

   $= 2 \csc^2 \alpha + (\cot^4 \alpha - \csc^4 \alpha)$

   $= 2 \csc^2 \alpha + (\cot^2 \alpha - \csc^2 \alpha)(\cot^2 \alpha + \csc^2 \alpha)$

   $= 2 \csc^2 \alpha + (-1)(\cot^2 \alpha + \csc^2 \alpha)$

   $= 2 \csc^2 \alpha - \cot^2 \alpha - \csc^2 \alpha$

   $= \csc^2 \alpha - \cot^2 \alpha$

   $= 1$

18. $\dfrac{\tan z}{\sin z} = \dfrac{\frac{\sin z}{\cos z}}{\sin z}$

   $\qquad = \dfrac{\sin z}{\cos z} \cdot \dfrac{1}{\sin z}$

   $\qquad = \dfrac{1}{\cos z}$

   $\qquad = \sec z$

19. $\tan A \csc A = \dfrac{\sin A}{\cos A} \cdot \dfrac{1}{\sin A}$

   $\qquad = \dfrac{1}{\cos A}$

   $\qquad = \sec A$

PAGES 362–363   EXERCISES

20. $\tan \theta = \dfrac{1}{\cot \theta}$ 21. $\csc \theta = \dfrac{1}{\sin \theta}$

   $\qquad = \dfrac{1}{2}$ $\qquad = \dfrac{1}{0}$

   $\qquad\qquad\qquad\qquad$ undefined

22. $\cos \theta = \dfrac{1}{\sec \theta}$ 23. $\tan \theta = \dfrac{1}{\cot \theta}$

   $\qquad = \dfrac{1}{4.5}$ $\qquad = \dfrac{1}{1}$

   $\qquad = \dfrac{1}{\frac{9}{2}}$ $\qquad = 1$

   $\qquad = \dfrac{2}{9}$

24. $\cos^2 \theta = 1 - \sin^2 \theta$ 25. $\sec^2 \theta = \tan^2 \theta + 1$

   $\cos \theta = \sqrt{1 - \sin^2 \theta}$ $\sec \theta = \sqrt{\tan^2 \theta + 1}$

   $\qquad = \sqrt{1 - \left(\frac{1}{2}\right)^2}$ $\qquad = \sqrt{\left(\frac{\sqrt{3}}{2}\right)^2 + 1}$

   $\qquad = \sqrt{\frac{3}{4}}$ $\qquad = \sqrt{\frac{7}{4}}$

   $\qquad = \dfrac{\sqrt{3}}{2}$ $\qquad = \dfrac{\sqrt{7}}{2}$

26. $\csc^2 \theta = 1 + \cot^2 \theta$ 27. $\sec^2 \theta = \tan^2 \theta + 1$

   $\csc \theta = \sqrt{1 + \cot^2 \theta}$ $\sec \theta = \sqrt{\tan^2 \theta + 1}$

   $\qquad = \sqrt{1 + (0.8)^2}$ $\qquad = \sqrt{\left(\frac{\sqrt{11}}{2}\right)^2 + 1}$

   $\qquad = \sqrt{1 + \left(\frac{8}{10}\right)^2}$ $\qquad = \sqrt{\frac{15}{4}}$

   $\qquad = \sqrt{\frac{164}{100}}$ $\qquad = \dfrac{\sqrt{15}}{2}$

   $\qquad = \dfrac{2\sqrt{41}}{10}$

   $\qquad = \dfrac{\sqrt{41}}{5}$

28. $\tan \theta = \dfrac{\sin \theta}{\cos \theta}$ 29. $\csc \theta = \dfrac{1}{\sin \theta}$

   $\qquad = \dfrac{\sin \theta}{\sqrt{1 - \sin^2 \theta}}$ $\qquad = \dfrac{1}{\sqrt{1 - \cos^2 \theta}}$

   $\qquad = \dfrac{\frac{40}{41}}{\sqrt{1 - \left(\frac{40}{41}\right)^2}}$ $\qquad = \dfrac{1}{\sqrt{1 - \left(\frac{2}{3}\right)^2}}$

   $\qquad = \dfrac{\frac{40}{41}}{\sqrt{\frac{81}{1681}}}$ $\qquad = \dfrac{1}{\sqrt{\frac{5}{9}}}$

   $\qquad = \dfrac{\frac{40}{41}}{\frac{9}{41}}$ $\qquad = \dfrac{1}{\frac{\sqrt{5}}{3}}$

   $\qquad\qquad\qquad$ $\qquad = \dfrac{3}{\sqrt{5}} \cdot \dfrac{\sqrt{5}}{\sqrt{5}}$

   $\qquad = \dfrac{40}{9}$ $\qquad = \dfrac{3\sqrt{5}}{5}$

30. $\tan \theta = \dfrac{\sin \theta}{\cos \theta}$ 31. $\sec^2 \theta = \tan^2 \theta + 1$

   $\qquad = \dfrac{\sqrt{1 - \cos^2 \theta}}{\cos \theta}$ $\sec \theta = \sqrt{\tan^2 \theta + 1}$

   $\qquad = \dfrac{\sqrt{1 - \left(\frac{3}{5}\right)^2}}{\frac{3}{5}}$ $\qquad = \sqrt{\left(\frac{7}{2}\right)^2 + 1}$

   $\qquad = \dfrac{\sqrt{\frac{16}{25}}}{\frac{3}{5}}$ $\qquad = \sqrt{\frac{53}{4}}$

   $\qquad = \dfrac{\frac{4}{5}}{\frac{3}{5}}$ $\qquad = \dfrac{\sqrt{53}}{2}$

   $\qquad = \dfrac{4}{3}$

32. $\cot \theta = \dfrac{\cos \theta}{\sin \theta}$

$= \dfrac{\cos \theta}{\sqrt{1 - \cos^2 \theta}}$

$= \dfrac{\dfrac{3}{10}}{\sqrt{1 - \left(\dfrac{3}{10}\right)^2}}$

$= \dfrac{\dfrac{3}{10}}{\sqrt{\dfrac{91}{100}}}$

$= \dfrac{3}{\sqrt{91}} \cdot \dfrac{\sqrt{91}}{\sqrt{91}}$

$= \dfrac{3\sqrt{91}}{91}$

33. $\sin \theta = \sqrt{1 - \cos^2 \theta}$

$= \sqrt{1 - \dfrac{1}{\sec^2 \theta}}$

$= \sqrt{1 - \dfrac{1}{(\tan^2 \theta + 1)}}$

$= \sqrt{1 - \dfrac{1}{\left(\dfrac{1}{2}\right)^2 + 1}}$

$= \sqrt{1 - \dfrac{1}{\dfrac{5}{4}}}$

$= \sqrt{1 - \dfrac{4}{5}}$

$= \sqrt{\dfrac{1}{5}}$

$= \dfrac{1}{\sqrt{5}} \cdot \dfrac{\sqrt{5}}{\sqrt{5}}$

$= \dfrac{\sqrt{5}}{5}$

34. $\sin 665°$

$= (720° - 55°)$

$= (360°(2) - 55°)$

$= -\sin 55°$

35. $\cos 562°$

$= \cos (22° + 540°)$

$= \cos (22° + 180(3))$

$= -\cos 22°$

36. $\tan (-342°)$

$= \dfrac{\sin (-342°)}{\cos (-342°)}$

$= \dfrac{\sin (18° + (-360°))}{\cos (18° + (-360°))}$

$= \dfrac{\sin 18°}{\cos 18°}$

$= \tan 18°$

37. $\sin (-792°)$

$= \sin (-360°(2) - 72°)$

$= -\sin 72°$

38. $\csc 850°$

$= \dfrac{1}{\sin (900° - 50°)}$

$= \dfrac{1}{\sin 50°}$

$= \csc 50°$

39. $\sec (-210°)$

$= \dfrac{1}{\cos (-210°)}$

$= \dfrac{1}{-\cos 30°}$

$= -\sec 30°$

40. $\dfrac{\tan x \csc x}{\sec x}$

$= \dfrac{\dfrac{\sin x}{\cos x} \cdot \dfrac{1}{\sin x}}{\dfrac{1}{\cos x}}$

$= \dfrac{\dfrac{1}{\cos x}}{\dfrac{1}{\cos x}}$

$= 1$

41. $\dfrac{\cos \theta}{\sec \theta - \tan \theta}$

$= \dfrac{\cos \theta}{\dfrac{1}{\cos \theta} - \dfrac{\sin \theta}{\cos \theta}}$

$= \dfrac{\cos \theta}{\dfrac{1 - \sin \theta}{\cos \theta}}$

$= \cos \theta \cdot \dfrac{\cos \theta}{1 - \sin \theta}$

$= \dfrac{\cos^2 \theta}{1 - \sin \theta}$

$= \dfrac{1 - \sin^2 \theta}{1 - \sin \theta}$

$= \dfrac{(1 - \sin \theta)(1 + \sin \theta)}{1 - \sin \theta}$

$= 1 + \sin \theta$

42. $\tan A \cos^2 A$

$= \dfrac{\sin A}{\cos A} \cdot \cos^2 A$

$= \sin A \cos A$

43. $\sin A \cdot \cot A$

$= \sin A \cdot \dfrac{\cos A}{\sin A}$

$= \cos A$

44. $\dfrac{\tan \beta}{\cot \beta} = \dfrac{\tan \beta}{\dfrac{1}{\tan \beta}}$

$= \tan^2 \beta$

45. $\cos x \tan x \csc x$

$= \cos x \cdot \dfrac{\sin x}{\cos x} \cdot \dfrac{1}{\sin x}$

$= \dfrac{\cos x \sin x}{\cos x \sin x}$

$= 1$

46. $\dfrac{1}{\sin^2 \theta} - \dfrac{\cos \theta}{\sin^2 \theta}$

$= \dfrac{1 - \cos^2 \theta}{\sin^2 \theta}$

$= \dfrac{\sin^2 \theta}{\sin^2 \theta}$

$= 1$

47. $\dfrac{\cos^2 A}{1 + \sin A}$

$= \dfrac{1 - \sin^2 A}{1 + \sin A}$

$= \dfrac{(1 - \sin A)(1 + \sin A)}{1 + \sin A}$

$= 1 - \sin A$

48. $\dfrac{\csc \beta}{1 + \cot^2 \beta}$

$= \dfrac{\csc \beta}{\csc^2 \beta}$

$= \sin \beta$

49. $\sin^2 A \cos^2 A + \sin^4 A$

$= \sin^2 A (\cos^2 A + \sin^2 A)$

$= \sin^2 A (1)$

$= \sin^2 A$

50. $(1 - \sin x)(1 + \sin x) = 1 - \sin^2 x = \cos^2 x$

51. $\cos^4 \alpha + 2 \cos^2 \alpha \sin^2 \alpha + \sin^4 \alpha$

$= (\cos^2 \alpha + \sin^2 \alpha)$

$= 1$

52. $\sin x + \cos x \tan x$

$= \sin x + \cos x \cdot \dfrac{\sin x}{\cos x}$

$= \sin x + \sin x$

$= 2 \sin x$

53. $\cos \theta = \pm \sqrt{1 - \sin^2 \theta}$

54. $\sec \theta = \pm\sqrt{\tan^2 \theta + 1}$

$\quad = \pm\sqrt{\dfrac{1}{\cot^2 \theta} + 1}$

$\quad = \pm\sqrt{\dfrac{1 + \cot^2 \theta}{\cot^2 \theta}}$

$\quad = \pm\dfrac{\sqrt{1 + \cot^2 \theta}}{\cot \theta}$

55. $\tan \theta = \dfrac{\sin \theta}{\cos \theta}$

$\quad = \dfrac{\pm\sqrt{1 - \cos^2 \theta}}{\cos \theta}$

56. $\csc \theta = \dfrac{1}{\sin \theta}$

$\quad = \dfrac{1}{\pm\sqrt{1 - \cos^2 \theta}}$

$\quad = \pm\dfrac{\sqrt{1 - \cos^2 \theta}}{1 - \cos^2 \theta}$

57. Case 3: $\sin (k \cdot 360° - A) = -\sin A$ and
$\quad\quad\quad \cos (k \cdot 360° - A) = \cos A;$

Case 4: $\sin ((2k - 1)180° - A) = \sin A$ and
$\quad\quad\quad \cos ((2k - 1)180° - A) = -\cos A;$

See students' work for explanations.

58. $\sin \theta = \dfrac{EF}{OE} = \dfrac{EF}{1} = EF$ because circle O is a unit circle.

$\cos \theta = OF$ because circle O is a unit circle.

$\tan \theta = CD$: $\triangle EOF \sim \triangle COD$, so $\dfrac{EF}{OF} = \dfrac{CD}{OD}$.

$OD = 1$ since circle O is a unit circle.

$\sin \theta = EF$, $\cos \theta = OF$, so $\dfrac{\sin \theta}{\cos \theta} = \dfrac{CD}{1}$. By definition, $\tan \theta = CD$.

$\sec \theta = CO$: $\triangle EOF \sim \triangle COD$, so $\dfrac{EO}{OF} = \dfrac{CO}{OD}$. $OD = EO = 1$ since circle O is a unit circle and $\cos \theta = OF$, so $\dfrac{1}{\cos \theta} = \dfrac{CO}{1}$. Substituting $\sec \theta = CO$.

$\cot \theta = BA$: $\triangle EOF \sim \triangle OBA$, so $\dfrac{OF}{EF} = \dfrac{BA}{OA}$.

$OA = 1$ since circle O is a unit circle, $\sin \theta = EF$, $\cos \theta = OF$, so $\dfrac{\cos \theta}{\sin \theta} = \dfrac{BA}{1}$.

By quotient identity, $\cot \theta = BA$.

$\csc \theta = OB$: $\triangle EOF \sim \triangle OBA$, so $\dfrac{EO}{EF} = \dfrac{OB}{OA}$. $OA = EO = 1$ since circle O is a unit circle and $\sin \theta = EF$, so $\dfrac{1}{\sin \theta} = \dfrac{OB}{1}$.

By reciprocal identity, $\csc \theta = OB$.

59. See students' work.

60. $d = \sqrt{(x_2 - x_1)^2 + (y_2 - y_1)^2}$

$\quad = \sqrt{(8 - 2)^2 + (-2 - (-5))^2}$

$\quad = \sqrt{6^2 + 3^2}$

$\quad = \sqrt{45}$

$\quad = 3\sqrt{5}$

$m = \dfrac{y_2 - y_1}{x_2 - x_1}$

$\quad = \dfrac{-2 + 5}{8 - 2}$

$\quad = \dfrac{3}{6} = \dfrac{1}{2}$

61. Symmetric with respect to y-axis?

$y \overset{?}{=} 5(-x)^3 + 2x + 5$

$\quad \neq 5x^3 - 2x + 5$

no

Symmetric with respect to x-axis?

$-y \overset{?}{=} 5x^3 - 2x + 5 = y$

no

neither

62. as $x \to \infty$, $y \to \infty$

as $x \to -\infty$, $y \to \infty$

63. positive: 1

$f(-x) = x^4 - 2x^3 + 6x - 1$

negative: 1 or 3

64. $\dfrac{15\pi}{16} \cdot \dfrac{180}{\pi} = \dfrac{675}{4} = 168°45'$

65. $\sin 25° = \dfrac{x}{30}$

$30 \sin 25° = x$

$12.7 \approx x$

$\cos 25° = \dfrac{y}{30}$

$30 \cos 25° = y$

$27.2 \approx y$

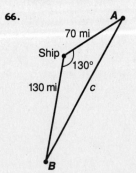

The diagonals are $2x$ or about 25.4 units and $2y$ or about 54.4 units long.

66.

$c^2 = a^2 + b^2 - 2ab \cos C$

$\quad = 130^2 + 70^2 - 2(130)(70) \cos 130°$

$\quad \approx 21,800 + 11,698.7$

$\quad \approx 33,498.73$

$c \approx 183$ miles

67. $K = \frac{1}{2} ab \sin C$

$\qquad = \frac{1}{2}(6.2)(7.5) \sin 97°$

$\qquad \approx 23.1$ units^2

68. $y = -6 \cos \pi t$

69. Let x = least, y = second, and z = greatest.

$3x = 2z + 3$ By substitution,

$z = x + 4$ $3x = 2(x + 4) + 3$

$\qquad\qquad 3x = 2x + 8 + 3$

$\qquad\qquad\quad x = 11$

$\qquad\qquad\quad z = 15$

7-2 Verifying Trigonometric Identities

PAGE 366   **CHECKING FOR UNDERSTANDING**

1. When you are trying to verify a possible trigonometric identity, you must work as though the two expressions are not equal. If you perform an operation to both sides, this assumes that they are equal.

2. See students' work.

3. $\tan^2 x \cos^2 x \stackrel{?}{=} 1 - \cos^2 x$

$\dfrac{\sin^2 x}{\cos^2 x} \cdot \cos^2 x \stackrel{?}{=} 1 - \cos^2 x$

$\qquad\qquad \sin^2 x \stackrel{?}{=} 1 - \cos^2 x$

$\qquad 1 - \cos^2 x = 1 - \cos^2 x$

4. $\csc A \sec A \stackrel{?}{=} \cot A + \tan A$

$\csc A \sec A \stackrel{?}{=} \dfrac{\cos A}{\sin A} + \dfrac{\sin A}{\cos A}$

$\csc A \sec A \stackrel{?}{=} \dfrac{\cos^2 A + \sin^2 A}{\sin A \cos A}$

$\csc A \sec A \stackrel{?}{=} \dfrac{1}{\sin A \cos A}$

$\csc A \sec A = \csc A \sec A$

5. $\tan \beta \csc \beta \stackrel{?}{=} \sec \beta$

$\dfrac{\sin \beta}{\cos \beta} \cdot \dfrac{1}{\sin \beta} \stackrel{?}{=} \sec \beta$

$\qquad \dfrac{1}{\cos \beta} \stackrel{?}{=} \sec \beta$

$\qquad \sec \beta = \sec \beta$

6. $\csc \alpha \cos \alpha \tan \alpha \stackrel{?}{=} 1$

$\dfrac{1}{\sin \alpha} \cdot \cos \alpha \cdot \dfrac{\sin \alpha}{\cos \alpha} \stackrel{?}{=} 1$

$\qquad \dfrac{\sin \alpha \cos \alpha}{\sin \alpha \cos \alpha} \stackrel{?}{=} 1$

$\qquad\qquad\qquad 1 = 1$

7. $\sin \theta \sec \theta \cot \theta \stackrel{?}{=} 1$

$\sin \theta \cdot \dfrac{1}{\cos \theta} \cdot \dfrac{\cos \theta}{\sin \theta} \stackrel{?}{=} 1$

$\qquad \dfrac{\sin \theta \cos \theta}{\sin \theta \cos \theta} \stackrel{?}{=} 1$

$\qquad\qquad\qquad 1 = 1$

8. $\sec^2 y - \tan^2 y \stackrel{?}{=} \tan y \cot y$

$\dfrac{1}{\cos^2 y} - \dfrac{\sin^2 y}{\cos^2 y} \stackrel{?}{=} \tan y \cot y$

$\dfrac{1 - \sin^2 y}{\cos^2 y} \stackrel{?}{=} \tan y \cot y$

$\dfrac{\cos^2 y}{\cos^2 y} \stackrel{?}{=} \tan y \cot y$

$\dfrac{\cos y}{\cos y} \stackrel{?}{=} \tan y \cot y$

$\dfrac{\cos y}{\cos y} \cdot \dfrac{\sin y}{\sin y} \stackrel{?}{=} \tan y \cot y$

$\dfrac{\sin y}{\cos y} \cdot \dfrac{\cos y}{\sin y} \stackrel{?}{=} \tan y \cot y$

$\tan y \cot y = \tan y \cot y$

9-12. Sample answers are given.

9. $\sin x = \tan x$

$1 = \dfrac{\tan x}{\sin x}$

$1 = \dfrac{\sin x}{\cos x} \cdot \dfrac{1}{\sin x}$

$\; = \dfrac{1}{\cos x}$

$\; = \sec x$

10. $2 \tan x = \cot x$

$2 \dfrac{\sin x}{\cos x} = \dfrac{\cos x}{\sin x}$

$\dfrac{2 \sin^2 x}{\cos^2 x} = 1$

$\dfrac{\sin^2 x}{\cos^2 x} = \dfrac{1}{2}$

$\tan^2 x = \dfrac{1}{2}$

$\tan x = \pm \sqrt{\dfrac{1}{2}}$

$\tan x = \pm \dfrac{\sqrt{2}}{2}$

11. $\sin x = 2 \cos x$

$\dfrac{\sin x}{\cos x} = 2$

$\tan x = 2$

12. $\tan x \cos x = \dfrac{1}{2}$

$\dfrac{\sin x}{\cos x} \cdot \cos x = \dfrac{1}{2}$

$\sin x = \dfrac{1}{2}$

PAGES 367-368   **EXERCISES**

13. $\dfrac{1}{\sec^2 \theta} + \dfrac{1}{\csc^2 \theta} \stackrel{?}{=} 1$

$\dfrac{1}{\frac{1}{\cos^2 \theta}} + \dfrac{1}{\frac{1}{\sin^2 \theta}} \stackrel{?}{=} 1$

$\cos^2 \theta + \sin^2 \theta \stackrel{?}{=} 1$

$\qquad\qquad\qquad 1 = 1$

14. $\dfrac{\tan x \cos x}{\sin x} \stackrel{?}{=} 1$

$\tan x \cdot \dfrac{\cos x}{\sin x} \stackrel{?}{=} 1$

$\dfrac{\sin x}{\cos x} \cdot \dfrac{\cos x}{\sin x} \stackrel{?}{=} 1$

$\qquad\qquad\qquad 1 = 1$

15. $\dfrac{\sin A}{\csc A} + \dfrac{\cos A}{\sec A} \stackrel{?}{=} 1$

$\dfrac{\sin A}{\frac{1}{\sin A}} + \dfrac{\cos A}{\frac{1}{\cos A}} \stackrel{?}{=} 1$

$\sin^2 A + \cos^2 A \stackrel{?}{=} 1$

$\qquad\qquad\qquad 1 = 1$

16. $\dfrac{1 + \tan^2 \theta}{\csc^2 \theta} \overset{?}{=} \tan^2 \theta$

$\quad\dfrac{\sec^2 \theta}{\csc^2 \theta} \overset{?}{=} \tan^2 \theta$

$\quad\dfrac{\dfrac{1}{\cos^2 \theta}}{\dfrac{1}{\sin^2 \theta}} \overset{?}{=} \tan^2 \theta$

$\quad\dfrac{\sin^2 \theta}{\cos^2 \theta} \overset{?}{=} \tan^2 \theta$

$\quad\tan^2 \theta = \tan^2 \theta$

17. $\dfrac{1 + \tan \gamma}{1 + \cot \gamma} \overset{?}{=} \dfrac{\sin \gamma}{\cos \gamma}$

$\dfrac{1 + \dfrac{\sin \gamma}{\cos \gamma}}{1 + \dfrac{\cos \gamma}{\sin \gamma}} \overset{?}{=} \dfrac{\sin \gamma}{\cos \gamma}$

$\dfrac{\dfrac{\cos \gamma + \sin \gamma}{\cos \gamma}}{\dfrac{\sin \gamma + \cos \gamma}{\sin \gamma}} \overset{?}{=} \dfrac{\sin \gamma}{\cos \gamma}$

$\dfrac{\sin \gamma + \cos \gamma}{\cos \gamma} \cdot \dfrac{\sin \gamma}{\sin \gamma + \cos \gamma} \overset{?}{=} \dfrac{\sin \gamma}{\cos \gamma}$

$\dfrac{\sin \gamma}{\cos \gamma} = \dfrac{\sin \gamma}{\cos \gamma}$

18. $\dfrac{\sec \alpha}{\sin \alpha} - \dfrac{\sin \alpha}{\cos \alpha} \overset{?}{=} \cot \alpha$

$\dfrac{\dfrac{1}{\cos \alpha}}{\sin \alpha} - \dfrac{\sin \alpha}{\cos \alpha} \overset{?}{=} \cot \alpha$

$\dfrac{1}{\sin \alpha \cos \alpha} - \dfrac{\sin^2 \alpha}{\sin \alpha \cos \alpha} \overset{?}{=} \cot \alpha$

$\dfrac{1 - \sin^2 \alpha}{\sin \alpha \cos \alpha} \overset{?}{=} \cot \alpha$

$\dfrac{\cos^2 \alpha}{\sin \alpha \cos \alpha} \overset{?}{=} \cot \alpha$

$\dfrac{\cos \alpha}{\sin \alpha} \overset{?}{=} \cot \alpha$

$\cot \alpha = \cot \alpha$

19. $\cos^2 x + \tan^2 x \cos^2 x \overset{?}{=} 1$

$\cos^2 x + \dfrac{\sin^2 x}{\cos^2 x} \cdot \cos^2 x \overset{?}{=} 1$

$\cos^2 x + \sin^2 x \overset{?}{=} 1$

$1 = 1$

20. $\tan^2 \theta - \sin^2 \theta \overset{?}{=} \tan^2 \theta \sin^2 \theta$

$\dfrac{\sin^2 \theta}{\cos^2 \theta} - \dfrac{\sin^2 \theta \cos^2 \theta}{\cos^2 \theta} \overset{?}{=} \tan^2 \theta \sin^2 \theta$

$\dfrac{\sin^2 \theta (1 - \cos^2 \theta)}{\cos^2 \theta} \overset{?}{=} \tan^2 \theta \sin^2 \theta$

$\dfrac{\sin^2 \theta}{\cos^2 \theta} \cdot \sin^2 \theta \overset{?}{=} \tan^2 \theta \sin^2 \theta$

$\tan^2 \theta \sin^2 \theta = \tan^2 \theta \sin^2 \theta$

21. $1 - \cot^4 x \overset{?}{=} 2 \csc^2 x - \csc^4 x$

$1 - \cot^4 x \overset{?}{=} \csc^2 x (2 - \csc^2 x)$

$1 - \cot^4 x \overset{?}{=} (1 + \cot^2 x)(2 - (1 + \cot^2 x))$

$1 - \cot^4 x \overset{?}{=} (1 + \cot^2 x)(1 - \cot^2 x)$

$1 - \cot^4 x = 1 - \cot^4 x$

22. $\sin \theta + \cos \theta \overset{?}{=} \dfrac{1 + \tan \theta}{\sec \theta}$

$\sin \theta + \cos \theta \overset{?}{=} \dfrac{1 + \dfrac{\sin \theta}{\cos \theta}}{\dfrac{1}{\cos \theta}}$

$\sin \theta + \cos \theta \overset{?}{=} \dfrac{\dfrac{\cos \theta + \sin \theta}{\cos \theta}}{\dfrac{1}{\cos \theta}}$

$\sin \theta + \cos \theta \overset{?}{=} \dfrac{\sin \theta + \cos \theta}{\cos \theta} \cdot \cos \theta$

$\sin \theta + \cos \theta = \sin \theta + \cos \theta$

23. $\dfrac{\sec x - 1}{\sec x + 1} + \dfrac{\cos x - 1}{\cos x + 1} \overset{?}{=} 0$

$\dfrac{\dfrac{1}{\cos x} - 1}{\dfrac{1}{\cos x} + 1} + \dfrac{\cos x - 1}{\cos x + 1} \overset{?}{=} 0$

$\dfrac{1 - \cos x}{1 + \cos x} + \dfrac{\cos x - 1}{\cos x + 1} \overset{?}{=} 0$

$\dfrac{1 - \cos x + \cos x - 1}{1 + \cos x} \overset{?}{=} 0$

$0 = 0$

24. $\sec^4 \alpha - \sec^2 \alpha \overset{?}{=} \dfrac{1}{\cot^4 \alpha} + \dfrac{1}{\cos^2 \alpha}$

$\sec^4 \alpha - \sec^2 \alpha \overset{?}{=} \tan^4 \alpha + \tan^2 \alpha$

$\sec^4 \alpha - \sec^2 \alpha \overset{?}{=} \tan^2 \alpha (\tan^2 \alpha + 1)$

$\sec^4 \alpha - \sec^2 \alpha \overset{?}{=} (\sec^2 \alpha - 1)[(\sec^2 \alpha - 1) + 1]$

$\sec^4 \alpha - \sec^2 \alpha \overset{?}{=} (\sec^2 \alpha - 1) \sec^2 \alpha$

$\sec^4 \alpha - \sec^2 \alpha = \sec^4 \alpha - \sec^2 \alpha$

25. $\dfrac{\cos x}{1 + \sin x} + \dfrac{\cos x}{1 - \sin x} \overset{?}{=} 2 \sec x$

$\dfrac{\cos x (1 - \sin x) + \cos x (1 + \sin x)}{1 - \sin^2 x} \overset{?}{=} 2 \sec x$

$\dfrac{(1 - \sin x) + (1 + \sin x)}{\cos x} \overset{?}{=} 2 \sec x$

$\dfrac{2}{\cos x} \overset{?}{=} 2 \sec x$

$2 \sec x = 2 \sec x$

26. $\dfrac{\sec B}{\cos B} - \dfrac{\tan B}{\cot B} \overset{?}{=} 1$

$\dfrac{\sec B}{\dfrac{1}{\sec B}} - \dfrac{\tan B}{\dfrac{1}{\tan B}} \overset{?}{=} 1$

$\sec^2 B - \tan^2 B \overset{?}{=} 1$

$(\tan^2 B + 1) - \tan^2 B \overset{?}{=} 1$

$1 = 1$

27. $1 + \sec^2 x \sin^2 x \overset{?}{=} \sec^2 x$

$1 + \dfrac{1}{\cos^2 x} \sin^2 x \overset{?}{=} \sec^2 x$

$1 + \tan^2 x \overset{?}{=} \sec^2 x$

$\sec^2 x = \sec^2 x$

28. $\dfrac{1 - 2\cos^2 \theta}{\sin \theta \cos \theta} \overset{?}{=} \tan \theta - \cot \theta$

$\dfrac{1 - 2\cos^2 \theta}{\sin \theta \cos \theta} \overset{?}{=} \dfrac{\sin \theta}{\cos \theta} - \dfrac{\cos \theta}{\sin \theta}$

$\dfrac{1 - 2\cos^2 \theta}{\sin \theta \cos \theta} \overset{?}{=} \dfrac{\sin^2 \theta \; \cos^2 \theta}{\sin \theta \cos \theta}$

$\dfrac{1 - 2\cos^2 \theta}{\sin \theta \cos \theta} \overset{?}{=} \dfrac{1 - \cos^2 \theta - \cos^2 \theta}{\sin \theta \cos \theta}$

$\dfrac{1 - 2\cos^2 \theta}{\sin \theta \cos \theta} = \dfrac{1 - 2\cos^2 \theta}{\sin \theta \cos \theta}$

29.-34. Sample answers are given.

29. $2 \sin^2 x = 3 \cos^2 x$

$\dfrac{\sin^2 x}{\cos^2 x} = \dfrac{3}{2}$

$\tan^2 x = \dfrac{3}{2}$

$\tan x = \sqrt{\dfrac{3}{2}}$

$\tan x = \pm \dfrac{\sqrt{6}}{2}$

30. $\dfrac{\tan x}{\sin x} = \sqrt{2}$

$\dfrac{\sin x}{\cos x} \cdot \dfrac{1}{\sin x} = \sqrt{2}$

$\dfrac{1}{\cos x} = \sqrt{2}$

$\sec x = \sqrt{2}$

31. $1 - \sin^2 x = \dfrac{1}{9}$

$\cos^2 x = \dfrac{1}{9}$

$\cos x = \pm \dfrac{1}{3}$

32. $\dfrac{\sin x \; \sec x}{\cot x} = \dfrac{9}{16}$

$\sin x \cdot \dfrac{1}{\cos x} \cdot \tan x = \dfrac{9}{16}$

$\tan x \cdot \tan x = \dfrac{9}{16}$

$\tan^2 x = \dfrac{9}{16}$

$\tan x = \pm \dfrac{3}{4}$

33. $1 + \tan^2 x = \sin^2 x + \dfrac{1}{\sec^2 x}$

$\sec^2 x = 1 - \cos^2 x + \dfrac{1}{\sec^2 x}$

$\sec^2 x = 1 - \dfrac{1}{\sec^2 x} + \dfrac{1}{\sec^2 x}$

$\sec^2 x = 1$

$\sec x = \pm 1$

34. $\dfrac{\cos x \; \tan x}{\csc x} = \dfrac{1}{9}$

$\cos x \cdot \dfrac{\sin x}{\cos x} \cdot \sin x = \dfrac{1}{9}$

$\sin^2 x = \dfrac{1}{9}$

$\sin x = \pm \dfrac{1}{3}$

35. $\sin 420° \approx 0.8660254038$

$\cos 420° = 0.5$

$\tan 420° \approx 1.732050808$

$\csc 420° \approx 1.154700538$

$\sec 420° = 2$

$\cot 420° \approx 0.5773502692$

36. $\sin(-650°) \approx 0.9396926208$

$\cos(-650°) \approx 0.3420201433$

$\tan(-650°) \approx 2.747477419$

$\csc(-650°) \approx 1.064177772$

$\sec(-650°) \approx 2.9238044$

$\cot(-650°) \approx 0.3639702343$

37. a. Since $0° \le x \le 90°$, then $\sin x \ge 0$ and $\cos x \ge 0$.

Thus, $\sin x \cdot \cos x \ge 0$

$2 \sin x \cdot \cos x \ge 0$

$1 + 2 \sin x \cos x \ge 1$

$\sin^2 x + 2 \sin x \cos x + \cos^2 x \ge 1$

$(\sin x + \cos x)^2 \ge 1$

$\sin x + \cos x \ge 1$

b. $(\sin x - \cos x)^2 \ge 0$

$\sin^2 x + \cos^2 x - 2 \sin x \cos x \ge 0$

$\sin^2 x + \cos^2 x \ge 2 \sin x \cos x$

Since $0° < x < 90°$, $\sin x > 0$ and $\cos x > 0$.
Thus, $\sin x \cdot \cos x > 0$.
Divide by $\sin x \cos x$.

$\dfrac{\sin^2 x}{\sin x \cos x} + \dfrac{\cos^2 x}{\sin x \cos x} \ge 2$

$\dfrac{\sin x}{\cos x} + \dfrac{\cos x}{\sin x} \ge 2$

$\tan x + \cot x \ge 2$

38. a. $F_w = \mu_s N$

$\dfrac{F_w}{N} = \mu_s$

$\dfrac{w \sin \theta}{w \cos \theta} = \mu_s$

$\tan \theta = \mu_s$

b. $\mu_s = \tan \theta$

$\mu_s = \tan 24°$

$\mu_s \approx 0.45$

39. a.

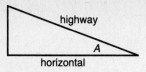

highway

horizontal

A

b. $\dfrac{d^2 - d^2 \cos^2 A}{d^2 - d^2 \sin A} = \dfrac{9}{400}$

$\dfrac{d^2(1 - \cos^2 A)}{d^2(1 - \sin^2 A)} = \dfrac{9}{400}$

$\dfrac{1 - \cos^2 A}{1 - \sin^2 A} = \dfrac{9}{400}$

$\dfrac{\sin^2 A}{\cos^2 A} = \dfrac{9}{400}$

$\tan^2 A = \dfrac{9}{400}$

$\tan A = \pm \dfrac{3}{20}$

40. $[f \circ g](x) = f(g(x))$

$= f(x^2 - 6x + 9)$

$= \dfrac{2}{3}\left(x^2 - 6x + 9\right) - 2$

$= \dfrac{2}{3}x^2 - 4x + 6 - 2$

$= \dfrac{2}{3}x^2 - 4x + 4$

$[g \circ f](x) = g(f(x))$

$= g\left(\dfrac{2}{3}x - 2\right)$

$= \left(\dfrac{2}{3}x - 2\right)^2 - 6\left(\dfrac{2}{3}x - 2\right) + 9$

$= \dfrac{4}{9}x^2 - \dfrac{4}{3}x - \dfrac{4}{3}x + 4 - 4x + 12 + 9$

$= \dfrac{4}{9}x^2 - \dfrac{20}{3}x + 25$

41. $P(5) = 5^4 - 4(5)^3 - 2(5)^2 - 1$

$= 625 - 500 - 50 - 1$

$= 74$

no

42. $x + y \le 50$

$x \le 30$

$y \le 50$

$P(x, y) = 18x + 6y$

$P(30, 0) = 18 \cdot 30 + 0 = 540$

$P(0, 50) = 18(0) + 6(50) = 300$

$P(30, 20) = 18(30) + 6(20) = 660$

Maximum profit would be 30 preschoolers and
20 school-age.

43. $s = r\theta$

$11.5 = 12\theta$

$\dfrac{11.5}{12} = \theta$

$\dfrac{11.5}{12} \cdot \dfrac{180}{\pi} \approx 54.9°$

44. $4 \csc \theta \cos \theta \tan \theta = 4 \dfrac{1}{\sin \theta} \cdot \cos \theta \cdot \dfrac{\sin \theta}{\cos \theta}$

$= 4 \dfrac{\sin \theta \cos \theta}{\sin \theta \cos \theta}$

$= 4$

45. Need to know more about the fraction. E

7-2B Graphing Calculators: Verifying Trigonometric Identities

PAGE 370 EXERCISES

1. yes

2. no

3. yes

4. no

5. no

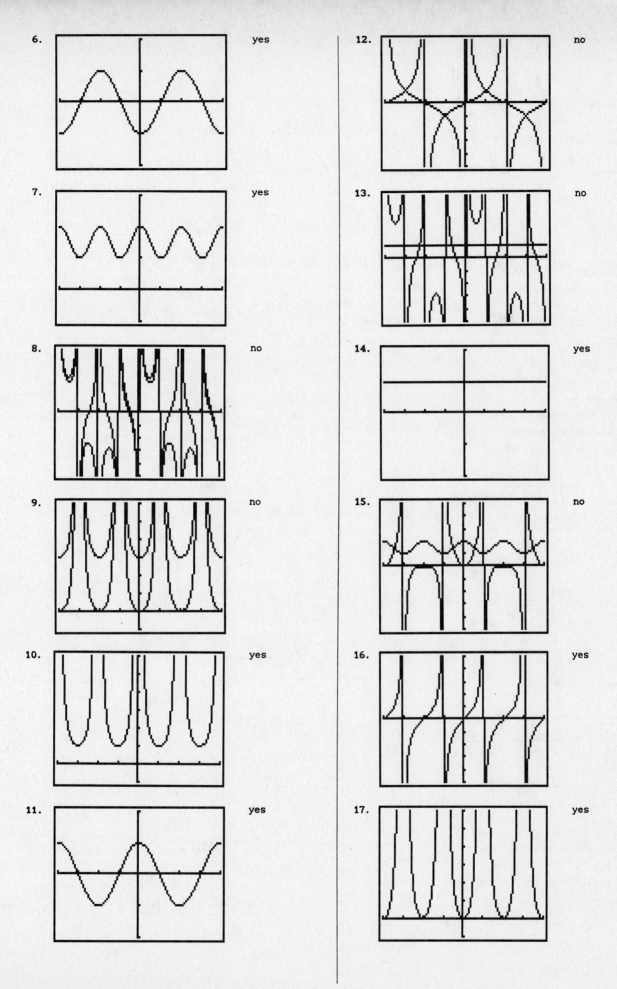

6.   yes

7.   yes

8.   no

9.   no

10.   yes

11.   yes

12.   no

13.   no

14.   yes

15.   no

16.   yes

17.   yes

18. 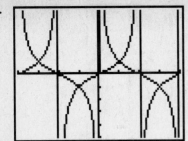   no

---

7-3   Sum and Difference Identities

1. no; $\cos (A + B) = \cos A \cos B - \sin A \sin B$

2. Use the sum identity for the sine function to find $\sin (60° + 45°)$.

$\sin (60° + 45°) = \sin 60° \cos 45° + \cos 60° \sin 45°$

$\qquad = \dfrac{\sqrt{3}}{2} \cdot \dfrac{\sqrt{2}}{2} + \dfrac{1}{2} \cdot \dfrac{\sqrt{2}}{2}$

$\qquad = \dfrac{\sqrt{6} + \sqrt{2}}{4}$

3. The sign changes because $\sin (-\beta) = -\sin \beta$.

4. $\cos 105° = \cos (60° + 45°)$

$\qquad = \cos 60° \cos 45° - \sin 60° \sin 45°$

$\qquad = \dfrac{1}{2} \cdot \dfrac{\sqrt{2}}{2} - \dfrac{\sqrt{3}}{2} \cdot \dfrac{\sqrt{2}}{2}$

$\qquad = \dfrac{\sqrt{2}}{4} - \dfrac{\sqrt{6}}{4} = \dfrac{\sqrt{2} - \sqrt{6}}{4}$

5. $\sin 150° = \sin (120° + 30°)$

$\qquad = \sin 120° \cos 30° + \sin 30° \cos 120°$

$\qquad = \dfrac{\sqrt{3}}{2} \cdot \dfrac{\sqrt{3}}{2} + \dfrac{1}{2} \cdot \dfrac{-1}{2}$

$\qquad = \dfrac{3}{4} - \dfrac{1}{4} = \dfrac{1}{2}$

6. $\tan 75° = \tan (45° + 30°)$

$\qquad = \dfrac{\tan 45° + \tan 30°}{1 - \tan 45° \tan 30°}$

$\qquad = \dfrac{1 + \dfrac{\sqrt{3}}{3}}{1 - 1\left(\dfrac{\sqrt{3}}{3}\right)}$

$\qquad = \dfrac{3 + \sqrt{3}}{3 - \sqrt{3}} \cdot \dfrac{3 + \sqrt{3}}{3 + \sqrt{3}}$

$\qquad = \dfrac{12 + 6\sqrt{3}}{6} = 2 + \sqrt{3}$

7. $\cos 150° = \cos (180° - 30°)$

$\qquad = \cos 180° \cos 30° + \sin 180° \sin 30°$

$\qquad = -1 \cdot \dfrac{\sqrt{3}}{2} + 0 \cdot \dfrac{1}{2}$

$\qquad = -\dfrac{\sqrt{3}}{2}$

8. $\sin (x + y) = \sin x \cos y + \sin y \cos x$

$\qquad = \dfrac{4}{5} \cdot \dfrac{3}{5} + \dfrac{3}{5} \cdot \dfrac{4}{5}$

$\qquad = \dfrac{12}{25} + \dfrac{12}{25}$

$\qquad = \dfrac{24}{25}$

9. $\cos (x - y) = \cos x \cos y + \sin x \sin y$

$\qquad = \dfrac{3}{5} \cdot \dfrac{3}{5} + \dfrac{4}{5} \cdot \dfrac{4}{5}$

$\qquad = \dfrac{9}{25} + \dfrac{16}{25}$

$\qquad = \dfrac{25}{25} = 1$

10. $\tan (x + y) = \dfrac{\tan x + \tan y}{1 - \tan x \tan y}$

$\qquad = \dfrac{\dfrac{4}{3} + \dfrac{4}{3}}{1 - \left(\dfrac{4}{3}\right)\left(\dfrac{4}{3}\right)}$

$\qquad = \dfrac{\dfrac{8}{3}}{\dfrac{-7}{9}} = -\dfrac{24}{7}$

11. $\sin (180° - \theta) \overset{?}{=} \sin \theta$

$\sin 180° \cos \theta - \cos 180° \sin \theta \overset{?}{=} \sin \theta$

$0 \cdot \cos \theta - (-1) \sin \theta \overset{?}{=} \sin \theta$

$\sin \theta = \sin \theta$

12. $\cos \left(\dfrac{3\pi}{2} + \theta\right) \overset{?}{=} \sin \theta$

$\cos \dfrac{3\pi}{2} \cos \theta - \sin \dfrac{3\pi}{2} \sin \theta \overset{?}{=} \sin \theta$

$0 \cdot \cos \theta - (-1) \sin \theta \overset{?}{=} \sin \theta$

$\sin \theta = \sin \theta$

13. $\tan (270° - x) \overset{?}{=} \cot x$

$\dfrac{\sin (270° - x)}{\cos (270° - x)} \overset{?}{=} \cot x$

$\dfrac{\sin 270° \cos x - \sin x \cos 270°}{\cos 270° \cos x + \sin 270° \sin x} \overset{?}{=} \cot x$

$\dfrac{(-1) \cos x - \sin x \cdot 0}{0 \cdot \cos x + (-1) \sin x} \overset{?}{=} \cot x$

$\dfrac{-\cos x}{-\sin x} \overset{?}{=} \cot x$

$\cot x = \cot x$

14. $\cos (360° - \theta) \overset{?}{=} \cos \theta$

$\cos 360° \cos \theta + \sin 360° \sin \theta \overset{?}{=} \cos \theta$

$1 \cdot \cos \theta + 0 \cdot \sin \theta \overset{?}{=} \cos \theta$

$\cos \theta = \cos \theta$

15. $\sin 195° = \sin (150° + 45°)$

$\qquad = \sin 150° \cos 45° + \sin 45° \cos 150°$

$\qquad = \dfrac{1}{2} \cdot \dfrac{\sqrt{2}}{2} + \dfrac{\sqrt{2}}{2} \cdot \left(-\dfrac{\sqrt{3}}{2}\right)$

$\qquad = \dfrac{\sqrt{2} - \sqrt{6}}{4}$

16. $\cos 255° = \cos (30° + 225°)$

$= \cos 30° \cos 225° - \sin 30° \sin 225°$

$= \dfrac{\sqrt{3}}{2}\left(-\dfrac{\sqrt{2}}{2}\right) - \dfrac{1}{2}\left(-\dfrac{\sqrt{2}}{2}\right)$

$= \dfrac{-\sqrt{6} + \sqrt{2}}{4}$

$= \dfrac{\sqrt{2} - \sqrt{6}}{4}$

17. $\tan (-105°) = \tan (45° - 150°)$

$= \dfrac{\tan 45° - \tan 150°}{1 + \tan 45° \tan 150°}$

$= \dfrac{1 + \dfrac{\sqrt{3}}{3}}{1 - \dfrac{\sqrt{3}}{3}}$

$= \dfrac{3 + \sqrt{3}}{3 - \sqrt{3}} \cdot \dfrac{3 + \sqrt{3}}{3 + \sqrt{3}}$

$= \dfrac{12 + 6\sqrt{3}}{6} = 2 + \sqrt{3}$

18. $\sin 75° = \sin (45° + 30°)$

$= \sin 45° \cos 30° + \sin 30° \cos 45°$

$= \dfrac{\sqrt{2}}{2} \cdot \dfrac{\sqrt{3}}{2} + \dfrac{1}{2} \cdot \dfrac{\sqrt{2}}{2}$

$= \dfrac{\sqrt{6} + \sqrt{2}}{4}$

19. $\tan (-195°) = \tan (-150° - 45°)$

$= \dfrac{\tan (-150°) - \tan 45°}{1 + \tan (-150°) \tan 45°}$

$= \dfrac{\dfrac{\sqrt{3}}{3} - 1}{1 + \dfrac{\sqrt{3}}{3} \cdot 1}$

$= \sqrt{3} - 2$

20. $\cos 195° = \cos (150° + 45°)$

$= \cos 150° \cos 45° - \sin 150° \sin 45°$

$= -\dfrac{\sqrt{3}}{2} \cdot \dfrac{\sqrt{2}}{2} - \dfrac{1}{2} \cdot \dfrac{\sqrt{2}}{2}$

$= \dfrac{-\sqrt{6} - \sqrt{2}}{4}$

21. $\tan 165° = \tan (45° + 120°)$

$= \dfrac{\tan 45° - \tan 120°}{1 - \tan 45° \tan 120°}$

$= \dfrac{1 - \sqrt{3}}{1 + \sqrt{3}} \cdot \dfrac{1 - \sqrt{3}}{1 - \sqrt{3}}$

$= \dfrac{4 - 2\sqrt{3}}{-2}$

$= -2 + \sqrt{3} = \sqrt{3} - 2$

22. $\cos 345° = \cos (45° + \cos 300°)$

$= \cos 45° \cos 300° - \sin 45° \sin 300°$

$= \dfrac{\sqrt{2}}{2} \cdot \dfrac{1}{2} + \dfrac{\sqrt{2}}{2} \cdot \dfrac{\sqrt{3}}{2}$

$= \dfrac{\sqrt{6} + \sqrt{2}}{4}$

23. $\sin 285° = \sin (45° + 240°)$

$= \sin 45° \cos 240° + \sin 240° \cos 45°$

$= \dfrac{\sqrt{2}}{2}\left(-\dfrac{\sqrt{3}}{2}\right) + \dfrac{\sqrt{2}}{2}\left(-\dfrac{1}{2}\right)$

$= \dfrac{-\sqrt{6} - \sqrt{2}}{4}$

24. $\cos (\alpha + \beta) = \cos \alpha \cos \beta - \sin \alpha \sin \beta$

$= \dfrac{12}{13} \cdot \dfrac{4}{5} - \dfrac{5}{13} \cdot \dfrac{3}{5}$

$= \dfrac{48}{65} - \dfrac{15}{65}$

$= \dfrac{33}{65}$

25. $\sin (\alpha - \beta) = \sin \alpha \cos \beta - \sin \beta \cos \alpha$

$= \dfrac{4}{5} \cdot \dfrac{5}{13} - \dfrac{12}{13} \cdot \dfrac{3}{5}$

$= \dfrac{20}{65} - \dfrac{36}{65}$

$= -\dfrac{16}{65}$

26. $\tan (\alpha + \beta) = \dfrac{\tan \alpha + \tan \beta}{1 - \tan \alpha \tan \beta}$

$= \dfrac{\dfrac{\sin \alpha}{\cos \alpha} + \dfrac{\sin \beta}{\cos \beta}}{1 - \dfrac{\sin \alpha}{\cos \alpha} \cdot \dfrac{\sin \beta}{\cos \beta}}$

$= \dfrac{\sin \alpha \cos \beta + \sin \beta \cos \alpha}{\cos \alpha \cos \beta - \sin \alpha \sin \beta}$

$= \dfrac{\dfrac{12}{13} \cdot \dfrac{35}{37} + \dfrac{12}{37} \cdot \dfrac{5}{13}}{\dfrac{35}{37} \cdot \dfrac{5}{13} - \dfrac{12}{13} \cdot \dfrac{12}{37}}$

$= \dfrac{\dfrac{480}{481}}{\dfrac{31}{481}} = \dfrac{480}{31}$

27. $\cos (\alpha - \beta) = \cos \alpha \cos \beta - \sin \alpha \sin \beta$

$= \dfrac{15}{17} \cdot \dfrac{24}{25} + \dfrac{8}{17} \cdot \dfrac{7}{25}$

$= \dfrac{360}{425} + \dfrac{56}{425}$

$= \dfrac{416}{425}$

28. $\tan (\alpha + \beta) = \dfrac{\tan \alpha + \tan \beta}{1 - \tan \alpha \tan \beta}$

$= \dfrac{\dfrac{5}{12} + \dfrac{3}{4}}{1 - \dfrac{5}{12} \cdot \dfrac{3}{4}}$

$= \dfrac{\dfrac{14}{12}}{\dfrac{33}{48}}$

$= \dfrac{14}{12} \cdot \dfrac{48}{33}$

$= \dfrac{56}{33}$

29. $\sin (\alpha - \beta) = \sin \alpha \cos \beta - \sin \beta \cos \alpha$

$= \dfrac{8}{17} \cdot \dfrac{24}{25} - \dfrac{7}{25} \cdot \dfrac{15}{17}$

$= \dfrac{192}{425} - \dfrac{105}{425}$

$= \dfrac{87}{425}$

30.
$$\sin(270° + x) \overset{?}{=} -\cos x$$
$$\sin 270° \cos x + \sin x \cos 270° \overset{?}{=} -\cos x$$
$$(-1)\cos x + 0 \cdot \sin x \overset{?}{=} -\cos x$$
$$-\cos x = -\cos x$$

31.
$$\cos(90° + \theta) \overset{?}{=} -\sin \theta$$
$$\cos 90° \cos \theta - \sin 90° \sin \theta \overset{?}{=} -\sin \theta$$
$$0 \cdot \cos \theta - 1 \cdot \sin \theta \overset{?}{=} -\sin \theta$$
$$-\sin \theta = -\sin \theta$$

32.
$$\tan(90° + \theta) \overset{?}{=} -\cot \theta$$
$$\frac{\sin(90° + \theta)}{\cos(90° + \theta)} \overset{?}{=} -\cot \theta$$
$$\frac{\sin 90° \cos \theta + \sin \theta \cos 90°}{\cos 90° \cos \theta - \sin 90° \sin \theta} \overset{?}{=} -\cot \theta$$
$$\frac{1 \cdot \cos \theta + \sin \theta \cdot 0}{0 \cdot \cos \theta - 1 \cdot \sin \theta} \overset{?}{=} -\cot \theta$$
$$\frac{\cos \theta}{-\sin \theta} \overset{?}{=} -\cot \theta$$
$$-\cot \theta = -\cot \theta$$

33.
$$\sin\left(\frac{\pi}{2} + x\right) \overset{?}{=} \cos x$$
$$\sin\frac{\pi}{2} \cos x + \cos\frac{\pi}{2} \sin x \overset{?}{=} \cos x$$
$$1 \cdot \cos x + 0 \cdot \sin x \overset{?}{=} \cos x$$
$$\cos x = \cos x$$

34.
$$-\cos \theta \overset{?}{=} \cos(\pi + \theta)$$
$$-\cos \theta \overset{?}{=} \cos \pi \cos \theta - \sin \pi \sin \theta$$
$$-\cos \theta \overset{?}{=} (-1)\cos \theta - 0 \cdot \sin \theta$$
$$-\cos \theta = -\cos \theta$$

35.
$$\tan(\pi - \theta) \overset{?}{=} -\tan \theta$$
$$\frac{\tan \pi - \tan \theta}{1 + \tan \pi \tan \theta} \overset{?}{=} -\tan \theta$$
$$\frac{0 - \tan \theta}{1 + 0 \cdot \tan \theta} \overset{?}{=} -\tan \theta$$
$$-\tan \theta = -\tan \theta$$

36.
$$-\sin \theta \overset{?}{=} \cos\left(\frac{\pi}{2} + \theta\right)$$
$$-\sin \theta \overset{?}{=} \cos\frac{\pi}{2} \cos \theta - \sin\frac{\pi}{2} \sin \theta$$
$$-\sin \theta \overset{?}{=} 0 \cdot \cos \theta - 1 \cdot \sin \theta$$
$$-\sin \theta = -\sin \theta$$

37.
$$\frac{\sin(\beta - \alpha)}{\sin \alpha \sin \beta} \overset{?}{=} \cot \alpha - \cot \beta$$
$$\frac{\sin \beta \cos \alpha - \sin \alpha \cos \beta}{\sin \alpha \sin \beta} \overset{?}{=} \cot \alpha - \cot \beta$$
$$\frac{\cos \alpha}{\sin \alpha} - \frac{\cos \beta}{\sin \beta} \overset{?}{=} \cot \alpha - \cot \beta$$
$$\cot \alpha - \cot \beta = \cot \alpha - \cot \beta$$

38.
$$\sin^2 \alpha - \sin^2 \beta \overset{?}{=} \sin(\alpha + \beta)\sin(\alpha - \beta)$$
$$\sin^2 \alpha - \sin^2 \beta \overset{?}{=} [\sin \alpha \cos \beta + \sin \beta \cos \alpha]$$
$$\cdot [\sin \alpha \cos \beta - \sin \beta \cos \alpha]$$
$$\sin^2 \alpha - \sin^2 \beta \overset{?}{=} (\sin \alpha \cos \beta)^2 - (\sin \beta \cos \alpha)^2$$
$$\sin^2 \alpha - \sin^2 \beta \overset{?}{=} \sin^2 \alpha \cos^2 \beta - \sin^2 \beta \cos^2 \alpha$$
$$\sin^2 \alpha - \sin^2 \beta \overset{?}{=} \sin^2 \alpha (1 - \sin^2 \beta)$$
$$- \sin^2 \beta (1 - \sin^2 \alpha)$$
$$\sin^2 \alpha - \sin^2 \beta \overset{?}{=} \sin^2 \alpha - \sin^2 \alpha \sin^2 \beta$$
$$- \sin^2 \beta + \sin^2 \alpha \sin^2 \beta$$
$$\sin^2 \alpha - \sin^2 \beta = \sin^2 \alpha - \sin^2 \beta$$

39.
$$\cos(30° - x) + \cos(30° + x) \overset{?}{=} \sqrt{3} \cos x$$
$$\cos 30° \cos x + \sin 30° \sin x$$
$$+ \cos 30° \cos x - \sin 30° \sin x \overset{?}{=} \sqrt{3} \cos x$$
$$2 \cos 30° \cos x \overset{?}{=} \sqrt{3} \cos x$$
$$2 \cdot \frac{\sqrt{3}}{2} \cos x \overset{?}{=} \sqrt{3} \cos x$$
$$\sqrt{3} \cos x = \sqrt{3} \cos x$$

40.
$$\cos(\alpha + \beta) + \cos(\alpha - \beta) \overset{?}{=} 2 \cos \alpha \cos \beta$$
$$\cos \alpha \cos \beta - \sin \alpha \sin \beta$$
$$+ \cos \alpha \cos \beta + \sin \alpha \sin \beta \overset{?}{=} 2 \cos \alpha \cos \beta$$
$$2 \cos \alpha \cos \beta = 2 \cos \alpha \cos \beta$$

41.
$$\cot(\alpha + \beta) = \frac{1}{\tan(\alpha + \beta)}$$
$$= \frac{1 - \tan \alpha \tan \beta}{\tan \alpha + \tan \beta}$$
$$= \frac{1 - \dfrac{1}{\cot \alpha \cot \beta}}{\dfrac{1}{\cot \alpha} + \dfrac{1}{\cot \beta}}$$
$$= \frac{\cot \alpha \cot \beta - 1}{\cot \alpha + \cot \beta}$$

42.
$$\sin(\alpha + \beta + \gamma)$$
$$= \sin[(\gamma + \beta) + \gamma]$$
$$= \sin(\alpha + \beta)\cos \gamma + \sin \gamma \cos(\alpha + \beta)$$
$$= (\sin \alpha \cos \beta + \sin \beta \cos \alpha)\cos \gamma$$
$$+ \sin \gamma (\cos \alpha \cos \beta - \sin \alpha \sin \beta)$$
$$= \sin \alpha \cos \beta \cos \gamma + \sin \beta \cos \alpha \cos \gamma$$
$$+ \sin \gamma \cos \alpha \cos \beta - \sin \gamma \sin \alpha \sin \beta$$

43. It is given that $(3M + 3)(2N + 2) = 12$,
$M = \tan \alpha$, and $N = \tan \beta$.
$$3(M + 1) \cdot 2(N + 1) = 12$$
$$(M + 1)(N + 1) = 2$$
$$MN + M + N + 1 = 2$$
$$\tan \alpha \tan \beta + \tan \alpha + \tan \beta + 1 = 2$$
$$\tan \alpha + \tan \beta = 1 - \tan \alpha \tan \beta$$
$$\frac{\tan \alpha + \tan \beta}{1 - \tan \alpha \tan \beta} = 1$$

Thus, $\tan(\alpha + \beta) = 1$ or $\alpha + \beta = \arctan 1$.

Therefore, $\alpha + \beta = \frac{\pi}{4} + n\pi$ where n is any integer.

160

44. $n = \dfrac{\sin\left[\frac{1}{2}(\alpha + \beta)\right]}{\sin\left(\frac{\beta}{2}\right)}$

$= \dfrac{\sin\left[\frac{1}{2}(\alpha + 60°)\right]}{\sin\left(\frac{60°}{2}\right)}$

$= \dfrac{\sin\left(\frac{\alpha}{2} + 30°\right)}{\sin 30°}$

$= \dfrac{\sin\frac{\alpha}{2}\cos 30° + \sin 30°\cos\frac{\alpha}{2}}{\frac{1}{2}}$

$= 2\left(\dfrac{\sqrt{3}}{2}\sin\frac{\alpha}{2} + \dfrac{1}{2}\cos\frac{\alpha}{2}\right)$

$= \sqrt{3}\sin\frac{\alpha}{2} + \cos\frac{\alpha}{2}$

45. $\tan\theta = \dfrac{m_2 - m_1}{1 - m_2 m_1}$

46. $5x - 2y = 9$
$y = 3x - 1$
$5x - 2(3x - 1) = 9$
$5x - 6x + 2 = 9$
$\quad\quad\quad\quad x = -7$
$y = 3(-7) - 1$
$y = -22$
$(-7, -22)$

47. $f(x) = \frac{1}{2}x^2 - 2x + 1$
$f'(x) = x - 2$
$f'(4) = 4 - 2 = 2$
$y - y_1 = m(x - x_1)$
$y - 1 = 2(x - 4)$
$y - 1 = 2x - 8$
$\quad\quad y = 2x - 7$

48. $y = 4x^2 - 6x + 11$

$x = \dfrac{-b \pm \sqrt{b^2 - 4ac}}{2a}$

$= \dfrac{6 \pm \sqrt{(-6)^2 - 4(4)(11)}}{2(4)}$

$= \dfrac{6 \pm \sqrt{-140}}{8}$

$= \dfrac{6 \pm 2i\sqrt{35}}{8}$

$= \dfrac{3 \pm i\sqrt{35}}{4}$

49. $\csc 270° = \dfrac{1}{\sin 270°} = \dfrac{1}{-1} = -1$

50. $a^2 = b^2 + c^2 - 2bc\cos A$
$7^2 = 9^2 + 13^2 - 2(9)(13)\cos A$
$0.8590 \approx \cos A$
$\quad A \approx 30°48'$

$\dfrac{7}{\sin 30°48'} \approx \dfrac{9}{\sin B}, \ B \approx 41°10'$

$C \approx 360° - 30°48' - 41°10' \approx 108°2'$

51. $2\sec^2 x \overset{?}{=} \dfrac{1}{1 + \sin x} + \dfrac{1}{1 - \sin x}$

$\overset{?}{=} \dfrac{(1 - \sin x) + (1 + \sin x)}{(1 + \sin x)(1 - \sin x)}$

$\overset{?}{=} \dfrac{2}{1 - \sin^2 x}$

$\overset{?}{=} \dfrac{2}{\cos^2 x}$

$2\sec^2 x = 2\sec^2 x$

52. For all x, $7x + 1$ will be greater than $7x - 1$.
Quantity A is greater. A

$\boxed{\textbf{7-4}}$ **Double-Angle and Half-Angle Identities**

PAGE 381   CHECKING FOR UNDERSTANDING

1. Answers may vary. A sample answer is to choose $\cos 2\theta = 1 - 2\sin^2\theta$ when you know $\sin\theta$ and $\cos 2\theta = 2\cos\theta - 1$ when you know $\cos\theta$.

2. The sign is determined by the quadrant in which the terminal side of 2θ falls and by which function you are finding.

3. **a.** III or IV
b. I or II
c. I, II, III, IV

4. $\cos 2A = 1 - 2\sin^2\theta$

$= 1 - 2\left(\dfrac{3}{5}\right)^2$

$= 1 - \dfrac{18}{25}$

$= \dfrac{7}{25}$

5. $\tan A = \dfrac{\sin A}{\cos A}$

$= \dfrac{\frac{3}{5}}{\frac{4}{5}} = \dfrac{3}{4}$

$\tan 2A = \dfrac{2\tan A}{1 - \tan^2 A}$

$= \dfrac{2\left(\frac{3}{4}\right)}{1 - \left(\frac{3}{4}\right)^2}$

$= \dfrac{\frac{3}{2}}{\frac{7}{16}} = \dfrac{24}{7}$

6. $\sin 2A = 2 \sin A \cos A$

$\qquad = 2 \cdot \dfrac{3}{5} \cdot \dfrac{4}{5}$

$\qquad = \dfrac{24}{25}$

7. $\sin \dfrac{A}{2} = \pm\sqrt{\dfrac{1 - \cos A}{2}}$

$\qquad = \pm\sqrt{\dfrac{1 - \frac{4}{5}}{2}}$

$\qquad = \sqrt{\dfrac{1}{10}}$

$\qquad = \dfrac{\sqrt{10}}{10}$

8. $\cos \dfrac{A}{2} = \pm\sqrt{\dfrac{1 + \cos A}{2}}$

$\qquad = \pm\sqrt{\dfrac{1 + \frac{4}{5}}{2}}$

$\qquad = \sqrt{\dfrac{9}{10}}$

$\qquad = \dfrac{3\sqrt{10}}{10}$

9. $\tan \dfrac{A}{2} = \pm\sqrt{\dfrac{1 - \cos A}{1 + \cos A}}$

$\qquad = \pm\sqrt{\dfrac{1 - \frac{4}{5}}{1 + \frac{4}{5}}}$

$\qquad = \sqrt{\dfrac{1}{9}}$

$\qquad = \dfrac{1}{3}$

10. $\sin 22°30' = \sin \dfrac{45°}{2}$

$\qquad = \pm\sqrt{\dfrac{1 - \cos 45°}{2}}$

$\qquad = \sqrt{\dfrac{1 - \frac{\sqrt{2}}{2}}{2}}$

$\qquad = \sqrt{\dfrac{2 - \sqrt{2}}{4}}$

$\qquad = \dfrac{\sqrt{2 - \sqrt{2}}}{2}$

11. $\cos 22°30' = \cos \dfrac{45°}{2}$

$\qquad = \pm\sqrt{\dfrac{1 + \cos 45°}{2}}$

$\qquad = \sqrt{\dfrac{1 + \frac{\sqrt{2}}{2}}{2}}$

$\qquad = \sqrt{\dfrac{2 + \sqrt{2}}{4}}$

$\qquad = \dfrac{\sqrt{2 + \sqrt{2}}}{2}$

12. $\tan 22°30' = \tan \dfrac{45°}{2}$

$\qquad = \pm\sqrt{\dfrac{1 - \cos 45°}{1 + \cos 45°}}$

$\qquad = \sqrt{\dfrac{1 - \frac{\sqrt{2}}{2}}{1 + \frac{\sqrt{2}}{2}}}$

$\qquad = \sqrt{\dfrac{2 - \sqrt{2}}{2 + \sqrt{2}}} \cdot \sqrt{\dfrac{2 - \sqrt{2}}{2 - \sqrt{2}}}$

$\qquad = \sqrt{\dfrac{4 - 4\sqrt{2} + 2}{4 - 2}}$

$\qquad = \sqrt{\dfrac{6 - 4\sqrt{2}}{2}}$

$\qquad = \sqrt{3 - 2\sqrt{2}}$

13. $\dfrac{1}{2} \sin 2A \overset{?}{=} \dfrac{\tan A}{1 + \tan^2 A}$

$\qquad \overset{?}{=} \dfrac{\frac{\sin A}{\cos A}}{\sec^2 A}$

$\qquad \overset{?}{=} \dfrac{\sin A}{\cos A} \cdot \cos^2 A$

$\qquad \overset{?}{=} \dfrac{2 \sin A \cos A}{2}$

$\dfrac{1}{2} \sin 2A = \dfrac{1}{2} \sin 2A$

14. $\tan 2x \tan x + 2 \overset{?}{=} \dfrac{\tan 2x}{\tan x}$

$\left(\dfrac{2 \tan x}{1 - \tan^2 x}\right) \tan x + 2 \overset{?}{=} \dfrac{\tan 2x}{\tan x}$

$\dfrac{2 \tan^2 x + 2(1 - \tan^2 x)}{1 - \tan^2 x} \overset{?}{=} \dfrac{\tan 2x}{\tan x}$

$\dfrac{2(\tan^2 x + 1 - \tan^2 x)}{1 - \tan^2 x} \overset{?}{=} \dfrac{\tan 2x}{\tan x}$

$\dfrac{2}{1 - \tan^2 x} \overset{?}{=} \dfrac{\tan 2x}{\tan x}$

$\dfrac{2 \tan x}{(1 - \tan^2 x) \tan x} \overset{?}{=} \dfrac{\tan 2x}{\tan x}$

$\dfrac{\tan 2x}{\tan x} = \dfrac{\tan 2x}{\tan x}$

15. $\sin 2x \overset{?}{=} 2 \cot x \sin^2 x$

$\sin 2x \overset{?}{=} 2 \dfrac{\cos x}{\sin x} \cdot \sin^2 x$

$\sin 2x \overset{?}{=} 2 \cos x \sin x$

$\sin 2x = \sin 2x$

16. $\sin^2 \theta \overset{?}{=} \dfrac{1}{2}(1 - \cos 2\theta)$

$\sin^2 \theta \overset{?}{=} \dfrac{1}{2}(1 - (1 - 2 \sin^2 \theta))$

$\sin^2 \theta \overset{?}{=} \dfrac{1}{2}(2 \sin^2 \theta)$

$\sin^2 \theta = \sin^2 \theta$

17. $\sin 2y = 2 \sin y \cos y$

$\quad = 2 \cdot \dfrac{-5}{13} \cdot \dfrac{-12}{13}$

$\quad = \dfrac{120}{169}$

18. $\tan 2y = \dfrac{2 \tan y}{1 - \tan^2 y}$

$\quad = \dfrac{2\left(\dfrac{5}{12}\right)}{1 - \left(\dfrac{5}{12}\right)^2}$

$\quad = \dfrac{10}{12} \cdot \dfrac{144}{119}$

$\quad = \dfrac{120}{119}$

19. $\sin \dfrac{y}{2} = \pm\sqrt{\dfrac{1 - \cos y}{2}}$

$\quad = \sqrt{\dfrac{1 + \dfrac{12}{13}}{2}}$

$\quad = \sqrt{\dfrac{25}{26}}$

$\quad = \dfrac{5\sqrt{26}}{26}$

20. $\cos 2y = 1 - 2 \sin^2 y$

$\quad = 1 - 2\left(-\dfrac{5}{13}\right)^2$

$\quad = 1 - \dfrac{50}{169}$

$\quad = \dfrac{119}{169}$

21. $\tan \dfrac{y}{2} = \pm\sqrt{\dfrac{1 - \cos y}{1 + \cos y}}$

$\quad = -\sqrt{\dfrac{1 + \dfrac{12}{13}}{1 - \dfrac{12}{13}}}$

$\quad = -\sqrt{\dfrac{25}{1}}$

$\quad = -5$

22. $\cos \dfrac{y}{2} = \pm\sqrt{\dfrac{1 + \cos y}{2}}$

$\quad = -\sqrt{\dfrac{1 - \dfrac{12}{13}}{2}}$

$\quad = -\sqrt{\dfrac{1}{26}}$

$\quad = -\dfrac{\sqrt{26}}{26}$

23. $\sin 105^\circ = \sin \dfrac{210^\circ}{2}$

$\quad = \pm\sqrt{\dfrac{1 - \cos 210^\circ}{2}}$

$\quad = \sqrt{\dfrac{1 + \dfrac{\sqrt{3}}{2}}{2}}$

$\quad = \sqrt{\dfrac{2 + \sqrt{3}}{4}}$

$\quad = \dfrac{\sqrt{2 + \sqrt{3}}}{2}$

24. $\cos \dfrac{13\pi}{12} = -\cos 15^\circ$

$\quad = -\cos \dfrac{30^\circ}{2}$

$\quad = -\sqrt{\dfrac{1 + \cos 30^\circ}{2}}$

$\quad = -\sqrt{\dfrac{1 + \dfrac{\sqrt{3}}{2}}{2}}$

$\quad = -\dfrac{\sqrt{2 + \sqrt{3}}}{2}$

25. $\tan 195^\circ = \tan \dfrac{390^\circ}{2}$

$\quad = \sqrt{\dfrac{1 - \cos 390^\circ}{1 + \cos 390^\circ}}$

$\quad = \sqrt{\dfrac{1 - \dfrac{\sqrt{3}}{2}}{1 + \dfrac{\sqrt{3}}{2}}}$

$\quad = \dfrac{\sqrt{2 - \sqrt{3}}}{\sqrt{2 + \sqrt{3}}} \cdot \dfrac{\sqrt{2 - \sqrt{3}}}{\sqrt{2 - \sqrt{3}}}$

$\quad = 2 - \sqrt{3}$

26. $\cos \dfrac{19\pi}{12} = \cos \dfrac{570^\circ}{2}$

$\quad = \cos \dfrac{210^\circ}{2}$

$\quad = \sqrt{\dfrac{1 + \cos 210^\circ}{2}}$

$\quad = \sqrt{\dfrac{1 - \dfrac{\sqrt{3}}{2}}{2}}$

$\quad = \dfrac{\sqrt{2 - \sqrt{3}}}{2}$

27. $\sin \dfrac{7\pi}{8} = \sin \dfrac{315^\circ}{2}$

$\quad = \sqrt{\dfrac{1 - \cos 315^\circ}{2}}$

$\quad = \sqrt{\dfrac{1 - \dfrac{\sqrt{2}}{2}}{2}}$

$\quad = \dfrac{\sqrt{2 - \sqrt{2}}}{2}$

28. $\tan \dfrac{13\pi}{12} = \tan \dfrac{390^\circ}{2}$

$\quad = \tan \dfrac{30^\circ}{2}$

$\quad = \sqrt{\dfrac{1 - \cos 30^\circ}{1 + \cos 30^\circ}}$

$\quad = 2 - \sqrt{3}$

29.
$$1 + \cos 2A \overset{?}{=} \frac{2}{1 + \tan^2 A}$$
$$1 + \cos 2A \overset{?}{=} \frac{2}{\sec^2 A}$$
$$1 + \cos 2A \overset{?}{=} 2(\cos^2 A)$$
$$1 + \cos 2A \overset{?}{=} 1 + 2\cos^2 A - 1$$
$$1 + \cos 2A = 1 + \cos 2A$$

30.
$$\cos^2 2x + 4\sin^2 x \cos^2 x \overset{?}{=} 1$$
$$\cos^2 2x + (2\sin x \cos x)^2 \overset{?}{=} 1$$
$$\cos^2 2x + (\sin 2x)^2 \overset{?}{=} 1$$
$$\cos^2 2x + \sin^2 2x \overset{?}{=} 1$$
$$1 = 1$$

31.
$$\csc A \sec A \overset{?}{=} 2\csc 2A$$
$$\frac{1}{\sin A \cos A} \overset{?}{=} 2\csc 2A$$
$$\frac{2}{2\sin A \cos A} \overset{?}{=} 2\csc 2A$$
$$\frac{2}{\sin 2A} \overset{?}{=} 2\csc 2A$$
$$2\csc 2A = 2\csc 2A$$

32.
$$\frac{1 - \tan^2 \theta}{1 + \tan^2 \theta} \overset{?}{=} \cos 2\theta$$
$$\frac{1 - \dfrac{\sin^2 \theta}{\cos^2 \theta}}{\sec^2 \theta} \overset{?}{=} \cos 2\theta$$
$$\cos^2 \theta \left(1 - \frac{\sin^2 \theta}{\cos^2 \theta}\right) \overset{?}{=} \cos 2\theta$$
$$\cos^2 \theta - \sin^2 \theta \overset{?}{=} \cos 2\theta$$
$$\cos 2\theta = \cos 2\theta$$

33.
$$\cot X \overset{?}{=} \frac{\sin 2X}{1 - \cos 2X}$$
$$\cot X \overset{?}{=} \frac{2\sin X \cos X}{1 - (1 - 2\sin^2 X)}$$
$$\cot X \overset{?}{=} \frac{2\sin X \cos X}{2\sin^2 X}$$
$$\cot X \overset{?}{=} \frac{\cos X}{\sin X}$$
$$\cot X = \cot X$$

34.
$$\frac{1 + \cos x}{\sin x} \overset{?}{=} \cot \frac{x}{2}$$
$$\frac{1 + \cos x}{\sin x} \overset{?}{=} \frac{\cos \dfrac{x}{2}}{\sin \dfrac{x}{2}}$$
$$\frac{1 + \cos x}{\sin x} \overset{?}{=} \frac{\sqrt{\dfrac{1 + \cos x}{2}}}{\sqrt{\dfrac{1 - \cos x}{2}}}$$
$$\frac{1 + \cos x}{\sin x} \overset{?}{=} \sqrt{\frac{1 + \cos x}{1 - \cos x}}$$
$$\frac{1 + \cos x}{\sin x} \overset{?}{=} \sqrt{\frac{(1 + \cos x)^2}{1 - \cos^2 x}}$$

$$\frac{1 + \cos x}{\sin x} \overset{?}{=} \sqrt{\frac{(1 + \cos x)^2}{\sin^2 x}}$$
$$\frac{1 + \cos x}{\sin x} = \frac{1 + \cos x}{\sin x}$$

35.
$$\sin 2B\,(\cot B + \tan B) \overset{?}{=} 2$$
$$2\sin B \cos B \left(\frac{\cos B}{\sin B} + \frac{\sin B}{\cos B}\right) \overset{?}{=} 2$$
$$2\sin B \cos B \left(\frac{\cos^2 B + \sin^2 B}{\sin B \cos B}\right) \overset{?}{=} 2$$
$$2 = 2$$

36.
$$1 - \sin A \overset{?}{=} \left(\sin \frac{A}{2} - \cos \frac{A}{2}\right)^2$$
$$1 - \sin A \overset{?}{=} \sin^2 \frac{A}{2} - 2\sin \frac{A}{2} \cos \frac{A}{2} + \cos^2 \frac{A}{2}$$
$$1 - \sin A \overset{?}{=} 1 - 2\sin \frac{A}{2} \cos \frac{A}{2}$$
$$1 - \sin A = 1 - \sin A$$

37.
$$\cot \frac{\alpha}{2} \overset{?}{=} \frac{\sin \alpha}{1 - \cos \alpha}$$
$$\frac{1}{\tan \dfrac{\alpha}{2}} \overset{?}{=} \frac{\sin \alpha}{1 - \cos \alpha}$$
$$\frac{1}{\sqrt{\dfrac{1 - \cos \alpha}{1 + \cos \alpha}}} \overset{?}{=} \frac{\sin \alpha}{1 - \cos \alpha}$$
$$\frac{1}{\sqrt{\dfrac{(1 - \cos \alpha)^2}{1 - \cos^2 \alpha}}} \overset{?}{=} \frac{\sin \alpha}{1 - \cos \alpha}$$
$$\frac{1}{\sqrt{\dfrac{(1 - \cos \alpha)^2}{\sin^2 \alpha}}} \overset{?}{=} \frac{\sin \alpha}{1 - \cos \alpha}$$
$$\frac{1}{\dfrac{1 - \cos \alpha}{\sin \alpha}} \overset{?}{=} \frac{\sin \alpha}{1 - \cos \alpha}$$
$$\frac{\sin \alpha}{1 - \cos \alpha} = \frac{\sin \alpha}{1 - \cos \alpha}$$

38.
$$\tan \frac{x}{2} \overset{?}{=} \frac{\sin x}{1 + \cos x}$$
$$\frac{\sin \dfrac{x}{2}}{\cos \dfrac{x}{2}} \overset{?}{=} \frac{\sin x}{1 + \cos x}$$
$$\frac{\sqrt{\dfrac{1 - \cos x}{2}}}{\sqrt{\dfrac{1 + \cos x}{2}}} \overset{?}{=} \frac{\sin x}{1 + \cos x}$$
$$\sqrt{\frac{1 - \cos x}{1 + \cos x}} \overset{?}{=} \frac{\sin x}{1 + \cos x}$$
$$\sqrt{\frac{1 - \cos^2 x}{(1 + \cos x)^2}} \overset{?}{=} \frac{\sin x}{1 + \cos x}$$
$$\sqrt{\frac{\sin^2 x}{(1 + \cos x)^2}} \overset{?}{=} \frac{\sin x}{1 + \cos x}$$
$$\frac{\sin x}{1 + \cos x} = \frac{\sin x}{1 + \cos x}$$

39.
$$\frac{\cos 2A}{1 + \sin 2A} \overset{?}{=} \frac{\cot A - 1}{\cot A + 1}$$

$$\frac{\cos 2A}{1 + \sin 2A} \overset{?}{=} \frac{\dfrac{\cos A}{\sin A} - 1}{\dfrac{\cos A}{\sin A} + 1}$$

$$\overset{?}{=} \frac{\cos A - \sin A}{\cos A + \sin A}$$

$$\overset{?}{=} \frac{\cos^2 A - \sin^2 A}{\cos^2 A + 2 \sin A \cos A + \sin^2 A}$$

$$\overset{?}{=} \frac{\cos 2A}{1 + 2 \sin A \cos A}$$

$$= \frac{\cos 2A}{1 + \sin 2A}$$

40.
$$\frac{\sin \alpha + \sin 3\alpha}{\cos \alpha + \cos 3\alpha} \overset{?}{=} \tan 2\alpha$$

$$\frac{\sin \alpha + \sin (2\alpha + \alpha)}{\cos \alpha + \cos (2\alpha + \alpha)} \overset{?}{=} \tan 2\alpha$$

$$\frac{\sin \alpha + \sin 2\alpha \cos \alpha + \cos 2\alpha \sin \alpha}{\cos \alpha + \cos 2\alpha \cos \alpha - \sin 2\alpha \sin \alpha} \overset{?}{=} \tan 2\alpha$$

$$\frac{\begin{array}{c}\sin \alpha + 2 \sin \alpha \cos \alpha \cos \alpha \\ + \sin \alpha \, (2 \cos^2 \alpha - 1)\end{array}}{\begin{array}{c}\cos \alpha + (2 \cos^2 \alpha - 1) \cos \alpha \\ - 2 \sin \alpha \cos \alpha \sin \alpha\end{array}} \overset{?}{=} \tan 2\alpha$$

$$\frac{\sin \alpha \, (1 + 2 \cos^2 \alpha + 2 \cos^2 \alpha - 1)}{\cos \alpha \, (1 + 2 \cos^2 \alpha - 1 - 2 \sin^2 \alpha)} \overset{?}{=} \tan 2\alpha$$

$$\frac{\sin \alpha \, (4 \cos^2 \alpha)}{\cos \alpha \, (2)(\cos^2 \alpha - \sin^2 \alpha)} \overset{?}{=} \tan 2\alpha$$

$$\frac{2 \cos \alpha \sin \alpha}{\cos^2 \alpha - \sin^2 \alpha} \overset{?}{=} \tan 2\alpha$$

$$\frac{\sin 2\alpha}{\cos 2\alpha} \overset{?}{=} \tan 2\alpha$$

$$\tan 2\alpha = \tan 2\alpha$$

41. $\sin 3\alpha$

$= \sin (2\alpha + \alpha)$

$= \sin 2\alpha \cos \alpha + \cos 2\alpha \sin \alpha$

$= (2 \sin \alpha \cos \alpha) \cos \alpha + \sin \alpha \, (1 - 2 \sin^2 \alpha)$

$= 2 \sin \alpha \cos^2 \alpha + \sin \alpha - 2 \sin^3 \alpha$

$= 2 \sin \alpha \, (1 - \sin^2 \alpha) + \sin \alpha - 2 \sin^3 \alpha$

$= 2 \sin \alpha - 2 \sin^3 \alpha + \sin \alpha - 2 \sin^3 \alpha$

$= 3 \sin \alpha - 4 \sin^3 \alpha$

42. $\cos 3\alpha$

$= \cos (2\alpha + \alpha)$

$= \cos 2\alpha \cos \alpha - \sin 2\alpha \sin \alpha$

$= (2 \cos^2 \alpha - 1) \cos \alpha - (2 \sin \alpha \cos \alpha) \sin \alpha$

$= 2 \cos^3 \alpha - \cos \alpha - 2 \sin^2 \alpha \cos \alpha$

$= 2 \cos^3 \alpha - \cos \alpha - 2(1 - \cos^2 \alpha) \cos \alpha$

$= 2 \cos^3 \alpha - \cos \alpha - 2 \cos \alpha + 2 \cos^3 \alpha$

$= 4 \cos^3 \alpha - 3 \cos \alpha$

43. Use the half-angle formula to first find $\sin 2x$ and then to find $\sin x$.

$$\left(\frac{2}{3}\right)^2 + \cos^2 4x = 1$$

$$\cos^2 4x = 1 - \frac{4}{9}$$

$$\cos^2 4x = \frac{5}{9}$$

$$\cos 4x = \frac{-\sqrt{5}}{3}$$

$$\sin 2x = \sin \frac{4x}{2} = \sqrt{\frac{1 - \left(-\dfrac{\sqrt{5}}{3}\right)}{2}}$$

$$= \sqrt{\frac{3 + \sqrt{5}}{6}} \cdot \frac{\sqrt{6}}{\sqrt{6}}$$

$$= \frac{\sqrt{18 + 6\sqrt{5}}}{6}$$

$$\left(\frac{\sqrt{18 + 6\sqrt{5}}}{6}\right)^2 + \cos^2 2x = 1$$

$$\cos^2 2x = 1 - \frac{18 + 6\sqrt{5}}{36}$$

$$\cos^2 2x = \frac{18 - 6\sqrt{5}}{36}$$

$$\cos 2x = \frac{\sqrt{18 + 6\sqrt{5}}}{6}$$

$$\sin x = \sin \frac{2x}{2}$$

$$= \sqrt{\frac{1 - \dfrac{\sqrt{18 + 6\sqrt{5}}}{6}}{2}}$$

$$= \sqrt{\frac{\dfrac{6 - \sqrt{18 - 6\sqrt{5}}}{6}}{2}}$$

$$= \sqrt{\frac{6 - \sqrt{18 - 6\sqrt{5}}}{12}} \cdot \frac{\sqrt{12}}{\sqrt{12}}$$

$$= \frac{\sqrt{72 - 12\sqrt{18 - 6\sqrt{5}}}}{12}$$

$$= \frac{2\sqrt{18 - 3\sqrt{18 - 6\sqrt{5}}}}{12}$$

$$= \frac{\sqrt{18 - 3\sqrt{18 - 6\sqrt{5}}}}{6}$$

44. a. $d = \dfrac{v_o^2}{g} \sin 2\theta$

$$= \frac{v_o^2}{g} \cdot 2 \sin \theta \cos \theta$$

$$= \frac{2 v_o^2}{g} \sin \theta \cos \theta$$

b. $d = \dfrac{2(100)^2}{32} \sin 60° \cos 60°$

$ = \dfrac{25}{4} \cdot \dfrac{1}{2} \cdot \dfrac{\sqrt{3}}{2}$

$ \approx 270.6$ feet

c. $45°$; The greatest value of the sine function is 1 and $\sin 2\theta = 1$ when $\theta = 45°$.

45. $n = \dfrac{\sin\left(\dfrac{\alpha + \beta}{2}\right)}{\sin\left(\dfrac{\alpha}{2}\right)}$

$= \dfrac{\sqrt{\dfrac{1 - \cos(\alpha + \beta)}{2}}}{\sqrt{\dfrac{1 - \cos\alpha}{2}}}$

$= \dfrac{\sqrt{\dfrac{1 - (\cos\alpha\cos\beta - \sin\alpha\sin\beta)}{2}}}{\sqrt{\dfrac{1 - \cos\alpha}{2}}}$

$= \dfrac{\sqrt{\dfrac{1 - (\cos\alpha\cos\beta + \sin\alpha\sin\beta)}{2}}}{\sqrt{\dfrac{1 - \cos\alpha}{2}}}$

$= \sqrt{\dfrac{1 - \cos\alpha\cos\beta + \sin\alpha\sin\beta}{1 - \cos\alpha}}$

46. $D = \{-1, 0, 3\}$
$R = \{-6, 0, 4, 7\}$
no

47. $3x - y = 10$
$3x - 10 = y$
slope $= m = 3$
$\quad y - y_1 = m(x - x_1)$
$\quad y + 2 = 3(x - 0)$
$\quad y + 2 = 3x$
$3x - y - 2 = 0$

48. $4x^3 + 3x^2 - x = 0$
$x(4x^2 + 3x - 1) = 0$
$x(4x - 1)(x + 1) = 0$
$x = 0 \quad 4x - 1 = 0 \quad x + 1 = 0$
$\qquad\qquad x = \dfrac{1}{4} \qquad x = -1$
$0, \dfrac{1}{4}, -1$

49. $A \geq 90°$
$a < b$
no triangle

50. $\sin\theta = \sqrt{1 - \cos^2\theta}$

$= \sqrt{1 - \left(\dfrac{2}{3}\right)^2}$

$= \sqrt{\dfrac{5}{9}}$

$= \dfrac{\sqrt{5}}{3}$

51. $\tan 150° = \tan(180° - 30°)$

$= \dfrac{\tan 180° - \tan 30°}{1 + \tan 180° \tan 30°}$

$= \dfrac{0 - \dfrac{\sqrt{3}}{3}}{1}$

$= -\dfrac{\sqrt{3}}{3}$

52. $8^2 = 4^3 = 64$
The best answer is B.

Mid-Chapter Review

PAGE 383

1. $\cos\theta = \pm\sqrt{1 - \sin^2\theta}$

$= \sqrt{1 - \left(\dfrac{4}{5}\right)^2}$

$= \sqrt{\dfrac{9}{25}}$

$= \dfrac{3}{5}$

2. $\tan^2\theta = \sec^2\theta - 1$

$\dfrac{2}{25} = \dfrac{1}{\cos^2\theta} - 1$

$\dfrac{27}{25} = \dfrac{1}{\cos^2\theta}$

$\dfrac{25}{27} = \cos^2\theta$

$\dfrac{5}{3\sqrt{3}} = \cos\theta$

$\dfrac{5\sqrt{3}}{9} = \cos\theta$

3. $\dfrac{1 - \sin^2\alpha}{\sin^2\alpha} = \dfrac{\cos^2\alpha}{\sin^2\alpha}$

$= \cot^2\alpha$

4. $\cos\beta\csc\beta$

$= \cos\beta \cdot \dfrac{1}{\sin\beta}$

$= \cot\beta$

5. $\sin\theta(1 + \cot^2\theta) \overset{?}{=} \csc\theta$

$\sin\theta(\csc^2\theta) \overset{?}{=} \csc\theta$

$\dfrac{1}{\csc\theta}(\csc^2\theta) \overset{?}{=} \csc\theta$

$\csc\theta = \csc\theta$

6. $\cos^2 A \overset{?}{=} (1 - \sin A)(1 + \sin A)$

$\cos^2 A \overset{?}{=} 1 - \sin^2 A$

$\cos^2 A = \cos^2 A$

7. $-\cos\theta \overset{?}{=} \cos(180° - \theta)$

$-\cos\theta \overset{?}{=} \cos 180° \cos\theta + \sin 180° \sin\theta$

$-\cos\theta \overset{?}{=} (-1)\cos\theta + 0\sin\theta$

$-\cos\theta = -\cos\theta$

8. $\dfrac{\cos A + \sin A}{\cos A - \sin A} \overset{?}{=} \dfrac{1 + \sin 2A}{\cos 2A}$

$\dfrac{(\cos A + \sin A)(\cos A + \sin A)}{(\cos A - \sin A)(\cos A + \sin A)} \overset{?}{=} \dfrac{1 + \sin 2A}{\cos 2A}$

$\dfrac{\cos^2 A + 2\cos A\sin A + \sin^2 A}{\cos^2 A - \sin^2 A} \overset{?}{=} \dfrac{1 + \sin 2A}{\cos 2A}$

$\dfrac{1 + \sin 2A}{\cos 2A} = \dfrac{1 + \sin 2A}{\cos 2A}$

9. $\sin^2 \theta \overset{?}{=} \frac{1}{2}(1 - \cos 2\theta)$

$\sin^2 \theta \overset{?}{=} \frac{1}{2}[1 - (1 - 2 \sin^2 \theta)]$

$\sin^2 \theta \overset{?}{=} \frac{1}{2}[2 \sin^2 \theta]$

$\sin^2 \theta = \sin^2 \theta$

10. $\sin 2x \overset{?}{=} 2 \cot x \sin^2 x$

$\sin 2x \overset{?}{=} 2 \frac{\cos x}{\sin x} \sin^2 x$

$\sin 2x \overset{?}{=} 2 \cos x \sin x$

$\sin 2x = \sin 2x$

Technology: Double and Half Angles

PAGE 384   EXERCISES

1. 0.866, 0.5

2. −0.785, −0.620

3. −0.988, 0.155

4. −0.020, 1.000

5.
```
10  INPUT "ENTER THE VALUE OF COS X:   "; C1
20  INPUT "ENTER THE QUADRANT OF ANGLE X:   "; Q
30  S1 = SQR (1 - C1 ^ 2)
40  IF Q = 1 THEN 70
50  IF Q = 2 THEN 70
60  S1 = (-1) * S1
70  PRINT "SIN 2X =   "; 2 * S1 * C1
80  PRINT "COS 2X =   "; 1 - 2 * S1 ^ 2
90  END
```

6. −0.866, −0.5

7. −0.96, 0.28

8.
```
10  INPUT "ENTER THE VALUE OF SIN X:   "; S1
20  INPUT "ENTER THE QUADRANT OF ANGLE X:   "; Q
30  C1 = SQR (1 - S1 ^ 2)
40  IF Q = 1 THEN 70
50  IF Q = 4 THEN 70
60  C1 = (-1) * C1
70  PRINT "SIN (1/2) X =   "; SQR ((1 - C1)/2)
80  C2 = SQR ((1 + C1)/2)
90  IF Q < 3 THEN 110
100 C2 = (-1) * C2
110 PRINT "COS (1/2) X =   "; C2
120 END
```

Graphing Calculators: Solving Trigonometric Equations

PAGE 386   EXERCISES

1.
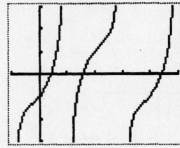

38.2°, 142.3°

2.
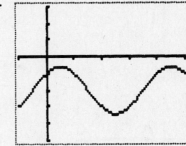

no solutions

3.
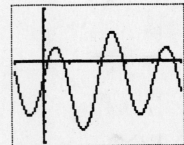

17.3°, 65.6°, 192.8°, 262.6°

4.
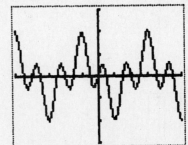

−360°, −315°, −225°, −180°, −135°, −45°, 0°,
45°, 135°, 180°, 225°, 315°, 360°

5.

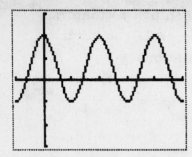

55.7°, 125.3°, 234.7°, 305.2°

6.

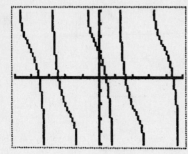

-321.8°, -218.1°, 38.0°, 142.2°

7.

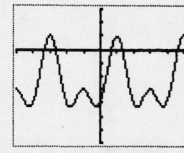

-300°, -240°, 60°, 120°

8.

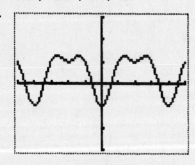

-308°, -52°, 52°, 308°

9.

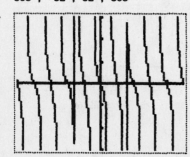

-360°, -270°, -180°, -90°, 0°, 90°, 180°, 270°, 360°

10.

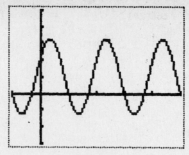

90°, 153.4°, 270°, 333.4°

7-5   Solving Trigonometric Equations

PAGES 389-390   CHECKING FOR UNDERSTANDING

1. Answers may vary. A sample answer is that in solving an equation you may perform the same operation on both sides of the equation, but while verifying an identity you may not.

2. **a.** infinitely many

   b. one

   c. none

3. $2 \sin x + 1 = 0$

   $2 \sin x = -1$

   $\sin x = -\dfrac{1}{2}$

       $x = -30°$

4. $2 \cos x - 1 = 0$

   $2 \cos x = 1$

   $\cos x = \dfrac{1}{2}$

       $x = 60°$

5. $\sqrt{2} \sin x - 1 = 0$

   $\sqrt{2} \sin x = 1$

   $\sin x = \dfrac{1}{\sqrt{2}}$

         $= \dfrac{\sqrt{2}}{2}$

         $= 45°$

6. $2 \cos x + 1 = 0$

   $2 \cos x = -1$

   $\cos x = -\dfrac{1}{2}$

       $x = 120°$

7. $2 \cos x - \sqrt{3} = 0$

   $\cos x = \dfrac{\sqrt{3}}{2}$

       $x = 30°$

8.
$$\sin 2x - 1 = 0$$
$$2 \sin x \cos x - 1 = 0$$
$$2 \sin x \cos x = 1$$
$$\sin^2 x \cos^2 x = \frac{1}{4}$$
$$\sin^2 x (1 - \sin^2 x) = \frac{1}{4}$$
$$\sin^2 x - \sin^4 x - \frac{1}{4} = 0$$
$$\sin^4 x - \sin^2 x + \frac{1}{4} = 0$$
$$\left(\sin^2 x - \frac{1}{2}\right)\left(\sin^2 x - \frac{1}{2}\right) = 0$$
$$\sin^2 x = \frac{1}{2}$$
$$\sin x = \frac{1}{\sqrt{2}} = \frac{\sqrt{2}}{2}$$
$$x = 45°$$

9. $\cos 3x - 0.5 = 0$

$\qquad \cos 3x = 0.5$

$\qquad\qquad 3x = 60° + 360k°$ or $300° + 360k°$

$\qquad\qquad x = 20°, 140°, 100°$

10. $\qquad\qquad \tan 2x - \sqrt{3} = 0$

$\qquad\qquad\qquad \tan 2x = \sqrt{3}$

$\qquad\qquad \dfrac{2 \tan x}{1 - \tan^2 x} = \sqrt{3}$

$\qquad\qquad\qquad 2 \tan x = \sqrt{3}(1 - \tan^2 x)$

$\qquad\qquad\qquad 2 \tan x = \sqrt{3} - \sqrt{3} \tan^2 x$

$\qquad \sqrt{3} \tan^2 x + 2 \tan x - \sqrt{3} = 0$

$\qquad (\sqrt{3} \tan x - 1)(\tan x + \sqrt{3}) = 0$

$\qquad \sqrt{3} \tan x - 1 = 0 \qquad \tan x + \sqrt{3} = 0$

$\qquad\qquad \tan x = \dfrac{1}{\sqrt{3}} \qquad\qquad \tan x = -\sqrt{3}$

$\qquad\qquad\qquad\qquad\qquad\qquad\qquad x = -60°$

$\qquad\qquad\qquad = \dfrac{\sqrt{3}}{3}$

$\qquad\qquad\qquad x = 30°$

11. $\qquad\qquad \cos 2x = \cos x$

$\qquad\qquad 2 \cos^2 x - 1 = \cos x$

$\qquad 2 \cos^2 x - \cos x - 1 = 0$

$\qquad (2 \cos x + 1)(\cos x - 1) = 0$

$\qquad 2 \cos x = -1 \qquad\qquad \cos x = 1$

$\qquad\qquad\qquad\qquad\qquad\qquad\qquad x = 0°$

$\qquad \cos x = -\dfrac{1}{2}$

$\qquad\qquad x = 120°, 240°$

$\qquad x = 0° + 120k°$

12. $\qquad\qquad \sin x = \tan x$

$\qquad\qquad \sin x = \dfrac{\sin x}{\cos x}$

$\qquad \sin x \cos x = \sin x$

$\quad \sin x \cos x - \sin x = 0$

$\qquad \sin x (\cos x - 1) = 0$

$\quad \sin x = 0 \qquad\qquad \cos x = 1$

$\qquad\quad x = 0° \qquad\qquad\qquad x = 0°$

$\quad x = 0° + 180k°$

13. $\sin x + \sin x \cos x = 0$

$\quad \sin x (1 + \cos x) = 0$

$\sin x = 0 \qquad\qquad \cos x = -1$

$\quad x = 0° \qquad\qquad\qquad x = 180°$

$\quad x = 0° + 360k° \qquad\qquad x = 180° + 360k°$

So, $x = 0° + 180k°$.

14. $\sin x = \cos x$

$\quad x = 45° + 180k°$

15. $\qquad \cos 2x + \cos x + 1 = 0$

$\quad 2 \cos^2 x - 1 + \cos x + 1 = 0$

$\qquad\qquad 2 \cos^2 x + \cos x = 0$

$\qquad \cos x (2 \cos x + 1) = 0$

$\qquad \cos x = 0 \qquad 2 \cos x = -1$

$\qquad\qquad\qquad\qquad\qquad \cos x = -\dfrac{1}{2}$

$x = 90° + 180k°$

$x = 120° + 360k°$

$x = 240° + 360k°$

16. $\tan^2 x - \sqrt{3} \tan x = 0$

$\quad \tan x (\tan x - \sqrt{3}) = 0$

$\quad \tan x = 0 \qquad\qquad \tan x = \sqrt{3}$

$\qquad x = 0° + 180k° \qquad x = 60° + 180k°$

17. $\sin^2 x - 3 = 0$

$\qquad \sin^2 x = \dfrac{3}{4}$

$\qquad \sin x = \pm \dfrac{\sqrt{3}}{2}$

$\qquad\qquad x = 60°, 120°$

18. $\qquad 2 \sin^2 x + \sin x = 0$

$\quad \sin x (2 \sin x + 1) = 0$

$\quad \sin x = 0 \qquad \sin x = -\dfrac{1}{2}$

$\qquad x = 0° \qquad\qquad x = 180°$

19. $\sqrt{3} \tan x + 1 = 0$ $\qquad\qquad$ 20. $\sqrt{2} \cos x - 1 = 0$

$\qquad \tan x = -\dfrac{1}{\sqrt{3}}$ $\qquad\qquad\qquad \cos x = \dfrac{1}{\sqrt{2}}$

$\qquad \tan x = -\dfrac{\sqrt{3}}{3}$ $\qquad\qquad\qquad \cos x = \dfrac{\sqrt{2}}{2}$

$\qquad\qquad x = 150°$ $\qquad\qquad\qquad\qquad x = 45°$

21. $\qquad \tan 2x = \cot x$

$\qquad \dfrac{\tan x}{1 - \tan^2 x} = \dfrac{1}{\tan x}$

$\qquad\qquad \tan^2 x = 1 - \tan^2 x$

$\qquad\qquad 2 \tan^2 x = 1$

$\qquad\qquad \tan^2 x = \dfrac{1}{2}$

$\qquad\qquad \tan x = \dfrac{1}{\sqrt{2}} = \dfrac{\sqrt{2}}{2}$

$\qquad\qquad x = 30°, 90°, 150°$

22. $\qquad 2 \cos^2 x = \sin x + 1$

$\quad 2(1 - \sin^2 x) = \sin x + 1$

$\quad 2 - 2 \sin^2 x = \sin x + 1$

$\qquad\qquad 0 = 2 \sin^2 x + \sin x - 1$

$\qquad\qquad 0 = (2 \sin x - 1)(\sin x + 1)$

$\quad \sin x = \dfrac{1}{2} \qquad\qquad \sin x = 1$

$\qquad x = 30°, 150°$

23. $\qquad\qquad \sin 2x = \cos x$

$\qquad 2 \sin x \cos x = \cos x$

$\quad \cos x (2 \sin x - 1) = 0$

$\quad \cos x = 0 \qquad \sin x = \dfrac{1}{2}$

$\qquad x = 90° \qquad\qquad x = 30°, 150°$

24. $\sin^2 x - 3 \sin x + 2 = 0$

$\quad (\sin x - 2)(\sin x - 1) = 0$

$\sin x = 2 \qquad\qquad \sin x = 1$

$\qquad\qquad\qquad\qquad\qquad x = 90°$

25.
$$\sin x + \cos x = 0$$
$$\sin x = -\cos x$$
$$\sin^2 x = \cos^2 x$$
$$\sin^2 x - \cos^2 x = 0$$
$$\sin^2 x - 1 + \sin^2 x = 0$$
$$2 \sin^2 x - 1 = 0$$
$$\sin^2 x = \frac{1}{2}$$
$$\sin x = \frac{1}{\sqrt{2}} = \frac{\sqrt{2}}{2}$$
$$x = 135°$$

26.
$$\cos^2 x - \frac{7}{2} \cos x - 2 = 0$$
$$(\cos x - 4)\left(\cos x + \frac{1}{2}\right) = 0$$
$$\cos x = 4 \qquad \cos x = -\frac{1}{2}$$
$$x = 120°$$

27.
$$3 \cos 2x - 5 \cos x = 1$$
$$3(2 \cos^2 x - 1) - 5 \cos x = 1$$
$$6 \cos^2 x - 5 \cos x - 4 = 0$$
$$(3 \cos x - 4)(2 \cos x + 1) = 0$$
$$\cos x = \frac{4}{3} \qquad \cos x = -\frac{1}{2}$$
$$x = 120°$$

28.
$$\tan^2 x = 3 \tan x$$
$$\tan^2 x - 3 \tan x = 0$$
$$\tan x (\tan x - 3) = 0$$
$$\tan x = 0 \qquad \tan x = 3$$
$$x = 0°, 180° \qquad x \approx 71°34'$$

29.
$$3 \tan^2 x + 4 \sec x = -4$$
$$3(\sec^2 x - 1) + 4 \sec x = -4$$
$$3 \sec^2 x + 4 \sec x + 1 = 0$$
$$(3 \sec x + 1)(\sec x + 1) = 0$$
$$\sec x = \frac{-1}{3} \qquad \sec x = -1$$
$$x = 180°$$

30.
$$\sin 2x = \cos 3x$$
$$2 \sin x \cos x = 4 \cos^3 x - 3 \cos x$$
$$2 \sin x = 4 \cos^2 x - 3$$
$$2 \sin x = 4(1 - \sin^2 x) - 3$$
$$2 \sin x = 4 - 4 \sin^2 x - 3$$
$$4 \sin^2 x + 2 \sin x - 1 = 0$$
$$\sin x = \frac{-2 \pm \sqrt{4 + 16}}{8}$$
$$= \frac{-1 \pm \sqrt{5}}{4}$$
$$x = 18°, 90°, 162°$$

31.
$$\sin 2x \sin x + \cos 2x \cos x = 1$$
$$2 \sin x \cos x \sin x + (2 \cos^2 x - 1) \cos x = 1$$
$$2 \cos x (1 - \cos^2 x) + 2 \cos^3 x - \cos x = 1$$
$$2 \cos x - 2 \cos^3 x + 2 \cos^3 x - \cos x = 1$$
$$\cos x = 1$$
$$x = 0°$$

32.
$$3 \sin^2 x - \cos^2 x = 0$$
$$3 \sin^2 x - 1 + \sin^2 x = 0$$
$$4 \sin^2 x = 1$$
$$\sin^2 x = \frac{1}{4}$$
$$\sin x = \frac{1}{2}$$
$$x = 30°, 150°$$

33.
$$\cos 2x + 3 \cos x - 1 = 0$$
$$2 \cos^2 x - 1 + 3 \cos x - 1 = 0$$
$$2 \cos^2 x + 3 \cos x - 2 = 0$$
$$(2 \cos x - 1)(\cos x + 2) = 0$$
$$\cos x = \frac{1}{2} \qquad \cos x = -2$$
$$x = 60°$$

34.
$$4 \tan x + \sin 2x = 0$$
$$4 \frac{\sin x}{\cos x} + 2 \sin x \cos x = 0$$
$$4 \sin x + 2 \sin x \cos^2 x = 0$$
$$2 \sin x + \sin x (1 - \sin^2 x) = 0$$
$$2 \sin x + \sin x - \sin^3 x = 0$$
$$3 \sin x - \sin^3 x = 0$$
$$\sin x (3 - \sin^2 x) = 0$$
$$\sin x = 0 \qquad \sin^2 x = 3$$
$$\sin x = \sqrt{3}$$
$$x = 0°, 180°$$

35.
$$2 \sin x \cos x + 4 \sin x = \cos x + 2$$
$$2 \sin x (\cos x + 2) = \cos x + 2$$
$$2 \sin x = 1$$
$$\sin x = \frac{1}{2}$$
$$x = 30°, 150°$$

36.
$$\sqrt{3} \cot x \sin x + 2 \cos^2 x = 0$$
$$\sqrt{3} \cdot \frac{\cos x}{\sin x} \cdot \sin x + 2 \cos^2 x = 0$$
$$\sqrt{3} \cos x + 2 \cos^2 x = 0$$
$$\cos x (\sqrt{3} + 2 \cos x) = 0$$
$$\cos x = 0 \qquad \cos x = \frac{-\sqrt{3}}{2}$$
$$x = 90° \qquad x = 150°$$

37.
$$2 \sin^2 x - 1 = 0$$
$$\sin^2 x = \frac{1}{2}$$
$$\sin x = \frac{\pm\sqrt{2}}{2}$$
$$x = 45° + 90k°$$

38. $\cos x - 2 \cos x \sin x = 0$

$\cos x (1 - 2 \sin x) = 0$

$\cos x = 0 \qquad\qquad \sin x = \frac{1}{2}$

$x = 90° + 180k° \qquad x = 30° + 360k°$

$\qquad\qquad\qquad\qquad x = 150° + 360k°$

39. $\sin^2 x - 2 \sin x - 3 = 0$

$(\sin x - 3)(\sin x + 1) = 0$

$\sin x = 3 \qquad \sin x = -1$

$\qquad\qquad\quad x = 270° + 360k°$

40. $\qquad 3 \cos 2x - 5 \cos x = 1$

$\quad 3(2 \cos^2 x - 1) - 5 \cos x = 1$

$\quad 6 \cos^2 x - 5 \cos x - 4 = 0$

$(3 \cos x - 4)(2 \cos x + 1) = 0$

$\cos x = \frac{4}{3} \qquad \cos x = -\frac{1}{2}$

$\qquad\qquad\qquad x = 120° + 360k°$

$\qquad\qquad\qquad x = 240° + 360k°$

41. $\cos x \tan x - \sin^2 x = 0$

$\cos x \cdot \dfrac{\sin x}{\cos x} - \sin^2 x = 0$

$\sin x (1 - \sin x) = 0$

$\sin x = 0 \qquad\qquad \sin x = 1$

$x = 0° + 180k° \qquad x = 90° + 360k°$

42. $\sin^2 x - \sin x = 0$

$\sin x (\sin x - 1) = 0$

$\sin x = 0 \qquad\qquad \sin x = 1$

$x = 0° + 180k° \qquad x = 90° + 360k°$

43. $4 \cos^2 x - 4 \cos x + 1 = 0$

$(2 \cos x - 1)(2 \cos x - 1) = 0$

$\qquad\qquad\qquad \cos x = \frac{1}{2}$

$\qquad\qquad\qquad x = 60° + 360k°$

$\qquad\qquad\qquad x = 300° + 360k°$

44. $\cos x = 3 \cos x - 2$

$\quad 2 = 2 \cos x$

$\quad 1 = \cos x$

$\quad x = 0° + 360k°$

45. $\qquad \dfrac{\tan x - \sin x}{\tan x + \sin x} = \dfrac{\sec x - 1}{\sec x + 1}$

$\dfrac{\frac{\sin x}{\cos x} - \sin x}{\frac{\sin x}{\cos x} + \sin x} = \dfrac{\frac{1}{\cos x} - 1}{\frac{1}{\cos x} + 1}$

$\dfrac{\sin x - \sin x \cos x}{\sin x + \sin x \cos x} = \dfrac{1 - \cos x}{1 + \cos x}$

$\dfrac{\sin x (1 - \cos x)}{\sin x (1 + \cos x)} = \dfrac{1 - \cos x}{1 + \cos x}$

$\dfrac{1 - \cos x}{1 + \cos x} = \dfrac{1 - \cos x}{1 + \cos x}$

true for all reals except $90k°$ where k is any integer

46. a. $y = 2 \sin \left(3\pi - \dfrac{\pi}{2}\right)$

$= 2 \sin (2.5\pi)$

$= 2 \sin 450°$

$= 2 \cdot 1$

$= 2$

2 inches above the equilibrium

b. $0 = 2 \sin \left(\pi t - \dfrac{\pi}{2}\right)$

$0 = \sin \left(\dfrac{2\pi t - \pi}{2}\right)$

$= \sin \left(\dfrac{\pi(2t - 1)}{2}\right)$

$= \sin (180° t - 90°)$

$= [\sin (180° t) \cos (180° t)$

$\quad - \sin 90° \cos 90°]$

$= [\sin (180° t) \cos (180° t)]$

$= [\sin^2 (180° t)(1 - \sin^2 (180° t))]$

$\sin^2 (180° t) = 0 \qquad 1 - \sin^2 (180° t) = 0$

$t = 0.5 + k$ seconds where k is any integer

c.

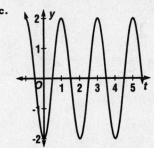

47. a. $\qquad n_1 \sin i = n_2 \sin r$

$1.0 \sin 10° = 1.5 \sin r$

$\dfrac{\sin 10°}{1.5} = \sin r$

$0.1158 \approx \sin r$

$r \approx 6.6°$

b. $1.5 \sin 10° = 1.33 \sin r$

$\dfrac{1.5 \sin 10°}{1.33} = \sin r$

$0.1958 \approx \sin r$

$r \approx 7.5$

c. same as it enters, $10°$

48. Measure the angles of refracted light to determine the index of refraction. If the index is 2.42, the diamond is genuine.

49. $2(9) - 4(3) \overset{?}{\leq} 7, \qquad 2(-1) - 4(2) \overset{?}{\leq} 7,$

$\qquad\quad 6 \leq 7 \qquad\qquad\qquad\quad -9 \leq 7$

$\qquad\quad$ yes $\qquad\qquad\qquad\qquad\quad$ yes

$2(2) - 4(-2) \overset{?}{\leq} 7$

$\qquad 12 \not\leq 7$

$\qquad$ no

50. $y = 2x^3 + 1$ is $y = 2x^3$ shifted 1 unit up.

51. $f(x) = x^3 - 4x^2 + 4x + 6$

$f'(x) = 3x^2 - 8x + 4$ $\qquad$ $f''(x) = 6x - 8$

$0 = (3x - 2)(x - 2)$ $\qquad$ $0 = 6x - 8$

$x = \dfrac{2}{3}, \; x = 2$ $\qquad$ $x = \dfrac{4}{3}$

$f\left(\dfrac{2}{3}\right) = \left(\dfrac{2}{3}\right)^3 - 4\left(\dfrac{2}{3}\right)^2 + 4\left(\dfrac{2}{3}\right) + 6 = \dfrac{194}{27} = 7\dfrac{5}{27}$

$f(2) = 8 - 16 + 8 + 6 = 6$

$f\left(\dfrac{4}{3}\right) = \dfrac{64}{27} - \dfrac{64}{9} + \dfrac{16}{3} + 6 = \dfrac{178}{27} = 6\dfrac{16}{27}$

Test points on both sides of each critical point.

$\left(\dfrac{2}{3}, \; 7\dfrac{5}{27}\right)$ is a maximum, $(2,6)$ is a minimum,

and $\left(\dfrac{4}{3}, \; 6\dfrac{16}{27}\right)$ is a point of inflection.

52. $2^2 + 3^2 = y^2$

$13 = y^2$

$y = \sqrt{13}$

$\sin \theta = \dfrac{2}{\sqrt{13}} = \dfrac{2\sqrt{13}}{13}$

$\cos \theta = -\dfrac{3}{\sqrt{13}} = -\dfrac{3\sqrt{13}}{13}$

$\tan \theta = -\dfrac{2}{3}$

$\csc \theta = \dfrac{\sqrt{13}}{2}$

$\sec \theta = -\dfrac{\sqrt{13}}{3}$

$\cot \theta = -\dfrac{3}{2}$

53. $\sec\left(\cos^{-1}\dfrac{2}{5}\right)$

$= \sec\left(\sec^{-1}\dfrac{5}{2}\right)$

$= \dfrac{5}{2}$

54. $\sin \theta = \dfrac{1}{\csc \theta}$

$= \dfrac{1}{3}$

55. $\cos 7°30' = \cos \dfrac{15°}{2}$

$= \pm\sqrt{\dfrac{1 + \cos 15°}{2}}$

$= \sqrt{\dfrac{1 + \dfrac{\sqrt{2 + \sqrt{3}}}{2}}{2}}$

$= \sqrt{\dfrac{2 + \sqrt{2 + \sqrt{3}}}{4}}$

$= \dfrac{\sqrt{2 + \sqrt{2 + \sqrt{3}}}}{2}$

56. $4^3 - 4 - [(-3)^3 - (-3)] = 60 + 27 - 3 = 84$

The best answer is A.

Case Study Follow-Up

PAGE 391

1. The cycle appears to be about 12 years long, ranging between a maximum of about +12% in 1980 and a minimum of about +2% in 1986.

2. around 1998

3. Answers may vary. A sample answer is the sine function. $f(1983)$ is halfway between the extreme values of the function, as $\sin 0°$ is halfway between the extreme values of the sine function.

<table>
<tr><td>7-6</td><td></td></tr>
</table>

Normal Form of a Linear Equation

1.

Quadrant	I	II	III	IV
coefficient of x ($\cos \phi$)	+	−	−	+
coefficient of y ($\sin \phi$)	+	+	−	−

2. $x \cos \phi + y \sin \phi - p = 0$

Substitute $225°$ for ϕ and 7 for p.

$x \cos 225° + y \sin 225° - 7 = 0$

Simplify.

$-\dfrac{\sqrt{2}}{2}x + \left(-\dfrac{\sqrt{2}}{2}y\right) - 7 = 0$

Multiply each side by $-\sqrt{2}$.

$x + y - 7\sqrt{2} = 0$

3. $x \cos 45° + y \sin 45° - 11 = 0$

$\dfrac{\sqrt{2}}{2}x + \dfrac{\sqrt{2}}{2}y - 11 = 0$

$x + y - 11\sqrt{2} = 0$

4. $x \cos 60° + y \sin 60° - 3 = 0$

$\dfrac{1}{2}x + \dfrac{\sqrt{3}}{2}y - 3 = 0$

$x + \sqrt{3}y - 6 = 0$

5. $x \cos 135° + y \sin 135° = 0$

$-\dfrac{\sqrt{2}}{2}x + \dfrac{\sqrt{2}}{2}y = 0$

$x - y = 0$

6. $x \cos 225° + y \sin 225° - 6 = 0$

$-\dfrac{\sqrt{2}}{2}x - \dfrac{\sqrt{2}}{2}y - 6 = 0$

$x + y + 6\sqrt{2} = 0$

7. $x \cos 30° + y \sin 30° - 2 = 0$

$\dfrac{\sqrt{3}}{2}x + \dfrac{1}{2}y - 2 = 0$

$\sqrt{3}x + y - 4 = 0$

8. $x \cos 135° + y \sin 135° - 1 = 0$

$-\dfrac{\sqrt{2}}{2}x + \dfrac{\sqrt{2}}{2}y - 1 = 0$

$x - y + \sqrt{2} = 0$

9. $x \cos 270° + y \sin 270° - 4 = 0$

$ x(0) + y(-1) - 4 = 0$

$ -y - 4 = 0$

10. $-\sqrt{A^2 + B^2} = -\sqrt{5^2 + (-1)^2} = -\sqrt{26}$

$\dfrac{5x}{-\sqrt{26}} - \dfrac{y}{-\sqrt{26}} + \dfrac{3}{-\sqrt{26}} = 0$

$-\dfrac{5}{\sqrt{26}}x + \dfrac{1}{\sqrt{26}}y - \dfrac{3}{\sqrt{26}} = 0$

$p = \dfrac{3}{\sqrt{26}} \approx 0.6$

$\sin \phi = \dfrac{1}{\sqrt{26}}, \ \cos \phi = -\dfrac{5}{\sqrt{26}}$

$\tan \phi = \dfrac{-1}{5}$

$ = -0.2$

$ \phi \approx 169°$

11. $\sqrt{A^2 + B^2} = \sqrt{9 + 1} = \sqrt{10}$

$\dfrac{3x}{\sqrt{10}} - \dfrac{y}{\sqrt{10}} - \dfrac{4}{\sqrt{10}} = 0$

$p = \dfrac{4}{\sqrt{10}} \approx 1.3$

$\sin \phi = \dfrac{-1}{\sqrt{10}}, \ \cos \phi = \dfrac{3}{\sqrt{10}}$

$\tan \phi = -\dfrac{1}{3}$

$ \phi \approx 342°$

12. $\sqrt{A^2 + B^2} = \sqrt{25 + 1} = \sqrt{26}$

$\dfrac{5x}{\sqrt{26}} + \dfrac{y}{\sqrt{26}} - \dfrac{7}{\sqrt{26}} = 0$

$p = \dfrac{7}{\sqrt{26}} \approx 1.4$

$\sin \phi = \dfrac{1}{\sqrt{26}}, \ \cos \phi = \dfrac{5}{\sqrt{26}}$

$\tan \phi = \dfrac{1}{5}$

$ \phi \approx 11°$

PAGES 396-397   EXERCISES

13. $x \cos 45° + y \sin 45° - 5 = 0$

$ \dfrac{\sqrt{2}}{2}x + \dfrac{\sqrt{2}}{2}y - 5 = 0$

$ x + y - 5\sqrt{2} = 0$

14. $x \cos 60° + y \sin 60° - 3 = 0$

$ x \cdot \dfrac{1}{2} + y \cdot \dfrac{\sqrt{3}}{2} - 3 = 0$

$ x + \sqrt{3}y - 6 = 0$

15. $x \cos 225° + y \sin 225° - 25 = 0$

$ -\dfrac{\sqrt{2}}{2}x - \dfrac{\sqrt{2}}{2}y - 25 = 0$

$ x + y + 25\sqrt{2} = 0$

16. $x \cos 150° + y \sin 150° - 2 = 0$

$ x \cdot \dfrac{-\sqrt{3}}{2} + y \cdot \dfrac{1}{2} - 2 = 0$

$ \sqrt{3}x - y + 4 = 0$

17. $x \cos 240° + y \sin 240° - 8 = 0$

$ -\dfrac{1}{2}x - \dfrac{\sqrt{3}}{2}y - 8 = 0$

$ x + \sqrt{3}y + 16 = 0$

18. $x \cos 120° + y \sin 120° - 32 = 0$

$ -\dfrac{1}{2}x + \dfrac{\sqrt{3}}{2}y - 32 = 0$

$ x - \sqrt{3}y + 64 = 0$

19. $\sqrt{A^2 + B^2} = \sqrt{(-1)^2 + 1^2} = \sqrt{2}$

$-\dfrac{x}{\sqrt{2}} + \dfrac{y}{\sqrt{2}} - \dfrac{6}{\sqrt{2}} = 0$

$p = \dfrac{6}{\sqrt{2}} \approx 4.24$

$\sin \phi = \dfrac{1}{\sqrt{2}}, \ \cos \phi = -\dfrac{1}{\sqrt{2}}$

$\tan \phi = -1$

$ \phi = 135°$

20. $\sqrt{A^2 + B^2} = \sqrt{2^2 + (-3)^2} = \sqrt{13}$

$\dfrac{2x}{\sqrt{13}} - \dfrac{3y}{\sqrt{13}} - \dfrac{1}{\sqrt{13}} = 0$

$p = \dfrac{1}{\sqrt{13}} \approx 0.28$

$\cos \phi = \dfrac{2}{\sqrt{13}}, \ \sin \phi = \dfrac{-3}{\sqrt{13}}$

$\tan \phi = \dfrac{-2}{3}$

$ \phi \approx -56°19'$

21. $\sqrt{A^2 + B^2} = \sqrt{1^2 + 1^2} = \sqrt{2}$

$\dfrac{x}{\sqrt{2}} + \dfrac{y}{\sqrt{2}} - \dfrac{8}{\sqrt{2}} = 0$

$p = \dfrac{8}{\sqrt{2}} \approx 5.66$

$\sin \phi = \dfrac{1}{\sqrt{2}}, \ \cos \phi = \dfrac{1}{\sqrt{2}}$

$\tan \phi = 1$

$ \phi = 45°$

22. $\sqrt{A^2 + B^2} = \sqrt{3^2 + 4^2} = \sqrt{25} = 5$

$\dfrac{3}{5}x + \dfrac{4}{5}y - \dfrac{1}{5} = 0$

$p = \dfrac{1}{5}$

$\sin \phi = \dfrac{4}{5}, \ \cos \phi = \dfrac{3}{5}$

$\tan \phi = \dfrac{4}{3}$

$ \approx 53°8'$

23. $\sqrt{A^2 + B^2} = \sqrt{1^2 + (-3)^2} = \sqrt{10}$

$\dfrac{x}{\sqrt{10}} - \dfrac{3y}{\sqrt{10}} - \dfrac{2}{\sqrt{10}} = 0$

$p = \dfrac{2}{\sqrt{10}} \approx 0.63$

$\sin \phi = \dfrac{-3}{\sqrt{10}}, \quad \cos \phi = \dfrac{1}{\sqrt{10}}$

$\tan \phi = -3$

$\phi \approx -71°34'$

24. $\sqrt{A^2 + B^2} = \sqrt{6^2 + (-8)^2} = \sqrt{100} = 10$

$\dfrac{6}{10}x - \dfrac{8}{10}y - \dfrac{15}{10} = 0$

$\dfrac{3}{5}x - \dfrac{4}{5}y - \dfrac{3}{2} = 0$

$p = \dfrac{3}{2}$

$\sin \phi = -\dfrac{4}{5}, \quad \cos \phi = \dfrac{3}{5}$

$\tan \phi = -\dfrac{4}{3}$

$\phi \approx -53°8'$

25. $\sqrt{A^2 + B^2} = \sqrt{(-4)^2 + 4^2} = \sqrt{32} = p$

$\cos \phi = \dfrac{OM}{p} = \dfrac{-4}{\sqrt{32}}, \quad \sin \phi = \dfrac{MC}{p} = \dfrac{4}{\sqrt{32}}$

$x \cos \phi + y \sin \phi - p = 0$

$\dfrac{-4}{\sqrt{32}}x + \dfrac{4}{\sqrt{32}}y - \sqrt{32} = 0$

$-4x + 4y - 32 = 0$

$x - y + 8 = 0$

26. $\sqrt{A^2 + B^2} = \sqrt{3^2 + 3^2} = \sqrt{18}$

$\cos \phi = \dfrac{OM}{p} = \dfrac{3}{\sqrt{18}}, \quad \sin \phi = \dfrac{MC}{p} = \dfrac{3}{\sqrt{18}}$

$x \cos \phi + y \sin \phi - p = 0$

$\dfrac{3}{\sqrt{18}}x + \dfrac{3}{\sqrt{18}}y - \sqrt{18} = 0$

$3x + 3y - 18 = 0$

$x + y - 6 = 0$

27. $p = 1$

$\cos \phi = \dfrac{1}{2} \text{ and } -\dfrac{1}{2}$

$\sin \phi = \dfrac{\sqrt{3}}{2} \text{ and } -\dfrac{\sqrt{3}}{2}$

$\dfrac{1}{2}x + \dfrac{\sqrt{3}}{2}y - 1 = 0 \qquad \dfrac{-1}{2}x - \dfrac{\sqrt{3}}{2}y - 1 = 0$

$x + \sqrt{3}y - 2 = 0 \qquad\qquad x + \sqrt{3}y + 2 = 0$

28. $p = 3$

$\cos \phi = \pm\dfrac{\sqrt{2}}{2}, \quad \sin \phi = \pm\dfrac{\sqrt{2}}{2}$

$\dfrac{\sqrt{2}}{2}x + \dfrac{\sqrt{2}}{2}y - 3 = 0 \qquad -\dfrac{\sqrt{2}}{2}x - \dfrac{\sqrt{2}}{2}y - 3 = 0$

$x + y - 3\sqrt{2} = 0 \qquad\qquad x + y + 3\sqrt{2} = 0$

29. $p = \sqrt{4^2 + 3^2} = \sqrt{25} = 5$

$\cos \phi = \dfrac{4}{5}, \quad \sin \phi = \dfrac{3}{5}$

$\dfrac{4}{5}x + \dfrac{3}{5}y - 5 = 0$

$4x + 3y - 25 = 0$

$p = \sqrt{(-3)^2 + 1^2} = \sqrt{10}$

$\cos \phi = \dfrac{-3}{\sqrt{10}}, \quad \sin \phi = \dfrac{1}{\sqrt{10}}$

$\dfrac{-3}{\sqrt{10}}x + \dfrac{1}{\sqrt{10}}y - \sqrt{10} = 0$

$-3x + y - 10 = 0$

$4x + 3y - 25 = 0 \qquad 4\left(-\dfrac{5}{13}\right) + 3y - 25 = 0$

$\dfrac{-3(-3x + y - 10 = 0)}{13x \qquad\quad + 5 = 0} \qquad\qquad y = \dfrac{115}{13}$

$x = -\dfrac{5}{13}$

Point of intersection is at $\left(-\dfrac{5}{13}, \dfrac{115}{13}\right)$.

30. $2\sqrt{2}x - y - 18 = 0$

$\sqrt{A^2 + B^2} = \sqrt{2(2)^2 + (-1)^2} = \sqrt{9} = 3$

$\dfrac{2\sqrt{2}}{3}x - \dfrac{1}{3}y - \dfrac{18}{3} = 0$

$p = \dfrac{18}{3} = 6$

radius = 6

31. a.

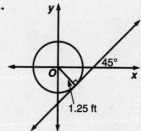

b. $p = 1.25, \quad \phi = 45°$

$x \cos(-45°) + y \sin(-45°) - 1.25 = 0$

$\dfrac{\sqrt{2}}{2}x - \dfrac{\sqrt{2}}{2}y - 1.25 = 0$

$x - y - 1.25\sqrt{2} = 0$

32. $m = \dfrac{2 - 4}{5 + 4} = -\dfrac{2}{9}$

$y - 2 = -\dfrac{2}{9}(x - 5)$

$y = -\dfrac{2}{9}x + \dfrac{10}{9} + \dfrac{18}{9}$

$y = -\dfrac{2}{9}x + \dfrac{28}{9}$

33. no

34. 3 roots

$$\frac{1}{2}\begin{array}{|rrrr} 4 & -4 & 13 & -6 \\ & 2 & -1 & 6 \\ \hline 4 & -2 & 12 & 0 \end{array}$$

$$4x^2 - 2x + 12 = 0$$

$$2x^2 - x + 6 = 0$$

$$x = \frac{-(-1) \pm \sqrt{1 - 4(2)(6)}}{2(2)}$$

$$= \frac{1 \pm \sqrt{-47}}{4}$$

$$= \frac{1 \pm i\sqrt{47}}{4}$$

$$x = \frac{1}{2}, \quad \frac{1 \pm i\sqrt{47}}{4}$$

35. $\tan S \cos S = \frac{1}{2}$

$$\frac{\sin S}{\cos S} \cdot \cos S = \frac{1}{2}$$

$$\sin S = \frac{1}{2}$$

36. $\tan x + \cot x = 2$

$$\tan x + \frac{1}{\tan x} = 2$$

$$\tan^2 x + 1 = 2\tan x$$

$$\tan^2 x - 2\tan x + 1 = 0$$

$$(\tan x - 1)(\tan x - 1) = 0$$

$$\tan x = 1$$

$$x = 45°$$

37. $\dfrac{\frac{a-b}{a+b}}{\frac{b-a}{b+a}} = \dfrac{a-b}{a+b} \cdot \dfrac{b+a}{b-a}$

$$= \frac{a-b}{b-a}$$

$$= \frac{a-b}{(-1)a - b}$$

$$= \frac{1}{(-1)}$$

$$= -1$$

The best answer is D.

7-7 Distance from a Point to a Line

1. yes, $Ax_1 + By_1 + C = 0$ if the point is on the line, so the distance is 0.

2. The prediction for Linda's systolic blood pressure was too low and the prediction for her father was too high.

3. $\dfrac{6(4) - 8(2) + 1}{-\sqrt{6^2 + 8^2}} = \dfrac{9}{-\sqrt{100}}$

$$= -\frac{9}{10}$$

$$= -0.9, \quad |d| = 0.9$$

4. $\dfrac{12(-3) + 5(5) - 3}{\sqrt{12^2 + 5^2}} = \dfrac{-14}{\sqrt{169}}$

$$= -\frac{14}{13}, \quad |d| = \frac{14}{13}$$

5. $\dfrac{3(-1) - 7(4) - 1}{\sqrt{3^2 + (-7)^2}} = \dfrac{-32}{\sqrt{58}}$

$$= \frac{-32\sqrt{58}}{58}$$

$$= \frac{-16\sqrt{58}}{29}$$

$$\approx -4.2, \quad |d| \approx 4.2$$

6. $\dfrac{1(-5) - 3(0) + 11}{-\sqrt{(-5)^2 + 0^2}} = \dfrac{6}{-\sqrt{1^2 + (-3)^2}}$

$$= \frac{6}{-\sqrt{10}}$$

$$= \frac{-6\sqrt{10}}{10}$$

$$= \frac{-3\sqrt{10}}{5}$$

$$\approx -1.9, \quad |d| \approx 1.9$$

7. (0, 9)

$$d = \frac{6(0) - 2(9) - 4}{\sqrt{6^2 + (-2)^2}}$$

$$= \frac{-22}{\sqrt{40}}$$

$$= \frac{-22\sqrt{40}}{40}$$

$$= \frac{-11\sqrt{10}}{10}$$

$$\approx -3.48, \quad |d| \approx 3.48$$

8. (0, -2)

$$d = \frac{2(0) + 4(-2) - 7}{\sqrt{2^2 + 4^2}}$$

$$= \frac{-15}{\sqrt{20}} = -\frac{3\sqrt{5}}{2}$$

$$\approx -3.35, \quad |d| \approx 3.35$$

9. (0, -4)

$$d = \frac{2(0) - 6(-4) - 4}{\sqrt{2^2 + (-6)^2}}$$

$$= \frac{20}{\sqrt{40}}$$

$$= \frac{10\sqrt{10}}{10}$$

$$= \sqrt{10}$$

$$\approx 3.16$$

10. (-1, 1)

$$d = \frac{2(-1) - 7(1) - 9}{\sqrt{2^2 + (-7)^2}}$$

$$= \frac{-18}{\sqrt{53}}$$

$$\approx -2.47, \quad |d| \approx 2.47$$

11. $d_1 = \dfrac{4x_1 - 3y_1 + 12}{-\sqrt{4^2 + (-3)^2}} = \dfrac{4x_1 - 3y_1 + 12}{-5}$

$d_2 = \dfrac{5x_1 + 12y_1 - 1}{\sqrt{5^2 + 12^2}} = \dfrac{5x_1 + 12y_1 - 1}{13}$

$\dfrac{4x_1 - 3y_1 + 12}{-5} = -\dfrac{5x_1 + 12y_1 - 1}{13}$

$52x_1 - 39y_1 + 156 = -25x_1 + 60y_1 - 5$

$27x + 99y + 161 = 0$

12. $d_1 = \dfrac{9x_1 + 40y_1 - 1}{\sqrt{9^2 + 40^2}} = \dfrac{9x_1 + 40y_1 - 1}{41}$

$d_2 = \dfrac{\frac{3}{4}x_1 + y_1 + 2}{-\sqrt{\left(\frac{3}{4}\right)^2 + 1^2}} = \dfrac{\frac{3}{4}x_1 + y_1 + 2}{-\sqrt{\frac{25}{16}}}$

$= \dfrac{3x_1 + 4y_1 + 8}{-5}$

$\dfrac{9x_1 + 40y_1 - 1}{41} = \dfrac{3x_1 + 4y_1 + 8}{-5}$

$-45x_1 - 200y_1 + 5 = 123x_1 + 164y_1 + 328$

$168x + 364y + 323 = 0$

13. $d_1 = \dfrac{y_1 - 5}{\sqrt{0^2 + 1^2}} = y_1 - 5$

$d_2 = \dfrac{x_1 - y_1 + 2}{-\sqrt{1^2 + (-1)^2}} = \dfrac{x_1 - y_1 + 2}{-\sqrt{2}}$

$y_1 - 5 = -\dfrac{x_1 - y_1 + 2}{-\sqrt{2}}$

$-\sqrt{2}y_1 + 5\sqrt{2} = -x_1 + y_1 - 2$

$0 = x - (1 + \sqrt{2})y + 2 + 5\sqrt{2}$

14. $d_1 = \dfrac{x_1 - y_1 + 3}{-\sqrt{2}}$

$d_2 = \dfrac{2x_1 + y_1 - 1}{\sqrt{5}}$

$\dfrac{x_1 - y_1 + 3}{-\sqrt{2}} = \dfrac{2x_1 + y_1 - 1}{\sqrt{5}}$

$\sqrt{5}x_1 - \sqrt{5}y_1 + 3\sqrt{5} = -2\sqrt{2}x_1 - \sqrt{2}y_1 + \sqrt{2}$

$(\sqrt{5} + 2\sqrt{2})x - (\sqrt{5} - \sqrt{2})y + 3\sqrt{5} - \sqrt{2} = 0$

15. $\dfrac{1(-4) - 7(2) + 4}{-\sqrt{1^2 + (-7)^2}} = \dfrac{-14}{-\sqrt{50}}$

$= \dfrac{14}{5\sqrt{2}}$

$= \dfrac{7\sqrt{2}}{5}$

≈ 1.98

16. $\dfrac{3(0) - 1(0) + 1}{-\sqrt{9 + 1}} = \dfrac{1}{-\sqrt{10}}$

$= \dfrac{-\sqrt{10}}{10}$

$\approx -0.32, \; |d| \approx 0.32$

17. $\dfrac{2(2) + 3(-2) + 2}{-\sqrt{4 + 9}} = \dfrac{0}{-\sqrt{13}}$

$= 0$

The point is on the line.

18. $\dfrac{6(-3) - 5(2) - 2}{\sqrt{36 + 25}} = \dfrac{-30}{\sqrt{61}}$

$= \dfrac{-30\sqrt{61}}{61}$

$\approx -3.84, \; |d| \approx 3.84$

19. (4, 0)

$d = \dfrac{6(4) - 8(0) - 48}{\sqrt{36 + 64}} = \dfrac{-24}{10}$

$= -2.4, \; |d| = 2.4$

20. (1, 0)

$d = \dfrac{1(1) + 1(0) - 6}{\sqrt{2}} = \dfrac{-5}{\sqrt{2}}$

$= \dfrac{-5\sqrt{2}}{2}$

$\approx -3.54, \; |d| \approx 3.54$

21. (1, 1)

$d = \dfrac{3(1) - 2(1) - 5}{\sqrt{4 + 9}}$

$= \dfrac{-4}{\sqrt{13}}$

$= \dfrac{-4\sqrt{13}}{13}$

$\approx -1.11, \; |d| \approx 1.11$

22. (2, 1)

$d = \dfrac{3(2) - 5(1) + 7}{-\sqrt{9 + 25}}$

$= \dfrac{8}{-\sqrt{34}}$

$= \dfrac{-8\sqrt{34}}{34}$

$= \dfrac{-4\sqrt{34}}{17}$

$\approx -1.37, \; |d| \approx 1.37$

23. $d_1 = \dfrac{x_1 + y_1 - 8}{\sqrt{2}}, \; d_2 = \dfrac{2x_1 - y_1 - 4}{\sqrt{5}}$

$\dfrac{x_1 + y_1 - 8}{\sqrt{2}} = -\dfrac{2x_1 - y_1 - 4}{\sqrt{5}}$

$\sqrt{5}x_1 + \sqrt{5}y_1 - 8\sqrt{5} = -2\sqrt{2}x_1 + \sqrt{2}y_1 + 4\sqrt{2}$

$(\sqrt{5} + 2\sqrt{2})x + (\sqrt{5} - \sqrt{2})y - 8\sqrt{5} - 4\sqrt{2} = 0$

24. $d_1 = \dfrac{4x_1 + y_1 + 3}{-\sqrt{17}}$, $d_2 = \dfrac{x_1 + y_1 + 2}{-\sqrt{2}}$

$\dfrac{4x_1 + y_1 + 3}{-\sqrt{17}} = -\dfrac{x_1 + y_1 + 2}{-\sqrt{2}}$

$4\sqrt{2}x_1 + \sqrt{2}y_1 + 3\sqrt{2} = -\sqrt{17}x_1 - \sqrt{17}y_1 - 2\sqrt{17}$

$(\sqrt{17} + 4\sqrt{2})x + (\sqrt{17} + \sqrt{2})y + 3\sqrt{2} + 2\sqrt{17} = 0$

25. $d_1 = \dfrac{x_1 - y_1 + 4}{-\sqrt{2}}$, $d_2 = \dfrac{x_1 + 4y_1 + 6}{-\sqrt{17}}$

$\dfrac{x_1 - y_1 + 4}{-\sqrt{2}} = \dfrac{x_1 + 4y_1 + 6}{-\sqrt{17}}$

$-\sqrt{17}x_1 + \sqrt{17}y_1 - 4\sqrt{17} = \sqrt{2}x_1 - 4\sqrt{2}y_1 - 6\sqrt{2}$

$(\sqrt{2} - \sqrt{17})x + (\sqrt{17} + 4\sqrt{2})y - 4\sqrt{17} + 6\sqrt{2} = 0$

26. $d_1 = \dfrac{3x_1 + 2y_1 - 2}{\sqrt{13}}$, $d_2 = \dfrac{2x_1 + 3y_1 + 2}{-\sqrt{13}}$

$\dfrac{3x_1 + 2y_1 - 2}{\sqrt{13}} = \dfrac{2x_1 + 3y_1 + 2}{-\sqrt{13}}$

$3x_1 + 2y_1 - 2 = -2x_1 - 3y_1 - 2$

$5x_1 + 5y_1 = 0$

$x + y = 0$

27. $d_1 = \dfrac{x_1 + y_1 - 5}{\sqrt{2}}$, $d_2 = \dfrac{x_1 - 5}{1}$

$\dfrac{x_1 + y_1 - 5}{\sqrt{2}} = x_1 - 5$

$x_1 + y_1 - 5 = \sqrt{2}x_1 - 5\sqrt{2}$

$(1 - \sqrt{2})x + y - 5 + 5\sqrt{2} = 0$

28. $\dfrac{3x_1 + y_1 - 7}{\sqrt{1}} = -\dfrac{2x_1 + 5y_1 + 3}{-\sqrt{29}}$

$3\sqrt{29}x_1 + \sqrt{29}y_1 - 7\sqrt{29} = 2\sqrt{10}x_1 + 5\sqrt{10}y_1 + 3\sqrt{10}$

$0 = (3\sqrt{29} - 2\sqrt{10})x + (\sqrt{29} - 5\sqrt{10})y - 7\sqrt{29} - 3\sqrt{10}$

29. $\dfrac{6x_1 + y_1 - 3}{\sqrt{37}} = -\dfrac{x_1 + 3y_1 + 1}{-\sqrt{10}}$

$6\sqrt{10}x_1 + \sqrt{10}y_1 - 3\sqrt{10} = \sqrt{37}x_1 + 3\sqrt{37}y_1 + \sqrt{37}$

$0 = (6\sqrt{10} - \sqrt{37})x + (\sqrt{10} - 3\sqrt{37})y - \sqrt{37} - 3\sqrt{10}$

30. $\dfrac{3x_1 - y_1 - 1}{\sqrt{10}} = -\dfrac{x_1 + y_1 + 2}{-\sqrt{2}}$

$3\sqrt{2}x_1 - \sqrt{2}y_1 - \sqrt{2} = \sqrt{10}x_1 + \sqrt{10}y_1 + 2\sqrt{10}$

$0 = (3\sqrt{2} - \sqrt{10})x - (\sqrt{10} + \sqrt{2})y - \sqrt{2} - 2\sqrt{10}$

31. $3 = \dfrac{x - 5y + 10}{-\sqrt{26}}$

$-3\sqrt{26} = x - 5y + 10$

$0 = x - 5y + 10 + 3\sqrt{26}$

$-3 = \dfrac{x - 5y + 10}{-\sqrt{26}}$

$3\sqrt{26} = x - 5y + 10$

$0 = x - 5y + 10 - 3\sqrt{26}$

32. $m_1 = \dfrac{3 + 4}{5 - 1} = \dfrac{7}{4}$ $\qquad$ $m_2 = \dfrac{3 - 1}{5 + 4} = \dfrac{2}{9}$

$y + 4 = \dfrac{7}{4}(x - 1)$ $\qquad$ $y - 1 = \dfrac{2}{9}(x + 4)$

$y = \dfrac{7}{4}x - \dfrac{23}{4}$ $\qquad$ $9y - 9 = 2x + 8$

$4y = 7x - 23$ $\qquad\qquad$ $9y = 2x + 17$

$a_1 = \dfrac{7(-4) - 4(1) - 23}{\sqrt{65}}$ $\qquad$ $a_2 = \dfrac{2(1) - 9(-4) + 17}{\sqrt{85}}$

$= \dfrac{-55\sqrt{65}}{65}$ $\qquad\qquad$ $= \dfrac{55}{\sqrt{85}}$

$= \dfrac{-11\sqrt{65}}{13}$ $\qquad\qquad$ $= \dfrac{55\sqrt{85}}{85}$

≈ -6.82 $\qquad\qquad\qquad$ $= \dfrac{11\sqrt{85}}{17}$

$|a_1| \approx 6.82$ $\qquad\qquad$ ≈ 5.97

$m_3 = \dfrac{-4 - 1}{1 + 4} = -1$

$y - 1 = -1(x + 4)$

$y - 1 = -x - 4$

$y = -x - 3$

$a_3 = \dfrac{(-1)5 - (1)(3) - 3}{\sqrt{2}}$

$= \dfrac{-11}{\sqrt{2}}$

$= -\dfrac{11\sqrt{2}}{2}$

≈ -7.78, $|a_3| \approx 7.78$

33. a. 5.1 units $\qquad$ b. -13.2 units

c. 3.6 units $\qquad$ d. 0 units

34. radius of circle $P = \sqrt{[(-5) - (-2)]^2 + (6 - 2)^2}$

$= \sqrt{(-3)^2 + 4^2}$

$= 5$

Find the distance between the line and the center of circle P.

$d = \dfrac{5(-5) + (-12)6 + 32}{-\sqrt{5^2 + (-12)^2}}$ $= \dfrac{-65}{-13}$ $= 5$

Since the distance from the line to the center of the circle is 5, and the definition of a circle is the set of all points in the plane that are 5 units from the center, the line and the circle have one point in common. Therefore, the line is a tangent by definition.

35. a. $d = \dfrac{3(16) - 72 + 28}{\sqrt{10}}$

$= \dfrac{4}{\sqrt{10}}$

$= \dfrac{2\sqrt{10}}{5} \approx 1.26$ units

$d = \dfrac{3(18) - 84 + 28}{\sqrt{10}}$

$= \dfrac{-2}{\sqrt{10}}$

$= -\dfrac{\sqrt{10}}{5}$

≈ -0.63 units, $|d| \approx 0.63$

$d = \dfrac{3(16) - 76 + 28}{\sqrt{10}}$

$= \dfrac{0}{\sqrt{10}}$

$= 0$ units

b. $(16, 76)$ **c.** $(16, 72)$

36. $8x + 2y = 35.10$

$3x + y = 14.30 \rightarrow y = -3x + 14.30$

$8x + 2(-3x + 14.3) = 35.10$

$\qquad\qquad\quad 2x = 6.5$

$\qquad\qquad\quad\; x = 3.25$

$y = -3(3.25) + 14.3$

$= 4.55$

$\$3.25,\ \$4.55$

37. $y = \dfrac{x - 2}{x(x + 2)(x - 2)}$

38.

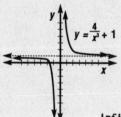

$y = \dfrac{4}{x^3} + 1$

infinite discontinuity

39. $\dfrac{1 - \sin^2 \alpha}{\sin^2 \alpha} = \dfrac{\cos^2 \alpha}{\sin^2 \alpha} = \cot^2 \alpha$

40. $-\sqrt{4 + 25} = -\sqrt{29}$

$-\dfrac{2x}{\sqrt{29}} + \dfrac{5y}{\sqrt{29}} - \dfrac{3}{\sqrt{29}} = 0$

$p = \dfrac{3}{\sqrt{29}} \approx 0.56$

$\sin \phi = \dfrac{-2}{\sqrt{29}},\ \cos \phi = \dfrac{5}{\sqrt{29}}$

$\tan \phi = \dfrac{-2}{5}$

$\phi \approx 112°$

41. $A = \pi r^2$

$A = \pi 3^2 = 9\pi$

$A = \pi 5^2 - 9\pi = 16\pi$

$16\pi > 9\pi$

Quantity A is greater. A

Chapter 7 Summary and Review

PAGES 406-408   SKILLS AND CONCEPTS

1. $\csc \theta = \dfrac{1}{\sin \theta}$

$= \dfrac{1}{\frac{1}{2}}$

$= 2$

2. $\tan^2 \theta = \sec^2 \theta - 1$

$16 = \sec^2 \theta - 1$

$17 = \sec^2 \theta$

$\sqrt{17} = \sec \theta$

3. $\sin \theta = \dfrac{1}{\csc \theta}$

$= \dfrac{1}{\frac{5}{3}}$

$= \dfrac{3}{5}$

$\cos \theta = \sqrt{1 - \sin^2 \theta}$

$= \sqrt{1 - \dfrac{9}{25}}$

$= \sqrt{\dfrac{16}{25}}$

$= \dfrac{4}{5}$

4. $\tan \theta = \dfrac{\sin \theta}{\cos \theta}$

$= \dfrac{\sqrt{1 - \cos^2 \theta}}{\cos \theta}$

$= \dfrac{\sqrt{1 - \dfrac{16}{25}}}{\dfrac{4}{5}}$

$= \dfrac{\sqrt{\dfrac{9}{25}}}{\dfrac{4}{5}}$

$= \dfrac{\dfrac{3}{5}}{\dfrac{4}{5}}$

$= \dfrac{3}{4}$

5. $\cos^2 x + \tan^2 x \cos^2 x \overset{?}{=} 1$

$\cos^2 x + \left(\dfrac{\sin^2 x}{\cos^2 x}\right) \cos^2 x \overset{?}{=} 1$

$\cos^2 x + \sin^2 x \overset{?}{=} 1$

$1 = 1$

6. $\dfrac{1 - \cos \theta}{1 + \cos \theta} \overset{?}{=} (\csc \theta - \cot \theta)^2$

$\dfrac{1 - \cos \theta}{1 + \cos \theta} \overset{?}{=} \left(\dfrac{1}{\sin \theta} - \dfrac{\cos \theta}{\sin \theta}\right)^2$

$\dfrac{1 - \cos \theta}{1 + \cos \theta} \overset{?}{=} \left(\dfrac{1 - \cos \theta}{\sin \theta}\right)^2$

$\dfrac{1 - \cos \theta}{1 + \cos \theta} \overset{?}{=} \dfrac{(1 - \cos \theta)^2}{\sin^2 \theta}$

$\dfrac{1 - \cos \theta}{1 + \cos \theta} \overset{?}{=} \dfrac{(1 - \cos \theta)^2}{1 - \cos^2 \theta}$

$\dfrac{1 - \cos \theta}{1 + \cos \theta} \overset{?}{=} \dfrac{(1 - \cos \theta)^2}{(1 - \cos \theta)(1 + \cos \theta)}$

$\dfrac{1 - \cos \theta}{1 + \cos \theta} = \dfrac{1 - \cos \theta}{1 + \cos \theta}$

7. $\dfrac{\sec \theta + 1}{\tan \theta} \overset{?}{=} \dfrac{\tan \theta}{\sec \theta - 1}$

$\dfrac{\sec \theta + 1}{\tan \theta} \overset{?}{=} \dfrac{\tan \theta(\sec \theta + 1)}{\sec^2 \theta - 1}$

$\dfrac{\sec \theta + 1}{\tan \theta} \overset{?}{=} \dfrac{\tan \theta (\sec \theta + 1)}{\tan^2 \theta}$

$\dfrac{\sec \theta + 1}{\tan \theta} = \dfrac{\sec \theta + 1}{\tan \theta}$

8.
$$\frac{\sin^4 x - \cos^4 x}{\sin^2 x} \overset{?}{=} 1 - \cot^2 x$$

$$\frac{(\sin^2 x - \cos^2 x)(\sin^2 x + \cos^2 x)}{\sin^2 x} \overset{?}{=} 1 - \cot^2 x$$

$$\frac{\sin^2 x - \cos^2 x}{\sin^2 x} \overset{?}{=} 1 - \cot^2 x$$

$$1 - \frac{\cos^2 x}{\sin^2 x} \overset{?}{=} 1 - \cot^2 x$$

$$1 - \cot^2 x = 1 - \cot^2 x$$

9. $\cos 240° = \cos(180° + 60°)$

$$= \cos 180° \cos 60° - \sin 180° \sin 60°$$

$$= (-1) \cdot \frac{1}{2} - 0 \cdot \frac{\sqrt{3}}{2}$$

$$= -\frac{1}{2}$$

10. $\cos 15° = \cos(60° - 45°)$

$$= \cos 60° \cos 45° + \sin 60° \sin 45°$$

$$= \frac{1}{2} \cdot \frac{\sqrt{2}}{2} + \frac{\sqrt{3}}{2} \cdot \frac{\sqrt{2}}{2}$$

$$= \frac{\sqrt{2} + \sqrt{6}}{4}$$

11. $\sin(-255°) = \sin(-120° - 135°)$

$$= \sin(-120°) \cos(135°)$$
$$- \sin 135° \cos(-120°)$$

$$= \frac{-\sqrt{3}}{2} \cdot \frac{-\sqrt{2}}{2} - \left(\frac{\sqrt{2}}{2}\right) \cdot \frac{-1}{2}$$

$$= \frac{\sqrt{6} + \sqrt{2}}{4}$$

12. $\tan 165° = \tan(135° + 30°)$

$$= \frac{\tan 135° + \tan 30°}{1 - \tan 135° + \tan 30°}$$

$$= \frac{-1 + \frac{\sqrt{3}}{3}}{1 + \frac{\sqrt{3}}{3}}$$

$$= \frac{-3 + \sqrt{3}}{3 + \sqrt{3}}$$

$$= \frac{(-3 + \sqrt{3})(3 - \sqrt{3})}{6}$$

$$= \frac{-9 + 6\sqrt{3} - 3}{6}$$

$$= \frac{-12 + 6\sqrt{3}}{6}$$

$$= -2 + \sqrt{3}$$

13.
$$\cos(90° - \theta) \overset{?}{=} \sin \theta$$
$$\cos 90° \cos \theta + \sin 90° \sin \theta \overset{?}{=} \sin \theta$$
$$(0) \cos \theta + (1) \sin \theta \overset{?}{=} \sin \theta$$
$$\sin \theta = \sin \theta$$

14.
$$\cos(60° + \theta) + \cos(60° - \theta) \overset{?}{=} \cos \theta$$
$$(\cos 60° \cos \theta - \sin 60° \sin \theta)$$
$$+ (\cos 60° \cos \theta + \sin 60° \sin \theta) \overset{?}{=} \cos \theta$$
$$\frac{1}{2} \cos \theta - \frac{\sqrt{3}}{2} \sin \theta + \frac{1}{2} \cos \theta + \frac{\sqrt{3}}{2} \sin \theta \overset{?}{=} \cos \theta$$
$$\cos \theta = \cos \theta$$

15. $\sin 2\theta = 2 \sin \theta \cos \theta$

$$= 2 \cdot \frac{4}{5} \cdot \frac{3}{5}$$

$$= \frac{24}{25}$$

16. $\cos 2\theta = 2 \cos^2 \theta - 1$

$$= 2\left(\frac{3}{5}\right)^2 - 1$$

$$= \frac{18}{25} - 1$$

$$= -\frac{7}{25}$$

17. $\sin \frac{\theta}{2} = \pm\sqrt{\frac{1 - \cos \theta}{2}}$

$$= \sqrt{\frac{1 - \frac{3}{5}}{2}}$$

$$= \sqrt{\frac{\frac{2}{5}}{2}}$$

$$= \sqrt{\frac{1}{5}}$$

$$= \frac{\sqrt{5}}{5}$$

18. $\cos \frac{\theta}{2} = \pm\sqrt{\frac{1 + \cos \theta}{2}}$

$$= \sqrt{\frac{1 + \frac{3}{5}}{2}}$$

$$= \sqrt{\frac{\frac{8}{5}}{2}}$$

$$= \sqrt{\frac{4}{5}}$$

$$= \frac{2\sqrt{5}}{5}$$

19. $\tan 2\theta = \frac{2 \tan \theta}{1 - \tan^2 \theta}$

$$= \frac{2\left(\frac{4}{3}\right)}{1 - \left(\frac{4}{3}\right)^2}$$

$$= \frac{\frac{8}{3}}{1 - \frac{16}{9}}$$

$$= \frac{\frac{8}{3}}{\frac{-7}{9}}$$

$$= -\frac{24}{7}$$

20. $\tan \dfrac{\theta}{2} = \pm\sqrt{\dfrac{1 - \cos \theta}{1 + \cos \theta}}$

$$= \sqrt{\dfrac{1 - \dfrac{3}{5}}{1 + \dfrac{3}{5}}}$$

$$= \sqrt{\dfrac{\dfrac{2}{5}}{\dfrac{8}{5}}}$$

$$= \sqrt{\dfrac{2}{8}}$$

$$= \sqrt{\dfrac{1}{4}}$$

$$= \dfrac{1}{2}$$

21.
$$\tan x + 1 = \sec x$$
$$\tan^2 x + 2 \tan x + 1 = \sec^2 x$$
$$\tan^2 x + 2 \tan x + 1 = \tan^2 x + 1$$
$$2 \tan x = 0$$
$$\tan x = 0$$
$$x = 0 + 360k°$$

22.
$$\sin^2 x + \cos 2x - \cos x = 0$$
$$(1 - \cos^2 x) + (2 \cos^2 x - 1) - \cos x = 0$$
$$\cos^2 x - \cos x = 0$$
$$\cos x (\cos x - 1) = 0$$

$\cos x = 0 \qquad\qquad \cos x = 1$

$x = 90° + 180k° \qquad x = 0° + 360k°$

23. $\sin x \tan x = 0$

$\tan x (\sin x - 1) = 0$

$\tan x = 0 \qquad\qquad \sin x = 1$

$x = 0 + 180k°$

24.
$$\cos 2x \sin x = 1$$
$$(1 - 2 \sin^2 x) \sin x = 1$$
$$\sin x - 2 \sin^3 x - 1 = 0$$
$$2 \sin^3 x - \sin x + 1 = 0$$
$$(\sin x + 1)(2 \sin^2 x) - 2 \sin x + 1 = 0$$

$2 \sin^2 x - 2 \sin x + 1 = 0$: imaginary solution

$\sin x = -1$

$x = 270° + 360k°$

25. $\sqrt{A^2 + B^2} = \sqrt{7^2 + 3^2} = \sqrt{58}$

$\dfrac{7x}{\sqrt{58}} + \dfrac{3y}{\sqrt{58}} - \dfrac{8}{\sqrt{58}} = 0$

$p = \dfrac{8}{\sqrt{58}} \approx 1.1$

$\tan \theta = \dfrac{3}{7}$

$\theta \approx 23°$

26. $\sqrt{A^2 + B^2} = \sqrt{6^2 + (-4)^2} = \sqrt{52} = -2\sqrt{13}$

$\dfrac{6x}{-2\sqrt{13}} - \dfrac{4y}{-2\sqrt{13}} + \dfrac{5}{-2\sqrt{13}} = 0$

$\dfrac{-3x}{\sqrt{13}} + \dfrac{2y}{\sqrt{13}} - \dfrac{5}{2\sqrt{13}} = 0$

$p = \dfrac{5}{2\sqrt{13}} \approx 0.7$

$\tan \theta = -\dfrac{2}{3}$

$\theta \approx 146°$

27. $\sqrt{A^2 + B^2} = \sqrt{9^2 + 5^2} = \sqrt{106}$

$\dfrac{9x}{\sqrt{106}} + \dfrac{5y}{\sqrt{106}} - \dfrac{3}{\sqrt{106}} = 0$

$p = \dfrac{3}{\sqrt{106}} \approx 0.3$

$\tan \phi = \dfrac{5}{9}$

$\phi \approx 29°$

28. $-\sqrt{A^2 + B^2} = -\sqrt{1 + 49} = -\sqrt{50} = -5\sqrt{2}$

$\dfrac{x}{-5\sqrt{2}} + \dfrac{7y}{5\sqrt{2}} - \dfrac{5}{5\sqrt{2}} = 0$

$\dfrac{-x}{5\sqrt{2}} + \dfrac{7y}{5\sqrt{2}} - \dfrac{1}{\sqrt{2}} = 0$

$p = \dfrac{1}{\sqrt{2}} \approx 0.7$

$\tan \phi = -7$

$\phi \approx 98°$

29. $d = \dfrac{2(5) - 3(6) + 2}{-\sqrt{2^2 + 3^2}}$

$= \dfrac{-6}{-\sqrt{13}}$

≈ 1.7

30. $\dfrac{2(-4) + 3(-3) - 6}{\sqrt{3^2 + 2^2}} = d$

$\dfrac{-23}{\sqrt{13}} = d$

$-6.4 \approx d, \ |d| \approx 6.4$

31. $\dfrac{4(4) - 3(-2) + 1}{-\sqrt{4^2 + 3^2}} = d$

$\dfrac{23}{-\sqrt{25}} = d$

$-\dfrac{23}{5} = d$

$-4.6 \approx d, \ |d| \approx 4.6$

32.
$$\frac{20 - \frac{1}{3}(21) - 6}{\sqrt{1^2 + \left(\frac{1}{3}\right)^2}} = d$$

$$\frac{7}{\sqrt{\frac{10}{9}}} = d$$

$$\frac{21}{\sqrt{10}} = d$$

$$6.6 \approx d$$

33.
$$\frac{3x + y - 2}{\sqrt{3^2 + 1^2}} = -\left(\frac{x + 2y - 3}{\sqrt{1^2 + 2^2}}\right)$$

$$\frac{3x + y - 2}{\sqrt{10}} = -\left(\frac{x + 2y - 3}{\sqrt{5}}\right)$$

$$3\sqrt{5}x + \sqrt{5}y - 2\sqrt{5} = -\sqrt{10}x - 2\sqrt{10}y + 3\sqrt{10}$$

$$(3\sqrt{5} + \sqrt{10})x + (\sqrt{5} + 2\sqrt{10})y - 2\sqrt{5} - 3\sqrt{10} = 0$$

34.
$$\frac{3y - x + 18}{-\sqrt{3^2 + 1^2}} = \frac{4y - 3x - 8}{\sqrt{4^2 + 3^2}}$$

$$\frac{3y - x + 18}{-\sqrt{10}} = \frac{4y - 3x - 8}{5}$$

$$15y - 5x + 90 = -4\sqrt{10}y + 3\sqrt{10}x + 8\sqrt{10}$$

$$(5 + 3\sqrt{10})x - (15 + 4\sqrt{10})y - 90 + 8\sqrt{10} = 0$$

PAGE 408   APPLICATIONS AND PROBLEM SOLVING

35.
$$\frac{v_0^2 \sin^2 \theta}{2g} \stackrel{?}{=} \frac{v_0^2 \tan^2 \theta}{2g \sec^2 \theta}$$

$$\stackrel{?}{=} \frac{v_0^2 \frac{\sin^2 \theta}{\cos^2 \theta}}{2g \frac{1}{\cos^2 \theta}}$$

$$\stackrel{?}{=} \frac{v_0^2 \sin^2 \theta}{\cos^2 \theta} \cdot \frac{\cos^2 \theta}{2g}$$

$$= \frac{v_0^2 \sin^2 \theta}{2g}$$

The formulas are equivalent.

36.
$$\sin 30° = \frac{x}{100} \qquad 30° + 45° + \theta = 90°$$

$$100 \sin 30° = x \qquad\qquad \theta = 15°$$

$$50 = x$$

$$\cos \theta = \frac{x}{y}$$

$$\cos 15° = \frac{50}{y}$$

$$y = \frac{50}{\cos 15°}$$

$$y \approx 51.76$$

Ms. Jones is about 51.76 yards from the telephone pole.

Chapter 7 Test

PAGE 409

1.
$$\cos \theta = \sqrt{1 - \sin^2 \theta}$$

$$= \sqrt{1 - \left(\frac{1}{2}\right)^2}$$

$$= \sqrt{\frac{3}{4}}$$

$$= \frac{\sqrt{3}}{2}$$

2.
$$\sin \theta = \frac{1}{\csc \theta}$$

$$= \frac{3}{5}$$

$$\cos \theta = \sqrt{1 - \sin^2 \theta}$$

$$= \sqrt{1 - \left(\frac{3}{5}\right)^2}$$

$$= \sqrt{\frac{16}{25}}$$

$$= \frac{4}{5}$$

3.
$$\tan^2 \theta = \sec^2 \theta \cdot 1$$

$$= 3^2 - 1$$

$$= 8$$

$$\tan \theta = \sqrt{8} = 2\sqrt{2}$$

4.
$$\sec \theta = \frac{1}{\cos \theta}$$

$$= \frac{1}{\sqrt{1 - \sin^2 \theta}}$$

$$= \frac{1}{\sqrt{1 - \left(\frac{4}{5}\right)^2}}$$

$$= \frac{1}{\sqrt{\frac{9}{25}}}$$

$$= \frac{5}{3}$$

5.
$$\tan \theta (\cot \theta + \tan \theta) \stackrel{?}{=} \sec^2 \theta$$

$$\tan \theta \cot \theta + \tan^2 \theta \stackrel{?}{=} \sec^2 \theta$$

$$1 + \tan^2 \theta \stackrel{?}{=} \sec^2 \theta$$

$$\sec^2 \theta = \sec^2 \theta$$

6.
$$\sin^2 A \cot^2 A \stackrel{?}{=} (1 - \sin A)(1 + \sin A)$$

$$\sin^2 A \frac{\cos^2 A}{\sin^2 A} \stackrel{?}{=} (1 - \sin A)(1 + \sin A)$$

$$\cos^2 A \stackrel{?}{=} (1 - \sin A)(1 + \sin A)$$

$$1 - \sin^2 A \stackrel{?}{=} (1 - \sin A)(1 + \sin A)$$

$$(1 - \sin A)(1 + \sin A) = (1 - \sin A)(1 + \sin A)$$

7.
$$\frac{\sec x}{\sin x} - \frac{\sin x}{\cos x} \stackrel{?}{=} \cot x$$

$$\frac{\sec x \cos x - \sin^2 x}{\sin x \cos x} \stackrel{?}{=} \cot x$$

$$\frac{1 - \sin^2 x}{\sin x \cos x} \stackrel{?}{=} \cot x$$

$$\frac{\cos^2 x}{\sin x \cos x} \stackrel{?}{=} \cot x$$

$$\frac{\cos x}{\sin x} \stackrel{?}{=} \cot x$$

$$\cot x = \cot x$$

181

8.
$$\frac{\cos x}{1 + \sin x} + \frac{\cos x}{1 - \sin x} \overset{?}{=} 2 \sec x$$

$$\frac{\cos x - \cos x \sin x + \cos x + \sin x \cos x}{1 - \sin^2 x} \overset{?}{=} 2 \sec x$$

$$\frac{2 \cos x}{1 - \sin^2 x} \overset{?}{=} 2 \sec x$$

$$\frac{2 \cos x}{\cos^2 x} \overset{?}{=} 2 \sec x$$

$$\frac{2}{\cos x} \overset{?}{=} 2 \sec x$$

$$2 \sec x = 2 \sec x$$

9. $\sin 255° = \sin (135° + 120°)$

$= \sin 135° \cos 120° + \sin 120° \cos 135°$

$= \frac{\sqrt{2}}{2} \cdot \frac{-\sqrt{3}}{2} + \frac{\sqrt{2}}{2} \cdot \frac{-1}{2}$

$= \frac{-\sqrt{6} - \sqrt{2}}{4}$

10. $\cos 165° = \cos (135° + 30°)$

$= \cos 135° \cos 30° - \sin 135° \sin 30°$

$= -\frac{\sqrt{2}}{2} \cdot \frac{\sqrt{3}}{2} - \frac{\sqrt{2}}{2} \cdot \frac{1}{2}$

$= \frac{-\sqrt{6} - \sqrt{2}}{4}$

11. $\sin (-195°)$

$= \sin (-135° - 60°)$

$= \sin (-135°) \cos (60°) - \sin 60° \cos (-135°)$

$= \frac{-\sqrt{2}}{2} \cdot \frac{1}{2} - \frac{\sqrt{3}}{2} \cdot \frac{-\sqrt{2}}{2}$

$= \frac{-\sqrt{2}}{4} + \frac{\sqrt{6}}{4}$

$= \frac{\sqrt{6} - \sqrt{2}}{4}$

12. $\sin 2x = 2 \sin x \cos x$

$= 2 \cdot \frac{-\sqrt{7}}{4} \cdot \frac{3}{4}$

$= -\frac{3\sqrt{7}}{8}$

13. $\cos \frac{x}{2} = \pm\sqrt{\frac{1 + \cos x}{2}}$

$= -\sqrt{\frac{1 + \frac{3}{4}}{2}}$

$= -\frac{\sqrt{14}}{4}$

14. $\tan 2x = \frac{-2 \tan x}{1 - \tan^2 x}$

$= \frac{-2 \cdot \frac{\sqrt{7}}{3}}{1 - \left(\frac{\sqrt{7}}{3}\right)^2}$

$= \frac{-2\sqrt{7}}{3} \cdot \frac{9}{2}$

$= -3\sqrt{7}$

15. $\sin x - \cos x = 0$

$\sin x = \cos x$

$\sin^2 x = \cos^2 x$

$\sin^2 x - \cos^2 x = 0$

$\sin^2 x - 1 + \sin^2 x = 0$

$2 \sin^2 x = 1$

$\sin^2 x = \frac{1}{2}$

$\sin x = \frac{\sqrt{2}}{2}$

$x = 45°$

16. $2 \cos^2 x + 3 \sin x - 3 = 0$

$2(1 - \sin^2 x) + 3 \sin x - 3 = 0$

$-2 \sin^2 x + 3 \sin x - 1 = 0$

$2 \sin^2 x - 3 \sin x + 1 = 0$

$(2 \sin x - 1)(\sin x - 1) = 0$

$\sin x = \frac{1}{2} \qquad\qquad \sin x = 1$

$x = 30°, 150° \qquad\quad x = 90°$

17. $\tan^2 x - \sqrt{3} \tan x = 0$

$\tan x (\tan x - \sqrt{3}) = 0$

$\tan x = 0 \qquad\qquad \tan x = \sqrt{3}$

$x = 0°, 180° \qquad\quad x = 60°$

18. $\tan 2x \cot x - 3 = 0$

$\frac{\tan x}{1 - \tan^2 x} \cdot \frac{1}{\tan x} - 3 = 0$

$\frac{1}{1 - \tan^2 x} = 3$

$1 = 3 - 3 \tan^2 x$

$\frac{1}{3} = -3 \tan^2 x$

$\frac{1}{9} = \tan^2 x$

$\frac{1}{3} = \tan x$

$x = 30°, 150°$

19. $\sqrt{A^2 + B^2} = \sqrt{2}$

$-\frac{x}{\sqrt{2}} + \frac{y}{\sqrt{2}} - \frac{3}{\sqrt{2}} = 0$

$p = \frac{3}{\sqrt{2}} \approx 2.1$

$\tan \phi = -1$

$\phi = 135°$

20. $\sqrt{A^2 + B^2} = \sqrt{3^2 + 6^2} = \sqrt{45} = 3\sqrt{5}$

$$\frac{3x}{3\sqrt{5}} + \frac{6y}{3\sqrt{5}} - \frac{7}{3\sqrt{5}} = 0$$

$$\frac{x}{\sqrt{5}} + \frac{2y}{\sqrt{5}} - \frac{7}{3\sqrt{5}} = 0$$

$$p = \frac{7}{3\sqrt{5}} \approx 1.0$$

$$\tan \phi = 2$$

$$\phi \approx 63°$$

21. $-\sqrt{A^2 + B^2} = \sqrt{10^2 + 5^2} = \sqrt{125} = 5\sqrt{5}$

$$\frac{-10x}{5\sqrt{5}} + \frac{5y}{5\sqrt{5}} + \frac{5}{5\sqrt{5}} = 0$$

$$\frac{-2x}{\sqrt{5}} + \frac{y}{\sqrt{5}} + \frac{1}{\sqrt{5}} = 0$$

$$\frac{2x}{\sqrt{5}} - \frac{y}{\sqrt{5}} - \frac{1}{\sqrt{5}} = 0$$

$$p = \frac{1}{\sqrt{5}} \approx 0.4$$

$$\tan \phi = -\frac{1}{2}$$

$$\phi \approx 333°$$

22. $d = \dfrac{2(-5) + 8 - 6}{\sqrt{2^2 + 1^2}}$

$$= \frac{-8}{\sqrt{5}}$$

$$\approx -3.6, \ |d| \approx 3.6$$

23. $d = \dfrac{-3(-6) - 4(8) - 2}{\sqrt{3^2 + 4^2}}$

$$= \frac{-16}{\sqrt{25}}$$

$$= -\frac{16}{5}$$

$$= -3.2, \ |d| \approx 3.2$$

24. $\dfrac{5x + 2y - 7}{\sqrt{5^2 + 2^2}} = \dfrac{3x + 4y - 4}{\sqrt{3^2 + 4^2}}$

$$\frac{5x + 2y - 7}{\sqrt{29}} = \frac{3x + 4y - 4}{5}$$

$$25x + 10y - 35 = 3\sqrt{29}x + 4\sqrt{29}y - 4\sqrt{29}$$

$$(25 - 3\sqrt{29})x + (10 - 4\sqrt{29})y - 35 + 4\sqrt{29} = 0$$

25. $R = \dfrac{v_o^2}{g} \sin 2\theta$

$$= \frac{88^2}{32} \, 2 \sin \theta \cos \theta$$

$$= \frac{88^2}{32} \cdot 2 \cdot \frac{3}{5} \cdot \frac{4}{5}$$

$$= \frac{5808}{25}$$

$$= 232.32 \text{ feet}$$

PAGE 409   BONUS

$$\sec \theta = \sqrt{\tan^2 \theta + 1}$$

$$= \sqrt{\frac{1}{\cot^2 \theta} + 1}$$

$$= \sqrt{\left(\frac{2xy}{x^2 - y^2}\right)^2 + 1}$$

$$= \sqrt{\frac{4x^2y^2 + x^4 - 2x^2y^2 + y^4}{x^4 - 2x^2y^2 + y^4}}$$

$$= \left(\frac{x^4 + 2x^2y^2 + y^4}{x^4 - 2x^2y^2 + y^4}\right)^{\frac{1}{2}}$$

$$= \sqrt{\frac{(x^2 + y^2)^2}{(x^2 - y^2)^2}}$$

$$= \frac{x^2 + y^2}{x^2 - y^2}$$

Chapter 8   Vectors and Parametric Equations

Geometric Vectors

PAGES 417-418   CHECKING FOR UNDERSTANDING

1. A vector has magnitude and direction. A line segment only has length. A vector can be represented by a directed line segment.

2.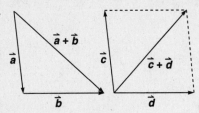

3. No, they are opposites.

4. any two or more vectors whose sum is the given vector

5.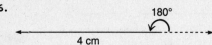
1 cm 50°

6.
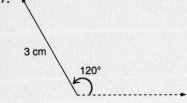
180°
4 cm

7.
3 cm
120°

8. 270°

2.5 cm

9. 18 mm
45°

10.
35 mm

65°

11.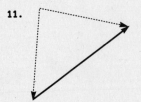

12.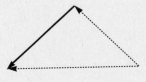

13.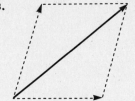

14. $\sin 30° = \dfrac{v}{2.2}$ $\tan 30° = \dfrac{1.1}{h}$

   $2.2 \sin 30° = v$

   $1.1 \text{ cm} = v$ $h = \dfrac{1.1}{\tan 30°}$

   $h \approx 1.9 \text{ cm}$

15. Using the Pythagorean theorem,

   $13^2 + 7^2 = c^2$

   $218 = c^2$

   $14.8 \text{ km} \approx c$

PAGES 418-419   EXERCISES

16-28. Answers may vary slightly.

16. 5.2 cm, 53°   17. 3.4 cm, 85°   18. 2.8 cm, 142°

19. 5.0 cm, 3°   20. 3.0 cm, 135°

21. 8.1 cm, 60°   22. 9.8 cm, 335°

23. 0.7 cm, 306°   24. 5.0 cm, 153°

25. 2.7 cm, 14°   26. 7.1 cm, 17°

27. 2.9 cm, 286°   28. 11.1 cm, 79°

29. $\sin 60° = \dfrac{v}{2.7}$ $\cos 60° = \dfrac{h}{2.7}$

   $2.7 \sin 60° = v$ $2.7 \cos 60° = h$

   $2.3 \text{ cm} \approx v$ $1.4 \text{ cm} \approx h$

30. $\sin 45° = \dfrac{v}{1.5}$ $\cos 45° = \dfrac{h}{1.5}$

   $1.5 \sin 45° = v$ $1.5 \cos 45° = h$

   $1.1 \text{ cm} \approx v$ $1.1 \text{ cm} \approx h$

31. $\sin 45° = \dfrac{v}{2.5}$ $\cos 45° = \dfrac{h}{2.5}$

   $2.5 \sin 45° = v$ $2.5 \cos 45° = h$

   $1.8 \text{ cm} \approx v$ $1.8 \text{ cm} \approx h$

32.
$$\sin 30° = \frac{v}{4.2} \qquad \cos 30° = \frac{h}{4.2}$$
$$4.2 \sin 30° = v \qquad 4.2 \cos 30° = h$$
$$2.1 \text{ cm} \approx v \qquad 3.6 \text{ cm} \approx h$$

33.
$$8.8^2 + 7.3^2 = c^2$$
$$130.73 = c^2$$
$$11.4 \text{ m} \approx c$$

34. yes

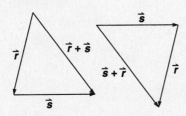

35. The difference; sample answer: the other diagonal would be the sum of one of the vectors and the opposite of the other vector, so it is the difference between the original two.

36. Yes, if they are opposite vectors; yes, if they form a closed triangle when placed tip-to-tail.

37. a.

↓5 m/s

100 m/s

b.
$$100^2 + 5^2 = c^2$$
$$10,025 = c^2$$
$$100.12 \text{ m/s} \approx c$$

38. a.
$$\cos 60° = \frac{h}{95} \qquad \sin 60° = \frac{v}{95}$$
$$95 \cos 60° = h \qquad 95 \sin 60° = v$$
$$48 \text{ N} \approx h \qquad 82 \text{ N} \approx v$$

b.
$$\cos 30° = \frac{h}{95} \qquad \sin 30° = \frac{v}{95}$$
$$95 \cos 30° = h \qquad 95 \sin 30° = v$$
$$82 \text{ N} \approx h \qquad 48 \text{ N} \approx v$$

39. a.

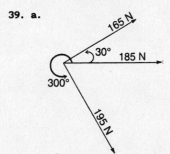

165 N

30°

185 N

300°

195 N

b. 434.1 N at 349°

40.
$$m = 1$$
$$y - 1 = x + 3$$
$$-4 = x - y$$

41.
$$f'(x) = 6x$$
$$f'(2) = 6(2)$$
$$= 12$$
$$y - 12 = 12(x - 2)$$
$$y - 12 = 12x - 24$$
$$y = 12x - 12$$

42.
$$2x^3 + 5x^2 - 12x = 0$$
$$x(2x^2 + 5x - 12) = 0$$
$$x(2x - 3)(x + 4) = 0$$
$$x = 0 \quad 2x - 3 = 0 \quad x + 4 = 0$$
$$x = \frac{3}{2} \qquad x = -4$$

43.
$$A = \frac{1}{2}r^2\theta$$
$$= \frac{1}{2}(6)^2(65°)\left(\frac{\pi}{180°}\right)$$
$$\approx 20.42 \text{ ft}^2$$

44. $y = 3 \sin \pi t$

45. If $y = 1$ and $x = 3$, then $z = 6$. If $y = 2$ and $x = 6$, then $z = 12$. There is not enough information to determine whether z or 10 is greater. **D**

<table>
<tr><td>

8-2

</td><td>

Algebraic Vectors

</td></tr>
</table>

PAGES 422-423   CHECKING FOR UNDERSTANDING

1. No, the magnitude of the resultant could be equal to the magnitude of one component if the other component is zero. But if both components are nonzero, the magnitude of the resultant must be greater since it is the hypotenuse of the right triangle formed by the three vectors.

2. They have the same magnitude, but different directions.

3. No, their directions may not be the same.

4. No, their magnitudes may not be the same.

5. $|(4, 3)| = \sqrt{4^2 + 3^2}$
$$= \sqrt{25}$$
$$= 5$$
$$4\vec{i} + 3\vec{j}$$

6. $|(6, 7)| = \sqrt{6^2 + 7^2}$
$$= \sqrt{85}$$
$$6\vec{i} + 7\vec{j}$$

7. $|(-2, -3)| = \sqrt{(-2)^2 + (-3)^2}$
$$= \sqrt{13}$$
$$-2\vec{i} - 3\vec{j}$$

8. $|(-5, 15)| = \sqrt{(-5)^2 + 15^2}$
$$= \sqrt{250}$$
$$= 5\sqrt{10}$$
$$-5\vec{i} + 15\vec{j}$$

9. $\overrightarrow{AB} = (2 - 4, 8 - 2)$
$$= (-2, 6)$$
$$|\overrightarrow{AB}| = \sqrt{(-2)^2 + 6^2}$$
$$= \sqrt{40}$$
$$= 2\sqrt{10}$$

10. $\overrightarrow{AB} = (3 - 0, 1 - 4)$
$$= (3, -3)$$
$$|\overrightarrow{AB}| = \sqrt{3^2 + (-3)^2}$$
$$= \sqrt{18}$$
$$= 3\sqrt{2}$$

11. $\vec{AB} = (1 - (-4), 9 - 0)$
$= (5, 9)$
$|\vec{AB}| = \sqrt{5^2 + 9^2}$
$= \sqrt{106}$

12. $\vec{AB} = (-1 - (-5), 2 - 7)$
$= (4, -5)$
$|\vec{AB}| = \sqrt{4^2 + (-5)^2}$
$= \sqrt{41}$

13. $(4, 5) + (2, 1) = (4 + 2, 5 + 1) = (6, 6)$

14. $(-1, 2) + (3, 5) = (-1 + 3, 2 + 5) = (2, 7)$

15. $(-1, 6) + (-8, -5) = (-1 + -8, 6 + -5) = (-9, 1)$

16. $(2, 4) + (-2, -3) = (2 + -2, 4 + -3) = (0, 1)$

17. $\vec{i} + \vec{j} = (1, 0) + (0, 1)$
$= (1 + 0, 0 + 1)$
$= (1, 1)$

18. $2\vec{i} - \vec{j} = 2(1, 0) - (0, 1)$
$= (2, 0) - (0, 1)$
$= (2 - 0, 0 - 1)$
$= (2, -1)$

19. $5\vec{i} + 7\vec{j} = 5(1, 0) + 7(0, 1)$
$= (5, 0) + (0, 7)$
$= (5 + 0, 0 + 7)$
$= (5, 7)$

20. $4\vec{i} - \vec{j} = 4(1, 0) - (0, 1)$
$= (4, 0) - (0, 1)$
$= (4 - 0, 0 - 1)$
$= (4, -1)$

PAGES 423-424   EXERCISES

21. $\vec{AB} = (-2 - 7, -2 - 7)$
$= (-9, -9)$
$|\vec{AB}| = \sqrt{(-9)^2 + (-9)^2}$
$= \sqrt{162}$
$= 9\sqrt{2}$

22. $\vec{AB} = (1 - (-2), 3 - 5)$
$= (3, -2)$
$|\vec{AB}| = \sqrt{3^2 + (-2)^2}$
$= \sqrt{13}$

23. $\vec{AB} = (-5 - 0, 0 - 5)$
$= (-5, -5)$
$|\vec{AB}| = \sqrt{(-5)^2 + (-5)^2}$
$= \sqrt{50}$
$= 5\sqrt{2}$

24. $\vec{AB} = (7 - 5, 6 - 0)$
$= (2, 6)$
$|\vec{AB}| = \sqrt{2^2 + 6^2}$
$= \sqrt{40}$
$= 2\sqrt{10}$

25. $\vec{AB} = (5 - 4, -4 - (-5))$
$= (1, 1)$
$|\vec{AB}| = \sqrt{1^2 + 1^2}$
$= \sqrt{2}$

26. $\vec{AB} = (-4 - (-9), -3 - 2)$
$= (5, -5)$
$|\vec{AB}| = \sqrt{5^2 + (-5)^2}$
$= \sqrt{50}$
$= 5\sqrt{2}$

27. $\vec{AB} = (8 - 7, 6 - 6)$
$= (1, 0)$
$|\vec{AB}| = \sqrt{1^2 + 0^2}$
$= \sqrt{1}$
$= 1$

28. $\vec{AB} = (19 - 12, 1 - (-4))$
$= (7, 5)$
$|\vec{AB}| = \sqrt{7^2 + 5^2}$
$= \sqrt{74}$

29. $\vec{u} = (4, -3) + (-6, 2)$
$= (4 + -6, -3 + 2)$
$= (-2, -1)$

30. $\vec{u} = (4, -3) - (-6, 2)$
$= (4 - (-6), -3 - 2)$
$= (10, -5)$

31. $\vec{u} = 3(4, -3)$
$= (12, -9)$

32. $\vec{u} = 4(-6, 2)$
$= (-24, 8)$

33. $\vec{u} = (-6, 2) - 2(4, -3)$
$= (-6, 2) - (8, -6)$
$= (-6 - 8, 2 - (-6))$
$= (-14, 8)$

34. $\vec{u} = (4, -3) - 3(-6, 2)$
$= (4, -3) - (-18, 6)$
$= (4 - (-18), -3 - 6)$
$= (22, -9)$

35. $\vec{u} = 2(4, -3) + 3(-6, 2)$
$= (8, -6) + (-18, 6)$
$= (8 + -18, -6 + 6)$
$= (-10, 0)$

36. $\vec{u} = 4(-6, 2) - 3(4, -3)$
$= (-24, 8) - (12, -9)$
$= (-24 - 12, 8 - (-9))$
$= (-36, 17)$

37. $\vec{u} = 6(-6, 2) - 2(4, -3)$
$= (-36, 12) - (8, -6)$
$= (-36 - 8, 12 - (-6))$
$= (-44, 18)$

38. Let $\vec{a} = (a_1, a_2)$ and $\vec{b} = (b_1, b_2)$.

$\vec{a} + \vec{b} = (a_1, a_2) + (b_1, b_2)$

$= (a_1 + b_1, a_2 + b_2)$ vector addition

$= (b_1 + a_1, b_2 + a_2)$ Addition of real numbers is commutative.

$= (b_1, b_2) + (a_1, a_2)$

$= \vec{b} + \vec{a}$

39. (0, 0)

40. a. They are opposites.

b. It is a parallelogram.

41.
$\cos 42° = \dfrac{h}{110}$ $\sin 42° = \dfrac{v}{110}$

$110 \cos 42° = h$ $110 \sin 42° = v$

$81.7 \text{ N} \approx h$ $73.6 \text{ N} \approx v$

42. Tug A: $\cos 30° = \dfrac{h}{6}$ $\sin 30° = \dfrac{v}{6}$

$6 \cos 30° = h$ $6 \sin 30° = v$

$5.2 \approx h$ $3 = v$

Tug B: $\cos 330° = \dfrac{h}{6}$ $\sin 330° = \dfrac{v}{6}$

$6 \cos 330° = h$ $6 \sin 330° = v$

$5.2 \approx h$ $-3 = v$

$\vec{A} = (5.2, 3)$ $\vec{B} = (5.2, -3)$

$\vec{A} + \vec{B} = (5.2 + 5.2, 3 + -3) = (10.4, 0)$

$|\vec{A} + \vec{B}| = \sqrt{10.4^2 + 0^2} = 10.4$ tons

43. The vertical would decrease and the horizontal would increase.

44. $y^2 = 121 - x^2$

$x^2 + y^2 = 121$

The graph is a circle having center (0, 0) and radius 11. It is symmetric with respect to all.

45. $x = \dfrac{8 \pm \sqrt{(-8)^2 - 4(5)(12)}}{10}$

$= \dfrac{8 \pm \sqrt{-176}}{10}$

$= \dfrac{8 \pm 4i\sqrt{11}}{10}$

$= \dfrac{4 \pm 2i\sqrt{11}}{5}$

46.
$\dfrac{x + 3}{x + 2} = 2 - \dfrac{3}{x^2 + 5x + 6}$

$(x + 2)(x + 3)\left(\dfrac{x + 3}{x + 2}\right) =$

$(x + 2)(x + 3)\left(2 - \dfrac{3}{x^2 + 5x + 6}\right)$

$(x + 3)^2 = 2(x + 2)(x + 3) - 3$

$x^2 + 6x + 9 = 2x^2 + 10x + 12 - 3$

$0 = x^2 + 4x$

$0 = x(x + 4)$

$x = 0$ $x + 4 = 0$

$x = -4$

47. $2 \tan x - 4 = 0$

$2 \tan x = 4$

$\tan x = 2$

$x \approx 63.43°$

$x \approx 63°26'$

48. $8^2 + 5^2 = c^2$

$89 = c^2$

$9.4 \text{ m/s} \approx c$

$58°$ west of south

49. $a(b + 1) = c$

$ab + a = c$

$ab = c - a$

$b = \dfrac{c - a}{a}$

$b = \dfrac{c}{a} - 1$

The best answer is D.

8-3   ### Vectors in Three-Dimensional Space

PAGES 427–428   **CHECKING FOR UNDERSTANDING**

1. First find 3 on the x-axis, -1 on the y-axis, and 2 on the z-axis. Then imagine a plane perpendicular to the x-axis at 3 and planes perpendicular to the y- and z-axes at -1 and 2. The three planes will intersect at (3, -1, 2).

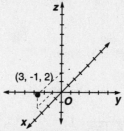

2. The radicand for the magnitude of a vector in space contains another squared term, $(z_2 - z_1)^2$.

3. $\vec{i} = (1, 0, 0, 0)$, $\vec{j} = (0, 1, 0, 0)$, $\vec{k} = (0, 0, 1, 0)$, and $\vec{\ell} = (0, 0, 0, 1)$

4.

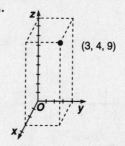

(3, 4, 9)

$|(3, 4, 9)| = \sqrt{3^2 + 4^2 + 9^2}$

$= \sqrt{106}$

5.

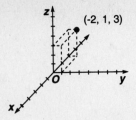

$|(-2, 1, 3)| = \sqrt{(-2)^2 + 1^2 + 3^2}$

$\qquad = \sqrt{14}$

6.

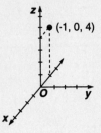

$|(-1, 0, 4)| = \sqrt{(-1)^2 + 0^2 + 4^2}$

$\qquad = \sqrt{17}$

7.

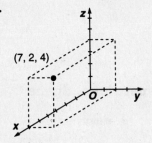

$|(7, 2, 4)| = \sqrt{7^2 + 2^2 + 4^2}$

$\qquad = \sqrt{69}$

8.

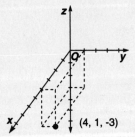

$|(4, 1, -3)| = \sqrt{4^2 + 1^2 + (-3)^2}$

$\qquad = \sqrt{26}$

9.

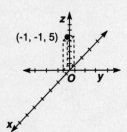

$|(-1, -1, 5)| = \sqrt{(-1)^2 + (-1)^2 + 5^2}$

$\qquad = \sqrt{27}$

$\qquad = 3\sqrt{3}$

10. $\overrightarrow{AB} = (3 - 2, \ 1 - 5, \ 0 - 4)$

$\qquad = (1, \ -4, \ -4)$

$\qquad = \vec{i} - 4\vec{j} - 4\vec{k}$

11. $\overrightarrow{AB} = (3 - (-1), \ -5 - 3, \ -4 - 10)$

$\qquad = (4, \ -8, \ -14)$

$\qquad = 4\vec{i} - 8\vec{j} - 14\vec{k}$

12. $\overrightarrow{AB} = (0 - (-11), \ -2 - 4, \ 13 - (-2))$

$\qquad = (11, \ -6, \ 15)$

$\qquad = 11\vec{i} - 6\vec{j} + 15\vec{k}$

13. $\overrightarrow{AB} = (4 - (-3), \ 3 - 0, \ -1 - 0)$

$\qquad = (7, \ 3, \ -1)$

$\qquad = 7\vec{i} + 3\vec{j} - \vec{k}$

PAGES 428-429   EXERCISES

14. $\overrightarrow{AB} = (4 - 8, \ 0 - 1, \ 1 - 1)$

$\qquad = (-4, \ -1, \ 0)$

$\qquad |\overrightarrow{AB}| = \sqrt{(-4)^2 + (-1)^2 + 0^2}$

$\qquad\qquad = \sqrt{17}$

$\qquad\qquad \approx 4.123$

15. $\overrightarrow{AB} = (5 - 3, \ 7 - 7, \ 2 - (-1))$

$\qquad = (2, \ 0, \ 3)$

$\qquad |\overrightarrow{AB}| = \sqrt{2^2 + 0^2 + 3^2}$

$\qquad\qquad = \sqrt{13}$

$\qquad\qquad \approx 3.606$

16. $\overrightarrow{AB} = (3 - (-2), \ 9 - 5, \ -3 - 8)$

$\qquad = (5, \ 4, \ -11)$

$\qquad |\overrightarrow{AB}| = \sqrt{5^2 + 4^2 + (-11)^2}$

$\qquad\qquad = \sqrt{162}$

$\qquad\qquad = 9\sqrt{2} \approx 12.728$

17. $\overrightarrow{AB} = (-3 - (-2), \ 5 - 4, \ 2 - 7)$

$\qquad = (-1, \ 1, \ -5)$

$\qquad |\overrightarrow{AB}| = \sqrt{(-1)^2 + 1^2 + (-5)^2}$

$\qquad\qquad = \sqrt{27}$

$\qquad\qquad = 3\sqrt{3} \approx 5.196$

18. $\overrightarrow{AB} = (20 - (-2), \ 5 - (-4), \ 11 - 1)$

$\qquad = (22, \ 9, \ 10)$

$\qquad |\overrightarrow{AB}| = \sqrt{22^2 + 9^2 + 10^2}$

$\qquad\qquad = \sqrt{665}$

$\qquad\qquad \approx 25.788$

19. $\overrightarrow{AB} = (3 - (-12), \ -21 - 3, \ 4 - 0)$

$\qquad = (15, \ -24, \ 4)$

$\qquad |\overrightarrow{AB}| = \sqrt{15^2 + (-24)^2 + 4^2}$

$\qquad\qquad = \sqrt{817}$

$\qquad\qquad \approx 28.583$

20. $9\vec{i} + 3\vec{j} - \vec{k}$ **21.** $3\vec{i} + \vec{k}$

22. $2\vec{j} - 2\vec{k}$ **23.** $-5\vec{i} - 8\vec{j} + \vec{k}$

24. $-15\vec{i} + 7\vec{j}$ **25.** $8\vec{i} - 3\vec{j} + 11\vec{k}$

26. $\vec{u} = (1, \ -3, \ -8) + (3, \ 9, \ -1)$

$\qquad = (1 + 3, \ -3 + 9, \ -8 + (-1))$

$\qquad = (4, \ 6, \ -9)$

27. $\vec{u} = (3, 9, -1) - (1, -3, -8)$

   $= (3 - 1, 9 - (-3), -1 - (-8))$

   $= (2, 12, 7)$

28. $\vec{u} = 3(1, -3, -8) + (3, 9, -1)$

   $= (3, -9, -24) + (3, 9, -1)$

   $= (3 + 3, -9 + 9, -24 + -1)$

   $= (6, 0, -25)$

29. $\vec{u} = (1, -3, -8) - 2(3, 9, -1)$

   $= (1, -3, -8) - (6, 18, -2)$

   $= (1 - 6, -3 - 18, -8 - (-2))$

   $= (-5, -21, -6)$

30. $\vec{u} = 4(1, -3, -8) - 3(3, 9, -1)$

   $= (4, -12, -32) - (9, 27, -3)$

   $= (4 - 9, -12 - 27, -32 - (-3))$

   $= (-5, -39, -29)$

31. $\vec{u} = 2(3, 9, -1) - 5(1, -3, -8)$

   $= (6, 18, -2) - (5, -15, -40)$

   $= (6 - 5, 18 - (-15), -2 - (-40))$

   $= (1, 33, 38)$

32. $|\overrightarrow{P_1P_2}| = \sqrt{(x_2 - x_1)^2 + (y_2 - y_1)^2 + (z_2 - z_1)^2}$

   $= \sqrt{(x_1 - x_2)^2 + (y_1 - y_2)^2 + (z_1 - z_2)^2} = |\overrightarrow{P_2P_1}|$

   because $(x - y)^2 = (y - x)^2$ for all real numbers x and y.

33. If $\vec{a} = (a_1, a_2, a_3)$, then $|\vec{a}| = $

   $\sqrt{(a_1)^2 + (a_2)^2 + (a_3)^2}$. If $-\vec{a} = $

   $(-a_1, -a_2, -a_3)$, then $|\vec{a}| = $

   $(-a_1)^2 + (-a_2)^2 + (-a_3)^2$. Since $a_1^2 = $

   $(-a_1^2)$, $a_2^2 = (-a_2)^2$, and $a_3^2 = (-a_3)^2$,

   $|-\vec{a}| = |\vec{a}|$.

34. $|\vec{a}| = \sqrt{1^2 + 1^2 + (-1)^2}$

   $= \sqrt{3}$

   $\frac{1}{\sqrt{3}}\vec{i} + \frac{1}{\sqrt{3}}\vec{j} - \frac{1}{\sqrt{3}}\vec{k}$

35. $|\vec{b}| = \sqrt{4^2 + (-3)^2 + (-12)^2}$

   $= \sqrt{169}$

   $= 13$

   $\frac{4}{13}\vec{i} - \frac{3}{13}\vec{j} - \frac{12}{13}\vec{k}$

36. $F = \dfrac{(1.6 \times 10^{-19})(-1.6 \times 10^{-19})}{4\pi(8.854 \times 10^{-12})(2 \times 10^{-11})^2} \cdot (0, 1, 0)$

   $\approx -5.7522 \times 10^{-7}\vec{j}$

37. a. $(-132, -3454, 0)$

   b. $(3, -2, 4) + (6, 2, 5) + (x, y, z)$

   $= (0, 0, 0)$

   $(9 + x, 0 + y, 9 + z) = (0, 0, 0)$

   $x = -9, y = 0, z = -9$

   $(-9, 0, -9)$

38. Let x = number of sweatshirts.

   Let y = number of sweatpants.

   $x \geq 0, y \geq 0$

   $x + 1.5y \leq 100$

   $2.5x + 2y \leq 180$

   $1.5x + 3y \leq 195$

   possible solutions: $(0, 65), (72, 0), (0, 0)$,

   $(10, 60), (33.33, 48.34)$

   $P(x, y) = 5.5x + 4y$

   $P(0, 65) = \$260$

   $P(72, 0) = \$396 \leftarrow$ maximum

   $P(0, 0) = \$0$

   $P(10, 60) = \$295$

   $P(33.33, 48.34) = \$376.68$

   72 shirts and 0 pants

39. $\quad x = \dfrac{y + 1}{3y}$

   $x = \dfrac{y}{3y} + \dfrac{1}{3y}$

   $x = \dfrac{1}{3} + \dfrac{1}{3y}$

   $x - \dfrac{1}{3} = \dfrac{1}{3y}$

   $\dfrac{3x - 1}{3} = \dfrac{1}{3y}$

   $3y = \dfrac{3}{3x - 1}$

   $y = \dfrac{1}{3x - 1} \neq \dfrac{3x}{x + 1}$, no

40. $f'(x) = 2x^3 + 12x^2 - 14x \qquad f(0) = 1$

   $0 = 2x^3 + 12x^2 - 14x \qquad f(-7) = -513.5$

   $0 = 2x(x^2 + 6x - 7) \qquad f(1) = -1.5$

   $0 = 2x(x + 7)(x - 1) \qquad f(3.03) \approx 90.15$

   $x = 0, -7, 1 \qquad f(-7.03) \approx -513.45$

   $f''(x) = 6x^2 + 24x - 14$

   $0 = 6x^2 + 24x - 14$

   $0 = 3x^2 + 12x - 7$

   $x = \dfrac{-12 \pm \sqrt{12^2 - 4(3)(-7)}}{2(3)}$

   $x = \dfrac{-6 \pm 2\sqrt{57}}{3}$

   critical points: $(0, 1), (-7, -513.5)$,

   $(1, -1.5), (3.03, 90.15), (-7.03, -513.45)$

   $f(-0.01) \approx 0.9993 \qquad f(-7.04) \approx -513.41$

   $f(0.01) \approx 0.9993 \qquad f(-7.02) \approx -513.48$

   $f(0.99) \approx -1.4992 \qquad f(-7.01) \approx -513.49$

   $f(1.01) \approx -1.4992 \qquad f(-6.99) \approx -513.49$

   $f(3.02) \approx 88.92$

   $f(3.04) \approx 91.39$

   So $(0, 1)$ is a maximum; $\left(1, -\dfrac{3}{2}\right)$ and

   $(-7, -513.5)$ are minimums; and $(3.03, 90.15)$ and

   $(-7.03, -513.45)$ are points of inflection.

41. $\cos 2\theta = 1 - 2 \sin^2 \theta$

So, $1 - 2 \sin^2 10° = \cos 20°$.

42. $x \cos \phi + y \sin \phi - p = 0$

$x \cos 60° + y \sin 60° - 3 = 0$

$\frac{1}{2}x + \frac{\sqrt{3}}{2}y - 3 = 0$

$x + \sqrt{3}y - 6 = 0$

43. $\vec{AB} = (6 - 5, -5 - (-6))$

$= (1, 1)$

$|\vec{AB}| = \sqrt{1^2 + 1^2}$

$= \sqrt{2}$

≈ 1.414

44. $(x^a)^b = x^{ab}$ and $x^a x^b = x^{a+b}$

We don't know which is larger, ab or $a + b$. D

8-4   Perpendicular Vectors

PAGE 433   CHECKING FOR UNDERSTANDING

1. They are not perpendicular.

2. No; a vector cannot be perpendicular to itself.

3. $\vec{i} = (1, 0, 0); \vec{j} = (0, 1, 0); \vec{k} = (0, 0, 1)$

$\vec{i} \times \vec{j} = \begin{vmatrix} \vec{i} & \vec{j} & \vec{k} \\ 1 & 0 & 0 \\ 0 & 1 & 0 \end{vmatrix}$

$= \begin{vmatrix} 0 & 0 \\ 1 & 0 \end{vmatrix}\vec{i} - \begin{vmatrix} 1 & 0 \\ 0 & 0 \end{vmatrix}\vec{j} + \begin{vmatrix} 1 & 0 \\ 0 & 1 \end{vmatrix}\vec{k}$

$= 0\vec{i} - 0\vec{j} + 1\vec{k}$

$= \vec{k}$

4. $(3, 5) \cdot (4, -2) = 3 \cdot 4 + 5 \cdot -2 = 2$, no

5. $(8, 4) \cdot (2, 4) = 8 \cdot 2 + 4 \cdot 4 = 32$, no

6. $(5, -1) \cdot (2, 3) = 5 \cdot 2 + (-1) \cdot 3 = 7$, no

7. $(-6, 3) \cdot (1, 2) = -6 \cdot 1 + 3 \cdot 2 = 0$, yes

8. $(4, 2) \cdot (-3, 6) = 4 \cdot -3 + 2 \cdot 6 = 0$, yes

9. $(11, 2) \cdot (-3, 16) = 11 \cdot -3 + 2 \cdot 16 = -1$, no

10. $(7, -2, 4) \cdot (3, 8, 1) = 7 \cdot 3 + -2 \cdot 8 + 4 \cdot 1$
$= 9$, no

11. $(-2, 4, 8) \cdot (16, 4, 2)$

$= -2 \cdot 16 + 4 \cdot 4 + 8 \cdot 2$

$= 0$, yes

12.
$(7, 2, 1) \times (2, 5, 3) = \begin{vmatrix} \vec{i} & \vec{j} & \vec{k} \\ 7 & 2 & 1 \\ 2 & 5 & 3 \end{vmatrix}$

$= 1\vec{i} - 19\vec{j} + 31\vec{k}$

$= (1, -19, 31)$

13.
$(-2, -3, 1) \times (2, 3, -4) = \begin{vmatrix} \vec{i} & \vec{j} & \vec{k} \\ -2 & -3 & 1 \\ 2 & 3 & -4 \end{vmatrix}$

$= 9\vec{i} - 6\vec{j} + 0\vec{k}$

$= (9, -6, 0)$

14.
$(1, -3, 2) \times (5, 1, -2) = \begin{vmatrix} \vec{i} & \vec{j} & \vec{k} \\ 1 & -3 & 2 \\ 5 & 1 & -2 \end{vmatrix}$

$= 4\vec{i} + 12\vec{j} + 16\vec{k}$

$= (4, 12, 16)$

15.
$(-1, 0, 4) \times (5, 2, -1) = \begin{vmatrix} \vec{i} & \vec{j} & \vec{k} \\ -1 & 0 & 4 \\ 5 & 2 & -1 \end{vmatrix}$

$= -8\vec{i} + 19\vec{j} - 2\vec{k}$

$= (-8, 19, -2)$

PAGES 433-435   EXERCISES

16. $(-6, 1) \cdot (-1, 2) = -6 \cdot -1 + 1 \cdot 2 = 8$, no

17. $(2, 0) \cdot (0, 4) = 2 \cdot 0 + 0 \cdot 4 = 0$, yes

18. $(2, -2) \cdot (5, -5) = 2 \cdot 5 + (-2) \cdot (-5) = 20$, no

19. $(2, 5) \cdot (0, 1) = 2 \cdot 0 + 5 \cdot 1 = 5$, no

20. $(5, 2) \cdot (-3, 7) = 5 \cdot -3 + 2 \cdot 7 = -1$, no

21. $(-8, 2) \cdot (4.5, 18) = -8 \cdot 4.5 + 2 \cdot 18 = 0$, yes

22. $(3, -2, 4) \cdot (1, -4, 0)$

$= 3 \cdot 1 + (-2) \cdot (-4) + 4 \cdot 0$

$= 11$, no

23. $(-4, 9, 8) \cdot (3, 2, -2)$

$= -4 \cdot 3 + 9 \cdot 2 + 8 \cdot -2$

$= -10$, no

24. $(4, 9, -3) \cdot (-6, 7, 5)$

$= 4 \cdot -6 + 9 \cdot 7 + -3 \cdot 5$

$= 24$, no

25. $(-6, 2, 10) \cdot (4, 1, 9)$

$= -6 \cdot 4 + 2 \cdot 1 + 10 \cdot 9$

$= 68$, no

26.
$(1, 3, 2) \times (2, -1, -1) = \begin{vmatrix} \vec{i} & \vec{j} & \vec{k} \\ 1 & 3 & 2 \\ 2 & -1 & -1 \end{vmatrix}$

$= -1\vec{i} + 5\vec{j} - 7\vec{k}$

$= (-1, 5, -7)$

$(1, 3, 2) \cdot (-1, 5, -7)$

$= 1 \cdot -1 + 3 \cdot 5 + 2 \cdot -7$

$= 0$, yes

$(2, -1, -1) \cdot (-1, 5, -7)$

$= 2 \cdot -1 + -1 \cdot 5 + -1 \cdot -7$

$= 0$, yes

27.
$(2, 1, 2) \times (1, -1, 3) = \begin{vmatrix} \vec{i} & \vec{j} & \vec{k} \\ 2 & 1 & 2 \\ 1 & -1 & 3 \end{vmatrix}$

$= 5\vec{i} - 4\vec{j} - 3\vec{k}$

$= (5, -4, -3)$

$(2, 1, 2) \cdot (5, -4, -3)$

$= 2 \cdot 5 + 1 \cdot -4 + 2 \cdot -3$

$= 0$, yes

$(1, -1, 3) \cdot (5, -4, -3)$

$= 1 \cdot 5 + (-1) \cdot (-4) + 3 \cdot -3$

$= 0$, yes

28.

$$(1, -3, 2) \times (-2, 1, -5) = \begin{vmatrix} \vec{i} & \vec{j} & \vec{k} \\ 1 & -3 & 2 \\ -2 & 1 & -5 \end{vmatrix}$$

$$= 13\vec{i} + 1\vec{j} - 5\vec{k}$$

$$= (13, 1, -5)$$

$(1, -3, 2) \cdot (13, 1, -5)$

$= 1 \cdot 13 + -3 \cdot 1 + 2 \cdot -5$

$= 0$, yes

$(-2, 1, -5) \cdot (13, 1, -5)$

$= -2 \cdot 13 + 1 \cdot 1 + -5 \cdot -5$

$= 0$, yes

29.

$$(4, 0, -2) \times (-7, 1, 0) = \begin{vmatrix} \vec{i} & \vec{j} & \vec{k} \\ 4 & 0 & -2 \\ -7 & 1 & 0 \end{vmatrix}$$

$$= 2\vec{i} + 14\vec{j} + 4\vec{k}$$

$$= (2, 14, 4)$$

$(4, 0, -2) \cdot (2, 14, 4)$

$= 4 \cdot 2 + 0 \cdot 14 + -2 \cdot 4$

$= 0$, yes

$(-7, 1, 0) \cdot (2, 14, 4)$

$= -7 \cdot 2 + 1 \cdot 14 + 0 \cdot 4$

$= 0$, yes

30. Sample answer: $(-20, -31, 25)$

31. Sample answer: $(1, -8, 5)$

32. $\vec{a} \cdot \vec{b} = (a_1, a_2) \cdot (b_1, b_2)$

$\qquad = a_1 b_1 + a_2 b_2$

$\qquad = b_1 a_1 + b_2 a_2$

$\qquad = (b_1, b_2) \cdot (a_1, a_2)$

$\qquad = \vec{b} \cdot \vec{a}$

33. $\vec{a} \cdot \vec{b} = (a_1, a_2, a_3) \cdot (b_1, b_2, b_3)$

$\qquad = a_1 b_1 + a_2 b_2 + a_3 b_3$

$\qquad = b_1 a_1 + b_2 a_2 + b_3 a_3$

$\qquad = (b_1, b_2, b_3) \cdot (a_1, a_2, a_3)$

$\qquad = \vec{b} \cdot \vec{a}$

34.

$$\vec{a} \times \vec{a} = \begin{vmatrix} a_2 & a_3 \\ a_2 & a_3 \end{vmatrix}\vec{i} - \begin{vmatrix} a_1 & a_3 \\ a_1 & a_3 \end{vmatrix}\vec{j} + \begin{vmatrix} a_1 & a_2 \\ a_1 & a_2 \end{vmatrix}\vec{k}$$

$$= (a_2 a_3 - a_2 a_3)\vec{i} - (a_1 a_3 - a_1 a_3)\vec{j} +$$

$$(a_1 a_2 - a_1 a_2)\vec{k}$$

$$= 0$$

35.

$$\vec{a} \times (\vec{b} + \vec{c}) = \begin{vmatrix} \vec{i} & \vec{j} & \vec{k} \\ a_1 & a_2 & a_3 \\ (b_1 + c_1) & (b_2 + c_2) & (b_3 + c_3) \end{vmatrix}$$

$$= \begin{vmatrix} a_2 & a_3 \\ (b_2 + c_2) & (b_3 + c_3) \end{vmatrix}\vec{i} - \begin{vmatrix} a_1 & a_3 \\ (b_1 + c_1) & (b_3 + c_3) \end{vmatrix}\vec{j} + \begin{vmatrix} a_1 & a_2 \\ (b_1 + c_1) & (b_2 + c_2) \end{vmatrix}\vec{k}$$

$$= [a_2(b_3 + c_3) - a_3(b_2 + c_2)]\vec{i} -$$

$$[a_1(b_3 + c_3) - a_3(b_1 + c_1)]\vec{j} +$$

$$[a_1(b_2 + c_2) - a_2(b_1 + c_1)]\vec{k}$$

$$= [(a_2 b_3 + a_2 c_3) - (a_3 b_2 + a_3 c_2)]\vec{i} -$$

$$[(a_1 b_3 + a_1 c_3) - (a_3 b_1 + a_3 c_1)]\vec{j} +$$

$$[(a_1 b_2 + a_1 c_2) - (a_2 b_1 + a_2 c_1)]\vec{k}$$

$$= [(a_2 b_3 - a_3 b_2) + (a_2 c_3 - a_3 c_2)]\vec{i} -$$

$$[(a_1 b_3 - a_3 b_1) + (a_1 c_3 - a_3 c_1)]\vec{j} +$$

$$[(a_1 b_2 - a_2 b_1) + (a_1 c_2 - a_2 c_1)]\vec{k}$$

$$= (a_2 b_3 - a_3 b_2)\vec{i} + (a_2 c_3 - a_3 c_2)\vec{i} -$$

$$(a_1 b_3 - a_3 b_1)\vec{j} - (a_1 c_3 - a_3 c_1)\vec{j} +$$

$$(a_1 b_2 - a_2 b_1)\vec{k} + (a_1 c_2 - a_2 c_1)\vec{k}$$

$$= [(a_2 b_3 - a_3 b_2)\vec{i} - (a_1 b_3 - a_3 b_1)\vec{j} +$$

$$(a_1 b_2 - a_2 b_1)\vec{k}] + [(a_2 c_3 - a_3 c_2)\vec{i} -$$

$$(a_1 c_3 - a_3 c_1)\vec{j} + (a_1 c_2 - a_2 c_1)\vec{k}]$$

$$= \left[\begin{vmatrix} a_2 & a_3 \\ b_2 & b_3 \end{vmatrix}\vec{i} - \begin{vmatrix} a_1 & a_3 \\ b_1 & b_3 \end{vmatrix}\vec{j} + \begin{vmatrix} a_1 & a_2 \\ b_1 & b_2 \end{vmatrix}\vec{k} \right] +$$

$$\left[\begin{vmatrix} a_2 & a_3 \\ c_2 & c_3 \end{vmatrix}\vec{i} - \begin{vmatrix} a_1 & a_3 \\ c_1 & c_3 \end{vmatrix}\vec{j} + \begin{vmatrix} a_1 & a_2 \\ c_1 & c_2 \end{vmatrix}\vec{k} \right]$$

$$= \vec{a} \times \vec{b} + \vec{a} \times \vec{c}$$

36. No, $\vec{a} \times \vec{b}$ and $\vec{b} \times \vec{a}$ have the same magnitude but opposite directions.

37. a. $(4, -4, -4)$

b. $(47, -4, 33)$

38.
$$\vec{a} \cdot \vec{b} = \vec{a} \cdot \vec{c}$$

$\vec{a} \cdot \vec{b} - \vec{a} \cdot \vec{c} = 0$

$\vec{a} \cdot (\vec{b} - \vec{c}) = 0$

So, $\vec{a} \perp (\vec{b} - \vec{c})$.

$$\vec{a} \times \vec{b} = \vec{a} \times \vec{c}$$

$\vec{a} \times \vec{b} - \vec{a} \times \vec{c} = 0$

$\vec{a} \times (\vec{b} - \vec{c}) = 0$

So, $\vec{a} = (\vec{b} - \vec{c})$, $\vec{a} = 0$, or $(\vec{b} - \vec{c}) = 0$.

Since the inner products are equal, we conclude that $\vec{a} \perp (\vec{b} - \vec{c})$, so it cannot be that $\vec{a} = (\vec{b} - \vec{c})$. We are given that $\vec{a} \neq 0$, so it must be that $(\vec{b} - \vec{c}) = 0$.

$\vec{b} - \vec{c} = 0$

$\vec{b} = \vec{c}$

Yes, $\vec{b} = \vec{c}$.

39. a. The point where the force is applied is

$(1.5 \cos 30°, 0, 1.55 \sin 30°)$

$= (1.30, 0, 0.75)$.

$\overrightarrow{PQ} = (1.30 - 0, 0 - 0, 0.75 - 0)$

$\quad = (1.30, 0, 0.75)$

$\vec{F} = -55\vec{k}$

$\quad = (0, 0, -55)$

$\vec{M} = \overrightarrow{PQ} \times \vec{F}$

$\quad = \begin{vmatrix} \vec{i} & \vec{j} & \vec{k} \\ 1.30 & 0 & 0.75 \\ 0 & 0 & -55 \end{vmatrix}$

$\quad = 0\vec{i} + 71.5\vec{j} + 0\vec{k}$

$\quad = (0, 71.5, 0)$

b. $|\vec{M}| = \sqrt{0^2 + 71.5^2 + 0^2} = 71.5$ lb/ft

c. the y-axis

40. distance between A and B

$= \sqrt{(5 - 2)^2 + (3 - (-1))^2} = \sqrt{9 + 16} = 5$

distance between B and C

$= \sqrt{(-3 - 5)^2 + (11 - 3)^2} = \sqrt{64 + 64} \approx 11.31$

distance between A and C

$= \sqrt{(2 - (-3))^2 + (-1 - 11)^2} = \sqrt{25 + 144} = 13$

perimeter $\approx 5 + 11.31 + 13 \approx 29.31$ units

41. As $x \to +\infty$, $y \to -\infty$; as $x \to -\infty$, $y \to +\infty$.

42. -1.3, -0.6

43. Let $\theta = \mathrm{Tan}^{-1} \dfrac{\sqrt{33}}{4}$.

$\mathrm{Tan}\,\theta = \dfrac{\sqrt{33}}{4}$

$\theta \approx 55.15°$

$\cos 55.15° \approx 0.57$

$\quad \approx \dfrac{4}{7}$

44. $\overrightarrow{AB} = (0 - 5, -11 - 7, 8 - (-2))$

$\quad = (-5, -18, 10)$

45. $\sqrt{12} + \sqrt{27} = 2\sqrt{3} + 3\sqrt{3} = 5\sqrt{3}$

The best answer is B.

Mid-Chapter Review

PAGE 435

1. $\cos 65° = \dfrac{h}{1}$

$\quad 0.4$ cm $\approx h$

$\sin 65° = \dfrac{v}{1}$

$\quad 0.9$ cm $\approx v$

1 cm

2. $\cos 15° = \dfrac{h}{3.1}$

$3.1 \cos 15° = h$

$\quad 3.0$ cm $\approx h$

$\sin 15° = \dfrac{v}{3.1}$

$3.1 \sin 15° = v$

$\quad 0.8$ cm $\approx v$

3.1 cm

3. $\cos 120° = \dfrac{h}{0.8}$

$0.8 \cos 120° = h$

$\quad 0.4 \approx h$

$\sin 120° = \dfrac{v}{0.8}$

$0.8 \sin 120° = v$

$\quad 0.7$ cm $\approx v$

0.8 cm

4. $\cos 160° = \dfrac{h}{2.2}$

$2.2 \cos 160° = h$

$\quad 2.1 \approx h$

$\sin 160° = \dfrac{v}{2.2}$

$2.2 \sin 160° = v$

$\quad 0.8$ cm $\approx v$

2.2 cm

5. $\overrightarrow{AB} = (-3 - 5, 3 - 2)$

$\quad = (-8, 1)$

$|\overrightarrow{AB}| = \sqrt{(-8)^2 + 1^2}$

$\quad = \sqrt{65}$

$\quad \approx 8.062$

6. $\overrightarrow{AB} = (-3 - (-4), 3 - 3)$

$\quad = (1, 0)$

$|\overrightarrow{AB}| = \sqrt{1^2 + 0^2}$

$\quad = 1$

7. $\overrightarrow{AB} = (-2 - 8, 5 - (-7))$

$\quad = (-10, 12)$

$|\overrightarrow{AB}| = \sqrt{(-10)^2 + 12^2}$

$\quad = \sqrt{244}$

$\quad = 2\sqrt{61}$

$\quad \approx 15.620$

8. $\overrightarrow{AB} = (4 - 3, 0 - 1, -1 - (-2))$

$\quad = (1, -1, 1)$

$|\overrightarrow{AB}| = \sqrt{1^2 + (-1)^2 + 1^2}$

$\quad = \sqrt{3}$

$\quad \approx 1.732$

9. $\overrightarrow{AB} = (-2 - 6, 4 - 10, -12 - (-11))$

$\quad = (-8, -6, -1)$

$|\overrightarrow{AB}| = \sqrt{(-8)^2 + (-6)^2 + (-1)^2}$

$\quad = \sqrt{101}$

$\quad \approx 10.050$

10. $\vec{u} = (-2, 7) + (7, -10)$

$\quad = (-2 + 7, 7 + (-10))$

$\quad = (5, -3)$

11. $\vec{u} = 2(-2, 7) - 4(7, -10)$

$\quad = (-4, 14) - (28, -40)$

$\quad = (-4 - 28, 14 - (-40))$

$\quad = (-32, 54)$

12. $\vec{u} = 2(7, -10) - (-2, 7)$

$\quad = (14, -20) - (-2, 7)$

$\quad = (14 - (-2), -20 - 7)$

$\quad = (16, -27)$

13. $\vec{u} = (-2, 1, 3) + (-1, -1, 5)$

$\quad = (-2 + (-1), 1 + (-1), 3 + 5)$

$\quad = (-3, 0, 8)$

14. $\vec{u} = (-1, -1, 5) - 2(-2, 1, 3)$

$\quad = (-1, -1, 5) - (-4, 2, 6)$

$\quad = (-1 - (-4), -1 - 2, 5 - 6)$

$\quad = (3, -3, -1)$

15. $\vec{u}$ = 4(-1, -1, 5)

    = (-4, -4, 20)

16. (2, -1) · (3, 4) = 2 · 3 + -1 · 4 = 2, no

17. (-1, 5) · (10, 2) = -1 · 10 + 5 · 2 = 0, yes

18. (9, 2, -4) · (2, -7, 3)

    = 9 · 2 + 2 · (-7) + (-4) · 3

    = -8, no

19. Sample answer: (-6, -36, -24)

8-5   Applications with Vectors

PAGES 438-439   CHECKING FOR UNDERSTANDING

1. They are in equilibrium; or they are opposite.

2. more

3.

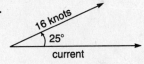

16 knots
25°
current

4.

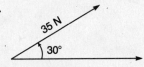

35 N
30°

5.

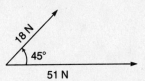

18 N
45°
51 N

6. magnitude = $\sqrt{40^2 + 45^2} \approx 60.2$ N

    direction: $\tan \theta = \dfrac{45}{40}$

                       $\theta \approx 48.37°$ or $48°22'$

7. magnitude = $\sqrt{30^2 + (-15)^2} \approx 33.5$ km/h

    direction: $\tan \theta = \dfrac{15}{30}$

                       $\theta \approx 26.57$

   $360° - \theta \approx 333.43°$ or $333°26'$

8. $|\vec{r}|^2 = 23^2 + 23^2 - 2(23)(23) \cos 120°$

       = 1587

   $|\vec{r}| \approx 39.8$ N

   $\dfrac{39.8}{\sin 120°} \approx \dfrac{23}{\sin \theta}$

      $\sin \theta \approx \dfrac{23 \sin 120°}{39.8}$

      $\sin \theta \approx 0.50$

           $\theta \approx 30°$ $30° + 60° = 90°$

9. $|\vec{r}|^2 = 250^2 + 45^2 - 2(250)(45) \cos 45°$

   $|\vec{r}|^2 \approx 48,615.1$

   $|\vec{r}| \approx 220.5$ km/h

   $\dfrac{220.5}{\sin 45°} \approx \dfrac{250}{\sin \theta}$

     $\sin \theta \approx \dfrac{250 \sin 45°}{220.5}$

         $\theta \approx 126.7$ or $126°42'$

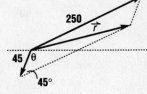

250
$\vec{r}$
45 θ
45°

The direction of the resultant is $126°42' - 110°$ or $16°42'$.

PAGES 439-441   EXERCISES

10. $|\vec{r}|^2 = 10^2 + 10^2 - 2(10)(10) \cos 150°$

    $|\vec{r}|^2 \approx 373.21$

    $|\vec{r}| \approx 19.3$ lb

11. $|\vec{r}|^2 = 10^2 + 10^2 - 2(10)(10) \cos 90°$

    $|\vec{r}|^2 = 200$

    $|\vec{r}| \approx 14.1$ lb

12. $|\vec{r}|^2 = 10^2 + 10^2 - 2(10)(10) \cos 60°$

    $|\vec{r}|^2 = 100$

    $|\vec{r}| = 10$ lb

13. $|\vec{r}|^2 = 10^2 + 10^2 - 2(10)(10) \cos 45°$

    $|\vec{r}|^2 \approx 58.58$

    $|\vec{r}| \approx 7.65$ lb

14. $|\vec{r}|^2 = 10^2 + 10^2 - 2(10)(10) \cos 10°$

    $|\vec{r}|^2 \approx 3.04$

    $|\vec{r}| \approx 1.7$ lb

15. $|\vec{r}|^2 = 10^2 + 10^2 - 2(10)(10) \cos 0°$

    $|\vec{r}|^2 = 0$

    $|\vec{r}| = 0$ lb

16. $|\vec{r}|^2 = 100^2 + 50^2 - 2(100)(50) \cos 90°$

    $|\vec{r}|^2 = 12,500$

    $|\vec{r}| \approx 111.8$ N

    $\dfrac{111.8}{\sin 90°} \approx \dfrac{100}{\sin \theta}$

      $\sin \theta \approx \dfrac{100 \sin 90°}{111.8}$

      $\sin \theta \approx 0.89$

        $\theta \approx 63.44°$ or $63°26'$

17. $\sin 40° = \dfrac{F_1}{25}$

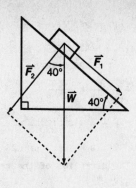

$\quad F_1 = 25 \sin 40°$

$\quad F_1 \approx 16.07 \text{ lb}$

$\quad W = mg$

$\quad 25 = m(32)$

$\quad \dfrac{25}{32} = m$

$\quad 0.78 \approx m$

$\quad F = ma$

$16.07 \approx 0.78a$

$\quad a \approx 20.6 \text{ ft/s}^2$

18. $\quad \cos 30° = \dfrac{h}{18} \qquad\qquad \sin 30° = \dfrac{v}{18}$

$\quad 18 \cos 30° = h \qquad\quad 18 \sin 30° = v$

$\quad 15.6 \text{ N} \approx h \qquad\qquad 9 \text{ N} = v$

19. $|\vec{r}|^2 = 33^2 + 44^2 - 2(33)(44) \cos 150°$

$\quad |\vec{r}|^2 \approx 5539.94$

$\quad |\vec{r}| \approx 74 \text{ N}$

$\quad \dfrac{74}{\sin 150°} \approx \dfrac{44}{\sin \theta}$

$\qquad \sin \theta \approx \dfrac{44 \sin 150°}{74}$

$\qquad\quad \theta \approx 17°$

The direction of the equilibriant should be
$180° + (90° - \theta)$ or $253°$.

20. $|\vec{r}|^2 = 48^2 + 36^2 - 2(48)(36) \cos 22°$

$\quad |\vec{r}|^2 \approx 395.65$

$\quad |\vec{r}| \approx 19.9 \text{ N}$

$\quad \dfrac{19.9}{\sin 22°} \approx \dfrac{48}{\sin \theta}$

$\qquad \sin \theta \approx \dfrac{48 \sin 22°}{19.9}$

$\qquad\quad \theta \approx 64.63° \approx 64°38'$

$\quad$ or $\theta \approx 115.37° \approx 115°22'$

$\quad 115°22' - 20° = 95°22'$

$\quad 5°22'$ west of south

21. $\sin 22° = \dfrac{F_1}{300}$

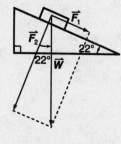

$\quad F_1 = 300 \sin 22°$

$\quad F_1 \approx 112.4 \text{ lb}$

$\quad \tan 22° \approx \dfrac{112.4}{F_2}$

$\quad\quad F_2 \approx \dfrac{112.4}{\tan 22°}$

$\qquad\quad \approx 278.2 \text{ lb}$

22. First find $\vec{x}$, the resultant of $\vec{OA}$ and $\vec{OB}$.

$\quad |\vec{x}|^2 = 11^2 + 7^2 - 2 \cdot 11 \cdot 7 \cos 75°$

$\quad |\vec{x}| \approx 11.4 \text{ N}$

$\quad \dfrac{11}{\sin \angle BOD} \approx \dfrac{11.4}{\sin 75°}, \quad m\angle BOD \approx 68°45'$

The angle between $\vec{x}$ and $\vec{OC}$ is $68°45' + 108°$,
or $176°45'$.

Then find $\vec{r}$, the resultant of $\vec{x}$ and $\vec{OC}$.

$\quad |\vec{r}|^2 \approx (11.4)^2 + 15^2 - 2(11.4)(15) \cos 3°15'$

$\quad |\vec{r}| \approx 3.7 \text{ N}$

$\quad \dfrac{3.7}{\sin 3°15'} \approx \dfrac{11.4}{\sin \theta}, \quad \theta \approx 10°2'$

a. No, the vectors are not in equilibrium.

b. The resultant is a force of 3.7 N, $10°2'$
east of south.

23. The forces acting at 90° and 270° are opposite.
Their resultant is a force of 20 N at 270°.
The forces acting at 0° and 180° are equal and
opposite, so their resultant is zero.
To find the resultant of all five forces, add
the force of 50 N at 60° with the resultant of
20 N at 270°.

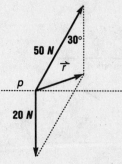

$|\vec{r}|^2 = 50^2 + 20^2 - 2(50)(20) \cos 30°$

$\quad |\vec{r}|^2 \approx 1167$

$\quad |\vec{r}| \approx 34 \text{ N}$

$\quad \dfrac{50}{\sin \theta} \approx \dfrac{34}{\sin 30°}$

$\qquad \theta \approx 133°$

The resultant force is 34 N at 43°. So a force
of 34 N at 223° would produce equilibrium.

24. Method b is better. Vectors show that when the
rope is nearly straight then the force exerted
by the car and the tree are much greater than
Jeff could exert on his own.

25. $|\vec{r}|^2 = (210)^2 + (100)^2 - 2(210)(100) \cos 110°$

$\quad |\vec{r}|^2 \approx 68,464.846$

$\quad |\vec{r}| \approx 261.66 \text{ km}$

$\quad \dfrac{261.66}{\sin 110°} \approx \dfrac{100}{\sin \theta}$

$\qquad \sin \theta \approx \dfrac{100 \sin 110°}{261.66}$

$\qquad\quad \theta \approx 21.05°$

$\qquad\quad \approx 21°3' \text{ SE}$

26. a. speed $= \sqrt{35^2 + 55^2}$

   $= \sqrt{4250}$

   $= 65$ m/s

   b. $\sin \theta = \frac{55}{65}$

   $\theta = 58°$

27. $\sin \theta = \frac{4}{12}$

   $\theta \approx 19.47$

   $\theta \approx 19°28'$

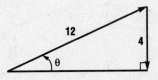

28. $\cos 30° = \frac{h}{40}$ $\sin 30° = \frac{v}{40}$

   $40 \cos 30° = h$ $40 \sin 30° = v$

   34.6 lb $= h$ 20 lb $= v$

29. $|\vec{r}|^2 = 85^2 + 125^2 - 2(85)(125) \cos 108°$

   $|\vec{r}|^2 \approx 29,416.61$

   $|\vec{r}| \approx 171.5$ N

   $\frac{171.51}{\sin 108°} \approx \frac{85}{\sin \theta}$

   $\sin \theta \approx \frac{85 \sin 108°}{171.5}$

   $\theta \approx 28.12°$ or $28°7'$

30. $260^2 + 16^2 = c^2$ 31. $\cos 25° = \frac{120}{F}$

   $67,856 = c^2$ $F = \frac{120}{\cos 25°}$

   260.5 mph $\approx c$ $F \approx 132.4$ lb

   $\sin \theta \approx \frac{16}{260.5}$

   $\theta \approx 3.52°$

   $\theta \approx 3°31'$ NW

32. $|\vec{r}|^2 = 16^2 + 260^2 - 2 \cdot 16 \cdot 260 \cos 70°$

   $|\vec{r}| \approx 255.0$ mph

   $\frac{16}{\sin \theta} \approx \frac{255.0}{\sin 70°}$, $\theta \approx 3°23'$

   The direction is $3°23'$

   east of north.

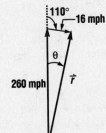

33. $2(6) - 3(12) + 6(15) = 66$

34.

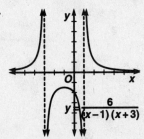

35. possible roots: ±2, $\pm\frac{2}{3}$, ±1, $\pm\frac{1}{3}$

   $f(2) = 0$ $f(1) = -4$

   $f(-2) = -28$ $f(-1) = 0$

   $f\left(\frac{2}{3}\right) \approx -2.22$ $f\left(\frac{1}{3}\right) = 0$

   $f\left(-\frac{2}{3}\right) \approx 2.67$ $f\left(-\frac{1}{3}\right) \approx 3.11$

   roots: 2, -1, $\frac{1}{3}$

36. $\tan (-75°) = \tan (-30° + -45°)$

   $= \dfrac{\tan (-30)° + \tan (-45°)}{1 - \tan (-30°) \tan (-45°)}$

   $= \dfrac{-\frac{\sqrt{3}}{3} + (-1)}{1 - \left(-\frac{\sqrt{3}}{3}\right)(-1)}$

   $= \dfrac{\frac{-\sqrt{3} - 3}{3}}{\frac{3 - \sqrt{3}}{3}}$

   $= \dfrac{-\sqrt{3} - 3}{3 - \sqrt{3}} \cdot \dfrac{3 + \sqrt{3}}{3 + \sqrt{3}}$

   $= \dfrac{-3\sqrt{3} - 3 - 9 - 3\sqrt{3}}{6}$

   $= \dfrac{-12 - 6\sqrt{3}}{6}$

   $= -2 - \sqrt{3}$

37. $(4, -1, 8) \cdot (-5, 2, 2)$

   $= 4 \cdot (-5) + (-1) \cdot 2 + 8 \cdot 2$

   $= -6$, no

38. $m\angle EOD = 180° - (85° + 15°) = 80°$

   Since $EO = DO$, $m\angle OED = m\angle ODE = \frac{180° - 80°}{2} = 50°$.

   $m\angle ODC = 180° - 50° = 130°$

   So, $m\angle ECA = 180° - (130° + 15°) = 35°$.

   The best answer is D.

Case Study Follow-Up

PAGE 441

1. $\frac{450,000}{250,000,000} \times 10,000 = 18$ tons

   18 tons $= 36,000$ lb

2. $\cos 52° = \frac{h}{36,000}$

   $36,000 \cos 52° = h$

   $22,164$ lb $\approx h$

3. $\cos \theta = \frac{32,000}{36,000}$

   $\theta \approx 27°$

4. See students' work.

Vectors and Parametric Equations

1. The direction vector $\overrightarrow{P_1P_2}$ is the ordered pair $(x_2 - x_1, y_2 - y_1)$. The slope of a line through P_1 and P_2 would be $m = \dfrac{y_2 - y_1}{x_2 - x_1}$.

2. about 5.4 minutes

3. 4 hours after the race started

4. a. $(x - (-5), y - 8) = t(3, 7)$
   $(x + 5, y - 8) = t(3, 7)$
   b. $x + 5 = 3t \qquad y - 8 = 7t$
   $x = -5 + 3t \qquad y = 8 + 7t$
   c. $t = \dfrac{x + 5}{3} \qquad t = \dfrac{y - 8}{7}$
   $\dfrac{x + 5}{3} = \dfrac{y - 8}{7}$
   $7(x + 5) = 3(y - 8)$
   $7x + 35 = 3y - 24$
   $7x + 59 = 3y$
   $\dfrac{7}{3}x + \dfrac{59}{3} = y$

5. a. $(x - (-1), y - (-5)) = t(3, 7)$
   $(x + 1, y + 5) = t(3, 7)$
   b. $x + 1 = 3t \qquad y + 5 = 7t$
   $x = -1 + 3t \qquad y = -5 + 7t$
   c. $t = \dfrac{x + 1}{3} \qquad t = \dfrac{y + 5}{7}$
   $\dfrac{x + 1}{3} = \dfrac{y + 5}{7}$
   $7(x + 1) = 3(y + 5)$
   $7x + 7 = 3y + 15$
   $7x - 8 = 3y$
   $\dfrac{7}{3}x - \dfrac{8}{3} = y$

6. a. $(x - 6, y - 2) = t(3, 7)$
   b. $x - 6 = 3t \qquad y - 2 = 7t$
   $x = 6 + 3t \qquad y = 2 + 7t$
   c. $t = \dfrac{x - 6}{3} \qquad t = \dfrac{y - 2}{7}$
   $\dfrac{x - 6}{3} = \dfrac{y - 2}{7}$
   $7(x - 6) = 3(y - 2)$
   $7x - 42 = 3y - 6$
   $7x - 36 = 3y$
   $\dfrac{7}{3}x - 12 = y$

7. a. $(x - 5, y - (-9)) = t(3, 7)$
   $(x - 5, y + 9) = t(3, 7)$
   b. $x - 5 = 3t \qquad y + 9 = 7t$
   $x = 5 + 3t \qquad y = -9 + 7t$
   c. $t = \dfrac{x - 5}{3} \qquad t = \dfrac{y + 9}{7}$
   $\dfrac{x - 5}{3} = \dfrac{y + 9}{7}$
   $7(x - 5) = 3(y + 9)$
   $7x - 35 = 3y + 27$
   $7x - 62 = 3y$
   $\dfrac{7}{3}x - \dfrac{62}{3} = y$

8. a. $(x - (-6), y - 0) = t(3, 7)$
   $(x + 6, y) = t(3, 7)$
   b. $x + 6 = 3t \qquad y = 7t$
   $x = -6 + 3t$
   c. $t = \dfrac{x + 6}{3} \qquad t = \dfrac{y}{7}$
   $\dfrac{x + 6}{3} = \dfrac{y}{7}$
   $7(x + 6) = 3y$
   $7x + 42 = 3y$
   $\dfrac{7}{3}x + 14 = y$

9. a. $(x - 11, y - (-4)) = t(3, 7)$
   $(x - 11, y + 4) = t(3, 7)$
   b. $x - 11 = 3t \qquad y + 4 = 7t$
   $x = 11 + 3t \qquad y = -4 + 7t$
   c. $t = \dfrac{x - 11}{3} \qquad t = \dfrac{y + 4}{7}$
   $\dfrac{x - 11}{3} = \dfrac{y + 4}{7}$
   $7(x - 11) = 3(y + 4)$
   $7x - 77 = 3y + 12$
   $7x - 89 = 3y$
   $\dfrac{7}{3}x - \dfrac{89}{3} = y$

10. $x = t$
    $y = 9t - 1$

11. $x = t$
    $y = 3t + 11$

12. $x = t$
    $y = -2t + 6$

13. $(x - (-4), y - (-11)) = t(-3, 8)$
    $(x + 4, y + 11) = t(-3, 8)$
    $x + 4 = -3t \qquad y + 11 = 8t$
    $x = -4 - 3t \qquad y = -11 + 8t$

14. $(x - 1, y - 5) = t(-7, 2)$
    $x - 1 = -7t \qquad y - 5 = 2t$
    $x = 1 - 7t \qquad y = 5 + 2t$

15. $(x - (-1), y - 0) = t(3, 2)$
    $(x + 1, y) = t(3, 2)$
    $x + 1 = 3t \qquad y = 2t$
    $x = -1 + 3t$

16. $(x - (-4), y - 1) = t(-6, 10)$
    $(x + 4, y - 1) = t(-6, 10)$
    $x + 4 = -6t \qquad y - 1 = 10t$
    $x = -4 - 6t \qquad y = 1 + 10t$

17. $x = t$
    $y = -2t + 3$

18. $x = t$
    $y = 4t - 2$

19. $x = t$

$3x + 2y = 5$

$2y = -3x + 5$

$y = -\frac{3}{2}x + \frac{5}{2}$

$y = -\frac{3}{2}t + \frac{5}{2}$

20. $x = 3t - 5 \rightarrow \dfrac{x + 5}{3} = t$

$y = -2t + 7 \rightarrow \dfrac{7 - y}{2} = t$

$\dfrac{x + 5}{3} = \dfrac{7 - y}{2}$

$2(x + 5) = 3(7 - y)$

$2x + 10 = 21 - 3y$

$2x - 11 = -3y$

$-\frac{2}{3}x + \frac{11}{3} = y$

21. $x = -t + 6 \rightarrow 6 - x = t$

$y = t + 2 \rightarrow y - 2 = t$

$6 - x = y - 2$

$-x + 8 = y$

22. $x = -4t + 3 \rightarrow \dfrac{3 - x}{4} = t$

$y = 5t - 3 \rightarrow \dfrac{y + 3}{5} = t$

$\dfrac{3 - x}{4} = \dfrac{y + 3}{5}$

$5(3 - x) = 4(y + 3)$

$15 - 5x = 4y + 12$

$3 - 5x = 4y$

$-\frac{5}{4}x + \frac{3}{4} = y$

23. $x = 4t - 11 \rightarrow \dfrac{x + 11}{4} = t$

$y = t + 3 \rightarrow y - 3 = t$

$\dfrac{x + 11}{4} = y - 3$

$4(y - 3) = x + 11$

$4y - 12 = x + 11$

$4y = x + 23$

$y = \frac{1}{4}x + \frac{23}{4}$

24. $x = 9t \rightarrow \dfrac{x}{9} = t$

$y = 4t + 2 \rightarrow \dfrac{y - 2}{4} = t$

$\dfrac{x}{9} = \dfrac{y - 2}{4}$

$4x = 9(y - 2)$

$4x = 9y - 18$

$4x + 18 = 9y$

$\frac{4}{9}x + 2 = y$

25. $x = 8$

26.

t	x	y
-1	-2	-2
0	2	-1
1	6	0

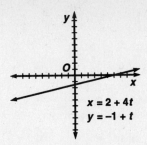

$x = 2 + 4t$
$y = -1 + t$

27.

t	x	y
-1	-8	6
0	-3	2
1	2	-2

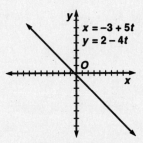

$x = -3 + 5t$
$y = 2 - 4t$

28.

t	x	y
0	1	1
1	2	0
2	3	-1

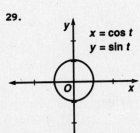

$x = 1 + t$
$y = 1 - t$

29.

$x = \cos t$
$y = \sin t$

30.

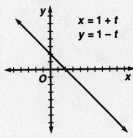

$x = 4 \cos t$
$y = 7 \sin t$

31. $m = \dfrac{2 - (-3)}{5 - (-4)} = \dfrac{5}{9}$

$y + 3 = \frac{5}{9}(x + 4)$

$y + 3 = \frac{5}{9}x + \frac{20}{9}$

$y = \frac{5}{9}x - \frac{7}{9}$

So, if $x = t$, $y = \frac{5}{9}t - \frac{7}{9}$. (sample answer)

32. See students' work.

33. Truck 1: $x = 50t$

$ y = 1$

Truck 2: $x = 54(t - 1)$

$ y = 2$

a. 13.5 h

b. at $t = 13.5$, $x = 675$ miles

c. Truck 1 drives 1125 miles in 22.5 hours +
   3 hour break = 25.5 hours $\rightarrow$ 9:30 AM
   Truck 2 drives 1125 miles in 20.83 hours +
   3 hour break = 23.83 hours $\rightarrow$ 8:50 AM

d. $1125 + x = 21.83$
   $x \approx 51.53$, at least 1.53 mph

34. $3x = -12$ $3x = 12$

     $x = -4$ $x = 4$

35. $\begin{bmatrix} 4 & -1 & 6 \\ 4 & 0 & 2 \end{bmatrix} \begin{bmatrix} 0 & 3 \\ 2 & -2 \\ 5 & 1 \end{bmatrix} = \begin{bmatrix} 28 & 20 \\ 10 & 14 \end{bmatrix}$

36. Let h = height.

Let x = distance from first spot to cliff.

$\tan 60° = \dfrac{h}{x} \rightarrow 1.7321 \approx \dfrac{h}{x}$

$\tan 52° = \dfrac{h}{x + 45} \rightarrow 1.2799 \approx \dfrac{h}{45 + x}$

$x \approx \dfrac{h}{1.7321}$ $45 + x \approx \dfrac{h}{1.2799}$

                      $x \approx \dfrac{h - 57.5955}{1.2799}$

$\dfrac{h}{1.7321} = \dfrac{h - 57.5955}{1.2799}$

$1.2799h = 1.7321h - 99.7612$

$99.7612 = 0.4522h$

$221 \text{ ft} = h$

37. 8, 360°, 30°

38. $\cos 60° = \dfrac{h}{30}$ $\sin 60° = \dfrac{v}{30}$

   $30 \cos 60° = h$ $30 \sin 60° = v$

      $15 \text{ lb} = h$ $15\sqrt{3} \text{ lb} = v$

39. $x^2 + x - 20 = (x + 5)(x - 4)$

The best answer is A.

Technology:
Using Parametric Equations

1. about 63 feet

2. yes

8-7   Using Parametric Equations to Model Motion

1. The relative vertical position of the ball varies due to the effects of gravity slowing the vertical velocity on the way up and increasing it on the way down.

2. The hockey players want all of the velocity to be in the horizontal direction to keep the puck on the ice.

3. The projectile is launched straight up; it travels no distance in the horizontal direction; sample answers: toy rockets, a tip-off in a basketball game.

4. gravity

5. Zero; for a moment, it is not going up or down.

6. equal magnitude with opposite directions

7. a. $x = t|\vec{v}| \cos \theta$

      $= 75t \cos 25°$

    $y = 5 + t|\vec{v}| \sin \theta + \dfrac{1}{2}gt^2$

      $= 5 + 75t \sin 25° + \dfrac{1}{2}(-32)t^2$

      $= 5 + 75t \sin 25° - 16t^2$

   b. See students' work.

   c. $y = 0$ when $t = ?$

     $0 = 5 + 75t \sin 25° - 16t^2$

     $0 \approx -16t^2 + 31.7t + 5$

     $t \approx \dfrac{-31.7 \pm \sqrt{(31.7)^2 - 4(-16)(5)}}{-32}$

       ≈ 2.13

     When $t \approx 2.13$, $x \approx 145$ ft.

   d. from graph, 20.7 ft

   e. No, x will never be 215 ft.

8. $\sin 40° = \dfrac{v}{50}$ 9. $\cos 42° = \dfrac{h}{62}$

   $50 \sin 40° = v$ $62 \cos 42° = h$

   $32.14 \text{ ft/s} \approx v$ $46.07 \text{ ft/s} \approx h$

10. a. 300 mph = 440 ft/s

     $x = t|\vec{v}| \cos \theta$

     $= 440t \cos 0°$

     $= 440t$

    $y = 3500 + t|\vec{v}| \sin \theta + \dfrac{1}{2}gt^2$

     $= 3500 + 440t \sin 0° + \dfrac{1}{2}(-32)t^2$

     $= 3500 - 16t^2$

   b. See students' graphs.

   c. $y = 0$ when $t = ?$

     $16t^2 = 3500$

      $t^2 = 218.75$

       $t \approx 14.8$ s

   d. when $t \approx 14.8$, $x \approx 440(14.8)$

                    ≈ 6512 feet

                    ≈ 1.23 miles

11. a. $x = 100t \cos 10°$

    $y = 100t \sin 10° - 16t^2$

    $y = 0$ when $t = ?$

     $0 = 17.36t - 16t^2$

     $0 = t(17.36 - 16t)$

     $t = 0,\ 17.36 - 16t = 0$

                 $17.36 = 16t$

                 $1.09 \approx t$

    $x \approx 100(1.09) \cos 10°$

      ≈ 107 ft

b. $x = 100t \cos 30°$

$y = 100t \sin 30° - 16t^2$

$y = 0$ when $t = ?$

$0 = 50t - 16t^2$

$0 = t(50 - 16t)$

$t = 0,\ 50 - 16t = 0$

$\qquad\qquad 50 = 16t$

$\qquad\qquad 3.12 \approx t$

$x \approx 100(3.12) \cos 30° \approx 270$ ft

c. $x = 100t \cos 45°$

$y = 100t \sin 45° - 16t^2$

$y = 0$ when $t = ?$

$0 = 70.7t - 16t^2$

$0 = t(70.7 - 16t)$

$t = 0,\ 70.7 - 16t = 0$

$\qquad\qquad 70.7 = 16t$

$\qquad\qquad 4.4 \approx t$

$x \approx 100(4.4) \cos 45° \approx 313$ ft

d. $x = 100t \cos 60°$

$y = 100t \sin 60° - 16t^2$

$y = 0$ when $t = ?$

$0 = 86.6t - 16t^2$

$0 = t(86.6 - 16t)$

$t = 0,\ 86.6 - 16t = 0$

$\qquad\qquad 86.6 = 16t$

$\qquad\qquad 5.4 \approx t$

$x \approx 100(5.4) \cos 60° \approx 271$ ft

e. $x = 100t \cos 80°$

$y = 100t \sin 80° - 16t^2$

$y = 0$ when $t = ?$

$0 = 98.5t - 16t^2$

$0 = t(98.5 - 16t)$

$t = 0,\ 98.5 - 16t = 0$

$\qquad\qquad 98.5 = 16t$

$\qquad\qquad 6.2 \approx t$

$x \approx 100(6.2) \cos 80° \approx 107$ ft

f. $x = 100t \cos 90°$

$y = 100t \sin 90° - 16t^2$

$y = 0$ when $t = ?$

$0 = 100t - 16t^2$

$0 = t(100 - 16t)$

$t = 0,\ 100 - 16t = 0$

$\qquad\qquad 100 = 16t$

$\qquad\qquad 6.25 = t$

$x = 100(6.25) \cos 90° = 0$ ft

12. $45°$. Answers may vary.

13. The range is the same for projectiles fired at angles of $\alpha°$ and $(90 - \alpha)°$. But the time in the air is greater when the angle is greater.

14. a. They both reach the ground at the same time because their vertical displacements are the same. They are both $850 - 16t^2$.

b. first stone: $x = 0$

second stone: $x = 45t \cos 0° = 45t$

stone lands: $850 - 16t^2 = 0$

$\qquad\qquad 850 = 16t^2$

$\qquad\qquad 53.125 = t^2$

$\qquad\qquad 7.3 \approx t$

second stone: $x \approx 45(7.3) \approx 328$ ft

The stones will be 328 feet apart.

15. a. See students' work.

b. See students' work.

16. $x = 88t \cos 30°$

$y = 88t \sin 30° - 16t^2$

a. $y = 0$ when $t = ?$

$0 = 44t - 16t^2$

$0 = t(44 - 16t)$

$t = 0,\ 44 - 16t = 0$

$\qquad\qquad 44 = 16t$

$\qquad\qquad t = 2.75$ s

b. $x = 88(2.75) \cos 30°$

$\quad \approx 209.58$ ft or 69.86 yd

$30 + 69.86 = 99.86$ yard line. This is 0.14 yard or about 5 inches from the Cowboys' goal line.

c. $y' = 44 - 32t$

$0 = 44 - 32t$

$32t = 44$

$t = 1.375$ s

$y = 88(1.375) \sin 30° - 16(1.375)^2$

$\quad = 30.24$ ft

17. a. $x = 155t \cos 22°$

$y = 155t \sin 22° - 16t^2 + 3$

b. $420 = 155t \cos 22°$

$t = \dfrac{420}{155 \cos 22°}$

$t \approx 2.92$

$y = 155(2.92) \sin 22° - 16(2.92)^2 + 3$

$\quad \approx 36.12$ ft

It will clear the fence.

c. $0 = 155t \sin 22° - 16t^2 + 3$

$0 \approx -16t^2 + 58.06t + 3$

Use the quadratic equation.

$t \approx \dfrac{-58.06 \pm \sqrt{(58.06)^2 - 4(-16)(3)}}{2(-16)}$

$t \approx -0.05$ or 3.68

$x = 155t \cos 22°$

$x \approx 155(3.68) \cos 22°$

$x \approx 528.87$ ft

18. a. increase

b. reduce or increase depending on initial angle and velocity.

19. No, the projectile will travel four times as far.

20. a. Maximum range is achieved when $\theta = 45°$.

$x = 1200t \cos 45°$

$y = 1200t \sin 45° - 16t^2 + 5$

$0 = 1200t \sin 45° - 16t^2 + 5$

$0 \approx -16t^2 + 848.53t + 5$

Use the quadratic formula.

$t \approx \dfrac{-848.53 \pm \sqrt{(848.53)^2 - 4(-16)(5)}}{2(-16)}$

$t \approx -0.0059$ or 53.0390

$x \approx 1200(53.039) \cos 45° \approx 45,005$ feet

b. $t \approx 53$ seconds

21. a. $y = |\vec{v}|t \sin 85° - 16t^2$

$250 = 4|\vec{v}| \sin 85° - 16(4)^2$

$250 = 3.98|\vec{v}| - 256$

$506 = 3.98|\vec{v}|$

$\vec{v} = 127$ ft/s

b. $x = 127t \cos 85°$

$x = 127(4) \cos 85°$

$= 44.3$ ft or 14.8 yd

$14.8 + 100 = 114.8$ yd

22. $(f \circ g)(x) = f(g(x))$

$= \left(\dfrac{1}{2}x + 6\right)^2 - 4$

$= \dfrac{1}{4}x^2 + 6x + 36 - 4$

$= \dfrac{1}{4}x^2 + 6x + 32$

$(g \circ f)(x) = g(f(x))$

$= \dfrac{1}{2}(x^2 - 4) + 6$

$= \dfrac{1}{2}x^2 - 2 + 6$

$= \dfrac{1}{2}x^2 + 4$

23.

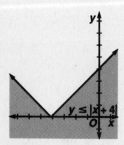

$y \leq |x| + 4$

24. car 1: when $x = 135$, $y = 20.25$

car 2: when $x = 245$, $y = 5.95$

Car 1 prediction is closer to actual.

25. $x = 4t + 1 \rightarrow t = \dfrac{x - 1}{4}$

$y = 5t - 7 \rightarrow t = \dfrac{y + 7}{5}$

$\dfrac{x - 1}{4} = \dfrac{y + 7}{5}$

$5(x - 1) = 4(y + 7)$

$5x - 5 = 4y + 28$

$5x - 4y - 33 = 0$

26. Let x = additional money.

$(0.05)(2400) + 0.08x = 0.06(2400 + x)$

$120 + 0.08x = 144 + 0.06x$

$0.02x = 24$

$x = \$1200$

Chapter 8 Summary and Review

PAGES 456-458   SKILLS AND CONCEPTS

1-4. Answers may vary due to measurement.

1. 4.1 cm, 25°   **2.** 5.7 cm, 25°

3. 5.9 cm, 357°   **4.** 5 cm, 70°

5. $\cos 50° = \dfrac{h}{1.3}$ $\sin 50° = \dfrac{v}{1.3}$

$1.3 \cos 50° = h$ $1.3 \sin 50° = v$

0.8 cm $= h$ 1 cm $= v$

6. $\cos 10° = \dfrac{h}{2.7}$ $\sin 10° = \dfrac{v}{2.7}$

$2.7 \cos 10° = h$ $2.7 \sin 10° = v$

2.7 cm $= h$ 0.5 cm $= v$

7. $\vec{CD} = (7 - 2, 15 - 3)$

$= (5, 12)$

$|\vec{CD}| = \sqrt{5^2 + 12^2}$

$= 13$

8. $\vec{CD} = (4 - (-2), 12 - 8)$

$= (6, 4)$

$|\vec{CD}| = \sqrt{6^2 + 4^2}$

$= \sqrt{52}$

$= 2\sqrt{13}$

9. $\vec{CD} = (0 - 2, 9 - (-3))$

$= (-2, 12)$

$|\vec{CD}| = \sqrt{(-2)^2 + (12)^2}$

$= \sqrt{148}$

$= 2\sqrt{37}$

10. $\vec{CD} = (-5 - (-6), -4 - 4)$

$= (1, -8)$

$|\vec{CD}| = \sqrt{1^2 + (-8)^2}$

$= \sqrt{65}$

11. $\vec{u} = (2, -5) + (3, -1)$

$= (2 + 3, -5 + (-1))$

$= (5, -6)$

12. $\vec{u} = (2, -5) - (3, -1)$

$= (2 - 3, -5 - (-1))$

$= (-1, -4)$

13. $\vec{u} = 3(2, -5) + 2(3, -1)$

$= (6, -15) + (6, -2)$

$= (6 + 6, -15 + (-2))$

$= (12, -17)$

14. $\vec{u} = 3(2, -5) - 2(3, -1)$

$= (6, -15) - (6, -2)$

$= (6 - 6, -15 - (-2))$

$= (0, -13)$

15. $\overrightarrow{EF} = (6 - 2, -2 - (-1), 1 - 4)$

$= (4, -1, -3)$

$= 4\vec{i} - \vec{j} - 3\vec{k}$

16. $\overrightarrow{EF} = (-1 - 9, 5 - 8, 11 - 5)$

$= (-10, -3, 6)$

$= -10\vec{i} - 3\vec{j} + 6\vec{k}$

17. $\overrightarrow{EF} = (2 - (-4), -1 - (-3), 7 - 0)$

$= (6, 2, 7)$

$= 6\vec{i} + 2\vec{j} + 7\vec{k}$

18. $\overrightarrow{EF} = (-4 - 3, 0 - 7, 5 - (-8))$

$= (-7, -7, 13)$

$= -7\vec{i} - 7\vec{j} + 13\vec{k}$

19. $(5, -1) \cdot (-2, 6) = 5 \cdot (-2) + (-1) \cdot 6$

$= -16$

20. $(4, 1, -2) \cdot (3, -4, 4)$

$= 4 \cdot 3 + 1 \cdot (-4) + (-2) \cdot 4$

$= 0$

21.

$(2, -1, 4) \times (6, -2, 1) = \begin{vmatrix} \vec{i} & \vec{j} & \vec{k} \\ 2 & -1 & 4 \\ 6 & -2 & 1 \end{vmatrix}$

$= 7\vec{i} + 22\vec{j} + 2\vec{k}$

$= (7, 22, 2)$

22.

$(5, 2, -1) \times (2, -4, -4) = \begin{vmatrix} \vec{i} & \vec{j} & \vec{k} \\ 5 & 2 & -1 \\ 2 & -4 & -4 \end{vmatrix}$

$= -12\vec{i} + 18\vec{j} - 24\vec{k}$

$= (-12, 18, -24)$

23. $|\vec{r}|^2 = 26^2 + 32^2 - 2(26)(32) \cos 98°$

≈ 1931.58

$|\vec{r}| \approx 43.95 \text{ lb}$

$\dfrac{43.95}{\sin 98°} \approx \dfrac{26}{\sin \theta}$

$\sin \theta \approx \dfrac{26 \sin 98°}{43.95}$

$\theta \approx 35.86° \text{ or } 35°52'$

24. $|\vec{r}|^2 = 30^2 + 12^2 - 2(30)(12) \cos 154°$

≈ 1691.13

$|\vec{r}| \approx 41.12 \text{ m/s}$

$\dfrac{41.12}{\sin 154°} \approx \dfrac{30}{\sin \theta}$

$\sin \theta \approx \dfrac{30 \sin 154°}{41.12}$

$\theta \approx 18.65 \text{ or } 18°39'$

25. $(x - 3, y + 5) = t(4, 2)$

$x = 3 + 4t$

$y = -5 + 2t$

26. $(x + 1, y - 9) = t(-7, -5)$

$x = -1 - 7t$

$y = 9 - 5t$

27. $(x - 4, y) = t(3, -6)$

$x = 4 + 3t$

$y = -6t$

28. $(x + 2, y + 7) = t(0, 8)$

$x = -2$

$y = -7 + 8t$

29. $x = 30t \cos 28°$

$y = 30t \sin 28° - 16t^2$

30. $0 = 30t \sin 28° - 16t^2$

$0 = 14.08t - 16t^2$

$0 = t(14.08 - 16t)$

$t = 0, \quad 14.08 - 16t = 0$

$14.08 = 16t$

$0.88 = t$

$x = 30(0.88) \cos 28°$

PAGE 458   APPLICATIONS AND PROBLEM SOLVING

31. $\overrightarrow{PQ} = (\cos 60°, 0, \sin 60°)$

$= (0.5, 0, 0.87)$

$\vec{F} = -50\vec{k}$

$= (0, 0, -50)$

$\vec{M} = \overrightarrow{PQ} \times \vec{F}$

$= \begin{vmatrix} \vec{i} & \vec{j} & \vec{k} \\ 0.5 & 0 & 0.87 \\ 0 & 0 & -50 \end{vmatrix}$

$= 0\vec{i} + 25\vec{j} + 0\vec{k}$

$|\vec{M}| = \sqrt{0^2 + 25^2 + 0^2} = 25 \text{ lb/ft}$

32. $|\vec{r}|^2 = 70^2 + 90^2 - 2(70)(90) \cos 150°$

$\approx 23{,}911.92$

$|\vec{r}| \approx 154.6 \text{ N}$

$\dfrac{154.6}{\sin 150°} \approx \dfrac{70}{\sin \theta}$

$\sin \theta \approx \dfrac{70 \sin 150°}{154.6}$

$\theta \approx 13.08° \text{ or } 13°5'$

33. $x = 38t \cos 40°$

$y = 38t \sin 40° - 16t^2 + 2$

when $t = 0.5$,

$y = 38(0.5) \sin 40° - 16(0.5)^2 + 2$

$= 10.2 \text{ feet}$

Chapter 8 Test

PAGE 459

1. $\approx 3.1 \text{ cm}, \approx 69°$ 2. $\approx 9.5 \text{ cm}, \approx -8°$

3. $\cos 30° = \dfrac{h}{2.9}$ $\sin 30° = \dfrac{v}{2.9}$

$2.9 \cos 30° = h$ $2.9 \sin 30° = v$

$2.5 \text{ cm} = h$ $1.5 \text{ cm} = v$

4. $\cos 135° = \frac{h}{2}$　　　$\sin 135° = \frac{v}{2}$

$2 \cos 135° = h$　　　$2 \sin 135° = v$

$-1.4 \text{ cm} = h$　　　$1.4 \text{ cm} = v$

$1.4 \text{ cm} = |h|$

5. $\vec{AB} = (-1 - 3, \ 9 - 6)$

$= (-4, 3)$

6. $\vec{AB} = (3 - (-2), \ 10 - 7)$

$= (5, 3)$

7. $\vec{AB} = (9 - 2, \ -3 - (-4), \ 7 - 5)$

$= (7, 1, 2)$

8. $\vec{AB} = (-8 - (-4), \ -10 - (-8), \ 2 - (-2))$

$= (-4, -2, 4)$

9. $\vec{r} - \vec{s} = (-1, 3, 4) - (4, 3, -6)$

$= (-5, 0, 10)$

10. $3\vec{s} - 2\vec{r} = 3(4, 3, -6) - 2(-1, 3, 4)$

$= (12, 9, -18) - (-2, 6, 8)$

$= (14, 3, -26)$

11. $\vec{r} + 3\vec{s} = (-1, 3, 4) + 3(4, 3, -6)$

$= (-1, 3, 4) + (12, 9, -18)$

$= (11, 12, -14)$

12. $|\vec{r}| = \sqrt{(-1)^2 + 3^2 + 4^2} = \sqrt{26}$

13. $|\vec{s}| = \sqrt{4^2 + 3^2 + (-6)^2} = \sqrt{61}$

14. $-\vec{i} + 3\vec{j} + 4\vec{k}$

15. $4\vec{i} + 3\vec{j} - 6\vec{k}$

16. $\vec{r} \cdot \vec{s} = (-1, 3, 4) \cdot (4, 3, -6)$

$= (-1) \cdot 4 + 3 \cdot 3 + 4 \cdot (-6)$

$= -19$

17. $\vec{r} \times \vec{s} = \begin{vmatrix} \vec{i} & \vec{j} & \vec{k} \\ -1 & 3 & 4 \\ 4 & 3 & -6 \end{vmatrix}$

$= -30\vec{i} + 10\vec{j} - 15\vec{k}$

$= (-30, 10, -15)$

18. No, $\vec{r} \cdot \vec{s} \neq 0$.

19. $x = 3 + 2t$　　　**20.** $x = -2 + t$

$y = 11 - 5t$　　　　　　$y = 9t$

21. $x = 12 - 4t$

$y = -8 - 7t$

22. $x = -2t + 6 \rightarrow \dfrac{6 - x}{2} = t$

$y = 9t - 8 \rightarrow \dfrac{y + 8}{9} = t$

$\dfrac{6 - x}{2} = \dfrac{y + 8}{9}$

$9(6 - x) = 2(y + 8)$

$54 - 9x = 2y + 16$

$38 - 9x = 2y$

$-\dfrac{9}{2}x + 19 = y$

23. a.

$|\vec{r}|^2 = 16^2 + 3^2 - 2(16)(3) \cos 35°$

≈ 186.36

$|\vec{r}| \approx 13.7 \text{ knots}$

b. $\dfrac{16}{\sin \theta} \approx \dfrac{13.7}{\sin 35°}$

$\sin \theta \approx \dfrac{16 \sin 35°}{13.7}$

$\theta \approx 138°$

$\tan (180° - \theta) \approx \dfrac{250}{y}$

$y \approx \dfrac{250}{\tan 42°}$

$y \approx 277.7 \text{ m}$

24. $\vec{PQ} = (1.5 \cos 60°, \ 0, \ 1.5 \sin 60°)$

$= (0.75, 0, 1.30)$

$\vec{F} = -110\vec{k}$

$= (0, 0, -110)$

$\vec{M} = \vec{PQ} \times \vec{F}$

$= \begin{vmatrix} \vec{i} & \vec{j} & \vec{k} \\ 0.75 & 0 & 1.30 \\ 0 & 0 & -110 \end{vmatrix}$

$= 82.5 \, \vec{j}$

$= (0, 82.5, 0)$

$|\vec{M}| = \sqrt{0^2 + 82.5^2 + 0^2} = 82.5 \text{ lb/ft}$

25. $x = 28t \cos 35°$

$y = 28t \sin 35° - 16t^2$

when $y = 0, \ t = ?$

$0 = 28t \sin 35° - 16t^2$

$0 = 16.06t - 16t^2$

$0 = t(16.06 - 16t)$

$t = 0, \ 16.06 - 16t = 0$

$16.06 = 16t$

$1 \approx t$

$x \approx 28(1) \cos 35° \approx 23 \text{ ft}$

PAGE 459　　BONUS

Let $\vec{u} = (u_1, 0)$ and $\vec{v} = (v_1, v_2)$.

$\vec{u} \cdot \vec{v} < 0$

$u_1 v_1 + u_2 v_2 < 0$

$u_1 v_1 + 0(v_2) < 0$

$u_1 v_1 < 0$

So, $u_1 < 0$ and $v_1 > 0$ or $u_1 > 0$ and $v_1 < 0$

Therefore, $90° < \theta < 270°$ or $\cos \theta < 0$.

Unit 2 Review

PAGES 460-461

1. $\frac{\pi}{2} \cdot \frac{180}{\pi} = \frac{180\pi}{2\pi}$

$\qquad = 90°$

2. $\frac{3\pi}{4} \cdot \frac{180}{\pi} = \frac{540\pi}{4\pi}$

$\qquad = 135°$

3. $\frac{7\pi}{2} \cdot \frac{180}{\pi} = \frac{1260\pi}{2\pi}$

$\qquad = 630°$

4. $-\frac{7\pi}{12} \cdot \frac{180}{\pi} = \frac{-1260\pi}{12\pi}$

$\qquad = -105°$

5. $\theta = 60° \cdot \frac{\pi}{180} = \frac{\pi}{3}$

$s = r\theta$

$s = 6\left(\frac{\pi}{3}\right)$

$\quad = 2\pi$

$\quad \approx 6.28$ inches

6. $x = 2, \ y = 3, \ r = \sqrt{2^2 + 3^2} = \sqrt{13}$

$\cos \theta = \frac{x}{r} = \frac{2}{\sqrt{13}} = \frac{2\sqrt{13}}{13}$

7. $x = 10, \ y = 2, \ r = \sqrt{10^2 + 2^2} = 2\sqrt{26}$

$\tan \theta = \frac{y}{x} = \frac{2}{10} = \frac{1}{5}$

8. $x = -4, \ y = 1, \ r = \sqrt{(-4)^2 + 1^2} = \sqrt{17}$

$\sin \theta = \frac{y}{r} = \frac{1}{\sqrt{17}} = \frac{\sqrt{17}}{17}$

9. $x = 1, \ y = 0, \ r = \sqrt{1^2 + 0^2} = 1$

$\sec \theta = \frac{r}{x} = \frac{1}{1} = 1$

10. $\sin \pi = 0$

11. $\cot \frac{\pi}{3} = \frac{1}{\tan \frac{\pi}{3}} = \frac{1}{\sqrt{3}} = \frac{\sqrt{3}}{3}$

12. $\sec \frac{3\pi}{4} = \dfrac{1}{\cos \frac{3\pi}{4}}$

$= \dfrac{1}{-\cos \frac{\pi}{4}}$

$= \dfrac{1}{-\frac{\sqrt{2}}{2}}$

$= -\dfrac{2}{\sqrt{2}}$

$= \dfrac{-2\sqrt{2}}{2}$

$= -\sqrt{2}$

13. $\csc \frac{-2\pi}{3} = \dfrac{1}{\sin\left(-\frac{2\pi}{3}\right)}$

$= \dfrac{1}{-\sin \frac{\pi}{3}}$

$= \dfrac{1}{-\frac{\sqrt{3}}{2}}$

$= -\dfrac{2}{\sqrt{3}}$

$= \dfrac{-2\sqrt{3}}{3}$

14. $A = 25°, \ C = 90°, \ B = 180° - 25° - 90°$

$\qquad\qquad\qquad\qquad = 65°$

$\sin 25° = \frac{a}{c}$

$c = \dfrac{12.1}{\sin 25°}$

$c \approx 28.6$

$\cos 25° = \frac{b}{c}$

$b \approx 28.6 \cos 25°$

$b \approx 25.9$

15. $\tan A = \frac{3}{5}$

$A \approx 30.96°$ or $30°58'$

$C = 90°, \ B \approx 180° - 30°58' - 90° \approx 59°2'$

$c = \sqrt{a^2 + b^2} = \sqrt{3^2 + 5^2} = \sqrt{34} \approx 5.8$

16. $B = 63°, \ C = 90°, \ A = 180° - 63° - 90° = 27°$

$\sin 27° = \frac{a}{24}$

$10.9 \approx a$

$a^2 + b^2 = c^2$

$(10.9)^2 + b^2 \approx 24^2$

$b^2 \approx 457.19$

$b \approx 21.4$

17. $A = 46°, \ a = 86, \ c = 200$

$c \sin A = 200 \sin 46° = 143.9$

$a < c \sin A \rightarrow$ No solution exists.

18. $a = 19, \ b = 20, \ A = 65°$

$b \sin A = 20 \sin 65° = 18.13$

$b \sin A < a < b$, so two solutions exist.

$\dfrac{19}{\sin 65°} = \dfrac{20}{\sin B}$

$\qquad B \approx 72°33'$ or $107°27'$

$C_1 \approx 180° - 65° - 72°33' \approx 42°27'$

$C_2 \approx 180° - 65° - 107°27' \approx 7°33'$

$\dfrac{c_1}{\sin 42°24'} \approx \dfrac{19}{\sin 65°} \qquad \dfrac{c_2}{\sin 7°33'} \approx \dfrac{19}{\sin 65°}$

$\qquad c_1 \approx 14.1 \qquad\qquad\qquad c_2 \approx 2.8$

19. $A = 73°, \ B = 65°, \ b = 38$

$b \sin A = 38 \sin 73° \approx 36.3$

$\dfrac{38}{\sin 65°} = \dfrac{a}{\sin 73°}$

$a \approx 40.1$

$a > b \sin A$ and $a > b$ so one solution exists.

$C = 180° - 73° - 65° = 42°$

$\dfrac{c}{\sin 42°} = \dfrac{38}{\sin 65°}$

$c \approx 28.1$

20. $s = \frac{1}{2}(5 + 9 + 6) = 10$

$K = \sqrt{10(10 - 5)(10 - 9)(10 - 6)} \approx 14.1$

21. $C = 180° - 63° - 17° = 100°$

$\dfrac{22}{\sin 63°} = \dfrac{b}{\sin 17°}$

$b \approx 7.22$

$K = \frac{1}{2}ab \sin C$

$\quad \approx \frac{1}{2}(22)(7.22) \sin 100°$

$\quad \approx 78.2$

22. 2, $\frac{360°}{3} = 120°, \ 0°$

23. none, $\frac{180°}{5} = 36°, \ 0°$

203

24. none, $\dfrac{180°}{\frac{1}{2}} = 360°$, $\dfrac{-90°}{\frac{1}{2}} = -180°$

25.

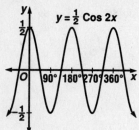

$y = \frac{1}{2}\text{Cos }2x$

26.

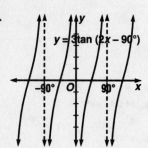

$y = 3\tan(2x - 90°)$

27.

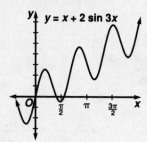

$y = x + 2\sin 3x$

28. Let $\theta = \arccos \frac{1}{4}$.

$\cos \theta = \frac{1}{4}$

29. Let $\theta = \cos^{-1} \frac{2}{3}$.

$\cos \theta = \frac{2}{3}$

$\theta = 48.2°$

$\cot 48.2° \approx 0.89 = \frac{2\sqrt{5}}{5}$

30. Let $\alpha = \sin^{-1} 0$ and $\beta = \tan^{-1} 0$.

$\sin \alpha = 0 \qquad \tan \beta = 0$

$\alpha = 0° \qquad \beta = 0°$

$\cos 0° + \sin 0° = 1 + 0 = 1$

31. Let $\theta = \text{Arccos } \frac{1}{2}$.

$\text{Cos } \theta = \frac{1}{2}$

32. Let $\theta = \text{Tan}^{-1} 1$.

$\text{Tan } \theta = 1$

$\theta = 45°$

$\sin \theta = \frac{\sqrt{2}}{2}$

33. Let $\theta = \text{Arccot } \frac{\sqrt{3}}{3}$.

$\text{Cot } \theta = \frac{\sqrt{3}}{3}$

$\theta = \frac{\pi}{3}$

$\cos\left(\frac{\pi}{2} - \frac{\pi}{3}\right) = \cos\left(\frac{\pi}{6}\right) = \frac{\sqrt{3}}{2}$

34. $y = \arccos x \qquad\qquad x = \arccos y$

$\cos x = y$

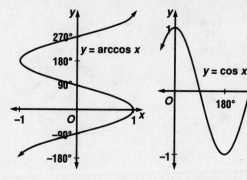

35. $y = \cot x \qquad\qquad x = \cot y$

$\text{arccot } x = y$

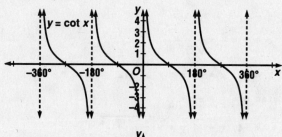

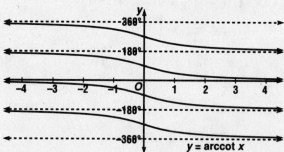

36. $y = \text{Tan } x \qquad\qquad x = \text{Tan } y$

$\text{Arctan } x = y$

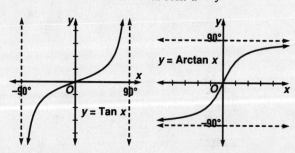

37. $y = \text{Arcsin } 2x \qquad\qquad x = \text{Arcsin } 2y$

$\text{Sin } x = 2y$

$\frac{1}{2}\text{Sin } x = y$

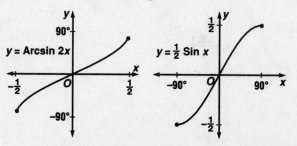

38. $\cos \theta = \dfrac{1}{\sec \theta} = \dfrac{1}{\frac{4}{3}} = \dfrac{3}{4}$

39. $\sin^2 \theta + \cos^2 \theta = 1$

$\sin^2 \theta + \left(\dfrac{1}{3}\right)^2 = 1$

$\sin^2 \theta = \dfrac{8}{9}$

$\sin \theta = \sqrt{\dfrac{8}{9}}$

$= \dfrac{2\sqrt{2}}{3}$

40. $1 + \cot^2 \theta = \csc^2 \theta$

$1 + \cot^2 \theta = \dfrac{1}{\sin^2 \theta}$

$1 + \cot^2 \theta = \dfrac{1}{\left(\frac{1}{2}\right)^2}$

$1 + \cot^2 \theta = 4$

$\cot^2 \theta = 3$

$\cot \theta = \sqrt{3}$

41. $\tan x + \tan x \cot^2 x \overset{?}{=} \sec x \csc x$

$\tan x(1 + \cot^2 x) \overset{?}{=} \sec x \csc x$

$\tan x(\csc^2 x) \overset{?}{=} \sec x \csc x$

$\left(\dfrac{\sin x}{\cos x}\right)\left(\dfrac{1}{\sin^2 x}\right) \overset{?}{=} \sec x \csc x$

$\left(\dfrac{1}{\cos x}\right)\left(\dfrac{1}{\sin x}\right) \overset{?}{=} \sec x \csc x$

$\sec x \csc x = \sec x \csc x$

42.
$\sin (180° - \theta) \overset{?}{=} \tan \theta \cos \theta$

$\sin 180° \cos \theta - \cos 180° \sin \theta \overset{?}{=} \tan \theta \cos \theta$

$0 (\cos \theta) - (-1) \sin \theta \overset{?}{=} \tan \theta \cos \theta$

$\sin \theta \overset{?}{=} \tan \theta \cos \theta$

$\sin \theta \left(\dfrac{\cos \theta}{\cos \theta}\right) \overset{?}{=} \tan \theta \cos \theta$

$\dfrac{\sin \theta}{\cos \theta} \cdot \cos \theta \overset{?}{=} \tan \theta \cos \theta$

$\tan \theta \cos \theta = \tan \theta \cos \theta$

43. $\sin 105° = \sin (45° + 60°)$

$= \sin 45° \cos 60° + \cos 45° \sin 60°$

$= \left(\dfrac{\sqrt{2}}{2}\right)\left(\dfrac{1}{2}\right) + \left(\dfrac{\sqrt{2}}{2}\right)\left(\dfrac{\sqrt{3}}{2}\right)$

$= \dfrac{\sqrt{2} + \sqrt{6}}{4}$

44. $\cos 135° = \cos (90° + 45°)$

$= \cos 90° \cos 45° - \sin 90° \sin 45°$

$= 0 \cdot \dfrac{\sqrt{2}}{2} - 1 \cdot \dfrac{\sqrt{2}}{2}$

$= -\dfrac{\sqrt{2}}{2}$

45. $\cos 15° = \cos (45° - 30°)$

$= \cos 45° \cos 30° + \sin 45° \sin 30°$

$= \dfrac{\sqrt{2}}{2} \cdot \dfrac{\sqrt{3}}{2} + \dfrac{\sqrt{2}}{2} \cdot \dfrac{1}{2}$

$= \dfrac{\sqrt{6} + \sqrt{2}}{4}$

46. $\sin (-210°) = -\sin 210°$

$= -\sin (180° + 30°)$

$= -(\sin 180° \cos 30° + \cos 180° \sin 30°)$

$= -\left(0 \cdot \dfrac{\sqrt{3}}{2} + (-1)\left(\dfrac{1}{2}\right)\right)$

$= \dfrac{1}{2}$

47. $\cos 2x = 1 - 2 \sin^2 x$

$= 1 - 2\left(\dfrac{2}{5}\right)^2$

$= 1 - \dfrac{8}{25}$

$= \dfrac{17}{25}$

48. $\sin \dfrac{x}{2} = \sqrt{\dfrac{1 - \cos x}{2}}$

If $\sin x = \dfrac{2}{5}$, $\cos x = \dfrac{\sqrt{21}}{5}$.

$\sin \dfrac{x}{2} = \sqrt{\dfrac{1 - \frac{\sqrt{21}}{5}}{2}} = \sqrt{\dfrac{5 - \sqrt{21}}{10}}$

49. $\tan \dfrac{x}{2} = \sqrt{\dfrac{1 - \cos x}{1 + \cos x}}$

$= \sqrt{\dfrac{1 - \frac{\sqrt{21}}{5}}{1 + \frac{\sqrt{21}}{5}}}$

$= \sqrt{\dfrac{5 - \sqrt{21}}{5 + \sqrt{21}}}$

50. $\sin 2x = 2 \sin x \cos x$

$= 2\left(\dfrac{2}{5}\right)\left(\dfrac{\sqrt{21}}{5}\right)$

$= \dfrac{4\sqrt{21}}{25}$

51. $\sin^2 x - \sin x = 0$

$\sin x (\sin x - 1) = 0$

$\sin x = 0 \qquad \sin x - 1 = 0$

$x = 0°, 180° \qquad \sin x = 1$

$x = 90°$

52.
$\cos 2x = 4 \cos x - 3$

$2 \cos^2 x - 1 = 4 \cos x - 3$

$2 \cos^2 x - 4 \cos x + 2 = 0$

$\cos^2 x - 2 \cos x + 1 = 0$

$(\cos x - 1)(\cos x - 1) = 0$

$\cos x - 1 = 0$

$\cos x = 1$

$x = 0°$

53. $5 \cos x + 1 = 3 \cos 2x$

$5 \cos x + 1 = 3(2 \cos^2 x - 1)$

$5 \cos x + 1 = 6 \cos^2 x - 3$

$0 = 6 \cos^2 x - 5 \cos x - 4$

$0 = (3 \cos x - 4)(2 \cos x + 1)$

$3 \cos x - 4 = 0 \qquad 2 \cos x + 1 = 0$

$3 \cos x = 4 \qquad 2 \cos x = -1$

$\cos x = \dfrac{4}{3} \qquad \cos x = -\dfrac{1}{2}$

$\varnothing \qquad\qquad x = 120°$

54. $\sqrt{A^2 + B^2} = \sqrt{2^2 + 3^2} = \sqrt{13}$

$\dfrac{2x}{\sqrt{13}} + \dfrac{3y}{\sqrt{13}} - \dfrac{2}{\sqrt{13}} = 0$

$\cos \phi = \dfrac{2}{\sqrt{13}}, \ \sin \phi = \dfrac{3}{\sqrt{13}}$

$p = \dfrac{2}{\sqrt{13}} \text{ or } \dfrac{2\sqrt{13}}{13} \qquad \tan \phi = \dfrac{3}{2}$

$\phi \approx 56°$

55. $5x + 2y - 8 = 0$

$\sqrt{A^2 + B^2} = \sqrt{5^2 + 2^2} = \sqrt{29}$

$\dfrac{5x}{\sqrt{29}} + \dfrac{2y}{\sqrt{29}} - \dfrac{8}{\sqrt{29}} = 0$

$\cos \phi = \dfrac{5}{\sqrt{29}}, \ \sin \phi = \dfrac{2}{\sqrt{29}}$

$p = \dfrac{8}{\sqrt{29}} \text{ or } \dfrac{8\sqrt{29}}{29} \qquad \tan \phi = \dfrac{2}{5}$

$\phi \approx 22°$

56. $3x - y - 7 = 0$

$\sqrt{A^2 + B^2} = \sqrt{3^2 + (-1)^2} = \sqrt{10}$

$\dfrac{3x}{\sqrt{10}} - \dfrac{y}{\sqrt{10}} - \dfrac{7}{\sqrt{10}} = 0$

$\cos \phi = \dfrac{3}{\sqrt{10}}, \ \sin \phi = -\dfrac{1}{\sqrt{10}}$

$p = \dfrac{7}{\sqrt{10}} \text{ or } \dfrac{7\sqrt{10}}{10} \qquad \tan \phi = \dfrac{-1}{3}$

$\phi \approx -18°$

57. $d = \dfrac{Ax_1 + By_1 + C}{-\sqrt{A^2 + B^2}}$

$= \dfrac{2(2) - 2(5) + 3}{-\sqrt{2^2 + (-2)^2}}$

$= \dfrac{-3}{-2.8}$

≈ 1.1

58. $d = \dfrac{Ax_1 + By_1 + C}{-\sqrt{A^2 + B^2}}$

$= \dfrac{-(-2) + 4(2) + 6}{-\sqrt{(-1)^2 + 4^2}}$

$= \dfrac{16}{-4.1}$

≈ -3.9

59. $d = \dfrac{Ax_1 + By_1 + C}{\sqrt{A^2 + B^2}}$

$= \dfrac{4(1) - (-3) - 1}{\sqrt{4^2 + (-1)^2}}$

$= \dfrac{6}{4.1}$

≈ 1.5

60–61. Answers may vary slightly.

60. 4.5 cm, 94°   **61.** 1 cm, 1.8 cm

62. $\vec{u} = (1, -3) + (2, -2)$

$= (3, -5)$

63. $\vec{u} = (2, -2) - (1, -3)$

$= (2 - 1, -2 - (-3))$

$= (1, 1)$

64. $\vec{u} = 3(1, -3) + 2(2, -2)$

$= (3, -9) + (4, -4)$

$= (7, -13)$

65. $\vec{u} = -3(1, -3) + (2, -2)$

$= (-3, 9) + (2, -2)$

$= (-1, 7)$

66. $\vec{u} = 2(3, 1, -1) + (-5, 2, 3)$

$= (6, 2, -2) + (-5, 2, 3)$

$= (1, 4, 1)$

$= \vec{i} + 4\vec{j} + \vec{k}$

67. $\vec{u} = (3, 1, -1) - 2(-5, 2, 3)$

$= (3, 1, -1) - (-10, 4, 6)$

$= (13, -3, -7)$

$= 13\vec{i} - 3\vec{j} - 7\vec{k}$

68. $\vec{u} = 3(3, 1, -1) + 3(-5, 2, 3)$

$= (9, 3, -3) + (-15, 6, 9)$

$= (-6, 9, 6)$

$= -6\vec{i} + 9\vec{j} + 6\vec{k}$

69. $\vec{u} = 4(3, 1, -1) - 2(-5, 2, 3)$

$= (12, 4, -4) - (-10, 4, 6)$

$= (22, 0, -10)$

$= 22\vec{i} - 10\vec{k}$

70. $(4, -2) \cdot (-2, 3) = 4 \cdot (-2) + (-2) \cdot 3 = -14$

71. $(3, -4, 1) \cdot (4, -2, 2)$

$= 3 \cdot 4 + (-4)(-2) + 1 \cdot 2$

$= 22$

72.

$(5, -2, 5) \times (-1, 0, 3) = \begin{vmatrix} \vec{i} & \vec{j} & \vec{k} \\ 5 & -2 & 5 \\ -1 & 0 & -3 \end{vmatrix}$

$= 6\vec{i} + 10\vec{j} - 2\vec{k}$

$= (6, 10, -2)$

73. $(x - 0, y - 5) = t(-1, 5)$

$(x, y - 5) = t(-1, 5)$

$x = -t$

$y = 5 + 5t$

74. $(x - 4, y - (-3)) = t(-2, -2)$

$(x - 4, y + 3) = t(-2, -2)$

$x = 4 - 2t$

$y = -3 - 2t$

Unit 3 Advanced Functions and Graphing
Chapter 9 Polar Coordinates and Complex Numbers

9-1 Polar Coordinates

PAGE 470   CHECKING FOR UNDERSTANDING

1. North Pole, South Pole

2. because the graph of reference angles and/or negative radii can result in the same point

3. The points 2 units from the origin in the opposite direction are on the circle where $r = 2$.

4.

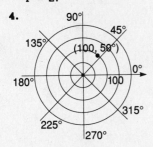

$$(r, \theta + 360k^{\circ})$$
$$\rightarrow (100, 50^{\circ} + (-1)360^{\circ}) \rightarrow (100, -310^{\circ})$$
$$(-r, \theta + (2k + 1)180^{\circ})$$
$$\rightarrow (-100, 50^{\circ} + (1)180^{\circ}) \rightarrow (-100, 230^{\circ})$$
$$\rightarrow (-100, 50^{\circ} + (-1)180^{\circ}) \rightarrow (-100, -130^{\circ})$$

5.

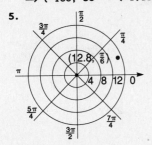

$$(r, \theta + 2k\pi)$$
$$\rightarrow \left(12.8, \frac{\pi}{6} + 2(-1)\pi\right) \rightarrow \left(12.8, -\frac{11\pi}{6}\right)$$
$$(-r, \theta + (2k + 1)\pi)$$
$$\rightarrow \left(-12.8, \frac{\pi}{6} + (1)\pi\right) \rightarrow \left(-12.8, \frac{7\pi}{6}\right)$$
$$\rightarrow \left(-12.8, \frac{\pi}{6} + (-1)\pi\right) \rightarrow \left(-12.8, -\frac{5\pi}{6}\right)$$

6.

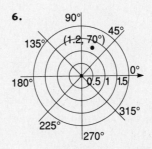

$$(r, \theta + 360k^{\circ})$$
$$\rightarrow (1.2, 70^{\circ} + (-1)360^{\circ}) \rightarrow (1.2, -290^{\circ})$$
$$(-r, \theta + (2k + 1)180^{\circ})$$
$$\rightarrow (-1.2, 70^{\circ} + (1)180^{\circ}) \rightarrow (-1.2, 250^{\circ})$$
$$\rightarrow (-1.2, 70^{\circ} + (-1)180^{\circ}) \rightarrow (-1.2, -110^{\circ})$$

7.   8.

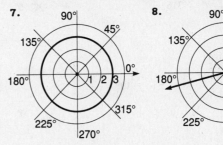

9.

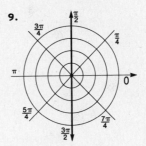

PAGES 470–471   EXERCISES

10.   11.

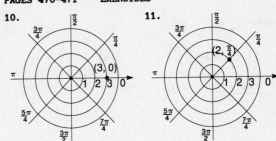

207

12.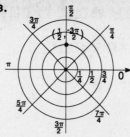

13.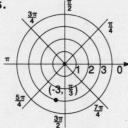

14.

15.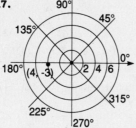

16.

17.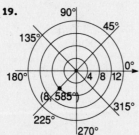

18.

19.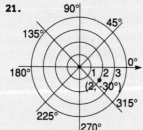

20.

21.

22. Sample answer: $\left(2, \dfrac{\pi}{6}\right)$

$(r, \theta + 2k\pi) \rightarrow \left(2, \dfrac{\pi}{6} + 2(-1)\pi\right) \rightarrow \left(2, -\dfrac{11\pi}{6}\right)$

$(-r, \theta + (2k+1)\pi) \rightarrow \left(-2, \dfrac{\pi}{6} + \pi\right) \rightarrow \left(-2, \dfrac{7\pi}{6}\right)$

$\rightarrow \left(-2, \dfrac{\pi}{6} - \pi\right) \rightarrow \left(-2, -\dfrac{5\pi}{6}\right)$

23. Sample answer: $\left(-2, -\dfrac{\pi}{3}\right)$

$(r, \theta + 2k\pi) \rightarrow \left(-2, -\dfrac{\pi}{3} + 2\pi\right) \rightarrow \left(-2, \dfrac{5\pi}{3}\right)$

$(-r, \theta + (2k+1)\pi)$

$\rightarrow \left(-(-2), -\dfrac{\pi}{3} + \pi\right) \rightarrow \left(2, \dfrac{2\pi}{3}\right)$

$\rightarrow \left(-(-2), -\dfrac{\pi}{3} - \pi\right) \rightarrow \left(2, -\dfrac{4\pi}{3}\right)$

24. Sample answer: $(100, 208°)$

$(r, \theta + 360k°)$

$\rightarrow (100, 208° - 360°) \rightarrow (100, -152°)$

$(-r, \theta + (2k+1)180°)$

$\rightarrow (-100, 208° - 540°) \rightarrow (-100, -332°)$

$\rightarrow (-100, 208° - 180°) \rightarrow (-100, 28°)$

25.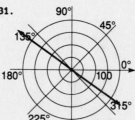

26.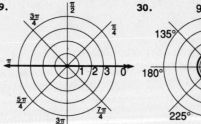

27.

28.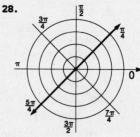

29.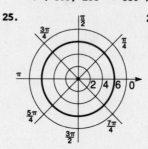

30.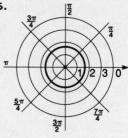

31.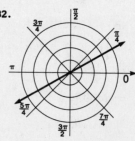

32.

33.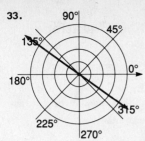

34.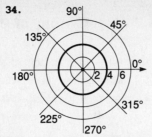

35.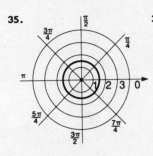

36.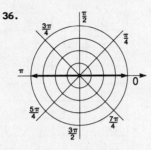

37. $r = \sqrt{(-3)^2 + 4^2} = 5$

$\sin \theta = \frac{4}{5}, \theta \approx 53°$

$180° - 53° = 127°$

Sample answer: $(5, 127°)$

38. The internal triangle $\triangle MNL$ is an equilateral triangle with sides of length 8. Since the sides of external $\triangle ABC$ are parallel to those of $\triangle MNL$, the measure of each angle of $\triangle ABC$ is

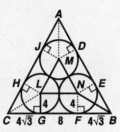

$60°$, Therefore, $\triangle ABC$ is an equilateral triangle. Now, $\angle LCG = 30° = \angle NBF$, so $\angle CLG = 60° = \angle BNF$ and $CG = BF = 4\sqrt{3}$. Also, $GF = LN = 4 + 4 = 8$. Thus each side of $\triangle ABC$ is $4\sqrt{3} + 8 + 4\sqrt{3} = 8 + 8\sqrt{3}$. If h is the height of $\triangle ABC$,

$\sin C - \sin 60° = \dfrac{h}{8 + 8\sqrt{3}}$

$\dfrac{\sqrt{3}}{2} = \dfrac{h}{8 + 8\sqrt{3}}$

$h = 4\sqrt{3} + 12.$

Area $= \frac{1}{2}(8 + 8\sqrt{3})(4\sqrt{3} + 12) = 64\sqrt{3} + 96.$

Therefore, the area of $\triangle ABC$ is $64\sqrt{3} + 96$ square units.

39. a. $(90, 0°), (90, 90°)$ **b.** $(60.5, 45°)$

40. a. due north   **b.** 5 miles

41. $x = \dfrac{-(-9) \pm \sqrt{(-9)^2 - 4(4)(5)}}{2(4)}$

$= \dfrac{9 \pm \sqrt{1}}{8}$

$= \dfrac{9 \pm 1}{8}$

$x = \dfrac{10}{8}$ or $x = \dfrac{8}{8}$

$= 1.25$ $= 1$

42. $\dfrac{3\pi}{8} \cdot \dfrac{180°}{\pi} = 67.5° = 67°30'$

43. $\cos 20° + \sin 50° \approx 1.7057$

$\cos 80° + \sin 40° \approx 0.8164$

$\cos 20° + \sin 50°$ is greater.

44. $\cot \theta = \dfrac{5}{\sqrt{2}} = \dfrac{5\sqrt{2}}{2}$

45. $x = t|\vec{v}|\cos \theta$

$= 0.5(60)\cos 60°$

$= 15$ ft

$y = t|\vec{v}|\sin \theta + \frac{1}{2}gt^2$

$= 0.5(60)\sin 60° + \frac{1}{2}(-32)(0.5)^2$

≈ 22 ft

46. 2 h 12 min $= 2.2$ h

$(2.2 \text{ h})\left(\dfrac{360°}{12 \text{ h}}\right) = 66°$

The best answer is A.

9-2A Graphing Calculators: Graphing Polar Equations

PAGE 474   EXERCISES

1. $x = (0.5\theta)\cos \theta, \ y = (0.5\theta)\sin \theta$

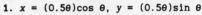

2. $x = (3\sqrt{\cos 2\theta})\cos \theta, \ y = (3\sqrt{\cos 2\theta})\sin \theta$

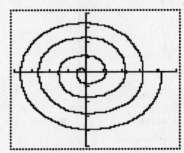

3. $x = (6 + 6 \sin \theta)\cos \theta, \ y = (6 + 6 \sin \theta)\sin \theta$

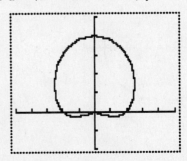

209

4. $x = (7 + 4 \cos \theta) \cos \theta$, $y = (7 + 4 \cos \theta) \sin \theta$

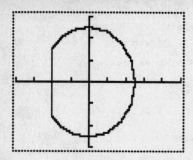

5. $x = (8 \sin 4\theta) \cos \theta$, $y = (8 \sin 4\theta) \sin \theta$

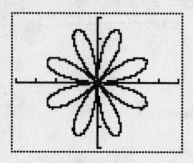

6. $x = (4\sqrt{\sin 2\theta}) \cos \theta$, $y = (4\sqrt{\sin 2\theta}) \sin \theta$

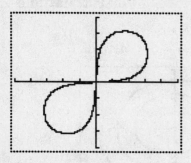

7. $x = (1 + 2 \sin \theta) \cos \theta$, $y = (1 + 2 \sin \theta) \sin \theta$

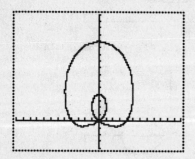

8. $x = (10 + 10 \cos \theta) \cos \theta$,
   $y = (10 + 10 \cos \theta) \sin \theta$

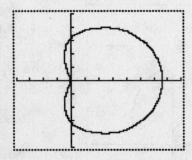

PAGES 479-480   CHECKING FOR UNDERSTANDING

1. the spiral of Archimedes

2. r must be a real number, thus requiring the use
   of radians, which are real numbers.

3.

θ	$\cos \theta$	$8 \cos \theta$	(r, θ)
$0°$	1	8	$(8, 0°)$
$30°$	0.9	6.9	$(6.9, 30°)$
$60°$	0.5	4	$(4, 30°)$
$90°$	0	0	$(0, 90°)$
$120°$	−0.5	−4	$(−4, 120°)$
$150°$	−0.9	−6.9	$(−6.9, 150°)$
$180°$	−1	−8	$(−8, 180°)$
$210°$	−0.9	−6.9	$(−6.9, 210°)$
$240°$	−0.5	−4	$(−4, 240°)$
$270°$	0	0	$(0, 270°)$
$300°$	0.5	4	$(4, 300°)$
$330°$	0.9	6.9	$(6.9, 330°)$

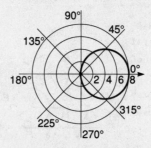

4.

θ	$\sin \theta$	$2 + 2 \sin \theta$	(r, θ)
$0°$	0	2	$(2, 0°)$
$30°$	0.5	3	$(3, 30°)$
$60°$	0.9	3.7	$(3.7, 60°)$
$90°$	1	4	$(4, 90°)$
$120°$	0.9	3.7	$(3.7, 120°)$
$150°$	0.5	3	$(3, 150°)$
$180°$	0	2	$(2, 180°)$
$210°$	−0.5	1	$(1, 210°)$
$240°$	−0.9	0.3	$(0.3, 240°)$
$270°$	−1	0	$(0, 270°)$
$300°$	−0.9	0.3	$(0.3, 300°)$
$330°$	−0.5	1	$(1, 330°)$

5. cardioid

6.

spiral of Archimedes

7.

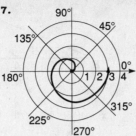

spiral of Archimedes

8.

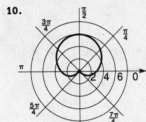

limaçon

9.

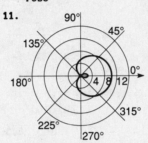

rose

10.

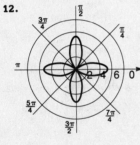

cardioid

11.

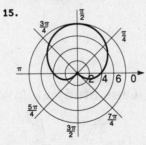

limaçon

12.

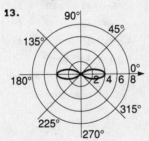

rose

13.

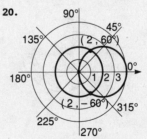

lemniscate

14.

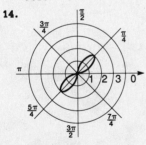

lemniscate

15.

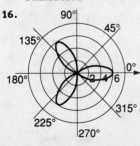

cardioid

16.

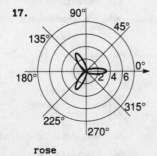

rose

17.

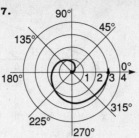

rose

18.

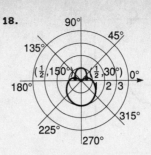

Substitute sin θ for r in second equation.

$\sin θ = 1 - \sin θ$

$\sin θ = \dfrac{1}{2}$

$θ = 30°$ or $150°$

$r = \sin θ$

$r = \sin 30°$ or $r = \sin 150°$

$= \dfrac{1}{2}$ $\qquad = \dfrac{1}{2}$

$\left(\dfrac{1}{2}, 30°\right), \left(\dfrac{1}{2}, 150°\right)$

19.

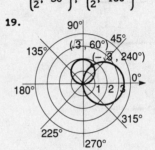

Substitute $2\sqrt{3} \cos θ$ for r in second equation.

$2\sqrt{3} \cos θ = 2 \sin θ$

$\dfrac{\cos θ}{\sin θ} = \dfrac{2}{2\sqrt{3}}$

$\cot θ = \dfrac{\sqrt{3}}{3}$

$θ = 60°$ or $240°$

$r = 2 \sin θ$

$r = 2 \sin 60°$ or $r = 2 \sin 240°$

$= \sqrt{3}$ $\qquad = -\sqrt{3}$

$(\sqrt{3}, 60°), (-\sqrt{3}, 240°)$

20.

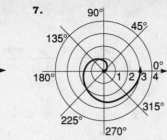

Substitute $4 \cos θ$ for r in second equation.

$4 \cos θ = 2 \sin 90°$

$4 \cos θ = 2$

$\cos θ = \dfrac{1}{2}$

$θ = 60°$ or $-60°$

$r = 2 \sin 90° = 2$

$(2, 60°), (2, -60°)$

211

21.

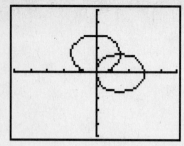

(2.1, 0.8)

22.

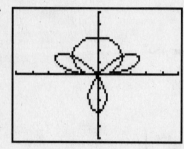

(0, 0), (2.0, 0.8), (2.1, 1.3)

23.

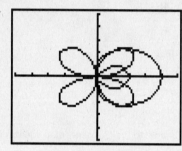

(3.0, -0.9), (1.8, 0.3), (3.0, 0.9), (2.2, -1.2)

24. length of petal = $|a|$ units

25. If n is odd, the rose has n petals, each of which is traced twice from 0 to 2π. If n is even, the rose has $2n$ petals, each of which is traced once from 0 to 2π.

26. The graph is the same as that of the sine but rotated counterclockwise.

27. 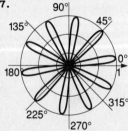 **28.**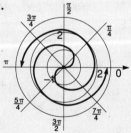

a rose with 10 petals

29. See students' work.

30.

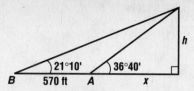

$$\tan 36°40' = \frac{h}{x} \qquad \tan 21°10' = \frac{h}{x + 570}$$

$$x \tan 36°40' = h \quad (x + 570)\tan 21°10' = h$$

$$x \tan 36°40' = (x + 570)\tan 21°10'$$

$$0.7445x \approx 0.3872x + 220.71$$

$$0.3573x \approx 220.71$$

$$x \approx 617.72$$

$$\tan 36°40' \approx \frac{h}{617.72}$$

$$h \approx 460$$

The peak is about 460 feet above the plain.

31. $\sin 255° = \sin (300° - 45°)$

$= \sin 300° \cos 45° - \cos 300° \sin 45°$

$= -\frac{\sqrt{3}}{2} \cdot \frac{\sqrt{2}}{2} - \frac{1}{2} \cdot \frac{\sqrt{2}}{2}$

$= \frac{-\sqrt{6} - \sqrt{2}}{4}$

32. $(3, -2, 4) \cdot (1, -4, 0) = 3(1) + (-2)(-4) + 4(0)$

$= 11$

No, the vectors are not perpendicular.

33. $(r, \theta + 360k°)$

$\rightarrow (10, -20° + (1)360°) \rightarrow (10, 340°)$

$(-r, \theta + (2k + 1)180°)$

$\rightarrow (-10, -20° + (1)180°) \rightarrow (-10, 160°)$

$\rightarrow (-10, -20° + (-1)180°) \rightarrow (-10, -200°)$

34. least common multiple of 3, 4, and 5:

$3 \cdot 4 \cdot 5 = 60$

To have a remainder of 2 when dividing by each of these numbers, add 2 to 60. The answer is 62.

Case Study Follow-Up

PAGE 481

1. increase in radius: 20%

   increase in area of hole: 80%

2. 1989: a lemniscate and two cardioids

   1991: a limaçon

3. Assuming the increase from 9300 deaths per year to 200,000 deaths per year is constant over the next 50 years:

   $$50\left(\frac{9300 + 200,000}{2}\right) = 5,232,500$$

   About 5.2 million deaths can be expected.

4. See students' work.

Technology:
Graphing Polar Equations

1.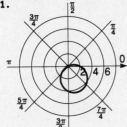

2.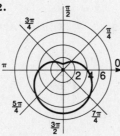

3.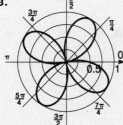

4.

9-3	**Polar and Rectangular Coordinates**

PAGE 486   CHECKING FOR UNDERSTANDING

1. Since $r = \pm 5$, they are both circles of radius 5.

2. Add π to the value of θ.

3. $\frac{\pi}{4} \approx 0.79$ **4.** 1.35   **5.** 1.18

6. $r = \sqrt{5^2 + 12^2} = 13$

$\theta = \text{Arctan}\, \frac{12}{5} \approx 1.18$

$(13, 1.18)$

7. $r = \sqrt{(-2)^2 + (-2)^2} = 2\sqrt{2}$

$\theta = \text{Arctan}\, \frac{-2}{-2} + \pi \approx 3.93$

$(2\sqrt{2}, 3.93)$

8. $r = \sqrt{(-1)^2 + (-3)^2} = \sqrt{10}$

$\theta = \text{Arctan}\, \frac{-3}{-1} + \pi \approx 4.39$

$(\sqrt{10}, 4.39)$

9. $x = 3 \cos \frac{\pi}{2}$ $y = 3 \sin \frac{\pi}{2}$

$= 3(0)$ $= 3(1)$

$= 0$ $= 3$

$(0, 3)$

10. $x = -2 \cos \frac{\pi}{4}$ $y = -2 \sin \frac{\pi}{4}$

$= -2\left(\frac{\sqrt{2}}{2}\right)$ $= -2\left(\frac{\sqrt{2}}{2}\right)$

$= -\sqrt{2}$ $= -\sqrt{2}$

$(-\sqrt{2}, -\sqrt{2})$

---

11. $x = 2.5 \cos 2$ $y = 2.5 \sin 2$

≈ -1.04 ≈ 2.27

$(-1.04, 2.27)$

12. $x^2 + y^2 = 9$

$(r \cos \theta)^2 + (r \sin \theta)^2 = 9$

$r^2(\cos^2 \theta + \sin^2 \theta) = 9$

$r^2 = 9$

$r = \pm 3$

The polar equation is $r = 3$ or $r = -3$.

13. $\sqrt{x^2 + y^2} = 7$

$x^2 + y^2 = 49$

PAGES 486-487   EXERCISES

14. $r = \sqrt{0^2 + 1.5^2} = 1.5$

$\theta = \text{Arctan}\, \frac{1.5}{0} = \frac{\pi}{2}$

$\left(1.5, \frac{\pi}{2}\right)$

15. $r = \sqrt{0^2 + 3^2} = 3$

$\theta = \text{Arctan}\, \frac{3}{0} = \frac{\pi}{2}$

$\left(3, \frac{\pi}{2}\right)$

16. $r = \sqrt{\left(\frac{\sqrt{3}}{2}\right)^2 + \left(\frac{1}{2}\right)^2} = 1$

$\theta = \text{Arctan}\, \frac{\sqrt{3}}{3} = \frac{\pi}{6}$

$\left(1, \frac{\pi}{6}\right)$

17. $r = \sqrt{2^2 + 0^2} = 2$

$\theta = \text{Arctan}\, \frac{0}{2} = 0$

$(2, 0)$

18. $r = \sqrt{(-0.25)^2 + 0^2} = 0.25$

$\theta = \text{Arctan}\, \frac{0}{-0.25} + \pi = \pi$

$(0.25, \pi)$

19. $r = \sqrt{(-\sqrt{2})^2 + (-\sqrt{2})^2} = 2$

$\theta = \text{Arctan}\, \frac{-\sqrt{2}}{-\sqrt{2}} + \pi = \frac{5\pi}{4}$

$\left(2, \frac{5\pi}{4}\right)$

20. $x = \sqrt{2} \cos 45°$ $y = \sqrt{2} \sin 45°$

$= 1$ $= 1$

$(1, 1)$

21. $x = 5 \cos 0.93$ $y = 5 \sin 0.93$

≈ 2.99 ≈ 4.01

$(2.99, 4.01)$

22. $x = \sqrt{29} \cos (-1.19)$ $y = \sqrt{29} \sin (-1.19)$

≈ 2.00 ≈ -5.00

$(2.00, -5.00)$

23. $x = \sqrt{2} \cos 4.39$ $y = \sqrt{2} \sin 4.39$

≈ -0.45 ≈ -1.34

$(-0.45, -1.34)$

24. $x = \sqrt{13} \cos (-0.59)$ $y = \sqrt{13} \sin (-0.59)$

≈ 3.00 ≈ -2.01

$(3.00, -2.01)$

25. $x = 3.464 \cos 2.09$ $y = 3.464 \sin 2.09$

≈ -1.72 ≈ 3.01

$(-1.72, 3.01)$

26. $y = -5$
$r \sin \theta = -5$
$r = -5 \csc \theta$

27. $x = 10$
$r \cos \theta = 10$
$r = 10 \sec \theta$

28.
$x^2 + y^2 = 7$
$(r \cos \theta)^2 + (r \sin \theta)^2 = 7$
$r^2(\cos^2 \theta + \sin^2 \theta) = 7$
$r^2 = 7$
$r = \sqrt{7}$ or $r = \sqrt{-7}$

29.
$2x^2 + 2y^2 = 5y$
$2(r \cos \theta)^2 + 2(r \sin \theta)^2 = 5(r \sin \theta)$
$2r^2(\cos^2 \theta + \sin^2 \theta) = 5r \sin \theta$
$2r^2 = 5r \sin \theta$
$r = \dfrac{5}{2} \sin \theta$

30. $r = 12$
$\sqrt{x^2 + y^2} = 12$
$x^2 + y^2 = 144$

31. $\theta = -45°$
$\text{Arctan } \dfrac{y}{x} = -45°$
$\text{Tan}(-45°) = \dfrac{y}{x}$
$-1 = \dfrac{y}{x}$
$y = -x$

32. $r \sin \theta = 4$
$y = 4$

33. $r = -2 \sec \theta$
$r = -2\dfrac{1}{\cos \theta}$
$r \cos \theta = -2$
$x = -2$

34. $x = y$
$r \cos \theta = r \sin \theta$
$\cos \theta = \sin \theta$
$\tan \theta = 1$
$\theta = 45°$

35. $r = \cos \theta + \sin \theta$
$r^2 = r \cos \theta + r \sin \theta$
$x^2 + y^2 = x + y$

36. $r = \dfrac{5}{3 \cos \theta + 8 \sin \theta}$
$r(3 \cos \theta + 8 \sin \theta) = 5$
$3r \cos \theta + 8r \sin \theta = 5$
$3x + 8y = 5$
$3x + 8y - 5 = 0$

37. Let the coordinates of $P(r, \theta)$ be (x, y).
Thus $PR = y$ and $OR = x$.
$\sin \theta = \dfrac{y}{r}$, so $y = r \sin \theta$
$\cos \theta = \dfrac{x}{r}$, so $x = r \cos \theta$

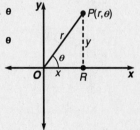

38. $A = \dfrac{\ell^2 \pi}{4k}$
$4380 = \dfrac{132^2 \cdot \pi}{4k}$
$k \approx 3.124$
So, $r \approx 132 \cos 3.124\theta$.

39. $A = \dfrac{\ell^2 \pi}{4k}$
$7542 = \dfrac{\ell^2 \pi}{4.5}$
$\ell^2 \approx 48{,}013$
$\ell \approx 219$ meters

40. a. $F = W \cos 60° = 0.5W$
  b. The rider feels only half his or her weight, and the rider comes out of his or her seat.

41. $y = \dfrac{x^4(x + 2)}{x(x + 2)}$

42. $d_1 = \dfrac{x - y + 2}{\sqrt{2}}$ $d_2 = \dfrac{y - 5}{1}$
Since $d_1 = d_2$: $\dfrac{x - y + 2}{\sqrt{2}} = y - 5$
$x - y + 2 = \sqrt{2}y - 5\sqrt{2}$
$x - (1 + \sqrt{2})y + 2 + 5\sqrt{2} = 0$

43. equal

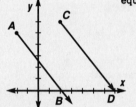

44. $(r, \theta + 360k°)$
$\rightarrow (90, 208° + (0)360°) \rightarrow (90, 208°)$
$\rightarrow (90, 208° + (-1)360°) \rightarrow (90, -152°)$
$(-r, \theta + (2k + 1)180°)$
$\rightarrow (-90, 208° + (-1)180°) \rightarrow (-90, 28°)$

45.

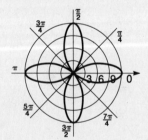

46. $\dfrac{\dfrac{1}{8} + \dfrac{6}{4}}{\dfrac{3}{16}} \cdot \dfrac{16}{16} = \dfrac{2 + 24}{3} = \dfrac{26}{3}$

$\dfrac{\dfrac{2}{12} + \dfrac{1}{3}}{\dfrac{12}{16}} \cdot \dfrac{48}{48} = \dfrac{8 + 16}{36} = \dfrac{24}{36}$

Quantity A is greater. A

9-4 Polar Form of a Linear Function

PAGE 491   CHECKING FOR UNDERSTANDING

1. When you find the values of the sine and cosine functions, use their signs to determine in which quandrant the normal lies.

2. because all possible values of $\cos \theta$ are contained in that range

3. $\sqrt{2^2 + 3^2} = \sqrt{13}$

$\dfrac{2x}{\sqrt{13}} + \dfrac{3y}{\sqrt{13}} - \dfrac{5}{\sqrt{13}} = 0$

4. $-\sqrt{2^2 + 1^2} = -\sqrt{5}$

$-\dfrac{2x}{\sqrt{5}} + \dfrac{y}{\sqrt{5}} - \dfrac{6}{\sqrt{5}} = 0$

5. $\dfrac{x}{\sqrt{10}} - \dfrac{3y}{\sqrt{10}} - \dfrac{4}{\sqrt{10}} = 0$

$\cos \phi = \dfrac{1}{\sqrt{10}}$, $\sin \phi = -\dfrac{3}{\sqrt{10}}$, $p = \dfrac{4}{\sqrt{10}}$ or $\dfrac{2\sqrt{10}}{5}$

$\phi = \arctan(-3)$

$\phi \approx -72°$

$p = r \cos (\theta - \phi)$

$\dfrac{2\sqrt{10}}{5} = r \cos (\theta + 72°)$

6. $2 = r \cos \left(\theta - \dfrac{\pi}{4}\right)$

$2 = r \left(\cos \theta \cos \dfrac{\pi}{4} + \sin \theta \sin \dfrac{\pi}{4}\right)$

$2 = \dfrac{\sqrt{2}}{2} r \cos \theta + \dfrac{\sqrt{2}}{2} r \sin \theta$

$2 = \dfrac{\sqrt{2}}{2}x + \dfrac{\sqrt{2}}{2}y$

$0 = x + y - 2\sqrt{2}$

7.

θ	20°	25°	50°	60°
r	2.31	2.44	4	5.85

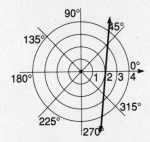

8.

θ	10°	25°	40°	60°
r	3.46	4.24	6	17.3

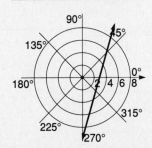

PAGES 492-493   EXERCISES

9.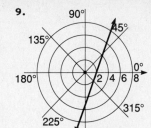

10.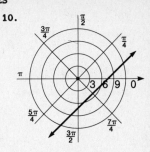

11.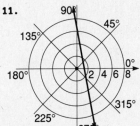

12.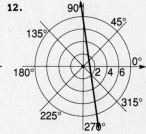

13.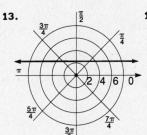

14.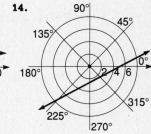

15. $x = 12$

$r \cos \theta = 12$

16. $-\dfrac{x}{\sqrt{2}} + \dfrac{y}{\sqrt{2}} = 0$

$\cos \phi = -\dfrac{\sqrt{2}}{2}$, $\sin \phi = \dfrac{\sqrt{2}}{2}$, $p = 0$

$\phi = \arctan 1$

$\phi = 45°$

Since $\cos \phi$ is negative and $\sin \phi$ is positive,

$\phi = 135°$.

$p = r \cos (\theta - \phi)$

$0 = r \cos (\theta - 135°)$

17. $-\dfrac{3x}{\sqrt{10}} + \dfrac{y}{\sqrt{10}} - \dfrac{4}{\sqrt{10}} = 0$

$\cos \phi = -\dfrac{3}{\sqrt{10}}$, $\sin \phi = \dfrac{1}{\sqrt{10}}$, $p = \dfrac{4}{\sqrt{10}}$ or $\dfrac{2\sqrt{10}}{5}$

$\phi = \arctan\left(-\dfrac{1}{3}\right)$

$\phi \approx -18°$

Since $\cos \phi$ is negative and $\sin \phi$ is positive,

$\phi \approx 162°$.

$\dfrac{2\sqrt{10}}{5} = r \cos (\theta - 162°)$

18. $\dfrac{2x}{\sqrt{5}} + \dfrac{y}{\sqrt{5}} - \dfrac{5}{\sqrt{5}} = 0$

$\cos \phi = \dfrac{2}{\sqrt{5}}, \ \sin \phi = \dfrac{1}{\sqrt{5}}, \ p = \dfrac{5}{\sqrt{5}} \text{ or } \sqrt{5}$

$\phi = \arctan \dfrac{1}{2}$

$\phi \approx 27°$

$\sqrt{5} = r \cos (\theta - 27°)$

19. $r \cos \left(\theta + \dfrac{\pi}{2} \right) = 0$

$r \left(\cos \theta \cos \dfrac{\pi}{2} - \sin \theta \sin \dfrac{\pi}{2} \right) = 0$

$-r \sin \theta = 0$

$y = 0$

20. $r = \dfrac{1}{\cos \theta}$ 21. $r \cos \theta - 3 = 0$

$r \cos \theta = 1$ $x - 3 = 0$

$x = 1$ $x = 3$

22. $r \cos \left(\theta - \dfrac{\pi}{3} \right) - 4 = 0$

$r \left(\cos \theta \cos \dfrac{\pi}{3} + \sin \theta \sin \dfrac{\pi}{3} \right) - 4 = 0$

$\dfrac{1}{2} r \cos \theta + \dfrac{\sqrt{3}}{2} r \sin \theta - 4 = 0$

$\dfrac{1}{2} x + \dfrac{\sqrt{3}}{3} y - 4 = 0$

$x + \sqrt{3} y - 8 = 0$

23. $m = \dfrac{3 - (-4)}{1 - 2} = -7$

$-4 = -7(2) + b$

$b = 10$

$y = -7x + 10 \longrightarrow 7x + y - 10 = 0$

$\dfrac{7x}{5\sqrt{2}} + \dfrac{y}{5\sqrt{2}} - \dfrac{2}{\sqrt{2}} = 0$

$\cos \phi = \dfrac{7}{5\sqrt{2}}, \ \sin \phi = \dfrac{1}{5\sqrt{2}}, \ p = \dfrac{2}{\sqrt{2}} \text{ or } \sqrt{2}$

$\phi = \arctan \dfrac{1}{7}$

$\phi \approx 8°$

$\sqrt{2} = r \cos (\theta - 8°)$

24. $m = \dfrac{4 - 0}{2 - 0} = 2$

$0 = 2(0) + b$

$b = 0$

$y = 2x \longrightarrow 2x - y = 0$

$\dfrac{2x}{\sqrt{5}} - \dfrac{y}{\sqrt{5}} = 0$

$\cos \phi = \dfrac{2}{\sqrt{5}}, \ \sin \phi = -\dfrac{1}{\sqrt{5}}, \ p = 0$

$\phi = \arctan (-2)$

$\phi \approx -63°$

$0 = r \cos (\theta + 63°)$

25. $y = 0.6x + 4 \longrightarrow -0.6x + y - 4 = 0$

$-3x + 5y - 20 = 0$

$-\dfrac{3x}{\sqrt{34}} + \dfrac{5y}{\sqrt{34}} - \dfrac{20}{\sqrt{34}} = 0$

$\cos \phi = -\dfrac{3}{\sqrt{34}}, \ \sin \phi = \dfrac{5}{\sqrt{34}}, \ p = \dfrac{20}{\sqrt{34}} \text{ or } \dfrac{10\sqrt{34}}{17}$

$\phi = \arctan \dfrac{5}{3}$

$\phi \approx 59°$

Since $\cos \phi$ is negative and $\sin \phi$ is positive, $\phi \approx 121°$.

$\dfrac{10\sqrt{34}}{17} = r \cos (\theta - 121°)$

26. $-2 = -\dfrac{1}{2}(3) + b$

$b = -\dfrac{1}{2}$

$y = -\dfrac{1}{2}x - \dfrac{1}{2} \longrightarrow x + 2y + 1 = 0$

$-\dfrac{x}{\sqrt{5}} - \dfrac{2y}{\sqrt{5}} - \dfrac{1}{\sqrt{5}} = 0$

$\cos \phi = \dfrac{1}{\sqrt{5}}, \ \sin \phi = -\dfrac{2}{\sqrt{5}}, \ p = \dfrac{1}{\sqrt{5}} \text{ or } \dfrac{\sqrt{5}}{5}$

$\phi = \arctan 2$

$\phi \approx 63°$

Since $\cos \phi$ is negative and $\sin \phi$ is negative, $\phi \approx 243°$.

$\dfrac{\sqrt{5}}{5} = r \cos (\theta - 243°)$

27. The MODE settings should be the standard default settings except for DEGREE and PARAM. The RANGE settings will vary. Suggested settings are: Tmin: 0, Tmax: 360, Tstep: 5; X min: -6, Xmax: 6; Xscl: 1, Ymin: -4, Y max: 4, Yscl: 1

28. $2 = r \cos (\theta + 20°)$

$r = \dfrac{2}{\cos(\theta + 20°)}$

parametric equations:

$x = \dfrac{2}{\cos(t + 20°)} \cdot \cos t,$

$y = \dfrac{2}{\cos(t + 20°)} \cdot \sin t$

29.

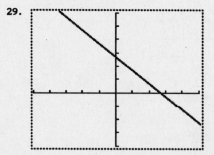

30. Since the angle the normal makes with the line dictates the slope of the line, a normal at 135° provides a line that makes an angle of 45° with the positive direction of the polar axis. In order to have a line at a 90° angle with the given line, it must have its normal at an angle of 90° with the normal of the first line. One such equation might be $3 = r \cos (\theta - 45°)$. For graphs, see students' work.

31. Leonnard Euler

32. $8 = 13r \cos (\theta - 67°)$

   $8 = 13r(\cos \theta \cos 67° + \sin \theta \sin 67°)$

   $8 \approx 5r \cos \theta + 12r \sin \theta$

   $8 \approx 5x + 12y$

   $0 \approx 5x + 12y - 8$

33. $\cos\left(\arcsin \dfrac{\sqrt{3}}{2}\right) = \cos 60°$

   $\qquad\qquad\qquad = \dfrac{1}{2}$ or 0.5

34. $\theta = 2t$

   $x = 3 \cos 2t$

   $y = 3 \sin 2t$

   $(3 \cos 2t, 3 \sin 2t)$

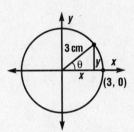

35.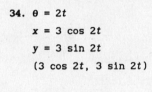

36. $\qquad r = 6$

   $\sqrt{x^2 + y^2} = 6$

   $x^2 + y^2 = 36$

37. area of paper = 9×12 or 108 in^2

   area of typed page = $(9 - 2)(12 - 3)$

   $\qquad\qquad\qquad = 63$ in^2

   $\dfrac{63}{108} = \dfrac{7}{12}$

   The best answer is B.

Mid-Chapter Review

PAGE 493

1.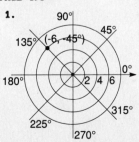

   $(r, \theta + 360k°)$

   $\rightarrow (-6, -45° + (1)360°) \rightarrow (-6, 315°)$

   $(-r, \theta + (2k + 1)180°)$

   $\rightarrow (6, -45° + 180°) \rightarrow (6, 135°)$

   $\rightarrow (6, -45° - 180°) \rightarrow (6, -225°)$

2. 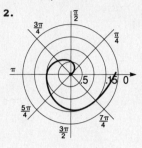   3.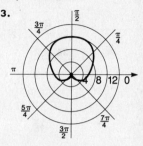

   $\qquad\qquad\qquad\qquad$ cardioid

4. $x = r \cos \theta \qquad\quad y = r \sin \theta$

   $\quad = \sqrt{2} \cos 135° \qquad = \sqrt{2} \sin 135°$

   $\quad = \sqrt{2}\left(-\dfrac{\sqrt{2}}{2}\right) \qquad = \sqrt{2}\left(\dfrac{\sqrt{2}}{2}\right)$

   $\quad = -1 \qquad\qquad\quad = 1$

   $(-1, 1)$

5. $r = \sqrt{1^2 + (\sqrt{3})^2} = 2$

   $\theta = \text{Arctan } \dfrac{\sqrt{3}}{1} = 60°$

   $(2, 60°)$ or $\left(2, \dfrac{\pi}{3}\right)$

6. $\dfrac{x}{\sqrt{2}} + \dfrac{y}{\sqrt{2}} - \dfrac{6}{\sqrt{2}} = 0$

   $\cos \phi = \dfrac{1}{\sqrt{2}}, \sin \phi = \dfrac{1}{\sqrt{2}}, p = \dfrac{6}{\sqrt{2}}$ or $3\sqrt{2}$

   $\phi = \arctan 1$

   $\quad = \dfrac{\pi}{4}$

   $3\sqrt{2} = r \cos \left(\theta - \dfrac{\pi}{4}\right)$

| 9-5 | **Simplifying Complex Numbers** |

PAGE 498 CHECKING FOR UNDERSTANDING

1. See students' work.

2. The real numbers are a subset of the complex numbers. A real number occurs when $b = 0$ in $a + bi$.

3. voltage: volts, current: amps, impedance: ohms

4. $i^{15} + i^{28} = (i^2)^7 i + (i^4)^7$

   $\qquad\qquad = -i + 1$ or $1 - i$

5. $(4 + 5i) + (3 + 2i) = 7 + 7i$

6. $(8 + 3i) - (1 - 6i) = 7 + 9i$

7. $(4 + 3i)(2 - i) = 8 + 2i - 3i^2 = 11 + 2i$

8. $(i - 6)^2 = i^2 - 12i + 36 = 35 - 12i$

9. $\dfrac{1 + i}{3 + 2i} = \left(\dfrac{1 + i}{3 + 2i}\right)\left(\dfrac{3 - 2i}{3 - 2i}\right)$

$\quad = \dfrac{3 + i - 2i^2}{9 - 4i^2}$

$\quad = \dfrac{5 + i}{13}$

10. $\dfrac{2}{12 + i} = \left(\dfrac{2}{12 + i}\right)\left(\dfrac{12 - i}{12 - i}\right)$

$\quad = \dfrac{24 - 2i}{144 - i^2}$

$\quad = \dfrac{24 - 2i}{145}$

11. $\dfrac{7i}{-5i} = -\dfrac{7}{5}$ or $-1\dfrac{2}{5}$

PAGES 499-500   EXERCISES

12. $i^{24} + i^{61} = (i^4)^6 + (i^4)^{15}i = 1 + i$

13. $i^4(7 + 2i) = 1(7 + 2i) = 7 + 2i$

14. $(7 - 6i) + (9 + 11i) = 16 + 5i$

15. $(-5 + 2i\sqrt{7}) - (2 - 7i\sqrt{7}) = -7 + 9i\sqrt{7}$

16. $(-3 - 10i) - (-5 - 4i) = 2 - 6i$

17. $-6(2 - 8i) + 3(5 + 7i)$

$\quad = (-12 + 48i) + (15 + 21i)$

$\quad = 3 + 69i$

18. $4(7 - i) - 5(2 - 6i) = (28 - 4i) - (10 - 30i)$

$\qquad\qquad\qquad\qquad\qquad = 18 + 26i$

19. $(3 + 5i)(4 - i) = 12 + 17i - 5i^2 = 17 + 17i$

20. $(4 - 2i\sqrt{3})(1 + 5i\sqrt{3}) = 4 + 18i\sqrt{3} - 10i^2(3)$

$\qquad\qquad\qquad\qquad\qquad = 34 + 18i\sqrt{3}$

21. $(3 - 4i)^2 = 9 - 24i + 16i^2$

$\qquad\quad = -7 - 24i$

22. $(\sqrt{5} + 2i)^2 = 5 + 4i\sqrt{5} + 4i^2$

$\qquad\qquad = 1 + 4i\sqrt{5}$

23. $(8 - \sqrt{-11})(8 + \sqrt{-11}) = (8 - i\sqrt{11})(8 + i\sqrt{11})$

$\qquad\qquad\qquad\qquad\qquad = 64 - 11i^2$

$\qquad\qquad\qquad\qquad\qquad = 75$

24. $(6 - 4i)(6 + 4i) = 36 - 16i^2 = 52$

25. $(5 + \sqrt{-8}) + (-13 + 4\sqrt{-2})$

$\quad = (5 + 2i\sqrt{2}) + (-13 + 4i\sqrt{2})$

$\quad = -8 + 6i\sqrt{2}$

26. $\dfrac{2 - 4i}{1 + 3i} = \dfrac{2 - 4i}{1 + 3i}\left(\dfrac{1 - 3i}{1 - 3i}\right)$

$\quad = \dfrac{2 - 10i + 12i^2}{1 - 9i^2}$

$\quad = \dfrac{-10 - 10i}{10}$

$\quad = -1 - i$

27. $\dfrac{3 - i}{2 - i} = \left(\dfrac{3 - i}{2 - i}\right)\left(\dfrac{2 + i}{2 + i}\right)$

$\quad = \dfrac{6 + i - i^2}{4 - i^2}$

$\quad = \dfrac{7 + i}{5}$

28. $x^2 - x + 1 = 0$

$x = \dfrac{-(-1) \pm \sqrt{(-1)^2 - 4(1)(1)}}{2(1)}$

$\quad = \dfrac{1 \pm \sqrt{-3}}{2}$

$\quad = \dfrac{1 \pm i\sqrt{3}}{2}$

29. $x^2 + 4x + 29 = 0$

$x = \dfrac{-4 \pm \sqrt{(4)^2 - 4(1)(29)}}{2(1)}$

$\quad = \dfrac{-4 \pm \sqrt{-100}}{2}$

$\quad = \dfrac{-4 \pm 10i}{2}$

$\quad = -2 \pm 5i$

30. $3x - 5yi = 15 - 20i$

$\quad 3x = 15 \qquad\qquad -5yi = -20i$

$\quad\ x = 5 \qquad\qquad\quad\ y = \dfrac{-20i}{-5i}$

$\qquad\qquad\qquad\qquad\qquad\quad y = 4$

31. $\sqrt{3}x + 7yi = 6 - 2i$

$\quad \sqrt{3}x = 6 \qquad\qquad 7yi = -2i$

$\quad\ x = 2\sqrt{3} \qquad\qquad y = -\dfrac{2}{7}$

32. $(x - y) + (2x + y)i = -3 + 9i$

$\quad x - y = -3 \qquad\qquad x - y = -3$

$\quad \underline{2x + y = 9} \qquad\qquad 2 - y = -3$

$\quad\ 3x\quad\ = 6 \qquad\qquad\quad y = 5$

$\qquad\ x = 2$

33. $(2x - y) + (x + y)i = -4 - 5i$

$\quad 2x - y = -4 \qquad\qquad x + y = -5$

$\quad \underline{x + y = -5} \qquad\qquad -3 + y = -5$

$\quad\ 3x\quad\ = -9 \qquad\qquad\quad y = -2$

$\qquad\ x = -3$

34. $(3 - i)(1 + 2i)(2 + 3i) = (3 + 5i - 2i^2)(2 + 3i)$

$\qquad\qquad\qquad\qquad\qquad = (5 + 5i)(2 + 3i)$

$\qquad\qquad\qquad\qquad\qquad = 10 + 25i + 15i^2$

$\qquad\qquad\qquad\qquad\qquad = -5 + 25i$

35. $(4 + 3i)(2 - 5i)(4 - 3i) = (16 - 9i^2)(2 - 5i)$

$\qquad\qquad\qquad\qquad\qquad = 25(2 - 5i)$

$\qquad\qquad\qquad\qquad\qquad = 50 - 125i$

36. $\dfrac{3}{\sqrt{2} - 5i} = \left(\dfrac{3}{\sqrt{2} - 5i}\right)\left(\dfrac{\sqrt{2} + 5i}{\sqrt{2} + 5i}\right)$

$\quad = \dfrac{3\sqrt{2} + 15i}{2 - 25i^2}$

$\quad = \dfrac{3\sqrt{2} + 15i}{27}$

$\quad = \dfrac{\sqrt{2} + 5i}{9}$

37. $\dfrac{2 + i\sqrt{3}}{12 + i\sqrt{3}} = \left(\dfrac{2 + i\sqrt{3}}{12 + i\sqrt{3}}\right)\left(\dfrac{12 - i\sqrt{3}}{12 - i\sqrt{3}}\right)$

$= \dfrac{24 + 10i\sqrt{3} - 3i^2}{144 - 3i^2}$

$= \dfrac{27 + 10i\sqrt{3}}{147}$

38. $\dfrac{(1 - 2i)^2}{(2 - i)^2} = \dfrac{1 - 4i + 4i^2}{4 - 4i + i^2}$

$= \dfrac{-3 - 4i}{3 - 4i}$

$= \left(\dfrac{-3 - 4i}{3 - 4i}\right)\left(\dfrac{3 + 4i}{3 + 4i}\right)$

$= \dfrac{-9 - 24i - 16i^2}{9 - 16i^2}$

$= \dfrac{7 - 24i}{25}$

39. $\dfrac{2 + i}{(1 - i)^2} = \dfrac{2 + i}{1 - 2i + i^2}$

$= \dfrac{2 + i}{-2i}$

$= \left(\dfrac{2 + i}{-2i}\right)\left(\dfrac{2i}{2i}\right)$

$= \dfrac{4i + 2i^2}{-4i^2}$

$= \dfrac{-2 + 4i}{4}$

$= \dfrac{-1 + 2i}{2}$

40. The addition of vectors, when expressed in terms of their unit vector components, behave exactly like the addition of imaginary numbers. When adding vectors you add the horizontal components together and then the vertical components. This parallels adding the real parts and then the imaginary parts.

41. a. $1.5 + 1.5 = 3$ volts

b. $E = I \cdot Z$

$3 = (1 + j\sqrt{3})Z$

$Z = \dfrac{3}{1 + j\sqrt{3}}$

$= \left(\dfrac{3}{1 + j\sqrt{3}}\right)\left(\dfrac{1 - j\sqrt{3}}{1 - j\sqrt{3}}\right)$

$= \dfrac{3 - 3j\sqrt{3}}{1 - 3j^2}$

$= \dfrac{3 - 3j\sqrt{3}}{4}$

$= 0.75(1 - j\sqrt{3})$ ohms

42. $E = I \cdot Z$

$= (6 - 8j)(14 + 8j)$

$= 84 - 112j + 48j - 64j^2$

$= 148 - 64j$ volts

43. $E = I \cdot Z$

$70 + 226j = I(6 + 8j)$

$I = \dfrac{70 + 226j}{6 + 8j}$

$= \left(\dfrac{70 + 226j}{6 + 8j}\right)\left(\dfrac{6 - 8j}{6 - 8j}\right)$

$= \dfrac{420 + 1356j - 560j - 1808j^2}{36 - 64j^2}$

$= \dfrac{2228 + 796j}{100}$

$= 22.28 + 7.96j$ amps

44. $E = I \cdot Z$

$-50 + 100j = (-6 - 2j)Z$

$Z = \dfrac{-50 + 100j}{-6 - 2j}$

$= \left(\dfrac{-50 + 100j}{-6 - 2j}\right)\left(\dfrac{-6 + 2j}{-6 + 2j}\right)$

$= \dfrac{300 - 600j - 100j + 200j^2}{36 - 4j^2}$

$= \dfrac{100 - 700j}{40}$

$= 2.5 - 17.5j$ ohms

45. $2x + 5y - 10 = 0$

$5y = -2x + 10$

$y = -\dfrac{2}{5}x + 2$

$m = -\dfrac{2}{5}$, y-intercept $= 2$

46. $\begin{bmatrix} 1 & 1 & 1 & 6 \\ 2 & -3 & 4 & 3 \\ 4 & -8 & 4 & 12 \end{bmatrix} \longrightarrow \begin{bmatrix} 1 & 1 & 1 & 6 \\ 0 & -5 & 2 & -9 \\ 0 & -12 & 0 & -12 \end{bmatrix} \longrightarrow$

$\begin{bmatrix} 1 & 1 & 1 & 6 \\ 0 & -12 & 0 & -12 \\ 0 & -5 & 2 & -9 \end{bmatrix} \longrightarrow \begin{bmatrix} 1 & 1 & 1 & 6 \\ 0 & 1 & 0 & 1 \\ 0 & -5 & 2 & -9 \end{bmatrix} \longrightarrow$

$\begin{bmatrix} 1 & 1 & 1 & 6 \\ 0 & 1 & 0 & 1 \\ 0 & 0 & 2 & -4 \end{bmatrix} \longrightarrow \begin{bmatrix} 1 & 1 & 1 & 6 \\ 0 & 1 & 0 & 1 \\ 0 & 0 & 1 & -2 \end{bmatrix} \longrightarrow$

$\begin{bmatrix} 1 & 0 & 0 & 7 \\ 0 & 1 & 0 & 1 \\ 0 & 0 & 1 & -2 \end{bmatrix}$ $(7, 1, -2)$

47. a. Let x = number of short answer questions answered.

Let y = number of essay questions answered.

$x \geq 0,\ y \geq 0$

$2x + 12y \leq 60$

$x + y \leq 20$

$S(x, y) = 5x + 15y$

$S(0, 0) = 5(0) + 15(0) = 0$

$S(20, 0) = 5(20) + 15(0) = 100$

$S(18, 2) = 5(18) + 15(2) = 120$

$S(0, 5) = 5(0) + 15(5) = 75$

18 short answers, 2 essay for a score of 120

b. $x \geq 0,\ y \geq 0$

$\qquad 2x + 12y \leq 120$

$\qquad x + y \leq 20$

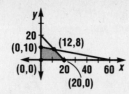

$S(0,\ 0) = 5(0) + 15(0) = 0$

$S(20,\ 0) = 5(20) + 15(0) = 100$

$S(12,\ 8) = 5(12) + 15(8) = 180$

$S(0,\ 10) = 5(0) + 15(10) = 150$

12 short answer, 8 essay for a score of 180

48. $y = \arccos x$

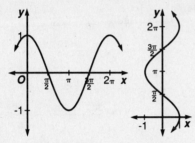

49. $\sin^4 A + \cos^2 A = (\sin^2 A)^2 + \cos^2 A$

$\qquad = (1 - \cos^2 A)^2 + \cos^2 A$

$\qquad = (1 - 2\cos^2 A + \cos^4 A) + \cos^2 A$

$\qquad = \cos^4 A + 1 - \cos^2 A$

$\qquad = \cos^4 A + \sin^2 A$

50. $(3,\ 5) + (-1,\ 2) = (2,\ 7)$

51. $x^2 + y^2 = 25$

$\qquad r^2 = 25$

$\qquad r = 5 \text{ or } r = -5$

52.

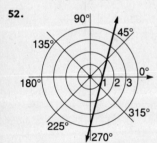

53. area of larger triangle $= \frac{1}{2} \cdot 9 \cdot 7 = 31.5$

area of smaller triangle $= \frac{1}{2} \cdot 5 \cdot 3 = 7.5$

area of shaded region $= 31.5 - 7.5 = 24$

Quantity B is greater. B

9-6 Polar Form of Complex Numbers

1. Modulus is the length of the radius vector for the polar form of a complex number. The modulus is equal to $\sqrt{x^2 + y^2}$ for $x + yi$.

2. angle formed by the polar axis and the radius vector

3. Answers may vary. Sample answer: It is easier to write and it is shorter.

4. Their measures will differ by some multiple of 2π.

5.

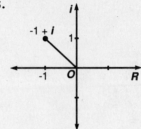

$r = \sqrt{(-1)^2 + 1^2} = \sqrt{2}$

$\theta = \arctan \dfrac{1}{-1} + \pi = \dfrac{3\pi}{4}$

$\sqrt{2}\left(\cos \dfrac{3\pi}{4} + i \sin \dfrac{3\pi}{4}\right)$

6.

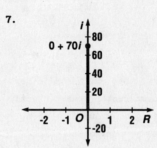

$-2(1 - i) = -2 + 2i$

$r = \sqrt{(-2)^2 + 2^2} = 2\sqrt{2}$

$\theta = \arctan \dfrac{2}{-2} + \pi = \dfrac{3\pi}{4}$

$2\sqrt{2}\left(\cos \dfrac{3\pi}{4} + i \sin \dfrac{3\pi}{4}\right)$

7.

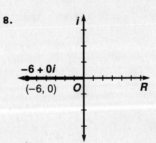

$r = \sqrt{0^2 + 70^2} = 70$

$\theta = \arctan \dfrac{70}{0} = \dfrac{\pi}{2}$

$70\left(\cos \dfrac{\pi}{2} + i \sin \dfrac{\pi}{2}\right)$

8.

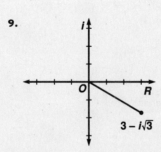

$r = \sqrt{(-6)^2 + 0^2} = 6$

$\theta = \arctan \dfrac{0}{-6} + \pi = \pi$

$6(\cos \pi + i \sin \pi)$

9.

$r = \sqrt{3^2 + (-\sqrt{3})^2} = 2\sqrt{3}$

$\theta = \arctan \dfrac{-\sqrt{3}}{3} = \dfrac{5\pi}{6}$

$2\sqrt{3}\left(\cos \dfrac{5\pi}{6} + i \sin \dfrac{5\pi}{6}\right)$

10.

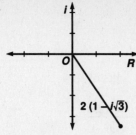

$2(1 - i\sqrt{3}) = 2 - 2i\sqrt{3}$

$r = \sqrt{2^2 + (-2\sqrt{3})^2} = 4$

$\theta = \arctan\left(\dfrac{-2\sqrt{3}}{2}\right) = \arctan(-\sqrt{3}) = \dfrac{5\pi}{3}$

$4\left(\cos\dfrac{5\pi}{3} + i\sin\dfrac{5\pi}{3}\right)$

11.

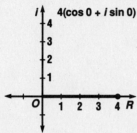

$x = r\cos\theta \qquad\qquad y = r\sin\theta$

$\quad = 4\cos 0 \qquad\qquad\quad = 4\sin 0$

$\quad = 4 \qquad\qquad\qquad\quad = 0$

$4 + 0i = 4$

12.

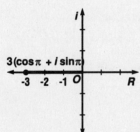

$x = 3\cos\pi \qquad\qquad y = 3\sin\pi$

$\quad = -3 \qquad\qquad\qquad\quad = 0$

$-3 + 0i = -3$

13.

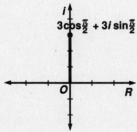

$x = 3\cos\dfrac{\pi}{2} \qquad\qquad y = 3\sin\dfrac{\pi}{2}$

$\quad = 0 \qquad\qquad\qquad\quad = 3$

$0 + 3i = 3i$

14.

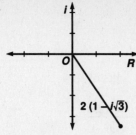

$x = 0.5\cos\dfrac{5\pi}{6} \qquad y = 0.5\sin\dfrac{5\pi}{6}$

$\quad = -\dfrac{\sqrt{3}}{4} \qquad\qquad\quad = \dfrac{1}{4}$

$-\dfrac{\sqrt{3}}{4} + \dfrac{1}{4}i$

PAGES 504–505   EXERCISES

15. $r = \sqrt{(-1)^2 + (-1)^2} = \sqrt{2}$

$\theta = \arctan\dfrac{-1}{-1} + \pi = \dfrac{5\pi}{4}$

$\sqrt{2}\left(\cos\dfrac{5\pi}{4} + i\sin\dfrac{5\pi}{4}\right)$

16. $r = \sqrt{0^2 + 6^2} = 6$

$\theta = \arctan\dfrac{6}{0} = \dfrac{\pi}{2}$

$6\left(\cos\dfrac{\pi}{2} + i\sin\dfrac{\pi}{2}\right)$

17. $r = \sqrt{0^2 + 10^2} = 10$

$\theta = \arctan\dfrac{10}{0} = \dfrac{\pi}{2}$

$10\left(\cos\dfrac{\pi}{2} + i\sin\dfrac{\pi}{2}\right)$

18. $r = \sqrt{(-5)^2 + (-1)^2} = \sqrt{26}$

$\theta = \arctan\dfrac{-1}{-5} + \pi \approx 3.34$

$\sqrt{26}(\cos 3.34 + i\sin 3.34)$

19. $r = \sqrt{4^2 + 3^2} = 5$

$\theta = \arctan\dfrac{3}{4} \approx 0.64$

$5(\cos 0.64 + i\sin 0.64)$

20. $r = \sqrt{(2\sqrt{3})^2 + (-3)^2} = \sqrt{21}$

$\theta = \arctan\dfrac{-3}{2\sqrt{3}} \approx -0.71$

$\sqrt{21}[\cos(-0.71) + i\sin(-0.71)]$

21. $r = \sqrt{1^2 + (\sqrt{3})^2} = 2$ **22.** $r = \sqrt{0^2 + (-4)^2} = 4$

$\theta = \arctan\dfrac{\sqrt{3}}{1} = \dfrac{\pi}{3} \qquad\qquad \theta = \arctan\dfrac{-4}{0} = \dfrac{3\pi}{2}$

$2\left(\cos\dfrac{\pi}{3} + i\sin\dfrac{\pi}{3}\right) \qquad\quad 4\left(\cos\dfrac{3\pi}{2} + i\sin\dfrac{3\pi}{2}\right)$

23. $r = \sqrt{(-5)^2 + 0^2} = 5$

$\theta = \arctan\dfrac{0}{-5} + \pi = \pi$

$5(\cos\pi + i\sin\pi)$

24. $x = 6 \cos \dfrac{3\pi}{2}$ $\qquad y = 6 \sin \dfrac{3\pi}{2}$

$\quad = 0 \qquad\qquad\qquad = -6$

$0 + (-6)i = -6i$

25. $x = 24 \cos \dfrac{5\pi}{3}$ $\qquad y = 24 \sin \dfrac{5\pi}{3}$

$\quad = 24 \cos \dfrac{\pi}{3} \qquad\quad = -24 \sin \dfrac{\pi}{3}$

$\quad = 24\left(\dfrac{1}{2}\right) \qquad\quad = -24 \cdot \dfrac{\sqrt{3}}{2}$

$\quad = 12 \qquad\qquad\quad = -12\sqrt{3}$

$12 - 12i\sqrt{3}$

26. $x = \sqrt{2} \cos \dfrac{5\pi}{4}$ $\qquad y = \sqrt{2} \sin \dfrac{5\pi}{4}$

$\quad = \sqrt{2}\left(-\dfrac{\sqrt{2}}{2}\right) \qquad = \sqrt{2}\left(-\dfrac{\sqrt{2}}{2}\right)$

$\quad = -1 \qquad\qquad\qquad = -1$

$-1 - i$

27. $x = 3 \cos 2$ $\qquad\quad y = 3 \sin 2$

$\quad \approx -1.25 \qquad\qquad \approx 2.73$

$-1.25 + 2.73i$

28. $x = 4 \cos 3$ $\qquad\quad y = 4 \sin 3$

$\quad \approx -3.96 \qquad\qquad \approx 0.56$

$-3.96 + 0.56i$

29. $x = 2 \cos \dfrac{\pi}{6}$ $\qquad y = 2 \sin \dfrac{\pi}{6}$

$\quad = \sqrt{3} \qquad\qquad\quad = 1$

$\sqrt{3} + i$

30. $x = \sqrt{2} \cos \left(-\dfrac{\pi}{2}\right)$ $\qquad y = \sqrt{2} \sin \left(-\dfrac{\pi}{2}\right)$

$\quad = 0 \qquad\qquad\qquad = -\sqrt{2}$

$0 + (-\sqrt{2})i = -i\sqrt{2}$

31. $x = 5 \cos \dfrac{17\pi}{6}$ $\qquad y = 5 \sin \dfrac{17\pi}{6}$

$\quad = -5 \cos \dfrac{\pi}{6} \qquad\quad = 5 \sin \dfrac{\pi}{6}$

$\quad = -5\left(\dfrac{\sqrt{3}}{2}\right) \qquad\quad = 5\left(\dfrac{1}{2}\right)$

$\quad = \dfrac{-5\sqrt{3}}{2} \qquad\qquad = \dfrac{5}{2}$

$\dfrac{-5\sqrt{3}}{2} + \dfrac{5}{2}i$

32. If C is a real number, then $y = 0$, $|C| = |x|$,

and $r = \sqrt{x^2}$ or $|x|$.

33. The sum of two complex numbers A and B can be graphed by graphing each complex number and drawing OA and OB. Complete a parallelogram whose sides include OA and OB. If C is the fourth vertex of the parallelogram, then C represents the sum of A and B.

34. $x = \dfrac{-(-4) \pm \sqrt{(-4)^2 - 4(1)(8)}}{2(1)}$

$\quad = \dfrac{4 \pm \sqrt{-16}}{2}$

$\quad = \dfrac{4 \pm 4i}{2}$

$\quad = 2 \pm 2i$

35. $E = I \cdot Z$

$70 + 226j = I(6 + 8j)$

$\quad I = \dfrac{70 + 226j}{6 + 8j}$

$\quad\quad = \left(\dfrac{70 + 226j}{6 + 8j}\right)\left(\dfrac{6 - 8j}{6 - 8j}\right)$

$\quad\quad = \dfrac{420 + 796j + 1808j^2}{36 - 64j^2}$

$\quad\quad = \dfrac{2228 + 796j}{100}$

$\quad\quad = 22.28 + 7.96j$

$E: \ r = \sqrt{70^2 + 226^2} \approx 236.59$

$\quad \theta = \arctan \dfrac{226}{70} \approx 1.27$

$\quad 236.59(\cos 1.27 + i \sin 1.27)$

$Z: \ r = \sqrt{6^2 + 8^2} = 10$

$\quad \theta = \arctan \dfrac{8}{6} \approx 0.93$

$\quad 10(\cos 0.93 + i \sin 0.93)$

$I: \ r = \sqrt{22.28^2 + 7.96^2} \approx 23.66$

$\quad \theta = \arctan \dfrac{7.96}{22.28} \approx 0.34$

$\quad 23.66(\cos 0.34 + i \sin 0.34)$

36. $V = \ell w h$

$192 = \ell w(6)$

$\quad \ell = \dfrac{32}{w}$

$C(w) = 0.05(2\ell h) + 0.10(2wh) + 0.20(\ell w)$

$\quad\quad = 0.10\left(\dfrac{32}{w}\right)(6) + 0.20w(6) + 0.20\left(\dfrac{32}{w}\right)w$

$\quad\quad = 19.2w^{-1} + 1.2w + 6.4$

$C'(w) = -19.2w^{-2} + 1.2$

$\quad 0 = -19.2w^{-2} + 1.2$

$\quad \dfrac{19.2}{w^2} = 1.2$

$\quad\quad w = 4$

$C(4.01) \approx 16.00003$

$C(4.00) = 16$

$C(3.99) \approx 16.00003$

$(4, 16)$ is a minimum point.

$\ell = \dfrac{32}{w} = \dfrac{32}{4}$ or 8

The dimensions are 4 in. by 8 in. by 6 in.

37. $\tan 42° = \dfrac{y}{x}$ $\qquad$ $\tan 56° = \dfrac{40 + y}{x}$

$\qquad y = x \tan 42°$ $\qquad\qquad y = x \tan 56° - 40$

$\qquad\qquad x \tan 42° = x \tan 56° - 40$

$\qquad\qquad\quad 0.9004x \approx 1.4826x - 40$

$\qquad\qquad\qquad 0.5822x \approx 40$

$\qquad\qquad\qquad\qquad x \approx 68.7$

$\quad y = x \tan 42°$

$\qquad \approx 68.7 \tan 42°$

$\qquad \approx 61.9$ feet

$61.9 + 40 = 101.9$ feet

No, the height of the building is approximately 61.9 feet, making a total of 101.9 feet with the tower, which is over the city's limit.

38. $\qquad\quad \sin 2x + 2 \sin x = 0$

$\quad 2 \sin x \cos x + 2 \sin x = 0$

$\qquad\quad 2 \sin x(\cos x + 1) = 0$

$\qquad\qquad \sin x(\cos x + 1) = 0$

$\sin x = 0 \qquad$ or $\quad \cos x + 1 = 0$

$\quad x = 0°, 360° \qquad\qquad \cos x = -1$

$\qquad\qquad\qquad\qquad\qquad x = 180°$

39. $\vec{u} = (2, -5, -3) + (-3, 4, -7)$

$\qquad = (-1, -1, -10)$

$\qquad = -\vec{i} - \vec{j} - 10\vec{k}$

40.

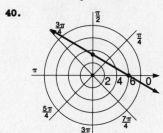

41. $X = X_L - X_C$

$8i = X_L - 7i$

$X_L = 15i$

42. $C_1 = 9\pi, C_2 = 6\pi$

$(9\pi)(120) = (6\pi)v$

$\qquad\qquad v = 180$ rpm

The best answer is D.

9-7	**Products and Quotients of Complex Numbers in Polar Form**

PAGE 508 $\qquad$ CHECKING FOR UNDERSTANDING

1. Find the product of $8 \text{ cis } \dfrac{3\pi}{4} \cdot 2 \text{ cis } \dfrac{5\pi}{4}$.

$16 \text{ cis}\left(\dfrac{3\pi}{4} + \dfrac{5\pi}{4}\right) = 16 \text{ cis } 2\pi$

2. Square its modulus and double its amplitude.

$(r \text{ cis } \theta)^2 = r^2 \text{ cis } 2\theta$

---

3. $5(\cos \pi + i \sin \pi) \cdot 6(\cos 2\pi + i \sin 2\pi)$

$= 5 \cdot 6[\cos (\pi + 2\pi) + i \sin (\pi + 2\pi)]$

$= 30(\cos 3\pi + i \sin 3\pi)$

$= 30(-1 + i \cdot 0)$

$= -30$

4. $3\left(\cos \dfrac{3\pi}{4} + i \sin \dfrac{3\pi}{4}\right) \cdot 8\left(\cos \dfrac{\pi}{2} + i \sin \dfrac{\pi}{2}\right)$

$= 8 \cdot 3\left[\cos \left(\dfrac{3\pi}{4} + \dfrac{\pi}{2}\right) + i \sin \left(\dfrac{3\pi}{4} + \dfrac{\pi}{2}\right)\right]$

$= 24\left(\cos \dfrac{5\pi}{4} + i \sin \dfrac{5\pi}{4}\right)$

$= 24\left(-\dfrac{\sqrt{2}}{2} + i \left(-\dfrac{\sqrt{2}}{2}\right)\right)$

$= -12\sqrt{2} - 12i\sqrt{2}$

$= -17.0 - 17.0i$

5. $15(\cos 2\pi + i \sin 2\pi) + 5(\cos \pi + i \sin \pi)$

$= \dfrac{15}{5}[\cos (2\pi - \pi) + i \sin (2\pi - \pi)]$

$= 3(\cos \pi + i \sin \pi)$

$= 3(-1 + i \cdot 0)$

$= -3$

6. $6\left(\cos \dfrac{\pi}{6} + i \sin \dfrac{\pi}{6}\right) + 2\left(\cos \dfrac{2\pi}{3} + i \sin \dfrac{2\pi}{3}\right)$

$= \dfrac{6}{2}\left[\cos \left(\dfrac{\pi}{6} - \dfrac{2\pi}{3}\right) + i \sin \left(\dfrac{\pi}{6} - \dfrac{2\pi}{3}\right)\right]$

$= 3\left(\cos - \dfrac{3\pi}{6} + i \sin - \dfrac{3\pi}{6}\right)$

$= 3\left(\cos \dfrac{3\pi}{2} + i \sin \dfrac{3\pi}{2}\right)$

$= 3(0 + i \cdot (-1))$

$= -3i$

PAGES 508-509 $\qquad$ EXERCISES

7. $(-1 - i)(1 + i) = -1 - 2i - i^2 = -2i$

8. $(-4 - 4i\sqrt{3}) + 2i$

$= \dfrac{-4}{2i} - \dfrac{4i\sqrt{3}}{2i}$

$= -\dfrac{4}{2i}\left(\dfrac{i}{i}\right) - 2\sqrt{3}$

$= -\dfrac{4i}{2i^2} - 2\sqrt{3}$

$= 2i - 2\sqrt{3}$ or $-2\sqrt{3} + 2i$

9. $(3 + 3i) + (-2 + 2i)$

$= \dfrac{3 + 3i}{-2 + 2i}$

$= \dfrac{3 + 3i}{-2 + 2i}\left(\dfrac{-2 - 2i}{-2 - 2i}\right)$

$= \dfrac{-6 - 12i - 6i^2}{4 - 4i^2}$

$= \dfrac{-12i}{8}$

$= -\dfrac{3}{2}i$

10. $(-2 + 2i)(\sqrt{3} + i) = -2\sqrt{3} + 2i\sqrt{3} - 2i + 2i^2$

$= -2\sqrt{3} - 2 + 2i\sqrt{3} - 2i$

$= -2(\sqrt{3} + 1) - 2i(1 - \sqrt{3})$

$\approx -5.46 + 1.46i$

11. $3(\cos 30° + i \sin 30°) \cdot 2(\cos 60° + i \sin 60°)$

$= 6(\cos 90° + i \sin 90°)$

$= 6(0 + i \cdot 1)$

$= 6i$

12. $2\left(\cos \frac{2\pi}{3} + i \sin \frac{2\pi}{3}\right) \cdot 3\left(\cos \frac{7\pi}{6} + i \sin \frac{7\pi}{6}\right)$

$= 6\left(\cos \frac{11\pi}{6} + i \sin \frac{11\pi}{6}\right)$

$= 6\left(\frac{\sqrt{3}}{2} + i\left(-\frac{1}{2}\right)\right)$

$= 3\sqrt{3} - 3i$

$= 5.2 - 3i$

13. $4\left(\cos \frac{3\pi}{4} + i \sin \frac{3\pi}{4}\right) + \sqrt{2}\left(\cos \frac{2\pi}{3} + i \sin \frac{2\pi}{3}\right)$

$= 2\sqrt{2}\left(\cos \frac{\pi}{12} + i \sin \frac{\pi}{12}\right)$

$\approx 2\sqrt{2}(0.9659 + 0.2588i)$

$\approx 2.7 + 0.7i$

14. $6\left(\cos \frac{\pi}{6} + i \sin \frac{\pi}{6}\right) \cdot 2\left(\cos \frac{2\pi}{3} + i \sin \frac{2\pi}{3}\right)$

$= 12\left(\cos \frac{5\pi}{6} + i \sin \frac{5\pi}{6}\right)$

$= 12\left(-\frac{\sqrt{3}}{2} + i \cdot \frac{1}{2}\right)$

$= -6\sqrt{3} + 6i$

$\approx -10.4 + 6i$

15. $3\left(\cos \frac{7\pi}{6} + i \sin \frac{7\pi}{6}\right) \cdot 6\left(\cos \frac{\pi}{6} + i \sin \frac{\pi}{6}\right)$

$= 18\left(\cos \frac{4\pi}{3} + i \sin \frac{4\pi}{3}\right)$

$= 18\left(-\frac{1}{2} + i\left(-\frac{\sqrt{3}}{2}\right)\right)$

$= -9 - 9i\sqrt{3}$

16. $3\sqrt{2}\left(\cos \frac{\pi}{4} + i \sin \frac{\pi}{4}\right) + \sqrt{2}\left(\cos \frac{\pi}{6} + i \sin \frac{\pi}{6}\right)$

$= 3\left(\cos \frac{\pi}{12} + i \sin \frac{\pi}{12}\right)$

$\approx 2.90 + 0.78i$

17. $2\left(\cos \frac{\pi}{4} + i \sin \frac{\pi}{4}\right) \cdot 3\left(\cos \frac{\pi}{2} + i \sin \frac{\pi}{2}\right)$

$= 6\left(\cos \frac{3\pi}{4} + i \sin \frac{3\pi}{4}\right)$

$= 6\left(-\frac{\sqrt{2}}{2} + i \cdot \frac{\sqrt{2}}{2}\right)$

$= -3\sqrt{2} + 3i\sqrt{2}$

18. $12(\cos \pi + i \sin \pi) + 4\left(\cos \frac{\pi}{6} + i \sin \frac{\pi}{6}\right)$

$= 3\left(\cos \frac{5\pi}{6} + i \sin \frac{5\pi}{6}\right)$

$= 3\left(-\frac{\sqrt{3}}{2} + i \cdot \frac{1}{2}\right)$

$= -\frac{3\sqrt{3}}{2} + \frac{3}{2}i$

19. $9.24(\cos 1.8 + i \sin 1.8)$

$+ 3.1(\cos 0.7 + i \sin 0.7)$

$\approx 2.98(\cos 1.1 + i \sin 1.1)$

$\approx 1.35 + 2.66i$

20. $2(\cos 0.8 + i \sin 0.8)$

$\cdot 3.2(\cos 1.5 + i \sin 1.5)$

$= 6.4(\cos 2.3 + i \sin 2.3)$

$\approx -4.26 + 4.77i$

21. $\frac{1}{3}\left(\cos \frac{7\pi}{8} + i \sin \frac{7\pi}{8}\right)$

$\cdot 3\sqrt{3}\left[\cos \left(-\frac{\pi}{4}\right) + i \sin \left(-\frac{\pi}{4}\right)\right]$

$= \sqrt{3}\left(\cos \frac{5\pi}{8} + i \sin \frac{5\pi}{8}\right)$

$\approx -0.66 + 1.60i$

22. $6\sqrt{3}\left(\cos \frac{5\pi}{4} + i \sin \frac{5\pi}{4}\right) + \sqrt{3}\left(\cos \frac{\pi}{6} + i \sin \frac{\pi}{6}\right)$

$= 6\left(\cos \frac{13\pi}{12} + i \sin \frac{13\pi}{12}\right)$

$\approx -5.80 - 1.55i$

23. $8\left(\cos \frac{3\pi}{2} + i \sin \frac{3\pi}{2}\right) + \frac{4}{5}\left(\cos \frac{\pi}{2} + i \sin \frac{\pi}{2}\right)$

$= 10(\cos \pi + i \sin \pi)$

$= 10(-1 + i \cdot 0)$

$= -10$

24. $a + bi = \sqrt{a^2 + b^2}(\cos \theta_1 + i \sin \theta_1)$

$\theta_2 = \arctan \frac{\sqrt{3}}{1} = 60°$

$1 + i\sqrt{3} = 2(\cos 60° + i \sin 60°)$

$(a + bi)(1 + i\sqrt{3})$

$= 2\sqrt{a^2 + b^2}[\cos (\theta_1 + 60°) + \sin (\theta_2 + 60°)]$

It is rotated 60°.

25. Since $\cos \frac{\pi}{4} = \frac{\sqrt{2}}{2}$, $\sin \frac{\pi}{4} = \frac{\sqrt{2}}{2}$, $\cos \left(-\frac{\pi}{4}\right) = \frac{\sqrt{2}}{2}$,

and $\sin\left(-\frac{\pi}{4}\right) = -\frac{\sqrt{2}}{2}$,

$s_1 = 4\sqrt{2}\left(\frac{\sqrt{2}}{2} + i\frac{\sqrt{2}}{2}\right)$ or $4 + 4i$, and

$s_2 = 4\sqrt{2}\left(\frac{\sqrt{2}}{2} + i\left(-\frac{\sqrt{2}}{2}\right)\right)$ or $4 - 4i$.

$s_1 + s_2 = 4 + 4i + 4 - 4i = 8$

$-\frac{b}{a} = -\frac{-8}{1} = 8$

$s_1 s_2 = (4 + 4i)(4 - 4i) = 16 - 16i^2$ or 32

$\frac{c}{a} = \frac{32}{1} = 32$

26. $E = I \cdot Z$

$161(\cos 337° + i \sin 337°)$

$= I \cdot 32(\cos 300° + i \sin 300°)$

$I = 161(\cos 337° + i \sin 337°)$

$+ 32(\cos 300° + i \sin 300°)$

$I \approx 5(\cos 37° + i \sin 37°)$ amps

27. $a^2 = 400^2 + 600^2 - 2(400)(600)\cos 46°20'$

$a \approx 434$

perimeter $\approx 400 + 600 + 434 \approx 1434$ ft

$s = \frac{1}{2}(400 + 600 + 434) = 717$

$K = \sqrt{717(717 - 400)(717 - 600)(717 - 434)}$

$\approx 86{,}751$ ft^2

28.

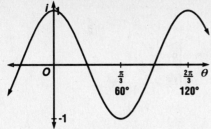

29. $2(4 - 3i)(7 - 2i) = 2(28 - 29i + 6i^2)$
$$= 2(22 - 29i)$$
$$= 44 - 58i$$

30. $x = 5 \cos \frac{5\pi}{6}$ $\qquad$ $y = 5 \sin \frac{5\pi}{6}$

$\quad = 5\left(-\frac{\sqrt{3}}{2}\right)$ $\qquad = 5\left(\frac{1}{2}\right)$

$\quad = -\frac{5\sqrt{3}}{2}$ $\qquad\quad = \frac{5}{2}$

$\quad = -\frac{5\sqrt{3}}{2} + \frac{5}{2}i$

31. $(0.20)\frac{6}{10} + (0.60)\frac{4}{10} = 0.12 + 0.24$
$$= 0.36 \text{ or } 36\%$$

The best answer is A.

9-8 Powers and Roots of Complex Numbers

PAGES 515-516

1. $(1 + i)(1 + i)(1 + i)(1 + i)(1 + i)$

$= (1 + 2i + i^2)(1 + 2i + i^2)(1 + i)$

$= (2i)(2i)(1 + i)$

$= -4(1 + i)$

$= -4 - 4i$

$r = \sqrt{1^2 + 1^2} = \sqrt{2}$

$\theta = \arctan \frac{1}{1} = \frac{\pi}{4}$

$(1 + i)^5 = \left[\sqrt{2}\left(\cos \frac{\pi}{4} + i \sin \frac{\pi}{4}\right)\right]^5$

$\qquad = (\sqrt{2})^5\left[\cos\left(5 \cdot \frac{\pi}{4}\right) + i \sin\left(5 \cdot \frac{\pi}{4}\right)\right]$

$\qquad = 4\sqrt{2}\left[\cos \frac{5\pi}{4} + i \sin \frac{5\pi}{4}\right]$

$\qquad = 4\sqrt{2}\left(-\frac{\sqrt{2}}{2} - \frac{\sqrt{2}}{2}i\right)$

$\qquad = -4 - 4i$

Same results, $-4 - 4i$. Answers may vary.

2. a. equilateral triangle $\quad$ **b.** square

$\quad$ **c.** regular hexagon

3. $360° \div 6 = 60°$ intervals

$\qquad 64^{\frac{1}{6}} = 2$

---

4. $\left(\cos \frac{\pi}{6} + i \sin \frac{\pi}{6}\right)^4 = \cos\left(4 \cdot \frac{\pi}{6}\right) + i \sin\left(4 \cdot \frac{\pi}{6}\right)$

$\qquad\qquad = \cos \frac{2\pi}{3} + i \sin \frac{2\pi}{3}$

$\qquad\qquad = -\frac{1}{2} + \frac{\sqrt{3}}{2}i$

5. $\left[3\left(\cos \frac{\pi}{3} + i \sin \frac{\pi}{3}\right)\right]^2$

$= 3^2\left[\cos\left(2 \cdot \frac{\pi}{3}\right) + i \sin\left(2 \cdot \frac{\pi}{3}\right)\right]$

$= 9\left(\cos \frac{2\pi}{3} + i \sin \frac{2\pi}{3}\right)$

$= 9\left(-\frac{1}{2} + \frac{\sqrt{3}}{2}i\right)$

$= -\frac{9}{2} + \frac{9\sqrt{3}}{2}i$

6. $r = \sqrt{(\sqrt{2})^2 + (\sqrt{2})^2} = 2$

$\theta = \arctan \frac{\sqrt{2}}{\sqrt{2}} = \frac{\pi}{4}$

$(\sqrt{2} + i\sqrt{2})^5 = \left[2\left(\cos \frac{\pi}{4} + i \sin \frac{\pi}{4}\right)\right]^5$

$\qquad = 2^5\left[\cos\left(5 \cdot \frac{\pi}{4}\right) + i \sin\left(5 \cdot \frac{\pi}{4}\right)\right]$

$\qquad = 32\left(\cos \frac{5\pi}{4} + i \sin \frac{5\pi}{4}\right)$

$\qquad = 32\left(-\frac{\sqrt{2}}{2} - \frac{\sqrt{2}}{2}i\right)$

$\qquad = -16\sqrt{2} - 16i\sqrt{2}$

7. $r = \sqrt{\left(-\frac{\sqrt{3}}{2}\right)^2 + \left(-\frac{1}{2}\right)^2} = 1$

$\theta = \arctan \frac{\sqrt{3}}{3} = \frac{7\pi}{6}$

$\left(-\frac{\sqrt{3}}{2} - \frac{i}{2}\right)^3 = \left(\cos \frac{7\pi}{6} + i \sin \frac{7\pi}{6}\right)^3$

$\qquad = \cos\left(3 \cdot \frac{7\pi}{6}\right) + i \sin\left(3 \cdot \frac{7\pi}{6}\right)$

$\qquad = \cos \frac{7\pi}{2} + i \sin \frac{7\pi}{2}$

$\qquad = 0 + i(-1)$

$\qquad = -i$

8. $(4i)^{\frac{1}{2}} = (0 + 4i)^{\frac{1}{2}}$

$\qquad = \left[4\left(\cos \frac{\pi}{2} + i \sin \frac{\pi}{2}\right)\right]^{\frac{1}{2}}$

$\qquad = 4^{\frac{1}{2}}\left[\cos\left(\frac{1}{2} \cdot \frac{\pi}{2}\right) + i \sin\left(\frac{1}{2} \cdot \frac{\pi}{2}\right)\right]$

$\qquad = 2\left(\cos \frac{\pi}{4} + i \sin \frac{\pi}{4}\right)$

$\qquad = 2\left(\frac{\sqrt{2}}{2} + \frac{\sqrt{2}}{2}i\right)$

$\qquad = \sqrt{2} + i\sqrt{2}$

9. $[-1(\cos \pi + i \sin \pi)]^{\frac{1}{3}} = (-1)^{\frac{1}{3}}\left(\cos \frac{\pi}{3} + i \sin \frac{\pi}{3}\right)$

$\qquad\qquad = -1\left(\frac{1}{2} + \frac{\sqrt{3}}{2}i\right)$

$\qquad\qquad = -\frac{1}{2} - \frac{\sqrt{3}}{2}i$

10. $r = \sqrt{1^2 + (-1)^2} = \sqrt{2}$

$\theta = \arctan \frac{1}{-1} = \frac{7\pi}{4}$

$(1 - i)^5 = \left[\sqrt{2}\left(\cos \frac{7\pi}{4} - i \sin \frac{7\pi}{4}\right)\right]^5$

$= (\sqrt{2})^5\left(\cos \frac{35\pi}{4} - i \sin \frac{35\pi}{4}\right)$

$= 4\sqrt{2}\left(\cos \frac{3\pi}{4} + i \sin \frac{3\pi}{4}\right)$

$= 4\sqrt{2}\left(-\frac{\sqrt{2}}{2} + i\frac{\sqrt{2}}{2}\right)$

$= -4 + 4i$

11. $r = \sqrt{3^2 + 4^2} = 5$

$\theta = \arctan \frac{4}{3} \approx 0.9273$

$(3 + 4i)^4 \approx [5(\cos 0.9273 + i \sin 0.9273)]^4$

$\approx 625(\cos 3.7092 + i \sin 3.7092)$

$\approx -527 - 336i$

12. $r = \sqrt{1^2 + (-1)^2} = \sqrt{2}$

$\theta = \arctan \frac{-1}{1} = \frac{7\pi}{4}$

$[-3(1 - i)]^3 = \left[-3\sqrt{2}\left(\cos \frac{7\pi}{4} + i \sin \frac{7\pi}{4}\right)\right]^3$

$= (-3\sqrt{2})^3\left(\cos \frac{21\pi}{4} + i \sin \frac{21\pi}{4}\right)$

$= -54\sqrt{2}\left(-\frac{\sqrt{2}}{2} - \frac{\sqrt{2}}{2}i\right)$

$= 54 + 54i$

13. $(1 + i)^{20} = \left[\sqrt{2}\left(\cos \frac{\pi}{4} + i \sin \frac{\pi}{4}\right)\right]^{20}$

$= (\sqrt{2})^{20}(\cos 5\pi + i \sin 5\pi)$

$= 1024(-1 + 0i)$

$= -1024$

14. $r = \sqrt{(-2)^2 + (2\sqrt{3})^2} = 4$

$\theta = \arctan -\sqrt{3} = \frac{2\pi}{3}$

$(-2 + 2i\sqrt{3})^4 = \left[4\left(\cos \frac{2\pi}{3} + i \sin \frac{2\pi}{3}\right)\right]^4$

$= 256\left(\cos \frac{8\pi}{3} + i \sin \frac{8\pi}{3}\right)$

$= 256\left(-\frac{1}{2} + \frac{\sqrt{3}}{2}i\right)$

$= -128 + 128i\sqrt{3}$

15. $r = \sqrt{12^2 + (-5)^2} = 13$

$\theta = \arctan \frac{12}{-5} \approx -1.1760 \text{ or } 5.1072$

$(-5 + 12i)^2 = [13(\cos 5.1072 + i \sin 5.1072)]^2$

$= 169(\cos 10.2144 + i \sin 10.2144)$

$= -119 - 120i$

16. $(0 + 8i)^{\frac{1}{3}} = \left[8\left(\cos \frac{\pi}{2} + i \sin \frac{\pi}{2}\right)\right]^{\frac{1}{3}}$

$= 2\left(\cos \frac{\pi}{6} + i \sin \frac{\pi}{6}\right)$

$= 2\left(\frac{\sqrt{3}}{2} + \frac{1}{2}i\right)$

$= \sqrt{3} + i \text{ or } 1.73 + i$

17. $[-2(1 + i)]^{\frac{1}{4}} = [2(-1 - i)]^{\frac{1}{4}}$

$= \left[2\sqrt{2}\left(\cos \frac{5\pi}{4} + i \sin \frac{5\pi}{4}\right)\right]^{\frac{1}{4}}$

$= 2^{\frac{3}{2}\cdot\frac{1}{4}}\left(\cos \frac{5\pi}{16} + i \sin \frac{5\pi}{16}\right)$

$\approx 1.297(0.5556 + 0.8315i)$

$\approx 0.72 + 1.08i$

18. $\sqrt[10]{-4i} = (-4i)^{\frac{1}{10}}$

$= [4(0 - i)]^{\frac{1}{10}}$

$= \left[4\left(\cos \frac{3\pi}{2} + i \sin \frac{3\pi}{2}\right)\right]^{\frac{1}{10}}$

$= 4^{\frac{1}{10}}\left(\cos \frac{3\pi}{20} + i \sin \frac{3\pi}{20}\right)$

$\approx 1.149(0.8910 + 0.4540i)$

$\approx 1.02 + 0.52i$

19. $(0 + 1i)^{\frac{1}{3}} = \left(\cos \frac{\pi}{2} + i \sin \frac{\pi}{2}\right)^{\frac{1}{3}}$

$= 1^{\frac{1}{3}}\left(\cos \frac{\pi}{6} + i \sin \frac{\pi}{6}\right)$

$= \frac{\sqrt{3}}{2} + \frac{1}{2}i \text{ or } 0.87 + 0.5i$

20. $(-1)^{\frac{1}{5}} = (-1 + 0i)^{\frac{1}{5}}$

$= (\cos \pi + i \sin \pi)^{\frac{1}{5}}$

$= 1^{\frac{1}{5}}\left(\cos \frac{\pi}{5} + i \sin \frac{\pi}{5}\right)$

$\approx 0.81 + 0.59i$

21. $\sqrt[4]{-2 + 2i\sqrt{3}} = (-2 + 2i\sqrt{3})^{\frac{1}{4}}$

$= [2(-1 + i\sqrt{3})]^{\frac{1}{4}}$

$= \left[2 \cdot 2\left(\cos \frac{2\pi}{3} + i \sin \frac{2\pi}{3}\right)\right]^{\frac{1}{4}}$

$= 4^{\frac{1}{4}}\left(\cos \frac{\pi}{6} + i \sin \frac{\pi}{6}\right)$

$= \sqrt{2}\left(\frac{\sqrt{3}}{2} + \frac{1}{2}i\right)$

$= \frac{\sqrt{6}}{2} + \frac{\sqrt{2}}{2}i$

$\approx 1.22 + 0.71i$

22. $x^3 + 1 = 0$

$\qquad x^3 = -1$

$\qquad -1 + 0i = \cos \pi + i \sin \pi$

$\qquad (-1 + 0i)^{\frac{1}{3}} = [\cos(\pi + 2n\pi) + i \sin(\pi + 2n\pi)]^{\frac{1}{3}}$

$\qquad\qquad = \cos \dfrac{\pi + 2n\pi}{3} + i \sin \dfrac{\pi + 2n\pi}{3}$

Let $n = 0$: $x_1 = \cos \dfrac{\pi}{3} + i \sin \dfrac{\pi}{3} = \dfrac{1}{2} + \dfrac{\sqrt{3}}{2}i$

Let $n = 1$: $x_2 = \cos \pi + i \sin \pi = -1$

Let $n = 2$: $x_3 = \cos \dfrac{5\pi}{3} + i \sin \dfrac{5\pi}{3} = \dfrac{1}{2} - \dfrac{\sqrt{3}}{2}i$

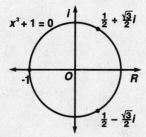

23. $x^5 = 1$

$\qquad 1 + 0i = \cos 0 + i \sin 0$

$\qquad (1 + 0i)^{\frac{1}{5}} = [\cos(0 + 2n\pi) + i \sin(0 + 2n\pi)]^{\frac{1}{5}}$

$\qquad\qquad = \cos \dfrac{2n\pi}{5} + i \sin \dfrac{2n\pi}{5}$

Let $n = 0$: $x_1 = \cos 0 + i \sin 0 = 1$

Let $n = 1$: $x_2 = \cos \dfrac{2\pi}{5} + i \sin \dfrac{2\pi}{5} \approx 0.31 + 0.95i$

Let $n = 2$: $x_3 = \cos \dfrac{4\pi}{5} + i \sin \dfrac{4\pi}{5} \approx -0.81 + 0.59i$

Let $n = 3$: $x_4 = \cos \dfrac{6\pi}{5} + i \sin \dfrac{6\pi}{5} \approx -0.81 - 0.59i$

Let $n = 4$: $x_5 = \cos \dfrac{8\pi}{5} + i \sin \dfrac{8\pi}{5} \approx 0.31 - 0.95i$

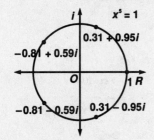

24. $x^3 - 8 = 0$

$\qquad x^3 = 8$

$\qquad 8 + 0i = 8(\cos 0 + i \sin 0)$

$\qquad (8 + 0i)^{\frac{1}{3}} = [8(\cos(0 + 2n\pi) + i \sin(0 + 2n\pi))]^{\frac{1}{3}}$

$\qquad\qquad = 2\left(\cos \dfrac{2n\pi}{3} + i \sin \dfrac{2n\pi}{3}\right)$

Let $n = 0$: $x_1 = 2(\cos 0 + i \sin 0) = 2$

Let $n = 1$: $x_2 = 2\left(\cos \dfrac{2\pi}{3} + i \sin \dfrac{2\pi}{3}\right) = -1 + i\sqrt{3}$

Let $n = 2$: $x_3 = 2\left(\cos \dfrac{4\pi}{3} + i \sin \dfrac{4\pi}{3}\right) = -1 - i\sqrt{3}$

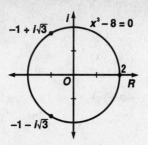

25. $x^6 = -1$

$\qquad -1 + 0i = \cos \pi + i \sin \pi$

$\qquad (-1 + 0i)^{\frac{1}{6}} = [\cos(\pi + 2n\pi) + i \sin(\pi + 2n\pi)]^{\frac{1}{6}}$

$\qquad\qquad = \cos \dfrac{\pi + 2n\pi}{6} + i \sin \dfrac{\pi + 2n\pi}{6}$

Let $n = 0$: $x_1 = \cos \dfrac{\pi}{6} + i \sin \dfrac{\pi}{6} = \dfrac{\sqrt{3}}{2} + \dfrac{1}{2}i$

Let $n = 1$: $x_2 = \cos \dfrac{\pi}{2} + i \sin \dfrac{\pi}{2} = i$

Let $n = 2$: $x_3 = \cos \dfrac{5\pi}{6} + i \sin \dfrac{5\pi}{6} = -\dfrac{\sqrt{3}}{2} + \dfrac{1}{2}i$

Let $n = 3$: $x_4 = \cos \dfrac{7\pi}{6} + i \sin \dfrac{7\pi}{6} = -\dfrac{\sqrt{3}}{2} - \dfrac{1}{2}i$

Let $n = 4$: $x_5 = \cos \dfrac{3\pi}{2} + i \sin \dfrac{3\pi}{2} = -i$

Let $n = 5$: $x_6 = \cos \dfrac{11\pi}{6} + i \sin \dfrac{11\pi}{6} = \dfrac{\sqrt{3}}{2} - \dfrac{1}{2}i$

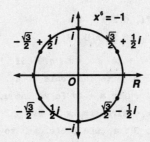

26. $x^4 + 1 = 2$

$\qquad x^4 = 1$

$\qquad 1 + 0i = \cos 0 + i \sin 0$

$\qquad (1 + 0i)^{\frac{1}{4}} = [\cos(0 + 2n\pi) + i \sin(0 + 2n\pi)]^{\frac{1}{4}}$

$\qquad\qquad = \cos \dfrac{n\pi}{2} + i \sin \dfrac{n\pi}{2}$

Let $n = 0$: $\cos 0 + i \sin 0 = 1$

Let $n = 1$: $\cos \dfrac{\pi}{2} + i \sin \dfrac{\pi}{2} = i$

Let $n = 2$: $\cos \pi + i \sin \pi = -1$

Let $n = 3$: $\cos \dfrac{3\pi}{2} + i \sin \dfrac{3\pi}{2} = -i$

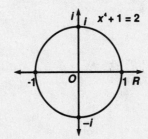

27. $x^5 - 6 = -7$

$x^5 = -1$

$-1 + 0i = \cos \pi + i \sin \pi$

$(-1 + 0i)^{\frac{1}{5}} = [\cos (\pi + 2n\pi) + i \sin (\pi + 2n\pi)]^{\frac{1}{5}}$

$\qquad = \cos \dfrac{\pi + 2n\pi}{5} + i \sin \dfrac{\pi + 2n\pi}{5}$

Let $n = 0$: $\cos \dfrac{\pi}{5} + i \sin \dfrac{\pi}{5} \approx 0.81 + 0.59i$

Let $n = 1$: $\cos \dfrac{3\pi}{5} + i \sin \dfrac{3\pi}{5} \approx -0.31 + 0.95i$

Let $n = 2$: $\cos \pi + i \sin \pi = -1$

Let $n = 3$: $\cos \dfrac{7\pi}{5} + i \sin \dfrac{7\pi}{5} \approx -0.31 - 0.95i$

Let $n = 4$: $\cos \dfrac{9\pi}{5} + i \sin \dfrac{9\pi}{5} \approx 0.81 - 0.59i$

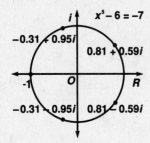

28. $-1, 1 - i, i$

29. $\pm 1 + 0i, -0.5 \pm 0.87i, 0.5 \pm 0.87i$

30. $1 + 0i, 0.31 \pm 0.95i, -0.81 \pm 0.59i$

31. a. $2 + 11i$ b. $-7 + 24i$ c. 6561

    d. This program will compute the roots of a complex number given in $a + bi$ form. The use must indicate the desired roots by using 2 for square roots, 3 for cube roots, and so on.

```
Prgm 14: CPLXROOT
:ClrHome
:Deg
:Disp "REAL PART="
:Input A
:Disp "IMAGINARY PART="
:Input B
:Disp "ROOTS (2,3,etc.)"
:Input P
:R▶P(A,B)
:0→N
:Lbl 1
:R^(1/P)cos((θ + 360N)/P)→X
:Disp "REAL PART="
:Disp X
:R^(1/P)sin((θ + 360N)/P)→Y
:Disp "IMAGINARY PART="
:Disp Y
:Pause
:If N = P1
:Goto 2
```

```
:N + 1→N
:Goto 1
:Lbl 2
:End
```

32. Since $42^3 = 2^3 \cdot 3^3 \cdot 7^3$, $2^a \cdot 3^b \cdot 7^c$ are the divisors of 42^3, where a, b, c are integers between 0 and 3 inclusive. Therefore, there are four choices for the exponent on 2 and four choices for the exponent on 3 and four choices for the exponent on 7. There are $4 \cdot 4 \cdot 4 = 4^3 = 64$ distinct divisors. Thus, excluding 1 and 42^3, there are 62 different divisors of 42^3.

33. a. $\dfrac{360°}{n}$

    b. a regular n-gon with one vertex at $(1, 0)$

34.

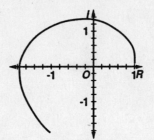

35. $f(x) = -2x^2 + 3x + 1$

$f'(x) = -4x + 3$

$\qquad = -4(1) + 3$

$\qquad = -1$

The slope is -1.

36. $\tan 21° = \dfrac{200}{x}$

$\qquad x \approx 521$ ft

37. a. $\sin 22° = \dfrac{300}{F_1}$

$\qquad F_1 \approx 800.8$ kg

    b. $\cos 22° = \dfrac{F_2}{300}$

$\qquad F_2 \approx 278.2$ kg

38. $x = \sqrt{2} \cos \left(-\dfrac{\pi}{2}\right)$ $y = \sqrt{2} \sin \left(-\dfrac{\pi}{2}\right)$

$\quad = \sqrt{2}(0)$ $= \sqrt{2}(-1)$

$\quad = 0$ $= -\sqrt{2}$

$0 - i\sqrt{2}$

39. $r = 5 \cdot 2 = 10$, $\theta = \dfrac{3\pi}{4} + \dfrac{2\pi}{3} = \dfrac{17\pi}{12}$

$5\left(\cos \dfrac{3\pi}{4} + i \sin \dfrac{3\pi}{4}\right) \cdot 2\left(\cos \dfrac{2\pi}{3} + i \sin \dfrac{2\pi}{3}\right)$

$= 10\left(\cos \dfrac{17\pi}{12} + i \sin \dfrac{17\pi}{12}\right)$

$\approx 10(-0.2588 - 0.9659i)$

$\approx -2.59 - 9.66i$

40. $*2 = 2^2 - 2(2) = 0$

$*1 = 1^2 - 2(1) = -1$

$*2 - *1 = 0 - (-1) = 1$

The best answer is C.

Chapter 9 Summary and Review

PAGES 518-520   SKILLS AND CONCEPTS

1.

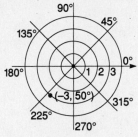

$(r, \theta + 360k°)$
$\rightarrow (-3, 50° + (-1)360°) \rightarrow (-3, -310°)$
$(-r, \theta + (2k + 1)180°)$
$\rightarrow (3, 50° + 180°) \rightarrow (3, 230°)$
$\rightarrow (3, 50° - 180°) \rightarrow (3, -130°)$

2.

$(r, \theta + 360k°) \rightarrow (1.5, -110° + 360°) \rightarrow (1.5, 250°)$
$(-r, \theta + (2k + 1)180°)$
$\rightarrow (-1.5, -110° + 180°) \rightarrow (-1.5, 70°)$
$\rightarrow (-1.5, -110° - 180°) \rightarrow (-1.5, -290°)$

3.

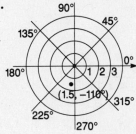

$(r, \theta + 2k\pi) \rightarrow \left(2, \frac{\pi}{2} - 2\pi\right) \rightarrow \left(2, -\frac{7\pi}{4}\right)$
$(-r, \theta + (2k + 1)\pi) \rightarrow \left(-2, \frac{\pi}{4} + \pi\right) \rightarrow \left(-2, \frac{5\pi}{4}\right)$
$\rightarrow \left(-2, \frac{\pi}{4} - \pi\right) \rightarrow \left(-2, -\frac{3\pi}{4}\right)$

4.

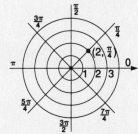

$(r, \theta + 2k\pi) \rightarrow \left(-3, -\frac{\pi}{2} + 2\pi\right) \rightarrow \left(-3, \frac{3\pi}{2}\right)$
$(-r, \theta + (2k + 1)\pi) \rightarrow \left(3, -\frac{\pi}{2} + \pi\right) \rightarrow \left(3, \frac{\pi}{2}\right)$
$\rightarrow \left(3, -\frac{\pi}{2} - \pi\right) \rightarrow \left(3, -\frac{3\pi}{2}\right)$

5.

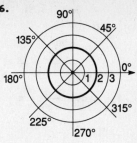

6.

7.

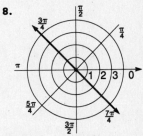

8.

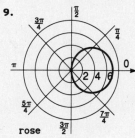

9.

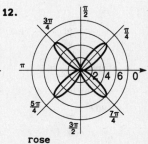

rose

10.

limaçon

11.

spiral of Archimedes

12.

rose

13. $x = r \cos \theta$ $y = r \sin \theta$

$\quad = 6 \cos \frac{\pi}{4}$ $= 6 \sin \frac{\pi}{4}$

$\quad = 6\left(\frac{\sqrt{2}}{2}\right)$ $= 6\left(\frac{\sqrt{2}}{2}\right)$

$\quad = 3\sqrt{2}$ $= 3\sqrt{2}$

$(3\sqrt{2}, 3\sqrt{2})$

14. $x = 2 \cos \left(-\frac{\pi}{6}\right)$ $y = 2 \sin \left(-\frac{\pi}{6}\right)$

$\quad = 2\left(\frac{\sqrt{3}}{2}\right)$ $= 2\left(-\frac{1}{2}\right)$

$\quad = \sqrt{3}$ $= -1$

$(\sqrt{3}, -1)$

15. $x = -2 \cos 2.3$ $y = -2 \sin 2.3$

$\quad \approx -2(-0.6663)$ $\approx -2(0.7457)$

$\quad \approx 1.33$ ≈ -1.49

$(1.33, -1.49)$

16. $x = -1 \cos (-4.5)$ $y = -1 \sin (-4.5)$
    ≈ 0.21 ≈ -0.98
    $(0.21, -0.98)$

17. $r = \sqrt{(-\sqrt{3})^2 + (-3)^2} = 2\sqrt{3}$
    $\theta = \text{Arctan } \dfrac{-3}{-\sqrt{3}} + \pi = \dfrac{4\pi}{3}$
    $\left(2\sqrt{3}, \dfrac{4\pi}{3}\right)$

18. $r = \sqrt{5^2 + 5^2} = 5\sqrt{2}$
    $\theta = \text{Arctan } \dfrac{5}{5} = \dfrac{\pi}{4}$
    $\left(5\sqrt{2}, \dfrac{\pi}{4}\right)$

19. $r = \sqrt{3^2 + (-2)^2} = \sqrt{13} \approx 3.61$
    $\theta = \text{Arctan } \dfrac{-2}{3} \approx -0.59$
    $(3.61, -0.59)$

20. $r = \sqrt{(-4)^2 + 2^2} = 2\sqrt{5} \approx 4.47$
    $\theta = \text{Arctan } \dfrac{2}{-4} + \pi \approx 2.68$
    $(4.47, 2.68)$

21. $2x + y + 3 = 0$
    $-\dfrac{2x}{\sqrt{5}} - \dfrac{y}{\sqrt{5}} - \dfrac{3}{\sqrt{5}} = 0$
    $\cos \phi = -\dfrac{2x}{\sqrt{5}}, \ \sin \phi = -\dfrac{1}{\sqrt{5}}, \ p = \dfrac{3}{\sqrt{5}} \text{ or } \dfrac{3\sqrt{5}}{5}$
    $\phi = \arctan \dfrac{1}{2} = 27°$
    Since $\cos \phi$ is negative and $\sin \phi$ is negative,
    $\phi = 207°$.
    $\dfrac{3\sqrt{5}}{5} = r \cos (\theta - 207°)$

22. $y = -3x - 4$
    $3x + y + 4 = 0$
    $-\dfrac{3}{\sqrt{10}} - \dfrac{y}{\sqrt{10}} - \dfrac{4}{\sqrt{10}} = 0$
    $\cos \phi = -\dfrac{3}{\sqrt{10}}, \ \sin \phi = -\dfrac{1}{\sqrt{10}}, \ p = \dfrac{4}{\sqrt{10}} \text{ or } \dfrac{2\sqrt{10}}{5}$
    $\phi = \arctan \dfrac{1}{3} \approx 18°$
    Since $\cos \phi$ is negative and $\sin \phi$ is negative,
    $\phi = 198°$.
    $\dfrac{2\sqrt{10}}{5} = r \cos (\theta - 198°)$

23. $3 = r \cos \left(\theta - \dfrac{\pi}{3}\right)$
    $3 = r\left(\cos \theta \cos \dfrac{\pi}{3} + \sin \theta \sin \dfrac{\pi}{3}\right)$
    $3 = \dfrac{1}{2}r \cos \theta + \dfrac{\sqrt{3}}{2} r \sin \theta$
    $3 = \dfrac{1}{2}x + \dfrac{\sqrt{3}}{2}y$
    $0 = x + \sqrt{3}y - 6$

24. $4 = r \cos \left(\theta + \dfrac{\pi}{2}\right)$
    $4 = r\left(\cos \theta \cos \dfrac{\pi}{2} - \sin \theta \sin \dfrac{\pi}{2}\right)$
    $4 = -r \sin \theta$
    $4 = -y$
    $y + 4 = 0$

25. $(2 + 3i) + (4 - 4i) = 6 - i$

26. $(-3 - i) - (2 + 7i) = -5 - 8i$

27. $i^{10} \cdot i^{25} = i^{35} = (i^4)^8 i^3 = -i$

28. $i^3(4 - 3i) = 4i^3 - 3i^4 = -4i - 3 \text{ or } -3 - 4i$

29. $(-i - 7)(i - 7) = -i^2 + 49 = -(-1) + 49 = 50$

30. $\dfrac{4 + i}{5 - 2i} = \left(\dfrac{4 + i}{5 - 2i}\right)\left(\dfrac{5 + 2i}{5 + 2i}\right)$
    $= \dfrac{20 + 13i + 2i^2}{25 - 4i^2}$
    $= \dfrac{18 + 13i}{29}$

31. $\dfrac{5}{\sqrt{2} - 4i} = \left(\dfrac{5}{\sqrt{2} - 4i}\right)\left(\dfrac{\sqrt{2} - 4i}{\sqrt{2} - 4i}\right)$
    $= \dfrac{5\sqrt{2} + 20i}{2 - 16i^2}$
    $= \dfrac{5\sqrt{2} + 20i}{18}$

32. $\dfrac{8 - i}{2 + 3i} = \left(\dfrac{8 - i}{2 + 3i}\right)\left(\dfrac{2 - 3i}{2 + 3i}\right)$
    $= \dfrac{16 - 26i + 3i^2}{4 - 9i^2}$
    $= \dfrac{13 - 26i}{13}$
    $= 1 - 2i$

33. $r = \sqrt{(-2)^2 + (2\sqrt{3})^2} = 4$
    $\theta = \text{Arctan } \dfrac{2\sqrt{3}}{-2} + \pi = \dfrac{2\pi}{3}$
    $4\left(\cos \dfrac{2\pi}{3} + i \sin \dfrac{2\pi}{3}\right)$

34. $r = \sqrt{6^2 + (-8)^2} = 10$
    $\theta = \text{Arctan } \dfrac{-8}{6} \approx -0.93$
    $10[\cos (-0.93) + i \sin (-0.93)]$

35. $x = 4 \cos \dfrac{5\pi}{6}$ $y = 4 \sin \dfrac{5\pi}{6}$
    $= 4\left(-\dfrac{\sqrt{3}}{2}\right)$ $= 4\left(\dfrac{1}{2}\right)$
    $= -2\sqrt{3}$ $= 2$
    $-2\sqrt{3} + 2i$

36. $x = 8 \cos \dfrac{7\pi}{4}$ $y = 8 \sin \dfrac{7\pi}{4}$
    $= 8\left(\dfrac{\sqrt{2}}{2}\right)$ $= 8\left(-\dfrac{\sqrt{2}}{2}\right)$
    $= 4\sqrt{2}$ $= -4\sqrt{2}$
    $4\sqrt{2} - 4i\sqrt{2}$

37. $r = 2 \cdot 4 = 8$, $\theta = \frac{\pi}{3} + \frac{\pi}{3} = \frac{2\pi}{3}$

$2\left(\cos \frac{\pi}{3} + i \sin \frac{\pi}{3}\right) \cdot 4\left(\cos \frac{\pi}{3} + i \sin \frac{\pi}{3}\right)$

$= 8\left(\cos \frac{2\pi}{3} + i \sin \frac{2\pi}{3}\right)$

$= 8\left(-\frac{1}{2} + \frac{\sqrt{3}}{2}i\right)$

$= -4 + 4i\sqrt{3}$

38. $r = 1.9 \cdot 3 = 5.7$, $\theta = 2.1 + 0.8 = 2.9$

$1.9(\cos 2.1 + i \sin 2.1)$

$\cdot 3(\cos 0.8 + i \sin 0.8)$

$= 5.7(\cos 2.9 + i \sin 2.9)$

$\approx 5.7(-0.9710 + 0.2392i)$

$\approx -5.53 + 1.36i$

39. $r = \frac{8}{2} = 4$, $\theta = \frac{7\pi}{6} - \frac{5\pi}{3} = -\frac{3\pi}{6}$ or $-\frac{\pi}{2}$

$8\left(\cos \frac{7\pi}{6} + i \sin \frac{7\pi}{6}\right) + 2\left(\cos \frac{5\pi}{3} + i \sin \frac{5\pi}{3}\right)$

$= 4\left[\cos \left(-\frac{\pi}{2}\right) + i \sin \left(-\frac{\pi}{2}\right)\right]$

$= 4(0 + (-1)i)$

$= -4i$

40. $r = \frac{6}{4} = \frac{3}{2}$, $\theta = \frac{\pi}{2} - \frac{\pi}{6} = \frac{\pi}{3}$

$6\left(\cos \frac{\pi}{2} + i \sin \frac{\pi}{2}\right) + 4\left(\cos \frac{\pi}{6} + i \sin \frac{\pi}{6}\right)$

$= \frac{3}{2}\left(\cos \frac{\pi}{3} + i \sin \frac{\pi}{3}\right)$

$= \frac{3}{2}\left(\frac{1}{2} + \frac{\sqrt{3}}{2}i\right)$

$= \frac{3}{4} + \frac{3\sqrt{3}}{4}i$

41. $r = \frac{2.2}{4.4} = 0.5$, $\theta = 1.5 - 0.6 = 0.9$

$2.2(\cos 1.5 + i \sin 1.5)$

$+ 4.4(\cos 0.6 + i \sin 0.6)$

$= 0.5(\cos 0.9 + i \sin 0.9)$

$\approx 0.5(0.6216 + 0.7833i)$

$\approx 0.31 + 0.39i$

42. $r = \sqrt{2^2 + 2^2} = 2\sqrt{2}$

$\theta = \text{Arctan} \frac{2}{2} = \frac{\pi}{4}$

$2 + 2i = 2\sqrt{2}\left[\cos \frac{\pi}{4} + i \sin \frac{\pi}{4}\right]$

$(2 + 2i)^8 = (2\sqrt{2})^8\left(\cos \left(8 \cdot \frac{\pi}{4}\right) + i \sin \left(8 \cdot \frac{\pi}{4}\right)\right)$

$= 4096(\cos 2\pi + i \sin 2\pi)$

$= 4096(1 + 0i)$

$= 4096$

43. $r = \sqrt{(\sqrt{3})^2 + (-1)^2} = 2$

$\theta = \text{Arctan} \frac{-1}{\sqrt{3}} = -\frac{\pi}{6}$

$\sqrt{3} - i = 2 \cos\left[\left(-\frac{\pi}{6}\right) + i \sin \left(-\frac{\pi}{6}\right)\right]$

$(\sqrt{3} - i)^7 = 2^7\left[\cos \left(-\frac{7\pi}{6}\right) + i \sin \left(-\frac{7\pi}{6}\right)\right]$

$= 128\left(-\frac{\sqrt{3}}{2} + \frac{1}{2}i\right)$

$= -64\sqrt{3} + 64i$

44. $r = \sqrt{(-1)^2 + 1^2} = \sqrt{2}$

$\theta = \text{Arctan} \frac{1}{-1} + \pi = \frac{3\pi}{4}$

$-1 + i = \sqrt{2}\left[\cos \frac{3\pi}{4} + i \sin \frac{3\pi}{4}\right]$

$(-1 + i)^4 = (\sqrt{2})^4\left(\cos \left(4 \cdot \frac{3\pi}{4}\right) + i \sin\left(4 \cdot \frac{3\pi}{4}\right)\right)$

$= 4(\cos 3\pi + i \sin 3\pi)$

$= 4(-1 + 0i)$

$= -4$

45. $r = \sqrt{(-2)^2 + (-2\sqrt{3})^2} = 4$

$\theta = \text{Arctan} \frac{-2\sqrt{3}}{-2} + \pi = \frac{4\pi}{3}$

$-2 - 2i\sqrt{3} = 4\left[\cos \frac{4\pi}{3} + i \sin \frac{4\pi}{3}\right]$

$(-2 - 2i\sqrt{3})^3 = 4^3\left(\cos \left(3 \cdot \frac{4\pi}{3}\right) + i \sin \left(3 \cdot \frac{4\pi}{3}\right)\right)$

$= 64(\cos 4\pi + i \sin 4\pi)$

$= 64(1 + 0i)$

$= 64$

46. $\sqrt[4]{i} = i^{\frac{1}{4}}$

$= (0 + i)^{\frac{1}{4}}$

$= \left[1\left(\cos \frac{\pi}{2} + i \sin \frac{\pi}{2}\right)\right]^{\frac{1}{4}}$

$= 1^{\frac{1}{4}}\left[\cos \left(\frac{1}{4} \cdot \frac{\pi}{2}\right) + i \sin \left(\frac{1}{4} \cdot \frac{\pi}{2}\right)\right]$

$= \cos \frac{\pi}{8} + i \sin \frac{\pi}{8}$

$\approx 0.92 + 0.38i$

47. $(\sqrt{3} + i)^{\frac{1}{3}} = \left[2\left(\cos \frac{\pi}{6} + i \sin \frac{\pi}{6}\right)\right]^{\frac{1}{3}}$

$= 2^{\frac{1}{3}}\left[\cos \left(\frac{1}{3} \cdot \frac{\pi}{6}\right) + i \sin \left(\frac{1}{3} \cdot \frac{\pi}{6}\right)\right]$

$\approx 1.260\left(\cos \frac{\pi}{18} + i \sin \frac{\pi}{18}\right)$

$\approx 1.260(0.9848 + 0.1736i)$

$\approx 1.24 + 0.22i$

48. $x^5 - 32 = 0$

$$x^5 = 32$$

$$32 + 0i = 32(\cos 0 + i \sin 0)$$

$$(32 + 0i)^{\frac{1}{5}}$$

$$= [32(\cos (0 + 2n\pi) + i \sin (0 + 2n\pi))]^{\frac{1}{5}}$$

$$= 2\left(\cos \frac{2n\pi}{5} + i \sin \frac{2n\pi}{5}\right)$$

Let $n = 0$: $x_1 = 2(\cos 0 + i \sin 0) = 2$

Let $n = 1$: $x_2 = 2\left(\cos \frac{2\pi}{5} + i \sin \frac{2\pi}{5}\right)$

$= 0.62 + 1.90i$

Let $n = 2$: $x_3 = 2\left(\cos \frac{4\pi}{5} + i \sin \frac{4\pi}{5}\right)$

$= -1.62 + 1.18i$

Let $n = 3$: $x_4 = 2\left(\cos \frac{6\pi}{5} + i \sin \frac{6\pi}{5}\right)$

$= -1.62 - 1.18i$

Let $n = 4$: $x_5 = 2\left(\cos \frac{8\pi}{5} + i \sin \frac{8\pi}{5}\right)$

$= 0.62 - 1.90i$

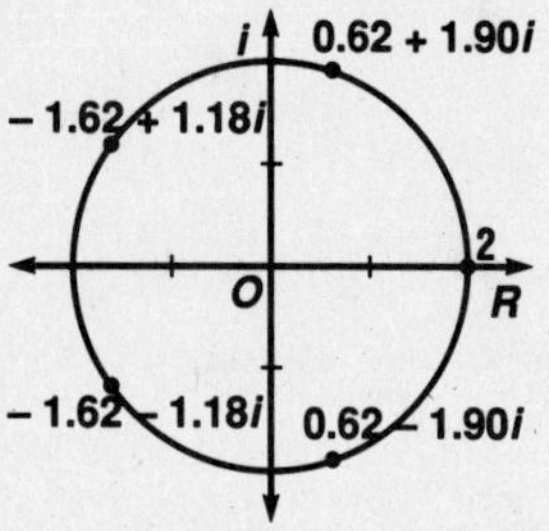

49. $x^6 - 1 = 0$

$$x^6 = 1$$

$$1 + 0i = \cos 0 + i \sin 0$$

$$(1 + 0i)^{\frac{1}{6}} = [\cos (0 + 2n\pi) + i \sin (0 + 2n\pi)]^{\frac{1}{6}}$$

$$= \cos \frac{n\pi}{3} + i \sin \frac{n\pi}{3}$$

Let $n = 0$: $x_1 = \cos 0 + i \sin 0 = 1$

Let $n = 1$: $x_2 = \cos \frac{\pi}{3} + i \sin \frac{\pi}{3} = \frac{1}{2} + \frac{\sqrt{3}}{2}i$

Let $n = 2$: $x_3 = \cos \frac{2\pi}{3} + i \sin \frac{2\pi}{3} = -\frac{1}{2} + \frac{\sqrt{3}}{2}i$

Let $n = 3$: $x_4 = \cos \pi + i \sin \pi = -1$

Let $n = 4$: $x_5 = \cos \frac{4\pi}{3} + i \sin \frac{4\pi}{3} = -\frac{1}{2} - \frac{\sqrt{3}}{2}i$

Let $n = 5$: $x_6 = \cos \frac{5\pi}{3} + i \sin \frac{5\pi}{3} = \frac{1}{2} - \frac{\sqrt{3}}{2}i$

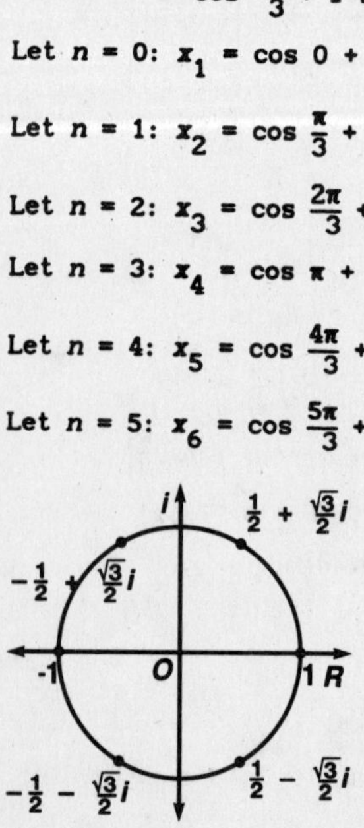

PAGE 520 APPICATIONS AND PROBLEM SOLVING

50. lemniscate

51.
$$E = I \cdot Z$$

$$50 + 180j = I(4 + 5j)$$

$$I = \frac{50 + 180j}{4 + 5j}$$

$$= \left(\frac{50 + 180j}{4 + 5j}\right)\left(\frac{4 - 5j}{4 + 5j}\right)$$

$$= \frac{20 + 695j - 900j^2}{16 - 25j^2}$$

$$= \frac{920 + 695j}{41}$$

$$\approx 22.44 + 16.95j$$

Chapter 9 Test

PAGE 521

1.

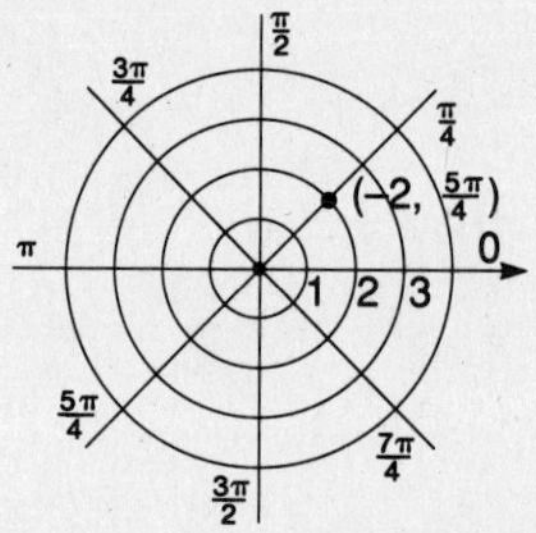

$$(r, \theta + 2k\pi) \rightarrow \left(-2, \frac{5\pi}{4} - 2\pi\right) \rightarrow \left(-2, -\frac{3\pi}{4}\right)$$

$$(-r, \theta + (2k + 1)\pi) \rightarrow \left(2, \frac{5\pi}{4} - \pi\right) \rightarrow \left(2, \frac{\pi}{4}\right)$$

$$\rightarrow \left(2, \frac{5\pi}{4} - 3\pi\right) \rightarrow \left(2, -\frac{7\pi}{4}\right)$$

2.

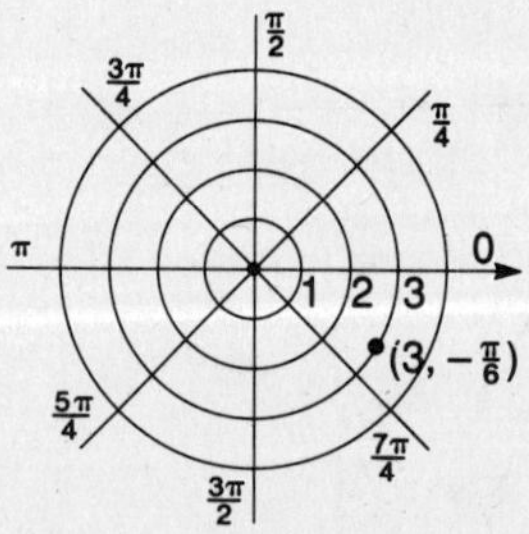

$$(r, \theta + 2k\pi) \rightarrow \left(3, -\frac{\pi}{6} + 2\pi\right) \rightarrow \left(3, \frac{11\pi}{6}\right)$$

$$(-r, \theta + (2k + 1)\pi) \rightarrow \left(-3, -\frac{\pi}{6} + \pi\right) \rightarrow \left(-3, \frac{5\pi}{6}\right)$$

$$\rightarrow \left(-3, -\frac{\pi}{6} - \pi\right) \rightarrow \left(-3, -\frac{7\pi}{6}\right)$$

3.

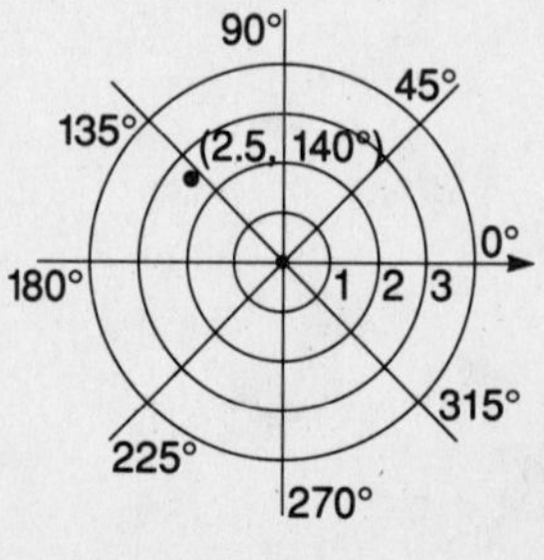

$(r, \theta + 360k°)$

$\rightarrow (2.5, 140° - 360°) \rightarrow (2.5, -220°)$

$(-r, \theta + (2k + 1)180°)$

$\rightarrow (-2.5, 140° - 180°) \rightarrow (-2.5, -40°)$

$\rightarrow (-2.5, 140° + 180°) \rightarrow (-2.5, 320°)$

4.

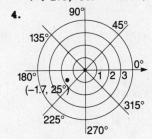

$(r, \theta = 360k°)$

$\rightarrow (-1.7, 25° - 360°) \rightarrow (-1.7, -335°)$

$(-r, \theta + (2k + 1)180°)$

$\rightarrow (1.7, 25° + 180°) \rightarrow (1.7, 205°)$

$\rightarrow (1.7, 25° - 180°) \rightarrow (1.7, -155°)$

5.   **6.**

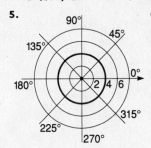

7.   **8.**

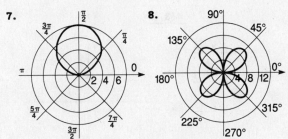

9.   **10.**

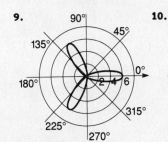

11. $x = r \cos \theta$ $y = r \sin \theta$

$= 3 \cos \left(- \dfrac{5\pi}{4}\right)$ $= 3 \sin \left(- \dfrac{5\pi}{4}\right)$

$= 3 \left(- \dfrac{\sqrt{2}}{2}\right)$ $= 3 \left(\dfrac{\sqrt{2}}{2}\right)$

$= - \dfrac{3\sqrt{2}}{2}$ $= \dfrac{3\sqrt{2}}{2}$

$\left(- \dfrac{3\sqrt{2}}{2}, \dfrac{3\sqrt{2}}{2}\right)$

12. $x = -4 \cos 1.4$ $y = -4 \sin 1.4$

≈ -0.68 ≈ -3.94

$(-0.68, -3.94)$

---

13. $x = 2\sqrt{2} \cos \dfrac{\pi}{4}$ $y = 2\sqrt{2} \sin \dfrac{\pi}{4}$

$= 2\sqrt{2}\left(\dfrac{\sqrt{2}}{2}\right)$ $= 2\sqrt{2}\left(\dfrac{\sqrt{2}}{2}\right)$

$= 2$ $= 2$

$(2, 2)$

14. $5x + 6y + 3 = 0$

$- \dfrac{5x}{\sqrt{61}} - \dfrac{6y}{\sqrt{61}} - \dfrac{3}{\sqrt{61}} = 0$

$\cos \phi = - \dfrac{5}{\sqrt{61}}, \sin \phi = - \dfrac{6}{\sqrt{61}}, p = \dfrac{3}{\sqrt{61}}$ or $\dfrac{3\sqrt{61}}{61}$

$\phi = \arctan \dfrac{6}{5} \approx 50°$

Since $\cos \phi$ is negative and $\sin \phi$ is negative,

$\phi = 230°$.

$\dfrac{3\sqrt{61}}{61} = r \cos (\theta - 230°)$

15. $2x - 4y - 1 = 0$

$\dfrac{2x}{2\sqrt{5}} - \dfrac{4y}{2\sqrt{5}} - \dfrac{1}{2\sqrt{5}} = 0 \rightarrow \dfrac{x}{\sqrt{5}} - \dfrac{2y}{\sqrt{5}} - \dfrac{1}{2\sqrt{5}} = 0$

$\cos \phi = \dfrac{1}{\sqrt{5}}, \sin \phi = - \dfrac{2}{\sqrt{5}}, p = \dfrac{1}{2\sqrt{5}}$ or $\dfrac{\sqrt{5}}{10}$

$\phi = \arctan \dfrac{-4}{2} \approx - 63°$

$\dfrac{\sqrt{5}}{10} = r \cos (\theta + 63°)$

16. $y = - \dfrac{1}{3}x + 2$

       $3y = -x + 6$

$x + 3y - 6 = 0$

$\dfrac{x}{\sqrt{10}} + \dfrac{3y}{\sqrt{10}} - \dfrac{6}{\sqrt{10}} = 0$

$\cos \phi = \dfrac{1}{\sqrt{10}}, \sin \phi = \dfrac{3}{\sqrt{10}}, p = \dfrac{6}{\sqrt{10}}$ or $\dfrac{3\sqrt{10}}{5}$

$\phi = \arctan \dfrac{3}{1} \approx 72°$

$\dfrac{3\sqrt{10}}{5} = r \cos (\theta - 72°)$

17. $i^{93} = (i^4)^{23}i = i$

18. $(2 - 5i) + (-2 + 4i) = 0 - 1i = -i$

19. $(-4 + i) - (4 - 2i) = -8 + 3i$

20. $(3 + 5i)(3 - 2i) = 9 + 9i - 10i^2 = 19 + 9i$

21. $(7 + i)^2 = 49 + 14i + i^2 = 48 + 14i$

22. $\dfrac{6 - 2i}{2 + i} = \left(\dfrac{6 - 2i}{2 + i}\right)\left(\dfrac{2 - i}{2 - i}\right)$

       $= \dfrac{12 - 10i + 2i^2}{4 - i^2}$

       $= \dfrac{10 - 10i}{5}$

       $= 2 - 2i$

23. $r = \sqrt{(-4)^2 + 4^2} = 4\sqrt{2}$

       $\theta = \text{Arctan} \dfrac{4}{-4} + \pi = \dfrac{3\pi}{4}$

       $4\sqrt{2}\left(\cos \dfrac{3\pi}{4} + i \sin \dfrac{3\pi}{4}\right)$

24. $r = \sqrt{(-5)^2 + 0^2} = 5$

$\theta = \text{Arctan} \dfrac{0}{-5} + \pi = \pi$

$5(\cos \pi - i \sin \pi)$

25. $r = \sqrt{6^2 + (-6\sqrt{3})^2} = 12$

$\theta = \text{Arctan} \dfrac{-6\sqrt{3}}{6} = \text{Arctan} (-\sqrt{3}) = -\dfrac{\pi}{3}$

$12\left[\cos\left(-\dfrac{\pi}{3}\right) + i \sin\left(-\dfrac{\pi}{3}\right)\right]$

26. $r = 4 \cdot 3 = 12, \quad \theta = \dfrac{3\pi}{2} + \dfrac{\pi}{4} = \dfrac{7\pi}{4}$

$4\left(\cos\dfrac{3\pi}{2} + i\sin\dfrac{3\pi}{2}\right) \cdot 3\left(\cos\dfrac{\pi}{4} + i\sin\dfrac{\pi}{4}\right)$

$= 12\left(\cos\dfrac{7\pi}{4} + i\sin\dfrac{7\pi}{4}\right)$

$= 12\left(\dfrac{\sqrt{2}}{2} - \dfrac{\sqrt{2}}{2}i\right)$

$= 6\sqrt{2} - 6i\sqrt{2}$

27. $(\sqrt{3} - 3i)(\sqrt{3} + i) = 3 - 3i\sqrt{3} + i\sqrt{3} - 3i^2$

$= 6 - 2i\sqrt{3}$

28. $r = \dfrac{2\sqrt{3}}{\sqrt{3}} = 2, \quad \theta = \dfrac{2\pi}{3} - \dfrac{\pi}{6} = \dfrac{\pi}{2}$

$2\sqrt{3}\left(\cos\dfrac{2\pi}{3} + i\sin\dfrac{2\pi}{3}\right) + \sqrt{3}\left(\cos\dfrac{\pi}{6} + i\sin\dfrac{\pi}{6}\right)$

$= 2\left(\cos\dfrac{\pi}{2} + i\sin\dfrac{\pi}{2}\right)$

$= 2(0 + i)$

$= 2i$

29. $r = \sqrt{1^2 + (-1)^2} = \sqrt{2}$

$\theta = \text{Arctan} \dfrac{-1}{1} = -\dfrac{\pi}{4}$

$1 - i = \sqrt{2}\left[\cos\left(-\dfrac{\pi}{4}\right) + i\sin\left(-\dfrac{\pi}{4}\right)\right]$

$(1 - i)^8 = \left[\sqrt{2}\left(\cos\left(-\dfrac{\pi}{4}\right) + i\sin\left(-\dfrac{\pi}{4}\right)\right)\right]^8$

$= (\sqrt{2})^8\left[\cos\left(-\dfrac{8\pi}{4}\right) + i\sin\left(-\dfrac{8\pi}{4}\right)\right]$

$= 16(\cos(-2\pi) + i\sin(-2\pi))$

$= 16(1 + 0i)$

$= 16$

30. $\sqrt[3]{-8i} = (-8i)^{\frac{1}{3}}$

$= [-8(0 + i)]^{\frac{1}{3}}$

$= \left[-8\left(\cos\dfrac{\pi}{2} + i\sin\dfrac{\pi}{2}\right)\right]^{\frac{1}{3}}$

$= (-8)^{\frac{1}{3}}\left[\cos\left(\dfrac{1}{3}\cdot\dfrac{\pi}{2}\right) + i\sin\left(\dfrac{1}{3}\cdot\dfrac{\pi}{2}\right)\right]$

$= -2\left(\cos\dfrac{\pi}{6} + i\sin\dfrac{\pi}{6}\right)$

$= -2\left(\dfrac{\sqrt{3}}{2} + \dfrac{1}{2}i\right)$

$= -\sqrt{3} - i \text{ or } -1.73 - i$

31. $x^8 - 1 = 0$

$x^8 = 1$

$x = (1 + 0i)^{\frac{1}{8}} = (\cos 2n\pi + i\sin 2n\pi)^{\frac{1}{8}}$

$= \cos\dfrac{2n\pi}{8} + i\sin\dfrac{2n\pi}{8}$

Let $n = 0$: $x_1 = \cos 0 + i\sin 0 = 1$

Let $n = 1$: $x_2 = \cos\dfrac{\pi}{4} + i\sin\dfrac{\pi}{4} = \dfrac{\sqrt{2}}{2} + \dfrac{\sqrt{2}}{2}i$

Let $n = 2$: $x_3 = \cos\dfrac{\pi}{2} + i\sin\dfrac{\pi}{2} = i$

Let $n = 3$: $x_4 = \cos\dfrac{3\pi}{4} + i\sin\dfrac{3\pi}{4} = -\dfrac{\sqrt{2}}{2} + \dfrac{\sqrt{2}}{2}i$

Let $n = 4$: $x_5 = \cos\pi + i\sin\pi = -i$

Let $n = 5$: $x_6 = \cos\dfrac{5\pi}{4} + i\sin\dfrac{5\pi}{4} = -\dfrac{\sqrt{2}}{2} - \dfrac{\sqrt{2}}{2}i$

Let $n = 6$: $x_7 = \cos\dfrac{3\pi}{2} + i\sin\dfrac{3\pi}{2} = -1$

Let $n = 7$: $x_8 = \cos\dfrac{7\pi}{4} + i\sin\dfrac{7\pi}{4} = \dfrac{\sqrt{2}}{2} - \dfrac{\sqrt{2}}{2}i$

32. $E = I \cdot Z$

$= 8(\cos 307° + j\sin 307°)$

$\cdot 20(\cos 115° + j\sin 115°)$

$= (8 \cdot 20)[\cos(307° + 115°)$

$+ j\sin(307° + 115°)]$

$= 160(\cos 422° + j\sin 422°)$

$= 160(\cos 62° + j\sin 62°)$

33. $x = \dfrac{-6 \pm \sqrt{6^2 - 4(3)(7)}}{2(3)}$

$= \dfrac{-6 \pm \sqrt{-48}}{6}$

$= \dfrac{-6 \pm 4i\sqrt{3}}{6}$

$= -1 \pm \dfrac{2i\sqrt{3}}{3}$

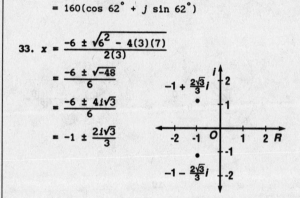

PAGE 521   BONUS

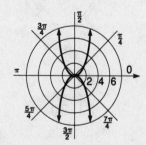

234

Chapter 10   Conics

PAGE 529   CHECKING FOR UNDERSTANDING

1. Answers will vary. Answers should be in the form, $(x + 2)^2 + (y - 6)^2 = r^2$ with r being the random value.

2. Both are 1.

3. Expand the factored form of the x and y terms. Combine the constant terms. Write the terms in order of degree and set equal to zero.

4. A geosynchronous orbit is one in which the satellite travels around Earth but remains above the same point on Earth at all times. The edge of Earth modeled by a circle and the circle representing a geosynchronous orbit are concentric circles.

5. $x^2 + y^2 = 81$

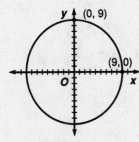

6. $x^2 + y^2 = 6$

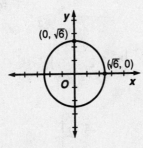

7. $(x - 2)^2 + (y + 7)^2 = 100$

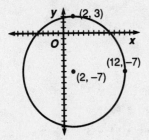

8. $(x - 3)^2 + (y + 2)^2 = 49$

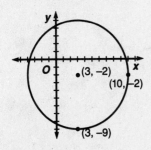

9. $(4, 3)$, 3

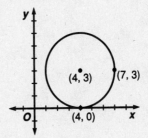

10. $(-4, 7)$, $\sqrt{7}$

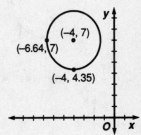

11. $(x - 3)^2 + (y - 2)^2 = \dfrac{10}{4}$

$(3, 2)$, $\dfrac{\sqrt{10}}{2}$

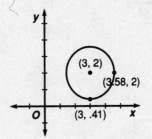

12. $9(x + 5)^2 + 9(y + 3)^2 = 4$

$(x + 5)^2 + (y + 3)^2 = \dfrac{4}{9}$

$(-5, -3)$, $\dfrac{2}{3}$

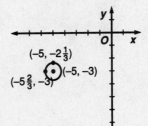

13. $0^2 + 0^2 + D \cdot 0 + E \cdot 0 + F = 0 \rightarrow \qquad F = 0$

$2.8^2 + 0^2 + 2.8D + E \cdot 0 + F \rightarrow 7.84 + 2.8D + F = 0$

$5^2 + 2^2 + 5D + 2E + F = 0 \rightarrow 29 + 5D + 2E + F = 0$

$7.84 + 2.8D = 0 \rightarrow D = -\dfrac{7.84}{2.8} = -2.8$

$29 + 5(-2.8) + 2E = 0 \rightarrow 2E = -15 \rightarrow E = -7.5$

$x^2 + y^2 - 2.8x - 7.5y = 0$

$(x^2 - 2.8x + 1.4^2) + (y^2 - 13.5y + 3.75^2)$

$\qquad\qquad = 0 + 1.4^2 + 3.75^2$

$(x - 1.4)^2 + (y - 3.75)^2 = 16.02$

14. $(x + 3)^2 + (y + 5)^2 = 16$

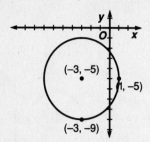

15. $(x - 7)^2 + (y - 4)^2 = 5$

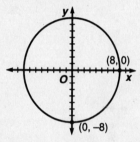

16. $x^2 + y^2 = 64$

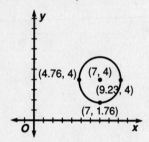

17.
$$x^2 + x + y^2 = \frac{3}{4}$$
$$\left(x^2 + x + \left(\frac{1}{2}\right)^2\right) + y^2 = \frac{3}{4} + \frac{1}{4}$$
$$\left(x + \frac{1}{2}\right)^2 + y^2 = 1$$

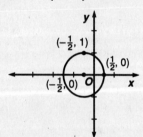

18.
$$x^2 - 4x + y^2 + 6y - 12 = 0$$
$$(x^2 - 4x + 4) + (y^2 + 6y + 9) = 12 + 4 + 9$$
$$(x - 2)^2 + (y + 3)^2 = 25$$

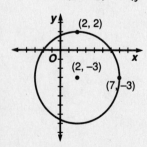

19. $3x^2 + 3y^2 = 27$
$$x^2 + y^2 = 9$$

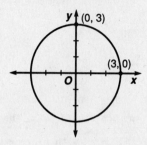

20.
$$x^2 + 8x + y^2 + 2y - 8 = 0$$
$$(x^2 + 8x + 16) + (y^2 + 2y + 1) = 8 + 16 + 1$$
$$(x + 4)^2 + (y + 1)^2 = 25$$

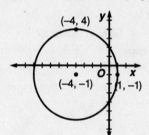

21.
$$16x^2 + 8x + 16y^2 - 32y = 127$$
$$x^2 + \frac{1}{2}x + y^2 - 2y = \frac{127}{16}$$
$$\left(x^2 + \frac{1}{2}x + \frac{1}{16}\right) + (y^2 - 2y + 1)^2 = \frac{127}{16} + \frac{1}{16} + 1$$
$$\left(x + \frac{1}{4}\right)^2 + (y - 1)^2 = 9$$

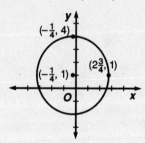

22.
$$6x^2 - 12x + 6y^2 + 36y = 36$$
$$x^2 - 2x + y^2 + 6y = 6$$
$$(x^2 - 2x + 1) + (y^2 + 6y + 9) = 6 + 1 + 9$$
$$(x - 1)^2 + (y + 3)^2 = 16$$

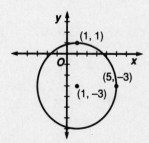

23.
$$16x^2 - 48x + 16y^2 + 8y = 75$$
$$x^2 - 3x + y^2 + \frac{1}{2}y = \frac{75}{16}$$
$$(x^2 - 3x + 2.25) + \left(y^2 + \frac{1}{2}y + \frac{1}{16}\right) = \frac{75}{16} + \frac{1}{16} + 2.25$$
$$(x - 1.5)^2 + \left(y + \frac{1}{4}\right)^2 = 7$$

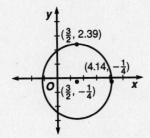

24.
$$x^2 - 4x + y^2 - 12y = -30$$
$$(x^2 - 4x + 4) + (y^2 - 12y + 36) = -30 + 4 + 36$$
$$(x - 2)^2 + (y - 6)^2 = 10$$

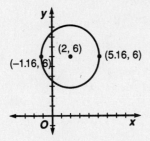

25.
$$x^2 + 14x + y^2 + 24y = -157$$
$$(x^2 + 14x + 49) + (y^2 + 24y + 144) = -157 + 49 + 144$$
$$(x + 7)^2 + (y + 12)^2 = 36$$

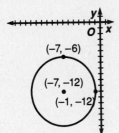

26. $7^2 + (-1)^2 + 7D - E + F = 0 \rightarrow 7D - E + F = -50$

$11^2 + (-5)^2 + 11D - 5E + F = 0 \rightarrow 11D - 5E + F = -146$

$3^2 + (-5)^2 + 3D - 5E + F = 0 \rightarrow 3D - 5E + F = -34$

$11D - 5E + F = -146$	$-98 - E + F = -50$
$\underline{3D - 5E + F = -34}$	$\underline{-154 - 5E + F = -146}$
$8D = -112$	$56 + 4E = 96$
$D = -14$	$E = 10$

$$7(-14) - 10 + F = -50$$
$$-108 + F = -50$$
$$F = 58$$
$$x^2 + y^2 - 14x + 10y + 58 = 0$$
$$(x^2 - 14x + 49) + (y^2 + 10y + 25) = -58 + 49 + 25$$
$$(x - 7)^2 + (y + 5)^2 = 16$$

center (7, -5), radius 4

27. $1^2 + 3^2 + D + 3E + F = 0 \rightarrow D + 3E + F = -10$

$5^2 + 5^2 + 5D + 5E + F = 0 \rightarrow 5D + 5E + F = -50$

$5^2 + 3^2 + 5D + 3E + F = 0 \rightarrow 5D + 3E + F = -34$

$5D + 5E + F = -50$	$D + F = 14$
$\underline{5D + 3E + F = -34}$	$\underline{5D + F = -10}$
$2E = -16$	$-4D = 24$
$E = -8$	$D = -6$

$$-6 + -24 + F = -10$$
$$F = 20$$
$$x^2 + y^2 - 6x - 8y + 20 = 0$$
$$(x^2 - 6x + 9) + (y^2 - 8y + 16) = -20 + 9 + 16$$
$$(x - 3)^2 + (y - 4)^2 = 5$$

(3, 4); $\sqrt{5}$

28. $5^2 + 3^2 + 5D + 3E + F = 0 \rightarrow 5D + 3E + F = -34$

$(-2)^2 + 2^2 - 2D + 2E + F = 0 \rightarrow -2D + 2E + F = -8$

$(-1)^2 + (-5)^2 - D - 5E + F = 0 \rightarrow -D - 5E + F = -26$

$-2D + 2E + F = -8$	$5D + 3E + F = -34$
$\underline{-D - 5E + F = -26}$	$\underline{-D - 5E + F = -26}$
$-D + 7E = 18$	$6D + 8E = -8$
$D = 7E - 18$	$6(7E - 18) + 8E = -8$
	$50E = 100$
	$E = 2$

$$D = 7(2) - 18 = -4$$
$$4 - 10 + F = -26$$
$$F = -20$$
$$x^2 + y^2 - 4x + 2y - 20 = 0$$
$$(x^2 - 4x + 4) + (y^2 + 2y + 1) = 20 + 4 + 1$$
$$(x - 2)^2 + (y + 1)^2 = 25$$

(2, -1), 5

29. $7^2 + (-1)^2 + 7D - E + F = 0 \rightarrow 7D - E + F = -50$

$7^2 + 5^2 + 7D + 5E + F = 0 \rightarrow 7D + 5E + F = -74$

$1^2 + (-1)^2 + D - E + F = 0 \rightarrow D - E + F = -2$

$7D - E + F = -50$	$7D + F = -54$
$\underline{7D + 5E + F = -74}$	$\underline{D + F = -6}$
$-6E = 24$	$6D = -48$
$E = -4$	$D = -8$

$$-8 + 4 + F = -2$$
$$F = 2$$
$$x^2 + y^2 - 8x - 4y + 2 = 0$$
$$(x^2 - 8x + 16) + (y^2 - 4y + 4) = -2 + 16 + 4$$
$$(x - 4)^2 + (y - 2)^2 = 18$$

(4, 2), $\sqrt{18} = 3\sqrt{2}$

30. $(-10)^2 + (-5)^2 - 10D - 5E + F = 0 \rightarrow$
$-10D - 5E + F = -125$

$(-2)^2 + 7^2 - 2D + 7E + F = 0 \rightarrow$
$-2D + 7E + F = -53$

$(-9)^2 + 0^2 - 9D + 0 \cdot E + F = 0 \rightarrow$
$-9D + F = -81$

$F = -81 + 9D$

$-70D - 35E + 7F = -875 \qquad F = -81 + 9(-6)$

$\underline{-10D + 35E + 5F = -265} \qquad = -135$

$-80D + 12F = -1140$

$-80D + 12(-81 + 9D) = -1140$

$28D = -168$

$D = -6$

$-2(-6) + 7E - 135 = -53$

$7E = 70$

$E = 10$

$x^2 + y^2 - 6x + 10y - 135 = 0$

$(x^2 - 6x + 9) + (y^2 + 10y + 25) = 135 + 9 + 25$

$(x - 3)^2 + (y + 5)^2 = 169$

$(3, -5); 13$

31. $2^2 + (-1)^2 + 2D - E + F = 0 \rightarrow 2D - E + F = -5$

$(-3)^2 + 0^2 - 3D - 0 \cdot E + F = 0 \rightarrow -3D + F = -9$

$1^2 + 4^2 + D + 4E + F = 0 \rightarrow D + 4E + F = -17$

$8D - 4E + 4F = -20$

$\underline{D + 4E + F = -17} \qquad F = -9 + 3\left(\frac{1}{3}\right)$

$9D + 5F = -37 \qquad\qquad = -8$

$9D + 5(-9 + 3D) = -37 \qquad \frac{1}{3} + 4E + (-8) = -17$

$24D = 8 \qquad\qquad 4E = -\frac{28}{3}$

$D = \frac{1}{3} \qquad\qquad E = -\frac{7}{3}$

$x^2 + y^2 + \frac{1}{3}x - \frac{7}{3}y - 8 = 0$

$\left(x^2 + \frac{1}{3}x + \frac{1}{36}\right) + \left(y^2 - \frac{7}{3}y + \frac{49}{36}\right) = 8 + \frac{1}{36} + \frac{49}{36}$

$\left(x + \frac{1}{6}\right)^2 + \left(y - \frac{7}{6}\right)^2 = \frac{169}{18}$

$\left(-\frac{1}{6}, \frac{7}{6}\right), \frac{13}{3\sqrt{2}} = \frac{13\sqrt{2}}{6}$

32. $r = \sqrt{(7 + 2)^2 + (-1 - 4)^2}$
$= \sqrt{81 + 25}$
$= \sqrt{106} \qquad (x + 2)^2 + (y - 4)^2 = 106$

33. $r = \sqrt{(0 + 3)^2 + (0 - 4)^2}$
$= \sqrt{9 + 16}$
$= 5 \qquad (x + 3)^2 + (y - 4)^2 = 25$

34. $d = \sqrt{(-2 - 4)^2 + (-3 - 5)^2}$
$= \sqrt{36 + 64}$
$= \sqrt{100} = 10 \qquad \frac{1}{2}d = r = s$

midpoint: $\frac{-2 + 4}{2} = 1, \frac{-3 + 5}{2} = 1$

$(x - 1)^2 + (y - 1)^2 = 25$

35. $d = \sqrt{(-3 - 2)^2 + (4 - 1)^2}$
$= \sqrt{25 + 9} \qquad = \sqrt{34}$

$\frac{1}{2}d = r = \frac{\sqrt{34}}{2}$

midpoint: $\frac{-3 + 2}{2} = -\frac{1}{2}, \frac{4 + 1}{2} = \frac{5}{2}$

$\left(x + \frac{1}{2}\right)^2 + \left(y - \frac{5}{2}\right)^2 = \frac{34}{4}$

36. $1 = \sqrt{\left(\frac{\sqrt{2}}{2} - x\right)^2 + \left(\frac{\sqrt{2}}{2} - 0\right)^2}$

$1 = \left(\frac{\sqrt{2}}{2} - x\right)^2 + \frac{2}{4}$

$\frac{1}{2} = \left(\frac{\sqrt{2}}{2} - x\right)^2$

$\frac{1}{2} = \frac{2}{4} - \sqrt{2}x + x^2$

$0 = x^2 - \sqrt{2}x$

$0 = x(x - \sqrt{2})$

$x = 0$ or $x = \sqrt{2}$

center: $(0, 0)$ or $(\sqrt{2}, 0)$

$x^2 + y^2 = 1$ or $(x - \sqrt{2})^2 + y^2 = 1$

37. $2x - y = -3$
$y = 2x + 3$

line perpendicular to $y = 2x + 3$, passing through $(5, 12)$:

$y = -\frac{1}{2}x + b$

$12 = -\frac{1}{2}(5) + b$

$\frac{29}{2} = b \qquad\qquad$ So, $y = -\frac{1}{2}x + \frac{29}{2}$.

$y = 2x + 3 \qquad\qquad y = 2x + 3$

$y = -\frac{1}{2}x + \frac{29}{2} \quad\rightarrow\quad \dfrac{4y = -2x + 58}{5y = 61}$

$\qquad\qquad\qquad\qquad y = \frac{61}{5}$

$\frac{61}{5} = 2x + 3$

$\frac{46}{5} = 2x$

$\frac{23}{5} = x$

$\left(\frac{23}{5}, \frac{61}{5}\right)$ is the point at which $2x - y = -3$ is tangent to the circle.

$d = \sqrt{\left(\frac{23}{5} - 5\right)^2 + \left(\frac{61}{5} - 12\right)^2}$

$= \sqrt{\left(-\frac{2}{5}\right)^2 + \left(\frac{1}{5}\right)^2}$

$= \sqrt{\frac{5}{25}}$ or $\sqrt{\frac{1}{5}} \qquad (x - 5)^2 + (y - 12)^2 = \frac{1}{5}$

38.

39.

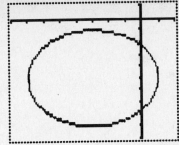

40.

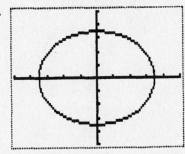

41.

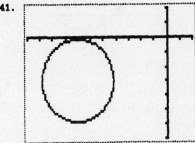

42. a. (0, 3); 5   **b.** (-1, 0); 3.3166

43.
$$x^2 - 2x + y^2 + 4y = -5$$
$$(x^2 - 2x + 1) + (y^2 + 4y + 4) = -5 + 1 + 4$$
$$(x - 1)^2 + (y + 2)^2 = 0$$

$r = 0$, $C(1, -2)$ It is a point.

44. $(x - k)^2 + (y - k)^2 = 64$

All the families of circles have centers located on the line $x - y = 0$.

45. It passes through the origin; the center is at (h, k) and the radius is $\sqrt{h^2 + k^2}$.

46. $v = \sqrt{\dfrac{GM}{r}}$

$\quad = \sqrt{\dfrac{(6.67 \times 10^{-11})(5.98 \times 10^{24})}{42,250,474.3}}$

$\quad \approx \sqrt{9440509.405}$

$\quad \approx 3072.54 \quad \approx 3.07 \times 10^3$ m/s

47. $v = \sqrt{\dfrac{GM}{r}}$

$\quad = \sqrt{\dfrac{(6.67 \times 10^{-11})(0.012 \times 5.98 \times 10^{24})}{(110 + 1740) \times 1,000}}$

$\quad \approx \sqrt{2587238.919} \quad \approx 1608.5$ m/s

48. a. $60° \times \dfrac{\pi}{180°} \approx 1.047$ **b.** $-105° \times \dfrac{\pi}{180°} \approx -1.833$

c. $1000° \times \dfrac{\pi}{180°} \approx 17.46$ **d.** $-90° \times \dfrac{\pi}{180°} \approx -1.571$

49. $\sin 100° = \sin 80° > \sin 10°$

50. $\cos \theta = \dfrac{1}{\sec \theta} = \dfrac{3}{5}$, $\tan \theta = \dfrac{\frac{4}{5}}{\frac{3}{5}} = \dfrac{4}{3}$

51. $(-3, 3) - (5, 2) = (-8, 1)$

52. $(\sqrt{2} + i)(4\sqrt{2} + i) = 4 \times 2 + \sqrt{2}i + 4\sqrt{2}i + i^2$
$\qquad\qquad\qquad\quad = 8 + 5\sqrt{2}i - 1$
$\qquad\qquad\qquad\quad = 7 + 5i\sqrt{2}$

53. $(2\sqrt{3} + 2i)^{\frac{1}{5}} = 1.31 + 0.14i$

54. surface area of 1 small cube = 1 in^2

$\dfrac{\text{surface area of large cube}}{8} = \dfrac{2 \cdot 2}{8} = \dfrac{1}{2}$

Quantity A is greater.   A

10-2A   Graphing Calculators: Locating the Vertex of a Parabola

PAGE 533   EXERCISES

1.

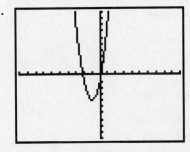

(-2, -10)

2.

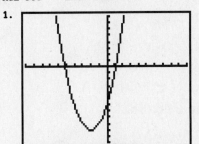

(3, 7)

3.

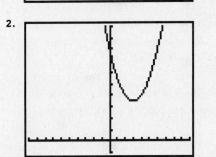

(-1, -4)

4.

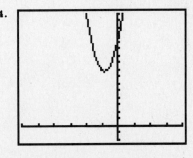

(-0.8, 7.8)

5.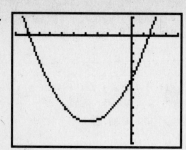

(-3.7, -240.9)

6.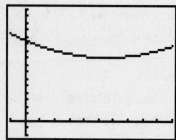

(11.0, 228.5)

10-2 **The Parabola**

PAGE 539   CHECKING FOR UNDERSTANDING

1. If p is positive the graph will curve up or to the right. If p is negative the graph will curve down or to the left.

2. If y is the variable squared, the directrix is parallel to the y-axis. If x is the variable squared, the directrix is parallel to the x-axis.

3. An equation for a parabola only has one squared term.

4. $x^2 = 16(y - 4)$

$(x - 0)^2 = 4(4)(y - 4)$

$(0, 4)$, $p = 4$, up

5. $(y + 12)^2 = 4(5)(x - 9)$

$(9, -12)$, $p = 5$, right

6. $(x - 3)^2 = -2(4)(y + 4)$

$(3, -4)$, $p = -2$, down

7. $(x - 6)^2 = 4\left(\frac{1}{2}\right)(y + 8)$

$(6, -8)$, $p = \frac{1}{2}$, up

---

8. $(x - 0)^2 = 8y$

$(x - 0)^2 = 4(2)(y - 0)$

vertex: $(0, 0)$; focus $(0, 2)$;

directrix: $y = -2$

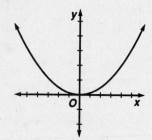

9. $(x - 2)^2 = 4(2)(y + 1)$

vertex: $(2, -1)$, focus $(2, 1)$;

directrix: $y = -3$

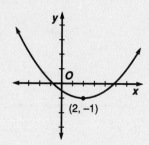

10. $(y + 2)^2 = -4(4)(x - 3)$

vertex: $(3, -2)$, focus $(-1, -2)$;

directrix: $x = 7$

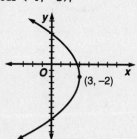

11. $y^2 - 6y = -9 + 4x$

$y^2 - 6y + 9 = -9 + 4x + 9$

$(y - 3)^2 = 4x$

12. $y^2 + 12y = 16x + 12$

$(y^2 + 12y + 36) = 16x + 12 + 36$

$(y + 6)^2 = 16x + 48$

$(y + 6)^2 = 16(x + 3)$

PAGES 540-541   EXERCISES

13. a. $y^2 - 4y + 4 = x - 7$

$(y - 2)^2 = x - 7$

b. vertex: $(7, 2)$

focus: $\left(7\frac{1}{4}, 2\right)$

directrix: $x = 6\frac{3}{4}$

axis: $y = 2$

c.

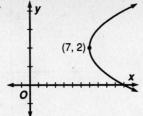

(7, 2)

14. a. $-4(x - 1) = (y + 5)^2$

  b. vertex: $(1, -5)$
    focus: $(0, -5)$
    directrix: $x = 2$
    axis: $y = -5$

  c.

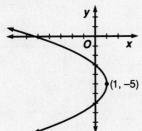

(1, −5)

15. a. $\qquad x^2 + 8x = -4y - 8 + 16$

$\qquad (x^2 + 8x + 16) = -4(y - 2)$

$\qquad\qquad (x + 4)^2 = -4(y - 2)$

  b. vertex: $(-4, 2)$
    focus: $(-4, 1)$
    directrix: $y = 3$
    axis: $x = -4$

  c.

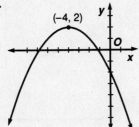

(−4, 2)

16. a. $\qquad x^2 - 2x = 12y - 13$

$\qquad (x^2 - 2x + 1) = 12y - 13 + 1$

$\qquad\qquad (x - 1)^2 = 12(y - 1)$

  b. vertex: $(1, 1)$
    focus: $(1, 4)$
    directrix: $y = -2$
    axis: $x = 1$

  c.

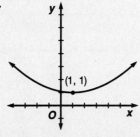

(1, 1)

17. a. $y^2 + 2x = 0$

$\qquad y^2 = -2x$

  b. vertex: $(0, 0)$
    focus: $\left(-\frac{1}{2}, 0\right)$
    directrix: $x = \frac{1}{2}$
    axis: $y = 0$

  c.

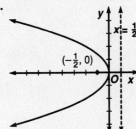

$x = \frac{1}{2}$

$\left(-\frac{1}{2}, 0\right)$

18. a. $3x^2 = 19y$

$\qquad x^2 = \frac{19}{3}y$

  b. vertex: $(0, 0)$
    focus: $\left(0, \frac{19}{12}\right)$
    directrix: $y = -\frac{19}{12}$
    axis: $x = 0$

  c.

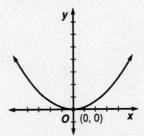

(0, 0)

19. a. $\qquad 4x^2 - 24x = 40y + 4$

$\qquad\qquad x^2 - 6x = 10y + 1$

$\qquad (x^2 - 6x + 9) = 10y + 1 + 9$

$\qquad\qquad (x - 3)^2 = 10(y + 1)$

  b. vertex: $(3, -1)$
    focus: $\left(3, \frac{6}{4}\right) = \left(3, \frac{3}{2}\right)$
    directrix: $y = -\frac{14}{4} = -\frac{7}{2}$
    axis: $x = 3$

  c.

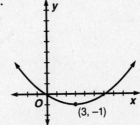

(3, −1)

20. a.
$$x^2 + 4x = -2y - 10$$
$$x^2 + 4x + 4 = -2y - 10 + 4$$
$$(x + 2)^2 = -2(y + 3)$$

b. vertex: $(-2, -3)$

focus: $\left(-2, -3\frac{1}{2}\right)$

directrix: $y = -2\frac{1}{2}$

axis: $x = -2$

c.

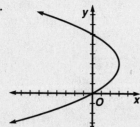

21. a.
$$y^2 - 6y = -3x$$
$$y^2 - 6y + 9 = -3x + 9$$
$$(y - 3)^2 = -3(x - 3)$$

b. vertex: $(3, 3)$

focus: $\left(\frac{9}{4}, 3\right)$

directrix: $x = \frac{15}{4}$

axis: $y = 3$

c.

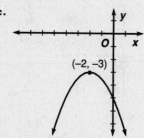

22. a.
$$x^2 - 8x = -8y - 32$$
$$(x^2 - 8x + 16) = -8y - 32 + 16$$
$$(x - 4)^2 = -8(y + 2)$$

b. vertex: $(4, -2)$

focus: $(4, -4)$

directrix: $y = 0$

axis: $x = 4$

c.

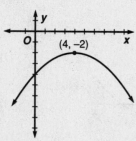

23. $(y - 0)^2 = 4(-3)(x - 0)$
$$y^2 = -12x$$

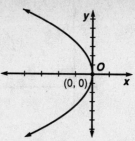

24. vertex: $(3, 5)$, $p = -1$
$$(y - 5)^2 = -4(x - 3)$$

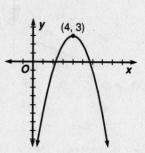

25. max at $(4, 3) \rightarrow$ vertex
$$(x - 4)^2 = 4p(y - 3)$$
$$(5 - 4)^2 = 4p(2 - 3)$$
$$1 = -4p$$
$$-\frac{1}{4} = p$$
$$(x - 4)^2 = -1(y - 3)$$

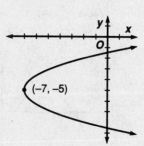

26. $(y + 5)^2 = 4p(x + 7)$
$$(-1 + 5)^2 = 4p(2 + 7)$$
$$16 = 36p$$
$$\frac{4}{9} = p$$
$$(y + 5)^2 = \frac{16}{9}(x + 7)$$

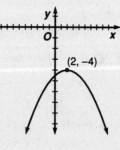

27. vertex: $(2, -6 + 2)$
$$(2, -4)$$
$$(x - 2)^2 = 4(-2)(y + 4)$$
$$(x - 2)^2 = -8(y + 4)$$

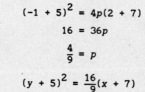

28. $p = 2$, opens up

vertex: $(3, -2)$
$$(x - 3)^2 = 4(2)(y + 2)$$
$$(x - 3)^2 = 8(y + 2)$$

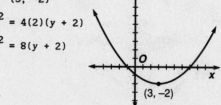

29. vertex $(-1, 2)$

$(y - 2)^2 = 4p(x + 1)$

$(0 - 2)^2 = 4p(0 + 1)$

$4 = 4p$

$1 = p$

$(y - 2)^2 = 4(x + 1)$

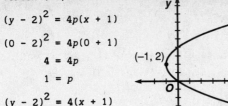

30.

$0^2 + D(0) + E(0) + F = 0 \rightarrow \qquad F = 0$

$3^2 + D(3) + E(-2) + F = 0 \rightarrow \quad 3D - 2E + F = -9$

$(-2)^2 + D(-2) + E(2) + F = 0 \rightarrow -2D + 2E + F = -4$

$\begin{array}{r} 3D - 2E + F = -9 \\ -2D + 2E + F = -4 \\ \hline \end{array}$

$\begin{array}{rl} 3(-13) - 2E & = -9 \\ -2E & = 30 \\ E & = -15 \end{array}$

$\begin{array}{r} D \quad + 2F = -13 \\ D \quad + 2(0) = -13 \\ D = -13 \end{array}$

$x^2 - 13x - 15y = 0$

$x^2 - 13x + \left(\dfrac{13}{2}\right)^2 = 15y + \dfrac{169}{4}$

$\left(x - \dfrac{13}{2}\right)^2 = 15\left(y + \dfrac{169}{60}\right)$

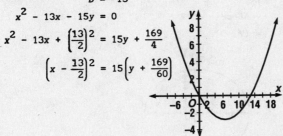

31. a. The opening becomes narrower.

b. The opening becomes wider.

32. $(2, -4)$, yes

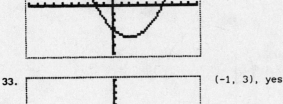

33. $(-1, 3)$, yes

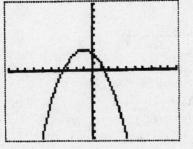

34. $(5, -1)$, no

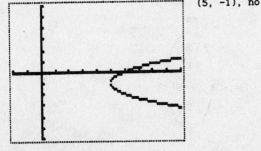

35. $(7, -3)$, no

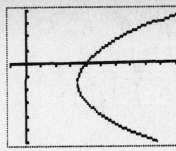

36. $p = 1$ or -1

$(y - 1)^2 = 4(x + 2)$

or

$(y - 1)^2 = -4(x + 2)$

37. focus: $(4, 3)$

$p = 2$

latus rectum: $4(2) = 8$

radius: $\dfrac{1}{2}(8) = 4$

focus = vertex

$(x - 4)^2 + (y - 3)^2 = 4^2$

$(x - 4)^2 + (y - 3)^2 = 16$

38. a. $\dfrac{f}{D} > 0.45$ \qquad **b.** $0.3 \le \dfrac{f}{10} \le 0.45$

$\dfrac{f}{10} > 0.45$ \qquad\qquad $3 \le f \le 4.5$ feet

$f > 4.5$ feet

c. $\dfrac{f}{D} < 0.3$

$\dfrac{f}{10} < 0.3$

$f < 3$ feet

39. a. Let $y =$ income and $x =$ number of $\$1.00$ increases.

income = (number of customers) · (cost of a ticket)

$y = (500 - 50x)(4 + x)$

$y = 2000 + 300x - 50x^2$

$y - 2000 = -50(x^2 - 6x)$

$y - 2000 - 450 = -50(x^2 - 6x + 9)$

$(y - 2450) = -50(x - 3)^2$

The vertex of the parabola is $(3, 2450)$, and because p is negative, it opens downward. An increase of $\$3$ will give a maximum profit. The price of each ticket should be $4 + 3$ or $\$7$.

b. The maximum income will be $\$2,450$.

40. a.

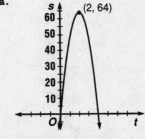

b. vertex: $(2, 64)$

c. the maximum height

d. \qquad $2 = 64t - 16t^2$

$16t^2 - 64t + 2 = 0$

$t = 4$ seconds

41.

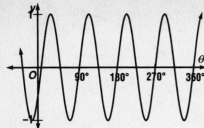

42. $\csc \theta \cos \theta \tan \theta \overset{?}{=} 1$

$\dfrac{1}{\sin \theta} \cdot \cos \theta \cdot \dfrac{\sin \theta}{\cos \theta} \overset{?}{=} 1$

$\dfrac{\sin \theta}{\sin \theta} \cdot \dfrac{\cos \theta}{\cos \theta} \overset{?}{=} 1$

$1 = 1$

43. $\vec{u} = \vec{v} + \vec{w} = (3, -5) + (-4, 2)$

$= (-1, -3)$

44. $\dfrac{1}{3}\left[\cos \dfrac{7\pi}{8} + i \sin \dfrac{7\pi}{8}\right] \cdot 3\sqrt{3}\left[\cos \left(-\dfrac{\pi}{4}\right) + \right.$

$\left. i \sin \left(-\dfrac{\pi}{4}\right)\right]$

$= \sqrt{3}\left[\cos \dfrac{5\pi}{8} + i \sin \dfrac{5\pi}{8}\right]$

$= -0.66 + 1.60i$

45. $(x - 7)^2 + (y - 4)^2 = 2$

46. $75 \times 42 = 3150$ ft^2

$\dfrac{7.48}{12} \approx 0.623$ g/in.

$0.623 \times 4 \approx 2.50$

$2.50 \times 3150 \approx 7854$ gallons

The best answer is B.

10-3   **The Ellipse**

1. If the a^2 is the denominator of the x terms, the major axis is parallel to the x-axis. If it is the denominator of the y terms, the major axis is parallel to the y-axis.

2. Solve the equation for y. This will result in two equations. Graph both equations on the same screen.

3. a circle

4. $a^2 = b^2 + c^2$

5. center: $(0, 0)$

$c = \sqrt{9 - 4} = \sqrt{5}$

foci: $(0, \pm\sqrt{5})$

vertices: $(0, \pm3), (\pm2, 0)$

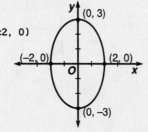

6. center: $(4, -6)$

$c = \sqrt{16 - 9} = \sqrt{7}$

foci: $(4 \pm \sqrt{7}, -6)$

vertices: $(4 \pm 4, -6), (4, -6 \pm 3)$

$= (8, -6), (0, -6), (4, -3), (4, -9)$

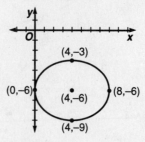

7. center: $(-2, 0)$

$c = \sqrt{81 - 49} = \sqrt{32} = 4\sqrt{2}$

foci: $(-2 \pm 4\sqrt{2}, 0)$

vertices: $(-2 \pm 9, 0), (-2, 0 \pm 7)$

$= (7, 0), (-11, 0), (-2, 7), (-2, -7)$

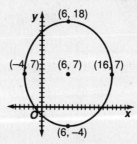

8. center: $(6, 7)$

$c = \sqrt{121 - 100} = \sqrt{21}$

foci: $(6, 7 \pm \sqrt{21})$

vertices: $(6 \pm 10, 7), (6, 7 \pm 11)$

$= (-4, 7), (16, 7), (6, -4), (6, 18)$

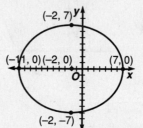

9. center: $(0, -9)$

$c = \sqrt{64 - 16} = \sqrt{48} = 4\sqrt{3}$

foci: $(0, -9 \pm 4\sqrt{3})$

vertices: $(0 \pm 4, -9), (0, -9 \pm 8)$

$= (4, -9), (-4, -9), (0, -1), (0, -17)$

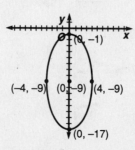

10. center: $(-10, 9)$

$c = \sqrt{225 - 64} = \sqrt{161}$

foci: $(-10 \pm \sqrt{161}, 9)$

vertices: $(-10 \pm 15, 9)$, $(-10, 9 \pm 8)$

$= (5, 9)$, $(-25, 9)$, $(-10, 1)$, $(-10, 17)$

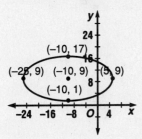

11. center: $(0, 0)$

$b = 3$, $a = 6$

$\dfrac{x^2}{9} + \dfrac{y^2}{36} = 1$

12. center: $(-2, 0)$

$a = 4$, $b = 2$

$\dfrac{(x + 2)^2}{16} + \dfrac{y^2}{4} = 1$

13. center: $(0, -5)$

$a = 7$, $b = 5$

$\dfrac{x^2}{49} + \dfrac{(y + 5)^2}{25} = 1$

14. center: $(-3, 4)$

$a = 8$, $b = 5$

$\dfrac{(x + 3)^2}{25} + \dfrac{(y - 4)^2}{64} = 1$

PAGES 548-550   EXERCISES

15. center: $(3, 4)$

$c = \sqrt{25 - 16} = \sqrt{9} = 3$

foci: $(3 \pm 3, 4) = (0, 4)$, $(6, 4)$

vertices: $(3 \pm 5, 4)$, $(3, 4 \pm 4)$

$= (-2, 4)$, $(8, 4)$, $(3, 0)$, $(3, 8)$

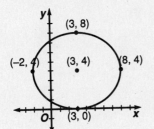

16. center: $(-2, 1)$

$c = \sqrt{25 - 4} = \sqrt{21}$

foci: $(-2, 1 \pm \sqrt{21})$

vertices: $(-2 \pm 2, 1)$, $(-2, 1 \pm 5)$

$= (-4, 1)$, $(0, 1)$, $(-2, -4)$, $(-2, 6)$

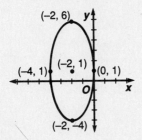

17. $4x^2 + 9y^2 = 36$

$\dfrac{x^2}{9} + \dfrac{y^2}{4} = 1$

center: $(0, 0)$

$c = \sqrt{9 - 4} = \sqrt{5}$

foci: $(\pm\sqrt{5}, 0)$

vertices: $(0 \pm 3, 0)$, $(0, 0 \pm 2)$

$= (-3, 0)$, $(3, 0)$, $(0, -2)$, $(0, 2)$

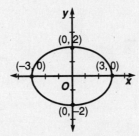

18. $9x^2 - 18x + 4y^2 + 16y = 11$

$9(x^2 - 2x + 1) + 4(y^2 + 4y + 4) = 11 + 9 + 16$

$9(x - 1)^2 + 4(y + 2)^2 = 36$

$\dfrac{(x - 1)^2}{4} + \dfrac{(y + 2)^2}{9} = 1$

center: $(1, -2)$

$c = \sqrt{9 - 4} = \sqrt{5}$

foci: $(1, -2 \pm \sqrt{5})$

vertices: $(1 \pm 2, -2)$, $(1, -2 \pm 3)$

$= (-1, -2)$, $(3, -2)$, $(1, -5)$, $(1, 1)$

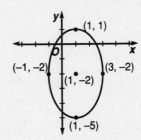

19. $4y^2 - 8y + 9x^2 - 54x = -49$

$4(y^2 - 2y + 1) + 9(x^2 - 6x + 9) = -49 + 4 + 81$

$4(y - 1)^2 + 9(x - 3)^2 = 36$

$\dfrac{(y - 1)^2}{9} + \dfrac{(x - 3)^2}{4} = 36$

center: $(3, 1)$

$c = \sqrt{9 - 4} = \sqrt{5}$

foci: $(3, 1 \pm \sqrt{5})$

vertices: $(3 \pm 2, 1)$, $(3, 1 \pm 3)$

$= (1, 1)$, $(5, 1)$, $(3, -2)$, $(3, 4)$

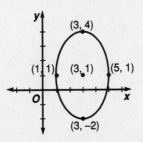

20.
$$x^2 - 2x + y^2 - 2y = 6$$
$$(x^2 - 2x + 1) + (y^2 - 2y + 1) = 6 + 1 + 1$$
$$(x - 1)^2 + (y - 1)^2 = 8$$
circle; center: (1, 1)
radius = $\sqrt{8} = 2\sqrt{2}$

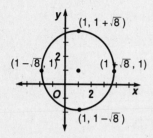

21. $4x^2 - 56x + 9y^2 + 108y = -484$
$$4(x^2 - 14x + 49) + 9(y^2 + 12y + 36)$$
$$= -484 + 196 + 324$$
$$4(x - 7)^2 + 9(y + 6)^2 = 36$$
$$\frac{(x - 7)^2}{9} + \frac{(y + 6)^2}{4} = 1$$
center: (7, -6)
$c = \sqrt{9 - 4} = \sqrt{5}$
foci: $(7 \pm \sqrt{5}, -6)$
vertices: $(7 \pm 3, -6)$, $(7, -6 \pm 2)$
= (4, -6), (10, -6), (7, -8), (7, -4)

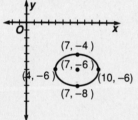

22. $18x^2 - 144x + 12y^2 - 48y = -120$
$$18(x^2 - 8x + 16) + 12(y^2 - 4y + 4)$$
$$= -120 + 288 + 48$$
$$18(x - 4)^2 + 12(y - 2)^2 = 216$$
$$\frac{(x - 4)^2}{12} + \frac{(y - 2)^2}{18} = 1$$
center: (4, 2)
$c = \sqrt{18 - 12} = \sqrt{6}$
foci: $(4, 2 \pm \sqrt{6})$
vertices: $(4 \pm \sqrt{12}, 2)$, $(4, 2 \pm \sqrt{18})$
= $(4 \pm 2\sqrt{3}, 2)$, $(4, 2 \pm 3\sqrt{2})$

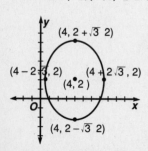

23. $\dfrac{y^2}{64} + \dfrac{x^2}{36} = 1$

24. $a = 5, b = 7$
$$\frac{(x + 3)^2}{49} + \frac{(y + 1)^2}{25} = 1$$

25. $b = \dfrac{2}{3} \cdot 6 = 4$
$$\frac{x^2}{36} + \frac{y^2}{16} = 1$$

26. $\dfrac{1}{2} = \dfrac{c}{a} \rightarrow c = \dfrac{1}{2}a$
$a = 10, c = 5,$
$b = \sqrt{10^2 - 5^2} = \sqrt{75}$
$$\frac{x^2}{100} + \frac{y^2}{75} = 1$$

27. $c = 2, a = 7$
$a^2 - c^2 = b^2$
$49 - 4 = 45$
major axis: x-axis
$$\frac{x^2}{49} + \frac{y^2}{45} = 1$$

28. $a = 4, c = 3$
center: (2, 3 - 3) = (2, 0)
major axis: y-axis
$b^2 = a^2 - c^2 = 16 - 9 = 7$
$$\frac{y^2}{16} + \frac{(x - 2)^2}{7} = 1$$

29. ellipse; 2 squared terms, $A \neq C$

30. parabola; one squared term

31. parabola; one squared term

32. circle; two squared terms, $A = C$

33. ellipse; two squared terms, $A \neq C$

34. circle; two squared terms, $A = C$

35. $c = 3$, center (1, 2)
$a^2 - b^2 = 9$
$$\frac{(x - 1)^2}{b^2} + \frac{(y - 2)^2}{a^2} = 1$$
$$\frac{(4 - 1)^2}{b^2} + \frac{(2 - 2)^2}{a^2} = 1$$
$$\frac{9}{b^2} + \frac{0}{a^2} = 1$$
$$\frac{9}{b^2} = 1$$
$$9 = b^2$$
$a^2 - 9 = 9$
$a^2 = 18$
$$\frac{(x - 1)^2}{9} + \frac{(y - 2)^2}{18} = 1$$

36. $a = \dfrac{1}{2} \cdot 20 = 10$
$b^2 = 10^2(1 - 0.7^2)$
$= 51$
$$\frac{y^2}{100} + \frac{(x - 3)^2}{51} = 1$$

37. $a = 7$, $b = 3$

$$\frac{(x + 3)^2}{9} + \frac{(y - 7)^2}{49} = 1$$

$$49(x + 3)^2 + 9(y - 7)^2 = 441$$

$$49(x^2 + 6x + 9) + 9(y^2 - 14y + 49) = 441$$

$$49x^2 + 294x + 441 + 9y^2 - 126y + 441 = 441$$

$$49x^2 + 9y^2 + 294x - 126y + 441 = 0$$

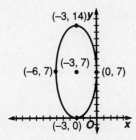

38. $y = \pm \dfrac{\sqrt{36 - 4(x - 2)^2}}{3} - 1$

$(-1, -1)$, $(5, -1)$, $(2, -3)$, $(2, 1)$

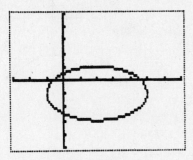

39. $y = \pm \dfrac{\sqrt{4 - (x - 3)^2}}{2} - 3$

$(5, -3)$, $(1, -3)$, $(3, -2)$, $(3, -4)$

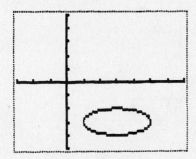

40. $y = \pm \dfrac{\sqrt{400 - 16(x + 1)^2}}{5} + 3$

$(4, 3)$, $(-6, 3)$, $(-1, 7)$, $(-1, -1)$

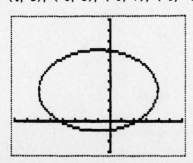

41. $y = \pm\sqrt{4 - 4(x - 1)^2} + 1$

$(0, 1)$, $(2, 1)$, $(1, -1)$, $(1, 3)$

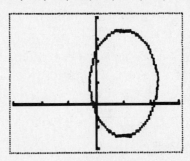

42. The semi-minor axis has length = 2 so the radius of the internal circle is equal to 2. The semi-major axis has length = 3 so the radius of the external circle is 3. The two equations are $x^2 + y^2 = 4$ and $x^2 + y^2 = 9$.

43. total distance = 46 + 70 = 116 million km

44. a. major axis = $9.1 \times 10^7 + 9.3 \times 10^7$

= 1.84×10^8 miles

b. distance = $9.3 \times 10^7 - 9.1 \times 10^7$

= 2.0×10^6 miles

45.

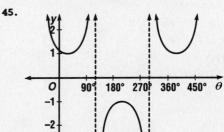

46. $\cos (A + B) = \cos A \cos B - \sin A \sin B$

$= \dfrac{5}{13} \cdot \dfrac{35}{37} - \dfrac{12}{13} \cdot \dfrac{12}{37}$

$= \dfrac{175}{481} - \dfrac{144}{481}$

$= \dfrac{31}{481}$

47. $c^2 = 110^2 + 425^2 - 2(110)(425) \cos 30°$

$c \approx 334.3$ mph

$110^2 \approx (334.3)^2 + 425^2 - 2(334.3)(425) \cos \theta$

$\theta \approx 170.53°$ or $170°32'$

$180° - 170°32' \approx 9°28'$ SW

48. $r = \sqrt{(-5)^2 + (-1)^2} = \sqrt{26}$

$\theta = \text{Arctan } \dfrac{-1}{-5} + \pi \approx 3.34$

$-5 - i = \sqrt{26} (\cos 3.34 + i \sin 3.34)$

49. $0^2 + (-9)^2 + 0 \cdot D - 9E + F = 0 \rightarrow$

$81 - 9E + F = 0$

$7^2 + (-2)^2 + 7D - 2E + F = 0 \rightarrow$

$53 + 7D - 2E + F = 0$

$(-5)^2 + (-10)^2 - 5D - 10E + F = 0 \rightarrow$

$125 - 5D - 10E + F = 0$

$\underline{265 + 35D - 10E + 5F = 0}$

$\underline{875 - 35D - 70E + 7F = 0}$

$1140 - 80E + 12F = 0$

$1140 - 80E + 12(9E - 81) = 0$

$168 + 28E = 0$

$E = -6$

$F = 9(-6) - 81$

$= -135$

$53 + 7D - 2(-6) + (-135) = 0$

$7D - 70 = 0$

$7D = 70$

$D = 10$

$x^2 + y^2 + 10x - 6y - 135 = 0$

$(x^2 + 10x + 25) + (y^2 - 6y + 9) = 135 + 25 + 9$

$(x + 5)^2 + (y - 3)^2 = 169$

50. vertex: $(-5, 0)$

focus: $(-5, 0 + 3) = (-5, 3)$

directrix: $y = -3$

51. $(x + 0.3x)(y - 0.2y) = A$

$(1.3x)(0.8y) = A$

$(1.04xy) = A$

$(xy + 0.04xy) = A$

4 percent

Case Study Follow-Up

1. in the U.S. Capitol in Washington, D.C.

2. $a = 22.2$, $b = 17.8$

$c^2 = a^2 - b^2$

$= 492.84 - 316.84$

$= 176$

$c \approx 13.3$

$2c \approx 26.6$ ft

3. See students' work.

10-4 **The Hyperbola**

PAGES 556–557   CHECKING FOR UNDERSTANDING

1. Write the equation in standard form. If the first expression contains x, the transverse axis is horizontal. If the first expression contains y, then the transverse axis is vertical.

2. Answers will vary. Sample answer: $xy = 64$. The graph is not symmetric with respect to a horizontal or vertical line.

3. **a.** It decreases.   **b.** It increases.

4. center: $(0, 0)$

$a = 6$, $b = 7$

$c = \sqrt{a^2 + b^2} = \sqrt{36 + 49} = \sqrt{85}$

foci: $(0, 0 \pm \sqrt{85})$

vertices: $(0, 6)$, $(0, -6)$

asymptotes: $y = \pm \frac{a}{b}x$

$y = \pm \frac{6}{7}x$

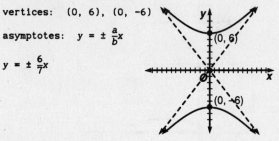

5. center: $(-3, 4)$

$a = 5$, $b = 7$

$c = \sqrt{25 + 49} = \sqrt{74}$

foci: $(-3 \pm \sqrt{74}, 4)$

vertices: $(-3 \pm 5, 4) = (-8, 4), (2, 4)$

asymptotes: $(y - 4) = \pm \frac{7}{5}(x + 3)$

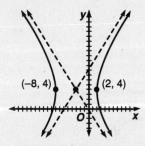

6. center: $(0, 5)$

$a = 4$, $b = 9$, $c = \sqrt{16 + 81} = \sqrt{97}$

foci: $(0 \pm \sqrt{97}, 5) = (\pm\sqrt{97}, 5)$

vertices: $(0 \pm 4, 5) = (-4, 5), (4, 5)$

asymptotes: $(y - 5) = \pm \frac{9}{4}x$

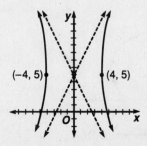

7. center: (8, 5)

$a = 2$, $b = 10$, $c = \sqrt{4 + 100} = \sqrt{104}$

foci: $(8, 5 \pm \sqrt{104})$

vertices: $(8, 5 \pm 2) = (8, 3)$, $(8, 7)$

asymptotes: $y - 5 = \pm \frac{1}{5}(x - 8)$

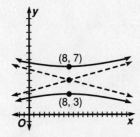

8. center: (-12, 0)

$a = 13$, $b = 17$, $c = \sqrt{169 + 289} = \sqrt{458}$

foci: $(-12, \pm\sqrt{458})$

vertices: $(-12, \pm 13) = (-12, -13)$, $(-12, 13)$

asymptotes: $y = \pm \frac{13}{17}(x + 12)$

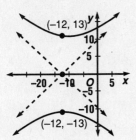

9. center: (-11, -7)

$a = 12$, $b = 6$, $c = \sqrt{144 + 36} = \sqrt{180}$

foci: $(-11 \pm \sqrt{180}, -7)$

vertices: $(-11 \pm 12, -7) = (-23, -7)$, $(1, -7)$

asymptotes: $y + 7 = \pm \frac{6}{12}(x + 11)$

$$y + 7 = \pm \frac{1}{2}(x + 11)$$

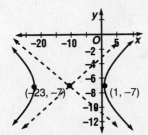

10. center: (0, 5)

$a = 5$, $b = 3$

$$\frac{x^2}{25} - \frac{(y - 5)^2}{9} = 1$$

11. center: (4, 3)

$a = 4$, $b = 3$

$$\frac{(y - 3)^2}{16} - \frac{(x - 4)^2}{9} = 1$$

12. center: (-4, 0)

$a = 2$, $b = 1$

$$\frac{y^2}{4} - \frac{(x + 4)^2}{1} = 1$$

13. center: (0, 0)

$a = 3$, $b = 3$

$$\frac{x^2}{9} - \frac{y^2}{9} = 1$$

14.

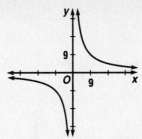

PAGES 557-559   EXERCISES

15. center: (0, 0)

$a = 5$, $b = 4$, $c = \sqrt{25 + 16} = \sqrt{41}$

foci: $(\pm\sqrt{41}, 0)$

vertices: $(5, 0)$, $(-5, 0)$

asymptotes: $y = \pm \frac{4}{5}x$

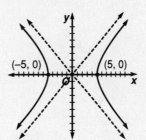

16. center: (2, 3)

$a = 4$, $b = 5$, $c = \sqrt{16 + 25} = \sqrt{41}$

foci: $(2, 3 \pm \sqrt{41})$

vertices: $(2, 3 \pm 4) = (2, -1)$, $(2, 7)$

asymptotes: $y - 3 = \pm \frac{4}{5}(x - 2)$

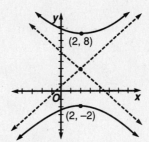

17. $\frac{x^2}{36} - \frac{y^2}{81} = 1$

center: (0, 0)

$a = 6$, $b = 9$, $c = \sqrt{36 + 81} = \sqrt{117}$

foci: $(\pm\sqrt{117}, 0)$

vertices: $(6, 0)$, $(-6, 0)$

asymptotes: $y = \pm \frac{9}{6}x$

$$= \pm \frac{3}{2}x$$

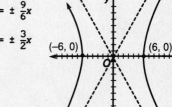

18. $\dfrac{(x + 6)^2}{36} - \dfrac{(y + 3)^2}{9} = 1$

center: $(-6, -3)$

$a = 6, \; b = 3, \; c = \sqrt{36 + 9} = \sqrt{45} = 3\sqrt{5}$

foci: $(-6 \pm 3\sqrt{5}, -3)$

vertices: $(-6 \pm 6, -3) = (0, -3), \; (-12, -3)$

asymptotes:

$y + 3 = \pm \dfrac{3}{6}(x + 6)$

$\qquad = \pm \dfrac{1}{2}(x + 6)$

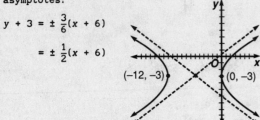

19. $\qquad\qquad 9x^2 - 54x - 4y^2 - 40y = 55$

$9(x^2 - 6x + 9) - 4(y^2 + 10y + 25) = 55 + 81 - 100$

$\qquad\qquad 9(x - 3)^2 - 4(y + 5)^2 = 36$

$\qquad\qquad \dfrac{(x - 3)^2}{4} - \dfrac{(y + 5)^2}{9} = 1$

center: $(3, -5)$

$a = 2, \; b = 3, \; c = \sqrt{4 + 9} = \sqrt{13}$

foci: $(3 \pm \sqrt{13}, -5)$

vertices: $(3 \pm 2, -5) = (1, -5), \; (5, -5)$

asymptotes: $\; y + 5 = \pm \dfrac{3}{2}(x - 3)$

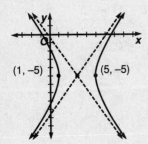

20. $y^2 - 5(x^2 - 4x + 4) = 50 - 20$

$\qquad y^2 - 5(x - 2)^2 = 30$

$\qquad \dfrac{y^2}{30} - \dfrac{(x - 2)^2}{6} = 1$

$c = \sqrt{6 + 30} = \sqrt{36} = 6$

center: $(2, 0)$

foci: $(2, \pm 6) = (2, 6), \; (2, -6)$

vertices: $(2, \pm\sqrt{30})$

asymptotes:

$y = \pm \dfrac{\sqrt{30}}{\sqrt{6}}(x - 2)$

$\quad = \pm\sqrt{5}(x - 2)$

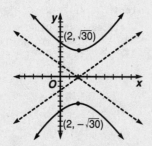

21. $9(x^2 - 10x + 25) - 4(y^2 + 6y + 9)$

$\qquad = 153 + 225 - 36$

$\qquad 9(x - 5)^2 - 4(y + 3)^2 = 36$

$\qquad \dfrac{(x - 5)^2}{4} - \dfrac{(y + 3)^2}{9} = 1$

center: $(5, -3)$

$a = 2, \; b = 3, \; c = \sqrt{4 + 9} = \sqrt{13}$

foci: $(5 \pm \sqrt{13}, -3)$

vertices: $(5 \pm 2, -3) = (7, -3), \; (3, -3)$

asymptotes: $\; y + 3 = \pm \dfrac{3}{2}(x - 5)$

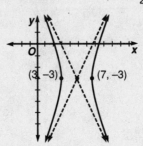

22. $49(x^2 + 6x + 9) - 25(y^2 - 8y + 16)$

$\qquad\qquad\qquad = 1184 + 441 - 400$

$\qquad 49(x + 3)^2 - 25(y - 4)^2 = 1225$

$\qquad \dfrac{(x + 3)^2}{25} - \dfrac{(y - 4)^2}{49} = 1$

center: $(-3, 4)$

$a = 5, \; b = 7, \; c = \sqrt{25 + 49} = \sqrt{74}$

foci: $(-3 \pm \sqrt{74}, 4)$

vertices: $(-3 \pm 5, 4) = (-8, 4), \; (2, 4)$

asymptotes: $\; y - 4 = \pm \dfrac{7}{5}(x + 3)$

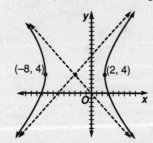

23. ellipse $\qquad$ **24.** hyperbola $\qquad$ **25.** circle

26. parabola $\qquad$ **27.** ellipse $\qquad$ **28.** hyperbola

29.

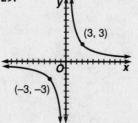

30.

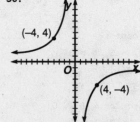

31.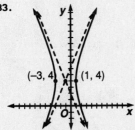
$\left(-\frac{3}{2}, \frac{3}{2}\right)$
$\left(\frac{3}{2}, -\frac{3}{2}\right)$

32.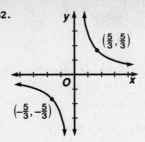
$\left(\frac{5}{3}, \frac{5}{3}\right)$
$\left(-\frac{5}{3}, -\frac{5}{3}\right)$

33.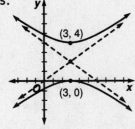
$(-3, 4)$ $(1, 4)$

34.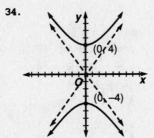
$(0, 4)$
$(0, -4)$

35.
$(3, 4)$
$(3, 0)$

36. $\dfrac{(x + 1)^2}{4} - \dfrac{(y - 4)^2}{9} = 1$

37. $2a = 8 \rightarrow a = 4$

$c = 5$

center: $(0, 0)$

$b = \sqrt{25 - 16} = \sqrt{9} = 3$

$\dfrac{y^2}{16} - \dfrac{x^2}{9} = 1$

38. $2b = 6 \rightarrow b = 3$

$a = 2$

center: $(3, 2)$

$\dfrac{(y - 2)^2}{4} - \dfrac{(x - 3)^2}{9} = 1$

39. $a = 3$

center: $(3, 3)$

$c = 5$

$b = \sqrt{25 - 9} = \sqrt{16} = 4$

$\dfrac{(x - 3)^2}{9} - \dfrac{(y - 3)^2}{16} = 1$

40. center: $(0, 0)$

$c = 8$

$a = b$ since equilateral

so $a^2 + a^2 = c^2$

$2a^2 = 64$

$a^2 = 32$

$\dfrac{x^2}{32} - \dfrac{y^2}{32} = 1$

41. center: $(0, 0)$

$c = 5$

$a = b$ so $a^2 + a^2 = c^2$

$2a^2 = 25$

$a^2 = \dfrac{25}{2}$

$\dfrac{y^2}{\frac{25}{2}} - \dfrac{x^2}{\frac{25}{2}} = 1$

$\dfrac{2y^2}{25} - \dfrac{2x^2}{25} = 1$

42. $3y = 2x - 9$

$3y + 3 = 2x - 9 + 3$

$3(y + 1) = 2x - 6$

$3(y + 1) = 2(x - 3)$

$(y + 1) = \dfrac{2}{3}(x - 3)$

center: $(3, -1)$

Since vertex is at $(6, -1)$, transverse axis is parallel to x-axis.

$b = 2, a = 3$

$\dfrac{(x - 3)^2}{9} - \dfrac{(y + 1)^2}{4} = 1$

43. center: $(4, 2)$

$4y + 4 = 3x$

$4y + 4 - 12 = 3x - 12$

$4y - 8 = 3(x - 4)$

$4(y - 2) = 3(x - 4)$

$(y - 2) = \dfrac{3}{4}(x - 4)$

$a = 3, b = 4$

$\dfrac{(y - 2)^2}{9} - \dfrac{(x - 4)^2}{16} = 1$

44. center: $(1, 0)$

$c = 3$

$\dfrac{b}{a} = \pm 4$

$b = 4a$

$c^2 = (4a)^2 + a^2$

$9 = 17a^2$

$\dfrac{9}{17} = a^2$

$b^2 = 16 \cdot \dfrac{9}{17} = \dfrac{144}{17}$

$\dfrac{(x - 1)^2}{\frac{9}{17}} - \dfrac{y^2}{\frac{144}{17}} = 1$

$\dfrac{17(x - 1)^2}{9} - \dfrac{17y^2}{144} = 1$

45. center: (1, 1)

$c = 4$

$\dfrac{a}{b} = \pm 2$

$a = 2b$

$c^2 = (2b)^2 + b^2$

$16 = 5b^2$

$\dfrac{16}{5} = b^2$

$a^2 = 4 \cdot \dfrac{16}{5} = \dfrac{64}{5}$

$\dfrac{(y - 1)^2}{\frac{64}{5}} - \dfrac{(x - 1)^2}{\frac{16}{5}} = 1$

$\dfrac{5(y - 1)^2}{64} - \dfrac{5(x - 1)^2}{16} = 1$

46.

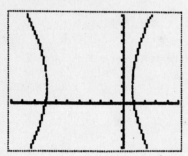

hyperbola

47.

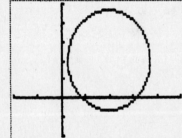

ellipse

48.

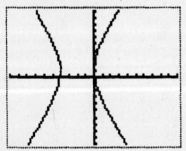

hyperbola

49.

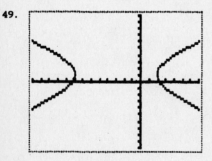

hyperbola

50. center: (0, 0)

$a^2 = b^2 \rightarrow a = b$

$\pm \dfrac{b}{a} = \pm 1$

$y = \pm 1x$

$y = \pm x$

51. $x - 2y = 0 \rightarrow \dfrac{1}{2}x = y$

$x + 2y = 0 \rightarrow -\dfrac{1}{2}x = y$

center: (0, 0)

passes through (2, 0) so x is transverse axis

$b = 1$, $a = 2$

$\dfrac{x^2}{4} - \dfrac{y^2}{1} = 1$

$\dfrac{x^2}{4} - y^2 = 1$

52. To find the center, find the intersection of the asymptotes.

$y = 2x$ and $y = -2x + 4$

$2x = -2x + 4$

$4x = 4$

$x = 1$

$y = 2 \cdot 1$

$y = 2$

The center is (1, 2).

Notice that (4, 2) must be a vertex and a equals 4 - 1 or 3.

Point A has an x-coordinate of 4.

Since $y = 2x$, the y-coordinate is 2 · 4 or 8.

The value of b is 8 - 2 or 6.

The equation is $\dfrac{(x - 1)^2}{9} - \dfrac{(y - 2)^2}{36} = 1$.

53. a.

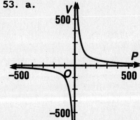

b. $10,440 = 90V$

$V = 116$ cm^3

c. $10,440 = 180V$

$V = 58$ cm^3

d. $V = \dfrac{1}{2}$ (original V)

54. a.

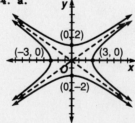

b. They are the same lines.

c. $\dfrac{(x - 3)^2}{9} - \dfrac{(y - 5)^2}{25} = 1$

d.

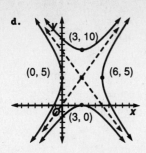

55. a.
$$d = rt$$
$$4.58 \times 10^9 = (4.69 \times 10^4)t$$
$$t = 9.77 \times 10^4 \text{ hours or } 4070 \text{ days}$$

b. March 2, 1972 + 4070 days

4070 days = 11 yrs, 55 days

May 1983

(actual: June 13, 1983)

56. $\sin(\arctan\sqrt{3}) = \sin(60°) = \dfrac{\sqrt{3}}{2}$

57. $\cot X \overset{?}{=} \dfrac{\sin 2X}{1 - \cos 2X}$

$\cot X \overset{?}{=} \dfrac{2\sin X \cos X}{1 - \cos^2 X + \sin^2 X}$

$\cot X \overset{?}{=} \dfrac{2\sin X \cos X}{2\sin^2 X}$

$\cot X \overset{?}{=} \dfrac{\cos X}{\sin X}$

$\cot X = \cot X$

58. $\begin{vmatrix} \vec{i} & \vec{j} & \vec{k} \\ 5 & 2 & 3 \\ -2 & 5 & 0 \end{vmatrix} = \begin{vmatrix} 2 & 3 \\ 5 & 0 \end{vmatrix}\vec{i} - \begin{vmatrix} 5 & 3 \\ -2 & 0 \end{vmatrix}\vec{j} + \begin{vmatrix} 5 & 2 \\ -2 & 5 \end{vmatrix}\vec{k}$

59. $0 = r\cos(\theta - 135°)$

60. $-\dfrac{x}{\sqrt{2}} + \dfrac{y}{\sqrt{2}} - \dfrac{4}{\sqrt{2}} = 0$

61. $y^2 + 2y - 4x = -5$

$(y^2 + 2y + 1) = 4x - 5 + 1$

$(y + 1)^2 = 4(x - 1)$

62. $4x^2 + 25(y^2 + 10y + 25) = -525 + 625$

$4x^2 + 25(y + 5)^2 = 100$

$\dfrac{x^2}{25} + \dfrac{(y + 5)^2}{4} = 1$

center: $(0, -5)$

vertices: $(5, -5), (-5, -5), (0, -3), (0, -7)$

63. $6 + \dfrac{1}{6} + 4 + \dfrac{1}{4} + 2 + \dfrac{1}{2} = 12 + \dfrac{2}{12} + \dfrac{3}{12} + \dfrac{6}{12}$

$= 12\dfrac{11}{12}$

The best answer is C.

Mid-Chapter Review

PAGE 559

1. $(x - 2)^2 = (y + 7)^2 = 81$

2.

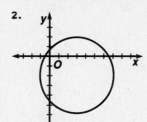

3. $(y - 3)^2 = 4x$

vertex: $(0, 3)$

focus: $(1, 3)$

directrix: $x = -1$

4.

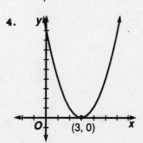

5.
$$x^2 - 6x + 16y^2 - 64y = -57$$
$$(x - 6x + 9) + 16(y^2 - 4y + 4) = -57 + 9 + 64$$
$$(x - 3)^2 + 16(y - 2)^2 = 16$$
$$\dfrac{(x - 3)^2}{16} + \dfrac{(y - 2)^2}{1} = 1$$

center: $(3, 2)$

$c = \sqrt{16 - 1} = \sqrt{15}$

foci: $(3 \pm \sqrt{15}, 2)$

major axis: $2 \cdot 4 = 8$

minor axis: $2 \cdot 1 = 2$

6.

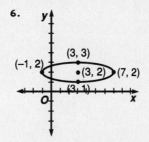

7. maximum distance $= b$

minimum distance $= a = 200$

$$\dfrac{x^2}{90,000} + \dfrac{y^2}{40,000} = 1$$

$$40,000x^2 + 90,000y^2 = 3,600,000,000$$

8. $3(y^2 + 8y + 16) - (x^2 + 2x + 1) = -41 + 48 - 1$

$$3(y + 4)^2 - (x + 1)^2 = 6$$

$$\dfrac{(y + 4)^2}{2} - \dfrac{(x + 1)^2}{6} = 1$$

hyperbola

9.

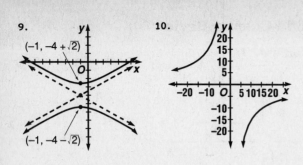

$(-1, -4 + \sqrt{2})$

O

$(-1, -4 - \sqrt{2})$

10.

Technology:
Asymptotes of a Hyperbola

1.

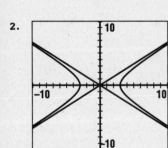

$y = \pm \dfrac{4}{7}x$

2.

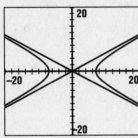

$y = \pm \dfrac{2}{3}x$

3.

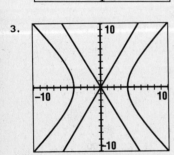

$y = \pm \dfrac{7}{4}x$

4.

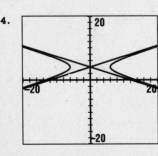

$y = 4 \pm \dfrac{1}{3}x$

10-5	**Conic Sections**

1. Answers will vary. A conic section is the intersection of a plane with a pair of conical surfaces placed vertex to vertex.

2. a. A and C have the same sign and $A \neq C$.

   b. A and C have opposite signs.

   c. $A = C$

   d. either $A = 0$ or $C = 0$

3. A circle is an ellipse in which $A = C$.

4. $e = \dfrac{c}{a}$, so $ae = c$ and $a^2 e^2 = c^2$.

   But $c^2 = a^2 + b^2$.

   So, $a^2 e^2 = a^2 + b^2$

   $a^2 e^2 - a^2 = b^2$

   $a^2(e^2 - 1) = b^2$

5. parabola   6. circle

7. hyperbola   8. ellipse

9. circle

   $x^2 - 8x + 16 + y^2 = -11 + 16$

   $(x - 4)^2 + y^2 = 5$

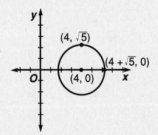

$(4, \sqrt{5})$

$(4 + \sqrt{5}, 0)$

O $(4, 0)$

10. ellipse

   $9x^2 - 54x + 25y^2 - 50y = 119$

   $9(x^2 - 6x + 9) + 25(y^2 - 2y + 1) = 119 + 81 + 25$

   $9(x - 3)^2 + 25(y - 1)^2 = 225$

   $\dfrac{(x - 3)^2}{25} + \dfrac{(y - 1)^2}{9} = 1$

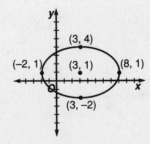

$(3, 4)$

$(-2, 1)$ $(3, 1)$ $(8, 1)$

$(3, -2)$

11. parabola

$$4\left(y^2 + y + \frac{1}{4}\right) = 15 - 8x + 1$$

$$4\left(y + \frac{1}{2}\right)^2 = 16 - 8x$$

$$4\left(y + \frac{1}{2}\right)^2 = -8(x - 2)$$

$$\left(y + \frac{1}{2}\right)^2 = -2(x - 2)$$

$\left(2, -\frac{1}{2}\right)$

12. hyperbola

$$x^2 + 2x - 3(y^2 + 8y) = 41$$

$$(x + 2x + 1) - 3(y^2 + 8y + 16) = 41 - 48 + 1$$

$$(x + 1)^2 - 3(y + 4)^2 = -6$$

$$\frac{(y + 4)^2}{2} - \frac{(x + 1)^2}{6} = 1$$

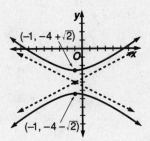

$(-1, -4 + \sqrt{2})$

$(-1, -4 - \sqrt{2})$

13. $e = \frac{c}{a}$

$$\frac{3}{4} = \frac{c}{2}$$

$$\frac{3}{2} = c$$

$$b^2 = a^2 - c^2 = 4 - \frac{9}{4} = \frac{7}{4} = 1.75$$

$$\frac{y^2}{4} + \frac{x^2}{1.75} = 1$$

PAGES 566-567   EXERCISES

14. parabola, so $e = 1$

15. $4(y^2 - 2y + 1) + 9(x^2 - 6x + 9) = -49 + 81 + 4$

$$4(y - 1)^2 + 9(x - 3)^2 = 36$$

$$\frac{(y - 1)^2}{9} + \frac{(x - 3)^2}{4} = 1$$

$$a^2 = 9,\ b^2 = 4$$

$$c = \sqrt{9 - 4} = \sqrt{5}$$

$$e = \frac{c}{a} = \frac{\sqrt{5}}{3}$$

16. $\frac{x^2}{9} - \frac{y^2}{5} = 1$

$$a^2 = 9,\ b^2 = 5$$

$$c = \sqrt{9 + 5} = \sqrt{14}$$

$$e = \frac{c}{a} = \frac{\sqrt{14}}{3}$$

17. $\frac{(x + 5)^2}{100} + \frac{(y - 1)^2}{100} = 1$

$$a^2 = 100,\ b^2 = 100$$

$$c = \sqrt{100 - 100} = 0$$

$$e = \frac{0}{10} = 0$$

18. $25(x^2 - 4x + 4) + (y^2 + 6y + 9) = -84 + 100 + 9$

$$25(x - 2)^2 + (y + 3)^2 = 25$$

$$\frac{(x - 2)^2}{1} + \frac{(y + 3)^2}{25} = 1$$

$$c = \sqrt{25 - 1} = \sqrt{24}$$

$$e = \frac{c}{a} = \frac{\sqrt{24}}{5}$$

19. $x^2 - (y^2 - 2y + 1) = 5 - 1$

$$x^2 - (y - 1)^2 = 4$$

$$\frac{x^2}{4} - \frac{(y - 1)^2}{4} = 1$$

$$c = \sqrt{4 + 4} = \sqrt{8} = 2\sqrt{2}$$

$$e = \frac{c}{a} = \frac{2\sqrt{2}}{2} = \sqrt{2}$$

20. parabola

$$y^2 = 8x - 8$$

$$y^2 = 8(x - 1)$$

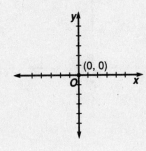

$(1, 0)$

21. hyperbola

$$xy = \frac{4}{9}$$

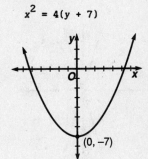

22. point, (0, 0)

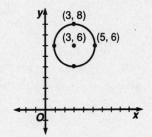

$(0, 0)$

23. parabola

$$x^2 = 4(y + 7)$$

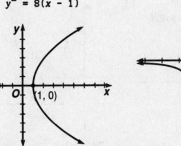

$(0, -7)$

24. circle

$$(x^2 - 6x + 9) + (y^2 - 12y + 36) = -41 + 9 + 36$$

$$(x - 3)^2 + (y - 6)^2 = 4$$

$(3, 8)$

$(3, 6)$ $(5, 6)$

25. hyperbola

$$(x^2 - 4x + 4) - (y^2 + 4y + 4) = 5 + 4 - 4$$

$$(x - 2)^2 - (y + 2)^2 = 5$$

$$\frac{(x - 2)^2}{5} - \frac{(y + 2)^2}{5} = 1$$

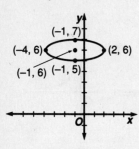

$(2 - \sqrt{5}, -2)$ $(2 + \sqrt{5}, -2)$

26. ellipse

$$\frac{(x + 1)^2}{9} + (y - 6)^2 = 1$$

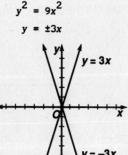

$(-1, 7)$ $(-4, 6)$ $(2, 6)$ $(-1, 6)$ $(-1, 5)$

27. parabola

$$x^2 - 8x + 16 = y$$

$$(x - 4)^2 = y$$

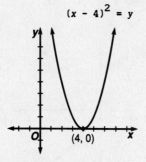

$(4, 0)$

28. intersecting lines

$$y^2 = 9x^2$$

$$y = \pm 3x$$

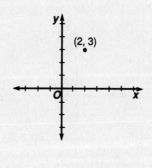

$y = 3x$ $y = -3x$

29. point $(2, 3)$

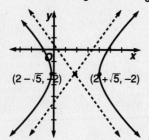

$(2, 3)$

30. $e = \dfrac{c}{a}$

$$\frac{1}{3} = \frac{c}{6}$$

$$c = 2$$

$$b^2 = 6^2 - 2^2 = 32$$

$$\frac{(x - 3)^2}{32} + \frac{(y - 1)^2}{36} = 1$$

31. $e = \dfrac{c}{a} = \dfrac{1}{4}$

$$c = 1$$

$$a = \frac{1}{\frac{1}{4}} = 4$$

center $(2, 5)$

$$b^2 = 16 - 1 = 15$$

$$\frac{(x - 2)^2}{16} + \frac{(y - 5)^2}{15} = 1$$

32. $e = \dfrac{c}{a} = \dfrac{5}{3}$

$$c = 5$$

$$a = \frac{c}{e} = \frac{5}{\frac{5}{3}} = 3$$

$$b^2 = c^2 - a^2 = 25 - 9 = 16$$

$$\frac{x^2}{9} - \frac{y^2}{16} = 1$$

33. center $(0, 0)$

$$c = 8$$

$$a = \frac{c}{e} = \frac{8}{\frac{4}{3}} = 6$$

$$b^2 = c^2 - a^2 = 64 - 36 = 28$$

$$\frac{y^2}{36} - \frac{x^2}{28} = 1$$

34. $e = \dfrac{5}{4}$, $c = 5$

$$a = \frac{c}{e} = \frac{5}{\frac{5}{4}} = 4$$

$$b^2 = 25 - 16 = 9$$

center $(0, 4)$

$$\frac{(y - 4)^2}{16} - \frac{x^2}{9} = 1$$

35. $2a = 20$

$$a = 10$$

$$c = ae \quad 10\left(\frac{7}{10}\right) = 7$$

$$b^2 = 100 - 49 = 51$$

$$\frac{y^2}{100} + \frac{(x - 3)^2}{51} = 1$$

36. $c = 3$

$$a = \frac{c}{e} = \frac{3}{1.5} = 2$$

$$b^2 = c^2 - a^2$$

$$= 9 - 4 = 5$$

$$\frac{(y + 1)^2}{4} - \frac{(x - 3)^2}{5} = 1$$

37. $c = 3$

center $(1, 2)$

$$a^2 = c^2 + b^2$$

$$\frac{(2 - 2)^2}{9 - b^2} + \frac{(4 - 1)^2}{b^2} = 1$$

$$\frac{9}{b^2} = 1$$

$$9 = b^2$$

$$a^2 = c^2 + b^2 = 9 + 9 = 18$$

$$\frac{(y - 2)^2}{18} + \frac{(x - 1)^2}{9} = 1$$

38. $c = 5$

center: $(1, 1)$

$c^2 = a^2 + b^2$

$\dfrac{(y - 1)^2}{25 - b^2} - \dfrac{(x - 1)^2}{25 - a^2} = 1$

$\dfrac{(4 - 1)^2}{a^2} - \dfrac{(1 - 1)^2}{25 - a^2} = 1$

$\dfrac{9}{a^2} = 1$

$9 = a^2$

$e = \dfrac{c}{a} = \dfrac{5}{3}$

39. $c = 3$, center: $(0, 0)$

$\dfrac{y^2}{a^2} - \dfrac{x^2}{9 - a^2} = 1$

$\dfrac{2}{a^2} = 1$

$a^2 = 2$

$e = \dfrac{c}{a} = \dfrac{3}{2} = 1.5$

40. Ellipse; axes are not parallel to coordinate axes.

41. $2a = 10,440$

$a = 5220$

a. $\dfrac{1}{2} \cdot 7920 = 3960 = r$

$e = \dfrac{c}{a}$

$0.16 = \dfrac{c}{5220}$

$835.2 = c$

$5220 - (3960 + 835.2) = 424.8$

$5220 - 3960 + 835.2 = 2095.2$

b. $b^2 = a^2 - c^2$

$= 27,248,400 - 697,559.04$

$= 26,550,840.96$

$\dfrac{x^2}{27,248,400} + \dfrac{y^2}{26,550,840.96} = 1$

42. a. $2a = 120$

$a = 60$

$b = 50$

$\dfrac{x^2}{3600} + \dfrac{y^2}{2500} = 1$

b. $\dfrac{(x - 60)^2}{3600} + \dfrac{y^2}{2500} = 1$

or $\dfrac{(x + 60)^2}{3600} + \dfrac{y^2}{2500} = 1$

depending on which end is used

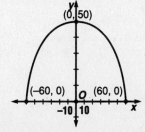

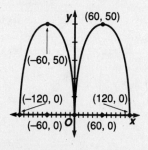

43. $r = 6.7$

$\tan 26°20' = \dfrac{x}{6.7}$

$x \approx 3.05$ cm

44. Arccos $\dfrac{\sqrt{3}}{2} = x$

$\cos x = \dfrac{\sqrt{3}}{2}$

$x = 30°$

45.
$$\sin^2 A = \cos A - 1$$
$$1 - \cos^2 A = \cos A - 1$$
$$\cos^2 A + \cos A - 2 = 0$$
$$(\cos A + 2)(\cos A - 1) = 0$$

$\cos A + 2 = 0 \qquad \cos A - 1 = 0$

$\cos A = -2 \qquad \cos A = 1$

no solution $\qquad\qquad A = 0°$

46.

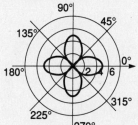

47. $c = 3$, $e = \dfrac{c}{a} \rightarrow a = \dfrac{c}{e} = \dfrac{3}{1.5} = 2$

$b^2 = c^2 - a^2 = 9 - 4 = 5$

$\dfrac{(y + 1)^2}{4} - \dfrac{(x - 3)^2}{5} = 1$

48. You need to know how many students. The best answer is E.

10-6A | **Graphing Calculators: Conic Sections**

PAGE 569   EXERCISES

1.
$$x - 22 = y^2 + 5y$$
$$x - 22 + \dfrac{25}{4} = \left(y^2 + 5y + \dfrac{25}{4}\right)$$
$$x - 15.75 = \left(y + \dfrac{5}{2}\right)^2$$
$$\pm\sqrt{x - 15.75} = y + \dfrac{5}{2}$$
$$y = -2.5 \pm \sqrt{x - 15.75}$$

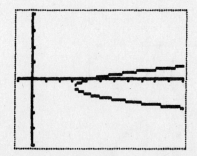

2. $(y - 3)^2 = 4 - x^2$

$\quad y - 3 = \pm\sqrt{4 - x^2}$

$\quad\quad y = 3 \pm \sqrt{4 - x^2}$

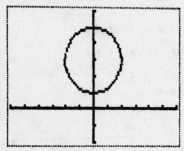

3. $10y^2 = 150 - 5x^2$

$\quad y^2 = 15 - 0.5x^2$

$\quad y = \pm\sqrt{15 - 0.5x^2}$

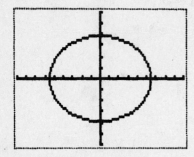

4. $4y^2 = 44 + 2x - 12x^2$

$\quad y^2 = 11 + 0.5x - 3x^2$

$\quad y = \pm\sqrt{11 + 0.5x - 3x^2}$

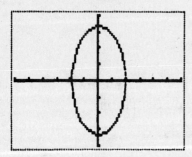

5. $\quad\quad\quad\quad 4x^2 + 24x + 12 = y^2 + 8y$

$4x^2 + 24x + 36 - 36 + 12 + 16 = y^2 + 8y + 16$

$\quad\quad\quad\quad (2x + 6)^2 + 8 = (y + 4)^2$

$\quad\quad\quad\quad \pm\sqrt{(2x + 6)^2 - 8} = y + 4$

$\quad\quad\quad -4 \pm \sqrt{(2x + 6)^2 - 8} = y$

6. $\quad\quad 4x^2 - 16x - 540 = 9y^2 - 144y$

$4x^2 - 16x + 16 - 16 - 540 + 576$

$\quad\quad\quad\quad\quad = 9(y^2 - 16y + 64)$

$\quad\quad (2x - 4)^2 + 20 = 9(y - 8)^2$

$\quad\quad \dfrac{(2x - 4)^2 + 20}{9} = (y - 8)^2$

$\quad \pm\dfrac{\sqrt{(2x - 4)^2 + 20}}{3} = y - 8$

$8 \pm \dfrac{\sqrt{(2x - 4)^2 + 20}}{3} = y$

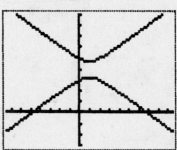

10-6 Transformations of Conics

PAGES 574-575 CHECKING FOR UNDERSTANDING

1. $\begin{bmatrix} -4 & -4 & -4 & -4 & -4 & -4 \\ 4 & 4 & 4 & 4 & 4 & 4 \end{bmatrix}$

2.
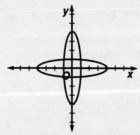

3. Write the equation in terms of $ay^2 + by + c = 0$.

$5y^2 + (4x)y + (8x^2 - 40) = 0$. Then use $a = 5$,

$b = 4x$, and $c = 8x^2 - 40$ in the quadratic

formula.

$y = \dfrac{-4x \pm \sqrt{(4x)^2 - 4(5)(8x^2 - 40)}}{2(5)}$

Graph the two equations on the same screen.

4. $\frac{x^2}{5} + \frac{y^2}{4} = 1$ ellipse

$$\begin{bmatrix} -\sqrt{5} & \sqrt{5} & 0 & 0 \\ 0 & 0 & 2 & -2 \end{bmatrix} + \begin{bmatrix} -5 & -5 & -5 & -5 \\ 6 & 6 & 6 & 6 \end{bmatrix} =$$

$$\begin{bmatrix} -5 - \sqrt{5} & -5 + \sqrt{5} & -5 & -5 \\ 6 & 6 & 8 & 4 \end{bmatrix}$$

center $(-5, 6)$

$$\frac{(x - 5)^2}{5} + \frac{(y - 6)^2}{4} = 1$$

$$4(x - 5)^2 + 5(y - 6)^2 = 20$$

$$4x^2 + 5y^2 + 40x - 60y + 260 = 0$$

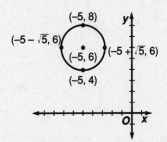

5. $3x^2 + 3y^2 = 16$

$$x^2 + y^2 = \frac{16}{3}$$

circle

$$(x + 5)^2 + (y - 6)^2 = \frac{16}{3}$$

$$3(x + 5)^2 + 3(y - 6)^2 = 16$$

$$3x^2 + 3y^2 + 30x - 36y + 167 = 0$$

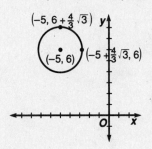

6. center $(-5, 6)$

hyperbola

$$3(y - 6)^2 - 7(x + 5)^2 = 21$$

$$7x^2 - 3y^2 + 70x + 36y + 88 = 0$$

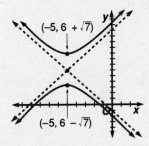

7. parabola

$$(x + 5)^2 = 4(y - 6)^2$$

$$x^2 + 16x - 4y + 88 = 0$$

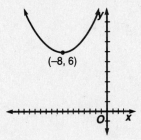

8. $(x \cos 90° + y \sin 90°)^2 -$
   $8(-x \sin 90° + y \cos 90°) = 0$

$$x \cdot 0 + y^2 + 8x - 8 \cdot 0 = 0$$

$$y^2 + 8x = 0$$

9. $6(x \cos 60° + y \sin 60°)^2 +$
   $5(-x \sin 60° + y \cos 60°) = 30$

$$6\left(\frac{1}{2}x + \frac{\sqrt{3}}{2}y\right)^2 + 5\left(-x\frac{\sqrt{3}}{2} + \frac{1}{2}y\right)^2 = 30$$

$$6\left(\frac{1}{4}x^2 + \frac{2\sqrt{3}}{4}xy + \frac{3}{4}y^2\right) + 5\left(\frac{3}{4}x^2 - \frac{2\sqrt{3}}{4}xy + \frac{1}{4}y^2\right) = 30$$

$$\frac{3}{2}x^2 + 3\sqrt{3}xy + \frac{9}{2}y^2 + \frac{15}{4}x^2 - \frac{10\sqrt{3}}{4}xy + \frac{5}{4}y^2 = 30$$

$$\frac{21}{4}x^2 + \frac{\sqrt{3}}{2}xy + \frac{23}{4}y^2 = 30$$

$$21x^2 + 2\sqrt{3}xy + 23y^2 = 120$$

10. $49\left(x \cos \frac{\pi}{4} + y \sin \frac{\pi}{4}\right)^2 - 16\left(-x \sin \frac{\pi}{4} + y \cos \frac{\pi}{4}\right)^2$
$$= 784$$

$$49\left(\frac{\sqrt{2}}{2}x + \frac{\sqrt{2}}{2}y\right)^2 - 16\left(-\frac{\sqrt{2}}{2}x + \frac{\sqrt{2}}{2}y\right)^2 = 784$$

$$49\left(\frac{1}{2}x^2 + xy + \frac{1}{2}y^2\right) - 16\left(\frac{1}{2}x^2 - xy + \frac{1}{2}y^2\right) = 784$$

$$\frac{33}{2}x^2 + 65xy + \frac{33}{2}y^2 = 784$$

$$33x^2 + 130xy + 33y^2 = 1568$$

11. $\left(-x \sin \frac{\pi}{6} + y \cos \frac{\pi}{6}\right)^2 + 8\left(x \cos \frac{\pi}{6} + y \sin \frac{\pi}{6}\right) = 0$

$$\left(-x \cdot \frac{1}{2} + y \cdot \frac{\sqrt{3}}{2}\right)^2 + 8\left(x \cdot \frac{\sqrt{3}}{2} + y \cdot \frac{1}{2}\right) = 0$$

$$\frac{1}{4}x^2 - \frac{\sqrt{3}}{2}xy + \frac{3}{4}y^2 + 4\sqrt{3}x + 4y = 0$$

$$x^2 - 2\sqrt{3}xy + 3y^2 + 16\sqrt{3}x + 16y = 0$$

12. $B^2 - 4AC = (4)^2 - 4(8)(5) = -144$

ellipse

$$\tan 2\theta = \frac{B}{A - C} = \frac{4}{8 - 5} = \frac{4}{3}$$

$$2\theta \approx 53.13°$$

$$\theta \approx 26.6°$$

13. circle

$$(x - 2)^2 + (y - 3)^2 = 6$$
$$x^2 - 4x + 4 + y^2 - 6y + 9 = 6$$
$$x^2 + y^2 - 4x - 6y + 7 = 0$$

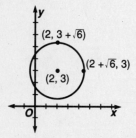

14. hyperbola

$$9(x)^2 - 25(y + 5)^2 = 225$$
$$9x^2 - 25y^2 - 250y - 625 = 225$$
$$9x^2 - 25y^2 - 250y - 850 = 0$$

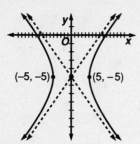

15. parabola

$$y + 4 = 2(x + 3)^2 - 7(x + 3) + 5$$
$$y + 4 = 2(x^2 + 6x + 9) - 7x - 21 + 5$$
$$y + 4 = 2x^2 + 12x + 18 - 7x - 21 + 5$$
$$y = 2x^2 + 5x - 2$$

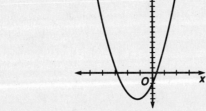

16. ellipse

$$3(x + 1)^2 + (y - 2)^2 = 9$$
$$3(x^2 + 2x + 1) + (y^2 - 4y + 4) = 9$$
$$3x^2 + 6x + 3 + y^2 - 4y + 4 = 9$$
$$3x^2 + y^2 + 6x - 4y - 2 = 0$$

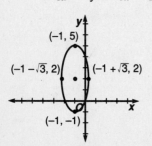

17. $(x \cos 45° + y \sin 45°)^2 -$
$$(-x \sin 45° + y \cos 45°)^2 = 9$$
$$\left(\frac{\sqrt{2}}{2}x + \frac{\sqrt{2}}{2}y\right)^2 - \left(-\frac{\sqrt{2}}{2}x + \frac{\sqrt{2}}{2}y\right)^2 = 9$$
$$\frac{1}{2}x^2 + xy + \frac{1}{2}y^2 + \frac{1}{2}x^2 + xy - \frac{1}{2}y^2 = 9$$
$$2xy = 9$$

18. $\left(x \cos \frac{\pi}{4} + y \sin \frac{\pi}{4}\right)^2 - 5\left(x \cos \frac{\pi}{4} + y \sin \frac{\pi}{4}\right) +$
$$\left(-x \sin \frac{\pi}{4} + y \cos \frac{\pi}{4}\right)^2 = 3$$
$$\left(\frac{\sqrt{2}}{2}x + \frac{\sqrt{2}}{2}y\right)^2 - 5\left(\frac{\sqrt{2}}{2}x + \frac{\sqrt{2}}{2}y\right) + \left(-\frac{\sqrt{2}}{2}x + \frac{\sqrt{2}}{2}y\right)^2 = 3$$
$$\frac{1}{2}x^2 + xy + \frac{1}{2}y^2 - \frac{5\sqrt{2}}{2}x - \frac{5\sqrt{2}}{2}y + \frac{1}{2}x^2 - xy + \frac{1}{2}y^2 = 3$$
$$x^2 + y^2 - \frac{5\sqrt{2}}{2}x - \frac{5\sqrt{2}}{2}y = 3$$
$$2x^2 + 2y^2 - 5\sqrt{2}x - 5\sqrt{2}y = 6$$

19. $\left(x \cos \frac{\pi}{4} + y \sin \frac{\pi}{4}\right)\left(-x \sin \frac{\pi}{4} + y \cos \frac{\pi}{4}\right) = -6$
$$\left(\frac{\sqrt{2}}{2}x + \frac{\sqrt{2}}{2}y\right)\left(-\frac{\sqrt{2}}{2}x + \frac{\sqrt{2}}{2}y\right) = -6$$
$$-\frac{1}{2}x^2 + \frac{1}{2}xy - \frac{1}{2}xy + \frac{1}{2}y^2 = -6$$
$$-\frac{1}{2}x^2 + \frac{1}{2}y^2 = -6$$
$$x^2 - y^2 = 12$$

20. $7(x \cos 30° + y \sin 30°) -$
$6\sqrt{3}(x \cos 30° + y \sin 30°) \cdot$
$(-x \sin 30° + y \cos 30°) +$
$13(-x \sin 30° + y \cos 30°) = 16$
$$7\left(\frac{\sqrt{3}}{2}x + \frac{1}{2}y\right)^2 - 6\sqrt{3}\left(\frac{\sqrt{3}}{2}x + \frac{1}{2}y\right)\left(-\frac{1}{2}x + \frac{\sqrt{3}}{2}y\right) +$$
$$13\left(-\frac{1}{2}x + \frac{\sqrt{3}}{2}y\right)^2 = 16$$
$$7\left(\frac{3}{4}x^2 + \frac{2\sqrt{3}}{4}xy + \frac{1}{4}y^2\right) -$$
$$6\sqrt{3}\left(-\frac{\sqrt{3}}{4}x^2 + \frac{3}{4}xy - \frac{1}{4}xy + \frac{\sqrt{3}}{4}y^2\right) +$$
$$13\left(\frac{1}{4}x^2 - \frac{2\sqrt{3}}{4}xy + \frac{3}{4}y^2\right) = 16$$
$$\frac{21}{4}x^2 + \frac{14\sqrt{3}}{4}xy + \frac{7}{4}y^2 + \frac{18}{4}x^2 - \frac{12\sqrt{3}}{4}xy - \frac{18}{4}y^2 +$$
$$\frac{13}{4}x^2 - \frac{26\sqrt{3}}{4}xy + \frac{39}{4}y^2 = 16$$
$$\frac{52}{4}x^2 - \frac{24\sqrt{3}}{4}xy + \frac{28}{4}y^2 = 16$$
$$13x^2 - 6\sqrt{3}xy + 7y^2 = 16$$

21. $B^2 - 4AC = 5^2 - 4(8)(-4) = 153$
hyperbola
$$\tan 2\theta = \frac{5}{8 + 4} = \frac{5}{12}$$
$$2\theta \approx 22.62°$$
$$\theta \approx 11°$$

22. $B^2 - 4AC = 16 - 4(9)(6) = -200$

ellipse

$\tan 2\theta = \frac{4}{9 - 6} = \frac{4}{3}$

$2\theta \approx 53.13^\circ$

$\theta \approx 27^\circ$

23. $B^2 - 4AC = 81 - 4(2)(14) = -31$

ellipse

$\tan 2\theta = \frac{9}{2 - 14} = -\frac{9}{12}$

$2\theta \approx -36.8^\circ$

$\theta \approx -18^\circ$

24. $B^2 - 4AC = 4 - 4(1)(1) = 0$

parabola

$\theta = \frac{\pi}{4} = 45^\circ$

25. $B^2 - 4AC = 48 - 4(2)(6) = 0$

parabola

$\tan 2\theta = \frac{4\sqrt{3}}{2 - 6} = -\sqrt{3}$

$2\theta = -60^\circ$

$\theta = -30^\circ$

26. $B^2 - 4AC = 16 - 4(2)(2) = 0$

parabola

$\theta = \frac{\pi}{4} = 45^\circ$

27. point

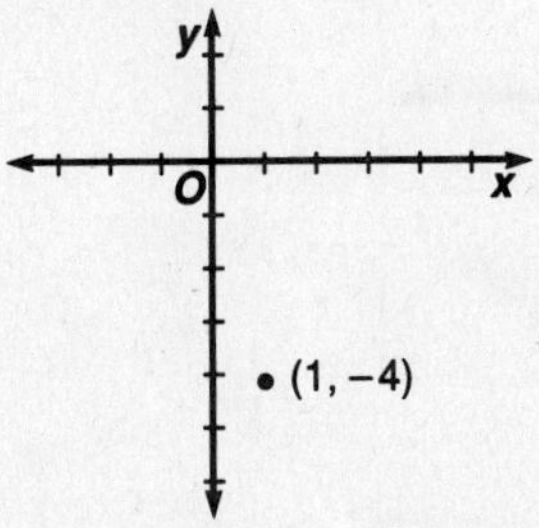

28. intersecting lines

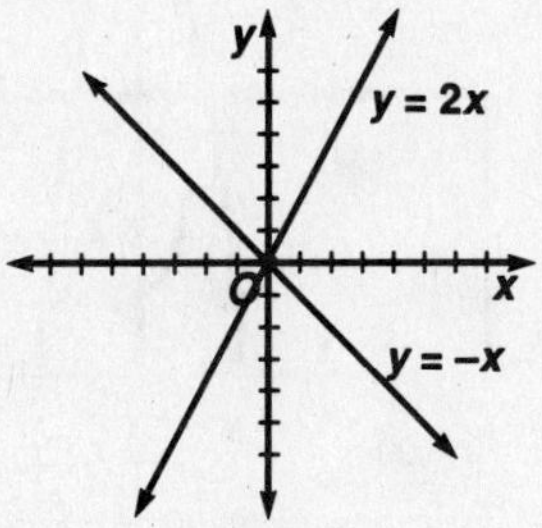

29. line

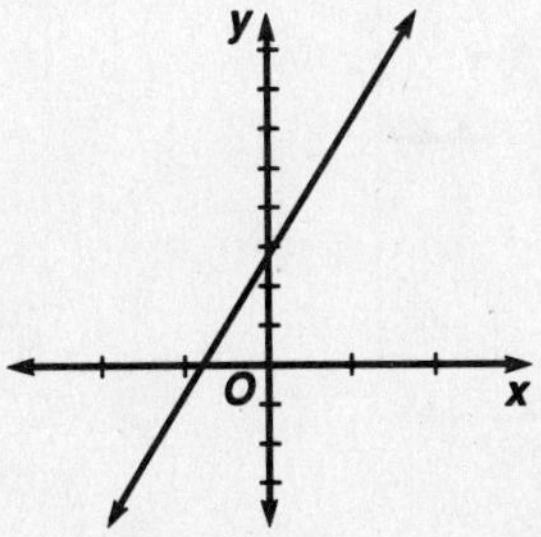

30. point

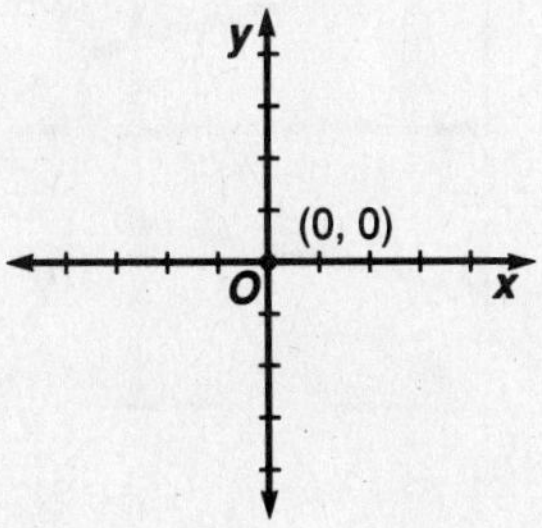

31.

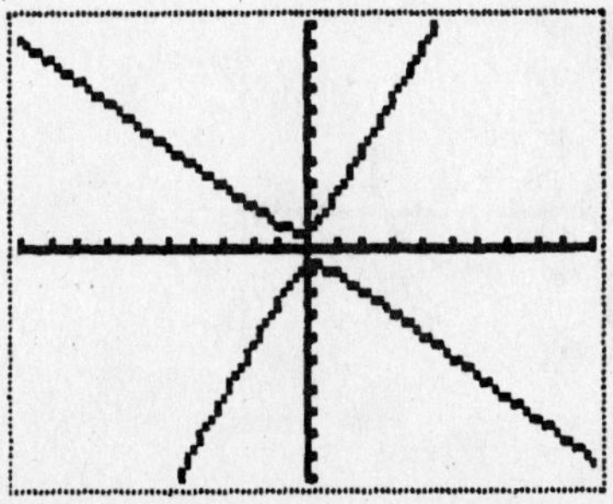

32.

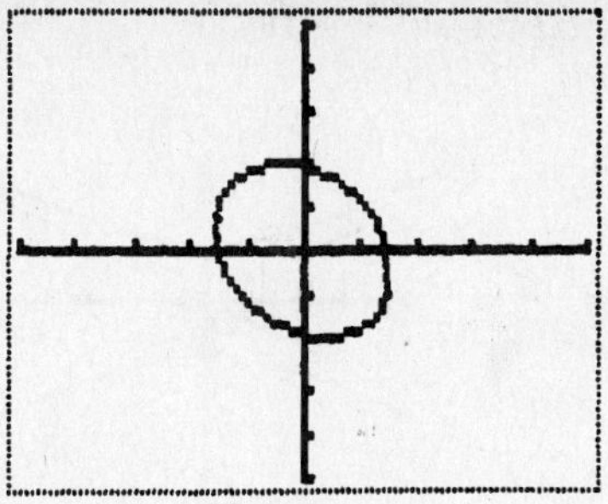

33.

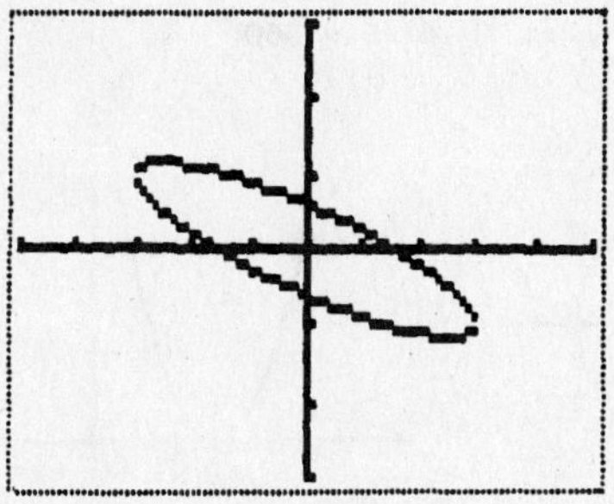

34.

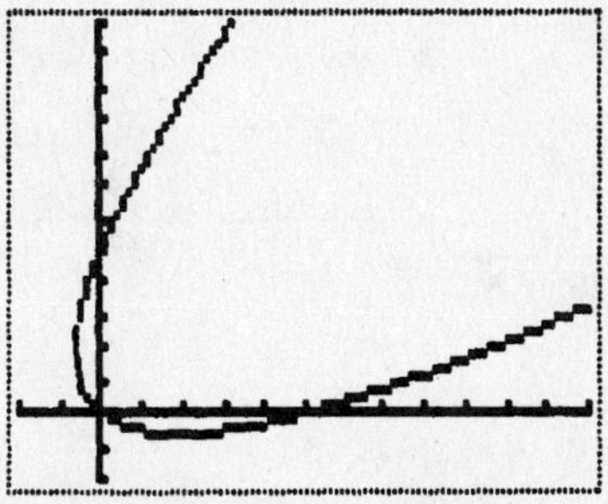

35.

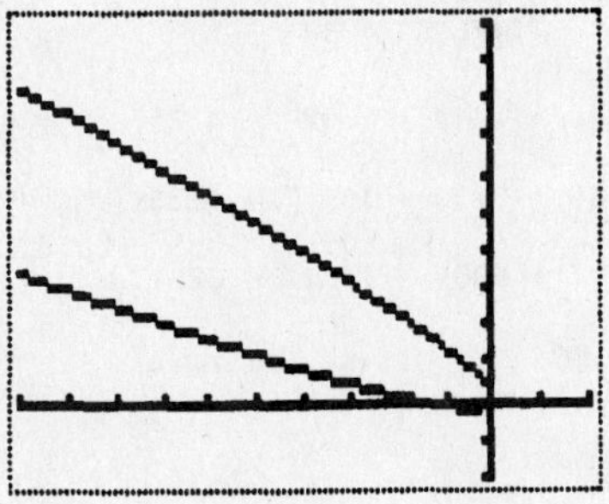

36.

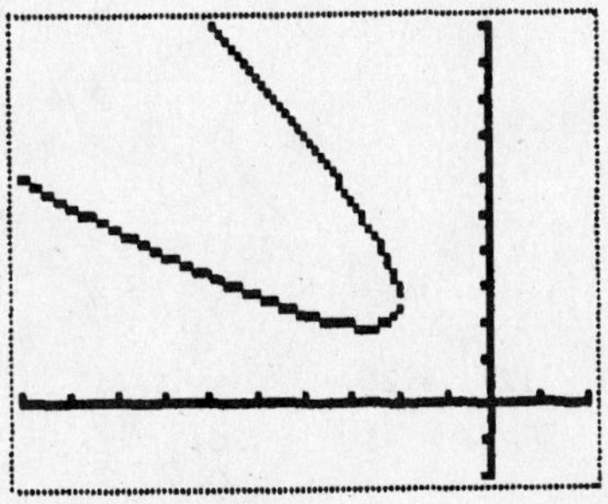

37. $5x^2 + 4xy + 8y^2 - 36 = 0$ is the equation of an ellipse whose center is the origin. Rotation:

$\tan 2\theta = \frac{4}{5 - 8} = -\frac{4}{3}$

$2\theta \approx -53^\circ$

$\theta \approx -26^\circ 30'$

38. **a.** $\theta = 180°$ **b.** $\theta = 180°$

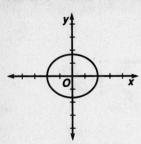   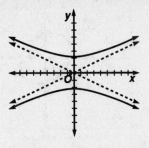

c. θ = any degree   **d.** $\theta = 360°$

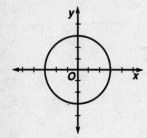   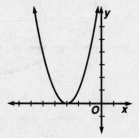

39. a.

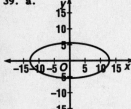

b. $169 - 25 = 144 = c^2$

$c = \pm12$

$\dfrac{(x + 12)^2}{169} + \dfrac{y^2}{25} = 1$

c. $\dfrac{(y + 12)^2}{169} + \dfrac{x^2}{25} = 1$

$25(y^2 + 24y + 144) + 169x^2 = 4225$

$25y^2 + 600y + 3600 + 169x^2 = 4225$

$25y^2 + 600y + 169x^2 = 625$

40. $x^2 + z^2 = 11.56$ **41.** no triangle

42. $y = 3 \sin \pi t$ **43.**

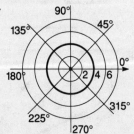

44. $(-5 + 12i)(-5 + 12i) = 25 - 120i + 144i^2$

$= -119 - 120i$

45. $(x^2 - 8x + 16) + y^2 = -11 + 16$

$(x - 4)^2 + y^2 = 5$

circle

46. If $x > 1$, $(\sqrt{x})^2 > \dfrac{1}{x^2}$.

If $x = 1$, $(\sqrt{x})^2 = \dfrac{1}{x^2}$.

If $0 < x < 1$, $(\sqrt{x})^2 < \dfrac{1}{x^2}$.

You need to know more about x to determine the relationship.   D

10-7A   Graphing Calculators: Solving Quadratic Systems

PAGE 578   EXERCISES

1.

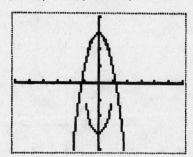

$(\pm2.31, 0.82)$, $(\pm2.31, -0.82)$

2.

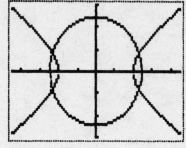

$(0, 3)$

3.

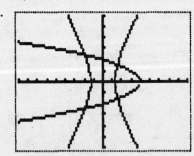

$(1.57, \pm1.56)$, $(-1.91, \pm2.43)$

4.

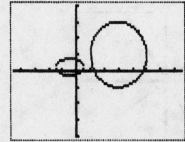

no solution

5.

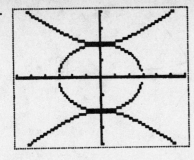

(0, ±2)

6.

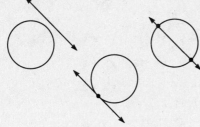

(3.16, ±0.18)

Systems of Second-Degree Equations and Inequalities

PAGES 582–583   CHECKING FOR UNDERSTANDING

1.

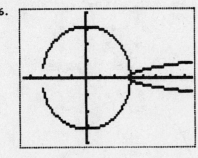

2.

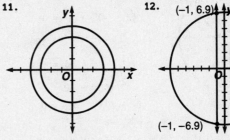

3. Negative values for width are not appropriate for this application.

---

4. Graph each inequality. The region in which the graphs overlap represents solution to the system.

5. 4   6. 2   7. 3   8. none   9. 1   10. 2

11.

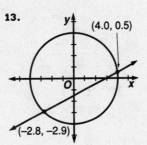

$x^2 + y^2 = 16$

$\underline{x^2 + y^2 = 9}$

$0 + 0 = 7$

no solution

12.

(−1, 6.9)

(−1, −6.9)

$x^2 + y^2 = 49$

$x + 1 = 0 \rightarrow x = -1$

$(-1)^2 + y^2 = 49$

$y^2 = 48$

$y = \pm\sqrt{48} \approx \pm6.9$

(−1, 6.9), (−1, −6.9)

13.

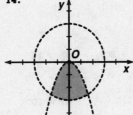

(4.0, 0.5)

(−2.8, −2.9)

$2y - x + 3 = 0 \rightarrow 2y + 3 = x$

$x^2 = 16 - y^2 \longrightarrow x^2 + y^2 = 16$

$(2y + 3)^2 + y^2 = 16$

$4y^2 + 12y + 9 + y^2 = 16$

$5y^2 + 12y - 7 = 0$

$y = \dfrac{-12 \pm \sqrt{144 - 4(5)(-7)}}{10}$

$= \dfrac{-12 \pm \sqrt{284}}{10}$

$y \approx 0.5, -2.9$

$x = 2(0.5) + 3 \qquad x = 2(-2.9) + 3$

$= 4 \qquad\qquad\quad = (-2.8)$

(4, 0.5), (−2.8, −2.9)

14.

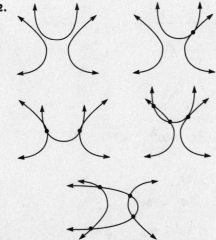

15.

263

16.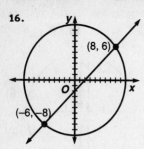

$x^2 + y^2 = 100$

$x = 2 + y$

$(2 + y)^2 + y^2 = 100$

$4 + 4y + y^2 + y^2 = 100$

$2y^2 + 4y - 96 = 0$

$y^2 + 2y - 48 = 0$

$(y - 6)(y + 8) = 0$

$y = 6, -8$

$x = 2 + 6 \quad x = 2 - 8$

$= 8 \qquad\quad = -6$

$(8, 6), (-6, -8)$

17.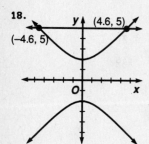

$y = 7 - x$

$y^2 + x^2 = 9$

$(7 - x)^2 + x^2 = 9$

$49 - 14x + x^2 + x^2 = 9$

$2x^2 - 14x + 40 = 0$

$x^2 - 7x + 20 = 0$

$x = \dfrac{7 \pm \sqrt{49 - 4(1)(20)}}{2}$

$= \dfrac{7 \pm \sqrt{-31}}{2}$

no solution

18.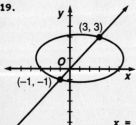

$y^2 - x^2 = 4$

$y = 5$

$5^2 - x^2 = 4$

$x^2 = 21$

$x \approx \pm 4.6$

$(4.6, 5), (-4.6, 5)$

19.

$x = y$

$5(x - 1)^2 + 20(y - 1)^2 = 100$

$5(y - 1)^2 + 20(y - 1)^2 = 100$

$(y - 1)^2(5 + 20) = 100$

$25(y^2 - 2y + 1) = 100$

$y^2 - 2y + 1 = 4$

$y^2 - 2y - 3 = 0$

$(y - 3)(y + 1) = 0$

$y = 3, -1$

$x = 3, -1$

$(3, 3), (-1, -1)$

20.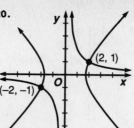

$xy = 2 \rightarrow y = \dfrac{2}{x}$

$x^2 - y^2 = 3$

$x^2 - \left(\dfrac{2}{x}\right)^2 = 3$

$x^2 - \dfrac{4}{x^2} = 3$

$x^4 - 4 = 3x^2$

$x^4 - 3x^2 - 4 = 0$

$(x^2 - 4)(x^2 + 1) = 0$

$x^2 = 4 \qquad x^2 = -1$

$x = \pm 2$

$y = \dfrac{2}{2} \qquad y = \dfrac{2}{-2}$

$= 1 \qquad\quad = -1$

$(2, 1), (-2, -1)$

21.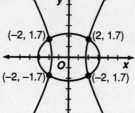

$x^2 + 2y^2 = 10 \longrightarrow x^2 + 2y^2 = 10$

$3x^2 - y^2 = 9 \longrightarrow 6x^2 - 2y^2 = 18$

$7x^2 = 28$

$x^2 = 4$

$x = \pm 2$

$3(2)^2 - y^2 = 9, \quad 3(-2)^2 - y^2 = 9$

$12 - y^2 = 9 \qquad\quad 12 - y^2 = 9$

$y^2 = 3 \qquad\qquad y^2 = 3$

$y \approx \pm 1.7 \qquad\qquad y \approx \pm 1.7$

$(2, \pm 1.7), (-2, \pm 1.7)$

22.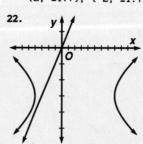

$(x - 2)^2 - 9(y + 3)^2 = 36$

$x = y$

$(y - 2)^2 - 9(y + 3)^2 = 36$

$y^2 - 4y + 4 - 9y^2 - 54y - 81 = 36$

$8y^2 + 58y + 113 = 0$

$y = \dfrac{-58 \pm \sqrt{3364 - 4(113)(8)}}{16} = \dfrac{-58 \pm \sqrt{-252}}{16}$

no solution

23.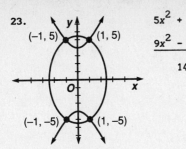

$5x^2 + y^2 = 30$

$\underline{9x^2 - y^2 = -16}$

$14x^2 = 14$

$x^2 = 1$

$x = \pm 1$

$5(1)^2 + y^2 = 30 \qquad 5(-1)^2 + y^2 = 30$

$\qquad y^2 = 25 \qquad\qquad\qquad y^2 = 25$

$\qquad y = \pm 5 \qquad\qquad\qquad y = \pm 5$

$(1, \pm 5), \; (-1, \pm 5)$

24.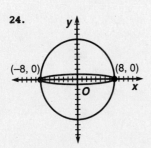

$x^2 + y^2 = 64 \longrightarrow -x^2 - y^2 = -64$

$x^2 + 64y^2 = 64 \longrightarrow \underline{x^2 + 64y^2 = 64}$

$\qquad\qquad\qquad\qquad\qquad 63y^2 = 0$

$\qquad\qquad\qquad\qquad\qquad\quad y^2 = 0$

$\qquad\qquad\qquad\qquad\qquad\quad\; y = 0$

$x^2 + 0^2 = 64$

$\quad x^2 = 64$

$\quad\; x = \pm 8$

$(\pm 8, \; 0)$

25.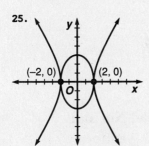

$9x^2 + 4y^2 = 36$

$\underline{9x^2 - 4y^2 = 36}$

$18x^2 = 72$

$x^2 = 4$

$x = \pm 2$

$9(2)^2 + 4y^2 = 36 \qquad 9(-2)^2 + 4y^2 = 36$

$\qquad\quad 4y^2 = 0 \qquad\qquad\qquad\quad 4y^2 = 0$

$\qquad\qquad y = 0 \qquad\qquad\qquad\qquad y = 0$

$(\pm 2, \; 0)$

26.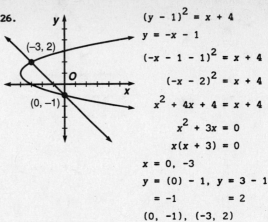

$(y - 1)^2 = x + 4$

$y = -x - 1$

$(-x - 1 - 1)^2 = x + 4$

$(-x - 2)^2 = x + 4$

$x^2 + 4x + 4 = x + 4$

$x^2 + 3x = 0$

$x(x + 3) = 0$

$x = 0, \; -3$

$y = (0) - 1, \quad y = 3 - 1$

$\quad = -1 \qquad\qquad = 2$

$(0, \; -1), \; (-3, \; 2)$

27.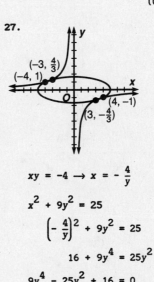

$xy = -4 \longrightarrow x = -\dfrac{4}{y}$

$x^2 + 9y^2 = 25$

$\left(-\dfrac{4}{y}\right)^2 + 9y^2 = 25$

$16 + 9y^4 = 25y^2$

$9y^4 - 25y^2 + 16 = 0$

$y^2 = \dfrac{25 \pm \sqrt{625 - 9(4)(16)}}{18}$

$\quad = \dfrac{25 \pm \sqrt{49}}{18}$

$\quad = \dfrac{25 \pm 7}{18}$

$y^2 = 1 \qquad\qquad y^2 = \dfrac{32}{18}$

$y = \pm 1 \qquad\qquad y = \pm \dfrac{4\sqrt{2}}{3\sqrt{2}} = \pm \dfrac{4}{3}$

$x(1) = -4 \qquad\qquad x(-1) = -4$

$\quad x = -4 \qquad\qquad\qquad x = 4$

$(-4, \; 1), \qquad\qquad (4, \; -1)$

$x\left(\dfrac{4}{3}\right) = -4 \qquad x\left(-\dfrac{4}{3}\right) = -4$

$\quad x = -3 \qquad\qquad\qquad x = 3$

$\left(-3, \; \dfrac{4}{3}\right), \qquad\qquad \left(3, \; -\dfrac{4}{3}\right)$

28. **29.**

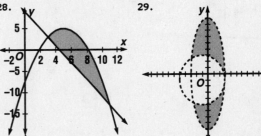

265

30.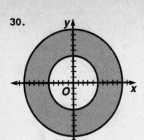

31.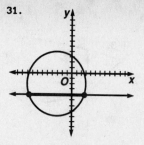

32.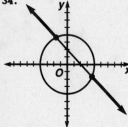

33.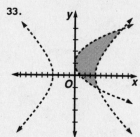

34.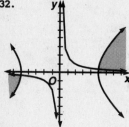

35.

36. $x^2 + y^2 = 1$

$y = 3x + 1$

$x^2 + (y + 1)^2 = 4$

$x = 0,\ y = 3(0) + 1 = 1$

$x = -\frac{3}{5},\ \left(-\frac{3}{5}\right)^2 + y^2 = 1$

$\frac{9}{25} + y^2 = 1$

$y^2 = \frac{16}{25}$

$y = \pm\frac{4}{5}$

$x^2 + (3x + 1)^2 = 1$

$x^2 + 9x^2 + 6x + 1 = 1$

$10x^2 + 6x = 0$

$x(10x + 6) = 0$

$x = 0,\ x = -\frac{6}{10} = -\frac{3}{5}$

Check $\left(-\frac{3}{5},\ \frac{4}{5}\right)$: $\left(-\frac{3}{5}\right)^2 + \left(\frac{4}{5} + 1\right)^2 \overset{?}{=} 4$

$\frac{9}{25} + \frac{81}{25} \overset{?}{=} 4$

$\frac{90}{25} \neq 4$

Check $\left(-\frac{3}{5},\ -\frac{4}{5}\right)$: $\left(-\frac{3}{5}\right)^2 + \left(-\frac{4}{5} + 1\right)^2 \overset{?}{=} 4$

$\frac{9}{25} + \frac{1}{25} \overset{?}{=} 4$

$\frac{10}{25} \neq 4$

Check $(0, 1)$: $0^2 + (1 + 1)^2 \overset{?}{=} 4$

$4 = 4$

Solution: $(0, 1)$

37. $\ell \cdot w = 216$

$2\ell + 2w = 60 \rightarrow \ell + w = 30 \rightarrow \ell = 30 - w$

$(30 - w)w = 216$

$30w - w^2 = 216$

$w^2 - 30w + 216 = 0$

$(w - 18)(w - 12) = 0$

$w = 18,\ w = 12$

$\ell \cdot 18 = 216$

$\ell = 12$

$12\ \text{ft} \times 18\ \text{ft}$

38. a.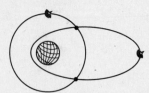

b. 2 times

c. See students' work.

39. $319 \sin 42°12' = d$

$d \approx 214.9$ meters

40. $y = \cos x$

$y = \arccos x$

41. $\overrightarrow{AB} = (5,\ 3,\ 2) - (3,\ 3,\ -1)$

$= (2,\ 0,\ 3)$

42. $6\left(\cos\frac{5\pi}{8} + i\sin\frac{5\pi}{8}\right) + 12\left(\cos\frac{\pi}{2} + i\sin\frac{\pi}{2}\right)$

$= 0.5\left(\cos\frac{5\pi}{8} + i\sin\frac{5\pi}{8}\right) + \left(\cos\frac{4\pi}{8} + i\sin\frac{4\pi}{8}\right)$

$= 0.5\left(\cos\frac{\pi}{8} + i\sin\frac{\pi}{8}\right)$

$= 0.46 + 0.10i$

43. $(y - 3 - 5) = (x + 4 + 3)^2$

$(y - 8) = (x + 7)^2$

$(-7,\ 8)$

44. $\frac{8}{14}(6) + \frac{6}{14}(8) = \frac{48}{14} + \frac{48}{14}$

$= \frac{96}{14} \approx 6.86$

| 10-8 | **Tangents and Normals to the Conic Sections** |

PAGES 589–590   CHECKING FOR UNDERSTANDING

1.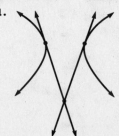

2. You use the slope of the tangent to determine the coordinates of the point of tangency. Then substitute that value into the equation of the circle.

3. $m = \dfrac{x - h}{2p}$

$\quad = \dfrac{0 - (-4)}{2 \cdot 2}$

$\quad = \dfrac{4}{4} = 1$

$\quad$ normal $= \dfrac{-1}{1} = -1$

4. $m = -\dfrac{(x - h)}{(y - k)}$

$\quad = -\dfrac{(-1 - 2)}{(2 - 3)}$

$\quad = -\left(\dfrac{-3}{-1}\right) = -3$

$\quad$ normal: $\dfrac{1}{3}$

5. $m = -\dfrac{b^2(x - h)}{a^2(y - k)}$

$\quad = -\dfrac{25(3 - 3)}{4(-4 - 1)}$

$\quad = -\dfrac{0}{-20}$

$\quad = 0$

$\quad$ normal: undefined

6. $m = -\dfrac{b^2(x - h)}{a^2(y - k)}$

$\quad = -\dfrac{9(-2 - (-2))}{36(6 - 3)}$

$\quad = -\dfrac{0}{108}$

$\quad = 0$

$\quad$ normal: undefined

7. $m = \dfrac{2p}{y - k}$

$\quad = \dfrac{2(2)}{2 - (-2)}$

$\quad = \dfrac{4}{4}$

$\quad = 1$

$\quad$ normal: -1

8. $m = \dfrac{b^2(x - h)}{a^2(y - k)}$

$\quad = \dfrac{9(-4 - 0)}{8(-3 - 0)}$

$\quad = \dfrac{-36}{-24}$

$\quad = \dfrac{3}{2}$

$\quad$ normal: $-\dfrac{2}{3}$

9. tangent: $xx_1 + yy_1 - r^2 = 0$

$\quad\quad\quad 9x - 8y - 145 = 0$

$\quad$ normal: $m = -\dfrac{8}{9}$

$\quad (y + 8) = \dfrac{-8}{9}(x - 9)$

$\quad\quad y = \dfrac{-8}{9}x + 8 - 8$

$\quad 9y + 8x = 0$

10. $x^2 + 4x - y + 1 = 0 \quad\quad (0, 1)$

$\quad (x^2 + 4x + 4) = y - 1 + 4$

$\quad\quad (x + 2)^2 = y + 3$

$\quad m = \dfrac{x - h}{2p} = \dfrac{0 + 2}{2 \cdot \frac{1}{4}} = \dfrac{2}{\frac{1}{2}} = 4$

$\quad$ tangent: $\quad y - 1 = 4(x - 0)$

$\quad\quad\quad\quad y - 1 = 4x$

$\quad\quad\quad 4x - y + 1 = 0$

$\quad$ normal: $\quad y - 1 = -\dfrac{1}{4}(x - 0)$

$\quad\quad\quad\quad y - 1 = -\dfrac{1}{4}x$

$\quad\quad\quad x + 4y - 4 = 0$

11. $m = -\dfrac{b^2(x - h)}{a^2(y - k)} = -\dfrac{9(4 - 0)}{25(1.8 - 0)} = -\dfrac{36}{45} = -\dfrac{4}{5}$

$\quad$ tangent: $\quad (y - 1.8) = -\dfrac{4}{5}(x - 4)$

$\quad\quad\quad\quad y = -\dfrac{4}{5}x + \dfrac{16}{5} + 1.8$

$\quad\quad\quad\quad y = -\dfrac{4}{5}x + 5$

$\quad\quad\quad 5y + 4x - 25 = 0$

$\quad$ normal: $\quad (y - 1.8) = \dfrac{5}{4}(x - 4)$

$\quad\quad\quad\quad y = \dfrac{5}{4}x - 3.2$

$\quad\quad\quad 25x - 20y - 64 = 0$

12. $m = \dfrac{b^2(x - h)}{a^2(y - k)} = \dfrac{1(2)}{4(0 - 0)} \quad\quad$ undefined

$\quad$ tangent: When slope is undefined, the tangent is a vertical line. In this case, $x = 2$ or $x - 2 = 0$.

$\quad$ normal: $m = 0$

$\quad y - 0 = 0(x - 2)$

$\quad\quad y = 0$

PAGES 590–591   EXERCISES

13. tangent: $2x + \sqrt{21}y - 25 = 0$

$\quad$ normal: $m = \dfrac{\sqrt{21}}{2}$

$\quad (y - \sqrt{21}) = \dfrac{\sqrt{21}}{2}(x - 2)$

$\quad\quad\quad y = \dfrac{\sqrt{21}}{2}x - \sqrt{21} + \sqrt{21}$

$\quad \dfrac{\sqrt{21}}{2}x - y = 0$

14. tangent: $\sqrt{13}x + 6y - 49 = 0$

$\quad$ normal: $m = \dfrac{6}{\sqrt{13}}$

$\quad\quad (y - 6) = \dfrac{6}{\sqrt{13}}(x - \sqrt{13})$

$\quad\quad\quad y = \dfrac{6}{\sqrt{13}}x - 6 + 6$

$\quad\quad \sqrt{13}y = 6x$

$\quad 13y - 6\sqrt{13}x = 0$

15. tangent: $x^2 + y^2 = 116$

$\quad -10x - 4y - 116 = 0$

$\quad 10x + 4y + 116 = 0$

$\quad$ normal: $m = \dfrac{4}{10} = \dfrac{2}{5}$

$\quad y + 4 = \dfrac{2}{5}(x + 10)$

$\quad\quad y = \dfrac{2}{5}x + 4 - 4$

$\quad 5y - 2x = 0$

16. tangent: $x^2 + y^2 = \frac{5}{3}$

$x + \frac{\sqrt{6}}{3}y - \frac{5}{3} = 0$

$3x + \sqrt{6}y - 5 = 0$

normal: $m = \frac{\sqrt{6}}{3}$

$\left(y - \frac{\sqrt{6}}{3}\right) = \frac{\sqrt{6}}{3}(x - 1)$

$y = \frac{\sqrt{6}}{3}x - \frac{\sqrt{6}}{3} + \frac{\sqrt{6}}{3}$

$3y - \sqrt{6}x = 0$

17. $y^2 + y = x + 5$

$\left(y + \frac{1}{2}\right)^2 = x + \frac{21}{4}$

$m = \frac{2p}{y - k} = \frac{2 \cdot \frac{1}{4}}{-3 + \frac{1}{2}} = \frac{\frac{1}{2}}{-\frac{5}{2}} = -\frac{1}{5}$

tangent: $(y + 3) = -\frac{1}{5}(x - 1)$

$y + 3 = -\frac{1}{5}x + \frac{1}{5}$

$5y = -x - 14$

$x + 5y + 14 = 0$

normal: $(y + 3) = 5(x - 1)$

$y = 5x - 5 - 3$

$5x - y - 8 = 0$

18. $m = -\frac{a^2(x - h)}{b^2(y - k)} = -\frac{36(\sqrt{3} - 0)}{4(6 - 3)} = -\frac{36\sqrt{3}}{12} = -3\sqrt{3}$

tangent: $(y - 6) = -3\sqrt{3}(x - \sqrt{3})$

$y - 6 = -3\sqrt{3}x + 9$

$3\sqrt{3}x + y - 15 = 0$

normal: $(y - 6) = \frac{1}{3\sqrt{3}}(x - \sqrt{3})$

$3\sqrt{3}y - 18\sqrt{3} = x - \sqrt{3}$

$0 = x - 3\sqrt{3}y + 17\sqrt{3}$

19. $m = -\frac{(x - h)}{(y - k)} = -\frac{(-4 + 2)}{(\sqrt{5} - 0)} = \frac{2}{\sqrt{5}}$

tangent: $(y - \sqrt{5}) = \frac{2}{\sqrt{5}}(x + 4)$

$y = \frac{2\sqrt{5}}{5}x + \frac{8\sqrt{5}}{5} + \sqrt{5}$

$\sqrt{5}y = 2x + 13$

$2x - \sqrt{5}y + 13 = 0$

normal: $(y - \sqrt{5}) = -\frac{\sqrt{5}}{2}(x + 4)$

$y = -\frac{\sqrt{5}}{2}x - 2\sqrt{5} + \sqrt{5}$

$y = -\frac{\sqrt{5}}{2}x - \sqrt{5}$

$2y + \sqrt{5}x + 2\sqrt{5} = 0$

20. $2\left(x^2 - \frac{7}{2}x + \frac{49}{16}\right) = 11 - 5y$

$2\left(x - \frac{7}{4}\right)^2 = -5y + 11 + \frac{49}{8}$

$\left(x - \frac{7}{4}\right)^2 = \frac{1}{2}\left(-5y + \frac{137}{8}\right)$

$\left(x - \frac{7}{4}\right)^2 = -\frac{5}{2}\left(y - \frac{137}{40}\right)$

$m = \frac{x - h}{2p} = \frac{-1 - \frac{7}{4}}{2\left(-\frac{5}{8}\right)} = \frac{-\frac{11}{4}}{-\frac{5}{4}} \cdot \frac{4}{-5} = \frac{11}{5}$

tangent: $y - \frac{2}{5} = \frac{11}{5}(x + 1)$

$y = \frac{11}{5}x + \frac{11}{5} + \frac{2}{5}$

$11x - 5y + 13 = 0$

normal: $\left(y - \frac{2}{5}\right) = -\frac{5}{11}(x + 1)$

$y = -\frac{5}{11}x - \frac{5}{11} + \frac{2}{5}$

$5x + 11y + \frac{3}{5} = 0$

21. $m = -\frac{b^2(x - h)}{a^2(y - k)} = -\frac{4(7 - 4)}{12(1 - 0)} = -1$

tangent: $(y - 1) = -1(x - 7)$

$y = -x + 8$

$x + y - 8 = 0$

normal: $(y - 1) = 1(x - 7)$

$y = x - 6$

$x - y - 6 = 0$

22. $m = -\frac{(x - h)}{(y - k)} = -\frac{(8 - 4)}{(3 - 3)} = -\frac{4}{0}$

undefined

tangent: $x = 8$

normal: $y - 3 = 0(x - 8)$

$y = 3$

23. $m = \frac{b^2(x - h)}{a^2(y - k)} = \frac{9(-4 - 1)}{25(-3 + 3)} = -\frac{45}{0}$

undefined

tangent: $x = -4$

normal: $y + 3 = 0(x + 4)$

$y = -3$

24. $m = \frac{b^2(x - h)}{a^2(y - k)} = \frac{64(-4 - 2)}{18(-7 - 1)} = \frac{-384}{-144} = \frac{8}{3}$

tangent: $y + 7 = \frac{8}{3}(x + 4)$

$y = \frac{8}{3}x + \frac{32}{3} - \frac{21}{3}$

$8x - 3y + 11 = 0$

normal: $y + 7 = -\frac{3}{8}(x + 4)$

$y = -\frac{3}{8}x - \frac{12}{8} - \frac{56}{8}$

$3x + 8y + 68 = 0$

25. $t = \sqrt{(x_1 - h)^2 + (y_1 - k)^2 - r^2}$

$= \sqrt{(6 - 0)^2 + (2 - 0)^2 - 37}$

$= \sqrt{3}$

≈ 1.73

26. $t = \sqrt{(4 + 3)^2 + (-1)^2 - 4}$

$= \sqrt{46}$

≈ 6.78

27. $x(x - 6) + y(y - 8) = 0$

$x^2 - 6x + 9 + y^2 - 8y + 16 = 9 + 16$

$(x - 3)^2 + (y - 4)^2 = 25$

$t = \sqrt{(10 - 3)^2 + (1 - 4)^2 - 25}$

$= \sqrt{33}$

≈ 5.74

28. $(x + 3)^2 + (y - 2)^2 = 4$

$t = \sqrt{(-7 + 3)^2 + (2 - 2)^2 - 4}$

$= \sqrt{8}$

$= 2\sqrt{3}$

≈ 3.46

29. radius = 5

$y = \pm 5$

30. radius = 7

$x = \pm 7$

31. ellipse; semi-major axis has length 8

$y = \pm 8$

32. If tangents are vertical, slope of normals = 0.
So equation of the normal is $y = 0$ since center
of ellipse is at origin.

33. slope $= -\dfrac{3}{4}$

$m = -\dfrac{x - h}{y - k}$

$-\dfrac{3}{4} = -\dfrac{x}{y}$

$\dfrac{3}{4} = \dfrac{x}{y}$

$\dfrac{3}{4}y = x$

$\left(\dfrac{3}{4}y\right)^2 + y^2 = 64$

$\dfrac{9}{16}y^2 + y^2 = 64$

$\dfrac{25}{16}y^2 = 64$

$y^2 = \pm\dfrac{1024}{25}$

$y = \pm\dfrac{32}{5}$

$x = \dfrac{3}{4} \cdot \dfrac{32}{5}$ $\qquad x = \dfrac{3}{4} \cdot \left(-\dfrac{32}{5}\right)$

$= \dfrac{24}{5}$ $\qquad\qquad = -\dfrac{24}{5}$

$\left(\dfrac{24}{5}, \dfrac{32}{5}\right), \left(-\dfrac{24}{5}, -\dfrac{32}{5}\right)$

$y - \dfrac{32}{5} = -\dfrac{3}{4}\left(x - \dfrac{24}{5}\right), \; y + \dfrac{32}{5} = -\dfrac{3}{4}\left(x + \dfrac{24}{5}\right)$

$y = -\dfrac{3}{4}x + \dfrac{18}{5} + \dfrac{32}{5}$ $\quad y = -\dfrac{3}{4}x - \dfrac{18}{5} - \dfrac{32}{5}$

$y = -\dfrac{3}{4}x + 10$ $\qquad\quad y = -\dfrac{3}{4}x - 10$

34. $m = \dfrac{16 - 0}{2 - 0} = 8$ $\qquad$ **b.** $y - 0 = 8(x - 0)$

a. $y = 8x + b$ $\qquad\qquad\qquad y = 8x$

35. slope = 3

$4 + 4y = (x^2 + 4x + 4) - 16$

$20 + 4y = (x + 2)^2$

$4(y + 5) = (x + 2)^2$

$3 = \dfrac{(x - h)}{2p}$

$3 = \dfrac{(a + 2)}{2 \cdot 1}$

$6 = a + 2$

$4 = a$

36. $p = \dfrac{1}{4}$ and slope = 2

$m = \dfrac{x - h}{2p}$

$2 = \dfrac{2 - h}{2 \cdot \frac{1}{4}}$

$2 = \dfrac{2 - h}{\frac{1}{2}}$

$1 = 2 - h$

$h = 1$

$(x - 1)^2 = 4\left(\dfrac{1}{4}\right)(y - k)$

$(2 - 1)^2 = 1(4 - k)$

$1 = 4 - k$

$k = 3$

$(x - 1)^2 = (y - 3)$

$x^2 - 2x + 1 = y - 3$

$x^2 - 2x + 4 = y$

So, $a = -2$ and $b = 4$.

37. $x^2 - 6x = 2y - 1$

$(x^2 - 6x + 9) = 2y - 1 + 9$

$(x - 3)^2 = 2(y - 4)$

$m = \dfrac{x - h}{2p}$

$1 = \dfrac{x - 3}{2 \cdot \frac{1}{2}}$

$1 = x - 3$

$x = 4$

$4^2 - 6 \cdot 4 - 2y + 1 = 0$

$16 - 24 - 2y + 1 = 0$

$-2y - 7 = 0$

$-2y = 7$

$y = -3.5$

$(4, -3.5)$

38. $x + y = 4 \rightarrow y = -x + 4$

$m = -1$

It is only true for $x = y$.

So, $x + x = 4$

$2x = 4$

$x = 2.$

$y = 2$

So, $xy = 2 \cdot 2 = 4$ and $k = 4$.

39.

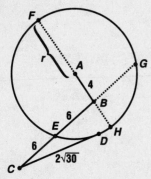

Extend $\overrightarrow{AB}$ to intersect $\odot A$ at points F and H.

Also, extend $\overrightarrow{CB}$ to intersect $\odot A$ at point G.

Given that $\overrightarrow{CD}$ is a tangent segment and since $\overrightarrow{CG}$ is a secant segment: $(CE)(CG) = (CD)^2$

$$6(12 + BG) = (2\sqrt{30})^2$$

$$BG = 8.$$

Note that $\overrightarrow{HF}$ and $\overrightarrow{EG}$ are chords and $\overrightarrow{HF}$ is a diameter. Thus, $(BG)(EB) = (BH)(BF)$

$$\text{or } (8)(6) = (r - 4)(r + 4)$$

$$48 = r^2 - 16$$

$$64 = r^2$$

$$r = 8.$$

Therefore, the radius of circle A is 8 units.

40. a.

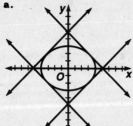

b. $a = 4$, $b = 3$

$$\frac{x^2}{16} + \frac{y^2}{9} = 1$$

$$y = \pm 2$$

$$\frac{x^2}{16} + \frac{4}{9} = 1$$

$$\frac{x^2}{16} = \frac{5}{9}$$

$$x^2 = \frac{80}{9}$$

$$x = \pm \frac{2\sqrt{20}}{3} \approx \pm 2.98$$

$$m \approx -\frac{9(\pm 2.98)}{16(2)} \approx \pm 0.84$$

c. $(2.98, 2)$, $m = -0.84$

$$y = mx + b$$

$$2 = (-0.84)(2.98) + b$$

$$2 = -2.50 + b$$

$$4.50 = b$$

$$y = -0.84x + 4.50$$

$(-2.98, 2)$, $m = 0.84$

$$y = mx + b$$

$$2 = (0.84)(-2.98) + b$$

$$2 = -2.50 + b$$

$$4.50 = b$$

$$y = 0.84x + 4.50$$

$(-2.98, -2)$, $m = -0.84$

$$y = mx + b$$

$$-2 = (-0.84)(-2.98) + b$$

$$-2 = 2.50 + b$$

$$-4.50 = b$$

$$y = -0.84x - 4.50$$

$(2.98, -2)$, $m = 0.84$

$$y = mx + b$$

$$-2 = (0.84)(2.98) + b$$

$$-2 = 2.50 + b$$

$$-4.50 = b$$

$$y = 0.84x - 4.50$$

41. a.

b. $(y - k)^2 = 4p(x - h)$

$$(3 - 0)^2 = 4p(2 - 0)$$

$$9 = 8p$$

$$\frac{9}{8} = p$$

$$m = \frac{2p}{y - k} = \frac{2\left(\frac{9}{8}\right)}{3 - 0} = \frac{\frac{9}{4}}{3} = \frac{3}{4}$$

$$y = mx + b$$

$$3 = \frac{3}{4}(2) + b$$

$$3 = \frac{3}{2} + b$$

$$\frac{3}{2} = b$$

$$y = \frac{3}{4}x + \frac{3}{2}$$

$$4y = 3x + 6$$

$$4y - 3x - 6 = 0$$

42. $k = \frac{1}{2}bc \sin A$

$24 = \frac{1}{2}(6)(10) \sin A$

$24 = 30 \sin A$

$\frac{24}{30} = \sin A$

$\frac{4}{5} = \sin A$

$A \approx 53°8'$

43.

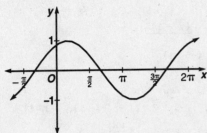

44. $\dfrac{2x - 3y + 9}{\sqrt{13}} = \dfrac{x + 4y + 4}{-\sqrt{17}}$

$\sqrt{13}x + 4\sqrt{13}y + 4\sqrt{13} = -2\sqrt{17}x + 3\sqrt{17}y - 9\sqrt{17}$

$(2\sqrt{17} + \sqrt{13})x + (4\sqrt{13} - 3\sqrt{17})y + 9\sqrt{17} + 4\sqrt{13} = 0$

45. $(3i + 5)(3i + 5) = 9i^2 + 30i + 25$

$= 16 + 30i$

46. $5\left(-\dfrac{\sqrt{3}}{2} + i \cdot \dfrac{1}{2}\right)$

$= -\dfrac{5\sqrt{3}}{2} + \dfrac{5}{2}i$

47.

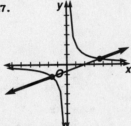

48. $(7x)^2 + (7x)^2 = c^2$

$98x^2 = c^2$

$\sqrt{98x^2} = c$

$c = 7x\sqrt{2}$ in.

The best answer is B.

Chapter 10 Summary and Review

PAGES 592–594   SKILLS AND CONCEPTS

1. $3x^2 + 3y^2 = 81$

$x^2 + y^2 = 27$

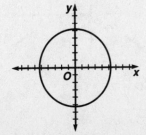

2. $x^2 + y^2 - 6y + 9 = 9$

$x^2 + (y - 3)^2 = 9$

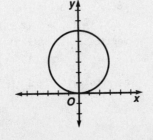

3. $x^2 + 3x + \dfrac{9}{4} + y^2 + y + \dfrac{1}{4} = 12 + \dfrac{9}{4} + \dfrac{1}{4}$

$\left(x + \dfrac{3}{2}\right)^2 + \left(y + \dfrac{1}{2}\right)^2 = \dfrac{29}{2}$

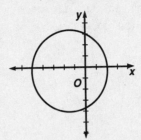

4. $x^2 + 14x + 49 + y^2 + 6y + 9 = 23 + 49 + 9$

$(x + 7)^2 + (y + 3)^2 = 81$

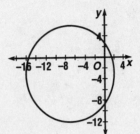

5. $p = 2$

vertex: $(7, 3)$

focus: $(7, 5)$

directrix: $y = 1$

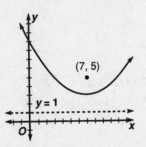

6. $p = -4$

vertex: $(1, -4)$

focus: $(-3, -4)$

directrix: $x = 5$

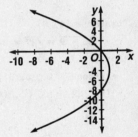

7. $y^2 + 6y + 9 = 4x - 25 + 9$

$(y + 3)^2 = 4(x - 4)$

$p = 1$

vertex: $(4, -3)$

focus: $(5, -3)$

directrix: $x = 3$

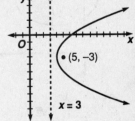

8. $x^2 + 4x + 4 = y - 8 + 4$

$(x + 2)^2 = y - 4$

$p = \dfrac{1}{4}$

vertex: $(-2, 4)$

focus: $\left(-2, \dfrac{17}{4}\right)$

directrix: $y = \dfrac{15}{4}$

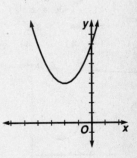

9. center: (3, -1)

$c = \sqrt{a^2 - b^2} = \sqrt{25 - 4} = \sqrt{21}$

foci: $(3 \pm \sqrt{21}, -1)$

vertices: $(3 \pm 5, -1)$, $(3, -1 \pm 2)$

= (-2, -1), (8, -1), (3, -3), (3, 1)

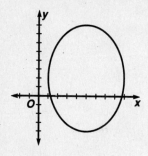

10. center: (5, 2)

$c = \sqrt{36 - 16} = \sqrt{20} = 2\sqrt{5}$

foci: $(5, 2 \pm 2\sqrt{5})$

vertices: $(5 \pm 4, 2)$, $(5, 2 \pm 6)$

= (1, 2), (9, 2), (5, -4), (5, 8)

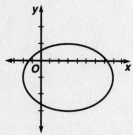

11. center: (4, 6)

$c = \sqrt{36 - 9} = \sqrt{27} = 3\sqrt{3}$

foci: $(4 \pm 3\sqrt{3}, 6)$

vertices: $(4 \pm 6, 6)$, $(4, 6 \pm 3)$

= (-2, 6), (10, 6), (4, 9), (4, 3)

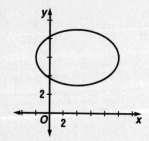

12. center: (-3, 4)

$c = \sqrt{6 - 4} = \sqrt{2}$

foci: $(-3, 4 \pm \sqrt{2})$

vertices: $(-3 \pm 2, 4)$, $(-3, 4 \pm \sqrt{6})$

= (-5, 4) (-1, 4), $(-3, 4 \pm \sqrt{6})$

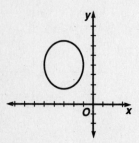

13. center: (0, 0)

$c = \sqrt{4 + 8} = \sqrt{12} = 2\sqrt{3}$

foci: $(\pm 2\sqrt{3}, 0)$

vertices: $(\pm 2, 0)$

asymptotes: $y = \pm \dfrac{\sqrt{8}}{2}x$

$= \pm\sqrt{2}x$

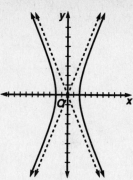

14. $\dfrac{(x + 5)^2}{4} - \dfrac{(y - 1)^2}{8} = 1$

center: (-5, 1)

$c = \sqrt{4 + 8} = \sqrt{12} = 2\sqrt{3}$

foci: $(-5 \pm 2\sqrt{3}, 1)$

vertices: $(-5 \pm 2, 1) = (-7, 1), (-3, 1)$

asymptotes: $y - 1 = \pm \dfrac{\sqrt{8}}{2}(x + 5)$

$= \pm\sqrt{2}(x + 5)$

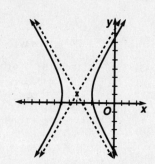

15. $y^2 - 5(x^2 - 4x + 4) = 50 - 20$

$y^2 - 5(x - 2)^2 = 30$

$\dfrac{y^2}{30} - \dfrac{(x - 2)^2}{6} = 1$

center: (2, 0)

$c = \sqrt{30 + 6} = 6$

foci: $(2, \pm 6)$

vertices: $(2, \pm\sqrt{30})$

asymptotes: $y = \pm \dfrac{\sqrt{30}}{\sqrt{6}}(x - 2)$

$= \pm\sqrt{5}(x - 2)$

16. $9(x^2 - 4x + 4) - 16(y^2 - 6y + 9)$

$= -36 + 36 - 144$

$\dfrac{(y - 3)^2}{9} - \dfrac{(x - 2)^2}{16} = 1$

center: (2, 3)

$c = \sqrt{16 + 9} = 5$

foci: $(2, 3 \pm 5)$

$= (2, 8), (2, -2)$

vertices: $(2, 3 \pm 3)$

$= 2, 6), (2, 0)$

asymptotes: $y - 3 = \pm \dfrac{3}{4}(x - 2)$

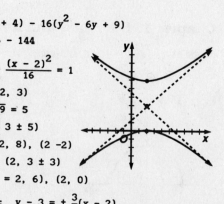

17. ellipse

$4(x^2 - 2x + 1) + y^2 = 12 + 4$

$$\frac{(x - 1)^2}{4} + \frac{y^2}{16} = 1$$

$$\frac{y^2}{16} + \frac{(x - 1)^2}{4} = 1$$

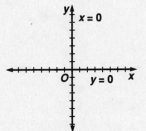

18. degenerate hyperbola

$x = 0, \ y = 0$

19. circle

$2(x - 4)^2 + 2(y - 1)^2 = 8$

$(x - 4)^2 + (y - 1)^2 = 4$

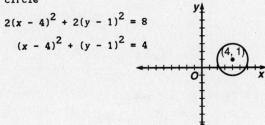

20. parabola

$x^2 - 8x + 16 = 6y - 16 + 16$

$(x - 4)^2 = 6y$

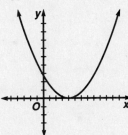

21. $(x + 3)^2 + (y - 2)^2 = 3$

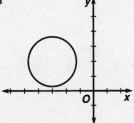

22. $4(x - 1)^2 - 16(y + 1)^2 = 64$

$(x - 1)^2 - 4(y + 1)^2 = 16$

23. $4\left(x \cos \frac{\pi}{6} + y \sin \frac{\pi}{6}\right)^2 + 9\left(-x \sin \frac{\pi}{6} + y \cos \frac{\pi}{6}\right)^2 = 36$

$$4\left(\frac{\sqrt{3}}{2}x + \frac{1}{2}y\right)^2 + 9\left(-\frac{1}{2}x + \frac{\sqrt{3}}{2}y\right)^2 = 36$$

$$4\left(\frac{3}{4}x^2 + \frac{2\sqrt{3}}{4}xy + \frac{1}{4}y^2\right) + 9\left(\frac{1}{4}x^2 - \frac{2\sqrt{3}}{4}xy + \frac{3}{4}y^2\right) = 36$$

$$3x^2 + 2\sqrt{3}xy + y^2 + \frac{9}{4}x^2 - \frac{18\sqrt{3}}{4}xy + \frac{27}{4}y^2 = 36$$

$$12x^2 + 8\sqrt{3}xy + 4y^2 + 9x^2 - 18\sqrt{3}xy + 27y^2 = 144$$

$$21x^2 - 10\sqrt{3}xy + 31y^2 = 144$$

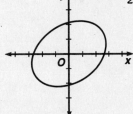

24. $(-x \sin 45° + y \cos 45°)^2 +$

$2(-x \sin 45° + y \cos 45°) -$

$4(x \cos 45° + y \sin 45°) + 7 = 0$

$$\left(-\frac{\sqrt{2}}{2}x + \frac{\sqrt{2}}{2}y\right)^2 + 2\left(-\frac{\sqrt{2}}{2}x + \frac{\sqrt{2}}{2}y\right) - 4\left(\frac{\sqrt{2}}{2}x + \frac{\sqrt{2}}{2}y\right) + 7 = 0$$

$$\left(\frac{1}{2}x^2 - xy + \frac{1}{2}y^2\right) + -\sqrt{2}x + \sqrt{2}y - 2\sqrt{2}x - 2\sqrt{2}y + 7 = 0$$

$$\frac{1}{2}x^2 - xy + \frac{1}{2}y^2 - 3\sqrt{2}x - \sqrt{2}y + 7 = 0$$

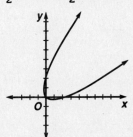

25.

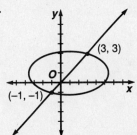

$(y - 1)^2 + 4(y - 1)^2 = 20$

$(y - 1)^2(1 + 4) = 20$

$(y - 1)^2 = 4$

$y^2 - 2y + 1 = 4$

$y^2 - 2y - 3 = 0$

$(y - 3)(y + 1) = 0$

$y = 3, \ -1$

$x = 3, \ -1 \qquad (3, 3), \ (-1, -1)$

26.

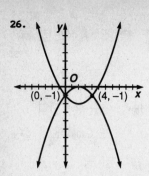

$$(x^2 - 4x + 4) = 4y + 4 + 4$$
$$(x - 2)^2 = 4(y + 2)$$
$$-4y = 4y + 8$$
$$y = -1$$
$$(x - 2)^2 = -4(-1)$$
$$(x - 2)^2 = 4$$
$$x^2 - 4x + 4 = 4$$
$$x^2 - 4x = 0$$
$$x(x - 4) = 0$$
$$x = 0, \; x = 4$$
$$(0, -1), \; (4, -1)$$

27.

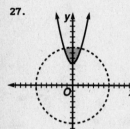

28.

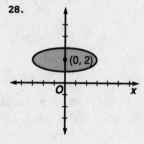

29. $(x^2 + 2x + 1) - 4(y^2 - 2y + 1) = 7 + 1 - 4$

$$(x + 1)^2 - 4(y - 1)^2 = 4$$
$$\frac{(x + 1)^2}{4} - (y - 1)^2 = 1$$
$$m = \frac{b^2(x - h)}{a^2(y - k)} = \frac{1(1 + 1)}{4(1 - 1)} = \frac{2}{0}$$

undefined $\rightarrow$ vertical line

tangent: $x = 1$

normal: $y = 1$

30. $\dfrac{x^2}{9} - \dfrac{y^2}{4} = 1$

$$m = \frac{b^2(x - h)}{a^2(y - k)} = \frac{4(6)}{9(2\sqrt{3})} = \frac{24}{18\sqrt{3}} = \frac{4\sqrt{3}}{9}$$

tangent: $y - 2\sqrt{3} = \dfrac{4\sqrt{3}}{9}(x - 6)$

$$y = \frac{4\sqrt{3}}{9}x - \frac{8\sqrt{3}}{3} + 2\sqrt{3}$$
$$y = \frac{4\sqrt{3}}{9}x - \frac{2\sqrt{3}}{3}$$
$$9y - 4\sqrt{3}x + 6\sqrt{3} = 0$$
$$4x - 3\sqrt{3}y - 6 = 0$$

normal: $y - 2\sqrt{3} = \dfrac{-9}{4\sqrt{3}}(x - 6)$

$$y = \frac{-9}{4\sqrt{3}}x + \frac{54}{4\sqrt{3}} + 2\sqrt{3}$$
$$4\sqrt{3}y = -9x + 78$$
$$9x + 4\sqrt{3}y - 78 = 0$$

31. $(x + 1)^2 = -\dfrac{1}{4}y$

$$m = \frac{x - h}{2p} = \frac{-2 + 1}{2 \cdot \left(-\dfrac{1}{16}\right)} = \frac{-1}{-\dfrac{1}{8}} = 8$$

tangent: $y + 4 = 8(x + 2)$

$$y = 8x + 12$$
$$0 = 8x - y + 12$$

normal: $y + 4 = -\dfrac{1}{8}(x + 2)$

$$8y + 32 = -x - 2$$
$$x + 8y + 34 = 0$$

32. $\dfrac{x^2}{25} + \dfrac{y^2}{9} = 1$

$$m = -\frac{b^2(x - h)}{a^2(y - k)} = -\frac{9 \cdot 4}{25\left[\dfrac{9}{5}\right]} = -\frac{36}{45} = -\frac{4}{5}$$

tangent: $y - \dfrac{9}{5} = -\dfrac{4}{5}(x - 4)$

$$y = -\frac{4}{5}x + \frac{16}{5} + \frac{9}{5}$$
$$= -\frac{4}{5}x + 5$$
$$4x + 5y - 25 = 0$$

normal: $y - \dfrac{9}{5} = \dfrac{5}{4}(x - 4)$

$$y = \frac{5}{4}x - 5 + \frac{9}{5}$$
$$25x - 20y - 64 = 0$$

PAGE 594   APPLICATIONS AND PROBLEM SOLVING

33. at the foci: $2a = 5, \; a = \dfrac{5}{2}, \; b = 2$

$$c = \sqrt{a^2 - b^2} = \sqrt{(2.5)^2 - 2^2} = 1.5$$

1.5 feet from the center

34. $e = \dfrac{c}{a}$

$$0.2 = \frac{c}{6000}$$
$$c = 1200$$
$$b^2 = 6000^2 - 1200^2 = 34{,}560{,}000$$
$$\frac{x^2}{36{,}000{,}000} + \frac{y^2}{34{,}560{,}000} = 1$$

Chapter 10 Test

PAGE 595

1. parabola

$$(x + 3)^2 = 8(y + 2)$$

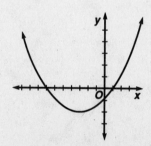

2. degenerate hyperbola

$4x^2 - y^2 = 0$

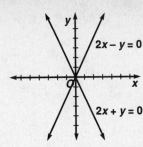

$2x - y = 0$

$2x + y = 0$

3. hyperbola

$$\frac{2x^2}{5} - \frac{13y^2}{5} = -1$$

$$\frac{y^2}{\frac{5}{13}} - \frac{x^2}{\frac{5}{2}} = 1$$

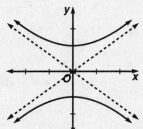

4. ellipse

$$\frac{(x-3)^2}{81} + \frac{(y+4)^2}{16} = 1$$

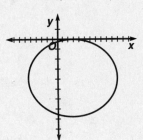

5. parabola

$$(y^2 + 10y + 25) = 2x - 27 + 25$$

$$(y+5)^2 = 2(x-1)$$

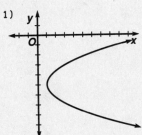

6. hyperbola

$$\frac{(x-4)^2}{36} - \frac{(y-5)^2}{4} = 1$$

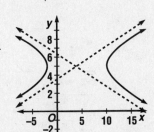

7. ellipse

$$(x^2 + 2x + 1) + 2(y^2 - 6y + 9) = -11 + 1 + 18$$

$$(x+1)^2 + 2(y-3)^2 = 8$$

$$\frac{(x+1)^2}{8} + \frac{(y-3)^2}{4} = 1$$

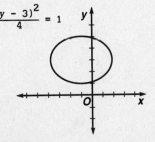

8. circle

$$(x^2 + 4x + 4) + y^2 = 6 + 4$$

$$(x+2)^2 + y^2 = 10$$

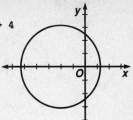

9. $r = \sqrt{(-8+6)^2 + (3+4)^2}$

$= \sqrt{4 + 49}$

$= \sqrt{53}$

$(x+8)^2 + (y-3)^2 = 53$

10. $p = \frac{3}{2}$

vertex: $\left(3, -\frac{7}{2}\right)$

$(x-3)^2 = -4 \cdot \frac{3}{2}\left(y + \frac{7}{2}\right)$

$(x-3)^2 = -6\left(y + \frac{7}{2}\right)$

11. $e = \frac{c}{a}$

$\frac{1}{2}a = \frac{1}{2}$

$a = 1$

$b^2 = 1 - \left(\frac{1}{2}\right)^2 = \frac{3}{4}$

$\dfrac{x^2}{1} + \dfrac{y^2}{\frac{3}{4}} = 1$

$x^2 + \dfrac{4y^2}{3} = 1$

12. $c = 3$

center: $(-5, 1)$

$e = \frac{c}{a}$

$\frac{3}{2} = \frac{3}{a}$

$a = 2$

$b^2 = c^2 - a^2$

$= 9 - 4 = 5$

$\dfrac{(y-1)^2}{4} - \dfrac{(x+5)^2}{5} = 1$

13. $\begin{bmatrix} -1 \\ 3 \end{bmatrix} + \begin{bmatrix} 3 \\ -5 \end{bmatrix} = \begin{bmatrix} 2 \\ -2 \end{bmatrix}$

$4(x-2)^2 + (y+2)^2 = 36$

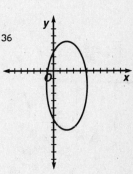

14. $2(x \cos 60° + y \sin 60°)^2 -$

$$(-x \sin 60° + y \cos 60°)^2 = 8$$

$$2\left(\frac{1}{2}x + \frac{\sqrt{3}}{2}y\right)^2 - \left(-\frac{\sqrt{3}}{2}x + \frac{1}{2}y\right)^2 = 8$$

$$2\left(\frac{1}{4}x^2 + \frac{\sqrt{3}}{2}xy + \frac{3}{4}x^2\right) - \frac{3}{4}x^2 + \frac{\sqrt{3}}{2}xy - \frac{1}{4}y^2 = 8$$

$$2x^2 + 4\sqrt{3}xy + 6y^2 - 3x^2 + 2\sqrt{3}xy - y^2 = 32$$

$$-x^2 + 6\sqrt{3}xy + 5y^2 = 32$$

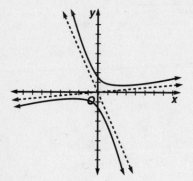

15.

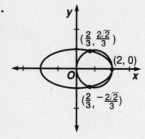

$$x^2 + 4y^2 = 4$$

$$(x - 1)^2 + y^2 = 1 \rightarrow y^2 = 1 - (x - 1)^2$$

$$x^2 + 4(1 - (x - 1)^2) = 4$$

$$x^2 + 4 - 4(x^2 - 2x + 1) = 4$$

$$x^2 + 4 - 4x^2 + 8x - 4 = 4$$

$$-3x^2 + 8x - 4 = 0$$

$$(-3x + 2)(x - 2) = 0$$

$$x = \frac{2}{3}, \ 2$$

$$\left(\frac{2}{3}\right)^2 + 4y^2 = 4 \qquad 2^2 + 4y^2 = 4$$

$$4y^2 = \frac{32}{9} \qquad\qquad 4y^2 = 0$$

$$y^2 = \frac{32}{36} \qquad\qquad y = 0$$

$$y = \pm \frac{2\sqrt{2}}{3}$$

$$\left(\frac{2}{3}, \ \frac{2\sqrt{2}}{3}\right), \ \left(\frac{2}{3}, \ -\frac{2\sqrt{2}}{3}\right), \ (2, \ 0)$$

16.

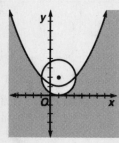

17. $(x^2 + 6x + 9) + y^2 - 10y + 25 = 0 + 9 + 25$

$$(x + 3)^2 + (y - 5)^2 = 34$$

$$m = -\frac{(x - h)}{(y - k)} = -\frac{(2 + 3)}{(1 - 5)} = \frac{5}{4}$$

tangent: $\quad y - 1 = \frac{5}{4}(x - 2)$

$$y = \frac{5}{4}x - \frac{5}{2} + \frac{2}{2}$$

$$y = \frac{5}{4}x - \frac{3}{2}$$

$$4y - 5x + 6 = 0$$

normal: $\quad m = -\frac{4}{5}$

$$y - 1 = -\frac{4}{5}(x - 2)$$

$$y = -\frac{4}{5}x + \frac{8}{5} + \frac{5}{5}$$

$$y = -\frac{4}{5}x + \frac{13}{5}$$

$$5y + 4x - 13 = 0$$

18. $16x^2 - (y^2 + 4y + 4) = 20 - 4$

$$16x^2 - (y + 2)^2 = 16$$

$$\frac{x^2}{1} - \frac{(y + 2)^2}{16} = 1$$

$$m = \frac{b^2(x - h)}{a^2(y - k)} = \frac{16(\sqrt{2} - 0)}{1(2 + 2)} = \frac{16\sqrt{2}}{4} = 4\sqrt{2}$$

tangent: $\quad y - 2 = 4\sqrt{2}(x - \sqrt{2})$

$$y = 4\sqrt{2}x - 8 + 2$$

$$y = 4\sqrt{2}x - 6$$

$$4\sqrt{2}x - y - 6 = 0$$

normal: $\quad m = -\frac{1}{4\sqrt{2}}$

$$y - 2 = -\frac{1}{4\sqrt{2}}(x - \sqrt{2})$$

$$y - 2 = -\frac{\sqrt{2}}{8}x + \frac{1}{4}$$

$$y = -\frac{\sqrt{2}}{8}x + \frac{9}{4}$$

$$8y + \sqrt{2}x - 18 = 0$$

19. $d = \sqrt{(-2 - 4)^2 + (3 - 5)^2}$

$$= \sqrt{36 + 4}$$

$$= \sqrt{40}$$

$$= 2\sqrt{10}$$

$$\frac{1}{2}d = r = \sqrt{10}$$

center: $\left(\frac{-2 + 4}{2}, \ \frac{3 + 5}{2}\right) = (1, \ 4)$

$$(x - 1)^2 + (y - 4)^2 = 10$$

20. $y = 2x - 3$

$$x^2 + y^2 = 90$$

$$x^2 + (2x - 3)^2 = 90$$

$$x^2 + 4x^2 - 12x + 9 = 90$$

$$5x^2 - 12x - 81 = 0$$

$$(5x - 27)(x + 3) = 0$$

$$x = \frac{27}{5}, \ x = -3$$

$$y = 2(-3) - 3 = -9$$

$$(-3, \ -9)$$

PAGE 595   BONUS

Given the equations $x^2 + y^2 = k$ and $x + y = 2k$ or $y = 2k - x$, then by substitution, $x^2 + (2k - x)^2 = k$ or $2x^2 - 4kx + (4k^2 - k) = 0$. Since the line is tangent to the circle, the roots of this equation must be equal. This implies that the discriminant of the quadratic formula equals zero. Thus,

$$b^2 - 4ac = (-4k)^2 - 4(2)(4k^2 - k) = 0.$$

$$8k - 16k^2 = 0$$

$$k(1 - 2k) = 0$$

$$k = 0 \text{ or } k = \frac{1}{2}$$

Therefore, the value of k is $\frac{1}{2}$.

277

Chapter 11 Exponential and Logarithmic Functions

Rational Exponents

1. If the base were negative and the denominator were even, then we would be taking an even root of a negative number, which is undefined.

2. $46^{\frac{1}{3}}$

3. No; for a number to be in scientific notation the exponent on 10 must be an integer.

4. add; subtract

5. $81^{\frac{1}{2}} = \sqrt{81}$
   $= 9$

6. $27^{-\frac{2}{3}} = \dfrac{1}{27^{\frac{2}{3}}}$
   $= \left(\dfrac{1}{\sqrt[3]{27}}\right)^2$
   $= \dfrac{1}{3^2}$
   $= \dfrac{1}{9}$

7. $7^{\frac{1}{4}} \cdot 7^{\frac{7}{4}} = 7^{\frac{1}{4} + \frac{7}{4}}$
   $= 7^{\frac{8}{4}}$
   $= 7^2$
   $= 49$

8. $\sqrt[4]{a} = a^{\frac{1}{4}}$

9. $\sqrt{xy^3} = (xy^3)^{\frac{1}{2}}$
   $= x^{\frac{1}{2}}y^{\frac{3}{2}}$

10. $\sqrt[3]{8x^3y^6} = (8x^3y^6)^{\frac{1}{3}}$
    $= 8^{\frac{1}{3}}(x^3)^{\frac{1}{3}}(y^6)^{\frac{1}{3}}$
    $= 2xy^{\frac{6}{3}}$
    $= 2xy^2$

11. $15^{\frac{1}{5}} = \sqrt[5]{15}$

12. $25^{\frac{1}{3}} = \sqrt[3]{25}$

13. $a^{\frac{3}{4}}y^{\frac{1}{4}} = (a^3y)^{\frac{1}{4}} = \sqrt[4]{a^3y}$

14. $\sqrt[3]{125} = 5$

15. $3^{-4} \cdot 3^8 = 3^{-4 + 8}$
    $= 3^4$
    $= 81$

16. $\sqrt[4]{16^2} = 16^{\frac{2}{4}}$
    $= 16^{\frac{1}{2}}$
    $= 4$

17. $\left(5^{\frac{3}{4}}\right)^4 = 5^{\frac{3}{4} \cdot 4}$
    $= 5^3$
    $= 125$

18. $\left(169^{\frac{1}{2}}\right)^0 = 13^0$
    $= 1$

19. $\left(8^{-\frac{1}{2}}\right)^{-\frac{2}{3}} = 8^{-\frac{1}{2} \cdot \left(-\frac{2}{3}\right)}$
    $= 8^{\frac{1}{3}}$
    $= 2$

20. $\left(\sqrt[3]{216}\right)^2 = 6^2$
    $= 36$

21. $\left(3^{-1} + 3^{-2}\right)^{-1} = \left(\dfrac{1}{3} + \dfrac{1}{9}\right)^{-1}$
    $= \left(\dfrac{3}{9} + \dfrac{1}{9}\right)^{-1}$
    $= \left(\dfrac{4}{9}\right)^{-1}$
    $= \dfrac{9}{4}$

22. $81^{\frac{1}{2}} - 81^{-\frac{1}{2}} = 9 - \dfrac{1}{81^{\frac{1}{2}}}$
    $= 9 - \dfrac{1}{9}$
    $= 8\dfrac{8}{9}$

23. $\dfrac{16^{\frac{3}{4}}}{16^{\frac{1}{4}}} = 16^{\frac{3}{4} - \frac{1}{4}}$
    $= 16^{\frac{1}{2}}$
    $= 4$

24. $\left(\sqrt[3]{343}\right)^{-2} = 7^{-2}$
    $= \dfrac{1}{7^2}$
    $= \dfrac{1}{49}$

25. $\dfrac{27}{27^{\frac{2}{3}}} = 27^{1 - \frac{2}{3}}$
    $= 27^{\frac{1}{3}}$
    $= 3$

26. $\sqrt{a^6b^3} = (a^6b^3)^{\frac{1}{2}}$
    $= a^{\frac{6}{2}}b^{\frac{3}{2}}$
    $= a^3b^{\frac{3}{2}}$

27. $\sqrt[6]{b^3} = (b^3)^{\frac{1}{6}}$
    $= b^{\frac{3}{6}}$
    $= b^{\frac{1}{2}}$

28. $\sqrt{25a^4b^{10}} = (25a^4b^{10})^{\frac{1}{2}}$
    $= 5a^{\frac{4}{2}}b^{\frac{10}{2}}$
    $= 5a^2b^5$

29. $\sqrt[3]{125a^2b^3} = (125a^2b^3)^{\frac{1}{3}}$
    $= 5a^{\frac{2}{3}}b^{\frac{3}{3}}$
    $= 5a^{\frac{2}{3}}b$

30. $\sqrt[3]{64s^9t^{15}} = (64s^9t^{15})^{\frac{1}{3}}$

$\qquad = 4s^{\frac{9}{3}}t^{\frac{15}{3}}$

$\qquad = 4s^3t^5$

31. $\sqrt[4]{24a^{12}b^{16}} = (24a^{12}b^{16})^{\frac{1}{4}}$

$\qquad = 24^{\frac{1}{4}}a^{\frac{12}{4}}b^{\frac{16}{4}}$

$\qquad = 24^{\frac{1}{4}}a^3b^4$

32. $\sqrt{169x^5} = (169x^5)^{\frac{1}{2}}$

$\qquad = 13x^{\frac{5}{2}}$

33. $\sqrt[5]{32x^5y^8} = (32x^5y^8)^{\frac{1}{5}}$

$\qquad = 2x^{\frac{5}{5}}y^{\frac{8}{5}}$

$\qquad = 2xy^{\frac{8}{5}}$

34. $\sqrt[5]{15x^3y^{15}} = (15x^3y^{15})^{\frac{1}{5}}$

$\qquad = 15^{\frac{1}{5}}x^{\frac{3}{5}}y^{\frac{15}{5}}$

$\qquad = 15^{\frac{1}{5}}x^{\frac{3}{5}}y^3$

35. $64^{\frac{1}{6}} = \sqrt[6]{64}$

$\qquad = 2$

36. $x^{\frac{2}{3}} = (x^2)^{\frac{1}{3}}$

$\qquad = \sqrt[3]{x^2}$

37. $4^{\frac{1}{3}}a^{\frac{2}{3}}y^{\frac{4}{3}} = (4a^2y^4)^{\frac{1}{3}}$

$\qquad = \sqrt[3]{4a^2y^4}$

$\qquad = y\sqrt[3]{4a^2y}$

38. $x^{\frac{4}{7}}y^{\frac{3}{7}} = (x^4y^3)^{\frac{1}{7}}$

$\qquad = \sqrt[7]{x^4y^3}$

39. $(rt^2)^{\frac{3}{5}}v^{\frac{3}{5}} = (rt^2v^3)^{\frac{1}{5}}$

$\qquad = \sqrt[5]{rt^2v^3}$

40. $a^{\frac{1}{6}}b^{\frac{4}{6}}c^{\frac{3}{6}} = (ab^4c^3)^{\frac{1}{6}}$

$\qquad = \sqrt[6]{ab^4c^3}$

41. $\dfrac{x^{\frac{2}{3}}}{x^{\frac{1}{3}}} = x^{\frac{2}{3} - \frac{1}{3}}$

$\qquad = x^{\frac{1}{3}}$

$\qquad = \sqrt[3]{x}$

42. $15x^{\frac{1}{3}}y^{\frac{1}{5}} = 15x^{\frac{5}{15}}y^{\frac{3}{15}}$

$\qquad = 15(x^5y^3)^{\frac{1}{15}}$

$\qquad = 15\sqrt[15]{x^5y^3}$

43. $(x^{10}y^2)^{\frac{1}{5}}a^{\frac{2}{5}} = x^{\frac{10}{5}}y^{\frac{2}{5}}a^{\frac{2}{5}}$

$\qquad = x^2(y^2a^2)^{\frac{1}{5}}$

44. $4x^2(4x)^{-2} = \dfrac{4x^2}{(4x)^2}$

$\qquad = \dfrac{4x^2}{16x^2}$

$\qquad = \dfrac{1}{4}$

45. $x^6 \cdot x^{-3} \cdot x^2 = x^{6-3+2}$

$\qquad = x^5$

46. $(y^{-2})^4 \cdot y^8 = y^{-8} \cdot y^8$

$\qquad = y^{-8+8}$

$\qquad = y^0$

$\qquad = 1$

47. $\left(5x^{\frac{1}{3}}\right)^3 = 5^3\left(x^{\frac{1}{3}}\right)^3$

$\qquad = 125x^{\frac{3}{3}}$

$\qquad = 125x$

48. $((2x)^4)^{-2} = (2x)^{-8}$

$\qquad = \dfrac{1}{(2x)^8}$

$\qquad = \dfrac{1}{256x^8}$

49. $(4y^4)^{\frac{3}{2}} = 4^{\frac{3}{2}}(y^4)^{\frac{3}{2}}$

$\qquad = 4^{\frac{3}{2}}y^6$

$\qquad = 8y^6$

50. $\sqrt{a^3b^2} \cdot \sqrt{a^4b^5} = \sqrt{a^3b^2 \cdot a^4b^5}$

$\qquad = \sqrt{a^7b^7}$

$\qquad = (a^7b^7)^{\frac{1}{2}}$

$\qquad = a^{\frac{7}{2}}b^{\frac{7}{2}}$

$\qquad = a^3b^3\left(a^{\frac{1}{2}}b^{\frac{1}{2}}\right)$

$\qquad = a^3b^3\sqrt{ab}$

51. $\left(a^{\frac{1}{2}}b^{-2}c^{\frac{5}{4}}\right)^{-4} = a^{-\frac{4}{2}}b^8c^{-5}$

$\qquad = a^{-2}b^8c^{-5}$

$\qquad = \dfrac{b^8}{a^2c^5}$

52. $(5ac)^{\frac{1}{3}}(a^2c^3)^{\frac{1}{3}} = (5a^3c^4)^{\frac{1}{3}}$

$\qquad = ac(5c)^{\frac{1}{3}}$

$\qquad = ac\sqrt[3]{5c}$

53. $\dfrac{3^{60}}{9^{30}} = \dfrac{3^{60}}{(3^2)^{30}}$

$\qquad = \dfrac{3^{60}}{3^{60}}$

$\qquad = 1$

54. $7.5 = 0.094\sqrt{A^3}$

$\qquad \dfrac{7.5}{0.094} = \sqrt{A^3}$

$\qquad \left(\dfrac{7.5}{0.094}\right)^2 = A^3$

$\qquad \sqrt[3]{\left(\dfrac{7.5}{0.094}\right)^2} = A$

$\qquad 18.53 \text{ cm}^2 \approx A$

55. $r = \sqrt[3]{\dfrac{Gm_e t^2}{4\pi^2}}$

$= \sqrt[3]{\dfrac{(6.67 \times 10^{-11})(5.98 \times 10^{24})(5400)^2}{4\pi^2}}$

$\approx 6{,}654{,}032.7$ meters or about 6654 km

distance above Earth $\approx 6654 - 6400$

≈ 254 km

56. $r = (1.3 \times 10^{-15})(12)^{\frac{1}{3}}$

$\approx 2.98 \times 10^{-15}$ m

57.

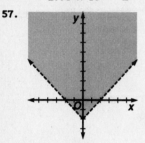

58. $27x^2 + 15x - 8 = 0$

$(9x + 8)(3x - 1) = 0$

$9x + 8 = 0 \qquad 3x - 1 = 0$

$x = -\dfrac{8}{9} \qquad x = \dfrac{1}{3}$

59. possible rational roots: $\pm 4, \pm 2, \pm 1, \pm\dfrac{1}{2}$

at $x = 4$, $f(x) = 108$

at $x = -4$, $f(x) = -84$

at $x = 2$, $f(x) = 0$

at $x = -2$, $f(x) = 0$

at $x = 1$, $f(x) = -9$

at $x = -1$, $f(x) = 3$

at $x = \dfrac{1}{2}$, $f(x) = -7.5$

at $x = -\dfrac{1}{2}$, $f(x) = 0$

rational roots: $-2, -\dfrac{1}{2}, 2$

60. $\dfrac{\pi}{24} \times \dfrac{180}{\pi} = \dfrac{180}{24} = 7.5°$

61. Let x = distance flown in 15 seconds.

$\tan 60° = \dfrac{9000}{x}$

$x = \dfrac{9000}{\tan 60°}$

$x \approx 5196$ m

So, $\dfrac{x}{15} \approx 346$ m/s.

62.

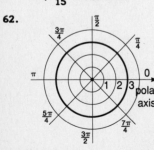

63. $(-3 + i)(-3 + i) = 9 - 6i - 1 = 8 - 6i$

$(8 - 6i)(8 - 6i) = 64 - 96i - 36 = 28 - 96i$

64. $x^2 - 4y^2 - 12x - 16y = -16$

$x^2 - 12x - 4y^2 - 16y = -16$

$(x - 6)^2 - 4(y + 2)^2 = -16 + 36 - 16$

$(x - 6)^2 - 4(y + 2)^2 = 4$

center: $(6, -2)$

foci: $(6 \pm \sqrt{5}, -2)$

vertices: $(8, -2), (4, -2)$

asymptotes: $y = \dfrac{1}{2}x - 5$, $y = -\dfrac{1}{2}x + 1$

65. $t = \sqrt{(-1 - 5)^2 + (-1 + 1)^2 - 4} = \sqrt{32} = 4\sqrt{2}$

66. The sum of the measures of the angles in <u>any</u> triangle are 180°, so the quantities are equal.

C

11-2A Graphing Calculators: Graphing Exponential Functions

PAGE 605   EXERCISES

1.

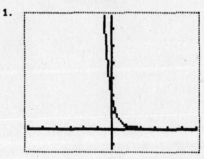

2.

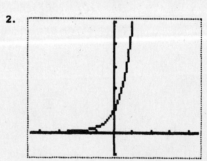

3.

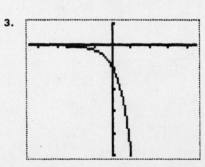

4.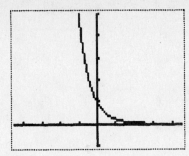

5.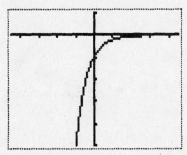

6.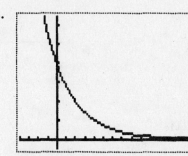

7.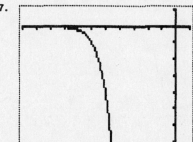

8.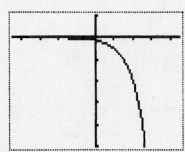

9.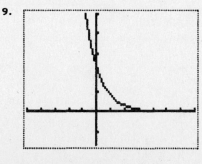

PAGE 611   CHECKING FOR UNDERSTANDING

1. The graph of $y = 4^x - 3$ is the graph of $y = 4^x$ shifted 3 units downward.

2. The graphs of $y = a^x$ and $y = \left(\dfrac{1}{a}\right)^x$ are reflections of each other across the y-axis.

3. An annuity is a series of equal payments made at equal intervals of time. Some examples are retirement plans, Christmas club accounts, mortgages, and car loans.

4. **a.** decreases   **b.** increases

5. $2^{\sqrt{6}} \approx 5.4622$ 6. $5^{\sqrt{2}} \approx 9.7385$

7. $\left(\dfrac{1}{3}\right)^{\pi} \approx 0.0317$

8. 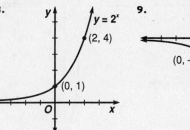   9.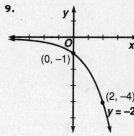

10.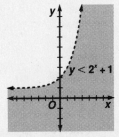

11. The graph of Exercise 9 is the graph of Exercise 8 reflected over the x-axis. The graph of Exercise 10 is the graph of Exercise 8 reflected across the y-axis.

12.

$y < 2^x + 1$

13. $P_n = P\left[\dfrac{1 - (1 + i)^{-n}}{i}\right]$

$P_n = 1000\left[\dfrac{1 - (1 + 0.05)^{-18}}{0.05}\right]$

$\approx \$11{,}689.59$

14. $7^{\sqrt{5}} \approx 77.5705$ 15. $8^{\sqrt{3}} \approx 36.6604$

16. $5^{\sqrt{10}} \approx 162.3070$

17.
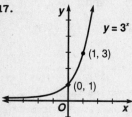
$y = 3^x$
(1, 3)
(0, 1)

18.
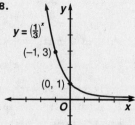
$y = \left(\frac{1}{3}\right)^x$
(−1, 3)
(0, 1)

19.
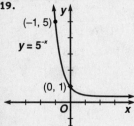
(−1, 5)
$y = 5^{-x}$
(0, 1)

20.
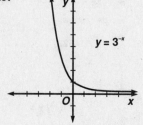
$y = 3^{-x}$

21.
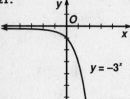
$y = -3^x$

22.
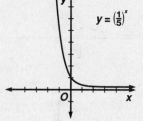
$y = \left(\frac{1}{5}\right)^x$

23.
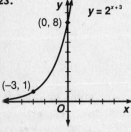
$y = 2^{x+3}$
(0, 8)
(−3, 1)

24.
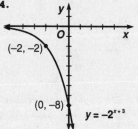
(−2, −2)
(0, −8)
$y = -2^{x+3}$

25.
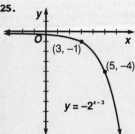
(3, −1)
(5, −4)
$y = -2^{x-3}$

26. They are reflections of each other across the
    y-axis.

27. They have similar shape, but the graph of
    Exercise 19 is steeper.

28. The graph of Exercise 24 is the graph of
    Exercise 23 reflected across the x-axis. The
    graph of Exercise 25 is the graph of Exercise 24
    shifted 6 places to the right.

29.
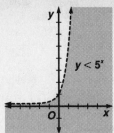
$y < 5^x$

30.
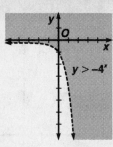
$y > -4^x$

31.
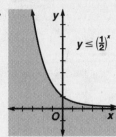
$y \leq \left(\frac{1}{2}\right)^x$

32.
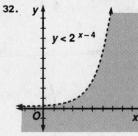
$y < 2^{x-4}$

33.
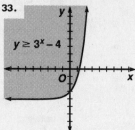
$y \geq 3^x - 4$

34.
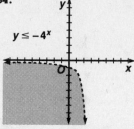
$y \leq -4^x$

35. They are reflections over the x-axis.

36. They are reflections over the y-axis.

37. a. $54.23   b. $434.85   c. $1005.78

38.
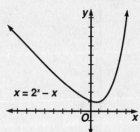
$x = 2^x - x$

39. $F_n = 1000 \left[\dfrac{(1 + 0.03)^{24} - 1}{0.03}\right]$

    $\approx \$34,426.47$

40. $P_n = 173,076.92 \left[\dfrac{1 - (1 + 0.05)^{-26}}{0.05}\right]$

    $\approx \$2,488,012.84$

    Note: $4,500,000 ÷ 26 = $173,076.92

41. structure 1:

$$F_n = 500\left[\frac{(1 + 0.006)^{360} - 1}{0.006}\right]$$

$\approx \$634{,}612.72$ over 30 years

$$F_n = 500\left[\frac{(1 + 0.006)^{60} - 1}{0.006}\right]$$

$\approx \$35{,}982.37$ over 5 years

structure 2:

$$F_n = 1500\left[\frac{(1 + 0.01825)^{120} - 1}{0.01825}\right]$$

$\approx \$637{,}851.56$ over 30 years

$$F_n = 1500\left[\frac{(1 + 0.01825)^{20} - 1}{0.01825}\right]$$

$\approx \$35{,}817.66$

Over 30 years, structure 2 is better; over 5 years, structure 1 is better.

42. $20{,}000 = P\left[\dfrac{(1 + 0.0051)^{60} - 1}{0.0051}\right]$

$20{,}000 \approx P[69.9856]$

$\$285.77 \approx P$

43. $120{,}000 = P\left[\dfrac{(1 + 0.035)^{8} - 1}{0.035}\right]$

$120{,}000 \approx P[9.0517]$

$\$13{,}257.20 \approx P$

44. domain: $\{-7, -2, 0, 4, 9\}$;

range: $\{-3, -2, 0, 2, 11\}$;

yes

45. $7(2) - (-3)(8) + 5(8) = 78$

46. $f(x) = x^3 - 7x^2 + 8x - 2$

$f'(x) = 3x^2 - 14x + 8 \qquad f''(x) = 6x - 14$

$0 = 3x^2 - 14x + 8 \qquad\quad 0 = 6x - 14$

$0 = (3x - 2)(x - 4) \qquad\quad x = \dfrac{7}{3}$

$3x - 2 = 0 \qquad x - 4 = 0$

$x = \dfrac{2}{3} \qquad\quad x = 4$

$f\left(\dfrac{2}{3}\right) = \left(\dfrac{2}{3}\right)^3 - 7\left(\dfrac{2}{3}\right)^2 + 8\left(\dfrac{2}{3}\right) - 2 = \dfrac{14}{27} \approx 0.5185$

$f(4) = 4^3 - 7(4)^2 + 8(4) - 2 = -18$

$f\left(\dfrac{7}{3}\right) = \left(\dfrac{7}{3}\right)^3 - 7\left(\dfrac{7}{3}\right)^2 + 8\left(\dfrac{7}{3}\right) - 2 = -\dfrac{236}{27} \approx -8.7407$

critical points: $\left(\dfrac{2}{3}, \dfrac{14}{27}\right)$, $(4, -18)$, $\left(\dfrac{7}{3}, -\dfrac{236}{27}\right)$

$f(0.65) \approx 0.5171 \qquad f(2.32) \approx -8.6296$

$f(0.68) \approx 0.5176 \qquad f(2.35) \approx -8.8796$

$f(3.99) \approx -17.9995$

$f(4.01) \approx -17.9995$

So, maximum at $\left(\dfrac{2}{3}, \dfrac{14}{27}\right)$; minimum at $(4, -18)$; and

point of inflection at $\left(\dfrac{7}{3}, -\dfrac{236}{27}\right)$.

47. $\cos 2\theta = \cos^2 \theta - \sin^2 \theta$

$= \left(\dfrac{\sqrt{15}}{8}\right)^2 - \left(\dfrac{7}{8}\right)^2$

$= \dfrac{15}{64} - \dfrac{49}{64}$

$= -\dfrac{34}{64}$

$= -\dfrac{17}{32}$

48. $\overrightarrow{AB} = (0 - 8, -2 - 3) = (-8, -5)$

$|\overrightarrow{AB}| = \sqrt{(-8)^2 + (-5)^2} = \sqrt{89}$

49. $-6 + 6i = r(\cos \theta + i \sin \theta)$

$r = \sqrt{(-6)^2 + (6)^2} = \sqrt{72} = 6\sqrt{2}$

$\theta = \text{Arctan} \dfrac{6}{-6} + \pi = -\dfrac{\pi}{4} + \pi = \dfrac{3\pi}{4}$

So, $-6 + 6i = 6\sqrt{2}\left(\cos \dfrac{3\pi}{4} + i \sin \dfrac{3\pi}{4}\right)$.

50. $\sqrt{20a^4b^{12}} = (20a^4b^{12})^{\frac{1}{2}}$

$= 20^{\frac{1}{2}} a^{\frac{4}{2}} b^{\frac{12}{2}}$

$= 20^{\frac{1}{2}} a^2 b^6$

51. 7 ft 9 in. = 93 in.

$93 + 3 = 31$ in.

$= 2$ ft 7 in.

The best answer is C.

11-3   The Number e

1. See students' work.

2. They are reflections across the y-axis.

3. Continuously; interest compounds faster, so it has a higher yield.

4. $e^{2.1} \approx 8.2$ **5.** $e^{3.3} \approx 27.1$

6. $e^{0.4} \approx 1.5$ **7.** $\sqrt{e} \approx 1.6$

8. $e^{-5.1} - 1 \approx -1.0$ **9.** $(2e)^{2.8} \approx 114.5$

10. increasing from $-\infty$ to ∞

11. $A = P\left(1 + \dfrac{r}{n}\right)^{nt}$

$= 1200\left(1 + \dfrac{0.075}{2}\right)^{2(4.5)}$

$\approx \$1671.38$

12. $e^{1.6} \approx 4.9530$ **13.** $e^{4.3} \approx 73.6998$

14. $\sqrt[3]{e} \approx 1.3956$ **15.** $2\sqrt[4]{e^3} \approx 4.2340$

16. $4\sqrt[3]{e^2} \approx 7.7909$ **17.** $e^0 = 1.0000$

18. decreasing from $-\infty$ to -1;
    increasing from -1 to ∞

19. increasing from $-\infty$ to ∞

20. increasing from $-\infty$ to ∞

21. increasing from $-\infty$ to ∞

22. decreasing from $-\infty$ to ∞

23. decreasing from $-\infty$ to 0, increasing from 0 to ∞

24.

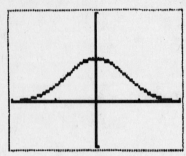

25. $A = P\left(1 + \dfrac{r}{n}\right)^{nt}$

    $= 1000\left(1 + \dfrac{0.10}{12}\right)^{12 \cdot 4}$

    $\approx \$1489.35$

26. $A = P\left(1 + \dfrac{r}{n}\right)^{nt}$

    $= 3200\left(1 + \dfrac{0.06}{4}\right)^{4 \cdot 5\frac{1}{2}}$

    $\approx \$4440.20$

27. $A = Pe^{rt}$

    $= 750e^{(0.055)\left(3\frac{1}{6}\right)}$

    $\approx \$892.69$

28. $A = P\left(1 + \dfrac{r}{n}\right)^{nt}$

    $= 45,000\left(1 + \dfrac{0.072}{365}\right)^{365 \cdot 30}$

    $\approx \$390,118.09$

29.

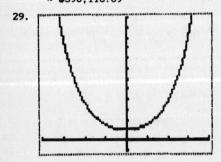

30. $y = ae^{-kt} + c$

    $= 128e^{-(0.01)(180)} + 72$

    $\approx 93°F$

31. $A = Pe^{rt}$, $A = P\left(1 + \dfrac{i}{n}\right)^{nt}$, $t = 1$

    $Pe^{r} = P\left(1 + \dfrac{i}{12}\right)^{12}$

    $e^{r} = \left(1 + \dfrac{i}{12}\right)^{12}$

    $e^{0.0378} = \left(1 + \dfrac{i}{12}\right)^{12}$

    $1.0385 \approx \left(1 + \dfrac{i}{12}\right)^{12}$

    $0.0032 \approx \dfrac{i}{12}$

    $i \approx 0.03786$ or 3.786%

32. $y = 6.7e^{-\frac{48.1}{t}}$

    a. $y = 6.7e^{-\frac{48.1}{15}}$

    ≈ 0.271292 millions of ft^3

    $\approx 271,292\ ft^3$

    b. $y = 6.7e^{-\frac{48.1}{50}}$

    ≈ 2.560257 millions of ft^3

    $\approx 2,560,257\ ft^3$

    c. no

33. a. $y = 434e^{-\frac{2(15)}{25}} \approx 131$

    b. $y = 434e^{-\frac{2(30)}{25}} \approx 39$

    c. 2050; No, this is 85 years and the legislator would have to be more than 100 years old then.

34. $D = 2.2e^{-\frac{(1.3)(0.5)}{0.4}}$

    ≈ 0.4332 mg

35. The graph is a logarithmic graph that approaches 0 as x becomes more negative, has y-intercept approximately 9.5, and curves sharply upward for the positive values of x.

36. a. $A = P(1 + E)$

    $P\left(1 + \dfrac{r}{n}\right)^{n} = P(1 + E)$

    $\left(1 + \dfrac{r}{n}\right)^{n} = 1 + E$

    $\left(1 + \dfrac{r}{n}\right)^{n} - 1 = E$

    b. $A = P(1 + E)$

    $Pe^{r} = P(1 + E)$

    $e^{r} = 1 + E$

    $e^{r} - 1 = E$

    c. $E = \left(1 + \dfrac{0.056}{12}\right)^{12} - 1 \approx 0.0575$ or 5.75%

    $E = e^{0.056} - 1 \approx 0.0576$ or 5.76%

37. for $n = 5$: 2.48832

for $n = 100$: 2.704813829

for $n = 500$: 2.715568521

for $n = 10,000$: 2.718145927

38. $m = 4$

$y - 1 = 4(x + 2)$

$y - 1 = 4x + 8$

$0 = 4x - y + 9$

39. 45 mi/hr = 792 in./s

$C = 2\pi r$

$= 2\pi(7)$

≈ 43.9823

$792 + 43.9823 \approx 18$ rps

40. $d = \dfrac{9(-3) - 2 - 3}{-\sqrt{81 + 1}}$

$= \dfrac{-32}{-\sqrt{82}}$

≈ 3.53

41. $15 = r \sin \theta$

42. $x^2 - 4x + y^2 - 6y = 3$

$(x - 2)^2 + (y - 3)^2 = 3 + 4 + 9$

$(x - 2)^2 + (y - 3)^2 = 16$

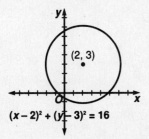

$(x - 2)^2 + (y - 3)^2 = 16$

43. $90,000 = P\left[\dfrac{1 - \left(1 + \dfrac{0.115}{12}\right)^{-360}}{\left(\dfrac{0.115}{12}\right)}\right]$

$\$891.26 \approx P$

44. $\dfrac{c^2 - d^2}{c + d} = \dfrac{(c + d)(c - d)}{c + d} = c - d$

So, $c - d = \dfrac{48}{12} = 4$.

Case Study Follow-Up

PAGE 619

1. $A = Pe^{rt}$

$= 13,000e^{(0.20)(10)}$

$\approx \$96,057.73$, about $\$96,000$

2. \$3 trillion ÷ \$96,000 ≈ 31 million

3. See students' work.

Technology: Compound Interest

PAGE 620   EXERCISES

1. expand the spreadsheet to contain 50 rows instead of 24

2. You could add a column to give the amounts for a second rate and then add another column subtracting one amount from the other.

11-4A Graphing Calculators: Graphing Logarithmic Functions

PAGE 621   EXERCISES

1.

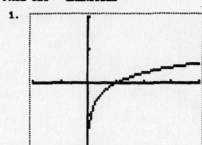

domain: $x > 0$

range: all reals

2.

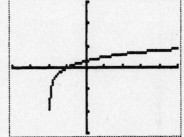

domain: $x > -2$

range: all reals

3.

domain: $x < 0$

range: all reals

4.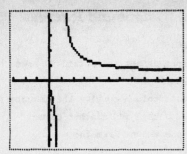

domain: $x > 0$
range: all reals

5.

domain: $x > -4$
range: all reals

6.

domain: $x < 3$
range: all reals

7.

domain: all reals except 0
range: all reals

8. cannot be graphed

11-4 **Logarithmic Functions**

PAGE 626   CHECKING FOR UNDERSTANDING

1. In the equation $y = a^x$, x is the logarithm.

2. See students' work.

3. Let $b^x = m$, then $\log_b m = x$.

$$(b^x)^p = m^p$$
$$b^{xp} = m^p$$
$$\log_b b^{xp} = \log_b m^p$$
$$xp = \log_b m^p$$
$$p\log_b m = \log_b m^p$$

---

4. $\log_4 64 = 3$

5. $\log_6 \left(\dfrac{1}{36}\right) = -2$

6. $\log_{49} 7 = \dfrac{1}{2}$

7. $27^{\frac{1}{3}} = 3$

8. $16^{\frac{1}{2}} = 4$

9. $9^{\frac{3}{2}} = 27$

10. $\log_2 32 = 5$

11. $\log_{10} 1000 = 3$

12. $\log_7 \dfrac{1}{343} = -3$

13. $\log_6 x + \log_6 9 = \log_6 54$

$$\log_6 9x = \log_6 54$$
$$9x = 54$$
$$x = 6$$

14. $\log_7 n = \dfrac{2}{3}\log_7 8$

$$\log_7 n = \log_7 8^{\frac{2}{3}}$$
$$\log_7 n = \log_7 4$$
$$n = 4$$

15. $4\log_2 x + \log_2 5 = \log_2 405$

$$\log_2 x^4 + \log_2 5 = \log_2 405$$
$$\log_2 5x^4 = \log_2 405$$
$$5x^4 = 405$$
$$x^4 = 81$$
$$x = 3$$

16. $\log_8 48 - \log_8 w = \log_8 4$

$$\log_8 \dfrac{48}{w} = \log_8 4$$
$$\dfrac{48}{w} = 4$$
$$12 = w$$

17.

$y = \log_3(x + 1)$

18.

$y < \log_2 x$

PAGES 626-628   EXERCISES

19. $\log_2 16 = 4$

20. $\log_5 \dfrac{1}{25} = -2$

21. $\log_3 \dfrac{1}{27} = -3$

22. $\log_{10} 1,000,000 = 6$

23. $\log_8 \dfrac{1}{4} = -\dfrac{2}{3}$

24. $\log_4 1 = 0$

25. $2^3 = 8$

26. $5^3 = 125$

27. $10^4 = 10,000$

28. $7^{-4} = \dfrac{1}{2401}$

---

29. $8^{\frac{1}{3}} = 2$

30. $(\sqrt{6})^4 = 36$

31. $\log_9 9^6 = 6$

32. $\log_{10} 0.01 = -2$

33. $12^{\log_{12} 5} = 5$

34. $\log_2 \frac{1}{16} = -4$

35. $\log_6 6^5 = 5\log_6 6$

$= 5$

36. $\log_8 16 = \frac{4}{3}$

37. $\log_a a^{10} = 10\log_a a$

$= 10$

38. $\log_{11} 11 = 1$

39. $10^{4\log_{10} 2} = 16$

40. $\log_x 49 = 2$

$x^2 = 49$

$x = 7$

41. $\log_5 0.04 = x$

$5^x = 0.04$

$5^x = \frac{1}{25}$

$x = -2$

42. $\log_6 (4x + 4) = \log_6 64$

$4x + 4 = 64$

$4x = 60$

$x = 15$

43. $\log_3 (3x) = \log_3 36$

$3x = 36$

$x = 12$

44. $\log_x 16 = -4$

$x^{-4} = 16$

$x = \frac{1}{2}$

45. $\log_6 216 = x$

$6^x = 216$

$x = 3$

46. $\log_{10} \sqrt[3]{10} = x$

$10^x = \sqrt[3]{10}$

$10^x = 10^{\frac{1}{3}}$

$x = \frac{1}{3}$

47. $\log_2 4 + \log_2 6 = \log_2 x$

$\log_2 24 = \log_2 x$

$24 = x$

48. $2\log_6 4 - \frac{1}{4}\log_6 16 = \log_6 x$

$\log_6 4^2 - \log_6 16^{\frac{1}{4}} = \log_6 x$

$\log_6 16 - \log_6 2 = \log_6 x$

$\log_6 8 = \log_6 x$

$8 = x$

49. $\log_3 12 - \log_3 x = \log_3 3$

$\log_3 \frac{12}{x} = \log_3 3$

$\frac{12}{x} = 3$

$x = 4$

50. $3\log_7 4 + 4\log_7 3 = \log_7 x$

$\log_7 4^3 + \log_7 3^4 = \log_7 x$

$\log_7 64 + \log_7 81 = \log_7 x$

$\log_7 5184 = \log_7 x$

$5184 = x$

51. $\log_4 (x - 3) + \log_4 (x + 3) = 2$

$\log_4 [(x - 3)(x + 3)] = 2$

$(x - 3)(x + 3) = 4^2$

$x^2 - 9 = 16$

$x^2 - 25 = 0$

$x^2 = 25$

$x = 5$

52. $\log_6 x = \frac{1}{2}\log_6 9 + \frac{1}{3}\log_6 27$

$\log_6 x = \log_6 9^{\frac{1}{2}} + \log_6 27^{\frac{1}{3}}$

$\log_6 x = \log_6 3 + \log_6 3$

$\log_6 x = \log_6 9$

$x = 9$

53. $\log_9 5x = \log_9 6 + \log_9 (x - 2)$

$\log_9 5x = \log_9 [6(x - 2)]$

$5x = 6x - 12$

$12 = x$

54. $\log_{10} x + \log_{10} x + \log_{10} x = \log_{10} 8$

$3\log_{10} x = \log_{10} 8$

$\log_{10} x^3 = \log_{10} 8$

$x^3 = 8$

$x = 2$

55.

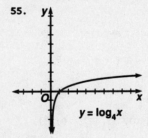

$y = \log_4 x$

56.

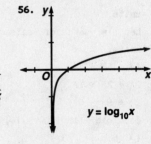

$y = \log_{10} x$

57.

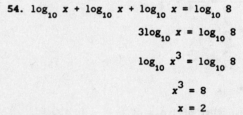

$y = \log_{\frac{1}{2}} x$

58.

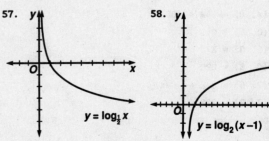

$y = \log_2 (x - 1)$

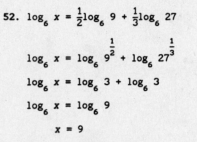

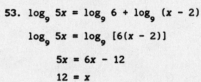

59.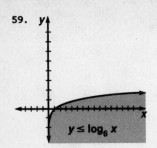

$y \le \log_6 x$

60.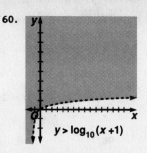

$y > \log_{10}(x+1)$

61. All powers of 1 are 1, so the inverse is not a function.

62. $16 = \dfrac{t}{3.3\log_2 256}$

$16 = \dfrac{t}{(3.3)(8)}$

$t = (16)(3.3)(8)$

$t = 422.4$ h

$t = 17$ days 14 h 24 min

63. a. $O = 100(3^0)$

$= 100$ units

b. $2700 = 100\left(3^{\frac{3s}{5}}\right)$

$27 = 3^{\frac{3s}{5}}$

$3 = \dfrac{3s}{5}$

$15 = 3s$

$s = 5$ ft/s

64. $m = \dfrac{0 - 5}{-6 - 8} = \dfrac{-5}{-14} = \dfrac{5}{14}$

$y - 0 = \dfrac{5}{14}(x + 6)$

$y = \dfrac{5}{14}x + \dfrac{30}{14}$

$y = \dfrac{5}{14}x + \dfrac{15}{7}$

65. Let A = number of units of type A in 100 ft units.

Let B = number of units of type B in 100 ft units.

$4A + 6B \le 48$

$2A + 2B \le 18$

$2A + B \le 16$

possible solutions: $(0, 0)$, $(8, 0)$, $(0, 8)$, $(3, 6)$, $(7, 2)$

$P(A, B) = 34A + 40B$

$P(0, 0) = 0$

$P(8, 0) = 272$

$P(0, 8) = 320$

$P(3, 6) = 342 \leftarrow$ max

$P(7, 2) = 318$

300 feet of A, 600 feet of B

66. $y = 7 - 8x^2$

$x = 7 - 8y^2$

$x + 7 = -8y^2$

$\dfrac{7 - x}{8} = y^2$

$\pm\sqrt{\dfrac{7 - x}{8}} = y$

67. $F'(x) = 2x - 6$

$F'(-1) = -8$

$y - 11 = -8(x + 1)$

$y = -8x + 3$

68. $\dfrac{-4}{x - 1} = \dfrac{7}{2 - x} + \dfrac{3}{x + 1}$

$\dfrac{-4}{x - 1} = \dfrac{7(x + 1) + 3(2 - x)}{(2 - x)(x + 1)}$

$\dfrac{-4}{x - 1} = \dfrac{4x + 13}{-x^2 + x + 2}$

$-4(-x^2 + x + 2) = (x - 1)(4x + 13)$

$4x^2 - 4x - 8 = 4x^2 + 9x - 13$

$-4x - 8 = 9x - 13$

$5 = 13x$

$x = \dfrac{5}{13}$

69. $\cos 90° = 0$

70. $\cos 2x + \sin x = 1$

$\cos^2 x - \sin^2 x + \sin x = 1$

$-\sin^2 x + \sin x = 1 - \cos^2 x$

$-\sin^2 x + \sin x = \sin^2 x$

$0 = 2\sin^2 x - \sin x$

$0 = \sin x(2\sin x - 1)$

$\sin x = 0 \qquad 2\sin x - 1 = 0$

$x = 0° \qquad\qquad \sin x = \dfrac{1}{2}$

$\qquad\qquad\qquad x = 30°$

71. $\vec{u} \cdot \vec{v} = (9) \cdot (-3) + (5)(2) + (3)(5)$

$= -27 + 10 + 15$

$= -2$, no

72. $(8 - 2i)(2 + 6i) = 16 + 44i + 12$

$= 28 + 44i$

73. $x^2 - 4x - 4y^2 = 0$

$(x - 2)^2 - 4y^2 = 4$

$\dfrac{(x - 2)^2}{4} - \dfrac{y^2}{1} = 1$; hyperbola

74. $A = Pe^{rt}$

$= 600e^{(0.06)(15)}$

$\approx \$1475.76$

75. $6\sqrt{45} + 3\sqrt{5} = 18\sqrt{5} + 3\sqrt{5}$

$= 6$

The best answer is D.

Mid-Chapter Review

1. $81^{\frac{3}{4}} = (\sqrt[4]{81})^3$
   $= 3^3$
   $= 27$

2. $\dfrac{25^{\frac{3}{4}}}{25^{\frac{1}{4}}} = 25^{\frac{3}{4} - \frac{1}{4}}$
   $= 25^{\frac{1}{2}}$
   $= 5$

3. $\sqrt[3]{\sqrt{27}} = \sqrt[3]{3\sqrt{3}}$
   $= 3^{\frac{1}{3}}3^{\frac{1}{6}}$
   $= 3^{\frac{2}{6}}3^{\frac{1}{6}}$
   $= 3^{\frac{3}{6}}$
   $= 3^{\frac{1}{2}}$
   $= \sqrt{3}$

4.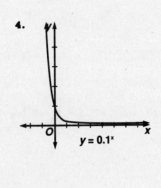
   $y = 0.1^x$

5. $F_n = 2500\left[\dfrac{(1 + 0.09)^{25} - 1}{0.09}\right]$
   $\approx \$211,752.24$

6. $e^{3.8} \approx 44.7012$

7. $5\sqrt{3}e \approx 14.2783$

8. $e^{\frac{2}{5}} \approx 1.4918$

9. $P = 760e^{-0.125(4.3)}$
   ≈ 443.9973
   about 444 mm of mercury

10. $\log_x 512 = 3$
    $x^3 = 512$
    $x = 8$

11. $\log_{\sqrt{5}} 5 = x$
    $(\sqrt{5})^x = 5$
    $x = 2$

12. $\log_5 (x^2 - 30) = \log_5 6$
    $x^2 - 30 = 6$
    $x^2 - 36 = 0$
    $x^2 = 36$
    $x = \pm 6$

11-5 Common Logarithms

1. They are the same.
2. exponential
3. 1000; 10,000
4. 1.9921
5. 2.6274
6. 0.3856
7. 354.73
8. 2.75
9. 0.01
10. 100 and 1000
11. 10,000 and 100,000

12. 0.001 and 0.01

13. $\log(784 \times 47.9 \times 0.0748) = \log 784 + \log 47.9$
    $+ \log 0.0748$
    ≈ 3.4486
    $784 \times 47.9 \times 0.0748 \approx 2809$

14. $\log\left(\dfrac{6.39 \times 1.54}{3.78}\right) = \log 6.39 + \log 1.54$
    $- \log 3.78$
    ≈ 0.4155
    $\dfrac{6.39 \times 1.54}{3.78} \approx 2.6$

15. $\log\left((1.69)^4 \times 221\right) = \log (1.69)^4 + \log 221$
    $= 4 \log 1.69 + \log 221$
    ≈ 3.2559
    $(1.69)^4 \times 221 \approx 1802.8$

16. $\log (7.32 \div \sqrt[4]{0.0743}) = \log 7.32 - \log (0.0743)^{\frac{1}{4}}$
    $= \log 7.32 - \dfrac{1}{4} \log 0.0743$
    ≈ 1.1468
    $7.32 \div \sqrt[4]{0.0743} \approx 14.0$

17. 2.9515
18. -0.1052
19. -2.2676
20. -0.0600
21. 4.3597
22. 7.6435
23. 1.81
24. 0.55
25. 0.01
26. 0.19
27. 84,004.01
28. 1.02

29. $\log (754 \times 24.5 \times 0.0128) = \log 754 + \log 24.5$
    $+ \log 0.0128$
    ≈ 2.3737
    $754 \times 24.5 \times 0.0128 \approx 236.5$

30. $\log\left(\dfrac{5.43 \times 7.12}{2.28}\right) = \log 5.43 + \log 7.12$
    $- \log 2.28$
    ≈ 1.2293
    $\dfrac{5.43 \times 7.12}{2.28} \approx 17.0$

31. $\log (642 \times (2.01)^3) = \log 642 + \log (2.01)^3$
    $= \log 642 + 3 \log 2.01$
    ≈ 3.7171
    $642 \times (2.01)^3 \approx 5213.4$

32. $\log (5.81 \times 71.1)^{\frac{1}{2}} = \dfrac{1}{2} \log (5.81 \times 71.1)$
    $= \dfrac{1}{2} (\log 5.81 + \log 71.1)$
    ≈ 1.3080
    $\sqrt{5.81 \times 71.1} \approx 20.3$

33. $\log (3.05 \times 730)^{\frac{1}{3}} = \frac{1}{3}(\log (3.05 \times 730))$

$= \frac{1}{3}(\log 3.05 + \log 730)$

≈ 1.1159

$\sqrt[3]{(3.05)(730)} \approx 13.1$

34. $\log [(8.83) \div \sqrt[5]{0.4218}] = \log 8.83 - \log (0.4218)^{\frac{1}{5}}$

$= \log 8.83 - \frac{1}{5} \log 0.4218$

≈ 1.0209

$8.83 \div \sqrt[5]{0.4218} \approx 10.5$

35. $\log \left(\frac{1}{0.7891}\right)^4 = 4 \log \left(\frac{1}{0.7891}\right)$

≈ 0.4115

$\left(\frac{1}{0.7891}\right)^4 \approx 2.6$

36. $\log (\sqrt[6]{82.9}) = \log (82.9)^{\frac{1}{6}}$

$= \frac{1}{6} \log 82.9$

≈ 0.3198

$\sqrt[6]{82.9} \approx 2.1$

37. $\log \sqrt{\frac{8.4}{0.31}} = \log \left(\frac{8.4}{0.31}\right)^{\frac{1}{2}}$

$= \frac{1}{2}(\log 8.4 - \log 0.31)$

≈ 0.7165

$\sqrt{\frac{8.4}{0.31}} \approx 5.2$

38. $\log \left[\frac{37.9\sqrt{488}}{(1.28)^3}\right] = \log 37.9 + \log (488)^{\frac{1}{2}}$

$- \log (1.28)^3$

$= \log 37.9 + \frac{1}{2} \log 488$

$- 3 \log 1.28$

≈ 2.6012

$\frac{37.9\sqrt{488}}{(1.28)^3} \approx 399.2$

39. $(3x)^{\log 3} - (5x)^{\log 5} = 0$

$3^{\log 3} \cdot x^{\log 3} = 5^{\log 5} \cdot x^{\log 5}$

$\frac{3^{\log 3}}{5^{\log 5}} = \frac{x^{\log 5}}{x^{\log 3}}$

$\log 3^{\log 3} - \log 5^{\log 5} = \log x^{\log 5} - \log 3$

$(\log 3)^2 - (\log 5)^2 = (\log 5 - \log 3)\log x$

$(\log 3 + \log 5)(\log 3 - \log 5)$

$= -(\log 3 - \log 5)\log x$

$\log 3 + \log 5 = -\log x$

$-\log 15 = \log x$

$\log \frac{1}{15} = \log x$

$x = \frac{1}{15}$

40. a. $M = 5.3 + 5 + 5 \log 0.018 \approx 1.58$

b. $5.3 = 8.6 + 5 + 5 \log p$

$-1.66 = \log p$

$0.0219 \approx p$

41. a. $R = \log \left(\frac{200}{1.6}\right) + 4.2 = 6.3$

b. 10 times

42. $d = \sqrt{(11 + 9)^2 + (-4 - 6)^2}$ $m = \frac{-4 - 6}{11 - (-9)}$

$= \sqrt{400 + 100}$ $= \frac{-10}{20}$

$= \sqrt{500}$ $= -\frac{1}{2}$

$= 10\sqrt{5}$

43. $A + B = \begin{bmatrix} 8 & 8 & -1 \\ 2 & -8 & -3 \end{bmatrix}$

44. $c^2 = 71^2 + 55^2 - 2(71)(55) \cos 106°$

$c^2 \approx 10,218.73$

$c \approx 101.1$

$c^2 = 71^2 + 55^2 - 2(71)(55) \cos 74°$

$c^2 \approx 5913.72$

$c \approx 76.9$

45. $\frac{\sin^2 x}{\cos^4 x + \cos^2 x \sin^2 x} \overset{?}{=} \tan^2 x$

$\frac{\sin^2 x}{\cos^2 x (\cos^2 x + \sin^2 x)} \overset{?}{=} \tan^2 x$

$\frac{\sin^2 x}{\cos^2 x} \overset{?}{=} \tan^2 x$

$\tan^2 x = \tan^2 x$

46. $\vec{AB} = (0 - 12, -11 + 5, 21 - 18)$

$= (-12, -6, 3)$

47. $\frac{(x - 2)^2}{4} + \frac{(y - 6)^2}{3} = 1$

48. $\log_5 (7x) = \log_5 (5x + 16)$

$7x = 5x + 16$

$2x = 16$

$x = 8$

49. price/lb $= \dfrac{d}{3}$

Let p = the number of pounds.

$$0.80 = \frac{d}{3}p$$

$$\frac{3(0.80)}{d} = p$$

$$\frac{2.4}{p} = p$$

The best answer is B.

11-6A Graphing Calculators: Exponential and Logarithmic Equations and Inequalities

PAGE 635   EXERCISES

1. 6.57

2. -0.77, 2, 4

3. 18.64

4. 174.83

5. -1.39, 2.89

6. 0.34

7. no solution

8. -8.04

9. no solution

10. $x \geq -1$

11. $x > \dfrac{1}{2}$

12. $3.5 < x < 4$

13. $x \leq 0.68,\ x \geq 7.41$

14. all real numbers

11-6 Exponential and Logarithmic Equations

PAGE 639   CHECKING FOR UNDERSTANDING

1. If $a^{x_1} = a^{x_2}$ and $a \neq 1$, then $x_1 = x_2$.

2. The constant of proportionality will be positive when the formula describes growth and negative when it describes decay.

3. An equation involving a variable as an exponent. no

4.
$$3^x = 72$$
$$\log 3^x = \log 72$$
$$x \log 3 = \log 72$$
$$x = \frac{\log 72}{\log 3}$$
$$\approx 3.89$$

5.
$$7^x = 98$$
$$\log 7^x = \log 98$$
$$x \log 7 = \log 98$$
$$x = \frac{\log 98}{\log 7}$$
$$\approx 2.36$$

6.
$$6^{2x} = 63$$
$$\log 6^{2x} = \log 63$$
$$2x \log 6 = \log 63$$
$$x = \frac{\log 63}{2 \log 6}$$
$$\approx 1.16$$

7.
$$x = \log_5 121$$
$$5^x = 121$$
$$\log 5^x = \log 121$$
$$x \log 5 = \log 121$$
$$x = \frac{\log 121}{\log 5}$$
$$\approx 2.98$$

8.
$$2^{-x} = 10$$
$$\log 2^{-x} = \log 10$$
$$-x \log 2 = \log 10$$
$$x = -\frac{\log 10}{\log 2}$$
$$\approx -3.32$$

9.
$$x = \log_3 16$$
$$3^x = 16$$
$$\log 3^x = \log 16$$
$$x \log 3 = \log 16$$
$$x = \frac{\log 16}{\log 3}$$
$$\approx 2.52$$

10.
$$5^{3x} = 128$$
$$\log 5^{3x} = \log 128$$
$$3x \log 5 = \log 128$$
$$x = \frac{\log 128}{3 \log 5}$$
$$\approx 1.00$$

11.
$$3^{-x} = 18$$
$$\log 3^{-x} = \log 18$$
$$-x \log 3 = \log 18$$
$$x = -\frac{\log 18}{\log 3}$$
$$\approx -2.63$$

12.
$$3^x = 3\sqrt{2}$$
$$\log 3^x = \log 3\sqrt{2}$$
$$x \log 3 = \log 3\sqrt{2}$$
$$x = \frac{\log 3\sqrt{2}}{\log 3}$$
$$\approx 1.32$$

13.
$$2^x > 14$$
$$\log 2^x > \log 14$$
$$x \log 2 > \log 14$$
$$x > \frac{\log 14}{\log 2}$$
$$x > 3.807$$

14.
$$5^x \leq 7\sqrt{6}$$
$$\log 5^x \leq \log 7\sqrt{6}$$
$$x \log 5 \leq \log 7\sqrt{6}$$
$$x \leq \frac{\log 7\sqrt{6}}{\log 5}$$
$$x \leq 1.766$$

15.
$$10^{x-3} \geq 52$$
$$\log 10^{x-3} \geq \log 52$$
$$(x-3) \log 10 \geq \log 52$$
$$x \log 10 - 3 \log 10 \geq \log 52$$
$$x - 3 \geq \log 52$$
$$x \geq \log 52 + 3$$
$$x \geq 4.716$$

PAGES 639-640   EXERCISES

16.
$$6^x = 72$$
$$\log 6^x = \log 72$$
$$x \log 6 = \log 72$$
$$x = \frac{\log 72}{\log 6}$$
$$x \approx 2.39$$

17.
$$2^x = 27$$
$$\log 2^x = \log 27$$
$$x \log 2 = \log 27$$
$$x = \frac{\log 27}{\log 2}$$
$$x \approx 4.75$$

18.
$$4.3^x < 76.2$$
$$\log 4.3^x < \log 76.2$$
$$x \log 4.3 < \log 76.2$$
$$x < \frac{\log 76.2}{\log 4.3}$$
$$x < 2.97$$

19.
$$2.2^{x-5} = 9.32$$
$$\log 2.2^{x-5} = \log 9.32$$
$$(x-5)\log 2.2 = \log 9.32$$
$$x\log 2.2 - 5\log 2.2 = \log 9.32$$
$$x\log 2.2 = \log 9.32 + 5\log 2.2$$
$$x = \frac{\log 9.32 + 5\log 2.2}{\log 2.2}$$
$$x \approx 7.83$$

20.
$$9^{x-4} = 7.13$$
$$\log 9^{x-4} = \log 7.13$$
$$(x-4)\log 9 = \log 7.13$$
$$x\log 9 - 4\log 9 = \log 7.13$$
$$x\log 9 = \log 7.13 + 4\log 9$$
$$x = \frac{\log 7.13 + 4\log 9}{\log 9}$$
$$x \approx 4.89$$

21.
$$6^{3x} = 81$$
$$\log 6^{3x} = \log 81$$
$$3x\log 6 = \log 81$$
$$x = \frac{\log 81}{3\log 6}$$
$$x \approx 0.82$$

22.
$$x < \log_3 52.7$$
$$3^x < 52.7$$
$$\log 3^x < \log 52.7$$
$$x\log 3 < \log 52.7$$
$$x < \frac{\log 52.7}{\log 3}$$
$$x < 3.61$$

23.
$$x = \log_4 19.5$$
$$4^x = 19.5$$
$$\log 4^x = \log 19.5$$
$$x\log 4 = \log 19.5$$
$$x = \frac{\log 19.5}{\log 4}$$
$$x \approx 2.14$$

24.
$$x^{\frac{2}{3}} \geq 27.6$$
$$\log x^{\frac{2}{3}} \geq \log 27.6$$
$$\frac{2}{3}\log x \geq \log 27.6$$
$$\log x \geq \frac{\log 27.6}{\frac{2}{3}}$$
$$\log x \geq 2.16$$
$$x \geq 145$$

25.
$$x^{\frac{2}{5}} = 17.3$$
$$\log x^{\frac{2}{5}} = \log 17.3$$
$$\frac{2}{5}\log x = \log 17.3$$
$$\log x = \frac{\log 17.3}{\frac{2}{5}}$$
$$\log x = 3.10$$
$$x \approx 1244.84$$

26.
$$5^{x-1} = 2^x$$
$$\log 5^{x-1} = \log 2^x$$
$$(x-1)\log 5 = x\log 2$$
$$x\log 5 - \log 5 = x\log 2$$
$$x(\log 5 - \log 2) = \log 5$$
$$x = \frac{\log 5}{\log 5 - \log 2}$$
$$x \approx 1.76$$

27.
$$3^{2x} = 7^{x-1}$$
$$\log 3^{2x} = \log 7^{x-1}$$
$$2x\log 3 = (x-1)\log 7$$
$$2x\log 3 = x\log 7 - \log 7$$
$$x(2\log 3 - \log 7) = -\log 7$$
$$x = \frac{-\log 7}{2\log 3 - \log 7}$$
$$x \approx -7.74$$

28.
$$6^{x-2} = 4^x$$
$$\log 6^{x-2} = \log 4^x$$
$$(x-2)\log 6 = x\log 4$$
$$x\log 6 - 2\log 6 = x\log 4$$
$$x(\log 6 - \log 4) = 2\log 6$$
$$x = \frac{2\log 6}{\log 6 - \log 4}$$
$$x \approx 8.84$$

29.
$$12^{x-4} = 3^{x-2}$$
$$\log 12^{x-4} = \log 3^{x-2}$$
$$(x-4)\log 12 = (x-2)\log 3$$
$$x\log 12 - 4\log 12 = x\log 3 - 2\log 3$$
$$x\log 12 - x\log 3 = 4\log 12 - 2\log 3$$
$$x(\log 12 - \log 3) = 4\log 12 - 2\log 3$$
$$x = \frac{4\log 12 - 2\log 3}{\log 12 - \log 3}$$
$$x \approx 5.58$$

30. $\log_2 x = -3$
$$2^{-3} = x$$
$$0.13 = x$$

31. $\log_x 6 > 1$
$$x^1 < 6$$
$$1 < x < 6$$

32. $\log_{27} \frac{1}{3} = x$
$$27^x = \frac{1}{3}$$
$$x = -\frac{1}{3}$$
$$\approx -0.33$$

33.
$$2^x > \sqrt{3^{x-2}}$$
$$\log 2^x > \log (3^x - 2)^{\frac{1}{2}}$$
$$x\log 2 > \frac{1}{2}(x-2)\log 3$$
$$x\log 2 > \frac{x}{2}\log 3 - \log 3$$
$$x\left(\log 2 - \frac{1}{2}\log 3\right) > -\log 3$$
$$x > -\frac{\log 3}{\log 2 - \frac{1}{2}\log 3}$$
$$x > -7.64$$

34.

$$6^{x^2 - 2} < 48$$

$$\log 6^{x^2 - 2} < \log 48$$

$$(x^2 - 2)\log 6 < \log 48$$

$$x^2 \log 6 < \log 48 + 2 \log 6$$

$$x^2 < \frac{\log 48 + 2 \log 6}{\log 6}$$

$$x^2 < 4.16$$

$$-2.04 < x < 2.04$$

35. $\log_3 \sqrt[4]{5} = x$

$$3^x = 5^{\frac{1}{4}}$$

$$\log 3^x = \log 5^{\frac{1}{4}}$$

$$x \log 3 = \frac{1}{4} \log 5$$

$$x = \frac{\frac{1}{4}\log 5}{\log 3}$$

$$x \approx 0.37$$

36.

$$\sqrt[3]{4^{x-1}} = 6^{x-2}$$

$$4^{\frac{x-1}{3}} = 6^{x-2}$$

$$\log 4^{\frac{x-1}{3}} = \log 6^{x-2}$$

$$\frac{x-1}{3}(\log 4) = (x-2)\log 6$$

$$\frac{x}{3}\log 4 - \frac{1}{3}\log 4 = x \log 6 - 2 \log 6$$

$$x\left(\frac{1}{3}\log 4 - \log 6\right) = \frac{1}{3}\log 4 - 2 \log 6$$

$$x = \frac{\frac{1}{3}\log 4 - 2 \log 6}{\frac{1}{3}\log 4 - \log 6}$$

$$x \approx 2.35$$

37. 13.57   **38.** 5.66

39. $x > 9.05$ **40.** It is steeper.

41. $2^{2a+3} - 2^{a+3} - 2^a + 1 = 0$

$$2^{2a}2^3 - 2^a 2^3 - 2^a + 1 = 0$$

$$8(2^{2a}) - 8(2^a) - 2^a + 1 = 0$$

$$8(2^a)^2 - 9(2^a) + 1 = 0$$

$$2^a = \frac{9 \pm \sqrt{81 - 32}}{16}$$

$$2^a = \frac{9 \pm 7}{16}$$

$$2^a = 1 \qquad \text{or} \qquad 2^a = \frac{1}{8}$$

$$\log 2^a = \log 1 \qquad\qquad \log 2^a = \frac{\log 1}{8}$$

$$a = \frac{\log 1}{\log 2} \qquad\qquad a \log 2 = \log \frac{1}{8}$$

$$= 0 \qquad\qquad\qquad a = \frac{\log \frac{1}{8}}{\log 2}$$

$$\qquad\qquad\qquad\qquad\qquad = -3$$

42. a. $A = 12{,}000(1 - 0.15)^5$

$$\approx \$5324.46$$

b. $124{,}000 = 89{,}000(1 + 0.04)^t$

$$1.39 = 1.04^t$$

$$\log 1.39 = \log 1.04^t$$

$$\log 1.39 = t \log 1.04$$

$$\frac{\log 1.39}{\log 1.04} = t$$

$$8.5 \approx t$$

8.5 years or 8 years 6 months

c. $1.85 = 1.35(1 + 0.035)^t$

$$1.37 = (1.035)^t$$

$$\log 1.37 = \log 1.035^t$$

$$\log 1.37 = t \log 1.035$$

$$\frac{\log 1.37}{\log 1.035} = t$$

$$9.2 \approx t$$

9.2 years or 9 years 2 months

43.

$$y = y \cdot c^{\frac{t}{T}}$$

$$2.1 = 7\left(\frac{1}{2}\right)^{\frac{13}{T}}$$

$$0.3 = \left(\frac{1}{2}\right)^{\frac{13}{T}}$$

$$\log 0.3 = \log \left(\frac{1}{2}\right)^{\frac{13}{T}}$$

$$\log 0.3 = \frac{13}{T}\log \frac{1}{2}$$

$$T = \frac{13 \log \frac{1}{2}}{\log 0.3}$$

$$T \approx 7.48 \text{ years}$$

44. a. $q = \left(\frac{1}{2}\right)0.8^7$

$q \approx 0.86471$ hundreds of thousands

$$\approx 86{,}471 \text{ units}$$

b. $0.64171 = \left(\frac{1}{2}\right)0.8^t$

$$\log 0.64171 = \log \left(\frac{1}{2}\right)0.8^t$$

$$\log 0.64171 = 0.8^t \log \frac{1}{2}$$

$$\frac{\log 0.64171}{\log \frac{1}{2}} = 0.8^t$$

$$0.64 \approx 0.8^t$$

$$\log 0.64 \approx \log 0.8^t$$

$$\log 0.64 \approx t \log 0.8$$

$$\frac{\log 0.64}{\log 0.8} \approx t$$

$$t \approx 2 \text{ yr}$$

45.

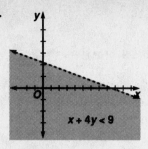

$x + 4y < 9$

46. $2x^2 + 7x - 4 = 0$

$2x^2 + 7x = 4$

$x^2 + \frac{7}{2}x = 2$

$x^2 + \frac{7}{2}x + \frac{49}{16} = 2 + \frac{49}{16}$

$\left(x + \frac{7}{4}\right)^2 = \frac{81}{16}$

$x + \frac{7}{4} = \pm \frac{9}{4}$

$x + \frac{7}{4} = \frac{9}{4} \qquad x + \frac{7}{4} = -\frac{9}{4}$

$x = \frac{2}{4} \qquad\qquad x = -\frac{16}{4}$

$x = \frac{1}{2} \qquad\qquad x = -4$

47. $y = \pm 17 \sin(8x + 480°)$

48. $\dfrac{\tan^2 t}{1 - \sec^2 t} = \dfrac{\tan^2 t}{-\tan^2 t} = -1$

49. $x = r \cos \theta \qquad\qquad y = r \sin \theta$

$x = 0.25 \cos \pi \qquad y = 0.25 \sin \pi$

$x = -0.25 \qquad\qquad y = 0$

50. $x^2 = -12y$

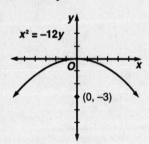

$x^2 = -12y$

$(0, -3)$

51. Let $A = \left(\dfrac{1}{0.381}\right)^2$.

$\log A = \log \left(\dfrac{1}{0.381}\right)^2$

$\log A = 2 \log \dfrac{1}{0.381}$

$\log A = 0.84$

$A \approx 6.89$

52. $6.02 \times 10^3 = 6020$

The best answer is B.

PAGE 643 **CHECKING FOR UNDERSTANDING**

1. Negative; for the value of y to decrease, the exponent of e must be negative.

2. Both equations find the final amount of something that is added at the same rate over and over again. So the formulas are the same with $A = y$, $P = n$, and $r = k$.

3. $\ln 9.32 \approx 2.2322$ **4.** $\ln 4.01 \approx 1.3888$

5. $\ln 0.21 \approx -1.5606$ **6.** antiln $2.84 \approx 17.1158$

7. antiln $0.7831 \approx 2.1882$

8. antiln $-3.874 \approx 0.0208$

9. $9 = e^x$ **10.** $18 = e^{3x}$

   $\ln 9 = \ln e^x$ $\ln 18 = \ln e^{3x}$

   $\ln 9 = x$ $\ln 18 = 3x \ln e$

   $2.1972 \approx x$ $\dfrac{\ln 18}{3} = x$

                 $0.9635 \approx x$

11. $65 = e^{6x}$ **12.** $y = ne^{kt}$

   $\ln 65 = \ln e^{6x}$ $250 = 15e^{0.658t}$

   $\ln 65 = 6x \ln e$ $16.67 \approx e^{0.658t}$

   $\dfrac{\ln 65}{6} = x$ $\ln 16.67 \approx \ln e^{0.658t}$

   $0.6957 \approx x$ $\ln 16.67 \approx 0.658t \ln e$

                 $\dfrac{\ln 16.67}{0.658} \approx t$

                   $t \approx 4.28$ hrs

PAGES 643-645   **EXERCISES**

13. $\ln 56.8 \approx 4.0395$ **14.** $\ln 0.0198 \approx -3.9221$

15. $\ln 980 \approx 6.8876$ **16.** $\ln 0.0089 \approx -4.7217$

17. $\ln 1 = 0$ **18.** $\ln \left(\dfrac{1}{0.32}\right) \approx 1.1394$

19. antiln $4.987 \approx 146.4963$

20. antiln $2.94 \approx 18.9158$

21. antiln $0.62 \approx 1.8589$

22. antiln $-0.053 \approx 0.9484$

23. antiln $0 = 1$ **24.** antiln $-2.81 \approx 0.0602$

25. $1600 = 4e^{0.045t}$

     $400 = e^{0.045t}$

   $\ln 400 = \ln e^{0.045t}$

   $\ln 400 = 0.045t \ln e$

   $\dfrac{\ln 400}{0.045} = t$

   $133.14 \approx t$

26. $10 = 5e^{5k}$

$2 = e^{5k}$

$\ln 2 = \ln e^{5k}$

$\ln 2 = 5k \ln e$

$\dfrac{\ln 2}{5} = k$

$0.14 \approx k$

27. $\ln 4.5 = \ln e^{0.031t}$

$\ln 4.5 = 0.031t \ln e$

$\dfrac{\ln 4.5}{0.031} = t$

$48.52 \approx t$

28. $25 = e^{0.075y}$

$\ln 25 = \ln e^{0.075y}$

$\ln 25 = 0.075y \ln e$

$\dfrac{\ln 25}{0.075} = y$

$42.92 \approx y$

29. $\ln 40.5 = \ln e^{0.21t}$

$\ln 40.5 = 0.21t \ln e$

$\dfrac{\ln 40.5}{0.21} = t$

$17.63 \approx t$

30. $\ln 60.3 = \ln e^{0.21t}$

$\ln 60.3 = 0.21t \ln e$

$\dfrac{\ln 60.3}{0.21} = t$

$19.52 \approx t$

31. $y = ne^{kt}$

$\dfrac{1}{2} = e^{k(1800)}$

$\ln \dfrac{1}{2} = \ln e^{1800k}$

$\ln \dfrac{1}{2} = 1800k \ln e$

$\dfrac{\ln \frac{1}{2}}{1800} = k$

$-0.000385 \approx k$

32. $10,000 = Pe^{0.08(19)}$

$10,000 = Pe^{1.52}$

$\dfrac{10,000}{e^{1.52}} = P$

$\$2,187.12 \approx P$

33. $y = ne^{kt}$

a. $0.90 = e^{5k}$

$\ln 0.90 = \ln e^{5k}$

$\ln 0.90 = 5k \ln e$

$\dfrac{\ln 0.90}{5} = k$

$-0.0211 \approx k$

b. $\dfrac{y}{n} = e^{-0.0211(10)}$

$\dfrac{y}{n} \approx 0.81 \qquad 81\%$

c. $0.25 = e^{-0.0211t}$

$\ln 0.25 = \ln e^{-0.0211t}$

$\ln 0.25 = -0.0211t \ln e$

$\dfrac{\ln 0.25}{-0.0211} = t$

$65.7 \approx t$

$1972 + 65 = 2037$

34. a. $s = s_0 \cdot e^{-at}$

$37,000 = 45,000e^{-a}$

$0.82 \approx e^{-a}$

$\ln 0.82 \approx \ln e^{-a}$

$\ln 0.82 \approx -a \ln e$

$-\ln 0.82 \approx a$

$0.196 \approx a$

b. $s = 45,000e^{-0.196(3)}$

$s \approx 24,995$

c. $15,000 = 45,000e^{-0.196t}$

$\dfrac{1}{3} = e^{-0.196t}$

$\ln \dfrac{1}{3} = \ln e^{-0.196t}$

$\ln \dfrac{1}{3} = -0.196t \ln e$

$\dfrac{\ln \frac{1}{3}}{-0.196} = t$

$t \approx 5.6 \text{ yr}$

35. $A = Pe^{rt}$

a. $2 = e^{0.056t}$

$\ln 2 = \ln e^{0.056t}$

$\ln 2 = 0.056t \ln e$

$\dfrac{\ln 2}{0.056} = t$

$t \approx 12.4 \text{ yr}$

b. Answers may vary.

36. a. $p = 760e^{-0.125(3.3)}$

$p \approx 503.1 \text{ mm}$

b. $450 = 760e^{-0.125a}$

$0.59 = e^{-0.125a}$

$\ln 0.59 = \ln e^{-0.125a}$

$\ln 0.59 = -0.125a \ln e$

$\dfrac{\ln 0.59}{-0.125} = a$

$a \approx 4.2 \text{ km}$

37. $p = 1 - e^{-\mu t}$

  a. $p = 1 - e^{-3\left(\frac{25}{60}\right)}$

    $p \approx 0.713$

  b. $0.90 = 1 - e^{-3T}$

    $e^{-3T} = 0.10$

    $\ln e^{-3T} = \ln 0.10$

    $-3T \ln e = \ln 0.10$

    $T = \dfrac{\ln 0.10}{-3}$

    $T \approx 0.77$ hr

    $T \approx$ about 46 min

38. a. $p = \dfrac{\frac{1}{15}e^{0.1(14)}}{1 - \frac{1}{15}\left(1 - e^{0.1(14)}\right)}$

    $\approx \dfrac{0.2703}{1.2037}$

    ≈ 0.225

  b. $0.20 = \dfrac{0.15e^{2k}}{1 - 0.15(1 - e^{2k})}$

    $0.20(1 - 0.15(1 - e^{2k})) = 0.15e^{2k}$

    $0.20 - 0.03(1 - e^{2k}) = 0.15e^{2k}$

    $0.20 - 0.03 + 0.03e^{2k} = 0.15e^{2k}$

    $0.17 = 0.12e^{2k}$

    $1.42 = e^{2k}$

    $\ln 1.42 = \ln e^{2k}$

    $\ln 1.42 = 2k \ln e$

    $\dfrac{\ln 1.42}{2} = k$

    $0.174 = k$

39. a. $g(15) = \dfrac{0.1}{1.25} + \left(0.07 - \dfrac{0.1}{1.25}\right)e^{-1.25(15)}$

    $= 0.08 + (-0.01)(0.000000007)$

    $= 0.08$ g

  b. $0.046 = \dfrac{c}{1.28} + \left(0.08 - \dfrac{c}{1.28}\right)e^{-1.28(2)}$

    $0.046 = \dfrac{c}{1.28} + 0.08e^{-2.56} - \dfrac{c}{1.28}e^{-2.56}$

    $0.046 = \dfrac{c}{1.28}(1 - e^{-2.56}) + 0.0062$

    $0.0398 = \dfrac{c}{1.28}(1 - e^{-2.56})$

    $0.0398 = \dfrac{c}{1.28}(0.9227)$

    $0.055 \approx c$

40. $e^{2x} - 2e^x + 1 = 0$

    $(e^x)^2 - 2e^x + 1 = 0$

    $e^x = \dfrac{2 \pm \sqrt{4 - 4}}{2}$

    $e^x = 1$

    $\ln e^x = \ln 1$

    $x \ln e = \ln 1$

    $x = 0$

41. $e^{-2x} - 4e^{-x} + 3 = 0$

    $(e^{-x})^2 - 4e^{-x} + 3 = 0$

    $e^{-x} = \dfrac{4 \pm \sqrt{16 - 12}}{2}$

    $e^{-x} = \dfrac{4 \pm \sqrt{4}}{2}$

    $e^{-x} = \dfrac{4 \pm 2}{2}$

$e^{-x} = 3$	or	$e^{-x} = 1$
$\ln e^{-x} = \ln 3$		$\ln e^{-x} = \ln 1$
$-x \ln e = \ln 3$		$-x \ln e = \ln 1$
$x = -\ln 3$		$x = -\ln 1$
$x \approx -1.10$		$x = 0$

42. $(f \circ g)(x) = f(g(x))$

    $= 8(2 - x^2)$

    $= 16 - 8x^2$

    $(g \circ f)(x) = g(f(x))$

    $= 2 - (8x)^2$

    $= 2 - 64x^2$

43. $(-8, 9)$

44. $s = \dfrac{1}{2}(10 + 10 + 12) = 16$

  $A = 2K$

    $= 2\sqrt{16(16 - 10)(16 - 10)(16 - 12)}$

    $= 2\sqrt{2304}$

    $= 96$ cm^2

45. Sample answer: $y = 12 \sin \pi t$

46. $x = 11 - t$ $y = 8 - 6t$

    $t = 11 - x$ $6t = 8 - y$

                            $t = \dfrac{8 - y}{6}$

          $11 - x = \dfrac{8 - y}{6}$

          $66 - 6x = 8 - y$

               $y = 6x - 58$

47.

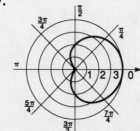

48. $3.6^x = 58.9$

$\ln 3.6^x = \ln 58.9$

$x \ln 3.6 = \ln 58.9$

$x = \dfrac{\ln 58.9}{\ln 3.6}$

$x \approx 3.182$

49. $\dfrac{\frac{1}{x} + \frac{1}{y}}{3} = \dfrac{\frac{y + x}{xy}}{3}$

$= \dfrac{x + y}{3xy}$

The best answer is D.

Chapter 11 Summary and Review

PAGES 646-648   SKILLS AND CONCEPTS

1. $\left(\dfrac{1}{64}\right)^{\frac{1}{6}} = \dfrac{1}{2}$

2. $27^{\frac{4}{3}} = \left(\sqrt[3]{27}\right)^4$

$= 3^4$

$= 81$

3. $\left(9^{\frac{3}{4}}\right)^{\frac{2}{3}} = 9^{\frac{6}{12}}$

$= 9^{\frac{1}{2}}$

$= 3$

4. $\left(\dfrac{216}{729}\right)^{\frac{2}{3}} = \left(\sqrt[3]{\dfrac{216}{729}}\right)^2$

$= \left(\dfrac{6}{9}\right)^2$

$= \left(\dfrac{2}{3}\right)^2$

$= \dfrac{4}{9}$

5. $3x^2(3x)^{-2} = \dfrac{3x^2}{9x^2}$

$= \dfrac{1}{3}$

6. $\left(6a^{\frac{1}{3}}\right)^3 = 6^3 a^{\frac{3}{3}}$

$= 216a$

7. $\left(\dfrac{1}{2}x^4\right)^3 = \dfrac{1}{8}x^{12}$

8. $(2a)^{\frac{1}{3}}(a^2 b)^{\frac{1}{3}} = 2^{\frac{1}{3}} a^{\frac{1}{3}} a^{\frac{2}{3}} b^{\frac{1}{3}}$

$= 2^{\frac{1}{3}} a^{\frac{1}{3}} a^{\frac{3}{3}} b^{\frac{1}{3}}$

$= 2^{\frac{1}{3}} ab^{\frac{1}{3}}$

9.
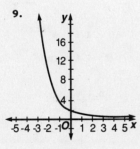

10.
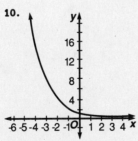

11.
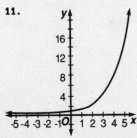

12.
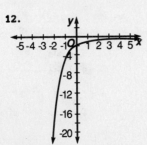

13. $e^{2.34} \approx 10.3812$

14. $\sqrt[5]{e} \approx 1.2214$

15. $3\sqrt[4]{e^3} \approx 6.3510$

16. $\dfrac{1}{4}\sqrt{e^5} \approx 3.0456$

17. $\log_x 81 = 4$

$81 = x^4$

$\sqrt[4]{81} = x$

$3 = x$

18. $\log_{\frac{1}{2}} x = -4$

$x = \left(\dfrac{1}{2}\right)^{-4}$

$x = 16$

19. $\log_3 3 + \log_3 x = \log_3 45$

$\log_3 3x = \log_3 45$

$3x = 45$

$x = 15$

20. $2 \log_6 4 - \dfrac{1}{3} \log_6 8 = \log_6 x$

$\log_6 4^2 - \log_6 8^{\frac{1}{3}} = \log_6 x$

$\log_6 16 - \log_6 2 = \log_6 x$

$\log_6 \dfrac{16}{2} = \log_6 x$

$\log_6 8 = \log_6 x$

$8 = x$

21. $\log_2 x = \dfrac{1}{3} \log_2 27$

$\log_2 x = \log_2 27^{\frac{1}{3}}$

$\log_2 x = \log_2 3$

$x = 3$

22. -1.3382

23. 1.6314

24. 42.80

25. 0.70

26. $\log [(4.22)^3 \times 0.629)] = \log 4.22^3 + \log 0.629$

$= 3 \log 4.22 + \log 0.629$

≈ 1.6746

$(4.22)^3 \times 0.629 \approx 47.27$

27. $\log \sqrt{9.12^2 \times 5.51} = \dfrac{1}{2}(\log 9.12^2 + \log 5.51)$

$= \dfrac{1}{2}(2 \log 9.12 + \log 5.51)$

≈ 1.3306

$\sqrt{9.12^2 \times 5.51} \approx 21.41$

28. $\log \left(\dfrac{6.32}{8.67}\right)^3 = 3(\log 6.32 - \log 8.67)$

≈ -0.4119

$\left(\dfrac{6.32}{8.67}\right)^3 \approx 0.39$

29. $\log\left(\dfrac{43.9\sqrt{54.8}}{(1.29)4}\right)$

$$= \log 43.9 + \log 54.8^{\frac{1}{2}} - \log 1.29^4$$

$$= \log 43.9 + \frac{1}{2}\log 54.8 - 4\log 1.29$$

$$\approx 2.0695$$

$$\frac{43.9\sqrt{54.8}}{(1.29)4} \approx 117.35$$

30. $2.5^x = 65.7$

$\log 2.5^x = \log 65.7$

$x \log 2.5 = \log 65.7$

$x = \dfrac{\log 65.7}{\log 2.5}$

$x \approx 4.57$

31. $x = \log_3 8.9$

$3^x = 8.9$

$\log 3^x = \log 8.9$

$x \log 3 = \log 8.9$

$x = \dfrac{\log 8.9}{\log 3}$

$x \approx 1.99$

32. $4^{y+3} = 28.4$

$\log 4^{y+3} = \log 28.4$

$(y+3)\log 4 = \log 28.4$

$y \log 4 = \log 28.4 - 3\log 4$

$y = \dfrac{\log 28.4 - 3\log 4}{\log 4}$

$y \approx -0.59$

33. $7^{x-2} = 5^{3-x}$

$\log 7^{x-2} = \log 5^{3-x}$

$(x-2)\log 7 = (3-x)\log 5$

$x \log 7 + x \log 5 = 2\log 7 + 3\log 5$

$x = \dfrac{2\log 7 + 3\log 5}{\log 7 + \log 5}$

$x \approx 2.45$

34. $2.3^{x^2} = 66.6$

$\log 2.3^{x^2} = \log 66.6$

$x^2 \log 2.3 = \log 66.6$

$x^2 = \dfrac{\log 66.6}{\log 2.3}$

$x^2 \approx 5.04$

$x \approx \pm 2.25$

35. $\sqrt{3^x} = 2^{x+1}$

$3^{\frac{x}{2}} = 2^{x+1}$

$\log 3^{\frac{x}{2}} = \log 2^{x+1}$

$\dfrac{x}{2}\log 3 = (x+1)\log 2$

$\dfrac{x}{2}\log 3 = x\log 2 + \log 2$

$x\left(\dfrac{1}{2}\log 3 - \log 2\right) = \log 2$

$x = \dfrac{\log 2}{\frac{1}{2}\log 3 - \log 2}$

$x \approx -4.82$

36. $\ln 8.63 \approx 2.1552$ 37. $\ln 403 \approx 5.9989$

38. antiln $3.7015 \approx 40.5080$

39. antiln $7.1121 \approx 1226.7210$

40. $4500 = 3e^{0.061t}$

$1500 = e^{0.061t}$

$\ln 1500 = \ln e^{0.061t}$

$\ln 1500 = 0.061t \ln e$

$\dfrac{\ln 1500}{0.061} = t$

$119.89 \approx t$

41. $16 = 5e^{0.4k}$

$3.2 = e^{0.4k}$

$\ln 3.2 = \ln e^{0.4k}$

$\ln 3.2 = 0.4k \ln e$

$\dfrac{\ln 3.2}{0.4} = k$

$2.91 \approx k$

42. $\ln 19.8 = \ln e^{0.083t}$

$\ln 19.8 = 0.083t \ln e$

$\dfrac{\ln 19.8}{0.083} = t$

$35.97 \approx t$

43. $\ln 6.2 = \ln e^{0.55t}$

$\ln 6.2 = 0.55t \ln e$

$\dfrac{\ln 6.2}{0.55} = t$

$3.32 \approx t$

44. $6.6 = 1.5e^{210k}$

$4.4 = e^{210k}$

$\ln 4.4 = \ln e^{210k}$

$\ln 4.4 = 210k \ln e$

$\dfrac{\ln 4.4}{210} = k$

$0.01 \approx k$

PAGE 648   APPLICATIONS AND PROBLEM SOLVING

45. a. $N = 65 - 30e^{-0.20(2)}$

≈ 45 words per minute

b. $N = 65 - 30e^{-0.20(15)}$

≈ 64 words per minute

c.
$$50 = 65 - 30e^{-0.20t}$$
$$-15 = -30e^{-0.20t}$$
$$\frac{1}{2} = e^{-0.20t}$$
$$\ln \frac{1}{2} = \ln e^{-0.20t}$$
$$\ln \frac{1}{2} = -0.20t \ln e$$
$$\frac{\ln \frac{1}{2}}{-0.20} = t$$
$$t = 3.5 \text{ wk}$$

46. a. $\beta = 10 \cdot \log \dfrac{1.15 \times 10^{-10}}{10^{-12}}$

≈ 20.6 db

b. $\beta = 10 \cdot \log \dfrac{9 \times 10^{-9}}{10^{-12}}$

≈ 39.5 db

c. $\beta = 10 \cdot \log \dfrac{8.95 \times 10^{-3}}{10^{-12}}$

≈ 99.5 db

47.
$$y = y_0 \cdot c^{\frac{t}{T}}$$
$$0.65 = 0.5^{\frac{t}{5730}}$$
$$\log 0.65 = \log 0.5^{\frac{t}{5730}}$$
$$\log 0.65 = \frac{t}{5730} \log 0.5$$
$$\frac{5730 \log 0.65}{\log 0.5} = t$$
$$3561 \approx t$$

48.
$$200{,}000 = 142{,}000 \, e^{0.014t}$$
$$1.41 = e^{0.014t}$$
$$\ln 1.41 = \ln e^{0.014t}$$
$$\ln 1.41 = 0.014t \ln e$$
$$\frac{\ln 1.41}{0.014} = t$$
$$24 \approx t$$
$$1970 + 24 \approx 1994$$

Chapter 11 Test

PAGE 649

1. $343^{\frac{2}{3}} = (\sqrt[3]{343})^2$

$= 7^2$

$= 49$

2. $(0.064)^{-\frac{1}{3}} = \dfrac{1}{\sqrt[3]{0.064}}$

$= \dfrac{1}{0.4}$

$= 2.5$

3. $49^{\frac{3}{2}} + 49^{-\frac{1}{2}} = (\sqrt{49})^3 + \dfrac{1}{\sqrt{49}}$

$= 343 + \dfrac{1}{7}$

$= 343\dfrac{1}{7}$

4. $((29)^3)^{-2} = (8a^3)^{-2}$

$= \dfrac{1}{(8a^3)^2}$

$= \dfrac{1}{64a^6}$

5. $\left(x^{\frac{3}{2}}y^2 a^{\frac{5}{4}}\right)^4 = x^{\frac{12}{2}}y^8 a^{\frac{20}{4}}$

$= x^6 y^8 a^5$

6. $\sqrt{a^2 b} \cdot \sqrt{a^3 b^5} = \sqrt{a^5 b^6}$

$= a^{\frac{5}{2}} b^3$

7. 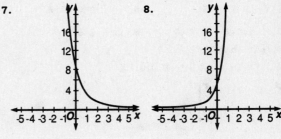 8.

9. $\log_x \sqrt[3]{8} = \dfrac{1}{3}$

$x^{\frac{1}{3}} = 2$

$x = 2^3$

$x = 8$

10. $\log_5 (2x) = \log_5 (3x - 4)$

$2x = 3x - 4$

$4 = x$

11. $\dfrac{1}{2} \log_3 64 - \log_3 x = \log_3 4$

$\log_3 64^{\frac{1}{2}} - \log_3 x = \log_3 4$

$\log_3 8 - \log_3 x = \log_3 4$

$\log_3 \dfrac{8}{x} = \log_3 4$

$\dfrac{8}{x} = 4$

$2 = x$

12.
$$3.6^x = 72.4$$
$$\log 3.6^x = \log 72.4$$
$$x \log 3.6 = \log 72.4$$
$$x = \frac{\log 72.4}{\log 3.6}$$
$$x \approx 3.34$$

13.
$$4^{x + 3} = 25.8$$
$$\log 4^{x + 3} = \log 25.8$$
$$(x + 3) \log 4 = \log 25.8$$
$$x \log 4 = \log 25.8 - 3 \log 4$$
$$x = \frac{\log 25.8 - 3 \log 4}{\log 4}$$
$$x \approx -0.66$$

14.
$$6^{x - 1} = 8^{2 - x}$$
$$\log 6^{x - 1} = \log 8^{2 - x}$$
$$(x - 1) \log 6 = (2 - x) \log 8$$
$$x \log 6 - \log 6 = 2 \log 8 - x \log 8$$
$$x(\log 6 + \log 8) = \log 6 + 2 \log 8$$
$$x = \frac{\log 6 + 2 \log 8}{\log 6 + \log 8}$$
$$x \approx 1.54$$

15. $\frac{e^2}{5} \approx 1.4778$

16. $\frac{1}{2}\sqrt[5]{e^2} \approx 0.7459$

17. $\log 542 \approx 2.7340$

18. $\ln 0.248 \approx -1.3943$

19. antiln $1.1217 \approx 3.0701$

20. antiln $(-1.9101) \approx 0.0123$

21. $A = P\left(1 + \frac{r}{n}\right)^{nt}$
$$= 3000\left(1 + \frac{0.08}{4}\right)^{4.6}$$
$$\approx \$4825.31$$

22. $A = Pe^{rt}$
$$= 6000\, e^{0.12(2)}$$
$$\approx \$7627.49$$

23. $n = 208(1.9)^{-0.11(3)}$
$$\approx 168 \text{ gaps}$$

24.
$$y = ne^{kt}$$
$$3 = e^{6k}$$
$$\ln 3 = \ln e^{6k}$$
$$\ln 3 = 6k \ln e$$
$$\frac{\ln 3}{6} = k$$
$$0.1831 = k$$
$$8 = e^{0.1831t}$$
$$\ln 8 = \ln e^{0.1831t}$$
$$\ln 8 = 0.1831t \ln e$$
$$\frac{\ln 8}{0.1831} = t$$
$$t \approx 11.36 \text{ hr}$$
$$t \approx 11 \text{ hrs } 21 \text{ min}$$

25.
$$4.5 = 10\, e^{-0.3x}$$
$$0.45 = e^{-0.3x}$$
$$\ln 0.45 = \ln e^{-0.3x}$$
$$\ln 0.45 = -0.3x \ln e$$
$$\frac{\ln 0.45}{-0.3} = x$$
$$2.66 \text{ m} \approx x$$

PAGE 649   BONUS

$$\log_2 (\log_3 (\log_a x)) = 1$$
$$\log_3 (\log_a x) = 2$$
$$\log_a x = 3^2$$
$$\log_a x = 9$$
$$x = a^9$$

Unit 3 Review

PAGES 650–651

1.

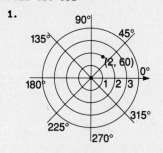

$(r, \theta + 360k°)$
$\rightarrow (2, 60° - 360°) \rightarrow (2, -300°)$
$(-r, \theta + (2k + 1)180°)$
$\rightarrow (-2, 60° + 180°) \rightarrow (-2, 240°)$
$\rightarrow (-2, 60° - 180°) \rightarrow (-2, -120°)$

2.

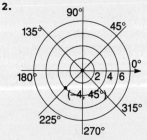

$(r, \theta + 360k°)$
$\rightarrow (-4, 45° - 360°) \rightarrow (-4, -315°)$
$(-r, \theta + (2k + 1)180°)$
$\rightarrow (4, 45° + 180°) \rightarrow (4, 225°)$
$\rightarrow (4, 45° - 180°) \rightarrow (4, -135°)$

3.

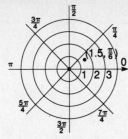

$(r, \theta + 2k\pi)$

$\rightarrow \left(1.5, \dfrac{\pi}{6} - 2\pi\right) \rightarrow \left(1.5, -\dfrac{11\pi}{6}\right)$

$(r, \theta + (2k + 1)\pi)$

$\rightarrow \left(-1.5, \dfrac{\pi}{6} + \pi\right) \rightarrow \left(-1.5, \dfrac{7\pi}{6}\right)$

$\rightarrow \left(-1.5, \dfrac{\pi}{6} - \pi\right) \rightarrow \left(-1.5, -\dfrac{5\pi}{6}\right)$

4.

$(r, \theta + 2k\pi)$

$\rightarrow \left(-2, \dfrac{-2\pi}{3} + 2\pi\right) \rightarrow \left(-2, \dfrac{4\pi}{3}\right)$

$(-r, \theta + (2k + 1)\pi)$

$\rightarrow \left(2, \dfrac{-2\pi}{3} + \pi\right) \rightarrow \left(2, \dfrac{\pi}{3}\right)$

$\rightarrow \left(2, \dfrac{-2\pi}{3} - \pi\right) \rightarrow \left(2, -\dfrac{5\pi}{3}\right)$

5.

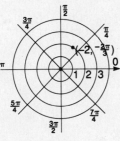

6.

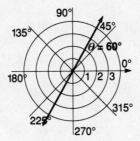

7.

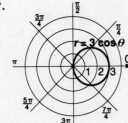

8.

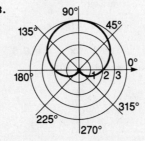

9. $r = \sqrt{(-2)^2 + (-2)^2} = 2\sqrt{2} \approx 2.83$

$\theta = \text{Arctan}\ \dfrac{-2}{-2} + \pi \approx 3.93$

$(2.83,\ 3.93)$

10. $r = \sqrt{2^2 + 2^2} = 2\sqrt{2} \approx 2.83$

$\theta = \text{Arctan}\ \dfrac{2}{2} \approx 0.79$

$(2.83,\ 0.79)$

11. $r = \sqrt{2^2 + (-3)^2} = \sqrt{13} \approx 3.61$

$\theta = \text{Arctan}\ \dfrac{-3}{2} \approx -0.98$

$(3.61,\ -0.98)$

12. $r = \sqrt{(-3)^2 + 1^2} = \sqrt{10} \approx 3.16$

$\theta = \text{Arctan}\ \dfrac{1}{-3} + \pi \approx 2.82$

$(3.16,\ 2.82)$

13. $2 = r \cos\left(\theta - \dfrac{\pi}{2}\right)$

$2 = r\left(\cos\theta \cos\dfrac{\pi}{2} + \sin\theta \sin\dfrac{\pi}{2}\right)$

$2 = r(0 + \sin\theta)$

$2 = r\sin\theta$

$2 = y$

14. $4 = r\cos\left(\theta + \dfrac{\pi}{3}\right)$

$4 = r\left(\cos\theta \cos\dfrac{\pi}{3} - \sin\theta \sin\dfrac{\pi}{3}\right)$

$4 = r\left(\dfrac{1}{2}\cos\theta - \dfrac{\sqrt{3}}{2}\sin\theta\right)$

$4 = \dfrac{1}{2}r\cos\theta - \dfrac{\sqrt{3}}{2}r\sin\theta$

$4 = \dfrac{1}{2}x - \dfrac{\sqrt{3}}{2}y$

$8 = x - \sqrt{3}y$

$0 = x - \sqrt{3}y - 8$

15. $i^{45} = (i^4)^{11} \cdot i = (1)^{11} \cdot i = i$

16. $(3 + 2i) + (3 - 3i) = 6 - i$

17. $i^4(3 + 3i) = (1)(3 + 3i) = 3 + 3i$

18. $(-i - 5)(i - 5) = -i^2 - 5i + 5i + 25$

$= 1 + 25$

$= 26$

19. $\dfrac{2 + i}{2 - 3i} = \dfrac{2 + i}{2 - 3i}\left(\dfrac{2 + 3i}{2 + 3i}\right)$

$= \dfrac{4 + 8i + 3i^2}{4 - 9i^2}$

$= \dfrac{1 + 8i}{13}$

20. $\dfrac{3}{\sqrt{2} - 2i} = \dfrac{3}{\sqrt{2} - 2i}\left(\dfrac{\sqrt{2} + 2i}{\sqrt{2} + 2i}\right)$

$= \dfrac{3\sqrt{2} + 6i}{2 - 4i^2}$

$= \dfrac{3\sqrt{2} + 6i}{6}$

$= \dfrac{\sqrt{2} + 2i}{2}$

21. $r = \sqrt{0^2 + (-3)^2} = 3$

$\theta = \text{Arctan} \frac{-3}{0} + \pi = \frac{3\pi}{2}$

$3\left(\cos \frac{3\pi}{2} + i \sin \frac{3\pi}{2}\right)$

22. $r = \sqrt{3^2 + 3^2} = \sqrt{18} = 3\sqrt{2}$

$\theta = \text{Arctan} \frac{3}{3} = \frac{\pi}{4}$

$3\sqrt{2}\left(\cos \frac{\pi}{4} + i \sin \frac{\pi}{4}\right)$

23. $r = \sqrt{(-1)^2 + 2^2} = \sqrt{5}$

$\theta = \text{Arctan} \frac{2}{-1} + \pi \approx 2.03$

$\sqrt{5}(\cos 2.03 + i \sin 2.03)$

24. $r = \sqrt{4^2 + (-5)^2} = \sqrt{41}$

$\theta = \text{Arctan} \frac{-5}{4} \approx -0.90$

$\sqrt{41}(\cos (-0.9) + i \sin (-0.9))$

25. $r = 2 \cdot 4 = 8$

$\theta = \frac{\pi}{2} + \frac{\pi}{2} = \pi$

$2\left(\cos \frac{\pi}{2} + i \sin \frac{\pi}{2}\right) \cdot 4\left(\cos \frac{\pi}{2} + i \sin \frac{\pi}{2}\right)$

$= 8(\cos \pi + i \sin \pi)$

$= 8(-1 + 0i)$

$= -8$

26. $r = (1.5)(2) = 3$

$\theta = 3.1 + 0.5 = 3.6$

$1.5(\cos 3.1 + i \sin 3.1) \cdot 2(\cos 0.5 + i \sin 0.5)$

$= 3(\cos 3.6 + i \sin 3.6)$

$\approx 3(-0.897 + i(-0.443))$

$\approx -2.69 - 1.33i$

27. $r = \sqrt{1^2 + 1^2} = \sqrt{2}$

$\theta = \text{Arctan} \frac{1}{1} = \frac{\pi}{4}$

$1 + i = \sqrt{2}\left(\cos \frac{\pi}{4} + i \sin \frac{\pi}{4}\right)$

$(1 + i)^7 = \left[\sqrt{2}\left(\cos \frac{\pi}{4} + i \sin \frac{\pi}{4}\right)\right]^7$

$= (\sqrt{2})^7\left[\cos \left(7 \cdot \frac{\pi}{4}\right) + i \sin \left(7 \cdot \frac{\pi}{4}\right)\right]$

$= 8\sqrt{2}\left(\cos \frac{7\pi}{4} + i \sin \frac{7\pi}{4}\right)$

$= 8\sqrt{2}\left(\frac{\sqrt{2}}{2} - \frac{\sqrt{2}}{2}i\right)$

$= 8 - 8i$

28. $x^5 - 1 = 0$

$x^5 = 1$

$1 + 0i = \cos 0 + i \sin 0$

$(1 + 0i)^{\frac{1}{5}} = [\cos (0 + 2n\pi) + i \sin (0 + 2n\pi)]^{\frac{1}{5}}$

$= \cos \frac{2n\pi}{5} + i \sin \frac{2n\pi}{5}$

Let $n = 0$: $x_1 = \cos 0 + i \sin 0 = 1$

Let $n = 1$: $x_2 = \cos \frac{2\pi}{5} + i \sin \frac{2\pi}{5}$

$= 0.31 + 0.95i$

Let $n = 2$: $x_3 = \cos \frac{4\pi}{5} + i \sin \frac{4\pi}{5}$

$= -0.81 + 0.59i$

Let $n = 3$: $x_4 = \cos \frac{6\pi}{5} + i \sin \frac{6\pi}{5}$

$= -0.81 - 0.59i$

Let $n = 4$: $x_5 = \cos \frac{8\pi}{5} + i \sin \frac{8\pi}{5}$

$= 0.31 - 0.95i$

29. $4x^2 + 4y^2 = 49$

$x^2 + y^2 = \frac{49}{4}$

$(0, 0), \frac{7}{2}$

30. $ x^2 + 10x + y^2 + 8y = 20$

$(x^2 + 10x + 25) + (y^2 + 8y + 16) = 20 + 25 + 16$

$(x + 5)^2 + (y + 4)^2 = 61$

$(-5, -4), \sqrt{61}$

31. $x^2 + y^2 + 9x - 8y + 4 = 0$

$\left(x^2 + 9x + \left(\frac{9}{2}\right)^2\right) + (y^2 - 8y + 16)$

$ = 0 + \left(\frac{9}{2}\right)^2 + 16 - 4$

$\left(x + \frac{9}{2}\right)^2 + (y - 4)^2 = \frac{129}{4}$

$\left(-\frac{9}{2}, 4\right), \frac{\sqrt{129}}{2}$

32. $(x - 2)^2 = 2(y - 4)$

vertex: $(2, 4)$

focus: $\left(2, 4 + \frac{2}{4}\right) = (2, 4.5)$

directrix: $y = 3.5$

axis: $x = 2$

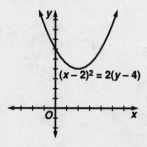

$(x-2)^2 = 2(y-4)$

33. $y^2 + 2y - 5x + 18 = 0$

$(y^2 + 2y + 1) = 5x - 18 + 1$

$(y + 1)^2 = 5(x - 3.4)$

vertex: $(3.4, -1)$

focus: $\left(3.4 + \dfrac{5}{4}, -1\right) = (4.65, -1)$

directrix: $x = 2.15$

axis: $y = -1$

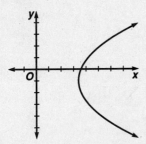

34. $(x - 1)^2 + 2(y - 3)^2 = 25$

$\dfrac{(x - 1)^2}{25} + \dfrac{(y - 3)^2}{\frac{25}{2}} = 1$

center: $(1, 3)$

$c = \sqrt{25 - \dfrac{25}{2}} = \sqrt{\dfrac{25}{2}} = \dfrac{5\sqrt{2}}{2}$

foci: $\left(1 \pm \dfrac{5\sqrt{2}}{2}, 3\right)$

vertices: $(1 \pm 5, 3)$, $\left(1, 3 \pm \dfrac{5\sqrt{2}}{2}\right)$

$= (6, 3), (-4, 3), (1, 6.54), (1, -0.54)$

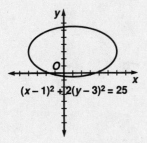

$(x - 1)^2 + 2(y - 3)^2 = 25$

35. $4(x + 2)^2 + 25(y - 2)^2 = 100$

$\dfrac{(x + 2)^2}{25} + \dfrac{(y - 2)^2}{4} = 1$

center: $(-2, 2)$

$c = \sqrt{25 - 4} = \sqrt{21}$

foci: $(-2 \pm \sqrt{21}, 2)$

vertices: $(-2 \pm 5, 2), (-2, 2 \pm 2)$

$= (-7, 2), (3, 2), (-2, 4), (-2, 0)$

$4(x + 2)^2 + 25(y - 2)^2 = 100$

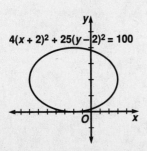

36. $4x^2 - y^2 = 27$

$\dfrac{x^2}{\frac{27}{4}} - \dfrac{y^2}{27} = 1$

center: $(0, 0)$

$c = \sqrt{\dfrac{27}{4} + 27} = \sqrt{\dfrac{135}{4}} = \dfrac{3\sqrt{15}}{2}$

foci: $\left(\pm \dfrac{3\sqrt{15}}{2}, 0\right)$

vertices: $\left(0 \pm \sqrt{\dfrac{27}{4}}, 0\right) = \left(\pm \dfrac{3\sqrt{3}}{2}, 0\right)$

asymptotes: $y = \pm 2x$

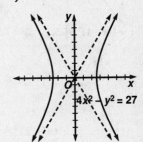

$4x^2 - y^2 = 27$

37. $\dfrac{(x + 1)^2}{4} - \dfrac{(y + 3)^2}{9} = 1$

center: $(-1, -3)$

$c = \sqrt{4 + 9} = \sqrt{13}$

foci: $(-1, -3 \pm \sqrt{13})$

vertices: $(-1, -3 \pm 3) = (-1, 0), (-1, -6)$

asymptotes:

$y + 3 = \pm \dfrac{4}{9}(x + 1)$

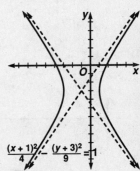

$\dfrac{(x + 1)^2}{4} - \dfrac{(y + 3)^2}{9} = 1$

38. parabola

$12y - 3x + 2x^2 + 1 = 0$

$2x^2 - 3x = -12y - 1$

$x^2 - \dfrac{3}{2}x = -6y - \dfrac{1}{2}$

$\left(x^2 - \dfrac{3}{2}x + \left(\dfrac{3}{4}\right)^2\right) = -6y - \dfrac{1}{2} + \left(\dfrac{3}{4}\right)^2$

$\left(x - \dfrac{3}{4}\right)^2 = -6y + \dfrac{1}{16}$

$\left(x - \dfrac{3}{4}\right)^2 = -6\left(y - \dfrac{1}{96}\right)$

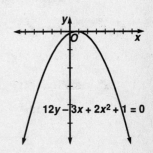

$12y - 3x + 2x^2 + 1 = 0$

39. hyperbola

$$4(x - 1)^2 = 25(y + 3)^2 + 100$$

$$4(x - 1)^2 - 25(y + 3)^2 = 100$$

$$\frac{(x - 1)^2}{25} - \frac{(y + 3)^2}{4} = 1$$

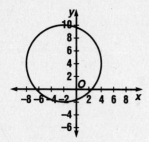

$4(x-1)^2 = 25(y+3)^2 + 100$

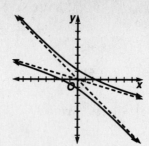

40. circle

$$x^2 + 4x + y^2 - 12y + 4 = 0$$

$$(x^2 + 4x + 4) + (y^2 - 12y + 36) = -4 + 4 + 36$$

$$(x + 2)^2 + (y - 6)^2 = 36$$

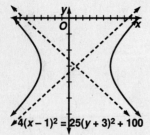

43.

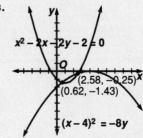

$x^2 - 2x - 2y - 2 = 0$

$(2.58, -0.25)$
$(0.62, -1.43)$

$(x - 4)^2 = -8y$

$x^2 - 2x - 2y - 2 = 0 \rightarrow 4x^2 - 8x - 8y - 8 = 0$

$(x - 4)^2 = -8y \qquad \rightarrow \underline{\quad x^2 - 8x + 8y + 16 = 0 \quad}$

$$5x^2 - 16x + 8 = 0$$

$$x = \frac{16 \pm \sqrt{(-16)^2 - 4(5)(8)}}{2(5)}$$

$$x = \frac{16 \pm \sqrt{96}}{10}$$

$$x \approx 0.62 \text{ or } 2.58$$

$$y \approx -1.43 \text{ or } -0.25$$

$$(0.62, -1.43), (2.58, -0.25)$$

41. $x - 1 = 3(y + 7)^2 + 1$

$x - 2 = 3(y + 7)^2$

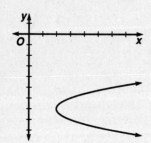

44.

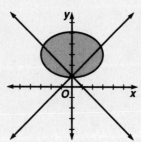

45. $m = -\dfrac{(x - h)}{(y - k)} = -\dfrac{(2 - 1)}{(-1 + 2)} = -1$

tangent: $y - (-1) = -1(x - 2)$

$y + 1 = -x + 2$

$y = -x + 1$

normal: $y - (-1) = 1(x - 2)$

$y + 1 = x - 2$

$y = x - 3$

42.

$$x^2 - \frac{y^2}{16} = 1$$

$$16x^2 - y^2 = 16$$

$$16\left(x \cos \frac{\pi}{3} + y \sin \frac{\pi}{3}\right)^2 - \left(-x \sin \frac{\pi}{3} + y \cos \frac{\pi}{3}\right)^2 = 16$$

$$16\left(\frac{1}{2}x + \frac{\sqrt{3}}{2}y\right)^2 - \left(-\frac{\sqrt{3}}{2}x + \frac{1}{2}y\right)^2 = 16$$

$$16\left(\frac{1}{4}x^2 + \frac{\sqrt{3}}{2}xy + \frac{3}{4}y^2\right) - \left(\frac{3}{4}x^2 - \frac{\sqrt{3}}{2}xy + \frac{1}{4}y^2\right) = 16$$

$$4x^2 + 8\sqrt{3}xy + 12y^2 - \frac{3}{4}x^2 + \frac{\sqrt{3}}{2}xy - \frac{1}{4}y^2 = 16$$

$$16x^2 + 32\sqrt{3}xy + 48y^2 - 3x^2 + 2\sqrt{3}xy - y^2 = 64$$

$$13x^2 + 34\sqrt{3}xy + 47y^2 - 64 = 0$$

46. $m = \dfrac{2p}{y - k} = \dfrac{2\left(\frac{1}{2}\right)}{0 - 4} = -\dfrac{1}{4}$

tangent: $y - 0 = -\dfrac{1}{4}(x - 5)$

$y = -\dfrac{1}{4}x + \dfrac{5}{4}$

normal: $y - 0 = 4(x - 5)$

$y = 4x - 20$

47. $m = \dfrac{a^2(x - h)}{b^2(y - k)} = \dfrac{25(2 - 2)}{16(8 - 3)} = 0$

tangent: $y - 8 = 0(x - 2)$

$\qquad\qquad y = 8$

normal: $x = 2$

48. $\sqrt{16x^2y^7} = (16x^2y^7)^{\frac{1}{2}}$

$\qquad\qquad = 16^{\frac{1}{2}}x^{\frac{2}{2}}y^{\frac{7}{2}}$

$\qquad\qquad = 4|x|y^3\sqrt{y}$

49. $\sqrt[3]{54a^4b^3c^8} = (54a^4b^3c^8)^{\frac{1}{3}}$

$\qquad\qquad = 54^{\frac{1}{3}}a^{\frac{4}{3}}b^{\frac{3}{3}}c^{\frac{8}{3}}$

$\qquad\qquad = (3^3 \cdot 2)^{\frac{1}{3}}a^{\frac{3}{3}}a^{\frac{1}{3}}b^{\frac{3}{3}}c^{\frac{6}{3}}c^{\frac{2}{3}}$

$\qquad\qquad = 3abc^2\sqrt[3]{2ac^2}$

50. $(3^2c^3d^5)^{\frac{1}{5}} = 3^{\frac{2}{5}}c^{\frac{3}{5}}d^{\frac{5}{5}}$

$\qquad\qquad = d\sqrt[5]{3^2c^3}$

$\qquad\qquad = d\sqrt[5]{9c^3}$

51. $(3x)^2(3x^2)^{-2} = (3^2x^2)(3^{-2}x^{-4})$

$\qquad\qquad = (3^{2-2})(x^{2-4})$

$\qquad\qquad = 1x^{-2}$

$\qquad\qquad = \dfrac{1}{x^2}$

52.   53.

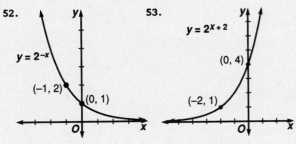

$y = 2^{-x}$

$(-1, 2)$

$(0, 1)$

$y = 2^{x+2}$

$(0, 4)$

$(-2, 1)$

54. $e^{2.3} \approx 9.9742$

55. $\sqrt[3]{8e} \approx 2.7912$

56. $\dfrac{e^3}{4} \approx 5.0214$

57. $e^{-4.7} \approx 0.0091$

58. $\log_x 36 = 2$

$\quad x^2 = 36$

$\quad x = 6$

59. $\log_2 (2x) = \log_2 27$

$\quad 2x = 27$

$\quad x = \dfrac{27}{2}$

60. $\log_5 x = \dfrac{1}{3} \log_5 64 + 2 \log_5 3$

$\qquad = \log_5 \left(64^{\frac{1}{3}}\right) + \log_5 (3^2)$

$\qquad = \log_5 4 + \log_5 9$

$\qquad = \log_5 (4 \cdot 9)$

$\qquad = \log_5 36$

$\quad x = 36$

61. $\log \left[(4.32)^2 \times (8.13)^3\right]$

$= 2 \log 4.32 + 3 \log 8.13$

≈ 4.00123913

antilog $4.00123913 \approx 10{,}028.573$

62. $\log \left[(6.1)^3(10.3)\right]^{\frac{1}{2}} = \dfrac{1}{2}(3 \log 6.1 + \log 10.3)$

$\qquad\qquad\qquad \approx 1.684413365$

antilog $1.684413365 \approx 48.352$

63. $\log \left(\dfrac{5.4\sqrt{7.8}}{(1.4)^3}\right) = \log 5.4 + \dfrac{1}{2} \log 7.8 - 3 \log 1.4$

$\qquad\qquad\qquad \approx 0.740056954$

antilog $0.740056954 \approx 5.496$

64. $\qquad 2.3^x = 23.4$

$\log (2.3^x) = \log 23.4$

$x \log 2.3 = \log 23.4$

$\qquad x = \dfrac{\log 23.4}{\log 2.3}$

$\qquad\quad \approx 3.79$

65. $x = \log_4 16$

$\quad = \dfrac{\log 16}{\log 4}$

$\quad = 2$

66. $\qquad 5^{x - 2} = 2^x$

$\log (5^{x - 2}) = \log (2^x)$

$(x - 2) \log 5 = x \log 2$

$x \log 5 - 2 \log 5 = x \log 2$

$x \log 5 - x \log 2 = 2 \log 5$

$x(\log 5 - \log 2) = 2 \log 5$

$\qquad\qquad x = \dfrac{2 \log 5}{\log 5 - \log 2}$

$\qquad\qquad x \approx 3.51$

67. $\quad 46 = e^x$

$\ln 46 = \ln (e^x)$

$\ln 46 = x \ln e$

$\ln 46 = x$

$\quad 3.83 \approx x$

68. $\quad 18 = e^{4k}$

$\ln 18 = \ln (e^{4k})$

$\ln 18 = 4k \ln e$

$\ln 18 = 4k$

$\dfrac{\ln 18}{4} = k$

$0.72 \approx k$

69. $\quad 519 = 3e^{0.035t}$

$\quad 173 = e^{0.035t}$

$\ln 173 = 0.035t \ln e$

$\ln 173 = 0.035t$

$\dfrac{\ln 173}{0.035} = t$

$147.24 \approx t$

Unit 4   Discrete Mathematics

Chapter 12   Sequences and Series

<table>
<tr><td>

| **12-1** | **Arithmetic Sequences and Series** |

1. a. $S_n = \frac{n}{2}[2a_1 + (n-1)d]$

   b. $S_n = \frac{14}{2}[2(3) + (14-1)3]$

   $= 7(6 + 39)$

   $= 7(45)$

   $= 315$

   c. a linear function

2. negative

3. n equals 7 because there are five arithmetic means, a first term, and a last term. Therefore, there are $1 + 5 + 1$ or 7 terms in the sequence.

4. a. yes

   b. The number of weeks cannot be negative.

5. $d = 9 - 5 = 4$

   $13 + 4 = 17$, $17 + 4 = 21$, $21 + 4 = 25$,

   $25 + 4 = 29$, $29 + 4 = 33$

   17, 21, 25, 29, 33

6. $d = -2 - (-9) = 7$

   $5 + 7 = 12$, $12 + 7 = 19$, $19 + 7 = 26$,

   $26 + 7 = 33$, $33 + 7 = 40$

   12, 19, 26, 33, 40

7. $d = -1 - 5 = -6$

   $-7 + (-6) = -13$, $-13 - 6 = -19$, $-19 - 6 = -25$,

   $-25 - 6 = -31$, $-31 - 6 = -37$

   $-13, -19, -25, -31, -37$

8. $d = 7 - 0 = 7$

   $14 + 7 = 21$, $21 + 7 = 28$, $28 + 7 = 35$,

   $35 + 7 = 42$, $42 + 7 = 49$

   21, 28, 35, 42, 49

9. $d = 3 - 1.5 = 1.5$

   $4.5 + 1.5 = 6$, $6 + 1.5 = 7.5$, $7.5 + 1.5 = 9$,

   $9 + 1.5 = 10.5$, $10.5 + 1.5 = 12$

   6, 7.5, 9, 10.5, 12

10. $d = a + 3 - a = 3$

   $a + 6 + 3 = a + 9$, $a + 9 + 3 = a + 12$,

   $a + 12 + 3 = a + 15$, $a + 15 + 3 = a + 18$,

   $a + 18 + 3 = a + 21$

   $a + 9$, $a + 12$, $a + 15$, $a + 18$, $a + 21$

11. $d = 0 - (-n) = n$

   $n + n = 2n$, $2n + n = 3n$, $3n + n = 4n$,

   $4n + n = 5n$, $5n + n = 6n$

   $2n, 3n, 4n, 5n, 6n$

</td><td>

12. $d = 2x - x = x$

   $3x + x = 4x$, $4x + x = 5x$, $5x + x = 6x$,

   $6x + x = 7x$, $7x + x = 8x$

   $4x$, $5x$, $6x$, $7x$, $8x$

13. $d = -b - b = -2b$

   $-3b - 2b = -5b$, $-5b - 2b = -7b$, $-7b - 2b = -9b$,

   $-9b - 2b = -11b$, $-11b - 2b = -13b$

   $-5b, -7b, -9b, -11b, -13b$

14. $d = -k - 5k = -6k$

   $-k - 6k = -7k$, $-7k - 6k = -13k$,

   $-13k - 6k = -19k$, $-19k - 6k = -25k$,

   $-25k - 6k = -31k$

   $-7k, -13k, -19k, -25k, -31k$

15. $a_n = a_1 + (n-1)d$

   $a_{79} = -7 + (79 - 1)(3)$

   $= -7 + 234$

   $= 227$

16. $a_n = a_1 + (n-1)d$

   $38 = a_1 + (15 - 1)(-3)$

   $38 = a_1 + (-42)$

   $80 = a_1$

17. $a_n = a_1 + (n-1)d$

   $21 = 12 + (3 - 1)d$

   $21 = 12 + 2d$

   $9 = 2d$

   $4.5 = d$

   $12 + 4.5 = 16.5$

   12, 16.5, 21

18. $s_n = \frac{n}{2}[2a_1 + (n-1)d]$

   $= \frac{63}{2}[2(-19) + (63 - 1)6]$

   $= 31.5[-38 + 372]$

   $= 31.5[334]$

   $= 10{,}521$

19. $a_n = a_1 + (n-1)d$

   $a_{19} = 11 + (19 - 1)(-2)$

   $= 11 + (-36)$

   $= -25$

</td></tr>
</table>

20. $a_n = a_1 \ (n - 1)d$

$a_{16} = 1.5 + (16 - 1)0.5$

$\quad\quad = 1.5 + 7.5$

$\quad\quad = 9$

21. $a_n = a_1 + (n - 1)d$

$37 = (-13) + (n - 1)5$

$37 = -13 + 5n - 5$

$55 = 5n$

$11 = n$

22. $633 = 9 + (n - 1)24$

$633 = 9 + 24n - 24$

$648 = 24n$

$27 = n$

23. $a_7 = a_1 + (7 - 1)(-2)$

$3 = a_1 + (-12)$

$15 = a_1$

24. $a_8 = a_1 + (8 - 1)\left(\dfrac{2}{3}\right)$

$15 = a_1 + \dfrac{14}{3}$

$\dfrac{31}{3} = a_1$

$10\dfrac{1}{3} = a_1$

25. $64 = 4 + (11 - 1)d$

$64 = 4 + 10d$

$60 = 10d$

$6 = d$

26. $20 = -6 + (29 - 1)d$

$20 = -6 + 28d$

$26 = 28d$

$\dfrac{13}{14} = d$

27. $d = -1 - (-2 + \sqrt{3}) = 1 - \sqrt{3}$

$a_6 = (-2 + \sqrt{3}) + (6 - 1)(1 - \sqrt{3})$

$\quad\quad = -2 + \sqrt{3} + 5 - 5\sqrt{3}$

$\quad\quad = 3 - 4\sqrt{3}$

28. $d = 2 - i - (1 + i) = 1 - 2i$

$a_7 = (1 + i) + (7 - 1)(1 - 2i)$

$\quad\quad = 1 + i + 6 - 12i$

$\quad\quad = 7 - 11i$

29. $d = (-15) - (-19) = 4$

$a_{43} = (-19) + (43 - 1)4$

$\quad\quad = (-19) + 168$

$\quad\quad = 149$

30. $d = 4 - 10 = -6$

$a_{58} = 10 + (58 - 1)(-6)$

$\quad\quad = 10 + (-342)$

$\quad\quad = -332$

31. $a_n = a_1 + (n - 1)d$

$48 = 36 + (3 - 1)d$

$12 = 2d$

$6 = d$

$36 + 6 = 42$

$36, \ 42, \ 48$

32. $5 = (-4) + (4 - 1)d$

$9 = 3d$

$3 = d$

$(-4) + 3 = (-1)$

$(-1) + 3 = 2$

$-4, \ -1, \ 2, \ 5$

33. $10 = \sqrt{2} + (4 - 1)d$

$10 - \sqrt{2} = 3d$

$\dfrac{10 - \sqrt{2}}{6} = d$

$\sqrt{2} + \dfrac{10 - \sqrt{2}}{3} = \dfrac{3\sqrt{2} + 10 - \sqrt{2}}{3} = \dfrac{10 + 2\sqrt{2}}{3}$

$\dfrac{10 + 2\sqrt{2}}{3} + \dfrac{10 - \sqrt{2}}{3} = \dfrac{20 + \sqrt{2}}{3}$

$\sqrt{2}, \ \dfrac{10 + 2\sqrt{2}}{3}, \ \dfrac{20 + \sqrt{2}}{3}, \ 10$

34. $4 = 1 + (5 - 1)d$

$3 = 4d$

$\dfrac{3}{4} = d$

$1 + \dfrac{3}{4} = 1.75$

$1.75 + 0.75 = 2.5$

$2.5 + 0.75 = 3.25$

$1, \ 1.75, \ 2.5, \ 3.25, \ 4$

35. $S_n = \dfrac{n}{2}(2a_1 + (n - 1)d)$

$S_{11} = \dfrac{11}{2}[2(-3) + (11 - 1)2]$

$\quad\quad = \dfrac{11}{2}(14)$

$\quad\quad = 77$

36. $S_{32} = \dfrac{32}{2}[2(0.5) + (32 - 1)(0.25)]$

$\quad\quad = 16[8.75]$

$\quad\quad = 140$

37. $S_n = \dfrac{n}{2}[2a_1 + (n - 1)d]$

$-14 = \dfrac{n}{2}[2(-7) + (n - 1)(1.5)]$

$-28 = -14n + 1.5n^2 - 1.5n$

$0 = 1.5n^2 - 15.5n + 28$

$0 = (3n - 7)(0.5n - 4)$

$3n = 7$ or $0.5n = 4$

$n = \dfrac{7}{3} \quad\quad\quad n = 8$

Since n must be a positive integer, $n = 8$.

38. $440 = \dfrac{n}{2}[2(5) + (n - 1)3]$

$880 = 10n + 3n^2 - 3n$

$0 = 3n^2 + 7n - 880$

$0 = (3n + 55)(n - 16)$

$3n = -55$ or $n = 16$

$n = -18\dfrac{1}{3}$

Since n must be a positive integer, $n = 16$.

39. $a_1 = 129, \ a_n = 159$

$\dfrac{n}{2}(129 + 159) = 180(n - 2)$

$\dfrac{n}{2}(288) = 180(n - 2)$

$144n = 180n - 360$

$-36n = -360$

$n = 10$

40. $S_n = a_1 + a_2 + (a_{3-1} - a_{3-2})$

$\qquad + (a_{4-1} - a_{4-2}) + (a_{5-1} - a_{5-2}) + \ldots$

$\qquad = a_1 + a_2 + a_2 - a_1 + a_3 - a_2 + a_4$

$\qquad \quad - a_3 + \ldots$

$\qquad = a_1 + a_2 + a_2 - a_1 + (a_2 - a_1) - a_2 + a_3$

$\qquad \quad - a_2 - a_3 + \ldots$

$\qquad = 0$

Each term can be reduced to a_1, a_2.

41. $S_n = a_1 + a_2 + \ldots + a_n$

$\qquad = 1 + 2 + 3 + 4 + 5 + \ldots + 21$

$\qquad = \dfrac{n(a_1 + a_2)}{2}$

$\qquad = \dfrac{21(7 + 21)}{2}$

$\qquad = 231$ cans

42. positive: $\qquad\qquad$ negative:

$S_n = \dfrac{n}{2}(a_1 + a_n) \qquad S_n = \dfrac{n}{2}(a_1 + a_n)$

$\quad = \dfrac{100}{2}(2 + 200) \qquad = \dfrac{100}{2}(1 + 199)$

$\quad = 10{,}100 \qquad\qquad\quad = 10{,}000$

Sums are not the same. They differ by 100.
Each of the first 100 even integers is 1
greater than each of the first 100 odd integers.

43. a. $a_n = 31$

$\quad$ **b.** $S_n = \dfrac{31}{2}[2(1) + (31 - 1)1]$

$\qquad\qquad = \dfrac{31}{2}(32)$

$\qquad\qquad = 496$

44. $d = 5$, $S_n = 650$, $a_1 = 20$

$\qquad S_n = \dfrac{n}{2}[2a_1 + (n - 1)d]$

$\qquad 650 = \dfrac{n}{2}[40 + (n - 1)5]$

$\qquad 1300 = n(40 + 5n - 5)$

$\qquad 0 = 35n + 5n^2 - 1300$

$\qquad 0 = n^2 + 7n - 260$

$\qquad\quad = (n - 20)(n - 13)$

$\qquad n = -20,\ n = 13$

13 weeks

45. $[f \circ g](4) = f(4 - 2)$

$\qquad\qquad\quad = f(2)$

$\qquad\qquad\quad = 2^2 - 4 \cdot 2 + 5$

$\qquad\qquad\quad = 1$

$\quad [g \circ f](4) = g[4^2 - 4(4) + 5]$

$\qquad\qquad\quad = g(5)$

$\qquad\qquad\quad = 5 - 2$

$\qquad\qquad\quad = 3$

46. $a \leq 10$, $b \leq 9$

$\qquad 3a + 5b \leq 55$

$\qquad a + 5b \leq 45$

Possible solutions: (0, 9), (5, 8), (10, 5),
(10, 0), (0, 0)

$P(a, b) = 320a + 500b$

$P(0, 9) = 4500$

$P(5, 8) = 5600$

$P(10, 5) = 5700 \leftarrow$ maximum

$P(10, 0) = 3200$

$P(0, 0) = 0$

10 cases of A, 5 cases of B

47. $r = \dfrac{1}{2}d = 3.65$

$\qquad \dfrac{360°}{5} = 72°, \dfrac{72°}{2} = 36°$

$\qquad \sin 54° = \dfrac{a}{3.65}$

$\qquad\quad a = 3.65 \sin 54°$

$\qquad \cos 54° = \dfrac{b}{3.65}$

$\qquad\quad b = 3.65 \cos 54°$

$\qquad\quad 2b = 7.3 \cos 54°$

$\quad A = \dfrac{1}{2}Pa$

$\quad A = \dfrac{1}{2}(5 \times 7.3 \cos 54°)(3.65 \sin 54°)$

$\quad A \approx 31.68$ cm^2

48. $\dfrac{\tan^2 \theta - \sin^2 \theta}{\tan^2 \theta \sin^2 \theta} = \dfrac{\dfrac{\sin^2 \theta - \sin^2 \theta \cos^2 \theta}{\cos^2 \theta}}{\dfrac{\sin^4 \theta}{\cos^2 \theta}}$

$\qquad\qquad\qquad = \dfrac{\sin^2 \theta (1 - \cos^2 \theta)}{\sin^4 \theta}$

$\qquad\qquad\qquad = \dfrac{\sin^2 \theta (\sin \theta)}{\sin^4 \theta}$

$\qquad\qquad\quad = 1$

49. $(2 + i)(3 - 4i)(1 + 2i) = (6 - 8i + 3i - 4i^2) \cdot$

$\qquad\qquad\qquad\qquad\qquad (1 + 2i)$

$\qquad\qquad\qquad = (10 - 5i)(1 + 2i)$

$\qquad\qquad\qquad = 10 + 20i - 5i - 10i^2$

$\qquad\qquad\qquad = 20 + 15i$

50. $\quad 45.9 = e^{0.075t}$

$\qquad \ln 45.9 = 0.075t \ln e$

$\qquad \dfrac{\ln 45.9}{0.075} = t$

$\qquad\quad 51.02 \approx t$

51. $\dfrac{x}{y} > 1$

$\qquad x > y$

So, $\dfrac{y}{x} < 1$.

The best answer is D.

Case Study Follow-Up

PAGE 662

1. Monthly income = $\frac{70,000}{12}$ = 5833.33

   $(0.28)5833.3 = 1633.33$

   Yes, 28% of their gross monthly income is $1633.33, which is greater than the monthly payment of $1622.82.

2. $a_1 = \$1622.82$

   $d = 0$

   number of terms = $15 \times 12 = 180$

   $S = \frac{180}{2}(1622.82 + 1622.82)$

   $S = \$292,107.60$

3. See students' work.

12-2 Geometric Sequences and Series

PAGES 667-668   CHECKING FOR UNDERSTANDING

1. If the common ratio were equal to 1, the sequence would be of the form $x, x, x, \ldots$, which would be a sequence of the same number. A common ratio of 0 is impossible.

2. If the first term in a geometric sequence were zero, then finding the common ratio would mean dividing by zero. Division by zero is undefined.

3. Arithmetic and geometric sequences are recursive because if you know the previous terms, you can find the next term.

4. a.

Beginning of Month	1	2	3	4	5
Height	3	3.21	3.43	3.68	3.93

6	7	8	9
4.21	4.50	4.82	5.15

b. an exponential function

5. $S_n = \frac{a_1 - a_1 r^n}{1 - r}$

   $F_n = \frac{P - Pr^n}{1 - r}$ Substitute the principal P for a_1 and the future value F_n for S_n.

   $F_n = \frac{Pr^n - P}{r - 1}$ Factor out -1.

   $F_n = \frac{P(r^n - 1)}{r - 1}$ Factor out P.

   $F_n = \frac{P[(1 + i)^n - 1]}{(1 + i) - 1}$ Substitute $1 + i$ for r.

   $F_n = P\frac{(1 + i)^n - 1}{i}$ Simplify.

6. $r = \frac{3}{2}$

   $3 \cdot \frac{3}{2} = \frac{9}{2}, \frac{9}{2} \cdot \frac{3}{2} = \frac{27}{4}, \frac{27}{4} \cdot \frac{3}{2} = \frac{81}{8}, \frac{81}{8} \cdot \frac{3}{2} = \frac{243}{16}$

   $\frac{9}{2}, \frac{27}{4}, \frac{81}{8}, \frac{243}{16}$

7. $r = \frac{3.5}{7} = \frac{1}{2}$

   $3.5(0.5) = 1.75, 1.75(0.5) = 0.875,$

   $0.875(0.5) = 0.4375, 0.4375(0.5) = 0.21875$

   $1.75, 0.875, 0.4375, 0.21875$

8. $r = \frac{3.6}{1.2} = 3$

   $3.6(3) = 10.8, 10.8(3) = 32.4, 32.4(3) = 97.2,$

   $97.2(3) = 291.6$

   $10.8, 32.4, 97.2, 291.6$

9. $r = \frac{2}{\sqrt{2}}$

   $2\left(\frac{2}{\sqrt{2}}\right) = \frac{4}{\sqrt{2}}$

   $= \frac{4\sqrt{2}}{2}$

   $= 2\sqrt{2}$

   $= \sqrt{8}$

   yes

10. $r = \frac{3}{\sqrt[3]{3^2}}$

    $3\left(\frac{3}{\sqrt[3]{3^2}}\right) = \frac{9}{\sqrt[3]{3^2}}$

    $= \frac{9\sqrt[3]{3}}{3}$

    $= \sqrt[3]{3}$

    yes

11. $r = \frac{t^{-1}}{t^{-2}}$

    $= \frac{t^2}{t}$

    $= t$

    $t^{-1}(t) = \frac{1}{t} \cdot t$

    $= 1$

    yes

12. $a_n = a_1 r^{n-1}$

    $a_9 = \left(\frac{1}{2}\right)\left(\frac{2}{3}\right)^{9-1}$

    $= \left(\frac{1}{2}\right)\left(\frac{256}{6561}\right)$

    $= \frac{128}{6561}$

13. $a_n = a_1 r^{n-1}$

    $24 = a_1(2)^4$

    $24 = 16a_1$

    $\frac{3}{2} = a_1$

14. $a_n = a_1 r^{n-1}$

    $a_4 = a_1 r^3$

    $54 = (-2)r^3$

    $-27 = r^3$

    $-3 = r$

    $(-2)(-3) = 6$

    $6(-3) = -18$

    $-2, 6, -18, 54$

15. $S_n = \frac{a_1 - a_1 r^n}{1 - r}, r = \frac{5}{\frac{5}{3}} = 3$

    $S_5 = \frac{\frac{5}{3} - \frac{5}{3}r^5}{1 - r}$

    $= \frac{\frac{5}{3} - \frac{5}{3}(3)^5}{1 - 3}$

    $= \frac{\frac{-1210}{3}}{-2}$

    $= \frac{605}{3} \quad = 201\frac{2}{3}$

16. $-3\left(\dfrac{2}{3}\right) = (-2)$, $(-2)\left(\dfrac{2}{3}\right) = -\dfrac{4}{3}$, $-\dfrac{4}{3}\left(\dfrac{2}{3}\right) = -\dfrac{8}{9}$,

$-\dfrac{8}{9}\left(\dfrac{2}{3}\right) = -\dfrac{16}{27}$

$-2, -\dfrac{4}{3}, -\dfrac{8}{9}, -\dfrac{16}{27}$

17. $8\left(\dfrac{3}{2}\right) = 12$, $12\left(\dfrac{3}{2}\right) = 18$, $18\left(\dfrac{3}{2}\right) = 27$

12, 18, 27

18. $r = \dfrac{2}{\sqrt{2}} = \sqrt{2}$

$a_9 = a_1 r^{9-1}$

$= \sqrt{2}(\sqrt{2})^8$

$= 16\sqrt{2}$

19. $r = \dfrac{0.1}{10} = 0.01$

$a_6 = a_1 r^{6-1}$

$= 10(0.01)^5$

$= 10^{-9}$

20. $a_5 = a_1 r^{5-1}$

$32\sqrt{2} = a_1(-\sqrt{2})^4$

$8\sqrt{2} = a_1$

$8\sqrt{2}(-\sqrt{2}) = -16$, $-16(-\sqrt{2}) = 16\sqrt{2}$,

$16\sqrt{2}(-\sqrt{2}) = -32$

$8\sqrt{2}, -16, 16\sqrt{2}, -32$

21. $a_4 = a_1 r^{4-1}$

$2.5 = a_1(2)^3$

$\dfrac{2.5}{8} = a_1$

$0.3125 = a_1$

$0.3125(2) = 0.625$, $0.625(2) = 1.25$

$0.3125, 0.625, 1.25$

22. $a_3 = a_1 r^{3-1}$

$4 = \dfrac{1}{4}r^2$

$16 = r^2$

$\pm 4 = r$

$\left(\dfrac{1}{4}\right)(\pm 4) = \pm 1$

$\dfrac{1}{4}, \pm 1, 4$

23. $a_4 = a_1 r^{4-1}$

$27 = 1r^3$

$27 = r^3$

$3 = r$

$1(3) = 3$, $3(3) = 9$

1, 3, 9, 27

24. $r = \dfrac{\frac{1}{4}}{\frac{1}{2}} = \dfrac{1}{2}$

$S_7 = \dfrac{(0.5) - (0.5)(0.5)}{1 - (0.5)}$

$= 2\left(\dfrac{1}{2} - \dfrac{1}{256}\right)$

$= 2\left(\dfrac{127}{256}\right)$

$= \dfrac{127}{128}$

25. $r = \dfrac{3}{2} = 1.5$

$S_6 = \dfrac{2 - 2(1.5)^6}{1 - 1.5}$

$= 41.5625$

26. $r = \dfrac{1}{0.5} = 2$

$S_9 = \dfrac{0.5 - (0.5)2^9}{1 - 2}$

$= \dfrac{0.5 - 256}{-1}$

$= 255.5$

27. $r = \dfrac{\sqrt{2}}{1} = \sqrt{2}$

$S_{10} = \dfrac{1 - 1(\sqrt{2})^{10}}{1 - \sqrt{2}}$

$= \dfrac{-31(1 + \sqrt{2})}{(1 - \sqrt{2})(1 + \sqrt{2})}$

$= 31(1 + \sqrt{2})$

28. The sum of the first six terms is

$\dfrac{a(r^6 - 1)}{r - 1} = 252$.

$\dfrac{a(r^6 - 1)}{(r - 1)a(r + 1)} = \dfrac{252}{12}$

$\dfrac{(r^2 - 1)(r^4 + r^2 + 1)}{(r^2 - 1)} = 21$

$r^4 + r^2 - 20 = 0$

$(r^2 - 4)(r^2 + 5) = 0$

$r^2 = 4$ or $r^2 = -5$

Reject $r^2 = -5$ since r cannot be a complex number. Therefore, the sum of the first four terms is:

$a + ar + ar^2 + ar^3 = (a + ar)(1 + r^2)$

$= (12)(1 + 4)$

$= 60$

The sum of the first four terms is 60.

29. $r = 1.14$, $a_1 = 180{,}000$

$a_{10} = a_1 r^9 = 180{,}000(1.14)^9 \approx \$585{,}350.73$

$a_{20} = 180{,}000(1.14)^{19} \approx \$2{,}170{,}024.72$

$a_{30} = 180{,}000(1.14)^{29} \approx \$8{,}044{,}761.88$

$a_{40} = 180{,}000(1.14)^{39} \approx \$29{,}823{,}712.71$

$a_{50} = 180{,}000(1.14)^{49} \approx \$110{,}563{,}103.40$

30. $r = 1 - 0.18 = 0.82$

$a_1 = 13{,}500$

$a_5 = a_1 r^4 = 13{,}500(0.82)^4 \approx \$6103.64$

31. $r = 2$ per half hour

$a_1 = 150$

12 hours = 24 half hours

$a_{24} = a_1 r^{23} = 150(2)^{23} \approx 1.258 \times 10^9$

$a_{48} = a_1 r^{47} = 150(2)^{47} \approx 2.111 \times 10^{16}$

32. $r = 1.095, a_1 = 5000$

$$S_n = \frac{a_1 - a_1 r^n}{1 - r}$$

$$= \frac{5000 - 5000(1.095)^{20}}{1 - 1.095}$$

$$\approx \$270,611.16$$

33. a. third pile: $(0.010) + (0.010) = 0.02$ cm

fourth pile: 8 pieces = $4(0.010) = 0.04$ cm

b. Each piece is $\frac{0.01}{2}$ cm high or 0.005 cm.

The pile doubles each time, so the formula is $0.005(2)^{n-1}$.

c. 10th pile: $0.005(2)^9 = 2.56$ cm

100th pile: $0.005(2)^{99} \approx 3.169 \times 10^{27}$ cm

34. $d_1 = \sqrt{(5 - 11)^2 + (9 - 4)^2}$

$$= \sqrt{36 + 25} \approx 7.8 \text{ units}$$

$$d_2 = \sqrt{(14 - 2)^2 + (9 - 4)^2}$$

$$= \sqrt{144 + 25} = 13 \text{ units}$$

35.

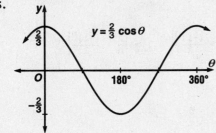

36. $25 + 5D + F = 0 \quad \rightarrow \quad 5D + F = -25$

$1 + 4 + D - 2E + F = 0 \quad \rightarrow \quad D - 2E + F = -5$

$16 + 9 + 4D - 3E + F = 0 \quad \rightarrow \quad 4D - 3E + F = -25$

$$\begin{array}{l} 3D - 6E + 3F = -15 \\ \underline{-8D + 6E - 2F = 50} \\ -5D + F = 35 \end{array} \qquad \begin{array}{l} 5D + 35 + 5D = -25 \\ 10D = -60 \\ D = -6 \end{array}$$

$$F = 35 + 5D$$

$$5(-6) + F = -25$$

$$F = 5$$

$$-6 - 2E + 5 = -5$$

$$E = 2$$

$$x^2 + y^2 - 6x + 2y + 5 = 0$$

$$(x^2 - 6x + 9) + (y^2 + 2y + 1) = -5 + 9 + 1$$

$$(x - 3)^2 + (y + 1)^2 = 5$$

37. a. $d = 5$ **b.** $T = 80 - 5n$

80, 75, 70, ...

c. $T = -125 + 5(40) = 75°F$

38. $\frac{1}{2} \cdot \frac{2}{3} \cdot \frac{3}{4} \cdot \frac{4}{5} \cdot \frac{5}{6} \cdot \frac{6}{7} = \frac{1}{7}$

The best answer is A.

Technology: Amortization

1. The principal is less each month. Therefore, the amount of interest due on the principal is less.

2. 3 months early

12-3   Infinite Sequences and Series

1. Each succeeding term is smaller than the one preceding it since the succeeding terms are equal to the preceding term multiplied by a number that is less than 1. Therefore, the terms of the sequence are getting smaller and smaller, and thus, approach 0.

2. b

3. greater than, does not

less than, does

See students' work for examples.

4. Since the terms of an arithmetic series do not approach zero as $n \rightarrow \infty$, infinite arithmetic series do not have limits.

5. $r = 2$ **6.** $d = 2$

$a_n = a_1 r^{n-1}$ $a_n = a_1 + (n - 1)d$

$ = 1(2)^{n-1}$ $ = 5 + (n - 1)2$

$ = 2^{n-1}$ $ = 3 + 2n$

7. $r = \frac{2}{3}$ **8.** numerator, add 2

$a_n = 3\left(\frac{2}{3}\right)^{n-1}$ denominator, add 1

$ \quad a_n = \frac{2n + 1}{n}$

9. $\lim\limits_{n \to \infty} \dfrac{1 - 2n}{5n} = \lim\limits_{n \to \infty} \left(\dfrac{1}{5n} - \dfrac{2}{5}\right)$

$$= 0 - \frac{2}{5}$$

$$= -\frac{2}{5}$$

10. $\lim\limits_{n \to \infty} \dfrac{n + 1}{n} = \lim\limits_{n \to \infty} \left(1 + \dfrac{1}{n}\right)$

$$= 1 + 0$$

$$= 1$$

11. $\lim\limits_{n \to \infty} \dfrac{3n - 5}{n} = \lim\limits_{n \to \infty} \left(3 - \dfrac{5}{n}\right)$

$$= 3 - 0$$

$$= 3$$

12. $r = 2\sqrt{2}$ **13.** $r = \frac{1}{2}$

$S_n = \infty$

does not exist $S_n = \dfrac{\dfrac{1}{20}}{1 - \dfrac{1}{2}}$

$$= \frac{1}{20} \cdot \frac{2}{1}$$

$$= \frac{1}{10}$$

14. $0.\overline{45} = \dfrac{45}{100} + \dfrac{45}{10{,}000} + \cdots$

$a_1 = \dfrac{45}{100}, \ r = \dfrac{1}{100}$

$S_n = \dfrac{\dfrac{45}{100}}{1 - \dfrac{1}{100}}$

$ = \dfrac{45}{100} \cdot \dfrac{100}{99}$

$ = \dfrac{45}{99}$

$ = \dfrac{5}{11}$

15. $0.888\ldots = \dfrac{8}{10} + \dfrac{8}{100} + \cdots$

$a_1 = \dfrac{8}{10}, \ r = \dfrac{1}{10}$

$S_n = \dfrac{\dfrac{8}{10}}{1 - \dfrac{1}{10}}$

$ = \dfrac{8}{9}$

16. $7.259259\ldots = 7 + \dfrac{259}{1000} + \dfrac{259}{1{,}000{,}000} + \cdots$

$a_1 = \dfrac{259}{1000}, \ r = \dfrac{1}{1000}$

$S_n = 7 + \dfrac{\dfrac{259}{1000}}{1 - \dfrac{1}{1000}}$

$ = 7 + \dfrac{259}{999}$

$ = 7\dfrac{7}{27}$

17. $\lim\limits_{n\to\infty} \dfrac{1}{3^n} = 0$

18. $\lim\limits_{n\to\infty} \dfrac{2n^2 - 6n}{5n^2} = \lim\limits_{n\to\infty} \left(\dfrac{2}{5} - \dfrac{6}{5n}\right)$

$\phantom{\lim\limits_{n\to\infty} \dfrac{2n^2 - 6n}{5n^2}} = \dfrac{2}{5} - 0$

$\phantom{\lim\limits_{n\to\infty} \dfrac{2n^2 - 6n}{5n^2}} = \dfrac{2}{5}$

19. $\lim\limits_{n\to\infty} \dfrac{n^2 - 4}{2n} = \lim\limits_{n\to\infty} \left(\dfrac{n}{2} - \dfrac{2}{n}\right)$

$\phantom{\lim\limits_{n\to\infty} \dfrac{n^2-4}{2n}} = \lim\limits_{n\to\infty} \left(\dfrac{n}{2} - 0\right)$

$\phantom{\lim\limits_{n\to\infty} \dfrac{n^2-4}{2n}} = \lim\limits_{n\to\infty} \dfrac{n}{2}$

does not exist

20. $\lim\limits_{n\to\infty} \dfrac{2n^2 + 3n - 2}{n^2} = \lim\limits_{n\to\infty} \left(2 + \dfrac{3}{n} - \dfrac{2}{n^2}\right)$

$\phantom{\lim\limits_{n\to\infty} \dfrac{2n^2+3n-2}{n^2}} = 2 + 0 + 0$

$\phantom{\lim\limits_{n\to\infty} \dfrac{2n^2+3n-2}{n^2}} = 2$

21. $\lim\limits_{n\to\infty} \left(\dfrac{n^2}{n^2} + \dfrac{n}{n^2} - \dfrac{3}{n^2}\right) = \lim\limits_{n\to\infty} \left(1 + \dfrac{1}{n} - \dfrac{3}{n^2}\right)$

$\phantom{\lim\limits_{n\to\infty} \left(\dfrac{n^2}{n^2}\right)} = 1 + 0 - 0$

$\phantom{\lim\limits_{n\to\infty} \left(\dfrac{n^2}{n^2}\right)} = 1$

22. $\lim\limits_{n\to\infty} \dfrac{3n + 1}{n - 3} = \lim\limits_{n\to\infty} \dfrac{\dfrac{3n}{n} + \dfrac{1}{n}}{\dfrac{n}{n} - \dfrac{3}{n}}$

$\phantom{\lim\limits_{n\to\infty} \dfrac{3n+1}{n-3}} = \dfrac{3 + 0}{1 - 0}$

$\phantom{\lim\limits_{n\to\infty} \dfrac{3n+1}{n-3}} = 3$

23. $\lim\limits_{n\to\infty} \dfrac{\dfrac{4n^2}{n^2} + \dfrac{5}{n^2}}{\dfrac{3n^2}{n^2} + \dfrac{2n}{n^2}} = \dfrac{4 + 0}{3 + 0}$

$\phantom{\lim\limits_{n\to\infty}} = \dfrac{4}{3}$

24. $\lim\limits_{n\to\infty} \dfrac{\dfrac{2n^3}{n^3}}{\dfrac{n^2}{n^3} + \dfrac{4n}{n^3}} = \dfrac{2}{0 + 0}$

does not exist

25. $\lim\limits_{n\to\infty} \left(\dfrac{2n}{n^2} + \dfrac{(-1)^n}{n^2}\right) = \lim\limits_{n\to\infty} \left(\dfrac{2}{n} + \dfrac{(-1)^n}{n^2}\right)$

$\phantom{\lim\limits_{n\to\infty} \left(\dfrac{2n}{n^2}\right)} = 0 + 0$

$\phantom{\lim\limits_{n\to\infty} \left(\dfrac{2n}{n^2}\right)} = 0$

26. $0.555\ldots = \dfrac{5}{10} + \dfrac{5}{100} + \cdots$

$a_1 = \dfrac{5}{10}, \ r = \dfrac{1}{10}$

$S_n = \dfrac{\dfrac{5}{10}}{1 - \dfrac{1}{10}}$

$ = \dfrac{5}{9}$

27. $0.2727\ldots = \dfrac{27}{100} + \dfrac{27}{10{,}000} + \cdots$

$a_1 = \dfrac{27}{100}, \ r = \dfrac{1}{100}$

$S_n = \dfrac{\dfrac{27}{100}}{1 - \dfrac{1}{100}}$

$ = \dfrac{27}{99}$

$ = \dfrac{3}{11}$

28. $0.370370\ldots = \dfrac{370}{1000} + \dfrac{370}{1{,}000{,}000} + \cdots$

$a_1 = \dfrac{370}{1000}, \ r = \dfrac{1}{1000}$

$S_n = \dfrac{\dfrac{370}{1000}}{1 - \dfrac{1}{1000}}$

$ = \dfrac{370}{999}$

$ = \dfrac{10}{27}$

29. $0.3181818\ldots = 0.3 + \dfrac{18}{1000} + \dfrac{18}{100,000} + \cdots$

$a_1 = \dfrac{18}{1000}, \quad r = \dfrac{1}{100}$

$S_n = 0.3 + \dfrac{\dfrac{18}{1000}}{1 - \dfrac{1}{100}}$

$= \dfrac{3}{10} + \dfrac{18}{990}$

$= \dfrac{3}{10} + \dfrac{2}{110}$

$= \dfrac{35}{110}$

$= \dfrac{7}{22}$

30. $3.2424\ldots = 3 + \dfrac{24}{100} + \dfrac{24}{10,000} + \cdots$

$a_1 = \dfrac{24}{100}, \quad r = \dfrac{1}{100}$

$S_n = 3 + \dfrac{\dfrac{24}{100}}{1 - \dfrac{1}{100}}$

$= 3 + \dfrac{24}{99}$

$= 3\dfrac{8}{33}$

31. $2.205205\ldots = 2 + \dfrac{205}{1000} + \dfrac{205}{1,000,000} + \cdots$

$a_1 = \dfrac{205}{1000}, \quad r = \dfrac{1}{1000}$

$S_n = 2 + \dfrac{\dfrac{205}{1000}}{1 - \dfrac{1}{1000}}$

$= 2 + \dfrac{205}{999}$

$= 2\dfrac{205}{999}$

32. $r = \dfrac{\dfrac{1}{3}}{\dfrac{2}{3}} = \dfrac{1}{2}$

$S_n = \dfrac{a_1}{1 - r}$

$= \dfrac{\dfrac{2}{3}}{1 - \dfrac{1}{2}}$

$= \dfrac{2}{3} \cdot \dfrac{2}{1}$

$= \dfrac{4}{3}$

33. $r = \dfrac{1}{\sqrt{3}} = \dfrac{\sqrt{3}}{3}$

$S_n = \dfrac{\sqrt{3}}{1 - \dfrac{\sqrt{3}}{3}}$

$= \dfrac{3\sqrt{3}}{3 - \sqrt{3}} \cdot \dfrac{(3 + \sqrt{3})}{(3 + \sqrt{3})}$

$= \dfrac{9\sqrt{3} + 9}{9 - 3}$

$= \dfrac{9(\sqrt{3} + 1)}{6}$

$= \dfrac{3}{2}(\sqrt{3} + 1)$

34. $r = \dfrac{\dfrac{4}{7}}{\dfrac{2}{7}} = 2$

a_n is getting increasingly larger.

S_n does not exist.

35. $r = \dfrac{0.02}{0.2} = 0.1$

$S_n = \dfrac{0.2}{1 - 0.1} = \dfrac{2}{9}$

36. $r = \dfrac{5}{10} = \dfrac{1}{2}$

$S_n = \dfrac{10}{1 - \dfrac{1}{2}} = 20$

37. a_n is getting increasingly larger.

S_n does not exist.

38. $\displaystyle\lim_{n \to \infty} \dfrac{\sqrt{n}}{\sqrt{n} + 1} = \lim_{n \to \infty} \dfrac{\dfrac{n^{\frac{1}{2}}}{n^{\frac{1}{2}}}}{\dfrac{n^{\frac{1}{2}}}{n^{\frac{1}{2}}} + \dfrac{1}{n^{\frac{1}{2}}}}$

$= \displaystyle\lim_{n \to \infty} \dfrac{1}{1 + \dfrac{1}{\sqrt{n}}}$

$= \dfrac{1}{1 + 0}$

$= 1$

39. $42\% = 21(0.42) = 8.82$

$8.82 = 21(0.8)^n$

$0.42 = (0.8)^n$

$\ln 0.42 = n \ln 0.8$

$n \approx 4$ strokes

40. $r = 0.70, \quad a_1 = 12$

first bounce: $S_n = \dfrac{12}{1 - 0.7} = 40$

second bounce: $S_n = \dfrac{8.4}{1 - 0.7} = 28$

$40 + 28 = 68$ feet

41. $r = \dfrac{1}{2}, \quad a_1 = 1$

Sequence: $1, \dfrac{1}{2}, \dfrac{1}{4}, \dfrac{1}{8}, \ldots$

$S_n = \dfrac{1}{1 - \dfrac{1}{2}} = 2$

One bug is at $(0, 2)$ and the other is at $(2, 0)$.

$d = \sqrt{(0 - 2)^2 + (2 - 0)^2} = \sqrt{4 + 4} = 2\sqrt{2}$

42. $\dfrac{1}{2}\begin{bmatrix} 9 & -3 \\ -6 & 6 \end{bmatrix} = \begin{bmatrix} \dfrac{9}{2} & \dfrac{-3}{2} \\ -3 & 3 \end{bmatrix}$

43. $k = \dfrac{-b \pm \sqrt{b^2 - 4ac}}{2a}$

$= \dfrac{-3 \pm \sqrt{9 - 4(3)(2)}}{2(3)}$

$= \dfrac{-3 \pm \sqrt{-15}}{6}$

$= \dfrac{-3 \pm i\sqrt{15}}{6}$

44. $r^2 = 50^2 + 150^2 - 2(50)(150) \cos 85°$

$= 25,000 - 15,000 \cos 85°$

$r \approx 162.2$ km/h

$\dfrac{50}{\sin \theta} = \dfrac{162.2}{\sin 85°}$

$\theta = 17°53'$

$17°53' + 30° = 47°53'$ SE

45. $S_n = \frac{n}{2}[2a_1 + (n-1)d]$

$S_{14} = \frac{14}{2}[2(3.2) + (14-1)1.5]$

$\quad = 7[6.4 + 19.5]$

$\quad = 181.3$

46. $a_1 = 2$, $a_5 = \frac{1}{8}$

$a_n = a_1 r^{n-1}$

$\frac{1}{8} = 2r^{5-1}$

$\frac{1}{16} = r^4$

$\pm \frac{1}{2} = r$

$a_2 = 2\left(\frac{1}{2}\right) = 1$ or $a_2 = 2\left(-\frac{1}{2}\right) = -1$

$a_3 = 1\left(\frac{1}{2}\right) = \frac{1}{2}$ $\quad a_3 = -1\left(-\frac{1}{2}\right) = \frac{1}{2}$

$a_4 = \frac{1}{2}\left(\frac{1}{2}\right) = \frac{1}{4}$ $\quad a_4 = \frac{1}{2}\left(-\frac{1}{2}\right) = -\frac{1}{4}$

$2, \pm 1, \frac{1}{2}, \pm\frac{1}{4}, \frac{1}{8}$

47. positive odd factors: 1, 13

positive even factors: 2, 26

The two quantities are equal. C

12-4 Convergent and Divergent Series

1. a.-c. See students' work.

d. Infinite arithmetic series do not converge because they do not approach zero as $n \to \infty$.

2. a.-c. See students' work.

d. In a geometric series where $|r| > 1$, each succeeding term is larger than the one preceding it. Therefore, the series approaches ∞ and thus, does not converge.

3. Sample answer: comparison test

4. arithmetic, divergent   **5.** neither, convergent

6. geometric,   **7.** arithmetic,
$r = \frac{1}{4} \to$ converge   divergent

8. geometric,   **9.** geometric,
$r = \frac{4}{3} \to$ divergent $r = \frac{1}{2} \to$ convergent

10. $a_n = \frac{1}{n^n}$, $a_{n+1} = \frac{1}{(n+1)^{n+1}}$

$r = \lim_{n\to\infty} \frac{a_{n+1}}{a_n} = \lim_{n\to\infty} \frac{\frac{1}{(n+1)^{n+1}}}{\frac{1}{n^n}}$

$\quad = \lim_{n\to\infty} \frac{n^n}{(n+1)^{n+1}} = 0$

convergent

---

11. $a_n = \frac{1}{1 \cdot 2 \cdot 3 \cdot \ldots \cdot n}$,

$a_{n+1} = \frac{1}{1 \cdot 2 \cdot 3 \cdot \ldots \cdot n \cdot (n+1)}$

$r = \lim_{n\to\infty} \frac{a_{n+1}}{a_n}$

$\quad = \lim_{n\to\infty} \frac{\frac{1}{1 \cdot 2 \cdot 3 \cdot \ldots \cdot n \cdot (n+1)}}{\frac{1}{1 \cdot 2 \cdot 3 \cdot \ldots \cdot n}}$

$\quad = \lim_{n\to\infty} \frac{1}{n+1}$

$\quad = 0$

convergent

12. The general term is $\frac{(n+1)}{n} > \frac{1}{n}$, so the series is divergent.

13. $a_n = \frac{n}{2^n}$, $a_{n+1} = \frac{n+1}{2^{n+1}}$

$r = \lim_{n\to\infty} \frac{a_{n+1}}{a_n}$

$\quad = \lim_{n\to\infty} \frac{\frac{n+1}{2^{n+1}}}{\frac{n}{2^n}}$

$\quad = \lim_{n\to\infty} \frac{(n+1)2^n}{n2^{n+1}}$

$\quad = \lim_{n\to\infty} \frac{(n+1)}{2n}$

$\quad = \lim_{n\to\infty} \left(\frac{1}{2} + \frac{1}{2n}\right)$

$\quad = \frac{1}{2}$

convergent

14. $a_n = \frac{1}{n \cdot 2^n}$, $a_{n+1} = \frac{1}{(n+1)2^{n+1}}$

$r = \lim_{n\to\infty} \frac{\frac{1}{(n+1)2^{n+1}}}{\frac{1}{n2^n}}$

$\quad = \lim_{n\to\infty} \frac{n2^n}{(n+1)2^{n+1}}$

$\quad = \lim_{n\to\infty} \frac{n}{2(n+1)}$

$\quad = \lim_{n\to\infty} \frac{\frac{n}{n}}{2\left(\frac{n}{n} + \frac{1}{n}\right)}$

$\quad = \frac{1}{2(1+0)}$

$\quad = \frac{1}{2}$

convergent

15. $a_n = \dfrac{1}{(2n - 1)2n}$,

$a_{n+1} = \dfrac{1}{[2(n + 1) - 1][2(n + 1)]}$

$\phantom{a_{n+1}} = \dfrac{1}{(2n + 1)(2n + 2)}$

$r = \lim\limits_{n \to \infty} \dfrac{\dfrac{1}{(2n + 1)(2n + 2)}}{\dfrac{1}{(2n - 1)2n}}$

$ = \lim\limits_{n \to \infty} \dfrac{(2n - 1)2n}{(2n + 1)(2n + 2)}$

$ = \lim\limits_{n \to \infty} \dfrac{4n^2 - 2n}{4n^2 + 6n + 2}$

$ = \lim\limits_{n \to \infty} \dfrac{4 - \dfrac{2}{n}}{4 + \dfrac{6}{n} + \dfrac{2}{n^2}}$

$ = \dfrac{4 - 0}{4 + 0 + 0}$

$ = 1$

cannot tell

16. $a_n = \dfrac{10^n}{1 \cdot 2 \cdot \ldots \cdot n}$,

$a_{n+1} = \dfrac{10^{n+1}}{1 \cdot 2 \cdot \ldots \cdot (n + 1)}$

$r = \lim\limits_{n \to \infty} \dfrac{\dfrac{10^{n+1}}{1 \cdot 2 \cdot \ldots \cdot (n + 1)}}{\dfrac{10^n}{1 \cdot 2 \cdot \ldots \cdot n}}$

$ = \lim\limits_{n \to \infty} \dfrac{(10^{n+1})(1 \cdot 2 \cdot \ldots \cdot n)}{(10^n)(1 \cdot 2 \cdot \ldots \cdot (n + 1))}$

$ = \lim\limits_{n \to \infty} \dfrac{10}{n + 1}$

$ = 0$

convergent

17. $a_n = \dfrac{n}{1 \cdot 2 \cdot \ldots \cdot (2n - 1)}$,

$a_{n+1} = \dfrac{n + 1}{1 \cdot 2 \cdot \ldots \cdot (2n + 1)}$

$r = \lim\limits_{n \to \infty} \dfrac{\dfrac{n + 1}{1 \cdot 2 \cdot \ldots \cdot (2n + 1)}}{\dfrac{n}{1 \cdot 2 \cdot \ldots \cdot (2n - 1)}}$

$ = \lim\limits_{n \to \infty} \dfrac{(n + 1)(1 \cdot 2 \cdot \ldots \cdot 2n - 1)}{n(1 \cdot 2 \cdot \ldots \cdot 2n + 1)}$

$ = \lim\limits_{n \to \infty} \dfrac{n + 1}{n(2n)(2n + 1)}$

$ = \lim\limits_{n \to \infty} \dfrac{n + 1}{4n^3 + 2n^2}$

$ = \lim\limits_{n \to \infty} \dfrac{\dfrac{n}{n^3} + \dfrac{1}{n^3}}{\dfrac{4n^3}{n^3} + \dfrac{2n^2}{n^3}}$

$ = \dfrac{0 + 0}{4 + 0}$

$ = 0$

convergent

18. $a_n = \dfrac{1}{1 \cdot 2 \cdot \ldots \cdot (2n)}$,

$a_{n+1} = \dfrac{1}{1 \cdot 2 \cdot \ldots \cdot 2(n + 1)}$

$r = \lim\limits_{n \to \infty} \dfrac{\dfrac{1}{1 \cdot 2 \cdot \ldots \cdot 2(n + 1)}}{\dfrac{1}{1 \cdot 2 \cdot \ldots \cdot 2n}}$

$ = \lim\limits_{n \to \infty} \dfrac{1 \cdot 2 \cdot \ldots \cdot 2n}{1 \cdot 2 \cdot \ldots \cdot 2(n + 1)}$

$ = \lim\limits_{n \to \infty} \dfrac{1}{(2n + 1)(2n + 2)}$

$ = \lim\limits_{n \to \infty} \dfrac{1}{4n^2 + 6n + 2}$

$ = \lim\limits_{n \to \infty} \dfrac{\dfrac{1}{n^2}}{\dfrac{4n^2}{n^2} + \dfrac{6n}{n^2} + \dfrac{2}{n^2}}$

$ = \dfrac{0}{4 + 0 + 0}$

$ = 0$

convergent

19. The general term is $\dfrac{1}{(2n - 1)^2}$.

$\dfrac{1}{(2n - 1)^2} < \dfrac{1}{n^2}$, so convergent

20. The general term is $\dfrac{1}{2}\left(\dfrac{1}{n}\right)$.
arithmetic, so divergent

21. The general term is $\dfrac{n}{(n + 1)}$.
arithmetic, so divergent

22. The general germ is $\dfrac{(n + 1)}{n}$.

$\dfrac{n + 1}{n} > \dfrac{1}{n}$, so divergent

23. geometric; $r = \dfrac{3}{4}$, so convergent

24. geometric; $r = \dfrac{1}{3}$, so convergent

25. The general term is $\dfrac{1}{3 + n^2}$.

$\dfrac{1}{3 + n^2} < \dfrac{1}{n^2}$, so convergent

26. $a_n = \dfrac{1}{1 \cdot 2 \cdot \ldots \cdot (2n - 1)}$,

$a_{n+1} = \dfrac{1}{1 \cdot 2 \cdot \ldots \cdot (2n + 1)}$

$r = \lim\limits_{n \to \infty} \dfrac{1 \cdot 2 \cdot \ldots \cdot (2n - 1)}{1 \cdot 2 \cdot \ldots \cdot (2n + 1)}$

$ = \lim\limits_{n \to \infty} \dfrac{1}{2n(2n + 1)}$

$ = \lim\limits_{n \to \infty} \dfrac{1}{4n^2 + 2n}$

$ = 0$

convergent

27.

$$5^x = 390,625$$

$$x \log 5 = \log 390,625$$

$$x = 8$$

$$5^{\frac{1}{7}} \cdot 5^{\frac{2}{7}} \cdot 5^{\frac{3}{7}} \cdot \ldots \cdot 5^{\frac{n}{7}} > 5^8$$

$$\frac{1}{7} + \frac{2}{7} + \frac{3}{7} + \ldots + \frac{n}{7} > 8$$

$$\frac{n}{2}\left[2\left(\frac{1}{7}\right) + (n-1)\frac{1}{7}\right] > 8$$

$$\frac{n}{14} + \frac{n^2}{14} > 8$$

$$n + n^2 > 112$$

$$n^2 + n - 112 > 0$$

$$n > \frac{-1 \pm \sqrt{1 + 448}}{2}$$

$$n > 10.09$$

The least positive number for n is 11.

28. Stern: $2000 + (2000 + 120) + \ldots$, $d = 120$

Adams: $2000 + 2000(1.05) + 2000(1.05)^2 + \ldots$,

$r = 1.05$

a. Stern: $a_{12} = a_1 + 11(120)$

$$= 2000 + 1320 = \$3320$$

Adams: $a_{12} = a_1 r^{11} = 2000(1.05)^{11} \approx \$3420.68$

Adams is greater.

b. Stern: $S_n = \frac{n}{2}[2a_1 + (n-1)d]$

$$= \frac{12}{2}[2(2000) + (11)(120)]$$

$$= 6[5320]$$

$$= \$31,920$$

Adams: $S_n = \frac{a_1 - a_1 r^n}{1 - r}$

$$= \frac{2000 - 2000(1.05)^{12}}{1 - 1.05}$$

$$\approx \$31,834.25$$

Mr. Stern's income is greater than Ms. Adams'.

29. $a_1 = 20$, $r = 0.90$, $20(0.9) = 18$

first bounce: $S_n = \dfrac{20}{1 - 0.9} = 200$

second bounce: $S_n = \dfrac{18}{1 - 0.9} = 180$

$200 + 180 = 380$ feet

30. symmetric to all

31.

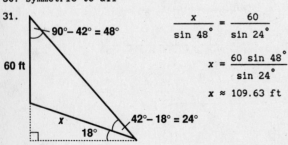

$90° - 42° = 48°$

60 ft

$42° - 18° = 24°$

$18°$

$$\frac{x}{\sin 48°} = \frac{60}{\sin 24°}$$

$$x = \frac{60 \sin 48°}{\sin 24°}$$

$$x \approx 109.63 \text{ ft}$$

32.

θ	0°	15°	30°	70°
r	2.31	2.83	4	-11.52

33. $\displaystyle \lim_{n\to\infty} \frac{n-1}{n} = \lim_{n\to\infty} \frac{\frac{n}{n} - \frac{1}{n}}{\frac{n}{n}} = \frac{1-0}{1} = 1$

34. $\dfrac{0.25 + 0.25 + 0.25 + 0.25}{4} = \dfrac{4(0.25)}{4} = 0.25$

Mid-Chapter Review

PAGE 684

1. Answers may vary. One such sequence is 5, $6\frac{1}{2}$, 8, $9\frac{1}{2}$, 11, $12\frac{1}{2}$, 14, $15\frac{1}{2}$, 17.

2. $S_{23} = \frac{n}{2}[2a_1 + (n-1)d]$

$$= \frac{23}{2}[2(-3) + 22(6)]$$

$$= 1449$$

3. $a_5 = a_1 r^4$

$$\frac{1}{3} = 2r^4$$

$$\frac{1}{16} = r^4$$

$$\pm \frac{1}{2} = r$$

$2\left(\pm\frac{1}{2}\right) = \pm1$, $2\left(\pm\frac{1}{2}\right)^2 = \frac{1}{2}$, $2\left(\pm\frac{1}{2}\right)^3 = \pm\frac{1}{4}$

2, ±1, $\frac{1}{2}$, $\pm\frac{1}{4}$, $\frac{1}{8}$

4. $r = \frac{1}{2}$

$$S_9 = \frac{a_1 - a_1 r^9}{1 - r}$$

$$= \frac{\frac{2}{3} - \frac{2}{3}\left(\frac{1}{2}\right)^9}{1 - \frac{1}{2}}$$

$$= \frac{\frac{2}{3} - \frac{1}{768}}{\frac{1}{2}}$$

$$= 2\left(\frac{511}{768}\right)$$

$$= \frac{511}{384}$$

5. $\displaystyle \lim_{n\to\infty} \frac{3n^2 + 4}{2n} = \lim_{n\to\infty} \left(\frac{3n}{2} + \frac{2}{n}\right)$

$$= \infty$$

limit does not exist

6. $r = \frac{2}{5}$

$S_n = \frac{a_1}{1 - r}$

$= \frac{1}{1 - \frac{2}{5}}$

$= \frac{5}{3}$

$= 1\frac{2}{3}$

7. $0.3636\ldots = \frac{36}{100} + \frac{36}{10,000} + \ldots$

$a_1 = \frac{36}{100}, \quad r = \frac{1}{100}$

$S_n = \frac{\frac{36}{100}}{1 - \frac{1}{100}}$

$= \frac{36}{99}$

$= \frac{4}{11}$

8. $r = \frac{1}{5}, \quad |r| < 1$

convergent

9. $S_n = \frac{a_1 - a_1 r^n}{1 - r}$

$= \frac{2000 - 2000(1.08)^{42}}{1 - 1.08}$

$\approx \$608,487.05$

12-5   Sigma Notation and the nth Term

1. Yes; $\sum\limits_{n=0}^{14} (2n + 10)$ also represents the series

$10 + 12 + 14 + \ldots + 38$.

2. a. 6   b. 101   c. 9

3. the number of terms in the series

4. Sample answers: $\sum\limits_{k=0}^{5} (4k + 7), \quad \sum\limits_{k=2}^{7} (4k - 1)$

5. $\sum\limits_{j=1}^{4} (j + 2) = (1 + 2) + (2 + 2) + (3 + 2)$
$+ (4 + 2) = 18$

6. $\sum\limits_{a=4}^{7} 2a = 2(4) + 2(5) + 2(6) + 2(7) = 44$

7. $\sum\limits_{p=5}^{7} (3p + 2) = [3(5) + 2] + [3(6) + 2]$
$+ [3(7) + 2] = 60$

8. $\sum\limits_{a=0}^{4} (0.5 + 2^a) = (0.5 + 2^0) + (0.5 + 2^1)$
$+ (0.5 + 2^2) + (0.5 + 2^3)$
$+ (0.5 + 2^4) = 33.5$

9. $\sum\limits_{b=0}^{\infty} 6\left(\frac{1}{2}\right)^b = 6\left(\frac{2}{3}\right)^0 + 6\left(\frac{2}{3}\right)^1 + 6\left(\frac{2}{3}\right)^2$
$+ 6\left(\frac{2}{3}\right)^3 + \ldots + 6\left(\frac{2}{3}\right)^\infty$

$S_n = \frac{a}{1 - r} = \frac{6}{1 - \frac{2}{3}} = 18$

10.-13. Sample answers given.

10. $\sum\limits_{n=1}^{4} 3n$

11. $\sum\limits_{n=1}^{5} \frac{32}{2^n}$

12. $\sum\limits_{n=0}^{4} (20 - 2^n)$

13. $\sum\limits_{n=2}^{\infty} \frac{n}{5}$

14. $7! = 7 \times 6 \times 5 \times 4 \times 3 \times 2 \times 1 = 5040$

15. $3(6!) = 3 \times 6 \times 5 \times 4 \times 3 \times 2 \times 1 = 2160$

16. $\frac{12!}{10!} = \frac{12 \cdot 11 \cdot 10 \cdot 9 \cdot 8 \cdot 7 \cdot 6 \cdot 5 \cdot 4 \cdot 3 \cdot 2 \cdot 1}{10 \cdot 9 \cdot 8 \cdot 7 \cdot 6 \cdot 5 \cdot 4 \cdot 3 \cdot 2 \cdot 1}$
$= 12 \times 11 = 132$

17. $9! = 9 \times 8 \times 7 \times 6 \times 5 \times 4 \times 3 \times 2 \times 1 = 362,880$

18. $2(5!) = 2 \times 5 \times 4 \times 3 \times 2 \times 1 = 240$

19. $3!4! = 3 \times 2 \times 1 \times 4 \times 3 \times 2 \times 1 = 144$

20. $5!3! = 5 \times 4 \times 3 \times 2 \times 1 \times 3 \times 2 \times 1 = 720$

21. $\frac{10!}{8!} = 10 \times 9 = 90$

22. $\frac{6!}{4!3!} = \frac{6 \times 5 \times 4 \times 3 \times 2 \times 1}{4 \times 3 \times 2 \times 1 \times 3 \times 2 \times 1} = \frac{6 \times 5}{3 \times 2 \times 1} = 5$

23. $\sum\limits_{r=1}^{3} (r - 3) = (1 - 3) + (2 - 3) + 3 - 3) = -3$

24. $\sum\limits_{k=5}^{8} 3k = 3(5) + 3(6) + 3(7) + 3(8) = 78$

25. $\sum\limits_{b=4}^{8} (4 - 2b) = [4 - 2(4)] + [4 - 2(5)]$
$+ [4 - 2(6)] + [4 - 2(7)]$
$+ [4 - 2(8)] = -40$

26. $\sum\limits_{z=1}^{9} (10 - z) = (10 - 1) + (10 - 2) + (10 - 3)$
$+ (10 - 4) + (10 - 5) + (10 - 6)$
$+ (10 - 7) + (10 - 8) + (10 - 9)$
$= 45$

27. $\sum\limits_{b=2}^{7} (b^2 + b) = (2^2 + 2) + (3^2 + 3) + (4^2 + 4)$
$+ (5^2 + 5) = 68$

28. $\sum\limits_{k=2}^{7} (5 - 2k) = [5 - 2(2)] + [5 - 2(3)]$
$+ [5 - 2(4)] + [5 - 2(5)]$
$+ [5 - 2(6)] + [5 - 2(7)] = -24$

29. $\sum\limits_{n=3}^{6} (3^n + 1) = (3^3 + 1) + (3^4 + 1) + (3^5 + 1)$
$+ (3^6 + 1) = 1084$

30. $\sum\limits_{n=1}^{4} 4^n = 4^1 + 4^2 + 4^3 + 4^4 = 340$

31. $\sum\limits_{p=1}^{4} \left(3^{p-1} + \frac{1}{2}\right) = \left(3^{1-1} + \frac{1}{2}\right) + \left(3^{2-1} + \frac{1}{2}\right)$
$+ \left(3^{3-1} + \frac{1}{2}\right) + \left(3^{4-1} + \frac{1}{2}\right) = 42$

32. $\sum\limits_{r=0}^{\infty} 5(0.2)^r = 5(0.2)^0 + 5(0.2)^1 + 5(0.2)^2$
$+ \ldots + 5(0.2)^\infty$

$S_n = \frac{a}{1 - r} = \frac{5}{1 - 0.2} = 6.25$

33. $\displaystyle\sum_{k=1}^{\infty} 4\left(\frac{1}{2}\right)^k = 4\left(\frac{1}{2}\right)^1 + 4\left(\frac{1}{2}\right)^2 + 4\left(\frac{1}{2}\right)^3 + \ldots + 4\left(\frac{1}{2}\right)^\infty$

$S_n = \dfrac{a}{1 - r} = \dfrac{4\left(\frac{1}{2}\right)}{1 - \frac{1}{2}} = 4$

34. $\displaystyle\sum_{j=0}^{\infty} 5\left(\frac{3}{4}\right)^j = 5\left(\frac{3}{4}\right)^0 + 5\left(\frac{3}{4}\right)^1 + 5\left(\frac{3}{4}\right)^2 + \ldots + 5\left(\frac{3}{4}\right)^\infty$

$S_n = \dfrac{a}{1 - r} = \dfrac{5}{1 - \frac{3}{4}} = 20$

35. $\displaystyle\sum_{k=1}^{5} 10k$　　　　**36.** $\displaystyle\sum_{k=1}^{5} 2^k$

37. $\displaystyle\sum_{k=0}^{4} 3 \cdot 2^k$　　　　**38.** $r = 10$

$\displaystyle\sum_{k=0}^{3} 3 \cdot 10^k$

39. $\displaystyle\sum_{k=2}^{10} \frac{1}{k}$　　　　**40.** $\displaystyle\sum_{k=1}^{7} \frac{1}{2k}$

41. $d = 2$　　　　**42.** $\displaystyle\sum_{k=0}^{3} (-2)^{3-k}$

$\displaystyle\sum_{k=0}^{3} (11 - 2k)$

43. $d = 2$　　　　**44.** $d = 5$

$\displaystyle\sum_{k=1}^{\infty} 2k$　　　　$\displaystyle\sum_{k=1}^{\infty} (5k - 1)$

45. $\displaystyle\sum_{k=3}^{\infty} \frac{2}{k}$　　　　**46.** $\displaystyle\sum_{k=1}^{\infty} 5^k$

47. $\displaystyle\sum_{k=0}^{\infty} \frac{k!}{k+1}$　　　　**48.** $\displaystyle\sum_{k=2}^{\infty} \frac{k!2^k}{k^2 - 1}$

49. $\dfrac{x!}{(x - 2)!} = \dfrac{x(x - 1)(x - 2)!}{(x - 2)!} = x(x - 1)$

50. $\dfrac{(x + 1)!}{(x - 1)!} = \dfrac{(x + 1)(x + 1 - 1)(x + 1 - 2)!}{(x - 1)!}$

$= \dfrac{(x + 1)x(x - 1)!}{(x - 1)!} = x(x + 1)$

51. $\dfrac{(x - y)!}{(x - y - 1)!} = \dfrac{(x - y)(x - y - 1)!}{(x - y - 1)!} = x - y$

52. a. 26　　　　**b.** 45　　　　**c.** 44

53. $\displaystyle\sum_{k=0}^{5} a^k + \sum_{n=6}^{10} a^n = (a^0 + a^1 + \ldots + a^5)$

$+ (a^6 + a^7 + \ldots + a^{10})$

$= \displaystyle\sum_{b=0}^{10} a^b$

true

54. $\displaystyle\sum_{r=3}^{7} 3^r + \sum_{a=7}^{9} 3^a = (3^3 + 3^4 + \ldots + 3^7)$

$+ (3^7 + 3^8 + 3^9)$

$= 3^7 + \displaystyle\sum_{j=3}^{9} 3^j$

false

55. $\displaystyle\sum_{n=1}^{10} (5 + n) \overset{?}{=} \sum_{m=0}^{9} (4 + m)$

$6 + 7 + 8 + \ldots + 15 \overset{?}{=} 4 + 5 + 6 + \ldots + 13$

$105 \neq 85$

false

56. $\displaystyle\sum_{r=2}^{8} (2r - 3) \overset{?}{=} \sum_{s=3}^{9} (2s - 5)$

$1 + 3 + 5 + \ldots + 13 \overset{?}{=} 1 + 3 + 5 + \ldots + 13$

$49 = 49$

true

57. $2\displaystyle\sum_{k=3}^{7} k^2 \overset{?}{=} \sum_{k=3}^{7} 2k^2$

$2(3^2 + 4^2 + \ldots + 7^2) \overset{?}{=} 2 \cdot 3^2 + 2 \cdot 4^2$

$+ \ldots + 2 \cdot 7^2$

$270 = 270$

true

58. $3\displaystyle\sum_{n=1}^{5} (n + 3) \overset{?}{=} \sum_{n=1}^{15} (n + 3)$

$3(4 + 5 + \ldots + 8) \overset{?}{=} (4 + 5 + 6 + \ldots + 18)$

$90 \neq 165$

false

59. year 1: $1500(1.08) + 1500(1.08)^{\frac{1}{2}} \approx 3178.85$

year 2: $3178.85(1.08) + 1500(1.08) + 1500(1.08)^{\frac{1}{2}}$

≈ 6612.00

year 3: $6612.00(1.08) + 3178.85 \approx 10{,}319.81$

year 4: $10{,}319.81(1.08) + 3178.85 \approx 14{,}324.25$

year 5: $14{,}324.25(1.08) + 3178.85 \approx 18{,}649.04$

year 6: $18{,}649.04(1.08) + 3178.85 \approx 23{,}319.81$

year 7: $23{,}319.81(1.08) + 3178.85 \approx 28{,}364.25$

year 8: $28{,}364{,}25(1.08) + 3178.85 \approx 33{,}812.24$

year 9: $33{,}812.24(1.08) + 3178.85 \approx 39{,}696.07$

year 10: $39{,}696.07(1.08) + 3178.85 \approx 46{,}050.61$

year 11: $46{,}050.61(1.08) + 3178.85 \approx 52{,}913.50$

year 12: $52{,}913.50(1.08) + 3178.85 \approx 60{,}325.43$

year 13: $60{,}325.43(1.08) + 3178.85 \approx 68{,}330.31$

year 14: $68{,}330.31(1.08) + 3178.85 \approx 76{,}975.59$

year 15: $76{,}975.59(1.08) + 3178.85 \approx 86{,}312.49$

year 16: $86{,}312.49(1.08) + 3178.85 \approx 96{,}396.34$

year 17: $96{,}396.34(1.08) + 3178.85 \approx 107{,}286.90$

year 18: $107{,}286.90(1.08) + 3178.85 \approx 119{,}048.70$

year 19: $119{,}048.70(1.08) + 3178.85 \approx 131{,}751.44$

year 20: $131{,}751.44(1.08) + 3178.85 \approx 145{,}470.41$

year 21: $145{,}470.41(1.08) + 3178.85 \approx 160{,}286.89$

year 22: $160{,}286.89(1.08) + 3178.85 \approx 176{,}288.69$

year 23: $176{,}288.69(1.08) + 3178.85 \approx 193{,}570.64$

year 24: $193{,}570.64(1.08) + 3178.85 \approx 212{,}235.14$

year 25: $212{,}235.14(1.08) + 3178.85 \approx 232{,}392.80$

year 26: $232{,}392.80(1.08) + 3178.85 \approx 254{,}163.08$

year 27: $254,163.08(1.08) + 3178.85 \approx 277,674.97$

year 28: $277,674.97(1.08) + 3178.85 \approx 303,067.82$

year 29: $303,067.82(1.08) + 3178.85 \approx 330,492.09$

year 30: $330,492.09(1.08) + 3178.85 \approx 360,110.31$

60. a. $a_1 = 90$, $r = 0.7$ b. $S_n = \dfrac{a}{1 - r}$

$S_8 = \dfrac{90 - 90(0.7)^8}{1 - 0.7}$ $= \dfrac{90}{1 - }$

≈ 282.71 feet $= 300$ feet

61. a. $P = (120 + 10x)(0.48 - 0.03)x$

$P = -0.3x^2 + 1.2x + 57.6$

$P = -0.3(x^2 - 4x) + 57.6$

$P = -0.3(x^2 - 4x + 4) + 57.6 + 1.2$

$P - 58.8 = -0.3(x - 2)^2$

The parabola opens downward and the vertex is (2, 58.8). Ms. Hoffman will receive the maximum profit in 2 weeks.

b. The maximum profit is \$58.80 per tree.

62. $2\underline{|}$ 1   8 K

        2   20

    $\overline{1 \quad 10 \quad 0}$

$K = -20$

63. $\sin (\tan^{-1} 1 - \sin^{-1} 1)$

$= \sin (45° - 90°)$

$= \sin (-45°)$

$= -\dfrac{\sqrt{2}}{2}$

64. $(1, 3) \cdot (3, -2) = 1(3) + 3(-2) = -3$, no

65. $a = -3$

$(y - k)^2 = 4a(x - h)$

$(y + 1)^2 = -12(x - 6)$

66. $\sqrt[6]{64a^6 b^{-2}} = 64^{\frac{1}{6}} a^{6\left(\frac{1}{6}\right)} b^{-2\left(\frac{1}{6}\right)} = 2ab^{-\frac{1}{3}}$

67. $0.222\ldots = \dfrac{2}{10} + \dfrac{2}{100} + \ldots$

$a_1 = \dfrac{2}{10}$, $r = \dfrac{1}{10}$

$S_n = \dfrac{a_1}{1 - r}$

$= \dfrac{\frac{2}{10}}{1 - \frac{1}{10}}$

$= \dfrac{\frac{2}{10}}{\frac{9}{10}}$

$= \dfrac{2}{9}$

68. This is a geometric series with $r = \dfrac{1}{3}$. Since $|r| < 1$ the series is convergent.

69. $2x + 4y = 8$ $3x + 6y = 12$ $4x + 8y = 8$

$x + 2y = 4$ $x + 2y = 4$ $x + 2y = 2$

$6x + 12 = 16$

$x + 2 = \dfrac{8}{3}$

I + II are equivalent. The best answer is A.

12-6   The Binomial Theorem

PAGE 694   CHECKING FOR UNDERSTANDING

1. See students' work.

2. 9th: 1   8   28   56   70   56   28   8   1

    10th: 1   9   36   84   126   126   84   36   9   1

3. 2^{n-1} 4. $n + 1$, n

5. $(a + b)^7 = a^7 + 7a^6 b + 21a^5 b^2 + 35a^4 b^3$

$+ 35a^3 b^4 + 21a^2 b^5 + 7ab^6 + b^7$

6. $(n + 2)^7 = n^7 + 14n^6 + 84n^5 + 280n^4 + 560n^3$

$+ 672n^2 + 448n + 128$

7. $(4 - b)^4 = 256 - 256b + 96b^2 - 16b^3 + b^4$

8. $(2x - 3y)^3 = 8x^3 - 36x^2 y + 54xy^2 - 27y^3$

9. $(a + b)^7 = \displaystyle\sum_{r=0}^{7} \dfrac{7!}{r!\,(7 - r)!} a^{7-r} b^r$

4th term $= \dfrac{7!}{3!\,(7 - 3)!} a^{7-3} b^3$

$= \dfrac{7 \cdot 6 \cdot 5 \cdot 4!}{3!\,4!} a^4 b^3$

$= 35a^4 b^3$

10. $(a - \sqrt{2})^8 = \displaystyle\sum_{r=0}^{8} \dfrac{8!}{r!\,(8 - r)!} a^{8-r} (-\sqrt{2})^r$

4th term $= \dfrac{8!}{3!\,(8 - 3)!} a^{8-3} (-\sqrt{2})^3$

$= \dfrac{8 \cdot 7 \cdot 6 \cdot 5!}{3!\,5!} a^5 (-2\sqrt{2})$

$= -112\sqrt{2} a^5$

PAGES 694-695   EXERCISES

11. $(x + y)^5 = x^5 + 5x^4 y + 10x^3 y^2 + 10x^2 y^3 + 5xy^4$

$+ y^5$

12. $(r - s)^6 = r^6 - 6r^5 s + 15r^4 s^2 - 20r^3 s^3 + 15r^2 s^4$

$- 6rs^5 + s^6$

13. $(x - 2)^7 = x^7 - 14x^6 + 84x^5 - 280x^4 + 560x^3$

$- 672x^2 + 448x - 128$

14. $(2a + b)^7 = 128a^7 + 448a^6 b + 672a^5 b^2 + 560a^4 b^3$

$+ 280a^3 b^4 + 84a^2 b^5 + 14ab^6 + b^7$

15. $(x + 3)^6 = x^6 + 3 \cdot 6x^5 + \dfrac{3^2 \cdot 6 \cdot 5}{1 \cdot 2} x^4$

$$+ \dfrac{3^3 \cdot 6 \cdot 5 \cdot 4}{1 \cdot 2 \cdot 3} x^3$$

$$+ \dfrac{3^4 \cdot 6 \cdot 5 \cdot 4 \cdot 3}{1 \cdot 2 \cdot 3 \cdot 4} x^2$$

$$+ \dfrac{3^5 \cdot 6 \cdot 5 \cdot 4 \cdot 3 \cdot 2}{1 \cdot 2 \cdot 3 \cdot 4 \cdot 5} x$$

$$+ \dfrac{3^6 \cdot 6 \cdot 5 \cdot 4 \cdot 3 \cdot 2 \cdot 1}{1 \cdot 2 \cdot 3 \cdot 4 \cdot 5 \cdot 6}$$

$$= x^6 + 18x^5 + 135x^4 + 540x^3 + 1215x^2$$

$$+ 1458x + 729$$

16. $(2 + d)^4 = 2^4 + 4 \cdot 2^3 d + \dfrac{4(3)2^2}{2 \cdot 1} d^2$

$$+ \dfrac{4 \cdot 3 \cdot 2 \cdot 2^1}{1 \cdot 2 \cdot 3} d^3$$

$$+ \dfrac{4 \cdot 3 \cdot 2 \cdot 1 \cdot 2^0}{1 \cdot 2 \cdot 3 \cdot 4} d^4$$

$$= 16 + 32d + 24d^2 + 8d^3 + d^4$$

17. $(2x + y)^6 = (2x)^6 + 6(2x)^5 y + \dfrac{6 \cdot 5 \cdot (2x)^4}{1 \cdot 2} y^2$

$$+ \dfrac{6 \cdot 5 \cdot 4 \cdot (2x)^3}{1 \cdot 2 \cdot 3} y^3$$

$$+ \dfrac{6 \cdot 5 \cdot 4 \cdot 3 \cdot (2x)^2}{1 \cdot 2 \cdot 3 \cdot 4} y^4$$

$$+ \dfrac{6 \cdot 5 \cdot 4 \cdot 3 \cdot 2 \cdot (2x)}{1 \cdot 2 \cdot 3 \cdot 4 \cdot 5} y^5$$

$$+ \dfrac{6 \cdot 5 \cdot 4 \cdot 3 \cdot 2 \cdot 1 \cdot (2x)^0}{1 \cdot 2 \cdot 3 \cdot 4 \cdot 5 \cdot 6} y^6$$

$$= 64x^6 + 192x^5 y + 240x^4 y^2 + 160x^3 y^3$$

$$+ 60x^2 y^4 + 12xy^5 + y^6$$

18. $(3x - y)^5 = (3x)^5 + 5(3x)^4 (-y)$

$$+ \dfrac{5 \cdot 4 \cdot (3x)^3}{1 \cdot 2} (-y)^2$$

$$+ \dfrac{5 \cdot 4 \cdot 3 \cdot (3x)^2}{1 \cdot 2 \cdot 3} (-y)^3$$

$$+ \dfrac{5 \cdot 4 \cdot 3 \cdot 2 \cdot (3x)}{1 \cdot 2 \cdot 3 \cdot 4} (-y)^4$$

$$+ \dfrac{5 \cdot 4 \cdot 3 \cdot 2 \cdot (3x)^0}{1 \cdot 2 \cdot 3 \cdot 4 \cdot 5} (-y)^5$$

$$= 243x^5 - 405x^4 y + 270x^3 y^2 - 90x^2 y^3$$

$$+ 15xy^4 - y^5$$

19. $(2x + \sqrt{3})^4 = (2x)^4 + 4(2x)^3 (\sqrt{3})$

$$+ \dfrac{4 \cdot 3 \cdot (2x)^2}{1 \cdot 2} (\sqrt{3})^2$$

$$+ \dfrac{4 \cdot 3 \cdot 2 \cdot (2x)}{1 \cdot 2 \cdot 3} (\sqrt{3})^3$$

$$+ \dfrac{4 \cdot 3 \cdot 2 \cdot 1 \cdot (2x)^0}{1 \cdot 2 \cdot 3 \cdot 4} (\sqrt{3})^4$$

$$= 16x^4 + 32\sqrt{3}x^3 + 72x^2 + 24\sqrt{3}x + 9$$

20. $(3a^2 - 2b)^4 = (3a^2)^4 + 4(3a^2)^3 (-2b)$

$$+ \dfrac{4 \cdot 3 \cdot (3a^2)^2}{1 \cdot 2} (-2b)^2$$

$$+ \dfrac{4 \cdot 3 \cdot 2 \cdot (3a^2)}{1 \cdot 2 \cdot 3} (-2b)^3$$

$$+ \dfrac{4 \cdot 3 \cdot 2 \cdot 1 \cdot (3a^2)^0}{1 \cdot 2 \cdot 3 \cdot 4} (-2b)^4$$

$$= 81a^8 - 216a^6 b + 216a^4 b^2 - 96a^2 b^3$$

$$+ 16b^4$$

21. $\dfrac{9!}{r!(9 - r)!} (2x)^{9-r} (-y)^r$

$$= \dfrac{9!}{4!(9 - 4)!} (2x)^{9-4} (-y)^4$$

$$= \dfrac{9 \cdot 8 \cdot 7 \cdot 6 \cdot 5!}{4!5!} (2x)^5 (y)^4$$

$$= \dfrac{9 \cdot 8 \cdot 7 \cdot 6}{4!} 32x^5 y^4$$

$$= 4032x^5 y^4$$

22. $\dfrac{8!}{r!(8 - r)!} (2a)^{8-r} (-3b)^r$

$$= \dfrac{8!}{4!(8 - 4)!} (2a)^{8-4} (-3b)^4$$

$$= \dfrac{8 \cdot 7 \cdot 6 \cdot 5 \cdot 4!}{4!4!} (2a)^4 (-3b)^4$$

$$= \dfrac{8 \cdot 7 \cdot 6 \cdot 5}{4!} 16a^4 81b^4$$

$$= 90{,}720a^4 b^4$$

23. $\dfrac{10!}{r!(10 - r)!} (x)^{10-r} \left(-\dfrac{1}{2}y\right)$

$$= \dfrac{10!}{6!(10 - 6)!} (x)^{10-6} \left(-\dfrac{1}{2}y\right)^6$$

$$= \dfrac{10 \cdot 9 \cdot 8 \cdot 7 \cdot 6!}{6!4!} x^4 \left(\dfrac{1}{2}y\right)^6$$

$$= 210x^4 \left(\dfrac{1}{64}y^6\right)$$

$$= \dfrac{105}{32} x^4 y^6$$

24. $\dfrac{11!}{r!(11 - r)!} (3x)^{11-r} (-2y)^r$

$$= \dfrac{11!}{5!(11 - 5)!} (3x)^{11-5} (-2y)^5$$

$$= \dfrac{11 \times 10 \times 9 \times 8 \times 7 \times 6!}{5!6!} (3x)^6 (-2y)^5$$

$$= 462(729)x^6 (-32)y^5$$

$$= -10{,}777{,}536x^6 y^5$$

25. Since the binomial expansion of $(4x - 1)^{16}$ would be a polynomial $p(x)$, the sum of the coefficients of the polynomial would be $p(1)$. Thus, $p(1) = (4 \cdot 1 - 1)^{16} = 3^{16} = 43{,}046{,}721$ is the sum of the coefficients of the binomial expansion of $(4x - 1)^{16}$.

26. $\sqrt{6} = \sqrt{4 + 2} = 2\sqrt{1 + \frac{2}{4}} = 2\left(1 + \frac{1}{2}\right)^{\frac{1}{2}}$

$2\left(1 + \frac{1}{2}\right)^{\frac{1}{2}} = 2\left[1^{\frac{1}{2}} + \frac{1}{2}(1)^{\frac{-1}{2}}\left(\frac{1}{2}\right)\right.$

$+ \frac{\frac{1}{2}\left(\frac{1}{2} - 1\right)}{2}(1)^{-\frac{3}{2}}\left(\frac{1}{2}\right)^2$

$+ \frac{\frac{1}{2}\left(\frac{1}{2} - 1\right)\left(\frac{1}{2} - 2\right)}{2 \cdot 3}$

$\left. \cdot (1)^{-\frac{5}{2}}\left(\frac{1}{2}\right)^3 + \ldots \right]$

$= 2\left[1 + \frac{1}{4} + \left(-\frac{1}{32}\right) + \frac{1}{128} \ldots\right]$

$= 2\left[\frac{128 + 32 - 4 + 1 \ldots}{128}\right]$

$= \frac{2(157)}{128}$

$\sqrt{6} \approx 2.45$

27. $(g + b)^6 = g^6 + 6g^5b + 15g^4b^2 + 20g^3b^3 + 15g^2b^4$

   $+ 6gb^5 + b^6$

   at least 2 boys: $15 + 20 + 15 + 6 + 1$
   $= 57$ groups

28. possible: $H^4 + 4H^3T + 6H^2T^2 + 4HT^3 + T^4$
   a. 1   b. 4   c. 6   d. 4

29. 50%, 25%, 1.56%, $100[1 - (0.5)^d]$%

30. $f(9) = 4 + 6(9) - (9)^3 = -671$

31. $\csc 180° = \frac{1}{\sin 180°} = \frac{1}{0}$; undefined

32. $(40, -30°)$, $(40, 330°)$, $(-40, -210°)$,
   $(-40, 150°)$

33. $\sum_{n=1}^{\infty} 3\left(\frac{1}{2}\right)^{n+1} = 3\left(\frac{1}{2}\right)^2 + 3\left(\frac{1}{2}\right)^3 + 3\left(\frac{1}{2}\right)^4 + \ldots + 3\left(\frac{1}{2}\right)^{\infty}$

   $S_n = \frac{a_1}{1 - r} = \frac{3}{1 - \frac{1}{2}} = 1.5$

34. perimeter of $\triangle XYZ = 4 + 9 + 8 = 21$
   Equilateral implies equal sides: $21 \div 3 = 7$.
   $AB = 7$
   The best answer is C.

12-7 Special Sequences and Series

1. See students' work.

2. $a_{n+1} = a_n + a_{n-1}$ for $n \geq 2$

3. the trigonometric series and the exponential series

4. $e^{i\pi} = \cos \pi + i \sin \pi = -1 + i \cdot 0 = -1$

5. See students' work.

6. 1, 1, 2, 3, 5, 8, 13, 21, 34, 55, 89, 144, 233, 377, 610, 987, 1597, 2584, 4181, 6765

7. $\frac{1}{1} = 1$, $\frac{2}{1} = 2$, $\frac{3}{2} = 1.5$, $\frac{5}{3} \approx 1.667$, $\frac{8}{5} = 1.6$,

   $\frac{13}{8} = 1.625$, $\frac{21}{13} \approx 1.615$, $\frac{34}{21} \approx 1.619$, $\frac{55}{34} \approx 1.618$;

   They approach 1.618.

8. about 1.618

9. $e^{1.1} = 1 + 1.1 + \frac{(1.1)^2}{2!} + \frac{(1.1)^3}{3!} + \frac{(1.1)^4}{4!}$

   $\approx 1 + 1.1 + 0.605 + 0.222 + 0.06$

   ≈ 2.99

10. $e^{-0.5} = 1 + (-0.5) + \frac{(-0.5)^2}{2!} + \frac{(-0.5)^3}{3!} + \frac{(-0.5)^4}{4!}$

    $\approx 1 - 0.5 + 0.125 - 0.021 + 0.003$

    ≈ 0.61

11. $e^{0.95} = 1 + (0.95) + \frac{(0.95)^2}{2!} + \frac{(0.95)^3}{3!} + \frac{(0.95)^4}{4!}$

    $\approx 1 + 0.95 + 0.45 + 0.14 + 0.03$

    ≈ 2.58

12. $2\left(\cos \frac{\pi}{3} + i \sin \frac{\pi}{3}\right) = 2e^{i\frac{\pi}{3}}$

13. $5\left(\cos \frac{5\pi}{3} + i \sin \frac{5\pi}{3}\right) = 3e^{i\frac{5\pi}{3}}$

14. $\sqrt{2}\left(\cos \frac{5\pi}{4} + i \sin \frac{5\pi}{4}\right) = \sqrt{2}e^{i\frac{5\pi}{4}}$

15. $12\left(\cos \frac{\pi}{6} + i \sin \frac{\pi}{6}\right) = 12e^{i\frac{\pi}{6}}$

16. $i = \cos \frac{\pi}{2} + i \sin \frac{\pi}{2} = e^{i\frac{\pi}{2}}$

17. $6i = 6\left(\cos \frac{\pi}{2} + i \sin \frac{\pi}{2}\right) = 6e^{i\frac{\pi}{2}}$

18. $\ln (-4) = \ln (-1) + \ln 4 \approx i\pi + 1.3863$

19. $\ln (-0.0082) = \ln (-1) + \ln (0.0082)$

    $\approx i\pi + (-4.8036)$

    $\approx i\pi - 4.8036$

20. $e^{1.5} = 1 + (1.5) + \frac{(1.5)^2}{2!} + \frac{(1.5)^3}{3!} + \frac{(1.5)^4}{4!}$

    $\approx 1 + 1.5 + 1.125 + 0.5625 + 0.21$

    ≈ 4.40

21. $e^{0.45} = 1 + (0.45) + \frac{(0.45)^2}{2!} + \frac{(0.45)^3}{3!} + \frac{(0.45)^4}{4!}$

    $\approx 1 + 0.45 + 0.10 + 0.015 + 0.002$

    ≈ 1.57

22. $e^{4.6} = 1 + (4.6) + \frac{(4.6)^2}{2!} + \frac{(4.6)^3}{3!} + \frac{(4.6)^4}{4!}$

    $\approx 1 + 4.6 + 10.58 + 16.22 + 18.66$

    ≈ 51.06

23. $e^{2.3} = 1 + 2.3 + \dfrac{(2.3)^2}{2!} + \dfrac{(2.3)^3}{3!} + \dfrac{(2.3)^4}{4!}$

$\approx 1 + 2.3 + 2.65 + 2.03 + 1.17$

≈ 9.14

24. $e^{0.8} = 1 + 0.8 + \dfrac{(0.8)^2}{2!} + \dfrac{(0.8)^3}{3!} + \dfrac{(0.8)^4}{4!}$

$\approx 1 + 0.8 + 0.32 + 0.08 + 0.017$

≈ 2.22

25. $e^{1.9} = 1 + 1.9 + \dfrac{(1.9)^2}{2!} + \dfrac{(1.9)^3}{3!} + \dfrac{(1.9)^4}{4!}$

$\approx 1 + 1.9 + 1.805 + 1.143 + 0.54$

≈ 6.39

26. $\sin x \approx x - \dfrac{x^3}{3!} + \dfrac{x^5}{5!} - \dfrac{x^7}{7!} + \dfrac{x^9}{9!}$

$\sin \pi \approx \sin 3.1416$

$\approx 3.1416 - \dfrac{(3.1416)^3}{3!} + \dfrac{(3.1416)^5}{5!} - \dfrac{(3.1416)^7}{7!}$

$+ \dfrac{(3.1416)^9}{9!}$

$\approx 3.1416 - 5.1677 + 2.5502 - 0.5993 + 0.0821$

≈ 0.0069

actual value: $\sin \pi = 0$

27. $\cos x \approx 1 - \dfrac{x^2}{2!} + \dfrac{x^4}{4!} - \dfrac{x^6}{6!} + \dfrac{x^8}{8!}$

$\cos \pi \approx \cos 3.1416$

$\approx 1 - \dfrac{(3.1416)^2}{2!} + \dfrac{(3.1416)^4}{4!} - \dfrac{(3.1416)^6}{6!}$

$+ \dfrac{(3.1416)^8}{8!}$

$\approx 1 - 4.9348 + 4.0588 - 1.3353 + 0.2353$

≈ -0.9760

actual value: $\cos \pi = -1$

28. $\cos \dfrac{\pi}{4} \approx \cos (0.7854)$

$\approx 1 - \dfrac{(0.7854)^2}{2!} + \dfrac{(0.7854)^4}{4!} - \dfrac{(0.7854)^6}{6!}$

$+ \dfrac{(0.7854)^8}{8!}$

$\approx 1 - 0.3084 + 0.0158 - 0.0003 + 0.0000$

≈ 0.7071

actual value: $\cos \dfrac{\pi}{4} = \dfrac{\sqrt{2}}{2} \approx 0.7071$

29. $1\left(\cos \dfrac{\pi}{4} + i \sin \dfrac{\pi}{4}\right) = 1e^{i\frac{\pi}{4}} = e^{i\frac{\pi}{4}}$

30. $3\left(\cos \dfrac{3\pi}{4} + i \sin \dfrac{3\pi}{4}\right) = 3e^{i\frac{3\pi}{4}}$

31. $4 - 4i = 4(1 - i)$

$= 4\sqrt{2}\left(\dfrac{\sqrt{2}}{2} - i\dfrac{\sqrt{2}}{2}\right)$

$= 4\sqrt{2}\left(\cos \dfrac{7\pi}{4} - i \sin \dfrac{7\pi}{4}\right)$

$= 4\sqrt{2}e^{i\frac{7\pi}{4}}$

32. $-1 + i\sqrt{3} = 2\left(-\dfrac{1}{2} + i\dfrac{\sqrt{3}}{2}\right)$

$= 2\left(\cos \dfrac{2\pi}{3} + i \sin \dfrac{2\pi}{3}\right)$

$= 2e^{i\frac{2\pi}{3}}$

33. $3 + 3i\sqrt{3} = 6\left(\dfrac{1}{2} + i\dfrac{\sqrt{3}}{2}\right)$

$= 6\left(\cos \dfrac{\pi}{3} + i \sin \dfrac{\pi}{3}\right)$

$= 6e^{i\frac{\pi}{3}}$

34. $-2\sqrt{3} - 2i = 4\left(-\dfrac{\sqrt{3}}{2} - \dfrac{1}{2}i\right)$

$= 4\left(\cos \dfrac{7\pi}{6} - i \sin \dfrac{7\pi}{6}\right)$

$= 4e^{i\frac{7\pi}{6}}$

35. $\ln (-7) = \ln (-1) + \ln 7$

$\approx i\pi + 1.9459$

36. $\ln (-6.2) = \ln (-1) + \ln (6.2)$

$\approx i\pi + 1.8245$

37. $\ln (-5.23) = \ln (-1) + \ln (5.23)$

$\approx i\pi + 1.6544$

38. $\ln (-48.2) = \ln (-1) + \ln (48.2)$

$\approx i\pi + 3.8754$

39. $\ln (-0.036) = \ln (-1) + \ln (0.036)$

$\approx i\pi - 3.3242$

40. $\ln (-4320) = \ln (-1) + \ln(4320)$

$\approx i\pi + 8.3710$

41. If you add the numbers on the diagonal lines as shown, the sums are the terms of the Fibonacci sequence.

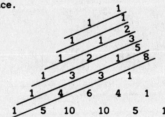

42. 1 month: 1 adult

2 months: 1 adult, 1 newborn

3 months: 2 adults, 1 newborn

4 months: 3 adults, 2 newborn

5 months: 5 adults, 3 newborn

6 months: 8 adults, 5 newborn

a. 6 months: 13 pairs; 9 months: 55 pairs; 12 months; 233 pairs

b.

Month	Pairs of Newborn Rabbits	Pairs of Adult Rabbits	Total Pairs of Rabbits
1	1	0	1
2	0	1	1
3	1	1	2
4	1	2	3
5	2	3	5
6	3	5	8
7	5	8	13
8	8	13	21
9	13	21	34
10	21	34	55
11	34	55	89
12	55	89	144

Use the table above to follow the growth of
the rabbit population. The Fibonacci
sequence occurs in each population column.

43. a. neither

b. 21, 28, 36, 45, 55

c. $\dfrac{n(n + 1)}{2}$

d. 50th term $= \dfrac{50(50 + 1)}{2} = 1275$

44. $y = x^3$

$= \dfrac{x^4}{x}$, hole at zero

$= \dfrac{x^4(x + 2)}{x(x + 2)}$, hole at (-2) and 0

45. $\sin^2 x = \cos x - 1$

$1 - \cos^2 x = \cos x - 1$

$0 = \cos^2 x + \cos x - 2$

$= (\cos x - 1)(\cos x + 2)$

$\cos x = 1 \qquad \cos x = -2$

$x = 0° \qquad$ undefined

46.

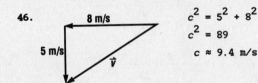

$c^2 = 5^2 + 8^2$

$c^2 = 89$

$c \approx 9.4$ m/s

47. $A = Pe^{rt}$

$A = (100)e^{(0.07 \times 15)}$

$A \approx 285.77$

48. $(x - 3y)^5 = \dfrac{n!}{r!(n - r)!} x^{n-r} y^r$

$= \dfrac{5!}{2!(5 - 2)!} x^{5-2}(-3y)^2$

$= \dfrac{5 \cdot 4 \cdot 3!}{2!3!} x^3 9y^2$

$= 90x^3 y^2$

49. $\sqrt{2}\% = \dfrac{\sqrt{2}}{100} \approx 0.014$

$0.014 \times 3\sqrt{2} \approx 0.06$

The best answer is A.

12-8 Mathematical Induction

PAGE 704   CHECKING FOR UNDERSTANDING

1. $n(n + 1)$

2. Verify S_n is valid for $n = 1$.

3. $n = k, \; n = k + 1$

4. $1 + 2 + 3 + \ldots + n = \dfrac{n(n + 1)}{2}$

5. $1 + 4 + 7 + \ldots + 148$

$148 = 3n - 2$

$n = 50$

$S_n = \dfrac{n(3n - 1)}{2} = \dfrac{50[3(50) - 1]}{2} = 3725$

6. $30 + 32 + 34 + \ldots + 50 = n(n + 1)$

$50 = 2n$

$n = 25$

The sum of the terms up to 28:

$S_{14} = (14)(14 + 1) = 210.$

The sum up to 50:

$S_{25} = 25(25 + 1) = 650$

$650 - 210 = 440$

7. $1^2 + 3^2 + 5^2 + \ldots + [n + (n + 1)]^2$

$= 1^2 + 3^2 + 5^2 + \ldots + (2n - 1)^2$

$1^2 + 3^2 = 10$

$1^2 + 3^2 + 5^2 = 35$

$1^2 + 3^2 + 5^2 + 7^2 = 84$

$S_n = \dfrac{n(2n - 1)(2n + 1)}{3}$

$S_9 = \dfrac{9(2 \cdot 9 - 1)(2 \cdot 9 + 1)}{3}$

$= 969$

8. $2^5 + 2^6 + 2^7 + 2^8 + \ldots + 2^{n-1}$

$2^0 = 1$

$2^0 + 2^1 = 3$

$2^0 + 2^1 + 2^2 = 7$

$S_n = 2^n - 1$

The sum of the first 11 terms is $2^{11} - 1 = 2047.$

The sum of the first 5 terms is $2^5 - 1 = 31.$

$2047 - 31 = 2016$

9. Step 1: Verify that the formula is valid for $n = 1$. Since $S_1 = 2$ and $1(1 + 1) = 2$, the formula is valid for $n = 1$.

Step 2: Assume the formula is valid for $n = k$ and derive a formula for $n = k + 1$.

$2 + 4 + 6 + \ldots + 2k + 2(k + 1)$
$$= k(k + 1) + 2(k + 1)$$
$$= (k + 1)(k + 2)$$

Apply the original formula for $n = k + 1$

S_{k+1}: $(k + 1)[(k + 1) + 1] = (k + 1)(k + 2)$

The formula gives the same result as adding the $(k + 1)$ term directly. Thus, if the formula is valid for $n = k$, it is also valid for $n = k + 1$. Since the formula is valid for $n = 1$, it is also valid for $n = 2$. Since it is valid for $n = 2$, it is also valid for $n = 3$, and so on, indefinitely. Thus, the formula is valid for all positive integral values of n.

10. Step 1: Verify that the formula is valid for $n = 1$. Since $S_1 = 1$ and $\dfrac{1(1 + 1)(1 + 2)}{6} = 1$, the formula is valid for $n = 1$.

Step 2: Assume the formula is valid for $n = k$ and derive the formula for $n = k + 1$.

$1 + 3 + 6 + \ldots + \dfrac{k(k + 1)}{2} = \dfrac{k(k + 1)(k + 2)}{6}$

$1 + 3 + 6 + \ldots + \dfrac{k(k + 1)}{2} + \dfrac{(k + 1)(k + 2)}{2}$

$$= \dfrac{k(k + 1)(k + 2)}{6} + \dfrac{(k + 1)(k + 2)}{2}$$

$$= \dfrac{k(k + 1)(k + 2) + 3(k + 1)(k + 2)}{6}$$

$$= \dfrac{(k + 1)(k + 2)(k + 3)}{6}$$

Apply the original formula for $n = k + 1$.

S_{k+1}: $\dfrac{(k + 1)[(k + 1) + 1][(k + 2) + 1]}{6}$

$$= \dfrac{(k + 1)(k + 2)(k + 3)}{6}$$

The formula gives the same result as adding the $(k + 1)$ term directly. Thus, if the formula is valid for $n = k$, it is also valid for $n = k + 1$. Since the formula is valid for $n = 1$, it is also valid for $n = 2$. Since it is valid for $n = 2$, it is also valid for $n = 3$, and so on, indefinitely. Thus, the formula is valid for all positive integral values of n.

11. Step 1: Verify that the formula is valid for $n = 1$. Since $S_1 = \dfrac{1}{2}$ and $1 - \dfrac{1}{2^1} = \dfrac{1}{2}$, the formula is valid for $n = 1$.

Step 2: Assume that the formula is valid for $n = k$ and derive a formula for $n = k + 1$.

$\dfrac{1}{2} + \dfrac{1}{2^2} + \dfrac{1}{2^3} + \ldots + \dfrac{2}{2^k} = 1 - \dfrac{1}{2^k}$

$\dfrac{1}{2} + \dfrac{1}{2^2} + \dfrac{1}{2^3} + \ldots + \dfrac{1}{2^k} + \dfrac{1}{2^{k+1}}$

$$= 1 - \dfrac{1}{2^k} + \dfrac{1}{2^{k+1}}$$

$$= 1 - \dfrac{2}{2 \cdot 2^k} + \dfrac{1}{2^{k+1}}$$

$$= 1 - \dfrac{2}{2^{k+1}} + \dfrac{2}{2^{k+1}}$$

$$= 1 - \dfrac{1}{2^{k+1}}$$

When the original formula is applied for $n = k + 1$, the same result is obtained. Thus, if the formula is valid for $n = k$, it is also valid for $n = k + 1$. Since the formula is valid for $n = 1$, it is also valid for $n = 2$. Since it is valid for $n = 2$, it is also valid for $n = 3$, and so on, indefinitely. Thus, the formula is valid for all positive integral values of n.

PAGES 704-705   EXERCISES

12. Step 1: Verify that the formula if valid for $n = 1$. Since $S_1 = 1$ and $\dfrac{1(1 + 1)(2 \cdot 1 + 1)}{6} = 1$, the formula is valid for $n = 1$.

Step 2: Assume that the formula is valid for $n = k$ and derive a formula for $n = k + 1$.

$1^2 + 2^2 + 3^2 + \ldots + k^2 = \dfrac{k(k + 1)(2k + 1)}{6}$

$1^2 + 2^2 + 3^2 + \ldots + k^2 + (k + 1)^2$

$$= \dfrac{k(k + 1)(2k + 1)}{6} + (k + 1)^2$$

$$= \dfrac{k(k + 1)(2k + 1) + 6(k + 1)^2}{6}$$

$$= \dfrac{(k + 1)[k(2k + 1) + 6(k + 1)]}{6}$$

$$= \dfrac{(k + 1)(2k^2 + 7k + 6)}{6}$$

$$= \dfrac{(k + 1)(k + 2)(2k + 3)}{6}$$

Apply the original formula for $n = k + 1$.

$S_{k+1} = \dfrac{(k + 1)[(k + 1) + 1][2(k + 1) + 1]}{6}$

$$= \dfrac{(k + 1)(k + 2)(2k + 3)}{6}$$

The formula gives the same result as adding the $(k + 1)$ term directly. Thus, if the formula is valid for $n = k$, it is also valid for $n = k + 1$. Since the formula is valid for $n = 1$, it is also valid for $n = 2$. Since it is valid for $n = 2$, it is also valid for $n = 3$, and so on, indefinitely. Thus, the formula is valid for all positive integral values of n.

324

13. Step 1: Verify that the formula is valid for $n = 1$. Since $S_1 = 1$, and $\frac{1^2(1 + 1)^2}{4} = 1$, the formula is valid for $n = 1$.

Step 2: Assume that the formula is valid for $n = k$ and derive a formula for $n = k + 1$.

$$1^3 + 2^3 + 3^3 + \ldots + k^3 = \frac{k^2(k + 1)^2}{4}$$

$$1^3 + 2^3 + 3^3 + \ldots + k^3 + (k + 1)^3$$

$$= \frac{k^2(k + 1)^2}{4} + (k + 1)^3$$

$$= \frac{k^2(k + 1)^2 + 4(k + 1)^3}{4}$$

$$= \frac{(k + 1)^2[k^2 + 4(k + 1)]}{4}$$

$$= \frac{(k + 1)^2(k^2 + 4k + 4)}{4}$$

$$= \frac{(k + 1)^2(k + 2)^2}{4}$$

When the original formula is applied for $n = k + 1$, the same result is obtained. Thus, if the formula is valid for $n = k$, it is also valid for $n = k + 1$. Since the formula is valid for $n = 1$, it is also valid for $n = 2$. Since it is valid for $n = 2$, it is also valid for $n = 3$, and so on, indefinitely. Thus, the formula is valid for all positive integral values of n.

14. Step 1: Verify that the formula is valid for $n = 1$. Since $S_1 = 1$ and

$$\frac{1(2 \cdot 1 - 1)(2 \cdot 1 + 1)}{3} = 1,$$ the formula is valid for $n = 1$.

Step 2: Assume that the formula is valid for $n = k$ and derive a formula for $n = k + 1$.

$$1^2 + 3^2 + 5^2 + \ldots + (2k - 1)^2$$

$$= \frac{k(2k - 1)(2k + 1)}{3}$$

$$1^2 + 3^2 + 5^2 + \ldots + (2k - 1)^2 + (2k + 1)^2$$

$$= \frac{k(2k - 1)(2k + 1)}{3} + (2k + 1)^2$$

$$= \frac{k(2k - 1)(2k + 1) + 3(2k + 1)^2}{3}$$

$$= \frac{[k(2k - 1) + 3(2k + 1)](2k + 1)}{3}$$

$$= \frac{(2k^2 + 5k + 3)(2k + 1)}{3}$$

$$= \frac{(2k + 3)(k + 1)(2k + 1)}{3}$$

When the original formula is applied for $n = k + 1$, the same result is obtained. Thus, if the formula is valid for $n = k$, it is also valid for $n = k + 1$. Since the formula is valid for $n = 1$, it is also valid for $n = 2$. Since it is

valid for $n = 2$, it is also valid for $n = 3$, and so on, indefinitely. Thus, the formula is valid for all positive integral values of n.

15. Step 1: Verify that the formula is valid for $n = 1$. Since $S_1 = 1$ and $2^1 - 1 = 1$, the formula is valid for $n = 1$.

Step 2: Assume the formula is valid for $n = k$ and derive a formula for $n = k + 1$.

$$1 + 2 + 4 + \ldots + 2^{k-1} = 2^k - 1$$

$$1 + 2 + 4 + \ldots + 2^{k-1} + 2^k = 2^k - 1 + 2^k$$

$$= 2(2^k) - 1$$

$$= 2^{k+1} - 1$$

When the original formula is applied for $n = k + 1$, the same result is obtained. Thus, if the formula is valid for $n = k$, it is also valid for $n = k + 1$. Since the formula is valid for $n = 1$, it is also valid for $n = 2$. Since it is valid for $n = 2$, it is also valid for $n = 3$, and so on, indefinitely. Thus, the formula is valid for all positive integral values of n.

16. Step 1: Verify that the formula is valid for $n = 1$. Since $S_1 = -\frac{1}{2}$ and $\frac{1}{2^1} - 1 = -\frac{1}{2}$, the the formula is valid for $n = 1$.

Step 2: Assume that the formula is valid for $n = k$ and derive a formula for $n = k + 1$.

$$-\frac{1}{2} - \frac{1}{4} - \frac{1}{8} - \ldots - \frac{1}{2^k} = \frac{1}{2^k} - 1$$

$$-\frac{1}{2} - \frac{1}{4} - \frac{1}{8} - \ldots - \frac{1}{2^k} - \frac{1}{2^{k+1}}$$

$$= \frac{1}{2^k} - 1 - \frac{1}{2^{k+1}}$$

$$= \frac{2}{2 \cdot 2^k} - 1 - \frac{1}{2^{k+1}}$$

$$= \frac{2}{2^{k+1}} - 1 - \frac{1}{2^{k+1}}$$

$$= \frac{1}{2^{k+1}} - 1$$

When the original formula is applied for $n = k + 1$, the same result is obtained. Thus, if the formula is valid for $n = k$, it is also valid for $n = k + 1$. Since the formula is valid for $n = 1$, it is also valid for $n = 2$. Since it is valid for $n = 2$, it is also valid for $n = 3$, and so on, indefinitely. Thus, the formula is valid for all positive integral values of n.

17. Step 1: Verify that the formula is valid for
$n = 1$. Since $S_1 = 1$ and $\dfrac{6 + 15 + 10 - 1}{30} = 1$,
the formula is valid for $n = 1$.

Step 2: Assume that the formula is valid for
$n = k$ and derive a formula for $n = k + 1$.

$1^4 + 2^4 + 3^4 + \ldots + k^4$

$\qquad = \dfrac{6k^5 + 15k^4 + 10k^3 - k}{30}$

$1^4 + 2^4 + 3^4 + \ldots + k^4 + (k + 1)^4$

$\qquad = \dfrac{6k^5 + 15k^4 + 10k^3 - k}{30} + (k + 1)^4$

$\qquad = \dfrac{(k+1)(6k^4+9k^3+k^2-k)+30(k+1)(k^3+3k^2+3k+1)}{30}$

$\qquad = \dfrac{(k+1)(6k^4+9k^3+k^2-k+30k^3+90k^2+90k+30)}{30}$

$\qquad = \dfrac{(k+1)[6(k^4+4k^3+6k^2+4k+1)+15(k^3+3k^2+3k+1)+10(k^2+2k+1)-1]}{30}$

$\qquad = \dfrac{(k+1)[6(k+1)^4+15(k+1)^3+10(k+1)^2-1]}{30}$

$\qquad = \dfrac{6(k+1)^5+15(k+1)^4+10(k+1)^3-(k+1)}{30}$

When the original formula is applied for
$n = k + 1$, the same result is obtained. Thus, if
the formula is valid for $n = k$, it is also valid
for $n = k + 1$. Since the formula is valid for
$n = 1$, it is also valid for $n = 2$. Since it is
valid for $n = 2$, it is also valid for $n = 3$, and
so on, indefinitely. Thus, the formula is valid
for all positive integral values of n.

18. Step 1: Verify that the formula is valid for
$n = 1$. Since $S_1 = a$ and $\frac{1}{2}[2a + (1 - 1)d] = a$,
the formula is valid for $n = 1$.

Step 2: Assume that the formula is valid for
$n = k$ and derive a formula for $n = k + 1$.

$a + (a + d) + (a + 2d) + \ldots + [a + (k - 1)d]$

$\qquad\qquad\qquad = \dfrac{k}{2}[2a + (k - 1)d]$

$a + (a + d) + (a + 2d) + \ldots +$
$[a + (k - 1)d] + (a + kd)$

$\qquad = \dfrac{k}{2}[2a + (k - 1)d] + (a + kd)$

$\qquad = \dfrac{k[2a + (k - 1)d] + 2a + 2kd}{2}$

$\qquad = \dfrac{2ak + k(k - 1)d + 2a + 2kd}{2}$

$\qquad = \dfrac{(k + 1)(2a) + [k(k - 1) + 2k]d}{2}$

$\qquad = \dfrac{(k + 1)(2a) + k(k + 1)d}{2}$

$\qquad = \dfrac{(k + 1)}{2}(2a + kd)$

When the original formula is applied for
$n = k + 1$, the same result is obtained. Thus, if
the formula is valid for $n = k$, it is also valid
for $n = k + 1$. Since the formula is valid for
$n = 1$, it is also valid for $n = 2$. Since it is
valid for $n = 2$, it is also valid for $n = 3$,
and so on, indefinitely. Thus, the formula is
valid for all positive integral values of n.

19. Step 1: Verify that the formula is valid for
$n = 1$. Since $S_1 = \frac{1}{2}$ and $\dfrac{1}{1 + 1} = \frac{1}{2}$, the formula
is valid for $n = 1$.

Step 2: Assume that the formula is valid for
$n = k$ and derive a formula for $n = k + 1$.

$\dfrac{1}{1 \cdot 2} + \dfrac{1}{2 \cdot 3} + \dfrac{1}{3 \cdot 4} + \ldots + \dfrac{1}{k(k + 1)} = \dfrac{k}{(k + 1)}$

$\dfrac{1}{1 \cdot 2} + \dfrac{1}{2 \cdot 3} + \dfrac{1}{3 \cdot 4} + \ldots + \dfrac{1}{k(k + 1)}$

$\quad + \dfrac{1}{(k + 1)(k + 2)} = \dfrac{k}{(k + 1)} + \dfrac{1}{(k + 1)(k + 2)}$

$\qquad\qquad = \dfrac{k(k + 2) + 1}{(k + 1)(k + 2)}$

$\qquad\qquad = \dfrac{k^2 + 2k + 1}{(k + 1)(k + 2)}$

$\qquad\qquad = \dfrac{(k + 1)^2}{(k + 1)(k + 2)}$

$\qquad\qquad = \dfrac{k + 1}{k + 2}$

When the original formula is applied for
$n = k + 1$, the same result is obtained. Thus, if
the formula is valid for $n = k$, it is also valid
for $n = k + 1$. Since the formula is valid for
$n = 1$, it is also valid for $n = 2$. Since it is
valid for $n = 2$, it is also valid for $n = 3$, and
so on indefinitely. Thus, the formula is valid
for all positive integral values of n.

20. Step 1: Verify that S_n: $(x + y)^n = x^n + nx^{n-1}y$

$\quad + \dfrac{n(n - 1)}{2!}x^{n-2}y^2 + \dfrac{n(n - 1)(n - 2)}{3!}x^{n-3}y^3 +$

$\ldots + y^n$ is valid for $n = 1$.

Since $S_1 = (x + y)^1 = x^1 + 1x^0y^1 = x + y$, S_n is
valid for $n = 1$.

Step 2: Assume the formula is valid for $n = k$
and derive a formula for $n = k + 1$.

S_k: $(x + y)^k = x^k + kx^{k-1}y + \dfrac{k(k - 1)}{2!}x^{k-2}y^2$

$\qquad\qquad + \dfrac{k(k - 1)(k - 2)}{3!}x^{k-3}y^3$

$\qquad\qquad + \ldots + y^k$

S_{k+1}:

$(x + y)^k(x + y)$

$= (x + y)\left[x^k + kx^{k-1}y + \dfrac{k(k-1)}{2!}x^{k-2}y^2 + \ldots + y^k\right]$

$(x + y)^{k+1}$

$= x\left[x^k + kx^{k-1}y + \dfrac{k(k-1)}{2!}x^{k-2}y^2 + \ldots + y^k\right]$

$\quad + y\left[x^k + kx^{k-1}y + \dfrac{k(k-1)}{2!}x^{k-2}y^2 + \ldots + y^k\right]$

$= x^{k+1} + kx^ky + \dfrac{k(k-1)}{2!}x^{k-1}y^2 + \ldots + xy^k$

$\quad + x^ky + kx^{k-1}y^2 + \dfrac{k(k-1)}{2!}x^{k-2}y^3 + \ldots + y^{k+1}$

$= x^{k+1} + (k+1)x^ky + kx^{k-1}y^2 + \dfrac{k(k-1)}{2!}x^{k-1}y^2$

$\quad + \ldots + y^{k+1}$

$= x^{k+1} + (k+1)x^ky + \dfrac{k(k+1)}{2!}x^{k-1}y^2 + \ldots + y^{k+1}$

When the original formula is applied for $n = k + 1$, the same result is obtained. Thus, if the formula is valid for $n = k$, it is also valid for $n = k + 1$. Since the formula is valid for $n = 1$, it is also valid for $n = 2$. Since it is valid for $n = 2$, it is also valid for $n = 3$, and so on, indefinitely. Thus, the formula is valid for all positive integral values of n.

21. a. arithmetic

   b. $1 + 2 + 3 + 4 + \ldots + 12 = \dfrac{12}{2}(1 + 12) = 78$

   $2 \times 78 = 156$

22. a. infinite

   b. You spend $600(0.7) = 420$.

   People spend: $420(0.7) = 294$

   $\qquad\qquad\quad 294(0.7) = 205.8$

   $\qquad\qquad\quad 205.8(0.7) = 144.06$

   $\qquad\qquad\qquad\qquad \vdots$

   $S_n = \dfrac{a_1}{1 - r} = \dfrac{600}{1 - (0.7)} = \$2000$

23. a. geometric

   b. There have been $\dfrac{1993 - 1000}{30} = 33.1$ or about 33 generations.

   $n = 33$, $r = 2$

   $S_n = \dfrac{a_1 - a_1r^n}{1 - r}$

   $\quad = \dfrac{2 - 2(2)^{33}}{1 - 2}$

   $\quad = 1.718 \times 10^{10}$

24. $(-1)(-6) - 3(-2) = 6 + 6 = 12$

25. $\quad \dfrac{2}{(x + 2)} = \dfrac{x}{(2 - x)} + \dfrac{(x^2 + 4)}{(x^2 - 4)}$

   $\dfrac{2}{x + 2} = \dfrac{-x}{x - 2} + \dfrac{x^2 + 4}{(x - 2)(x + 2)}$

   $\dfrac{2(x - 2)}{(x + 2)(x - 2)} = \dfrac{-x(x + 2) + x^2 + 4}{(x - 2)(x + 2)}$

   $2(x - 2) = -x^2 - 2x + x^2 + 4$

   $2x - 4 = -2x + 4$

   $4x = 8$

   $x = 2$

   If $x = 2$, denominator = 0.

   no solution

26.

27. center $(0, 3)$

   $a = 4$, $b = 3$

   $c = \sqrt{16 - 9} = \sqrt{7}$

   foci: $(0, 3 \pm \sqrt{7})$

   vertices: $(0, 7)$, $(0, -1)$, $(3, 3)$, $(-3, 3)$

28. $-1 + i = \sqrt{2}\left(\dfrac{-\sqrt{2}}{2} + i\,\dfrac{\sqrt{2}}{2}\right)$

   $\qquad\quad = \sqrt{2}\left(\cos\dfrac{3\pi}{4} + i\sin\dfrac{3\pi}{4}\right)$

   $\qquad\quad = \sqrt{2}\,e^{i\frac{3\pi}{4}}$

29. Let x = number of cars each represents.

   $270 = 2x$

   $135 = x$

   Since $135 > 100$, quantity A is greater.   A

Chapter 12 Summary and Review

PAGES 706-708   SKILLS AND CONCEPTS

1. $d = 4.3 - 3 = 1.3$

   $5.6 + 1.3 = 6.9$

   $6.9 + 1.3 = 8.2$

   $8.2 + 1.3 = 9.5$

   $9.5 + 1.3 = 10.8$

   $10.8 + 1.3 = 12.1$

   $6.9, 8.2, 9.5, 10.8, 12.1$

2. $a_n = a + (n - 1)d$

   $a_{20} = 7 + (20 - 1)(-4)$

   $\qquad = -69$

3. $a_5 = a_1 + (n - 1)d$

   $-4 = 6 + (4)d$

   $-10 = 4d$

   $-2.5 = d$

   $6 - 2.5 = 3.5$

   $3.5 - 2.5 = 1$

   $1 - 2.5 = -1.5$

   $6,\ 3.5,\ 1,\ -1.5,\ -4$

4. $r = \dfrac{49}{343} = \dfrac{1}{7}$

   $7\left(\dfrac{1}{7}\right) = 1$

   $1\left(\dfrac{1}{7}\right) = \dfrac{1}{7}$

   $\dfrac{1}{7}\left(\dfrac{1}{7}\right) = \dfrac{1}{49}$

   $\dfrac{1}{49}\left(\dfrac{1}{7}\right) = \dfrac{1}{343}$

   $1,\ \dfrac{1}{7},\ \dfrac{1}{49},\ \dfrac{1}{343}$

5. $a_n = ar^{n-1}$

   $a_7 = 2.2(2)^{7-1}$

      $= 140.8$

6. Sample answer:

   $a_n = ar^{n-1}$

   $125 = 0.2r^{5-1}$

   $625 = r^4$

    $5 = r$

   $0.2(5) = 1$

   $1(5) = 5$

   $5(5) = 25$

   $0.2,\ 1,\ 5,\ 25,\ 125$

7. $\displaystyle\lim_{n\to\infty} \frac{2n}{5n + 1} = \lim_{n\to\infty} \frac{\frac{2n}{n}}{\frac{5n}{n} + \frac{1}{n}}$

              $= \dfrac{2}{5 + 0}$

              $= \dfrac{2}{5}$

8. $\displaystyle\lim_{n\to\infty} \frac{4n + 1}{n} = \lim_{n\to\infty} \frac{4n}{n} + \lim_{n\to\infty} \frac{1}{n}$

              $= 4 + 0$

              $= 4$

9. $\displaystyle\lim_{n\to\infty} \frac{(-1)^n n^2}{5n^2} = \lim_{n\to\infty} \frac{(-1)^n}{5}$

   does not exist

10. $\displaystyle\lim_{n\to\infty} \frac{4n^3 - 3n}{n^4 - 4n^3} = \lim_{n\to\infty} \frac{n(4n^2 - 3)}{n^3(n - 4)}$

         $= \displaystyle\lim_{n\to\infty} \frac{4n^2 - 3}{n^3 - 4n^2}$

         $= \displaystyle\lim_{n\to\infty} \frac{\frac{4n^2}{n^3} - \frac{3}{n^3}}{\frac{n^3}{n^3} - \frac{4n^2}{n^3}}$

         $= \displaystyle\lim_{n\to\infty} \frac{\frac{4}{n} - \frac{3}{n^3}}{1 - \frac{4}{n}}$

         $= \dfrac{0 - 0}{1 - 0}$

         $= \dfrac{0}{1}$

         $= 0$

11. The general term is $\dfrac{(n + 5)}{n}$.

   $\dfrac{n + 5}{n} > \dfrac{1}{n}$, so the series is divergent.

12. The general term is $\dfrac{1}{n^3}$.

   $\dfrac{1}{n^3} < \dfrac{1}{n^2}$, so the series is convergent.

13. The general term is $\dfrac{2}{n}$.

   $\dfrac{2}{n} > \dfrac{1}{n}$, so the series is divergent.

14. $\displaystyle\sum_{a=5}^{11} (2a - 4) = (2 \cdot 5 - 4) + (2 \cdot 6 - 4)$

              $+ (2 \cdot 7 - 4) + (2 \cdot 8 - 4)$

              $+ (2 \cdot 9 - 4) + (2 \cdot 10 - 4)$

              $+ (2 \cdot 11 - 4)$

          $= 6 + 8 + 10 + 12 + 14 + 16 + 18$

          $= 84$

15. $\displaystyle\sum_{k=1}^{\infty} (0.4)^k = 0.4 + (0.4)^2 + (0.4)^3 + \ldots$

             $= 0.4 + 0.16 + 0.064 + \ldots$

   $S_n = \dfrac{a}{1 - r} = \dfrac{0.4}{1 - 0.4} = \dfrac{2}{3}$

16. $-1 + 1 + 3 + 5 + \ldots = \displaystyle\sum_{n=0}^{\infty} (2n - 1)$

17. $2 + 5 + 10 + 17 + \ldots + 82 = \displaystyle\sum_{n=1}^{9} (n^2 + 1)$

18. $(a - x)^6$

   $= a^6 + \dfrac{6!}{1!(6 - 1)!} a^5(-x)^1 + \dfrac{6!}{2!(6 - 2)!} a^4(-x)^2$

   $+ \dfrac{6!}{3!(6 - 3)!} a^3(-x)^3 + \dfrac{6!}{4!(6 - 4)!} a^2(-x)^4$

   $+ \dfrac{6!}{5!(6 - 5)!} a^1(-x)^5 + \dfrac{6!}{6!(6 - 6)!} a^0(-x)^6$

   $= a^6 - 6a^5x + 15a^4x^2 - 20a^3x^3 + 15a^2x^4$

    $- 6ax^5 + x^6$

19. $(12r + 3s)^4$

   $= (2r)^4 + \dfrac{4!}{1!(4 - 1)!} (2r)^3(3s)^1$

   $+ \dfrac{4!}{2!(4 - 2)!} (2r)^2(3s)^2$

   $+ \dfrac{4!}{3!(4 - 3)!} (2r)(3s)^3$

   $+ \dfrac{4!}{4!0!} (2r)^0(3s)^4$

   $= 16r^4 + 96r^3s + 216r^2s^2 + 216rs^3 + 81s^4$

20. $(x - 1)^{15} = \displaystyle\sum_{r=0}^{15} \frac{15!}{r!(15 - r)!} x^{15-r}(-1)^r$

   5th term $= \dfrac{15!}{4!(15 - 4)!} x^{15-4}(-1)^4$

            $= 1365x^{11}$

21. $(x + 3y)^{10} = \displaystyle\sum_{r=0}^{10} \frac{10!}{r!(10 - r)!} x^{10-r}(3y)^r$

   8th term $= \dfrac{10!}{7!(10 - 7)!} x^{10-7}(3y)^7$

            $= 262{,}440x^3y^7$

22. $4i = 4\left(\cos \dfrac{\pi}{2} + i \sin \dfrac{\pi}{2}\right)$

$= 4e^{i\frac{\pi}{2}}$

23. $2 - 2i = 2(1 - i)$

$= 2\sqrt{2}\left(\dfrac{\sqrt{2}}{2} - i\dfrac{\sqrt{2}}{2}\right)$

$= 2\sqrt{2}\left(\cos \dfrac{7\pi}{4} + i \sin \dfrac{7\pi}{4}\right)$

$= 2\sqrt{2}e^{i\frac{7\pi}{4}}$

24. $-5 - 5\sqrt{3}i = 5(-1 - \sqrt{3}i)$

$= 10\left(-\dfrac{1}{2} - i\dfrac{\sqrt{3}}{2}\right)$

$= 10\left(\cos \dfrac{4\pi}{3} + i \sin \dfrac{4\pi}{3}\right)$

$= 10e^{i\frac{4\pi}{3}}$

25. $3\sqrt{3} + 3i = 3(\sqrt{3} + i)$

$= 6\left(\dfrac{\sqrt{3}}{2} + \dfrac{1}{2}i\right)$

$= 6\left(\cos \dfrac{\pi}{6} + i \sin \dfrac{\pi}{6}\right)$

$= 6e^{i\frac{\pi}{6}}$

26. Step 1: Verify that the formula is valid for $n = 1$. Since $\dfrac{1(1 + 1)}{2} = \dfrac{1(2)}{2} = \dfrac{2}{2} = 1$, the formula is valid for $n = 1$.

Step 2: Assume that the formula is valid for $n = k$ and derive a formula for $n = k + 1$.

$1 + 2 + 3 + \ldots + k = \dfrac{k(k + 1)}{2}$

$1 + 2 + 3 + \ldots + k + (k + 1)$

$= \dfrac{k(k + 1)}{2} + (k + 1)$

$= \dfrac{k(k + 1)}{2} + \dfrac{2(k + 1)}{2}$

$= \dfrac{k^2 + 3k + 2}{2}$

$= \dfrac{(k + 1)(k + 2)}{2}$

$= \dfrac{(k + 1)[(k + 1) + 1]}{2}$

When the original formula is applied for $n = k + 1$, the same result is obtained. Thus, if the formula is valid for $n = k$, it is also valid for $n = k + 1$. Since the formula is valid for $n = 1$, it is also valid for $n = 2$. Since it is valid for $n = 2$, it is also valid for $n = 3$, and so on, indefinitely. Thus, the formula is valid for all positive integral values of n.

27. Step 1: Verify that the formula is valid for $n = 1$. Since $1(1 + 2) = 1(3) = 3$ and since $\dfrac{1(1 + 1)(2 \cdot 1 + 7)}{6} = \dfrac{1(2)(2 + 7)}{6} = 3$, the formula is valid for $n = 1$.

Step 2: Assume the formula is valid for $n = k$ and derive a formula for $n = k + 1$.

$3 + 8 + 15 + \ldots + k(k + 2) = \dfrac{k(k + 1)(2k + 7)}{6}$

$3 + 8 + 15 + \ldots + k(k + 2) + (k + 1)(k + 3)$

$= \dfrac{k(k + 1)(2k + 7)}{6} + (k + 1)(k + 3)$

$= \dfrac{k(k + 1)(2k + 7)}{6} + \dfrac{6(k + 1)(k + 3)}{6}$

$= \dfrac{(k + 1)[k(2k + 7) + 6(k + 3)]}{6}$

$= \dfrac{(k + 1)(2k^2 + 13k + 18)}{6}$

$= \dfrac{(k + 1)(k + 2)(2k + 9)}{6}$

$= \dfrac{(k + 1)[(k + 1) + 1][2(k + 1) + 7]}{6}$

When the original formula is applied for $n = k + 1$, the same result is obtained. Thus, if the formula is valid for $n = k$, it is also valid for $n = k + 1$. Since the formula is valid for $n = 1$, it is also valid for $n = 2$. Since it is valid for $n = 2$, it is also valid for $n = 3$, and so on, indefinitely. Thus, the formula is valid for all positive integral values of n.

PAGE 708   APPLICATIONS AND PROBLEM SOLVING

28. $r = 1 - 0.12 = 0.88$

$a_1 = 150,000,000$

$a_n = a_1 r^{n-1}$

$a_6 = 150,000,000(0.88)^{6-1}$

$\approx \$79,159,787.52$

29. $r = 0.5$, $a_1 = 100$

$S_n = \dfrac{a_1 - a_1 r^n}{1 - r}$

$S_5 = \dfrac{100 - 100(0.5)^5}{1 - 0.5}$

$= 193.75$ feet

Chapter 12 Test

1. $d = 4.5 - 3 = 1.5$

    $6 + 1.5 = 7.5$

    $7.5 + 1.5 = 9$

    $9 + 1.5 = 10.5$

    $10.5 + 1.5 = 12$

    $12 + 1.5 = 13.5$

    $7.5, 9, 10.5, 12, 13.5$

2. $r = \dfrac{\frac{1}{10}}{\frac{1}{4}} = \dfrac{2}{5}$

    $\dfrac{2}{125} \cdot \dfrac{3}{5} = \dfrac{4}{625}$

    $\dfrac{4}{625} \cdot \dfrac{2}{5} = \dfrac{8}{3125}$

    $\dfrac{8}{3125} \cdot \dfrac{2}{5} = \dfrac{16}{15,625}$

    $\dfrac{16}{15,625} \cdot \dfrac{2}{5} = \dfrac{32}{78,125}$

    $\dfrac{4}{625}, \dfrac{8}{3125}, \dfrac{16}{15,625}, \dfrac{32}{78,125}$

3. $a_5 = 8$, $a_1 = -4$

    $a_n = a_1 + (n - 1)d$

    $8 = -4 + (5 - 1)d$

    $12 = 4d$

    $3 = d$

    $-4 + 3 = -1$, $-1 + 3 = 2$,

    $2 + 3 = 5$,

    $-4, -1, 2, 5, 8$

4. Sample answer:

    $a_1 = 16$, $a_5 = 1$

    $a_n = a_1 r^{n-1}$

    $1 = 16r^{5-1}$

    $\dfrac{1}{16} = r^4$

    $\pm\dfrac{1}{2} = r$

    $16\left(\dfrac{1}{2}\right) = 8$, $8\left(\dfrac{1}{2}\right) = 4$,

    $4\left(\dfrac{1}{2}\right) = 2$

    $16, 8, 4, 2, 1$

5. $d = -1 - (-6) = 5$

    $a_{24} = a_1 + (n - 1)d$

    $a_{24} = -6 + (24 - 1)5$

    $\quad = 109$

6. $r = \dfrac{\frac{3}{4}}{\frac{1}{2}} = \dfrac{3}{2}$

    $a_8 = a_1 r^{8-1}$

    $\quad = \dfrac{1}{2}\left(\dfrac{3}{2}\right)^7$

    $\quad = \dfrac{2187}{256}$

7. $S_n = \dfrac{n}{2}[2a_1 + (n - 1)d]$

    $345 = \dfrac{n}{2}[2(12) + (n - 1)5]$

    $690 = n(24 + 5n - 5)$

    $690 = n(19n + 5n)$

    $0 = 5n^2 + 19n - 690$

    $\quad = (5n + 69)(n - 10)$

    $5n = -69 \quad n = 10$

    $n = \dfrac{-69}{5}$

    not possible

8. $r = \dfrac{5}{\frac{5}{2}} = 2$

    $S_n = \dfrac{a_1 - a_1 r^n}{1 - r}$

    $S_{10} = \dfrac{\frac{5}{2} - \frac{5}{2}(2)^{10}}{1 - 2}$

    $\quad = 2557\dfrac{1}{2}$

9. $\displaystyle\lim_{n\to\infty} \dfrac{n^3 + 3}{3n^2 + 1} = \lim_{n\to\infty} \dfrac{\frac{n^3}{n^3} + \frac{3}{n^3}}{\frac{3n^2}{n^3} - \frac{1}{n^3}}$

    $\quad = \dfrac{1 + 0}{0 + 0}$

    $\quad = \dfrac{1}{0}$

    does not exist

10. $\displaystyle\lim_{n\to\infty} \dfrac{n^3 + 4}{2n^3 + 3n} = \lim_{n\to\infty} \dfrac{\frac{n^3}{n^3} + \frac{4}{n^3}}{\frac{2n^3}{n^3} + \frac{3n}{n^3}}$

    $\quad = \dfrac{1 + 0}{2 + 0}$

    $\quad = \dfrac{1}{2}$

11. The general term is $\dfrac{1}{3 \cdot n^2} = \dfrac{1}{3n^2}$.

    $\dfrac{1}{3n^2} < \dfrac{1}{n^2}$, so the series is convergent.

12. arithmetic series, divergent

13. $\displaystyle\sum_{k=1}^{19} 5k$

14. $\displaystyle\sum_{k=4}^{\infty} (2k - 1)$

15. $(a + 2)^{10} = \displaystyle\sum_{r=0}^{10} \dfrac{10!}{r!(10 - r)!} a^{10-r}(2)^r$

    6th term: $= \dfrac{10!}{5!(10 - 5)!} a^{10-5}(2)^5$

    $\quad = 8064a^5$

16. $(3x - y)^8 = \displaystyle\sum_{r=0}^{8} \dfrac{8!}{r!(8 - r)!} (3x)^{8-r}(-y)^r$

    5th term $= \dfrac{8!}{4!(8 - 4)!} (3x)^{8-4}(-y)^4$

    $\quad = 5670x^4 y^4$

17. $-2 + 2i = 2(-1 + i)$

    $\quad = 2\sqrt{2}\left(-\dfrac{\sqrt{2}}{2} + \dfrac{\sqrt{2}}{2}i\right)$

    $\quad = 2\sqrt{2}\left(\cos\dfrac{3\pi}{4} + i\sin\dfrac{3\pi}{4}\right)$

    $\quad = 2\sqrt{2}\, e^{i\frac{3\pi}{4}}$

18. Since $S_1 = 6$ and $\dfrac{1(1 + 1)(4 + 5)}{3} = 6$, the

formula is valid for $n = 1$. Assume the formula is valid for $n = k$ and derive a formula for $n = k + 1$.

$2 \cdot 3 + 4 \cdot 5 + 6 \cdot 7 + \ldots + 2k(2k + 1)$

$\quad = \dfrac{k(k + 1)(4k + 5)}{3}$

$2 \cdot 3 + 4 \cdot 5 + \ldots + 2k(2k + 1)$

$+ 2(k + 1)(2k + 3)$

$\qquad = \dfrac{k(k + 1)(4k + 5)}{3} + 2(k + 1)(2k + 3)$

$\qquad = \dfrac{k(k + 1)(4k + 5) + 6(k + 1)(2k + 3)}{3}$

$\qquad = \dfrac{(k + 1)[k(4k + 5) + 6(2k + 3)]}{3}$

$\qquad = \dfrac{(k + 1)(4k^2 + 17k + 18)}{3}$

$\qquad = \dfrac{(k + 1)(k + 2)(4k + 9)}{3}$

When the original formula is applied for $n = k + 1$, the same result is obtained. Thus, if the formula is valid for $n = k$, it is also valid for $n = k + 1$. Since the formula is valid for $n = 1$, it is also valid for $n = 2$. Since it is valid for $n = 2$, it is also valid for $n = 3$, and so on, indefinitely.

19. $r = 1.02$, $a_1 = 200$

$S_{10} = \dfrac{a_1 - a_1 r^{40}}{1 - r}$

$\qquad = \dfrac{200 - 200(1.02)^{40}}{1 - 1.02}$

$\qquad \approx \$12{,}080.40$

20. $\displaystyle\sum_{n=1}^{6} 2^n = 2^1 + 2^2 + 2^3 + 2^4 + 2^5 + 2^6$

$\qquad\qquad = 126$ ancestors

PAGE 709 BONUS

The geometric mean, x, between two values, a and b,

is $\dfrac{a}{x} = \dfrac{x}{b}$ or $ab = x^2$. Since the area of a

triangle is $A = \dfrac{1}{2}bc \, \mathrm{Sin} \, A$, then for $\triangle ABC$:

area $= \dfrac{1}{2} \cdot AB \cdot AC \cdot \mathrm{Sin} \, A$.

Also, $\dfrac{AB}{16} = \dfrac{16}{AC}$ or $AB \cdot AC = 16^2$.

Thus, $80 = \dfrac{1}{2} \cdot 16^2 \cdot \mathrm{Sin} \, A$

$\qquad 80 = \dfrac{1}{2}(256) \, \mathrm{Sin} \, A$

$\qquad \dfrac{80}{128} = \mathrm{Sin} \, A$

or $\mathrm{Sin} \, A = \dfrac{5}{8} = 0.625$.

Chapter 13   Iteration and Fractals

13-1   Iterating Functions with Real Numbers

PAGES 714–715   CHECKING FOR UNDERSTANDING

1. Iteration is the process of repeatedly passing the output from one application of a function back through the same function. An example of iteration is an amortized loan.

2. Iteration is the repeated composition of a function upon itself.

3. a. There are more animals than the environment can sustain. The population will decrease.
   b. Less than 1; see students' explanations.

4. The principal payment increases. It is the payment minus the interest, and the balance on which the interest is computed is getting smaller.

5. $f(x_0) = f(2)$
   $= 2(2) + 1$
   $= 5$
   $f(x_1) = f(5)$
   $= 2(5) + 1$
   $= 11$
   $f(x_2) = f(11)$
   $= 2(11) + 1$
   $= 23$

6. $f(x_0) = f(4)$
   $= 3(4) - 7$
   $= 5$
   $f(x_1) = f(5)$
   $= 3(5) - 7$
   $= 8$
   $f(x_2) = f(8)$
   $= 3(8) - 7$
   $= 17$

7. $f(x_0) = f(-1)$
   $= (-1)^2 - 1$
   $= 0$
   $f(x_1) = f(0)$
   $= (0)^2 - 1$
   $= -1$
   $f(x_2) = f(-1)$
   $= (-1)^2 - 1$
   $= 0$

8. $f(x_0) = f(6)$
   $= (6 - 5)^2$
   $= 1$
   $f(x_1) = f(1)$
   $= (1 - 5)^2$
   $= 16$
   $f(x_2) = f(16)$
   $= (16 - 5)^2$
   $= 121$

9. $f(x_0) = f(1)$
   $= -2(1)^3 + 5(1) - 4$
   $= -1$
   $f(x_1) = f(-1)$
   $= -2(-1)^3 + 5(-1) - 4$
   $= -7$
   $f(x_2) = f(-7)$
   $= -2(-7)^3 + 5(-7) - 4$
   $= 647$

10. $f(2.2) = 3(2.2) - 5$
    $= 1.6$
    $f(1.6) = 3(1.6) - 5$
    $= -0.2$
    $f(-0.2) = 3(-0.2) - 5$
    $= -5.6$
    $f(-5.6) = 3(-5.6) - 5$
    $= -21.8$
    $f(-21.8) = 3(-21.8) - 5$
    $= -70.4$
    $f(-70.4) = 3(-70.4) - 5$
    $= -216.2$
    $f(-216.2) = 3(-216.2) - 5$
    $= -653.6$
    $f(-653.6) = 3(-653.6) - 5$
    $= -1965.8$
    $f(-1965.8) = 3(-1965.8) - 5$
    $= -5902.4$
    $f(-5902.4) = 3(-5902.4) - 5$
    $= -17,712.2$

11. $f(-1) = -8$
    $f(-8) = -29$
    $f(-29) = -92$
    $f(-92) = -281$
    $f(-281) = -848$
    $f(-848) = -2549$
    $f(-2549) = -7652$
    $f(-7652) = -22,961$
    $f(-22,961) = -68,888$
    $f(-68,888) = -206,669$

12. $f(4.9) = 9.7$
    $f(9.7) = 24.1$
    $f(24.1) = 67.3$
    $f(67.3) = 196.9$
    $f(196.9) = 585.7$
    $f(585.7) = 1752.1$
    $f(1752.1) = 5251.3$
    $f(5251.3) = 15,748.9$
    $f(15,748.9) = 47,241.7$
    $f(47,241.7) = 141,720.1$

PAGE 715–716   EXERCISES

13. $f(-1) = (-1)^2 = 1$
    $f(1) = 1^2 = 1$
    $f(1) = 1^2 = 1$

14. $f(-2) = (-2)^2 = 4$
    $f(4) = 4^2 = 16$
    $f(16) = 16^2 = 256$

15. $f(1.1) = (1.1)^3 + 1 \approx 2.33$
    $f(2.33) = (2.33)^3 + 1 \approx 13.65$
    $f(13.65) = (13.65)^3 + 1 \approx 2544.30$

16. $f(2.1) = 2.1(3 - 2.1) = 1.89$
    $f(1.89) = 1.89(3 - 1.89) \approx 2.10$
    $f(2.10) = 2.10(3 - 2.10) = 1.89$

17. $f(0.2)$
$= 2.8(0.2)(1 - 0.2)$
≈ 0.45
$f(0.45) \approx 0.69$
$f(0.69) \approx 0.60$
$f(0.60) \approx 0.67$
$f(0.67) \approx 0.62$
$f(0.62) \approx 0.66$
$f(0.66) \approx 0.63$
$f(0.63) \approx 0.65$
$f(0.65) \approx 0.64$
$f(0.64) \approx 0.65$

18. $f(0.5)$
$= 2.8(0.5)(1 - 0.5)$
$= 0.7$
$f(0.7) \approx 0.59$
$f(0.59) \approx 0.68$
$f(0.68) \approx 0.61$
$f(0.61) \approx 0.67$
$f(0.67) \approx 0.62$
$f(0.62) \approx 0.66$
$f(0.66) \approx 0.63$
$f(0.63) \approx 0.65$
$f(0.65) \approx 0.64$

19. $f(0.9)$
$= 2.8(0.9)(1 - 0.9)$
≈ 0.25
$f(0.25) \approx 0.53$
$f(0.53) \approx 0.70$
$f(0.70) \approx 0.59$
$f(0.59) \approx 0.68$
$f(0.68) \approx 0.61$
$f(0.61) \approx 0.67$
$f(0.67) \approx 0.62$
$f(0.62) \approx 0.66$
$f(0.66) \approx 0.63$

20. $f(0.01)$
$= 2.8(0.01)(1 - 0.01)$
≈ 0.03
$f(0.03) \approx 0.08$
$f(0.08) \approx 0.21$
$f(0.21) \approx 0.46$
$f(0.46) \approx 0.70$
$f(0.70) \approx 0.59$
$f(0.59) \approx 0.68$
$f(0.68) \approx 0.61$
$f(0.61) \approx 0.67$
$f(0.67) \approx 0.62$

21. $f(0.2)$
$= 3.1(0.2)(1 - 0.2)$
≈ 0.50
$f(0.50) \approx 0.78$
$f(0.78) \approx 0.53$
$f(0.53) \approx 0.77$
$f(0.77) \approx 0.55$
$f(0.55) \approx 0.77$
$f(0.77) \approx 0.55$
$f(0.55) \approx 0.77$
$f(0.77) \approx 0.55$
$f(0.55) \approx 0.77$

22. $f(0.45)$
$= 3.1(0.45)(1 - 0.45)$
≈ 0.77
$f(0.77) \approx 0.55$
$f(0.55) \approx 0.77$
$f(0.77) \approx 0.55$
$f(0.55) \approx 0.77$
$f(0.77) \approx 0.55$
$f(0.55) \approx 0.77$
$f(0.77) \approx 0.55$
$f(0.55) \approx 0.77$
$f(0.77) \approx 0.55$

23. $f(0.9)$
$= 3.1(0.9)(1 - 0.9)$
≈ 0.28
$f(0.28) \approx 0.62$
$f(0.62) \approx 0.73$
$f(0.73) \approx 0.61$
$f(0.61) \approx 0.74$
$f(0.74) \approx 0.60$
$f(0.60) \approx 0.74$
$f(0.74) \approx 0.60$
$f(0.60) \approx 0.74$
$f(0.74) \approx 0.60$

24. $f(1) = 3.1(1)(1 - 1)$
$= 0$
$f(0) = 3.1(0)(1 - 0)$
$= 0$
next 8 iterates:
0, 0, 0, 0, 0, 0, 0, 0

25. a. $t_1 = \dfrac{2}{1} = 2$

   $t_2 = \dfrac{2}{2} = 1$

   $t_3 = \dfrac{2}{1} = 2$

   $t_4 = \dfrac{2}{2} = 1$

   $\vdots \quad \vdots \quad \vdots$

   $t_{10} = \dfrac{2}{2} = 1$

   b. $t_1 = \dfrac{2}{4} = \dfrac{1}{2}$

   $t_2 = \dfrac{2}{\frac{1}{2}} = 4$

   $t_3 = \dfrac{2}{4} = \dfrac{1}{2}$

   $t_4 = \dfrac{2}{\frac{1}{2}} = 4$

   $\vdots \quad \vdots \quad \vdots$

   $t_{10} = \dfrac{2}{\frac{1}{2}} = 4$

   c. $t_1 = \dfrac{2}{a}$

   $t_2 = \dfrac{2}{\frac{2}{a}} = a$

   $t_3 = \dfrac{2}{a}$

   $t_4 = \dfrac{2}{\frac{2}{a}} = a$

   $\vdots \quad \vdots \quad \vdots$

   $t_{10} = \dfrac{2}{\frac{2}{a}} = a$

   d. They repeat in pairs.

   e. yes, $\pm\sqrt{2}$

26. a. 0.64   b. period-2 attractor
   c. chaotic, unless $x_0 = 0.25, 0.5,$ or 0.75

27. $f(0.6) = 0.66$
   $f(0.66) = 0.666$
   $f(0.666) = 0.6666$
   $\vdots \qquad \vdots$
   The values approach $\dfrac{2}{3}$.

28. a. $p_1 = p_0 + rp_0$
   $= 4210 + (0.063)4210$
   $= \$4475.23$
   $p_2 = 4475.23 + (0.063)4475.23$
   $\approx \$4757.17$
   $p_3 = 4757.17 + (0.063)4757.17$
   $\approx \$5056.87$

   b. $A = P(1 + r)^t$
   $= 4210(1 + 0.063)^1$
   $= \$4475.23$
   $A = 4210(1 + 0.063)^2$
   $\approx \$4757.17$
   $A = 4210(1 + 0.063)^3$
   $\approx \$5056.87$
   yes

29. a. $p_{n+1} = p_n + 1.75p_n(1 - p_n)$

b. $p_n = \dfrac{240}{500} = 0.48$

$p_1 = 0.48 + 1.75(0.48)(1 - 0.48) = 0.9168$

$(0.9168)(500) \approx 458$ bears

$p_2 = 0.9168 + 1.75(0.9168)(1 - 0.9168)$
≈ 1.0503

$(1.0503)(500) \approx 525$ bears

$p_3 = 1.0503 + 1.75(1.0503)(1 - 1.0503)$
≈ 0.9578

$(0.9578)(500) \approx 479$ bears

$p_4 = 0.9578 + 1.75(0.9578)(1 - 0.9578)$
≈ 1.0285

$(1.0285)(500) \approx 514$ bears

$p_5 = 1.0285 + 1.75(1.0285)(1 - 1.0285)$
≈ 0.9772

$(0.9772)(500) \approx 489$ bears

$p_6 = 0.9772 + 1.75(0.9772)(1 - 0.9772)$
≈ 1.0162

$(1.0162)(500) \approx 508$ bears

$p_7 = 1.0162 + 1.75(1.0162)(1 - 1.0162)$
≈ 0.9874

$(0.9874)(500) \approx 494$ bears

$p_8 = 0.9874 + 1.75(0.9874)(1 - 0.9874)$
≈ 1.0092

$(1.0092)(500) \approx 505$ bears

$p_9 = 1.0092 + 1.75(1.0092)(1 - 1.0092)$
≈ 0.9930

$(0.9930)(500) \approx 496$ bears

$p_{10} = 0.9930 + 1.75(0.9930)(1 - 0.9930)$
≈ 1.0052

$(1.0052)(500) \approx 503$ bears

$p_{11} = 1.0052 + 1.75(1.0052)(1 - 1.0052)$
≈ 0.9961

$(0.9961)(500) \approx 498$ bears

$p_{12} = 0.9961 + 1.75(0.9961)(1 - 0.9961)$
≈ 1.0029

$(1.0029)(500) \approx 501$ bears

$p_{13} = 1.0029 + 1.75(1.0029)(1 - 1.0029)$
≈ 0.9978

$(0.9978)(500) \approx 499$

$p_{14} = 0.9978 + 1.75(0.9978)(1 - 0.9978)$
≈ 1.0016

$(1.0016)(500) \approx 501$

$p_{15} = 1.0016 + 1.75(1.0016)(1 - 1.0016)$
≈ 0.9988

$(0.9988)(500) \approx 499$ bears

c.

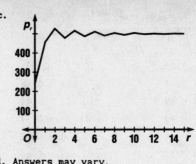

d. Answers may vary.

30. $c^2 = 9.2^2 + 12.5^2 - 2(9.2)(12.5) \cos 98°$

$c \approx 16.5$

$s = \dfrac{1}{2}(9.2 + 12.5 + 16.5) = 19.1$

$K = \sqrt{19.1(19.1 - 9.2)(19.1 - 12.5)(19.1 - 16.5)}$

≈ 56.9 square units

31. $r = \sqrt{2^2 + 1^2} = \sqrt{5}$

$\theta = \text{Arctan } \dfrac{-1}{2} \approx -0.4636$

$2 - i = \sqrt{5}(\cos(-0.4636) + i \sin(-0.4636))$

$(2 - i)^4 = [\sqrt{5}(\cos(-0.4636) + i \sin(-0.4636))]^4$

$= (\sqrt{5})^4(\cos 4(-0.4636) + i \sin 4(-0.4636))$

$= 25(\cos(-1.8546) + i \sin(-1.8546))$

$= 25(-0.28 - 0.96i)$

$= -7 - 24i$

32. $0^2 + 9^2 + D(0) + E(9) + F = 0 \rightarrow$
$9E + F + 81 = 0$

$(-7)^2 + 2^2 + D(-7) + E(2) + F = 0 \rightarrow$
$-7D + 2E + F + 53 = 0$

$0^2 + (-5)^2 + D(0) + E(-5) + F = 0 \rightarrow$
$-5E + F + 25 = 0$

$9E + F + 81 = 0 \qquad 9(-4) + F + 81 = 0$

$\underline{-5E + F + 25 = 0} \qquad\qquad F = -45$

$14E \quad + 56 = 0 \qquad -7D + 2(-4) + (-45) + 53 = 0$

$E = -4 \qquad\qquad D = 0$

$x^2 + y^2 + 0x - 4y - 45 = 0$

$x^2 + (y^2 - 4y + 4) = 45 + 4$

$x^2 + (y - 2)^2 = 49$

33. Subtract 0.6: 0.6, 0, −0.6, −1.2, −1.8

334

34. Show that for $n \in N$, $n^3 + (n + 1)^3 + (n + 2)^3$ is divisible by 9.

Let S equal the set of natural numbers for which the statement is true.

Suppose $n = 1$. Then $n^3 + (n + 1)^3 + (n + 2)^3 = 1^3 + 2^3 + 3^3$ or 36. 36 is divisible by 9, so $1 \in S$.

Assume that $k \in S$. Then $k^3 + (k + 1)^3 + (k + 2)^3$ is divisible by 9. Prove that $k + 1 \in S$.

$(k + 1)^3 + ((k + 1) + 1)^3 + ((k + 1) + 2)^3$
$= (k + 1)^3 + (k + 2)^3 + k^3 + 9k^2 + 27k + 27$
$= k^3 + (k + 1)^3 + (k + 2)^3 + 9(k^2 + 3k + 3)$

The expressions $[k^3 + (k + 1)^3 + (k + 2)^3]$ and $9(k^2 + 3k + 3)$ are each divisible by 9. So their sum must be also.

Therefore, if $k \in S$, $(k + 1) \in S$ also. The assertion is proved.

35. $\dfrac{1 + \frac{1}{x}}{\frac{y}{x}} = \left(\dfrac{1 + \frac{1}{x}}{\frac{y}{x}}\right)\left(\dfrac{\frac{x}{y}}{\frac{x}{y}}\right)$

$= \dfrac{x}{y} + \dfrac{1}{y}$

$= \dfrac{x + 1}{y}$

The best answer is A.

13-2 Graphical Iteration of Linear Functions

PAGES 719-720   CHECKING FOR UNDERSTANDING

1. A fixed point is a point that represents an initial value whose iterates for the function are constant. The fixed points are the points where the graphs of the function and $f(x) = x$ intersect.

2. It is an attractor.

3.
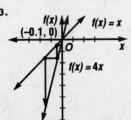

4.
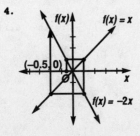

---

5. $f(x) = 6x + 2$
$f(x) = x$ ➡ $x = 6x + 2$
$-5x = 2$
$x = -\dfrac{2}{5}$

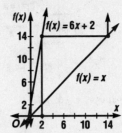

$-\dfrac{2}{5}$ is a repeller.

6. $f(x) = 0.2x - 1$
$f(x) = x$ ➡ $x = 0.2x - 1$
$0.8x = -1$
$x = -1.25$

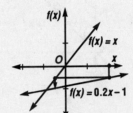

-1.25 is an attractor.

PAGES 720-721   EXERCISES

7.
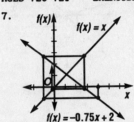

8.
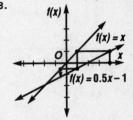

9.
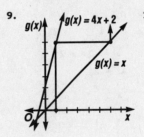
slope = 4
staircase out

10.
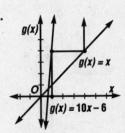
slope = 10
staircase out

11.
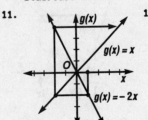
slope = -2
spiral out

12.
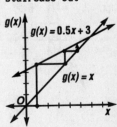
slope = 0.5
staircase in

335

13.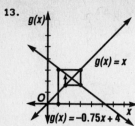

slope = -0.75

spiral in

14.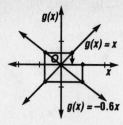

slope = -0.6

spiral in

15.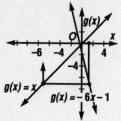

slope = -6

spiral out

16.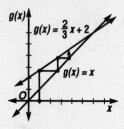

slope = $\frac{2}{3}$

staircase in

17.

slope = 10

staircase out

18.

slope = $-\frac{1}{4}$

spiral in

19. $-1 < m < 0$

20. $m < -1$

21. $0 < m < 1$

22. $m > 1$

23.
$$x = 2.5x + 4$$
$$-1.5x = 4$$
$$x = -2\frac{2}{3}$$
$$\left(-2\frac{2}{3}, -2\frac{2}{3}\right)$$

24.
$$x = -3x + 2$$
$$4x = 2$$
$$x = \frac{1}{2}$$
$$\left(\frac{1}{2}, \frac{1}{2}\right)$$

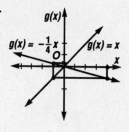

repeller

repeller

25.
$$x = 0.75x - 5$$
$$0.25x = -5$$
$$x = -20$$
$$(-20, -20)$$

26.
$$x = -0.8x - 18$$
$$1.8x = -18$$
$$x = -10$$
$$(-10, -10)$$

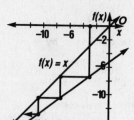

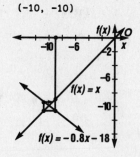

attractor

attractor

27. $f(x) = -3x + 2$ and $f(x) = -0.8x - 18$

28. Sample answer: $f(x) = 0.1x + 0.7$

29. Sample answer: $f(x) = 2x - 0.4$

30. Sample answer: $f(x) = -5x - 12$

31. $f(x) = x$

32. a. $p_n = p_n + rp_n$

$0 = rp_n$

$p_n = 0$

$(0, 0)$

b. $p_{n+1} = p_n + rp_n = (1 + r)p_n$

Since $r > 0$, then $1 + r > 1$. The slope is greater than 1, so $(0, 0)$ is a repeller.

33. a. $b_{n-1} = \left(1 + \frac{r}{12}\right)b_{n-1} - p$

$b_{n-1} = b_{n-1} + \frac{r}{12}b_{n-1} - p$

$0 = \frac{r}{12}b_{n-1} - p$

$b_{n-1} = \frac{12p}{r}$

$\left(\frac{12p}{r}, \frac{12p}{r}\right)$

The interest for a term is equal to the payment, so the principal is never reduced.

33. b. repeller

34. $-2\begin{bmatrix} 6 & -2 \\ 0 & -1 \end{bmatrix} = \begin{bmatrix} -2(6) & -2(-2) \\ -2(0) & -2(-1) \end{bmatrix} = \begin{bmatrix} -12 & 4 \\ 0 & 2 \end{bmatrix}$

35. possible rational roots: $\pm\frac{1}{12}$, $\pm\frac{1}{6}$, $\pm\frac{1}{4}$, $\pm\frac{1}{3}$, $\pm\frac{1}{2}$, ±1, $\pm\frac{2}{3}$, ±2, $\pm\frac{4}{3}$, ±4, $\pm\frac{3}{4}$, $\pm\frac{8}{3}$, ±8

root	12	-11	-54	-18	8
$-\frac{4}{3}$	12	-27	-18	6	0
$\frac{1}{4}$	12	-8	-56	-32	0

$-\frac{4}{3}$ and $\frac{1}{4}$ are the rational roots.

36. $\tan 81° = \frac{y}{50}$

$y \approx 316$

$316 + 6 = 322$ ft

37. $S_n = \dfrac{a_1 - a_1 r^n}{1 - r}$

$ = \dfrac{8 - 8\left(\dfrac{3}{4}\right)^6}{1 - \dfrac{3}{4}}$

$ = \dfrac{8 - 8\left(\dfrac{729}{4096}\right)}{\dfrac{1}{4}}$

$ = 4\left(8 - \dfrac{729}{512}\right)$

$ = 32 - \dfrac{729}{128}$

$ = 32 - 5\dfrac{89}{128}$

$ = 26\dfrac{39}{128}$

38. $f(0.7) = 6.5(0.7)(1 - 0.7)$

$ \approx 1.37$

$f(1.37) \approx -3.29$

$f(-3.29) \approx -91.74$

$f(-91.74) \approx -55{,}301.79$

39. $30\% = \dfrac{30}{100}$ or $\dfrac{3}{10}$

$10\% = \dfrac{10}{100}$ or $\dfrac{1}{10}$

$\dfrac{3}{10} \cdot \dfrac{1}{10} = \dfrac{3}{100}$ or 3%

13-3 Graphical Iteration of the Logistic Function

1. No; the behavior of one logistic function may be stable, while the behavior of another is chaotic.

2. Solve the system of equations of the function and $f(x) = x$.

3. The iterates repeat in a pattern of 4.

4. $a = 2 \rightarrow \left(\dfrac{1}{2}, \dfrac{2}{4}\right)$ or $(0.5, 0.5)$

5. $a = 3 \rightarrow \left(\dfrac{1}{2}, \dfrac{3}{4}\right)$ or $(0.5, 0.75)$

6. $a = 1.2 \rightarrow \left(\dfrac{1}{2}, \dfrac{1.2}{4}\right)$ or $(0.5, 0.3)$

7. $x = 2x(1 - x)$

$x = 2x - 2x^2$

$0 = 2x^2 - x$

$0 = x(2x - 1)$

$x = 0$ or $2x - 1 = 0$

$\phantom{x = 0 \text{ or } 2x - 1} x = \dfrac{1}{2}$

$(0, 0), (0.5, 0.5)$

attractor

8. $x = 3x(1 - x)$

$x = 3x - 3x^2$

$0 = 3x^2 - 2x$

$0 = x(3x - 2)$

$x = 0$ or $3x - 2 = 0$

$\phantom{x = 0 \text{ or } 3x - 2} x = \dfrac{2}{3}$

$(0, 0), \left(\dfrac{2}{3}, \dfrac{2}{3}\right)$

attractor

9. $x = 1.2x(1 - x)$

$x = 1.2x - 1.2x^2$

$0 = 1.2x^2 - 0.2x$

$0 = x(1.2x - 0.2)$

$x = 0$ or $1.2x - 0.2 = 0$

$\phantom{x = 0 \text{ or } 1.2x - 0.2} x = \dfrac{1}{6}$

$(0, 0), \left(\dfrac{1}{6}, \dfrac{1}{6}\right)$

attractor

10. $x = x(1 - x)$

$x = x - x^2$

$0 = x^2$

$x = 0$

$(0, 0)$

attractor

11. iterates: $0.661, 0.661, 0.661, \ldots$

fixed point attractor

12. iterates: $0.590, 0.738, 0.590, 0.738, \ldots$

period-2 attractor

13. $\left(\dfrac{1}{2}, \dfrac{2.4}{4}\right)$ or $(0.5, 0.6)$

14. $\left(\dfrac{1}{2}, \dfrac{0.4}{4}\right)$ or $(0.5, 0.1)$

15. $\left(\dfrac{1}{2}, \dfrac{4}{4}\right)$ or $(0.5, 1)$

16. $\left(\dfrac{1}{2}, \dfrac{0.64}{4}\right)$ or $(0.5, 0.16)$

17. $x = 1.6x(1 - x)$

$x = 1.6x - 1.6x^2$

$0 = 1.6x^2 - 0.6x$

$0 = x(1.6x - 0.6)$

$x = 0$ or $1.6x - 0.6 = 0$

$\phantom{x = 0 \text{ or } 1.6x - 0.6} x = \dfrac{3}{8}$

$(0, 0), \left(\dfrac{3}{8}, \dfrac{3}{8}\right)$

attractor

18. $x = 2.9x(1 - x)$

$x = 2.9x - 2.9x^2$

$0 = 2.9x^2 - 1.9x$

$0 = x(2.9x - 1.9)$

$x = 0$ or $2.9x - 1.9 = 0$

$\phantom{x = 0 \text{ or } 2.9x - 1.9} x \approx 0.655$

$(0, 0), (0.655, 0.655)$

attractor

19. $x = 3.2x(1 - x)$

$x = 3.2x - 3.2x^2$

$0 = 3.2x^2 - 2.2x$

$0 = x(3.2x - 2.2)$

$x = 0$ or $3.2x - 2.2 = 0$

$\phantom{x = 0 \text{ or } 3.2x - 2.2} x = \dfrac{11}{16}$

$(0, 0), \left(\dfrac{11}{16}, \dfrac{11}{16}\right)$

repeller

20. $x = 3.4x(1 - x)$

$x = 3.4x - 3.4x^2$

$0 = 3.4x^2 - 2.4x$

$0 = x(3.4x - 2.4)$

$x = 0$ or $3.4x - 2.4 = 0$

$$x = \frac{12}{17}$$

$(0, 0)$, $\left(\frac{12}{17}, \frac{12}{17}\right)$

repeller

21. iterates: 0.499, 0.810, 0.499, 0.810

period-2 attractor

22. iterates: 0.501, 0.875, 0.383, 0.827, 0.501,...

period-4 attractor

23. chaos

24. iterates: 0.545, 0.545, 0.545,...

fixed point attractor

25. iterates: 0.227, 0.657, 0.843, 0.496, 0.935, 0.227,...

period-5 attractor

26. chaos

27. a. $a \approx 3.0$ **b.** $a \approx 3.4495$

c. $a \approx 3.5441$ **d.** chaos

28. a. For $x_0 = 0.200$, the first ten iterates are

0.200, 0.640, 0.922, 0.289, 0.822, 0.585, 0.971, 0.113, 0.402, and 0.962.

For $x_0 = 0.201$, the first ten iterates are

0.201, 0.642, 0.919, 0.298, 0.837, 0.546, 0.992, 0.033, 0.129, and 0.449.

The tenth iterates are 0.962 and 0.449; yes.

b. See students' work.

29. a. $p_n = \frac{24}{40} = 0.6$

$p_1 = 0.6 + 1.75(0.6)(1 - 0.6) = 1.02$

$(1.02)(40) \approx 41$ antelope

$p_2 = 1.02 + 1.75(1.02)(1 - 1.02) = 0.9843$

$(0.9843)(40) \approx 39$ antelope

$p_3 = 0.9843 + 1.75(0.9843)(1 - 0.9843)$

≈ 1.0113

$(1.0113)(40) \approx 40$ antelope

$p_4 = 1.0113 + 1.75(1.0113)(1 - 1.0113)$

≈ 0.9913

$(0.9913)(40) \approx 40$ antelope

$p_5 = 0.9913 + 1.75(0.9913)(1 - 0.9913)$

≈ 1.0064

$(1.0064)(40) \approx 40$ antelope

The next 5 iterates are 40.

first ten iterates: 41, 39, 40, 40, 40, 40, 40, 40, 40, 40

b. fixed point attractor

c. period-4 attractor

30. See students' work.

31. $\dfrac{x}{x - 5} + \dfrac{17}{25 - x^2} = \dfrac{1}{x + 5}$

$(x - 5)(x + 5)\left(\dfrac{x}{x - 5} + \dfrac{17}{-(x - 5)(x + 5)}\right)$

$\qquad = \dfrac{1}{x + 5}(x - 5)(x + 5)$

$x(x + 5) - 17 = x - 5$

$x^2 + 4x - 12 = 0$

$(x + 6)(x - 2) = 0$

$x = -6$ or $x = 2$

32.

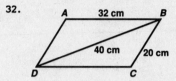

$40^2 = 20^2 + 32^2 - 2(20)(32) \cos A$

$176 = -1280 \cos A$

$\cos A = -0.1375$

$A \approx 97.90°$ or $97°54'$

$B \approx 180° - 97°54' \approx 82°6'$

33. $25x^2 + 4y^2 - 100x - 40y + 100 = 0$

$25(x^2 - 4x) + 4(y^2 - 10y) = -100$

$25(x^2 - 4x + 4) + 4(y^2 - 10y + 25)$

$\qquad\qquad\qquad = -100 + 100 + 100$

$25(x - 2)^2 + 4(y - 5)^2 = 100$

$\dfrac{(x - 2)^2}{4} + \dfrac{(y - 5)^2}{25} = 1$

ellipse

34. $|r| = 2$

Since $|r| > 0$, the sum does not exist.

35. $x = 1.36x + 2$

$-0.36x = 2$

$x = -\dfrac{50}{9}$

$\left(-\dfrac{50}{9}, -\dfrac{50}{9}\right)$

$m > 1$, so it is a repeller.

36. If $1 > y > 0$, then $\dfrac{1}{y} > 0$.

If $x = 1$ and $\dfrac{1}{y} > 0$, then $\dfrac{1}{y} > x$.

Quantity A is greater.

Mid-Chapter Review

PAGE 728

1. $f(8) = 5(8) - 3$
$\qquad = 37$

$f(37) = 5(37) - 3$
$\qquad = 182$

$f(182) = 5(182) - 3$
$\qquad = 907$

2. $f(0.9) = (0.9)^3$
$\qquad = 0.73$

$f(0.73) = (0.73)^3$
$\qquad = 0.39$

$f(0.39) = (0.39)^3$
$\qquad = 0.06$

3. $f(2) = 2^2 - 4(2) + 2$
$\qquad = -2$

$f(-2) = (-2)^2 - 4(-2) + 2$
$\qquad = 14$

$f(14) = (14)^2 - 4(14) + 2$
$\qquad = 142$

4. $f(0.6) = 0.6^2(1 - 2 \cdot 0.6)$
$\qquad = -0.07$

$f(-0.07) = (-0.07)^2(1 - 2(-0.07))$
$\qquad = 0.01$

$f(0.01) = (0.01)^2(1 - 2 \cdot 0.01)$
$\qquad = 0.00$

5.
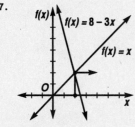
staircase out

6.
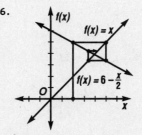
spiral in

7.

spiral out

8. Since $m < -1$, it is a repeller.

9. fixed point attractor

Technology: Graphical Iteration

PAGE 729   EXERCISES

1. fixed point repeller
2. fixed point attractor
3. fixed point attractor
4. period-2 attractor
5. chaos
6. period-4 attractor
7. fixed point attractor
8. chaos

13-4 **Complex Numbers and Iteration**

PAGES 731-732   CHECKING FOR UNDERSTANDING

1. It is the sequence of iterates produced when a complex number is iterated for a function $f(z)$.

2. $(a + bi)^2 = a^2 + 2abi + b^2i^2 = (a^2 - b^2) + 2abi$

Since $(a^2 - b^2) + 2abi$ is a complex number, the square of a complex number will always be a complex number; yes.

3. The methods are the same, but complex numbers are graphed on the complex plane and real numbers are graphed on the real plane.

4. $z_0 = 25 + 40i$

$z_1 = 0.6(25 + 40i) + 2i = 15 + 26i$

$z_2 = 0.6(15 + 26i) + 2i = 9 + 17.6i$

$z_3 = 0.6(9 + 17.6i) + 2i = 5.4 + 12.56i$

5. $z_0 = 5 - 10i$

$z_1 = 0.6(5 - 10i) + 2i = 3 - 4i$

$z_2 = 0.6(3 - 4i) + 2i = 1.8 - 0.4i$

$z_3 = 0.6(1.8 - 0.4i) + 2i = 1.08 + 1.76i$

6. $z_0 = 6i$

$z_1 = 0.6(6i) + 2i = 5.6i$

$z_2 = 0.6(5.6i) + 2i = 5.36i$

$z_3 = 0.6(5.36i) + 2i = 5.216i$

7. $z_0 = 2i$

$z_1 = (2i)^2 - 3i = 4i^2 - 3i = -4 - 3i$

$z_2 = (-4 - 3i)^2 - 3i$
$\qquad = 16 + 24i + 9i^2 - 3i = 7 + 21i$

$z_3 = (7 + 21i)^2 - 3i$
$\qquad = 49 + 294i + 441i^2 - 3i = -392 + 291i$

8. $z_0 = 1 - i$

$z_1 = (1 - i)^2 - 3i = 1 - 2i + i^2 - 3i = -5i$

$z_2 = (-5i)^2 - 3i = 25i^2 - 3i = -25 - 3i$

$z_3 = (-25 - 3i)^2 - 3i$
$\qquad = 625 + 150i + 9i^2 - 3i = 616 + 147i$

9. $z_0 = 1$

$z_1 = 1^2 - 3i = 1 - 3i$

$z_2 = (1 - 3i)^2 - 3i$
$\qquad = 1 - 6i + 9i^2 - 3i = -8 - 9i$

$z_3 = (-8 - 9i)^2 - 3i$
$\qquad = 64 + 144i + 81i^2 - 3i = -17 + 141i$

10. $z_0 = 0 - i$

$z_1 = (0 - i)^2 - 1 = i^2 - 1 = -2$

$z_2 = (-2)^2 - 1 = 4 - 1 = 3$

$z_3 = 3^2 - 1 = 8$

$z_4 = 8^2 - 1 = 63$

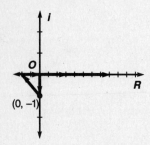

(0, −1)

11. $z_0 = 1 + 2i$

$z_1 = 2(1 + 2i) + i = 2 + 4i + i = 2 + 5i$

$z_2 = 2(2 + 5i) + i = 4 + 10i + i = 4 + 11i$

$z_3 = 2(4 + 11i) + i = 8 + 22i + i = 8 + 23i$

12. $z_0 = 5i$

$z_1 = 2(5i) + i = 11i$

$z_2 = 2(11i) + i = 23i$

$z_3 = 2(23i) + i = 47i$

13. $z_0 = 3$

$z_1 = 2(3) + i = 6 + i$

$z_2 = 2(6 + i) + i = 12 + 3i$

$z_3 = 2(12 + 3i) + i = 24 + 7i$

14. $z_0 = 4 - i$

$z_1 = 2(4 - i) + i = 8 - i$

$z_2 = 2(8 - i) + i = 16 - i$

$z_3 = 2(16 - i) + i = 32 - i$

15. $z_0 = \frac{1}{2} - \frac{1}{4}i$

$z_1 = 2\left(\frac{1}{2} - \frac{1}{4}i\right) + i = 1 + \frac{1}{2}i$

$z_2 = 2\left(1 + \frac{1}{2}i\right) + i = 2 + 2i$

$z_3 = 2(2 + 2i) + i = 4 + 5i$

16. $z_0 = 0.1i$

$z_1 = 2(0.1i) + i = 1.2i$

$z_2 = 2(1.2i) + i = 3.4i$

$z_3 = 2(3.4i) + i = 7.8i$

17. $z_0 = 1 + 2i$

$z_1 = 3(1 + 2i) + (2 - 3i)$

$= 3 + 6i + 2 - 3i = 5 + 3i$

$z_2 = 3(5 + 3i) + (2 - 3i)$

$= 15 + 9i + 2 - 3i = 17 + 6i$

$z_3 = 3(17 + 6i) + (2 - 3i)$

$= 51 + 18i + 2 - 3i = 53 + 15i$

18. $z_0 = -2 + 3i$

$z_1 = 3(-2 + 3i) + (2 - 3i)$

$= -6 + 9i + 2 - 3i = -4 + 6i$

$z_2 = 3(-4 + 6i) + (2 - 3i)$

$= -12 + 18i + 2 - 3i = -10 + 15i$

$z_3 = 3(-10 + 15i) + (2 - 3i)$

$= -30 + 45i + 2 - 3i = -28 + 42i$

19. $z_0 = 4 + i$

$z_1 = 3(4 + i) + (2 - 3i) = 12 + 3i + 2 - 3i = 14$

$z_2 = 3(14) + (2 - 3i) = 42 + 2 - 3i = 44 - 3i$

$z_3 = 3(44 - 3i) + (2 - 3i)$

$= 132 - 9i + 2 - 3i = 134 - 12i$

20. $z_0 = -1 + 2i$

$z_1 = 3(-1 + 2i) + (2 - 3i)$

$= -3 + 6i + 2 - 3i = -1 + 3i$

$z_2 = 3(-1 + 3i) + (2 - 3i)$

$= -3 + 9i + 2 - 3i = -1 + 6i$

$z_3 = 3(-1 + 6i) + (2 - 3i)$

$= -3 + 18i + 2 - 3i = -1 + 15i$

21. $z_0 = 0.5 - i$

$z_1 = 3(0.5 - i) + (2 - 3i)$

$= 1.5 - 3i + 2 - 3i = 3.5 - 6i$

$z_2 = 3(3.5 - 6i) + (2 - 3i)$

$= 10.5 - 18i + 2 - 3i = 12.5 - 21i$

$z_3 = 3(12.5 - 21i) + (2 - 3i)$

$= 37.5 - 63i + 2 - 3i = 39.5 - 66i$

22. $z_0 = \frac{1}{3} + \frac{2}{3}i$

$z_1 = 3\left(\frac{1}{3} + \frac{2}{3}i\right) + (2 - 3i)$

$= 1 + 2i + 2 - 3i = 3 - i$

$z_2 = 3(3 - i) + (2 - 3i)$

$= 9 - 3i + 2 - 3i = 11 - 6i$

$z_3 = 3(11 - 6i) + (2 - 3i)$

$= 33 - 18i + 2 - 3i = 35 - 21i$

23. $z_0 = 0,\ f(z) = z^2 + (1 + 2i)$

$z_1 = 0^2 + (1 + 2i) = 1 + 2i$

$z_2 = (1 + 2i)^2 + (1 + 2i)$

$= 1 + 4i + 4i^2 + 1 + 2i = -2 + 6i$

$z_3 = (-2 + 6i)^2 + (1 + 2i)$

$= 4 - 24i + 36i^2 + 1 + 2i = -31 - 22i$

$z_4 = (-31 - 22i)^2 + (1 + 2i)$

$= 961 + 1364i + 484i^2 + 1 + 2i = 478 + 1366i$

24. $z_0 = \frac{\sqrt{2}}{2} - \frac{\sqrt{2}}{2}i,\ f(z) = z^2$

$z_1 = \left(\frac{\sqrt{2}}{2} - \frac{\sqrt{2}}{2}i\right)^2 = \frac{1}{2} - i + \frac{1}{2}i^2 = -i$

$z_2 = (-i)^2 = -1$

$z_3 = 1^2 = 1$

$z_4 = 1^2 = 1$

25. $z_0 = 1 + 2i$, $f(z) = z^2 + (2 - 3i)$

$z_1 = (1 + 2i)^2 + (2 - 3i)$

$\quad = 1 + 4i + 4i^2 + 2 - 3i = -1 + i$

$z_2 = (-1 + i)^2 + (2 - 3i)$

$\quad = 1 - 2i + i^2 + 2 - 3i = 2 - 5i$

$z_3 = (2 - 5i)^2 + (2 - 3i)$

$\quad = 4 - 20i + 25i^2 + 2 - 3i = -19 - 23i$

$z_4 = (-19 - 23i)^2 + (2 - 3i)$

$\quad = 361 + 874i + 529i^2 + 2 - 3i = -166 + 871i$

26. $z_0 = i$, $f(z) = z^2 + (5 + 3i)$

$z_1 = i^2 + (5 + 3i) = -1 + 5 + 3i = 4 + 3i$

$z_2 = (4 + 3i)^2 + (5 + 3i)$

$\quad = 16 + 24i + 9i^2 + 5 + 3i = 12i + 27i$

$z_3 = (12 + 27i)^2 + (5 + 3i)$

$\quad = 144 + 648i + 729i^2 + 5 + 3i = -580 + 651i$

$z_4 = (-580 + 651i)^2 + (5 + 3i)$

$\quad = 336,400 - 755,160i + 423,801i^2 + 5 + 3i$

$\quad = -87,396 - 755,157i$

27. $z_0 = 1 + i$

$z_1 = (1 + i)^2 + (1 - i)$

$\quad = 1 + 2i + i^2 + 1 - i = 1 + i$

$z_2 = (1 + i)^2 + (1 - i) = 1 + i$

$z_3 = 1 + i$

$z_4 = 1 + i$

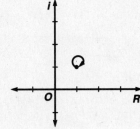

28. $z_0 = 0$

$z_1 = 0^2 + (1 - i) = 1 - i$

$z_2 = (1 - i)^2 + (1 - i)$

$\quad = 1 - 2i + i^2 + 1 - i = 1 - 3i$

$z_3 = (1 - 3i)^2 + (1 - i)$

$\quad = 1 - 6i + 9i^2 + 1 - i = -7 - 7i$

$z_4 = (-7 - 7i)^2 + (1 - i)$

$\quad = 49 + 98i + 49i^2 + 1 - i = 1 + 97i$

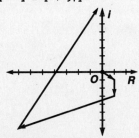

29. $z_0 = i$

$z_1 = i^2 + (1 - i) = -1 + 1 - i = -i$

$z_2 = (-i)^2 + (1 - i) = -1 + 1 - i = -i$

$z_3 = -i$

$z_4 = -i$

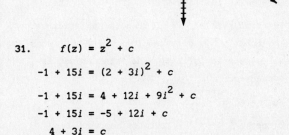

30. $z_0 = -2$

$z_1 = (-2)^2 + (1 - i) = 4 + 1 - i = 5 - i$

$z_2 = (5 - i)^2 + (1 - i)$

$\quad = 25 - 10i + i^2 + 1 - i = 25 - 11i$

$z_3 = (25 - 11i)^2 + (1 - i)$

$\quad = 625 - 550i + 121i^2 + 1 - i = 505 - 551i$

$z_4 = (505 - 551i)^2 + (1 - i)$

$\quad = 255,025 - 556,510i + 303,601i^2 + 1 - i$

$\quad = -48,575 - 556,511i$

31. $f(z) = z^2 + c$

$-1 + 15i = (2 + 3i)^2 + c$

$-1 + 15i = 4 + 12i + 9i^2 + c$

$-1 + 15i = -5 + 12i + c$

$4 + 3i = c$

32. See students' work.

33. $\begin{vmatrix} 5 & 3 & -2 \\ 0 & 2 & -2 \\ -3 & 0 & -1 \end{vmatrix} = 5\begin{vmatrix} 2 & -2 \\ 0 & -1 \end{vmatrix} - 3\begin{vmatrix} 0 & -2 \\ -3 & -1 \end{vmatrix} + (-2)\begin{vmatrix} 0 & 2 \\ -3 & 0 \end{vmatrix}$

$\quad = 5(-2) - 3(-6) - 2(6)$

$\quad = -4$

34. $A = \frac{1}{2}r^2\theta$

$\quad = \frac{1}{2}(25)^2\left(\frac{3\pi}{4}\right)$

$\quad \approx 736 \text{ ft}^2$

35. $\sqrt[4]{81x^4yz} = (81x^4yz)^{\frac{1}{4}} = 3xy^{\frac{1}{4}}z^{\frac{1}{4}}$

36. Answers may vary. A sample answer is $\sum\limits_{x=0}^{\infty} 5^x$.

37. iterates: $0.375, 0.375, 0.375, \ldots$

fixed point attractor

38. Let a = the number of questions answered
correctly.
$$4a - 1(25 - a) = 70$$
$$4a - 25 + a = 70$$
$$5a = 95$$
$$a = 19$$
The best answer is C.

Escape Points, Prisoner Points, and Julia Sets

PAGE 738   CHECKING FOR UNDERSTANDING

1. The prisoner set of a function is the set of all the points which do not approach infinity when iterated under the function.

2. If the prisoner set is connected, then the Julia set is the boundary between the prisoner set and the escape set. If the prisoner set is disconnected, then the Julia set is the prisoner set.

3. Iterate the initial point $0 + 0i$. If $0 + 0i$ escapes to infinity when iterated for the function $f(z) = z^2 + c$, then the prisoner set of the function is disconnected. If $0 + 0i$ does not escape to infinity, the prisoner set is connected.

4. $|z_0| = \sqrt{0.5^2 + 0.5^2} \approx 0.7071$

Since $|z_0| < 1$, the iterates approach 0.

prisoner set

5. $|z_0| = \sqrt{1^2 + 2^2} = \sqrt{5}$

Since $|z_0| > 1$, the iterates approach infinity.

escape set

6. $|z_0| = \sqrt{(-0.25)^2 + (-0.2)^2} \approx 0.1025$

Since $|z_0| < 1$, the iterates approach 0.

prisoner set

7. $|z_0| = \sqrt{(0.5)^2 + (-0.5\sqrt{3})^2} = 1$

Since $|z_0| = 1$, the iterates orbit around the unit circle.

Julia set

8. $|z_0| = \sqrt{(-1.5)^2 + 0^2} = 1.5$

Since $|z_0| > 1$, the iterates approach infinity.

escape set

9. $|z_0| = \sqrt{\left(\frac{2\sqrt{2}}{3}\right)^2 + \left(\frac{1}{3}\right)^2} = 1$

Since $|z_0| = 1$, the iterates orbit around the unit circle.

Julia set

10. $z_0 = 0 + 0i$

$z_1 = (0 + 0i)^2 + 2 + 2i = 2 + 2i$

$z_2 = (2 + 2i)^2 + 2 + 2i = 2 + 10i$

$z_3 = (2 + 10i)^2 + 2 + 2i = -94 + 42i$

$|z_0| = \sqrt{0^2 + 0^2} = 0$

$|z_1| = \sqrt{2^2 + 2^2} \approx 2.83$

$|z_2| = \sqrt{2^2 + 10^2} \approx 10.20$

$|z_3| = \sqrt{(-94)^2 + 42^2} \approx 102.96$

Since the iterates approach infinity, the Julia set is disconnected.

PAGES 738–739   EXERCISES

11. $z_0 = 1 + 2i$

$z_1 = (1 + 2i)^2 + (-5 + 0i)$
$\quad = 1 + 4i + 4i^2 - 5 = -8 + 4i$

$z_2 = (-8 + 4i)^2 + (-5 + 0i)$
$\quad = 64 - 64i + 16i^2 - 5 = 43 - 64i$

$z_3 = (43 - 64i)^2 + (-5 + 0i)$
$\quad = 1849 - 5504i + 4096i^2 - 5 = -2252 - 5504i$

escape set

12. $z_0 = 4 - 2i$

$z_1 = (4 - 2i)^2 + (-5 + 0i)$
$\quad = 16 - 16i + 4i^2 - 5 = 7 - 16i$

$z_2 = (7 - 16i)^2 + (-5 + 0i)$
$\quad = 49 - 224i + 256i^2 - 5 = -212 - 224i$

escape set

13. $z_0 = \frac{1 + \sqrt{21}}{2} + 0i$

$z_1 = \left(\frac{1 + \sqrt{21}}{2} + 0i\right)^2 + (-5 + 0i)$

$\quad = \frac{(1 + \sqrt{21})^2}{4} - 5$

$\quad = \frac{1 + 2\sqrt{21} + 21 - 20}{4}$

$\quad = \frac{2 + 2\sqrt{21}}{4}$

$\quad = \frac{1 + \sqrt{21}}{2}$

$z_2 = \frac{1 + \sqrt{21}}{2}$

$z_3 = \frac{1 + \sqrt{21}}{2}$ prisoner set

14. $z_0 = 1 + 1i$

$z_1 = (1 + 1i)^2 + (-1 + 0i)$

$\quad = 1 + 2i + i^2 - 1 = -1 + 2i$

$z_2 = (-1 + 2i)^2 + (-1 + 0i)$

$\quad = 1 - 4i + 4i^2 - 1 = -4 - 4i$

$z_3 = (-4 - 4i)^2 + (-1 + 0i)$

$\quad = 16 + 32i + 16i^2 - 1 = -1 + 32i$

escape set

15. $z_0 = 1 - 2i$

$z_1 = (1 - 2i)^2 + (-1 + 0i)$

$\quad = 1 - 4i + 4i^2 - 1 = -4 - 4i$

$z_2 = (-4 - 4i)^2 + (-1 + 0i)$

$\quad = 16 + 32i + 16i^2 - 1 = -1 + 32i$

$z_3 = (-1 + 32i)^2 + (-1 + 0i)$

$\quad = 1 - 64i + 1024i^2 - 1 = -1024 - 64i$

escape set

16. $z_0 = 0.5 + 0i$

$z_1 = (0.5 + 0i)^2 + (-1 + 0i) = 0.25 - 1 = -0.75$

$z_2 = (-0.75)^2 + (-1 + 0i) = 0.5625 - 1 = -0.4375$

$z_3 = (-0.4375)^2 + (-1 + 0i)$

$\quad \approx 0.1914 - 1 \approx -0.8086$

$z_4 = (-0.8086)^2 + (-1 + 0i)$

$\quad \approx 0.6538 - 1 \approx -0.3462$

prisoner set

17-26. Use the graphing calculator program on pages 737-738.

17. $z_0 = 0 + 0i \qquad |z_0| = \sqrt{0^2 + 0^2} = 0$

$z_1 = -1 \qquad\qquad |z_1| = \sqrt{(-1)^2 + 0^2} = 1$

$z_2 = 0 \qquad\qquad\; |z_2| = 0$

$z_3 = -1 \qquad\qquad |z_3| = 1$

$z_4 = 0 \qquad\qquad\; |z_4| = 0$

connected

18. $z_0 = 0 + 0i \qquad\quad |z_0| = 0$

$z_1 = -0.3 + 0.7i \qquad |z_1| \approx 0.762$

$z_2 = -0.7 + 0.28i \qquad |z_2| \approx 0.754$

$z_3 \approx 0.112 + 0.308i \qquad |z_3| \approx 0.328$

$z_4 \approx -0.382 + 0.769i \qquad |z_4| \approx 0.859$

$z_5 \approx -0.745 + 0.112i \qquad |z_5| \approx 0.753$

$\vdots \qquad\qquad\qquad\qquad \vdots$

$z_{13} \approx 895 - 1070i \qquad |z_{13}| \approx 1395$

disconnected

19. $z_0 = 0 + 0i \qquad\quad |z_0| = 0$

$z_1 = -1.25 \qquad\qquad |z_1| = 1.25$

$z_2 \approx 0.313 \qquad\qquad |z_2| \approx 0.313$

$z_3 \approx -1.152 \qquad\quad\; |z_3| \approx 1.152$

$z_4 \approx 0.078 \qquad\qquad |z_4| \approx 0.078$

$\vdots \qquad\qquad\qquad\qquad \vdots$

$z_{14} \approx 0.281 \qquad\qquad |z_{14}| \approx 0.281$

$z_{15} \approx -1.171 \qquad\quad |z_{15}| \approx 1.171$

connected

20. $z_0 = 0 + 0i \qquad\qquad |z_0| = 0$

$z_1 = -0.3 + 0.3i \qquad\quad |z_1| \approx 0.424$

$z_2 = -0.3 - 0.12i \qquad\; |z_2| \approx 0.323$

$z_3 = -0.224 - 0.228i \qquad |z_3| \approx 0.320$

$z_4 \approx -0.302 - 0.198i \qquad |z_4| \approx 0.361$

$\vdots \qquad\qquad\qquad\qquad\qquad \vdots$

$z_{14} \approx -0.268 - 0.196i \qquad |z_{14}| \approx 0.332$

$z_{15} \approx -0.267 - 0.195i \qquad |z_{15}| \approx 0.331$

connected

21. $z_0 = 0 + 0i \qquad\qquad |z_0| = 0$

$z_1 = -1 + 0.5i \qquad\qquad |z_1| \approx 1.118$

$z_2 = -0.250 - 0.500i \qquad |z_2| \approx 0.559$

$z_3 \approx -1.188 + 0.750i \qquad |z_3| \approx 1.405$

$z_4 \approx -0.152 - 1.281i \qquad |z_4| \approx 1.425$

$\vdots \qquad\qquad\qquad\qquad\qquad \vdots$

$z_8 \approx -1683 - 608i \qquad |z_8| \approx 1789$

disconnected

22. $z_0 = 0 + 0i \qquad\qquad |z_0| = 0$

$z_1 = 0.11 - 0.7i \qquad\qquad |z_1| \approx 0.709$

$z_2 \approx -0.368 - 0.854i \qquad |z_2| \approx 0.930$

$z_3 \approx -0.484 - 0.072i \qquad |z_3| \approx 0.489$

$z_4 \approx 0.339 - 0.631i \qquad\; |z_4| \approx 0.513$

$\vdots \qquad\qquad\qquad\qquad\qquad \vdots$

$z_{11} \approx -343 + 75i \qquad\qquad |z_{11}| \approx 351$

disconnected

23.
$$z_0 = 0 + 0i \qquad |z_0| = 0$$
$$z_1 = -1.2 + 0i \qquad |z_1| = 1.2$$
$$z_2 = 0.24 + 0i \qquad |z_2| = 0.24$$
$$z_3 \approx -1.142 + 0i \qquad |z_3| \approx 1.142$$
$$z_4 \approx 0.105 + 0i \qquad |z_4| \approx 0.105$$
$$\vdots \qquad\qquad \vdots$$
$$z_{14} \approx 0.188 + 0i \qquad |z_{14}| \approx 0.188$$
$$z_{15} \approx -1.165 + 0i \qquad |z_{15}| \approx 1.165$$
connected

24.
$$z_0 = 0 + 0i \qquad |z_0| = 0$$
$$z_1 = 0.4 + 0.5i \qquad |z_1| \approx 0.640$$
$$z_2 = 0.31 + 0.9i \qquad |z_2| \approx 0.952$$
$$z_3 \approx -0.314 + 1.058i \qquad |z_3| \approx 1.104$$
$$z_4 \approx -0.621 - 0.164i \qquad |z_4| \approx 0.889$$
$$\vdots \qquad\qquad \vdots$$
$$z_{10} \approx 2110 - 395i \qquad |z_{10}| \approx 2147$$
disconnected

25.
$$z_0 = 0 + 0i \qquad |z_0| = 0$$
$$z_1 = 4 + 0.5i \qquad |z_1| \approx 4.031$$
$$z_2 = 19.75 + 4.5i \qquad |z_2| \approx 20.256$$
$$z_3 \approx 374 + 178i \qquad |z_3| \approx 414$$
$$z_4 \approx 107{,}967 + 133{,}265i \qquad |z_4| \approx 171{,}512$$
disconnected

26.
$$z_0 = 0 + 0i \qquad |z_0| = 0$$
$$z_1 = 0.31 + 0.04i \qquad |z_1| \approx 0.312$$
$$z_2 = 0.405 + 0.065i \qquad |z_2| \approx 0.410$$
$$z_3 \approx 0.469 + 0.092i \qquad |z_3| \approx 0.478$$
$$z_4 \approx 0.522 + 0.127i \qquad |z_4| \approx 0.537$$
$$\vdots \qquad\qquad \vdots$$
$$z_{14} \approx 0.434 + 0.093i \qquad |z_{14}| \approx 0.444$$
$$z_{15} \approx 0.489 + 0.121i \qquad |z_{15}| \approx 0.504$$
connected

27-29. Answers will vary. Sample answers given.

27. prisoner set: $0 + 0i$
    escape set: $1 + i$

28. prisoner set: $0 + 0i$
    escape set: $0.5 + 0.5i$

29. prisoner set: $0.1 + 0.1i$
    escape set: $1 - i$

30. $f(z) = z^2 + (-3 + 0i)$
$$z = z^2 + (-3 + 0i)$$
$$0 = z^2 - z - 3$$
$$z = \frac{-(-1) \pm \sqrt{(-1)^2 - 4(1)(-3)}}{2(1)}$$
$$= \frac{1 \pm \sqrt{13}}{2}$$
So, $z_0 = \dfrac{1 \pm \sqrt{13}}{2}$.

31. See students' work. 32. See students' work.

33.
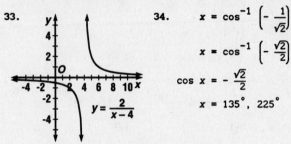
$$y = \frac{2}{x - 4}$$

34. $x = \cos^{-1}\left(-\dfrac{1}{\sqrt{2}}\right)$

$x = \cos^{-1}\left(-\dfrac{\sqrt{2}}{2}\right)$

$\cos x = -\dfrac{\sqrt{2}}{2}$

$x = 135°, 225°$

35. $\cos 2r = 2\cos^2 \theta - 1$
$$= 2(1 - \sin^2 \theta) - 1$$
$$= 2\left[1 - \left(\frac{3}{5}\right)^2\right] - 1$$
$$= 2\left(\frac{16}{25}\right) - 1$$
$$= \frac{32}{25} - 1$$
$$= \frac{7}{25}$$

36. $(n + 2)^4 = n^4 + 4n^3(2) + \dfrac{4(4 - 1)}{1 \cdot 2}n^2(2)^2$
$$+ \frac{4(4 - 1)(4 - 2)}{1 \cdot 2 \cdot 3}n(2)^3 + (2)^4$$
$$= n^4 + 8n^3 + 24n^2 + 32n + 16$$

37. $z_0 = 0$
$$z_1 = 0^2 + (1 - 3i) = 1 - 3i$$
$$z_2 = (1 - 3i)^2 + (1 - 3i)$$
$$= 1 - 6i + 9i^2 + 1 - 3i = -7 - 9i$$
$$z_3 = (-7 - 9i)^2 + (1 - 3i)$$
$$= 49 + 126i + 81i^2 + 1 - 3i = -31 + 123i$$
$$z_4 = (-31 + 123i)^2 + (1 - 3i)$$
$$= 961 - 7626i + 15{,}129i^2 + 1 - 3i$$
$$= -14{,}167 - 7629i$$

38. To find the value of $2a + b$, you need to know the value of a and b. The proportion $\dfrac{a}{b} = \dfrac{4}{5}$ can only be solved for one variable in terms of the other variable. Therefore, the value of $2a + b$ cannot be determined from the given information.
E

13-6   The Mandelbrot Set

1. If the iterations of the function $f(z) = z^2 + c$ for the initial point $z_0 = 0 + 0i$ do not escape to infinity, then the point c is in the Mandelbrot set.

2. A point is in the Mandelbrot set if its associated Julia set is connected.

3. If a point is in the Mandelbrot set, it is colored black. If a point escapes to infinity, then the color represents the number of iterations it takes to escape past a certain point.

4. The use of color in each case allows us to visualize the differences in areas of the land or the set.

5. The point escapes after 4 iterations.
   a. disconnected
   b. outside
   c. orange

6. c is a prisoner point.
   a. connected
   b. inside
   c. black

7. The point escapes after 11 iterations.
   a. disconnected
   b. outside
   c. light blue

8. The point escapes after 5 iterations.
   a. disconnected
   b. outside
   c. orange

9. The point escapes after 7 iterations.
   a. disconnected
   b. outside
   c. light blue

10. c is a prisoner point.
   a. connected
   b. inside
   c. black

11. The point escapes after 6 iterations.
   a. disconnected
   b. outside
   c. light blue

12. c is a prisoner point.
   a. connected
   b. inside
   c. black

13. c is a prisoner point.
   a. connected
   b. inside
   c. black

14. The point escapes after 4 iterations.
   a. disconnected
   b. outside
   c. orange

15. c is a prisoner point.
   a. connected
   b. inside
   c. black

16. The point escapes after 7 iterations.
   a. disconnected
   b. outside
   c. light blue

17. The point escapes after 12 iterations.
   a. disconnected
   b. outside
   c. light blue

18. The point escapes after 6 iterations.
   a. disconnected
   b. outside
   c. orange

19. c is a prisoner point.
   a. disconnected
   b. outside
   c. purple

20. The point escapes after 6 iterations.
   a. disconnected
   b. outside
   c. red

21. The point escapes after 13 iterations.
   a. disconnected
   b. outside
   c. light blue

22. The point escapes after 3 iterations.
   a. disconnected
   b. outside
   c. orange

23. c is a prisoner point.
   a. disconnected
   b. outside
   c. light blue

24. The point escapes after 9 iterations.
   a. disconnected
   b. outside
   c. light blue

25. outside the set

26. See students' work.

27. See students' work.

28. −2 to 1 on the real axis and −1 to 1 on the imaginary axis

29. See students' work.

30. Sample answer: The branches of the tree are small replicas of the entire tree. So the tree displays self-similarity.

31. $\overrightarrow{AB} = (5 - 8, -1 - (-3)) = (-3, 2)$

32. Don's stone:
$$y = t|\vec{v}| \sin\theta + \frac{1}{2}gt^2$$
$$-150 = t(35)\sin 0° + \frac{1}{2}(-32)t^2$$
$$-150 = -16t^2$$
$$t^2 = 9.375$$
$$t \approx 3.06$$
$$x = t|\vec{v}|\cos\theta = (3.06)(35)\cos 0° \approx 107 \text{ ft}$$
Joyce's stone:
$$x = t|\vec{v}|\cos\theta = t(0)\cos 270° = 0$$
distance between stones: 107 − 0 or 107 ft

33. $\log_{\frac{1}{3}} x = -3$
$$x = \left(\frac{1}{3}\right)^{-3}$$
$$x = 27$$

34. $a_n = \dfrac{n}{3^n},\ a_{n+1} = \dfrac{n+1}{3^{n+1}}$

$$r = \lim_{n\to\infty} \frac{a_{n+1}}{a_n}$$

$$= \lim_{n\to\infty} \frac{\dfrac{n+1}{3^{n+1}}}{\dfrac{n}{3^n}}$$

$$= \lim_{n\to\infty} \frac{n+1}{3n}$$

$$= \lim_{n\to\infty} \frac{1+\dfrac{1}{n}}{3}$$

$$= \frac{1}{3}$$

Since $r < 1$, the series is convergent.

35. $z_0 = 2 + 4i$

$z_1 = (2+4i)^2 + (0-i)$

$= 4 + 16i + 16i^2 + 0 - i = -12 + 15i$

$z_2 = (-12+15i)^2 + (0-i)$

$= 144 - 360i + 225i^2 + 0 - i = -81 - 361i$

$z_3 = (-81-361i)^2 + (0-i)$

$= 6561 + 58{,}482i + 130{,}321i^2 + 0 - i$

$= -123{,}760 + 58{,}481i$

escape set

36. $(2n+1) + (2n+3) + (2n+5) = 6n + 9$
$$= 3(2n+3)$$

The sum of three consecutive odd integers is always divisible by 3. The best answer is B.

Case Study Follow-Up

PAGE 745

1. $1.8 \times \dfrac{200}{1} = 360$ m

$17.3 \times \dfrac{50}{1} = 365$ m

$26.7 \times \dfrac{15}{1} = 400.5$ m; no

2-3. See students' work.

Chapter 13 Summary and Review

PAGES 746-748   SKILLS AND CONCEPTS

1. $f(3) = 5 - 2(3)$
$= -1$

$f(-1) = 5 - 2(-1)$
$= 7$

$f(7) = 5 - 2(7)$
$= -9$

2. $f(0) = 0^2 + 3$
$= 3$

$f(3) = 3^2 + 3$
$= 12$

$f(12) = 12^2 + 3$
$= 147$

3. $f(-1.3) = (-1.3 + 2)^3$
≈ 0.34

$f(0.34) \approx (0.34 + 2)^3$
≈ 12.81

$f(12.81) \approx (12.81 + 2)^3$
≈ 3248.37

4. $f(2.5) = 2.5^2 + 2.5 - 6$
$= 2.75$

$f(2.75) = 2.75^2 + 2.75 - 6$
≈ 4.31

$f(4.31) \approx 4.31^2 + 4.31 - 6$
≈ 16.89

5. $f(x) = 3x + 1$
$x = 3x + 1$
$x = -\dfrac{1}{2}$

6. $f(x) = 0.5x - 3$
$x = 0.5x - 3$
$x = -6$

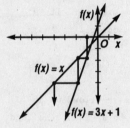

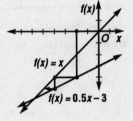

$-\dfrac{1}{2}$ is a repeller. -6 is an attractor.

7. $f(x) = -6x + 5$
$x = -6x + 5$
$x = \dfrac{5}{7}$

8. $f(x) = -2x + 0.3$
$x = -2x + 0.3$
$x = 0.1$

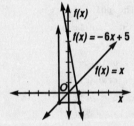

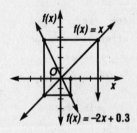

$\dfrac{5}{7}$ is a repeller. 0.1 is a repeller.

9. $f(x) = 2.7x(1 - x)$

$x = 2.7x(1 - x)$

$x = 2.7x - 2.7x^2$

$x = -2.7x^2 + 1.7x$

$0 = x(-2.7x + 1.7)$

$x = 0$ or $-2.7x + 1.7 = 0$
$x \approx 0.630$

$(0, 0), (0.630, 0.630)$

attractor

10. $f(x) = 1.9x(1 - x)$

$x = 1.9x(1 - x)$

$x = 1.9x - 1.9x^2$

$0 = -1.9x^2 + 0.9x$

$0 = x(-1.9x + 0.9)$

$x = 0$ or $-1.9x + 0.9 = 0$
$x \approx 0.474$

$(0, 0), (0.474, 0.474)$

attractor

11. $f(x) = 3.19x(1 - x)$

$\quad x = 3.19x(1 - x)$

$\quad x = 3.19x - 3.19x^2$

$\quad 0 = -3.19x^2 + 2.19x$

$\quad 0 = x(-3.19x + 2.19)$

$\quad x = 0$ or $-3.19x + 2.19 = 0$

$\qquad\qquad\qquad x \approx 0.687$

$(0, 0)$, $(0.687, 0.687)$

repeller

12. $f(x) = 3.35x(1 - x)$

$\quad x = 3.35x(1 - x)$

$\quad x = 3.35x - 3.35x^2$

$\quad 0 = -3.35x^2 + 2.35x$

$\quad 0 = x(-3.35x + 2.35)$

$\quad x = 0$ or $-3.35x + 2.35 = 0$

$\qquad\qquad\qquad x \approx 0.701$

$(0, 0)$, $(0.701, 0.701)$

repeller

13. iterates: $0.471, 0.830, 0.471, 0.830, \ldots$
period-2 attractor

14. iterates: $0.500, 0.500, 0.500, \ldots$
fixed point attractor

15. iterates: $0.512, 0.879, 0.373, 0.823, 0.512, \ldots$
period-4 attractor

16. chaos

17. $z_0 = 4i$

$\quad z_1 = 0.5(4i) + (4 - 2i) = 2i + 4 - 2i = 4$

$\quad z_2 = 0.5(4) + (4 - 2i) = 2 + 4 - 2i = 6 - 2i$

$\quad z_3 = 0.5(6 - 2i) + (4 - 2i)$

$\qquad = 3 - i + 4 - 2i = 7 - 3i$

18. $z_0 = -8$

$\quad z_1 = 0.5(-8) + (4 - 2i) = -4 + 4 - 2i = -2i$

$\quad z_2 = 0.5(-2i) + (4 - 2i) = -i + 4 - 2i = 4 - 3i$

$\quad z_3 = 0.5(4 - 3i) + (4 - 2i)$

$\qquad = 2 - 1.5i + 4 - 2i = 6 - 3.5i$

19. $z_0 = -4 + 6i$

$\quad z_1 = 0.5(-4 + 6i) + (4 - 2i)$

$\qquad = -2 + 3i + 4 - 2i = 2 + i$

$\quad z_2 = 0.5(2 + i) + (4 - 2i)$

$\qquad = 1 + 0.5i + 4 - 2i = 5 - 1.5i$

$\quad z_3 = 0.5(5 - 1.5i) + (4 - 2i)$

$\qquad = 2.5 - 0.75i + 4 - 2i = 6.5 - 2.75i$

20. $z_0 = 12 - 8i$

$\quad z_1 = 0.5(12 - 8i) + (4 - 2i)$

$\qquad = 6 - 4i + 4 - 2i = 10 - 6i$

$\quad z_2 = 0.5(10 - 6i) + (4 - 2i)$

$\qquad = 5 - 3i + 4 - 2i = 9 - 5i$

$\quad z_3 = 0.5(9 - 5i) + (4 - 2i)$

$\qquad = 4.5 - 2.5i + 4 - 2i = 8.5 - 4.5i$

21. $z_0 = 0 + 2i$

$\quad z_1 = (0 + 2i)^2 + (-1 + 0i) = 4i^2 - 1 + 0i = -5$

$\quad z_2 = (-5)^2 + (-1 + 0i) = 25 - 1 + 0i = 24$

$\quad z_3 = 24^2 + (-1 + 0i) = 576 - 1 + 0i = 575$

escape set

22. $z_0 = (0 + 0.7i)^2 + (-1 + 0i)$

$\qquad = 0.49i^2 - 1 + 0i = -1.49$

$\quad z_1 = (-1.49)^2 + (-1 + 0i)$

$\qquad = 2.220 - 1 + 0i \approx 1.220$

$\quad z_2 \approx (1.220)^2 + (-1 + 0i)$

$\qquad \approx 1.489 - 1 + 0i \approx 0.489$

$\quad z_3 = (0.489)^2 + (-1 + 0i)$

$\qquad \approx 0.239 - 1 + 0i \approx -0.761$

$\quad z_4 \approx (-0.761)^2 + (-1 + 0i)$

$\qquad \approx 0.579 - 1 + 0i \approx -0.421$

prisoner set

23. $z_0 = 1.628 + 0i$

$\quad z_1 = (1.628 + 0i)^2 + (-1 + 0i) \approx 1.650$

$\quad z_2 \approx (1.650)^2 + (-1 + 0i) \approx 1.723$

$\quad z_3 \approx (1.723)^2 + (-1 + 0i) \approx 1.969$

$\quad z_4 \approx (1.969)^2 + (-1 + 0i) \approx 2.877$

$\quad z_5 \approx (2.877)^2 + (-1 + 0i) \approx 7.277$

escape set

24. $z_0 = 0.5 - 0.5i$

$\quad z_1 = (0.5 - 0.5i)^2 + (-1 + 0i)$

$\qquad = 0.25 - 0.50i + 0.25i^2 - 1 + 0i$

$\qquad = -1 - 0.5i$

$\quad z_2 = (-1 - 0.5i)^2 + (-1 + 0i)$

$\qquad = 1 + i + 0.25i^2 - 1 + 0i$

$\qquad = -0.25 + i$

$\quad z_3 = (-0.25 + i)^2 + (-1 + 0i)$

$\qquad \approx 0.063 - 0.5i + i^2 - 1 + 0i$

$\qquad \approx -1.937 - 0.5i$

$\quad z_4 = (-1.937 - 0.5i)^2 + (-1 + 0i)$

$\qquad \approx 3.752 + 1.937i + 0.25i^2 - 1 + 0i$

$\qquad \approx 2.502 + 1.937i$

escape set

25-28. Use the graphing calculator program on pages 737-738.

25. $z_0 = 0 + 0i \qquad |z_0| = 0$

$\quad z_1 = -1 - i \qquad |z_1| = 1.414$

$\quad z_2 = -1 + i \qquad |z_2| = 1.414$

$\quad z_3 = -1 - 3i \qquad |z_3| = 3.162$

$\quad z_4 = -9 + 5i \qquad |z_4| = 10.296$

disconnected

26. $z_0 = 0 + 0i$ $\quad |z_0| = 0$

$z_1 = 0.2 + 0.2i$ $\quad |z_1| \approx 0.283$

$z_2 \approx 0.2 + 0.280i$ $\quad |z_2| \approx 0.344$

$z_3 \approx 0.162 + 0.312i$ $\quad |z_3| \approx 0.352$

$z_4 \approx 0.129 + 0.301i$ $\quad |z_4| \approx 0.327$

$\vdots$ $\qquad\qquad\qquad \vdots$

$z_{14} \approx 0.142 + 0.280i$ $\quad |z_{14}| \approx 0.314$

$z_{15} \approx 0.142 + 0.280i$ $\quad |z_{15}| \approx 0.314$

connected

27. $z_0 = 0 + 0i$ $\quad |z_0| = 0$

$z_1 = 0.5 + 0.1i$ $\quad |z_1| \approx 0.510$

$z_2 = 0.740 + 0.200i$ $\quad |z_2| \approx 0.767$

$z_3 \approx 1.008 + 0.396i$ $\quad |z_3| \approx 1.083$

$\vdots$ $\qquad\qquad\qquad \vdots$

$z_7 \approx -49 - 57i$ $\quad |z_7| \approx 75$

disconnected

28. $z_0 = 0 + 0i$ $\quad |z_0| = 0$

$z_1 = -0.3 - 0.2i$ $\quad |z_1| \approx 0.361$

$z_2 \approx -0.250 - 0.80i$ $\quad |z_2| \approx 0.838$

$z_3 \approx -0.244 - 0.160i$ $\quad |z_3| \approx 0.292$

$\vdots$ $\qquad\qquad\qquad \vdots$

$z_{14} \approx -0.253 - 0.133i$ $\quad |z_{14}| \approx 0.286$

$z_{15} \approx -0.253 - 0.133i$ $\quad |z_{15}| \approx 0.286$

connected

29. The point escapes after 8 iterations.   orange

30. The point escapes after 6 iterations. light blue

31. The point escapes after 12 iterations.   red

32. The point does not escape.   black

PAGE 748   APPLICATIONS AND PROBLEM SOLVING

33. a. $\dfrac{9.5\%}{12} = 0.00792$

$i_n = 0.00792(b_{n-1})$

$p_n = 714.73 - i_n = 714.73 - 0.00792b_{n-1}$

$b_n = b_{n-1} - p_n$

$b_n = b_{n-1} - (714.73 - 0.00792b_{n-1})$

$b_n = 1.00792b_{n-1} - 714.73$

b. $b_1 = 1.00792(85,000) - 714.73 = 84,958.48$

$b_2 = 1.00792(84,958.47) - 714.73 = 84,916.63$

$b_3 = 1.00792(84,916.61) - 714.73 = 84,874.45$

$b_4 = 1.00792(84,874.42) - 714.73 = 84,831.94$

34. a. $p_n = \dfrac{54}{72} = 0.75$

$p_1 = 0.75 + 1.9(0.75)(1 - 0.75) \approx 1.106$

$(1.106)(72) \approx 80$ otters

$p_2 = 1.106 + 1.9(1.106)(1 - 1.106) \approx 0.883$

$(0.883)(72) \approx 64$ otters

$p_3 = 0.883 + 1.9(0.883)(1 - 0.883) \approx 1.079$

$(1.079)(72) \approx 78$ otters

$p_4 = 1.079 + 1.9(1.079)(1 - 1.079) \approx 0.917$

$(0.917)(72) \approx 66$ otters

$p_5 = 0.917 + 1.9(0.917)(1 - 0.917) \approx 1.062$

$(1.062)(72) \approx 76$ otters

$p_6 = 1.062 + 1.9(1.062)(1 - 1.062) \approx 0.937$

$(0.937)(72) \approx 67$ otters

$p_7 = 0.937 + 1.9(0.937)(1 - 0.937) \approx 1.049$

$(1.049)(72) \approx 76$ otters

$p_8 = 1.049 + 1.9(1.049)(1 - 1.049) \approx 0.951$

$(0.951)(72) \approx 68$ otters

$p_9 = 0.951 + 1.9(0.951)(1 - 0.951) \approx 1.040$

$(1.040)(72) \approx 75$ otters

$p_{10} = 1.040 + 1.9(1.040)(1 - 1.040) \approx 0.961$

$(0.961)(72) \approx 69$ otters

b. fixed point attractor

Chapter 13 Test

PAGE 749

1. $f(2) = 4(2) - 5$
$\quad = 3$

$f(3) = 4(3) - 5$
$\quad = 7$

$f(4) = 4(7) - 5$
$\quad = 23$

2. $f(1.1) = (1.1 - 2)^2$
$\quad = 0.81$

$f(0.81) = (0.81 - 2)^2$
$\qquad \approx 1.42$

$f(1.42) = (1.42 - 2)^2$
$\qquad \approx 0.34$

3. $f(-2) = (-2)^3 + 7$
$\quad = -1$

$f(-1) = (-1)^3 + 7$
$\quad = 6$

$f(6) = 6^3 + 7$
$\quad = 223$

4. $f(x) = 2x - 5$
$x = 2x - 5$
$x = 5$
$(5, 5)$

repeller

5. $f(x) = 0.2x - 2$

$x = 0.2x - 2$

$x = -2.5$

$(-2.5, -2.5)$

6. $f(x) = -2x + 0.4$

$x = -2x + 0.4$

$x \approx 0.133$

$(0.133, 0.133)$

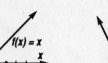

attractor   repeller

7. $-1 < m < 0$

8. $\left(\dfrac{1}{2}, \dfrac{1.6}{4}\right)$ or $(0.5, 0.4)$

$f(x) = 1.6x(1 - x)$

$x = 1.6x(1 - x)$

$x = 1.6x - 1.6x^2$

$0 = -1.6x^2 + 0.6x$

$0 = x(-1.6x + 0.6)$

$x = 0$ or $-1.6x + 0.6 = 0$

$x = 0.375$

$(0, 0), (0.375, 0.375)$

iterates: $0.375, 0.375, 0.375, \ldots$

fixed point attractor

9. $\left(\dfrac{1}{2}, \dfrac{3.48}{4}\right)$ or $(0.5, 0.87)$

$f(x) = 3.48x(1 - x)$

$x = 3.48x(1 - x)$

$x = 3.48x - 3.48x^2$

$x = -3.48x^2 + 2.48x$

$0 = x(-3.48x + 2.48)$

$x = 0$ or $-3.48x + 2.48 = 0$

$x \approx 0.713$

$(0, 0), (0.713, 0.713)$

iterates: $0.487, 0.869, 0.395, 0.832, 0.487, \ldots$

period-4 attractor

10. $\left(\dfrac{1}{2}, \dfrac{3.88}{4}\right)$ or $(0.5, 0.97)$

$f(x) = 3.88x(1 - x)$

$x = 3.88x(1 - x)$

$x = 3.88x - 3.88x^2$

$0 = -3.88x^2 + 2.88x$

$0 = x(-3.88x + 2.88)$

$x = 0$ or $-3.88x + 2.88 = 0$

$x \approx 0.742$

$(0, 0), (0.742, 0.742)$

chaos

11. $z_0 = 2i$

$z_1 = 2(2i) + (3 - i) = 4i + 3 - i = 3 + 3i$

$z_2 = 2(3 + 3i) + (3 - i)$

$\quad = 6 + 6i + 3 - i = 9 + 5i$

$z_3 = 2(9 + 5i) + (3 - i)$

$\quad = 18 + 10i + 3 - i = 21 + 9i$

12. $z_0 = -1 + 2i$

$z_1 = 2(-1 + 2i) + (3 - i)$

$\quad = -2 + 4i + 3 - i = 1 + 3i$

$z_2 = 2(1 + 3i) + (3 - i)$

$\quad = 2 + 6i + 3 - i = 5 + 5i$

$z_3 = 2(5 + 5i) + (3 - i)$

$\quad = 10 + 10i + 3 - i = 13 + 9i$

13. $z_0 = 0.5 + i$

$z_1 = 2(0.5 + i) + (3 - i)$

$\quad = 1 + 2i + 3 - i = 4 + i$

$z_2 = 2(4 + i) + (3 - i)$

$\quad = 8 + 2i + 3 - i = 11 + i$

$z_3 = 2(11 + i) + (3 - i)$

$\quad = 22 + 2i + 3 - i = 25 + i$

14-19. Use graphing calculator.

14. $z_0 = 1 + i$

$z_1 = -2 + 2i$

$z_2 = -2 - 8i$

$z_3 = -62 + 32i$

escape set

15. $z_0 = 0.8 + 0i$

$z_1 = -1.360$

$z_2 = -0.150$

$z_3 = -1.977$

$z_4 = 1.910$

$\vdots$

$z_{15} = 1.292$

prisoner set

16. $z_0 = 0.5 - 0.5i$

$z_1 = -2 - 0.5i$

$z_2 = 1.75 + 2i$

$z_3 = -2.938 + 7i$

$z_4 = -42.371 - 41.125i$

escape set

17. $z_0 = 0 + 0i$

$z_1 = -1 + i$

$z_2 = -1 - i$

$z_3 = -1 + 3i$

$z_4 = -9 - 5i$

$z_5 = 55 + 91i$

disconnected

18. $z_0 = 0 + 0i$

$z_1 = 0.2 - 0.2i$

$z_2 = 0.2 - 0.28i$

$z_3 = 0.162 - 0.312i$

$\vdots$

$z_{15} = 0.142 - 0.280i$

connected

19. $z_0 = 0 + 0i$

$z_1 = -0.6 + 0.4i$

$z_2 = -0.4 - 0.08i$

$z_3 = -0.446 + 0.464i$

$\vdots$

$z_{15} = -0.588 + 0.361i$

connected

20. outside; 15

21. outside; 11

22. outside; 7

23. outside; 6

24. inside the Mandelbrot set

25. $p_n = \frac{90}{120} = 0.75$

$p_1 = 0.75 + 2.1(0.75)(1 - 0.75) \approx 1.144$

$(1.144)(120) \approx 137$ eagles

$p_2 = 1.144 + 2.1(1.144)(1 - 1.144) \approx 0.798$

$(0.798)(120) \approx 96$ eagles

$p_3 = 0.798 + 2.1(0.798)(1 - 0.798) \approx 1.137$

$(1.137)(120) \approx 136$ eagles

$p_4 = 1.137 + 2.1(1.137)(1 - 1.137) \approx 0.810$

$(0.810)(120) \approx 97$ eagles

$p_5 = 0.810 + 2.1(0.810)(1 - 0.810) \approx 1.133$

$(1.133)(120) \approx 136$ eagles

PAGE 749   BONUS

$f(z) = z^2 + (2 + 2i)$

$7 - 10i = z_0^2 + (2 + 2i)$

$z_0^2 = 5 - 12i$

Since $(3 - 2i)(3 - 2i) = 9 - 12i + 4i^2$ or $5 - 12i$, $z_0 = 3 - 2i$.

Chapter 14   Combinatorics and Probability

14-1   Permutations

CHECKING FOR UNDERSTANDING

1. Events that do not affect each other are independent events.

2. Examples will vary. The basic counting principle allows us to determine the total number of ways independent events can happen in sequence given the number of choices for each event occurring. For example, if event A can happen in a ways, event B in b ways, and event C in c ways, then all three can happen in $a \cdot b \cdot c$ ways.

3. an arrangement in which order is important

4. Sample answer: $P(11, 5)$ or $55,440$

5. independent   6. dependent

7. independent

8. If a person can hold only one position, the choice is not dependent. If a person can hold more than one position, the choice is independent.

9. false   10. true

11. false   12. false

13. $P(4, 2) = \dfrac{4!}{(4-2)!}$

    $= \dfrac{4 \cdot 3 \cdot 2 \cdot 1}{2 \cdot 1}$

    $= 12$

14. $P(9, 1) = \dfrac{9!}{(9-1)!}$

    $= \dfrac{9 \cdot 8 \cdot 7 \cdot 6 \cdot 5 \cdot 4 \cdot 3 \cdot 2 \cdot 1}{8 \cdot 7 \cdot 6 \cdot 5 \cdot 4 \cdot 3 \cdot 2 \cdot 1}$

    $= 9$

15. $P(6, 3) = \dfrac{6!}{(6-3)!}$

    $= \dfrac{6 \cdot 5 \cdot 4 \cdot 3 \cdot 2 \cdot 1}{3 \cdot 2 \cdot 1}$

    $= 120$

PAGES 755-757   EXERCISES

16. $P(5, 3) = \dfrac{5!}{(5-3)!}$

    $= \dfrac{5 \cdot 4 \cdot 3 \cdot 2 \cdot 1}{2 \cdot 1}$

    $= 60$

17. $P(5, 5) = \dfrac{5!}{(5-5)!}$

    $= \dfrac{5 \cdot 4 \cdot 3 \cdot 2 \cdot 1}{1}$

    $= 120$

18. $P(7, 4) = \dfrac{7!}{(7-4)!}$

    $= \dfrac{7 \cdot 6 \cdot 5 \cdot 4 \cdot 3 \cdot 2 \cdot 1}{3 \cdot 2 \cdot 1}$

    $= 840$

19. $P(11, 10)$

    $= \dfrac{11!}{(11-10)!}$

    $= \dfrac{11 \cdot 10 \cdot 9 \cdot 8 \cdot 7 \cdot 6 \cdot 5 \cdot 4 \cdot 3 \cdot 2 \cdot 1}{1}$

    $= 39,916,800$

20. $\dfrac{P(6, 4)}{P(5, 3)} = \dfrac{\dfrac{6!}{(6-4)!}}{\dfrac{5!}{(5-3)!}}$

    $= \dfrac{6!}{5!}$

    $= \dfrac{6 \cdot 5 \cdot 4 \cdot 3 \cdot 2 \cdot 1}{5 \cdot 4 \cdot 3 \cdot 2 \cdot 1}$

    $= 6$

21. $\dfrac{P(6, 3) \cdot P(4, 2)}{P(5, 2)}$

    $= \dfrac{\dfrac{6!}{(6-3)!} \cdot \dfrac{4!}{(4-2)!}}{\dfrac{5!}{(5-2)!}}$

    $= \dfrac{\dfrac{6 \cdot 5 \cdot 4 \cdot 3 \cdot 2 \cdot 1 \cdot 4 \cdot 3 \cdot 2 \cdot 1}{3 \cdot 2 \cdot 1 \cdot 2 \cdot 1}}{\dfrac{5 \cdot 4 \cdot 3 \cdot 2 \cdot 1}{3 \cdot 2 \cdot 1}}$

    $= \dfrac{1440}{20}$

    $= 72$

22. $P(7, 7) = \dfrac{7!}{(7-7)!}$

    $= \dfrac{7 \cdot 6 \cdot 5 \cdot 4 \cdot 3 \cdot 2 \cdot 1}{1}$

    $= 5,040$

23. Using the basic counting principle, $2 \cdot 2 \cdot 2 = 8$.

24. Using the basic counting principle, $4 \cdot 3 \cdot 4 = 48$.

25. Using the basic counting principle, $26 \cdot 26 \cdot 26 \cdot 10 \cdot 10 \cdot 10 = 17,576,000$.

26. $P(12, 10)$

    $= \dfrac{12!}{(12-10)!}$

    $= \dfrac{12 \cdot 11 \cdot 10 \cdot 9 \cdot 8 \cdot 7 \cdot 6 \cdot 5 \cdot 4 \cdot 3 \cdot 2 \cdot 1}{2 \cdot 1}$

    $= 239,500,800$

27. 14

28.

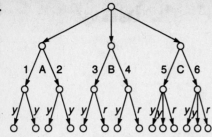

29. 4

30. 10

31. $P(4, 4) = \dfrac{4!}{(4 - 4)!}$

$= \dfrac{4 \cdot 3 \cdot 2 \cdot 1}{1}$

$= 24$

32. $P(2, 1) \cdot (4, 4) = \dfrac{2!}{(2 - 1)!} \cdot \dfrac{4!}{(4 - 4)!}$

$= \dfrac{2 \cdot 1}{1} \cdot \dfrac{4 \cdot 3 \cdot 2 \cdot 1}{1}$

$= 48$

33. $P(3, 1) \cdot P(4, 4) = \dfrac{3!}{(3 - 1)!} \cdot \dfrac{4!}{(4 - 4)!}$

$= \dfrac{3 \cdot 2 \cdot 1}{2 \cdot 1} \cdot \dfrac{4 \cdot 3 \cdot 2 \cdot 1}{1}$

$= 72$

34. Using the basic counting principle,
$4 \cdot 3 \cdot 1 \cdot 2 \cdot 1 = 24$.

35. $4 \cdot P(6, 3) = 4 \cdot \dfrac{6!}{(6 - 3)!}$

$= 4 \cdot \dfrac{6 \cdot 5 \cdot 4 \cdot 3 \cdot 2 \cdot 1}{3 \cdot 2 \cdot 1}$

$= 480$

36. Using the basic counting principle,
$1 \cdot 4 \cdot 8 \cdot 7 \cdot 6 = 1344$.

37. Using the basic counting principle,
$10 \cdot 10 \cdot 10 \cdot 10 \cdot 10 \cdot 24 \cdot 24 = 57{,}600{,}000$.

38. Using the basic counting principle,
$10 \cdot 10 \cdot 10 \cdot 10 \cdot 10 \cdot 26 \cdot 25 = 65{,}000{,}000$.

39. Using the basic counting principle,
$10 \cdot 10 \cdot 10 \cdot 10 \cdot 10 \cdot 25 \cdot 25 = 62{,}500{,}000$.

40. Using the basic counting principle, $10 \cdot 10 \cdot 10 \cdot 10 \cdot 10 \cdot 26 \cdot 26 - 1 = 67{,}599{,}999$.

41. $n[P(5, 3)] = P(7, 5)$

$n = \dfrac{P(7, 5)}{P(5, 3)}$

$= \dfrac{\dfrac{7!}{(7 - 5)!}}{\dfrac{5!}{(5 - 3)!}}$

$= \dfrac{7!}{5!}$

$= \dfrac{7 \cdot 6 \cdot 5 \cdot 4 \cdot 3 \cdot 2 \cdot 1}{5 \cdot 4 \cdot 3 \cdot 2 \cdot 1}$

$= 42$

42. $P(n, 4) = 3[P(n, 3)]$

$\dfrac{n!}{(n - 4)!} = 3\left[\dfrac{n!}{(n - 3)!}\right]$

$\dfrac{n!}{(n - 4)!} = \dfrac{3n!}{(n - 3)!}$

$n(n - 1)(n - 2)(n - 3) = 3(n)(n - 1)(n - 2)$

$n - 3 = 3$

$n = 6$

43. $7[P(n, 5)] = P(n, 3) \cdot P(9, 3)$

$7 \cdot \dfrac{n!}{(n - 5)!} = \dfrac{n!}{(n - 3)!} \cdot \dfrac{9!}{(n - 3)!}$

$7n(n - 1)(n - 2)(n - 3)(n - 4)$

$\qquad = n(n - 1)(n - 2)\dfrac{9!}{6!}$

$7(n - 3)(n - 4) = \dfrac{9 \cdot 8 \cdot 7 \cdot 6 \cdot 5 \cdot 4 \cdot 3 \cdot 2 \cdot 1}{6 \cdot 5 \cdot 4 \cdot 3 \cdot 2 \cdot 1}$

$7(n - 3)(n - 4) = 504$

$(n - 3)(n - 4) = 72$

$n^2 - 7n + 12 = 72$

$n^2 - 7n - 60 = 0$

$(n - 12)(n + 5) = 0$

$n - 12 = 0 \qquad n + 5 = 0$

$n = 12 \qquad n = -5$

Since n cannot be negative, $n = 12$.

44. $P(n, 4) = 40[P(n - 1, 2)]$

$\dfrac{n}{(n - 4)!} = 40\left[\dfrac{(n - 1)!}{(n - 1 - 2)!}\right]$

$n(n - 1)(n - 2)(n - 3) = 40(n - 1)(n - 2)$

$n(n - 3) = 40$

$n^2 - 3n - 40 = 0$

$(n - 8)(n + 5) = 0$

$n - 8 = 0 \qquad n + 5 = 0$

$n = 8 \qquad n = -5$

Since n cannot be negative, $n = 8$.

45. a. $37(7 + 3 + 6) = 592$

b. The pattern holds for all triples.

Let h, t, and u be the digits.

$100h + 10t + u$

$100h + 10u + t$

$100t + 10h + u$

$100t + 10u + h$

$100u + 10t + h$

$\underline{100u + 10h + t}$

$200(h + t + u) + 20(h + t + u) + 2(h + t + u)$

$= 222(h + t + u)$

$\dfrac{222(h + t + u)}{6} = 37(h + t + u)$

46. a. $P(8, 3) = \dfrac{8!}{(8 - 3)!}$

$= \dfrac{8 \cdot 7 \cdot 6 \cdot 5 \cdot 4 \cdot 3 \cdot 2 \cdot 1}{5 \cdot 4 \cdot 3 \cdot 2 \cdot 1}$

$= 336$

b. $P(8, 8) = \dfrac{8!}{(8 - 8)!}$

$\qquad\qquad = \dfrac{8 \cdot 7 \cdot 6 \cdot 5 \cdot 4 \cdot 3 \cdot 2 \cdot 1}{1}$

$\qquad\qquad = 40{,}320$

47. $P(46, 6) = \dfrac{46!}{(46 - 6)!}$

$\qquad\qquad = \dfrac{46!}{40!}$

$\qquad\qquad = 6{,}744{,}109{,}680$

48. neither

49. $y' = 4x$

At $x = -1$, $y' = 4(-1) = -4$.

50. Let $\theta = \cos^{-1} \dfrac{3}{5}$.

$\cos \theta = \dfrac{3}{5}$

$\tan \theta = \dfrac{4}{3}$

51. $(4 - 3i)(-4 + 3i) = -16 + 24i + 9$

$\qquad\qquad\qquad\quad = -7 + 24i$

52. $\qquad 25{,}000 = Pe^{0.09(5)}$

$\qquad 25{,}000 = P(1.5683)$

$\quad \$15{,}940.70 = P$

53. disconnected; outside

54. $x^2 + y^2 = 16$; $xy = 8 \rightarrow y = \dfrac{8}{x}$

$\qquad\qquad x^2 + \left(\dfrac{8}{x}\right)^2 = 16$

$\qquad\qquad x^2 + \dfrac{64}{x^2} = 16$

$\qquad\qquad x^4 + 64 = 16x^2$

$\qquad\qquad x^4 - 16x^2 + 64 = 0$

$\qquad\qquad (x^2 - 8)(x^2 - 8) = 0$

$\qquad\qquad\qquad x^2 - 8 = 0$

$\qquad\qquad\qquad\qquad x^2 = 8$

$\qquad\qquad\qquad\qquad x = \pm\sqrt{8}$

$\qquad\quad y = \dfrac{8}{\pm\sqrt{8}} = \pm\sqrt{8}$

$\quad (x + y)^2 = (\pm\sqrt{8} + (\pm\sqrt{8}))^2$

$\qquad\qquad\quad = (\pm 2\sqrt{8})^2$

$\qquad\qquad\quad = 32$

14-2 Permutations with Repetitions and Circular Permutations

PAGE 761   CHECKING FOR UNDERSTANDING

1. an arrangement of objects when one or more objects are repeated

2. A linear permutation has a beginning and an end; a circular permutation has neither.

3. Circular arrangements are considered to be alike if rotating a given arrangement clockwise or counterclockwise produces the other arrangement. In other words, all items are in the same position relative to each other in both arrangements.

4. If the arrangement can be physically turned over or flipped over, then reflection is possible; otherwise it is not reflective. For example, we can flip over a key ring, but not a football team in a huddle.

5. when there is a fixed reference point

6. circular, not reflective, $10! = 3{,}628{,}800$

7. circular, not reflective, $5! = 120$

8. circular, reflective, $\dfrac{7!}{2} = 2520$

9. linear, not reflective, $P(10, 10) = 3{,}628{,}800$

10. circular, not reflective

11. linear, not reflective

12. linear, not reflective

13. circular, not reflective

14. $P(6, 6) = \dfrac{6!}{(6 - 6)!} = 720$

15. $\dfrac{7!}{2!} = 2520$ \qquad 16. $\dfrac{8!}{2!3!} = 3360$

17. $\dfrac{9!}{2!2!} = 90{,}720$ \qquad 18. $\dfrac{7!}{2!3!} = 420$

19. $\dfrac{8!}{3!} = 6720$ \qquad 20. $\dfrac{9!}{2!} = 181{,}440$

21. $\dfrac{10!}{2!2!2!} = 453{,}600$ \qquad 22. $\dfrac{10!}{2!2!} = 907{,}200$

23. $\dfrac{6!}{2} = 360$ \qquad 24. $6! = 720$

25. $\dfrac{7!}{2} = 2520$ \qquad 26. $\dfrac{4!4!}{4} = 144$

27. $\dfrac{10!}{3!4!3!} = 4200$ \qquad 28. $\dfrac{6!}{2!2!} = 180$

29. $5!5! = 14{,}400$ \qquad 30. $6! = 720$

31. $\dfrac{(5 - 1)!}{2!} = \dfrac{4!}{2!} = 12$

32. $\dfrac{(20 - 1)!}{14!6!2} = \dfrac{19!}{14!6!2} = 969$

33. $3!3!2 = 6 \cdot 6 \cdot 2 = 72$

34. $3!3!4 = 6 \cdot 6 \cdot 4 = 144$

35. $3!3!2 = 6 \cdot 6 \cdot 2 = 72$

36. $\qquad \dfrac{n!}{3!(n - 3)!} = 35$

$\qquad \dfrac{n(n - 1)(n - 2)}{6} = 35$

$\qquad n(n - 1)(n - 2) = 210$

$n^3 - 3n^2 + 2n - 210 = 0$

$\qquad\qquad\qquad n = 7$

37. $\dfrac{6!}{4!2!} = 15$ **38.** $(5 - 1)! = 4! = 24$

39. Let x = percent of beef, y = percent of pork.

$x + y \leq 0.66$

$x \geq 0.30$

$y \geq 0.20$

$x \geq y$

possible solutions: (0.30, 0.20), (0.30, 0.30),
                    (0.33, 0.33), (0.46, 0.20)

$f(x, y) = 32(1.00 - x - y) + 140x + 90y$

$f(0.30, 0.20) = \$76$

$f(0.30, 0.30) = \$81.80$

$f(0.33, 0.33) = \$86.78$

$f(0.46, 0.20) = \$93.28$

minimum at (0.30, 0.20), cost = \$76

40. a. $\tan a = \dfrac{44}{24}$ **b.** $24^2 + 44^2 = c^2$

$a \approx 61.4°$ $2512 = c^2$

$c \approx 50.1$ inches

41. $c^2 = 6.11^2 + 5.84^2 - 2(6.11)(5.84) \cos 105°18'$

$c \approx 9.5$

$\dfrac{9.5}{\sin 105°18'} \approx \dfrac{6.11}{\sin A}, \; A \approx 38°20'$

$B \approx 180° - 105°18' - 38°20' \approx 36°22'$

42. $\cos 2x + \sin x = 1$

$1 - 2\sin^2 x + \sin x = 1$

$-2\sin^2 x + \sin x = 0$

$\sin x(-2 \sin x + 1) = 0$

$\sin x = 0$ $-2 \sin x + 1 = 0$

$x = 0°$ $\sin x = \dfrac{1}{2}$

$x = 30°$

43. $\dfrac{(y + 1)^2}{4} - \dfrac{(x - 3)^2}{5} = 1$

44. $6 \cdot 5 \cdot 2 = 60$ **45.** $\sqrt{0.4} = 0.6325$

$(0.4)2 = 0.8$

Quantity B is greater. B

14-3 Combinations

PAGE 766   CHECKING FOR UNDERSTANDING

1. A permutation is an arrangement in which the order is important. A combination is an arrangement in which order is not important.

2. $C(9, 5)$

3. Find the product of these two combinations, $C(8, 2)$ and $C(9, 3)$.

4. permutation   **5.** combination

6. combination   **7.** permutation

8. $C(4, 2) = \dfrac{4!}{(4 - 2)!2!} = 6$

9. $C(12, 7) = \dfrac{12!}{(12 - 7)!7!} = 792$

10. $C(6, 6) = \dfrac{6!}{(6 - 6)!6!} = 1$

11. $C(3, 2) \cdot C(8, 3) = \dfrac{3!}{(3 - 2)!2!} \cdot \dfrac{8!}{(8 - 3)!3!} = 168$

PAGES 766-767   EXERCISES

12. $C(20, 15) = \dfrac{20!}{(20 - 15)!15!} = 15,504$

13. $C(8, 5) \cdot C(7, 3) = \dfrac{8!}{(8 - 5)!5!} \cdot \dfrac{7!}{(7 - 3)!3!}$

$= 1960$

14. $C(8, 2) \cdot C(5, 1) \cdot C(4, 2)$

$= \dfrac{8!}{(8 - 2)!2!} \cdot \dfrac{5!}{(5 - 1)!1!} \cdot \dfrac{4!}{(4 - 2)!2!}$

$= 840$

15. $P(4, 2) \cdot C(13, 3) \cdot C(13, 2)$

$= \dfrac{4!}{(4 - 2)!} \cdot \dfrac{13!}{(13 - 3)!3!} \cdot \dfrac{13!}{(13 - 2)!2!}$

$= 267,696$

16. $C(10, 4) = \dfrac{10!}{(10 - 4)!4!} = 210$

17. $C(85, 2) = \dfrac{85!}{(85 - 2)!2!} = 3570$

18. $C(14, 9) = \dfrac{14!}{(14 - 9)!9!} = 2002$

19. $C(7, 4) \cdot C(9, 3) = \dfrac{7!}{(7 - 4)!4!} \cdot \dfrac{9!}{(9 - 3)!3!}$

$= 2940$

20. $C(8, 3) = \dfrac{8!}{(8 - 3)!3!} = 56$

21. a. $4 \cdot C(13, 5) = 4 \cdot \dfrac{13!}{(13 - 5)!5!} = 5148$

b. $C(13, 1) \cdot C(13, 1) \cdot C(13, 1) \cdot C(13, 1)$

$= [C(13, 1)]^4 = \left[\dfrac{13!}{(13 - 1)!1!}\right]^4 = 13^4 = 28,561$

22. $C(n, 12) = C(30, 18)$

$\dfrac{n!}{(n - 12)!12!} = \dfrac{30!}{(30 - 18)!18!}$

$\dfrac{n!}{(n - 12)!} = \dfrac{30!}{18!}$

$n = 30$

23. $C(14, 3) = C(n, 11)$

$\dfrac{14!}{(14 - 3)!3!} = \dfrac{n!}{(n - 11)!11!}$

$\dfrac{14!}{3!} = \dfrac{n!}{(n - 11)!}$

$n = 14$

24. $C(11, 8) = C(11, n)$

$\dfrac{11!}{(11 - 8)!8!} = \dfrac{11!}{(11 - n)!n!}$

$(11 - n)!n! = (11 - 8)!8!$

$n = 3$

25. $C(n, 5) = C(n, 7)$

$\dfrac{n!}{(n - 5)!5!} = \dfrac{n!}{(n - 7)!7!}$

$(n - 7)!7! = (n - 5)!5!$

$n = 12$

26. $C(6, 5) = \dfrac{6!}{(6 - 5)!5!} = 6$

27. $C(9, 5) = \dfrac{9!}{(9 - 5)!5!} = 126$

28. $C(9, 2) \cdot C(10, 3) = \dfrac{9!}{(9 - 2)!2!} \cdot \dfrac{10!}{(10 - 3)!3!}$
$= 4320$

29. $C(4, 2) \cdot C(6, 3) + C(4, 2) \cdot C(9, 3)$
$+ C(6, 2) \cdot C(4, 3) + C(6, 2) \cdot C(9, 3)$
$+ C(9, 2) \cdot C(4, 3) + C(9, 2) \cdot C(6, 3)$
$= 6 \cdot 20 + 6 \cdot 84 + 15 \cdot 4 + 15 \cdot 84 + 36 \cdot 4$
$+ 36 \cdot 20 = 2808$

30. $C(8, 5) = \dfrac{8!}{(8 - 5)!5!} = 56$

31. $C(8, 3) \cdot C(10, 2) = \dfrac{8!}{(8 - 3)!3!} \cdot \dfrac{10!}{(10 - 2)!2!}$
$= 2520$

32. $C(8, 1) \cdot C(10, 4) = \dfrac{8!}{(8 - 1)!1!} \cdot \dfrac{10!}{(10 - 4)!4!}$
$= 1680$

33. $C(10, 5) = \dfrac{10!}{(10 - 5)!5!} = 252$

34. $C(n, r) = \dfrac{n!}{(n - r)!r!}$ or $\dfrac{n!}{(n - r)!} \cdot \dfrac{1}{r!}$.

$P(n, r) = \dfrac{n}{(n - r)!}$. By substitution,

$C(n, r) = P(n, r) \cdot \dfrac{1}{r!}$ or $\dfrac{P(n, r)}{r!}$.

35. The pattern has a form of symmetry similar to a row in Pascal's triangle. For example, consider $C(12, r)$ as r goes from 0 to 12. The sequence of output values produced is: 1, 12, 66, 220, 495, 792, 924, 792, 495, 220, 66, 12, 1.

36. $C(10, 2) - 10 = \dfrac{10!}{(10 - 2)!2!} - 10 = 35$

37. $C(2, 1) \cdot C(6, 1) \cdot C(17, 7)$
$= \dfrac{2!}{(2 - 1)!1!} \cdot \dfrac{6!}{(6 - 1)!1!} \cdot \dfrac{17!}{(17 - 7)!7!}$
$= 233,376$

38. $18x^3 - 34x^2 + 16x = 0$
$2x(9x^2 - 17x + 8) = 0$
$2x(9x - 8)(x - 1) = 0$
$2x = 0 \qquad 9x - 8 = 0 \qquad x - 1 = 0$
$x = 0 \qquad\qquad x = \dfrac{8}{9} \qquad\quad x = 1$

39. $\overrightarrow{AB} = (3 - (-2), 9 - 5, -3 - 8) = (5, 4, -11)$

40. $\dfrac{5n - 1}{2n}$ \qquad 41. $(6 - 1)! = 5! = 120$

42. $x = 6k$
$\dfrac{x}{2} = \dfrac{6k}{2}$
$\dfrac{x}{2} = 3k$

If k is odd, $3k$ will also be odd.
The best answer is A.

Mid-Chapter Review

1. $2 \cdot 2 \cdot 2 \cdot 3 = 24$ \qquad 2. $\dfrac{7!}{3!2!} = 420$

3. $(5 - 1)! = 4!$
$= 24$

4. $P(13, 4) = \dfrac{13!}{(13 - 4)!}$
$= 17,160$

5. $C(13, 4) = \dfrac{13!}{(13 - 4)!4!} = 715$

14-4 Probability and Odds

1. Sample answer: Probability is the mathematical likelihood that either a success or a failure will happen.

2. The sum of these probabilities is always 1; they are complements of each other.

3. Sample answer: rolling a die that shows 9

4. Sample answer: The probability of the successful outcome of an event is the ratio of the number of successful outcomes to the total number of outcomes possible. The odds of the successful outcome of an event is the ratio of the probability of its success to the probability of its failure.

5. odds $= \dfrac{\frac{1}{2}}{\frac{1}{2}} = \dfrac{1}{1}$ \qquad 6. odds $= \dfrac{\frac{3}{4}}{\frac{1}{4}} = \dfrac{3}{1}$

7. odds $= \dfrac{\frac{7}{15}}{\frac{8}{15}} = \dfrac{7}{8}$ \qquad 8. odds $= \dfrac{\frac{3}{20}}{\frac{17}{20}} = \dfrac{3}{17}$

9. $P = \dfrac{3}{3 + 4} = \dfrac{3}{7}$ \qquad 10. $P = \dfrac{6}{6 + 5} = \dfrac{6}{11}$

11. $P = \dfrac{4}{4 + 9} = \dfrac{4}{13}$ \qquad 12. $P = \dfrac{1}{1 + 1} = \dfrac{1}{2}$

13. $P(2 \text{ consonants}) = \dfrac{4}{7} \cdot \dfrac{3}{6} = \dfrac{2}{7}$

14. $P(2 \text{ vowels}) = \dfrac{3}{7} \cdot \dfrac{2}{6} = \dfrac{1}{7}$

15. $P(1 \text{ vowel and 1 consonant}) = \dfrac{3}{7} \cdot \dfrac{4}{6} + \dfrac{4}{7} \cdot \dfrac{3}{6} = \dfrac{4}{7}$

16. $P(\text{win}) = \dfrac{7}{7 + 5} = \dfrac{7}{12}$

17. odds $= \dfrac{\frac{1}{4}}{\frac{3}{4}} = \dfrac{1}{3}$

18. $P(2 \text{ rap}) = \dfrac{5}{20} \cdot \dfrac{4}{19} = \dfrac{1}{19}$

19. $P(2 \text{ rock}) = \dfrac{9}{20} \cdot \dfrac{8}{19} = \dfrac{18}{95}$

355

20. $P(\text{2 country}) = \frac{4}{20} \cdot \frac{3}{19} = \frac{3}{95}$

21. $P(\text{1 rap and 1 rock}) = \frac{5}{20} \cdot \frac{9}{19} + \frac{9}{20} \cdot \frac{5}{19} = \frac{9}{38}$

22. $P(\text{no fives}) = \frac{5}{6} \cdot \frac{5}{6} = \frac{25}{36}$

$\text{odds} = \dfrac{\frac{25}{36}}{\frac{11}{36}} = \frac{25}{11}$

23. $P(\text{at least one five}) = \frac{1}{6} \cdot \frac{5}{6} + \frac{5}{6} \cdot \frac{1}{6} + \frac{1}{6} \cdot \frac{1}{6}$

$\qquad = \frac{11}{36}$

$\text{odds} = \dfrac{\frac{11}{36}}{\frac{25}{36}} = \frac{11}{25}$

24. $P(\text{both fives}) = \frac{1}{6} \cdot \frac{1}{6} = \frac{1}{36}$

$\text{odds} = \dfrac{\frac{1}{36}}{\frac{35}{36}} = \frac{1}{35}$

25. $P(\text{both have blue eyes}) = \frac{5}{17} \cdot \frac{4}{16} = \frac{5}{68}$

$\text{odds} = \dfrac{\frac{5}{68}}{\frac{63}{68}} = \frac{5}{63}$

26. $P(\text{neither has blue eyes}) = \frac{12}{17} \cdot \frac{11}{16} = \frac{33}{68}$

$\text{odds} = \dfrac{\frac{33}{68}}{\frac{35}{68}} = \frac{33}{35}$

27. $P(\text{at least one has blue eyes})$

$\qquad = \frac{5}{17} \cdot \frac{12}{16} + \frac{12}{17} \cdot \frac{5}{16} + \frac{5}{17} \cdot \frac{4}{16}$

$\qquad = \frac{35}{68}$

$\text{odds} = \dfrac{\frac{35}{68}}{\frac{33}{68}} = \frac{35}{33}$

28. $P(\text{all kings}) = 0$

$\text{odds} = \frac{0}{1} = 0$

29. $P(\text{all face cards})$

$\qquad = \frac{12}{52} \cdot \frac{11}{51} \cdot \frac{10}{50} \cdot \frac{9}{49} \cdot \frac{8}{48} \cdot \frac{7}{47} \cdot \frac{6}{46}$

$\qquad = \frac{99}{16,723,070}$

$\text{odds} = \dfrac{\frac{99}{16,723,070}}{\frac{16,722,971}{16,723,070}} = \frac{99}{16,722,971}$

30. $P(\text{all from one suit})$

$\qquad = 4 \cdot \frac{13}{52} \cdot \frac{12}{51} \cdot \frac{11}{50} \cdot \frac{10}{49} \cdot \frac{9}{48} \cdot \frac{8}{47} \cdot \frac{7}{46}$

$\qquad = \frac{33}{643,195}$

$\text{odds} = \dfrac{\frac{33}{643,195}}{\frac{643,162}{643,195}} = \frac{33}{643,162}$

31. $P(\text{4 from one suit and 3 from another})$

$\qquad = 4 \cdot \frac{13}{52} \cdot \frac{12}{51} \cdot \frac{11}{50} \cdot \frac{10}{49} \cdot 3 \cdot \frac{13}{48} \cdot \frac{12}{47} \cdot \frac{11}{46}$

$\qquad = \frac{4719}{9,004,730}$

$\text{odds} = \dfrac{\frac{4719}{9,004,730}}{\frac{9,000,011}{9,004,730}} = \frac{4719}{9,000,011}$

32. See students' work.

33.

Given a rope $\overrightarrow{PQ}$ and a random cut point, A, $AP{:}AQ = 1{:}8$. If AP is x inches long, then AQ is $8x$ inches long. Now, the cut must be made along $\overrightarrow{AP}$ so that the longer piece will be 8 or more times as long as the shorter piece. Thus, the probability that the cut is on $\overrightarrow{AP}$ is $\frac{x}{x + 8x} = \frac{1}{9}$. Since the cut can be made on either end of the rope, the actual probability is $\frac{2}{9}$.

34. $\frac{6}{48} \cdot \frac{5}{47} \cdot \frac{4}{46} \cdot \frac{3}{45} \cdot \frac{2}{44} \cdot \frac{1}{43} = \frac{1}{12,271,512}$

35. a. $P(\text{unemployed}) = \frac{184}{500} = \frac{46}{125}$

b. $P(\text{freshman employed part-time}) = \frac{55}{500} = \frac{11}{100}$

c. $P(\text{senior given that they are unemployed})$

$\qquad = \frac{18}{184} = \frac{9}{92}$

36. $y = \pm 2 \sin (2x - 90°)$

37. $\cos (\alpha + \beta) = \cos \alpha \cos \beta - \sin \alpha \sin \beta$

$\qquad = \frac{3}{5} \cdot \frac{5}{13} - \frac{4}{5} \cdot \frac{12}{13}$

$\qquad = \frac{-33}{65}$

38. $(1 + i, -1 + 2i)$, $(-1 + 2i, -4 + 4i)$,

$\quad (-4 + 4i, -1 + 32i)$, $(-1 + 32i, -1024 + 64i)$

39. $C(9, 4) = \frac{9!}{(9 - 4)!4!} = 126$

40.

$a + b = 8 \qquad\rightarrow \qquad -3a - 3b = -24$

$3b - 4 = -13a \quad\rightarrow \qquad \underline{13a + 3b = 4}$

$\qquad\qquad\qquad\qquad\qquad 10a = -20$

$\qquad\qquad\qquad\qquad\qquad\quad a = -2$

The best answer is C.

Case Study Follow-Up

1. According to figures cited in Case Study 3, thefts of motor vehicle accessories occur 15 times more often than purse thefts. Since the probability of Pilfer stealing a stereo is greater than either Filch or Pluder, it must be Pilfer.

2. See students' work.

14-5 Probabilities of Independent and Dependent Events

1. Sample answer: selecting one card from a deck of cards, replacing it, and then selecting another card

2. The outcome of one event does affect the outcome of the other.

3. Multiply the probability of the first times the probability of the second.

4. dependent; $\frac{4}{6} \cdot \frac{3}{5} = \frac{2}{5}$

5. independent; $\frac{5}{9} \cdot \frac{5}{9} = \frac{25}{81}$

6. independent; $\frac{1}{6} \cdot \frac{1}{6} = \frac{1}{36}$

7. dependent; $\frac{4}{15} \cdot \frac{4}{14} \cdot \frac{7}{13} = \frac{8}{195}$

8. independent; $\frac{4}{7} \cdot \frac{4}{7} \cdot \frac{4}{7} \cdot \frac{4}{7} = \frac{256}{2401}$

9. independent; $\frac{1}{2} \cdot \frac{3}{5} = \frac{3}{10}$

10. $P(\text{selecting 2 pennies}) = \frac{5}{21} \cdot \frac{4}{20} = \frac{1}{21}$

11. $P(\text{selecting 2 pennies}) = \frac{5}{21} \cdot \frac{5}{21} = \frac{25}{441}$

12. $P(\text{selecting same coin twice}) = 0$

13. $P(\text{breaking 2 picture frames}) = \frac{6}{16} \cdot \frac{5}{15} = \frac{1}{8}$

14. $P(\text{breaking 2 clocks}) = \frac{5}{16} \cdot \frac{4}{15} = \frac{1}{12}$

15. $P(\text{breaking a clock, then a candle})$

$= \frac{5}{16} \cdot \frac{5}{15} = \frac{5}{48}$

16. $P(\text{breaking a clock and a candle})$

$= \frac{5}{16} \cdot \frac{5}{15} + \frac{5}{16} \cdot \frac{5}{15} = \frac{5}{24}$

17. $P(\text{no 2s}) = \frac{5}{6} \cdot \frac{5}{6} = \frac{25}{36}$

18. $P(\text{two numbers alike}) = 6 \cdot \frac{1}{6} \cdot \frac{1}{6} = \frac{1}{6}$

19. $P(\text{two different numbers}) = \frac{6}{6} \cdot \frac{5}{6} = \frac{5}{6}$

20. $P(2 \text{ and any other number}) = \frac{1}{6} \cdot \frac{5}{6} = \frac{5}{36}$

21. a. $\frac{5}{16} \cdot \frac{4}{15} \cdot \frac{7}{14} = \frac{1}{24}$

    b. $\frac{5}{16} \cdot \frac{4}{16} \cdot \frac{7}{16} = \frac{35}{1024}$

22. a. $\frac{4}{9} \cdot \frac{3}{9} \cdot \frac{2}{9} = \frac{8}{243}$

    b. $\frac{4}{9} \cdot \frac{3}{8} \cdot \frac{2}{7} = \frac{1}{21}$

23. $P(\text{selecting 5 even numbers}) = \left(\frac{37}{75}\right)^5 \approx 0.029$

24. $P(\text{selecting 5 even numbers})$

$= \frac{37}{75} \cdot \frac{36}{74} \cdot \frac{35}{73} \cdot \frac{34}{72} \cdot \frac{33}{71}$

≈ 0.025

25. $P(\text{selecting 5 consecutive numbers})$

$= \frac{1}{75} \cdot \frac{1}{74} \cdot \frac{1}{73} \cdot \frac{1}{72} \cdot \frac{1}{71} \cdot C(71, 1)$

$= \frac{1}{29,170,800}$

26. $P(\text{all diamonds})$

$= \frac{13}{52} \cdot \frac{12}{51} \cdot \frac{11}{50} \cdot \frac{10}{49} \cdot \frac{9}{48} \cdot \frac{8}{47} \cdot \frac{7}{46} \cdot \frac{6}{45} \cdot \frac{5}{44}$

$\cdot \frac{4}{43} \cdot \frac{3}{42} \cdot \frac{2}{41} \cdot \frac{1}{40}$

$= \frac{1}{635,013,559,600}$

27. $P(\text{all one suit})$

$= \frac{52}{52} \cdot \frac{12}{51} \cdot \frac{11}{50} \cdot \frac{10}{49} \cdot \frac{9}{48} \cdot \frac{8}{47} \cdot \frac{7}{46} \cdot \frac{6}{45} \cdot \frac{5}{44}$

$= \cdot \frac{4}{43} \cdot \frac{3}{42} \cdot \frac{2}{41} \cdot \frac{1}{40}$

$= \frac{4}{635,013,559,600}$

28. $P(\text{all red cards})$

$= \frac{26}{52} \cdot \frac{25}{51} \cdot \frac{24}{50} \cdot \frac{23}{49} \cdot \frac{22}{48} \cdot \frac{21}{47} \cdot \frac{20}{46} \cdot \frac{19}{45} \cdot \frac{18}{44}$

$\cdot \frac{17}{43} \cdot \frac{16}{42} \cdot \frac{15}{41} \cdot \frac{14}{40}$

$= \frac{19}{1,160,054}$

29. $P(\text{all face cards}) = 0$

30. Dependent; if x and y are independent,

$P(x \text{ and } y) = \frac{3}{20}$.

31. $1 - \frac{P(26, n)}{26^n} > \frac{1}{2}$

For $n = 6$:

$1 - \frac{P(26, 6)}{26^6} = 1 - \frac{26 \cdot 25 \cdot 24 \cdot 23 \cdot 22 \cdot 21}{26^6}$

≈ 0.463

For $n = 7$:

$1 - \frac{P(26, 7)}{26^7} = 1 - \frac{26 \cdot 25 \cdot 24 \cdot 23 \cdot 22 \cdot 21 \cdot 20}{26^7}$

≈ 0.587

$n = 7$

32. $1 - \dfrac{P(366,\ n)}{366^n} > \dfrac{1}{2}$

For $n = 22$:

$1 - \dfrac{P(366,\ 22)}{366^{22}} \approx 0.476$

For $n = 23$:

$1 - \dfrac{P(366,\ 23)}{366^{23}} \approx 0.507$

$n = 23$

33. $\dfrac{C(96,\ 6)}{C(100,\ 6)} = \dfrac{\dfrac{96!}{(96-6)!6!}}{\dfrac{100!}{(100-6)!6!}} = \dfrac{\dfrac{96!}{90!}}{\dfrac{100!}{94!}} = \dfrac{435,643}{560,175}$

34. Rep: $2035 \times 0.37 \times 0.77 = 580$ vote Rep.

Dem: $2035 \times 0.40 \times 0.83 = 676$ vote Dem.

Ind: $2035 \times 0.21 \times 0.41 = 175$ vote Dem.

$2035 \times 0.21 \times 0.33 = 141$ vote Rep.

Total vote Dem: $676 + 175 = 851$

Total vote Rep: $580 + 141 = 721$

Glenn, $\dfrac{\dfrac{851}{1572}}{\dfrac{721}{1572}} = \dfrac{851}{721}$

35. origin   **36.** $y = 2$

37. $\sum\limits_{k=1}^{\infty} 3^k$

38. $P(\text{each a 3 given sum is 6}) = \dfrac{1}{5}$

$P = 2(1) + 2(w + 3) = 2(1) + 2w + 6$

39. An addition of 3 to each width will add 6 to the perimeter. The best answer is B.

14-6 Probabilities of Mutually Exclusive or Inclusive Events

PAGE 781   CHECKING FOR UNDERSTANDING

1. Mutually exclusive events cannot occur at the same time, mutually inclusive events can occur at the same time.

2. Sample answer: walking the dog and practicing the piano

3. Sample answer: watch TV and eat a snack

4.

Donated Food 35 | Both 30 | Donated Money 20

No Donation 115

5. a. exclusive, $\dfrac{5}{36} + \dfrac{4}{36} = \dfrac{1}{4}$

b. inclusive, $\dfrac{6}{36} + \dfrac{6}{36} - \dfrac{1}{36} = \dfrac{11}{36}$

6. a. inclusive, $\dfrac{4}{52} + \dfrac{26}{52} - \dfrac{2}{52} = \dfrac{7}{13}$

b. exclusive, $\dfrac{4}{52} + \dfrac{4}{52} = \dfrac{2}{13}$

7. inclusive, $\dfrac{1}{2} + \dfrac{2}{5} - \dfrac{1}{10} = \dfrac{4}{5}$

PAGES 782-783   EXERCISES

8. exclusive, $\dfrac{16}{32} = \dfrac{1}{2}$

9. inclusive, $\dfrac{15}{27} + \dfrac{11}{27} - \dfrac{6}{27} = \dfrac{20}{27}$

10. inclusive, $\dfrac{26}{52} + \dfrac{12}{52} - \dfrac{6}{52} = \dfrac{8}{13}$

11. $P(\text{shows either red or blue}) = \dfrac{2}{3}$

12. $P(\text{does not show red}) = \dfrac{2}{3}$

13. $P(\text{all 3 rock or all 3 rap})$

$= \dfrac{6}{11} \cdot \dfrac{5}{10} \cdot \dfrac{4}{9} + \dfrac{5}{11} \cdot \dfrac{4}{10} \cdot \dfrac{3}{9} = \dfrac{2}{11}$

14. $P(\text{exactly 2 rap}) = 3\left(\dfrac{5}{11} \cdot \dfrac{4}{10} \cdot \dfrac{6}{9}\right) = \dfrac{4}{11}$

15. $P(\text{at least 2 rap}) = 3\left(\dfrac{5}{11} \cdot \dfrac{4}{10} \cdot \dfrac{6}{9}\right) + \dfrac{5}{11} \cdot \dfrac{4}{10} \cdot \dfrac{3}{9}$

$= \dfrac{14}{33}$

16. $P(\text{at least 2 rock}) = 3\left(\dfrac{6}{11} \cdot \dfrac{5}{10} \cdot \dfrac{5}{9}\right) + \dfrac{6}{11} \cdot \dfrac{5}{10} \cdot \dfrac{4}{9}$

$= \dfrac{19}{33}$

17. $P(\text{both aces or both face cards})$

$= \left(\dfrac{4}{52} \cdot \dfrac{3}{51}\right) + \left(\dfrac{12}{52} \cdot \dfrac{11}{51}\right) = \dfrac{12}{221}$

18. $P(\text{both aces or both black})$

$= \left(\dfrac{4}{52} \cdot \dfrac{3}{51}\right) + \left(\dfrac{26}{52} \cdot \dfrac{25}{51}\right) - \left(\dfrac{2}{52} \cdot \dfrac{1}{51}\right) = \dfrac{55}{221}$

19. $P(\text{both black or both face cards})$

$= \left(\dfrac{26}{52} \cdot \dfrac{25}{51}\right) + \left(\dfrac{12}{52} \cdot \dfrac{11}{51}\right) - \left(\dfrac{6}{52} \cdot \dfrac{5}{51}\right) = \dfrac{188}{663}$

20. $P(\text{both either red or an ace}) = \left(\dfrac{28}{52} \cdot \dfrac{27}{51}\right) = \dfrac{63}{221}$

21. $P(\text{landing 3 heads or 2 tails})$

$= C(6,\ 3)\left(\dfrac{1}{2}\right)^6 + C(6,\ 2)\left(\dfrac{1}{2}\right)^6 = \dfrac{35}{64}$

22. $P(\text{landing at least 4 tails})$

$= C(6,\ 4)\left(\dfrac{1}{2}\right)^6 + C(6,\ 5)\left(\dfrac{1}{2}\right)^6 + C(6,\ 6)\left(\dfrac{1}{2}\right)^6 = \dfrac{11}{32}$

23. $P(\text{landing 4 heads or 1 tail})$

$= C(6,\ 4)\left(\dfrac{1}{2}\right)^6 + C(6,\ 5)\left(\dfrac{1}{2}\right)^6 = \dfrac{21}{64}$

24. $P(\text{landing all heads or all tails})$

$= 2\left(\dfrac{1}{2}\right)^6 = \dfrac{1}{32}$

25. $P(\text{all men or all women})$

$= \dfrac{C(7,\ 6)}{C(14,\ 6)} + \dfrac{C(7,\ 6)}{C(14,\ 6)}$

$= \dfrac{2}{429}$

26. P(5 men or 5 women)

$$= \frac{C(7, 5) \cdot C(7, 1)}{C(14, 6)} + \frac{C(7, 5) \cdot C(7, 1)}{C(14, 6)}$$

$$= \frac{14}{143}$$

27. P(3 men and 3 women)

$$= \frac{C(7, 3) \cdot C(7, 3)}{C(14, 6)}$$

$$= \frac{175}{429}$$

28. P(at least 4 women)

$$= \frac{C(7, 4) \cdot C(7, 2)}{C(14, 6)} + \frac{C(7, 5) \cdot C(7, 1)}{C(14, 6)}$$

$$+ \frac{C(7, 6)}{C(14, 6)}$$

$$= \frac{127}{429}$$

29. P(each is a 22) $= \frac{1}{25} \cdot \frac{1}{21} = \frac{1}{525}$

30. P(neither is a 25) $= \frac{24}{25} \cdot \frac{20}{21} = \frac{32}{35}$

31. P(at least one is a 23)

$$= \left(\frac{1}{25}\right)\left(\frac{20}{21}\right) + \left(\frac{24}{25}\right)\left(\frac{1}{21}\right) + \left(\frac{1}{25}\right)\left(\frac{1}{21}\right)$$

$$= \frac{3}{35}$$

32. P(each is greater than 10) $= \frac{15}{25} \cdot 1 = \frac{3}{5}$

33. There are 8 odds and 7 evens. In order for the sum to be odd, you must have 1 odd, 5 even, or 3 odd, 3 even, or 5 odd, 1 even.

$$P = \frac{C(8, 1) \cdot C(7, 5) + C(8, 3) \cdot C(7, 3) + C(8, 5) \cdot C(7, 1)}{C(15, 6)}$$

$$= \frac{72}{143}$$

34. $P = \frac{C(8, 1) \cdot C(5, 1) + C(8, 2) \cdot C(5, 0)}{C(13, 2)}$

$$= \frac{34}{39}$$

35. $\frac{93}{100} \cdot \frac{3}{100} + \frac{7}{100} \cdot \frac{97}{100} + \frac{93}{100} \cdot \frac{97}{100} = \frac{9979}{10,000}$

36. $s = r\theta$

$$\frac{s}{\theta} = r$$

$$\frac{0.25}{0.7854} \approx r$$

$$r \approx 0.3183 \text{ miles}$$

$$r \approx 1681 \text{ ft}$$

37. $\frac{(y - 1)^2}{36} + \frac{(x - 3)^2}{36} = 1$

38. $F_n = 2000 \left[\frac{(1 + 0.08)^{42} - 1}{0.08} \right]$

$$\approx \$608,487.05$$

39. $\frac{25}{50} \cdot \frac{24}{49} \cdot \frac{23}{48} \cdot \frac{22}{47} = \frac{253}{4606}$

40. for $(-4, 0)$, $d = \sqrt{(-8)^2 + 0^2} = 8$

for $(0, 4\sqrt{3})$, $d = \sqrt{(-4)^2 + (4\sqrt{3})^2} = 8$

for $(4, 8)$, $d = \sqrt{0^2 + 8^2} = 8$

for $(8, 0)$, $d = \sqrt{4^2 + 0^2} = 4$

for $(4, -8)$, $d = \sqrt{0^2 + (-8)^2} = 8$

The best answer is D.

14-7 Conditional Probability

1. Conditional probability is the probability some events will occur given that another event has already occurred.

2. No. Sample illustration: P(ace/red card) $= \frac{1}{13}$, P(red card/ace) $= \frac{1}{2}$.

3. Sample answer: the red cards of a standard deck of 52 cards

4. when A is a subset of B

5. Event A: one coin shows tails
   Event B: at least one coin shows heads

$$\frac{\frac{1}{2}}{\frac{3}{4}} = \frac{2}{3}$$

6. Event A: the member is a Democrat
   Event B: the member is a man

$$\frac{\frac{4}{12}}{\frac{8}{12}} = \frac{1}{2}$$

7. P(heart/red) $= \frac{\frac{13}{52}}{\frac{26}{52}} = \frac{1}{2}$

8. P(ace/red) $= \frac{\frac{2}{52}}{\frac{26}{52}} = \frac{1}{13}$

9. P(face card/red) $= \frac{\frac{6}{52}}{\frac{26}{52}} = \frac{3}{13}$

10. P(six of spades/red) $= 0$

11. P(six of hearts/red) $= \frac{\frac{1}{52}}{\frac{26}{52}} = \frac{1}{26}$

12. P(red six/red) $= \frac{\frac{2}{52}}{\frac{26}{52}} = \frac{1}{13}$

13. Event A: the girls are separated

Event B: a girl is on an end

$$\frac{\frac{3}{6}}{\frac{5}{6}} = \frac{3}{5}$$

14. Event A: marble came from the first bag

Event B: a blue marble is drawn

$$\frac{\frac{4}{16}}{\frac{10}{16}} = \frac{2}{5}$$

PAGES 787-789   EXERCISES

15. $P(\text{sum is 8}) = 0$

16. $P(\text{numbers match}) = \dfrac{\frac{2}{36}}{\frac{10}{36}} = \dfrac{1}{5}$

17. $P(\text{sum is 12}) = \dfrac{\frac{1}{36}}{\frac{10}{36}} = \dfrac{1}{10}$

18. $P(\text{sum is even}) = \dfrac{\frac{4}{36}}{\frac{10}{36}} = \dfrac{2}{5}$

19. $P(\text{sum is 9 or 10}) = \dfrac{\frac{7}{36}}{\frac{10}{36}} = \dfrac{7}{10}$

20. $P(\text{numbers match or sum is even}) = \dfrac{\frac{4}{36}}{\frac{10}{36}} = \dfrac{2}{5}$

21. $P(\text{all tails up/first coin tail}) = \dfrac{\frac{1}{8}}{\frac{4}{8}} = \dfrac{1}{4}$

22. $P(\text{all tails/one is a head}) = 0$

23. $P(\text{all tails/at least one tail}) = \dfrac{\frac{1}{8}}{\frac{7}{8}} = \dfrac{1}{7}$

24. $P(\text{all tails/at least two tails}) = \dfrac{\frac{1}{8}}{\frac{4}{8}} = \dfrac{1}{4}$

25. $P(\text{Fernando was selected, given that Becky was selected}) = \dfrac{\frac{4}{20}}{\frac{10}{20}} = \dfrac{2}{5}$

26. $P(\text{Emily was not selected, given that Andy and Cho were selected}) = \dfrac{\frac{3}{20}}{\frac{4}{20}} = \dfrac{3}{4}$

27. $P(\text{Becky and Cho were selected, given that Dan was not selected}) = \dfrac{\frac{3}{20}}{\frac{10}{20}} = \dfrac{3}{10}$

28. $P(\text{Cho and Andy were selected, given that neither Becky nor Emily were selected}) = \dfrac{\frac{2}{20}}{\frac{4}{20}} = \dfrac{1}{2}$

29. $P(\text{ends in 52, given even}) = \dfrac{\frac{6}{120}}{\frac{48}{120}} = \dfrac{1}{8}$

30. $P(\text{both odd, given sum even}) = \dfrac{\frac{10}{36}}{\frac{16}{36}} = \dfrac{5}{8}$

31. $P(\text{brown eyes, given brown hair}) = \dfrac{0.10}{0.60} = \dfrac{1}{6}$

32. $P(\text{no brown hair, given brown eyes}) = \dfrac{0.20}{0.30} = \dfrac{2}{3}$

33. $P(\text{sum greater than 18, given queen of hearts})$

$$= \frac{\frac{1}{52} \cdot \frac{19}{51}}{\frac{1}{52} \cdot \frac{51}{51}} = \frac{19}{51}$$

34. Event A: the sum of the cards is 7 or less.

Event B: at least one card is an ace.

Event B': both cards not an ace

$$P(B') = \frac{C(48, 2)}{C(52, 2)} = \frac{188}{221}$$

$$P(B) = 1 - P(B') = 1 - \frac{188}{221} = \frac{33}{221}$$

$$P(A \text{ and } B) = \frac{23}{C(52, 2)} = \frac{23}{1326}$$

$$P(A/B) = \frac{(P(A \text{ and } B)}{P(B)} = \frac{\frac{23}{1326}}{\frac{33}{221}} = \frac{23}{198}$$

35. Sample answer: when the number of possible outcomes becomes so large that it's not easy to list all of them

36. $P(A/B) = \dfrac{P(A \text{ and } B)}{P(B)}$ by definition. So, if

$P(A) = P(A/B)$ then by substitution

$$P(A) = \frac{P(A \text{ and } B)}{P(B)} \text{ or } P(A \text{ and } B) = P(A) \cdot P(B).$$

Therefore, events A and B are independent.

37. Let event A be that a person buys something. Let event B be that a person asks questions.

$$P(A/B) = \frac{P(A \text{ and } B)}{P(B)} = \frac{\frac{48}{200}}{\frac{60}{200}} \text{ or } \frac{4}{5}$$

Four out of five customers who ask questions will make a purchase. Therefore, they are more likely to buy something if they ask questions.

38. a. $\dfrac{130}{200} = \dfrac{13}{20}$ b. $\dfrac{68}{100} = \dfrac{17}{25}$ c. $\dfrac{62}{100} = \dfrac{31}{50}$

d. The new vaccine is slightly more effective than the conventional treatment.

39. a. $\dfrac{69}{70}$ b. $\dfrac{6}{75} = \dfrac{2}{25}$ c. $\dfrac{1}{25}$

40. $f(-2) = 2(-2)^2 - 2(-2) + 8 = 8 + 4 + 8 = 20$

41.
$$
\begin{array}{r|rrrrrr}
2 & 1 & 0 & 0 & -3 & 0 & -20 \\
  &   & 2 & 4 & 8 & 10 & 20 \\
\hline
  & 1 & 2 & 4 & 5 & 10 & 0
\end{array}
$$

$x^4 + 2x^3 + 4x^2 + 5x + 10$

42. $1{,}000{,}000 = P\left[\dfrac{1 - (1 + 0.12)^{-20}}{0.12}\right]$

$\$133{,}878.78 \approx P$

43. $f(-1) = (-1)^2 + 1 = 2$

    $f(2) = 2^2 + 1 = 5$

    $f(5) = 5^2 + 1 = 26$

44. $\dfrac{5}{26} + \dfrac{5}{26} - \dfrac{3}{26} = \dfrac{7}{26}$

45. 15% of 1400 = 210

    14% of 1500 = 210

    The two quantities are equal. C

14-8   The Binomial Theorem and Probability

1. Evaluate $C(5, 4)\left(\dfrac{1}{2}\right)^4\left(\dfrac{1}{2}\right)^1$.

2. A binomial experiment exists if and only if these conditions occur.
   - The experiment consists of n identical trials.
   - Each trial results in one of two outcomes.
   - The trials are independent.

3. binomial,

    $C(4, 2)\left(\dfrac{1}{2}\right)^2\left(\dfrac{1}{2}\right)^2 = 6\left(\dfrac{1}{4}\right)\left(\dfrac{1}{4}\right) = \dfrac{3}{8}$

4. a. binomial,

    $C(4, 4)\left(\dfrac{4}{52}\right)^4\left(\dfrac{48}{52}\right)^0 = 1 \cdot \dfrac{256}{7,311,616} \cdot 1$

                   $= \dfrac{1}{28,561}$

   b. not binomial

5. a. binomial,

    $C(2, 2)\left(\dfrac{8}{18}\right)^2\left(\dfrac{10}{18}\right)^0 = 1 \cdot \dfrac{64}{324} \cdot 1 = \dfrac{16}{81}$

   b. binomial,

    $C(2, 2)\left(\dfrac{4}{18}\right)^2\left(\dfrac{14}{18}\right)^0 = 1 \cdot \dfrac{16}{324} \cdot 1 = \dfrac{4}{81}$

   c. binomial,

    $C(2, 2)\left(\dfrac{6}{18}\right)^2\left(\dfrac{12}{18}\right)^0 = 1 \cdot \dfrac{36}{324} \cdot 1 = \dfrac{1}{9}$

   d. not binomial

   e. not binomial

   f. not binomial

6. $P(\text{all heads}) = C(3, 3)\left(\dfrac{1}{2}\right)^3\left(\dfrac{1}{2}\right)^0$

              $= 1 \cdot \dfrac{1}{8} \cdot 1$

              $= \dfrac{1}{8}$

7. $P(\text{exactly 2 tails}) = C(3, 2)\left(\dfrac{1}{2}\right)^2\left(\dfrac{1}{2}\right)^1$

                    $= 3 \cdot \dfrac{1}{4} \cdot \dfrac{1}{2}$

                    $= \dfrac{3}{8}$

8. $P(\text{at least 2 heads})$

  $= C(3, 2)\left(\dfrac{1}{2}\right)^2\left(\dfrac{1}{2}\right)^1 \cdot C(3, 3)\left(\dfrac{1}{2}\right)^3\left(\dfrac{1}{2}\right)^0$

  $= \dfrac{3}{8} + \dfrac{1}{8}$

  $= \dfrac{1}{2}$

9. $P(\text{only one 4}) = C(5, 1)\left(\dfrac{1}{6}\right)^1\left(\dfrac{5}{6}\right)^4$

              $= 5 \cdot \dfrac{1}{6} \cdot \dfrac{625}{1296}$

              $= \dfrac{3125}{7776}$

10. $P(\text{at least three 4s})$

  $= C(5, 3)\left(\dfrac{1}{6}\right)^3\left(\dfrac{5}{6}\right)^2 + C(5, 4)\left(\dfrac{1}{6}\right)^4\left(\dfrac{5}{6}\right)^1$

    $+ C(5, 5)\left(\dfrac{1}{6}\right)^5\left(\dfrac{5}{6}\right)^0$

  $= 10 \cdot \dfrac{1}{216} \cdot \dfrac{25}{36} + 5 \cdot \dfrac{1}{1296} \cdot \dfrac{5}{6} + 1 \cdot \dfrac{1}{7776} \cdot 1$

  $= \dfrac{276}{7776}$

  $= \dfrac{23}{648}$

11. $P(\text{no more than two 4s})$

  $= C(5, 0)\left(\dfrac{1}{6}\right)^0\left(\dfrac{5}{6}\right)^5 + C(5, 1)\left(\dfrac{1}{6}\right)^1\left(\dfrac{5}{6}\right)^5$

    $+ C(5, 2)\left(\dfrac{1}{6}\right)^2\left(\dfrac{5}{6}\right)^3$

  $= 1 \cdot 1 \cdot \dfrac{3125}{7776} + 5 \cdot \dfrac{1}{6} \cdot \dfrac{625}{1296} + 10 \cdot \dfrac{1}{36} \cdot \dfrac{125}{216}$

  $= \dfrac{7500}{7776}$

  $= \dfrac{625}{648}$

12. $P(\text{exactly five 4s}) = C(5, 5)\left(\dfrac{1}{6}\right)^5\left(\dfrac{5}{6}\right)^0$

                 $= 1 \cdot \dfrac{1}{7776} \cdot 1$

                 $= \dfrac{1}{7776}$

13. $P(\text{never the correct color}) = C(4, 0)\left(\dfrac{2}{3}\right)^0\left(\dfrac{1}{3}\right)^4$

                         $= 1 \cdot 1 \cdot \dfrac{1}{81}$

                         $= \dfrac{1}{81}$

14. $P(\text{correct at least 3 times})$

  $= C(4, 3)\left(\dfrac{2}{3}\right)^3\left(\dfrac{1}{3}\right)^1 + C(4, 4)\left(\dfrac{2}{3}\right)^4\left(\dfrac{1}{3}\right)^0$

  $= 4 \cdot \dfrac{8}{27} \cdot \dfrac{1}{3} + 1 \cdot \dfrac{16}{81} \cdot 1$

  $= \dfrac{16}{27}$

15. P(no more than 3 times correct)

$= 1 - P$(correct 4 times)

$= 1 - C(4, 4)\left(\frac{2}{3}\right)^4\left(\frac{1}{3}\right)^0$

$= 1 - 1 \cdot \frac{16}{81} \cdot 1$

$= 1 - \frac{16}{81}$

$= \frac{65}{81}$

16. P(correct exactly 2 times) $= C(4, 2)\left(\frac{2}{3}\right)^2\left(\frac{1}{3}\right)^2$

$= 6 \cdot \frac{4}{9} \cdot \frac{1}{9}$

$= \frac{8}{27}$

17. P(7 correct) $= C(10, 7)\left(\frac{1}{2}\right)^7\left(\frac{1}{2}\right)^3$

$= 120 \cdot \frac{1}{128} \cdot \frac{1}{8}$

$= \frac{15}{128}$

18. P(all incorrect) $= C(10, 0)\left(\frac{1}{2}\right)^0\left(\frac{1}{2}\right)^{10}$

$= 1 \cdot 1 \cdot \frac{1}{1024}$

$= \frac{1}{1024}$

19. P(at least 6 correct)

$= C(10, 6)\left(\frac{1}{2}\right)^6\left(\frac{1}{2}\right)^4 + C(10, 7)\left(\frac{1}{2}\right)^7\left(\frac{1}{2}\right)^3$

$+ C(10, 8)\left(\frac{1}{2}\right)^8\left(\frac{1}{2}\right)^2 + C(10, 9)\left(\frac{1}{2}\right)^9\left(\frac{1}{2}\right)^1$

$+ C(10, 10)\left(\frac{1}{2}\right)^{10}\left(\frac{1}{2}\right)^0$

$= 210 \cdot \frac{1}{64} \cdot \frac{1}{16} + 120 \cdot \frac{1}{128} \cdot \frac{1}{8} + 45 \cdot \frac{1}{256} \cdot \frac{1}{4}$

$+ 10 \cdot \frac{1}{512} \cdot \frac{1}{2} + 1 \cdot \frac{1}{1024} \cdot 1$

$= \frac{386}{1024}$

$= \frac{193}{512}$

20. P(at least half correct)

$= C(10, 5)\left(\frac{1}{2}\right)^5\left(\frac{1}{2}\right)^5 +$ answer to 19

$= 252 \cdot \frac{1}{32} \cdot \frac{1}{32} + \frac{386}{1024}$

$= \frac{252}{1024} + \frac{386}{1024}$

$= \frac{319}{512}$

21. P(exactly 1 hit) $= C(5, 1)\left(\frac{2}{10}\right)^1\left(\frac{8}{10}\right)^4$

$= 5 \cdot \frac{2}{10} \cdot \frac{4096}{10,000}$

$= \frac{256}{625}$

22. P(exactly 3 hits) $= C(5, 3)\left(\frac{2}{10}\right)^3\left(\frac{8}{10}\right)^2$

$= 10 \cdot \frac{8}{1000} \cdot \frac{64}{100}$

$= \frac{32}{625}$

23. P(at least 4 hits)

$= C(5, 4)\left(\frac{2}{10}\right)^4\left(\frac{8}{10}\right)^1 + C(5, 5)\left(\frac{2}{10}\right)^5\left(\frac{8}{10}\right)^0$

$= 5 \cdot \frac{16}{10,000} \cdot \frac{8}{10} + 1 \cdot \frac{32}{100,000} \cdot 1$

$= \frac{672}{100,000}$

$= \frac{21}{3125}$

24. P(3 heads) $= C(3, 3)\left(\frac{1}{2}\right)^3\left(\frac{1}{2}\right)^0$

$= 1 \cdot \frac{1}{8} \cdot 1$

$= \frac{1}{8}$

25. P(3 tails) $= C(3, 3)\left(\frac{1}{2}\right)^3\left(\frac{1}{2}\right)^0$

$= 1 \cdot \frac{1}{8} \cdot 1$

$= \frac{1}{8}$

26. P(at least 2 heads)

$= C(3, 2)\left(\frac{1}{2}\right)^2\left(\frac{1}{2}\right)^1 + C(3, 3)\left(\frac{1}{2}\right)^3\left(\frac{1}{2}\right)^0$

$= 3 \cdot \frac{1}{4} \cdot \frac{1}{2} + 1 \cdot \frac{1}{8} \cdot 1$

$= \frac{4}{8}$

$= \frac{1}{2}$

27. P(exactly 2 tails) $= C(3, 2)\left(\frac{1}{2}\right)^2\left(\frac{1}{2}\right)^1$

$= 3 \cdot \frac{1}{4} \cdot \frac{1}{2}$

$= \frac{3}{8}$

28. P(all point up) $= C(10, 10)\left(\frac{2}{5}\right)^{10}\left(\frac{3}{5}\right)^0$

$= 1 \cdot \frac{1024}{9,765,625} \cdot 1$

$= \frac{1024}{9,765,625}$

29. P(exactly 3 point up) $= C(10, 3)\left(\frac{2}{5}\right)^3\left(\frac{3}{5}\right)^7$

$= 120 \cdot \frac{8}{125} \cdot \frac{2187}{78,125}$

$= \frac{419,904}{1,953,125}$

30. P(exactly 5 point up) $= C(10, 5)\left(\frac{2}{5}\right)^5\left(\frac{3}{5}\right)^5$

$= 252 \cdot \frac{32}{3125} \cdot \frac{243}{3125}$

$= \frac{1,959,552}{9,765,625}$

31. P(at least 6 point up)

$= C(10, 6)\left(\frac{2}{5}\right)^6\left(\frac{3}{5}\right)^4 + C(10, 7)\left(\frac{2}{5}\right)^7\left(\frac{3}{5}\right)^3$

$\quad + C(10, 8)\left(\frac{2}{5}\right)^8\left(\frac{3}{5}\right)^2 + C(10, 9)\left(\frac{2}{5}\right)^9\left(\frac{3}{5}\right)^1$

$\quad + C(10, 10)\left(\frac{2}{5}\right)^{10}\left(\frac{3}{5}\right)^0$

$= 210 \cdot \frac{64}{15,625} \cdot \frac{81}{625} + 120 \cdot \frac{128}{78,125} \cdot \frac{27}{125}$

$\quad + 45 \cdot \frac{256}{390,625} \cdot \frac{9}{25} + 10 \cdot \frac{512}{1,953,125} \cdot \frac{3}{5}$

$\quad + 1 \cdot \frac{1024}{9,765,625} \cdot 1$

$= \frac{1,623,424}{9,765,625}$

32. a. $[C(5, 4) - 1]\left(\frac{1}{2}\right)^4\left(\frac{1}{2}\right)^1 = 4 \cdot \frac{1}{16} \cdot \frac{1}{2}$

$\qquad\qquad\qquad\qquad = \frac{1}{8}$ for each team

$\qquad 2 \cdot \frac{1}{8} = \frac{1}{4}$

b. $[C(5, 4) - 1]\left(\frac{3}{5}\right)^4\left(\frac{2}{5}\right)^1 = 4 \cdot \frac{81}{625} \cdot \frac{2}{5}$

$\qquad\qquad\qquad\qquad = \frac{648}{3125}$

33. P(4 do not collapse) $= C(6, 4)\left(\frac{4}{5}\right)^4\left(\frac{1}{5}\right)^2$

$\qquad\qquad\qquad\qquad = 15 \cdot \frac{256}{625} \cdot \frac{1}{25}$

$\qquad\qquad\qquad\qquad = \frac{768}{3125}$

34. a. P(all misses) $= C(12, 0)\left(\frac{9}{10}\right)^0\left(\frac{1}{10}\right)^{12}$

$\qquad\qquad\qquad = 1 \cdot 1 \cdot \frac{1}{1,000,000,000,000}$

$\qquad\qquad\qquad = \frac{1}{1,000,000,000,000}$

b. P(exactly 7 hits) $= C(12, 7)\left(\frac{9}{10}\right)^7\left(\frac{1}{10}\right)^5$

$\qquad\qquad\qquad = 792 \cdot \frac{4,782,969}{10,000,000} \cdot \frac{1}{100,000}$

$\qquad\qquad\qquad = \frac{3,788,111,448}{1,000,000,000,000}$

c. P(all hits) $= C(12, 12)\left(\frac{9}{10}\right)^{12}\left(\frac{1}{10}\right)^0$

$\qquad\qquad\quad = 1 \cdot \frac{282,429,536,481}{1,000,000,000,000} \cdot 1$

$\qquad\qquad\quad = \frac{282,429,536,481}{1,000,000,000,000}$

d. P(at least 10 hits)

$= C(12, 10)\left(\frac{9}{10}\right)^{10}\left(\frac{1}{10}\right)^2 + C(12, 11)\left(\frac{9}{10}\right)^{11}\left(\frac{1}{10}\right)^1$

$\quad + C(12, 12)\left(\frac{9}{10}\right)^{12}\left(\frac{1}{10}\right)^0$

$= 66 \cdot \frac{3,486,784,401}{10,000,000,000} \cdot \frac{1}{100}$

$\quad + 12 \cdot \frac{31,381,059,609}{100,000,000,000} \cdot \frac{1}{10}$

$\quad + 1 \cdot \frac{282,429,536,481}{1,000,000,000,000} \cdot 1$

$= \frac{889,130,022,255}{1,000,000,000,000} = \frac{177,826,004,451}{200,000,000,000}$

35. $C(13, 10)\left(\frac{5}{8}\right)^{10}\left(\frac{3}{8}\right)^3 = 286 \cdot \frac{9,765,625}{1,073,741,824} \cdot \frac{27}{512}$

$\qquad\qquad\qquad\qquad\qquad = \frac{7,541,015,625}{54,975,581,390}$

36. $AB = \begin{bmatrix} 59 & 38 \\ 74 & 47 \end{bmatrix}$

37. $\vec{u} \cdot \vec{v} = (2 \cdot 5) + (-1 \cdot 3) + (3 \cdot 0) = 7$

38. $\dfrac{x!(x - 3)!}{(x - 2)!(x - 1)!} = \dfrac{x!}{(x - 1)!} \cdot \dfrac{(x - 3)!}{(x - 2)!}$

$\qquad\qquad\qquad = x \cdot \dfrac{1}{x - 2}$

$\qquad\qquad\qquad = \dfrac{x}{x - 2}$

39. P(sum greater than 7, given numbers match)

$= \dfrac{\frac{3}{36}}{\frac{6}{36}} = \dfrac{1}{2}$

40. $a > b$

I. If you multiply each side by a negative number, the operation symbol is reversed. So, $ac < bc$ is true.

II. If you add the same number to each side, the operation symbol stays the same. So, $a + c > b + c$ is true.

III. If you subtract the same number from each side, the operation symbol stays the same. So, $a - c < b - c$ is false.

The best answer is C.

Technology: Dice Roll Simulation

PAGE 795   EXERCISES

1. See students' work.
2. See students' work.
3. See students' work.
4. The greater the number of rolls, the more likely it is that the experimental probability will approach the theoretical probability.

Chapter 14 Summary and Review

PAGES 796-798   SKILLS AND CONCEPTS

1. $P(6, 3) = \dfrac{6!}{(6 - 3)!} = 120$

2. $P(8, 6) = \dfrac{8!}{(8 - 6)!} = 20,160$

3. $\dfrac{P(4,\ 2) - P(6,\ 3)}{P(5,\ 3)} = \dfrac{\dfrac{4!}{(4-2)!} - \dfrac{6!}{(6-3)!}}{\dfrac{5!}{(5-3)!}}$

$= \dfrac{12 - 120}{60}$

$= \dfrac{-9}{5}$

4. $2 \cdot 5! = 240$ ways   5. $\dfrac{5!}{2!\,2!} = 30$

6. $\dfrac{10!}{2!\,3!\,3!} = 50,400$ 7. $\dfrac{8!}{2!} = 20,160$

8. $\dfrac{6!}{3!\,2!} = 60$ 9. $C(5,\ 3) = \dfrac{5!}{(5-3)!\,3!}$

$= 10$

10. $C(11,\ 8) = \dfrac{11!}{(11-8)!\,8!} = 165$

11. $C(5,\ 5) \cdot C(3,\ 2) = \dfrac{5!}{(5-5)!\,5!} \cdot \dfrac{3!}{(3-2)!\,2!}$

$= 1 \cdot 3$

$= 3$

12. $C(3,\ 2) \cdot C(7,\ 2) = \dfrac{3!}{(3-2)!\,2!} \cdot \dfrac{7!}{(7-2)!\,2!}$

$= 3 \cdot 21$

$= 63$ committees

13. odds $= \dfrac{\frac{4}{9}}{\frac{5}{9}} = \dfrac{4}{5}$ 14. odds $= \dfrac{\frac{1}{12}}{\frac{11}{12}} = \dfrac{1}{11}$

15. $P(\text{all 3 pennies}) = \dfrac{7}{16} \cdot \dfrac{7}{16} \cdot \dfrac{7}{16}$

$= \dfrac{343}{4096}$

16. $P(\text{2 pennies, 1 nickel}) = \dfrac{7}{16} \cdot \dfrac{7}{16} \cdot \dfrac{4}{16}$

$= \dfrac{49}{1024}$

17. $\dfrac{1}{6} \cdot \dfrac{5}{6} = \dfrac{5}{36}$ 18. $\dfrac{5}{6} \cdot \dfrac{5}{6} = \dfrac{25}{36}$

19. $\dfrac{6}{14} + \dfrac{3}{14} = \dfrac{9}{14}$ 20. $\dfrac{7}{14} + \dfrac{4}{14} - \dfrac{2}{14} = \dfrac{9}{14}$

21. $\dfrac{\frac{3}{36}}{\frac{1}{6}} = \dfrac{18}{36} = \dfrac{1}{2}$ 22. $\dfrac{\frac{4}{36}}{\frac{30}{36}} = \dfrac{4}{30} = \dfrac{2}{15}$

23. $C(4,\ 1)\left(\dfrac{1}{2}\right)^1 \left(\dfrac{1}{2}\right)^3 = 4 \cdot \dfrac{1}{2} \cdot \dfrac{1}{8}$

$= \dfrac{1}{4}$

24. $C(4,\ 0)\left(\dfrac{1}{2}\right)^0 \left(\dfrac{1}{2}\right)^4 = 1 \cdot 1 \cdot \dfrac{1}{16}$

$= \dfrac{1}{16}$

25. $C(4,\ 2)\left(\dfrac{1}{2}\right)^2 \left(\dfrac{1}{2}\right)^2 = 6 \cdot \dfrac{1}{4} \cdot \dfrac{1}{4}$

$= \dfrac{3}{8}$

26. $C(4,\ 3)\left(\dfrac{1}{2}\right)^3 \left(\dfrac{1}{2}\right)^1 + C(4,\ 4)\left(\dfrac{1}{2}\right)^4 \left(\dfrac{1}{2}\right)^0$

$= 4 \cdot \dfrac{1}{8} \cdot \dfrac{1}{2} + 1 \cdot \dfrac{1}{16} \cdot 1$

$= \dfrac{5}{16}$

27. $\dfrac{6!}{2} = \dfrac{720}{2} = 360$

28. $C(6,\ 4) = \dfrac{6!}{2!\,4!} = 15$ ways

29. a. $\dfrac{7}{15}$

b. $\dfrac{1}{15} \cdot \dfrac{7}{14} = \dfrac{7}{210} = \dfrac{1}{30}$

Chapter 14 Test

1. $P(6,\ 2) = \dfrac{6!}{(6-2)!} = 30$

2. $P(7,\ 5) = \dfrac{7!}{(7-5)!} = 2520$

3. $C(8,\ 3) = \dfrac{8!}{5!\,3!} = 56$

4. $C(5,\ 4) = \dfrac{5!}{1!\,4!} = 5$

5. $5! = 120$

6. $P(5,\ 3) = \dfrac{5!}{2!} = 60$ ways

7. $(7-1)! = 720$

8. $C(3,\ 1) \cdot C(12,\ 8) = \dfrac{3!}{2!\,1!} \cdot \dfrac{12!}{4!\,8!}$

$= 3 \cdot 495$

$= 1485$ teams

9. $C(4,\ 2) \cdot C(6,\ 3) = \dfrac{4!}{2!\,2!} \cdot \dfrac{6!}{3!\,3!}$

$= 6 \cdot 20$

$= 120$ ways

10. $C(20,\ 2) - 20 = \dfrac{20!}{18!\,2!} - 20$

$= 190 - 20$

$= 170$ diagonals

11. odds $= \dfrac{\frac{4}{7}}{\frac{3}{7}} = \dfrac{4}{3}$

12. $\dfrac{52}{52} \cdot \dfrac{12}{51} \cdot \dfrac{11}{50} \cdot \dfrac{10}{49} \cdot \dfrac{9}{48} = \dfrac{33}{16,660}$

13. $\dfrac{5}{36} \cdot \dfrac{3}{36} = \dfrac{15}{1296} = \dfrac{5}{432}$

14. $\dfrac{10 \cdot 10 \cdot 10 \cdot 10 \cdot 5 \cdot 5 \cdot 5}{10 \cdot 10 \cdot 10 \cdot 10 \cdot 10 \cdot 10 \cdot 10} = \dfrac{1}{8}$

15. $\dfrac{C(3,\ 3)}{C(12,\ 3)} + \dfrac{C(5,\ 3)}{C(12,\ 3)} = \dfrac{1}{220} + \dfrac{10}{220} = \dfrac{1}{20}$

16. $\dfrac{4}{52} + \dfrac{26}{52} - \dfrac{2}{52} = \dfrac{28}{52} = \dfrac{7}{13}$

17. $P(B) = \dfrac{18}{30}$

$P(A \text{ and } B) = \dfrac{5}{30}$

$P(A/B) = \dfrac{5}{18}$

364

18. $\dfrac{\frac{6}{36}}{\frac{26}{36}} = \dfrac{6}{26} = \dfrac{3}{13}$

19. $C(5,\ 0)\left(\dfrac{2}{3}\right)^0\left(\dfrac{1}{3}\right)^5 + C(5,\ 1)\left(\dfrac{2}{3}\right)^1\left(\dfrac{1}{3}\right)^4$

$\qquad + C(5,\ 2)\left(\dfrac{2}{3}\right)^2\left(\dfrac{1}{3}\right)^3$

$\qquad = 1 \cdot 1 \cdot \dfrac{1}{243} + 5 \cdot \dfrac{2}{3} \cdot \dfrac{1}{81} + 10 \cdot \dfrac{4}{9} \cdot \dfrac{1}{27}$

$\qquad = \dfrac{51}{243}$

$\qquad = \dfrac{17}{81}$

20. $C(7,\ 4)\left(\dfrac{4}{5}\right)^4\left(\dfrac{1}{5}\right)^3 = 35 \cdot \dfrac{256}{625} \cdot \dfrac{1}{125}$

$\qquad\qquad\qquad\qquad = \dfrac{1792}{15,625}$

PAGE 799   BONUS

There are 8 perfect squares less than or equal to 80 and 2 perfect squares between 80 and 120. Thus, the probability of choosing a perfect square is $8p + 2(2p)$ or $12p$. To find the value of p, recall that the sum of all the probabilities must equal 1, so

$80p + 40(2p) = 1$

$\qquad 80p + 80p = 1$

$\qquad\qquad\quad p = \dfrac{1}{160}$ or 0.00625.

Therefore, the probability that a perfect square is chosen is $12(0.00625)$ or 0.075.

Chapter 15   Statistics and Data Analysis

15-1   The Frequency Distribution

PAGES 806-807   CHECKING FOR UNDERSTANDING

1. It is similar to a histogram because it shows the graph of intervals of data. It is not a true histogram because the intervals are not equal.

2. to graph frequency distributions

3. Find the midpoint of the top of each bar and connect the midpoints with a broken line graph.

4. greatest: HBO, least: TMC

5. HBO, Cinemax, and Showtime have shown an increase in the number of subscribers. TMC has shown a decrease in the number of subscribers.

6. $32,000 - $26,000 = $6000

7. $0; $26,000; $32,000; $38,000; $44,000; $50,000

8. $13,000; $29,000; $35,000; $41,000; $47,000

9. $\frac{26}{100} \times 100 = 26\%$

10. $\frac{26 + 13}{100} \times 100 = 39\%$

11.

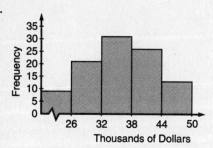

PAGES 807-810   EXERCISES

12. interval: 20 - 10 = 10

limits: 5, 15, 25, 35, 45, 55

13. interval: 1.2 - 1.1 = 0.1

limits: 1.05, 1.15, 1.25, 1.35, 1.45, 1.55, 1.65, 1.75

14. interval: 2.5

limits: 1.25, 3.75, 6.25, 8.75, 11.25, 13.75

15. interval: 1

limits: 24.5, 25.5, 26.5, 27.5, 28.5, 29.5, 30.5, 31.5, 32.5

16.

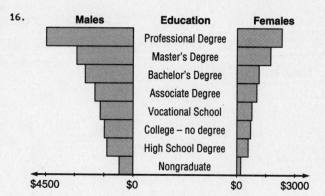

17. Women make less money than men for the same education.

18.

Class Limits	Class Marks	Tally	Frequency
65-75	70	||||	4
75-85	80	⦀ ⦀	10
85-95	90	⦀ ⦀ ⦀ |	16
95-105	100	⦀ ⦀ ⦀ ⦀ ⦀ ⦀ ⦀ ⦀ |||	38
105-115	110	⦀ ⦀ ⦀	15
115-125	120	⦀ ⦀ ||	12
125-135	130	|||	3
135-145	140	||	2

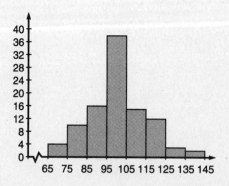

19.

Class Limits	Class Marks	Tally	Frequency
63-75	69	||||	4
75-87	81	卌 卌 ||	12
87-99	93	卌 卌 卌 卌 |||	23
99-111	105	卌 卌 卌 卌 卌 卌 卌 ||||	39
111-123	117	卌 卌 卌 |	16
123-135	129	||||	4
135-147	141	||	2

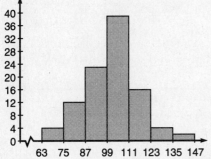

20. $144 - 66 = 78$, $\frac{78}{16} = 4.87$, interval = 5

Class Limits	Class Marks	Tally	Frequency
65-70	67.5	||	2
70-75	72.5	||	2
75-80	77.5	|||	3
80-85	82.5	卌 ||	7
85-90	87.5	卌 ||||	9
90-95	92.5	卌 ||	7
95-100	97.5	卌 卌 卌	15
100-105	102.5	卌 卌 卌 卌 |||	23
105-110	107.5	卌 ||	7
110-115	112.5	卌 |||	8
115-120	117.5	卌 |||	8
120-125	122.5	||||	4
125-130	127.5	|||	3
130-135	132.5		0
135-140	137.5	|	1
140-145	142.5	|	1

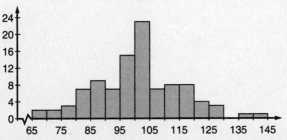

21. $\frac{144 - 66}{10} = 7.8$, interval = 8

Class Limits	Class Marks	Tally	Frequency
65-73	69	|||	3
73-81	77	卌	5
81-89	85	卌 卌 |||	13
89-97	93	卌 卌 |||	13
97-105	101	卌 卌 卌 卌 卌 卌 ||||	34
105-113	109	卌 卌 ||||	14
113-121	117	卌 卌 |	11
121-129	125	卌	5
129-137	133	|	1
137-145	141	|	1

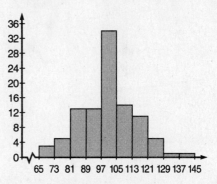

22. Sample answer: Need 4 intervals, freshman, sophomore, junior, senior.

$$\frac{144 - 66}{4} = \frac{78}{4} = 19.5$$

So interval needs to be 20, beginning with a class limit of 60.

23-25. Sample answers given.

23. highest = 2013.9, lowest: 2011.4

$2013.9 - 2011.4 = 2.5$, $\frac{2.5}{5} = 0.5$

Since all data begin with 20, disregard the first 2 digits.

Class Limits	Class Marks	Tally	Frequency
11.4-11.9	11.65	||||	4
11.9-12.4	12.15	卌 ||	7
12.4-12.9	12.65	卌 |||	8
12.9-13.4	13.15	|	1
13.4-13.9	13.65	||||	4

24.- 25.

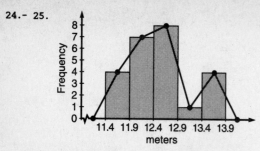

26. Probably discard it as a mistake since it is so different from the other measures.

27.

Population Change (in millions)

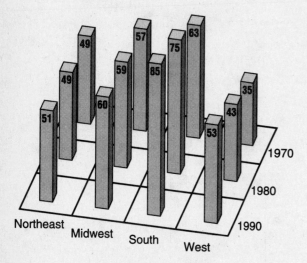

28.

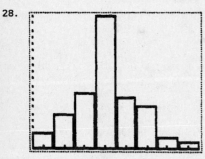

29.

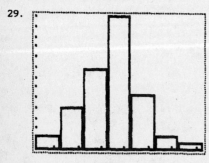

30.

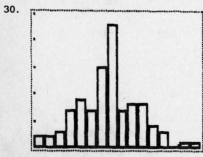

31.

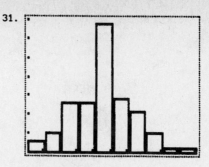

32. See students' work.

33. a.-c. See students' work.

34. a.

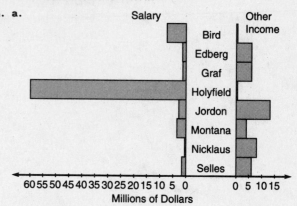

b. boxing

c. basketball

d. greatest: Holyfield, least: Graf

35. a.

Class Limits	Class Marks	Tally	Frequency
0–10	5	ⅣⅣ ⅣⅣ ⅣⅣ ⅣⅣ ⅣⅣ ⅣⅣ ⅢⅠ	33
10–20	15	ⅣⅣ ⅣⅣ ⅢⅠ	13
20–30	25	Ⅰ	1
30–40	35		0
40–50	45	ⅡⅠ	2

b.

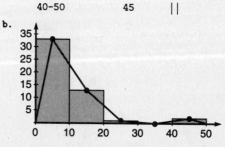

c. Because it differs greatly from the other data. If it was included, it would skew the intervals and the representation of the majority of the distribution.

36. $-\frac{13\pi}{3}$ is coterminal with $\frac{5\pi}{3}$ in Quadrant IV.

$\alpha' = 2\pi - \alpha = 2\pi - \frac{5\pi}{3} = \frac{\pi}{3}$

37. none

38. $a = 3$, focus: $(3,0)$ **39.** $a_4 = 216$, $a_1 = 125$

directrix: $x = -3$

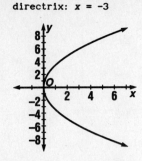

$$a_4 = a_1 r^{4-1}$$

$$216 = 125r^3$$

$$\frac{216}{125} = r^3$$

$$\frac{6}{5} = r$$

$$125\left(\frac{6}{5}\right) = 150$$

$$150\left(\frac{6}{5}\right) = 180$$

125, 150, 180, 216

40. $\frac{9}{10} \times \frac{9}{10} \times \frac{9}{10} \times \frac{9}{10} \times \frac{9}{10} = \frac{59,049}{100,000}$

41. $\frac{3}{8} + \frac{1}{6} + \frac{5}{12} = \frac{9}{24} + \frac{4}{24} + \frac{10}{24} = \frac{23}{24}$

$\frac{4}{15} + \frac{2}{25} + \frac{1}{3} = \frac{20}{75} + \frac{6}{75} + \frac{25}{75} = \frac{51}{75}$

$\frac{23}{24}x^2 > \frac{51}{75}x^2$ since x^2 is always positive.

Quantity A is greater. A

15-2   Measures of Central Tendency

PAGES 816-817   CHECKING FOR UNDERSTANDING

1. The mean of the corporate employees' salaries is $87,000.

2. $\frac{1}{25} \sum\limits_{i=1}^{25} x_i$

3. The greatest common place value is tens. So the stems will go from 8 to 13. The leaves will be the units digit for each stem.

4. mean

5.
```
1 | 0 5 5 5 5 7 7
2 | 0 0 0 5 5 5 5 7 8
3 | 0 0 5 5 5
4 | 6
5 | 5
```
1|0 means 10.

6. $\frac{1}{5}(3 + 3 + 3 + 6 + 12) = \frac{27}{5} = 5.4$, 3, 3

7. $\frac{1}{4}(10 + 10 + 45 + 58) = \frac{123}{4} = 30.75$

$M_d = \frac{10 + 45}{2} = \frac{55}{2} = 27.5$

Mode = 10

8. $\frac{1}{4}(140 + 150 + 160 + 170) = 155$

$M_d = \frac{150 + 160}{2} = 155$

no mode

9. $\frac{1}{12}(5 + 6 + 6 + 6 + 7 + 8 + 9 + 10 + 11 + 11 + 11 + 12) = 8.5$

$M_d = \frac{8 + 9}{2} = 8.5$

Mode: 6 and 11

10. **a.** $11 \times \$135 = \$1485$, $24 \times \$145 = \$3480$,
$30 \times \$155 = \$4650$, $10 \times \$165 = \$1650$,
$13 \times \$175 = \$2275$, $8 \times \$185 = \$1480$,
$4 \times \$195 = \$780$

b. $\$1485 + \$3480 + \$4650 + \$1650 + \$2275 + \$1480 + \$780 = \$15,800$

c. $11 + 24 + 30 + \ldots + 8 + 4 = 100$

d. $\frac{\$15,800}{100} = \$158$

e. 11
    35
    65
    75
    88
    96
    100

f. $\$150 - \$160$

g. $65 - 35 = 30$
    $50 - 35 = 15$
    interval: $160 - 150 = 10$
    $M_d - 150 = x$
    $\frac{30}{15} = \frac{10}{x}$
    $2x = 10$
    $x = 5$
    $M_d - 150 = 5$
        $M_d = 155$

PAGES 817-819   EXERCISES

11. **a.**
```
2 | 4 6 6 9
3 | 1 6 6 7 8 8
4 | 1 2 3
```
2|4 means 2.4 million.

b. $\overline{X} = \frac{2.6 + 2.4 + \ldots + 3.8 + 4.2}{13} = 3,438,500$

Median: 3,600,000

Mode: 2,600,000; 3,600,000; and 3,800,000

c. These are the years when the most babies were born. This large population is now adults in their 30s and 40s. They are an active group in commerce, politics, and other fields.

12. $\overline{X} = \frac{84 + 72 + 91 + 64 + 83}{5} = 78.8$

He was below average with 78.8.

13. **a.** convert to inches

$\overline{X} = \frac{67 + 56 + 73 + 64 + 84 + 79 + 64}{7}$

$\approx 69.57" \approx 5'9\frac{1}{2}"$

b. Answers will vary. The mean is not very representative because the mean is greater than the median (5'7") and the mode (5'4").

14. a. Order the data: 117, 124, 139, 142, 145, 151, 155, 160, 172

$$\bar{X} = \frac{117 + 124 + \ldots + 172}{9} = \frac{1305}{9} = 145$$

$$M_d = 145$$

$$\bar{X} - M_d = 145 - 145 = 0$$

b. Add 5 pounds to each.

15. a. Class Marks (X): 3, 7, 11, 15, 19, 23, 27, 31

$$\sum_{i=1}^{8} f_i X_i = 2(3) + 8(7) + 15(11) + 6(15)$$
$$+ 38(19) + 31(23) + 13(27) + 7(31)$$
$$= 2320$$

$$\bar{X} = \frac{2320}{2 + 8 + 15 + 6 + \ldots + 13 + 7} = \frac{2320}{120} \approx 19.3$$

b.

Visits	Cumulative Frequency	
1–5	2	
5–9	10	
9–13	25	
13–17	31	
17–21	69	$\leftarrow \quad 60 = \frac{1}{2}(120)$
21–25	100	
25–29	113	
29–33	120	

median class: 17–21

c.
$69 - 31 = 38 \qquad\qquad 21 - 17 = 4$

$60 - 31 = 29 \qquad\qquad M_d - 17 = x$

$$\frac{38}{29} = \frac{4}{x}$$

$$38x = 116$$

$$x \approx 3.1$$

$$M_d - 17 = x$$

$$M_d \approx 3.1 + 17 \approx 20.1$$

16. $7.5 = \dfrac{2 + 4 + 5 + 8 + x}{5}$

$37.5 = 19 + x$

$18.5 = x$

17. $6 = \dfrac{x + (2x - 1) + (2x) + (3x + 1)}{4}$

$24 = 8x$

$3 = x$

18. order data: 2, 3, 3.2, 8, 11, 13, 14, x

In order for middle score to be 8, $\dfrac{8 + x}{2} = 8$ or

$x = 8$.

19. $68 = \dfrac{60 + 72 + x + y + z}{5}$

$340 = 132 + x + y + z$

$208 = x + y + z$

20. Median = 50 cm so 50% has to be above 50 cm and 50% has to be below 50 cm. The sum of the distance from the left side of the median is 94. The sum of the distance on the right side is 76.

$94 = 76 + x$

$18 = x$

One more weight needs to be placed at $50 + 18 = 68$ cm from the end.

21. A 2-gram weight must be hung 34 cm from the end.

22. A: mode, since there are the most coins in this stack.

C: median, since there are more coins to the right.

So, B: mean.

23. a. $\bar{X} = \dfrac{\begin{array}{l}225(26.6) + 275(43.3) + \\ 325(69.3) + \ldots + 775(0.6)\end{array}}{26.6 + 43.3 + 69.3 + \ldots + 0.6}$

$$= \frac{227,050}{535} \approx 424.4$$

b. 26.6
69.9
139.2
228.2
327.0
410.1
465.2
500.0
520.5
530.4
534.4
535.0

c. 50% = 267.5
400–450

d. $327 - 228.2 = 98.8$
$267.5 - 228.2 = 39.3$
$450 - 400 = 50$
$M_d - 400 = x$

$$\frac{98.8}{39.3} = \frac{50}{x}$$

$98.8x = 1965x$

$x \approx 19.9$

$M_d = x + 400$

$\approx 19.9 + 400$

≈ 419.9

e. Lower; means differ because published average has access to each item of data whereas frequency distributions do not.

24. Convert heights to inches.

a. $\bar{X} = \dfrac{78 + 81 + 79 + 84 + 81 + \ldots + 73}{11}$

$= \dfrac{878}{11} \approx 79.82 \approx 6'7.8''$

6	1 6 6 7 7 7 9 9 9
7	0 1

$M_d = 6'7''$

Modes: $6'7''$ and $6'9''$

b. $\bar{X} = \dfrac{250 + 220 + \ldots + 175}{11} = \dfrac{2441}{11} \approx 221.91$ lb

17	5
19	8
21	0 5
22	0 0 2
23	5
24	0
25	0 6

$M_d = 220$ lb

Mode: 220 lb

c. median and mode of both heights and weights

25. $\dfrac{2 + i\sqrt{3}}{2 - i\sqrt{3}} \cdot \dfrac{2 + i\sqrt{3}}{2 + i\sqrt{3}} = \dfrac{4 + 4i\sqrt{3} + 3i^2}{4 + 3} = \dfrac{1 + 4i\sqrt{3}}{7}$

26. $\log_{10} 0.001 \rightarrow 0.001 = 10^x$

$$x = -3$$

27. Iteration is the process of repeated evaluation of a function using the result of the previous evaluation. Example: Let $f(x) = x^2$. Let $x_1 = 2$. Results: 4, 16, 256,...

28. $\dfrac{C(6, 3) \cdot C(7, 2)}{C(13, 5)} + \dfrac{C(6, 4) \cdot C(7, 1)}{C(13, 5)} +$

$\dfrac{C(6, 5) \cdot C(7, 0)}{C(13, 5)}$

$= \dfrac{(20)(21) + (15)(7) + (6)(1)}{1287} = \dfrac{531}{1287} = \dfrac{59}{143}$

29.

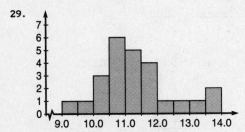

30. $A = (0.9h)(0.7w) = 0.63hw$

63% of original area remains.

15-3 Measures of Variability

1. 16 17 19 24 24 25 25 25 25 26

33 35 35 39 44 44 51 57 71 80

$M_d = \dfrac{26 + 33}{2} = 29.5$, $Q_1 = 24.5$, $Q_3 = 44$

$Q_R = 44 - 24.5 = 19.5$

$Q_1 - 1.5(19.5) = 24.5 - 29.25 = -4.75$

$Q_3 + 1.5(19.5) = 44 + 29.25 = 73.25$

outlier: 80

2. The non-frequency data is treated as individual pieces of data when finding the sum, mean, and so on. Frequency data is calculated using the products of the class marks and frequencies to find the sums, means, and so on.

3. The median of the data is $\dfrac{6 + 7}{2}$ or 6.5. $Q_1 = 3.5$ and $Q_3 = 9.5$. Plot these points on a number line and draw two side-by-side boxes that contain these points on their vertical sides. There are no outliers. The least extreme is 1 and the greatest extreme is 12. Plot these points and draw segments from each of these to its nearest quartile point.

4. It has less variability and is clustered more closely around the mean.

5. range = 350 - 145 = 205

6. 220　　　**7.** 25%　　　**8.** 320, 350

9. 50%　　　**10.** 75%　　　**11.** 50%

---

12. a. $\overline{X} = \dfrac{\begin{array}{c}(57 \times 3) + (65 \times 7) + (73 \times 11) + \\ (81 \times 38) + (89 \times 19) + (97 \times 12)\end{array}}{3 + 7 + 11 + 38 + 19 + 12}$

$= \dfrac{7362}{90}$

$= 81.8$

b. 77-85

c. $59 - 21 = 38$ 　　　 $85 - 77 = 8$

$45 - 21 = 24$ 　　　 $M_d - 77 = x$

$\dfrac{38}{24} = \dfrac{8}{x}$

$38x = 192$

$x \approx 5.1$

$M_d \approx 5.1 + 77 \approx 82.1$

d. $\sigma = \sqrt{\dfrac{\Sigma(X_i - \overline{X})^2 f_i}{\Sigma f_i}}$

$= \sqrt{\dfrac{(57 - 81.8)^2 \times 3 + (65 - 81.8)^2 \times 7 + ... + (97 - 81.8)^2 \times 12}{3 + 7 + ... + 12}}$

$= \sqrt{\dfrac{\begin{array}{c}1845.12 + 1975.7 + 851.84 + \\ 24.32 + 984.96 + 2772.48\end{array}}{90}}$

$= \sqrt{\dfrac{8454.42}{90}}$

≈ 9.69

---

13. a. $\overline{X} = \dfrac{(15.1 + 11.5 + ... + 6.2 + 5.8)}{10}$

$= 9.15$

b. 5.95, 2.35, 1.35, -0.15, -0.35, -0.65, -0.65, -1.55, -2.95, -3.35

c. $MD = \dfrac{1}{10}(|5.95| + |2.35| + ... + |-3.35|)$

$= 1.93$

d. $Q_1 = 10.5$, $Q_2 = \dfrac{8.8 + 8.5}{2} = 8.65$, $Q_3 = 7.6$

e. $Q_R = 10.5 - 7.6 = 2.9$

f. $Q_R = \dfrac{2.9}{2} = 1.45$

g. $SS = [(15.1 - 9.15)^2 + (11.5 - 9.15)^2 + ... + (5.8 - 9.15)^2]$

$= 66.065$

h. $\sigma = \sqrt{\dfrac{66.065}{10}} \approx 2.57$

i.

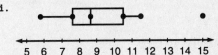

j. $Q_1 + 1.5(2.9) = 10.5 + 4.35 = 14.85$

$Q_3 - 1.5(2.9) = 7.6 - 4.35 = 3.25$

outlier: 15.1

14. a. $\overline{X} = \dfrac{46 + 42 + 29 + 29 + 26 + 28}{6} = 33.3$

$M_d = 29$

$\sigma = \sqrt{\dfrac{(46-33.3)^2+(42-33.3)^2+\ldots+(28-33.3)^2}{6}}$

≈ 7.7

b. $\overline{X} = \dfrac{31 + 29 + 30 + 35 + 33 + 32}{6} \approx 31.7$

$M_d = \dfrac{31 + 32}{2} = 31.5$

$\sigma = \sqrt{\dfrac{(31-31.7)^2+(29-31.7)^2+\ldots+(32-31.7)^2}{6}}$

≈ 1.97

c.

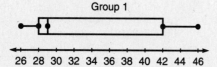

Group 2

Group 1

26 28 30 32 34 36 38 40 42 44 46

(1) similar

(2) very different

(3) Group 2

15. a. $\overline{X} = \dfrac{(10.6 + 13.2 + 14 + 13.2 + 10 + 9.2)}{6}$

≈ 11.7

$M_d = \dfrac{10.6 + 13.2}{2} = 11.9$

$\sigma = \sqrt{\dfrac{(10.6 - 11.7)^2 + (13.2 - 11.7)^2 + \ldots+ (9.2 - 11.7)^2}{6}}$

≈ 1.83

b. $\overline{X} = \dfrac{(11.9 + 11.9 + 12.8 + 13 + 11.9 + 11.9)}{6}$

≈ 12.23

$M_d = 11.9$

$\sigma = \sqrt{\dfrac{(11.9 - 12.23)^2 + (11.9 - 12.23)^2 + \ldots+ (11.9 - 12.23)^2}{6}}$

≈ 0.47

c.

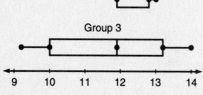

Group 4

Group 3

9   10   11   12   13   14

(1) similar

(2) very different

(3) Group 3

16. a. $\overline{X} = \dfrac{(80 \times 2) + (100 \times 11) +\ldots+ (180 \times 7)}{2 + 11 + 39 + 17 + 9 + 7}$

$= \dfrac{11,020}{85}$

≈ 129.65

b. $\sigma = \sqrt{\dfrac{(80 - 129.65)^2 \times 2 + (100 - 129.65) \times 11 +\ldots+ (180 - 129.65)^2 \times 7}{2 + 11 + 39 +\ldots+ 7}}$

≈ 23.29

c. It is 3.35 more than the mean, but very close to it considering the standard deviation.

17. a. range = 45 − 1 = 44

$\overline{X} = \dfrac{45 + 37 +\ldots+ 1 + 1}{20}$

$= 11.5$

$MD = \dfrac{1}{20}(|45 - 11.5| + |37 - 11.5| + \ldots+ |1 - 11.5|)$

$= 8.95$

IQ range $= \left(\dfrac{14 + 13}{2}\right) - (3) = 10.5$

$\sigma = \sqrt{\dfrac{(45-11.5)^2+(37-11.5)^2+\ldots+(1-11.5)^2}{20}}$

≈ 12.2

b. range = 38 − 3 = 35

$\overline{X} = \dfrac{38 + 34 +\ldots+ 7 + 4}{20}$

$= 10.8$

$MD = \dfrac{1}{20}(|38 - 10.8| + |34 - 10.8| + \ldots+ |4 - 10.8|)$

$= 7.3$

IQ range $= \left(\dfrac{12 + 9}{2}\right) - (5) = 5.5$

$\sigma = \sqrt{\dfrac{(38-10.8)^2+(34-10.8)^2+\ldots+(4-10.8)^2}{20}}$

≈ 9.74

c. Gold; **the interquartile** range is greater for **gold medals than for** silver.

18. Yes, when $\sigma < 1$ the variance is σ^2 so when $\sigma < 1$, $\sigma^2 < \sigma$.

19. When both have a value of 1, $\sigma^2 = \sigma = 1$.

20. p: ±1, ±3

q: ±1, ±2

$\dfrac{p}{q}$: $\pm\dfrac{1}{2}$, ± 1, $\pm\dfrac{3}{2}$, ± 3

21.

330 mi

60°

80°

40°

330 mi

c

$c^2 = 330^2 + 330^2 - 2(330)(330) \cos 80°$

$c \approx 424.24$ mi

22. $x = e^{0.346}$

  $x = 1.4$

23. $\dfrac{x + (2x - 1) + 2x + (3x + 1)}{4} = 6$

  $8x = 24$

  $x = 3$

24. Area of square $= 2 \times 2 = 4$ in^2

  Area of circle $= \pi r^2 = \pi(1)^2 = 3.14$ in^2

  $4 - 3.14 = 0.86$ in^2

  The best answer is C.

Case Study Follow-Up

PAGE 829

1. 37% of 14,475,630 = about 5.4 million

2. 5500 crimes

3. about 260

4. See students' work.

15-4   The Normal Distribution

PAGE 835   CHECKING FOR UNDERSTANDING

1. bell-shaped

2. See students' work.

3.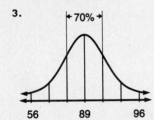

4.

5.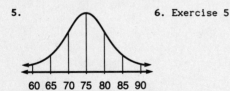

6. Exercise 5

7. $0.683(200) = 137$

8. $0.955(200) = 191$

9. $\dfrac{0.683}{2}(200) \approx 68$

10. $\dfrac{0.997}{2}(200) - \dfrac{0.955}{2}(200) \approx 4$

11. 68.3%

12. $27.5 = 24 + 3.5$, $20.5 = 24 - 3.5$

  $t\sigma = 3.5$

  $t(2) = 3.5$

  $t = 1.75$ 92.8%

13. $24 + 1.96\sigma$ and $24 - 1.96\sigma$

  $= 24 + 1.96(2)$ $= 24 - 1.96(2)$

  $= 27.9$ $= 20.1$

     $20.1\text{-}27.9$

14. $24 + 0.7(2) = 25.4$ and $24 - 0.7(2) = 22.6$

     $22.6\text{-}25.4$

PAGES 835-837   EXERCISES

15. 68.3%

16. $140 - 130 = 10$

  $t(20) = 10$

  $t = \dfrac{1}{2}$

     38.3%

17. $140 - 110 = 30$

  $t(20) = 30$

  $t = 1.5$

     86.6%

18. 100 is 2σ below 140.

  $0.5 - \dfrac{0.955}{2} = 0.0225$

     2.25%

19. $160 - 140 = 20$

  $0.5 - \dfrac{0.683}{2} = 0.1585$

     15.85%

20. $140 + t(20) = 200$ and $140 - 20t = 110$

  $20t = 60$ $30 = 20t$

  $t = 3$ $1.5 = t$

  $P = 0.997$ $P = 0.866$

  $P = \dfrac{0.997}{2} + \dfrac{0.866}{2} = 0.9315$

     93.15%

21. 90% is $t = 1.65$.

  $140 + 1.65(20) = 173$ and $140 - 165(20) = 107$

     107-173

22. 40% is above the mean, so $P = 80\%$ will give the value of $t = 1.3$.

  $140 + 1.3(20) = 166$

23. 68.3%

24. 1σ below the mean $= 34\%$

25. $355 - 351 = 4$

  $4 = 2t$

  $2 = t$

  0.955

  $0.5 + \dfrac{0.955}{2} = 0.9775$

  about 97.8%

26. $355 - 349 = 6$ and $363 - 355 = 8$

  $6 = 2t$ $2t = 8$

  $3 = t$ $t = 4$

  0.997 0.9999

  $\dfrac{0.997}{2} + \dfrac{0.9999}{2} = 0.998$

  $0.998 \times 1000 = 998$

27. $68\% \times (10{,}000) = 6800$

28. $40{,}000 - 30{,}000 = 2 \times 5000$

$t = 2$

$\dfrac{0.955}{2} = 0.4775$

$0.4775(10{,}000) = 4775$

29. $50\% \times (10{,}000) = 5000$

30. $50{,}000$ miles $= 2\sigma$ above mean.

$0.5 - \dfrac{0.955}{2} = 0.0225$

$0.0225 \times 10{,}000 = 225$

31. $40{,}000 - 25{,}000 = 15{,}000$

$15{,}000 = 3(5{,}000)$

$t = 3$

$0.5 - \dfrac{0.997}{2} = 0.0015$

$0.0015 \times 10{,}000 = 15$

32. 4 hours 30 min is 2σ below the mean.

$0.5 + \dfrac{0.955}{2} = 0.9775$

$0.9775 \times 1000 = 977.5$

about 978 logs

33. Answers will vary.

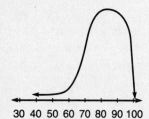

30 40 50 60 70 80 90 100

34. a. $19.88 - 17.72 = 2.16$

$2.16 = 1.42t$

$1.5 = t$

$P = 0.5 - \dfrac{0.866}{2} = 0.067$

6.7%

b. $19.88 - 18.9 = 0.98$

$0.98 = 1.42t$

$0.7 = t$

$P = \dfrac{0.516}{2} = 0.258$

25.8%

c. $20.47 - 19.88 = 0.59$ and $21.65 - 19.88 = 1.77$

$0.59 = 1.42t$ $1.77 = 1.42t$

$0.4 = t$ $t = 1.2$

above 20.47″:   above 21.65″:

$P = 0.5 - \dfrac{0.311}{2}$ $P = 0.5 - \dfrac{0.77}{2}$

$= 0.3445$ $= 0.115$

$P = 0.3445 - 0.115$

$= 0.2295$

$= 22.95\%$

d. $30 - 19.88 = 10.12$

$10.12 = 1.42t$

$7.1 = t$

about 7 standard deviations

35. A: $0.5 - \dfrac{0.866}{2} = 0.067,\ 6.7\%$

B: $\overline{X} + 0.5\sigma = 0.5 - \dfrac{0.383}{2} = 0.3085$

$\overline{X} + 1.5\sigma = 0.067$

$P = 0.3085 - 0.067 = 0.2415,\ 24.15\%$

C: $t = 0.5,\ P = 0.383$ or 38.3%

D: same as B: 24.15%

E: same as A: 6.7%

36.

$\begin{bmatrix} 3 & 7 \\ 8 & 9 \end{bmatrix} X - \begin{bmatrix} 2 & 7 \\ 6 & 9 \end{bmatrix} = \begin{bmatrix} 3 & 6 \\ 9 & 6 \end{bmatrix}$

$\begin{bmatrix} 3 & 7 \\ 8 & 9 \end{bmatrix} X = \begin{bmatrix} 5 & 13 \\ 15 & 15 \end{bmatrix}$

$-\dfrac{1}{29}\begin{bmatrix} 9 & -7 \\ -8 & 3 \end{bmatrix}\begin{bmatrix} 3 & 7 \\ 8 & 9 \end{bmatrix} X = -\dfrac{1}{29}\begin{bmatrix} 9 & -7 \\ -8 & 3 \end{bmatrix}\begin{bmatrix} 5 & 13 \\ 15 & 15 \end{bmatrix}$

$X = \begin{bmatrix} \dfrac{60}{29} & -\dfrac{12}{29} \\ -\dfrac{5}{29} & \dfrac{59}{29} \end{bmatrix}$

37.

$\sin^2 \phi \cot^2 \phi \stackrel{?}{=} (1 - \sin \phi)(1 + \sin \phi)$

$\sin^2 \phi \left(\dfrac{\cos \phi}{\sin \phi}\right)^2 \stackrel{?}{=} (1 - \sin \phi)(1 + \sin \phi)$

$\cos^2 \phi \stackrel{?}{=} (1 - \sin \phi)(1 + \sin \phi)$

$1 - \sin^2 \phi \stackrel{?}{=} (1 - \sin \phi)(1 + \sin \phi)$

$(1 - \sin \phi)(1 + \sin \phi) = (1 - \sin \phi)(1 + \sin \phi)$

38. tangent to the x-axis so radius $= 4$

$(x - 2)^2 + (y + 4)^2 = 16$

39. Only 4, 5, and 6 will have sum greater than 7.

Probability equals $\dfrac{1}{2}$.

40. a.

170 180 190 200 210 220 230 240 250 260

b. See students' work.

41. $\overline{X} = \dfrac{\Sigma X}{n}$

$n\overline{X} = \Sigma X$

$n \cdot 20 = 160$

$n = 8$

The best answer is A.

Mid-Chapter Review

PAGE 837

1.
Class Limits	Class Marks	Tally	Frequency
100-105	102.5	|||	3
105-110	107.5	⦀⦀ |||	8
110-115	112.5	⦀⦀ ⦀⦀ ⦀⦀ ||	17
115-120	117.5	⦀⦀ ⦀⦀ |||	13
120-125	122.5	⦀⦀ ||	7
125-130	127.5			1
130-135	132.5			1

2.
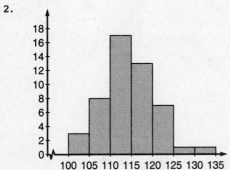

3.
```
10 | 0 0 4 5 5 5 6 7 8 9 9
11 | 0 0 0 0 1 1 2 2 2 2 3 3 4 4 4 4 4
     5 6 6 7 7 7 8 8 8 8 8 8 9
12 | 0 0 0 0 1 1 2 7
13 | 4
```

4. $\bar{X} = \dfrac{\Sigma X}{n} = \dfrac{112 + 116 + 118 + ... + 104}{50} \approx 113.88$

$M_d = 114$

Mode = 118

5. a. $Q_1 = 110$, $Q_3 = 118$

b. range = 134 - 100 = 34

c.
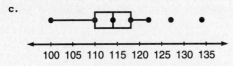

6. $\sigma = \sqrt{\dfrac{(100 - 113.88)^2 + (100 - 113.88)^2 + ... + (134 - 113.88)^2}{50}}$

≈ 6.427

7. 113.88 + 6.427 = 120, 113.88 - 6.427 = 107

107-120

15-5 Sample Sets of Data

PAGES 841-842   CHECKING FOR UNDERSTANDING

1. A population includes all possible items of data. A sample is only a representative portion of the population.

2. Sample answer: Group c, because freshmen usually are required to take beginning composition classes. Few freshmen take advanced physics and many athletes take fewer classes than the average student per year. The students on the third floor of the girls' dormitory may or may not be freshmen.

3. The standard error of the mean is a measure used to give a level of confidence about the sample mean.

4. There is a 99% probability that the true mean is within a certain range of the sample mean.

5. $\sigma_{\bar{X}} = \dfrac{40}{\sqrt{64}} = 5$

   1%: $\bar{X} = 200 \pm (2.58)(5)$
   187.1-212.9

   5%: $\bar{X} = 200 \pm (1.96)(5)$
   190.2-209.8

6. $\sigma_{\bar{X}} = \dfrac{5}{\sqrt{36}} \approx 0.83$

   1%: $\bar{X} = 45 \pm (2.58)(0.83)$
   42.86-47.14

   5%: $\bar{X} = 45 \pm (1.96)(0.83)$
   43.37-46.63

7. a. $\sigma_{\bar{X}} = \dfrac{1.4}{\sqrt{100}} = 0.14$ b. $\bar{X} = 4.6 \pm (2.58)(0.14)$
   4.239-4.961

   c. $\bar{X} = 4.6 \pm (0.67)(0.14)$
   4.506-4.694

   d. $\bar{X} = 4.6 \pm (1.65)(0.14)$
   4.369-4.831

PAGES 842-843   EXERCISES

8. $\sigma_{\bar{X}} = \dfrac{2.4}{\sqrt{100}} = 0.24$

   1%: $\bar{X} = 24 \pm (2.58)(0.24)$
   23.38-24.62

   5%: $\bar{X} = 24 \pm (1.96)(0.24)$
   23.53-24.47

9. $\sigma_{\bar{X}} = \dfrac{12}{\sqrt{200}} \approx 0.85$

   1%: $\bar{X} = 80 \pm (2.58)(0.85)$
   77.81-82.19

   5%: $\bar{X} = 80 \pm (1.96)(0.85)$
   78.33-81.67

10. a. $\sigma_{\bar{X}} = \dfrac{1.4}{\sqrt{50}} \approx 0.20$ b. $\bar{X} = 16.2 \pm (1.96)(0.2)$
    15.808-16.692

    c. $\bar{X} = 16.2 \pm (2.58)(0.2)$
    15.684-16.716

    d. $\bar{X} = 16.2 \pm (1.28)(0.2)$
    15.944-16.456

11. a. $\overline{X} = \dfrac{4(1) + 6(3) + 8(5) + \ldots + 20(2)}{1 + 3 + 5 + \ldots + 2}$

$= \dfrac{792}{64}$

≈ 12.38

$\sigma \approx \sqrt{\dfrac{(4 - 12.38)^2(1) + (6 - 12.38)^2(3) + \ldots + (20 - 12.38)^2(2)}{1 + 3 + 5 + \ldots + 2}}$

≈ 3.4

b. $\sigma_{\overline{X}} = \dfrac{3.4}{\sqrt{64}} = 0.425$

c. $\overline{X} = 12.38 \pm (1.96)(0.425)$

11.547–13.213

d. $13.38 = 12.38 + x(0.425)$

$x = 2.35$

$P = 0.982$

12. $\sigma_{\overline{X}} = \dfrac{8}{\sqrt{36}} \approx 1.33$

$\overline{X} + t(1.33) = \overline{X} + 1$

$t = \dfrac{1}{1.33}$

$t \approx 0.75$

$P = 0.546$

$P = 1 - 0.546 = 0.454$

13. $\overline{X} = 40$, $\sigma = 5$, $n = 81$

$30 = \overline{X} - t\sigma_{\overline{X}}$

$= 40 - t(5)$

$10 = 5\sigma$

$2 = \sigma$

$P = 0.955 = 95.5\%$

$100 - 95.5 = 4.5\%$ level of confidence

14. Sample answer: when the product sampled is very expensive; for example, jet engines.

15. a. $\sigma_{\overline{X}} = \dfrac{5.48}{\sqrt{100}} = 0.548$

b. $98.8 = 99.8 - t(0.548)$ $100.9 = 99.8 + 0.548t$

$-1 = -t(0.548)$ $1.1 = 0.548t$

$1.82 \approx t$ $2.0 = t$

$P = 0.928$ $P = 0.955$

$P = \dfrac{1}{2}(0.928) + \dfrac{1}{2}(0.955)$

$= 0.464 + 0.4775$

$= 0.9415$

16. $\$25 = \$25.75 - t\left(\dfrac{5.25}{\sqrt{100}}\right)$ $27 = 25.75 + t\left(\dfrac{5.25}{\sqrt{100}}\right)$

$-0.75 = -0.525t$ $1.25 = 0.525t$

$t \approx 1.43$ $2.38 \approx t$

$P = 0.838$ $P = 0.984$

$P = \dfrac{1}{2}(0.838) + \dfrac{1}{2}(0.984)$

$= 0.911$

17. $\sigma_{\overline{X}} = \dfrac{4.5}{\sqrt{81}} = 0.5$

$25 = 24.5 + 0.5t$

$t = 1.0$

$P = 0.5 - \dfrac{1}{2}(0.683) = 0.1585$

18. a. $\dfrac{1}{2}x + \dfrac{1}{4}y \le 4 \rightarrow 2x + y \le 16$

$\dfrac{1}{3}x + \dfrac{1}{2}y \le 6 \rightarrow 2x + 3y \le 36$

$\dfrac{1}{5}x + \dfrac{1}{6}y \le 8 \rightarrow 6x + 5y \le 240$

possible solutions: $(8, 0)$, $(0, 12)$, $(3, 10)$

$P(x, y) = 100x + 60y$

$P(8, 0) = 100(8) + 60(0) = 800$

$P(0, 12) = 100(0) + 60(12) = 720$

$P(3, 10) = 100(3) + 60(10) = 900 \leftarrow$ max

3 of Model 28, 10 of Model 74

b. \$900

19. $\tan \theta = \dfrac{500}{2500}$

$\theta \approx 11°28'$

20. $S_n = 1^3 + 2^3 + 3^3 + \ldots + 10^3$

$= 3025$

21. $160 = 140 + 20(t)$

$t = 1$

$P = 0.5 - \dfrac{1}{2}(0.683) = 0.1585$

22. Convert each number to a fraction with a common denominator and then compare the numerators.

(A) $\sqrt{3} = \dfrac{9\sqrt{3}}{9}$ **(B)** $\dfrac{1}{\sqrt{3}} = \dfrac{3\sqrt{3}}{9}$

(C) $\dfrac{\sqrt{3}}{3} = \dfrac{3\sqrt{3}}{9}$ **(D)** $\dfrac{1}{3} = \dfrac{3}{9}$

(E) $\dfrac{1}{3\sqrt{3}} = \dfrac{\sqrt{3}}{9}$

The smallest numerator is $\sqrt{3}$. The best answer is E.

Graphing Calculators: Scatter Plots and Lines of Regression

15-6A

PAGE 845   EXERCISES

1.

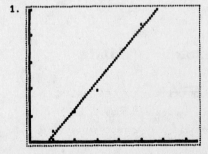

376

2.

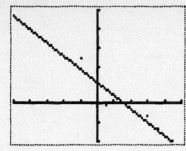

3. a.

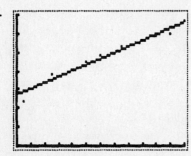

b. 3.8 ft

c.

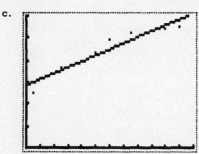

d. 5.2 ft

e. The regression line will be almost horizontal.

15-6 Scatter Plots

PAGE 851   CHECKING FOR UNDERSTANDING

1. One method is to select two points typical of the set of data and use the points to find the slope of the line passing through them. Then use the point-slope method to write the equation of the line. Another method is to separate the data into three equivalent sets and find a point that represents the average of the x-coordinates and the average of the y-coordinates for the points in each set. Then connect the three points with a line. The equation of the line can be found by using two of the points.

2. Its value will tell you whether the relation is negative or positive and to what degree.

3. positive   4. negative

5. positive   6. no correlation

7. negative   8. positive

---

9. a. ($5, $100), ($12, $149)

$$m = \frac{149 - 100}{12 - 5} = 7$$

b. $y - 100 = 7(x - 5)$ c. $s = 7p + 65,000,000$

$y = 7x + 65$

65 million

d. $s = 7(3) + 65$

$= 86$ million

10.

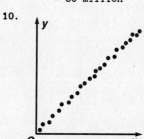

11.

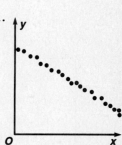

12.

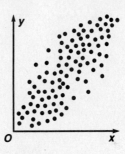

PAGES 851-854   EXERCISES

13. a.

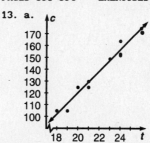

b. $m = \dfrac{175 - 130}{26 - 21} = \dfrac{45}{5} = 9$

$c - 130 = 9(t - 21)$

$c = 9t - 59$

c. $r = \dfrac{\Sigma XY - \dfrac{(\Sigma X)(\Sigma Y)}{n}}{\sqrt{\Sigma(X - \overline{X})^2 \Sigma(Y - \overline{Y})^2}} = 0.9844291973$

d. There is a strongly positive correlation between the temperature and the chirps per minute.

14. a.

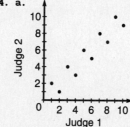

b. strongly positive

c. $r = 0.\overline{93}$

15. a.

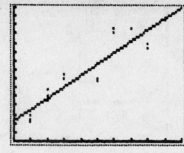

b. strongly negative

c. $r = -0.9\overline{63}$

d. Judges 1 and 2 seem very close in the scoring while judge 3 is not in synch with their opinions.

16. a.

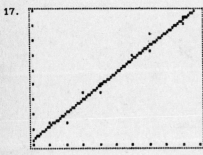

b. The older the machine, the more expensive maintenance is.

c. Sample answer:

$y = 22.6 + 12.67x$

d. $r = 0.9210450398$

e. The relationship between age of a machine and the cost of its maintenance is strongly positive.

17.

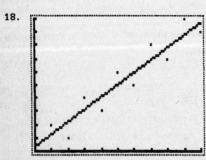

18.

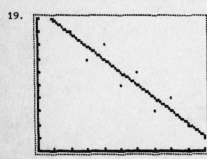

19.

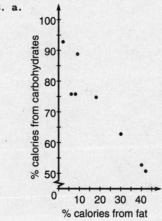

20.

21. a = the y-intercept of the line of regression, b = its slope

22. a.–c. Sample answers are given.

a. the space shuttle, because anything less than perfect may endanger the lives of the passengers

b. a medication that proves to help AIDS patients, because any positive correlation is better than none or a negative one

c. comparing a dosage of medicine to the growth factor of cancer cells, because the greater the dosage, the fewer cells produced would be good

23. a.

b. Sample answer: $y = -0.9x + 90$

c. extremely negative   **d.** $r = -0.939240534$

e. Sample answer: The greater the percentage of calories from fat, the lesser the percentage of calories from carbohydrates.

24. a.

Women – Small Frame

Women – Medium Frame

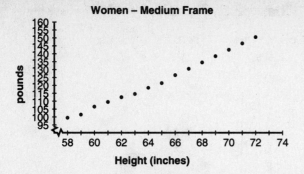

pounds vs. Height (inches)

Women – Large Frame

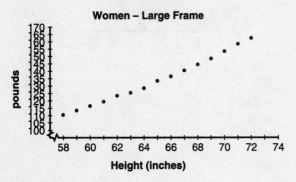

pounds vs. Height (inches)

Men – Small Frame

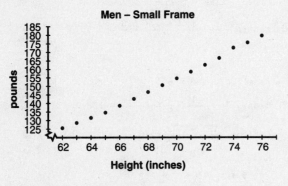

pounds vs. Height (inches)

Men – Medium Frame

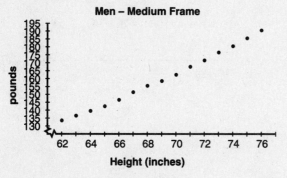

pounds vs. Height (inches)

Men – Large Frame

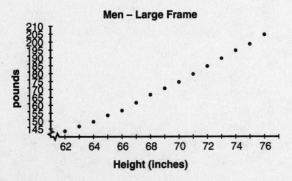

pounds vs. Height (inches)

b. x = height, y = weight

Women: small: $y = 3.386x - 103.2$

medium: $y = 3.675x - 114.8$

large: $y = 3.7x - 105.63$

Men: small: $y = 3.9x - 120.64$

medium: $y = 4.1x - 122.5$

large: $4.35x - 128.28$

c. Women: small: $r = 0.9947335131$

medium: $r = 0.9977127517$

large: $r = 0.99962987818$

Men: small: $r = 0.998566454$

medium: $r = 0.9980088523$

large: $r = 0.997233899$

25. $(f \circ g)(4) = f(g(4)) = f(0.5 \times 4 - 1)$

$$= f(1)$$
$$= 5 \cdot 1 + 9$$
$$= 14$$

$(g \circ f)(4) = g(f(4)) = g(5 \cdot 4 + 9)$

$$= g(29)$$
$$= 0.5(29) - 1$$
$$= 13.5$$

26.

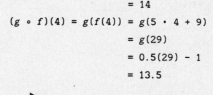

$$\tan 6°40' = \frac{x}{y}$$

$$y = \frac{x}{\tan 6°40'}$$

$$\tan 37°12' = \frac{x + 35}{y}$$

$$y = \frac{x + 35}{\tan 37°12'}$$

$$\frac{x}{\tan 6°40'} = \frac{x + 35}{\tan 37°12'}$$

$$(\tan 37°12')x = (\tan 6°40')x + 35 \tan 6°40'$$

$$x = \frac{35 \tan 6°40'}{\tan 37°12' - \tan 6°40'}$$

$$x \approx 6.37$$

$$\sin 6°40' \approx \frac{6.37}{s}$$

$$s \approx \frac{6.37}{\sin 6°40'}$$

$$s \approx 54.87 \text{ ft}$$

27. $3(3.4)^2 - 10 = 24.68$

$3(24.68)^2 - 10 = 1817.3072$

$3(1817.3072)^2 - 10 = 9{,}907{,}806.378$

$3(9{,}907{,}806.378)^2 - 10 = 2.944938816 \times 10^{14}$

$3(2.944938816 \times 10^{14})^2 - 10 = 2.60179939 \times 10^{29}$

28. $\overline{X} = 16.2 \pm \left(\dfrac{1.4}{\sqrt{50}}\right)(2.58)$

    15.684–16.716

29. $(4 + 6 + 7 + 8)4 = 100$

    The best answer is D.

Technology: Median-Fit Lines

PAGE 855   EXERCISES

1. **a.** 15.9 million   **b.** 28.0 million

    c. 36.4 million   **d.** 41.1 million

    e. 46.3 million

2. $y = 0.00840x + 0.43977$

15-6B   Graphing Calculators: Curve Fitting

PAGE 859   EXERCISES

1. polynomial

2. Polynomial regression; the Pearson product-moment correlation value is closer to -1.

3. $y = 0.568e^{1.0594x}$; $r = 0.9997$

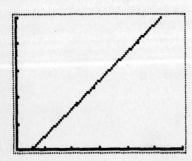

4. $y = 0.4848x^{2.5657}$; $r = 0.9921$

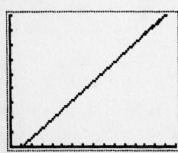

Chapter 15 Summary and Review

PAGES 860–862   SKILLS AND CONCEPTS

1. 0.5, 1.5, 2.5, 3.5, 4.5

2. 1.0

3.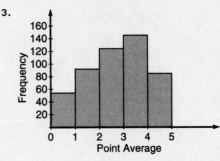

4. Mean $= \dfrac{4 + 8 + 2 + \ldots + 4}{9} = 5$

    Median: 5

    Mode: 4

5. Mean $= \dfrac{19 + 11 + \ldots + 16}{5} = 14.8$

    Median: 15

    Mode: none

6. Mean: $\dfrac{6.6 + 6.3 + \ldots + 6.3}{8} = 6.45$

    Median: $\dfrac{6.4 + 6.6}{2} = 6.5$

    Mode: 6.3 and 6.6

7. Mean: $\dfrac{130 + 135 + \ldots + 146}{8} = 133.25$

    Median: $\dfrac{131 + 133}{2} = 132$

    Mode: none

8. $\overline{X} = \dfrac{5 + 1 + 5 + \ldots + 1}{10}$

    $MD = \dfrac{1}{10}[|5 - 3.4| + |1 - 3.4| + \ldots + |1 - 3.4|]$

    $= 1.6$

9. $\sigma = \sqrt{\dfrac{1}{10}[(5-3.4)^2 + (1-3.4)^2 + \ldots + (1-3.4)^2]}$

    $= 1.74$

10. $Q_3 = 5$, $Q_1 = 2$

    $Q_R = \dfrac{5 - 2}{2} = 1.5$

11. $78 = 88 - t(5)$ $98 = 88 + t(5)$

    $t = 2$ $t = 2$

    $P = \dfrac{1}{2}(0.955)$ $P = \dfrac{1}{2}(0.955)$

            $P = 95.5\%$

12. $86 = 88 - t(5)$

    $-2 = -5t$

    $0.4 = t$

    $P = 0.311$

13. $P = 90\%$, $t = 1.65$

    $88 \pm 1.65(5) = 79.75$ and 96.25

14. $\sigma_{\overline{X}} = \dfrac{0.5}{\sqrt{200}} = 0.035$

15. $\bar{X} = 1.8 \pm 0.035(1.65)$

1.742–1.858

16. $\bar{X} = 1.8 \pm 0.035(1.96)$

1.7314–1.8686

17.

A scatter plot with a regression line. Y-axis "Final Grade" from 50 to 100, X-axis "Days Absent" from 0 to 6.

18. Sample answer: $y = -4.44x + 96.64$

19. $SP = \Sigma XY - \dfrac{(\Sigma X)(\Sigma Y)}{n}$

$= 1427 - \dfrac{18(596)}{7}$

$= -105.57$

$SS_X = [(0 - 2.6)^2 + (3 - 2.6)^2 + \ldots + (4 - 2.6)^2]$

$= 23.71$

$SS_Y = [(95-84.86)^2 + (88-84.86)^2 + \ldots + (77-84.86)^2]$

$= 470.86$

$r = \dfrac{-105.57}{\sqrt{(23.71)(470.86)}} = \dfrac{-105.57}{105.67} = -0.95$

20. strongly negative

PAGE 862   APPLICATIONS AND PROBLEM SOLVING

21. a.

```
1 | 0 3 5 6 7 9
2 | 1 3 4 5
3 | 9 9
```

1|0 means 10.

b. Mean: $\dfrac{10 + 13 + \ldots + 39}{12} = 21.75$

Median: $\dfrac{19 + 21}{2} = 20$

Mode: 39

22. a. Mean: $\dfrac{3.60 + 1.73 + \ldots + 1.42}{8} = 1.80$

Median: $\dfrac{1.55 + 1.56}{2} = 1.555$

b. $MD = \dfrac{1}{8}[|3.6-1.8| + |1.73+1.8| + \ldots + |1.42-1.8|]$

$= 0.45$

$\sigma = \sqrt{\dfrac{1}{8}[(3.6-1.8)^2 + (1.73-1.8)^2 + \ldots + (1.42-1.8)^2]}$

$= 0.69$

c.

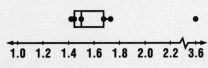

A box-and-whisker plot on a number line from 1.0 to 3.6.

outlier: 3.60

23. a.

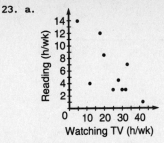

A scatter plot. Y-axis "Reading (h/wk)" from 2 to 14, X-axis "Watching TV (h/wk)" from 0 to 40.

b. $r = -0.72$

c. moderately negative

Chapter 15 Test

PAGE 863

1.

Class Limits	Class Marks	Tally	Frequency
0–3	1.5	|||	3
3–6	4.5	⊥⊥⊥⊥		6
6–9	7.5	⊥⊥⊥⊥ ⊥⊥⊥⊥ ⊥⊥⊥⊥		16
9–12	10.5	⊥⊥⊥⊥ ⊥⊥⊥⊥ ⊥⊥⊥⊥ ⊥⊥⊥⊥ ⊥⊥⊥⊥	25
12–15	13.5	⊥⊥⊥⊥ ⊥⊥⊥⊥ ⊥⊥⊥⊥ ||	17
15–18	16.5	⊥⊥⊥⊥ |||	8
18–21	19.5	⊥⊥⊥⊥	5

2.

A histogram. Y-axis "Frequency" from 0 to 25, X-axis "Days missed" from 0 to 21.

3. $\bar{X} = \dfrac{3(1.5) + 6(4.5) + \ldots + 5(19.5)}{3 + 6 + \ldots + 5}$

$= 10.438$

4. $M_d = \dfrac{10 + 10}{2} = 10$

5. $\sigma = \sqrt{\dfrac{(1.5 - 10.438)^2(3) + (4.5 - 10.438)^2(6) + \ldots + (19.5 - 10.438)^5}{80}}$

$= 4.210$

6. $\bar{X} = \dfrac{2.341 + 2.347 + \ldots + 2.344}{15}$

$= 2.344$

7. $M_d = 2.344$

8. Mode = 2.344

9. $Q_R = \dfrac{Q_3 - Q_1}{2} = \dfrac{2.347 - 2.341}{2} = \dfrac{0.006}{2} = 0.003$

10.

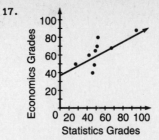

2.338 2.340 2.342 2.344 2.346 2.348 2.350

11. $MD = \frac{1}{15}(|2.341 - 2.344| + |2.347 - 2.344| + \ldots +$

$\qquad |2.344 - 2.344|)$

$\qquad = 0.0025$

12. $\sigma = \sqrt{\frac{1}{n}\left[\begin{array}{l}(2.341 - 2.344)^2 + (2.347 - 2.344)^2 + \\ \ldots + (2.344 - 2.344)^2\end{array}\right]}$

$\qquad = 0.0031$

13. $\bar{X} = 10.438 \pm (1.65)(4.21)$

$\qquad 3.47{-}17.33$

14. $8 = 10.438 - t(4.21)$, $\quad 12 = 10.438 + 4.21t$

$\qquad t = 0.6 \qquad\qquad\qquad t = 0.4$

$\qquad P = \dfrac{0.451}{2} \qquad\qquad P = \dfrac{0.311}{2}$

$\qquad\qquad P = 0.2255 + 0.1555$

$\qquad\qquad\quad = 0.381$

15. $\sigma_{\bar{X}} = \dfrac{\sigma}{\sqrt{n}} = \dfrac{4.21}{\sqrt{80}} = 0.4707$

16. $\bar{X} = 10.438 \pm (1.96)(0.4707)$

$\qquad 9.515{-}11.361$

17.

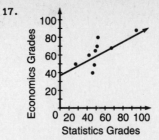

18. Let x = statistics grades, and y = economics grades.

$\qquad y = 0.59x + 32.06$

19. $r = 0.724$

20. moderately positive

PAGE 863   BONUS

The formula is the radicand of the standard deviation formula, or it is the square of the standard deviation.

variance $= (0.0031)^2 = 0.00000961$

Chapter 16   Graph Theory

16-1   Graphs

1. A multigraph can have loops and parallel edges; a simple graph cannot.

2. false

3. Sample answer:

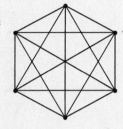

4. Every pair of vertices is not connected by exactly one edge.

5. t, u, and v

6. 1

7. B, C, E, and F

8. 2; x and y

9. 1; z

10. It is a multigraph because it has a loop and parallel edges.

11. $V = \{A, B, C, D, E, F\}$

12. $E = \{q, r, s, t, u, v, w, x, y, z\}$

13.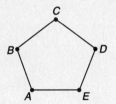

14.
$$A \quad B \quad C \quad D$$

15.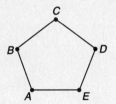

16.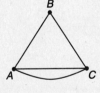

17.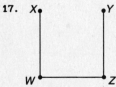

18.
$$L \qquad M$$

19.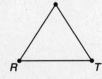

20.

21.

22.
$$R \quad\rule{1cm}{0.4pt}\quad T$$

23.
$$A \qquad B \quad\rule{1cm}{0.4pt}\quad C$$

24.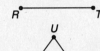

25.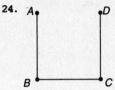

26.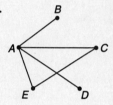

27.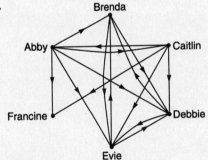

28.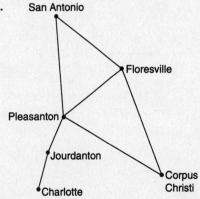

29.
$$A \quad\rule{3cm}{0.4pt}\quad B$$

30.

31.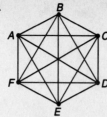

32. $\dfrac{5(5 - 1)}{2} = 10$

33. $\dfrac{7(7 - 1)}{2} = 21$

34. $\dfrac{10(10 - 1)}{2} = 45$

35. $\dfrac{n(n - 1)}{2}$

36. no; $\dfrac{3(3 - 1)}{2} = 3 \neq 4$

37. no; $\dfrac{4(4 - 1)}{2} = 6 \neq 5$

38. yes; $\dfrac{6(6 - 1)}{2} = 15$ **39.** yes; $\dfrac{10(10 - 1)}{2} = 45$

40. yes; $\dfrac{14(14 - 1)}{7} = 91$

41. no; $\dfrac{100(100 - 1)}{2} = 4950 \neq 4900$

42. 4, 2 loops on same vertex

43. yes; sample answer:

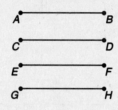

44. No, the sum of the degrees must be even.

45. sum of degrees = 2 · number of edges

$$= 2 \cdot 11$$
$$= 2 \cdot 22$$

Since each vertex has degree 2,
22 ÷ 2 = 11 vertices.

46. K_3

47. No; there would be $\dfrac{x^2 + 5x + 6}{2}$ edges, since

$$\dfrac{n(n - 1)}{2} = \dfrac{(x + 3)(x + 2)}{2}.$$

48. Sample answer:

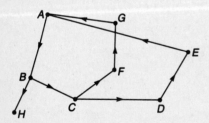

Descriptions may vary.

49. Sample answer:

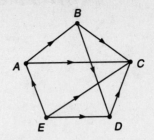

Descriptions may vary.

50. $y = x^2 - 6x + 14$

51. possible rational roots: ±1, ±2

$$f(1) = 1^3 - 1^2 - 1 - 2 = -3$$
$$f(-1) = (-1)^3 - (-1)^2 - (-1) - 2 = -3$$
$$f(2) = 2^3 - 2^2 - 2 - 2 = 0$$
$$f(-2) = (-2)^3 - (-2)^2 - (-2) - 2 = -12$$

rational root: 2

52.

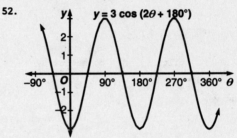

53. $|\sqrt{r}|^2 = 50^2 + 30^2 - 2(50)(30) \cos 140°$

$$\approx 2500 + 900 - 3000(-0.7660)$$
$$\approx 5698$$

$|\sqrt{r}| \approx 75.5 \text{ N}$

$$\dfrac{75.5}{\sin 140°} = \dfrac{30}{\sin \theta}$$

$$\sin \theta = \dfrac{30 \sin 140°}{75.5}$$

$$\approx 0.2554$$
$$\theta \approx 14°50'$$

54. Using $x^2 + y^2 + Dx + Ey + F = 0$,

$$4 + 1 + 2D - E + F = 0 \quad \rightarrow \quad 2D - E + F = -5$$
$$9 + 0 - 3D + F = 0 \quad \rightarrow \quad -3D + F = -9$$
$$1 + 16 + D + 4E + F = 0 \quad \rightarrow \quad D + 4E + F = -17$$

$$2D - E + F = -5 \qquad 3D - F = 9$$

$$\begin{array}{ll} \dfrac{3D \qquad - F = 9}{5D - E \qquad = 4} & \dfrac{D + 4E + F = -17}{4D + 4E \qquad = -8} \\ & D + E \qquad = -2 \end{array}$$

$$5D - E = 4 \qquad\qquad \tfrac{1}{3} + E = -2$$

$$\dfrac{D + E = -2}{6D \qquad = 2} \qquad\qquad E = -\tfrac{7}{3}$$

$$D \qquad = \tfrac{1}{3} \qquad\qquad -3\left(\tfrac{1}{3}\right) + F = -9$$

$$F = -8$$

So, $x^2 + y^2 + \tfrac{1}{3}x - \tfrac{7}{3}y - 8 = 0$

$$3x^2 + 3y^2 + x - 7y - 24 = 0.$$

55.

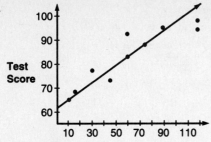

$m = \dfrac{83 - 65}{60 - 10} = \dfrac{18}{50} = 0.36$

Let x = minutes studied and y = test scores.

$y = 0.36x + b$

$65 = 0.36(10) + b$

$61.4 = b$

A prediction equation is $y = 61.4 + 0.36x$.

56. $\dfrac{x}{8} = 8$

$x = 8 \cdot 8$

$x = 64$

16-2   Walks and Paths

PAGE 874   CHECKING FOR UNDERSTANDING

1. In a walk, vertices and edges can be repeated. In a trail, vertices can be repeated but edges cannot be repeated. In a path, you cannot repeat anything.

2. because the set of paths is a subset of the set of walks

3. See students' work.

4. A bridge is an edge that, if removed, would cause the graph to no longer be connected.

5. trail, 7   6. 2

7. Multigraph; it has parallel edges.

8. yes   9. no

PAGES 874-876   EXERCISES

10. walk   11. cycle

12. trail   13. path

14. circuit   15. infinite number

16. 3

17. Answers will vary.

Sample answer: a, b, g, c, f

18. a, b, c, f

19. a. Sample answer: d; 1; b, c; 2; a, d; 2

    b. d; 1; b, c; 2

    c. d; b, c; d

20. a. Sample answer: a, c; 2; d, e; 2; a, b, d, f; 4

    b. a, c; 2; b, c; 2; d, e; 2; d, f; 2

    c. a, c; d, e; d, f

21. a. Sample answer: a; 1; b; 1; c; 1

    b. a; 1; b; 1; c; 1; d; 1

    c. a; b; c

22. 6   23. 21

24. 4   25. 7

26. No, K_1 is not connected, since it has no edges.

27. 3 cars; sample answer: U, Z; V, X; W, Y.

28. a.

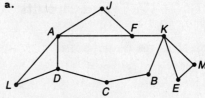

    b. 3 enclosures; sample answer: C, J, K, L; B, D, E, F; A, M.

29. $f(x) = x^4 - 8x^2 + 16$ $f''(x) = 12x^2 - 16$

$f'(x) = 4x^3 - 16x$

$0 = 4x^3 - 16x$ $0 = 12x^2 - 16$

$0 = 4x(x^2 - 4)$ $0 = 3x^2 - 4$

$0 = 4x(x - 2)(x + 2)$ $\dfrac{4}{3} = x^2$

$x = 0, 2, -2$ $\pm \dfrac{2\sqrt{3}}{3} = x$

$f(0) = 16$ $f\left(\dfrac{2\sqrt{3}}{3}\right) = \dfrac{64}{9}$

$f(2) = 0$

$f(-2) = 0$ $f\left(-\dfrac{2\sqrt{3}}{2}\right) = \dfrac{64}{9}$

critical points: $(0, 16)$, $(\pm2, 0)$, $\left(\pm \dfrac{2\sqrt{3}}{3}, \dfrac{64}{9}\right)$

Test points above and below the critical points. $(0, 16)$ is a maximum, $(\pm2, 0)$ are minimums, and $\left(\pm \dfrac{2\sqrt{3}}{3}, \dfrac{64}{9}\right)$ are points of inflection.

30. $-\sqrt{A^2 + B^2} = -\sqrt{3^2 + (-5)^2} = -\sqrt{34}$

$-\dfrac{3x}{\sqrt{34}} + \dfrac{5y}{\sqrt{34}} - \dfrac{5}{\sqrt{34}} = 0$

$\sin \phi = \dfrac{5}{\sqrt{34}}$, $\cos \phi = \dfrac{-3}{\sqrt{34}}$, $p = \dfrac{5}{\sqrt{34}}$

$\phi = \arctan \dfrac{B}{A}$

$= \arctan \left(-\dfrac{5}{3}\right)$

$\approx 121°$

$\dfrac{5}{\sqrt{34}} = r \cos (\theta - 121°)$

31. $C(6, 3) = \dfrac{6!}{(6 - 3)!3!} = 20$

32. F, H, J; 3

33. $x^2 = 36$ $2^{6-1} = 2^5$

       $x = \pm 6$ $= 32 \leftarrow E$

               $2^{-6-1} = 2^{-7}$

                      $= \dfrac{1}{128}$

The best answer is E.

16-3   Euler Paths and Circuits

PAGE 880   CHECKING FOR UNDERSTANDING

1. If the graph is not connected, at least one vertex will always be excluded from the path or circuit.

2. A Euler circuit is a path that includes each edge exactly once and has the same starting and ending vertex. A Euler path also includes each edge once and has different starting and ending vertices.

3. A connected graph contains an Euler circuit when the degree of each vertex is even.

4. A, C, D 5. C

6. A, D

7. Sample answer: $a, d, e, f, j, g, h, c, b, i$

8. yes

9. Sample answer: a, b, g, f, e, d, c

10. Connect edge a to the rest of the graph.

PAGES 881-882   EXERCISES

11. yes   12. no   13. yes

14. no   15. yes   16. yes

17. 11, 12, 14, 16   18. 11, 16   19. 12

20. No, it is not connected.

21. Yes; each vertex has even degree.

22-24. Answers may vary. Sample answers are given.

22.   23.

  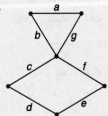

24.

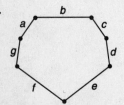

25. For $n - 1$ to be even, n must be odd. Thus, all complete graphs of the form K_n, where n is odd, contain an Euler circuit.

---

26. Yes; sample route: $y, k, b, m, n, h, a, c, d, e,$ $s, i, q, z, j, p, r, f, g, o, w.$

27. No; one, between New Jersey and Brooklyn

28. $d = \sqrt{(-1 - 3)^2 + (2 - (-5))^2}$

     $= \sqrt{16 + 49}$

     $= \sqrt{65}$

   $m = \dfrac{2 - (-5)}{-1 - 3} = -\dfrac{7}{4}$

29. $\sin 450° = 1$

30. $a_n = \dfrac{1}{n^n}$, $a_{n+1} = \dfrac{1}{(n + 1)^{n+1}}$

   $\lim\limits_{n \to \infty} \dfrac{\frac{1}{(n + 1)^{n+1}}}{\frac{1}{n^n}} = \lim\limits_{n \to \infty} \dfrac{n^n}{(n + 1)^{n+1}} = 0$

convergent

31. Sample answer: $f, 1; a, b, c, d, e, 5;$ $a, b, c, g, b, c, d, e, 8$

32. $\dfrac{8a + 12}{2} = \dfrac{8a}{2} + \dfrac{12}{2}$

            $= 4a + 6$

The two quantities are equal. C

Mid-Chapter Review

PAGE 882

1. yes   2. no

3. 4   4. $t, u, v,$ and y

5. $B, C,$ and E 6. circuit

7. no

8. Yes; sample answer: $r, s, u, t, z, x, y, v, w.$

16-4   Shortest Paths and Minimal Distances

PAGE 887   CHECKING FOR UNDERSTANDING

1. Since the minimal paths are weighted, the shortest path is not necessarily the minimal path.

2. Weighted multigraphs have values or weights assigned to their edges, multigraphs do not.

3. when the sum of the weights of the edges is the minimum weight

4. 4   5. 3

6. $A, B, D, I, G; A, C, D, I, G; A, B, D, F, G$ or A, C, D, F, G

7. $C, D, F, G;$ or C, D, I, G

8. yes   9. 6

10. P, B, C, D, E

11. because the path P, B, A is shorter

12. 6   13. C

14. None; A and Z are not connected.

15. 5; one path is A, G, K, M, I, Z.

16. 3; one path is A, F, I, Z.

17. 4; one path is A, C, Y, D, Z.

18. 4; one path is A, K, I, B, Z.

19. 7; one path is A, B, I, L, N, Q, F, Z.

20. 6; A, B, Z **21.** 7; A, G, K, Z

22. 6; A, C, S, Z **23.** 5; A, B, C, Z

24. 13; A, G, K, M, I, Z

25. 3; A, E, Z

26. 3 cities → 6 min = 3! min

   5 cities → 120 min = 5! min

   9! = 362,880 min = 252 days

27. a.

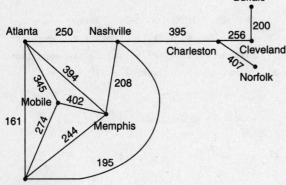

Buffalo

Atlanta 250 Nashville 395 256 200

Charleston Cleveland

394 407 Norfolk

345 208

Mobile 402

161 274 244 Memphis

195

Birmingham

b. Buffalo, Cleveland, Charleston, Nashville, Atlanta

c. Mobile, Birmingham, Nashville; 469 miles

28. 30¢; Kalispell, Missoula, Helena, Bozeman

29.

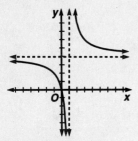

30. $\sin \theta = \dfrac{3}{4}$

$x = \sqrt{4^2 - 3^2}$ $y = 3, r = 4$

   $= \sqrt{7}$

$\sec \theta = \dfrac{4}{\sqrt{7}}$

   $= \dfrac{4\sqrt{7}}{7}$

31. Since $S_1 = 2$ and $2^{1+1} - 2 = 2$, the formula is valid for $n = 1$.

Assume the formula is valid for $n = k$ and derive a formula for $n = k + 1$.

$2 + 2^2 + 2^3 + \ldots + 2^k = 2^{k+1} - 2$

$2 + 2^2 + 2^3 + \ldots + 2^k + 2^{k+1} = 2^{k+1} - 2 + 2^{k+1}$

$= 2(2^{k+1}) - 2$

$= 2^{k+2} - 2$

When the original formula is applied for $n = k + 1$, the same result is obtained. Thus, if the formula is valid for $n = k$, it is also valid for $n = k + 1$. Since the formula is valid for $n = 1$, it is also valid for $n = 2$. Since it is valid for $n = 2$, it is also valid for $n = 3$, and so on indefinitely.

32. a, b, c, e, f, d

33. $x = -7 \rightarrow 2x = -14$

$\dfrac{1}{2y} = -14$

$2x = \dfrac{1}{2y}$

$2y = \dfrac{1}{2x}$

$y = \dfrac{1}{4x}$

The best answer is D.

Case Study Follow-Up

PAGE 890

1. This is at least 30% more participation than the national average.

2. a. Yes, it is possible since all vertices have an even degree.

b.

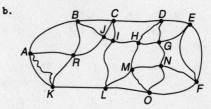

Sample answer: $R \rightarrow A \rightarrow B \rightarrow R \rightarrow J \rightarrow B \rightarrow C \rightarrow J \rightarrow I \rightarrow C \rightarrow D \rightarrow H \rightarrow I \rightarrow L \rightarrow M \rightarrow H \rightarrow G \rightarrow D \rightarrow E \rightarrow G \rightarrow N \rightarrow F \rightarrow E \rightarrow F \rightarrow O \rightarrow N \rightarrow M \rightarrow O \rightarrow L \rightarrow K \rightarrow A \rightarrow K \rightarrow R$

3. See students' work.

1. Sample answer:
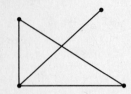

2. Sample answer:
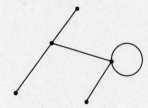

3. Sample answer:
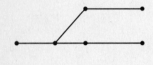

4. Sample answer:
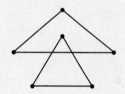

5. See students' work.

6. $21 = n - 1$
   $22 = n$, 22 vertices

7. $18 - 1 = 17$ edges

8. all

9. $7 - 1 = 6$ edges

10. at least 2 vertices

11. Sample answer: a, c, g, f, e

12.
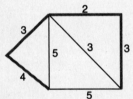

PAGES 893-895   EXERCISES

13. No; contains a cycle.

14. No; not connected.

15. yes

16-18. Answers may vary. Sample answers are given.

16. {V, X}, {X, Y}, {Y, D}, {D, B}, {B, Z}, {Z, H}, {H, G}, {G, F}, {F, C}, {E, A}, {A, V}

17. {Z, I}, {I, F}, {F, A}, {A, B}, {B, D}, {D, H}, {D, C}, {D, E}, {G, H}.

18. {A, B}, {B, I}, {I, L}, {L, C}, {C, D}, {D, E}, {E, N}, {N, Q}, {Q, F}, {F, Z}, {Z, M}, {M, S}, {S, R}, {R, T}, {T, K}, {K, J}, {J, P}, {P, O}, {O, H}, {H, G}

19. {B, A}, {A, E}, {E, F}, {F, D}, {D, C}, {C, Z}; 7

20. {E, D}, {D, A}, {A, B}, {B, C}, {B, Z}; 14

21. {H, G}, {G, A}, {A, B}, {B, E}, {E, C}, {C, D}, {D, Z}, {D, K}; 15

22. Sample answer:
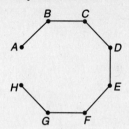

23. Sample answer:
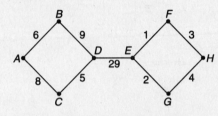

24. $66,000,000; See students' work.

25. See students' work; any spanning tree with fifteen vertices will satisfy the conditions.

26. False; sample answer: $x = 90°$.

   $\text{Tan}^{-1} 90° \approx 89.36$

   $\dfrac{1}{\text{Tan } 90°}$ = undefined

27. $(4 + 3)^2 + (-1)^2 - 4 = 46$
   $\sqrt{46} \approx 6.78$

28. $\dfrac{C(4, 0) \cdot C(6, 2)}{C(10, 2)} = \dfrac{1 \cdot 15}{45} = \dfrac{1}{3}$

29. A, B, C, D; 8

30. (A) $(-8)^{62} = 9.81 \times 10^{55}$
   (B) $(-8)^{75} = -5.39 \times 10^{67}$

   Quantity A is greater. A

16-6   Graphs and Matrices

1. Possible answers: Friendship patterns, authority structure in an organization, communication patterns, and cause-and-effect relationships.

2. Choose the longest path from the start.

3.

	A	B	C	D
A	0	0	1	1
B	1	0	0	0
C	1	1	0	0
D	1	0	1	0

4.
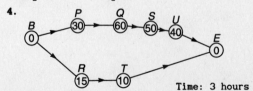

Time: 3 hours

5.

	A	B	C	D
A	0	1	1	1
B	1	0	1	1
C	1	1	0	1
D	1	1	1	0

6.

	J	K	L	M	N
J	0	0	1	1	0
K	0	0	0	1	1
L	1	0	0	0	1
M	1	1	0	0	0
N	0	1	1	0	0

16.

	E	F	G	H	I	J	K
E	0	1	0	0	0	0	0
F	0	0	0	1	0	0	0
G	0	1	0	1	0	0	0
H	0	0	0	0	1	0	0
I	0	0	0	0	0	0	1
J	0	0	0	0	1	0	0
K	1	1	0	0	0	1	0

7.

	Q	R	S	T	U	V
Q	0	1	1	1	1	1
R	1	0	1	0	0	0
S	1	1	0	1	0	0
T	1	0	1	0	1	0
U	1	0	0	1	0	1
V	1	0	0	0	1	0

17.

	Q	R	S	T	U	V	W	X	Y
Q	0	0	0	0	0	0	0	1	1
R	0	0	1	0	0	0	0	0	0
S	0	0	0	0	0	0	0	1	0
T	0	0	0	0	0	0	0	1	0
U	0	0	0	1	0	0	0	0	0
V	0	0	0	0	0	0	0	0	0
W	0	0	0	0	0	1	0	0	0
X	0	1	0	0	1	1	1	0	1
Y	0	0	0	0	0	0	0	0	0

8.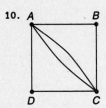

9.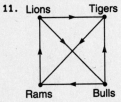

18.

	L	M	N	O	P
L	0	1	0	0	1
M	0	0	0	0	0
N	1	1	0	1	0
O	0	1	0	0	1
P	0	0	0	0	0

10.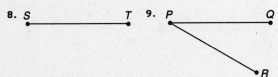

19.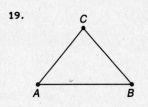

20.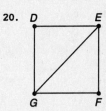

PAGES 901–903   EXERCISES

11.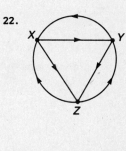

21.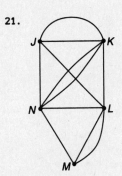

22.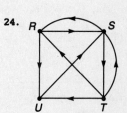

12.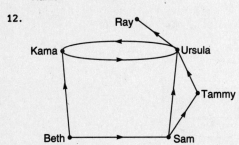

13.

	A	B	C	D
A	0	1	0	1
B	1	0	1	1
C	0	1	0	1
D	1	1	1	0

14.

	H	I	J	K	L
H	0	1	0	0	1
I	1	0	1	1	1
J	0	1	0	1	0
K	0	1	1	0	0
L	1	1	0	0	0

23.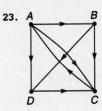

24.

15.

	X	Y	Z
X	0	2	0
Y	2	0	2
Z	0	2	0

25.

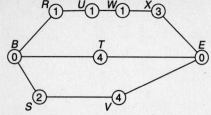

The path $B \to R \to U \to W \to X \to E$ and $B \to S \to V \to E$ are both critical. The minimum amount of time needed is 6 weeks.

26.

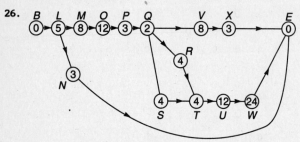

The path $B \to L \to M \to O \to P \to Q \to S \to T \to U \to W \to E$ is a critical path. The minimum amount of time needed is 74 days.

27. If the sum of each row and the sum of each column are even then G contains an Euler circuit.

28. a.

	A	B	C	D	E	F
A	0	0	0	0	0	1
B	1	0	1	1	0	0
C	0	0	0	1	0	0
D	0	0	0	0	0	0
E	1	0	0	1	0	0
F	0	0	0	0	1	0

b. Ben

29. a.

	A	C	D	H	M	S
A	0	1	0	0	0	1
C	0	0	1	0	1	0
D	0	0	0	1	1	0
H	1	0	0	0	0	1
M	0	0	0	0	0	1
S	0	0	1	0	1	0

b. 3, $D \to M \to S$; $D \to H \to A \to S$; $D \to H \to S$

c. yes; $C \to D \to H$; 2 flights

30.
$$d = \frac{Ax_1 + By_1 + C}{\sqrt{A^2 + B^2}}$$

$$= \frac{3(-1) + (-7)4 + (-1)}{\sqrt{3^2 + (-7)^2}}$$

$$= \frac{-32}{\sqrt{58}}$$

$$\approx -4.20$$

$$|d| \approx 4.20$$

31. $\log \dfrac{\sqrt[4]{0.0063}}{6.73} = \log (0.0063)^{\frac{1}{4}} - \log 6.73$

$$= \frac{1}{4} \log 0.0063 - \log 6.73$$

$$\approx -1.3782$$

$$\frac{\sqrt[4]{0.0063}}{6.73} \approx 0.042$$

32. Sample answer: {3, 4, 5, 6, 9, 9}

33. Sample answer: a, b, c, i, j, e

34.
$$(a - b)^2 = 64$$
$$a^2 - 2ab + b^2 = 64$$
$$a^2 + b^2 - 2ab = 64$$
$$a^2 + b^2 - 2(3) = 64$$
$$a^2 + b^2 = 70$$

The best answer is D.

Chapter 16 Summary and Review

PAGES 904–906   SKILLS AND CONCEPTS

1. no   **2.** 4

3. {A, B}, {A, C}, {A, E}   **4.** E and C

5. yes   **6.** walk

7. trail   **8.** cycle

9. circuit   **10.** u, w, v, x, z, y

11. Add a temporary edge parallel to v.

12. Path is A, D, E; distance is 40.

13.

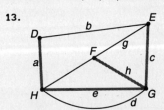

14. The weight is 75.

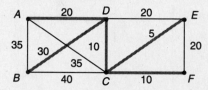

15.

	X	T	U	V	W
X	0	1	1	0	0
T	0	0	0	0	0
U	0	1	0	0	0
V	1	0	1	0	0
W	1	0	0	1	0

16.

$$\begin{array}{c} \\ H \\ I \\ J \\ K \\ L \\ M \end{array} \begin{array}{cccccc} H & I & J & K & L & M \\ \begin{bmatrix} 0 & 1 & 0 & 0 & 1 & 1 \\ 1 & 0 & 2 & 1 & 1 & 0 \\ 0 & 2 & 0 & 1 & 0 & 1 \\ 0 & 1 & 1 & 0 & 1 & 0 \\ 1 & 1 & 0 & 1 & 0 & 2 \\ 1 & 0 & 1 & 0 & 2 & 0 \end{bmatrix} \end{array}$$

17. Sample answer:

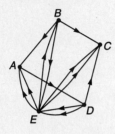

18. Sample answer:

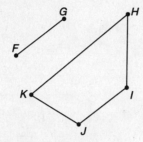

PAGE 906   APPLICATIONS AND PROBLEM SOLVING

19.

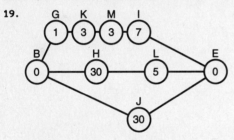

Critical path is B, H, L, E;
35 days.

Chapter 16 Test

PAGE 907

1. Simple graph; no loops or parallel edges.

2. 5

3. m, y, w, n, z, v

4. no

5. B, C, D

6. yes

7. circuit

8. Euler path: o, p, q, r, s, t, k, n, z, u, v, w, x, y, m, l

9. y, n, o, p

10. $\{A, C\}$, $\{C, D\}$, $\{D, B\}$, $\{D, I\}$, $\{I, F\}$, $\{F, E\}$, $\{I, G\}$, $\{I, J\}$, $\{J, K\}$, $\{I, H\}$

11.

	A	B	C	D	E	F	G	H	I	J	K
A	0	1	1	1	0	0	0	0	0	0	0
B	1	0	0	1	0	0	0	0	0	0	0
C	1	0	0	1	0	0	0	0	0	0	0
D	1	1	1	0	1	1	0	0	1	0	0
E	0	0	0	1	0	1	0	0	0	0	0
F	0	0	0	1	1	0	1	0	1	0	0
G	0	0	0	0	0	1	0	0	1	0	0
H	0	0	0	0	0	0	0	0	1	0	1
I	0	0	0	1	0	1	1	1	0	1	0
J	0	0	0	0	0	0	0	0	1	0	1
K	0	0	0	0	0	0	0	1	0	1	0

12. A multigraph may contain loops and/or parallel edges; a graph may not.

13.

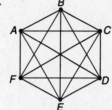

14. Sample answer:

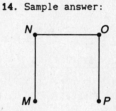

15. $6 - 1 = 5$ 16. true

17. A path may include any number of edges; an Euler path must include all of the edges.

18. at the vertices of odd degree

19. 3 cars

20. $39,000; Sarasota, Lakeland; Lakeland, Jacksonville; Lakeland, Daytona Beach; Daytona Beach, St. Augustine; St. Augustine, Bunnell

PAGE 907   BONUS

sum of the angles = $360°$

$45k = 360$

$k = 8$

Unit 4 Review

PAGES 908-909

1. $a_{20} = 3 + (20 - 1)(-2) = -35$

2. $S_9 = \dfrac{2 - 2(2)^9}{1 - 2} = 1022$

3. $\lim_{n \to \infty} \dfrac{4n + 1}{3n} = \dfrac{4}{3}$

4. $\lim_{n \to \infty} \dfrac{n^2 - 1}{n}$ does not exist

5. divergent, arithmetic series with $d = 3$

6. convergent, geometric series with $r = \dfrac{1}{3}$

Since $|r| < 1$, the series has a limit.

7. Using ratio test,

$$\lim_{n\to\infty} \frac{\dfrac{(n+1)^{n+1}}{n+1}}{\dfrac{n^n}{n}} = \lim_{n\to\infty} \frac{(n+1)n^n}{n(n+1)^{n+1}} = 0$$

convergent

8. $(3(2)-6) + (3(3)-6) + (3(4)-6) + (3(5)-6)$
$+ (3(6)-6) + (3(7)-6) + (3(8)-6)$
$= 0 + 3 + 6 + 9 + 12 + 15 + 18$
$= 63$

9. $7\left(\dfrac{1}{2}\right)^0 + 7\left(\dfrac{1}{2}\right)^1 + 7\left(\dfrac{1}{2}\right)^2 + 7\left(\dfrac{1}{2}\right)^3 + 7\left(\dfrac{1}{2}\right)^4 + 7\left(\dfrac{1}{2}\right)^5$

$+ 7\left(\dfrac{1}{2}\right)^6 = 7 + \dfrac{7}{2} + \dfrac{7}{4} + \dfrac{7}{8} + \dfrac{7}{16} + \dfrac{7}{32} + \dfrac{7}{64}$

$= \dfrac{889}{64}$

10. $\dfrac{9 \cdot 8 \cdot 7}{1 \cdot 2 \cdot 3} \cdot x^{9-3} = 84x^6$

11. $\dfrac{12 \cdot 11 \cdot 10 \cdot 9 \cdot 8 \cdot 7}{1 \cdot 2 \cdot 3 \cdot 4 \cdot 5 \cdot 6} x^{12-6} (2y)^6$

$= 59{,}136x^6y^6$

12. $f(1) = 4$
$f(4) = 13$
$f(13) = 40$

13. $f(-2) = -1$
$f(-1) = -4$
$f(-4) = 11$

14. $(-4, -4)$; repeller **15.** $(2, 2)$; attractor

16. $f(-i) = i$
$f(i) = 5i$
$f(5i) = 13i$

17. $f(3 - i) = 6 + i$
$f(6 + i) = 12 + 5i$
$f(12 + 5i) = 24 + 13i$

18. prisoner set **19.** escape set

20. $5! = 5 \cdot 4 \cdot 3 \cdot 2 \cdot 1 = 120$ patterns

21. $\dfrac{5!}{2!} = 5 \cdot 4 \cdot 3 = 60$ ways

22. $C(3, 2) \cdot C(5, 2) = \dfrac{3!}{(3-2)!2!} \cdot \dfrac{5!}{(5-2)!2!}$
$= 3 \cdot 10$
$= 30$ committees

23. odds $= \dfrac{\frac{2}{7}}{\frac{5}{7}} = \dfrac{2}{5}$ **24.** odds $= \dfrac{\frac{1}{14}}{\frac{13}{14}} = \dfrac{1}{13}$

25. $\dfrac{C(13, 3) \cdot C(39, 0)}{C(52, 3)} = \dfrac{286 \cdot 1}{22{,}100} = \dfrac{11}{850}$

26. $\dfrac{5}{36} \cdot \dfrac{1}{36} = \dfrac{5}{1296}$ **27.** $\dfrac{10}{36} = \dfrac{5}{18}$

28. $\dfrac{\frac{4}{52}}{\frac{12}{52}} = \dfrac{4}{12} = \dfrac{1}{3}$

29. 42, 65, 65, 66, 69, 70, 72, 76, 77, 77, 77, 80, 82, 82, 86, 89, 89, 91, 95, 99

30. range $= 99 - 42 = 57$

31. $\overline{X} = \dfrac{1}{20} \sum_{i=1}^{20} X_i$ **32.** $M_d = \dfrac{77 + 77}{2} = 77$

$= \dfrac{1}{20}(1549)$

$= 77.45$

33. mode $= 77$

34. $MD = \dfrac{1}{20} \sum_{i=1}^{20} |X_i - \overline{X}|$

$= \dfrac{1}{20}(35.45 + 12.45 + 12.45 + 11.45 + 8.45$
$+ 7.45 + 5.45 + 1.45 + 0.45 + 0.45 + 0.45$
$+ 2.55 + 4.55 + 4.55 + 8.55 + 11.55 + 11.55$
$+ 13.55 + 17.55 + 21.55)$
$= 9.595$

35. $Q_1 = \dfrac{69 + 70}{2}$ $\qquad Q_3 = \dfrac{86 + 89}{2}$
$= 69.5$ $\qquad\qquad = 87.5$

$Q_R = \dfrac{87.5 - 69.5}{2}$
$= 9$

36. $\sigma = \sqrt{\dfrac{1}{20} \sum_{i=1}^{20} (X_i - 77.45)^2}$

$= \sqrt{\dfrac{1}{20}[(42-77.45)^2+(65-77.45)^2+\ldots+(99-77.45)^2]}$

≈ 12.65

37. $\overline{x} + t\sigma = 65$ $\qquad\qquad \overline{x} + t\sigma = 75$
$70 + t(6) = 65$ $\qquad\qquad 70 + t(6) = 75$
$6t = -5$ $\qquad\qquad\qquad 6t = 5$
$t \approx 0.83333$ $\qquad\qquad t \approx 0.83333$

$P = 0.595$

38. $\overline{x} + 1.96\dfrac{\sigma}{\sqrt{n}} = 65.2 + 1.96\dfrac{(2.2)}{13}$
≈ 65.5

$\overline{x} - 1.96\dfrac{\sigma}{\sqrt{n}} = 65.2 - 1.96\dfrac{(2.2)}{13}$
≈ 64.9

64.9 inches to 65.5 inches

39.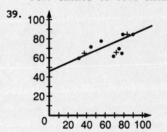

40.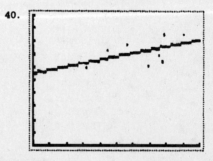

41. no **42.** 3

43. {A, D}, {A, C}, {A, B}

44. path **45.** cycle

46. trail

47. No; the degrees of vertices A and C are not even.

48. Paths A, B, I, E; A, F, I, E; and A, F, G, E have length 3.

Unit 5   An Introduction to Calculus

Chapter 17   Limits, Derivatives, and Integrals

17-1   Limits

PAGE 920   CHECKING FOR UNDERSTANDING

1. The limit of a function is the value of the function as the variable approaches a given value.

2. 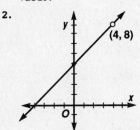   yes

3. Substitute s for x in $f(x)$. Then solve.

4. when the limit of one of the functions does not exist

5. $\lim\limits_{x\to0} x^2 = \lim\limits_{x\to0} (x \cdot x)$

   $= \lim\limits_{x\to0} x \cdot \lim\limits_{x\to0} x$

   $= 0 \cdot 0$

   $= 0$

6. $\lim\limits_{x\to3} (x - 1)^3 = \left[\lim\limits_{x\to3} (x - 1)\right]^3$

   $\lim\limits_{x\to3} (x - 1)^3 = \left[\lim\limits_{x\to3} (x - 1)\right] \cdot \left[\lim\limits_{x\to3} (x - 1)\right]$

   $\cdot \left[\lim\limits_{x\to3} (x - 1)\right]$

7. $\lim\limits_{x\to2} 6x = 6(2) = 12$

8. $\lim\limits_{x\to3} (x^2 + 4x - 5) = 3^2 + 4(3) - 5 = 16$

9. $\lim\limits_{x\to1} \dfrac{x - 2}{x + 2} = \dfrac{1 - 2}{1 + 2} = -\dfrac{1}{3}$

10. $\lim\limits_{x\to5} \sqrt{25 - x^2} = \sqrt{25 - 5^2} = 0$

11. $\lim\limits_{x\to3} \dfrac{x - 4}{x + 1} = \dfrac{3 - 4}{3 + 1} = -\dfrac{1}{4}$

12. $\lim\limits_{x\to-2} \dfrac{x^2 - 4}{x^2 + 4} = \dfrac{(-2)^2 - 4}{(-2)^2 + 4} = 0$

13. $\lim\limits_{x\to3} \dfrac{x^2 - x - 6}{x - 3} = \lim\limits_{x\to3} \dfrac{(x - 3)(x + 2)}{x - 3}$

   $= \lim\limits_{x\to3} (x + 2)$

   $= 3 + 2 \text{ or } 5$

14. $\lim\limits_{x\to0} \dfrac{2x^3}{x} = \lim\limits_{x\to0} 2x^2 = 2(0)^2 = 0$

15. $\lim\limits_{x\to-1} \dfrac{x^2 + 3x + 2}{x^2 + 4x + 3} = \lim\limits_{x\to-1} \dfrac{(x + 1)(x + 2)}{(x + 1)(x + 3)}$

   $= \lim\limits_{x\to-1} \dfrac{x + 2}{x + 3}$

   $= \dfrac{-1 + 2}{-1 + 3} \text{ or } \dfrac{1}{2}$

16. $\lim\limits_{x\to0} f[g(x)] = f[\lim\limits_{x\to0} (8x + 1)]$

   $= f(1)$

   $= 4(1) - 4 \text{ or } 0$

17. $\lim\limits_{x\to0} f[g(x)] = f[\lim\limits_{x\to0} (x^2 - 1)]$

   $= f(-1)$

   $= 5(-1) + 2 \text{ or } -3$

18. $\lim\limits_{x\to0} \dfrac{\sin^2 x}{x} = \left[\lim\limits_{x\to0} \sin x\right]\left[\lim\limits_{x\to0} \dfrac{\sin x}{x}\right]$

   $= 0 \cdot 1 \text{ or } 0$

19. $\lim\limits_{x\to0} \dfrac{\sin 3x}{5x} = \lim\limits_{x\to0} \left(\dfrac{3}{5} \cdot \dfrac{\sin 3x}{3x}\right)$

   $= \dfrac{3}{5} \cdot \lim\limits_{x\to0} \dfrac{\sin 3x}{3x}$

   $= \dfrac{3}{5} \cdot 1 \text{ or } \dfrac{3}{5}$

PAGES 920-922   EXERCISES

20. $\lim\limits_{x\to2} (x^2 - 4x + 1) = 2^2 - 4(2) + 1 = -3$

21. $\lim\limits_{x\to0} (4x + 1) = 4(0) + 1 = 1$

22. $\lim\limits_{x\to2} x^2 = 2^2 = 4$

23. $\lim\limits_{x\to1} \dfrac{x + 1}{x + 2} = \dfrac{1 + 1}{1 + 2} = \dfrac{2}{3}$

24. $\lim\limits_{x\to6} (7x - 22) = 7(6) - 22 = 20$

25. $\lim\limits_{x\to1} (x^2 + 4x + 3) = 1^2 + 4(1) + 3 = 8$

26. $\lim\limits_{n\to0} \left(5^n + \dfrac{1}{5^n}\right) = 5^0 + \dfrac{1}{5^0} = 2$

27. $\lim\limits_{x\to3} \dfrac{x^2 - 9}{x + 3} = \lim\limits_{x\to3} (x - 3) = 3 - 3 = 0$

28. $\lim\limits_{n\to3} \dfrac{n^2 - 9}{n - 3} = \lim\limits_{n\to3} (n + 3) = 3 + 3 = 6$

29. $\lim\limits_{x \to 2} \dfrac{x^2 - 4}{x^3 - 8} = \lim\limits_{x \to 2} \dfrac{x + 2}{x^2 + 2x + 4} = \dfrac{2 + 2}{2^2 + 2(2) + 4} = \dfrac{1}{3}$

30. $\lim\limits_{x \to 4} \dfrac{x - 4}{x^2 - 16} = \lim\limits_{x \to 4} \dfrac{1}{x + 4} = \dfrac{1}{4 + 4} = \dfrac{1}{8}$

31. $\lim\limits_{x \to -2} (x^4 - x^2 + x - 2) = (-2)^4 - (-2)^2 + (-2) - 2$
$$= 8$$

32. $\lim\limits_{x \to -2} \dfrac{x^3 - 8}{x - 2} = \lim\limits_{x \to -2} (x^2 + 2x + 4)$
$$= (-2)^2 + 2(-2) + 4 = 4$$

33. $\lim\limits_{x \to 2} \dfrac{x^2 - x - 2}{x^2 - 4} = \lim\limits_{x \to 2} \dfrac{x + 1}{x + 2} = \dfrac{2 + 1}{2 + 2} = \dfrac{3}{4}$

34. $\lim\limits_{x \to 0} \dfrac{(1 + x)^2 - 1}{x} = \lim\limits_{x \to 0} \dfrac{x^2 + 2x}{x}$
$$= \lim\limits_{x \to 0} (x + 2)$$
$$= 0 + 2 \text{ or } 2$$

35. $\lim\limits_{n \to 0} \dfrac{n^2}{n^4 + 1} = \dfrac{0^2}{0^4 + 1} = 0$

36. $\lim\limits_{x \to -1} \sqrt{x^2 - 1} = \sqrt{(-1)^2 - 1} = 0$

37. $\lim\limits_{x \to 1} \sqrt{\dfrac{2x + 1}{2x - 1}} = \sqrt{\dfrac{2(1) + 1}{2(1) - 1}} = \sqrt{3}$

38. $\lim\limits_{x \to 1} f[g(x)] = f[\lim\limits_{x \to 1} (x - 3)]$
$$= f(-2)$$
$$= 2(-2) + 1 \text{ or } -3$$

39. $\lim\limits_{x \to 1} f[g(x)] = f[\lim\limits_{x \to 1} (9x + 2)]$
$$= f(11)$$
$$= 7(11) - 2 \text{ or } 75$$

40. $\lim\limits_{x \to 1} f[g(x)] = f[\lim\limits_{x \to 1} (2x + 5)]$
$$= f(7)$$
$$= 3(7) - 4 \text{ or } 17$$

41. $\lim\limits_{x \to 1} f[g(x)] = f[\lim\limits_{x \to 1} (2x - 1)]$
$$= f(1)$$
$$= 1^2 + 3 \text{ or } 4$$

42. $\lim\limits_{x \to 0} \dfrac{\sin(-x)}{x} = -\lim\limits_{x \to 0} \dfrac{\sin(-x)}{-x} = -1$

43. $\lim\limits_{x \to 0} \dfrac{1 - \cos x}{x^2} = \lim\limits_{x \to 0} \dfrac{1 - \cos^2 x}{x^2(1 + \cos x)}$
$$= \lim\limits_{x \to 0} \dfrac{\sin^2 x}{x^2(1 + \cos x)}$$
$$= \lim\limits_{x \to 0} \left[\left(\dfrac{\sin x}{x} \right)^2 \cdot \left(\dfrac{1}{1 + \cos x} \right) \right]$$
$$= \left(\lim\limits_{x \to 0} \left(\dfrac{\sin x}{x} \right)^2 \right) \cdot \left(\lim\limits_{x \to 0} \dfrac{1}{1 + \cos x} \right)$$
$$= 1^2 \cdot \dfrac{1}{2} \text{ or } \dfrac{1}{2}$$

44. $\lim\limits_{x \to 0} \dfrac{\sin \sqrt[3]{x}}{\sqrt[3]{x}} = 1$

45. $\lim\limits_{x \to \frac{1}{2}} \dfrac{6x - 3}{x(1 - 2x)} = \lim\limits_{x \to \frac{1}{2}} \dfrac{3(2x - 1)}{x(1 - 2x)}$
$$= \lim\limits_{x \to \frac{1}{2}} \dfrac{-3}{x}$$
$$= -6$$

46. $\lim\limits_{x \to 0} \dfrac{\sin 6x}{x} = 6 \lim\limits_{x \to 0} \dfrac{\sin 6x}{6x}$
$$= 6 \cdot 1 \text{ or } 6$$

47. $\lim\limits_{x \to 4} \dfrac{\sqrt{x} - 2}{4 - x} = \lim\limits_{x \to 4} \dfrac{\sqrt{x} - 2}{(2 - \sqrt{x})(2 + \sqrt{x})}$
$$= \lim\limits_{x \to 4} \dfrac{-1}{2 + \sqrt{x}}$$
$$= \dfrac{-1}{2 + \sqrt{4}} \text{ or } -\dfrac{1}{4}$$

48. a. The function may have a limit of any number L such that $|L| < M$.

    b. If $f(x)$ is strictly increasing, then the limit of the function is M.

49. $S_n = \dfrac{a_1}{1 - r} = \dfrac{\frac{1}{2}}{1 - \frac{1}{2}} = 1$

50. $\lim\limits_{x \to \frac{2}{3}} \dfrac{x}{8 + 6x} = \dfrac{\frac{2}{3}}{8 + 6\left(\frac{2}{3}\right)} = \dfrac{1}{18}$

51. $\lim\limits_{t \to \infty} 30{,}000 + \dfrac{15{,}000}{(t + 3)^2}$
$$= \lim\limits_{t \to \infty} 30{,}000 + \lim\limits_{t \to \infty} \dfrac{15{,}000}{(t + 3)^2}$$
$$= 30{,}000 + 0 \text{ or } 30{,}000$$

52. $\begin{bmatrix} 5 & -3 \\ -1 & 0 \end{bmatrix} \cdot \begin{bmatrix} x \\ y \end{bmatrix} = \begin{bmatrix} 9 \\ -2 \end{bmatrix}$

    inverse: $\dfrac{1}{\begin{vmatrix} 5 & -3 \\ -1 & 0 \end{vmatrix}} \begin{bmatrix} 0 & 3 \\ 1 & 5 \end{bmatrix} = \dfrac{1}{-3} \begin{bmatrix} 0 & 3 \\ 1 & 5 \end{bmatrix}$

$$-\dfrac{1}{3} \begin{bmatrix} 0 & 3 \\ 1 & 5 \end{bmatrix} \begin{bmatrix} 5 & -3 \\ -1 & 0 \end{bmatrix} \begin{bmatrix} x \\ y \end{bmatrix} = -\dfrac{1}{3} \begin{bmatrix} 0 & 3 \\ 1 & 5 \end{bmatrix} \begin{bmatrix} 9 \\ -2 \end{bmatrix}$$
$$\begin{bmatrix} x \\ y \end{bmatrix} = -\dfrac{1}{3} \begin{bmatrix} -6 \\ -1 \end{bmatrix}$$
$$= \begin{bmatrix} 2 \\ \frac{1}{3} \end{bmatrix} \qquad \left(2, \dfrac{1}{3}\right)$$

53. $f(x) = 4x^2 - 8x + 9$
    $f'(x) = 8x - 8$

54. $r = \sqrt{2^2 + (-4)^2} = 2\sqrt{5}$

$\sin\theta = \dfrac{-4}{2\sqrt{5}} = \dfrac{-2}{\sqrt{5}} = \dfrac{-2\sqrt{5}}{5}$

$\cos\theta = \dfrac{2}{2\sqrt{5}} = \dfrac{1}{\sqrt{5}} = \dfrac{\sqrt{5}}{5}$

$\tan\theta = \dfrac{-4}{2} = -2$

$\sec\theta = \dfrac{2\sqrt{5}}{2} = \sqrt{5}$

$\csc\theta = \dfrac{2\sqrt{5}}{-4} = -\dfrac{\sqrt{5}}{2}$

$\cot\theta = \dfrac{2}{-4} = -\dfrac{1}{2}$

55. $d = \dfrac{6x + 2y - 1}{\sqrt{6^2 + 2^2}} = \dfrac{6(8) + 2(-3) - 1}{\sqrt{40}}$

$= \dfrac{41}{\sqrt{40}} \text{ or } \dfrac{41\sqrt{10}}{20}$

56. $\left(6^{\frac{2}{3}}\right)^3 = 6^2 = 36$

57. $e^{3.3} = 1 + 3.3 + \dfrac{3.3^2}{2!} + \dfrac{3.3^3}{3!} + \dfrac{3.3^4}{4!} \approx 20.68$

58. $C(10, 4) = \dfrac{10!}{(10 - 4)!\,4!} = \dfrac{10 \cdot 9 \cdot 8 \cdot 7}{4 \cdot 3 \cdot 2 \cdot 1}$

$= 210 \text{ groups}$

59. mean $= \dfrac{7.3 + 8.6 + 5.4 + 8.6 + 8.9 + 10.1 + 6.4}{7}$

$= 7.9$

median = 4th term = 8.6

mode = 8.6

60.

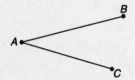

61. Triangle ABC is a 3-4-5 right triangle.

area of triangle $= \dfrac{1}{2}(6)(8) = 24$

area of rectangle $= \ell w$

$24 = \ell(3)$

$\ell = 8$

perimeter of rectangle $= 2(3) + 2(8) = 22$ inches

The best answer is C.

17-2 | **Derivatives and Differentiation Techniques**

PAGE 928   CHECKING FOR UNDERSTANDING

1. The limit of $\dfrac{f(a + h) - f(a)}{h}$ as h approaches 0 is the slope of the tangent through $(a, f(a))$.

2. $f'(x)$, $\dfrac{dy}{dx}$, $\displaystyle\lim_{\Delta x \to 0}\dfrac{\Delta y}{\Delta x}$

3. See students' work.

4. Answers may vary. A sample answer is given.

Use $\dfrac{d(uv)}{dx} = u\dfrac{dv}{dx} + v\dfrac{du}{dx}$.

$\dfrac{d(x^4(3x^5 - 2x^3))}{dx} = x^4(15x^4 - 6x^2)$

$+ (3x^5 - 2x^3)(4x^3)$

$= (15x^8 - 6x^6) + (12x^8 - 8x^6)$

$= 27x^8 - 14x^6$

Simplify the expression first.

$x^4(3x^5 - 2x^3) = 3x^9 - 2x^7$

$\dfrac{d(3x^9 - 2x^7)}{dx} = 3 \cdot 9x^{9-1} - 2 \cdot 7x^{7-1}$

$= 27x^8 - 14x^6$

5. the derivative of expression u with respect to x

6. $f(x) = 2x$

$f'(x) = 2 \cdot 1x^{1-1} = 2$

7. $f(x) = 7x - 3$

$f'(x) = 7 \cdot 1x^{1-1} - 0 = 7$

8. $f(x) = -x$

$f'(x) = -1 \cdot 1x^{1-1} = -1$

9. $f(x) = 2x^2$

$f'(x) = 2 \cdot 2x^{2-1} = 4x$

10. $f(x) = x^3$

$f'(x) = 3x^{3-1} = 3x^2$

11. $f(x) = 6x^2$

$f'(x) = 6 \cdot 2x^{2-1} = 12x$

12. $f(x) = (2x - 3)(x + 5)$

$f'(x) = (2x - 3)(1) + (2)(x + 5)$

$= 2x - 3 + 2x + 10$

$= 4x + 7$

13. $f(x) = (3x + 1)(2x^2 - 5x)$

$= (3x + 1)(4x - 5) + (3)(2x^2 - 5x)$

$= 12x^2 + 11x - 5 + 6x^2 - 15x$

$= 18x^2 - 26x - 5$

14. $f(x) = (x - 2x^2)^2$

$f'(x) = 2(x - 2x^2)(1 - 4x)$

$= 2x(1 - 2x)(1 - 4x)$

$= 2x(2x - 1)(4x - 1)$

15. $f(x) = x^2(x^2 + 1)^{-3}$

$f'(x) = x^2[-3(x^2 + 1)^{-4}(2x)] + (x^2 + 1)^{-3}(2x)$

$= x^2\left(\dfrac{-6x}{(x^2 + 1)^4}\right) + \dfrac{2x}{(x^2 + 1)^3}$

$= \dfrac{-6x^3}{(x^2 + 1)^4} + \dfrac{2x(x^2 + 1)}{(x^2 + 1)^4}$

$= \dfrac{-6x^3 + 2x^3 + 2x}{(x^2 + 1)^4}$

$= \dfrac{-2x(2x^2 - 1)}{(x^2 + 1)^4}$

16. $f(x) = \sqrt{4x^2 - 1} = (4x^2 - 1)^{\frac{1}{2}}$

$f'(x) = \dfrac{1}{2}(4x^2 - 1)^{-\frac{1}{2}}(8x)$

$= \dfrac{4x}{\sqrt{4x^2 - 1}}$

17. $f(x) = \dfrac{2x + 3}{4x - 1}$

$f'(x) = \dfrac{(4x - 1)(2) - (2x + 3)(4)}{(4x - 1)^2}$

$= \dfrac{8x - 2 - 8x - 12}{(4x - 1)^2}$

$= -\dfrac{14}{(4x - 1)^2}$

18. $f(x) = \dfrac{x^3 - 1}{x^4 + 1}$

$f'(x) = \dfrac{(x^4 + 1)(3x^2) - (x^3 - 1)(4x^3)}{(x^4 + 1)^2}$

$= \dfrac{3x^6 + 3x^2 - 4x^6 + 4x^3}{(x^4 + 1)^2}$

$= \dfrac{-x^6 + 4x^3 + 3x^2}{(x^4 + 1)^2}$

$= \dfrac{-x^2(x^4 - 4x - 3)}{(x^4 + 1)^2}$

19. $f(x) = -3x - \dfrac{6}{x + 2}$

$f'(x) = -3 - \dfrac{(x + 2)(0) - 6(1)}{(x + 2)^2}$

$= -3 + \dfrac{6}{(x + 2)^2}$

PAGES 928-930   EXERCISES

20. $f(x) = x$

$f'(x) = 1$

21. $f(x) = 6x - 4$

$f'(x) = 6$

22. $f(x) = -4x - 2$

$f'(x) = -4$

23. $f(x) = 5x^2 - x$

$f'(x) = 10x - 1$

24. $f(x) = x^4 - 2x^2$

$f'(x) = 4x^3 - 4x$

25. $f(x) = x^5 + 3$

$f'(x) = 5x^4$

26. $f(x) = x^{\frac{1}{2}}$

$f'(x) = \dfrac{1}{2}x^{-\frac{1}{2}} = \dfrac{1}{2\sqrt{x}}$

27. $f(x) = \sqrt[3]{x} = x^{\frac{1}{3}}$

$f'(x) = \dfrac{1}{3}x^{-\frac{2}{3}} = \dfrac{1}{3\sqrt[3]{x^2}}$

28. $f(x) = x^2(x^2 - 3)$

$f'(x) = x^2(2x) + (x^2 - 3)(2x)$

$= 2x^3 + 2x^3 - 6x$

$= 4x^3 - 6x$

29. $f(x) = (x^3 - 2x)(3x^2)$

$f'(x) = (x^3 - 2x)(6x) + 3x^2(3x^2 - 2)$

$= 6x^4 - 12x^2 + 9x^4 - 6x^2$

$= 15x^4 - 18x^2$

30. $f(x) = 8x^4(1 - 9x^2)$

$f'(x) = 8x^4(-18x) + (1 - 9x^2)(32x^3)$

$= -144x^5 + 32x^3 - 288x^5$

$= 32x^3 - 432x^5$

31. $f(x) = (x^2 + 4)^3$

$f'(x) = 3(x^2 + 4)^2(2x)$

$= 6x(x^2 + 4)^2$

32. $f(x) = (x^3 - 2x + 1)^4$

$f'(x) = 4(x^3 - 2x + 1)^3(3x^2 - 2)$

$= (12x^2 - 8)(x^3 - 2x + 1)^3$

33. $f(x) = \sqrt{x^2 - 1} = (x^2 - 1)^{\frac{1}{2}}$

$f'(x) = \dfrac{1}{2}(x^2 - 1)^{-\frac{1}{2}}(2x)$

$= \dfrac{x}{\sqrt{x^2 - 1}}$

34. $f(x) = x^2(x + 1)^{-1}$

$= x^2[-1(x + 1)^{-2}(1)] + (x + 1)^{-1}(2x)$

$= \dfrac{-x^2}{(x + 1)^2} + \dfrac{2x}{x + 1}$

$= \dfrac{-x^2}{(x + 1)^2} + \dfrac{2x(x + 1)}{(x + 1)^2}$

$= \dfrac{-x^2 + 2x^2 + 2x}{(x + 1)^2}$

$= \dfrac{x^2 + 2x}{(x + 1)^2}$

35. $f(x) = (x^2 - 4)^{-\frac{1}{2}}$

$f'(x) = -\frac{1}{2}(x^2 - 4)^{-\frac{3}{2}}(2x)$

$= \dfrac{-x}{\sqrt{(x^2 - 4)^3}}$

36. $f(x) = \dfrac{x + 1}{x^2 - 4}$

$f'(x) = \dfrac{(x^2 - 4)(1) - (x + 1)(2x)}{(x^2 - 4)^2}$

$= \dfrac{x^2 - 4 - 2x^2 - 2x}{(x^2 - 4)^2}$

$= \dfrac{-x^2 - 2x - 4}{(x^2 - 4)^2}$

37. $f(x) = \left(\dfrac{x + 1}{x - 1}\right)^2$

$f'(x) = 2\left(\dfrac{x + 1}{x - 1}\right)\left[\dfrac{(x - 1)(1) - (x + 1)(1)}{(x - 1)^2}\right]$

$= 2\left(\dfrac{x + 1}{x - 1}\right)\left[\dfrac{-2}{(x - 1)^2}\right]$

$= \dfrac{-4(x + 1)}{(x - 1)^3}$

38. $f(x) = x\sqrt{1 - x^3} = x(1 - x^3)^{\frac{1}{2}}$

$f'(x) = x\left[\dfrac{1}{2}(1 - x^3)^{-\frac{1}{2}}(-3x^2)\right] + (1 - x^3)^{\frac{1}{2}}(1)$

$= \dfrac{-3x^3}{2\sqrt{1 - x^3}} + \sqrt{1 - x^3}$

39. $f(x) = 2x^3 + \dfrac{2}{x^3}$

$f'(x) = 6x^2 + \dfrac{x^3(0) - 2(3x^2)}{(x^3)^2}$

$= 6x^2 + \dfrac{-6x^2}{x^6}$

$= 6x^2 - \dfrac{6}{x^4}$

40. $f(x) = \sqrt{2x} - \sqrt{2}x = (2x)^{\frac{1}{2}} - 2^{\frac{1}{2}}x$

$f'(x) = \dfrac{1}{2}(2x)^{-\frac{1}{2}}(2) - 2^{\frac{1}{2}}$

$= \dfrac{1}{(2x)^{\frac{1}{2}}} - 2^{\frac{1}{2}}$

$= \dfrac{1}{\sqrt{2x}} - \sqrt{2}$

41. $f(x) = \left(1 + \dfrac{1}{x}\right)\left(2 - \dfrac{1}{x}\right) = (1 - x^{-1})(2 - x^{-1})$

$f'(x) = (1 + x^{-1})(x^{-2}) + (2 - x^{-1})(-x^{-2})$

$= x^{-2} + x^{-3} - 2x^{-2} + x^{-3}$

$= -x^{-2} + 2x^{-3}$

$= -\dfrac{1}{x^2} + \dfrac{2}{x^3}$

42. $f(x) = 3x - \dfrac{\dfrac{2}{x} - \dfrac{3}{x - 1}}{x - 2}$

$= 3x - \dfrac{2}{x(x - 2)} - \dfrac{3}{(x - 1)(x - 2)}$

$= 3x - \dfrac{2}{x^2 - 2x} - \dfrac{3}{x^2 - 3x + 2}$

$f'(x) = 3 - \dfrac{(x^2 - 2x)(0) - 2(2x - 2)}{(x^2 - 2x)^2}$

$\qquad - \dfrac{(x^2 - 3x + 2)(0) - 3(2x - 3)}{(x^2 - 3x + 2)^2}$

$= 3 - \dfrac{-4x + 4}{x^2(x - 2)^2} - \dfrac{-6x + 9}{(x - 1)^2(x - 2)^2}$

$= 3 - \dfrac{(-4x + 4)(x - 1)^2 - (-6x + 9)(x^2)}{x^2(x - 1)^2(x - 2)^2}$

$= 3 - \dfrac{-4x^3 + 12x^2 - 12x + 4 + 6x^3 - 9x^2}{[x(x - 1)(x - 2)]^2}$

$= 3 - \dfrac{2x^3 + 3x^2 - 12x + 4}{[x(x - 1)(x - 2)]^2}$

43. Use $\dfrac{d\left(\dfrac{u}{v}\right)}{dx} = \dfrac{v\dfrac{du}{dx} - u\dfrac{dv}{dx}}{v^2}$ for $u = 1$. Then $\dfrac{du}{dx} = 0$.

$\dfrac{d\left(\dfrac{u}{v}\right)}{dx} = \dfrac{v\dfrac{du}{dx} - u\dfrac{dv}{dx}}{v^2}$

$= \dfrac{v(0) - (1)\dfrac{dv}{dx}}{v^2}$

$= \dfrac{-\dfrac{dv}{dx}}{v^2}$

44. a. $C(t) = 32.07 - 0.79t + 0.02142t^2 - 0.0001t^3$

$C'(t) = -0.79 + 0.04284t - 0.0003t^2$

b. $C'(70) = -0.79 + 0.04284(70) - 0.0003(70)^2$

$= 0.7388$

c. $0.6 = -0.79 + 0.04284t - 0.0003t^2$

$0 = -0.0003t^2 + 0.04284t - 1.39$

$t = \dfrac{-0.04284 \pm \sqrt{(0.04284)^2 - 4(-0.0003)(-1.39)}}{2(-0.0003)}$

$t \approx \dfrac{-0.04284 \pm 0.01293}{-0.0006}$

$t \approx 50$ or $t \approx 93$

45. a. $h(t) = 256 + 96t - 16t^2$

$h'(t) = 96 - 32t$

b. $h'(t) = 96 - 32(2) = 32$ ft/s

c. initial velocity = 96 ft/s

after 2 seconds, velocity = 32 ft/s

decreasing

d. $h(t) = 256 + 96t - 16t^2$

$0 = -16t^2 + 96t + 256$

$t = \dfrac{-96 \pm \sqrt{96^2 - 4(-16)(256)}}{2(-16)}$

$= 8$ s

$h'(t) = 96 - 32t$

$= 96 - 32(8)$

$= -160$ ft/s

46. a. $C(I) = \dfrac{5\left(2\sqrt{I^3} + 3\right)}{I + 10} = \dfrac{10I^{\frac{3}{2}} + 15}{I + 10}$

$\dfrac{dC}{dI} = \dfrac{(I + 10) \cdot 10\left(\frac{3}{2}\right)I^{\frac{1}{2}} - \left(10I^{\frac{3}{2}} + 15\right)(1)}{(I + 10)^2}$

$= \dfrac{15\sqrt{I}(I + 10) - \left(10\sqrt{I^3} + 15\right)}{(I + 10)^2}$

b. $\dfrac{dC}{dI} = \dfrac{15\sqrt{100}(100 + 10) - \left(10\sqrt{100^3} + 15\right)}{(100 + 10)^2}$

$= \dfrac{16,500 - 10,015}{12,100}$

≈ 0.536

c. $\dfrac{dC}{dI} = \dfrac{15\sqrt{150}(150 + 10) - \left(10\sqrt{150^3} + 15\right)}{(150 + 10)^2}$

$\approx \dfrac{29,394 - 18,386}{25,600}$

≈ 0.43

$1 - \dfrac{dC}{dI} \approx 1 - 0.43 \approx 0.57$

47. See students' work.

48. $d_1 = \sqrt{(8 - 0)^2 + (4 - 3)^2}$ $\qquad m_1 = \dfrac{4 - 3}{8 - 0}$

$= \sqrt{65}$ $\qquad\qquad\qquad\qquad = \dfrac{1}{8}$

$d_2 = \sqrt{(10 - 2)^2 + (-4 - (-5))^2}$ $\quad m_2 = \dfrac{-4 - (-5)}{10 - 2}$

$= \sqrt{65}$ $\qquad\qquad\qquad\qquad = \dfrac{1}{8}$

$d_3 = \sqrt{(10 - 8)^2 + (-4 - 4)^2}$ $\qquad m_3 = \dfrac{-4 - 4}{10 - 8}$

$= \sqrt{68}$ $\qquad\qquad\qquad\qquad = -4$

$d_4 = \sqrt{(2 - 0)^2 + (-5 - 3)^2}$ $\qquad m_4 = \dfrac{-5 - 3}{2 - 0}$

$= \sqrt{68}$ $\qquad\qquad\qquad\qquad = -4$

Since $d_1 = d_2$, $d_3 = d_4$, $m_1 = m_2$, and $m_3 = m_4$,

the figure is a parallelogram.

49. p: ± 1, ± 2

q: ± 1, ± 2, ± 4, ± 8

$\dfrac{p}{q}$: ± 1, $\pm\dfrac{1}{2}$, $\pm\dfrac{1}{4}$, $\pm\dfrac{1}{8}$, ± 2

50. $s = \dfrac{1}{2}(2.1 + 3.2 + 4.4) = 4.85$

$K = \sqrt{4.85(4.85 - 2.1)(4.85 - 3.2)(4.85 - 4.4)}$

≈ 3.1 units^2

51. phase shift $= -\dfrac{c}{k}$ $\qquad$ period $= \dfrac{2\pi}{k}$

$0 = -\dfrac{c}{k}$ $\qquad\qquad 4 = \dfrac{2\pi}{k}$

$c = 0$ $\qquad\qquad\quad k = \dfrac{\pi}{2}$

$y = A \sin (kt + c)$

$= 12 \sin \left(\dfrac{\pi}{2}t + 0\right)$

$= 12 \sin \dfrac{\pi t}{2}$

Sample answer: $y = 12 \sin \dfrac{\pi t}{2}$

52. $r = \dfrac{16}{4} = 4$, $\theta = \dfrac{\pi}{8} - \dfrac{\pi}{4} = -\dfrac{\pi}{8}$ or $\dfrac{15\pi}{8}$

$\dfrac{16\left(\cos \frac{\pi}{8} + i \sin \frac{\pi}{8}\right)}{4\left(\cos \frac{\pi}{4} + i \sin \frac{\pi}{4}\right)}$

$= 4\left(\cos \dfrac{15\pi}{8} + i \sin \dfrac{15\pi}{8}\right)$

53. $a_6 = a_1 r^{6 - 1}$

$a_6 = 9\left(-\dfrac{1}{3}\right)^5$

$= -\dfrac{1}{27}$

54. $\dfrac{5!}{r!(5 - r)!}p^{5 - r}q^r = \dfrac{5!}{5!(5 - 5)!}\left(\dfrac{1}{4}\right)^{5 - 5}\left(\dfrac{1}{4}\right)^5$

$= 1(1)\left(\dfrac{1}{4}\right)^5$

$= \dfrac{1}{1024}$

55. $\lim\limits_{x \to -1} \sqrt{x^2 - 1} = \sqrt{(-1)^2 - 1} = 0$

56. $2^n = 8$

$n = 3$

So, $3^{n + 2} = 3^{3 + 2} = 243$.

Case Study Follow-Up

PAGE 930

1. Generally well; In years 0, 2, 3, and 5, it produces a value within 0.1% of the actual value. In years 1 and 4, however, it is off by as much as 1.5%.

2. $f'(x) = -0.84x + 2.1$

3. $f'(2) = -0.84(2) + 2.1 = 0.42$

4. See students' work.

1. The upper sum is the sum of the areas of the rectangles above the curve and the lower sum is the sum of the areas of the rectangles below the curve. The sums give the interval in which the area of the region must fall.

2. The interval from 0 to 1 was divided into n rectangles, so each rectangle would be $\frac{1}{n}$ units wide.

3. $A = \lim\limits_{n \to \infty} \sum\limits_{i=1}^{n} \left(\frac{i}{n}\right)^2 \left(\frac{1}{n}\right)$

$= \lim\limits_{n \to \infty} \frac{1}{n^3}(1^2 + 2^2 + 3^2 + \ldots + n^2)$

$= \lim\limits_{n \to \infty} \frac{1}{n^3}\left(\frac{n(n+1)(2n+1)}{6}\right)$

$= \lim\limits_{n \to \infty} \frac{2n^3 + 3n^2 + n}{6n^3}$

$= \lim\limits_{n \to \infty} \left(\frac{1}{3} + \frac{1}{2n} + \frac{1}{6n^2}\right)$

$= \frac{1}{3}$

4. $A = \lim\limits_{n \to \infty} \sum\limits_{i=1}^{n} \left(\frac{4i}{n}\right)^2 \left(\frac{4}{n}\right)$

$= \lim\limits_{n \to \infty} \frac{64}{n^3}(1^2 + 2^2 + 3^2 + \ldots + n^2)$

$= \lim\limits_{n \to \infty} \frac{64}{n^3}\left(\frac{n(n+1)(2n+1)}{6}\right)$

$= \lim\limits_{n \to \infty} \frac{32}{3}\left(\frac{2n^3 + 3n^2 + n}{n^3}\right)$

$= \lim\limits_{n \to \infty} \frac{32}{3}\left(2 + \frac{3}{n} + \frac{1}{n^2}\right)$

$= \frac{64}{3}$

5. $A = \lim\limits_{n \to \infty} \sum\limits_{i=1}^{n} \left(\frac{i}{n}\right)\left(\frac{1}{n}\right)$

$= \lim\limits_{n \to \infty} \frac{1}{n^2}(1 + 2 + 3 + \ldots + n)$

$= \lim\limits_{n \to \infty} \frac{1}{n^2}\left(\frac{n(n+1)}{2}\right)$

$= \lim\limits_{n \to \infty} \frac{1}{2}\left(\frac{n^2 + n}{n^2}\right)$

$= \lim\limits_{n \to \infty} \frac{1}{2}\left(1 + \frac{1}{n}\right)$

$= \frac{1}{2}$

6. $A = \lim\limits_{n \to \infty} \sum\limits_{i=1}^{n} \left(\frac{4i}{n}\right)^2 \left(\frac{4}{n}\right) - \lim\limits_{n \to \infty} \sum\limits_{i=1}^{n} \left(\frac{i}{n}\right)^2 \left(\frac{1}{n}\right)$

$= \lim\limits_{n \to \infty} \frac{64}{n^3}\left(\frac{n(n+1)(2n+1)}{6}\right)$

$\quad - \lim\limits_{n \to \infty} \frac{1}{n^3}\left(\frac{n(n+1)(2n+1)}{6}\right)$

$= \lim\limits_{n \to \infty} \frac{32}{3}\left(\frac{2n^3 + 3n^2 + n}{n^3}\right) - \lim\limits_{n \to \infty} \frac{1}{6}\left(\frac{2n^3 + 3n^2 + n}{n^3}\right)$

$= \lim\limits_{n \to \infty} \frac{32}{3}\left(2 + \frac{3}{n} + \frac{1}{n^2}\right) - \lim\limits_{n \to \infty} \frac{1}{6}\left(2 + \frac{3}{n} + \frac{1}{n^2}\right)$

$= \frac{64}{3} - \frac{1}{3}$

$= \frac{63}{3}$ or 21

7. $A = \lim\limits_{n \to \infty} \sum\limits_{i=1}^{n} \left(\frac{5i}{n}\right)\left(\frac{5}{n}\right) - \lim\limits_{n \to \infty} \sum\limits_{i=1}^{n} \left(\frac{2i}{n}\right)\left(\frac{2}{n}\right)$

$= \lim\limits_{n \to \infty} \frac{25}{n^2}\left(\frac{n(n+1)}{2}\right) - \lim\limits_{n \to \infty} \frac{4}{n^2}\left(\frac{n(n+1)}{2}\right)$

$= \lim\limits_{n \to \infty} \frac{25}{2}\left(\frac{n^2 + n}{n^2}\right) - \lim\limits_{n \to \infty} 2\left(\frac{n^2 + n}{n^2}\right)$

$= \lim\limits_{n \to \infty} \frac{25}{2}\left(1 + \frac{1}{n}\right) - \lim\limits_{n \to \infty} 2\left(1 + \frac{1}{n}\right)$

$= \frac{25}{2} - 2$

$= \frac{21}{2}$

8. $A = \lim\limits_{n \to \infty} \sum\limits_{i=1}^{n} \left(\frac{2i}{n}\right)^3 \left(\frac{2}{n}\right)$

$= \lim\limits_{n \to \infty} \frac{16}{n^4}(1^3 + 2^3 + 3^3 + \ldots + n^3)$

$= \lim\limits_{n \to \infty} \frac{16}{n^4}\left(\frac{n^2(n+1)^2}{4}\right)$

$= \lim\limits_{n \to \infty} 4\left(\frac{(n+1)^2}{n^2}\right)$

$= \lim\limits_{n \to \infty} 4\left(\frac{n^2 + 2n + 1}{n^2}\right)$

$= \lim\limits_{n \to \infty} 4\left(1 + \frac{2}{n} + \frac{1}{n^2}\right)$

$= 4$

9. $A = \lim_{n\to\infty} \sum_{i=1}^{n} \left(\frac{2i}{n}\right)^2 \left(\frac{2}{n}\right)$

$= \lim_{n\to\infty} \frac{8}{n^3}\left(\frac{n(n+1)(2n+1)}{6}\right)$

$= \lim_{n\to\infty} \frac{4}{3}\left(\frac{2n^3 + 3n^2 + n}{n^3}\right)$

$= \lim_{n\to\infty} \frac{4}{3}\left(2 + \frac{3}{n} + \frac{1}{n^2}\right)$

$= \frac{8}{3}$

10. $A = \lim_{n\to\infty} \sum_{i=1}^{n} \left(\frac{10i}{n}\right)\left(\frac{10}{n}\right)$

$= \lim_{n\to\infty} \frac{100}{n^2}\left(\frac{n(n+1)}{2}\right)$

$= \lim_{n\to\infty} 50\left(\frac{n^2 + n}{n^2}\right)$

$= \lim_{n\to\infty} 50\left(1 + \frac{1}{n}\right)$

$= 50$

11. $A = \lim_{n\to\infty} \sum_{i=1}^{n} \left(\frac{i}{n}\right)^5 \left(\frac{1}{n}\right)$

$= \lim_{n\to\infty} \frac{1}{n^6}\left(\frac{2n^6 + 6n^5 + 5n^4 - n^2}{12}\right)$

$= \lim_{n\to\infty} \frac{1}{12}\left(2 + \frac{6}{n} + \frac{5}{n^2} - \frac{1}{n^4}\right)$

$= \frac{1}{6}$

12. $A = \lim_{n\to\infty} \sum_{i=1}^{n} \left(\frac{ai}{n}\right)^2 \left(\frac{a}{n}\right)$

$= \lim_{n\to\infty} \frac{a^3}{n^3}\left(\frac{n(n+1)(2n+1)}{6}\right)$

$= \lim_{n\to\infty} \frac{a^3}{6}\left(\frac{2n^3 + 3n^2 + n}{n^3}\right)$

$= \lim_{n\to\infty} \frac{a^3}{6}\left(2 + \frac{3}{n} + \frac{1}{n^2}\right)$

$= \frac{2a^3}{6}$ or $\frac{a^3}{3}$

13. $A = \lim_{n\to\infty} \sum_{i=1}^{n} \left(\frac{7i}{n}\right)^4\left(\frac{7}{n}\right) - \lim_{n\to\infty} \sum_{i=1}^{n} \left(\frac{4i}{n}\right)^4\left(\frac{4}{n}\right)$

$= \lim_{n\to\infty} \frac{16,807}{n^5}\left(\frac{6n^5 + 15n^4 + 10n^3 - n}{30}\right)$

$\quad - \lim_{n\to\infty} \frac{1024}{n^5}\left(\frac{6n^5 + 15n^4 + 10n^3 - n}{30}\right)$

$= \lim_{n\to\infty} \frac{16,807}{30}\left(\frac{6n^5 + 15n^4 + 10n^3 - n}{n^5}\right)$

$\quad - \lim_{n\to\infty} \frac{1024}{30}\left(\frac{6n^5 + 15n^4 + 10n^3 - n}{n^5}\right)$

$= \lim_{n\to\infty} \frac{16,807}{30}\left(6 + \frac{15}{n} + \frac{10}{n^2} - \frac{1}{n^4}\right)$

$\quad - \lim_{n\to\infty} \frac{1024}{30}\left(6 + \frac{15}{n} + \frac{10}{n^2} - \frac{1}{n^4}\right)$

$= \frac{16,807}{5} - \frac{1024}{5}$

$= \frac{15,783}{5}$ or $3156\frac{3}{5}$

14. $A = \lim_{n\to\infty} \sum_{i=1}^{n} \left(\frac{ai}{n}\right)^3\left(\frac{a}{n}\right)$

$= \lim_{n\to\infty} \frac{a^4}{n^4}\left(\frac{n^2(n+1)^2}{4}\right)$

$= \lim_{n\to\infty} \frac{a^4}{4}\left(\frac{(n+1)^2}{n^2}\right)$

$= \lim_{n\to\infty} \frac{a^4}{4}\left(\frac{n^2 + 2n + 1}{n^2}\right)$

$= \lim_{n\to\infty} \frac{a^4}{4}\left(1 + \frac{2}{n} + \frac{1}{n^2}\right)$

$= \frac{a^4}{4}$

15. $A = \lim_{n\to\infty} \sum_{i=1}^{n} \left(\frac{bi}{n}\right)^2\left(\frac{b}{n}\right) - \lim_{n\to\infty} \sum_{i=1}^{n} \left(\frac{ai}{n}\right)^2\left(\frac{a}{n}\right)$

$= \frac{b^3}{3} - \frac{a^3}{3}$

$= \frac{b^3 - a^3}{3}$

16. $A = \lim_{n\to\infty} \sum_{i=1}^{n} \left(\frac{2i}{n}\right)^2\left(\frac{2}{n}\right) + \lim_{n\to\infty} \sum_{i=1}^{n} \left(\frac{3i}{n}\right)^2\left(\frac{3}{n}\right)$

$= \lim_{n\to\infty} \frac{8}{n^3}\left(\frac{n(n+1)(2n+1)}{6}\right)$

$\quad + \lim_{n\to\infty} \frac{27}{n^3}\left(\frac{n(n+1)(2n+1)}{6}\right)$

$= \lim_{n\to\infty} \frac{4}{3}\left(\frac{2n^3 + 3n^2 + n}{n^3}\right) + \lim_{n\to\infty} \frac{9}{2}\left(\frac{2n^3 + 3n^2 + n}{n^3}\right)$

$= \lim_{n\to\infty} \frac{4}{3}\left(2 + \frac{3}{n} + \frac{1}{n^2}\right) + \lim_{n\to\infty} \frac{9}{2}\left(2 + \frac{3}{n} + \frac{1}{n^2}\right)$

$= \frac{8}{3} + 9$ or $\frac{35}{3}$

17. $A = \lim\limits_{n\to\infty} \sum\limits_{i=1}^{n} \left(\frac{4i}{n}\right)\left(\frac{4}{n}\right) + \lim\limits_{n\to\infty} \sum\limits_{i=1}^{n} \left(\frac{2i}{n}\right)\left(\frac{2}{n}\right)$

$= \lim\limits_{n\to\infty} \frac{16}{n^2}\left(\frac{n(n+1)}{2}\right) + \lim\limits_{n\to\infty} \frac{4}{n^2}\left(\frac{n(n+1)}{2}\right)$

$= \lim\limits_{n\to\infty} 8\left(\frac{n^2+n}{n^2}\right) + \lim\limits_{n\to\infty} 2\left(\frac{n^2+n}{n^2}\right)$

$= \lim\limits_{n\to\infty} 8\left(1 + \frac{1}{n}\right) + \lim\limits_{n\to\infty} 2\left(1 + \frac{1}{n}\right)$

$= 8 + 2$ or 10

18. $A = \lim\limits_{n\to\infty} \sum\limits_{i=1}^{n} \left(\frac{i}{n}\right)\left(\frac{1}{n}\right) - \lim\limits_{n\to\infty} \sum\limits_{i=1}^{n} \left(\frac{i}{n}\right)^2\left(\frac{1}{n}\right)$

$= \frac{1}{2} - \frac{1}{3}$

$= \frac{1}{6}$

19. $A = \lim\limits_{n\to\infty} \sum\limits_{i=1}^{n} \left(\frac{i}{n}\right)\left(\frac{1}{n}\right) - \lim\limits_{n\to\infty} \sum\limits_{i=1}^{n} \left(\frac{i}{n}\right)^3\left(\frac{1}{n}\right)$

$= \frac{1}{2} - \frac{1}{4}$

$= \frac{1}{4}$

20. $A = \lim\limits_{n\to\infty} \sum\limits_{i=1}^{n} \left(\frac{bi}{n}\right)\left(\frac{b}{n}\right) - \lim\limits_{n\to\infty} \sum\limits_{i=1}^{n} \left(\frac{ai}{n}\right)\left(\frac{a}{n}\right)$

$= \lim\limits_{n\to\infty} \frac{b^2}{n^2}\left(\frac{n(n+1)}{2}\right) - \lim\limits_{n\to\infty} \frac{a^2}{n^2}\left(\frac{n(n+1)}{2}\right)$

$= \lim\limits_{n\to\infty} \frac{b^2}{2}\left(\frac{n^2+n}{n^2}\right) - \lim\limits_{n\to\infty} \frac{a^2}{2}\left(\frac{n^2+n}{n^2}\right)$

$= \frac{b^2}{2} - \frac{a^2}{2}$ or $\frac{b^2 - a^2}{2}$

21. $A = \lim\limits_{n\to\infty} \sum\limits_{i=1}^{n} \left(\frac{bi}{n}\right)^3\left(\frac{b}{n}\right) - \lim\limits_{n\to\infty} \sum\limits_{i=1}^{n} \left(\frac{ai}{n}\right)^3\left(\frac{a}{n}\right)$

$= \frac{b^4 - a^4}{4}$

22. a. ≈ 21.33 units^2 **b.** 44.4 units^2

c. 5.60 units^2

23. a constant function

24. $A = \lim\limits_{n\to\infty} \sum\limits_{i=1}^{n} f\left(\frac{30i}{n}\right)\left(\frac{30}{n}\right) - \lim\limits_{n\to\infty} \sum\limits_{i=1}^{n} f\left(\frac{20i}{n}\right)\left(\frac{20}{n}\right)$

$= \lim\limits_{n\to\infty} \sum\limits_{i=1}^{n} \left(3 + 0.1\left(\frac{30i}{n}\right)\right)\left(\frac{30}{n}\right)$

$- \lim\limits_{n\to\infty} \sum\limits_{i=1}^{n} \left(3 + 0.1\left(\frac{20i}{n}\right)\right)\left(\frac{20}{n}\right)$

$= \lim\limits_{n\to\infty} \sum\limits_{i=1}^{n} \left(\frac{90}{n} + \frac{90i}{n^2}\right) - \lim\limits_{n\to\infty} \sum\limits_{i=1}^{n} \left(\frac{60}{n} + \frac{40i}{n^2}\right)$

$= \lim\limits_{n\to\infty} \left[\frac{90}{n} + \frac{90}{n^2}\left(\frac{n(n+1)}{2}\right)\right]$

$- \lim\limits_{n\to\infty} \left[\frac{60}{n} + \frac{40}{n^2}\left(\frac{n(n+1)}{2}\right)\right]$

$= \lim\limits_{n\to\infty} \left(\frac{90}{n} + 45 + \frac{45}{n}\right) - \lim\limits_{n\to\infty} \left(\frac{60}{n} + 20 + \frac{20}{n}\right)$

$= (0 + 45 + 0) - (0 + 20 + 0)$

$= \$25$

25. $A = \lim\limits_{n\to\infty} \sum\limits_{i=1}^{n} 0.5\left(\frac{6i}{n}\right)^2\left(\frac{6}{n}\right)$

$= \lim\limits_{n\to\infty} \frac{108}{n^3}\left(\frac{n(n+1)(2n+1)}{6}\right)$

$= \lim\limits_{n\to\infty} 18\left(\frac{2n^3 + 3n^2 + n}{n^3}\right)$

$= \lim\limits_{n\to\infty} 18\left(2 + \frac{3}{n} + \frac{1}{n^2}\right)$

$= 36$ feet

26. $(-3, 9) \cdot (2, 1) = -3 \cdot 2 + 9 \cdot 1 = 3$

no

27. general form of a parabola with a horizontal

axis: $y^2 + Dx + Ey + F = 0$

$0^2 + D(0) + E(0) + F = 0 \qquad \rightarrow \qquad F = 0$

$(-1)^2 + D(2) + E(-1) + F = 0 \rightarrow \quad 1 + 2D - E + F = 0$

$(-4)^2 + D(4) + E(-4) + F = 0 \rightarrow 16 + 4D - 4E + F = 0$

$\underline{\begin{array}{l} 1 + 2D - E = 0 \longrightarrow \quad -2 - 4D + 2E = 0 \\ 16 + 4D - 4E = 0 \longrightarrow \quad 16 + 4D - 4E = 0 \end{array}}$

$\qquad\qquad\qquad\qquad\qquad 14 \qquad\quad - 2E = 0$

$\qquad\qquad\qquad\qquad\qquad\qquad\qquad E = 7$

$1 + 2D - E = 0$

$1 + 2D - 7 = 0$

$\qquad D = 3$

The equation is $y^2 + 3x + 7y = 0$.

28. $|z_0| = \sqrt{(0.3)^2 + (0.4)^2} = 0.5$

Since $|z_0| < 1$, the iterates for the function

$f(z) = z^2$ will approach 0. Therefore,

$0.3 + 0.4i$ is in the prisoner set.

29. $f(x) = \left(1 + \dfrac{1}{x}\right)\left(2 - \dfrac{1}{x}\right) = (1 + x^{-1})(2 - x^{-1})$

$f'(x) = (1 + x^{-1})(x^{-2}) + (2 - x^{-1})(-x^{-2})$

$\quad\quad = x^{-2} + x^{-3} - 2x^{-2} + x^{-3}$

$\quad\quad = -\dfrac{1}{x^2} + \dfrac{2}{x^3}$

30. area of square $= s^2$

height of triangle: $s^2 + h^2 = (2s)^2$

$\quad\quad\quad\quad\quad\quad\quad h^2 = 4s^2 - s^2$

$\quad\quad\quad\quad\quad\quad\quad h = \sqrt{3}s$

area of triangle $= \frac{1}{2}(2s)(\sqrt{3}s)$

$\quad\quad\quad\quad\quad\quad = \sqrt{3}s^2$

Since $\sqrt{3}s^2 > s^2$, quantity B is greater. B

Mid-Chapter Review

PAGE 937

1. $\lim\limits_{x \to 5} (x^2 - 4x + 1) = 5^2 - 4(5) + 1 = 6$

2. $\lim\limits_{n \to 3} \dfrac{n^2 - 3n + 2}{n - 1} = \dfrac{3^2 - 3(3) + 2}{3 - 1} = 1$

3. $\lim\limits_{x \to -3} \dfrac{x^2 - 9}{x + 3} = \lim\limits_{x \to -3} (x - 3) = -6$

4. $\lim\limits_{n \to \infty} \dfrac{5n^2 - 1}{n^2} = \lim\limits_{n \to \infty} \left(5 - \dfrac{1}{n^2}\right) = 5$

5. $\lim\limits_{x \to \infty} \dfrac{(x - 4)(x + 1)}{x^2} = \lim\limits_{x \to \infty} \dfrac{x^2 - 3x - 4}{x^2}$

$\quad\quad\quad\quad\quad\quad = \lim\limits_{x \to \infty} 1 - \dfrac{3}{x} - \dfrac{4}{x^2}$

$\quad\quad\quad\quad\quad\quad = 1$

6. $\lim\limits_{x \to 0} \dfrac{(x + 2)^2 - 4}{x} = \lim\limits_{x \to 0} \dfrac{x^2 + 4x}{x} = \lim\limits_{x \to 0} (x + 4) = 4$

7. $\lim\limits_{x \to \frac{1}{2}} \dfrac{2x^2 + 5x - 3}{x^2 - x} = \dfrac{2\left(\frac{1}{2}\right)^2 + 5\left(\frac{1}{2}\right) - 3}{\left(\frac{1}{2}\right)^2 - \frac{1}{2}} = \dfrac{0}{-\frac{1}{4}} = 0$

8. $\lim\limits_{n \to 3} \sqrt{\dfrac{2n + 3}{3n - 5}} = \sqrt{\dfrac{2(3) + 3}{3(3) - 5}} = \sqrt{\dfrac{9}{4}} = \dfrac{3}{2}$

9. $\lim\limits_{x \to 1} \dfrac{x^2}{\sqrt[3]{(x^2 - 2)^2}} = \dfrac{1^2}{\sqrt[3]{(1^2 - 2)^2}} = \dfrac{1}{1} = 1$

10. $f(x) = 4x^2$

$f'(x) = 4 \cdot 2x^{2 - 1} = 8x$

11. $f(x) = (x - 1)^2$

$f'(x) = 2(x - 1)(1) = 2x - 2$

12. $f(x) = \dfrac{5}{1 - 3x}$

$f'(x) = \dfrac{(1 - 3x)(0) - 5(-3)}{(1 - 3x)^2} = \dfrac{15}{(1 - 3x)^2}$

13. $f(x) = -\dfrac{4}{x^9} = -4x^{-9}$

$f'(x) = -4(-9)x^{-10} = \dfrac{36}{x^{10}}$

14. $f(x) = \dfrac{x^2 - 5x + 4}{x^2 + x - 20} = \dfrac{x - 1}{x + 5}$

$f'(x) = \dfrac{(x + 5)(1) - (x - 1)(1)}{(x + 5)^2} = \dfrac{6}{(x + 5)^2}$

15. $f(x) = \dfrac{\sqrt{x^2 - 1}}{x} = \dfrac{(x^2 - 1)^{\frac{1}{2}}}{x}$

$f'(x) = \dfrac{x\left(\frac{1}{2}\right)(x^2 - 1)^{-\frac{1}{2}}(2x) - (x^2 - 1)^{\frac{1}{2}}(1)}{x^2}$

$\quad\quad = \dfrac{x^2(x^2 - 1)^{-\frac{1}{2}} - (x^2 - 1)^{\frac{1}{2}}}{x^2}$

$\quad\quad = (x^2 - 1)^{-\frac{1}{2}} - \dfrac{(x^2 - 1)^{\frac{1}{2}}}{x^2}$

$\quad\quad = \dfrac{1}{\sqrt{x^2 - 1}} - \dfrac{\sqrt{x^2 - 1}}{x^2}$

$\quad\quad = \dfrac{x^2 - (x^2 - 1)}{x^2\sqrt{x^2 - 1}}$

$\quad\quad = \dfrac{1}{x^2\sqrt{x^2 - 1}}$

16. $A = \lim\limits_{n \to \infty} \sum\limits_{i=1}^{n} 0.3\left(\dfrac{6i}{n}\right)^2\left(\dfrac{6}{n}\right)$

$\quad = \lim\limits_{n \to \infty} \sum\limits_{i=1}^{n} \dfrac{64.8i^2}{n^3}$

$\quad = \lim\limits_{n \to \infty} \dfrac{64.8}{n^3}\left(\dfrac{n(n + 1)(2n + 1)}{6}\right)$

$\quad = \lim\limits_{n \to \infty} 10.8\left(\dfrac{2n^3 + 3n^2 + n}{n^3}\right)$

$\quad = \lim\limits_{n \to \infty} 10.8\left(2 + \dfrac{3}{n} + \dfrac{1}{n^2}\right)$

$\quad = 21.6$ feet

Technology: Riemann Sums

PAGE 938   EXERCISES

1. 8.9688, 7.7188; 8.585, 8.085; 8.4588, 8.2088
   They are closer approximations of the area.

2. lower, yes   3. lower, upper

1. It is the area under the curve $f(x)$ between $x = a$ and $x = b$.

2. Integration is finding the antiderivative of a function.

3. Since $F'(x) = 5$ when $F(x) = 5x + C$, then

$$\int 5dx = 5x + C.$$

4. $\int 2xdx = 2 \int xdx = 2 \cdot \frac{x^2}{2} + C = x^2 + C$

5. $\int 3x^2dx = 3 \int x^2dx = 3 \cdot \frac{x^3}{3} + C = x^3 + C$

6. $\int (2x - 3)dx = \int 2xdx - \int 3dx$

$$= 2 \int xdx - \int 3dx$$

$$= 2 \cdot \frac{x^2}{2} + C_1 - 3x + C_2$$

$$= x^2 - 3x + C$$

7. $\int (5x^4 + 2x)dx = \int 5x^4dx + \int 2xdx$

$$= 5 \int x^4dx + 2 \int xdx$$

$$= 5 \cdot \frac{x^5}{5} + C_1 + 2 \cdot \frac{x^2}{2} + C_2$$

$$= x^5 + x^2 + C$$

8. $\int \sqrt{2x} \, dx = \sqrt{2} \int x^{\frac{1}{2}}dx$

$$= \sqrt{2} \cdot \frac{x^{\frac{3}{2}}}{\frac{3}{2}} + C$$

$$= \frac{2\sqrt{2}}{3} \cdot \sqrt{x^3} + C$$

$$= \frac{2\sqrt{2x^3}}{3} + C$$

9. $\int 10dx = 10x + C$

10. $\int (2x - 12)dx = \int 2xdx - \int 12dx$

$$= x^2 + C_1 - 12x + C_2$$

$$= x^2 - 12x + C$$

11. $\int (3x^2 - 8x^3 + 5x^4)dx$

$$= \int 3x^2dx - \int 8x^3dx + \int 5x^4dx$$

$$= 3 \cdot \frac{x^3}{3} + C_1 - 8 \cdot \frac{x^4}{4} + C_2 + 5 \cdot \frac{x^5}{5} + C_3$$

$$= x^3 - 2x^4 + x^5 + C$$

12. $\int (x^4 - 5)dx = \int x^4dx - \int 5dx$

$$= \frac{x^5}{5} + C_1 - 5x + C_2$$

$$= \frac{x^5}{5} - 5x + C$$

13. $\int 5x^3dx = 5 \cdot \frac{x^4}{4} + C = \frac{5}{4}x^4 + C$

14. $\int (\pi x + \sqrt{x})dx = \int \pi xdx + \int \sqrt{x} \, dx$

$$= \pi \cdot \frac{x^2}{2} + C_1 + \frac{x^{\frac{3}{2}}}{\frac{3}{2}} + C_2$$

$$= \frac{\pi x^2}{2} + \frac{2\sqrt{x^3}}{3} + C$$

15. Let $u = x + 5$. Then $du = 1dx$.

$$\int (x + 5)^{20} = \int u^{20}du$$

$$= \frac{u^{21}}{21} + C$$

$$= \frac{(x + 5)^{21}}{21} + C$$

16. Let $u = x + 1$. Then $du = 1dx$.

$$\int \sqrt{1 + x} \, dx = \int u^{\frac{1}{2}}du$$

$$= \frac{2}{3}u^{\frac{3}{2}} + C$$

$$= \frac{2\sqrt{(1 + x)^3}}{3} + C$$

17. $\int (-2x + 3)dx = \int -2xdx + \int 3dx$

$$= -2\frac{x^2}{2} + C_1 + 3x + C_2$$

$$= -x^2 + 3x + C$$

18. Let $u = 1 - x^2$. Then $du = -2x$.

$$\int \frac{-2x}{\sqrt{1 - x^2}}dx = \int u^{-\frac{1}{2}}du$$

$$= 2u^{\frac{1}{2}} + C$$

$$= 2\sqrt{1 - x^2} + C$$

19. Let $u = x - 1$. Then $du = 1dx$.

$$\int \frac{1}{x - 1}dx = \int u^{-1}du$$

$$= \ln |u| + C$$

$$= \ln |x - 1| + C$$

20. Let $u = x^2 + 2x + 2$. Then $du = (2x + 2)du = 2(x + 1)du$.

$$\int \frac{x + 1}{\sqrt[3]{x^2 + 2x + 2}}dx = \int u^{-\frac{1}{3}} \cdot \frac{1}{2}du$$

$$= \frac{1}{2} \cdot \frac{3}{2} \cdot u^{\frac{2}{3}} + C$$

$$= \frac{3}{4}\sqrt[3]{(x^2 + 2x + 2)^2} + C$$

21. $F(x) = 8 \cdot \frac{x^5}{5} + C = \frac{8}{5}x^5 + C$

22. $f(x) = 4x^{\frac{1}{3}}$

$$F(x) = 4 \cdot \frac{x^{\frac{4}{3}}}{\frac{4}{3}} + C = 3x^{\frac{4}{3}} + C = 3\sqrt[3]{x^4} + C$$

23. $f(x) = x^5 - \frac{1}{x^4} = x^5 - x^{-4}$

$$F(x) = \frac{x^6}{6} - \frac{x^{-3}}{-3} + C = \frac{x^6}{6} + \frac{1}{3x^3} + C$$

24. $f(x) = \frac{2}{x^3} = 2x^{-3}$

$$F(x) = 2 \cdot \frac{x^{-2}}{-2} + C = -\frac{1}{x^2} + C$$

25. $f(x) = \frac{2}{\sqrt{x}} = 2x^{-\frac{1}{2}}$

$$F(x) = 2 \cdot \frac{x^{\frac{1}{2}}}{\frac{1}{2}} + C = 4x^{\frac{1}{2}} + C = 4\sqrt{x} + C$$

26. Let $u = 1 - 4x$. Then $du = -4dx$.

$$F(x) = \int u^{-1} \cdot -\frac{1}{2}du$$

$$= -\frac{1}{2}\ln|u| + C$$

$$= -\frac{1}{2}\ln|1 - 4x| + C$$

27. Let $u = \frac{x + 1}{x}$. Then $du = \frac{x(1) - (x + 1)(1)}{x^2}$

$$= -\frac{1}{x^2}.$$

$$\int \frac{1}{x^2}\left(\frac{x + 1}{x}\right)dx = \int u^{\frac{1}{3}} \cdot (-du)$$

$$= -\frac{u^{\frac{4}{3}}}{\frac{4}{3}} + C$$

$$= -\frac{3}{4}u^{\frac{4}{3}} + C$$

$$= -\frac{3}{4}\left(\frac{x + 1}{x}\right)^{\frac{4}{3}} + C$$

28. a. $v(t) = 45$

$$s(t) = \int 45dt = 45t + C$$

b. $104 = 45(2) + C$

$C = 14$

$s(t) = 45t + 14$

c. $v(t) = -32t + 100$

$$s(t) = -32 \cdot \frac{t^2}{2} + 100t + C = -16t^2 + 100t + C$$

At 50 feet above ground:

$$50 = -16(0)^2 + 100(0) + C$$

$C = 50$

The equation is $s(t) = -16t^2 + 100t + 50$.

29. $m(x) = 4 - 0.02x$

$$r(x) = \int (4 - 0.02x)dx$$

$$= 4x - 0.02 \cdot \frac{x^2}{2} + C$$

$$= 4x - 0.01x^2 + C$$

$$-300 = 4(0) - 0.01(0)^2 + C$$

$C = -300$

The equation is $r(x) = 4x - 0.01x^2 - 300$.

30. a. $D'(x) = -3.2x + 20$

$$D(x) = \int (-3.2x + 20)dx$$

$$D(x) = -3.2 \cdot \frac{x^2}{2} + 20x + C$$

$$D(x) = -1.6x^2 + 20x + C$$

b. $65 = -1.6(0.85)^2 + 20(0.85) + C$

$C = 49.156$

$$D(x) = -1.6x^2 + 20x + 49.156$$

$$= -1.6(0.95)^2 + 20(0.95) + 49.156$$

$$\approx 67 \text{ loaves}$$

31. Let x = number of gallons of Autumn Wheat.

Let y = number of gallons of Harvest Brown.

$x \geq 0, y \geq 0$

$4x + 1y \leq 32$

$1x + 6y \leq 54$

possible solutions: $(0, 9)$, $(6, 8)$, $(8, 0)$

$f(x, y) = x + y$

$f(0, 0) = 0 + 0 = 0$

$f(8, 0) = 8 + 0 = 8$

$f(6, 8) = 6 + 8 = 14 \leftarrow$ max

$f(0, 9) = 0 + 9 = 9$

The maximum number of gallons is 14.

32.

$$1 + \sin 2x \stackrel{?}{=} (\sin x + \cos x)^2$$

$$1 + 2 \sin x \cos x \stackrel{?}{=} \sin^2 x + 2 \sin x \cos x$$
$$+ \cos^2 x$$

$$1 + 2 \sin x \cos x \stackrel{?}{=} (\sin^2 x + \cos^2 x)$$
$$+ 2 \sin x \cos x$$

$$1 + 2 \sin x \cos x = 1 + 2 \sin x \cos x$$

33. $7^{\log_7 2x} = 2x$

34. $f(8) = 0.5(8) - 1 = 3$

$f(3) = 0.5(3) - 1 = 0.5$

$f(0.5) = 0.5(0.5) - 1 = -0.75$

35. (vertices)(degrees) = 2(edges)

$$n \times 2 = 2 \times 15$$
$$n = 15$$

36. $A = \lim\limits_{n \to \infty} \sum\limits_{i=1}^{n} \left(\frac{7i}{n}\right)^2 \left(\frac{7}{n}\right) - \lim\limits_{n \to \infty} \sum\limits_{i=1}^{n} \left(\frac{2i}{n}\right)^2 \left(\frac{2}{n}\right)$

$= \lim\limits_{n \to \infty} \frac{343}{n^3}\left(\frac{n(n + 1)(2n + 1)}{6}\right)$

$\quad - \lim\limits_{n \to \infty} \frac{8}{n^3}\left(\frac{n(n + 1)(2n + 1)}{6}\right)$

$= \lim\limits_{n \to \infty} \frac{343}{6}\left(\frac{2n^3 + 3n^2 + n}{n^3}\right)$

$\quad - \lim\limits_{n \to \infty} \frac{4}{3}\left(\frac{2n^3 + 3n^2 + n}{n^3}\right)$

$= \lim\limits_{n \to \infty} \frac{343}{6}\left(2 + \frac{3}{n} + \frac{1}{n^2}\right) - \lim\limits_{n \to \infty} \frac{4}{3}\left(2 + \frac{3}{n} + \frac{1}{n^2}\right)$

$= \frac{343}{3} - \frac{8}{3}$

$= 111\frac{2}{3}$ units^2

37. $\frac{a}{a + c} \cdot b + \frac{c}{a + c} \cdot d + 10 = \frac{ab + cd}{a + c} + 10$

The best answer is A.

17-5 | The Fundamental Theorem of Calculus

PAGES 948-949   CHECKING FOR UNDERSTANDING

1. They are inverse operations.

2. Suppose you are evaluating the definite integral of $f(x)$ from $x = a$ to $x = b$. The value is $F(a) - F(b)$. If a constant is added to $F(a)$ and $F(b)$, it would have a net effect of zero.

3. since area can never be negative

4. $\int_1^3 5dx = 5x \Big|_1^3 = 5(3) - 5(1) = 10$ units^2

5. $\int_0^3 4dx = 4x \Big|_0^3 = 4(3) - 4(0) = 12$ units^2

6. $\int_0^5 xdx = \frac{x^2}{2}\Big|_0^5 = \frac{5^2}{2} - \frac{0^2}{2} = 12\frac{1}{2}$ units^2

7. $\int_0^2 x^2dx = \frac{x^3}{3}\Big|_0^2 = \frac{2^3}{3} - \frac{0^3}{3} = \frac{8}{3}$ units^2

8. $\int_0^9 \sqrt{x}dx = \frac{2}{3}x^{\frac{3}{2}}\Big|_0^9 = \frac{2}{3}(9)^{\frac{3}{2}} - \frac{2}{3}(0)^{\frac{3}{2}} = \frac{2}{3} \cdot 27$

$$= 18 \text{ units}^2$$

9. $\int_0^2 x^3dx = \frac{x^4}{4}\Big|_0^2 = \frac{2^4}{4} - \frac{0^4}{4} = 4$ units^2

10. $\int_0^1 (2x + 3)dx = x^2 + 3x \Big|_0^1$

$$= (1^2 + 3(1)) - (0^2 + 3(0))$$
$$= 4$$

11. $\int_0^1 (3x^2 + 6x + 1)dx = x^3 + 3x^2 + x \Big|_0^1$

$$= (1^3 + 3(1)^2 + 1)$$
$$- (0^3 + 3(0)^2 + 0)$$
$$= 5$$

12. $\int_0^3 \left(\frac{1}{2}x - 4\right)dx = \frac{x^2}{4} - 4x \Big|_0^3$

$$= \left(\frac{3^2}{4} - 4(3)\right) - \left(\frac{0^2}{4} - 4(0)\right)$$
$$= \frac{9}{4} - 12$$
$$= -\frac{39}{4}$$

13. $\int_{-4}^{-1} (5x + 14)dx = \frac{5x^2}{2} + 14x \Big|_{-4}^{-1}$

$$= \left(\frac{5(-1)^2}{2} + 14(-1)\right)$$
$$- \left(\frac{5(-4)^2}{2} + 14(-4)\right)$$
$$= \frac{5}{2} - 14 - 40 + 56$$
$$= \frac{9}{2}$$

14.

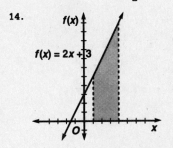

$f(x) = 2x + 3$

$\int_1^4 (2x + 3)dx = x^2 + 3x \Big|_1^4$

$$= (4^2 + 3(4)) - (1^2 + 3(1))$$
$$= 24 \text{ units}^2$$

15.

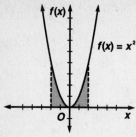

$$\int_{-2}^{2} x^2 dx = \frac{x^3}{3}\Big|_{-2}^{2}$$

$$= \frac{2^3}{3} - \frac{(-2)^3}{3}$$

$$= \frac{16}{3} \text{ units}^2$$

PAGES 949-951   EXERCISES

16. $\int_{-1}^{3} (3 - x)dx = 3x - \frac{x^2}{2}\Big|_{-1}^{3}$

$$= \left(3(3) - \frac{3^2}{2}\right) - \left(3(-1) - \frac{(-1)^2}{2}\right)$$

$$= 9 - \frac{9}{2} + 3 + \frac{1}{2}$$

$$= 8 \text{ units}^2$$

17. $\int_{1}^{4} (x + 3)dx = \frac{x^2}{2} + 3x\Big|_{1}^{4}$

$$= \left(\frac{4^2}{2} + 3(4)\right) - \left(\frac{1^2}{2} + 3(1)\right)$$

$$= 8 + 12 - \frac{1}{2} - 3$$

$$= 16\frac{1}{2} \text{ units}^2$$

18. $\left|\int_{0}^{6} \left(\frac{x}{2} - 3\right)dx\right| = \left|\frac{1}{4}x^2 - 3x\Big|_{0}^{6}\right|$

$$= \left|\left(\frac{1}{4}(6)^2 - 3(6)\right) - \left(\frac{1}{4}(0)^2 - 3(0)\right)\right|$$

$$= |9 - 18|$$

$$= 9 \text{ units}^2$$

19. $\int_{0}^{2} (2x - x^2)dx = x^2 - \frac{x^3}{3}\Big|_{0}^{2}$

$$= \left(2^2 - \frac{2^3}{3}\right) - \left(0^2 - \frac{0^3}{3}\right)$$

$$= 4 - \frac{8}{3}$$

$$= 1\frac{1}{3} \text{ units}^2$$

20. $\left|\int_{-2}^{2} (x^2 - 4)dx\right| = \left|\frac{x^3}{3} - 4x\Big|_{-2}^{2}\right|$

$$= \left|\left(\frac{2^3}{3} - 4(2)\right) - \left(\frac{(-2)^3}{3} - 4(-2)\right)\right|$$

$$= \left|\frac{8}{3} - 8 + \frac{8}{3} - 8\right|$$

$$= 10\frac{2}{3} \text{ units}^2$$

21. $\int_{1}^{3} \left(\frac{1}{2}x^2\right)dx = \frac{x^3}{6}\Big|_{1}^{3}$

$$= \frac{3^3}{6} - \frac{1^3}{6}$$

$$= \frac{26}{6} \text{ or } 4\frac{1}{3} \text{ units}^2$$

22. $\int_{0}^{3} x dx = \frac{x^2}{2}\Big|_{0}^{3}$

$$= \frac{3^2}{2} - \frac{0^2}{2}$$

$$= \frac{9}{2}$$

23. $\int_{-1}^{1} (x + 1)^2 dx = \int_{-1}^{1} (x^2 + 2x + 1)dx$

$$= \frac{x^3}{3} + x^2 + x\Big|_{-1}^{1}$$

$$= \left(\frac{1^3}{3} + 1^2 + 1\right)$$

$$- \left(\frac{(-1)^3}{3} + (-1)^2 + (-1)\right)$$

$$= \frac{7}{3} + \frac{1}{3}$$

$$= \frac{8}{3} \text{ or } 2\frac{2}{3}$$

24. $\int_{-1}^{1} (4x^3 + 3x^2)dx = x^4 + x^3\Big|_{-1}^{1}$

$$= (1^4 + 1^3) - ((-1)^4 + (-1)^3)$$

$$= 2 - 0$$

$$= 2$$

25. $\int_{1}^{4} \left(x^2 + \frac{2}{x^2}\right)dx = \frac{x^3}{3} + 2\frac{x^{-1}}{-1}\Big|_{1}^{4}$

$$= \frac{x^3}{3} - \frac{2}{x}\Big|_{1}^{4}$$

$$= \left(\frac{4^3}{3} - \frac{2}{4}\right) - \left(\frac{1^3}{3} - \frac{2}{1}\right)$$

$$= \frac{64}{3} - \frac{1}{2} - \frac{1}{3} + 2$$

$$= 22\frac{1}{2}$$

26. $\displaystyle\int_{-1}^{1} 12x(x+1)(x-1)\,dx = \int_{-1}^{1} (12x^3 - 12x)\,dx$

$$= 3x^4 - 6x^2 \Big|_{-1}^{1}$$

$$= (3(1)^4 - 6(1)^2)$$

$$\quad - (3(-1)^4 - 6(-1)^2)$$

$$= -3 - (-3)$$

$$= 0$$

27. $\displaystyle\int_{4}^{5} (x^2 + 6x - 7)\,dx = \frac{x^3}{3} + 3x^2 - 7x \Big|_{4}^{5}$

$$= \left(\frac{5^3}{3} + 3(5)^2 - 7(5)\right)$$

$$\quad - \left(\frac{4^3}{3} + 3(4)^2 - 7(4)\right)$$

$$= \frac{125}{3} + 75 - 35 - \frac{64}{3} - 48 + 28$$

$$= 40\frac{1}{3}$$

28. $\displaystyle\int_{0}^{2} (x - 4x^2)\,dx = \frac{x^2}{2} - \frac{4x^3}{3} \Big|_{0}^{2}$

$$= \left(\frac{2^2}{2} - \frac{4(2)^3}{3}\right) - \left(\frac{0^2}{2} - \frac{4(0)^3}{3}\right)$$

$$= 2 - \frac{32}{3}$$

$$= -8\frac{2}{3}$$

29. $\displaystyle\int_{-1}^{0} (1 - x^2)\,dx = x - \frac{x^3}{3} \Big|_{-1}^{0}$

$$= \left(0 - \frac{0^3}{3}\right) - \left((-1) - \frac{(-1)^3}{3}\right)$$

$$= 1 - \frac{1}{3}$$

$$= \frac{2}{3}$$

30. $\displaystyle\int_{1}^{4} (3x^2 - 6x)\,dx = x^3 - 3x^2 \Big|_{1}^{4}$

$$= (4^3 - 3(4)^2) - (1^3 - 3(1)^2)$$

$$= 64 - 48 - 1 + 3$$

$$= 18$$

31. $\displaystyle\int_{-2}^{3} (x+2)(x-3)\,dx = \int_{-2}^{3} (x^2 - x - 6)\,dx$

$$= \frac{x^3}{3} - \frac{x^2}{2} - 6x \Big|_{-2}^{3}$$

$$= \left(\frac{3^3}{3} - \frac{3^2}{2} - 6(3)\right)$$

$$\quad - \left(\frac{(-2)^3}{3} - \frac{(-2)^2}{2} - 6(-2)\right)$$

$$= 9 - \frac{9}{2} - 18 + \frac{8}{3} + 2 - 12$$

$$= -20\frac{5}{6}$$

32.

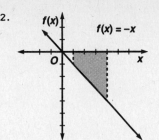

$$\left|\int_{1}^{4} -x\,dx\right| = \left|-\frac{x^2}{2} \Big|_{1}^{4}\right|$$

$$= \left|-\frac{4^2}{2} - \left(-\frac{1^2}{2}\right)\right|$$

$$= 7\frac{1}{2} \text{ units}^2$$

33.

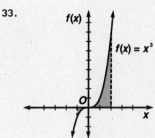

$$\int_{-1}^{2} x^3\,dx = \int_{0}^{2} x^3\,dx + \left|\int_{-1}^{0} x^3\,dx\right|$$

$$= \frac{x^4}{4} \Big|_{0}^{2} + \left|\frac{x^4}{4} \Big|_{-1}^{0}\right|$$

$$= \left(\frac{2^4}{4} - \frac{0^4}{4}\right) + \left(\frac{(-1)^4}{4} - \frac{0^4}{4}\right)$$

$$= 4 + \frac{1}{4}$$

$$= 4\frac{1}{4} \text{ units}^2$$

34.

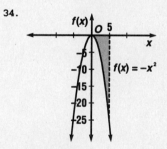

$$\left|\int_{0}^{5} -x^2\,dx\right| = \left|-\frac{x^3}{3} \Big|_{0}^{5}\right|$$

$$= \left|-\frac{5^3}{3} - \left(-\frac{0^3}{3}\right)\right|$$

$$= \frac{125}{3} \text{ units}^2$$

35.

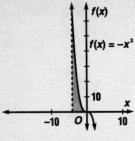

$$\int_{-4}^{0} -x^3 \, dx = -\frac{x^4}{4}\Big|_{-4}^{0}$$

$$= -\frac{0^4}{4} - \left(-\frac{(-4)^4}{4}\right)$$

$$= 64 \text{ units}^2$$

36.

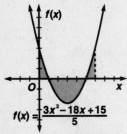

$$\int_{0}^{6} \frac{3x^2 - 18x + 15}{5} dx$$

$$= \int_{0}^{1} \left(\frac{3x^2}{5} - \frac{18x}{5} + 3\right)dx + \left|\int_{1}^{5} \left(\frac{3x^2}{5} - \frac{18x}{5} + 3\right)dx\right|$$

$$+ \int_{5}^{6} \left(\frac{3x^2}{5} - \frac{18x}{5} + 3\right)dx$$

$$= \frac{x^3}{5} - \frac{9x^2}{5} + 3x\Big|_{0}^{1} + \left|\frac{x^3}{5} - \frac{9x^2}{5} + 3x\Big|_{1}^{5}\right|$$

$$+ \frac{x^3}{5} - \frac{9x^2}{5} + 3x\Big|_{5}^{6}$$

$$= \left(\frac{1}{5} - \frac{9}{5} + 3\right) + \left|(25 - 45 + 15) - \left(\frac{1}{5} - \frac{9}{5} + 3\right)\right|$$

$$+ \left(\frac{216}{5} - \frac{324}{5} + 18\right) - (25 - 45 + 15)$$

$$= \frac{7}{5} + \left|-5 - \frac{7}{5}\right| + \left(-\frac{18}{5}\right) - (-5)$$

$$= 9\frac{1}{5} \text{ units}^2$$

37.

$$\int_{0}^{3} (9 - 3x^2) dx$$

$$= \int_{0}^{\sqrt{3}} (9 - 3x^2)dx + \left|\int_{\sqrt{3}}^{3} (9 - 3x^2)dx\right|$$

$$= 9x - x^3\Big|_{0}^{\sqrt{3}} + \left|9x - x^3\Big|_{\sqrt{3}}^{3}\right|$$

$$= (9\sqrt{3} - 3\sqrt{3}) + \left|(27 - 27) - (9\sqrt{3} - 3\sqrt{3})\right|$$

$$= 6\sqrt{3} + 6\sqrt{3}$$

$$\approx 20.8 \text{ units}^2$$

38. a. $\int_{a}^{b} x^3 dx = \frac{1}{4}x^4\Big|_{a}^{b}$

$$= \frac{1}{4}b^4 - \frac{1}{4}a^4$$

$$= \frac{1}{4}(b^4 - a^4)$$

b. $\int_{a}^{b} x^n dx = \frac{1}{n+1}(b^{n+1} - a^{n+1})$

39. a. $\ell(x) = 12{,}000\sqrt{100 - x}$

$$\left|\int_{18}^{21} 12{,}000(100 - x)^{\frac{1}{2}}\right|$$

$$= \left|12{,}000\left(-\frac{2}{3}\right)(100 - x)^{\frac{3}{2}}\Big|_{18}^{21}\right|$$

$$= \left|8000(100 - x)^{\frac{3}{2}}\Big|_{18}^{21}\right|$$

$$= \left|8000(100 - 21)^{\frac{3}{2}} - 8000(100 - 18)^{\frac{3}{2}}\right|$$

$$\approx \left|5{,}617{,}339 - 5{,}940{,}333\right|$$

$$\approx 322{,}994 \text{ people}$$

b. $\left|\int_{21}^{23} 12{,}000(100 - x)^{\frac{1}{2}}\right|$

$$= \left|8000(100 - x)^{\frac{3}{2}}\Big|_{21}^{23}\right|$$

$$= \left|8000(100 - 23)^{\frac{3}{2}} - 8000(100 - 21)^{\frac{3}{2}}\right|$$

$$= \left|5{,}405{,}378 - 5{,}617{,}339\right|$$

$$= 211{,}961 \text{ people}$$

40. Let $u = r^2 - x^2$. Then $du = -2x$.

$$V = \int_0^r \frac{k}{\ell}x(r^2 - x^2)dx$$

$$= \int_0^r \frac{k}{\ell}u\left(-\frac{1}{2}du\right)$$

$$= -\frac{k}{2\ell}\int_0^r u\,du$$

$$= -\frac{k}{2\ell}\cdot\frac{u^2}{2}\Big|_0^r$$

$$= -\frac{k}{4\ell}(r^2 - x^2)^2\Big|_0^r$$

$$= \left(-\frac{k}{4\ell}(r^2 - r^2)^2\right) - \left(-\frac{k}{4\ell}(r^2 - 0^2)^2\right)$$

$$= \frac{kr^4}{4\ell}$$

41. $W = (156,250\pi)\int_0^{100}(100 - y)dy$

$$= (156,250\pi)\left(100y - \frac{y^2}{2}\right)\Big|_0^{100}$$

$$= 156,250\pi\left[\left(100(100) - \frac{100^2}{2}\right) - \left(100(0) - \frac{0^2}{2}\right)\right]$$

$$= 156,250\pi(5000)$$

$$= 781,250,000\pi$$

$$\approx 2,454,369,261 \text{ foot-pounds}$$

42. $x = 7 - y^2$

$y^2 = 7 - x$

$y = \pm\sqrt{7 - x}$

43. $(x + 3)(x - 0.5)(x - 6)(x - 2) = 0$

$(x^2 + 2.5x - 1.5)(x^2 - 8x + 12) = 0$

$x^4 - 8x^3 + 12x^2 + 2.5x^3 - 20x^2 +$

$\qquad\qquad 30x - 1.5x^2 + 12x - 18 = 0$

$x^4 - 5.5x^3 - 9.5x^2 + 42x - 18 = 0$

$2x^4 - 11x^3 - 19x^2 + 84x - 36 = 0$

44. $\quad x = -5t - 1 \qquad\qquad y = 2t + 10$

$\quad 5t = -x - 1 \qquad\qquad 2t = y - 10$

$\quad t = \dfrac{-x - 1}{5} \qquad\qquad t = \dfrac{y - 10}{2}$

$$\frac{-x - 1}{5} = \frac{y - 10}{2}$$

$$-2x - 2 = 5y - 50$$

$$5y = -2x + 48$$

$$y = -\frac{2}{5}x + \frac{48}{5}$$

45. $\qquad 2x^2 - y^2 - 16x + 4y + 24 = 0$

$\quad 2(x^2 - 8x) - (y^2 - 4y) + 24 = 0$

$2(x^2 - 8x + 16) - (y^2 - 4y + 4) = -24 + 32 - 4$

$\qquad\qquad 2(x - 4)^2 - (y - 2)^2 = 4$

$$\frac{(x - 4)^2}{2} - \frac{(y - 2)^2}{4} = 1$$

center: $(4, 2)$

foci: $c^2 = a^2 + b^2$

$\qquad c^2 = 2 + 4$

$\qquad c = \sqrt{6}$

$\qquad (4 \pm \sqrt{6},\ 2)$

vertices: $a = \sqrt{2}$

$\qquad\qquad (4 \pm \sqrt{2},\ 2)$

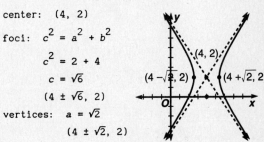

asymptotes: $y - k = \pm\dfrac{b}{a}(x - h)$

$\qquad\qquad\quad y - 2 = \pm\sqrt{2}(x - 4)$

46. $(5x - 1)^3 = (5x)^3 + 3(5x)^2(-1)$

$\qquad\qquad + \dfrac{3(3 - 1)}{1\cdot 2}(5x)^1(-1)^2$

$\qquad\qquad + \dfrac{3(3 - 1)(3 - 2)}{1\cdot 2\cdot 3}(5x)^0(-1)^3$

$\qquad = 125x^3 - 75x^2 + 15x - 1$

47. $100\% - 68.3\% = 31.7\%$

48. Let $u = 2 - 5x^4$. Then $du = -20x^3$.

$$\int x^3(2 - 5x^4)^7 dx = \int u^7\left(-\frac{1}{20}du\right)$$

$$= -\frac{1}{20}\int u^7 du$$

$$= -\frac{1}{20}\cdot\frac{u^8}{8} + C$$

$$= -\frac{1}{160}(2 - 5x^4)^8 + C$$

49. $m\angle BCD = 40°$

$\quad 40 = \dfrac{1}{2}m\overset{\frown}{BC}$

$\quad 80 = m\overset{\frown}{BC}$

$\quad m\angle BAC = \dfrac{1}{2}m\overset{\frown}{BC}$

$\quad m\angle BAC = \dfrac{1}{2}(80)$

$\quad m\angle BAC = 40°$

The best answer is C.

Chapter 17 Summary and Review

PAGES 952-954   SKILLS AND CONCEPTS

1. $\displaystyle\lim_{x\to 0}\left(4^x + \frac{1}{4^x}\right) = 4^0 + \frac{1}{4^0} = 1 + 1 = 2$

2. $\lim\limits_{x\to 0} \dfrac{\sqrt{x+4}-2}{x} = \lim\limits_{x\to 0} \dfrac{(\sqrt{x+4}-2)(\sqrt{x+4}+2)}{x(\sqrt{x+4}+2)}$

$\qquad\qquad\qquad = \lim\limits_{x\to 0} \dfrac{x+4-4}{x(\sqrt{x+4}+2)}$

$\qquad\qquad\qquad = \lim\limits_{x\to 0} \dfrac{x}{x(\sqrt{x+4}+2)}$

$\qquad\qquad\qquad = \lim\limits_{x\to 0} \dfrac{1}{\sqrt{x+4}+2}$

$\qquad\qquad\qquad = \dfrac{1}{\sqrt{0+4}+2} = \dfrac{1}{4}$

3. $\lim\limits_{x\to 0} \dfrac{3x^3-2x}{2x^2-3x} = \lim\limits_{x\to 0} \dfrac{3x^2-2}{2x-3} = \dfrac{3(0)^2-2}{2(0)-3} = \dfrac{2}{3}$

4. $\lim\limits_{x\to 0} \dfrac{\sqrt{3x^2+x+1}}{\sqrt[3]{3x^3-x+8}} = \dfrac{\sqrt{3(0)^2+0+1}}{\sqrt[3]{3(0)^3-0+8}} = \dfrac{\sqrt{1}}{\sqrt[3]{8}} = \dfrac{1}{2}$

5. $\lim\limits_{x\to 1} f[g(x)] = f[\lim\limits_{x\to 1}(-3x)]$

$\qquad\qquad\quad = f(-3)$

$\qquad\qquad\quad = -3+2 \text{ or } -1$

6. $\lim\limits_{x\to 1} f[g(x)] = f[\lim\limits_{x\to 1}(2x+1)]$

$\qquad\qquad\quad = f(3)$

$\qquad\qquad\quad = 3^2-1 \text{ or } 8$

7. $\lim\limits_{x\to 0} \dfrac{1-\cos^2 x}{x^2} = \lim\limits_{x\to 0} \dfrac{\sin^2 x}{x^2}$

$\qquad\qquad\quad = \lim\limits_{x\to 0} \dfrac{\sin x}{x} \cdot \lim\limits_{x\to 0} \dfrac{\sin x}{x}$

$\qquad\qquad\quad = 1 \cdot 1 \text{ or } 1$

8. $\lim\limits_{x\to 0} \left(x - \dfrac{\sin 3x}{x}\right) = \lim\limits_{x\to 0} x - \lim\limits_{x\to 0} \dfrac{\sin 3x}{x}$

$\qquad\qquad\qquad = \lim\limits_{x\to 0} x - 3\lim\limits_{x\to 0} \dfrac{\sin 3x}{3x}$

$\qquad\qquad\qquad = 0 - 3 \cdot 1 \text{ or } -3$

9. $f(x) = x^6$

$\quad f'(x) = 6x^5$

10. $f(x) = 4x^3$

$\quad f'(x) = 4 \cdot 3x^2 = 12x^2$

11. $f(x) = 3x + 4x^2$

$\quad f'(x) = 3 + 8x$

12. $f(x) = (x^4-3x^2)(5x^3)$

$\quad f'(x) = (x^4-3x^2)(15x^2) + (5x^3)(4x^3-6x)$

$\qquad\quad = 15x^6 - 45x^4 + 20x^6 - 30x^4$

$\qquad\quad = 35x^6 - 75x^4$

13. $f(x) = \sqrt{2x^3-6x} = (2x^3-6x)^{\frac{1}{2}}$

$\quad f'(x) = \dfrac{1}{2}(2x^3-6x)^{-\frac{1}{2}}(6x^2-6)$

$\qquad\quad = \dfrac{6x^2-6}{2\sqrt{2x^3-6x}}$

$\qquad\quad = \dfrac{3x^2-3}{\sqrt{2x^3-6x}}$

14. $f(x) = 4x + \dfrac{(x-1)^2}{2x}$

$\quad f'(x) = 4 + \dfrac{2x[2(x-1)(1)] - (x-1)^2(2)}{(2x)^2}$

$\qquad\quad = 4 + \dfrac{4x^2-4x-(2x^2-4x+2)}{4x^2}$

$\qquad\quad = 4 + \dfrac{2x^2-2}{4x^2}$

$\qquad\quad = 4 + \dfrac{1}{2} - \dfrac{1}{2x^2}$

$\qquad\quad = \dfrac{9}{2} - \dfrac{1}{2x^2}$

15. $A = \lim\limits_{n\to\infty} \sum\limits_{i=1}^{n} 2\left(\dfrac{2i}{n}\right)\left(\dfrac{2}{n}\right)$

$\qquad = \lim\limits_{n\to\infty} \dfrac{8}{n^2}\left(\dfrac{n(n+1)}{2}\right)$

$\qquad = \lim\limits_{n\to\infty} 4\left(\dfrac{n^2+n}{n^2}\right)$

$\qquad = \lim\limits_{n\to\infty} 4\left(1 + \dfrac{1}{n}\right)$

$\qquad = 4 \text{ units}^2$

16. $A = \lim\limits_{n\to\infty} \left(\dfrac{i}{n}\right)^3\left(\dfrac{1}{n}\right)$

$\qquad = \lim\limits_{n\to\infty} \dfrac{1}{n^4}\left(\dfrac{n^2(n+1)^2}{4}\right)$

$\qquad = \lim\limits_{n\to\infty} \dfrac{1}{4}\left(\dfrac{n^4+2n^3+n^2}{n^4}\right)$

$\qquad = \lim\limits_{n\to\infty} \dfrac{1}{4}\left(1 + \dfrac{2}{n} + \dfrac{1}{n^2}\right)$

$\qquad = \dfrac{1}{4} \text{ units}^2$

17. $A = \lim\limits_{n\to\infty} \sum\limits_{i=1}^{n} \left(\dfrac{4i}{n}\right)^2\left(\dfrac{4}{n}\right) - \lim\limits_{n\to\infty} \sum\limits_{i=1}^{n} \left(\dfrac{3i}{n}\right)^2\left(\dfrac{3}{n}\right)$

$\qquad = \lim\limits_{n\to\infty} \dfrac{64}{n^3}\left(\dfrac{n(n+1)(2n+1)}{6}\right)$

$\qquad\quad - \lim\limits_{n\to\infty} \dfrac{27}{n^3}\left(\dfrac{n(n+1)(2n+1)}{6}\right)$

$\qquad = \lim\limits_{n\to\infty} \dfrac{32}{3}\left(\dfrac{2n^3+3n^2+n}{n^3}\right) - \lim\limits_{n\to\infty} \dfrac{9}{2}\left(\dfrac{2n^3+3n^2+n}{n^3}\right)$

$\qquad = \lim\limits_{n\to\infty} \dfrac{32}{3}\left(2 + \dfrac{3}{n} + \dfrac{1}{n^2}\right) - \lim\limits_{n\to\infty} \dfrac{9}{2}\left(2 + \dfrac{3}{n} + \dfrac{1}{n^2}\right)$

$\qquad = \dfrac{64}{3} - 9$

$\qquad = \dfrac{37}{3} \text{ units}^2$

18. $A = \lim\limits_{n\to\infty} \sum\limits_{i=1}^{n} 6\left(\dfrac{2i}{n}\right)^2\left(\dfrac{2}{n}\right) - \lim\limits_{n\to\infty} \sum\limits_{i=1}^{n} 6\left(\dfrac{i}{n}\right)^2\left(\dfrac{1}{n}\right)$

$= \lim\limits_{n\to\infty} \dfrac{48}{n^3}\left(\dfrac{n(n+1)(2n+1)}{6}\right)$

$\quad - \lim\limits_{n\to\infty} \dfrac{6}{n^3}\left(\dfrac{n(n+1)(2n+1)}{6}\right)$

$= \lim\limits_{n\to\infty} 8\left(\dfrac{2n^3 + 3n^2 + n}{n^3}\right) - \lim\limits_{n\to\infty} \dfrac{2n^3 + 3n^2 + n}{n^3}$

$= \lim\limits_{n\to\infty} 8\left(2 + \dfrac{3}{n} + \dfrac{1}{n^2}\right) - \lim\limits_{n\to\infty}\left(2 + \dfrac{3}{n} + \dfrac{1}{n^2}\right)$

$= 16 - 2$ or 14 units^2

19. $\displaystyle\int \dfrac{4}{x^2}dx = \int 4x^{-2}dx = 4\dfrac{x^{-1}}{-1} + C = -\dfrac{4}{x} + C$

20. $\displaystyle\int 5x^3 dx = 5\dfrac{x^4}{4} + C$

21. $\displaystyle\int (1 - x)dx = \int 1dx - \int xdx$

$= x + C_1 - \left(\dfrac{x^2}{2} + C_2\right)$

$= x - \dfrac{x^2}{2} + C$

22. $\displaystyle\int \dfrac{1}{\sqrt{x+3}}dx = \int (x+3)^{-\frac{1}{2}}dx$

Let $u = x + 3$. Then $du = 1dx$.

$\displaystyle\int (x+3)^{-\frac{1}{2}}dx = \int u^{-\frac{1}{2}}du$

$= \dfrac{u^{\frac{1}{2}}}{\frac{1}{2}} + C$

$= 2\sqrt{x+3} + C$

23. $f(x) = 5(x+3)^9$

Let $u = x + 3$. Then $du = 1dx$.

$F(x) = \displaystyle\int 5u^9 du$

$= 5\dfrac{u^{10}}{10} + C$

$= \dfrac{(x+3)^{10}}{2} + C$

24. $f(x) = 1 - \dfrac{1}{x^2} = 1 - x^{-2}$

$F(x) = x - \dfrac{x^{-1}}{-1} + C = x + \dfrac{1}{x} + C$

25. $\displaystyle\int_2^4 6xdx = 6 \cdot \dfrac{x^2}{2}\Big|_2^4 = 3x^2\Big|_2^4 = 3(4)^2 - 3(2)^2 = 36$

26. $\displaystyle\int_{-3}^2 3x^2dx = 3 \cdot \dfrac{x^3}{3}\Big|_{-3}^2 = x^3\Big|_{-3}^2 = 2^3 - (-3)^3 = 35$

27. $\displaystyle\int_{-2}^2 (3x^2 - x + 5)dx = 3 \cdot \dfrac{x^3}{3} - \dfrac{x^2}{2} + 5x\Big|_{-2}^2$

$= (2^3 - 2^2 + 5(2))$

$\quad - ((-2)^3 - (-2)^2 + 5(-2))$

$= 14 - (-22)$

$= 36$

28. $\displaystyle\int_0^4 (x-2)(2x+3)dx = \int_0^4 (2x^2 - x - 6)dx$

$= \dfrac{2x^3}{3} - \dfrac{x^2}{2} - 6x\Big|_0^4$

$= \dfrac{2(4)^3}{3} - \dfrac{4^2}{2} - 6(4)$

$= \dfrac{128}{3} - 8 - 24$

$= 10\dfrac{2}{3}$

PAGE 954   APPLICATIONS AND PROBLEM SOLVING

29. $\lim\limits_{t\to 100} \dfrac{1}{2}m\left(\dfrac{50}{1+t^2}\right)^2 = \dfrac{1}{2}m\left(\dfrac{50}{1+100^2}\right)^2$

$\approx 0.0000125m$

30. $c(x) = -9x^5 + 135x^3 + 10{,}000$

$c'(x) = -45x^4 + 405x^2$

$= -45(2.6)^4 + 405(2.6)^2$

$\approx \$681.41$

31. a. $\dfrac{50 \text{ mi}}{h} \cdot \dfrac{h}{3600} \cdot \dfrac{5280}{\text{mi}} \approx 73.333$ ft/s

$\dfrac{73{,}333 \text{ ft/s}}{7 \text{ s}} \approx 10.48$ ft/s^2

b. $a(t) = 10.48$

$v(t) = \displaystyle\int 10.48dt = 10.48t + C_1$

c. $d(t) = \displaystyle\int (10.48t + C_1)dt$

$= 10.48 \cdot \dfrac{t^2}{2} + C_1 t + C_2$

$= 5.24t^2 + C_1 t + C_2$

32.

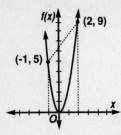

area inside = (area of trapezoid) −

(area below parabola)

area of trapezoid = $\frac{1}{2}h(b_1 + b_2)$

$= \frac{1}{2}(3)(6 + 9)$

$= 22.5$

area below parabola = $\int_{-1}^{2} (3x^2 - 2x + 1)dx$

$= x^3 - x^2 + x \Big|_{-1}^{2}$

$= (2^3 - 2^2 + 2)$

$- ((-1)^3 - (-1)^2 + (-1))$

$= 6 - (-3)$ or 9

area inside = $22.5 - 9 = 13.5$ units^2

Chapter 17 Test

PAGE 955

1. $\lim_{x \to 3} \frac{x^2 - 9}{x^3 - 27} = \lim_{x \to 3} \frac{x + 3}{x^2 + 3x + 9}$

$= \frac{3 + 3}{3^2 + 3(3) + 9}$

$= \frac{6}{27}$ or $\frac{2}{9}$

2. $\lim_{x \to 1} \frac{x^2 - 2x + 3}{3x^2 - 5} = \frac{1^2 - 2(1) + 3}{3(1)^2 - 5} = \frac{2}{-2} = -1$

3. $\lim_{x \to \infty} \frac{(x - 2)(x + 1)}{x^2} = \lim_{x \to \infty} \frac{x^2 - x - 2}{x^2}$

$= \lim_{x \to \infty} \left(1 - \frac{1}{x} - \frac{2}{x^2}\right)$

$= 1$

4. $\lim_{x \to 4} \sqrt{x}(x - 1)^2 = \sqrt{4}(4 - 1)^2 = 2 \cdot 3^2 = 18$

5. $\lim_{x \to 0} \frac{\sin(-2x)}{3x} = -\frac{2}{3} \lim_{x \to 0} \frac{\sin(-2x)}{-2x}$

$= -\frac{2}{3} \cdot 1$ or $-\frac{2}{3}$

6. $\lim_{x \to 1} \frac{x - 1}{x^3 - 1} = \lim_{x \to 1} \frac{1}{x^2 + x + 1} = \frac{1}{1^2 + 1 + 1} = \frac{1}{3}$

7. $\lim_{x \to 1} f[g(x)] = f[\lim_{x \to 1} (3x^2)]$

$= f(3)$

$= 3^3$ or 27

8. $f(x) = 4x^3 - 4$

$f'(x) = 12x^2$

9. $f(x) = (x + 3)^2$

$f'(x) = 2(x + 3)(1) = 2(x + 3)$

10. $f(x) = 6(x^4 - 5) = 6x^4 - 30$

$f'(x) = 24x^3$

11. $f(x) = (2x^4)(x^3 + 3x^2)$

$f'(x) = (2x^4)(3x^2 + 6x) + (x^3 + 3x^2)(8x^3)$

$= 6x^6 + 12x^5 + 8x^6 + 24x^5$

$= 14x^6 + 36x^5$

12. $f(x) = \frac{2x}{1 + x^2}$

$f'(x) = \frac{(1 + x^2)(2) - (2x)(2x)}{(1 + x^2)^2}$

$= \frac{2 + 2x^2 - 4x^2}{(1 + x^2)^2}$

$= \frac{2 - 2x^2}{1 + 2x^2 + x^4}$

13. $f(x) = \sqrt{4x^2 - 1} = (4x^2 - 1)^{\frac{1}{2}}$

$f'(x) = \frac{1}{2}(4x^2 - 1)^{-\frac{1}{2}}(8x) = \frac{4x}{\sqrt{4x^2 - 1}}$

14. $A = \lim_{n \to \infty} \sum_{i=1}^{n} \left(\frac{2i}{n}\right)3\left(\frac{2}{n}\right)$

$= \lim_{n \to \infty} \frac{16}{n^4}\left(\frac{n^2(n + 1)^2}{4}\right)$

$= \lim_{n \to \infty} 4\left(\frac{n^4 + 2n^3 + n^2}{n^4}\right)$

$= \lim_{n \to \infty} 4\left(1 + \frac{2}{n} + \frac{1}{n^2}\right)$

$= 4$ units^2

15. $A = \lim\limits_{n\to\infty} \sum\limits_{i=1}^{n} 3\left(\dfrac{3i}{n}\right)^2\left(\dfrac{3}{n}\right) - \lim\limits_{n\to\infty} \sum\limits_{i=1}^{n} 3\left(\dfrac{i}{n}\right)^2\left(\dfrac{1}{n}\right)$

$\quad = \lim\limits_{n\to\infty} \dfrac{81}{n^3}\left(\dfrac{n(n+1)(2n+1)}{6}\right)$

$\qquad - \lim\limits_{n\to\infty} \dfrac{3}{n^3}\left(\dfrac{n(n+1)(2n+1)}{6}\right)$

$\quad = \lim\limits_{n\to\infty} \dfrac{27}{2}\left(\dfrac{2n^3+3n^2+n}{n^3}\right) - \lim\limits_{n\to\infty} \dfrac{1}{2}\left(\dfrac{2n^3+3n^2+n}{n^3}\right)$

$\quad = \lim\limits_{n\to\infty} \dfrac{27}{2}\left(2+\dfrac{3}{n}+\dfrac{1}{n^2}\right) - \lim\limits_{n\to\infty} \dfrac{1}{2}\left(2+\dfrac{3}{n}+\dfrac{1}{n^2}\right)$

$\quad = 27 - 1$ or 26 units^2

16. $\displaystyle\int (1-2x)dx = x - 2\cdot\dfrac{x^2}{2} + C = x - x^2 + C$

17. $\displaystyle\int (3x^2+4x+7)dx = 3\cdot\dfrac{x^3}{3} + 4\cdot\dfrac{x^2}{2} + 7x + C$

$\qquad\qquad = x^3 + 2x^2 + 7x + C$

18. $\displaystyle\int \dfrac{1}{x^2}dx = \int x^{-2}dx$

$\qquad = \dfrac{x^{-1}}{-1} + C$

$\qquad = -\dfrac{1}{x} + C$

19. $f(x) = \sqrt[3]{x^2} = x^{\frac{2}{3}}$

$\quad F(x) = \dfrac{x^{\frac{5}{3}}}{\frac{5}{3}} + C = \dfrac{3}{5}\sqrt[3]{x^5} + C$

20. $f(x) = \dfrac{1}{2x^3} = \dfrac{1}{2}x^{-3}$

$\quad F(x) = \dfrac{1}{2}\cdot\dfrac{x^{-2}}{-2} + C = -\dfrac{1}{4x^2} + C$

21. $\displaystyle\int_0^1 (2x+3)dx = x^2 + 3x \Big|_0^1$

$\qquad = 1^2 + 3(1) - (0^2 + 3(0))$

$\qquad = 4$

22. $\displaystyle\int_1^3 (-x^2-x+3)dx = -\dfrac{x^3}{3} - \dfrac{x^2}{2} + 3x \Big|_1^3$

$\qquad = -\dfrac{3^3}{3} - \dfrac{3^2}{2} + 3(3)$

$\qquad\quad - \left(-\dfrac{1^3}{3} - \dfrac{1^2}{2} + 3(1)\right)$

$\qquad = -9 - \dfrac{9}{2} + 9 + \dfrac{1}{3} + \dfrac{1}{2} - 3$

$\qquad = -\dfrac{20}{3}$

23. $\displaystyle\int_1^4 \left(x^2 + \dfrac{2}{x^2}\right)dx = \dfrac{x^3}{3} + 2\cdot\dfrac{x^{-1}}{-1} \Big|_1^4$

$\qquad = \dfrac{x^3}{3} - \dfrac{2}{x} \Big|_1^4$

$\qquad = \dfrac{4^3}{3} - \dfrac{2}{4} - \left(\dfrac{1^3}{3} - \dfrac{2}{1}\right)$

$\qquad = \dfrac{64}{3} - \dfrac{1}{2} - \dfrac{1}{3} + 2$

$\qquad = 22\dfrac{1}{2}$

24. $T(\ell) = 2\pi\sqrt{\dfrac{\ell}{32}} = \dfrac{2\pi}{\sqrt{32}}\cdot\ell^{\frac{1}{2}}$

$\quad T'(\ell) = \dfrac{2\pi}{\sqrt{32}}\cdot\dfrac{1}{2}\ell^{-\frac{1}{2}} = \dfrac{\pi}{\sqrt{32\ell}}$

25. $V = \pi\displaystyle\int_{-2}^2 (2^2 - x^2)dx$

$\quad = \pi\left(4x - \dfrac{x^3}{3}\right)\Big|_{-2}^2$

$\quad = \pi\left(4(2) - \dfrac{2^3}{3}\right) - \pi\left(4(-2) - \dfrac{(-2)^3}{3}\right)$

$\quad = \pi\cdot\dfrac{16}{3} - \pi\cdot\left(-\dfrac{16}{3}\right)$

$\quad = \dfrac{32\pi}{3}$

PAGE 955   BONUS

$\lim\limits_{x\to 0} \dfrac{\tan x}{x} = \lim\limits_{x\to 0} \dfrac{\sin x}{x\cos x}$

$\qquad = \lim\limits_{x\to 0} \dfrac{\sin x}{x} \cdot \lim\limits_{x\to 0} \dfrac{1}{\cos x}$

$\qquad = 1\cdot 1$ or 1